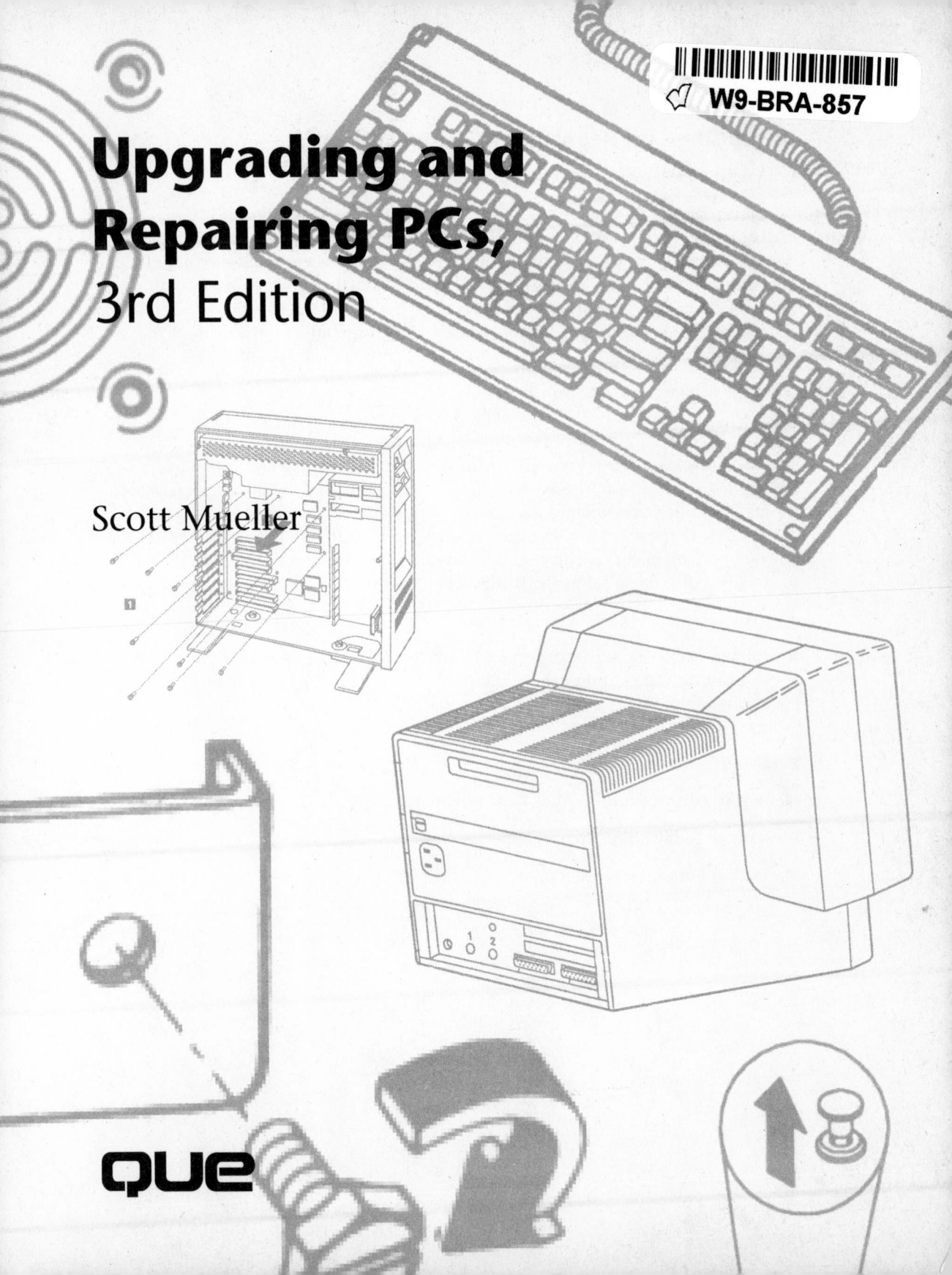

Upgrading and Repairing PCs,

3rd Edition

Scott Mueller

que

Upgrading and Repairing PCs, 3rd Edition

Library of Congress Catalog No.: 93-86245

ISBN: 1-56529-467-X

96 95 94   10 9 8 7 6 5 4

Interpretation of the printing code: the rightmost double-digit number is the year of the book's printing; the rightmost single-digit number, the number of the book's printing. For example, a printing code of 94-2 shows that the second printing of the book occurred in 1994.

Publisher: David P. Ewing

Managing Editor: Corinne Walls

Director of Publishing: Michael Miller

Marketing Manager: Ray Robinson

Dedication

To my mother.

Credits

Publishing Manager
Brad Koch

Acquisitions Editor
Tom Godfrey

Product Director
Steven M. Schafer

Production Editor
Mike La Bonne

Copy Editors
Judy Brunetti, Tom Hayes, Susan Ross
Moore, J. Christopher Nelson, Susan Pink

Technical Editors
Jerry L. Cox, John Little, John Ross

Book Designer
Amy Peppler-Adams

Cover Designer
Dan Armstrong

Editorial Assistant
Jill Stanley

Production Team
Jeff Baker
Angela Bannan
Danielle Bird
Paula Carroll
Charlotte Clapp
Anne Dickerson
Karen Dodson
Carla Hall
Heather Kaufman
Bob LaRoche
Beth Lewis
Shelly Palma
Caroline Roop
Amy L. Steed
Tina Trettin
Michelle Worthington
Lillian Yates

Indexers
Charlotte Clapp
Jeanne Clark
Michael Hughes
Joy Dean Lee
John Sleeva
Craig Small
Suzanne Snyder

Composed in *Stone Serif* and *MCPdigital* by Que Corporation

About the Author

Scott Mueller is president of Mueller Technical Research, an international personal computer research and corporate training firm. Since 1982, MTR has specialized in the industry's most accurate and effective documentation and corporate technical training seminars, maintaining a client list that includes Fortune 500 companies, the U.S. and foreign governments, major software and hardware corporations, as well as PC enthusiasts and entrepreneurs. He has logged millions of miles, presenting his seminars to thousands of PC professionals throughout North and South America, Canada, Europe, and Australia.

Mueller has many popular books, articles, and course materials to his credit in addition to *Upgrading and Repairing PCs*, which have sold more than 500,000 copies in previous editions. Other books include *Que's Guide to Data Recovery* and coauthorship of *The IBM PS/2 Handbook* and the newly released *Killer PC Utilities*. He is a regular contributor to the *Troubleshooter*, a monthly publication from Landmark International.

As an internationally recognized seminar director and renowned authority in deciphering technical information, Mueller has developed and presented personal computer training courses in all areas of PC hardware and software. He specializes in systems hardware, including upgrades, maintenance, troubleshooting, and repair. He is an expert in data-recovery techniques and strategies, local area networks, and major business applications software. Other areas of expertise include systems software, specifically, DOS, OS/2, Windows and Windows NT. Mueller's seminars are available in beginning, intermediate, and advanced levels and are offered both publicly and in custom on-site versions. A video presentation of Mueller's most popular seminar on PC troubleshooting and repair is currently being developed.

For more information about training seminars, or video availability, contact Mueller Technical Research, 21718 Mayfield Lane, Barrington, IL 60010-9733. Phone: 708-726-0709; Fax: 708-726-0710; CompuServe ID: 73145,1566.

Acknowledgments

This third edition is the product of nearly two years of additional research and development over the previous edition. Several people have helped me with both the research and production of this book. I would like to thank the following people:

First, a very special thanks to my Wife and partner, Lynn. This book has been an incredible burden on both our business and family life, and she has put up with a lot! Lynn has also been a tremendous help with many of the tables in the book as well as product research.

Thanks to Lisa Carlson of Mueller Technical Research for helping with most of the product research; Chris Huffman at Micro 2000, Mike Siewruk at Landmark, Alex Alexander at Ultra-X, and Robert Hurt at Data Depot for providing information and assistance on diagnostics products; Lloyd Nelson at IBM for providing access to IBM technical information; Brian Gatza at TCE for information on power supply and hard disk test products; John Rourke at Allied Computer for providing technical information; David Means at Great Falls Computer for several interesting technical tips; Tony Castillo at Aeronics for information on SCSI terminator products; Sue Hunt at Intel for documentation on 486 and Pentium processors; Skip Johnson at Sigma Data for information on CPU and disk upgrade products; Joe Antonelli for field use information and feedback about various products; and Alan Wyatt and Steve Konicki for assistance with updating several of the chapters.

Thanks to all of the other companies and people who have allowed me to evaluate and test their products, as well as those who have provided me with information and documentation.

Thanks to all of the people who have attended the Seminars that I have given; you may not realize how much I learn from each of you and your questions! Also thanks to those of you who have written to me with questions and suggestions concerning this book, I welcome all of your comments. Thanks to those of you on the many CompuServe forums with both questions and answers, from which I have also learned a great deal.

Trademarks

Contents at a Glance

Contents

4 IBM PS/2 and PS/1 System Hardware   119

5 IBM-Compatible Computers   309

III Hardware Considerations   345

6 System Teardown and Inspection   347

7 Primary System Components   399

8 Secondary System Components   465

9 Floppy Disk Drives   539

15 Software Troubleshooting Guide 935

16 A Final Word **995**

Appendix **1003**

Introduction

Welcome to *Upgrading and Repairing PCs*, 3rd Edition. This book is for people who want to upgrade, repair, maintain, and troubleshoot personal or company computers. This book covers the full range of IBM-compatible and IBM systems, and IBM's Personal System/2.

In addition, this book covers state-of-the-art hardware that makes the most modern personal computers easier, faster, and more productive to use. Hardware includes systems based on the 486 and Pentium CPU chips, local bus video, CD-ROM drives, tape backups, sound boards, PCMCIA devices for laptops, IDE and SCSI-interface devices, larger and faster hard drives, and increased system memory capacity.

The comprehensive coverage of the IBM-compatible personal computer in this book has consistently won acclaim. With the release of this 3rd edition, *Upgrading and Repairing PCs* takes its place as one of the most comprehensive, and easily used, references on even the most modern systems—those based on cutting-edge hardware and software. The book examines personal computer systems in depth, outlines the differences among them, and presents options for configuring each system at the time you purchase it.

Sections of this book provide detailed information about each internal component of a personal computer system, from the processor to the keyboard and video display. The book examines the options available in modern, high-performance PC configurations and how to use them to your advantage; it focuses on much of the hardware and software available today and specifies the optimum configurations for achieving maximum benefit for the time and money you spend. At a glance, here are the major system components and peripherals covered in *Upgrading and Repairing PCs*:

- Pentium, 486, and earlier central processing unit (CPU) chips.

- Special bus architectures and devices including VESA-Standard Local Bus (VLB), Expanded Industry Standard Architecture (EISA), Microchannel Architecture (MCA).

- Larger, faster hard drives and hard drive interfaces, including IDE and SCSI.

- Floppy drives, including 360K, 1.2M, 1.44M, and 2.88M drives.

- New storage devices like Bernoulli and magneto-optical drives.

- Increased system memory capacity.

- Large-screen Super VGA monitors and high-speed graphics adapter cards.

- Peripheral devices such as CD-ROM drives, sound boards, and tape backups.

- PCMCIA devices for laptops.

- Multimedia devices such as full-motion video.

This book also shows you how to troubleshoot the kind of hardware problems that can make PC upgrading and repairing difficult. Troubleshooting coverage includes DMA channel and IRQ problems, and memory address conflicts. This book tells you how to avoid these kinds of problems, and how to make installing a new adapter board in your computer a simple plug-and-play operation. This book also focuses on software problems, starting with the basics of how DOS or another operating system works with your system hardware to start up your system. You learn how to troubleshoot and avoid problems involving system hardware, the operating system, and applications software such as word processors or spreadsheets.

What Are the Main Objectives of This Book?

Upgrading and Repairing PCs focuses on several objectives. The primary objective is to help you learn how to maintain, upgrade, and repair your PC system. To that end, *Upgrading and Repairing PCs* helps you fully understand the family of computers that has grown from the original IBM PC, including IBM and IBM-compatible systems. This book discusses all areas of system improvement such as floppy disks, hard disks, central processing units, math coprocessors, and power-supply improvement. The book discusses proper system and component care; it specifies the most failure-prone items in different PC systems and tells you how to locate and identify a failing component. You'll learn about powerful diagnostics hardware and software that enables a system to help you determine the cause of a problem and how to repair it.

The IBM-compatible microcomputer family is moving forward rapidly in power and capabilities. Processor performance increases with every new chip design. *Upgrading and Repairing PCs* helps you gain an understanding of each of the CPU chips used in IBM and IBM-compatible computer systems.

This book covers the important differences between major system architectures—the original Industry Standard Architecture (ISA), Expanded Industry Standard Architecture (EISA), and IBM's proprietary Microchannel Architecture (MCA). The most modern systems use special bus architectures and adapter cards with special characteristics to get top speed from system peripherals like video adapter cards and hard drives. Besides ISA, EISA, and MCA, these special bus architectures include VESA-Standard Local Bus (VLB), and

Peripheral Component Interconnect (PCI) devices. *Upgrading and Repairing PCs* covers each of these system architectures and their adapter boards to enable you to make decisions about which kind of system you may want to buy in the future, and how to upgrade and troubleshoot such systems.

The amount of storage space available to modern PCs is increasing geometrically. *Upgrading and Repairing PCs* covers storage options ranging from larger, faster hard drives to state-of-the-art storage devices. In addition, this book provides detailed information on upgrading and troubleshooting system RAM.

When you finish reading this book, you should have the knowledge to perform repairs on nearly all systems and components.

Who Should Use This Book?

Upgrading and Repairing PCs is designed for people who want a good understanding of how their PC systems work. Each section fully explains common and not-so common problems, what causes problems, and how to handle problems when they arise. You will gain an understanding of disk configuration and interfacing, for example, that can improve your diagnostics and troubleshooting skills. You'll develop a feel for what goes on in a system that you can rely on your own judgment and observations and not some table of canned troubleshooting steps. This book is for people who are truly interested in their systems and how they operate.

Upgrading and Repairing PCs is written for people who will select, install, configure, maintain, and repair systems they or their companies use. To accomplish these tasks, you need a level of knowledge much higher than that of average system users. You must know exactly which tool to use for a task and how to use the tool correctly. This book can help you achieve this level of knowledge.

What Is in This Book?

Chapter 1 is an introduction to the development of the IBM PC and compatibles. Chapter 2 provides detailed information about the different types of systems you encounter and what separates one type of system from another, including the types of system bus that differentiates systems. Chapter 2 also explains the memory architecture of the different system types, including conventional, extended, and expanded memory. This information helps you build a foundation of knowledge essential for the remainder of the book.

Chapters 3 and 4 describe with considerable depth each IBM PC and PS/2 model and list differences among individual versions of each system. Technical specifications for each system are highlighted in these chapters also. This information is useful not only for supporting actual IBM equipment, but also for people whose IBM-compatible systems are not supplied with extensive documentation. You learn how to compare and contrast systems with the IBM standard.

Chapter 5 discusses IBM-compatible systems. It provides detailed information about differences in compatible systems and standard IBM systems, and also lists important features of different compatible systems. The chapter is useful especially if you make purchasing decisions. You can use Chapter 5 as a general guideline for features that make a certain compatible computer a good or bad choice.

The proper teardown, disassembly, and inspection procedures for a system are examined in Chapter 6. Each component that makes up a typical system, from the power supply to the microprocessor, is discussed in Chapter 7.

Chapter 8 discusses important system components such as the keyboard, mouse-pointing device, monitors and video display adapters, CD-ROM drives, SCSI interface devices, multimedia, sound boards, computer audio systems, memory, serial and parallel ports, and troubleshooting these devices. Also discussed are differences between serial-port designs that can affect performance, and newer high-speed modems.

Chapters 9 and 10 describe in detail floppy disk drives and hard disk drives. This information is invaluable when you install drives as either replacements or upgrades in a system, and if you troubleshoot and repair malfunctioning drives. You'll find especially interesting information about newer IDE and SCSI interface drives, used in most of the latest IBM and compatible systems.

Chapter 11 focuses on preventive maintenance and backup procedures. The chapter shows you how to develop your own preventive maintenance programs and how to put together a tool kit you'll use to work on your system. It also covers the basics of system care and cleaning and examines how to maintain a system to avoid common problems. It shows how to clean system adapter boards, reseat loose chips, avoid infection by computer viruses, and work with data backup.

Chapter 12 lists specific system upgrades and examines how to do them. It discusses how to add different floppy drives (such as 3 1/2-inch) to a system and how to expand a system by adding additional hard drives, or larger hard drives. It shows how to speed up a system by upgrading its processor, adding memory, and upgrading the motherboard (or using other hardware devices) to convert from one type of system to another (from an XT to an AT, or from a 286 AT to a 386, for example).

Chapter 13 focuses on system diagnostics and the required tools needed to perform such diagnostics. It describes manufacturer-provided diagnostics and different aftermarket diagnostics utilities. A new section in this edition discusses some of the hardware diagnostic boards.

Chapters 14 and 15 examine hardware and software troubleshooting. These chapters explain the most common problems and the procedures you use to discover the source of and resolve these problems. Chapter 16 concludes the book.

The appendix lists many tables and data with valuable reference information. You probably will refer to this section of the book repeatedly when you're troubleshooting system problems. The tables and charts are one of my most valuable reference sources. You'll also find useful information for upgrading and repairing IBM systems. Most of the information has never appeared all in one book.

I believe that *Upgrading and Repairing PCs* will prove to be the best book of its kind on the market. It offers not only the breadth of IBM and compatible equipment, but also much in-depth coverage of each topic. This book is valuable as a reference tool for understanding how various components in a system interact and operate, and as a guide to repairing and servicing problems you encounter. *Upgrading and Repairing PCs* is far more than just a repair manual. I sincerely hope that you enjoy it.

Part I

The Background and Features of Personal Computers

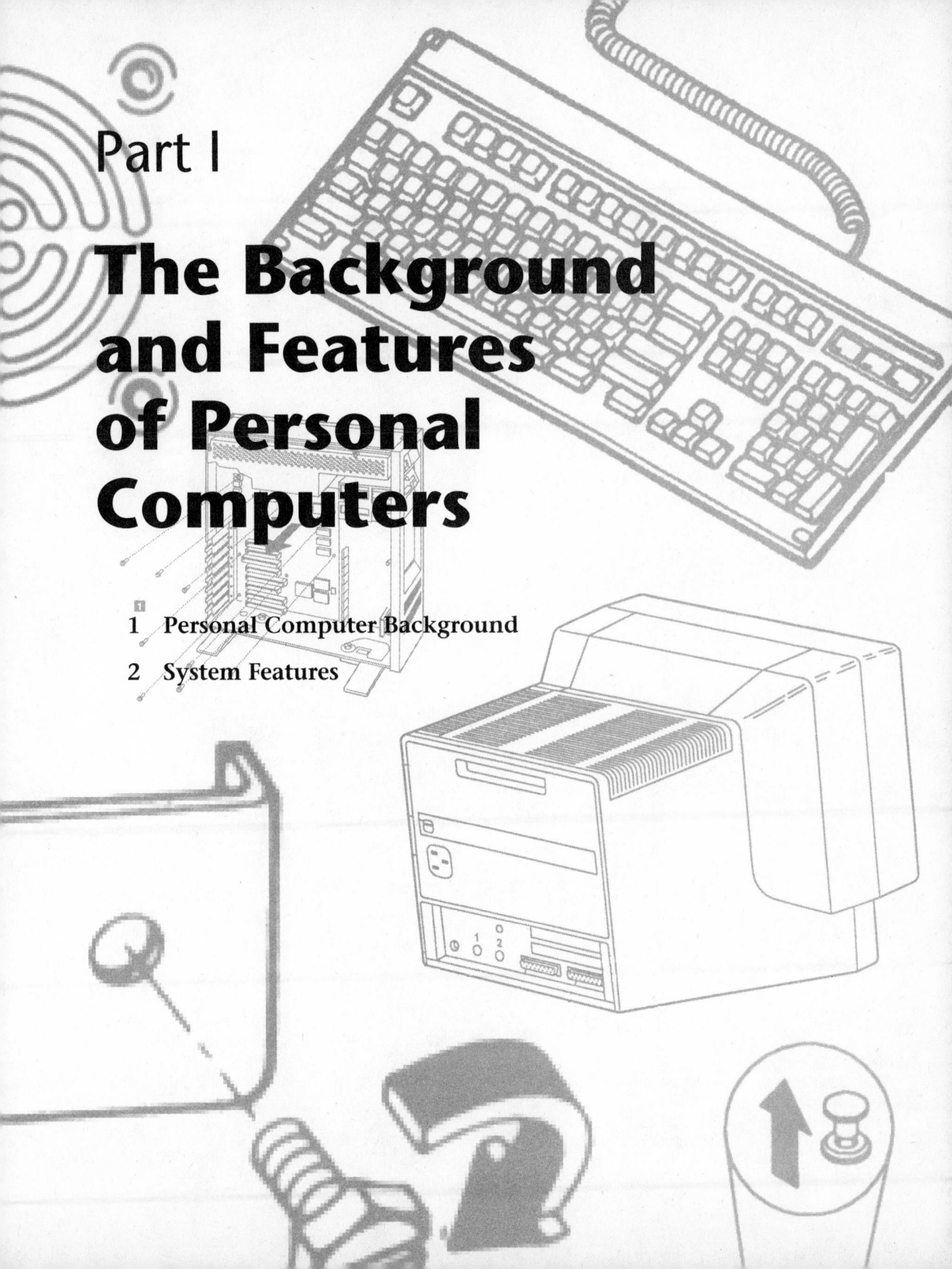

Chapter 1

Personal Computer Background

Many discoveries and inventions have contributed to the development of the machine known today as the personal computer. Examining a few important developmental landmarks can help bring the whole picture into focus.

Personal Computing History

A modern digital computer is largely a collection of electronic switches. These switches are used to represent as well as control the routing of data elements called *binary digits* (bits). Because of the on or off nature of the binary information and signal routing used by the computer, an efficient electronic switch was required. The first electronic computers used vacuum tubes as switches, and although the tubes worked, they had many problems.

The tube was inefficient as a switch. It consumed a great deal of electrical power and gave off enormous heat—a significant problem in the earlier systems. Tubes were notoriously unreliable also; one failed every two hours or so in the larger systems.

The invention of the transistor, or semiconductor, was one of the most important developments leading to the personal computer revolution. The transistor was invented in 1948 by John Bardeen, Walter Brattain, and William Shockley (engineers at Bell Laboratories). The transistor, essentially a solid-state electronic switch, replaced the much less suitable vacuum tube. Because the transistor consumed significantly less power, a computer system built with transistors was much smaller, faster, and more efficient than a computer system built with vacuum tubes.

The conversion to transistors began a trend toward miniaturization that continues to this day. Today's small laptop [or palmtop] PC systems, which run on batteries, have more computing power than many earlier systems that filled rooms and consumed huge amounts of electrical power.

In 1959, engineers at Texas Instruments invented the integrated circuit (IC), a semiconductor circuit that contains more than one transistor on the same base (or substrate material) and connects the transistors without wires. The first IC contained only six transistors. By comparison, the Intel Pentium microprocessor used in many of today's high-end systems has more than 3 million transistors! Today, there are many ICs with transistor counts in the multi-million range.

In 1969, Intel introduced a 1K-bit memory chip, which was much larger than anything else available at the time. (A 1K-bit equals 1,024 bits, and a byte equals 8 bits; this chip, therefore, stored 128 bytes—not much by today's standards.) Because of Intel's success in chip manufacturing and design, Busicomp, a Japanese calculator-manufacturing company, asked Intel to produce 12 different logic chips for one of its calculator designs. Rather than produce the 12 separate chips, Intel engineers included all the functions of the chips in a single chip. In addition to just incorporating all the functions and capabilities of the 12-chip design into one multipurpose chip, they designed the chip to be controlled by a program that could alter the function of the chip. The chip then was "generic" in nature: it could function in designs other than just a calculator. Previous designs were hard-wired for one purpose with built-in instructions; this chip would read from memory a variable set of instructions, which Intel already was producing. The idea was to design almost an entire computing device on one chip. The first microprocessor, the Intel 4004, a 4-bit processor, was introduced in 1971. The chip operated on 4 bits of data at a time. The 4004 chip's successor was the 8008 8-bit microprocessor in 1972.

In 1973, some of the first microcomputer kits based on the 8008 chip were developed. These kits were little more than demonstration tools and did little except blink lights. In late 1973, Intel introduced the 8080 microprocessor, which was 10 times faster than the earlier 8008 chip and addressed 64K of memory. This breakthrough was the one the personal computer industry was waiting for.

MITS introduced the Altair kit in a cover story in the January 1975 issue of *Popular Electronics* magazine. The Altair kit, considered to be the first personal computer, included an 8080 processor, a power supply, a front panel with a large number of lights, and 256 bytes (not kilobytes) of memory. The kit sold for $395 and had to be assembled. The computer included open architecture (slots) that prompted various add-ons and peripherals from aftermarket companies. The new processor inspired other companies to write programs, including the CP/M (Control Program for Microprocessors) operating system and the first version of Microsoft BASIC.

IBM introduced what can be called its first *personal computer* in 1975. The Model 5100 had 16K of memory, a built-in 16-line-by-64-character display, a built-in BASIC language interpreter, and a built-in DC-300 cartridge tape drive for storage. The system's $9,000 price placed it out of the mainstream personal computer marketplace, dominated by experimenters (affectionately referred to as hackers) who built low-cost kits ($500 or so) as a hobby. The IBM system obviously was not in competition for this low-cost market and did not sell well. The Model 5100 was succeeded by the 5110 and 5120 before IBM introduced the IBM Personal Computer (Model 5150). Although the 5100 series preceded the IBM PC, there was nothing in common between these older systems and the 5150

IBM PC released later. The PC it turned out was very closely related to the IBM System/23 DataMaster, an office computer system introduced in 1980.

In 1976, a new company, Apple Computer, introduced the Apple I (for $695). This system consisted of a main circuit board screwed to a piece of plywood. A case and power supply were not included. Only a handful of these computers were made, and they reportedly have sold to collectors for more than $20,000. The Apple II, introduced in 1977, helped set the standard for nearly all the important microcomputers to follow, including the IBM PC.

The microcomputer world was dominated in 1980 by two types of computer systems. One type, the Apple II, claimed a large following of loyal users and a gigantic software base that was growing at a fantastic rate. The other type consisted not of a single system but included all the many systems that evolved from the original MITS Altair. These systems were compatible with each other and were distinguished by their use of the CP/M operating system and expansion slots that followed the S-100 (for slots with 100 pins) standard. All these systems were built by a variety of companies and sold under various names. For the most part, however, these companies used the same software and plug-in hardware.

The IBM Personal Computer

At the end of 1980, IBM had decided to truly compete in the rapidly growing low-cost personal computer market. The company established what was then called the Entry Systems Division, in Boca Raton, Florida, to develop the new system. This small group consisted of 12 engineers and designers under the direction of Don Estridge. The team's chief designer was Lewis Eggebrecht. The division developed IBM's first real PC. (IBM considered the 5100 system, developed in 1975, to be an intelligent programmable terminal rather than a genuine computer, even though it truly was a computer.) Nearly all these engineers moved from working on the System/23 DataMaster project, a small, office computer system introduced in 1980 (and the direct predecessor of the IBM PC).

Much of the PC's design was influenced by the DataMaster's design. In the DataMaster's single-piece design, the display and keyboard were integrated into the unit. Because these features were limiting, they became external units on the PC—although the PC keyboard layout and electrical designs were copied from the DataMaster. Several other parts of the IBM PC system also were copied from the DataMaster, including the expansion bus, or input-output slots, which included not only the same physical 62-pin connector, but also the almost identical pin specifications. This copying was possible because the PC used the same interrupt controller and a similar direct memory access (DMA) controller as the DataMaster. Expansion cards already designed for the DataMaster could then be easily "ported" to the PC. The DataMaster used an Intel 8085 CPU, which had a 64K address limit, and an 8-bit internal and external data bus. This prompted the PC design team to use the Intel 8088 CPU in the PC, which offered a much larger 1M memory address limit, and had an internal 16-bit data bus, but only an 8-bit external data bus. The 8-bit external data bus and similar instruction set allowed the 8088 to be easily interfaced into the earlier DataMaster designs.

Estridge and the design team rapidly developed the design and specifications for the new system. In addition to borrowing from the System/23 DataMaster, the team also studied the marketplace, which also had enormous influence on the IBM PC's design. The designers looked at the prevailing standards, learned from the success of those systems, and incorporated into the new PC all the features of the popular systems—and more. With the parameters for design made obvious by the market, IBM produced a system that filled perfectly its niche in the market.

IBM brought its system from idea to delivery in one year by using existing designs, great autonomy within IBM, and purchasing as many components as possible from outside vendors. IBM contracted out the PC's languages and operating system, for example, to a small company named Microsoft. (IBM originally had contacted Digital Research, which invented CP/M, but that company apparently was not interested in the proposal. Microsoft was interested, however, and since has become one of the largest software companies in the world.) The use of outside vendors was also an open invitation for the aftermarket to jump in and support the system. And it did.

On Wednesday, August 12, 1981, a new standard took its place in the microcomputer industry with the debut of the IBM PC. Since then, IBM has sold more than 10 million PCs, and the PC has grown into a large family of computers and peripherals. More software has been written for this family than for any other system on the market.

The IBM-Compatible Marketplace 12 Years Later

In the more than 12 years since the original IBM PC was introduced, many changes have occurred. For example, the IBM compatible computer advanced from a 4.77 MHz 8088-based system to 66 MHz Pentium-based system—more than *100 times faster* than the original IBM PC (in actual processing speed, not just clock speed). The original PC could have only two 160K floppy drives for storage, whereas modern systems easily can have several gigabytes of hard disk storage. A rule of thumb in the computer industry is that available processor performance and disk storage capacity at least doubles every two to three years. Since the beginning of the PC industry this pattern shows no signs of changing.

In addition to performance and storage capacity, another major change since the original IBM PC was introduced is that IBM is not the only manufacturer of "IBM-compatible" systems. IBM invented the IBM-compatible standard, of course, and continues to set standards that compatible systems follow, but it does not dominate the market as before. As often as not, new standards in the PC industry are developed by companies and organizations other than IBM. Hundreds of system manufacturers produce computers compatible with IBM's systems, not to mention the thousands of peripheral manufacturers with components that expand and enhance IBM and IBM-compatible systems.

The IBM-compatible market continues to thrive and prosper. New technology will be integrated into these systems and enable them to grow with the times. Because of both the high value these types of systems can offer for the money and the large amount of software available to run on them, IBM and IBM-compatible systems likely will dominate the personal computer marketplace for perhaps the next ten years as well.

Chapter Summary

This chapter traced the development of personal computing from the transistor to the introduction of the IBM PC. Intel's continuing development of the integrated circuit led to a succession of microprocessors and reached a milestone with the 1973 introduction of the 8080 chip. In 1975, MITS introduced the Altair computer kit, based on the 8080 microprocessor. IBM jumped into the personal computer market with the Model 5100 in 1975.

In 1976, Apple sold its first computers, followed in 1977 by the enormously successful Apple II. Because of its success, the Apple II played a major role in setting standards and expectations for all later microcomputers.

Finally, in 1981, IBM introduced its Personal Computer to a microcomputer world dominated by the Apple II and the somewhat Apple-compatible computers that evolved from the Altair, both of which used the CP/M operating system. The IBM PC, designed with the needs of the market in mind and with many of its components produced by outside vendors, immediately set the new standard for the microcomputer industry. This standard has evolved to meet the needs of today's users, with more powerful systems that offer performance levels not even imagined in 1981.

Chapter 2, "System Features," describes the technical fundamentals of IBM personal computers and their compatibles; differences between 8-bit, 16-bit, 32-bit, and 64-bit systems; the structure and use of memory; and how to obtain and use technical reference and hardware maintenance and service manuals.

Chapter 2

System Features

This chapter discusses the system architecture of IBM-compatible systems including systems based on the new Pentium (586) CPU chip, and explains memory structure and use. Many types of IBM and compatible systems are on the market today. Most systems are similar to one another, but differences in system architecture have become increasingly important as operating environments such as Windows, Windows NT and OS/2 have become more and more popular, and DOS-based software applications, such as WordPerfect 6.0 for DOS, have become more demanding of your system.

Operating systems like OS/2 1.x require at least a 286 CPU platform on which to run, and OS/2 2.x requires at least a 386 CPU. Environments such as Windows offer different capabilities and operating modes based on the capabilities of the hardware platform you run it on. Windows NT requires at least a 386, but is practical for use only on 486- and Pentium-based systems. Running WordPerfect 6.0 for DOS in graphics mode requires at least a 386. Knowing and understanding the differences in these hardware platforms will allow you to plan for, install, and utilize modern operating systems and applications that make great demands on your hardware.

Types of Systems

Many types of IBM-compatible personal computers are on the market today and commonly identified by a strange code consisting of letters and numbers—PC, XT, AT, MCA, VLB, PCI, 8088, 80286, 80386, 80486, and Pentium. With such codes used to describe what is purportedly an easy-to-use device, no wonder so many people still are intimidated when they think about using a personal computer.

All IBM and compatible systems can be broken down into two basic system types, or classes. These system types are the following:

- PC and XT types of systems
- AT types of systems

The term PC is often used in a general sense whenever discussing an MS-DOS-compatible computer system, regardless of whether it is a PC/XT- or AT-type computer. However, when discussing PC/XT- vs. AT-types of systems, there are some lines of demarcation (such as the types of CPU, the operating modes of the CPU, and the number of Interrupt Request Lines (IRQs) and Direct Memory Access (DMA) channels). For example, the term PC can be used to describe systems based on the entire Intel family of chips, from the 8086 to the Pentium (and even the NEC V-20 and V-30). The term XT, however, always means a system based on the Intel 8088 CPU chip, and the term AT means a system based on the 80286 or higher.

Note

Over the years, various manufacturers have deviated from the basic PC/XT and AT standards and some manufacturers (and their customers) have suffered greatly due to this practice. Some manufacturers of well-known non-IBM compatible systems have been forced out of business by lack of consumer interest. Others struggled for years before producing a more or less fully compatible line of systems. If your system does not follow all the criteria listed for it, especially if it is an AT-type system, you can expect compatibility and operational problems.

Table 2.1 summarizes some of the most basic differences between a standard PC/XT system and an AT system. Other important differences between systems are covered throughout this book, including differences mandated by the capabilities of the CPU chip at the heart of each system. This table is important because it details the basic designs of older PC- and XT-type systems in contrast with today's high-powered AT-type systems.

Table 2.1 Differences between PC (or XT) and AT Systems

System attributes	PC or XT type	AT type
Supported processors	All Intel 80xx	286 or higher
Processor modes	Real	Real/protected/virtual real
Expansion-slot width	8-bit	16-bit/32-bit
Slot type	ISA	ISA/EISA/MCA/PCMCIA/VLB/PCI
Interrupts	8 + NMI	16 + NMI
DMA channels	4	8
Maximum RAM	1 megabyte	16 or 4096 megabytes
Motherboard ROM space	F0000-FFFFF	0E0000-0FFFFF/FE0000-FFFFFF
Floppy controller	250 KHz rate	250/300/500/1000 KHz rates
Boot floppy drive	360K or 720K	1.2M/1.44M/2.88M
Hard disk BIOS	Adapter	Motherboard or adapter
Keyboard interface	Unidirectional	Bidirectional
CMOS setup/clock	No	Yes
Serial port UART	8250B	16450/16550

Using the information in this table, you can properly categorize virtually any system as a PC type or AT type. For a system to match the true industry-standard definition of PC/XT- or AT-class system, it must match the characteristics of one of the system types listed in table 2.1. For example, the newest Pentium-based systems can be categorized as AT-type systems, as can 486, 386, and 286 systems. Because of its 16-bit slots and 80286 CPU chip type, IBM's XT Model 286 is actually categorized as an AT-type system, not a PC/XT-type system. A COMPAQ Deskpro is a PC system, and the Deskpro 286 and Deskpro 386 are AT-type systems. The AT&T 6300 qualifies as a PC-type system, and the 6310 is an AT-type system.

PC systems usually have double-density (DD) floppy controllers, but AT systems must have a controller capable of both high-density (HD) and double-density operation. Some newer systems, such as the PS/2 Model 57, also have a controller capable of extra-high density (ED). These systems can run the 2.88M floppy drive. Because of the different controller types, the boot floppy drive on a PC system must be the DD, 5 1/4-inch 360K or 3 1/2-inch 720K drives, but the AT needs the 5 1/4-inch 1.2M or the 3 1/2-inch 1.44M or 2.88M drives for proper operation. You can use a double-density disk drive as the boot drive in an AT system; the problem is that your boot drive is *supposed* to be a high-density drive. Many applications that run on only AT-type systems are packaged on high-density disks. The OS/2 operating system, for example, is packaged on high-density disks and cannot be loaded from double-density disks. The capability to boot and run OS/2 is a basic AT-compatibility test.

The AT architecture uses CMOS memory and a real-time clock, and PC/XT-type systems usually don't. (An exception is the PS/2 Model 30, which has a real-time clock even though it is an XT-class system.) A *real-time clock* is the built-in clock implemented by a special CMOS memory chip on the motherboard in an AT system. You can have a clock added on some expansion adapters in a PC system, but DOS does not recognize the clock unless a special program is run on bootup. The CMOS memory in the AT system also stores the systems basic configuration information including the amount of installed memory, the number and types of floppy drives and hard disks, and the type of video adapter. On a PC or XT type of system, these basic configuration options are set by using switches and jumpers on the motherboard, and various adapters.

The PC-type systems use a hard disk controller with an on-board hard disk ROM BIOS (Read-Only Memory/Basic Input-Output System). The controller ROM on such systems contains a set of built-in tables for supported drives or has an *autoconfigure* option that can configure a drive dynamically by building a table entry on the spot and storing it directly on the drive. On AT-type systems, the controller BIOS and the supported drive table are embedded in the Motherboard ROM. This motherboard-resident hard disk BIOS is designed for a particular type of controller, and other controllers used must look like or emulate the one expected by the motherboard code. This situation is especially true for ST-506/412 and ESDI interface drives.

To make modern AT-type systems as flexible as possible, the BIOS of AT-type systems built in the past few years usually offer a user-defined hard drive type that enables you to correctly configure your computer for nearly any hard drive. Most of today's Integrated

Drive Electronics (IDE) drives require the proper configuration of the system CMOS. Small Computer Systems Interface (SCSI) adapters normally have their own on-board BIOS because they commonly do not emulate the ST-506/412 or ESDI controllers.

Another difference between PC/XT and AT systems is in the keyboard interface. AT systems use a bidirectional keyboard interface with an Intel 8042 processor running the show. This processor has ROM built-in and can be considered a part of the total system ROM package. The PC/XT systems used an 8255 Programmable Peripheral Interface (PPI) chip, which supports only a unidirectional interface. A keyboard can be configured to work with only one of the interface designs. With many keyboards, you can alter the way the keyboard interfaces by flipping a switch on the bottom of the keyboard. Others, like IBM's Enhanced 101-key keyboard, detect which type of system they are plugged into and switch automatically. The older XT and AT keyboards work with only the type of system for which they were designed.

The serial-port control chip (UART) for the PC-type system is a National Semiconductor 8250B. AT systems use the newer NS 16450 or 16550 chips. Because these chips differ in subtle ways, the system BIOS must be designed for a specific UART chip.

PC systems set aside 64K of memory for the motherboard ROM, using the last segment in the 1M of total space. The actual addresses for this memory are F0000-FFFFF in hexadecimal. An AT system sets aside 128K at the end of the first megabyte and at the end of the last (16th) megabyte of memory. The addresses are 0E0000-0FFFFF and FE0000-FFFFFF in hexadecimal. In the AT system, each set of 128K bytes of ROM space is the same code: double mapped—only 128K total is available as the amount of actual memory, but the system has it positioned in two different places so that the total memory consumed is 256K. Double mapping is required in the AT systems because of the microprocessor design.

PC/XT systems include only four Direct Memory Access channels, compared with seven on a true AT design. Four of the AT-type system's DMA channels move data on an 8-bit path, like the PC/XT DMA channels, and the other three operate at 16-bits. The PC/XT type system provides eight interrupt request lines (IRQs), where AT systems have 15. The small number of IRQs on a PC/XT-type system severely limits the number of devices like a modem and mouse, which require the use of these resources.

This contrast of the basic types of systems, the PC/XT and AT, does not tell the whole story, however. Many possibilities are available, however. Some systems have the NEC V-20 or V-30 processors, but these processors are functionally identical to the Intel chips. A few PC or XT systems have an 80286 or 80386 processor for increased performance. These systems usually have one or more 8-bit slots of the same system-bus design featured in the original IBM PC.

A PC or XT cannot have more than 1M of processor-addressable memory, of which only 640K is available for user programs and data. These systems can run most software that runs under MS-DOS but cannot run OS/2 or any software designed to run under OS/2, nor can it run Windows in Standard or 386 Enhanced mode, and cannot be used to run Windows NT.

The PC/XT type of systems are based on what is termed the 8-bit Industry Standard Architecture (ISA) expansion slot. The AT-type system, however, can be equipped with a variety of expansion bus data widths. Here are the types of slots common on AT-type systems:

- 16-bit Industry Standard Architecture (ISA) bus

- 16-bit PS/2 Micro Channel Architecture (MCA) bus

- 32-bit PS/2 Micro Channel Architecture (MCA) bus

- 32-bit Extended Industry Standard Architecture (EISA) bus

- 32-bit VESA-Standard Local bus

- 32-bit Peripheral Component Interconnect (PCI) bus

The following sections begin by discussing some basics of system design, including the motherboard. Later sections detail the differences between the original PC/XT expansion bus and the various 16- and 32-bit width slots common in modern personal computers. These sections also detail the capabilities of various systems depending on their expansion bus type.

The Motherboard

The main circuitry of the personal computer is a large printed circuit board known as the motherboard. The motherboard is the single most important circuit board in your system because it contains the basic logic circuits of the system, as well as the brain of your computer—the central processing unit (CPU) chip. The CPU installed on the motherboard plays a central role in determining your system type. For example, a motherboard containing an 8088 CPU chip is a PC/XT type of system. A motherboard containing an 80286, 80386, 80486, or Pentium CPU chip can be termed an AT-type computer system. The different CPU chips installed in personal computers are detailed in Chapter 7, "Primary System Components."

The components of the motherboard have a significant effect on the performance of your system. For example, the motherboard of a personal computer based on the most modern CPU chip, the Pentium, is designed to provide much faster memory access than the original PC, which was based on the 8088 CPU chip. The motherboards designed for the Pentium chip also provide much greater system memory capacity than the original IBM PC. It is common for motherboards designed for the Pentium to be capable of holding as much as 1G of RAM chips where the original IBM PC contained only 64K of memory.

In addition, the motherboard contains a varying number of expansion slots, which enable you to plug additional devices into the motherboard such as controllers for fast hard drives or video cards. The following sections cover the different types of expansion slots.

The Expansion Bus

The expansion bus is basic to the understanding of personal computers. In a real sense, any device that controls the flow of electrical impulses from one point to another can be referred to as a *bus*. In a personal computer, the expansion bus is the collection of electronic components that determines how many bytes of data can flow between a system's central processing unit (CPU) chip and an adapter board at one time.

Expansion slots are needed on personal computers because the basic system cannot possibly be built to satisfy all the needs of the people who buy them. The main circuitry of the computer is contained on a large printed circuit board known as the motherboard. The expansion bus, which also is known as the expansion slot, or motherboard slot, enables you to add devices to your computer to expand its capabilities. The most basic computer components, like hard drive controllers and video adapter cards, are plugged into expansion slots, as are more specialized devices like sound boards and CD-ROM drive interface cards.

The data width of expansion slots determines how much information can flow at one time between the CPU and the adapter board plugged into the slot. The slots created by IBM for use on the first PC/XT- and AT-type systems later came to be known as the Industry Standard Architecture (ISA) slot. The original IBM PC and XT systems had an 8-bit expansion bus. The AT-type system increased the bus width to 16-bits. Systems based on the 386, 486, and Pentium chips frequently have 32-bit expansion slots. On many of these systems, the 32-bit adapter board is used, for example, to speed video and hard drive output. Various system architectures have been introduced that provide for 32-bit slots.

> **Note**
>
> Although systems based on the 386SX or SL chips have the full instruction-set capabilities of the full 32-bit 386DX processor, they have only a 16-bit hardware data path, and therefore, do not support 32-bit slots.

The development of these various bus types over the years is a fascinating study of personal computer technology. The basic 8- and 16-bit expansion buses, now known as ISA architecture, were developed by IBM, but were an open system architecture, which means any manufacturer is welcome to use them for a small licensing fee. The 8- and 16-bit ISA bus have been used by perhaps thousands of other manufacturers for use in compatible systems.

This lack of restrictions on the use of ISA bus architecture is an important reason IBM-compatible systems have dominated the personal computer marketplace. In fact, the ability of other manufacturers to use ISA architecture is often credited with the long-term success of IBM PCs and compatibles.

When IBM developed its much more sophisticated and powerful Micro Channel Architecture (MCA), the company charged a somewhat larger license fee to other system manufacturers, one reason often cited for the failure of MCA architecture to become a widespread industry standard. Another reason MCA has failed to be adopted universally for systems with 32-bit slots is that adapter cards designed for 8- and 16-bit ISA slots will not work in MCA systems. Compatibility between PC- and AT-type adapter boards has been an important consideration of consumers since the AT-class computer was introduced roughly a decade ago.

MCA consists of special 16- and 32-bit slots, with the 32-bit slots present in only 80386DX or higher systems. AT-type systems from other manufacturers based on 386 or higher CPU chips can include various types of 32-bit slots—the Extended Industry Standard Architecture (EISA) slot, the VESA-Standard Local Bus (VLB) slot or the Peripheral Component Interconnect (PCI) slot. Many EISA-based systems include 32-bit VESA-Standard slots for use by a video adapter card or IDE local bus hard drive interface.

In September 1988, more or less in response to IBM's introduction of Micro Channel Architecture, a consortium of manufacturers led by COMPAQ introduced a new slot system: Extended Industry Standard Architecture (EISA). EISA Architecture provides 32-bit slots for use with 386DX or higher systems. The EISA slot enables manufacturers to design adapter cards that have many of the same capabilities of MCA adapters. But the users of EISA systems also can use 16-bit ISA adapters in their systems. EISA provides markedly faster hard drive throughput when used with devices such as Small Computer System Interface (SCSI) bus mastering hard drive controllers. When compared with 16-bit ISA system architecture, EISA also enables greater system expansion with fewer adapter conflicts.

The capabilities of EISA systems are greatly expanded when these systems are equipped with VESA-Standard Local Bus (VLB) slots. The addition of the VLB slots enables EISA systems to take advantage of the latest in video card technology as well as fast 32-bit Integrated Drive Electronics (IDE) hard drive interface cards.

Not all 32-bit slots are compatible with MCA, EISA, VLB, or PCI standards. For example, manufacturers of early 386 (and some 486) systems integrated proprietary 32-bit slots in their non-Micro Channel AT systems. Usually, the only expansion boards available for these slots are memory boards produced by the system manufacturer itself. These proprietary slots are incompatible with today's high-speed hard drive controllers or 32-bit video adapter boards.

ISA Bus Architecture. The 8- and 16-bit ISA bus is the basis of the modern personal computer. Since 1982, when the first IBM PC was introduced, the bus which has come to be known as Industry Standard Architecture has made it possible for thousands of different manufacturers to build systems whose components (except for a few specialized parts) were interchangable. For example, floppy drives that worked in an IBM PC would also work in what came to be known as IBM "clones." Video adapters that worked in IBM ATs also worked in IBM compatible systems based on the 286 CPU chip. Importantly, the software applications that ran on IBM PC- and AT-type systems would also run on compatible systems designed by other manufacturers.

It is safe to say that one reason personal computers were little more than a specialty (or novelty) item before IBM introduced the first PC is that the software designed for one computer brand would not run on another maker's computers, nor would hardware devices designed for one computer brand work on another.

8-Bit ISA. Physically, the 8-bit ISA expansion slot works something like the way furniture makers once used tongue-and-groove to hold two pieces of wood together. An adapter card with 62 gold contacts on its bottom edge plugs into a slot on the motherboard with 62 matching gold contacts. Electronically, this slot provides 8 data lines and 20 addressing lines to allow the handling of 1M of memory.

Although the physical design of the bus is simple, IBM never published full specifications for the timings of the data and address lines, so manufacturers in the early days of IBM-compatibles had to do their best to figure out how to make adapter boards. This became less of a problem, however, as the IBM-compatible personal computer became more widely accepted as the industry standard and manufacturers had more time and incentive to build adapter boards that worked correctly with the bus.

All PC-motherboard configurations have had five expansion slots. The XT introduced later had eight slots. Because of the larger number, the slots had to be positioned closer together; they are approximately an inch apart in the PC and only .8 inches apart in the XT. Because of this design, some of the extremely thick, or double-stacked, expansion cards that fit well in a PC require two adjacent slots in an XT. The dimensions of XT adapter cards are as follows:

XT ISA card

4.2 inches (106.68 mm) high

13.13 inches (333.5 mm) long

0.5 inches (12.7 mm) wide

Because most board manufacturers realize that many of their boards will be installed in XTs and later systems, boards usually are designed for the width of XT slots. The only modern cards that seem to cause problems in XT systems are some hard disks on a card. But even among such hard cards, many are designed so that they do not occupy two slot spaces.

In the XT or Portable PC, the eighth slot—the one closest to the power supply—is a special slot; only certain cards can be installed there. A card installed in the eighth slot must supply to the motherboard on pin B8 a special card-selected signal, which few cards have been designed to do. (The IBM asynchronous adapter card and the keyboard/timer card from a 3270 PC are two examples of cards that fit in the eighth slot.) Additionally, the timing requirements for the eighth slot are stricter.

The reason this strange slot is in the XT is that IBM developed the system to support a special configuration called the 3270-PC, which is really an XT with three to six special adapter boards installed. The eighth slot was designed specifically to accept the keyboard/timer adapter from the 3270 PC. This board needed special access to the motherboard because it replaced the motherboard keyboard circuitry. Special timing and the card-selected signal made this access possible. (Contrary to what many users believe, the eighth slot has nothing to do with the IBM expansion chassis.) The IBM expansion chassis, by the way, is a box developed by IBM that looked like another system unit. Because the IBM XT had eight slots, one full-height floppy drive, and one full-height hard drive, the expansion gave room for more expansion slots and additional floppy and hard drives.

16-bit ISA. Like the XT, the AT has eight slots. Because of the 16-bit bus width of the 80286 CPU chip, however, some slots are equipped to handle many more signals than the PC or XT to tap the power and speed the processor is capable of providing. IBM took the safe route for the most part and kept the physical slot design the same, but added extension connectors providing an additional 36 connector pins to six of the slots to carry extra signals. Therefore, you can plug any standard PC or XT expansion card into the AT with no changes. Some XT-type cards do not work in 16-bit ISA slots, even though you can physically plug them in, because of problems with interrupts, DMA channels, ROM address conflicts, and so on.

The slot-extension connector physically interferes with cards that have a *skirt*, which is an extended area of the card that drops down toward the motherboard just after the connector. To handle these cards, IBM omitted the extension connector from two of the slots so that they could physically handle any skirted PC or XT expansion card. (Some XT cards, however, don't work properly in the AT even though you can physically plug them in.) Rather than use earlier PC or XT boards, most often you will purchase expansion cards designed specifically for the AT. Boards designed specifically for the AT take advantage of the full 16-bit slot; they can perform a 16-bit transfer rather than an 8-bit transfer and achieve greater speed. Some dedicated AT cards also take advantage of the fact that the AT is a larger box that supports cards a half-inch taller, thereby allowing more circuitry on the board.

The dimensions of a typical AT expansion board are shown in the following:

AT ISA card

4.8 inches (121.92 mm) high

13.13 inches (333.5 mm) long

0.5 inches (12.7 mm) wide

Actually, two heights are available for cards commonly found in AT systems: those that use the full 4.8 inches of available space and those that are only 4.2 inches tall. The shorter cards became an issue when IBM introduced the XT Model 286. Because this model has an AT motherboard in an XT case, it needs AT-type boards with the 4.2-inch maximum height. Most board makers trimmed down their boards a little; now many of them make only 4.2-inch-tall boards, used in either the standard AT or the XT Model 286.

32-bit EISA Slot. The slot is at the core of EISA systems, designed for backward compatibility with most 8- and 16-bit adapter boards while enabling EISA adapters to make use of the full 32-bit bus width of the 386 and later CPU chips. The EISA slot adds 90 new connections (55 new signals) without increasing the connector size. In fact, physically the 32-bit EISA slot looks much like the 16-bit ISA slot, and has the same connectors as the 16-bit slot. But the EISA slot also contains a second row of connectors. These connectors are located deeper in the slot than the ones common to both the 16-bit and EISA slots.

The EISA adapter card has two rows of connectors, the first row being of the same kind as a 16-bit ISA card and another, thinner row that extends from the 16-bit connectors. You can visualize the EISA edge connectors by remembering what it looks like to lay a 1x1 board on a 2x2 board in a lumber yard. The edge connector on an EISA board is about 0.2 inch longer than the connectors on an 8- or 16-bit adapter board of the additional row of 32-bit connectors on an EISA board. The longest (and thinnest) connectors on an EISA card pass completely through the 16-bit part of the slot and make contact with the EISA 32-bit connectors deeper in the slot. Simultaneously, the 16-bit connectors on the card contact the 16-bit connectors in the slot.

Special stops in the EISA slot prevent an 8- or 16-bit card from being inserted too far into an EISA slot, preventing older-style cards from shorting out the EISA connectors in the slot, which could damage the computer. Once the EISA adapter card is fully inserted, both the upper and lower sets of contacts are fully engaged in the EISA slot. The physical specifications of an EISA card are presented in the following:

> **EISA card**
>
> 5.0 inches (127.0 mm) high
>
> 13.13 inches (333.5 mm) long
>
> 0.5 inches (12.7 mm) wide

An EISA slot will accept most 8- and 16-bit bus adapter boards, but it will not accept cards that add a skirt, an area on the long bottom edge of the board used to obtain more component space. Such a skirt keeps an 8- and 16-bit card from plugging into an EISA slot. However, a short skirt or mini-skirt located between the expansion connector and card-retaining bracket does not interfere with the EISA slot.

The EISA specification calls for more than 45 watts at four different voltages to be available to each slot, a challenge to 200 watt or smaller power supplies. It takes more than 325 watts to fully power the eight EISA slots on a system. Most EISA adapters, however, do not use the full 45 watts available to them. In fact, most use about the same amount of power as 8- and 16-bit adapter boards.

The system clock on EISA motherboards runs at a fixed rate between 6 and 8.33 Mhz to help ensure compatibility with 8- and 16-bit adapter boards, most of which run at 8 to 10 MHz. The EISA slot does not enable adapters to run at the 33 MHz internal chip speeds of the fastest 486s, as does the VESA-Standard Local Bus (VLB) slot, one reason many EISA systems are equipped with VLB slots.

EISA use a technology called *bus mastering* to speed up the system. In essence, a bus master is an adapter with its own processor that can execute operations independently of the system's central processing unit (CPU). Bus mastering enables certain devices to make themselves a high system priority and when given the nod by the EISA arbitration unit, or *Integrated System Peripheral* chip (ISP), temporarily take control of the system. In essence, when given control, a bus master adapter takes control of the system as if it were the motherboard. For example, a bus mastering EISA hard drive controller achieves much greater data throughput with a fast drive because the controller is able to take over the computer to transfer data 32 bits at a time.

The ISP determines which device gains control through use of a four-level order of priority. The order, in terms of priority, is system memory refresh, DMA transfers, the CPU itself, and bus masters. A bus mastering adapter board notifies the ISP when it wants control of the system. Then, after the ISP has taken care of the needs of the higher-priority system memory refresh, DMA transfers, and the CPU itself, the ISP signals permission for the bus mastering adapter board to take control. Bus mastering adapter boards have built-in circuitry to keep them from taking over the system for periods of time that would interfere with first priority operations like memory refresh.

EISA systems also use an automated setup to deal with adapter board interrupts and addressing issues, which often cause problems when installing several different 8- and 16-bit adapter boards on a system based on AT architecture. EISA setup software seeks potential conflicts and automatically configures the system to avoid them. EISA does, however, enable you to do your own troubleshooting as well as jumper and switch board configuration.

MCA Bus. Three types of slots are involved in IBM's Micro Channel Architecture (MCA) design, the 16-bit slot, the 16-bit slot with video extensions, and the 32-bit slot. These slots are based on an all-new bus design, rather than being based on the 16-bit AT bus. Because these MCA slots are different, no adapters that plug into an ISA or EISA system will work in an MCA system, or vice versa. The number of pins, their signals, and even the physical dimensions of the new bus connectors are different from the old ISA bus design. The MCA slot design is superior in every way to the older ISA implementation and many think it superior to the EISA design. The physical dimensions of an MCA adapter card are as follows:

> **16-bit MCA card**
>
> 3.5 inches (88.2 mm) high
>
> 11.5 inches (292.1 mm) long

MCA runs asynchronously with the main processor. Because IBM has published strict timing requirements for boards that plug into an MCA slot, the "slot swapping" sessions often needed to resolve timing problems when adding a new board to an ISA-based system should become a thing of the past on MCA systems. MCA is much more reliable as far as these types of problems are concerned than the standard ISA or even EISA designs. MCA adapters, like certain EISA adapters can be bus masters, meaning that they can take control of the system according to another of priority in order to more rapidly do their job.

MCA systems achieve a new level of "ease of use," as anyone who has set up one of these systems can tell you. An MCA system has no jumpers and switches—neither on the motherboard nor on any expansion adapter. You don't need an electrical engineering degree to be able to plug a card into a PC. However, some of the fastest computer components available on the market today will not work with MCA systems, because these components were designed for ISA, EISA, or VLB slots.

16-Bit MCA. Every Micro Channel Architecture slot has a 16-bit connector. This connector is the primary MCA slot design, the one found in all MCA systems. This 16-bit MCA slot has connectors which are smaller than the connectors found on an ISA or EISA system. The slot itself is divided into two sections, one that handles 8-bit operations, and another for 16-bit operations.

32-Bit MCA. In addition to the basic 16-bit slot, MCA systems based on the 386DX or higher processor chips have several 32-bit slots designed to take advantage of the processors' increased communications and memory-addressing capabilities. Even though the 32-bit slot uses an extension to the original MCA connector, as the 16-bit ISA slot used an extension of the 8-bit ISA design, the 32-bit extension was designed at the same time as the rest of MCA. Because the extension connector was designed directly into MCA and not added later, the design is more integrated than the 16-bit extension connector in ISA systems.

MCA Video Extensions. The third type of MCA slot is a standard 16-bit MCA connector with an added special *video-extension connector*. This special slot is in almost every MCA system, and normally only one slot in each system would have this design. This slot, although it is not 32-bit like the VESA-Standard Local Bus Video slot for ISA- and EISA-based systems, speeds up your video subsystem. Unlike VLB, the MCA video extension connector takes advantage of special VGA circuitry built into the motherboard. MCA enables an MCA-compatible high-resolution video adapter card video card special access to this motherboard VGA circuitry so the new card does not need to duplicate this circuitry.

The MCA video slot goes beyond local bus in at least one way. No matter what new type of video board you add to an MCA system, all your programs will run because you never lose the built-in VGA circuits. The built-in VGA circuits do not have to be disabled. Instead, your new card coexists with the VGA circuits and can even "borrow" some things, such as the digital-to-analog converter, which can make the add-on video boards less expensive because they can use circuitry on the motherboard rather than built-in duplicates of that circuitry.

Local Bus. Local bus technology was introduced to overcome a traditional bottleneck in personal computers — the speed at which data can move between the CPU and subsystems like the video adapter and hard drive. The flow of information between the video card (and hard drive) and the CPU chip has long been a bottleneck because these devices were confined to using the 8 MHz speed of the original ISA bus, and its 16-bit data path.

Two technologies have emerged since the introduction of systems based on the 486 CPU chip that go a long way toward eliminating this bottleneck—the VESA-Standard Local Bus (also known as *VLB*) and the Intel Peripheral Component Interconnect (PCI) bus. The following sections discuss these two cutting-edge bus technologies, as well as some local bus implementations to steer away from.

Proprietary Local Bus Implementations. Shortly after the 486 CPU chip was introduced, manufacturers scrambled to provide technology that would enable the video subsystem and hard drive to keep up with the incredible speed of this new microprocessor chip. While the Video Electronics Standards Association (VESA) and Intel struggled to design a bus that would take advantage of the speed and data path width of the 486, various manufacturers began building systems based on what they hoped (or at least inferred) would be the new standard. Many manufacturers sold systems with these maverick local bus slots. Unfortunately, video cards and hard drive controllers were never produced for most of these proprietary designs, leaving the purchasers of these systems high and dry when it came time to speed up their video or hard drives. COMPAQ, Dell, and Hewlett-Packard, among others who chose not to use VLB, have shipped systems based on proprietary local bus technology. This decision may have been aided by the fact that Intel's PCI bus for the 486 was introduced long after the VLB slot was the hottest selling new bus design since the AT bus was introduced nearly a decade before.

With the introduction of the Pentium chip, some manufacturers are again taking the maverick approach to local bus. Instead of waiting until a standard is defined for access to the 64-bit path and 60- or 66-MHz speeds of the Pentium chip, these manufacturers are opting to produce systems based on what they think might become the standard. Those who are contemplating buying a fast system based on the Pentium chip, and want local bus technology, would be well advised to wait until VESA updates its VLB standard for the new chip, or systems become available based on the PCI bus.

VESA Standard Local Bus (VLB). During the time the 486 was the fastest system money could buy, the VESA Standard Local Bus enjoyed the position of king of the hill as far as cutting-edge bus technology was concerned. The VLB slot offers direct access to system memory at the speed of the processor itself. (For example, 33 MHz on a 486DX-33 or a clock-doubled 486DX2-66.) Although by inserting wait states, the VLB will work on a 50MHz DX system. The VLB bus can move data 32 bits at a time, enabling data to flow between the CPU and the video subsystem or hard drive at the full 32-bit width of the 486 chip. The maximum rated throughput of the VLB is 128-132M per second compared to the theoretical ISA bus maximum of 8M per second. In other words, local bus went a long way toward removing the major bottlenecks to faster video and hard drive throughput.

VLB-equipped systems have become especially popular with users of Windows and OS/2 because these slots are used for special 32-bit video accelerator cards that greatly speed the repainting of the graphics screens used in the icon- and menu-based interface of these operating systems. The performance of Windows and OS/2 suffer greatly from bottlenecks of even the best 16-bit VGA card. Where VGA cards may be capable of painting 600,000 pixels per second on-screen, manufacturers of local bus video adapters often advertise that their cards will paint 50-60 million pixels per second to the screen. Although performance typically is somewhat less in "real world" uses of computers equipped with these devices, the increase in speed is remarkable when compared with either a fast VGA card or a graphics accelerator card. A VLB video card often enables Windows and OS/2 to run as fast as DOS programs run on a similar system—a major accomplishment when scrolling through a word processing document involves the repainting of millions of pixels.

Additionally, VLB offers manufacturers of hard drive interface cards an opportunity to overcome another traditional bottleneck—the rate at which data can flow between the hard drive and the CPU. The average 16-bit IDE drive and interface can achieve up to 5M per second throughput, which means you can save a 1.5M file to disk almost instantly. This is much faster than hard drives of just a few years ago. VLB hard drive adapters for IDE drives are touted as providing throughput of as much as 8M per second in burst mode, which means that for a short period of time, the hard drive is able to move as much as 8M of data into or out of the CPU.

In real world situations, the true throughput of VLB hard drive adapters is somewhat less than 8M per second. But there is a substantial boost in hard drive data transfers on systems equipped with VLB hard drive adapters because they take advantage of the full 32-bit data path width of the CPU, as well as the native speed of the 486 and Pentium CPU chips local bus systems are built around. Drives linked to a local bus caching an IDE interface card with 8M or 16M of cache RAM can achieve significantly higher throughput than possible with a 16-bit IDE interface card.

Physically, the VESA-Standard slot is an extension to the 16-bit ISA slot, which enables the slot to be used either for a VLB-compatible device or a 16-bit adapter. The VESA extension is similar to a Micro Channel connector, and has 112 contacts. If the designer of an adapter card wishes, a board may be designed to connect only to the VESA extension and not the ISA 16-bit portion of the slot.

Most computer manufacturers produce systems with VESA-Standard slots, so if you are contemplating a local bus 486 computer, ensure it complies with the VESA standard. Proprietary designs are nearly worthless; a local bus video motherboard will mean significantly faster screen and hard drive response only if you can find a video card or hard drive adapter that works with it. At this time, VLB adapters are the only ones that conform with this criterion. If you are convinced that another local bus standard is superior, you should buy a motherboard that includes that slot standard only after you ensure you will be able to buy video cards and hard drive adapters that will take full advantage of this slot design.

There is one important consideration when purchasing VLB adapters: although VESA is a consortium of manufacturers, not all manufacturers who belong to the consortium adhere strictly to VESA specifications. The standards adopted by VESA are voluntary, and some manufacturers choose to only partially implement the VESA guidelines. Before you purchase a VESA-standard video card or hard drive adapter, ensure that the motherboard, the adapter card, and the monitor or hard drive you have in mind will all work with one another. For example, when purchasing a VLB video card, contact the manufacturer to see if the card has been tested with your system and that the card will support the monitor you wish to buy.

If you plan on purchasing a Pentium-based system, and want local bus, you may want to wait a short time. VESA has been hard at work updating its local bus standard for the 64-bit path of this CPU chip, VL-Bus/64, and Intel has introduced its own version of the local bus, called the Peripheral Component Interconnect (PCI) standard, which is optimized for the 64-bit path of the Pentium. A shootout between these standards is widely predicted for when both become available on Pentium systems.

Available VLB Adapters. Many manufacturers are producing VESA-compliant Local Bus Video boards, and selecting among them is difficult. However, two manufacturers are producing superior VLB video cards against which other cards are judged. ATI produces a VLB version of its Graphics Ultra Pro and Diamond produced a VLB card called the Viper. These video cards, as well as other VLB video adapters, are somewhat expensive, but when the cost of the board is weighed against productivity gains, many people decide they are worth it.

PCI Local Bus. Intel Corporation, the designer of the CPU chip on which all versions of the personal computer have been based, has a different local bus specification in mind, called the Peripheral Component Interconnect (PCI) standard. Intel's PCI has been slow to gain acceptance because of several factors. First it was introduced long after the VLB bus had been adopted by most system manufacturers for 486 systems. Second, the PCI bus, like the Micro Channel Architecture bus, is an all-new bus design, and VESA-standard adapter boards will not work in a PCI slot. Third, although PCI was slightly faster than VLB on a 486 system, it was pricey. With VLB dominating the 486 marketplace, many manufacturers and their customers saw the PCI bus as simply muddying the water as far as the peripheral bus was concerned.

However, Intel was first out of the gate with a local bus optimized for the Pentium and the PCI bus appears to be a different story as far as Pentium-based systems are concerned. On these systems, the PCI bus is capable of transferring data at approximately the same speed as the VESA-Standard local bus—128-to-132M per second.

PCI bypasses the standard Input/Output bus and uses the system bus to take full advantage of the Pentium's 64-bit data path. The PCI bus runs at the 60 MHz or 66 MHz speed of the processor (compared with the 33 MHz maximum speed of the VESA-Standard Local Bus). These two improvements are touted as virtually eliminating traditional PC bottlenecks. Hard drive throughput speeds are promised to be astonishing on PCI bus systems. Video response, when PCI video cards become available, is expected to leave 486-equipped VLB systems in the dust, although VESA is expected to catch up by releasing its 64-bit specifications in a very short time.

Background and Features

There is one catch where the PCI bus is concerned. Motherboard and peripheral manufacturers will have to redesign their products from the ground up because of the fact that the PCI bus is so different from the ISA or VLB bus, and this will add significantly to the cost of virtually all PCI-based systems and their adapters. For the forseeable future, PCI-based systems will be the workhorses of only the very few who crave the ultimate in speed and power—and don't mind paying the price. With the Pentium-optimized VESA Local Bus standard just around the corner, many who want to buy Pentium systems would be well advised to wait until both standards are available and their prices and performance can be compared.

PCI Bus Implementations. At this writing, PCI-based peripherals were more a promise than a reality. For example, various major manufacturers have announced that they will be producing PCI-compliant video adapters and hard drive subsystems that will take advantage of the wider data path of the Pentium chip. It is important to note that many PCI-compliant devices will take two PCI slots.

For example, Western Digital has shown IDE drives and interface cards supporting the PCI chip set. NCR is developing a PCI version of its Small Computer Systems Interface (SCSI). BusLogic has introduced Fast SCSI-2 hard drive controller electronics that the company says can achieve data throughput speeds of 10M per second when either incorporated into the motherboard itself or as an add-in card. However, SCSI bus mastering controllers that achieve 10M per second transfer rates are already available for 486 VLB systems. BusLogic says this adapter will also be produced in a 486 PCI-compatible version. The adapter uses a 20 MHz 80186 processor to control direct memory access functions.

Similarly, most of the video card manufacturers who produce VESA-Standard Local Bus video cards have announced they will produce video cards based on the standard. However, few of these products have been shown, and finding one at your local computer retailer or mail order outlet may be difficult for some time to come.

As far as PCI-compliant video cards are concerned, here are some general guidelines for comparing products. Look first at the video adapters produced by the leaders in VESA Local Bus video. For example, Diamond and ATI. Then look for cards produced by other major manufacturers based on video processing chips manufactured by ATI, S3, Weitek, and Tseng Labs.

PCMCIA Bus. In an effort to give laptop and notebook computers the kind of expandability users have grown used to with desktop systems, the Personal Computer Memory Card International Association has established several standards for credit card-sized expansion boards that fit into a small slot on laptops and notebooks. The PCMCIA standards, which were developed by a consortium of more than 300 manufacturers including IBM, Toshiba, and Apple, have been touted as a revolutionary advance in mobile computing because PCMCIA laptop and notebook slots enable you to add memory expansion cards, faxmodems, SCSI adapters, Local Area Network cards, and many other types of devices. The idea behind PCMCIA was to enable you to plug any manufacturer's PCMCIA peripheral into your notebook.

The promise of the 2.1-by-3.4 inch PCMCIA 68-pin cards is enormous. Marketers envision not only memory expansion cards, tiny hard drives, and wireless modems, which are already available, but wireless LAN connectors, PCMCIA sound cards, and CD-ROM controllers, along with tape backup drives and a host of other peripherals. As it now stands, the PCMCIA devices available cost roughly double what you would pay for the same device for an ISA desktop system. Under version 2.0 of the PCMCIA card standard, devices can be made physically lengthier, which will help in the design of some advanced peripheral cards.

There is just one drawback to PCMCIA: The standard has been only loosely followed by those who manufacture computers and peripheral devices. Anyone purchasing a laptop or notebook computer with an eye toward expandability must do their homework before buying the system. Some devices that are advertised as fully PCMCIA-compatible do not work with systems that also advertise themselves as fully PCMCIA compatible. The only way to be safe when buying PCMCIA cards if you already have a PCMCIA bus computer is to contact the device manufacturer and determine whether the device has been tested in your computer. Before you purchase a PCMCIA-compatible computer, you should get the manufacturer's list of devices with which the computer will work.

In an effort to solve these compatibility problems, the PCMCIA has continued to establish standards. In fact, as of this writing, there are four such standards: PCMCIA Type I, PCMCIA Type II, and PCMCIA Type III. PCMCIA Type IV is expected on the market early in 1994. Even with all the PCMCIA types, compatibility problems remain, mostly because PCMCIA standards are voluntary and some manufacturers do not fully implement these standards before advertising their products as PCMCIA-compatible. But these standards have helped make more and more PCMCIA computers and peripherals compatible with one another. Each of the PCMCIA standards is discussed in the following sections.

PCMCIA Type I. The original PCMCIA standard, now called Type I slots, can handle cards 3.3 millimeters thick. These slots work only with memory expansion cards. If shopping for a PCMCIA memory expansion card, check with your system manufacturer before buying to ensure that the card you buy will work with your system.

PCMCIA Type II . PCMCIA Type II slots hold cards that are 5mm thick but otherwise are the same physical form factor as Type I cards. PCMCIA Type II slots also can be used with Type I cards because the guides that hold the cards are the same thickness. It is the center portion of the slot that provides more room. Type II cards support virtually any type of expansion device, such as modems, or LAN adapters.

PCMCIA Type III. In late 1992, PCMCIA Type III was introduced. These slots are intended primarily for removable hard drive, and are 10.5mm thick. But they also are backwardly compatible with Type I and Type II cards.

PCMCIA Type IV . PCMCIA Type IV slots are due by the beginning of 1994 and are intended to be used with hard drives that are thicker than the 10.5mm Type III slot would allow. The exact dimensions of the slot have not yet been determined, but it is expected that Type IV slots will be backwardly compatible with Types I-III.

The System Memory Map

A total of 1M of memory was installed on the original PC, and the top half of that was reserved for use by the system. Placing this reserved space at the top (between 512K and 1024K instead of at the bottom, between 0K and 512K) has led to what today is often called the "conventional memory barrier." The shortsightedness of the designers of the original PC and the constant pressures on system and peripheral manufacturers to maintain compatibility by never breaking from the original memory scheme of the first PC has resulted in a system memory structure that is (to put it kindly) a mess. More than a decade after the first PC was introduced, even the newest Pentium-based systems are limited in important ways by the memory map of the first PCs.

Someone who wants to become knowledgable about personal computers must at one time or another come to terms with the types of memory installed on their system—the small and large pieces of different kinds of memory, some accessible by software application programs, and some not. The following sections detail the different kinds of memory installed on a modern PC. The kinds of memory covered in the following sections include these specific different kinds of memory:

- Conventional Memory

- Upper Memory

- High Memory

- Extended Memory

- Expanded Memory

- Video RAM Memory

- Adapter ROM and Special Purpose RAM

- Motherboard ROM

Subsequent sections also cover preventing memory conflicts and overlap, using memory managers to optimize your system's memory, making better use of wasted RAM, and finding missing RAM. Figure 2.1 is the memory map for an XT system and represents how the memory is likely to be allocated. Each symbol on a line is equal to 1K of memory. Each line or segment is 64K, and the entire map is 1,024K, or 1M.

These symbols are used in figure 2.1:

.	Program-accessible memory (user-installed RAM)
v	Video RAM
a	Adapter-board ROM and special-purpose RAM
r	Motherboard ROM BIOS
b	IBM Cassette BASIC (*r* on compatibles)

In an AT system, the memory map extends beyond the 1M boundary and can continue to 16M on a system based on the 286 CPU chip or 4G (4096M) on a 386 or higher. For this reason, in the computer industry, any memory greater than 1M is called *extended memory*. Figure 2.2 shows the memory map for an AT-type system (286) with 16M of memory.

```
 Conventional (base) memory
             : 0---1---2---3---4---5---6---7---8---9---A---B---C---D---E---F---
       00000: ................................................................
       10000: ................................................................
       20000: ................................................................
       30000: ................................................................
       40000: ................................................................
       50000: ................................................................
       60000: ................................................................
       70000: ................................................................
       80000: ................................................................
       90000: ................................................................
 Upper memory area (UMA)
       A0000: vvvvvvvvvvvvvvvvvvvvvvvvvvvvvvvvvvvvvvvvvvvvvvvvvvvvvvvvvvvvvvvvv
       B0000: vvvvvvvvvvvvvvvvvvvvvvvvvvvvvvvvvvvvvvvvvvvvvvvvvvvvvvvvvvvvvvvvvv
       C0000: aaaaaaaaaaaaaaaaaaaaaaaaaaaaaaaaaaaaaaaaaaaaaaaaaaaaaaaaaaaaaaaaa
       D0000: aaaaaaaaaaaaaaaaaaaaaaaaaaaaaaaaaaaaaaaaaaaaaaaaaaaaaaaaaaaaaaaaa
       E0000: rrrrrrrrrrrrrrrrrrrrrrrrrrrrrrrrrrrrrrrrrrrrrrrrrrrrrrrrrrrrrrrrr
       F0000: rrrrrrrrrrrrrrrrrrrrrrrrrbbbbbbbbbbbbbbbbbbbbbbbbbbbbbbrrrrrrrrrr
```

Fig. 2.1
The 1M memory map for PC/XT-type systems.

Conventional Memory. The original PC/XT type system was designed to make use of 1M of memory workspace, sometimes called RAM (random-access memory). This 1M of RAM is divided into several sections, some of which have special uses. DOS can read and write to the entire megabyte but can manage the loading of programs only in the portion of RAM space called *conventional memory*, which at the time the first PC was introduced was 512K. The other 512K was reserved for use by the system itself, including the motherboard and adapter boards plugged into the system slots.

Eventually IBM decided that only 384K was needed for these reserved uses and the company began marketing PCs with 640K of user memory. For a time, IBM offered the AT with only 512K conventional memory, but returned to the 640K configuration. Thus, 640K became the standard for memory that can be used by DOS for running programs, and is often termed the 640K memory barrier. The remaining memory after 640K is reserved for use by the graphics boards, other adapters, and the motherboard ROM BIOS.

Upper Memory. The term *upper memory* is used to describe the reserved 384K at the top of the first megabyte of system memory on a PC/XT and the first megabyte on an AT-type system. This memory has the addresses from A0000-to-F0000. The way the 384K of upper memory is used breaks down as follows:

- The first 128K after conventional memory is called *video RAM*. It is reserved for use by video adapters. When text and graphics are displayed on-screen, the electronic impulses that contain their images reside in this space.

- The next 128K is reserved for the software programs, or adapter BIOS, that reside in read-only memory chips on the adapter boards plugged into the system slots.

■ The last 128K of memory is reserved for motherboard BIOS, (the basic input-output system, which is stored in read-only RAM chips or ROM). The POST (Power-On Self Test) and bootstrap loader, which handles your system at bootup until DOS takes over, also reside in this space.

The following symbols are used in figure 2.2:

.   Program-accessible memory (user-installed RAM)

v   Video RAM

a   Adapter-board ROM and special-purpose RAM

r   Motherboard ROM BIOS

b   IBM Cassette BASIC (r on compatibles)

h   High-Memory Area (HMA, allocated by HIMEM.SYS)

Not all of the 384K of reserved memory is fully used on most AT-type systems. For example, according to IBM's definition of the PC standard, reserved video RAM begins at address A0000, which is right at the 640K boundary, but this reserved area may not be used, depending on which video adapter is installed in the system. Some adapters do not use the area beginning at A0000, instead using a higher address. Different video adapters also use varying amounts of RAM for their operations.

In fact, although the top 384K of the first megabyte is termed reserved memory, it is possible to use parts of this memory to load device drivers (like ANSI.SYS) and memory resident programs (like MOUSE.COM), which frees up the conventional memory they would otherwise require. The amount of upper memory will vary from system to system depending on the adapter cards installed on the system. For example, higher-resolution video adapters usually use more memory than those offering lower resolution because of the larger number of pixels (picture elements) and colors on the screen. For information on loading device drivers and memory resident programs into upper memory, see the section later in this chapter titled, "Configuring Unused Upper Memory with Memory Managers."

Video RAM Memory. A video adapter installed in your system uses some of your system's memory to hold graphics or character information for display. Some adapters, like the VGA, also have on-board BIOS mapped into the system's space reserved for such types of adapters. Generally, the higher the resolution and color capabilities of the video adapter, the more system memory the video adapter uses. It is important to note that most VGA or Super VGA adapters have additional on-board memory that is used to handle the information currently displayed on the screen and to speed screen refresh.

In the standard system-memory map, a total of 128K is reserved for use by the video card to store currently displayed information. The reserved video memory is located in segments A000 and B000. The video adapter ROM uses additional upper memory space in segment C000.

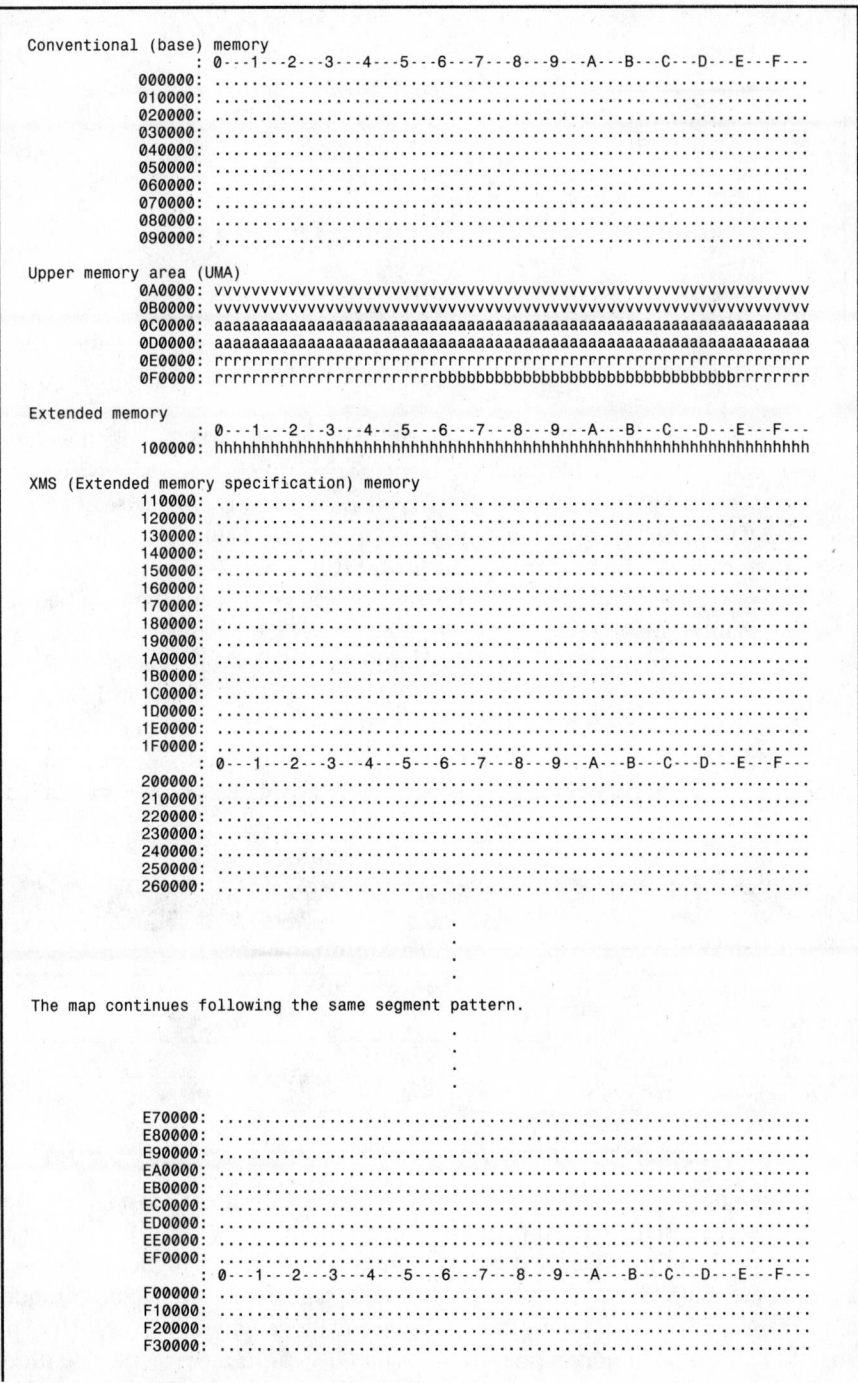

```
Conventional (base) memory
          : 0---1---2---3---4---5---6---7---8---9---A---B---C---D---E---F---
  000000: ................................................................
  010000: ................................................................
  020000: ................................................................
  030000: ................................................................
  040000: ................................................................
  050000: ................................................................
  060000: ................................................................
  070000: ................................................................
  080000: ................................................................
  090000: ................................................................
Upper memory area (UMA)
  0A0000: vvvvvvvvvvvvvvvvvvvvvvvvvvvvvvvvvvvvvvvvvvvvvvvvvvvvvvvvvvvvvvvvvv
  0B0000: vvvvvvvvvvvvvvvvvvvvvvvvvvvvvvvvvvvvvvvvvvvvvvvvvvvvvvvvvvvvvvvvvv
  0C0000: aaaaaaaaaaaaaaaaaaaaaaaaaaaaaaaaaaaaaaaaaaaaaaaaaaaaaaaaaaaaaaaaa
  0D0000: aaaaaaaaaaaaaaaaaaaaaaaaaaaaaaaaaaaaaaaaaaaaaaaaaaaaaaaaaaaaaaaaa
  0E0000: rrrrrrrrrrrrrrrrrrrrrrrrrrrrrrrrrrrrrrrrrrrrrrrrrrrrrrrrrrrrrrrrr
  0F0000: rrrrrrrrrrrrrrrrrrrrrrrrrrrrbbbbbbbbbbbbbbbbbbbbbbbbbbbbrrrrrrrrr
Extended memory
          : 0---1---2---3---4---5---6---7---8---9---A---B---C---D---E---F---
  100000: hhhhhhhhhhhhhhhhhhhhhhhhhhhhhhhhhhhhhhhhhhhhhhhhhhhhhhhhhhhhhhhhhh
XMS (Extended memory specification) memory
  110000: ................................................................
  120000: ................................................................
  130000: ................................................................
  140000: ................................................................
  150000: ................................................................
  160000: ................................................................
  170000: ................................................................
  180000: ................................................................
  190000: ................................................................
  1A0000: ................................................................
  1B0000: ................................................................
  1C0000: ................................................................
  1D0000: ................................................................
  1E0000: ................................................................
  1F0000: ................................................................
          : 0---1---2---3---4---5---6---7---8---9---A---B---C---D---E---F---
  200000: ................................................................
  210000: ................................................................
  220000: ................................................................
  230000: ................................................................
  240000: ................................................................
  250000: ................................................................
  260000: ................................................................
                          .
                          .
                          .
The map continues following the same segment pattern.
                          .
                          .
                          .
  E70000: ................................................................
  E80000: ................................................................
  E90000: ................................................................
  EA0000: ................................................................
  EB0000: ................................................................
  EC0000: ................................................................
  ED0000: ................................................................
  EE0000: ................................................................
  EF0000: ................................................................
          : 0---1---2---3---4---5---6---7---8---9---A---B---C---D---E---F---
  F00000: ................................................................
  F10000: ................................................................
  F20000: ................................................................
  F30000: ................................................................
```

Fig. 2.2 (continues)

The memory map on a system based on the 286 CPU chip.

```
         : 0---1---2---3---4---5---6---7---8---9---A---B---C---D---E---F---
 F00000:  ................................................................
 F10000:  ................................................................
 F20000:  ................................................................
 F30000:  ................................................................
 F40000:  ................................................................
 F50000:  ................................................................
 F60000:  ................................................................
 F70000:  ................................................................
 F80000:  ................................................................
 F90000:  ................................................................
 FA0000:  ................................................................
 FB0000:  ................................................................
 FC0000:  ................................................................
 FD0000:  ................................................................
 FE0000:  rrrrrrrrrrrrrrrrrrrrrrrrrrrrrrrrrrrrrrrrrrrrrrrrrrrrrrrrrrrrrrrr
 FF0000:  rrrrrrrrrrrrrrrrrrrrrrrrbbbbbbbbbbbbbbbbbbbbbbbbbbbbbbbbrrrrrrrrr
```

Fig. 2.2 (continued)

The location of video adapter RAM is responsible for the 640K DOS *conventional memory barrier*. DOS can use all available contiguous memory in the first megabyte—which means all—memory until the video adapter RAM is encountered. The use of adapters such as the MDA and CGA allows DOS access to more than 640K of system memory; the video memory *wall* begins at A0000 for the EGA, MCGA, and VGA systems but the MDA and CGA do not use as much video RAM, which leaves some space that can be used by DOS and programs. The previous figures show that the MDA adapter enables DOS to use an additional 64K of memory (all of segment A000), bringing the total for DOS program space to 704K. Similarly, the CGA enables a total of 736K of possible contiguous memory. The EGA, VGA, or MCGA is limited to the normal maximum of 640K of contiguous memory because of the larger amount used by video RAM. The maximum DOS-program memory workspace therefore depends on which video adapter is installed (see table 2.2).

Table 2.2 DOS Memory Limitations from Video Adapter	
Video adapter	**Maximum memory**
Monochrome Display Adapter (MDA)	704K
Color Graphics Adapter (CGA)	736K
Enhanced Graphics Adapter (EGA)	640K
Video Graphics Array (VGA)	640K
MultiColor Graphics Array (MCGA)	640K

Using this memory to 736K might be possible depending on the video adapter, the types of memory boards installed, ROM programs on the motherboard, and the type of system. You can use some of this memory if your system has an 80386 or higher processor. With special software, such as Quarterdeck's QEMM, that can operate these chips unique memory-management capabilities, you can remap extended memory to use this space. Systems that lack this memory-management capability cannot remap and use this memory. However, it is important to note that most application software is not designed to use the memory beyond 640K and will not attempt to locate itself or its data files in the area above the conventional memory barrier.

This section examines how standard video adapters use the system's memory. Figures 2.3 through 2.7 show where in a system the monochrome, EGA, VGA, and IBM PS/2 adapters use memory. Each symbol in these figures is equal to 1K of memory. This map is important because, although memory may be designated for use by a monochrome adapter, some VGA or Super VGA cards may use this space in order to speed their operation in interfaces like Windows or OS/2 or even in DOS.

Monochrome Display Adapter Memory (MDA). Figure 2.3 shows where the Monochrome Display Adapter (MDA) uses the system's memory. This adapter uses only a 4K portion of the reserved video RAM from B0000-B0FFF. Because the ROM code that is used to operate this adapter is actually a portion of the motherboard ROM, no additional ROM space is used in segment C000.

These symbols are used in figure 2.3:

.   Empty memory addresses

M   Monochrome Display Adapter (MDA) video RAM

```
        : 0---1---2---3---4---5---6---7---8---9---A---B---C---D---E---F---
  A0000: ................................................................
  B0000: MMMM............................................................
        : 0---1---2---3---4---5---6---7---8---9---A---B---C---D---E---F---
  C0000: ................................................................
  D0000: ................................................................
```

Fig. 2.3
The Monochrome card memory map.

Color Graphics Adapter (CGA) Memory. Figure 2.4 shows where the Color Graphics Adapter (CGA) uses the system's memory. The CGA uses a 16K portion of the reserved video RAM from B8000-BBFFF. Because the ROM code that is used to operate this adapter is a portion of the motherboard ROM, no additional ROM space is used in segment C000.

These symbols are used in figure 2.4:

.   Empty memory addresses

C   Color Graphics Adapter (CGA) video RAM

```
        : 0---1---2---3---4---5---6---7---8---9---A---B---C---D---E---F---
  A0000: ................................................................
  B0000: ................................CCCCCCCCCCCCCCCC................
        : 0---1---2---3---4---5---6---7---8---9---A---B---C---D---E---F---
  C0000: ................................................................
  D0000: ................................................................
```

Fig. 2.4
The CGA card memory map.

Enhanced Graphics Adapter (EGA) Memory. Figure 2.5 shows where the Enhanced Graphics Adapter (EGA) uses the systems memory. This adapter uses all 128K of the video RAM from A0000-BFFFF. The ROM code that is used to operate this adapter is on the adapter itself and consumes 16K of memory from C0000-C3FFF.

These symbols are used in figure 2.5:

.   Empty memory addresses

E   Enhanced Graphics Adapter (EGA) video RAM

R   Video adapter ROM BIOS addresses

```
      : 0---1---2---3---4---5---6---7---8---9---A---B---C---D---E---F---
A0000: EEEEEEEEEEEEEEEEEEEEEEEEEEEEEEEEEEEEEEEEEEEEEEEEEEEEEEEEEEEEEEEEEE
B0000: EEEEEEEEEEEEEEEEEEEEEEEEEEEEEEEEEEEEEEEEEEEEEEEEEEEEEEEEEEEEEEEEEE
      : 0---1---2---3---4---5---6---7---8---9---A---B---C---D---E---F---
C0000: RRRRRRRRRRRRRRRRR...............................................
D0000: ................................................................
```

Fig. 2.5
The EGA card memory map.

Video Graphics Array (VGA) Memory. Standard VGA (Video Graphics Array) cards use all 128K of the video RAM from A0000-BFFFF. Plus they use 32K of ROM memory space from C0000 to C7FFF. A standard VGA adapter memory map looks like figure 2.7.

PS/2 Adapter Memory. Figure 2.6 shows where the IBM PS/2 (Video Graphics Array) adapter uses system memory. The PS/2 adapter uses all of the 128K of video RAM from A0000-BFFFF. The ROM code that operates this adapter is on the adapter itself and consumes 24K of memory from C0000-C5FFF.

These symbols are used in figure 2.6:

.   Empty memory addresses

V   Video Graphics Array (VGA) or MultiColor Graphics Array (MCGA) video RAM

R   Video adapter ROM BIOS addresses

S   Scratch-pad memory

```
      : 0---1---2---3---4---5---6---7---8---9---A---B---C---D---E---F---
A0000: VVVVVVVVVVVVVVVVVVVVVVVVVVVVVVVVVVVVVVVVVVVVVVVVVVVVVVVVVVVVVVVVVV
B0000: VVVVVVVVVVVVVVVVVVVVVVVVVVVVVVVVVVVVVVVVVVVVVVVVVVVVVVVVVVVVVVVVVV
      : 0---1---2---3---4---5---6---7---8---9---A---B---C---D---E---F---
C0000: RRRRRRRRRRRRRRRRRRRRRRRRR..SSSSSS........SS......................
D0000: ................................................................
```

Fig. 2.6
IBM VGA card (PS/2 Display Adapter).

These symbols are used in figure 2.7:

.   Empty memory addresses

V   Video Graphics Array (VGA) or MultiColor Graphics Array (MCGA) video RAM

R   Video adapter ROM BIOS addresses

```
      : 0---1---2---3---4---5---6---7---8---9---A---B---C---D---E---F---
A0000: VVVVVVVVVVVVVVVVVVVVVVVVVVVVVVVVVVVVVVVVVVVVVVVVVVVVVVVVVVVVVVVVVV
B0000: VVVVVVVVVVVVVVVVVVVVVVVVVVVVVVVVVVVVVVVVVVVVVVVVVVVVVVVVVVVVVVVVVV
      : 0---1---2---3---4---5---6---7---8---9---A---B---C---D---E---F---
C0000: RRRRRRRRRRRRRRRRRRRRRRRRRRRRRRRRRRRRRR..........................
D0000: ................................................................
```

Fig. 2.7
Standard VGA card.

Note that the IBM PS/2 Display Adapter uses what is termed *scratch pad* memory, or additional memory. This memory use was not documented clearly in the technical-reference information for the adapter. In particular, the 2K of memory used at CA000 can cause problems with other cards if they are addressed in this area. If you try to install a hard disk controller with a 16K BIOS at C8000, for example, the system locks up during boot-up because of the conflict with the video-card memory. You can solve the problem by altering to D8000 the start address of the disk controller BIOS.

On PS/2 systems with the Video Graphics Array (VGA) or MultiColor Graphics Array (MCGA), the built-in display systems also use all 128K of the reserved video RAM space; because these display systems are built into the motherboard, however, the control BIOS code is built into the motherboard ROM BIOS and needs no space in segment C000. Figure 2.8 shows where such PS/2 systems use the system memory.

These symbols are used in figure 2.8:

.   Empty memory addresses

V   Video Graphics Array (VGA) or MultiColor Graphics Array (MCGA) video RAM.

```
A0000: VVVVVVVVVVVVVVVVVVVVVVVVVVVVVVVVVVVVVVVVVVVVVVVVVVVVVVVVVVVVVVVVVV
B0000: VVVVVVVVVVVVVVVVVVVVVVVVVVVVVVVVVVVVVVVVVVVVVVVVVVVVVVVVVVVVVVVVVV
      : 0---1---2---3---4---5---6---7---8---9---A---B---B---D---E---F---
C0000: ................................................................
D0000: ................................................................
```

Fig. 2.8
The PS/2 motherboard VGA and MCGA memory use.

As you can see in figures 2.3 to 2.8, each type of video adapter on the market uses two types of memory: video RAM, which stores the display information, and ROM code, which controls the adapter, must exist somewhere in the system's memory. The ROM code built into the motherboard ROM on standard PC and AT systems controls adapters such as the MDA and CGA. All the EGA and VGA adapters for the PC and AT systems use the full 128K of video RAM and some ROM space at the beginning of segment C000. IBM's technical-reference manuals say that the memory between C0000 and C7FFF is reserved specifically for ROM on video adapter boards. Note that the VGA and MCGA built into the motherboards of the PS/2 systems have the ROM-control software built into the motherboard ROM in segments E000 and F000 and require no other code space in segment C000.

Adapter ROM and Special Purpose RAM Memory. The second 128K of upper memory beginning at segment C000 is reserved for the software programs, or BIOS (basic input-output system), on the adapter boards plugged into the system slots. These BIOS programs are stored on special chips known as read-only memory (ROM), which have fused circuits so that the PC cannot alter them. ROM is useful for permanent programs that always must be present while the system is running. Graphics boards, hard disk controllers, communications boards, and expanded memory boards, for example, are adapter boards that might use some of this memory.

On systems based on the 386 CPU chip or higher, memory managers like QEMM or the DOS 6 MEMMAKER can load device drivers and memory resident programs into unused areas of the adapter BIOS area of upper memory. Some memory managers, such as QEMM, also can remap the BIOS of some adapters to more efficiently make use of this adapter BIOS memory area.

Video Adapter BIOS. Although 128K of upper memory beginning at segment C000 is reserved for use by the video adapter BIOS, not all of this space is used by various video adapters commonly found on PCs. The following details the amount of space used by the BIOS on each type of common video adapter card:

Type of Adapter	Adapter BIOS Memory Used
Monochrome Display Adapter (MDA)	None
Color Graphics Adapter (CGA)	None
Enhanced Graphics Adapter (EGA)	16K from C0000-to-C3FFF
Video Graphics Array (VGA)	32K from C0000-to-C7FFF

Some of the more advanced graphics accelerator cards on the market do use most or all of the 128K of upper memory beginning at segment C000 in order to speed the repainting of graphics displays in Windows, OS/2 or other graphical user interfaces (GUIs). In addition, these graphics cards may contain 2M of onboard memory in which to store currently displayed data and more quickly fetch new screen data as it is sent to the display by the CPU.

Hard Disk Controller BIOS. The upper memory addresses C000-to-D000 also are used for the BIOS contained on hard drive controllers. The following details the amount of memory and the addresses commonly used by the BIOS contained on hard drive adapter cards:

Adapter Type	Memory Use
XT 10M hard drive	8K at C8000
XT 20M hard drive	4K at C8000
ESDI	16K at C8000
Other hard drive controllers	16K at C8000

The hard drive adapter card used on a particular system may use a different amount of memory, but it is most likely to use the memory segment beginning at C800 since this address is considered part of the IBM standard for personal computers.

Network Adapter BIOS. Network adapter cards also use upper memory in segments C000 and D000. The exact amount of memory used, and the starting address for each network card varies with the type and manufacturer of the card. The following details some common types of network cards and the amout of memory and the addresses commonly used by their BIOS:

Network Card	Memory Use
Token Ring adapter ROM	8K at CC000
Token Ring adapter RAM	16K at D8000

Other ROMs in the Upper Memory Area. In addition to the BIOS for hard drive controllers and network cards, upper memory segments C000 and D000 are used by SCSI (small computer system interface) devices, sound boards, memory boards, and various other devices and adapter boards. For example, LIM expanded memory boards require 64K at D000. Some adapters may require memory only for BIOS information and others may require RAM in these upper memory segments. For information on a specific adapter, consult the manufacturer's documentation.

Motherboard BIOS Memory. The last 128K of reserved memory is used by the motherboard BIOS, (the basic input-output system, which is stored in a read-only RAM chip or ROM). The BIOS programs in ROM control the system during the boot-up procedure. Because these programs must be available immediately, they cannot be loaded from a device like a disk drive. In other words, the BIOS fare located in a read-only chip is responsible for controlling the system until the point at which DOS takes over. The main functions of the programs stored in the motherboard ROM are listed in the following:

■ *Power-On Self Test*, the POST, is a set of routines that tests the motherboard, memory, disk controllers, video adapters, keyboard, and other primary system components. This routine is useful when you troubleshoot system failures or problems.

■ The *basic input-output system* (BIOS) is the software interface, or master control program, to all the hardware in the system. With the ROM BIOS, a program easily can access features in the system by calling a ROM BIOS program module instead of talking directly to the device.

■ The *bootstrap loader* routine initiates a search for an operating system on a floppy disk or hard disk. If an operating system is found, it is loaded into memory and given control of the system.

Both segments E000 and F000 in the memory map are considered reserved for the motherboard ROM-BIOS, but only AT systems actually use this entire area. PC systems require only segment F000 and enable adapter card ROM or RAM to make use of segment E000. This information might be important when you attempt to install an adapter into a system that already has a full complement of other boards using memory in segments C000 and D000.

One thing that can be confusing is the difference between a segment address and a full address. For example, on a PS/2 system, a SCSI host adapter might have 16K ROM on the card addressed from D4000 to D7FFF. These numbers expressed in segment:offset form are D400:0000 to D700:0FFF. The segment portion is composed of the most significant four digits, and the offset portion is composed of the least significant four digits. Because each portion overlaps by one digit, the ending address of ts ROM can be expressed in four different ways:

    D000:7FFF = D0000+07FFF = D7FFF

    D700:0FFF = D7000+00FFF = D7FFF

    D7F0:00FF = D7F00+000FF = D7FFF

    D7FF:000F = D7FF0+0000F = D7FFF

Adding together the segment and offset numbers makes possible even more combinations:

    D500:2FFF = D5000+02FFF = D7FFF

    D6EE:111F = D6EE0+0111F = D7FFF

As you can see, several combinations are possible. The correct and generally accepted way to write this address is either D7FFF or D700:0FFF.

Many different ROM-interface programs are in the IBM motherboards, but the location of these programs is mostly consistent. Figures 2.9 through 2.12 show the memory use in segments E000 and F000.

Figure 2.9 shows the memory use in an IBM PC and XT with a 256K motherboard.

These symbols are used in figure 2.9:

    .   Empty memory addresses

    b   IBM ROM Cassette BASIC

    R   Motherboard ROM BIOS (CBIOS, for Compatibility BIOS)

    x   Decoded by motherboard (unavailable)

```
       : 0---1---2---3---4---5---6---7---8---9---A---B---C---D---E---F---
E0000: ................................................................
F0000: xxxxxxxxxxxxxxxxxxxxxxxxxxxbbbbbbbbbbbbbbbbbbbbbbbbbbbbbbbbbRRRRRRRR
       : 0---1---2---3---4---5---6---7---8---9---A---B---C---D---E---F---
```

Fig. 2.9

ROM-BIOS memory use in an IBM PC and XT with 256K.

Figure 2.10 shows the memory use in an XT with a 640K motherboard and in the PS/2
Model 25 and Model 30. These systems have additional BIOS code compared to the original PC and XT. Note that Cassette BASIC remains in the same addresses.

These symbols are used in figure 2.10:

.   Empty memory addresses (unavailable)

x   Empty memory decoded by motherboard (unavailable)

R   Video adapter ROM BIOS addresses

```
       : 0---1---2---3---4---5---6---7---8---9---A---B---C---D---E---F---
E0000: xxxxxxxxxxxxxxxxxxxxxxxxxxxxxxxxxxxxxxxxxxxxxxxxxxxxxxxxxxxxxxxxxx
F0000: RRRRRRRRRRRRRRRRRRRRRRRRRRbbbbbbbbbbbbbbbbbbbbbbbbbbbbbbbbbRRRRRRRR
```

Fig. 2.10

ROM-BIOS memory use in IBM XT and PS/2 Models 25 and 30 with a 640K.

Figure 2.11 shows the memory use in an IBM XT-286 and AT. Note that the system board
decodes segment E000 even though no code is there, because this area was planned for
future ROM expansion; the expansion was implemented later, in the PS/2 systems, for a
protected-mode BIOS called ABIOS (for Advanced BIOS).

These symbols are used in figure 2.11:

.   Empty memory (available for other uses)

R   Video adapter ROM BIOS addresses

b   IBM ROM Cassette BASIC

```
       : 0---1---2---3---4---5---6---7---8---9---A---B---C---D---E---F---
E0000: ................................................................
F0000: xxxxxxxxxxxxxxxxxxxxxxxxxxxxxxxxxxxxRRRRRRRRRRRRRRRRRRRRRRRRRRRRRRR
```

Fig. 2.11

ROM-BIOS memory use in an IBM XT-286 and AT.

IBM-Compatible ROM-BIOS. Systems produced by IBM and other companies have
different BIOS software installed in ROM. How close in function this software is to what
IBM has is a critical issue with any IBM-compatible. The ROM-BIOS software must duplicate the functionality of the programs contained in an IBM ROM in order for software to

run on the systems as it would on an equivalent IBM system. Fortunately, this software has been relatively easy to duplicate functionally. Modern compatibles are at no real disadvantage.

Figure 2.12 shows the ROM-BIOS memory use in most PC- or XT-compatible systems. These systems lack the Cassette BASIC found in IBM's BIOS.

These symbols are used in figure 2.12:

> x   Empty memory decoded by motherboard (unavailable)
>
> R   Motherboard ROM BIOS (CBIOS: Compatibility BIOS)
>
> b   IBM ROM Cassette BASIC

```
        : 0---1---2---3---4---5---6---7---8---9---A---B---C---D---E---F---
E0000: ...............................................................
F0000: RRRRRRRRRRRRRRRRRRRRRRRRRRRRbbbbbbbbbbbbbbbbbbbbbbbbbbbbbbbRRRRRRRR
```

Fig. 2.12
ROM-BIOS memory use in most PC- or XT-compatibles.

The ROM-BIOS memory use of most AT-compatible systems is shown in Figure 2.13.

These symbols are used in figure 2.13:

> x   Empty memory decoded by motherboard (unavailable)
>
> R   Motherboard ROM BIOS (CBIOS-Compatibility BIOS)

```
        : 0---1---2---3---4---5---6---7---8---9---A---B---C---D---E---F---
E0000: xxxxxxxxxxxxxxxxxxxxxxxxxxxxxxxxxxxxxxxxxxxxxxxxxxxxxxxxxxxxxx
F0000: RRRRRRRRRRRRRRRRRRRRRRRRRRRRRRRRRRRRRRRRRRRRRRRRRRRRRRRRRRRRRRRRRR
```

Fig. 2.13
ROM-BIOS memory use of most AT-compatible systems.

IBM PS/2 ROM-BIOS. ROM-BIOS memory usage on PS/2 Model 25 and Model 30 are shown previously, in figure 2.10. The ROM-BIOS memory use by PS/2 models with a 286 or higher processor, including ISA and MCA systems, is shown in table 2.14. Figure 2.14 shows that PS/2 systems use more of the allocated ROM space for their motherboard ROM BIOS. Segment E000 contains the Advanced BIOS (ABIOS), used in protected mode.

These symbols are used in figure 2.14:

> A   Advanced ROM BIOS (ABIOS: for protected-mode operation)
>
> R   Motherboard ROM BIOS (CBIOS: Compatibility BIOS)
>
> b   IBM ROM Cassette BASIC

```
         : 0---1---2---3---4---5---6---7---8---9---A---B---C---D---E---F---
   E0000: AAAAAAAAAAAAAAAAAAAAAAAAAAAAAAAAAAAAAAAAAAAAAAAAAAAAAAAAAAAAAAAAAA
   F0000: RRRRRRRRRRRRRRRRRRRRRRRRRRRbbbbbbbbbbbbbbbbbbbbbbbbbbbbbbbRRRRRRRR
```

Fig. 2.14
ROM-BIOS memory in 286 or higher PS/2s (ISA and MCA).

The PS/2 Models with 286 and higher processors each have an additional 64K of Advanced BIOS code, to be used when the systems are running protected-mode software, used by powerful operating systems such as OS/2. IBM has not placed all real mode BIOS code in segment F000 and protected-mode BIOS in segment E000, as one might imagine. The code in segment E000 in these systems is both Advanced BIOS (protected mode only) code and real mode. Similarly, Advanced BIOS and real mode code are distributed throughout segment F000. Earlier AT systems, which don't have the Advanced BIOS code, can run OS/2 but must load the equivalent of the Advanced BIOS software from disk rather than having it loaded from ROM.

Some compatible systems with a SCSI hard disk and host adapter need a special protected-mode driver in order for the adapter to work under OS/2, because the on-board BIOS runs in only real mode and not in protected mode. IBM SCSI adapters, however, include both real- and protected-mode BIOS software on-board, and operate hard disks under any operating system with no need for drivers.

IBM Cassette Basic. It may come as something of a surprise to some personal computer users, but before IBM systems supported a hard drive, they supported the loading of programs and data to or from a cassette tape recorder plugged into the cassette port on the back of an original of the system. The ROM maps of most IBM-compatibles equal the IBM system with which they are compatible, the exception being the Cassette BASIC portion, a special Microsoft version designed for the original IBM PC, with built-in ROM to enable diskless operation. Because no IBM system after the original PC (and virtually no compatible) has a cassette port (although all have the Cassette BASIC interpreter in ROM), this type of BASIC language interpreter by itself is useless. The disk version of BASIC from IBM uses Cassette BASIC as an overlay to save the duplication of the software code on the disk; IBM's BASICA.COM expects to find Cassette BASIC in ROM and does not work without it. Because no compatible system has Cassette BASIC in ROM, none will run IBM's BASICA.COM program from the PC DOS disk.

If you have a non-IBM system, you must get from your system's manufacturer an equivalent version of Microsoft BASIC called GW-BASIC (Graphics Workstation BASIC). The GWBASIC.EXE file has the equivalent program code of the IBM BASICA.COM file and enables interpreted BASIC programs to run exactly as they would on an IBM system.

DOS 5 and later versions from IBM still include the BASICA interpreter; however, non-IBM versions with the generic Microsoft MS-DOS no longer include the GW-BASIC interpreter. All DOS 5 and higher versions (IBM and others) have a crippled version of the Microsoft QuickBASIC Compiler. The compiler is crippled so that you can compile programs in memory but not create EXE files on disk. To do so, you must purchase a copy of QuickBASIC.

Extended Memory. As mentioned previously in this chapter, the memory map on a system based on the 286 CPU chip or higher can extend beyond the 1-megabyte boundary. On a 286 the extended memory limit is 16M; on a 386 or higher the extended memory limit is 4G (4096M). Figure 2.2, earlier in this chapter, shows the memory map for an AT-type system (286) with 16M of memory.

For an AT system to be able to address memory beyond the first megabyte, the processor must be in *protected mode*, the native mode of these processors. On a 286, only programs designed to run in protected mode can take advantage of extended memory. But 386 and higher processors offer another mode, called *virtual real mode*, which enables extended memory to be, in effect, chopped into 1 megabyte pieces (each with its own copy of DOS) and for several programs to run at once in these protected areas of memory. Although several DOS programs may be running at once, each still is limited to a maximum of 640K of memory (primarily because DOS programs are written to use only this amount of memory). Running several programs at once in virtual real mode, which is termed *multi-tasking*, requires software that can manage each program, keeping them from crashing into one another. Windows and DesqVIEW are two examples of such multitasking environments.

The 80286 and higher CPU chips also run in what is termed *real mode*, which enables full compatibility with the 8088 CPU chip installed on the PC/XT-type computer. Real mode enables you to run DOS programs one at a time on an AT-type system just like you would on a PC/XT. However, an AT-type system running in real mode, particularly a 386-, 486-, or Pentium-based system, is really functioning as little more than a turbo PC. The 80286 can emulate the 8086 or 8088, but it cannot operate in protected mode at the same time it is doing so.

XMS Memory. The extended memory specification (XMS) was developed in 1987 by Microsoft, Intel, AST Corp., and Lotus Development to specify how programs would use the memory in excess of 1M. The XMS specification functions on systems based on the 286 CPU chip or higher and allows real mode programs (those designed to run in DOS) to use extended memory and another block of memory usually out of the reach of DOS.

Extended memory can be made to conform to the XMS specification by installing a device driver in the CONFIG.SYS file. The most common XMS driver is HIMEM.SYS, which is included with Windows and recent versions of DOS, including DOS 6.0. Other memory managers, like QEMM, also convert extended memory into XMS-specification memory when you add their device drivers to CONFIG.SYS.

High Memory Area (HMA). An area of memory 64K in size minus 16 bytes at the beginning of the first megabyte of extended memory is termed the High Memory Area (HMA). It can be used by memory managers to load device drivers and memory resident programs, to free up conventional memory for use by real mode programs. Only one device driver or memory resident program can be loaded into HMA at one time, no matter its size.

The HMA area is extremely important to those who use DOS 5.0 or 6.0 because these DOS versions can move their own kernal (about 40K of program instructions) into this area if you load an XMS driver and add the line DOS=HIGH to your CONFIG.SYS. Taking advantage of this DOS capability frees another 40K of conventional memory for use by real mode programs.

Expanded Memory. Some systems incorporate *expanded memory*. Unlike conventional (the first megabyte) or extended (the second through 16th megabytes) memory, expanded memory is *not* directly addressable by the processor except through a small 64K window. Expanded memory is a segment-switching scheme in which a memory adapter has on-board a large number of 64K segments. The system uses one available segment to map into the board. After this 64K is filled with data, the board rotates the filled segment out and a new, empty one in to take its place.

Segment D000 in the first megabyte usually is used for mapping. Lotus, Intel, and Microsoft—founders of the LIM specification for expanded memory (LIM EMS)—decided to use this segment because it is largely unused by most adapters. Programs must be written specially to take advantage of this segment-swapping scheme, and then only data normally can be placed in this segment because it is above the area of contiguous memory (640K) that DOS can use. For example, a program cannot run while it is swapped out and therefore not visible by the processor. This type of memory generally is useful only in systems that do not have extended (processor-addressable) memory available to them.

To convert extended memory to LIM EMS, you must load a device driver in your CONFIG.SYS file. The expanded memory driver EMM386.EXE is included with DOS versions 5.0 and 6.0. Previous DOS versions also include expanded memory drivers.

Preventing ROM-BIOS Memory Conflicts and Overlap. As detailed in previous sections, C000 and D000 are reserved for use by adapter-board ROM and RAM. Table 2.3 is provided to enable you to see at a glance how typical adapter boards use space in these segments.

Table 2.3 Default Memory Use of Various Adapter Boards	
Adapter	**Memory Use**
IBM EGA ROM	16K at C0000
IBM PS/2 (VGA) display adapter ROM	24K at C0000
IBM PS/2 (VGA) display adapter scratch RAM	24K at CA000
Most other EGA/VGA adapter ROMs	32K at C0000
IBM XT 10M hard disk controller ROM	8K at C8000
IBM XT 20M hard disk controller ROM	4K at C8000
IBM ESDI fixed disk adapter/A	16K at C8000
Most other hard disk controller ROMs	16K at C8000
Token Ring network adapter ROM	8K at CC000
Token Ring network adapter RAM	16K at D8000
LIM expanded memory adapter RAM	64K at D0000

Note that some of the listed adapter boards would use the same memory addresses as other boards, which is not allowed in a single system. If two adapters have overlapping ROM or RAM addresses, usually neither board operates properly. Each board functions if you remove or disable the other one, but they do not work together.

With many adapter boards you can change the actual memory locations to be used with jumpers, switches, or driver software, which might be necessary to allow two boards to coexist in one system. This type of conflict can cause problems for troubleshooters. If you install a Token Ring network card and an Intel Above Board (an EMS board) and then follow the factory-set default configuration with each one, neither adapter card works in the same system. You must read the documentation for each adapter to find out what memory addresses the adapter uses and how to change the addresses to allow coexistence with another adapter. Most of the time, you can work around these problems by reconfiguring the board or changing jumpers, switch settings, or software-driver parameters. For the Token Ring card, you can change the software-driver parameters in the CONFIG.SYS file to move the memory the card uses from D8000 to something closer to C4000. This change enables the two boards to coexist and stay out of each others way.

The LIM EMS specification normally uses the entire segment D000 for expanded memory. The use of segment D000 by the LIM EMS cuts in half the amount of available ROM and RAM space for other adapters, forcing many adapters, such as the Token Ring network adapter, to be reconfigured so that their memory use excludes this segment.

Additionally, you must ensure that adapter boards do not use the same IRQ (interrupt request line) or DMA (direct memory access) channel. An IRQ is a hardware signal used by devices like the mouse and modem to signal the processor that the device needs CPU time and divert it temporarily to another process. As mentioned previously, the PC/XT-type system provides 8 interrupt request lines (IRQs) and AT-type systems have 15. No two devices can use the same interrupt at the same time. This becomes a problem only when you attempt to configure two devices, such as a modem and a mouse, to use the same IRQ. For example, COM1 normally uses IRQ 4. If you configure a modem to use COM1 and configure a mouse to use IRQ 4 at the same time, the two devices will conflict. Similarly, if you configure two devices to use the same DMA channel, one or both of the devices will not work properly.

You can easily avoid adapter board memory, IRQ and DMA channel conflicts by creating a chart or template to mock up the system's memory, IRQ and DMA channel configuration by penciling on the template the resources already used by each installed adapter. You end up with a picture of the system's memory, IRQ and DMA channel layout and the relationship of each adapter. This procedure helps you anticipate conflicts and ensures that you configure each adapter board correctly the first time. The template also becomes important documentation when you consider new adapter purchases. New adapters incorporating a ROM that the system must recognize must fit in the available workspace and if it uses IRQs or DMA channels, it must be configurable for those IRQs and DMA channels that are available.

Shadow RAM and ROM. Computers based on the 386 or higher CPU chip, which provide memory access on a 32- or 64-bit path, often use a 16-bit data path for system ROM-BIOS information. In addition, adapter cards with onboard BIOS may use an 8-bit path to system memory. On these high-end computers, using a 16- or 8-bit path to memory is a significant bottleneck to system performance.

Some computers enable you to use what is termed shadow memory for system ROM-BIOS and adapter card BIOS. Shadowing essentially moves the programming code from slow ROM chips into fast 32-bit system memory. In addition, some adapters, such as video cards, often include software device drivers that can move their BIOS from the slow ROM chip into system memory. Using shadow RAM on a system equipped for it can greatly speed up these BIOS routines—sometimes making them four to five times faster.

Total Installed Memory versus Total Usable Memory. It is not uncommon on a system that uses numerous memory resident programs and device drivers that instead of having nearly 640K of conventional memory available to DOS programs, the system instead has only 500K of available conventional memory, or even less. This problem is caused by the fact that each memory resident program and device driver you load in CONFIG.SYS and AUTOEXEC.BAT, the two text files that specify the programs loaded on system bootup, uses conventional memory. In addition, DOS itself uses conventional memory to store its own programming code.

It is not uncommon for computer users to fiddle endlessly with their CONFIG.SYS and AUTOEXEC.BAT files in an attempt to free up as much conventional memory as possible, and some computer users even use special utilities to keep track of different combinations of CONFIG.SYS and AUTOEXEC.BAT files that load different device drivers and memory resident programs only when they are needed.

One way to free up conventional memory, of course, is to remove from your CONFIG.SYS and AUTOEXEC.BAT files all but the most essential device drivers and memory resident programs. For example, removing ANSI.SYS from your CONFIG.SYS file would free up a small amount of conventional memory for use by DOS programs.

A solution to the problem of RAM-cram that is more acceptable to most computer users who have systems based on the 386 or higher CPU chip is to use a memory manager like the DOS 6.0 MEMMAKER utility, or Quarterdeck's QEMM to move device drivers and memory resident programs into available upper memory, thus freeing the conventional memory these drivers would use. In addition, DOS 5.0 and 6.0 enable you to use the command DOS=HIGH in your CONFIG.SYS to free-up as much as 40K of conventional memory by moving part of the DOS programming code into the HMA area.

Wasted Memory. A pragmatic view of conventional memory is that every byte of this 640K is so precious for running DOS programs, that any memory used by device drivers and memory resident programs that are not currently being used by the system is wasted memory. In other words, if you run Windows most of the time, and you also load MOUSE.COM in your AUTOEXEC.BAT, the memory used by MOUSE.COM would be considered wasted memory. This situation is because Windows does not need MOUSE.COM in order for the mouse to work properly in Windows programs, although a mouse driver is needed if you plan to use the mouse in DOS programs running under Windows.

Even if your view of conventional memory is not as strict as this pragmatic view, it is reasonable to consider as wasted memory any RAM used by device drivers or memory resident programs that are rarely needed by your system. For example, ANSI.SYS, a DOS device driver used to add color to batch files and other screens, as well as remap the keys on your keyboard, is generally not needed because most people will never want to remap their keyboard and DOS programs do not require ANSI.SYS to provide color. In other words, WordPerfect 6.0 will display its screens in color regardless of whether you have ANSI.SYS loaded in CONFIG.SYS.

It is a good idea any time you receive an out-of-memory error message to take a fresh look at your CONFIG.SYS and AUTOEXEC.BAT files with an eye toward removing device drivers and memory resident programs that are not absolutely essential. In addition, if you load pop-up programs in AUTOEXEC.BAT like SideKick or a similar utility, you should give thought to the idea of running these programs in non-memory-resident mode where available. By adding the directory of such programs to your DOS path, you can launch these type programs whenever you need them, but they will not be using system memory when they aren't being used.

Adapter Memory Configuration and Optimization. Ideally, adapter boards would be simple "plug-and-play" devices that would require you to merely plug the adapter into a motherboard slot and then use them. However, sometimes it almost seems that adapter boards (except on EISA and MCA systems) are designed as if they were the only adapter likely to be present on a system. Rather than adapter boards being plug-and-plays, they usually require you to know the upper memory addresses, IRQ lines and DMA channels already on your system and then to configure the new adapter so it will not conflict with your already-installed adapters.

Adapter boards use upper memory for their BIOS and as working RAM. If two boards attempt to use the same BIOS area or RAM area of upper memory, there is a conflict of the type that can keep your system from booting. The following sections cover ways to avoid these potential conflicts, and how to troubleshoot them if they do occur. In addition, these sections discuss moving adapter memory to resolve conflicts and provide some ideas on optimizing adapter memory use.

Adding adapters to EISA and MCA systems is somewhat more simple because these system architecture feature what is termed auto-configure adapter boards. In other words, EISA and MCA systems work with adapters to determine available upper memory addresses, IRQs and DMA channels and automatically configure all adapters to work optimally together.

How To Determine What Adapters Occupy Upper Memory Space. There are two basic ways to determine what adapters are using space in upper memory. They are listed in the following:

■ Study the documentation for each adapter on your system to determine the memory addresses they use.

■ Use a software utility that can quickly determine for you what upper memory areas your adapters are using.

The most simple way (although by no means always the most foolproof) is to use a software utility to determine the upper memory areas used by the adapters installed on your system. One such utility, MSD.EXE, comes with Windows 3.1 and MS-DOS 6.0. This utility examines your system configuration and determines not only the upper memory used by your adapters, but also the IRQs used by each of these adapters. Other utilities that accomplish the same task are available, although if you have Windows 3.1 or MS-DOS 6.0, there is no need to purchase a utility package simply to gain this diagnostic capability.

> **Note**
>
> If you have used MSD or another utility to determine the upper memory and IRQs used by your adapters, but still cannot isolate the problem, the next step is to study the documentation for the conflicting adapters. Comparing the memory, IRQ, and DMA needs of one adapter with the other should reveal a potential conflict.

Once you have run MSD or another utility to determine your system's upper memory configuration, make a printout of the memory addresses used by your adapters as well as the IRQs they use. Thereafter, you can quickly refer to the printout when you are adding a new adapter to ensure that the new board will not conflict with any devices already installed on your system.

Moving Adapter Memory to Resolve Conflicts. Once you have identified a conflict or potential conflict by studying the documentation for the adapter boards installed on your system or using a software diagnostic utility to determine the upper memory addresses, IRQs, and DMA channels used by all your adapter boards, you may have to reconfigure one or more of your adapters to move the upper memory space (as well as the IRQs and DMA channels) used by a problem adapter.

Most adapter boards make moving adapter memory a somewhat simple process, enabling you to change a few jumpers or switches in order to reconfigure the board to use available memory, IRQs, and DMA channels. The following steps will help you resolve nearly any conflict that arises because adapter boards conflict with one another:

1. Determine the upper memory addresses, IRQs and DMA channels used by all your adapter boards and write them down.

2. Determine the overlapping memory addresses, IRQs, or DMA channels used by your adapters.

3. Consult the documentation for your adapter boards to determine which boards can be reconfigured so that all adapters will have access to unique memory addresses, IRQs, or DMA channels.

4. Configure the affected adapter boards so that there is no conflict in memory addresses, IRQs, or DMA channels.

For example, if one adapter used the upper memory range C8000-CBFFF and another adapter used the range CA000-CBFFF you would have a potential address conflict. Similarly, if a bus mouse adapter were configured for COM1 and IRQ 4 and your modem also were configured for COM1 and IRQ 4, you would have a conflict if both the modem and mouse were to be used at the same time. If your sound board uses DMA channel 3 and another device also uses DMA channel 3, this conflict could lockup your system, and even threaten the integrity of any unsaved data when both devices were in use at the same time. In the case of the conflict between the mouse and modem, it would be a simple matter to change the jumpers on the bus mouse adapter to use COM2 and IRQ3 and thereby resolve the conflict. Of course, if COM2 or IRQ 3 were already in use by another adapter board, you would be faced with a dilemma: how to run all three devices without conflict. This problem is covered in Chapter 7, "Primary System Components."

Optimizing Adapter Memory Use. On an ideal PC, adapter boards would always come configured so that the upper memory addresses they use would meet the upper memory addresses used by the next adapter, but with no overlap that would cause conflicts. Such an upper memory arrangement would not only be "cleaner," but would make it much more simple to use available upper memory for loading device drivers and memory resident programs. However, this is not the case. Adapter boards often leave gaps of unused memory between one another, which is, of course, preferable to an overlap, but still is not the best use of upper memory.

Someone who wanted to make the most of their upper memory might consider studying the documentation for each adapter board installed on their system to determine if there were a way to compact the upper memory used by each of these devices. For example, if it were possible on a particular system, using the adapters installed on it, it could make the use of upper memory more simple if you configured your adapter boards so that the blocks of memory they use fit together like bricks in a wall, rather than like a slice of swiss cheese, as is the case on most systems.

Taking Advantage of Unused Upper Memory. On systems based on the 386 or higher CPU chip, memory resident programs and device drivers can be moved into the upper memory area by using a memory manager like the DOS 6.0 MEMMAKER or Quarterdeck's QEMM (version 7.01 or later). These memory management utilities examine the memory resident programs and device drivers installed on your system, and determine their memory needs, and then calculate the best way to move these drivers and programs into upper memory, thus freeing the conventional memory they used.

Using MEMMAKER and QEMM is quite simple. Make a backup of your CONFIG.SYS and AUTOEXEC.BAT files so you will have usable copies if you need them to restore your system configuration and then run either MEMMAKER from the DOS prompt or use the installation program on the QEMM diskette. Both programs install required device drivers in your CONFIG.SYS file and then begin optimizing your memory configuration.

Both do an outstanding job of freeing up conventional memory, although QEMM 7.01 can free considerably more conventional memory than any other memory management utility available as of this writing.

The following sections cover using memory management software to optimize conventional memory, as well as additional ways to configure your system memory to make your system run as efficiently as possible. It is important to note that the DOS HIMEM.SYS and EMM386.EXE play an integral role in MEMMAKER's ability to move device drivers and memory resident programs into upper memory. Such use of HIMEM.SYS and EMM386.EXE is covered in the section titled, "MS-DOS 6 MEMMAKER." The next two sections describe using HIMEM.SYS and EMM386.EXE to configure extended and expanded memory.

Using HIMEM.SYS (DOS). The DOS device driver HIMEM.SYS, which is included with Windows and recent versions of DOS including 4.0 and higher, is used to configure extended memory to the XMS specification. HIMEM.SYS is installed by adding a line invoking the device driver to your CONFIG.SYS file. Other memory managers, like QEMM, also convert extended memory into XMS-specification memory.

The XMS extended memory specification was developed by Microsoft, Intel, AST Corp., and Lotus Development in 1987 and specifies how programs may use memory beyond the first megabyte on systems based on the 286 CPU chip or higher. The XMS specification also allows real mode programs (those designed to run in DOS) to use extended memory.

Using EMM386.EXE (DOS). The program EMM386.EXE, which is included with MS-DOS 5.0 and 6.0, is used to convert all or part of the extended memory on a system to EMS version 4 memory, which can then be used by programs that need expanded memory. Earlier versions of DOS include other expanded memory drivers.

The EMM386.EXE program can be used from the DOS command prompt to create expanded memory as needed, and it can be turned off when the program that uses expanded memory is no longer being used. For more information on using EMM386.EXE to convert extended memory to expanded, consult Que's *Using MS-DOS 6* or your DOS manual.

MS-DOS 6 MEMMAKER. You can increase the amount of conventional memory available to software applications on systems based on the 386 CPU chip and above by running the DOS 6.0 utility MEMMAKER. In DOS 6.0 (as well as DOS 5.0), loading device drivers and memory resident programs into upper memory can result in more than 600K of free conventional memory because part of the DOS kernal, or program code, also can be moved from conventional memory. DOS 6.0 includes a special utility, MEMMAKER, which automatically performs the task of loading device drivers and memory resident programs into UMBs.

Over the course of months or years of use, the installation programs for various software utilities often install so many memory resident programs and device drivers in your AUTOEXEC.BAT and CONFIG.SYS files that you have too little conventional memory left to start all the programs you want to run. You may want to use MEMMAKER to free up more conventional memory for your programs. When you run the MEMMAKER utility, it automatically performs the following functions in order to free up more memory:

- Maps unused areas of reserved memory as *upper memory blocks*, or UMBs, into which MEMMAKER can then load device drivers and memory resident programs to free up the conventional memory these drivers and programs otherwise would use.

- Moves memory resident programs and device drivers into UMBs

- Moves the DOS kernal into the high memory area (HMA)

Before running MEMMAKER, it is a good idea to carefully examine your CONFIG.SYS and AUTOEXEC.BAT files to identify unnecessary device drivers and memory resident programs. For example, the DOS device driver ANSI.SYS is often loaded in CONFIG.SYS to enable you to use color in batch files and other DOS screens or remap the keys on your keyboard. Unless you frequently use ANSI.SYS to remap the keys on your keyboard, chances are you would be better off by removing ANSI.SYS from your CONFIG.SYS file to free up the memory the driver is using. Nearly all programs provide color screens without using ANSI.SYS.

Once you have stripped down CONFIG.SYS and AUTOEXEC.BAT to their bare essentials, and made backup copies of these important configuration files, you are ready to run MEMMAKER to optimize your system memory. To run MEMMAKER, exit from any other programs you are running, start your network or any memory resident programs and device drivers you absolutely need, and at the DOS prompt, type the following:

```
MEMMAKER
```

The MEMMAKER setup runs in two modes—Express and Custom. Express setup is preferable for those people who want to enable MEMMAKER to load device drivers and memory resident programs into high memory with the minimum amount of user input, unless they have an EGA or VGA (but not a Super VGA) monitor. If you have an EGA or VGA monitor, choose Custom Setup and answer Yes in the advanced options screen where it asks whether MemMaker should use monochrome region (B000-B7FF) for running programs. You should use the defaults for the rest of the options in Custom Setup unless you are sure that one of the defaults is not correct for your system. Custom setup is wrong for your system unless you are an expert on running MEMMAKER, or are knowledgable about optimizing system memory and particular device drivers and memory resident programs on the system.

When MEMMAKER has finished optimizing the system memory, the following three lines will have been added to CONFIG.SYS:

```
DEVICE=EMM386.EXE
```

```
DEVICE=HIMEM.SYS

DOS=HIGH,UMB
```

In addition, MEMMAKER will have modified each line in CONFIG.SYS and AUTOEXEC.BAT that loads a device driver or memory resident program now being loaded into UMBs. Various DEVICE= lines in your CONFIG.SYS have been changed to DEVICEHIGH= and various lines in your AUTOEXEC.BAT will have the LH command inserted in front of them. For example, the line DEVICE=ANSI.SYS will be changed to DEVICEHIGH=ANSI.SYS. In your AUTOEXEC.BAT, lines like C:\MOUSE\MOUSE.COM will be changed to LH C:\MOUSE\MOUSE.COM. The DEVICEHIGH and LH commands load the device drivers and memory-resident programs into UMBs. Memmaker also adds codes which it uses to specify where in upper memory each device will be loaded. For example, after you run MemMaker, a statment like this might be added to your AUTOEXEC.BAT:

```
LH /C:2 C:\MOUSE\MOUSE.COM
```

where /C:2 is the upper memory block the device is to be loaded into. On many systems MEMMAKER will free up 620K of conventional memory.

For detailed information on using the MEMMAKER utility, consult your DOS 6.0 manual or Que's *Using DOS 6.0*. You also can get help on MEMMAKER by typing **HELP MEMMAKER** at the DOS prompt.

IBM-DOS 6.1 RAMBoost. The IBM-DOS 6.1 RAMBoost utility, licensed from Central Point which supplies some of the MS-DOS 6.0 utilities, works much like MEMMAKER to free up additional conventional memory. After you have made backup copies of CONFIG.SYS and AUTOEXEC.BAT and stripped them down to only what you need to load, you enter the following at the DOS prompt:

```
RAMSETUP
```

RAMBoost calculates the best way to load your memory resident programs and device drivers into UMBs. RAMBoost gives results that are roughly equivalent to the MS-DOS 6.0 MEMMAKER utility. On many systems it will free up 620K of conventional memory.

Third-Party Memory Managers. Although MEMMAKER and RAMBoost do a good job of freeing-up conventional memory on most systems, memory management utilities like Quarterdeck's QEMM, and Qualitas' 386MAX do a considerably better job on many systems with more complex configurations, and therefore, numerous memory resident programs and device drivers. For example, on a system that MEMMAKER can free up only 620K of conventional memory, QEMM version 7.01 can give you 631K or more.

QEMM and 386MAX also enable you to shadow the computer ROM BIOS, video adapter ROM BIOS, or both. These software products use only as much upper memory as is necessary to accomplish the shadowing. If you use such a utility, ensure that you carefully follow the manufacturer's directions on shadowing ROM BIOS or video adapter BIOS. The following sections provide information about QEMM and 386MAX.

Quarterdeck QEMM. One of the strengths of QEMM version 7.01 is how simple it is to install and use. Before running the QEMM INSTALL program, make a backup of your CONFIG.SYS and AUTOEXEC.BAT files so you will have usable copies if you need them to restore your system configuration. Then exit any program you are running. At the DOS prompt, log to the drive where the QEMM install diskette is located and run the INSTALL program. QEMM will copy its files to the C:\QEMM directory (or another directory if you wish).

Then the INSTALL program will load the Optimize utility, which calculates the upper memory needed for your memory resident programs and device drivers and determines the proper region of upper memory for each. During this process, your system will be rebooted several times (or when prompted you may have to turn off your system and then restart it). When Optimize is finished, you can type MEM at the DOS prompt to find out how much free conventional memory your system has. You will find three lines at the beginning of CONFIG.SYS similar to the following:

```
DEVICE=C:\QEMM\DOSDATA.SYS

DEVICE=C:\QEMM\QEMM386.SYS R:2 dbf=2 RAM ST:m ARAM=CF80-CFFF

DEVICE=C:\QEMM\DOS-UP.SYS @C:\QEMM\DOS-UP.DAT
```

Like MEMMAKER, QEMM uses codes to specify into which UMB or upper memory region each device driver or memory resident program is loaded. For example, the following line loads the Microsoft CD-ROM extensions into upper memory:

```
c:\qemm\loadhi /r:2 /res=16208 /sqt=cb00-cbff
C:\dos\mscdex.exe/d:mscd0001 /L:g /e /m:20
```

The line in CONFIG.SYS that loads a device driver for a CD-ROM drive looks similar to the following:

```
DEVICE=c:\qemm\loadhi.sys /r:4 C:\dos\ULTRACD.SYS /D:MSCD0001
```

Once QEMM is installed and running on your system, each time you add a memory resident program or device driver, or any time you add or remove an adapter board (which might change the configuration of upper memory), you will need to again run OPTIMIZE. For additional information on installing and running QEMM, and for troubleshooting help, consult your QEMM user manual.

Qualitas 386MAX. Before running the 386MAX version 7.0 INSTALL program, take the precaution of making a backup copy of your CONFIG.SYS and AUTOEXEC.BAT files in case you need them later to restore your system. Then exit any program you are running, log to the drive with the 386MAX install diskette and run INSTALL. 386MAX will copy its files to the C:\386MAX subdirectory (or any directory you choose). Then the INSTALL program will load the MAXIMIZE utility which determines where in upper memory to place each memory resident program and device driver.

Once MAXIMIZE has finished, you can type MEM at the DOS prompt to find out how much free conventional memory your system has. You will find several new lines in your CONFIG.SYS file similar to the following:

```
Device=c:\386max\386max.sys pro=c:\386max\386max.pro

REM MAXIMIZE: ExtraDOS must come at the end of CONFIG.SYS

Device=C:\386MAX\ExtraDOS.max pro=C:\386MAX\ExtraDOS.PRO

Install=C:\386MAX\ExtraDOS.max
```

As with MEMMAKER and QEMM, 386MAX uses codes to specify which region of upper memory each memory resident program and device driver is loaded into. For example, a line similar to the following in your AUTOEXEC.BAT would load the Microsoft CD-ROM extensions:

```
c:\386max\386load size=72512 prgreg=2
prog=C:\dos\mscdex.exe/d:mscd0001 /L:g /e /m:20
```

The line in CONFIG.SYS that loaded your CD-ROM device driver would be similar to the following:

```
DEVICE=C:\386MAX\386load.sys size=15920 prgreg=2
flexframe prog=C:\dos\ULTRACD.SYS /D:MSCD0001
```

Whenever you add a news device driver or memory resident program to your system, or when you add or remove an adapter, you must again run MAXIMIZE.

Reviewing System-Memory Maps. You have learned how memory is used in systems compatible with the IBM standard. The reserved memory is deducted from what is available for programs and data because the reserved memory usually cannot be used by an operating system. Table 2.4 lists the maximum available memory for different systems.

Table 2.4 Maximum Addressable and Usable Memory	
System type	**Maximum addressable memory (RAM)**
PC/XT (or AT real mode)	1,024K (1M)
AT (protected mode)	16,384K (16M)
AT 386 or greater	4,194,304K (4,096M)

Even though the 386 and higher processors can address four gigabytes of memory, some 386DX and all 386SX systems are limited to 16 total megabytes of useful addressable memory. This limitation is primarily in the DMA controllers and not the processor. The memory beyond 16M usually can be used for *non-operating system memory*, used for adapters, caches, or other items not controlled by the operating system running on the machine. Because limitations in memory beyond 16M vary among computers, you should consult the manufacturer if you intend to use it.

Documentation. One of the biggest problems in troubleshooting, servicing, or upgrading a system is being able to find proper documentation. As with the system units, IBM has set the standard for the type of documentation a manufacturer makes available. Some manufacturers duplicate the size and content of IBM's manuals, and other manufacturers provide no documentation at all. Generally, the type of documentation provided for a system is proportionate to the size of the manufacturing company. (Large companies can afford to produce good documentation.) Some of this documentation unfortunately is essential for even the most basic troubleshooting and upgrading tasks. Other documentation is necessary only for software and hardware developers with special requirements.

Types of Documentation. Four types of documents are available for each system. Some manuals cover an entire range of systems, which can save money and shelf space. You can get these types of manuals:

■ Guide-to-operations (GTO) manuals (called quick-reference manuals for the PS/2)

■ Technical-reference (TR) manuals

■ Hardware-maintenance service (HMS) manuals

■ Hardware-maintenance reference (HMR) manuals

A guide-to-operations manual is included in the purchase of a system. For PS/2 systems, these manuals are called quick-reference manuals. They contain basic instructions for system setup, operation, testing, relocation, and option installation. A *customer-level* basic diagnostics disk (usually called a Diagnostics and Setup Disk) normally is included also in a system. For PS/2 machines, a special disk—the Reference Disk—contains the setup and configuration programs as well as both customer-level and technician-level diagnostics.

For PC and XT types of systems, you can find listings of all the jumper and switch settings for the motherboard. These settings specify the number of floppy disk drives, math-chip use, memory use, type of video adapter, and other items. For AT systems, the basic diagnostics disk also has the SETUP routine (used to set the date and time), installed memory, installed disk drives, and installed video adapters. This information is saved by the SETUP program into CMOS battery backed-up memory. For PS/2 systems, the included disk (called the Reference Disk) contains the special programmable option-select (POS) configuration routine and a hidden version of the advanced diagnostics.

Technical-Reference Manuals. The technical-reference manuals provide system-specific hardware and software interface information for the system. The manuals are intended for people who design hardware and software products to operate with these systems or people who must integrate other hardware and software into a system. Three types of technical-reference manuals are available: One is a technical-reference manual for a particular system; another covers all the options and adapters; and a third covers the ROM BIOS interface. For PS/2 systems, one hardware interface technical-reference manual covers all the PS/2 systems with updates for newer systems as they become available.

Each system has a separate technical-reference manual or an update to the hardware interface technical-reference manual. These publications provide basic interface and design information for the system units. They include information about the system board, math coprocessor, power supply, video subsystem, keyboard, instruction sets, and other features of the system. You need this information for integrating and installing aftermarket floppy and hard disk drives, memory boards, keyboards, network adapters, or virtually anything you want to plug into your system. This manual often contains schematic diagrams showing the circuit layout of the motherboard and pinouts for the various connectors and jumpers. It also includes listings of the floppy and hard disk drive tables, which show the range of drives that can be installed on a particular system. Power specifications for the power supply also are in this manual. You need these figures in order to determine whether the system has adequate current to power a particular add-on device.

The options and adapters technical-reference manual begins with a starter manual augmented with supplements. The basic manual covers a few IBM adapter cards, and supplements for new adapters and options are issued continually. These publications provide interface and design information about the options and adapters available for the various systems. This information includes a hardware description, programming considerations, interface specifications, and BIOS information.

The third manual is the BIOS interface technical-reference manual. This publication provides basic input-output system (BIOS) interface information. This compendium covers every BIOS that has been available in IBM's systems. The manual is designed for developers of hardware or software products that operate with the IBM PC and PS/2 products.

Hardware-Maintenance Manuals. Each hardware maintenance library consists of two manuals: a hardware-maintenance service manual and a hardware-maintenance reference manual. These real-service manuals are written for service technicians. IBM and local computer-retail outlets use these manuals to diagnose and service your system.

For IBM systems, two sets of manuals are available. One set covers the PC, XT, Portable PC, AT, and PS/2 Model 25 and Model 30. The other manual set covers the PS/2 systems except Model 25 and Model 30: these systems are considered as old PC or XT systems rather than as true PS/2 systems.

Manuals are purchased in starter form and then updated with supplements covering new systems and options. The PS/2 Model 25 and Model 30, for example, are covered by supplements that update the PC maintenance library; the PS/2 Model 80 is covered by a supplement to the PS/2 maintenance library.

The basic hardware-maintenance service manual for the PC or PS/2 contains all the information you need to troubleshoot and diagnose a failing system. This book contains special flowcharts that IBM calls maintenance-analysis procedures (MAPs), which can help you find a correct diagnosis in a step-by-step manner. It contains information about jumper positions and switch settings, a detailed parts catalog, and disks containing the advanced diagnostics. The hardware-maintenance service manual is an essential part of a troubleshooter's toolkit.

Many technicians with troubleshooting experience never need to use the maintenance-analysis procedures (MAPs), but when they have a tough problem, the MAPs help them organize a troubleshooting session. The MAPs tell you to check the switch and jumper settings before the cables, to check the cables before replacing the drive or controller, and so on. This type of information is extremely valuable and can work over a range of systems without getting too specific.

The basic hardware-maintenance reference manual for the PC or PS/2 contains general information about the systems. It describes the diagnostic procedures and field-replaceable unit (FRU) locations, system adjustments, and component removal and installation. The information in it is useful primarily to users with no experience in disassembling and reassembling a system or who have difficulty identifying components within the system. Most people do not need this manual after the first time they take down a system for service.

Obtaining Documentation. You cannot accurately troubleshoot or upgrade a system without the technical-reference manual. Because of the specific nature of the information in the manual, the information must be obtained from the manufacturer of the system. The IBM AT Technical Reference Manual, for example, is useless to a person with a COMPAQ Deskpro 286. A person with a Deskpro 286 must get the manual from COMPAQ.

The hardware-maintenance service manual also is a necessary item, but it is not available from most manufacturers. The manual is not nearly as system-specific as the technical-reference manual; the one from IBM works well for most compatibles. Some information, such as the parts catalog, is specific to IBM systems and does not apply to compatibles, but most of the book has general information.

Many knowledgeable reviewers use the IBM advanced diagnostics, included with the hardware-maintenance service manual, as an acid test for compatibility. If the system truly is compatible, it should pass the tests with flying colors. (Most systems pass.) Many manufacturers do not have or sell a book or disk equivalent to the hardware-maintenance service manual. COMPAQ, for example, has a service manual, but does not sell it or any parts to anyone who is not a COMPAQ-authorized dealer. Servicing or upgrading these systems therefore is more costly, and limited by how much your dealer helps you. Buyers are fortunate that sufficient third-party diagnostics work with most compatible systems such as the COMPAQ systems.

To get hardware-service documentation, contact the dealer who sold you the system and then, if necessary, contact the manufacturer. (Contacting the manufacturer is often more efficient because dealers rarely stock these items.) You can get the items easily from IBM. To order the IBM manuals, call this toll-free number:

    1-800-IBM-PCTB (1-800-426-7282)

TB is the abbreviation for technical books. The service is active Monday through Friday, from 8 a.m. to 8 p.m. Eastern time. When you call, you can request copies of the *Technical Directory*—a catalog listing all the part numbers and prices of available documentation. You can inquire also about the availability of technical-reference or service documentation covering newly announced products that might not be listed yet in this directory.

For other manufacturers' manuals, the process of obtaining these types of manuals might (or might not) be so easy. Most larger-name companies run responsible service and support operations that include providing technical documentation. Others either do not have or are unwilling to part with such documentation, to protect their service departments or their dealers' service departments from competition. Contact the manufacturer directly, and the manufacturer can direct you to the correct department so that you can inquire about this information.

Chapter Summary

This chapter has discussed the differences between the two basic types of IBM and compatible computers—the PC/XT, and the AT. This chapter also discussed the adapter bus designs common to modern PCs, including ISA, EISA, MCA VESA-Local Bus, PCI, PCMCIA, and proprietary bus designs.

The system-memory map was examined in detail to show how computers organize and use RAM and ROM. The differences between conventional, extended, and expanded memory were explained. The chapter has described DOS program memory and video memory and their operation. It also discussed memory management utilities like the MS-DOS 6.0 MEMMAKER, as well as QEMM and 386MAX. Also included was a discussion of avoiding and troubleshooting adapter board memory, IRQ and DMA channel conflicts and the use of memory templates to make installing adapter boards easier.

The chapter ended with a discussion about how to obtain the service manuals necessary for maintaining and upgrading your computer.

Part II

IBM PC, PS/2, and Compatible Systems

Chapter 3

IBM Personal Computer Family Hardware

This chapter explains and interprets IBM's original family of personal computer system units and accessories. It separates and identifies each personal computer system originally offered by IBM, including the complete original line of PC systems that have been discontinued. Because the entire original line has been discontinued, much of this chapter can be considered a history lesson. The information still is valuable, however, because many people still own and manage these older systems, which are more likely to break down than newer ones. The original line of systems often are called Industry Standard Architecture (ISA) systems, or *Classic* PCs. IBM calls them *Family/1* systems. The PS/2 (or *Family/2*) systems are examined in Chapter 4, "IBM Personal System/2 Family Hardware."

This chapter is a reference specific to the original line of true IBM PC, XT, and AT systems. IBM-compatible systems are examined separately in Chapter 5, "IBM-Compatible (and Incompatible) Computers," but even people who do not own IBM systems will find Chapter 5 filled with interesting and useful information. After all, the idea behind most "IBM-compatible" systems is to clone, copy, or emulate the features of a particular IBM system or combination of systems. For upgrade and repair purposes, most PC-compatible systems are treated in the same manner as IBM systems. Most compatible systems can exchange parts easily with IBM systems and vice versa. In fact, most of the parts that make up IBM systems are made by third-party companies, and you can purchase these same parts outside of IBM to save money.

In Chapter 2, "System Features," you learned that all systems can be broken down into two basic types: PC/XT or AT. AT types of systems often are broken down into several subtypes. These subtypes can be classified as systems that use 286 or 386/486 processors and systems with Industry Standard Architecture (ISA), Extended Industry Standard Architecture (EISA), or Micro Channel Architecture (MCA) slots. You can use this chapter to compare a compatible system with a specific IBM system in a feature-by-feature comparison. This kind of comparison is often interesting because compatibles usually offer many more features and options at a lower price.

System-Unit Features by Model

In the following sections, you learn the makeup of all the various versions or models of the specific systems and also technical details and specifications of each system. Every system unit has a few standard parts. The primary component is the motherboard, which has the CPU (central processing unit, or microprocessor) and other primary computer circuitry. Each unit also includes a case with an internal power supply, a keyboard, certain standard adapters or plug-in cards, and usually some form of a disk drive.

You receive an explanation of each system's various submodels and details about the differences between and features of each model. You learn about the changes from model to model and version to version of each system.

Included for your reference is part-number information for each system and option. This information is for comparison and reference purposes only because all these systems have been discontinued and generally are no longer available. IBM still stocks and sells component parts and assemblies, however, for even these discontinued units. You can (and usually should) replace failed components in these older systems with non-IBM replacement parts because you invariably can obtain upgraded or improved components compared to what IBM offers, or even get the exact same part at a greatly reduced price.

An Introduction to the PC

IBM introduced the IBM Personal Computer August 12, 1981, and officially withdrew the machine from marketing April 2, 1987. During the nearly six-year life of the PC, IBM made only a few basic changes to the system. The basic motherboard circuit design was changed in April 1983 to accommodate 64K RAM chips and a switch was made from single- to double-sided floppy drives. Three different ROM BIOS versions were used during the life of the system; most other specifications, however, remained unchanged. Because IBM no longer markets the PC system, and because of the PC's relatively limited expansion capability and power, the standard PC is obsolete by most standards.

The system unit supports only floppy disk drives unless the power supply is upgraded or an expansion chassis is used to house the hard disk externally. IBM never offered an internal hard disk for the PC, but many third-party companies stepped in to fill this void with upgrades. The system unit included many configurations with single or dual floppy disk drives. Early on, one version even was available with no disk drives, and others used single-sided floppy drives. The PC motherboard was based on the 16-bit Intel 8088 microprocessor and included the Microsoft Cassette BASIC language built into ROM. For standard memory, the PC offered configurations with as little as 16K of RAM (when the system was first announced) and as much as 256K on the motherboard. Two motherboard designs were used. Systems sold before March 1983 had a motherboard that supported a maximum of 64K of RAM, and later systems supported a maximum of 256K on the motherboard. In either case, you added more memory (as much as 640K) by installing memory cards in the expansion slots.

The first bank of memory chips in every PC is soldered to the motherboard. Soldered memory is reliable but not conducive to easy servicing because the solder prevents you from easily exchanging failing memory chips located in the first bank. The chips must be unsoldered and the defective chip replaced with a socket so that a replacement can be plugged in. When IBM services the defective memory, IBM advises you to exchange the entire motherboard. Considering today's value of these systems, replacing the motherboard with one of the many compatible motherboards on the market may be a better idea. Repairing the same defective memory chip in the XT system is much easier because all memory in an XT is socketed.

Although originally equipped with single-sided floppy drives, IBM quickly switched to using only double-sided (360K) floppy disk drives. You can install a maximum of two drives in the system unit by using IBM-supplied drives, or four using half-height third-party drives and mounting brackets.

The system unit has five slots that support expansion cards for additional devices, features, or memory. All these slots support full-length adapter cards. In most configurations, the PC included at least a floppy disk controller card. You need a second slot for a monitor adapter, which leaves three slots for adapter cards.

All models of the PC have a fan-cooled, 63.5-watt power supply. This low-output power supply doesn't support much in the way of system expansion, especially power-hungry items, such as hard disks. Usually, this low-output supply must be replaced by a higher-output unit, such as the one used in the XT. Figure 3.1 shows an interior view of a PC system unit.

An 83-key keyboard with an adjustable typing angle is standard equipment on the PC. The keyboard is attached to the rear of the system unit by a 6-foot coiled cable. Figure 3.2 shows the back panel of the PC.

Most model configurations of the PC system unit included these major functional components:

- Intel 8088 microprocessor
- ROM-based diagnostics (POST)
- BASIC language interpreter in ROM
- 256K of dynamic RAM
- Floppy disk controller
- One or two 360K floppy drives
- A 63.5-watt power supply
- Five I/O expansion slots
- Socket for the 8087 math coprocessor

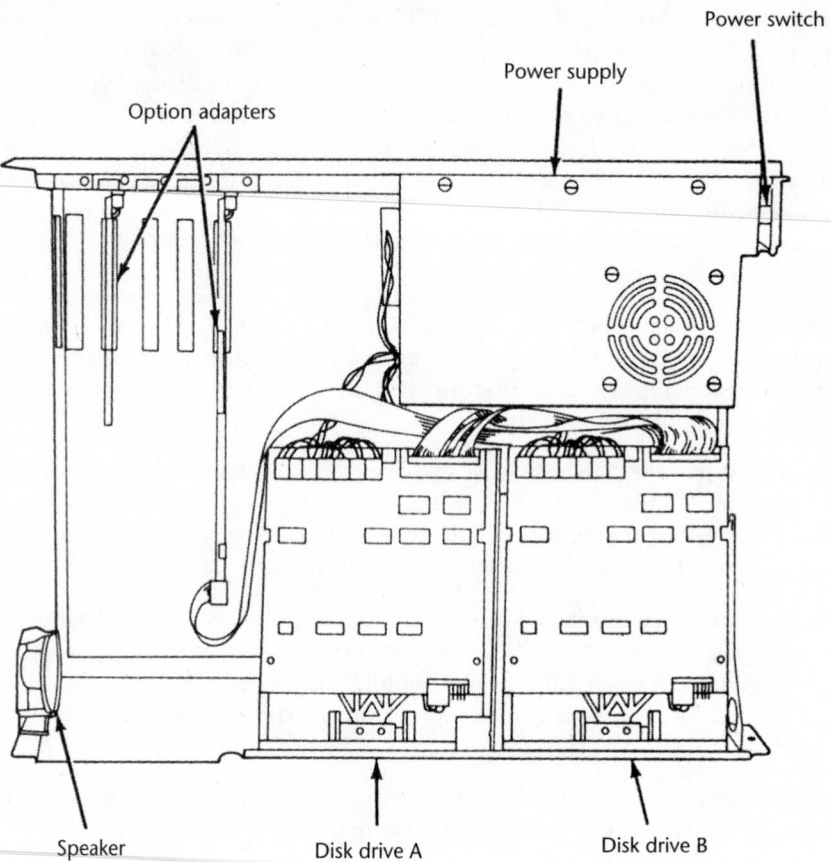

Fig. 3.1
The IBM PC system-unit interior view.

PC Models and Features

Although several early-model configurations of the IBM PC were available before March 1983, only two models were available after that time. The later models differ only in the number of floppy drives: one or two. IBM designated these models as follows:

> IBM PC 5150 Model 166: 256K RAM, one 360K drive
> IBM PC 5150 Model 176: 256K RAM, two 360K drives

The PC never was available with a factory-installed hard disk, primarily because the system unit has a limited base for expansion and offered few resources with which to work. After IBM started selling XTs with only floppy disk drives (on April 2, 1985), the PC became obsolete. The XT offered much more for virtually the same price. Investing in a PC after the XT introduction was questionable.

IBM finally withdrew the PC from the market April 2, 1987. IBM's plans for the system became obvious when the company didn't announce a new model with the Enhanced Keyboard, as it did with other IBM systems.

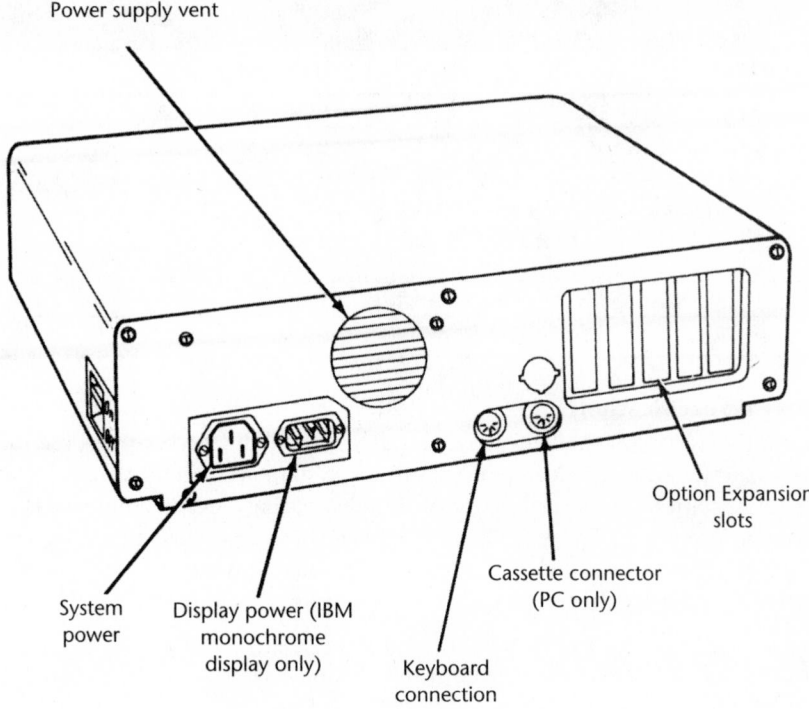

Power supply vent

Option Expansion slots

Cassette connector (PC only)

System power

Display power (IBM monochrome display only)

Keyboard connection

II

Compatible Systems

Fig. 3.2
The IBM PC system-unit rear view.

With some creative purchasing, you can make a usable system of a base PC by adding the requisite components, such as a full 640K of memory and hard and floppy drives. You still may have a slot or two to spare. Unfortunately, expanding this system requires re-placing many of the boards in the system unit with boards that combine the same functions in less space. Only you can decide when your money is better invested in a new system.

Before you can think of expanding a PC beyond even a simple configuration, and to allow for compatibility and reliability, you must address two major areas:

ROM BIOS level (version)

Power supply

In most cases, the power supply is the most critical issue because all PCs sold after March 1983 already have the latest ROM BIOS. If you have an earlier PC system, you also must upgrade the ROM because the early versions lack some required capabilities. Both prob-lems, and also other expansion issues related to all systems in the PC family, are ad-dressed in Chapter 7, "Primary System Components," and Chapter 12, "System Upgrades and Improvements." Table 3.1 shows the part numbers for the IBM PC system unit.

Table 3.1 IBM PC Part Numbers

Description	Number
PC system unit, 256K, one 360K drive	5150166
PC system unit, 256K, two 360K drives	5150176
Options	
PC expansion-unit Model 001 with 10M fixed disk	5161001
360K disk drive	1503810
8087 math coprocessor option	1501002
BIOS update kit	1501005

PC Technical Specifications

Technical information for the Personal Computer system and keyboard is described in this section. Here, you find information about the system architecture, memory configurations and capacities, standard system features, disk storage, expansion slots, keyboard specifications, and physical and environmental specifications. This kind of information may be useful in determining what parts you need when you are upgrading or repairing these systems. Figure 3.3 shows the layout and components on the PC motherboard.

System architecture	
Microprocessor	8088
Clock speed	4.77 MHz
Bus type	ISA (Industry Standard Architecture)
Bus width	8-bit
Interrupt levels	8
Type	Edge-Triggered
Shareable	No
DMA channels	3
DMA burst mode supported	No
Bus masters supported	No
Upgradeable processor complex	No

Memory	
Standard on system board	16K, 64K or 256K
Maximum on system board	256K
Maximum total memory	640K
Memory speed (ns) and type	200ns dynamic RAM
System board memory-socket type	16-pin DIP
Number of memory-module sockets	27 (3 banks of 9)
Memory used on system board	27 16Kx1-bit or 64Kx1-bit DRAM chips in 3 banks of 9, one soldered bank of 9 16Kx1-bit or 64Kx1-bit chips

Memory

Memory cache controller	No
Wait states:	
System board	1
Adapter	1

Standard features

ROM size	40K
ROM shadowing	No
Optional math coprocessor	8087
Coprocessor speed	4.77 MHz
Standard graphics	None standard
RS232C serial ports	None standard
UART chip used	NS8250B
Maximum speed (bits per second)	9,600 bps
Maximum number of ports supported	2
Pointing device (mouse) ports	None standard
Parallel printer ports	None standard
Bi-directional	No
Maximum number of ports supported	3
CMOS real-time clock (RTC)	No
CMOS RAM	None

Disk storage

Internal disk and tape drive bays	2 full-height
Number of 3 1/2-/5 1/4-inch bays	0/2
Standard floppy drives	1x360K
Optional floppy drives:	
5 1/4-inch 360K	Optional
5 1/4-inch 1.2M	No
3 1/2-inch 720K	Optional
3 1/2-inch 1.44M	No
3 1/2-inch 2.88M	No
Hard disk controller included	None

Expansion slots

Total adapter slots	5
Number of long and short slots	5/0
Number of 8-/16-/32-bit slots	5/0/0
Available slots (with video)	3

II

Compatible Systems

Keyboard specifications	
101-key enhanced keyboard	No, 83-key
Fast keyboard speed setting	No
Keyboard cable length	6 feet

Physical specifications	
Footprint type	Desktop
Dimensions:	
Height	5.5 inches
Width	19.5 inches
Depth	16.0 inches
Weight	25 pounds

Environmental specifications	
Power-supply output	63.5 watts
Worldwide (110/60,220/50)	No
Auto-sensing/switching	No
Maximum current:	
104-127 VAC	2.5 amps
Operating range:	
Temperature	60-90 degrees F
Relative humidity	8-80 percent
Maximum operating altitude	7,000 feet
Heat (BTUs/hour)	505
Noise (Average dB, operating, 1m)	43
FCC classification	Class B

Introduction to the PC Convertible

IBM marked its entry into the laptop computer market on April 2, 1986 by introducing the IBM 5140 PC Convertible. The system superseded the 5155 Portable PC (IBM's transportable system), which no longer was available. The IBM 5140 system wasn't a very successful laptop system. Other laptops offered more disk storage, higher processor speeds, more readable screens, lower cost, and more compact cases, which pressured IBM to improve the Convertible. Because the improvements were limited to the display, however, this system never gained respect in the marketplace.

The PC Convertible was available in two models. The Model 2 had a CMOS 80C88 4.77 Mhz microprocessor, 64K of ROM, 256K of Static RAM, an 80-column-by-25-line detachable liquid crystal display, two 3 1/2-inch floppy disk drives, a 78-key keyboard, an AC adapter, and a battery pack. Also included were software programs called Application Selector, SystemApps, Tools, Exploring the IBM PC Convertible, and Diagnostics. The

Model 22 is the same basic computer as the Model 2 but with the diagnostics software only. You can expand either system to 512K of RAM by using 128K RAM memory cards, and you can include an internal 1200bps modem in the system unit. With aftermarket memory expansion, the computers can reach 640K.

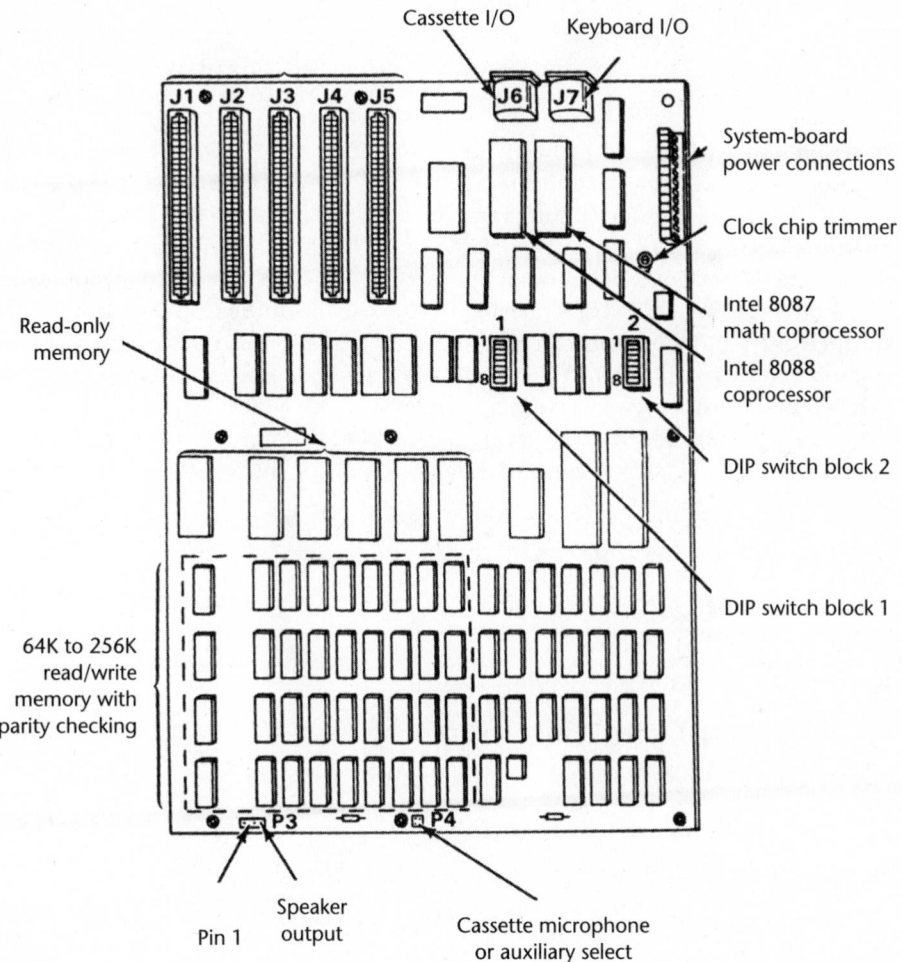

Fig. 3.3
The IBM PC system board.

Although the unit was painfully slow at 4.77 Mhz, one notable feature is the use of Static memory chips for the system's RAM. Static RAM does not require the refresh signal that normal Dynamic RAM requires, which would normally require about 7 percent of the processor's time (refresh overhead) in a standard PC or XT system. This feature means that the Convertible is about 7 percent faster than an IBM PC or XT even though they all operate at the same clock speed of 4.77 Mhz. Because of the increased reliability of the

Static RAM (compared to Dynamic RAM) used in the Convertible, as well as the desire to minimize power consumption, none of the RAM in the Convertible is parity checked.

At the back of each system unit is an extendable bus interface. This 72-pin connector enables you to attach the following options to the base unit: a printer, a serial or parallel adapter, and a CRT display adapter. Each feature is powered from the system unit. The CRT display adapter operates only when the system is powered from a standard AC adapter. A separate CRT display or a television set attached through the CRT display adapter requires a separate AC power source.

Each system unit includes a detachable liquid crystal display (LCD). When the computer is not mobile, the LCD screen can be replaced by an external monitor. When the LCD is latched in the closed position, it forms the cover for the keyboard and floppy disk drives. Because the LCD is attached with a quick-disconnect connector, you can remove it easily to place the 5140 system unit below an optional IBM 5144 PC Convertible monochrome or IBM 5145 PC Convertible color display. During the life of the Convertible, IBM offered three different LCD displays. The first display was a standard LCD, which suffered from problems with contrast and readability. Because of complaints, IBM changed the LCD to a Super Twisted type LCD display, which had much greater contrast. Finally, in the third LCD, IBM added a fluorescent backlight to the Super Twisted LCD display, which not only offered greater contrast, but also made the unit usable in low light situations.

The PC Convertible system unit has these standard features:

- Complementary Metal-Oxide Semiconductor (CMOS) 80C88 4.77Mhz microprocessor

- Two 32K CMOS ROMs containing these items:

  POST (Power-On Self Test) of system components

  BIOS (basic input-output system) support

  BASIC language interpreter

- 256K CMOS Static RAM (expandable to 512K)

- Two 3 1/2-inch 720K (formatted) floppy drives

- An 80-column-by-25-line detachable LCD panel (graphics modes: 640-by-200 resolution and 320-by-200 resolution)

- LCD controller

- 16K RAM display buffer

- 8K LCD font RAM

- Adapter for optional printer (#4010)

- Professional keyboard (78 keys)

- AC adapter

- Battery pack

The system-unit options for the 5140 are shown in this list:

- 128K Static RAM memory card (#4005)

- Printer (#4010)

- Serial/parallel adapter (#4015)

- CRT display adapter (#4020)

- PC Convertible Specifications and Highlights

This section lists some technical specifications for the IBM 5140 PC Convertible system. The weights of the unit and options are listed because weight is an important consideration when you carry a laptop system. Figure 3.4 shows the PC Convertible motherboard components and layout.

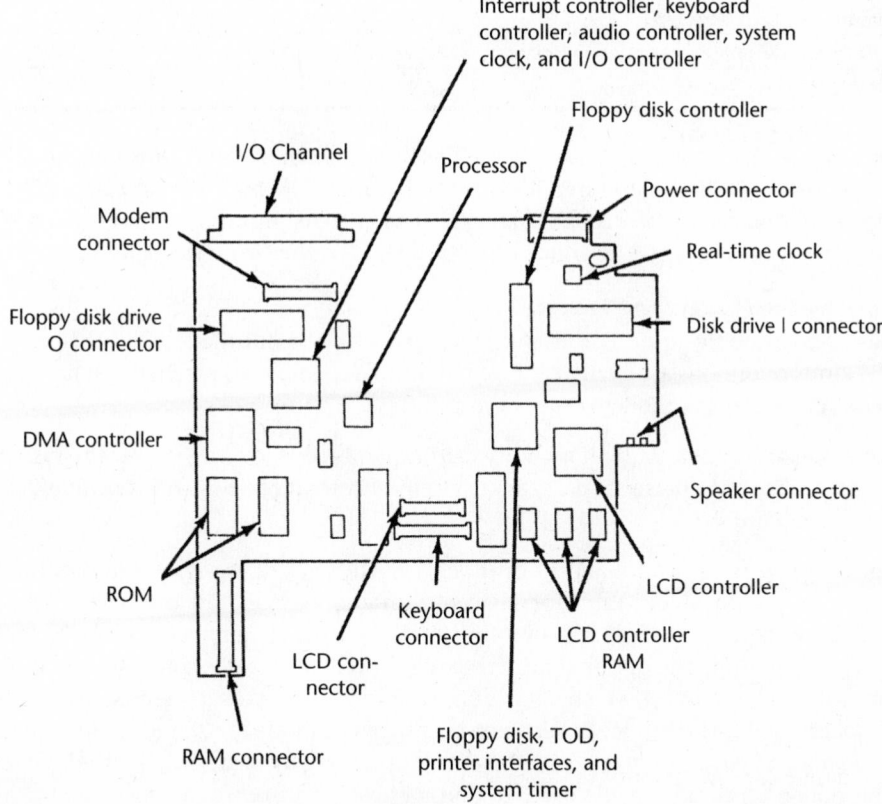

Fig. 3.4
The PC Convertible system board.

Dimensions	
Depth:	360 mm (14.17 inches)
	374 mm (14.72 inches) including handle
Width:	309.6 mm (12.19 inches)
	312 mm (12.28 inches) including handle
Height:	67 mm (2.64 inches)
	68 mm (2.68 inches) including footpads

Weight	
Models 2 and 22 (including battery)	5.5 kg (12.17 pounds)
128K/256K memory card	40 g (1.41 ounces)
Printer	1.6 kg (3.50 pounds)
Serial/parallel adapter	470 g (1.04 pounds)
CRT display adapter	630 g (1.40 pounds)
Internal modem	170 g (6 ounces)
Printer cable	227 g (8 ounces)
Battery charger	340 g (12 ounces)
Automobile power adapter	113 g (4 ounces)
5144 PC Convertible monochrome display	7.3 kg (16 pounds)
5145 PC Convertible color display	16.9 kg (37.04 pounds)

To operate the IBM 5140 PC Convertible properly, you must have PC DOS Version 3.2 or later. Previous DOS versions aren't supported because they don't support the 720K floppy drive. Using the CRT display adapter and an external monitor requires that the system unit be operated by power from the AC adapter rather from the battery.

PC Convertible Models and Features

This section covers the options and special features available for the PC Convertible. Several kinds of options are available, from additional memory to external display adapters, serial/parallel ports, modems, and even printers.

Memory Cards. A 128K or 256K memory card expands the base memory in the system unit. You can add two of these cards, for a system-unit total of 640K with one 256K card and one 128K card.

Optional Printers. An optional printer attaches to the back of the system unit or to an optional printer-attachment cable for adjacent printer operation. The printer's intelligent, microprocessor-based, 40 cps, non-impact dot-matrix design makes it capable of low-power operation. The optional printer draws power from and is controlled by the system unit. Standard ASCII 96-character, upper- and lowercase character sets were printed with a high-resolution, 24-element print head. A mode for graphics capability is provided also. You can achieve near-letter-quality printing by using either a thermal transfer ribbon on smooth paper or no ribbon on heat-sensitive thermal paper.

Serial/Parallel Adapters. A serial/parallel adapter attaches to the back of the system unit, a printer, or other feature module attached to the back of the system unit.

The adapter provides an RS-232C asynchronous communications interface and a parallel printer interface, both compatible with the IBM personal computer asynchronous communications adapter and the IBM personal computer parallel printer adapter.

CRT Display Adapters. A CRT display adapter attaches to the back of the system unit, printer, or other feature module attached to the back of the system unit. This adapter enables you to connect to the system a separate CRT display, such as the PC Convertible monochrome display or PC Convertible color display. By using optional connectors or cables, you can use the CRT display adapter also to attach a standard CGA type of monitor. Because composite video output is available, you can also use a standard television set.

Internal Modems. With an internal modem, you can communicate with compatible computers over telephone lines. It runs Bell 212A (1200 bps) or Bell 103A (300 bps) protocols. The modem comes as a complete assembly, consisting of two cards connected by a cable. The entire assembly is installed inside the system unit. Over the life of the system, IBM made two different internal modems for the Convertible. The original modem was made for IBM by Novation, and did not follow the Hayes standard for commands and protocols. This rendered the modem largely incompatible with popular software designed to use the Hayes command set. Later, IBM changed the modem to one that was fully Hayes-compatible, and this change resolved the problems with software. IBM never introduced a modem faster than 1200 bps for the Convertible. Fortunately, you still can operate a standard external modem through the serial port, although you lose the convenience of having it built in.

Printer Cables. The printer cable is 22 inches (0.6 meter) long with a custom 72-pin connector attached to each end. With this cable, you can operate the Convertible printer when it is detached from the system unit and place the unit for ease of use and visibility.

Battery Chargers. The battery charger is a 110-volt input device that charges the system's internal batteries. It does not provide sufficient power output for the system to operate while the batteries are being charged.

The IBM 5145 PC Convertible Color Display. The 5145 PC Convertible color display is a 13-inch color display attached to the system unit through the CRT display adapter. It comes with a display stand, an AC power cord, a signal cable that connects the 5145 to the CRT display adapter, and a speaker for external audio output. The monitor is a low-cost unit compatible with the standard IBM CGA type of display.

Special software available for the Convertible includes these programs:

- The *Application Selector* program, installed as an extension to DOS, provides a menu-driven interface to select and run applications software, the SystemApps, and Tools.

- The *SystemApps* program provides basic functions similar to many memory-resident programs on the market. This application, which includes Notewriter, Schedule, Phone List, and Calculator, is equivalent in function to the popular SideKick program.

II

Compatible Systems

■ You can use the menu-driven *Tools* program as a front end for DOS to control and maintain the system (copying and erasing files, copying disks, and so on). With DOS, additional functions are available, including printing, formatting, and configuring the Application Selector function keys. This program presents many DOS functions in an easy-to-use menu format.

This additional software, except system diagnostics, is not included with the Model 22. Table 3.2 shows the part numbers of the IBM Convertible system units.

Table 3.2 IBM Convertible Part Numbers	
5140 PC Convertible system units	**Number**
Two 720K drives, 256K RAM with system applications	5140002
Two 720K drives, 256K RAM without system applications	5140022

An Introduction to the XT

Introduced March 8, 1983, the PC XT with a built-in 10M hard disk (originally standard, later optional) caused a revolution in personal computer configurations. At the time, having even a 10M hard disk was something very special. XT stands for XTended (extended). IBM chose this name because the IBM PC XT system includes many features not available in the standard PC. The XT has eight slots, allowing increased expansion capabilities; greater power-supply capacity; completely socketed memory; motherboards that support memory expansion to 640K without using an expansion slot; and optional hard disk drives. To obtain these advantages, the XT uses a different motherboard circuit design than the PC.

The system unit was available in several models, with a variety of disk drive configurations: one 360K floppy disk drive, two 360K floppy disk drives, one floppy disk and one hard disk drive, or two floppy disk drives and one hard disk drive. The floppy disk drives were full-height drives in the earlier models, and half-height drives in more recent models. With the four available drive bays, IBM had standard configurations with two floppy drives and a single hard disk, with room for a second hard disk provided that all half-height units were used.

IBM-offered 10M and 20M, full-height hard disks. In some cases, IBM also installed half-height hard disks, but they were always installed in a bracket and cradle assembly that took up the equivalent space of a full-height drive. If you wanted half-height hard disks (to install two of them stacked, for example), then you had to use non-IBM supplied drives or modify the mounting of the IBM supplied half-height unit so that two could fit. Most aftermarket sources for hard disks had mounting kits that would work.

IBM also used double-sided Double Density (DD) 360K floppy disk drives in full- or half-height configurations. A 3 1/2-inch 720K floppy disk drive was available in more recent models. The 3 1/2-inch drives were available in a normal internal configuration or as an external device. You can install a maximum of two floppy disk drives and one hard disk drive in the system unit, using IBM-supplied drives. With half-height hard disks, you can install two hard drives in the system unit.

The XT is based on the same 8- and 16-bit Intel 8088 microprocessor (the CPU has 16-bit registers but only an 8-bit data bus) as the PC and runs at the same clock speed. Operationally, the XT systems are identical to the PC systems except for the hard disk. All models have at least one 360K floppy disk drive and a keyboard. For standard memory, the XT offers 256K or 640K on the main board. The hard disk models also include a serial adapter.

The system unit has eight slots that support cards for additional devices, features, or memory. Two of the slots support only short option cards because of physical interference from the disk drives. The XT has at least a disk drive adapter card in the floppy-disk-only models, and a hard disk controller card and serial adapter in the hard disk models. Either five or seven expansion slots (depending on the model) are available. Figure 3.5 shows the interior of an XT.

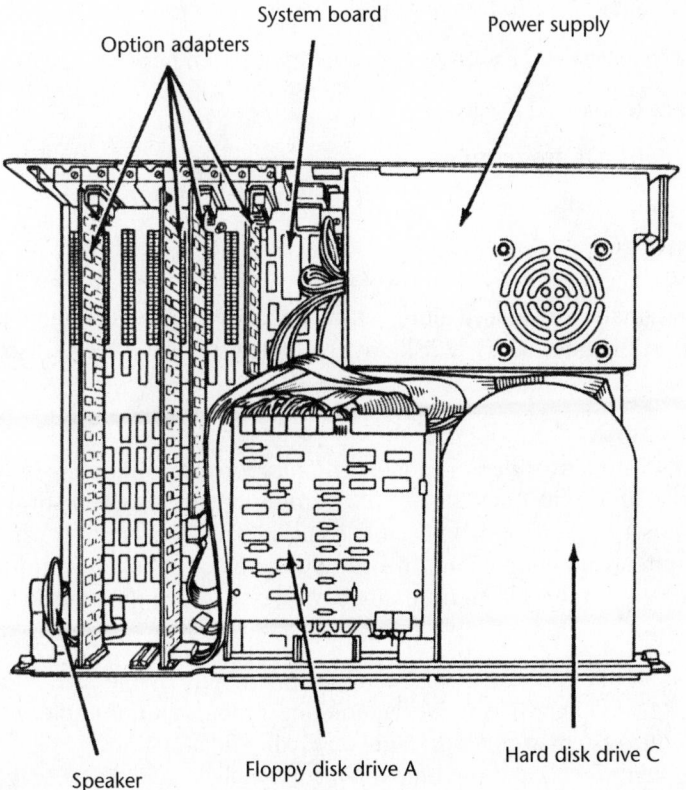

Fig. 3.5
The IBM PC XT interior.

II

Compatible Systems

All XT models include a heavy-duty, fan-cooled, 130-watt power supply to support the greater expansion capabilities and disk drive options. The power supply has more than double the capacity of the PC's supply, and can easily support hard disk drives as well as the full complement of expansion cards.

An 83-key keyboard was standard equipment with the early XT models, but was changed to an enhanced 101-key unit in the more recent models. The keyboard is attached to the system unit by a 6-foot coiled cable.

All models of the PC XT system unit contain these major functional components:

- Intel 8088 microprocessor
- ROM-based diagnostics (POST)
- BASIC language interpreter in ROM
- 256K or 640K of dynamic RAM
- Floppy disk controller
- One 360K floppy drive (full- or half-height)
- 10M or 20M hard disk drive with interface (enhanced models)
- Serial interface (enhanced models)
- Heavy-duty, 130-watt power supply
- Eight I/O expansion slots
- Socket for 8087 math coprocessor

The IBM XT was originally introduced along with DOS 2.0, which was required as a minimum to support the internal hard disk drive. All XT systems require DOS 2.x or later to function properly.

XT Models and Features

The XT was available in many different model configurations, but originally only one model was available. This model included a 10M hard disk, marking the first time that a hard disk was standard equipment in a personal computer and was properly supported by the operating system and peripherals. This computer helped change the industry standard for personal computers from normally having one or two floppy disk drives only to now including one or more hard disks.

Today, most people wouldn't consider a PC to be even remotely usable without a hard disk. The original XT was expensive, however, and buyers couldn't unbundle, or delete, the hard disk from the system at purchase time for credit and add it later. This fact distinguished the XT from the PC and misled many people to believe that the only difference between the two computers was the hard disk. People who recognized and wanted the greater capabilities of the XT without the standard IBM hard disk unfortunately had to wait for IBM to sell versions of the XT without the hard disk drive.

The original Model 087 of the XT included a 10M hard disk, 128K of RAM, and a standard serial interface. IBM later increased the standard memory in all PC systems to 256K. The XT reflected the change in Model 086, which was the same as the preceding 087 except for a standard 256K of RAM.

On April 2, 1985, IBM introduced new models of the XT without the standard hard disk. Designed for expansion and configuration flexibility, the new models enabled you to buy the system initially at a lower cost and add your own hard disk to the system later. The XT therefore could be considered in configurations that previously only the original PC could fill. The primary difference between the PC and the XT is the XT's expansion capability, provided by the larger power supply, eight slots, and better memory layout. These models cost only $300 more than equivalent PCs, rendering the original PC no longer a viable option.

The extra expense of the XT can be justified with the first power-supply replacement you make with an overworked PC. The IBM PC XT is available in two floppy disk models:

5160068 XT with one full-height 360K disk drive

5160078 XT with two full-height 360K disk drives

Both these models have 256K of memory and use the IBM PC XT motherboard, power supply, frame, and cover. The serial (asynchronous communications) adapter isn't included as a standard feature with these models.

IBM introduced several more models of the PC XT on April 2, 1986. These models were significantly different from previous models. The most obvious difference, the Enhanced Keyboard, was standard with these newer computers. A 20M (rather than 10M) hard disk and high-quality, half-height floppy disk drives were included. The new half-height floppy disk drives allow for two drives in the space that previously held only one floppy drive. With two drives, backing up floppy disks became easy. A new 3 1/2-inch floppy disk drive, storing 720K for compatibility with the PC Convertible laptop computer, was released also. These more recent XT system units were configured with a new memory layout allowing for 640K of RAM on the motherboard without an expansion slot. This feature conserves power, improves reliability, and lowers the cost of the system.

One 5 1/4-inch, half-height, 360K floppy disk drive and 256K of system-board memory was standard with the XT Models 267 and 268. Models 277 and 278 have a second 5 1/4-inch floppy disk drive. Models 088 and 089 were expanded PC XTs with all the standard features of the Models 267 and 268—a 20M hard disk, a 20M fixed disk drive adapter, a serial port adapter, and an additional 256K of system-board memory—adding up to 512K.

The following list shows the highlights of these new models:

- Enhanced Keyboard standard on Models 268, 278, and 089

    101 keys

    Recappable

Selectric typing section

Dedicated numeric pad

Dedicated cursor and screen control

Two additional function keys

9-foot cable

- Standard PC XT keyboard on Models 267, 277, and 088
- More disk capacity (20M)
- Standard 5 1/4-inch, half-height, 360K floppy drive
- Available 3 1/2-inch, half-height, 720K floppy drive
- Capacity for four half-height storage devices within the system unit
- Capacity to expand to 640K bytes memory on system board without using expansion slots

These newest XT models have an extensively changed ROM BIOS. The new BIOS is 64K and internally similar to the BIOS found in ATs. The ROM includes support for the new keyboard and 3 1/2-inch floppy disk drives. The POST also was enhanced.

The new XTs were originally incompatible in some respects with some software programs. These problems had centered on the new 101-key enhanced keyboard and the way the new ROM addresses the keys. These problems weren't major and were solved quickly by the software companies.

Seeing how much IBM changed the computer without changing the basic motherboard design is interesting. The ROM is different, and the board now can hold 640K of memory without a card in a slot. The memory trick is a simple one. IBM designed this feature into the board originally and chose to unleash it with these models of the XT.

During the past several years, I have modified many XTs to have 640K on the motherboard, using a simple technique designed into the system by IBM. A jumper and chip added to the motherboard can alter the memory addressing in the board to enable the system to recognize 640K. The new addressing is set up for 256K chips, installed in two of the four banks. The other two banks of memory contain 64K chips—adding up to 640K. Chapter 12 has a set of detailed instructions for modifying an IBM XT in this way.

XT Technical Specifications

Technical information for the XT system, described in this section, gives information about the system architecture, memory configurations and capacities, standard system features, disk storage, expansion slots, keyboard specifications, and also physical and environmental specifications. This information can be useful in determining what parts you need when you are upgrading or repairing these systems. Figure 3.6 shows the layout and components on the XT motherboard.

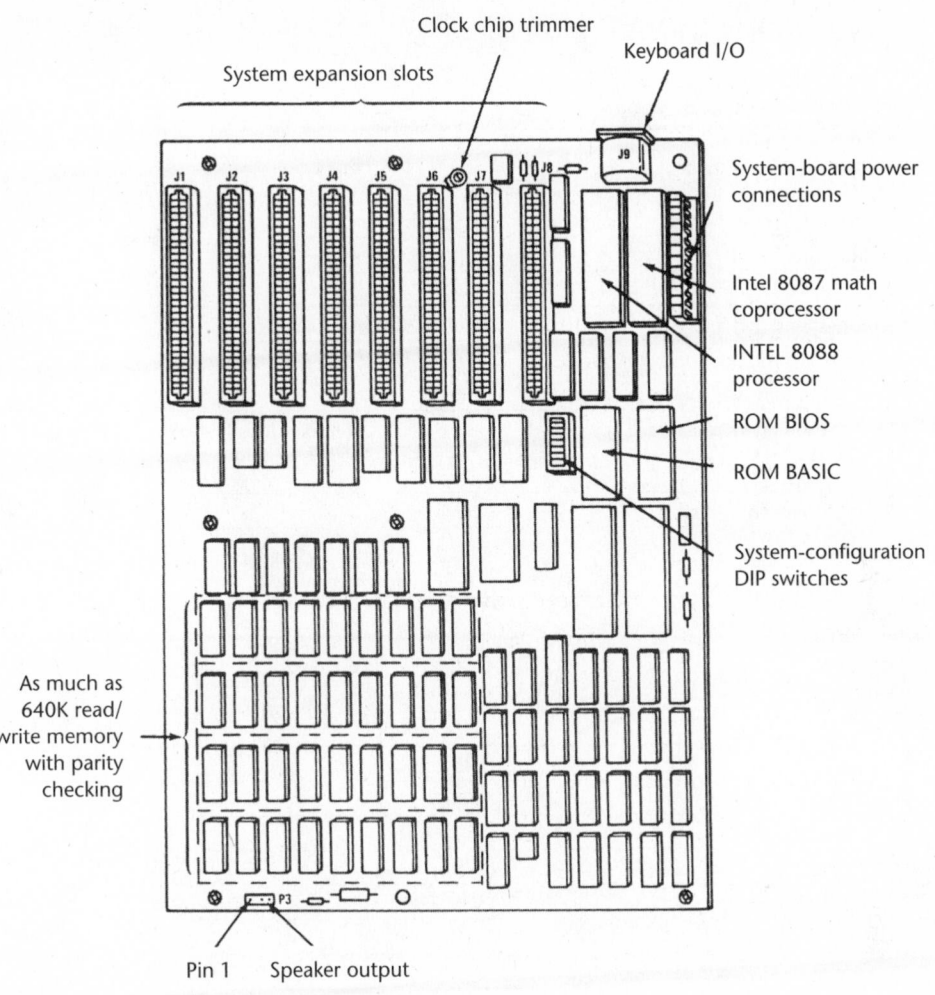

Clock chip trimmer

Keyboard I/O

System expansion slots

System-board power connections

Intel 8087 math coprocessor

INTEL 8088 processor

ROM BIOS

ROM BASIC

System-configuration DIP switches

As much as 640K read/ write memory with parity checking

Pin 1   Speaker output

Fig. 3.6

The XT system board.

System architecture	
Microprocessor	8088
Clock speed	4.77 MHz
Bus type	ISA (Industry Standard Architecture)
Bus width	8-bit
Interrupt levels	8
Type	Edge-triggered
Shareable	No
DMA channels	3
DMA burst mode supported	No

System architecture

Bus masters supported	No
Upgradeable processor complex	No

Memory

Standard on system board	256K or 640K
Maximum on system board	256K or 640K
Maximum total memory	640K
Memory speed (ns) and type	200ns dynamic RAM
System board memory-socket type	16-pin DIP
Number of memory-module sockets	36 (4 banks of 9)
Memory used on system board	36 64Kx1-bit DRAM chips in 4 banks of 9, or 2 banks of 9 256Kx1-bit and 2 banks of 9 64Kx1-bit chips
Memory cache controller	No
Wait states:	
System board	1
Adapter	1

Standard features

ROM size	40K or 64K
ROM shadowing	No
Optional math coprocessor	8087
Coprocessor speed	4.77 MHz
Standard graphics	None standard
RS232C serial ports	1 (some models)
UART chip used	NS8250B
Maximum speed (bits per second)	9,600 bps
Maximum number of ports supported	2
Pointing device (mouse) ports	None standard
Parallel printer ports	1 (some models)
Bi-directional	No
Maximum number of ports supported	3
CMOS real-time clock (RTC)	No
CMOS RAM	None

Disk storage

Internal disk and tape drive bays	2 full-height or 4 half-height
Number of 3 1/2 or 5 1/4-inch bays	0/2 or 0/4
Standard floppy drives	1x360K
Optional floppy drives:	

Disk storage

5 1/4-inch 360K	Optional	
5 1/4-inch 1.2M	No	
3 1/2-inch 720K	Optional	
3 1/2-inch 1.44M	No	
3 1/2-inch 2.88M	No	
Hard disk controller included:	ST-506/412 (Xebec Model 1210)	
ST-506/412 hard disks available	10/20M	
Drive form factor	5 1/4-inch	
Drive interface	ST-506/412	
Drive capacity	10M	20M
Average access rate (ms)	85	65
Encoding scheme	MFM	MFM
BIOS drive type number	1	2
Cylinders	306	615
Disk storage		
Heads	4	4
Sectors per track	17	17
Rotational speed (RPMs)	3600	3600
Interleave factor	6:1	6:1
Data transfer rate (kilobytes/second)	85	85
Automatic head parking	No	No

Expansion slots

Total adapter slots	8
Number of long/short slots	6/2
Number of 8-/16-/32-bit slots	8/0/0
Available slots (with video)	4

Keyboard specifications

101-key enhanced keyboard	Yes
Fast keyboard speed setting	No
Keyboard cable length	6 feet

Physical specifications

Footprint type	Desktop
Dimensions:	
Height	5.5 inches
Width	19.5 inches
Depth	16.0 inches
Weight	32 pounds

Environmental specifications	
Power-supply output	130 watts
Worldwide (110v/60Hz,220v/50Hz)	No
Auto-sensing/switching	No
Maximum current:	
90-137 VAC	4.2 amps
Operating range:	
Temperature	60-90 degrees F
Relative humidity	8-80 percent
Maximum operating altitude	7,000 feet
Heat (BTUs/hour)	717
Noise (Average dB, operating, 1m)	56
FCC classification	Class B

Table 3.3 shows the part numbers of the XT system units.

Table 3.3 IBM XT Model Part Numbers	
Description	**Number**
XT system unit/83-key keyboard, 256K:	
one full-height 360K drive	5160068
one half-height 360K drive	5160267
two full-height 360K drives	5160078
two half-height 360K drives	5160277
XT system unit/101-key keyboard, 256K:	
one half-height 360K drive	5160268
two half-height 360K drives	5160278
XT system unit/83-key keyboard, 256K, one serial, one full-height 360K drive, 10M hard disk	5160086
XT system unit/83-key keyboard, 640K, one serial, one half-height 360K drive, 20M fixed disk	5160088
XT system unit/101-key keyboard, 640K, one serial, one half-height 360K drive, 20M fixed disk	5160089
Option numbers	
PC expansion-unit Model 002, 20M fixed disk	5161002
20M fixed disk drive	6450326
20M fixed disk adapter	6450327
10M fixed disk drive	1602500
10M fixed disk adapter	1602501

Description	Number
5 1/4-inch, half-height, 360K drive	6450325
5 1/4-inch, full-height, 360K drive	1503810
3 1/2-inch, half-height, 720K internal drive	6450258
3 1/2-inch, half-height, 720K external drive	2683190
8087 math coprocessor option	1501002
Asynchronous serial adapter	1502074
Enhanced Keyboard accessories	
Clear keycaps (60) with paper inserts	6341707
Blank light keycaps	1351710
Blank dark keycaps	1351728
Paper inserts (300)	6341704
Keycap-removal tools (6)	1351717

An Introduction to the 3270 PC

On October 18, 1983, IBM announced a special version of the XT, the 3270 PC. The 3270 PC combines the functions of IBM's 3270 display system with those of the XT. This system was basically a standard XT system unit with three to six custom adapter cards added to the slots. The keyboard and display for this system also were unique and attach to some of the special adapter cards. The 3270 PC Control Program runs all this hardware. This combination can support as many as seven concurrent activities: one local PC DOS session, four remote mainframe sessions, and two local electronic notepads. With the help of the 3270 PC Control Program, information can be copied between windows, but a PC DOS window cannot receive information.

The 3270 PC included a new keyboard that addresses some complaints about the Personal Computer keyboard. The keyboard has more keys and an improved layout. The Enter and Shift keys are enlarged. The cursor keys are separate from the numeric keypad and form a small group between the main alphanumeric keys and the numeric keypad. At the top of the keyboard, 20 function keys are arranged in two rows of 10. To help clarify keystroke operations, the new keyboard is annotated. Blue legends designate PC-specific functions; black legends indicate 3270 functions. The keyboard is greatly improved, but most new keys and features don't work in PC mode. Often, you must obtain special versions of programs or disregard most of the new keys.

3270 PC Models and Features

The 3270 PC includes several specialized expansion boards that can be added to an XT. This section examines those expansion boards.

Compatible Systems

The 3270 System Adapter. The 3270 system adapter supports communication between the 3270 PC and the remote 3274 controller through a coaxial cable. One physical 3274 connection can support four logical connections.

The Display Adapter. A display adapter is used in place of the PC's monochrome or Color/Graphics Display Adapter and provides text-only displays in eight colors. The PC's extended-character graphics are available, but bit-mapped graphics capabilities were not supported unless you add the accessory extended graphics card.

The 3270 Extended Graphics Adapter. The 3270 Extended Graphics Adapter provides storage and controls necessary for displaying local graphics in high- or medium-resolution mode. High-resolution mode is available in two colors at 720-by-350 or 640-by-200 pixels. IBM originally called this adapter the XGA, but this is not the same as the newer XGA (eXtended Graphics Array), which is either available for, or included with, certain PS/2 systems.

Medium-resolution mode is available with a choice of two sets of four colors at 360-by-350 or 320-by-200 pixels. To run in medium-resolution mode, your system must have an available system-expansion slot adjacent to the display adapter card. If you install a Programmed Symbols feature (discussed in the following section) next to the display adapter, you must use the slot adjacent to the PS feature. Because the aspect ratio differs for each display monitor, applications programs must control the aspect ratio parameter; a circle on the 5150/5160 PC with the Color Graphics Adapter looks slightly elliptical on the 3270 PC with the 3270 Extended Graphics Adapter unless you change this parameter.

Programmed Symbols. The Programmed Symbols (PS) adapter provides graphics capabilities available on IBM 3278/3279 display stations. This card provides storage for as many as six 190-symbol sets whose shapes and codes were definable. Symbol sets were loaded (and accessed for display) under program control. To accept this board, your system must have an available system-expansion slot adjacent to the display adapter card. If a 3270 Extended Graphics Adapter feature is installed, you must use the slot adjacent to the 3270 Extended Graphics Adapter. The PS card is available in distributed-function terminal (DFT) mode only and can be used in one of the four host sessions.

The Keyboard Adapter. You use the keyboard adapter to adapt the 3270-style keyboard to the system unit. The keyboard connects to this board rather than to the motherboard, as it does for the PC. The board is short and must be installed in the special eighth slot in the XT system unit.

The standard XT system unit provides eight expansion slots; at least five of the slots normally were filled on delivery with the 3270 system adapter, the display adapter, the keyboard adapter, the disk drive adapter, and the hard disk controller. If you add options such as the graphics adapter and a memory multifunction card, you can see that even with the XT as a base, slots were at a premium in this system.

Software. The 3270 PC runs under control of the 3270 PC Control Program in conjunction with PC DOS and supports concurrent operation of as many as four remote-host interactive sessions, two local notepad sessions, and one PC DOS session. The Control

Program enables users to associate sessions with display screen windows and to manage the windows by a set of functions that IBM named *advanced screen management*.

Windows. You can define windows that permit viewing of all (as many as 2,000 characters) or part of a presentation space. In IBM's vocabulary, a *presentation space* is a logical display area presented by a single host. PC DOS presentation spaces are 2,000 characters (25 lines by 80 characters), remote host spaces are as many as 3,440 characters, and notepad presentation spaces are 1,920 characters.

As many as seven windows can appear on-screen at one time. Every window is associated with a distinct presentation space. Windows can be as large as the screen or as small as one character, and can be positioned at any point within their presentation space. A window 20 characters wide and four lines long, for example, shows the first 20 characters of the last four lines of a host session display. You can change window size and position in the presentation space at any time without affecting the content of the presentation space.

At any time, only one window on the 3270 PC screen can be the active window. When you enter information from the keyboard, the information is directed to the session associated with the active window. You can switch between active windows by using keystroke commands.

You can define the foreground and background colors of host session windows not using extended data-stream attributes. You can define the background color for the 5272 screen also (the color to be displayed in areas not occupied by windows).

Special Facilities. In addition to advanced screen-management functions, the Control Program offers a number of related special facilities that help you take further advantage of the 3270 environment.

Data can be copied within or between any presentation spaces except into the PC DOS screen. You copy by marking a block of data in one window and marking a destination in some other window, much the same as a block copy in a word processor.

You can think of the notepads as local electronic scratch pads you can use at your convenience. You can save and restore the contents of a notepad at any time by using PC DOS files as the storage medium.

You can define as many as 10 screen configurations, each of which describes a set of windows configured in any way, and they can display on command any one configuration. Use PC DOS files to store the configuration information.

You can print a full copy of the display screen on a local printer. Similarly, you can print a full copy of a PC DOS presentation space on a local printer. You also can print a full copy of any host presentation space on a local printer, a 3274 attached printer, or a 43xx display/printer.

The Control Program maintains at the bottom of the screen a status line that displays current configuration information, including the name of the active window. The program includes a help function and displays active workstation functions and sessions

II

Compatible Systems

and an on-line tutorial that explains and simulates system functions. The tutorial is a standard PC DOS program that can be run on any IBM PC.

The Control Program, assisted by a host-based IBM 3270 PC file-transfer program, can initiate transfers of ASCII, binary, and EBCDIC files to and from remote hosts.

A drawback to this software is that it is memory resident and consumes an enormous amount of space. The result is that in the PC DOS session, not many applications can run in the leftover workspace. Your only option—reboot the computer without loading the Control Program—is a clumsy and time-consuming procedure. Even with this tactic, the drastic differences in the display hardware and the keyboard still render this computer much less than "PC compatible." The AT version of this system offers a solution to the memory problem by enabling much of the Control Program to reside in the AT's extended memory, above the 1M memory limit of the PC and XT.

The Significance of the 3270. The 3270 PC is a great system to use if you are a corporate worker who deals every day with many information sources (most of which are available through an IBM mainframe SNA network). Corporate information managers greatly appreciate the concurrent access to several SNA-based databases. The 3270 PC provides essential tools for viewing, extracting, combining, and manipulating information: multiple concurrent-terminal sessions, cut-and-paste capability between sessions, PC productivity tools, and up- and downloading host files from PC DOS files.

For simple 3270 terminal-emulation capability, however, this system is more than you need. In addition, the display and keyboard make this system partially incompatible with the rest of the PC world. Many PC applications do not run properly on this system. If you depend more on PC DOS applications than on the mainframe, or if you consider the multiple mainframe sessions unimportant, using one of the simpler 3270 emulation adapters is more cost-effective.

An Introduction to the XT 370

On Oct. 18, 1983, IBM introduced another special version of the XT, the XT 370, consisting of a standard PC XT chassis with three special cards added. These adapters were special S/370-emulation cards that enable the computer to execute the mainframe system 370 instruction set. The boards enable you to run VM/CMS and emulate 4M of virtual memory. You can download programs and compilers from the mainframe and execute them directly on the XT. You switch between 370 mode and the standard XT by using a *hot key*, or special keystroke, sequence.

XT/370 Models and Features

The three cards that make up the XT 370—the PC 370-P card, the PC 370-M card, and the PC 3277-EM card—are examined in this section.

The P card implements an emulation of the 370 instruction set. The card has three microprocessors. One processor is a heavily modified Motorola 68000 produced under license to IBM. This chip implements the general-purpose registers, the PSW instruction fetch and decode logic, and 72 commonly used S/370 instructions.

A second processor is a slightly modified Motorola 68000, which is listed in Motorola's catalog. The chip emulates the remaining nonfloating-point instructions, manipulates the page table, handles exception conditions, and performs hardware housekeeping.

The third microprocessor, a modified Intel 8087 that executes S/370 floating-point instructions, is interfaced as a peripheral rather than the normal 8087 coprocessor linkage.

The M card has 512K of parity-checked RAM. You can access this memory from the P card or from the XT's native 8088 processor. Concurrent requests are arbitrated in favor of the 8088. The M card resides in an XT expansion slot but is connected to the P card by a special edge connector. Sixteen-bit-wide transfers between M card memory and the P card are carried out through this connector (normal XT memory transfers operate in 8-bit-wide chunks).

Operating in native PC mode, the M card's memory is addressed as contiguous memory beginning at the end of the 256K memory of the system's motherboard. In native PC mode, the XT 370 has 640K of usable RAM; some of the M card's memory is not used.

Operating in 370 mode, only the 512K RAM of the M card is usable (the memory on the motherboard is not available). The first 480K of this memory implements 480K of real S/370 space. The remaining 32K on the M card functions as a microcode control-storage area for the second P card microprocessor.

The first 64K (of 480K) of S/370 memory are consumed by VM/PC; 416K of real memory remains for user programs. User programs larger than 416K are handled through paging.

The PC 3277-EM card attaches the XT 370 to an S/370 mainframe by a local or remote 3274 control unit (connection through coaxial cable). When VM/PC is running, the EM card uses the IBM monochrome or color display. Under VM/PC, the EM card is used also to up- and download data between a host VM system and the XT 370.

The XT 370 can run in native PC XT mode or in S/370 mode under the VM/PC Control Program. Under VM/PC, the user can use a "hot key" to alternate between a local CMS session and a remote 3277 session (or, optionally, a 3101-emulation session). VM/PC does not offer a true VM-like environment. Rather, VM/PC provides an environment in which CMS applications can run. Non-CMS VM applications do not run on the XT 370.

The VM/PC system, which must be licensed, is provided on six floppy disks and includes the VM/PC Control Program, CMS, XEDIT, EXEC2, local and remote file-transfer utilities, and the 370 Processor Control package.

Estimations of the XT 370 CPU's performance indicate that it is about half of a 4331 when the XT 370 is running a commercial instruction mix. When the XT 370 is running scientific codes, you can expect twice the performance as from the 4331. The CPU generally is categorized as a 0.1 MIPS (million instructions per second) processor. This size

II

Compatible Systems

does not sound impressive when you're used to multi-MIPS, single-chip microprocessors, but remember that 0.1-million S/370 instructions likely will produce substantially more computing than 0.1-million instructions of your standard microprocessor chip.

The XT 370 running in S/370 mode can access the 512K on the M card. Of this 512K, 32K is reserved for microcode control storage, and 65K is used by the VM/PC Control Program; 416K remains for user programs. If a user program requires more memory than 416K, VM/PC uses a paging area on the XT 370's hard disk and swaps pieces of the program in and out of memory according to use.

Swapping on the small 10M or 20M hard disks is considerably slower than on the large disks used with mainframes. Programs larger than 416K, therefore, probably will run very slowly. Field test users report long delays in loading large programs into memory, even when the programs are well under the maximum for nonpaging operation. Delays are due to the relatively slow operation of the XT 370 hard disks. Because of size and speed problems, many users of these systems should consider larger and faster hard disks.

An Introduction to the Portable PC

IBM introduced the Portable PC on Feb. 16, 1984. The IBM Portable PC, a "transportable" personal computer, has a built-in, 9-inch, amber composite video monitor; one 5 1/4-inch, half-height floppy disk drive (with space for an optional second drive); an 83-key keyboard; two adapter cards; a floppy disk controller; and a Color Graphics Adapter (CGA). The unit has also a universal-voltage power supply capable of overseas operation on 220-volt power. Figure 3.7 shows the Portable PC exterior.

The system board used in the IBM Portable PC is the same board used in the original IBM XT's, with 256K of memory. Because the XT motherboard was used, eight expansion slots are available for the connection of adapter boards, although only two slots can accept a full-length adapter card because of internal space restrictions. The power supply is basically the same as an XT's, with physical changes for portability and a small amount of power drawn to run the built-in monitor. In function and performance, the Portable PC system unit has identical characteristics to an equivalently configured IBM PC XT system unit. Figure 3.8 shows the Portable PC interior view.

IBM withdrew the Portable PC from the market April 2, 1986, a date that coincides with the introduction of the IBM Convertible laptop PC. The Portable PC is rare because not many were sold. The system was largely misunderstood by the trade press and user community. Most people did not understand that the system was really a portable XT, and had more to offer than the standard IBM PC did. Maybe if IBM had called the system the Portable XT, it would have sold better.

The Portable PC system unit has these major functional components:

- Intel 8088 4.77 Mhz microprocessor

- ROM-based diagnostics (POST)

Keyboard cable connector

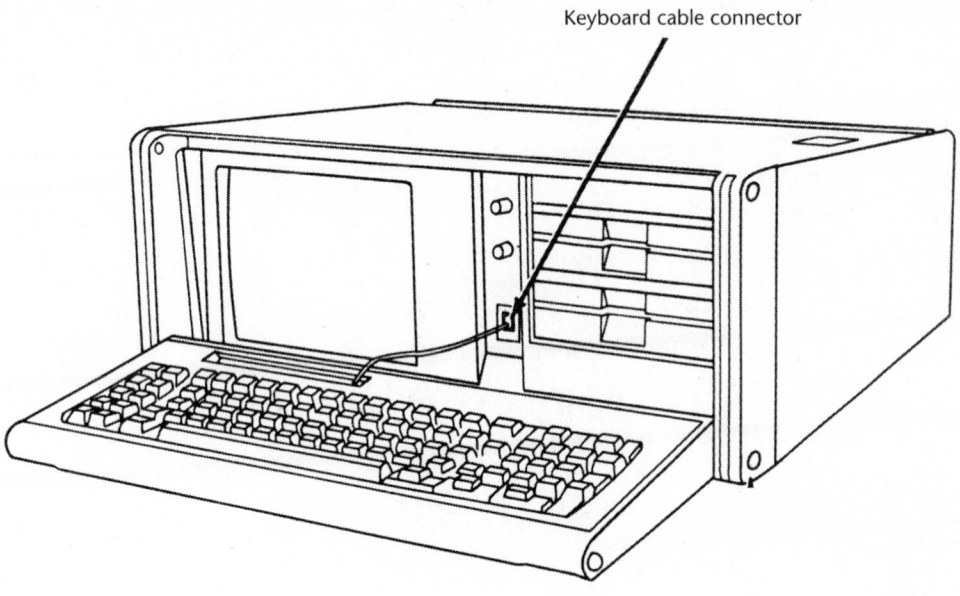

Fig. 3.7
The IBM Portable PC.

Color/Graphics
monitor adapter

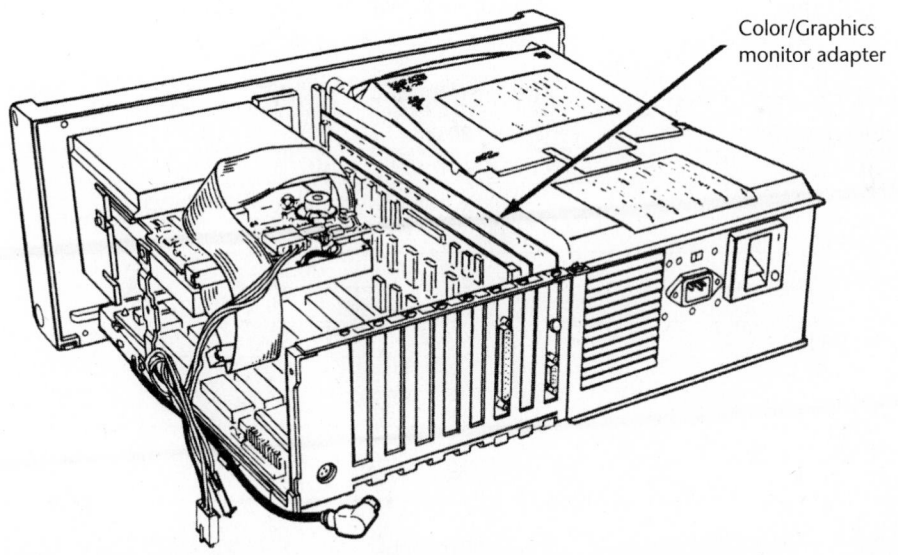

Fig. 3.8
The IBM Portable PC's interior.

- BASIC language interpreter in ROM

- 256K of dynamic RAM

- Eight expansion slots (two long slots, one 3/4-length slot, and five short slots)

- Socket for 8087 math coprocessor

- Color/Graphics Monitor Adapter

- 9-inch, amber, composite video monitor

- Floppy disk interface

- One or two half-height 360K floppy drives

- 114-watt universal power supply (115 V to 230 V, 50 Hz to 60 Hz)

- Lightweight 83-key keyboard

- Enclosure with carrying handle

- Carrying bag for the system unit

Portable PC Technical Specifications

The technical data for the Portable PC system is described in this section, which includes information about the system architecture, memory configurations and capacities, standard system features, disk storage, expansion slots, keyboard specifications, and also physical and environmental specifications. This information can be useful in determining what kinds of parts you need when you are upgrading or repairing these systems. Figure 3.6 previously showed the XT motherboard, also used in the Portable PC.

System architecture	
Microprocessor	8088
Clock speed	4.77 MHz
Bus type	ISA (Industry Standard Architecture)
Bus width	8-bit
Interrupt levels	8
Type	Edge-triggered
Shareable	No
DMA channels	3
DMA burst mode supported	No
Bus masters supported	No
Upgradeable processor complex	No

Memory	
Standard on system board	256K
Maximum on system board	256K

Memory

Maximum total memory	640K
Memory speed (ns) and type	200ns dynamic RAM
System board memory-socket type	16-pin DIP
Number of memory-module sockets	36 (4 banks of 9)
Memory used on system board	36 64Kx1-bit DRAM chips in 4 banks of 9 chips
Memory cache controller	No
Wait states:	
System board	1
Adapter	1

Standard features

ROM size	40K
ROM shadowing	No
Optional math coprocessor	8087
Coprocessor speed	4.77 MHz
Standard graphics	None standard
RS232C serial ports	None standard
UART chip used	NS8250B
Maximum speed (bits per second)	9,600 bps
Maximum number of ports supported	2
Pointing device (mouse) ports	None standard
Parallel printer ports	None standard
Bi-directional	No
Maximum number of ports supported	3
CMOS real-time clock (RTC)	No
CMOS RAM	None

Disk storage

Internal disk and tape drive bays	2 half-height
Number of 3 1/2-/5 1/4-inch bays	0/2
Standard floppy drives	1x360K
Optional floppy drives:	
5 1/4-inch 360K	Optional
5 1/4-inch 1.2M	No
3 1/2-inch 720K	Optional
3 1/2-inch 1.44M	No
3 1/2-inch 2.88M	No
Hard disk controller included	None

II

Compatible Systems

Expansion slots	
Total adapter slots	8
Number of long and short slots	5/3
Number of 8-/16-/32-bit slots	8/0/0
Available slots (with video)	6

Keyboard specifications	
101-key Enhanced Keyboard	No
Fast keyboard speed setting	No
Keyboard cable length	6 feet

Physical specifications	
Footprint type	Desktop
Dimensions:	
Height	8.0 inches
Width	20.0 inches
Depth	17.0 inches
Weight	31 pounds

Environmental specifications	
Power-supply output	114 watts
Worldwide (110/60,220/50)	Yes
Auto-sensing/switching	No
Maximum current:	
90-137 VAC	4.0 amps
Operating range:	
Temperature	60-90 degrees F
Relative humidity	8-80 percent
Maximum operating altitude	7,000 feet
Heat (BTUs/hour)	650
Noise (Average dB, operating, 1m)	42
FCC classification	Class B

Table 3.4 shows the part numbers for the Portable PC:

Table 3.4 IBM Portable PC Model Part Numbers	
Description	Number
256K, one 360K half-height drive	5155068
256K, two 360K half-height drives	5155076
Half-height 360K floppy disk drive	6450300

The disk drive used in the Portable PC was a half-height drive, the same unit specified for use in the PCjr. When the Portable PC was introduced, PCjr was the only one IBM sold with the half-height drive.

An Introduction to the AT

IBM introduced the Personal Computer AT (Advanced Technology) on Aug. 14, 1984. The IBM AT system included many features previously unavailable in IBM's PC systems such as increased performance, an advanced 16-bit microprocessor, high-density floppy disk and hard disk drives, larger memory space, and an advanced coprocessor. Despite its new design, the IBM AT incredibly retained compatibility with most existing hardware and software products for the earlier systems.

In most cases, IBM AT system performance was from three to five times faster than the IBM XT for single applications running DOS on both computers. The performance increase is due to the combination of a reduced cycle count for most instructions by the 80286 processor, an increased system clock rate, 16-bit memory, and faster hard disk and controller.

The AT system unit has been available in several models: a floppy-disk-equipped base model (068) and several hard-disk-enhanced models. Based on a high-performance, 16-bit, Intel 80286 microprocessor, each computer includes Cassette BASIC language in ROM and a CMOS (Complementary Metal Oxide Semiconductor) clock and calendar with battery backup. All models were equipped with a high-density (HD) 1.2M floppy disk drive, a keyboard, and a lock. For standard memory, the base model offers 256K, and the enhanced models offer 512K. In addition, the enhanced models have a 20M or a 30M hard disk drive and a serial/parallel adapter. Each system can be expanded through customer-installable options. You can add memory (to 512K) for the base model by adding chips to the system board. You can expand all models to 16M by installing memory cards.

Besides the standard drives included with the system, IBM offered only two different hard disks as upgrades for the AT: a 30M hard disk drive and a 20M hard disk drive. IBM also offered only three different types of floppy drives for the AT; a second, high-density (HD) 1.2M floppy disk drive; a double-density (DD) 360K floppy disk drive; and a new 3 1/2-inch 720K drive. The original 068 and 099 models of the AT did not support the 720K drive in the BIOS. You had to add a special driver (DRIVER.SYS; supplied with DOS) for the drive to work. The later model ATs supported not only the 720K 3 1/2-inch drive but also the 1.44M high-density (HD) 3 1/2-inch floppy drive, however IBM never sold or installed the 1.44M drives in a factory configuration. Also, the CMOS Setup program never offered the 1.44M drive as a selection even though the BIOS would support it. In that case, one could use an aftermarket or public domain CMOS Setup program which did offer the choice. These were available on many BBS (Bulletin Board Systems) as well as Compuserve.

You can install as many as two floppy disk drives and one hard disk drive or one floppy disk drive and two hard disk drives in the system unit. To use the high-density 5 1/4 inch floppy disk drives properly, you must have special floppy disks—5 1/4-inch, high-coercivity, double-sided, soft-sectored disks. Because of track width problems between the high-density 1.2M drives and the double density 360K drives, a double-density 360K floppy drive was available for complete compatibility with the standard PC or XT systems. You can exchange disks reliably between the 1.2M and the standard 360K drives if you use the proper method and understand the recording process. This information is covered in Chapter 9. For complete interchange reliability, however, IBM recommended you purchase the 360K drive.

The system unit has eight slots that support cards for additional devices, features, or memory. Six slots support the advanced 16-bit or 8-bit option cards. Two slots support only 8-bit option cards. All system-unit models, however, use one 16-bit slot for the fixed disk and floppy disk drive adapter. The enhanced models use an additional 8-bit slot for the serial/parallel adapter. The result is seven available expansion slots for the base model and six available expansion slots for enhanced models. Figure 3.9 shows the interior of an AT system unit.

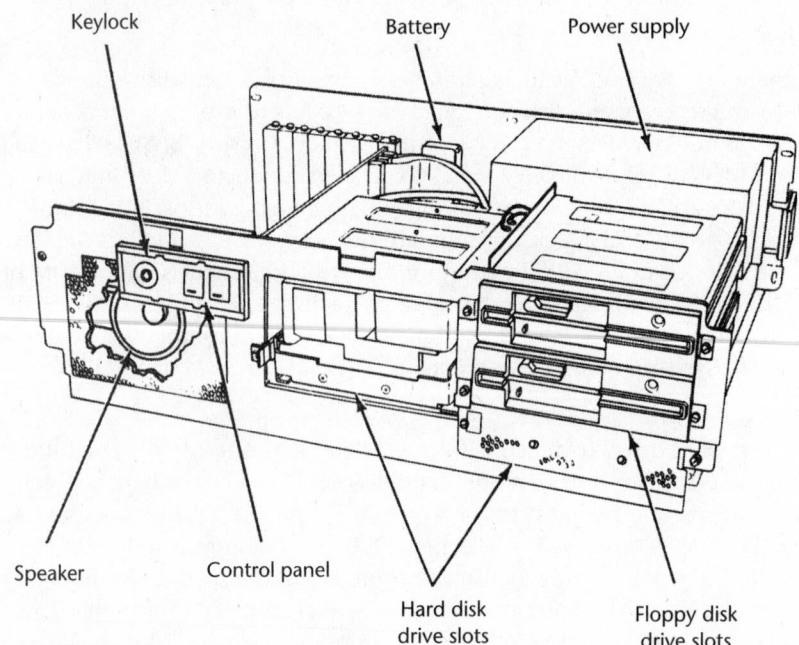

Fig. 3.9
The IBM AT system-unit interior.

All models include a universal power supply; a temperature-controlled, variable-speed cooling fan; and a security lock with key. The user selects the power supply for a country's voltage range. The cooling fan significantly reduces the noise in most environments; the fan runs slower when the system unit is cool and faster when the system unit is hot. When the system is locked, no one can remove the system-unit cover, boot the system, or enter commands or data from the keyboard, thereby enhancing the system's security.

The keyboard is attached to the system unit by a 9-foot, coiled cable that enables the AT to adapt to a variety of workspace configurations. The keyboard includes key-location enhancements and mode indicators for improved keyboard usability. Figure 3.10 shows the rear panel of an AT.

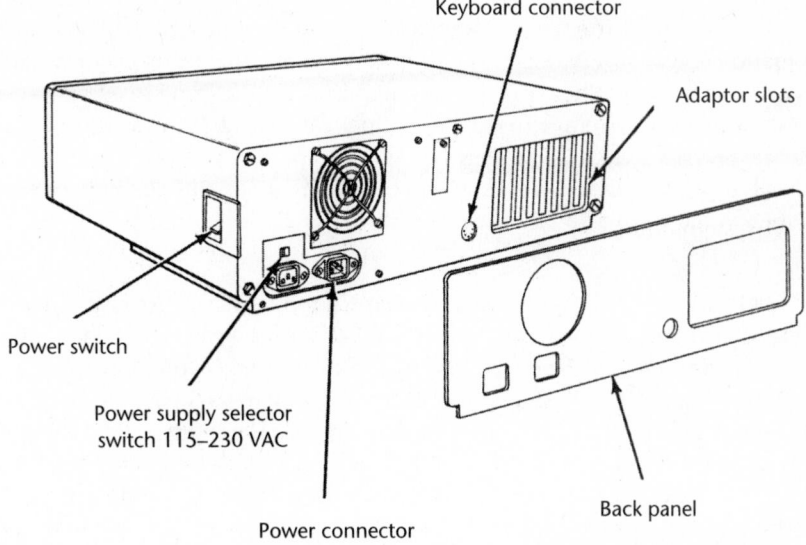

Fig. 3.10
The IBM AT rear view.

Every system unit for the AT models has these major functional components:

- Intel 80286 (6Mhz or 8Mhz) microprocessor
- Socket for 80287 math coprocessor
- 8086-compatible real mode
- Protected virtual address mode
- Eight I/O expansion slots (six 16-bit, two 8-bit)
- 256K of dynamic RAM (base model)
- 512K of dynamic RAM (enhanced models)
- ROM-based diagnostics (POST)
- BASIC language interpreter in ROM
- Hard/floppy disk controller
- 1.2M HD floppy drive

AT Models and Features

Since the introduction of the AT, several models have become available. First, IBM announced two systems: a base model (068) and an enhanced model (099). The primary difference between the two systems was the standard 20M hard disk that came with the enhanced model. IBM has introduced two other AT systems since the first systems, each offering new features.

The first generation of AT systems have a 6 MHz system clock that dictates the processor cycle time. The *cycle time*, the system's smallest interval of time, represents the speed at which operations occur. Every operation in a computer takes at least one or (usually) several cycles to complete. Therefore, if two computers are the same in every way except for the clock speed, the system with the faster clock rate executes the same operations in a shorter time proportional to the difference in clock speed. Cycle time and clock speed are two different ways of describing the same thing. Discussions of clock speed are significant when you consider buying the AT because not all models have the same clock speed.

All models of the AT included a combination hard/floppy disk controller that was really two separate controllers on the same circuit board. The board was designed by IBM and Western Digital, and manufactured for IBM by Western Digital. This controller had no on-board ROM BIOS like the Xebec hard disk controller used in the XT. In the AT, IBM built full support for the hard disk controller directly into the motherboard ROM BIOS. To support different types of hard disks, IBM encoded a table into the motherboard ROM that listed the parameters of various drives that could be installed. In the first version of the AT, with a ROM BIOS dated 01/10/84, only the first 14 types in the table were filled in. Type 15 was reserved for internal reasons, and was not usable. Other table entries from 16 through 47 were left unused and actually filled with zeros. Later versions of the AT added new drive types to the tables, starting from type 16 and up.

The first two AT models were the 068 (base) model, which had 256K on the motherboard and a single 1.2M floppy disk drive, and the model 099 (enhanced), which had a 20M hard disk drive, a serial/parallel adapter, and 512K on the motherboard. IBM designated the motherboard on these computers as Type 1, which is physically larger than the later Type 2 board and used an unusual memory layout. The memory is configured as four banks of 128K chips—512K on the board. This configuration sounds reasonable until you realize that a 128K chip does not really exist in the physical form factor that IBM used. IBM actually created this type of memory device by stacking a 64K chip on top of another one and soldering the two together. My guess is that IBM had many 64K chips to use, and the AT was available to take them.

On Oct. 2, 1985, IBM announced a new model of the AT, the Personal Computer AT Model 239. The system has all the standard features of the AT Model 099, but has also a 30M hard disk rather than a 20M hard disk. A second, optional 30M hard disk drive expands the Model 239's hard disk storage to 60M. This unit's motherboard, a second-generation design IBM calls Type 2, is about 25 percent smaller than the Type 1 but uses the same mounting location for physical compatibility. All important items, such as the slots and connectors, remain in the same locations. Other major improvements in this board are in the memory. The 128K memory chips have been replaced by 256K devices. Now only two banks of chips were needed to get the same 512K on the board.

The AT Model 239 includes these items:

- 512K of RAM (standard)

- 6 Mhz Type 2 motherboard with 256K memory chips

- Serial/parallel adapter (standard)

- 30M hard disk (standard)

- New ROM BIOS (dated 06/10/85)

    ROM supports 3 1/2-inch 720K floppy drives without using external driver programs

    ROM supports 22 hard disk types (up to type 23), including the supplied 30M disk

    POST fixes clock rate to 6 MHz

The Type 2 motherboard's design is much improved over Type 1's; the Type 2 motherboard has improved internal-circuit timing and layout. Improvements in the motherboard indicated that the system would be pushed to higher speeds—exactly what happened with the next round of introductions.

In addition to obvious physical differences, the Model 239 includes significantly different ROM software from the previous models. The new ROM supports more types of hard and floppy disks, and its new POST prevents alteration of the clock rate from the standard 6 MHz models. Because support for the 30M hard disk is built into the new ROM, IBM sells also a 30M hard disk upgrade kit that includes the new ROM for the original AT systems. This $1,795 kit represents unfortunately the only legal way to obtain the newer ROM.

The 30M hard disk drive upgrade kit for the Personal Computer AT Models 068 and 099 includes all the features in the 30M hard disk drive announced for the AT Model 239. The upgrade kit also has a new basic input-output subsystem (BIOS), essential to AT operation. The new ROM BIOS supports 22 drive types (compared to the original 14 in earlier ATs), including the new 30M drive. To support the 30M hard disk drive, a new diagnostics floppy disk and an updated guide-to-operations manual were shipped with this kit.

The 30M update kit included these items:

- 30M hard disk drive

- Two new ROM BIOS modules

- Channel keeper bar (a bracket for the fixed disk)

■ Data cable for the hard disk

■ Diagnostics and Setup disk

Some people were upset initially that IBM had "fixed the microprocessor clock" to 6 MHz in the new model, thereby disallowing any possible "hot rod" modifications. Many people realized that the clock crystal on all the AT models was socketed so that the crystal could be replaced easily by a faster one. More important, because the AT circuit design is modular, changing the clock crystal does not have repercussions throughout the rest of the system, as is the case in the PC and PC XT. For the price of a new crystal (about $1) and the time needed to plug it in, someone easily could increase an AT's speed by 30 percent, and sometimes more. Because the ROM now checked the CPU clock rate, you no longer could implement a simple speedup alteration without also changing the ROM BIOS as well.

Many people believed that this change was made to prevent the AT from being "too fast" and therefore competing with IBM's minicomputers. In reality, the earlier motherboard was run intentionally at 6 MHz because IBM did not believe that the ROM BIOS software and critical system timing was fully operational at a higher speed. Also, IBM used some components that were rated only for 6 Mhz operation, starting with the CPU. Users who increased the speed of their early computers often received DOS error messages from timing problems, and in some cases, total system lockups because of components not functioning properly at the higher speeds. Many companies selling speedup kits sold software to help smooth over some of these problems, but IBM's official solution was to improve the ROM BIOS software and motherboard circuitry and to introduce a complete new system running at the faster speed. If you want increased speed no matter what model you have, several companies used to sell clock-crystal replacements that were frequency synthesizers rather than a fixed type of crystal. The units can wait until the POST is finished and change midstream to an increased operating speed. Unfortunately, I know of nobody still making or selling these upgrades. If you are really interested in speeding up your AT in this manner, I discuss a technique for patching the existing ROM to ignore the speed test in Chapter 12, so that a faster crystal will still pass the POST procedure.

On April 2, 1986, IBM introduced the Personal Computer AT Models 319 and 339. These two similar systems were an enhancement of the earlier Model 239. The primary difference from the Model 239 is a faster clock crystal that provides 8 MHz operation. The Model 339 has a new keyboard, the Enhanced Keyboard, with 101 keys rather than the usual 84. Model 319 is the same as Model 339, but includes the original keyboard.

Highlights of the Models 319 and 339 are shown in this list:

■ Faster processor speed (8 MHz)

■ Type 2 motherboard, with 256K chips

■ 512K of RAM (standard)

■ Serial/parallel adapter (standard)

- 30M hard disk (standard)

- New ROM BIOS (dated 11/15/85)

- ROM Support for 22 types (up to type 23) of hard disks

- ROM Support for 3 1/2-inch drives, at both 720K and 1.44M capacities

- POST fixes clock rate to 8 MHz

- 101-key Enhanced Keyboard (standard on Model 339)

  Recappable keys

  Selectric typing section

  Dedicated numeric pad

  Dedicated cursor and screen controls

  12 function keys

  Indicator lights

  9-foot cable

The most significant physical difference in these new systems is the Enhanced Keyboard on the Model 339. The keyboard, similar to a 3270 keyboard, has 101 keys. It could be called the IBM "corporate" keyboard because it is standard on all new desktop systems. The 84-key PC keyboard still was available, with a new 8 MHz model, as the Model 319.

These new 8 MHz systems were available only in an enhanced configuration with a standard 30M hard drive. If you wanted a hard disk larger than IBM's 30M, you could either add a second drive or replace the 30M unit with something larger.

ROM support for 3 1/2-inch disk drives at both 720K and 1.44M exists only in Models 339 and 319. In particular, the 1.44M drive, although definitely supported by the ROM BIOS and controller, was not ever offered as an option by IBM. This shortcoming meant that the IBM Setup program found on the Diagnostics and Setup disk did not offer the 1.44M floppy drive as a choice when configuring the system! Anybody adding such a drive had to use one of the many Setup replacement programs available in the public domain, or "borrow" one from an IBM compatible system that used a floppy disk-based setup program. Adding the 1.44M drive became one of the most popular upgrades for the AT systems, because many newer systems came with that type of drive as standard equipment. Earlier AT systems still can use the 720K and 1.44M drives, but they would need to either upgrade the ROM to support it (recommended) or possibly use software drivers to make them work.

AT Technical Specifications

Technical information for the AT system is described in this section. You will find information about the system architecture, memory configurations and capacities, standard system features, disk storage, expansion slots, keyboard specifications, as well as physical

II

Compatible Systems

and environmental specifications. This type of information can be useful in determining what types of parts are needed when you are upgrading or repairing these systems. Figures 3.11 and 3.12 show the layout and components on the two different AT motherboards.

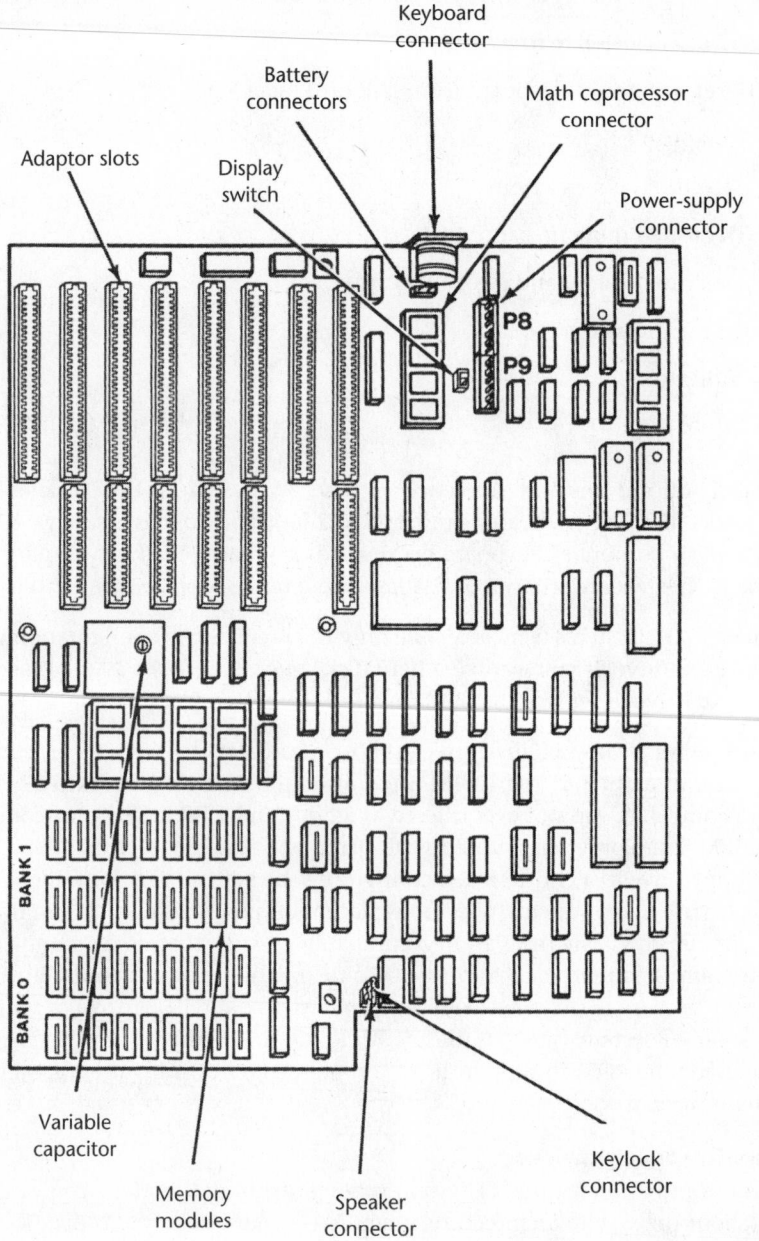

Fig. 3.11
The IBM AT Type 1 system board.

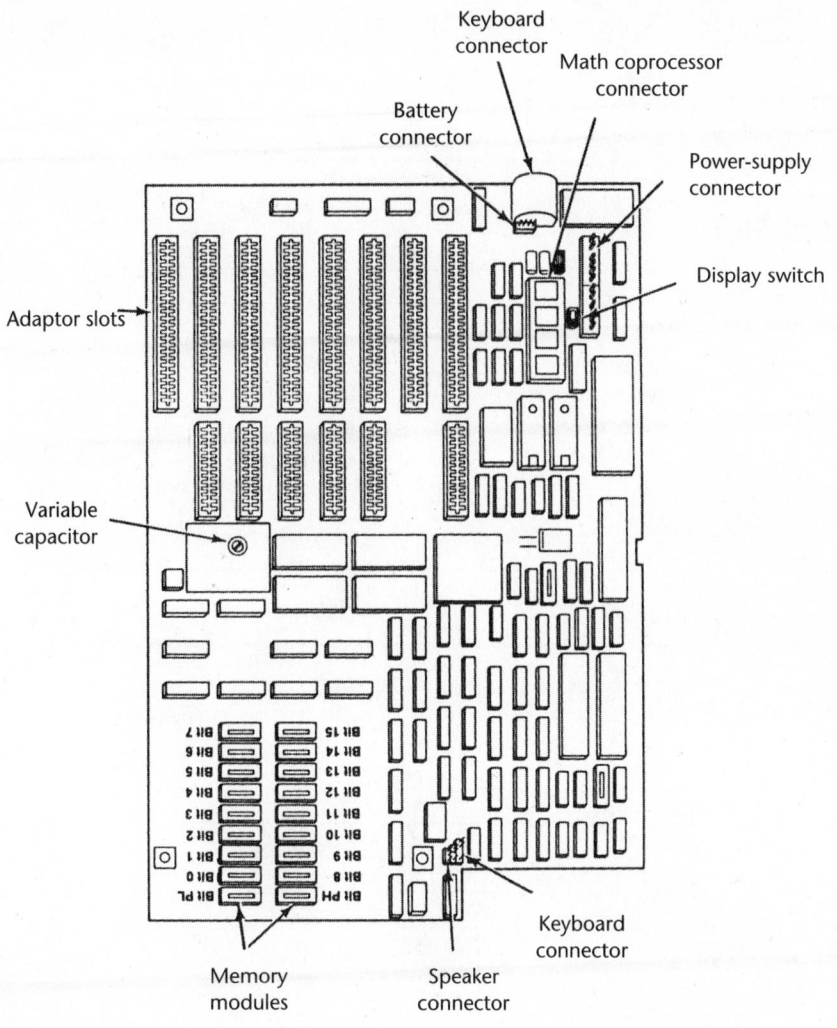

Fig. 3.12

The IBM AT Type 2 system board.

System architecture	
Microprocessor	80286
Clock speed	6 or 8 MHz
Bus type	ISA (Industry Standard Architecture)
Bus width	16-bit
Interrupt levels	16
Type	Edge-triggered
Shareable	No
DMA channels	7

Compatible Systems

System architecture

DMA burst mode supported	No
Bus masters supported	No
Upgradeable processor complex	No

Memory

Standard on system board	512K
Maximum on system board	512K
Maximum total memory	16M
Memory speed (ns) and type	150ns dynamic RAM
System board memory-socket type	16-pin DIP
Number of memory-module sockets	18 or 36 (1 or 2 banks of 18)
Memory used on system board	36 128Kx1-bit DRAM chips in 2 banks of 18, or 18 256Kx1-bit chips in one bank
Memory cache controller	No
Wait states:	
System board	1
Adapter	1

Standard features

ROM size	64K
ROM shadowing	No
Optional math coprocessor	80287
Coprocessor speed	4 or 5.33 MHz
Standard graphics	None standard
RS232C serial ports	1 (some models)
UART chip used	NS16450
Maximum speed (bits per second)	9,600 bps
Maximum number of ports supported	2
Pointing device (mouse) ports	None standard
Parallel printer ports	1 (some models)
Bi-directional	Yes
Maximum number of ports supported	3
CMOS real-time clock (RTC)	Yes
CMOS RAM	64 bytes
Battery life	5 years

Disk storage

Internal disk and tape drive bays	1 full-height and 2 half-height
Number of 3 1/2-, 5 1/4-inch bays	0/3
Standard floppy drives	1x1.2M
Optional floppy drives:	

Disk storage

5 1/4-inch 360K	Optional
5 1/4-inch 1.2M	Standard
3 1/2-inch 720K	Optional
3 1/2-inch 1.44M	Optional (8 MHz models)
3 1/2-inch 2.88M	No
Hard disk controller included:	ST-506/412 (Western Digital WD1002-WA2 or WD1003-WA2)
ST-506/412 hard disks available	20/30M
Drive form factor	5 1/4-inch
Drive interface	ST-506/412

Drive capacity	20M	30M
Average access rate (ms)	40	40
Encoding scheme	MFM	MFM
BIOS drive type number	2	20
Cylinders	615	733
Heads	4	5
Sectors per track	17	17
Rotational speed (RPMs)	3600	3600
Disk storage		
Interleave factor	3:1	3:1
Data transfer rate (kilobytes/second)	170	170
Automatic head parking	Yes	Yes

Expansion slots

Total adapter slots	8
Number of long and short slots	8/0
Number of 8-/16-/32-bit slots	2/6/0
Available slots (with video)	5

Keyboard specifications

101-key Enhanced Keyboard	Yes (8 MHz models)
Fast keyboard speed setting	Yes
Keyboard cable length	6 feet

Physical specifications

Footprint type	Desktop
Dimensions:	
Height	6.4 inches
Width	21.3 inches
Depth	17.3 inches
Weight	43 pounds

Environmental specifications	
Power-supply output	192 watts
Worldwide (110v/60Hz,220v/50Hz)	Yes
Auto-sensing/switching	No
Maximum current:	
90-137 VAC	5.0 amps
Operating range:	
Temperature	60-90 degrees F
Relative humidity	8-80 percent
Maximum operating altitude	7,000 feet
Heat (BTUs/hour)	1229
Noise (Average dB, operating, 1m)	42
FCC classification	Class B

Table 3.5 shows the AT system-unit part-number information.

Table 3.5 IBM AT Model Part Numbers	
Description	**Number**
AT 6 MHz/84-key keyboard, 256K: one 1.2M floppy drive	5170068
AT 6 MHz/84-key keyboard, 512K, serial/parallel: one 1.2M floppy drive, 20M hard disk	5170099
one 1.2M floppy drive, 30M hard disk	5170239
AT 8 MHz/84-key keyboard, 512K, serial/parallel: one 1.2M floppy drive, 30M hard disk	5170319
AT 8 MHz/101-key, 512K, serial/parallel: one 1.2M floppy drive, 30M hard disk	5170339
System options	
20M fixed disk drive	6450205
30M fixed disk	6450210
30M fixed disk drive upgrade kit	6450468
360K half-height floppy disk drive (AT)	6450207
1.2M high-density drive	6450206
3 1/2-inch, half-height, 720K external drive (AT)	2683191
Serial/parallel adapter	6450215
80287 math coprocessor option	6450211
Floor-standing enclosure	6450218

Description	Number
Enhanced Keyboard accessories	
Clear keycaps (60) with paper inserts	6341707
Blank light keycaps	1351710
Blank dark keycaps	1351728
Paper inserts (300)	6341704
Keycap-removal tools (6)	1351717

3270-AT

IBM announced the AT 3270 on June 18, 1985. This computer, basically the same as the original 3270 PC, is configured with an AT, rather than an XT, as the base. New software enhancements and adapter cards used the DOS memory space better and can place much of the Control Program in the extended-memory area, beyond the 1M boundary. Much of this capability comes from the *XMA card* from IBM. Because much of the Control Program can reside in the area above 1M, DOS can find more room for applications software. Although this configuration doesn't eliminate the incompatibilities in the display hardware or keyboard, it at least makes available the memory needed to run an application.

The AT 3270 system has the same basic adapters as the standard 3270 PC. This system differs, however, in the capability of enabling the Control Program to reside in the memory space above 1M (extended memory), which doesn't exist on a standard PC or XT. IBM made several changes in the Control Program for this system and in special memory adapters, such as the XMA card. These changes enhanced the compatibility of the AT 3270 system over the original 3270 PC.

For more information about the AT 3270 system, refer to the section on the 3270 PC in this chapter.

The AT-370

The AT-370 is basically the same system as the XT 370 except for its use of an AT as the base unit. The same three custom processor boards that convert an XT into an XT-370 also plug into an AT. This system is at least two to three times faster than the XT version. The custom processor boards also were available as an upgrade for existing ATs. For a more complete description of this system, refer to the section "XT/370 PC Models and Features" earlier in this chapter.

An Introduction to the XT Model 286

On Sept. 9, 1986, IBM introduced a new AT-type system disguised inside the chassis and case of an XT. This XT Model 286 system featured increased memory, an Intel 80286 microprocessor, and as many as three internal drives standard. The computer combined an XT's cost-effectiveness, flexibility, and appearance with the high-speed, high-performance technology of the Intel 80286 microprocessor. This model may have looked like an XT, but underneath the cover, it was all AT.

The IBM XT Model 286 can operate as much as three times faster than earlier models of the XT in most applications. It has a standard 640K of memory. Various memory-expansion options enable users to increase its memory to 16M.

Standard features in this system include a half-height, 1.2M, 5 1/4-inch, high density floppy disk drive; a 20M hard disk drive; a serial/parallel adapter card; and the IBM Enhanced Keyboard. You can select an optional, internal, second floppy disk drive from the following list:

- Half-height, 3 1/2-inch, 720K floppy drive

- Half-height, 3 1/2-inch, 1.44M floppy drive

- Half-height, 5 1/4-inch, 1.2M floppy drive

- Half-height, 5 1/4-inch, 360K floppy drive

The IBM XT Model 286's performance stems primarily from the AT motherboard design, with 16-bit I/O slots and an Intel 80286 processor running at 6 MHz. In addition to the type of processor used, clock speed and memory architecture are the primary factors in determining system performance. Depending on the model, the IBM AT's clock speed is 6 or 8 MHz, with 1 wait state, and the XT Model 286 processes data at 6 MHz, with 0 wait states. The elimination of a wait state improves performance by increasing processing speed for system memory access. The 0-wait-state design makes the XT Model 286 definitely faster than the original AT models that ran at 6 MHz and about equal in speed to the 8 MHz AT systems. Based on tests, the XT Model 286 also is about three times faster than an actual XT.

Because the XT Model 286 is an AT-class system, the processor supports both real and protected modes. Operating in real address mode, the 80286 is 8088 compatible; therefore, you can use most software that runs on the standard PC systems. In real address mode, the system can address as much as 1M of RAM. Protected mode provides a number of advanced features to facilitate multitasking operations. Protected mode provides separation and protection of programs and data in multitasking environments. In protected mode, the 80286 can address as much as 16M of real memory and 1G of virtual memory. In this mode, the XT Model 286 can run advanced operating systems such as OS/2 and UNIX. When the XT Model 286 was introduced, it was the least-expensive IBM system capable of running a true multitasking operating system.

The IBM XT Model 286 has a standard 640K of RAM. Memory options enable the system to grow to 15 1/2M, much higher than the 640K limit in other PC XTs. If you add an operating system such as OS/2 or Windows, you can take advantage of the larger memory capacities that the XT Model 286 provides.

A 20M hard disk drive is a standard feature in the XT Model 286, as is a 5 1/4-inch, 1.2M, high-density floppy disk drive. A similar floppy disk drive is standard on all models of the AT. Floppy disks formatted on a 1.2M floppy disk drive therefore can be read by an AT or an XT Model 286. The 1.2M floppy disk drive also can read floppy disks formatted with PC-family members that use a 360K floppy disk drive. Figure 3.13 shows the interior of an XT 286 system unit.

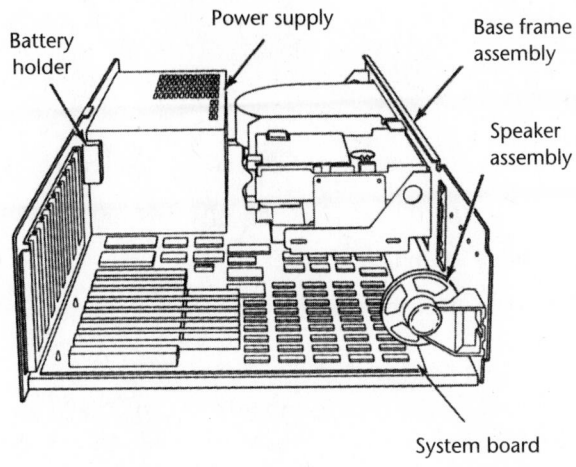

Fig. 3.13
The IBM XT-286 system unit interior.

The XT Model 286 features the IBM Enhanced Keyboard with indicator lights. Many IBM personal computers use the Enhanced Keyboard, but the XT Model 286 was the first PC XT to feature keyboard indicator lights. The Caps Lock, Num Lock, and Scroll Lock lights remind users of keyboard status, which helps to prevent keyboard-entry errors.

The IBM XT Model 286 has eight I/O slots, to accommodate peripheral-device adapter cards and memory-expansion options. Five slots support the advanced 16-bit cards or 8-bit cards; three support only 8-bit cards. Two of the three 8-bit slots support only short cards.

A hard disk and floppy drive adapter card were standard features in the XT Model 286. This multifunction card takes only one 16-bit slot and supports as many as four disk drives (two floppy disk drives and two hard disk drives).

The serial/parallel adapter, another standard feature, is a combination card that requires only one slot (either type) and provides a serial and a parallel port. The parallel portion of the adapter has the capacity to attach devices, such as a parallel printer, that accept eight bits of parallel data. The fully programmable serial portion supports asynchronous communications from 50 bps to 9600 bps, although even higher speeds were possible with the right software. The serial portion requires an optional serial-adapter cable or a serial-adapter connector. When one of these options is connected to the adapter, all the signals in a standard EIA RS-232C interface are available. You can use the serial port for interfacing a modem, a remote display terminal, a mouse, or other serial device. The XT Model 286 supports as many as two serial/parallel adapters.

A standard IBM XT Model 286 offers these features:

- 80286 processor at 6 MHz with 0 wait states
- 640K of motherboard memory
- 1.2M floppy drive
- 20M hard disk
- Five 16-bit and three 8-bit expansion slots
- Fixed disk/floppy disk drive adapter (occupies one 16-bit expansion slot)
- Serial/parallel adapter (occupies one 16-bit expansion slot)
- Enhanced Keyboard with indicator lights
- CMOS Time-and-date clock with battery backup

XT Model 286 Models and Features

The XT Model 286 processor is as much as 3 times faster internally than the preceding XT family and as much as 25 percent faster than the AT Model 239, depending on specific applications.

A 20M fixed disk and a 1.2M, 5 1/4-inch floppy disk drive were standard on the XT Model 286. One additional floppy disk drive can be installed internally as drive B.

You can add as a second half-height floppy drive any type of floppy drive, including both the double- and high-density versions of the 5 1/4- and 3 1/2-inch drives.

If you want to be able to read standard 5 1/4-inch data or program floppy disks created by the XT Model 286 on other PC systems, you might want to add a 5 1/4-inch 360K floppy disk drive, which provides full read/write compatibility with those systems. The 1.2M drives write a narrower track than the 360K drives, and would be unable to properly overwrite a floppy disk written on first by a 360K drive. If full read/write compatibility with 360K drives is not important, you can add a second, 1.2M, high-density floppy disk drive.

You can add any 3 1/2-inch drive, including the 720K and 1.44M versions. Because the 1.44M does not have any read/write compatibility problems with the 720K drives, however, and the 1.44M drives always can operate in 720K mode, I suggest adding only the 1.44M, 3 1/2-inch drives rather than the 720K versions. The higher-density drive is only a small extra expense compared to the double-density version. Most people do not know that full ROM BIOS support for these 1.44M drives is provided in the XT Model 286. Unfortunately, because IBM never offered the 1.44M drive as an option, the supplied Setup program will not offer the 1.44M drive as a choice in the Setup routine. Instead, you have to use one of the many available public domain AT type setup programs, or "borrow" such a program from an AT compatible system.

XT Model 286 Technical Specifications

The technical information for the XT 286 system described in this section covers the system architecture, memory configurations and capacities, standard system features, disk storage, expansion slots, keyboard specifications, and also physical and environmental specifications. You can use this information to determine the parts you need when you are upgrading or repairing these systems. Figure 3.14 shows the layout and components on the XT 286 motherboard.

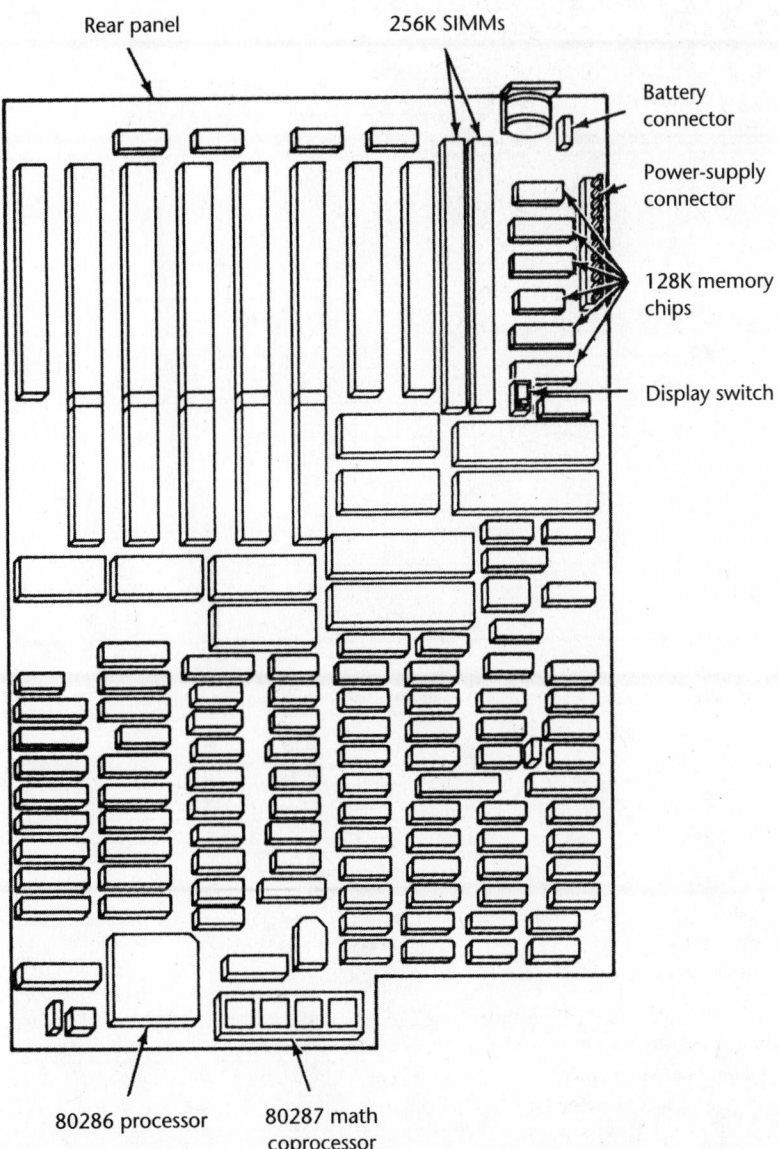

Rear panel

256K SIMMs

Battery connector

Power-supply connector

128K memory chips

Display switch

80286 processor

80287 math coprocessor

Fig. 3.14
The IBM XT 286 system board.

Compatible Systems

System architecture

Microprocessor	80286
Clock speed	6 MHz
Bus type	ISA (Industry Standard Architecture)
Bus width	16-bit
Interrupt levels	16
Type	Edge-triggered
Shareable	No
DMA channels	7
DMA burst mode supported	No
Bus masters supported	No
Upgradeable processor complex	No

Memory

Standard on system board	640K
Maximum on system board	640K
Maximum total memory	16M
Memory speed (ns) and type	150ns dynamic RAM
System board memory-socket type	9-bit SIMM
Number of memory-module sockets	2
Memory used on system board	One bank of 4 64Kx4-bit and 2 64Kx1-bit DRAM parity chips, and one bank of 2 9-bit SIMMs
Memory cache controller	No
Wait states:	
System board	0
Adapter	1

Standard features

ROM size	64K
ROM shadowing	No
Optional math coprocessor	80287
Coprocessor speed	4.77 MHz
Standard graphics	None standard
RS232C serial ports	1
UART chip used	NS16450
Maximum speed (bits per second)	9,600 bps
Maximum number of ports supported	2
Pointing device (mouse) ports	None standard
Parallel printer ports	1
Bi-directional	Yes
Maximum number of ports supported	3

Standard features

CMOS real-time clock (RTC)	Yes
CMOS RAM	64 bytes
Battery life	5 years

Disk storage

Internal disk and tape drive bays	1 full-height and 2 half-height
Number of 3 1/2-/5 1/4-inch bays	0/3
Standard floppy drives	1x1.2M
Optional floppy drives:	
5 1/4-inch 360K	Optional
5 1/4-inch 1.2M	Standard
3 1/2-inch 720K	Optional
3 1/2-inch 1.44M	Optional
3 1/2-inch 2.88M	No
Hard disk controller included:	ST-506/412 (Western Digital WD1003-WA2)
ST-506/412 hard disks available	20M
Drive form factor	5 1/4-inch
Drive interface	ST-506/412
Drive capacity	20M
Average access rate (ms)	65
Encoding scheme	MFM
BIOS drive type number	2
Cylinders	615
Heads	4
Sectors per track	17
Rotational speed (RPMs)	3600
Interleave factor	3:1
Data transfer rate (kilobytes/second)	170
Automatic head parking	No

Expansion slots

Total adapter slots	8
Number of long and short slots	6/2
Number of 8-/16-/32-bit slots	3/5/0
Available slots (with video)	5

Keyboard specifications

101-key Enhanced Keyboard	Yes
Fast keyboard speed setting	Yes
Keyboard cable length	6 feet

Physical specifications

Footprint type	Desktop
Dimensions:	
Height	5.5 inches
Width	19.5 inches
Depth	16.0 inches
Weight	28 pounds

Environmental specifications

Power-supply output	157 watts
Worldwide (110v/60Hz,220v/50Hz)	Yes
Auto-sensing/switching	Yes
Maximum current:	
90-137 VAC	4.5 amps
Operating range:	
Temperature	60-90 degrees F
Relative humidity	8-80 percent
Maximum operating altitude	7,000 feet
Heat (BTUs/hour)	824
Noise (Average dB, operating, 1m)	42
FCC classification	Class B

Table 3.6 lists the XT Model 286 system-unit part numbers.

Table 3.6 IBM XT-286 Model Part Numbers

Description	Number
XT Model 286 system unit, 6 MHz 0 wait state,	
640K, serial/parallel,	
1.2M floppy drive, one 20M hard disk	5162286
Optional accessories	
5 1/4-inch, half-height 360K drive	6450325
3 1/4-inch, half-height 720K internal drive	6450258
3 1/2-inch, half-height 720K external drive	2683190
80287 math coprocessor option	6450211
Enhanced Keyboard accessories	
Clear keycaps (60) with paper inserts	6341707
Blank light keycaps	1351710
Blank dark keycaps	1351728
Paper inserts (300)	6341704
Keycap removal tools (6)	1351717

Chapter Summary

This chapter has examined all the systems that make up the original line of IBM personal computers. Although these systems have long since been discontinued, I am amazed to find many of them still in everyday use. From individuals to large corporations to the U.S. Government, I regularly encounter many of these old systems in my training and consulting practice. Because these systems still are used, and probably will be for years, the information in this chapter is useful as a reference tool. I also consider much of this information as a sort of history lesson. It is easy to see how far IBM-compatible computing has come when you look over the specifications of these older systems.

The chapter has described the makeup of all the versions or models of each system, as well as their technical details and specifications. Each system unit's main components were listed also.

Each system's submodels were discussed, which should help you better understand the differences among systems that might look the same on the outside but differ internally.

Chapter 4 provides the same type of analysis found in this chapter for IBM's PS/2 system family.

II

Compatible Systems

IBM PS/2 and PS/1 System Hardware

This chapter identifies and describes each of the IBM Personal System/1 (PS/1) and Personal System/2 (PS/2) system units and standard features. The chapter begins by explaining the major differences between the IBM PC and the PS/1 and PS/2 systems—why the PS/2 is so similar to, yet so different from, the classic PC line.

The chapter continues with a discussion of the primary PS/2 models, which are based closely on the original PC line. These original systems sometimes are called Industry Standard Architecture (ISA) systems, and they include the standard ISA type of 8-bit and 16-bit I/O expansion slots.

The chapter also examines the PS/2 models and their respective submodels with the Micro Channel Architecture (MCA) slot design, which is dramatically different from the original ISA design.

Differences between PS/2 and PC Systems

Except for the obvious differences in appearance between PS/2 systems and the earlier "classic" (ISA) line of systems, the two types are quite similar. For troubleshooting and repair, you can consider the PS/2 as simply another type of PC-compatible system. All the troubleshooting techniques used on the other systems apply to the PS/2, although some repairs are conducted differently. For example, because each PS/2 motherboard includes a built-in floppy disk controller, if you determine that this controller is defective (using the same troubleshooting techniques as for the earlier systems), you must replace the entire mother-board. In contrast, on a PC system with the same problem, you replace only the floppy controller card, a much less costly operation.

After working on a PS/2 system for some time, you will discover several positive features of these systems:

■ The PS/2 is much more reliable than the earlier types of systems, for several reasons:

Robotic assembly of most of the system eliminates most human error during assembly.

The presence of fewer cables than other systems—or no cables at all—eliminates one of the biggest problem areas for repairs.

Better shielding than in other systems prevents reception and transmission of stray signals.

■ The PS/2 systems have no switches or jumpers to set, a feature that eliminates many service calls due to operator installation or configuration errors.

■ The systems can be taken apart and reassembled with no tools or only a few tools for special operations. Stripping down a PS/2 system to the motherboard usually takes less than one minute.

You will also discover several negative features as well:

■ Because the motherboard includes so many features, it is likely to be replaced more often than in other systems.

■ Parts are more expensive than for other systems, and items such as the motherboards, power supplies, and floppy drives can be much more expensive. Because of greatly reduced frequency of repair and the decreased labor required for each repair, however, maintaining a PS/2 system costs about half as much as maintaining other systems.

The primary areas of difference between PS/2 and PC systems are design and construction, video, and I/O adapter board slots.

Design and Construction

The design and construction of typical PS/2 systems is fascinating—they weren't designed in a day. The systems were designed with automated assembly in mind. Because parts and components are modular, technicians and users can remove and reinstall most of them without using any tools.

The no-tool disassembly concept carries over to the floppy and hard disk drives. To remove the floppy disk drive, you hold the front of the drive while bending a plastic tab and pull the drive from the system unit. To replace the drive, you slide the drive back into the case until it snaps into place. As a technician, you can amaze people who are unfamiliar with these systems when you open the system, remove a drive, replace it with a new unit, and close the system, all within 30 seconds. People who usually work on other types of systems, or who have never seen the inside of a PS/2, are usually quite impressed.

Parts and Availability. The small amount of labor required to service PS/2 systems is helping to change the repair and service industry. The modular construction should make labor less expensive than parts on the repair bill. Parts pricing and availability are much more important when you service a PS/2.

The availability and price of parts, however, can be a problem. A PS/2 system doesn't have many parts; the PS/2 motherboard contains many components that other systems house on expansion adapter cards. Furthermore, most PS/2 disk drives have integrated or built-in controllers, and items such as logic boards, which attach to the drives, are not available separately. Having so much integration makes PS/2s much easier to repair but may require replacing the motherboard more often than in earlier systems. Frequently, however, replacing an inexpensive adapter could solve a problem.

Because many of the custom chips used in the PS/2 boards are unavailable separately, PS/2 motherboards are very difficult to repair. Unlike motherboards in other systems, PS/2 motherboards usually must be replaced (or exchanged) rather than repaired. Although very little motherboard repair occurs even with non-PS/2 systems—because repairing a motherboard is usually more costly than replacing it—the repair or replacement issue is more important with PS/2s because the PS/2 motherboard contains so many more components (and therefore more potential places for things to go wrong) than other motherboards. IBM is the primary source of new or exchange motherboards for the PS/2.

Cables. Another design feature of the PS/2 is that several models contain no cables, which is amazing when you think of the earlier systems with their mazes of cables for carrying power and data. Eliminating cables makes components easier to install and also removes perhaps the largest single source of errors and problems. PS/2 systems are also much better shielded against stray signals because of their circuit and case design.

Video

The PS/2 video subsystem differs greatly from a PC subsystem. The original PC systems had a Monochrome Display Adapter (MDA), Color Graphics Adapter (CGA), or Enhanced Graphics Adapter (EGA) available as a plug-in board. The PS/2 Models 25 and 30 have on the motherboard a built-in video adapter: the MultiColor Graphics Array (MCGA). PS/2 Models 50 and up (as well as the 25-286 and 30-286) contain a built-in video subsystem: the Video Graphics Array (VGA), which is a higher-end system. The MCGA is a subset of the VGA and lacks color capability in the highest-resolution mode. Some newer systems, such as Models P75, 90, and 95, include eXtended Graphics Array (XGA) on either the motherboard or a card. The newer XGA standard is a super-VGA type of adapter that includes more resolution and colors than the standard VGA and retains backward compatibility.

The VGA and XGA support all video modes available in the earlier MDA, CGA, and EGA, as well as some newer VGA- and XGA-specific modes. Because this downward compatibility is almost 100 percent, few programs are unable to run on a VGA- or an XGA-equipped system, although programs not written specifically for VGA or XGA cannot take advantage of their extra resolution and color capability.

Because VGA and XGA supersede EGA and all other previous standards, IBM has stopped producing all other video adapters, including EGA. For a while, IBM sold a VGA card for upgrading PC systems to VGA; this 8-bit board, called the IBM PS/2 Display Adapter, plugged into any IBM PC or PC-compatible system. IBM discontinued the board, leaving only aftermarket boards available for upgrading older systems. Most video-card vendors have followed IBM's lead and have also discontinued EGA boards. These vendors have successfully cloned the VGA and XGA technology, providing many video-card choices for upgrading PC and PC-compatible systems. In fact, IBM has been assisting video board manufacturers in developing clones of the XGA.

In contrast to other graphics adapters, VGA and XGA have analog output and require displays that can accept this signal. Other graphics adapters use a digital signal and work with monitors designed to accept the signal. Therefore, if you are upgrading a system to VGA or XGA, you probably also need to add a new monitor to your shopping list. Some monitors, such as the NEC MultiSync and the Sony Multiscan, accept both digital and analog signals. These monitors offer a flexibility for working with older digital systems not found in IBM's monitors, but they can be more expensive. If you have such a monitor and are upgrading your system's video adapter to VGA or XGA, you do not need a new monitor.

The change to analog displays comes for two primary reasons: color and money. With an analog display, many colors become available without a big jump in cost. VGA is designed to display as many as 262,144 colors, which would require a digital interface design with at least 18 lines to transmit all this color information to the monitor. Using an interface with 18 digital driver circuits on the video card, running through a thick cable containing at least 18 shielded wires, to a monitor with 18 digital receiver circuits, would cost thousands of dollars. A much simpler and less costly approach is to convert the digital color information to analog information for transmission and use by the display. This approach reduces the amount of circuitry required and allows for a much smaller cable. Analog transmission can send the same color information through fewer wires and circuits.

Micro Channel Architecture (MCA) Slots

Perhaps the most important difference between PS/2 systems and other systems is the I/O adapter board interface bus, or slots. PS/2 Models 50 and higher incorporate a new bus interface called Micro Channel Architecture (MCA). MCA is a new slot design that is incompatible with the ISA slot system but offers improvements in many areas. The first consequence of this bus is that a design adapter that plugs into the ISA 8-bit or 8/16-bit slots cannot plug into MCA slots. MCA is both physically and electrically different from ISA.

MCA Advantages. MCA was designed to meet strict FCC regulations for Class B certification. These requirements are much stricter than for Class A, which covers allowable emissions in a location zoned as commercial or industrial. Class B requirements are for systems sold in residential environments and are designed to eliminate electrical interference with devices such as TV and radios. Meeting Class B requirements should give these systems a distinct advantage as clock rates (speeds) go ever higher. People in the communications and radio industry know that as the frequency of an oscillator increases, so does the problem of noise emissions. MCA has many ground connections for shielding, including a ground pin no further than one-tenth of an inch from any signal line in the slot. The Appendix of this book includes a pinout diagram of ISA and MCA bus slots.

MCA is designed to eliminate the bane of adapter board installers: setting jumpers and switches to configure the adapters. In surveys, IBM found that as many as 60 percent of all technician service calls were "no problem" calls; they were switch- and jumper-setting sessions. No wonder switches and jumpers are a problem, considering the number of switches and jumpers on some memory and multifunction boards. Setting them correctly can be very difficult, and nearly impossible without the board's original manual because each manufacturer's board is different. If you buy new boards, you might save money if you buy whatever board is on sale; you probably will end up with many different adapter boards, however, most with hard-to-read manuals and a bunch of jumpers and switches to set.

IBM's answer to this problem is called Programmable Option Selection (POS), a built-in feature on all MCA-equipped systems. The POS uses a special file called an Adapter Description File (with the file extension ADF) that comes with each adapter. The ADF file contains all possible setting attributes for the board and is read in by the system start-up disk or reference disk. The reference disk contains a special configuration routine that reads all the files and decides on nonconflicting settings for each board. The operator might need to select particular settings when two boards conflict. When the settings are set, they are stored in CMOS (battery-saved memory) and are available every time the system is started. The settings can be stored on disk also for backup, in case of a battery failure, or to quickly restore a configuration to several systems. The POS feature saves much labor and time, and is affecting the upgrade and repair industry: Many manufacturers have established switchless setups for their adapters to make them more "PS/2-like."

Finally, MCA-equipped systems are much more reliable than ISA-equipped systems, for several reasons. The rest of this section discusses the reliability of the MCA system, particularly timing considerations.

MCA Reliability. One reason that MCA-equipped systems are more reliable than those with ISA bus interfaces is that the MCA is well shielded. MCA-equipped systems therefore are more immune to noise from radio transmissions or any electrical noise.

This reason might be minor compared with the timing of the MCA bus. The MCA is asynchronous, which means that communication between adapters and the system board doesn't depend on timing. This feature solves a relatively common problem with bus systems. Have you ever had problems getting a system to work, only to find that moving a board to a different slot or switching two boards allows the system to operate normally? (By the way, I don't think that any IBM service manual officially suggests this solution.) The problem that moving or switching boards solves is one of timing. Each slot is supposed to carry the same signals as all the other slots, but that doesn't exactly happen. Effects on the bus, such as capacitance and signal propagation delays, can cause timing windows to "appear" differently in different slots, which can affect a board's functioning in that slot. MCA eliminates this type of problem; it is designed so that a board can tell it to "wait"—in effect, slowing the system by adding wait states until the board is ready.

Another timing-related problem is known to people who use some of the "turbo" IBM-compatible systems. In these "hypersystems," some boards cannot keep up with the system speed and do not work at all. On some systems, some of these boards can work if the system is slowed by adding wait states to operations or by reducing the speed of the system clock—but then the system doesn't really operate at its full performance capacity. Many communications, networking, and memory adapters can be speed-limiting in this way. With MCA, the bus cycles at a fixed, constant speed among all the systems, no matter what the microprocessor clock speed; the MCA always waits for a board, inserting wait states until the board is ready to proceed. Although this process might slow the system somewhat, the board and system work. Therefore, the same adapter functions in the 10 MHz Model 50 or the 50 MHz Model 90, regardless of their different clock speeds.

Other MCA design parameters for performance improvements exist, but they are more difficult to see. Most benchmarks have not proven any performance advantage in MCA systems over those with the standard ISA slots. IBM has demonstrated MCA coprocessing capabilities, however, which showed excellent performance. Taking full advantage of MCA's performance capabilities requires new bus master adapter designs. These new designs are adapters with processors that can function independently of the system or even take control of it. For now, MCA provides increased reliability and easy setup and use. The improvements incorporated into this bus make it the standard bus for the future; for now, however, many more systems in use still have the earlier ISA bus design.

Fortunately, most troubleshooting techniques and methods apply equally to the MCA and the ISA bus systems. The MCA systems suffer fewer failures overall, and are much easier to set up and install. The real question is, how much are customers willing to pay for these features?

PS/2 System-Unit Features by Model

This section provides a reference to all the PS/2 systems that IBM has produced. The standard parts included with each system unit include the items in this list:

- Motherboard with the CPU (central processing unit, or microprocessor) and other primary computer circuitry

- Case with internal power supply

- Keyboard

- Standard adapters or plug-in cards

- Some form of disk drive (usually)

This section also includes various kinds of information about each system unit:

- A listing of specific components

- Technical data and specifications

■ An explanation of each submodel, with details about differences and features of each model, including changes from model to model and version to version

■ Price of each system and option

Note

Prices shown are the IBM list prices and usually will not reflect true purchase prices. Normally, a standard discount of 30 percent is subtracted from the retail price. Retail prices are provided for comparison and reference only. If a model has been discontinued, the price given represents the retail list price at the time the system was withdrawn.

Decoding PS/2 Model Numbers

With the large variety of PS/2 systems now available, you might have difficulty telling from the model number how one differs from another. IBM's model-designation scheme started out with some reasoning behind it; but the increasingly large number of models made the original scheme difficult to adhere to and resulted in many inconsistencies in model designations. To restore consistency and enable greater understanding of the product line, IBM recently created a new model-designation scheme. This section provides an explanation of the older, inconsistent scheme, as well as the new method.

This list shows examples of the use of the old system:

Model	Meaning
Model 70-121	120M HD, one floppy disk drive
Model 30-E41	10 MHz 286, 45M HD, one floppy disk drive
Model 70-B61	25 MHz 486, 60M HD, one floppy disk drive

Table 4.1 describes the original PS/2 model designation meanings used by IBM for the PS/2 Models 25, 25-286, 30, 30-286, 50, 55, 60, 65, 70, P70, P75, and 80.

Table 4.1 PS/2 Model Designation Codes (for Original Models)

Model	Meaning
2	20M hard disk drive
3	30M hard disk drive (except A3*)
4	45M hard disk drive
6	60M hard disk drive
8	80M hard disk drive
**0	Medialess (no hard disk, no floppy disk drives)
**1	1 floppy disk drive
**1	Monochrome display (25 only)

(continues)

Table 4.1 Continued

Model	Meaning
**2	2 floppy disk drives
**4	Color display (25, 25-286 only)
**6	10 MHz 286; 1 floppy disk (25-286 only)
0**	Space-saving keyboard (25-286 only)
12*	120M hard disk drive
A2*	25 MHz 386; 120M hard disk drive
B2*	25 MHz 486; 120M hard disk drive
16*	160M hard disk drive
A16	160M hard disk drive
32*	320M hard disk drive
40*	400M hard disk drive
A**	25 MHz 386 processor
A3*	25 MHz 386 processor; 320M hard disk drive
B**	25 MHz 486 processor
C**	Color display
E**	10 MHz 286 (30-286 only)
E6*	16 MHz 386; 60M hard disk drive (70 only)
G**	Enhanced keyboard
L0*	Token-ring LAN adapter (25 only)
LE*	EtherNet LAN adapter (55 only)
LT*	16/4 token-ring LAN adapter (55 only)
M**	Monochrome display

* Represents any number or letter

Table 4.2 describes the new model-designation meanings used by IBM for the PS/2 Models 35, 40, L40, 56, 57, 90, and 95.

Table 4.2 PS/2 Model Designation Codes (for Newer Models)

Model	Meaning
0**	Standard processor complex design
1**	Advanced processor complex design
2**	16/4 token-ring LAN adapter
4	20 MHz 386SX
G	20 MHz 486SX
J	25 MHz 486
K	33 MHz 486
M	50 MHz 486

Model	Meaning
**0	No hard disk, one floppy disk drive
**3	40M hard disk drive
**4	60M hard disk drive
**5	80M hard disk drive
**9	160M hard disk drive
**D	320M hard disk drive
**F	400M hard disk drive
**X	Medialess (no hard disk, no floppy disk drives)

This list shows examples of the use of the new system:

Model	Meaning
Model 35-24X	Token ring, 20 MHz 386SX, no media
Model 40-040	20 MHz 386SX, 1 floppy disk drive, no hard disk
Model 95-0KF	33 MHz 486, 400M hard disk drive

Table 4.3 provides a reference list of all IBM PS/2 models that use the Industry Standard Architecture (ISA) bus and shows their standard.

PS/1

Announced June 26, 1990, the IBM PS/1 Computer was designed for consumers who have little or no knowledge about computers and who intend to use their computers at home. The PS/1 system is based on a 10 MHz 80286 processor with 512K or 1M of memory standard (depending on model). On October 7, 1991, IBM expanded its PS/1 product line by introducing several new PS/1 systems with 386SX processors. These newer systems address a broader market, including small businesses and the advanced computing requirements of second-time buyers. An upgrade is available from IBM. You can exchange the original systems for the new 386SX versions.

Each PS/1 system comes with an IBM Enhanced Keyboard, VGA display, IBM mouse, 2400 bps internal modem, IBM DOS, Microsoft Works, and tutorials that enable the purchaser to run a variety of applications immediately after setting up the system. Included with U.S. models is software to access the IBM PS/1 on-line Users' Club through the Prodigy on-line communications service. Several models are available so that you can select the type of display (black and white, or color) and the system-unit configuration (a single floppy drive with 512K of memory or a single floppy drive and 30M hard disk with 1M of memory).

Table 4.3 IBM PS/2 System Models with ISA Bus

Part number	CPU	MHz	PLANAR MEMORY Std.	Max.	STANDARD Floppy drive	Hard disk	Bus type
25							
8525-001	8086	8	512K	640K	1×720K	—	ISA/8
8525-G01	8086	8	512K	640K	1×720K	—	ISA/8
8525-004	8086	8	512K	640K	1×720K	—	ISA/8
8525-G04	8086	8	512K	640K	1×720K	—	ISA/8
25 LS							
8525-L01	8086	8	640K	640K	1×720K	—	ISA/8
8525-L04	8086	8	640K	640K	1×720K	—	ISA/8
30							
8530-001	8086	8	640K	640K	1×720K	—	ISA/8
8530-002	8086	8	640K	640K	2×720K	—	ISA/8
8530-021	8086	8	640K	640K	1×720K	20M	ISA/8
PS/1 286							
2011-M01	286	10	512K	2.5M	1×1.44M	—	ISA/16
2011-C01	286	10	512K	2.5M	1×1.44M	—	ISA/16
2011-M34	286	10	1M	2.5M	1×1.44M	30M	ISA/16
2011-C34	286	10	1M	2.5M	1×1.44M	30M	ISA/16
PS/1 SX							
2121-C42	386SX	16	2M	6M	1×1.44M	40M	ISA/16
2121-B82	386SX	16	2M	6M	1×1.44M	80M	ISA/16
2121-C92	386SX	16	2M	6M	1×1.44M	129M	ISA/16
25 286							
8525-006	286	10	1M	4M	1×1.44M	—	ISA/16
8525-G06	286	10	1M	4M	1×1.44M	—	ISA/16
8525-036	286	10	1M	4M	1×1.44M	30M	ISA/16
8525-G36	286	10	1M	4M	1×1.44M	30M	ISA/16
25 SX							
8525-K00	386SX	16	1M	16M	1×1.44M	—	ISA/16
8525-K01	386SX	16	4M	16M	1×1.44M	—	ISA/16
8525-L01	386SX	16	4M	16M	1×1.44M	—	ISA/16
30 286							
8530-E01	286	10	1M	4M	1×1.44M	—	ISA/16
8530-E21	286	10	1M	4M	1×1.44M	20M	ISA/16
8530-E31	286	10	1M	4M	1×1.44M	30M	ISA/16
8530-E41	286	10	1M	4M	1×1.44M	45M	ISA/16
35 SX							
8535-040	386SX	20	2M	16M	1×1.44M	—	ISA/16
8535-043	386SX	20	2M	16M	1×1.44M	40M	ISA/16

Total/ available slots	STANDARD Video	KB	Date introduced	Date withdrawn
2/2	MCGA	SS	08/04/87	—
2/2	MCGA	Enh	08/04/87	—
2/2	MCGA	SS	08/04/87	—
2/2	MCGA	Enh	08/04/87	—
2/1	MCGA	Enh	06/02/88	—
2/1	MCGA	Enh	06/02/88	—
3/3	MCGA	Enh	04/04/89	
3/3	MCGA	Enh	04/02/87	
3/3	MCGA	Enh	04/02/87	
0	VGA	Enh	06/26/90	—
0	VGA	Enh	06/26/90	—
0	VGA	Enh	06/26/90	—
0	VGA	Enh	06/26/90	—
0	VGA	Enh	10/07/91	—
2/2	VGA	Enh	10/07/91	—
2/2	VGA	Enh	10/07/91	—
2/2	VGA	SS	05/10/90	—
2/2	VGA	Enh	05/10/90	—
2/2	VGA	SS	05/10/90	—
2/2	VGA	Enh	05/10/90	—
2/2	VGA	Enh	01/21/92	—
2/1	VGA	Enh	01/21/92	—
2/1	VGA	Enh	01/21/92	—
3/3	VGA	Enh	09/13/87	05/04/92
3/3	VGA	Enh	09/13/88	09/11/91
3/3	VGA	Enh	09/26/89	01/17/92
3/3	VGA	Enh	04/23/91	05/04/92
3/3	VGA	Any	06/11/91	—
3/3	VGA	Any	06/11/91	—

Compatible Systems

(continues)

Table 4.3 Continued

Part number	CPU	MHz	PLANAR MEMORY Std.	Max.	STANDARD Floppy drive	Hard disk	Bus type
35 LS							
8535-14X	386SX	20	2M	16M	—	—	ISA/16
8535-24X	386SX	20	2M	16M	—	—	ISA/16
40 SX							
8540-040	386SX	20	2M	16M	1×1.44M	—	ISA/16
8540-043	386SX	20	2M	16M	1×1.44M	40M	ISA/16
8540-045	386SX	20	2M	16M	1×1.44M	80M	ISA/16
L40 SX							
8543-044	386SX	20	2M	18M	1×1.44M	60M	ISA/16

* Sales of this system unit are limited to the educational market. Suggested pricing was not available before press time.

Table 4.4 provides a reference list of all IBM PS/2 models that use the Micro Channel Architecture (MCA) bus and shows their standard features.

Table 4.4 IBM PS/2 System Models with MCA Bus

Part number	CPU	MHz	PLANAR MEMORY Std.	Max.	STANDARD Floppy drive	Hard disk	Bus type
50							
8550-021	286	10	1M	1M	1×1.44M	20M	MCA/16
50Z							
8550-031	286	10	1M	2M	1×1.44M	30M	MCA/16
8550-061	286	10	1M	2M	1×1.44M	60M	MCA/16
55 SX							
8555-031	386SX	16	2M	8M	1×1.44M	30M	MCA/16
8555-041	386SX	16	4M	8M	1×1.44M	40M	MCA/16
8555-061	386SX	16	2M	8M	1×1.44M	60M	MCA/16
8555-081	386SX	16	4M	8M	1×1.44M	80M	MCA/16
55 LS							
8555-LT0	386SX	16	4M	8M	—	—	MCA/16
8555-LE0	386SX	16	4M	8M	—	—	MCA/16

Total/ available slots	STANDARD Video	KB	Date introduced	Date withdrawn
3/2	VGA	Any	10/17/91	—
3/2	VGA	Any	06/11/91	—
5/5	VGA	Any	06/11/91	—
5/5	VGA	Any	06/11/91	—
5/5	VGA	Any	06/11/91	—
0	VGA	SS	03/26/91	07/21/92

Keyboards available include the Enhanced (101-key), Space-Saving (84-key), and Host-Connected (122-key). If "Any" is indicated, purchaser can choose any of the three.

Total available slots	STANDARD Video	KB	Date introduced	Date withdrawn
4/3	VGA	Enh	04/02/87	05/03/89
4/3	VGA	Enh	06/07/88	07/23/91
4/3	VGA	Enh	06/07/88	07/23/91
3/3	VGA	Enh	05/09/89	09/11/91
3/3	VGA	Enh	06/11/91	05/25/92
3/3	VGA	Enh	05/09/89	09/11/91
3/3	VGA	Enh	06/11/91	05/25/92
3/2	VGA	Enh	10/09/90	05/25/92
3/2	VGA	Enh	10/09/90	05/25/92

(continues)

II

Compatible Systems

Table 4.4 Continued

Part number	CPU	MHz	PLANAR MEMORY Std.	Max.	STANDARD Floppy drive	Hard disk	Bus type
56 SX							
8556-043	386SX	20	4M	16M	1×2.88M	40M	MCA/16
8556-045	386SX	20	4M	16M	1×2.88M	80M	MCA/16
56 SLC							
8556-055	386SLC	20	4M	16M	1×2.88M	80M	MCA/16
8556-059	386SLC	20	4M	16M	1×2.88M	160M	MCA/16
56 LS							
8556-14x	386SX	20	4M	16M	—	—	MCA/16
8556-24x	386SX	20	4M	16M	—	—	MCA/16
56 SLC LS							
8556-15x	386SLC	20	4M	16M	—	—	MCA/16
8556-25x	386SLC	20	4M	16M	—	—	MCA/16
57 SX							
8557-045	386SX	20	4M	16M	1×2.88M	80M	MCA/16
8557-049	386SX	20	4M	16M	1×2.88M	160M	MCA/16
57 SLC							
8557-055	386SLC	20	4M	16M	1×2.88M	80M	MCA/16
8557-059	386SLC	20	4M	16M	1×2.88M	160M	MCA/16
M57 SLC							
8557-255	386SLC	20	4M	16M	1×2.88M	80M	MCA/16
8557-259	386SLC	20	4M	16M	1×2.88M	160M	MCA/16
60							
8560-041	286	10	1M	1M	1×1.44M	44M	MCA/16
8560-071	286	10	1M	1M	1×1.44M	70M	MCA/16
65 SX							
8565-061	386SX	16	2M	8M	1×1.44M	60M	MCA/16
8565-121	386SX	16	2M	8M	1×1.44M	120M	MCA/16
8565-321	386SX	16	2M	8M	1×1.44M	320M	MCA/16
70 386							
8570-E61	386DX	16	2M	6M	1×1.44M	60M	MCA/32
8570-061	386DX	20	2M	6M	1×1.44M	60M	MCA/32

Total available slots	STANDARD Video	KB	Date introduced	Date withdrawn
3/3	VGA	Any	02/25/92	—
3/3	VGA	Any	02/25/92	—
3/3	VGA	Any	02/25/92	—
3/3	VGA	Any	02/25/92	—
3/2	VGA	Any	02/25/92	—
3/2	VGA	Any	02/25/92	—
3/2	VGA	Any	02/25/92	—
3/2	VGA	Any	02/25/92	—
5/5	VGA	Any	06/11/91	—
5/5	VGA	Any	06/11/91	—
5/5	VGA	Any	02/25/92	—
5/5	VGA	Any	02/25/92	—
5/3	XGA	Any	10/17/91	02/25/92
5/3	XGA	Any	02/25/92	—
8/7	VGA	Enh	04/02/87	10/31/90
8/7	VGA	Enh	04/02/87	10/31/90
8/7	VGA	Enh	03/20/90	07/23/91
8/7	VGA	Enh	03/20/90	07/23/91
8/7	VGA	Enh	10/30/90	07/23/91
3/3	VGA	Enh	06/07/88	07/23/91
3/3	VGA	Enh	09/26/89	09/11/91

(continues)

Compatible Systems

Table 4.4 Continued

Part number	CPU	MHz	PLANAR MEMORY Std.	Max.	STANDARD Floppy drive	Hard disk	Bus type
8570-081	386DX	20	4M	6M	1×1.44M	80M	MCA/32
8570-121	386DX	20	2M	6M	1×1.44M	120M	MCA/32
8570-161	386DX	20	4M	6M	1×1.44M	160M	MCA/32
8570-A61	386DX	25	2M	8M	1×1.44M	60M	MCA/32
8570-A81	386DX	25	4M	8M	1×1.44M	80M	MCA/32
8570-A21	386DX	25	2M	8M	1×1.44M	120M	MCA/32
8570-A16	386DX	25	4M	8M	1×1.44M	160M	MCA/32
70 486							
8570-B61	486DX	25	2M	8M	1×1.44M	60M	MCA/32
8570-B21	486DX	25	2M	8M	1×1.44M	120M	MCA/32
P70 386							
8573-031	386DX	16	2M	8M	1×1.44M	30M	MCA/32
8573-061	386DX	20	4M	8M	1×1.44M	60M	MCA/32
8573-121	386DX	20	4M	8M	1×1.44M	120M	MCA/32
P75 486							
8573-161	486DX	33	8M	16M	1×1.44M	160M	MCA/32
8573-401	486DX	33	8M	16M	1×1.44M	400M	MCA/32
80 386							
8580-041	386DX	16	1M	4M	1×1.44M	44M	MCA/32
8580-071	386DX	16	2M	4M	1×1.44M	70M	MCA/32
8580-081	386DX	20	4M	4M	1×1.44M	80M	MCA/32
8580-111	386DX	20	2M	4M	1×1.44M	115M	MCA/32
8580-121	386DX	20	2M	4M	1×1.44M	120M	MCA/32
8580-161	386DX	20	4M	4M	1×1.44M	160M	MCA/32
8580-311	386DX	20	2M	4M	1×1.44M	314M	MCA/32
8580-321	386DX	20	4M	4M	1×1.44M	320M	MCA/32
8580-A21	386DX	25	4M	8M	1×1.44M	120M	MCA/32
8580-A16	386DX	25	4M	8M	1×1.44M	160M	MCA/32
8580-A31	386DX	25	4M	8M	1×1.44M	320M	MCA/32
90 XP 486							
8590-0G5	486SX	20	4M	64M	1×1.44M	80M	MCA/32
8590-0G9	486SX	20	4M	64M	1×1.44M	160M	MCA/32
8590-0H5	486SX	25	4M	64M	1×1.44M	80M	MCA/32
8590-0H9	486SX	25	4M	64M	1×1.44M	160M	MCA/32

Total available slots	STANDARD Video	KB	Date introduced	Date withdrawn
3/3	VGA	Enh	06/11/91	—
3/3	VGA	Enh	09/26/89	09/11/91
3/3	VGA	Enh	06/11/91	—
3/3	VGA	Enh	09/26/89	09/11/91
3/3	VGA	Enh	06/11/91	01/17/92
3/3	VGA	Enh	09/26/89	09/11/91
3/3	VGA	Enh	06/11/91	—
3/3	VGA	Enh	09/26/89	09/11/91
3/3	VGA	Enh	06/20/89	09/11/91
2/2	VGA	Enh	03/20/90	07/23/91
2/2	VGA	Enh	05/09/89	07/23/91
2/2	VGA	Enh	05/09/89	—
4/4	XGA	Enh	11/12/90	—
4/4	XGA	Enh	11/12/90	—
8/7	VGA	Enh	04/02/87	10/31/90
8/7	VGA	Enh	04/02/87	10/31/90
8/7	VGA	Enh	10/30/90	—
8/7	VGA	Enh	04/02/87	12/27/90
8/7	VGA	Enh	03/20/90	01/29/91
8/7	VGA	Enh	10/30/90	—
8/7	VGA	Enh	08/04/87	12/27/90
8/7	VGA	Enh	03/20/90	—
8/7	VGA	Enh	03/20/90	01/29/91
8/7	VGA	Enh	10/30/90	—
8/7	VGA	Enh	03/20/90	—
4/3	XGA	Enh	04/23/91	01/17/92
4/3	XGA	Enh	04/23/91	01/17/92
4/3	XGA	Enh	10/17/91	—
4/3	XGA	Enh	10/17/91	—

Compatible Systems

(continues)

Table 4.4 Continued

Part number	CPU	MHz	PLANAR MEMORY Std.	Max.	STANDARD Floppy drive	Hard disk	Bus type
8590-0J5	486DX	25	8M	64M	1×1.44M	80M	MCA/32
8590-0J9	486DX	25	8M	64M	1×1.44M	160M	MCA/32
8590-0K9	486DX	33	8M	64M	1×1.44M	320M	MCA/32
8590-0KD	486DX	33	8M	64M	1×1.44M	320M	MCA/32
8590-0KF	486DX	33	8M	64M	1×1.44M	400M	MCA/32
95 XP 486							
8595-0G9	486SX	20	4M	64M	1×1.44M	160M	MCA/32
8595-0GF	486SX	20	4M	64M	1×1.44M	400M	MCA/32
8595-0H9	486SX	25	8M	64M	1×1.44M	160M	MCA/32
8595-0HF	486SX	25	8M	64M	1×1.44M	400M	MCA/32
8595-0J9	486DX	25	8M	64M	1×1.44M	160M	MCA/32
8595-0JD	486DX	25	8M	64M	1×1.44M	320M	MCA/32
8595-0JF	486DX	25	8M	64M	1×1.44M	400M	MCA/32
8595-0KD	486DX	33	8M	64M	1×1.44M	320M	MCA/32
8595-0KF	486DX	33	8M	64M	1×1.44M	400M	MCA/32

Keyboards available include the Enhanced (101-key), Space-Saving (84-key), and Host-Connected (122-key). If "Any" is indicated, the purchaser can choose any of the three.

Highlights of the PS/1 include the items in this list:

- 10 MHz 286 processor
- 12-inch Video Graphics Array (VGA) display (color or black-and-white)
- IBM mouse
- 101-key IBM keyboard
- Built-in 2400 bits-per-second (bps) modem
- Free three-month subscription to Prodigy
- PS/1 Club, an on-line customer support service
- Microsoft Works integrated application software
- Ease of set-up and use
- Preloaded DOS and menu interface (on hard disk models)
- Possibility of future expansion with PS/1 options
- Special IBM warranty

Total available slots	STANDARD Video	KB	Date introduced	Date withdrawn
4/3	XGA	Enh	10/30/90	01/17/92
4/3	XGA	Enh	10/30/90	01/17/92
4/3	XGA	Enh	10/17/91	—
4/3	XGA	Enh	10/30/90	—
4/3	XGA	Enh	10/17/91	—
8/6	XGA	Enh	04/23/91	01/17/92
8/6	XGA	Enh	04/23/91	01/17/92
8/6	XGA	Enh	10/17/91	—
8/6	XGA	Enh	10/17/91	—
8/6	XGA	Enh	10/30/90	01/17/92
8/6	XGA	Enh	10/30/90	01/17/92
8/6	XGA	Enh	04/23/91	01/17/92
8/6	XGA	Enh	10/30/90	—
8/6	XGA	Enh	04/23/91	—

The 386SX models also offer the following additional features:

- 16 MHz 386SX processor

- 2M RAM, expandable to 6M on the system board

- 12-inch Color Video Graphics Array (VGA) display

IBM has announced a special model (B84) of the PS/1 that will be similar to the B82 but will come preloaded with OS/2 version 2.0. With OS/2 version 2.0, PS/1 users will be able to run DOS, Windows, and OS/2 applications, exploiting virtually all software available, regardless of the environment for which the software was designed.

System Features. IBM designed the PS/1 to enable home consumers to buy everything in one convenient place. Most consumers can set up and use the PS/1 in 15 minutes. The setup is simple: Take the components out of the box, attach cables, plug in the system, and push one button. Because the user interface (in ROM) and DOS already are installed on the system, users select what they want to do from the first screen and (on the floppy-drive system) are prompted to insert the proper floppy disk or (on the hard-drive system) are presented with the program they select after the machine goes to the hard disk, on which all the software included with the PS/1 was preloaded.

One special feature of the PS/1 is its warranty. Although most repair service is available easily through IBM authorized dealers, you have also another option. IBM's Express Maintenance service provides parts directly to customers, normally within 48 hours. Because the PS/1 is a totally modular, snap-together unit, replacing any part of the system is a relatively easy task. You therefore have an alternate route for service if the dealer is too far away or does not have needed parts in stock.

The IBM PS/1 computer comes in several models. The following list includes the major features of each model.

286 models:

> 2011-M01: Black-and-white display, 512K memory
> 2011-C01: Color display, 512K memory
> 2011-M34: Black-and-white display, 30M hard disk, 1M memory
> 2011-C34: Color display, 30M hard disk, 1M memory

386SX models:

> 2121-C42: Color display, 40M hard disk, 2M memory
> 2121-B82: Color display, 80M hard disk, 2M memory
> 2121-C92: Color display, 129M hard disk, 2M memory

All PS/1 models also include a 2400 bps modem, software, and service—all in one box. On hard disk models, all the software and DOS are pre-loaded, and everything is configured for an immediate start after you plug in the system.

The more powerful PS/1models—the B82 and C92—also feature an 80 MB or 129MB hard drive, two 11-inch AT-compatible expansion slots and come preloaded with Microsoft Windows 3.0 and Productivity Pack for Windows customized for the PS/1. These systems deliver enough power to run the latest DOS, Windows, and OS/2 software applications. They are ideal for small businesses or home offices. With Microsoft Productivity Pack, customers easily can learn more about Windows 3.0. The design of these systems enables two hard drives to be stacked one on top of the other. By adding the new 129 M hard drive, you can expand the C92's storage capacity to 260 MB. *Note:* After its introduction, the C92, which has the 129M hard disk standard, was available only through Sears Brand Central outlets. All other dealers or retail outlets can sell only the B82 as the top model. IBM did not make clear how long this exclusive distribution of the highest-end PS/1 would last, so you should check whether other outlets will carry it when you are ready to purchase. The only difference between the B82 and C92 models is the 80MB versus 129MB standard hard disk.

IBM is offering a comprehensive 386SX upgrade package for owners of the 286-based PS/1 systems. This upgrade will be available from December 1991 through December 1992. The PS/1 upgrade package will enable current PS/1 owners to exchange their 286 system unit for the PS/1 386SX B82 system unit.

The standard service and support provided with the PS/1 system is excellent. Although, if necessary, most repair service can be obtained easily through IBM authorized dealers, another route is available. IBM has a special toll-free service called Express Maintenance, which provides parts directly to the customer, normally within 48 hours.

Support is available from the PS/1 Club, an on-line support service, exclusively available to PS/1 owners through Prodigy seven days a week, 18 hours a day, 365 days a year. PS/1 owners receive product support in four ways:

- ■ "Answer Bank," a database with answers to hundreds of commonly asked questions about computers

- ■ "Info Exchange," an electronic bulletin board where users can write to other PS/1 Club members or to an IBM expert who will reply within 24 hours

- ■ "Write to Us," where users can send comments and suggestions directly to IBM

- ■ "News to Use," an on-line posting of PS/1-related announcements and usability tips

The PS/1 is compatible with the PS/2 Model 30-286 at the BIOS level (although the BIOS is not identical) and at most hardware interfaces. The PS/1 also is compatible with the original IBM AT system. The 286 PS/1 is about 50 percent faster than the IBM AT, whereas the 386SX versions are more than twice as fast as an AT. All PS/1 systems incorporate many features that would have been extra-cost options on the original IBM AT system. Because the PS/1, like the PS/2, has many features integrated on its motherboard, many standard types of adapter cards—such as graphics adapters, some disk controllers, and many memory upgrades—do not work with it.

System Expansion and Restrictions. The PS/1 has some significant limitations and restrictions to expansion. The biggest limitation is that the system has no standard expansion slots! Several 386SX models have a larger chassis that includes 2 slots standard, but these slots accept only 3/4-length (11 inch) boards. For systems that do not have any standard slots, an optional extra-cost expansion chassis provides three slots, but none of them accepts full-length expansion cards. Two of the slots in the expansion unit accept 3/4-length cards and the third accepts only a 1/2-length board (8 inches). This setup effectively prevents the use of many types of expansion cards such as network adapters, memory boards, and many others, because many of those boards are the full 13.1 inches long. The expansion chassis cannot be used for additional slots on units that include two standard slots. These units will be limited to having only two slots.

The PS/1 has 512K or 2M of memory installed permanently on the motherboard, depending on the system. An additional connector especially for memory is available, which can be used to bring the installed memory up to as much as 16M; however, IBM offers a board with a maximum of only 4M for this connector. This connector is nonstandard, so industry standard memory devices such as 9-bit or 36-bit SIMMs cannot be used. Third-party companies now offer memory-expansion cards with larger amounts of memory for the PS/1.

The limited number and kinds of possible expansion slots is a serious limitation, but less of a problem than it might seem at first, because of the special connectors the PS/1 provides for various options. The modem that comes with the system plugs into a special motherboard connector and does not require a slot. An additional music and game adapter is optionally available that plugs into another special motherboard connector. Finally, a single hard disk and a second floppy disk drive can also be added without requiring an expansion slot.

Although the PS/1 offers many options for expansion that do not require the expansion chassis, the fact that the expansion chassis is an extra-cost item and supports only 1/2- and 3/4-length boards is nevertheless a significant limitation to the system.

A final limitation of the PS/1 is that the system's memory is not parity-checked as has been the standard in all other IBM systems since the original IBM PC. Parity-checked memory is memory that uses an extra bit for every eight bits of memory to allow a cross-check of memory accuracy. The status of parity is monitored continuously in most systems so that if a memory value contains an error, it is found immediately and does not go undetected.

On the PS/1, memory errors can go undetected more easily than in other IBM or IBM-compatible systems that do offer standard parity-checking. This statement might sound shocking and seem to reflect a seriously crippling feature of the system, but, in comparison, Apple Macintosh systems also do not have parity-checked memory as a standard feature. A computer does not require parity-checking to function, but the more "mission critical" that information accuracy is, the more parity-checking becomes an issue. The lack of parity-checking makes the PS/1 less suited for business applications use.

Table 4.5 describes the technical specifications for the 286 PS/1.

Table 4.5 PS/1 286 Technical Specifications	
System architecture	
Microprocessor	80286
Clock speed	10 MHz
Bus type	ISA (Industry Standard Architecture)
Bus width	16-bit
Interrupt levels	16
Type	Edge-triggered
Shareable	No
DMA channels	7
DMA burst mode supported	No
Bus masters supported	No
Upgradeable processor complex	No
Memory	
Standard on system board	512K (x01)
	1M (x34)
Maximum on system board	2.5M
Maximum total memory	8.5M

Memory

Memory speed and type	120ns dynamic RAM
System-board memory socket type	Proprietary card
Number of memory-module sockets	1
Number available in standard	0 (x34)
configuration	1 (x01)
Memory used on system board	Soldered 512K bank, 512K/2M cards
Parity-checked memory	No
Memory cache controller	No
Wait states:	
System board	1
Adapter	1

Standard features

ROM size	256K
ROM shadowing	No
User interface menu in ROM	Yes
Optional math coprocessor	No
Standard graphics	VGA (Video Graphics Array)
Standard display	Included
Monochrome	(M01,M34)
Color	(C01,C34)
Audio earphone jack	Yes
2400 bps modem	U.S./Canada only
Hayes-compatible	Yes
Phone cord and splitter included	Yes
RS232C serial ports	Optional, (requires expansion chassis)
UART chip used	NS16450

System architecture

Maximum speed (bits/second)	19,200 bps
DMA data transfer support	No
Maximum number of ports	1
Pointing device (mouse) ports	1
IBM mouse included	Yes
Parallel printer ports	1
Bidirectional	Yes
CMOS real-time clock (RTC)	Yes
CMOS RAM	64 bytes
Battery life	10 years
Replaceable	Yes (Dallas module)

(continues)

Table 4.5 Continued	
Disk storage	
Internal disk and tape drive bays	2
Number of 3 1/2- and 5 1/4-inch bays	2/0
Standard floppy disk drives	1×1.44M
Optional floppy disk drives:	
5 1/4-inch 360K	Optional
5 1/4-inch 1.2M	Optional
3 1/2-inch 720K	No
3 1/2-inch 1.44M	Standard
3 1/2-inch 2.88M	No
Hard disk controller included	IDE connector on system board
IDE hard disks available	30M
Drive form factor	3 1/2-inch
Drive interface	IDE
Average access rate (ms)	19
Encoding scheme	RLL
BIOS drive type number	35
Cylinders	921
Heads	2
Sectors per track	33
Rotational speed (RPM)	3600
Interleave factor	4:1
Data transfer rate (K/second)	248
Automatic head parking	Yes
Expansion slots	
Total adapter slots	0
Number of long and short slots	0/0
System architecture	
Number of 8-/16-/32-bit slots	0/0/0
Available slots	0
With optional expansion unit:	
Total adapter slots	3
Number of long and short slots	2/1
Number of 8-/16-/32-bit slots	0/3/0
Available slots	3

Keyboard specifications

101-key Enhanced Keyboard	Yes
Fast keyboard speed setting	Yes
Keyboard cable length	6 feet

Security features

Keylock:	
Locks cover	No
Locks keyboard	No
Keyboard password	No
Power-on password	No
Network server mode	No

Physical specifications

Footprint type	Desktop
Dimensions:	
Height	14.25 inches
Width footprint	10.75 inches
Width display	12.0 inches
Depth	17.0 inches
Weight:	
Color display	38.0 pounds
Mono display	31.0 pounds

Environmental specifications

Power supply:	
Worldwide (110/60, 220/50)	Yes
Auto-sensing and switching	Yes
Maximum current:	
90-137 VAC; color	2.5 amps
80-259 VAC; color	2.0 amps
90-137 VAC; mono	2.0 amps

System architecture

80-259 VAC; mono	1.25 amps
Operating range:	
Temperature	50-95 degrees F
Relative humidity	8 to 80 percent
Heat (BTUs/hour)	358
FCC classification	Class B

Table 4.6 describes the technical specifications for the 386SX PS/1.

Table 4.6 PS/1 386SX Technical Specifications

System architecture

Microprocessor	80386SX
Clock speed	16 MHz
Bus type	ISA (Industry Standard Architecture)
Bus width	16-bit
Interrupt levels	16
Type	Edge-triggered
Shareable	No
DMA channels	7
DMA burst mode supported	No
Bus masters supported	No
Upgradeable processor complex	No

Memory

Standard on system board	2M
Maximum on system board	6M
Maximum total memory	16M
Memory speed and type	100ns dynamic RAM
System-board memory socket type	Proprietary card
Number of memory-module sockets	1
Number available in standard configuration	1
Memory used on system board	Soldered 2M bank, 2M/4M cards
Parity-checked memory	No
Memory cache controller	No
Wait states:	
System board	0-2
Adapter	0-2

Standard features

ROM size	256K
ROM shadowing	Yes
User interface menu in ROM	Yes
Optional math coprocessor	387SX
Coprocessor speed	16 MHz
Standard graphics	VGA (Video Graphics Array)
Standard display	Color, included

Standard features

Audio earphone jack	Yes
2400 bps modem	U.S./Canada only
Hayes-compatible	Yes
Phone cord and splitter included	Yes
RS232C serial ports	Optional
UART chip used	NS16450
Maximum speed (bits/second)	19,200 bps
DMA data transfer support	No
Maximum number of ports	1
Pointing device (mouse) ports	1
IBM mouse included	Yes
Parallel printer ports	1
Bidirectional	Yes
CMOS real-time clock (RTC)	Yes
CMOS RAM	64 bytes
Battery life	10 years
Replaceable	Yes (Dallas module)

Disk storage

Internal disk and tape drive bays	2 (C42)
	3 (B82, C92)
Number of 3 1/2- and 5 1/4-inch bays	2/0 (C42)
	3/0 (B82, C92)
Standard floppy disk drives	1×1.44M
Optional floppy disk drives:	
5 1/4-inch 360K	Optional
5 1/4-inch 1.2M	Optional
3 1/2-inch 720K	No
3 1/2-inch 1.44M	Standard
3 1/2-inch 2.88M	No
Hard disk controller included	IDE connector on system
	board
IDE hard disks available	40M (C42)
	80M (B82)
	129M (C92)
Drive form factor	3 1/2-inch
Drive interface	IDE
Average access rate (ms)	21
Encoding scheme	RLL
Automatic head parking	Yes

(continues)

Table 4.6 Continued

Expansion slots

Total adapter slots	0 (C42)
	2 (B82, C92)
Number of long and short slots	0/0 (C42)
	0/2 (B82, C92)
Number of 8-/16-/32-bit slots	0/0/0 (C42)
	0/2/0 (B82, C92)
Available slots	0 (C42)
	2 (B82, C92)
With optional expansion unit:	
Total adapter slots	3 (C42)
Number of long and short slots	2/1 (C42)
Number of 8-/16-/32-bit slots	0/3/0 (C42)
Available slots	3 (C42)

Keyboard specifications

101-key Enhanced Keyboard	Yes
Fast keyboard speed setting	Yes
Keyboard cable length	6 feet

Security features

Keylock:	
Locks cover	No
Locks keyboard	No
Keyboard password	No
Power-on password	No
Network server mode	No

Physical specifications

Footprint type	Desktop
Dimensions:	
Height	14.25 inches (C42)
	15.75 inches (B82, C92)
Width footprint	10.75 inches
Width display	12.0 inches
Depth	17.0 inches
Weight:	
Color display	39.0 pounds

Environmental specifications

Power supply:	
Worldwide (110/60, 220/50)	Yes
Auto-sensing and switching	Yes
Maximum current:	
90-137 VAC; color	2.5 amps
80-259 VAC; color	2.0 amps
Operating range:	
Temperature	50-95 degrees F
Relative humidity	8 to 80 percent
Heat (BTUs/hour)	358
FCC classification	Class B

Table 4.7 shows the primary specifications and costs of the various PS/1 models, and table 4.8 shows the accessories available from IBM for the PS/1.

PS/2 Model 25

The PS/2 Model 25, the lowest-priced PS/2 family member, was introduced August 11, 1987 (see fig. 4.1). The Model 25 (8525) is a general-purpose system that incorporates the PC-style 8-bit slot architecture, enabling this system to accept most current adapters. The Model 25 uses the Intel 8086 processor and operates at 8 MHz with 0 wait states to read-only memory (ROM). This system is 40 percent smaller and more than twice as fast as the original IBM PC.

The Model 25's display is integrated into the system unit, which makes it look similar to the Apple Macintosh. With the Model 25, you can choose one of two keyboards: the IBM Space-Saving Keyboard or the IBM Enhanced Keyboard, which has a numeric keypad. You also can choose one of two displays: monochrome or color. A second 3 1/2-inch floppy disk drive, a 20M hard disk, and an additional 128K of RAM memory are available.

The Model 25 offers the same text and graphics capabilities as the IBM PS/2 Model 30. The built-in MultiColor Graphics Array (MCGA) can display as many as 256 colors on the system's color monitor (from a palette of more than 256,000 colors) or 64 shades of gray on the monochrome monitor.

Two 8-bit expansion slots enable you to attach many existing personal computer cards. A 12-inch analog display (color or monochrome), a display adapter, an RS-232C serial adapter, a parallel adapter, and a floppy disk drive adapter are standard, increasing the function of the standard unit. Figure 4.2 shows the rear panel of the Model 25.

II

Compatible Systems

Table 4.7 PS/1 Model Summary

Part number	CPU	MHz	PLANAR MEMORY Std.	Max.	STANDARD Floppy drive	Hard disk	Bus type
PS/1 286							
2011-M01	286	10	512K	2.5M	1×1.44M	—	ISA/16
2011-C01	286	10	512K	2.5M	1×1.44M	—	ISA/16
2011-M34	286	10	1M	2.5M	1×1.44M	30M	ISA/16
2011-C34	286	10	1M	2.5M	1×1.44M	30M	ISA/16
PS/1 SX							
2121-C42	386SX	16	2M	6M	1×1.44M	40M	ISA/16
2121-B82	386SX	16	2M	6M	1×1.44M	80M	ISA/16
2121-C92	386SX	16	2M	6M	1×1.44M	129M	ISA/16

Keyboards available include the Enhanced (101-key), Space-Saving (84-key), and Host-Connected (122-key). If "Any" is indicated, purchaser could choose any of the three. PS/1 Models Mxx have a built-in monochrome analog display, and Models Cxx have the Color Analog Display.

Table 4.8 PS/1 Special Accessories

Description	Part number	Price	Notes
PS/1 286 to 386SX upgrade	93F2059	$1,045	Trade in x01 Model for B82 Model
PS/1 286 to 386SX upgrade	93F2059	845	Trade in x34 Model for B82 Model
PS/1 color display upgrade	1057108	699	Upgrade for mono systems
PS/1 512K memory card	1057035	109	Upgrades to 1M on motherboard
PS/12M memory card	1057660	279	Upgrades to 2.5M on motherboard
PS/12M memory card	92F9935	279	Upgrades to 4M on 386SX motherboard
PS/14M memory card	92F9694	549	Upgrades to 6M on 386SX motherboard
5 1/4-inch 360K PS/1 286 drive	1057139	299	Attaches to PS/1
5 1/4-inch 360K PS/1 SX drive	92F9333	299	Attaches to PS/1
5 1/4-inch 1.2M PS/1 286 drive	1057191	299	Attaches to PS/1
5 1/4-inch 1.2M PS/1 SX drive	92F9334	299	Attaches to PS/1
3 1/2-inch 1.44M PS/1 drive	1057039	249	PS/1 internal drive

Total/ available slots	STANDARD Video	KB	Date introduced	Date withdrawn
0	VGA	Enh	06/26/90	—
0	VGA	Enh	06/26/90	—
0	VGA	Enh	06/26/90	—
0	VGA	Enh	06/26/90	—
0	VGA	Enh	10/07/91	—
2/2	VGA	Enh	10/07/91	—
2/2	VGA	Enh	10/07/91	—

Description	Part number	Price	Notes
30M 3 1/2-inch IDE drive	1057036	$ 599	For PS/1-M01/C01
80M 3 1/2-inch IDE drive	92F9937	1,060	For PS/1 386SX
129M 3 1/2-inch IDE drive	92F9938	1,500	For PS/1 386SX
PS/1 adapter expansion unit	1057028	169	Three slots: two 11-inch, one 9.5-inch
AT serial/parallel adapter	6450215	161	Requires expansion unit
Audio card/joystick connector	1057735	129	Attaches to 286 motherboard
Audio card/joystick connector	92F9932	129	Attaches to 386SX motherboard
Audio card/joystick for 286	1057064	249	Includes joystick, MIDI connector
Second joystick	1057109	39	Includes Y-cable for 1057064
PS/1 two-piece dust cover set	95F1136	20	Water-repellent, antistatic

The PS/1 286 to 386 upgrade is not sold through dealers and must be ordered by calling IBM Direct at 1-800-421-5448. This upgrade will be available through 12/92.

II

Compatible Systems

Each model of the PS/2 Model 25 includes these features:

- Approximately twice the speed of the IBM PC or IBM XT

- Two 8-bit expansion slots (one full-size and one 8-inch), which allows attachment of many existing PC cards

- Integrated MultiColor Graphics Array (MCGA) graphics

    Displays 256 colors from 262,144 possible colors

    Displays 64 shades of gray

- 512K of RAM standard, expandable to 640K on the motherboard

- Integrated floppy disk controller for as many as two 3 1/2-inch 720K drives

- One 3 1/2-inch (720K) floppy disk drive

- 12-inch analog display (color or monochrome)

- IBM Space-Saving Keyboard or Enhanced Keyboard

- Integrated serial port, parallel port, mouse port, and keyboard port

- Audio earphone connector

- Math coprocessor socket

- Advanced technology that eliminates jumpers and switches

Some PC adapters do not work in the Model 25 for various reasons. Because of the integrated functions on the Model 25 motherboard, certain options (such as PC types of memory upgrades, floppy controllers, and graphics adapters) might conflict with what is already present on the motherboard. Moreover, because of physical constraints, adapter cards thicker than 0.8 inch might not work, and one of the two slots is a half-length slot. The integrated MCGA does not support modes that support the 5151 Monochrome Display. The Model 25 has analog graphics output and does not support digital display devices. Figures 4.3 and 4.4 illustrate the locations of internal components of the PS/2 Model 25.

IBM has expanded the usefulness of the Model 25 in two main ways: by offering a version for use on a local area network (LAN) and by providing hard disks for data and program storage.

LAN Support. On June 2, 1988, IBM introduced a specially configured version of the Model 25, called the Model 25 LAN Station, or LS. This system is basically a standard Model 25 preconfigured with the IBM Token Ring Network PC Adapter for use in a LAN. The Model 25 LS is available in both monochrome (8525-L01) and color (8525-L04) versions. The Models L01 and L04 include the Enhanced Keyboard and 640K of RAM. Because the Token Ring Adapter II card uses the half-length expansion slot, the LS models have only a single full-length expansion slot remaining in the system unit for other adapter boards. Both models come with one 3 1/2-inch (720K) floppy disk drive. A second 720K floppy or a 20M hard drive is available.

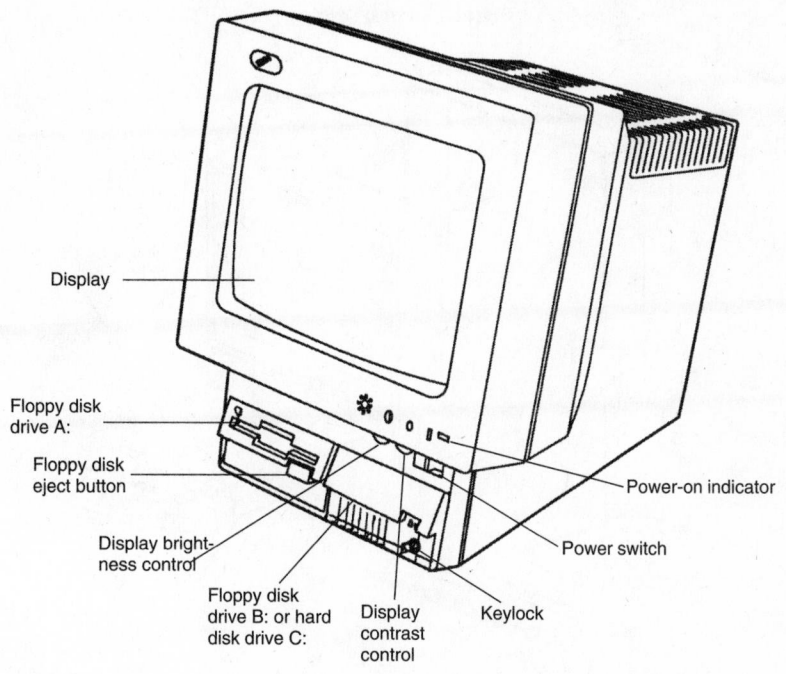

Fig. 4.1

PS/2 Model 25 (front view).

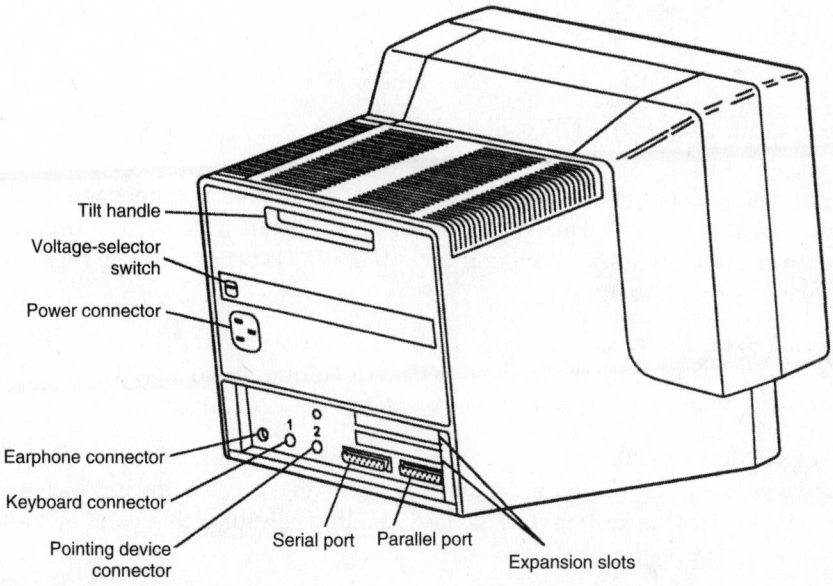

Fig. 4.2

PS/2 Model 25 (rear view).

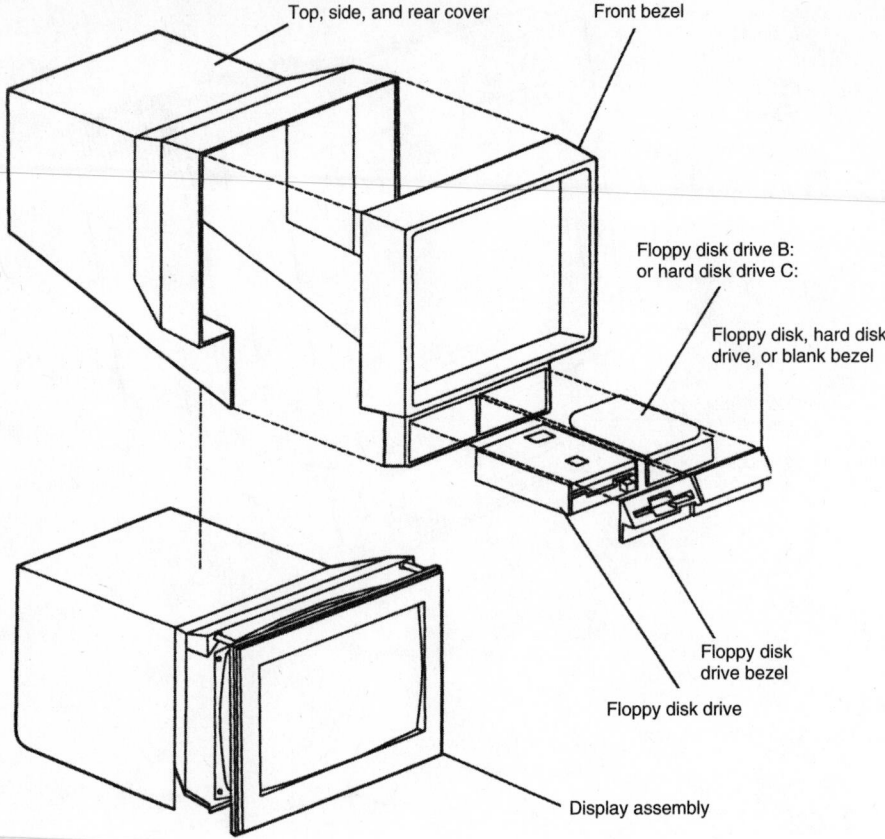

Fig. 4.3
PS/2 Model 25 interior (part 1).

LAN software for operating on a network is not supplied with this system and must be purchased separately. Because many people buy LAN software from a third party such as Novell, the fact that the software support is "unbundled" is beneficial. You then can choose which software to use.

Hard Disk Drives. For increased storage, IBM made a 20M hard disk drive for the Model 25. Each system has the capacity to use one hard disk drive. On models with two floppy disk drives, the 20M hard disk replaces the second floppy disk drive.

The IBM PS/2 Model 25 20M hard disk drive (78X8958) features 20M of storage, 3 1/2-inch hard disk technology, a stepper motor head-actuator mechanism, and a keylocked bezel, which disables the keyboard. It has also a built-in controller that plugs into a special

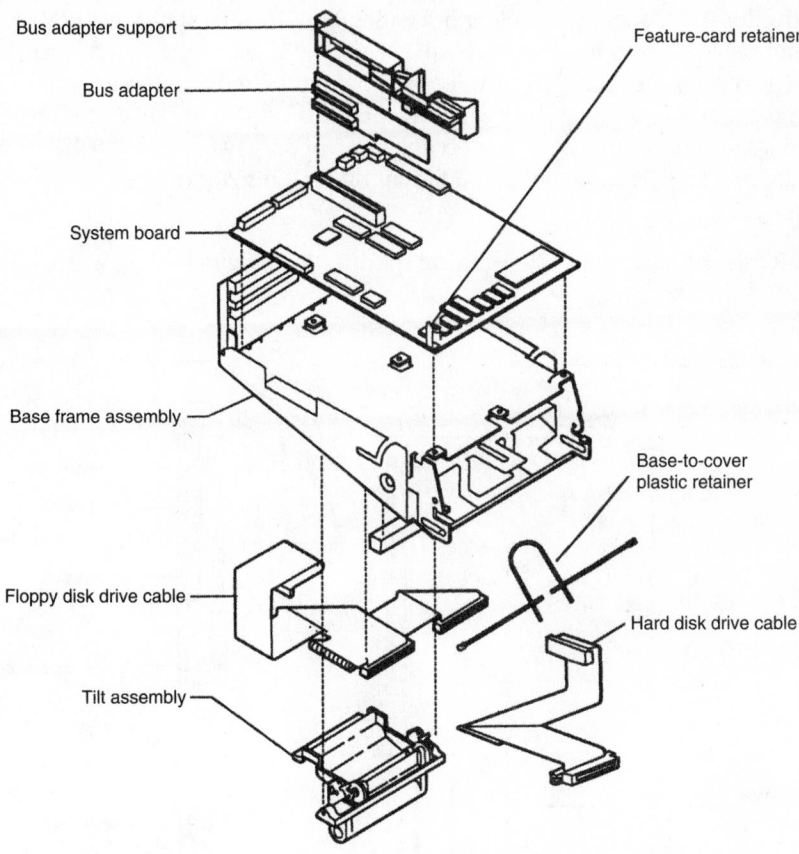

Fig. 4.4
PS/2 Model 25 interior (part 2).

port on the motherboard and does not occupy an expansion slot. (Because the controller is integrated on the drive, the term IDE—Integrated Drive Electronics—is used to describe this type of drive.) The hard disk drive is essentially the same one used in the Model 30. The built-in controller on this drive unit conserves a precious slot in the Model 25. Because the Model 25 has only two slots, conserving one of them is an important consideration.

IBM produced another hard disk for the Model 25—the 20M hard disk drive with adapter (27F4130). The controller uses RLL encoding and achieves higher data-transmission speeds than the built-in controller on the other hard drive. Like the currently available hard drive for the Model 25, the older drive uses 3 1/2-inch hard disk technology, a stepper motor head-actuator mechanism, and a keylocked bezel, which disables the keyboard. The older drive uses a higher-speed stepper motor and also has a special actuator that parks the heads automatically when the power is turned off. This drive, however, required a separate controller, which occupies one of only two slots available in the Model 25; probably because of this limitation, IBM has discontinued production of this hard disk drive.

Table 4.9 lists the PS/2 Model 25 technical specifications; figure 4.5 shows the PS/2 Model 25 system board.

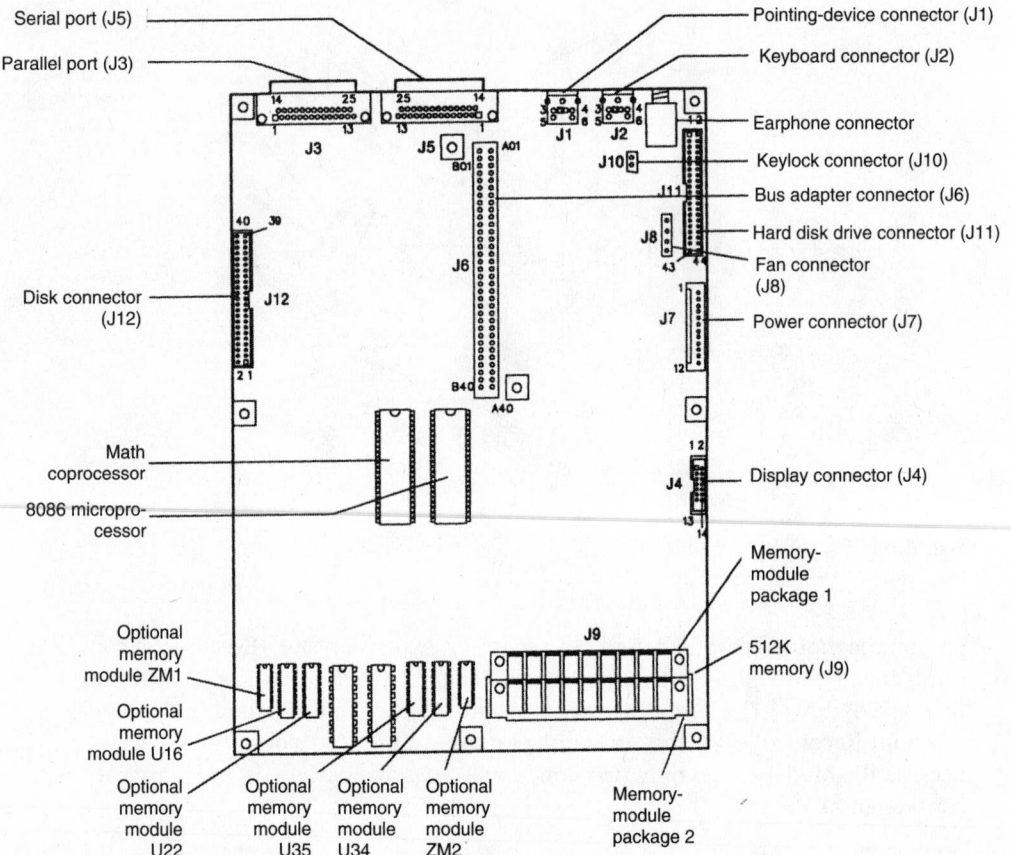

Fig. 4.5
The PS/2 Model 25 system board.

Table 4.9 PS/2 Model 25 Technical Specifications

System architecture

Microprocessor	8086
Clock speed	8 MHz
Bus type	ISA (Industry Standard Architecture)
Bus width	8-bit
Interrupt levels	8
Type	Edge-triggered
Shareable	No
DMA channels	3
DMA burst-mode supported	No
Bus masters supported	No
Upgradeable processor complex	No

Memory

Standard on system board	512K
Maximum on system board	640K
Maximum total memory	640K
Memory speed and type	150ns dynamic RAM
System board memory-socket type	9-bit SIMM (single in-line memory module)
Number of memory-module sockets	2
Number available in standard configuration	0
Memory used on system board	Two 256K 9-bit SIMMs, one socketed bank of four 64Kx4-bit and two 64Kx1-bit chips
Memory cache controller	No
Wait states:	
System board	0
Adapter	4

Standard features

ROM size	64K
ROM shadowing	No
Optional math coprocessor	8087
Coprocessor speed	8 MHz
Standard graphics	MCGA (MultiColor Graphics Array)
Built-in display	Yes
Monochrome	Model 8525-xx1
Color	Model 82525-xx4
Dot pitch (mm)	0.38
Audio earphone jack	Yes

(continues)

Compatible Systems

II

Table 4.9 Continued

Standard features

Color Model 8525-xx4	
Dot pitch (mm)	0.38
Audio earphone jack	Yes
RS232C serial ports	1
UART chip used	NS8250B
Maximum speed	9,600 bps
Maximum number ports	2
Pointing device (mouse) ports	1
Parallel printer ports	1
Bidirectional	Yes
Maximum number ports	2
CMOS real-time clock (RTC)	No
CMOS RAM	None

Disk storage

Internal disk and tape drive bays	2	
Number of 3 1/2- and 5 1/4-inch bays	2/0	
Standard floppy disk drives	1×720K	
Optional floppy disk drives:		
5 1/4-inch 360K	Optional	
5 1/4-inch 1.2M	No	
3 1/2-inch 720K	Standard	
3 1/2-inch 1.44M	No	
3 1/2-inch 2.88M	No	
Hard disk controller included:	(IDE connector on system board and/or an ST-506/412 RLL controller in the short slot)	
IDE/ST-506 hard disks available	20M	
Drive form factor	3 1/2-inch	
Drive interface	IDE	ST-506
Average access rate (ms)	80	38
Encoding scheme	MFM	RLL
BIOS drive type number	26	36
Cylinders	612	402
Heads	4	4
Sectors per track	17	26
Rotational speed (RPM)	3600	3600
Interleave factor	3:1	3:1
Data transfer rate (K/second)	170	260
Automatic head parking	No	Yes

Expansion slots

Total adapter slots	2
Number of long and short slots	1/1
Number of 8-/16-/32-bit slots	2/0/0
Available slots	2

Keyboard specifications

101-key Enhanced Keyboard	Yes (Gxx,Lxx)
84-key Space-Saving Keyboard	Yes (0xx)
Fast keyboard speed setting	No
Keyboard cable length:	
Space-Saving Keyboard	5 feet
Enhanced Keyboard	6 feet

Security features

Keylock:	
Locks cover	Yes (with optional hard disk)
Locks keyboard	Yes
Keyboard password	No
Power-on password	No
Network server mode	No

Physical specifications

Footprint type	Desktop
Dimensions:	
Height	15.0 inches
Width footprint	9.5 inches
Width display	12.6 inches
Depth	14.7 inches
Weight:	
001/G01	31.0 pounds
L01	32.0 pounds
004/G04	36.0 pounds
L04	37.0 pounds
Carrying case	Optional

Environmental specifications

Power-supply output	90 watts (001/G01) 115 watts (004/G04)
Worldwide (110/60,220/50)	Yes
Auto-sensing/switching	Manual switch

(continues)

Compatible Systems

Table 4.9 Continued	
Expansion slots	
Maximum current:	
90-137 VAC	2.8 amps
80-259 VAC	1.7 amps
Operating range:	
Temperature	60-90 degrees F
Relative humidity	8-80 percent
Maximum operating altitude	7,000 feet
Heat (BTUs/hour)	683
Noise (Avg dB, operating, 1m)	44 dB
FCC classification	Class B

Table 4.10 shows the primary specifications and costs of the different versions of PS/2 Model 25.

PS/2 Model 30

The IBM PS/2 Model 30 (IBM 8530), announced April 2, 1987, is a general-purpose system designed to offer more features and performance than the IBM PC and XT—especially in display graphics—and at a lower price. This system includes as standard many features built into the system board, including a graphics adapter, a parallel port, a serial port, a clock calendar, 640K of RAM, and a mouse port. The Model 30 also uses many existing PC adapter cards for further expansion due to its ISA 8-bit slots. Figure 4.6 shows a front view and figure 4.7 shows a rear-panel view of the Model 30. As of December 27, 1990, all versions of the PS/2 Model 30 have been discontinued and no longer are available.

Table 4.10 IBM PS/2 Model 25 Model Summary							
			PLANAR MEMORY		**STANDARD**		
Part number	**CPU**	**MHz**	**Std.**	**Max.**	**Floppy drive**	**Hard disk**	**Bus type**
25							
8525-001	8086	8	512K	640K	1×720K	—	ISA/8
8525-G01	8086	8	512K	640K	1×720K	—	ISA/8
8525-004	8086	8	512K	640K	1×720K	—	ISA/8
8525-G04	8086	8	512K	640K	1×720K	—	ISA/8
25 LS							
8525-L01	8086	8	640K	640K	1×720K	—	ISA/8
8525-L04	8086	8	640K	640K	1×720K	—	ISA/8

Models that end in xx1 have the monochrome analog display as a built-in feature; models that end in xx4 have the color display. The 25 LS models include also an IBM Token Ring Adapter II card in the half-length slot.

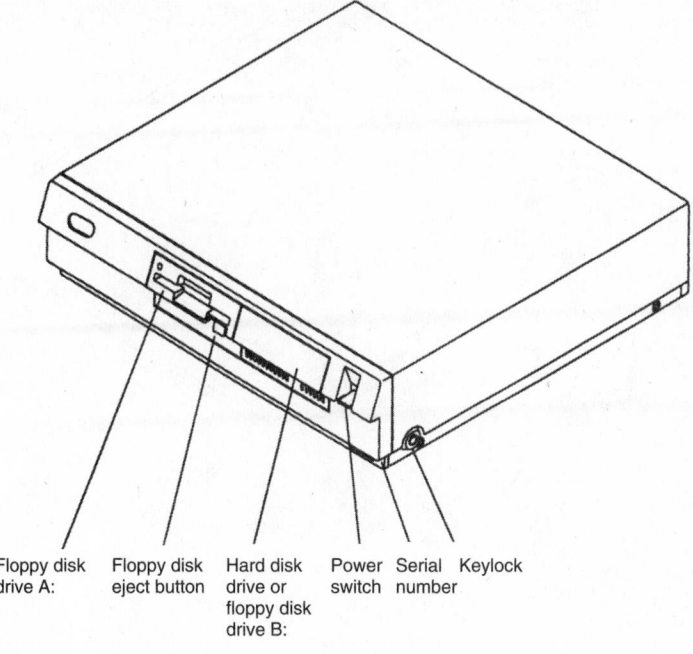

Floppy disk drive A: Floppy disk eject button   Hard disk drive or floppy disk drive B: Power switch   Serial number   Keylock

Fig. 4.6
PS/2 Model 30.

Total/ available slots	STANDARD Video	KB	Date introduced	Date withdrawn
2/2	MCGA	SS	08/04/87	—
2/2	MCGA	Enh	08/04/87	—
2/2	MCGA	SS	08/04/87	—
2/2	MCGA	Enh	08/04/87	—
2/1	MCGA	Enh	06/02/88	—
2/1	MCGA	Enh	06/02/88	—

Keyboards available include the Enhanced (101-key), Space-Saving (84-key), and Host-Connected (122-key). If "Any" is indicated, purchaser can choose any of the three.

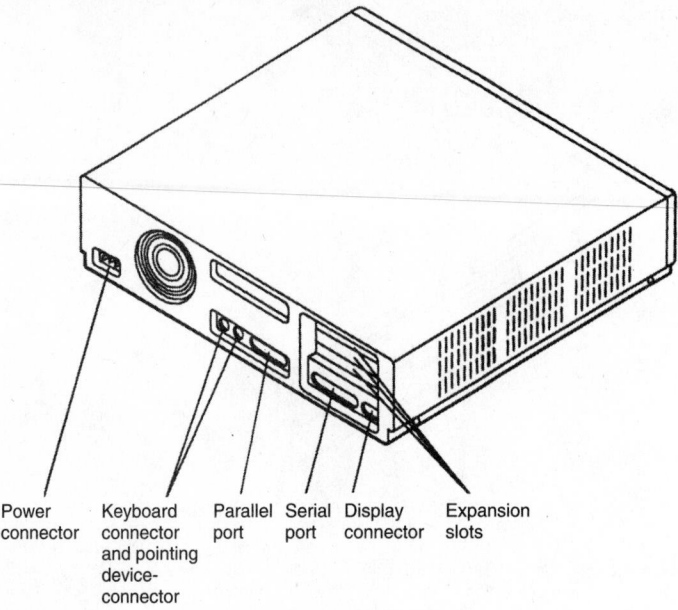

Power   Keyboard   Parallel   Serial   Display   Expansion
connector   connector   port   port   connector   slots
              and pointing
              device-
              connector

Fig. 4.7
PS/2 Model 30 (rear view).

The Model 30 is based on an 8086 microprocessor, running at 8 MHz with 0 wait states. Performance is enhanced by the use of a 16-bit-wide data path to the motherboard memory, which results in internal processing speed nearly comparable to a 6 MHz AT and more than twice as fast as the 8088-based PC or XT.

Major features of the Model 30 include the items in this list:

■ Many functions are integrated on the motherboard, including disk controllers, graphics, and ports

■ Integrated MCGA graphics displays as many as 256 colors or 64 shades of gray

■ Approximately twice the performance speed of 8088-based IBM PC and IBM XT systems

■ Smaller design, with reduced power requirements

■ Worldwide power supply

■ Switchless installation and configuration

■ 640K random-access memory (RAM)

■ 16-bit access to motherboard memory

■ Integrated floppy disk controller for two 720K drives

■ Integrated serial port, parallel port, mouse port, and keyboard port

- IBM Enhanced Keyboard

- Time-of-day clock with extended-life battery

- Socket for a math coprocessor

- Three expansion slots to accommodate PC or XT 8-bit adapter cards

Figure 4.8 shows an interior view of the Model 30.

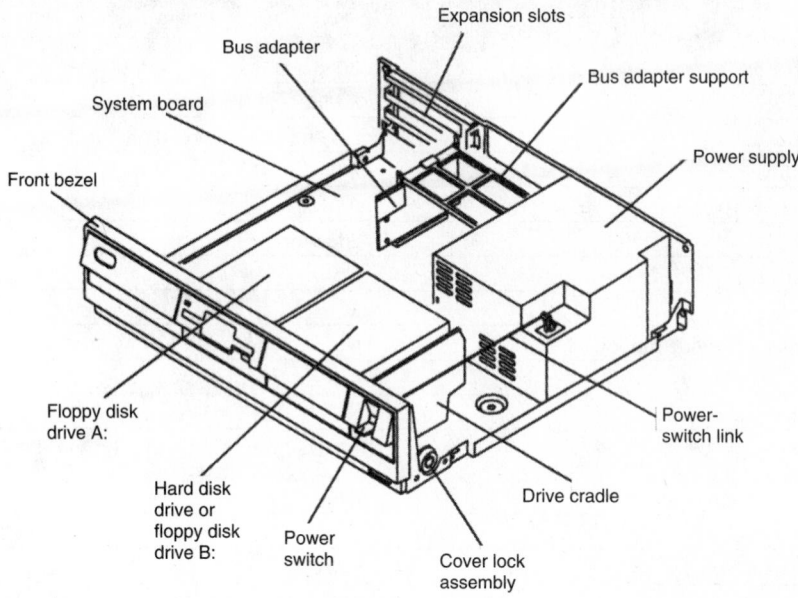

Fig. 4.8
PS/2 Model 30 interior.

The Model 30 was available in three versions: the 30-001, with one 3 1/2-inch (720K) floppy drive; the 30-002, with two 3 1/2-inch (720K) floppy drives; and the 30-021, with a 20M hard disk drive and a single 3 1/2-inch (720K) floppy drive. All models included 640K RAM.

Graphics Adapter. MultiColor Graphics Array (MCGA), the graphics adapter function integrated into the Model 30 motherboard, supports all Color Graphics Adapter (CGA) modes when an analog PS/2 display is attached. Other digital displays are incompatible. In addition to providing existing CGA mode support, MCGA supports four expanded modes, a subset of the VGA processor on Models 50 and higher:

    640×480 by 2 colors—all points addressable

    320×200 by 256 colors—all points addressable

    40×25 by 16 colors for text (8-by-16-character box)

    80×25 by 16 colors for text (8-by-16-character box)

Compatible Systems

The integrated graphics adapter automatically switches from color to 64 shades of gray when connected to a monochrome analog display. This feature allows users who prefer a monochrome display to execute color-based applications without compatibility problems or troublesome software reconfiguration.

Table 4.11 lists the PS/2 Model 30 technical specifications.

Table 4.11 PS/2 Model 30 Technical Specifications	
System architecture	
Microprocessor	8086
Clock speed	8 MHz
Bus type	ISA (Industry Standard Architecture)
Bus width	8-bit
Interrupt levels	8
Type	Edge-triggered
Shareable	No
DMA channels	3
DMA burst mode supported	No
Bus masters supported	No
Upgradeable processor complex	No
Memory	
Standard on system board	640K
Maximum on system board	640K
Maximum total memory	640K
Memory speed and type	150ns dynamic RAM
System board memory-socket type	9-bit SIMM (single in-line memory module)
Number of memory-module sockets	2
Number available in standard configuration	0
Memory used on system board	Two 256K 9-bit SIMMs, one soldered bank of four 64K×4-bit and two 64K×1-bit chips.
Memory cache controller	No
Wait states:	
System board	0
Adapter	4
Standard features	
ROM size	64K
ROM shadowing	No
Optional math coprocessor	8087
Coprocessor speed	8 MHz

System architecture

Standard graphics	MCGA (MultiColor Graphics Array)
RS232C serial ports	1
UART chip used	NS8250B
Maximum speed (bits per second)	9,600 bps
Maximum number of ports supported	2
Pointing device (mouse) ports	1
Parallel printer port	1
Bidirectional	Yes
Maximum number of ports supported	2
CMOS real-time clock (RTC)	Yes
CMOS RAM	None
Battery life	5 years
Replaceable	Yes (replace bus adapter)

Disk storage

Internal disk and tape drive bays	2
Number of 3 1/2- and 5 1/4-inch bays	2/0
Standard floppy drives	1×720K
	2×720K (002)
Optional floppy drives:	
5 1/4-inch 360K	Optional
5 1/4-inch 1.2M	No
3 1/2-inch 720K	Standard
3 1/2-inch 1.44M	No
3 1/2-inch 2.88M	No
Hard disk controller included	IDE connector on system board
IDE hard disks available	20M
Drive form factor	3 1/2-inch
Controller type	IDE
Average access rate (ms)	80
Encoding scheme	MFM
BIOS drive type number	26
Cylinders	612
Heads	4
Sectors per track	17

(continues)

II

Compatible Systems

Table 4.11 Continued

Disk storage

Rotational speed (RPM)	3600
Interleave factor	3:1
Data transfer rate (K/second)	170
Automatic head parking	No

Expansion slots

Total adapter slots	3
Number of long and short slots	3/0
Number of 8-/16-/32-bit slots	3/0/0
Available slots	3

Keyboard specifications

101-key Enhanced Keyboard	Yes
Fast keyboard speed setting	No
Keyboard cable length	3 feet

Security features

Keylock:	
Locks cover	Yes
Locks keyboard	Yes
Keyboard password	No

Security features

Power-on password	No
Network server mode	No

Table 4.12 shows the primary specifications and costs of the different versions of PS/2 Model 30.

Table 4.12 IBM PS/2 Model 30 Model Summary

Part number	CPU	MHz	PLANAR MEMORY Std.	Max.	STANDARD Floppy drive	Hard disk	Bus type
30							
8530-001	8086	8	640K	640K	1×720K	—	ISA/8
8530-002	8086	8	640K	640K	2×720K	—	ISA/8
8530-021	8086	8	640K	640K	1×720K	20M	ISA/8

All models of the 8530 have been discontinued and are no longer available from IBM.

Physical specifications

Footprint type	Desktop
Dimensions:	
Height	4.0 inches
Width	15.6 inches
Depth	16.0 inches
Weight:	
00x	17.5 pounds
021	21.0 pounds

Environmental specifications

Power-supply output	70 watts
Worldwide (110/60,220/50)	Yes
Auto-sensing/switching	Yes
Maximum current:	
90-137 VAC	1.5 amps
180-265 VAC	0.75 amps
Operating range:	
Temperature	60-90 degrees F
Relative humidity	8-80 percent
Maximum operating altitude	7,000 feet
Heat (BTUs/hour)	341
Noise (Average dB, operating, 1m)	37.5 dB
FCC classification	Class B

Total/ available slots	STANDARD Video	KB	Date introduced	Date withdrawn
3/3	MCGA	Enh	04/04/89	12/27/90
3/3	MCGA	Enh	04/02/87	07/05/89
3/3	MCGA	Enh	04/02/87	12/27/90

II

Compatible Systems

Figures 4.9 and 4.10 show the system boards for the PS/2 Model 30 (8530-001) and the standard PS/2 Model 30.

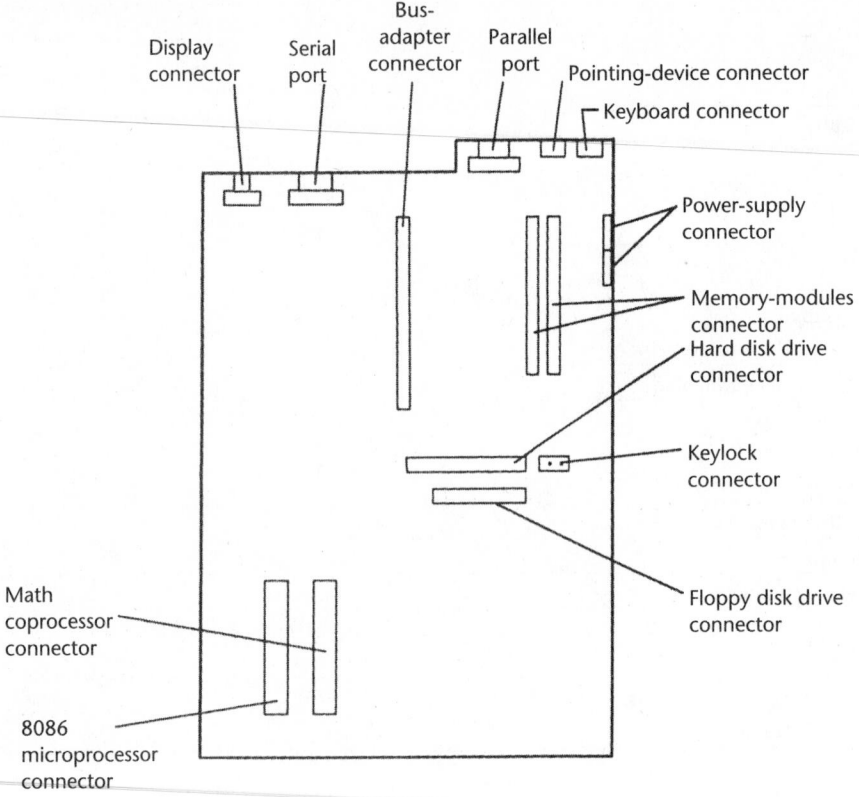

Fig. 4.9
PS/2 Model 30 (8530-001) system board.

PS/2 Model 25 286

Introduced on May 10, 1990 the PS/2 Model 25 286 (8525) unit is an enhanced version of the PS/2 Model 25. It is a standard Model 25 with an upgraded motherboard that makes it an AT-type system. This system features an 80286 microprocessor, expanded system-board memory (1M to 4M), high-density 3 1/2-inch (1.44M) floppy disk drives, and an integrated 12-inch VGA color monitor. The Model 25 286 utilizes the 80286 processor operating at 10 MHz with 1 wait state to system memory and has the following integrated functions: parallel port, serial port, pointing device port, keyboard port, an audio earphone connector, 1.44M floppy disk drive support, and VGA graphics. The Model 25 286 is offered in floppy drive only and 30M hard disk models with the IBM Enhanced (101-key) or Space-Saving (84-key) Keyboard. It features 1M standard memory, with a maximum of 4M on the system board. The Model 25 286 is physically very similar to the Model 25 (see figs. 4.1 through 4.4 earlier in this chapter, which show exterior and interior views of the Model 25).

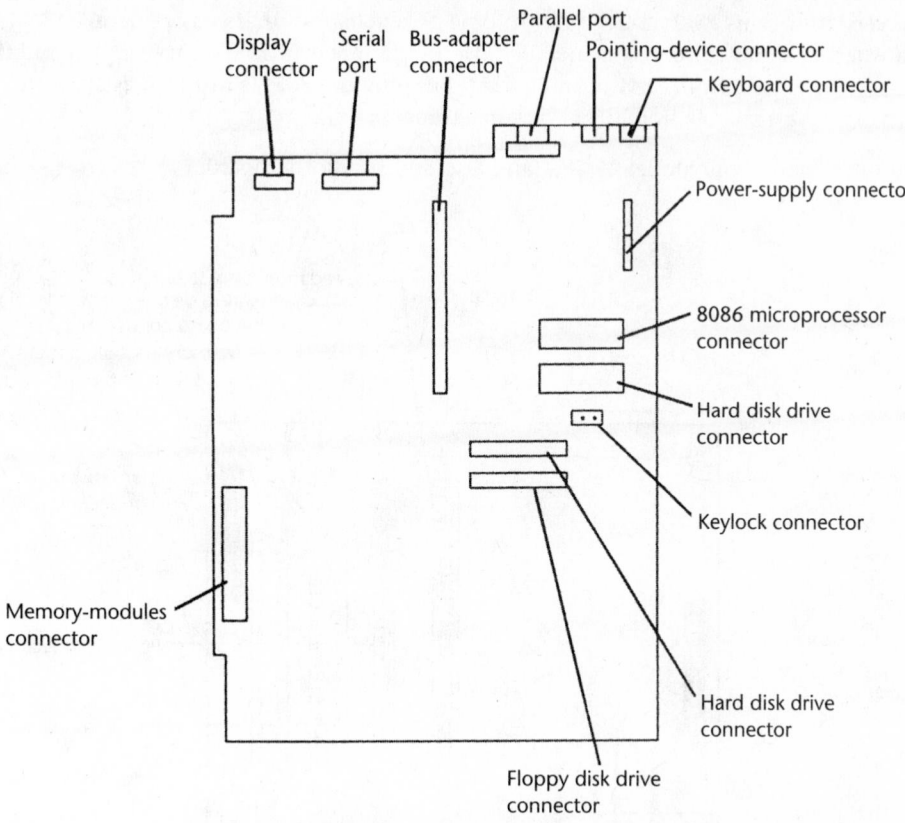

Fig. 4.10

Standard PS/2 Model 30 system board.

The Model 25 286 differs significantly from the Model 25: It is a full AT-class system, and the original Model 25 is a PC-class system. They differ in virtually every way except appearance. (Refer to figures 4.1 through 4.4.) The Model 25 286 has a high-density floppy disk controller and a full VGA adapter integrated on the system board. An integrated color display is the only one offered. System memory can be increased to 4M on the system board and can address a maximum of 16M, providing functionality with DOS and Windows. As an AT-class system, the Model 25 286 is capable of running OS/2; the Model 25 is not. The Model 25 286 makes a perfect LAN workstation, although it is not sold preconfigured as one.

Like the Model 25, the Model 25 286 is compatible with the IBM AT at the BIOS interface level (although the BIOS is not identical) and at most hardware interfaces. Because many features are integrated on the motherboard in this system, many cards—graphics adapters, some disk controllers, and others—do not work with this system, and memory adapters that are not flexible in setting the starting memory address might not work either.

The motherboard in this system is identical to that of the Model 30 286. The BIOS is the same as the Model 30 286 as well, at least for the later versions.

Compatible Systems

The versions of this PS/2 model differ in type of keyboard (Enhanced or Space-Saving) and whether a 30M hard disk is included. Hard disks are available from IBM that will fit this system in sizes from 20M through 45M, but only the 30M is installed as standard. Hard disks are available from other manufacturers as well.

Figure 4.11 shows the Model 25 286 (and also 30 286) motherboard.

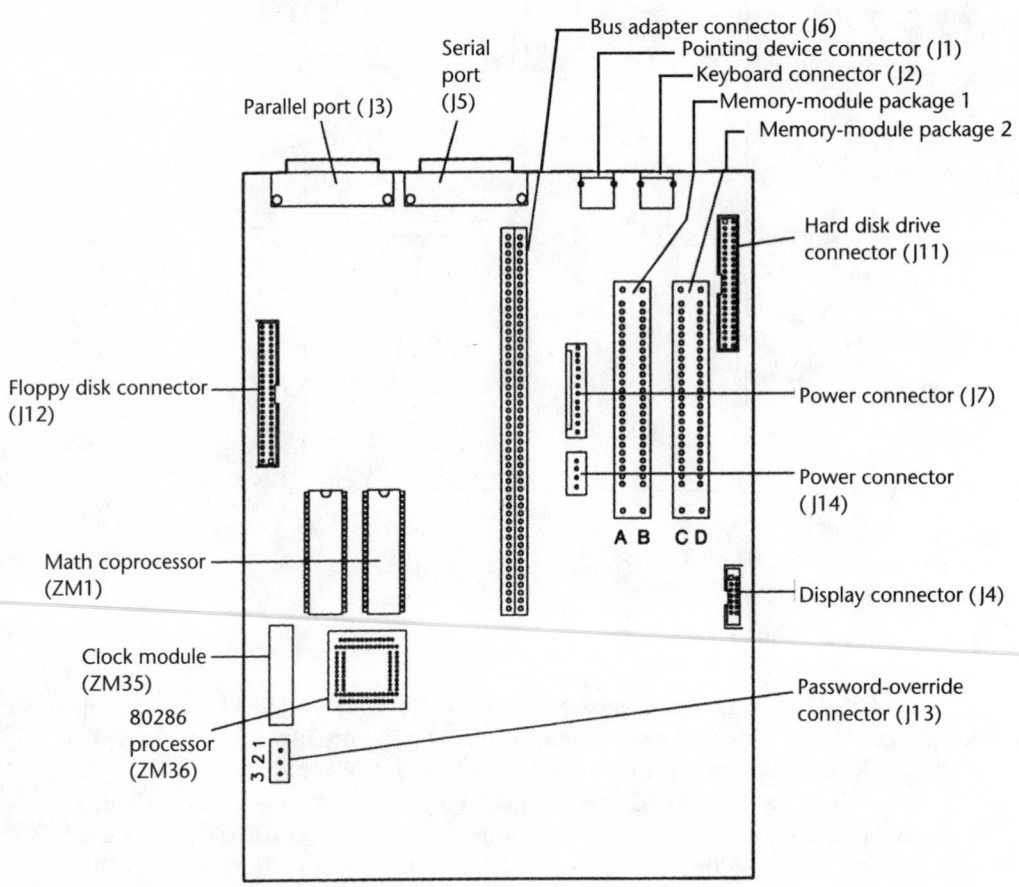

Fig. 4.11
PS/2 Model 25 286 (and 30 286) system board.

Table 4.13 lists the technical specifications for the PS/2 Model 25 286.

Table 4.13 PS/2 Model 25 286 Technical Specifications

System architecture

Microprocessor	80286
Clock speed	10 MHz
Bus type	ISA (Industry Standard Architecture)
Bus width	16-bit
Interrupt levels	16
Type	Edge-triggered
Shareable	No
DMA channels	7
DMA burst mode supported	No
Bus masters supported	No
Upgradeable processor complex	No

Memory

Standard on system board	1M
Maximum on system board	4M
Maximum total memory	16M
Memory speed and type	120ns dynamic RAM
System board memory-socket type	9-bit SIMM (single in-line memory module)
Number of memory-module sockets	4
Number available in standard configuration	2
Memory used on system board	256K/1M 9-bit SIMMs
Memory cache controller	No
Wait states:	
System board	1
Adapter	1

Standard features

ROM size	128K
ROM shadowing	No
Optional math coprocessor	80287
Coprocessor speed	6.67 MHz
Standard graphics	VGA (Video Graphics Array)
Built-in display	Yes
Monochrome	No
Color	(006,G06)
Dot pitch (mm)	.28
Audio earphone jack	Yes
RS232C serial ports	1
UART chip used	NS16450

(continues)

Table 4.13 Continued

Standard features

Maximum speed	19,200 bps
Maximum number of ports supported	2
Pointing device (mouse) ports	1
Parallel printer ports	1
Bidirectional	Yes
Maximum number of ports supported	2
CMOS real-time clock (RTC)	Yes
CMOS RAM	64 bytes
Battery life	10 years
Replaceable	Yes (Dallas module)

Disk storage

Internal disk and tape drive bays	2
Number of 3 1/2- and 5 1/4-inch bays	2/0
Standard floppy drives	1×1.44M
Optional floppy drives:	
5 1/4-inch 360K	Optional
5 1/4-inch 1.2M	No
3 1/2-inch 720K	No
3 1/2-inch 1.44M	Standard
3 1/2-inch 2.88M	No

Hard disk controller included:	IDE connector on system board				
IDE hard disks available	20/30/45M				
Drive form factor	3 1/2-inch				
Drive interface	IDE				
Drive capacity	20M	20M	30M	30M	45M
Average access rate (ms)	80	27	27	19	32
Encoding scheme	MFM	RLL	RLL	RLL	RLL
BIOS drive type number	26	34	33	35	37
Cylinders	612	775	614	921	580
Heads	4	2	4	2	6
Sectors per track	17	27	25	33	26
Rotational speed (RPM)	3600	3600	3600	3600	3600
Interleave factor	2:1	3:1	3:1	4:1	3:1
Data transfer rate (K/second)	255	270	250	248	260
Automatic head parking	No	No	No	Yes	Yes

Expansion slots

Total adapter slots	2
Number of long and short slots	1/1
Number of 8-/16-/32-bit slots	0/2/0
Available slots	2

Keyboard specifications

101-key Enhanced Keyboard	Yes (Gxx)
84-key Space-Saving Keyboard	Yes (0xx)
Fast keyboard speed setting	Yes
Keyboard cable length:	
Space-Saving Keyboard	5 feet
Enhanced Keyboard	6 feet

Security features

Keylock:	
Locks cover	Yes (x36)
Locks keyboard	No
Keyboard password	Yes
Power-on password	Yes
Network server mode	Yes

Physical specifications

Footprint type	Desktop
Dimensions:	
Height	15.0 inches
Footprint width	9.5 inches
Display width	12.6 inches
Depth	14.7 inches
Weight:	
x06	35.3 lbs
x36	37.0 lbs
Carrying case	Optional

Environmental specifications

Power-supply output	124.5 watts
Worldwide (110/60,220/50)	Yes
Auto-sensing/switching	Manual switch
Maximum current:	
90-137 VAC	3.0 amps
80-259 VAC	1.7 amps
Operating range:	
Temperature	60-90 degrees F

(continues)

Table 4.13 Continued	
Environmental specifications	
Relative humidity	8-80 percent
Maximum operating altitude	7,000 feet
Heat (BTUs/hour)	654
Noise (Average dB, operating, 1m)	51 dB
FCC classification	Class B

Table 4.14 shows the primary specifications and costs of the different versions of PS/2 Model 25 286.

PS/2 Model 30 286

The IBM PS/2 Model 30 286 (8530), introduced September 13, 1988, was the first PS/2 system with the full 16-bit ISA slot design in the original IBM AT and IBM XT 286 systems. Some people considered the Model 30 286 a reintroduction of the IBM AT; in slot design, it was. IBM supports both original Industry Standard Architecture (ISA) and Micro Channel Architecture (MCA). MCA-equipped PS/2 systems, however, are still (and will be for some time) IBM's primary platform. Figure 4.12 shows a front view and figure 4.13 shows a rear view of the Model 30 286.

The PS/2 Model 30 286 is a 80286 version of the Model 30. Although it shares the shape and form of the Model 30, its motherboard and circuitry are very different. The Model 30 is a PC-type system, and the Model 30 286 is an AT-type system. The Model 30 286 has processor performance equal to the Model 50 and includes a 1.44M floppy disk drive and VGA graphics. The Model 30 286 uses the Intel 80286 processor and operates at 10 MHz with 1 wait state to ROM. In addition to accepting most IBM PC and XT adapter cards, the Model 30 286 accepts most AT adapter cards. Figure 4.14 shows an interior view if the Model 30 286.

You can think of the Model 30 286 as equal to the Model 50, except that it uses ISA slots rather than MCA slots. The Model 30 286 is very similar to the Model 25 286. In fact, the

			PLANAR MEMORY		STANDARD		
Part number	**CPU**	**MHz**	**Std.**	**Max.**	**Floppy drive**	**Hard disk**	**Bus type**
25 286							
8525-006	286	10	1M	4M	1×1.44M	—	ISA/16
8525-G06	286	10	1M	4M	1×1.44M	—	ISA/16
8525-036	286	10	1M	4M	1×1.44M	30M	ISA/16
8525-G36	286	10	1M	4M	1×1.44M	30M	ISA/16

Keyboards available include the Enhanced (101-key), Space-Saving (84-key), and Host-Connected (122-key). If "Any" is indicated, purchaser could choose any of the three.

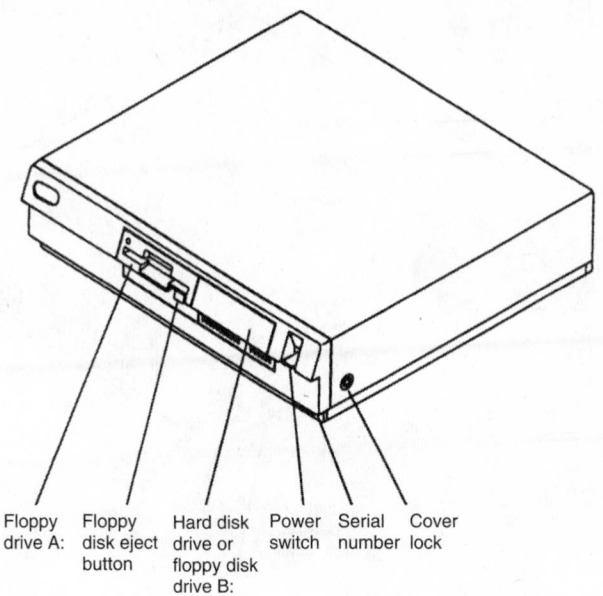

Floppy drive A: Floppy disk eject button   Hard disk drive or floppy disk drive B: Power switch   Serial number   Cover lock

Fig. 4.12
PS/2 Model 30 286.

motherboards in the two systems are identical. The Models 25 286 and 30 286 could be considered identical systems in hardware and BIOS; they differ only in physical shape and form.

The PS/2 Model 30 286 includes these standard features:

- Greatly improved performance over the XT, the AT, and 8086-based versions of the Model 25 and Model 30

- 10 MHz 80286 16-bit microprocessor, 1 wait state

- Optional 80287 coprocessor

Total/ available slots	STANDARD Video	KB	Date introduced	Date withdrawn
2/2	VGA	SS	05/10/90	—
2/2	VGA	Enh	05/10/90	—
2/2	VGA	SS	05/10/90	—
2/2	VGA	Enh	05/10/90	—

II

Compatible Systems

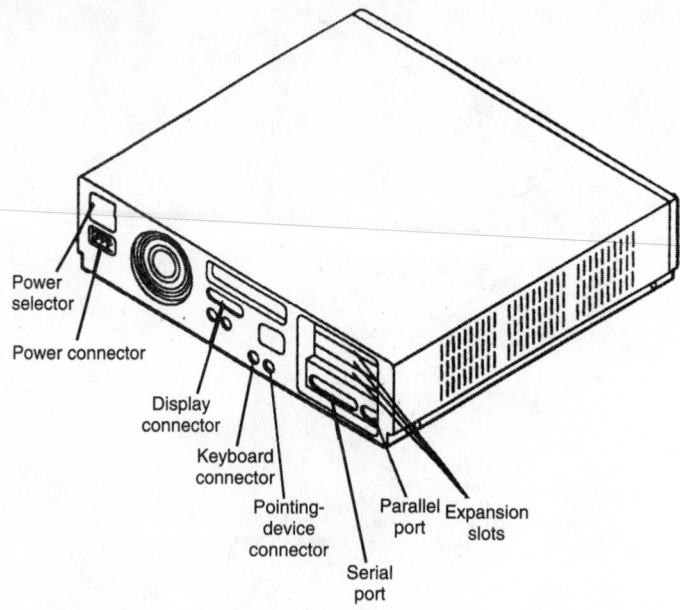

Fig. 4.13

PS/2 Model 30 286 (rear view).

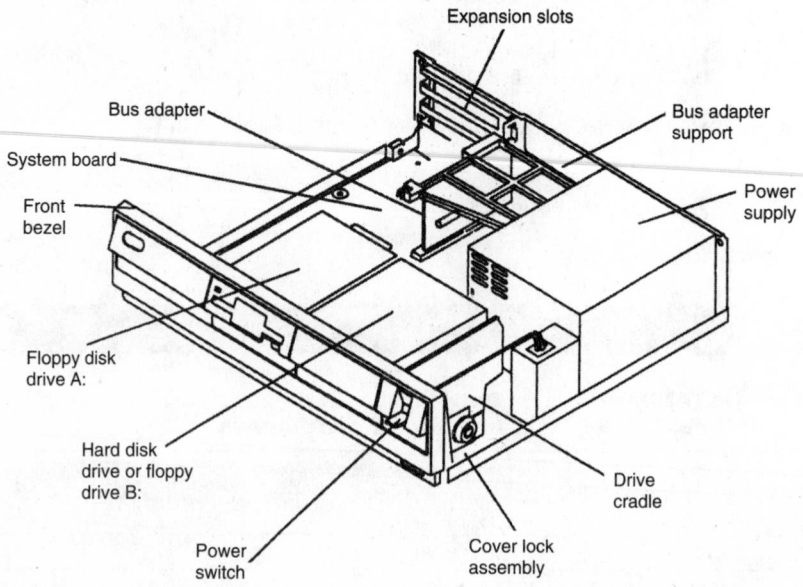

Fig. 4.14

PS/2 Model 30 286 (interior view).

- 16-bit ISA bus for adapters

- Three full-sized slots

- 1M random-access memory (RAM) standard

- Memory expansion to 4M on the system board

- 1.44M, 3 1/2-inch floppy disk drive

- Universal, automatic voltage-sensing power supply

- Keyboard port, serial/asynchronous port, parallel port, mouse port, and Video Graphics Array (VGA) port

- IBM Enhanced Keyboard

- Switchless installation and configuration

Several versions of the Model 30 286 have been available. The Model E01 (8530-E01) was a single floppy disk drive version of the Model 30 286 (without a hard disk drive). An optional 3 1/2-inch 20M hard disk drive (27F4969) was available for this model. The second model (8530-E21) included the 20M drive as a standard feature. Otherwise, these models were identical. The 30 286 was then available with 30M and 45M IDE (Integrated Drive Electronics) hard disk drives that plug into a modified slot connector on the motherboard. As of May 4, 1992, even these newer models have been discontinued. Currently, all 8530 systems have been withdrawn from marketing by IBM.

The PS/2 Model 30 286 is compatible with the PC, XT, and AT at the BIOS level and at most hardware interfaces. Because many components are included on the motherboard, however, many boards that could be used in the standard PC, XT, or AT systems do not work in the Model 30 286, even though it has the ISA-style slots. Boards not likely to work include graphics adapters, some memory adapters (especially those that are not flexible in setting the starting memory address), and some other cards. Because of the built-in VGA, an analog display is required.

Available versions of this model differ only in the standard hard disk supplied with the unit. Available models offer no hard drive, a 30M hard drive, or a 45M hard drive. Hard disks for installation after you purchase the system are available from other manufacturers.

Table 4.15 lists the technical specifications for the PS/2 Model 30 286.

Table 4.15 PS/2 Model 30 286 Technical Specifications

System architecture	
Microprocessor	80286
Clock speed	10 MHz
Bus type	ISA (Industry Standard Architecture)
Bus width	16-bit

(continues)

Compatible Systems

Table 4.15 Continued

System architecture

Interrupt levels	16
Type	Edge-triggered
Shareable	No
DMA channels	7
DMA burst mode supported	No
Bus masters supported	No
Upgradeable processor complex	No

Memory

Standard on system board	1M
Maximum on system board	4M
Maximum total memory	16M
Memory speed (ns) and type	120ns dynamic RAM
System board memory-socket type	9-bit SIMM (single in-line memory module)
Number of memory module sockets	4
Number available in standard configuration	2
Memory used on system board	256K/1M 9-bit SIMMs
Memory cache controller	No
Wait states:	
System board	1
Adapter	1

Standard features

ROM size 128K	
ROM shadowing	No
Optional math coprocessor	80287
Coprocessor speed	6.67 MHz
Standard graphics	VGA (Video Graphics Array)
RS232C serial ports	1
UART chip used	NS16450
Maximum speed (bits/second)	19,200 bps
Maximum number of ports	2
Pointing device (mouse) ports	1
Parallel printer ports	1
Bidirectional	Yes
Maximum number of ports	2

Standard features

CMOS real-time clock (RTC)	Yes
CMOS RAM	64 bytes
Battery life	10 years
Replaceable	Yes (Dallas module)

Disk storage

Internal disk and tape drive bays	2				
Number of 3 1/2- and 5 1/4-inch bays	2/0				
Standard floppy drives	1×1.44M				
Optional floppy drives:					
5 1/4-inch 360K	Optional				
5 1/4-inch 1.2M	No				
3 1/2-inch 720K	No				
3 1/2-inch 1.44M	Standard				
3 1/2-inch 2.88M	No				
Hard disk controller included:	IDE connector on system board				
IDE hard disks available	20/30/45M				
Drive form factor	3 1/2-inch				
Drive interface	IDE				
Drive capacity	20M	20M	30M	30M	45M
Average access rate (ms)	80	27	27	19	32
Encoding scheme	MFM	RLL	RLL	RLL	RLL
BIOS drive type number	26	34	33	35	37
Cylinders	612	775	614	921	580
Heads	4	2	4	2	6
Sectors per track	17	27	25	33	26
Rotational speed (RPM)	3600	3600	3600	3600	3600
Interleave factor	2:1	3:1	3:1	4:1	3:1
Data transfer rate (K/second)	255	270	250	248	260
Automatic head parking	No	No	No	Yes	Yes

Expansion slots

Total adapter slots	3
Number of long and short slots	3/0
Number of 8-/16-/32-bit slots	0/3/0
Available slots	3

Keyboard specifications

101-key Enhanced Keyboard	Yes
Fast keyboard speed setting	Yes
Keyboard cable length	6 feet

II

Compatible Systems

(continues)

Table 4.15 Continued	
Security features	
Keylock:	
Locks cover	Yes
Locks keyboard	No
Keyboard password	Yes
Power-on password	Yes
Network server mode	Yes
Physical specifications	
Footprint type	Desktop
Dimensions:	
Height	4.0 inches
Width	16.0 inches
Depth	15.6 inches
Weight	17.0 lbs (E01)
	19.0 lbs

PS/2 Model 35 SX

The PS/2 Model 35 SX (8535), introduced June 11, 1991, uses the 80386SX microprocessor operating at 20 MHz with 0 to 2 wait states and has the following integrated functions: parallel port, serial port, pointing device port, video graphics array (VGA 16-bit) port, keyboard port, 1.44M (million bytes) floppy disk drive support, math coprocessor socket, and three single in-line memory module (SIMM) sockets (two available for memory expansion). The PS/2 Model 35 SX is a three-slot, two-bay system; it is offered in floppy disk drive only (040) and a 40M hard disk model (043). All models come with 2M memory (expandable to 16M) standard on the system board. This system uses the 16-bit ISA for expansion, and its slots are full length. IBM's first 386 system using the ISA bus

Table 4.16 shows the primary specifications and costs of the various versions of PS/2 Model 30 286.

Table 4.16 IBM PS/2 Model 30 286 Model Summary							
			PLANAR MEMORY		STANDARD		
Part number	CPU	MHz	Std.	Max.	Floppy drive	Hard disk	Bus type
30 286							
8530-E01	286	10	1M	4M	1×1.44M	—	ISA/16
8530-E21	286	10	1M	4M	1×1.44M	20M	ISA/16
8530-E31	286	10	1M	4M	1×1.44M	30M	ISA/16
8530-E41	286	10	1M	4M	1×1.44M	45M	ISA/16

Note: *All the 30 286 models have been withdrawn and no longer are available from IBM.*

Environmental specifications

Power-supply output	90 watts
Worldwide (110/60,220/50)	Yes
Auto-sensing/switching	Manual switch
Maximum current:	
90-137 VAC	2.5 amps
180-265 VAC	1.3 amps
Operating range:	
Temperature	60-90 degrees F
Relative humidity	8-80 percent
Maximum operating altitude	7,000 feet
Heat (BTUs/hour)	438
Noise (Average dB, operating, 1m)	46 dB
FCC classification	Class B

shows that, although the company's emphasis is on the MCA bus, it continues to support and enhance its offerings in the ISA realm.

All versions of the PS/2 Model 35 are compatible with the IBM AT at the BIOS interface level (although the BIOS is not identical) and at most hardware interfaces. This system also uses the same motherboard as the PS/2 Model 40 SX. The only difference is that the bus adapter in the Model 40 supports five slots rather than three, as in the Model 35. Because many features are already integrated in these systems, many standard ISA adapters such as graphics, memory, disk controller, and other cards might not operate.

The PS/2 Floor Stand option is available if you want to install the system unit vertically.

Total/ available slots	STANDARD Video	KB	Date introduced	Date withdrawn
3/3	VGA	Enh	09/13/87	05/04/92
3/3	VGA	Enh	09/13/88	09/11/91
3/3	VGA	Enh	09/26/89	01/17/92
3/3	VGA	Enh	04/23/91	05/04/92

LAN Version. A special version of the Model 35, the Model 35 LS, provides a local area network (LAN) workstation solution and is available with all the standard features of the Model 35 SX, with this exception: No disk devices of any kind are installed in this medialess system; rather, a 16/4 token ring adapter or IBM EtherNet adapter with Remote Initial Program Load (RIPL) occupies one of the three adapter slots. The 35 LS-24X includes an IBM 16/4 token ring adapter as a standard feature; the 35 LS-14X model includes an IBM EtherNet adapter as a standard feature.

With the RIPL ROM, the system can "boot" DOS or OS/2 from the LAN server machine. The diskless Model 35 LS is fully upgradeable to the Model 35 SX configurations.

The Models 35 SX and LS both have a universal power supply with an autosense circuit. No manual switching is required. The Models 35 SX and LS, therefore, can easily be used worldwide.

Standard versions of Model 35 SX differ only in the choice of whether to have a hard disk; the LS version is completely diskless. In other respects, the models are similar.

Keyboard Options. Both the PS/2 Model 35 SX and 35 LS support the IBM Enhanced Keyboard (101/102 keys), Space-Saving Keyboard (84/85 keys), and the IBM Host-Connected Keyboard (122 keys). The Host-Connected Keyboard is similar to the 3270 keyboard offered with 3270 IBM PC and IBM AT systems. This keyboard is similar in design to that of a 3270 terminal keyboard and offers keys dedicated to 3270 functions. The Host-Connected Keyboard is supported by the BIOS in this system and cannot be retro-fitted to PS/2 systems that do not have the proper BIOS support. When you purchase a Model 35 SX or LS, you must choose any one of these three keyboards.

Floppy Drive Support. The Model 35 SX has BIOS support for the new 2.88M floppy drive. Although this drive does not come standard in this system, one is available from IBM. The Model 35 SX is one of the first systems to support this drive.

One very interesting feature of the Model 35 SX is its selectable-boot feature. As part of the system CMOS setup program, the user can specify which drive should be booted from and in which order the boot process should try each drive selected. The system supports an internally mounted 5 1/4-inch 1.2M drive in addition to the standard 3 1/2-inch 1.44M drive, and you can specify either drive as the primary boot device. You also can specify booting only from the hard disk, or even from a network file server (RIPL). This setup offers flexibility not found on many other systems.

The Model 35 SX system unit has two drive bays that can accommodate 5 1/4-inch or 3 1/2-inch devices, unlike many other PS/2 systems. Most older PS/2 systems cannot fit 5 1/4-inch devices internally.

Table 4.17 gives the specifications for the PS/2 model 35 SX.

Table 4.17 PS/2 Model 35 SX Technical Specifications

System architecture

Microprocessor	80386SX
Clock speed	20 MHz
Bus type	ISA (Industry Standard Architecture)
Bus width	16-bit
Interrupt levels	16
Type	Edge-triggered
Shareable	No
DMA channels	7
DMA burst mode supported	No
Bus masters supported	No
Upgradeable processor complex	No

Memory

Standard on system board	2M
Maximum on system board	16M
Maximum total memory	16M
Memory speed and type	85ns dynamic RAM
System-board memory socket type	36-bit SIMM (single in-line memory module)
Number of memory-module sockets	3
Number available in standard configuration	2
Memory used on system board	1M/2M/4M/8M 36-bit SIMMs
Memory cache controller	No
Wait states:	
System board	0-2
Adapter	1

Standard features

ROM size	128K
ROM shadowing	Yes
Optional math coprocessor	80387SX
Coprocessor speed	20 MHz
Standard graphics	VGA (Video Graphics Array)
8-/16-/32-bit controller	16-bit
Bus master	No
Video RAM (VRAM)	256K
RS232C serial ports	1
UART chip used	NS16450
Maximum speed (bits/second)	19,200 bps
Maximum number of ports	2

(continues)

Table 4.17 Continued

Standard features

Pointing device (mouse) ports	1
Parallel printer ports	1
Bidirectional	Yes
Maximum number of ports	2
CMOS real-time clock (RTC)	Yes
CMOS RAM	64 bytes
CMOS battery life	10 years
Replaceable battery	Yes (Dallas module)

Disk storage

Internal disk and tape drive bays	2	
Number of 3 1/2-/5 1/4-inch bays	0/2	
Selectable boot drive	Yes	
Bootable drives	All physical drives	
Standard floppy drives	1×1.44M	
None (24X)		
Optional floppy drives:		
5 1/4-inch 360K	Optional	
5 1/4-inch 1.2M	Optional	
3 1/2-inch 720K	No	
3 1/2-inch 1.44M	Standard	
3 1/2-inch 2.88M	Optional	
Hard disk controller included	IDE connector on system board	
IDE hard drives available	40/80M	
Drive form factor	3 1/2-inch	
Drive interface	IDE	
Drive capacity	40M	80M
Average access rate (ms)	17	17
Read-ahead cache	32K	32K
Encoding scheme	RLL	RLL
Cylinders	1038	1021
Heads	2	4
Sectors per track	39	39
Rotational speed (RPM)	3600	3600
Interleave factor	1:1	1:1
Data transfer rate (K/second)	1170	1170
Automatic head parking	Yes	Yes

Expansion slots

Total adapter slots	3
Number of long and short slots	3/0
Number of 8-/16-/32-bit slots	0/3/0
Available slots	3

Keyboard specifications

Keyboard choices	122-key Host-Connected Keyboard
	101-key Enhanced Keyboard
	84-key Space-Saving Keyboard
Fast keyboard speed setting	Yes
Keyboard cable length	10 feet

Security features

Keylock:	
Locks cover	Yes
Locks keyboard	No
Keyboard password	Yes
Power-on password	Yes
Network server mode	Yes

Physical specifications

Footprint type	Desktop
Orientation	Horizontal (vertical with optional stand)
Dimensions:	
Height	4.5 inches
Width	14.2 inches
Depth	15.6 inches
Weight:	
24X	22.4 lbs
040	23.8 lbs
043	20.9 lbs

Environmental specifications

Power-supply output	118 watts
Worldwide (110/60,220/50)	Yes
Auto-sensing/switching	Yes
Maximum current:	
90-137 VAC	3.5 amps
180-265 VAC	1.75 amps
Operating range:	
Temperature	50-95 degrees F

(continues)

Compatible Systems

Table 4.17 Continued	
Environmental specifications	
Relative humidity	8-80 percent
Maximum operating altitude	7,000 feet
Heat (BTUs/hour):	
24X	123
040	130
043	144
FCC classification	Class B

Table 4.18 shows the primary specifications and costs of the various versions of PS2/ Model 35 SX and LS.

PS/2 Model 40 SX

The PS/2 Model 40 SX (8540), introduced June 11, 1991, uses the 80386SX microprocessor operating at 20 MHz with 0 to 2 wait states to system memory. The Model 40 SX ships with 2M system board memory (expandable to 16M on planar), 3 1/2-inch drive options, and 16-bit VGA. The system also provides five full-size, customer-accessible, 8-/ 16-bit expansion card slots. The 80386SX microprocessor PS/2 Model 40 SX has the following integrated functions: parallel port, serial port, pointing device port, VGA port, keyboard port, 1.44M floppy disk drive support, math coprocessor socket, and three single in-line memory module (SIMM) sockets (two available for memory expansion).

The Model 40 SX has a universal power supply with an autosense circuit. No manual switching is required. Therefore, the Model 40 SX can easily be used worldwide.

The PS/2 Model 40 SX is compatible with the IBM AT at the BIOS interface level (although the BIOS is not identical) and at most hardware interfaces. This system also uses the same motherboard as the PS/2 Model 35 SX. The only difference is that the bus

			PLANAR MEMORY		STANDARD		
Part number	**CPU**	**MHz**	**Std.**	**Max.**	**Floppy drive**	**Hard disk**	**Bus type**
35 SX							
8535-040	386SX	20	2M	16M	1×1.44M	—	ISA/16
8535-043	386SX	20	2M	16M	1×1.44M	40M	ISA/16
35 LS							
8535-14X	386SX	20	2M	16M	—	—	ISA/16
8535-24X	386SX	20	2M	16M	—	—	ISA/16

Table 4.18 IBM PS/2 Model 35 SX/LS Model Summary

Keyboards available include the Enhanced (101-key), Space-Saving (84-key), and Host-Connected (122-key). If "Any" is indicated, purchaser could choose any of the three.

adapter in the Model 40 supports five slots rather than three, as in the Model 35. Because many features are already integrated in these systems, many standard ISA adapters such as graphics, memory, disk controller, and other cards might not operate.

The standard versions of the Model 40 SX differ only by whether and what kind of hard disk drive they provide: a floppy-drive-only model (8540-040), a 40M hard disk model (8540-043), or an 80M hard disk model (8540-045). In other respects the versions are similar.

The PS/2 Floor Stand option is available if you want to install the system unit vertically.

Keyboard Options. The PS/2 Model 40 SX supports the IBM Enhanced Keyboard (101/102 keys), Space-Saving Keyboard (84/85 keys), and the IBM Host-Connected Keyboard (122 keys). The Host-Connected Keyboard is similar to the 3270 keyboard offered with 3270 IBM PC and IBM AT systems. This keyboard is similar in design to a 3270 terminal keyboard and offers keys dedicated to 3270 functions. The Host-Connected Keyboard is supported by the BIOS in this system and cannot be retrofitted to PS/2 systems that do not have the proper BIOS support.

When you purchase a Model 40 SX, you can choose any of these three keyboards. The keyboard can be specified only in new equipment orders and cannot be ordered separately for on-order or installed equipment.

Floppy Drive Support. The Model 40 SX has BIOS support for the new 2.88M floppy drive. Although this drive does not come standard in this system, one is available from IBM. The Model 40 SX is one of the first systems to support this drive.

One very interesting feature of the Model 40 SX is its selectable-boot feature. As part of the system CMOS setup program, you can specify from which drive it should be booted and in which order the boot process should try each drive selected. The system supports an internally mounted 5 1/4-inch 1.2M drive in addition to the standard 3 1/2-inch 1.44M drive; you can specify either drive as the primary boot device. You also can specify

Total/ available slots	STANDARD Video	KB	Date introduced	Date withdrawn
3/3	VGA	Any	06/11/91	—
3/3	VGA	Any	06/11/91	—
3/2	VGA	Any	10/17/91	—
3/2	VGA	Any	06/11/91	—

The 35 LS-24X includes an IBM 16/4 Token Ring Adapter as a standard feature, whereas the 35 LS-4X model includes an IBM EtherNet Adapter as a standard feature.

booting only from the hard disk, or even from a network file server (RIPL). This setup offers flexibility not found on many other systems.

The Model 40 SX has two or three available drive bays (depending on whether the model has a hard disk) and supports up to two hard disks and a variety of optional floppy disk devices, including a 5 1/4-inch internally mounted 1.2M floppy drive or a 2.88M 3 1/2-inch floppy drive. Because of a selectable boot feature, you can boot the system from any installed drive.

Table 4.19 lists the technical specifications for the PS/2 model 40 SX.

Table 4.19 PS/2 Model 40 SX Technical Specifications	
System architecture	
Microprocessor	80386SX
Clock speed	20 MHz
Bus type	ISA (Industry Standard Architecture)
Bus width	16-bit
Interrupt levels	16
Type	Edge-triggered
Shareable	No
DMA channels	7
DMA burst mode supported	No
Bus masters supported	No
Upgradeable processor complex	No
Memory	
Standard on system board	2M
Maximum on system board	16M
Maximum total memory	16M
Memory speed and type	85ns dynamic RAM
System board memory-socket type	36-bit SIMM (single in-line memory module)
Number of memory-module sockets	3
Number available in standard configuration	2
Memory used on system board	1M/2M/4M/8M 36-bit SIMMs
Memory cache controller	No
Wait states:	
System board	0-2
Adapter	1
Standard features	
ROM size	128K
ROM shadowing	Yes

System architecture

Optional math coprocessor	80387SX
Coprocessor speed	20 MHz
Standard graphics	VGA (Video Graphics Array)
8-/16-/32-bit controller	16-bit
Bus master	No
Video RAM (VRAM)	256K
RS232C serial ports	1
UART chip used	NS16450
Maximum speed (bits per second)	19,200 bps
Maximum number of ports	2
Pointing device (mouse) ports	1
Parallel printer ports	1
Bidirectional	Yes
Maximum number of ports	2
CMOS real-time clock (RTC)	Yes
CMOS RAM	64 bytes
CMOS battery life	10 years
Replaceable	Yes (Dallas module)

Disk storage

Internal disk and tape drive bays	4	
Number of 3 1/2- and 5 1/4-inch bays	1/3	
Selectable boot drive	Yes	
Bootable drives	All physical drives	
Standard floppy drives	1x1.44M	
Optional floppy drives:		
5 1/4-inch 360K	Optional	
5 1/4-inch 1.2M	Optional	
3 1/2-inch 720K	No	
3 1/2-inch 1.44M	Standard	
3 1/2-inch 2.88M	Optional	
Hard disk controller included:	IDE connector on system board	
IDE hard drives available	40/80M	
Drive form factor	3 1/2-inch	
Drive interface	IDE	
Drive capacity	40M	80M
Average access rate (ms)	17	17
Read-ahead cache	32K	32K
Encoding scheme	RLL	RLL

(continues)

Table 4.19 Continued

Disk storage

Cylinders	1038	1021
Heads	2	4
Sectors per track	39	39
Rotational speed (RPM)	3600	3600
Interleave factor	1:1	1:1
Data transfer rate (K/second)	1170	1170
Automatic head parking	Yes	Yes

Expansion slots

Total adapter slots	5
Number of long and short slots	5/0
Number of 8-/16-/32-bit slots	0/5/0
Available slots	5

Keyboard specifications

Keyboard choices:	
122-key Host-Connected Keyboard	
101-key Enhanced Keyboard	
84-key Space-Saving Keyboard	
Fast keyboard speed setting	Yes
Keyboard cable length	10 feet

Security features

Keylock:	
Locks cover	Yes
Locks keyboard	No

Table 4.20 shows the primary specifications and costs of the various versions of PS/2 Model 40 SX.

Table 4.20 IBM PS/2 Model 40 SX Model Summary

Part number	CPU	MHz	PLANAR MEMORY Std.	Max.	STANDARD Floppy drive	Hard disk	Bus type
40 SX							
8540-040	386SX	20	2M	16M	1×1.44M	—	ISA/16
8540-043	386SX	20	2M	16M	1×1.44M	40M	ISA/16
8540-045	386SX	20	2M	16M	1×1.44M	80M	ISA/16

Keyboards available include the Enhanced (101-key), Space-Saving (84-key), and Host-Connected (122-key). If "Any" is indicated, the purchaser could choose any of the three.

Security features

Keyboard password	Yes
Power-on password	Yes
Network server mode	Yes

Physical specifications

Footprint type	Desktop
Orientation	Horizontal/vertical (stand included)
Dimensions:	
Height	6.7 inches
Width	17.3 inches
Depth	15.5 inches
Weight:	
	26.3 lbs (040)
	27.8 lbs

Environmental specifications

Power-supply output	197 watts
Worldwide (110/60,220/50)	Yes
Auto-sensing/switching	Manual switch
Maximum current:	
90-137 VAC	6.0 amps
180-265 VAC	3.0 amps
Operating range:	
Temperature	50-95 degrees F
Relative humidity	8-80 percent
Maximum operating altitude	7,000 feet
Heat (BTUs/hour)	190
FCC classification	Class B

Total/ available slots	STANDARD Video	KB	Date introduced	Date withdrawn
5/5	VGA	Any	06/11/91	12/21/92
5/5	VGA	Any	06/11/91	12/21/92
5/5	VGA	Any	06/11/91	12/21/92

Compatible Systems

II

PS/2 Model L40 SX

The PS/2 Model L40 SX, announced March 26, 1991, is a small, lightweight, battery-operated (AC/DC) portable laptop system. The PS/2 Model L40 SX is designed for people who want a high-function portable that is easy to carry and has the speed and capacity to support advanced applications. Standard features include a 20 MHz 80386SX processor; 2M of 80ns memory (expandable to 18M); 60M 2 1/2-inch hard disk; 3 1/2-inch 1.44M floppy disk drive; 10mm-thick, cold fluorescent, black-and-white LCD with VGA resolution; 84/85 key keyboard; and serial, parallel, keypad/mouse, VGA, and external expansion I/O ports for attaching external devices. In addition, each system includes an external 17-key numeric keypad, an AC adapter, a rechargeable battery pack, and a carrying case. Options for the PS/2 Model L40 SX include a one-slot expansion chassis, a data/fax modem (for the U.S. and Canada); a second serial adapter; a Trackpoint pointing device; 2M, 4M, or 8M memory upgrades; a quick charger; and a car-battery adapter.

The PS/2 Model L40 SX physical package is based on a clamshell design. It fits in most attaché cases and weighs 7.7 pounds, including the rechargeable battery pack. The PS/2 Model L40 SX features the familiar IBM keyboard size and layout; 80386SX architecture; large, easy-to-read display; high-capacity hard disk; and efficient battery-power management, while maintaining the light weight of a notebook portable. Compared to the IBM PS/2 Model P70, the PS/2 Model L40 SX adds battery operation, clamshell design, black-on-white LCD, and a smaller, lighter package.

System Expansion and Restrictions. The Model L40 SX is designed to be compatible with the IBM AT at the BIOS interface level and at most hardware interfaces, and the system is very expandable. Many I/O connections are provided as standard. An external numeric keypad, included with the unit, plugs into the standard mouse port. The numeric keypad has a mouse port to enable numeric keypad and mouse connections to operate concurrently. The L40 has a standard serial port, parallel port, VGA display port, and a special external expansion port reserved for an expansion chassis or base station called the Communications Cartridge I.

The PS/2 Communications Cartridge I is a one-slot expansion unit that you use with the Model L40 SX. The unit contains one half-size card slot that was especially designed to support Token-Ring, 3270 or 5250 communications adapter cards. Although the Communications Cartridge I was designed primarily for these communications adapters, other types of adapters should also work, but are technically not supported by IBM.

The expansion of the system has some limitations. Unless you purchase the Communications Cartridge I expansion chassis, for example, there are slots available for attaching adapters and cards other than the specific IBM PS/2 Model L40 SX options. Also, when the VGA port is operational, the integrated LCD is not operational—a drawback when you use the system for presentations with a large-screen projector. Additionally, because the IBM PS/2 internal data/fax modem for Model L40 SX and the IBM PS/2 serial adapter for Model L40 SX use the same internal connector, only one of these options can be installed per system. Finally, external keyboards are not supported.

Power Management. The L40 boasts very efficient power management. A suspend-resume function is provided. You suspend an application by closing the clamshell and leaving the power switch on. When the clamshell is opened, the application resumes at the point at which it was suspended. During suspension, system components are automatically powered off, except for the real-time clock and application memory. The system can be set to resume at a specific time. An internal backup battery is provided to prevent disruption of the application or system when the rechargeable battery pack is being changed.

To reduce the frequency of recharging the batteries, trickle recharging occurs during AC operation. To conserve and prolong battery life between recharges, a switch is provided for user selection of system speed under manual or automatic control. In automatic mode, the hardware initiates low clock-speed operation during idle periods. In manual mode, the processor runs at the default clock speed set by the user when the system is configured. The clock-speed settings are 20 MHz, 10 MHz, and 5 MHz.

In an effort to conserve even more battery power, the hardware supports sleep mode. Sleep mode conserves battery power during idle times between clock cycles and keystrokes by putting system components in an idle state that results in low power usage. (Sleep mode is not operational when an external display is attached.) This function is exploited by DOS and OS/2. The L40 SX has an informative LCD display that uses international symbols that indicate operational and environmental status. These status indicators include: a battery gauge, humidity, temperature-limit indicator, modem carrier detect, Numeric Lock, Scroll Lock, speaker enabled, suspend mode, floppy disk drive in use, and hard drive in use indicators.

Environmental Protection. The system's temperature and humidity sensors do not allow the unit to operate under incorrect environmental conditions. This feature is essential considering that a laptop system may spend time in a parked car, garage, or some other environment unsuitable for computer use. Few other systems offer this kind of protection.

Imagine leaving your system in your car for a few hours in the winter. After bringing the system inside, condensation forms on the circuitry and even on the hard disk platters. If you power up the system, the circuits or the hard drive might be destroyed. The L40 intervenes and does not allow the system to operate until safe temperature and humidity exist in the system's environment.

Table 4.21 lists the technical specifications for the PS/2 model L40 SX.

Table 4.21 PS/2 Model L40 SX Technical Specifications	
System architecture	
Microprocessor	80386SX
Clock speed	20/10/5 MHz
Bus type	ISA (Industry Standard Architecture)
Bus width	16-bit
Interrupt levels	16
Type	Edge-triggered

(continues)

Table 4.21 Continued	
System architecture	
Shareable	No
DMA channels	7
DMA burst mode supported	No
Bus masters supported	No
Upgradeable processor complex	No
Memory	
Standard on system board	2M
Maximum on system board	18M (16M + 2M EMS)
Maximum total memory	18M
Memory speed and type	80ns CMOS RAM
System board memory-socket type	36-bit CMOS SIMMs, specially keyed
Number system-board memory modules	2
Number available in standard configuration	2
Memory used on system board	2M soldered, and 2M/4M/8M 36-bit CMOS SIMMs
Memory cache controller	No
Wait states:	
System board	0-2
Standard features	
ROM size	128K
ROM shadowing	Yes
Optional math coprocessor	80387SX
Coprocessor speed	20 MHz
Standard graphics	VGA (Video Graphics Array)
8-/16-/32-bit controller	8-bit
Bus master	No
Video RAM (VRAM)	256K
Built-in display	Yes
Type	LCD
Dimensions (Diag/H×W)	10 inches/6 × 8 inches
Number of grayshades	32
Backlit/sidelit	Sidelit
Supertwisted	Yes
Contrast ratio	12:1
Detachable	No
External monitor port	Yes
External display disables LCD	Yes
LCD indicators	Yes
RS232C serial ports	1

Standard features	
UART chip used	NS16450
Maximum speed (bits/second)	19,200 bps
Maximum number of ports supported	2
Internal modem	Optional
Hayes-compatible	Yes
Asynchronous/synchronous	Yes/Yes
FAX capable	Yes
Group III compatible	Yes
FAX software included	Yes
Send/receive FAX	Yes/Yes
Maximum speed (bps):	
Data	2400 bps
FAX	9600 bps
Pointing device (mouse) ports	1
Parallel printer ports	1
Bidirectional	Yes
Maximum number of ports supported	1
CMOS real-time clock (RTC)	Yes
CMOS RAM	64 bytes
CMOS battery life	5 years
Replaceable	Yes

Disk storage	
Internal disk and tape drive bays	2
Number of 3 1/2-/5 1/4-inch bays	1/0
Standard floppy drives	1×1.44M
Hard disk controller included:	IDE connector on system board
IDE hard disks available	60M
Drive form factor	2 inches
Drive interface	IDE
Average access rate (ms)	19
Encoding scheme	RLL
Cylinders	822
Heads	4
Sectors per track	38
Rotational speed (RPM)	3600
Interleave factor	1:1
Data transfer rate (K/second)	1140
Automatic head parking	Yes

(continues)

II

Compatible Systems

Table 4.21 Continued	
Expansion slots	
Total adapter slots	0
Available slots	0
Keyboard specifications	
101-key Enhanced Keyboard	Yes (with external keypad)
84-key keyboard	Yes
Fast keyboard speed setting	Yes
Keyboard detachable	No
Security features	
Keylock:	
Locks cover	No
Locks keyboard	No
Keyboard password	Yes
Power-on password	Yes
Network server mode	Yes
Physical specifications	
Footprint type	Laptop
Dimensions:	
Height	2.1 inches
Width	12.8 inches
Depth	10.7 inches
Weight: with battery	7.7 lbs
Carrying case	Leather, included

Table 4.22 shows the primary specifications and costs of the PS/2 Model L40 SX.
Table 4.23 shows accessories available from IBM for the PS/2 Model L40 SX.

Table 4.22 IBM PS/2 Model L40 SX Model Summary							
			PLANAR MEMORY		**STANDARD**		
Part number	CPU	MHz	Std.	Max.	Floppy drive	Hard disk	Bus type
L40 SX							
8543-044	386SX	20	2M	18M	151.44M	60M	ISA/16

Environmental specifications

Power supply:	
Worldwide (110/60,220/50)	Yes
Auto-sensing/switching	Yes
Maximum current:	
90-265 VAC	2.7 amps
Operating range:	
Temperature	41-95 degrees F
Relative humidity	5-95 percent
Maximum operating altitude	8000 feet
Heat (BTUs/hour)	136
Noise (Average dB, operating, 1m)	32 dB
FCC classification	Class B

Miscellaneous

A/C adapter included	Yes
Quick charger	Optional
Car cigarette lighter adapter	Optional
Battery pack included	Yes
Battery charge duration	3 hours
Setup and power-management software	Yes
Speed-setting switch and software	Yes

Total/ available slots	STANDARD Video	KB	Date introduced	Date withdrawn
0	VGA	SS	03/26/91	07/21/92

Table 4.23 IBM PS/2 Model L40 SX Special Accessories

Description	Part number	Price	Notes
Communications Cartridge I	3541001	$595	One slot expansion chassis
Rechargeable battery pack	79F0197	130	3 hours use/up to 500 charges
Quick charger	79F0192	132	Charges in 2 1/2 hours rather than 8 hours
Car battery adapter	79F1012	165	Lighter socket runs and recharges L40
Leather carrying case	79F3981	71	Included with L40SX, black leather
Deluxe carrying case	79F0981	115	Cloth case, pockets and compartments
Airline travel hard case	79F3844	247	Plastic, padded, wheels, storage
Serial adapter for L40 SX	79F0979	119	Second serial, N/A with internal FAX or modem

PS/2 Model 50

The IBM PS/2 Model 50, which uses MCA, was introduced April 2, 1987, as an entry-level desktop system in the PS/2 family. Figure 4.15 shows a front view of the Model 50. As of July 23, 1991, all models of the 50 and 50 Z were discontinued and no longer are available from IBM.

The Model 50 features a 10 MHz 286 processor running with 0 or 1 wait state, depending on the model version, and 1M of memory on the system board. System-board memory can be expanded to 2M on Model 50 Z systems but is limited to 1M on the standard model (8550-021). As much as 16M of additional memory can be added with memory adapter cards. The IBM Model 50 comes standard with a 1.44M, 3 1/2-inch floppy disk drive; a 20M, 30M, or 60M hard disk drive (depending on the model); a serial port; a parallel port; a mouse port; and a Video Graphics Array (VGA) port. Figure 4.16 shows the rear panel of the Model 50.

The 80286 10 MHz 16-bit microprocessor running with 1 wait state enables the 50-021 to perform approximately 20 percent faster than the IBM XT 286 or the IBM AT Model 339. The Model 50 Z systems (8550-031 and 8550-061) run with 0 wait states to motherboard memory access, which translates into an additional 20 percent performance increase for most computational tasks.

The Model 50 has two levels of BIOS, which total 128K: a Compatibility BIOS (CBIOS) with memory addressability of up to 1M provides support for real-mode-based application programs. An additional version of BIOS, Advanced BIOS (ABIOS), provides support for protected-mode-based multitasking operating systems and has extended memory addressability of up to 16M.

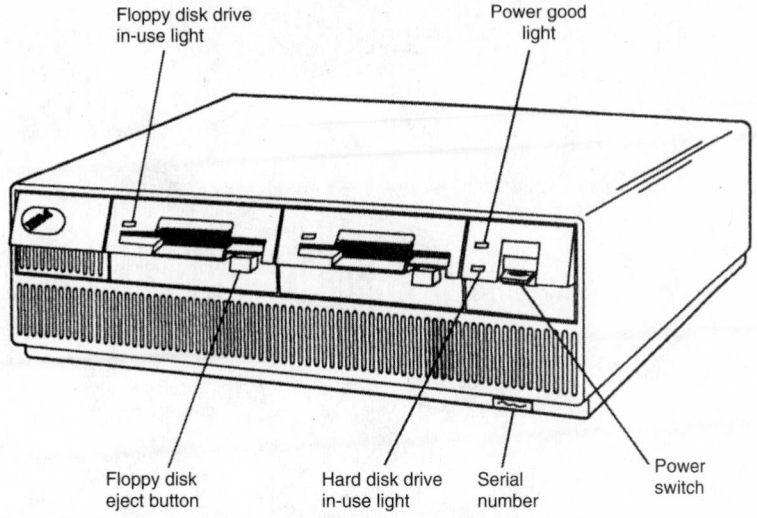

Floppy disk drive
in-use light

Power good
light

Floppy disk
eject button

Hard disk drive
in-use light

Serial
number

Power
switch

Fig. 4.15
PS/2 Model 50.

Note

Real mode is a mode in which the 80286 processor can emulate 8086 or 8088 processors for compatibility purposes. DOS runs under this mode. Protected mode, not found in the 8086 or 8088 processors, allows for specialized support of multitasking. Advanced multitasking operating systems such as OS/2 run under this mode.

Additional features of the system unit include four 16-bit I/O slots (with one slot occupied by the disk controller adapter); a 94-watt, automatic voltage-sensing, universal power supply; a time-and-date clock with battery backup; a socket for an 80287; an additional position for a second 3 1/2-inch floppy disk drive; and the IBM Enhanced Keyboard. Figure 4.17 shows an interior view of the Model 50.

Model 50 Z. On June 2, 1988, IBM introduced the PS/2 Model 50 Z (actually the 8550-031 and the 8550-061). These models offer improved performance and greater hard disk capacity. Higher-speed (85ns) memory provides 0-wait-state processor performance and can be upgraded to 2M on the system board. The 50 Z comes with a 30M or 60M hard disk drive, which provides greater capacity and improved average access time over the standard 20M hard disk in Model 50-021.

Floppy Drive Support. The standard 1.44M drive in all the Model 50 systems can format, read, and write to either 720K (double density) or 1.44M (high density) floppy disks. In double-density mode, this drive is fully compatible with the 720K (3 1/2-inch) floppy disk drive. In high-density mode, the standard drive doubles the data capability to 1.44M and the data rate to 500K bits per second.

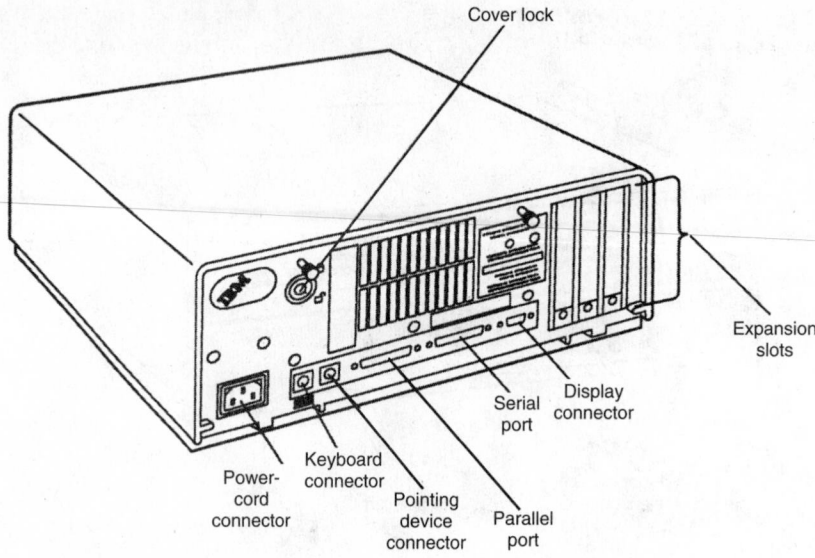

Fig. 4.16
PS/2 Model 50 rear panel view.

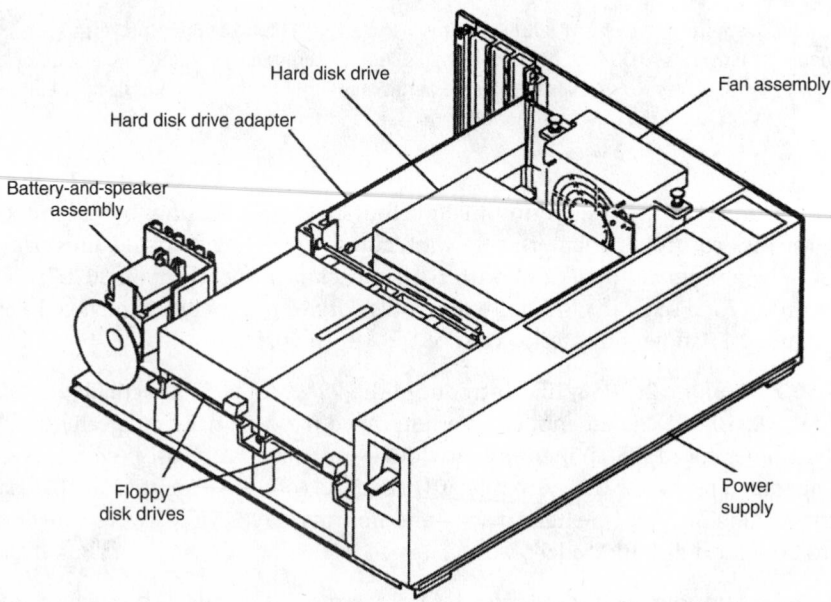

Fig. 4.17
PS/2 Model 50 interior view.

> **Note**
>
> Because of the capabilities and design of the disk media, you should not use the 1.44M drive to format a 720K (1M unformatted) disk as 1.44M, or to format a 1.44M (2M unformatted) disk as 720K.

A 5 1/4-inch external disk drive (360K) is available that enables you to convert or operate existing 5 1/4-inch applications. To operate, this drive requires the External Diskette Drive Adapter/A. The adapter card plugs into the connector for the 3 1/2-inch drive B. When the external drive is installed, it becomes drive B. Unfortunately, the external disk drive consumes one slot and the drive B position.

System Expansion. In response to user complaints about the storage capacity of the original 20M Model 50, IBM offers the PS/2 60M hard disk drive as an upgrade option. You can install this drive by replacing the existing 20M hard disk in the PS/2 Model 50 (8550-021) or 30M in the Model 50 Z (8550-031). No trade-in is available for the earlier drive. This drive provides 60M of storage and a faster access time of 27ms. The replacement adapter card required for the 50-021 is included.

For additional memory, IBM offers the PS/2 1-8M Memory Expansion Adapter/A and the PS/2 2-8M Memory Expansion Adapter/A—16-bit, full-length circuit cards. You can expand either card to a maximum of 8M by using optional memory kits. You can configure the adapter memory from 1M to 8M by using either the 0.5M memory module kit or the 2M memory module kit. These cards can be installed in any open expansion slot on the Model 50. The adapter is easy to set up because it contains no jumpers or hardware switches. An additional feature is an on-board ROM that contains a POST and microcode to initialize the card.

These memory cards also provide support for two different operating modes: expanded memory and extended memory. Used as expanded memory, the adapter card's memory is compatible with applications written to the LIM EMS V4.0 standard. In addition, you can use the adapter card's memory as extended memory for DOS or OS/2. By installing two adapters, each filled to 8M, a user can reach the system address limit of 16M for the Model 50.

Because of the 0 wait states on the 50 Z systems, IBM offers a special motherboard memory upgrade for only these systems. This upgrade consists of one 2M, 85ns memory kit, which you install on the system board of the 50-031 or 50-061, replacing the standard 1M of memory. This upgrade brings the system board to its maximum capacity of 2M for these models.

Table 4.24 lists the technical specifications for the PS/2 Model 50.

II

Compatible Systems

Table 4.24 PS/2 Model 50 Technical Specifications

System architecture

Microprocessor	80286
Clock speed	10 MHz
Bus type MCA	(Micro Channel Architecture)
Bus width	16-bit
Interrupt levels	16
Type	Level-sensitive
Shareable	Yes
DMA channels	15
DMA burst mode supported	Yes
Bus masters supported	15
Upgradeable processor complex	No

Memory

Standard on system board	1M
Maximum on system board	2M
	1M (021)
Maximum total memory	16M
Memory speed and type	85ns dynamic RAM
	150ns dynamic RAM (021)
System board memory-socket type	36-bit SIMM (single in-line memory module)
	9-bit SIMM (021)
Number of memory-module sockets	1
	2 (021)
Number available in standard configuration	0
Memory used on system board	1M/2M 36-bit SIMM
	512K 9-bit SIMMs (021)
Memory cache controller	No
Wait states:	
System board	0
	1 (021)
Adapter	0-1

Standard features

ROM size	128K
ROM shadowing	No
Optional math coprocessor	80287
Coprocessor speed	10 MHz

Standard features

Standard graphics	VGA (Video Graphics Array)
8-/16-/32-bit controller	8-bit
Bus master	No
Video RAM (VRAM)	256K
RS232C serial ports	1
UART chip used	NS16550
Maximum speed (bits per second)	19,200 bps
FIFO mode enabled	No
Maximum number of ports	8
Pointing device (mouse) ports	1
Parallel printer ports	1
Bidirectional	Yes
Maximum number of ports	8
CMOS real-time clock (RTC)	Yes
CMOS RAM	64 bytes
Battery life	5 years
Replaceable	Yes

Disk storage

Internal disk and tape drive bays	3		
Number of 3 1/2- and 5 1/4-inch bays	3/0		
Standard floppy drives	1×1.44M		
Optional floppy drives:			
5 1/4-inch 360K	Optional		
5 1/4-inch 1.2M	Optional		
3 1/2-inch 720K	No		
3 1/2-inch 1.44M	Standard		
3 1/2-inch 2.88M	No		
Hard disk controller included:	IDE connector on Interposer Card		
	ST-506 Controller (021)		
ST-506/IDE hard disks available	20/30/60M		
Drive form factor	3 1/2-inch		
Drive capacity	20M	30M	60M
Drive interface	ST-506	IDE	IDE
Average access rate (ms)	80	39	27
Encoding scheme	MFM	RLL	RLL
BIOS drive type number	30	33	None
Cylinders	611	614	762
Heads 4	4	6	
Sectors per track	17	25	26

(continues)

Compatible Systems

Table 4.24 Continued

Disk storage

Rotational speed (RPM)	3600	3600	3600
Interleave factor	1:1	1:1	1:1
Data transfer rate (K/second)	510	750	780
Automatic head parking	No	No	Yes

Expansion slots

Total adapter slots	3
Number of long and short slots	3/0
Number of 8-/16-/32-bit slots	0/3/0
Number of slots with video ext.	1
Available slots	3

Keyboard specifications

101-key Enhanced Keyboard	Yes
Fast keyboard speed setting	Yes
Keyboard cable length	6 feet

Security features

Keylock:	
Locks cover	Yes
Locks keyboard	No
Keyboard password	Yes
Power-on password	Yes
Network server mode	Yes

Physical specifications

Footprint type	Desktop
Dimensions:	
Height	5.5 inches
Width	14.2 inches
Depth	16.5 inches
Weight	23.0 lbs
	21.0 lbs (021)

Environmental specifications

Power-supply output	94 watts
Worldwide (110/60,220/50)	Yes
Auto-sensing/switching	Yes
Maximum current:	
90-137 VAC	2.7 amps
180-265 VAC	1.4 amps

Environmental specifications	
Operating range:	
Temperature	60-90 degrees F
Relative humidity	8-80 percent
Maximum operating altitude	7,000 feet
Heat (BTUs/hour)	494
Noise (Average dB, operating, 1m)	46 dB
FCC classification	Class B

Figures 4.18 and 4.19 show the layout and components on Model 50 and 50 Z motherboards, respectively.

Table 4.25 shows the primary specifications and costs of the different versions of PS/2 Model 50.

PS/2 Model 55 SX

The PS/2 Model 55 SX, introduced May 9, 1989, has been one of IBM's top-selling systems because of the system's reasonable performance, modular construction, low price, and compact, efficient design. Model 55 SX systems use the 386 SX processor running at 16 MHz. They have 2M as standard memory in the 30M and 60M hard drive configurations, and 4M as standard memory in the 40M and 80M hard drive configurations. These Model 55 SX systems have the capability of supporting up to 16M of memory and have offered hard disks from 30M to 80M. Additional features include 1.44M, 3 1/2-inch floppy disk drive; ports (keyboard, pointing device, serial/asynchronous, parallel, VGA); three MCA I/O slots, and an Enhanced Keyboard. Figure 4.20 shows a front view and figure 4.21 shows a rear panel view of a Model 55 SX.

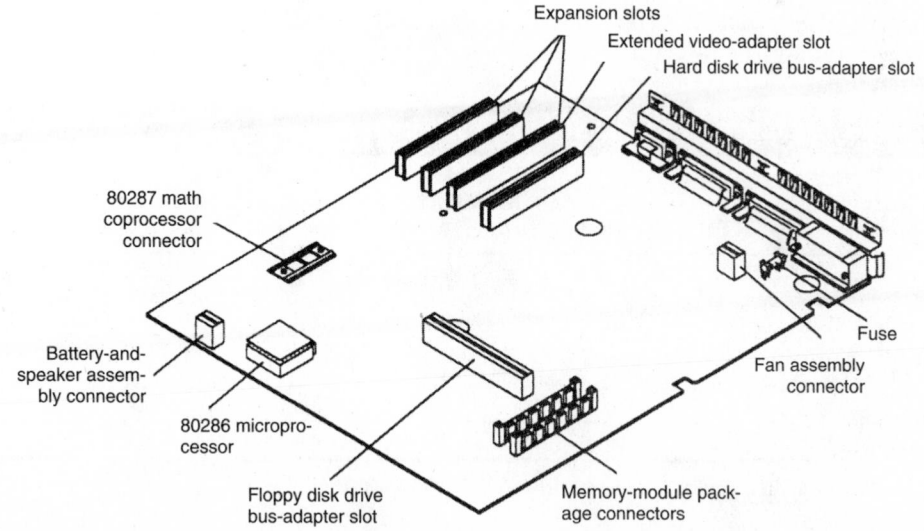

Fig. 4.18
PS/2 Model 50 system board.

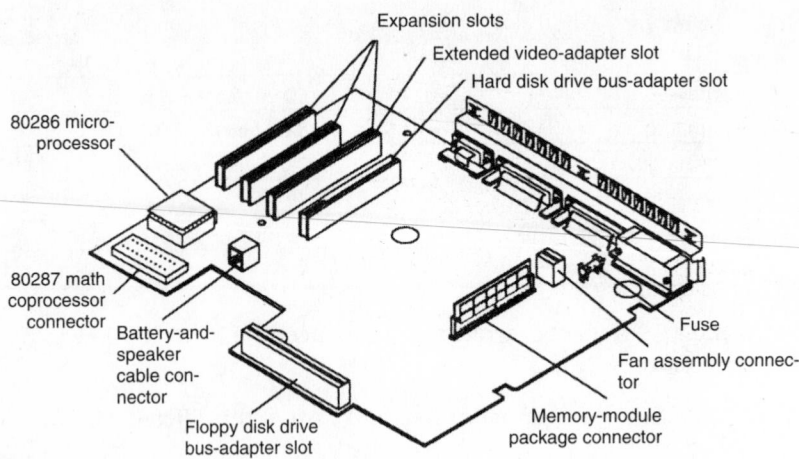

Fig. 4.19
PS/2 Model 50Z system board.

Also available are special diskless versions of the Model 55 SX with preinstalled IBM To-ken Ring or EtherNet Adapters. These "Lxx" versions are designed as LAN workstations and have the capability to boot directly from the LAN server system. The -LEx models include an IBM Ethernet Adapter, and the -LTx models include an IBM Token Ring Net-work Adapter. Although these models come without any drives, they can be upgraded later with both floppy and hard disk drives.

The PS/2 Model 55 SX is designed to maintain compatibility with many software prod-ucts currently operating under DOS and OS/2 on the IBM AT and the rest of the PS/2 family. These systems have full 80386 memory management capability, which means that they can operate in 32-bit software mode. Figure 4.22 shows an interior view of the Model 55 SX.

Table 4.25 IBM PS/2 Model 50 Model Summary

Part number	CPU	MHz	PLANAR MEMORY Std.	Max.	STANDARD Floppy drive	Hard disk	Bus type
50							
8550-021	286	10	1M	1M	1×1.44M	20M	MCA/16
50 Z							
8550-031	286	10	1M	2M	1×1.44M	30M	MCA/16
8550-061	286	10	1M	2M	1×1.44M	60M	MCA/16

Note: *All 50 and 50 Z models have been withdrawn from marketing by IBM.*

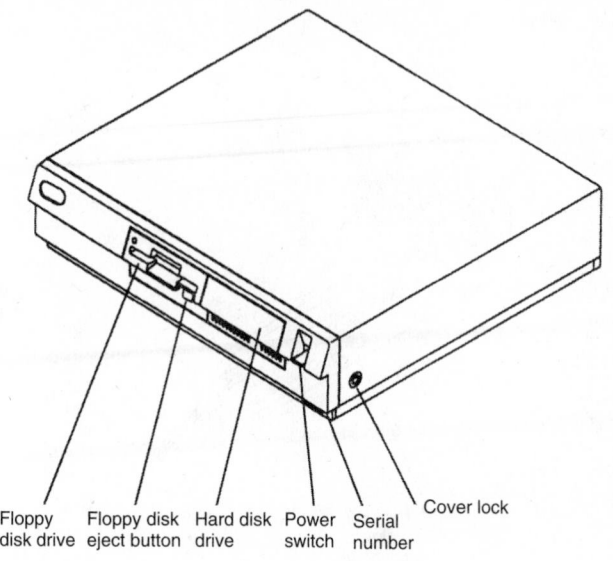

Floppy | Floppy disk | Hard disk | Power | Serial | Cover lock
disk drive | eject button | drive | switch | number

Fig. 4.20
PS/2 Model 55 SX.

The various models of the 55 SX differ only in the size of the preinstalled hard disk. Models have been available with 30M, 40M, 60M, and 80M drives. The 30M and 60M drive models have been discontinued by IBM, and the 40M and 80M models have taken their place.

Table 4.26 lists the technical specifications for the PS/2 model 55SX.

Total/available slots	STANDARD Video	KB	Date introduced	Date withdrawn
4/3	VGA	Enh	04/02/87	05/03/89
4/3	VGA	Enh	06/07/88	07/23/91
4/3	VGA	Enh	06/07/88	07/23/91

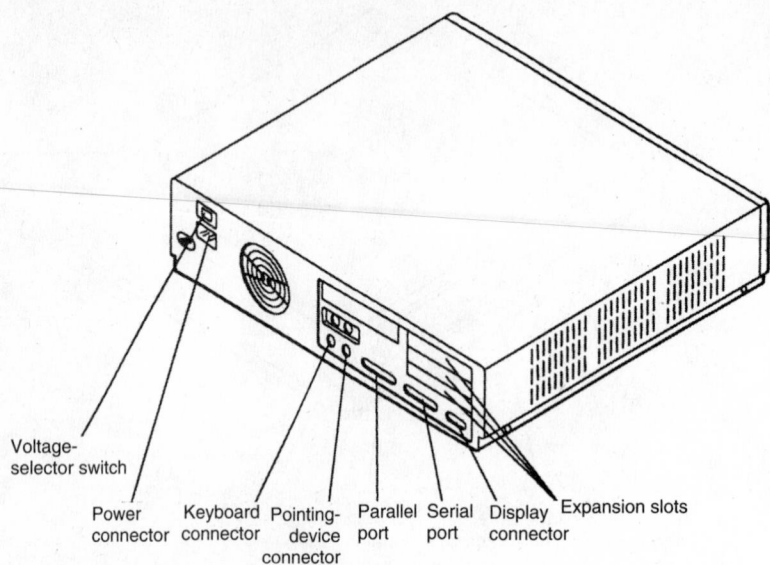

Voltage-
selector switch

Power   Keyboard Pointing- Parallel Serial Display   Expansion slots
connector   connector   device   port   port   connector
                          connector

Fig. 4.21
PS/2 Model 55 SX rear panel view.

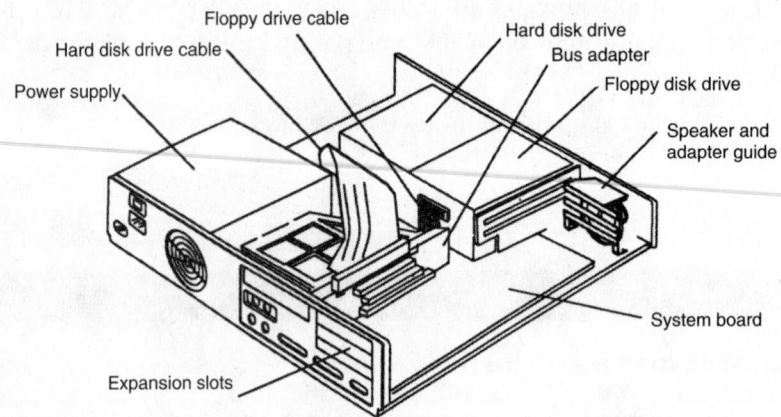

Floppy drive cable

Hard disk drive cable   Hard disk drive
                             Bus adapter
Power supply   Floppy disk drive

                             Speaker and
                             adapter guide

                             System board

Expansion slots

Fig. 4.22
PS/2 Model 55 SX interior view.

Table 4.26 PS/2 Model 55 SX Technical Specifications

System architecture

Microprocessor	80386SX
Clock speed	16 MHz
Bus type	MCA (Micro Channel Architecture)
Bus width	16-bit
Interrupt levels	16
Type	Level-sensitive
Shareable	Yes
DMA channels	15
DMA burst mode supported	Yes
Bus masters supported	15
Upgradeable processor complex	No

Memory

Standard on system board	4M
Maximum on system board	8M
Maximum total memory	16M
Memory speed and type	100ns dynamic RAM
System board memory socket type	36-bit SIMM (single in-line memory module)
Number of memory module sockets	2
Number available in standard configuration	1
Memory used on system board	1M/2M/4M 36-bit SIMMs
Memory cache controller	No
Wait states:	
System board	0-2
Adapter	0-4

Standard features

ROM size	128K
ROM shadowing	Yes
Optional math coprocessor	80387SX
Coprocessor speed	16 MHz
Standard graphics	VGA (Video Graphics Array)
8-/16-/32-bit controller	8-bit
Bus master	No
Video RAM (VRAM)	256K
RS232C serial ports	1
UART chip used	NS16550A
Maximum speed (bits/second)	19,200 bps

(continues)

Compatible Systems

II

Table 4.26 Continued

Standard features

FIFO mode enabled	Yes
Maximum number of ports	8
Pointing device (mouse) ports	1
Parallel printer ports	1
Bidirectional	Yes
Maximum number of ports	
supported	8
CMOS real-time clock (RTC)	Yes
CMOS RAM	64 bytes
Battery life	10 years
Replaceable	Yes (Dallas module)

Disk storage

Internal disk and tape drive bays	2
Number of 3 1/2- and 5 1/4-inch bays	2/0
Standard floppy drives	1×1.44M
	None (LT0,LE0)
Optional floppy drives:	
5 1/4-inch 360K	Optional
5 1/4-inch 1.2M	Optional
3 1/2-inch 720K	No
3 1/2-inch 1.44M	Standard
3 1/2-inch 2.88M	No

Hard disk controller included:	IDE connector on bus adapter			
IDE hard disks available	30M/40M/60M/80M			
Drive form factor	3 1/2-inch			
Drive interface	IDE			
Drive capacity	30M	40M	60M	80M
Average access rate (ms)	27	17	27	17
Read-ahead cache	No	32K	No	32K
Encoding scheme	RLL	RLL	RLL	RLL
BIOS drive type number	33	None	None	None
Cylinders	614	1038	762	1021
Heads	4	2	6	4
Sectors per track	25	39	26	39
Rotational speed (RPM)	3600	3600	3600	3600
Interleave factor	1:1	1:1	1:1	1:1
Actual transfer rate (K/second)	750	1170	780	1170
Automatic head parking	No	Yes	Yes	Yes

Expansion slots

Total adapter slots	3
Number of long and short slots	3/0
Number of 8-/16-/32-bit slots	0/3/0
Number of slots with video ext.	1
Available slots	3
Keyboard specifications:	
101-key Enhanced Keyboard	Yes
Fast keyboard speed setting	Yes
Keyboard cable length	6 feet

Security features

Keylock:	
Locks cover	Yes
Locks keyboard	No
Keyboard password	Yes
Power-on password	Yes
Network server mode	Yes

Physical specifications

Footprint type	Desktop
Dimensions:	
Height	4.0 inches
Width	16.0 inches
Depth	15.6 inches
Weight	15.5 lbs (LT0,LE0)
	19.0 lbs

Environmental specifications

Power-supply output	90 watts
Worldwide (110/60,220/50)	Yes
Auto-sensing/switching	Manual switch
Maximum current:	
90-137 VAC	2.5 amps
180-265 VAC	1.3 amps
Operating range:	
Temperature	60-90 degrees F
Relative humidity	8-80 percent
Maximum operating altitude	7,000 feet
Heat (BTUs/hour)	438

(continues)

Compatible Systems

II

Table 4.26 Continued	
Environmental specifications	
Noise (Average dB, operating, 1m)	40 dB
FCC classification	Class B

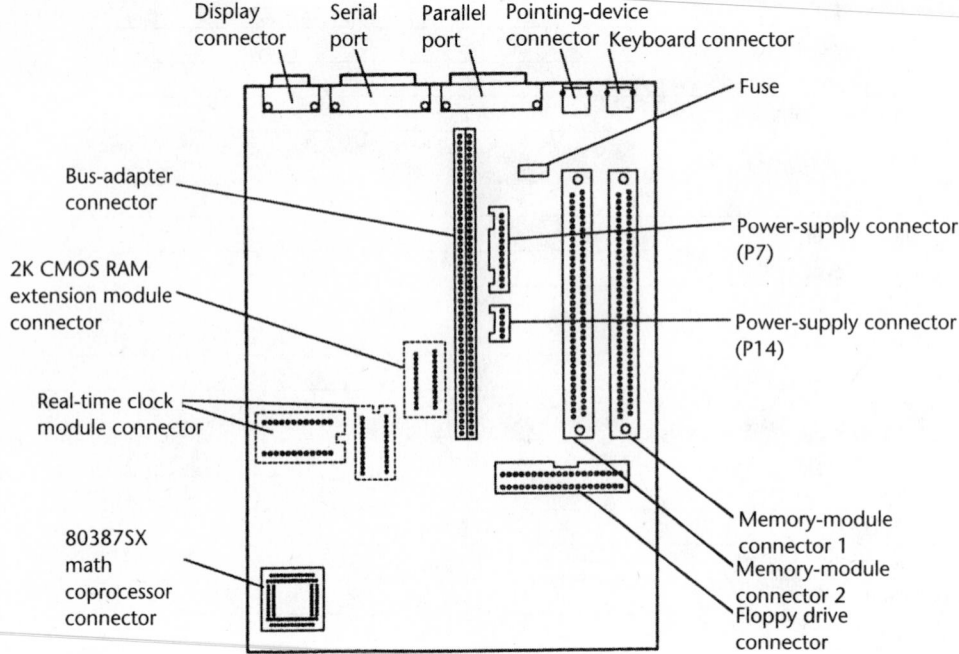

Fig. 4.23
PS/2 Model 55 SX system board.

Figure 4.23 shows the Model 55 SX motherboard components and layout.

Table 4.27 shows the primary specifications and costs of the various versions of PS/2 Model 55 SX.

PS/2 Model 56 SX, SLC, LS, and LS SLC

The PS/2 Model 56, introduced February 25, 1992, is an MCA system designed to replace the PS/2 Model 55 SX. The system has a 386SX or 386SLC 20 MHz processor, and offers improvements such as increased speed, configuration flexibility, and a Small Computer System Interface (SCSI) input/output interface. For improved graphics performance, video is provided through an enhanced 16-bit VGA controller integrated on the system board. Several models are offered including models with SCSI hard disk capacities of 80M and 160M, with or without the 386SLC processor option, and LAN versions with built-in token ring or EtherNet adapters.

The SLC models use a new custom, high-speed processor. The new IBM 386SLC processor is designed and manufactured in IBM's Burlington, Vermont, semiconductor facility. The 386SLC chip powers the PS/2 cached processor option. This processor includes a built-in cache controller and 8K cache similar to 486 processors. The 386SLC is up to 88 percent faster than the standard 386SX processor. The standard Model 56 SX systems can be upgraded to the SLC processor by adding the PS/2 cached processor option.

The PS/2 Model 56 is designed for desktop operation but ships with a vertical stand, allowing the customer the flexibility of horizontal or vertical orientation. The mechanical package allows for expansion with three 16-bit slots for MCA adapters and two bays for I/O devices. One of the bays contains an extra-high-density 3 1/2-inch 2.88M (million bytes) media sense floppy disk drive. Another bay contains an SCSI hard disk.

SCSI Standard. The SCSI controller is integrated in the system board, so a slot is not required, and the controller can support up to seven SCSI devices (including the standard SCSI hard disk). Two of the additional SCSI devices can be attached internally and the remaining devices externally with the external SCSI connector.

System Memory. The system ships with one 4M single in-line memory module (SIMM) located in the first SIMM socket on the motherboard. The PS/2 Model 56 supports up to 16M of 70ns memory on the system board in three SIMM sockets, all of which are addressable by direct memory address (DMA). Because the system board supports the full 16M, memory should not be installed via adapter cards in the bus. The Model 56 supports 2M, 4M, and 8M memory SIMMs (70ns only). To take advantage of enhanced performance via interleaved memory, SIMMs should be installed using all 2M or all 4M SIMMs. One, two, or three 2M SIMMs provide memory interleaving. Two or three 4M SIMMs also provide memory interleaving. The 8M SIMMs do not provide interleaving, but do allow the maximum capacity of 16M to be reached.

Keyboard Options. The PS/2 Model 56 supports the IBM Enhanced Keyboard (101/102 keys), Space-Saving Keyboard (84/85 keys), and the IBM Host-Connected Keyboard (122 keys). The Host-Connected Keyboard is similar to the 3270 keyboard offered with 3270 IBM PC and IBM AT systems. This keyboard is similar in design to that of a 3270 terminal keyboard and offers keys dedicated to 3270 functions. The Host-Connected Keyboard is supported by the BIOS in this system and cannot be retrofitted to PS/2 systems that do not have the proper BIOS support.

When you purchase a Model 56, you can choose any of these three keyboards. The keyboard can be specified only in new equipment orders and cannot be ordered separately for on-order or installed equipment.

Floppy Drive Support. The Model 56 includes a standard 2.88M floppy disk drive. This drive is fully compatible with 1.44M and 720K floppy disk drives. The drive includes a media sensor, which prevents accidentally formatting floppy disks to the wrong capacity (which can result in data loss).

II

Compatible Systems

Table 4.27 IBM PS/2 Model 55 SX Model Summary

Part number	CPU	MHz	PLANAR MEMORY Std.	Max.	STANDARD Floppy drive	Hard disk	Bus type
55 SX							
8555-031	386SX	16	2M	8M	1×1.44M	30M	MCA/16
8555-041	386SX	16	4M	8M	1×1.44M	40M	MCA/16
8555-061	386SX	16	2M	8M	1×1.44M	60M	MCA/16
8555-081	386SX	16	4M	8M	1×1.44M	80M	MCA/16
55 LS							
8555-LT0	386SX	16	4M	8M	—	—	MCA/16
8555-LE0	386SX	16	4M	8M	—	—	MCA/16

The LT0 model includes an IBM 16/4 Token Ring Adapter, and the LE0 model includes an IBM

DOS 5.0 is the minimum DOS version supported on this system. Because of the 2.88M floppy disk drive, versions of DOS prior to 5.0 (or other operating systems or applications) might not format floppy disk media correctly. Use of the proper level of operating system along with the new 2.88M floppy disk drive provides media sensing of 720K, 1.44M, and 2.88M floppy disks, giving greater ease in formatting, reading, and writing floppy disks.

Initial Microcode Load. One very special feature of the Model 56 is called Initial Microcode Load (IML). The ROM BIOS is stored on the hard disk in a protected 3M partition and loaded from the disk during a "pre-boot" process. The formatted capacity of the hard disk is reduced by 3M, and the total user-accessible capacity might vary slightly, based on operating environments. This partition is protected from normal access and does not appear to the system when it is running FDISK or FORMAT. In fact, the partition is so well protected that the system BIOS cannot even access this system partition with standard Int 13h commands. For all intents and purposes the hard disk is simply 3M smaller than it would normally be. The 3M system partition also contains a copy of the Reference disk, which means that the Setup program is effectively in ROM as well! The setup program is accessed by pressing Ctrl-Alt-Ins when the cursor shifts to the right-hand portion of the screen during a boot operation.

Having a disk-based ROM offers an unprecedented level of control over the system compared to other models. For example, updating the ROM BIOS to a new version simply requires booting from a newer Reference disk and selecting the option that updates the system partition. This feature enables IBM to keep in step with ROM upgrades for new features and fix bugs in the BIOS without the expense and hassle of replacing ROM chips.

The optional 386SLC processor was designed, developed, and manufactured by IBM under a long-standing agreement with Intel. This chip has the same 32-bit internal, 16-bit

Total/ available slots	STANDARD Video	KB	Date introduced	Date withdrawn
3/3	VGA	Enh	05/09/89	09/11/91
3/3	VGA	Enh	06/11/91	05/25/92
3/3	VGA	Enh	05/09/89	09/11/91
3/3	VGA	Enh	06/11/91	05/25/92
3/2	VGA	Enh	10/09/90	05/25/92
3/2	VGA	Enh	10/09/90	05/25/92

EtherNet adapter. Both of these models are also diskless.

external design as the Intel 386SX and is fully compatible with Intel 386 architecture. Intel participated in testing the 386SLC and determined the processor to be compatible with the Intel 386 architecture. IBM designed the 386SLC with 8K of internal cache and an internal cache controller, which improves performance by accessing data from high-speed cache memory rather than system memory, whenever possible. This is very similar to the 486 and is the primary reason for the increased performance. Performance has been further enhanced by optimizing commonly used instructions.

LS models are designed as LAN stations and include no disk drives. These diskless models are available in several versions, with or without the 386SLC processor. The -1xx models include an IBM EtherNet adapter in one of the three slots, and the -2xx models include an IBM Token Ring network adapter in one of the three slots.

Table 4.28 lists the technical specifications for the PS/2 Model 56.

Table 4.28 PS/2 Model 56 Technical Specifications

System architecture

Microprocessor	80386SX (04x)
	80386SLC (05x)
Optional microprocessor	80386SLC (04x)
Clock speed	20MHz
Bus type	MCA (Micro Channel Architecture)
Bus width	16-bit
Interrupt levels	16
Type	Level-sensitive

(continues)

Table 4.28 Continued

System architecture

Shareable	Yes
DMA channels	15
DMA burst mode supported	Yes
Bus masters supported	15
Upgradeable processor complex	No

Memory

Standard on system board	4M
Maximum on system board	16M
Maximum total memory	16M
Memory speed and type	70ns dynamic RAM
System board memory socket type	36-bit SIMM (single in-line memory module)
Number of memory module sockets	3
Number available in standard configuration	2
Memory used on system board	2M/4M/8M 36-bit SIMMs
Memory interleaving	Yes (2MB/4MB SIMMs only)
Memory cache controller	No
Wait states:	
System board	0-2
Adapter	0-4

Standard features

ROM size	128K
ROM shadowing	Yes
BIOS extensions stored on disk	Yes
Setup and Diagnostics stored on disk	Yes
Optional math coprocessor	80387SX
Coprocessor speed	20 MHz
Standard graphics	VGA
8-/16-/32-bit controller	16-bit
Bus master	No
Video RAM (VRAM)	256K
RS232C serial ports	1
UART chip used	Custom (compatible with NS16550A)
Maximum speed (bits/second)	345,600
FIFO mode enabled	Yes
Supports DMA data transfer	Yes
Maximum number of ports	8
Pointing device (mouse) ports	1

Standard features

Parallel printer ports	1
Bidirectional	Yes
Supports DMA data transfer	Yes
Maximum number of ports	8
CMOS real-time clock (RTC)	Yes
CMOS RAM	64 bytes + 2K extension
Battery life	10 years
Replaceable	Yes (Dallas module)

Disk storage

Internal disk and tape drive bays	4					
Number of 3 1/2-inch and	1/3					
5 1/4-inch bays						
Selectable boot drive	Yes					
Bootable drives	All physical drives					
Standard floppy drives	1×2.88M					
Optional floppy drives:						
5 1/4-inch 360K	Optional					
5 1/4-inch 1.2M	Optional					
3 1/2-inch 720K	No					
3 1/2-inch 1.44M	Optional					
3 1/2-inch 2.88M	Standard					
Hard disk controller included:	SCSI integrated on system board					
Bus master	Yes					
Devices supported per adapter	7					
Adapters supported per system	4					
SCSI hard disks available	60M/80M/120M/160M/320M/400M					
Drive form factor	3 1/2-inch					
Drive interface	SCSI					
Drive capacity	60M	80M	120M	160M	320M	400M
Average access rate (ms)	23	17	23	16	12.5	11.5
Read-ahead cache	32K	32K	32K	32K	64K	128K
SCSI transfer mode	Async	Async	Async	Async	Sync	Sync
Encoding scheme	RLL	RLL	RLL	RLL	RLL	RLL
Cylinders	920	1021	920	1021	949	1201
Heads	4	4	8	8	14	14
Sectors per track	32	39	32	39	48	48
Rotational speed (RPM)	3600	3600	3600	3600	4318	4318
Interleave factor	1:1	1:1	1:1	1:1	1:1	1:1

(continues)

Compatible Systems

Table 4.28 Continued						
Disk storage						
Data transfer rate (K/second)	960	1170	960	1170	1727	1727
Automatic head parking	Yes	Yes	Yes	Yes	Yes	Yes
Expansion slots						
Total adapter slots	3					
Number of long and short slots	3/0					
Number of 8-/16-/32-bit slots	0/3/0					
Number of slots with video ext.	1					
Available slots	3					
	2 (1xx, 2xx)					
Keyboard specifications						
Keyboard choices:						
	122-key Host-Connected Keyboard					
	101-key Enhanced Keyboard					
	84-key Space-Saving Keyboard					
Fast keyboard speed setting	Yes					
Keyboard cable length	10 feet					
Security features						
Keylock:						
Locks cover	Yes					
Locks keyboard	No					
Keyboard password	Yes					
Power-on password	Yes					
Network server mode	Yes					
Physical specifications						
Footprint type	Desktop					
Orientation	Horizontal/vertical					
Dimensions:						
Height	4.5 inches					
Width	14.2 inches					
Depth	15.6 inches					
Weight	24 lbs					

Environmental specifications	
Power-supply output	118 watts
Worldwide (110/60,220/50)	Yes
Auto-sensing/switching	Yes
Maximum current:	
90-137 VAC	3.5 amps
180-265 VAC	1.75 amps
Operating range:	
Temperature	50-95 degrees F
Relative humidity	8-80 percent
Maximum operating altitude	7,000 feet
Heat (BTUs/hour)	154
FCC classification	Class B

Table 4.29 shows the primary specifications and costs of the various
versions of PS/2 Model 56.

PS/2 Model 57 SX

The PS/2 Model 57 SX, introduced June 11, 1991, is an MCA system designed to complement and enhance the PS/2 Model 55 SX, the PS/2 Model 65 SX, and the low end of the
PS/2 Model 70 386 family. The system has a 386SX 20 MHz processor and offers improvements such as increased speed, configuration flexibility, and a Small Computer
System Interface (SCSI) input/output interface. For improved graphics performance,
video is provided through an enhanced 16-bit VGA controller integrated on the system
board. Several models are offered with SCSI hard disk capacities of 80M and 160M.

On October 17, 1991, IBM introduced a new custom, high-speed processor upgrade for
the Model 57. The new upgrade option utilizes the powerful IBM 386SLC processor,
designed and manufactured in IBM's Burlington, Vermont, semiconductor facility. The
386SLC chip powers the PS/2 cached processor option. This processor includes a built-in
cache controller and 8K cache similar to 486 processors. The 386SLC is up to 88 percent
faster than the standard 386SX processor.

II

Compatible Systems

Table 4.29 IBM PS/2 Model 56 Model Summary

Part number	CPU	MHz	PLANAR MEMORY Std.	Max.	STANDARD Floppy drive	Hard disk	Bus type
56 SX							
8556-043	386SX	20	4M	16M	1×2.88M	40M	MCA/16
8556-045	386SX	20	4M	16M	1×2.88M	80M	MCA/16
56 SLC							
8556-055	386SLC	20	4M	16M	1×2.88M	80M	MCA/16
8556-059	386SLC	20	4M	16M	1×2.88M	160M	MCA/16
56 LS							
8556-14x	386SX	20	4M	16M	—	—	MCA/16
8556-24x	386SX	20	4M	16M	—	—	MCA/16
56 SLC LS							
8556-15x	386SLC	20	4M	16M	—	—	MCA/16
8556-25x	386SLC	20	4M	16M	—	—	MCA/16

Keyboards available include the Enhanced (101-key), Space-Saving (84-key), and Host-Connected

The PS/2 Model 57 SX is designed for desktop operation but ships with a vertical stand, allowing the customer the flexibility of horizontal or vertical orientation. The mechanical package allows for expansion with five 16-bit slots for MCA adapters and four bays for I/O devices. One of the four bays contains an extra-high-density 3 1/2-inch 2.88M (million bytes) media sense floppy disk drive. Another bay contains a SCSI hard disk. Additional 5 1/4-inch and/or 3 1/2-inch devices, floppy disk drives, hard disks, tape and CD-ROM drives, and similar devices might be installed in the two remaining bays.

SCSI Standard. The SCSI controller is integrated in the system board, so a slot is not required, and the controller can support as many as seven SCSI devices (including the standard SCSI hard disk). Two of the additional SCSI devices can be attached internally and the remaining devices externally with the external SCSI connector.

System Memory. The system ships with one 4M single in-line memory module (SIMM) located in the first SIMM socket on the motherboard. The PS/2 Model 57 SX supports up to 16M of 70ns memory on the system board in three SIMM sockets, all of which are addressable by direct memory address (DMA). Because the system board supports the full 16M, memory should not be installed with adapter cards in the bus. The Model 57 SX

Total/ available slots	STANDARD Video	KB	Date introduced	Date withdrawn
3/3	VGA	Any	02/25/92	—
3/3	VGA	Any	02/25/92	—
3/3	VGA	Any	02/25/92	—
3/3	VGA	Any	02/25/92	—
3/3	VGA	Any	02/25/92	—
3/2	VGA	Any	02/25/92	—
3/2	VGA	Any	02/25/92	—
3/2	VGA	Any	02/25/92	—

(122-key). If "Any" is indicated, purchaser could choose any of the three.

supports 2M, 4M, and 8M memory SIMMs (70ns only). To take advantage of enhanced performance with interleaved memory, SIMMs should be installed using all 2M or all 4M SIMMs. One, two, or three 2M SIMMs provide memory interleaving. Two or three 4M SIMMs also provide memory interleaving. The 8M SIMMs do not provide interleaving, but do allow the maximum capacity of 16M to be reached.

Keyboard Options. The PS/2 Model 57 supports the IBM Enhanced Keyboard (101/102 keys), Space-Saving Keyboard (84/85 keys), and the IBM Host-Connected Keyboard (122 keys). The Host-Connected Keyboard is similar to the 3270 keyboard offered with 3270 IBM PC and IBM AT systems. This keyboard is similar in design to that of a 3270 terminal keyboard and offers keys dedicated to 3270 functions. The Host-Connected Keyboard is supported by the BIOS in this system and cannot be retrofitted to PS/2 systems that do not have the proper BIOS support.

When you purchase a Model 57, you can choose any of these three keyboards. The keyboard can be specified only in new equipment orders and cannot be ordered separately for on-order or installed equipment.

Compatible Systems

Floppy Drive Support. The Model 57 is the first system in the PC world to be shipped with a standard 2.88M floppy disk drive (although the drive is supported as an option in several other PS/2 systems). This drive is fully compatible with 1.44M and 720K floppy disk drives. The drive includes a media sensor, which prevents accidentally formatting floppy disks to the wrong capacity (which can result in data loss).

DOS 5.0 is the minimum DOS version supported on this system. Because of the 2.88M floppy disk drive, versions of DOS prior to 5.0 (or other operating systems or applications) might not format floppy disk media correctly. Use of the proper level of operating system along with the new 2.88M floppy disk drive provides media sensing of 720K, 1.44M, and 2.88M floppy disks, making it easier to format, read, and write floppy disks.

Initial Microcode Load. One special feature of the Model 57 is called Initial Microcode Load (IML). The ROM BIOS is stored on the hard disk in a protected 3M partition and loaded from the disk during a "pre-boot" process. The formatted capacity of the hard disk is reduced by 3M, and the total user-accessible capacity might vary slightly, based on operating environments. This partition is protected from normal access and does not appear to the system when running FDISK or FORMAT. In fact, the partition is so well protected that the system BIOS cannot even access this system partition with standard Int 13h commands. For all intents and purposes the hard disk is 3M smaller than it would normally be. The 3M system partition also contains a copy of the Reference disk, which means that the Setup program is effectively in ROM as well. The setup program is accessed by pressing Ctrl-Alt-Ins when the cursor shifts to the right-hand portion of the screen during a boot operation.

Having a disk-based ROM offers an unprecedented level of control over the system compared to other models. Updating the ROM BIOS to a new version, for example, simply requires booting from a newer Reference disk and selecting the option that updates the system partition. This feature enables IBM to keep in step with ROM upgrades for new features and fix bugs in the BIOS without the expense and hassle of replacing ROM chips.

The optional 386SLC processor was designed, developed, and manufactured by IBM under a long-standing agreement with Intel. This chip has the same 32-bit internal, 16-bit external design as the Intel 386SX and is fully compatible with Intel 386 architecture. Intel participated in testing the 386SLC and has determined the processor to be compatible with the Intel 386 architecture. IBM designed the 386SLC with 8K of internal cache and an internal cache controller that improves performance by accessing data from high-speed cache memory rather than system memory, whenever possible. This is very similar to the 486, and is the primary reason for the increased performance. Performance has been further enhanced by optimizing commonly used instructions.

Because of IBM's deal with Intel, you may see other compatible systems using the 386SLC processor. Until then, only IBM systems will contain the new chip. Because of the enhanced 486-like design, installation of this chip will allow the Model 57 to perform faster than nearly all 25 MHz 386DX-based systems from IBM and other manufacturers. The 386SLC processor option card installs easily in the math coprocessor socket on the Model 57 SX system board. There is a socket on the 386SLC module for installation of a math coprocessor if you want one, or one has already been installed in the system.

On October 17, 1991, IBM pre-announced the PS/2 Ultimedia Model M57 SLC (8557-255). This enhanced version of the 57 includes the 386SLC processor module, for performance nearly double that of the standard Model 57. It also includes OS/2 2.0, whose availability coincides with the availability of this system in March 1992. This system also has complete multimedia capability. It adds the following standard product improvements to the model standard Model 57:

- Multimedia front panel with stereo headphone jack, mono microphone jack, volume control, and enhanced loudspeaker.

- 16-bit eXtended Graphics Array (XGA) adapter card with 1M VRAM supports 640×480 with 65,000 colors or 1024×768 with 256 colors.

- 16-bit audio adapter card with I/O to the front panel supports FM-quality stereo.

- IBM PS/2 mouse.

- 160M SCSI fixed disk.

- A new CD-ROM/XA drive (PS/2 CD-ROM II) with connection to the multimedia front panel, supporting existing CD-ROM formats and enabled to support new CD-ROM/XA formats.

- A CD containing three operating systems or environments, a variety of multimedia application samplers, and an "Introducing Ultimedia" demonstration.

- Operating systems supplied on CD-ROM include IBM OS/2 Version 2.0, IBM DOS 5.0, and Microsoft Windows 3.0 with Microsoft Multimedia Windows Extensions 1.0.

The PS/2 Ultimedia Model M57 SLC (8557-255) includes the IBM 386 SLC microprocessor as a standard item. This system is designed for desktop and floor standing operation (a floor stand is included). The mechanical package has five Micro Channel slots and four bays for I/O devices. The Audio Capture and Playback Adapter and the XGA Adapter are installed in two of the slots, leaving three slots for future expansion. A 3 1/2-inch 2.88M media sense disk drive, an SCSI fixed disk, and a CD-ROM/XA drive are installed in three of the bays. An additional 5 1/4-inch or 3 1/2-inch device, optical disk drive, fixed disk drive, tape drive, CD-ROM drive, or a similar device can be installed in the one remaining bay.

II

Compatible Systems

The primary video in the Ultimedia is provided by the 16-bit IBM PS/2 XGA Display Adapter/A. Additionally, an enhanced VGA port is provided, for direct video display/ monitor connections or indirect connections via the video feature bus connections to Micro Channel slot #2.

With OS/2 Version 2.0 as a standard feature, users can run OS/2, DOS, and Windows applications. Multimedia applications supported in any of the operating systems can be used effectively by the PS/2 Ultimedia Model M57 SLC user. XGA graphics and CD-ROM/ XA are leading-edge technologies. They offer capabilities yet to be exploited, making this one of the most advanced multimedia systems available. IBM intends to make IBM mul- timedia extensions to OS/2 generally available in 1992. These extensions will exploit the CD-ROM Extended Architecture (CD-ROM/XA) capabilities for interleaved data and com- pressed audio enabled by the PS/2 CD-ROM II drive. IBM also intends to provide the new PS/2 CD-ROM II drive as an optional feature on all IBM SCSI-supported PS/2 systems in the future.

Table 4.30 lists the technical specifications for the PS/2 model 57 SX.

Table 4.30 PS/2 Model 57 SX Technical Specifications	
System architecture	
Microprocessor	80386SX (04x)
	80386SLC (05x)
Optional microprocessor	80386SLC (04x)
Clock speed	20MHz
Bus type	MCA (Micro Channel Architecture)
Bus width	16-bit
Interrupt levels	16
Type	Level-sensitive
Shareable	Yes
DMA channels	15
DMA burst mode supported	Yes
Bus masters supported	15
Upgradeable processor complex	No
Memory	
Standard on system board	4M
Maximum on system board	16M
Maximum total memory	16M
Memory speed and type	70ns dynamic RAM
System board memory socket type	36-bit SIMM (single in-line memory module)

Memory

Number of memory module sockets	3
Number available in standard configuration	2
Memory used on system board	2M/4M/8M 36-bit SIMMs
Memory Interleaving	Yes (2MB/4MB SIMMs only)
Memory cache controller	No
Wait states:	
System board	0-2
Adapter	0-4

Standard features

ROM size	128K
ROM shadowing	Yes
BIOS extensions stored on disk	Yes
Setup and Diagnostics stored on disk	Yes
Optional math coprocessor	80387SX
Coprocessor speed	20 MHz
Standard graphics	VGA
	XGA (255, 259)
8-/16-/32-bit controller	16-bit
Bus master	No
	Yes (XGA)
Video RAM (VRAM)	256K (1M on XGA)
RS232C serial ports	1
UART chip used	Custom (compatible with NS16550A)
Maximum speed (bits/second)	345,600
FIFO mode enabled	Yes
Supports DMA data transfer	Yes
Maximum number of ports	8
Pointing device (mouse) ports	1
Parallel printer ports	1
Bidirectional	Yes
Supports DMA data transfer	Yes
Maximum number of ports	8
CMOS real-time clock (RTC)	Yes
CMOS RAM	64 bytes + 2K extension
Battery life	5 years
Replaceable	Yes

(continues)

II

Compatible Systems

Table 4.30 Continued

Disk storage

Internal disk and tape drive bays	4
Number of 3 1/2-inch and 5 1/4-inch bays	1/3
Selectable boot drive	Yes
Bootable drives	All physical drives
Standard floppy drives	1×2.88M
Optional floppy drives:	
5 1/4-inch 360K	Optional
5 1/4-inch 1.2M	Optional
3 1/2-inch 720K	No
3 1/2-inch 1.44M	Optional
3 1/2-inch 2.88M	Standard
Hard disk controller included:	SCSI integrated on system board
Bus master	Yes
Devices supported per adapter	7
Adapters supported per system	4
SCSI hard disks available	60M/80M/120M/160M/320M/400M
Drive form factor	3 1/2-inch
Drive interface	SCSI

	60M	80M	120M	160M	320M	400M
Drive capacity	60M	80M	120M	160M	320M	400M
Average access rate (ms)	23	17	23	16	12.5	11.5
Read-ahead cache	32K	32K	32K	32K	64K	128K
SCSI transfer mode	Async	Async	Async	Async	Sync	Sync
Encoding scheme	RLL	RLL	RLL	RLL	RLL	RLL
Cylinders	920	1021	920	1021	949	1201
Heads	4	4	8	8	14	14
Sectors per track	32	39	32	39	48	48
Rotational speed (RPM)	3600	3600	3600	3600	4318	4318
Interleave factor	1:1	1:1	1:1	1:1	1:1	1:1
Data transfer rate (K/second)	960	1170	960	1170	1727	1727
Automatic head parking	Yes	Yes	Yes	Yes	Yes	Yes

PS/2 Ultimedia Model M57 SLC (8557-255)

CD-ROM/XA drive characteristics:	
Formats	CD-DA, CD-ROM, CD-ROM/XA
Capacity	Typically 600M, media-dependent
Access time	380ms
Burst (64K) transfer rate	1.5M/sec
Sustained transfer rate	150K/second
Latency	56ms to 150ms

Expansion slots

Total adapter slots	5
Number of long and short slots	5/0
Number of 8-/16-/32-bit slots	0/5/0
Number of slots with video ext.	1
Available slots	5

Keyboard specifications

Keyboard choices:	
	122-key Host-Connected Keyboard
	101-key Enhanced Keyboard
	84-key Space-Saving Keyboard
Fast keyboard speed setting	Yes
Keyboard cable length	10 feet

Security features

Keylock:	
Locks cover	Yes
Locks keyboard	No
Keyboard password	Yes
Power-on password	Yes
Network server mode	Yes

Physical specifications

Footprint type	Desktop
Orientation	Horizontal/vertical (stand included)
Dimensions:	
Height	6.7 inches
Width	17.3 inches
Depth	15.5 inches
Weight	32.0 lbs

Environmental specifications

Power-supply output	197 watts
Worldwide (110/60,220/50)	Yes
Auto-sensing/switching	Manual switch
Maximum current:	
90-137 VAC	6.0 amps
180-265 VAC	3.0 amps

(continues)

Compatible Systems

Environmental specifications	
Operating range:	
Temperature	50-95 degrees F
Relative humidity	8-80 percent
Maximum operating altitude	7,000 feet
Heat (BTUs/hour)	120
FCC classification	Class B

Table 4.31 shows the primary specifications and costs of the various versions of PS/2 Model 57 SX.

PS/2 Model 60

The IBM PS/2 Model 60, introduced April 2, 1987, is a midrange, desk-side system in the PS/2 family using 16-bit MCA I/O slots. As of October 31, 1990, IBM has withdrawn all versions of the Model 60, and the system is no longer available. Figure 4.24 shows a front view of the Model 60.

The system unit features a 10 MHz microprocessor running with 1 wait state, enabling the Model 60 to perform approximately 20 percent faster than the IBM XT 286 or the IBM AT Model 339. The system-board limit of 1M memory is provided. The Model 60 comes standard with a 1.44M, 3 1/2-inch floppy disk drive; a 44M or a 70M hard disk drive; a disk controller; a serial port; a parallel port; a mouse port; a VGA port; and an 80287 coprocessor socket.

The system has two levels of BIOS, which total 128K: a Compatibility BIOS (CBIOS) with memory addressability of up to 1M provides support for real-mode-based application programs, and Advanced BIOS (ABIOS) provides support for protected-mode-based multitasking operating systems and has extended memory addressability up to 16M.

Table 4.31 IBM PS/2 Model 57 SX Model Summary

Part number	CPU	MHz	PLANAR MEMORY Std.	Max.	STANDARD Floppy drive	Hard disk	Bus type
57 SX							
8557-045	386SX	20	4M	16M	1×2.88M	80M	MCA/16
8557-049	386SX	20	4M	16M	1×2.88M	160M	MCA/16
57 SLC							
8557-055	386SLC	20	4M	16M	1×2.88M	80M	MCA/16
8557-059	386SLC	20	4M	16M	1×2.88M	160M	MCA/16
M57 SLC							
8557-255	386SLC	20	4M	16M	1×2.88M	80M	MCA/16
8557-259	386SLC	20	4M	16M	152.88M	160M	MCA/16

Keyboards available include the Enhanced (101-key), Space-Saving (84-key), and Host-Connected

Additional features of the system unit include eight 16-bit MCA I/O slots (with one slot occupied by the disk controller adapter); an automatic voltage-sensing, universal power supply; a time-and-date clock with battery backup; an additional slot for a second 3 1/2-inch floppy disk drive; and the IBM Enhanced Keyboard. Figure 4.25 shows the rear panel and figure 4.26 shows the interior view of a Model 60.

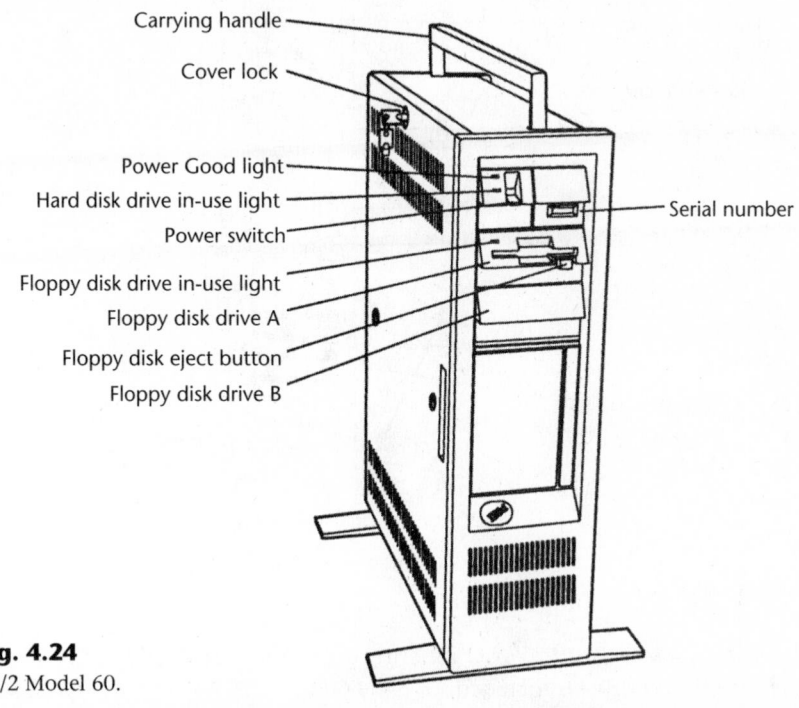

Fig. 4.24
PS/2 Model 60.

Total/ available slots	STANDARD Video	KB	Date introduced	Date withdrawn
5/5	VGA	Any	06/11/91	12/21/92
5/5	VGA	Any	06/11/91	12/21/92
5/5	VGA	Any	02/25/92	—
5/5	VGA	Any	02/25/92	—
5/3	XGA	Any	10/17/91	02/25/92
5/3	XGA	Any	02/25/92	—

(122-key). If "Any" is indicated, purchaser could choose any of the three.

Compatible Systems

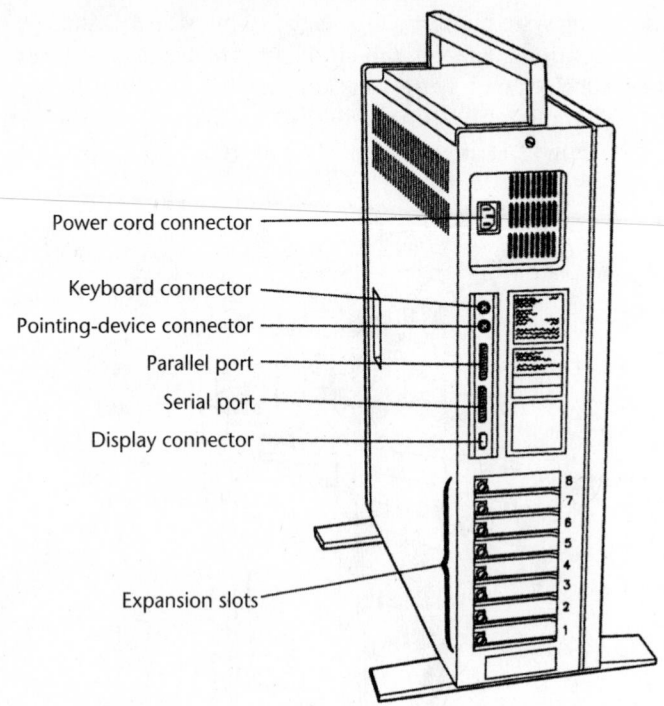

Power cord connector

Keyboard connector
Pointing-device connector
Parallel port
Serial port
Display connector

Expansion slots

Fig. 4.25
PS/2 Model 60 rear panel view.

IBM produced two versions of the Model 60, differing only in the hard disk and controller board supplied. The 70M drive is included with the 60-071 and also can be added as a second drive in that system. The 70M drive attaches using the high-performance Enhanced Small Device Interface (ESDI) disk adapter provided with the system unit and does not require an additional expansion slot. The ESDI adapter (standard in the 60-071) can connect up to two drives and allows for an extremely high data-transfer rate of 10 mbps (megabits per second) as well as increased reliability.

The standard Model 60-041 includes an ST-506/412 hard disk controller, which can connect up to two drives. The maximum transfer rate for this controller is 5 mbps (half that possible with the ESDI controller).

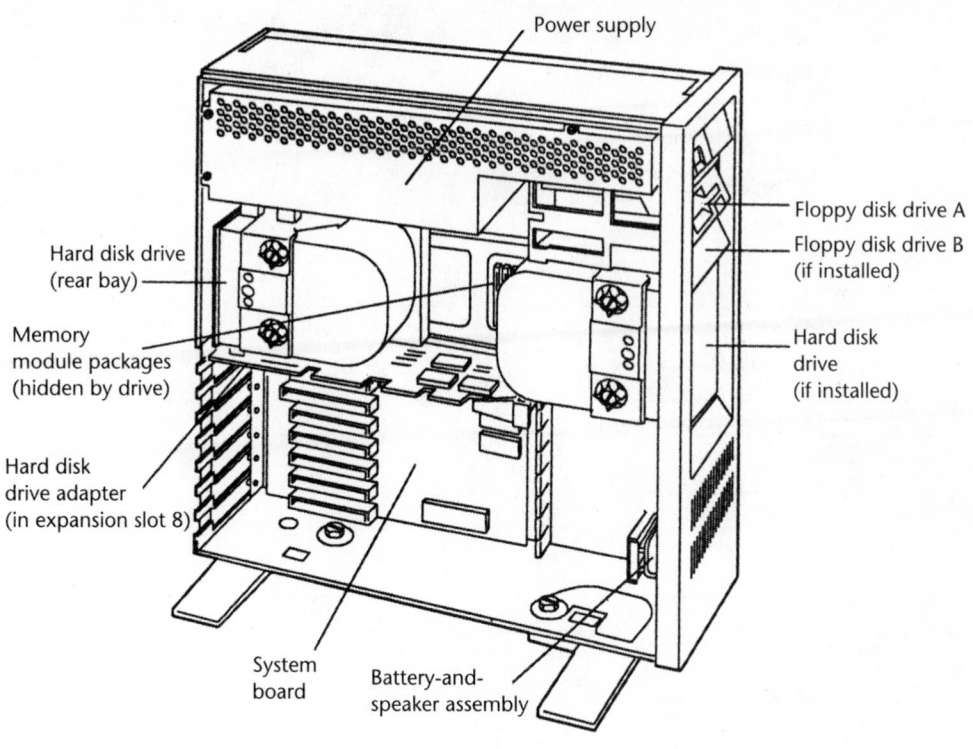

Power supply

Floppy disk drive A

Floppy disk drive B
(if installed)

Hard disk drive
(rear bay)

Hard disk
drive
(if installed)

Memory
module packages
(hidden by drive)

Hard disk
drive adapter
(in expansion slot 8)

System
board

Battery-and-
speaker assembly

Compatible Systems

Fig. 4.26
PS/2 Model 60 (interior view).

Table 4.32 lists the technical specifications for the PS/2 Model 60.

Table 4.32 PS/2 Model 60 Technical Specifications	
System architecture	
Microprocessor	80286
Clock speed	10 MHz
Bus type	MCA (Micro Channel Architecture)
Bus width	16-bit
Interrupt levels	16
Type	Level-sensitive
Shareable	Yes
DMA channels	15
DMA burst mode supported	Yes

(continues)

Table 4.32 Continued

System architecture

Bus masters supported	15
Upgradeable processor complex	No

Memory Architecture

Standard on system board	1M
Maximum on system board	1M
Maximum total memory	16M
Memory speed and type	150ns dynamic RAM
System board memory socket type	9-bit SIMM (single in-line memory module)
Number of memory module sockets	4
Number available in standard configuration	0
Memory used on system board	256K 9-bit SIMMs
Memory cache controller	No
Wait states:	
System board	1
Adapter	0-1

Standard features

ROM size	128K
ROM shadowing	No
Optional math coprocessor	80287
Coprocessor speed	10 MHz
Standard graphics	VGA (Video Graphics Array)
8-/16-/32-bit controller	8-bit
Bus master	No
Video RAM (VRAM)	256K
RS232C serial ports	1
UART chip used	NS16550
Maximum speed (bits/second)	19,200 bps
FIFO mode enabled	No
Maximum number of ports	8
Pointing device (mouse) ports	1
Parallel printer ports	1
Bidirectional	Yes
Maximum number of ports	8
CMOS real-time clock (RTC)	Yes
CMOS RAM	64 bytes + 2K extension
Battery life	5 years
Replaceable	Yes

Disk storage

Internal disk and tape drive bays	4				
Number of 3 1/2-/5 1/4-inch bays	2/2				
Standard floppy drives	1×1.44M				
Optional floppy drives:					
5 1/4-inch 360K	Optional				
5 1/4-inch 1.2M	Optional				
3 1/2-inch 720K	No				
3 1/2-inch 1.44M	Standard				
3 1/2-inch 2.88M	No				
Hard disk controller included:	ESDI controller				
	ST-506 controller (041)				
ST-506/ESDI hard disks available:	44M/70M/115M/314M				
Drive form factor	5 1/4-inch				
Drive capacity	44M	44M	70M	115M	314M
Drive interface	ST-506	ST-506	ESDI	ESDI	ESDI
Average access rate (ms)	40	40	30	28	23
Encoding scheme	MFM	MFM	RLL	RLL	RLL
BIOS drive type	31	32	None	None	None
Cylinders	733	1024	583	915	1225
Heads	7	5	7	7	15
Sectors per track	17	17	36	36	34
Rotational speed (RPM)	3600	3600	3600	3600	3600
Interleave factor	1:1	1:1	1:1	1:1	1:1
Data transfer rate (K/second)	510	510	1080	1080	1020
Automatic head parking	Yes	Yes	Yes	Yes	Yes

Expansion slots

Total adapter slots	8
Number of long and short slots	8/0
Number of 8-/16-/32-bit slots	0/8/0
Number of slots with video ext.	1
Available slots	7

Keyboard specifications

101-key Enhanced Keyboard	Yes
Fast keyboard speed setting	Yes
Keyboard cable length	10 feet

Security features

Keylock:	
Locks cover	Yes
Locks keyboard	No

(continues)

Compatible Systems

II

Table 4.32 Continued

Security features

Keyboard password	Yes
Power-on password	Yes
Network server mode	Yes

Physical specifications

Footprint type	Floor-standing
Dimensions:	
Height	23.5 inches
Width	6.5 inches
Depth	19.0 inches
Weight	47.0 lbs

Environmental specifications

Power-supply output	207 watts (041)
	225 watts (071)
Worldwide (110/60,220/50)	Yes
Auto-sensing/switching	Yes
Maximum current:	
90-137 VAC	5.3 amps
180-265 VAC	2.7 amps
Operating range:	
Temperature	60-90 degrees F
Relative humidity	8-80 percent
Maximum operating altitude	7,000 feet
Heat (BTUs/hour)	1240
Noise (Average dB, operating, 1m)	46 dB
FCC classification	Class B

Table 4.33 shows the primary specifications and costs of the various
versions of PS/2 Model 60.

Table 4.33 IBM PS/2 Model 60 Model Summary

Part CPU	MHz	Std.	PLANAR MEMORY Max.	drive	STANDARD Floppy disk	Hard type	Bus number
60							
8560-041	286	10	1M	1M	1×1.44M	44M	MCA/16
8560-071	286	10	1M	1M	1×1.44M	70M	MCA/16

Figure 4.27 shows the motherboard components and layout of a Model 60.

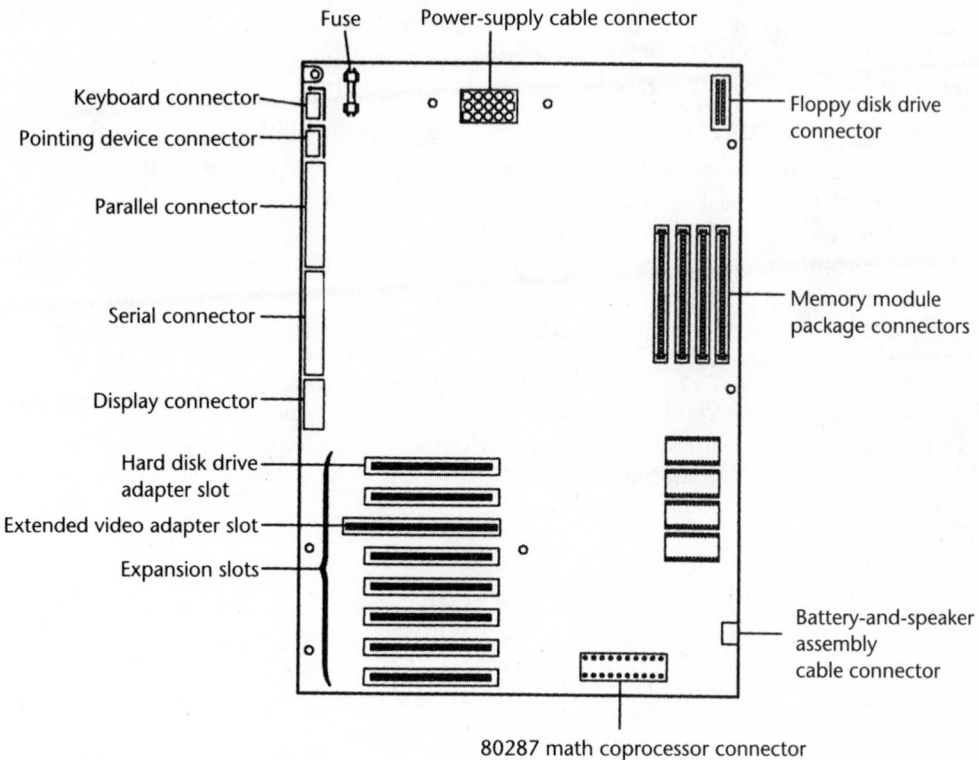

Fig. 4.27
PS/2 Model 60 system board.

Total/ available slots	STANDARD Video	KB	Date introduced	Date withdrawn
8/7	VGA	Enh	04/02/87	10/31/90
8/7	VGA	Enh	04/02/87	10/31/90

PS/2 Model 65 SX

The PS/2 Model 65 SX, introduced March 20, 1990, is based on the Intel 80386SX processor running at 16 MHz and uses 16-bit MCA I/O slots. All models of the Model 65 SX were discontinued on July 23, 1991, and are no longer available from IBM. Figure 4.28 and figure 4.29 show front and rear panel views of the Model 65, respectively.

Standard features of the Model 65 SX include a 1.44M, 3 1/2-inch, half-height floppy disk drive; VGA graphics adapter; 2M of memory; a 250-watt power supply; a time-and-date clock with battery backup; and the IBM Enhanced PC Keyboard. Two memory SIMM sockets are provided on the system board; one contains 2M of 100ns memory. Both versions of the Model 65 SX can be expanded to 8M of memory on the system board and support up to 16M total system memory. This can be done by removing the standard 2M SIMM and using 4M SIMMs instead. Figure 4.30 shows an interior view of the Model 65.

The hard disk drive controller is the PS/2 Micro Channel SCSI (Small Computer System Interface) Adapter. This bus master adapter provides additional expansion capability and an interface for the 3 1/2-inch, half-height SCSI hard disk drives of either 60M (8565-061) or 120M (8565-121).

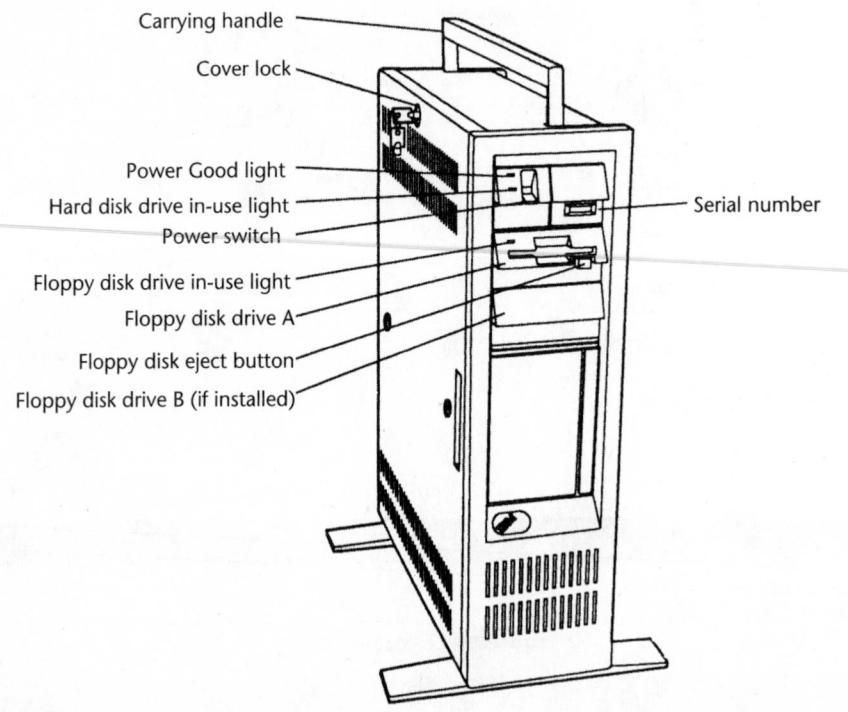

Fig. 4.28
PS/2 Model 65 SX.

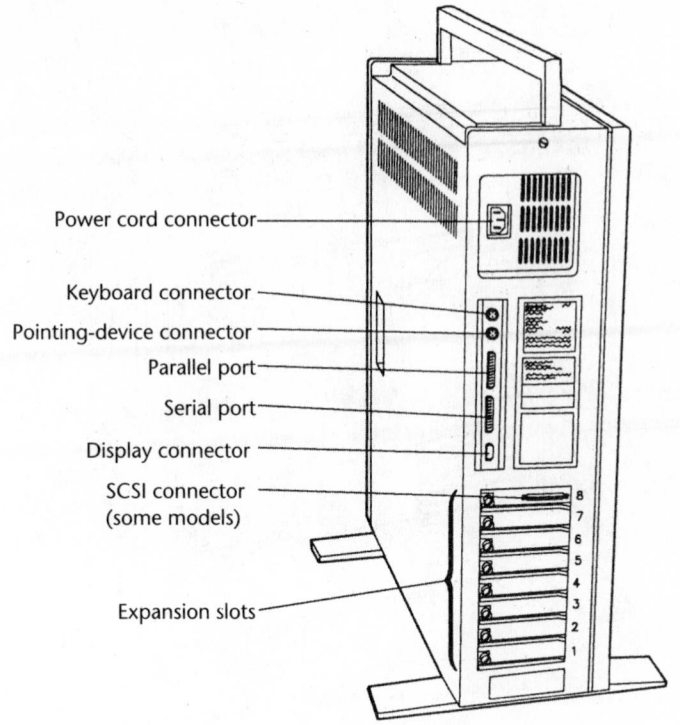

Power cord connector

Keyboard connector

Pointing-device connector

Parallel port

Serial port

Display connector

SCSI connector
(some models)

Expansion slots

Fig. 4.29
PS/2 Model 65 SX rear panel view.

The Model 65 SX has two levels of BIOS, which total 128K: a Compatibility BIOS (CBIOS) with memory addressability of up to 1M provides support for real-mode-based application programs, and Advanced BIOS (ABIOS) provides support for protected-mode-based multitasking operating systems and has extended memory addressability up to 16M.

Design enhancements to these systems offer significant advantages in configuration flexibility and expansion. In addition to providing seven available adapter slots, the standard configuration supports as many as five or six internal drives.

Drive Support. The PS/2 65 SX design provides five drive bays. The three bays in the front of the system are user-accessible; they can contain devices that require insertion and removal of media. The remaining two bays are designed for nonaccessible devices such as hard disks. The accessible bays consist of two 3 1/2-inch, half-height bays and one 5 1/4-inch, full-height bay. The top 3 1/2-inch, half-height bay contains a standard 1.44M floppy disk drive; the second 3 1/2-inch, half-height bay and the 5 1/4-inch, full-high bay are open for expansion purposes.

The standard hard disk drive configuration of the PS/2 Model 65 SX contains one SCSI hard disk drive located in one of the two nonaccessible bays. The other nonaccessible

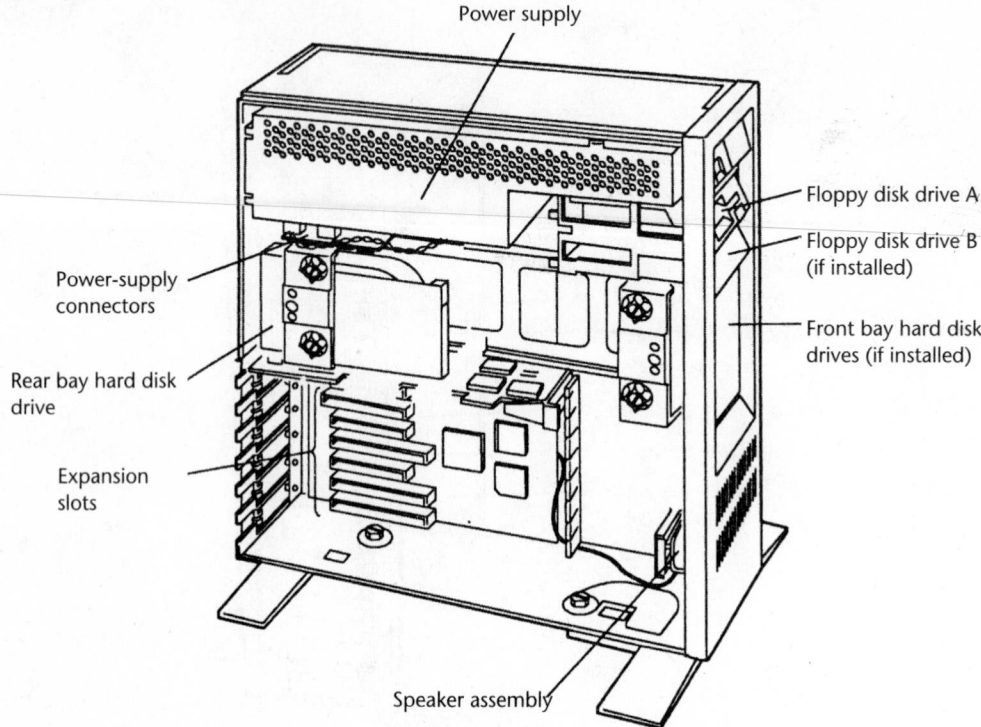

Power supply

Floppy disk drive A

Floppy disk drive B
(if installed)

Power-supply
connectors

Front bay hard disk
drives (if installed)

Rear bay hard disk
drive

Expansion
slots

Speaker assembly

Fig. 4.30
PS/2 Model 65 SX (interior view).

bay contains the necessary hardware to install a second IBM SCSI hard disk drive. The accessible 5 1/4-inch, full-height bay can be converted into two 3 1/2-inch, half-height bays through the use of the optional Fixed Disk Drive Kit A (1053) (6451053). This conversion allows the installation of third and fourth IBM SCSI hard disk drives.

The drive controller is the IBM PS/2 Micro Channel SCSI Adapter—a 16-bit MCA master adapter. Internal cabling is provided to support the standard hard disk drive and two additional internal SCSI devices. External SCSI devices attach directly to the IBM PS/2 Micro Channel SCSI Adapter external port, using the PS/2 card to option cable.

The specifications for the IBM PS/2 Micro Channel SCSI Adapter are as follows:

- Industry-standard interface (ANSI standard X3.131-1986)

- PS/2 16-bit intelligent bus master adapter

- Support for as many as seven physical SCSI devices

- Support for internal and external SCSI devices (single-ended)

- Micro Channel data transfer rate of up to 8.3M per second

- Support for asynchronous or synchronous SCSI devices

Table 4.34 lists the technical specifications for the PS/2 Model 65 SX.

Table 4.34 PS/2 Model 65 SX Technical Specifications

System architecture

Microprocessor	80386SX
Clock speed	16 MHz
Bus type	MCA (Micro Channel Architecture)
Bus width	16-bit
Interrupt levels	16

System architecture

Type	Level-sensitive
Shareable	Yes
DMA channels	15
DMA burst mode supported	Yes
Bus masters supported	15
Upgradeable processor complex	No

Memory

Standard on system board	2M
Maximum on system board	8M
Maximum total memory	16M
Memory speed and type	100ns dynamic RAM
System board memory socket type	36-bit SIMM (single in-line memory module)
Number of memory module sockets	2
Number available in standard configuration	1
Memory used on system board	1M/2M/4M 36-bit SIMMs
Memory cache controller	No
Wait states:	
System board	0-2
Adapters	0-4

Standard features

ROM size	128K
ROM shadowing	Yes
Optional math coprocessor	80387SX
Coprocessor speed	16 MHz
Standard graphics	VGA
8-/16-/32-bit controller	8-bit
Bus master	No

(continues)

Table 4.34 Continued

Standard features

Video RAM (VRAM)	256K
RS232C serial ports	1
UART chip used	NS16550A
Maximum speed (bits/second)	19,200 bps
FIFO mode enabled	Yes
Maximum number of ports	8
Pointing device (mouse) ports	1
Parallel printer ports	1
Bidirectional	Yes
Maximum number of ports	8
CMOS real-time clock (RTC)	Yes
CMOS RAM	64 bytes + 2K extension
Battery life	10 years
Replaceable	Yes (Dallas module)

Disk storage

Internal disk and tape drive bays	5 or 6 (reconfigurable)
Number of 3 1/2 and /5 1/4-inch bays	4/1 or 6/0 (reconfigurable)
Standard floppy drives	1×1.44M
Optional floppy drives:	
5 1/4-inch 360K	Optional
5 1/4-inch 1.2M	Optional
3 1/2-inch 720K	No
3 1/2-inch 1.44M	Standard
3 1/2-inch 2.88M	No
Hard disk controller included:	16-bit SCSI adapter
Bus master	Yes
Devices supported per adapter	7
Adapters supported per system	4
SCSI hard disks available:	60M/80M/120M/160M/320M/400M
Drive form factor	3 1/2-inch
Drive interface	SCSI

Drive capacity	60M	80M	120M	160M	320M	400M
Average access rate (ms)	23	17	23	16	12.5	11.5
Read-ahead cache	32K	32K	32K	32K	64K	128K
SCSI transfer mode	Async	Async	Async	Async	Sync	Sync
Encoding scheme	RLL	RLL	RLL	RLL	RLL	RLL
Cylinders	920	1021	920	1021	949	1201
Heads	4	4	8	8	14	14
Sectors per track	32	39	32	39	48	48

Disk storage

Rotational speed (RPM)	3600	3600	3600	3600	4318	4318
Interleave factor	1:1	1:1	1:1	1:1	1:1	1:1
Data transfer rate (K/sec)	960	1170	960	1170	1727	1727
Automatic head parking	Yes	Yes	Yes	Yes	Yes	Yes

Expansion slots

Total adapter slots	8
Number of long and short slots	8/0
Number of 8-/16-/32-bit slots	0/8/0
Number of slots with video ext.	1
Available slots	7

Keyboard specifications

101-key Enhanced Keyboard	Yes
Fast keyboard speed setting	Yes
Keyboard cable length	10 feet
Keylock:	
Locks cover	Yes
Locks keyboard	No
Keyboard password	Yes
Power-on password	Yes
Network server mode	Yes

Physical specifications

Footprint type:	Floor-standing
Dimensions:	
Height	23.5 inches
Width	6.5 inches
Depth	19.0 inches
Weight	52.0 lbs

Environmental specifications

Power-supply output	250 watts
Worldwide (110/60,220/50)	Yes
Auto-sensing/switching	Yes
Maximum current:	
90-137 VAC	5.3 amps
180-265 VAC	2.7 amps
Operating range:	
Temperature	60-90 degrees F
Relative humidity	8-80 percent
Maximum operating altitude	7,000 feet
Heat (BTUs/hour)	1218

(continues)

Compatible Systems

Table 4.34 Continued	
Enviornmental specifications	
Noise (Average dB, operating, 1m)	54 dB
FCC classification	Class B

Figure 4.31 shows the motherboard components and layout for the Model 65.

Table 4.35 shows the primary specifications and costs of the various versions of PS/2 Model 65 SX.

PS/2 Model 70 386

The PS/2 Model 70 386, introduced June 2, 1988, is a desktop, high-end system in the PS/2 family. The Model 70 386 includes Micro Channel Architecture (MCA). Figure 4.32 shows a front view of the Model 70.

The basic system features a 16 MHz, 20 MHz, or 25 MHz 80386 microprocessor and 2M or 4M of high-speed memory on the motherboard. Motherboard memory is expandable to 6M or 8M depending on the model; you can expand total memory to 16M with memory adapters. The Model 70 386 comes with a 1.44M, 3 1/2-inch floppy disk drive and either a 60M or 120M hard disk drive with integrated controller (IDE) as standard. A serial port, parallel port, mouse port, and VGA port also are standard. Figure 4.33 shows a rear panel view of the Model 70.

The top-of-the-line 70 386-Axx models feature a 25 MHz 80386 32-bit microprocessor and an Intel 82385 memory cache controller with a high-speed 64K static memory cache. This memory cache lets the Model 70 386 perform approximately 150 percent faster than the 20 MHz versions of the Model 80. The Model 70 386 is about 250 percent faster than the Model 50.

The Model 70 386 has two levels of BIOS, which total 128K: a Compatibility BIOS (CBIOS) with memory addressability of up to 1M provides support for real-mode-based application programs; and Advanced BIOS (ABIOS) provides support for protected-mode-based multitasking operating systems and has extended memory addressability up to 16M.

Table 4.35 IBM PS/2 Model 65 SX Model Summary

Part number	CPU	MHz	PLANAR MEMORY Std.	Max.	STANDARD Floppy drive	Hard disk	Bus type
65 SX							
8565-061	386SX	16	2M	8M	1×1.44M	60M	MCA/16
8565-121	386SX	16	2M	8M	1×1.44M	120M	MCA/16
8565-321	386SX	16	2M	8M	1×1.44M	320M	MCA/16

Note: *All Model 65 units are discontinued.*

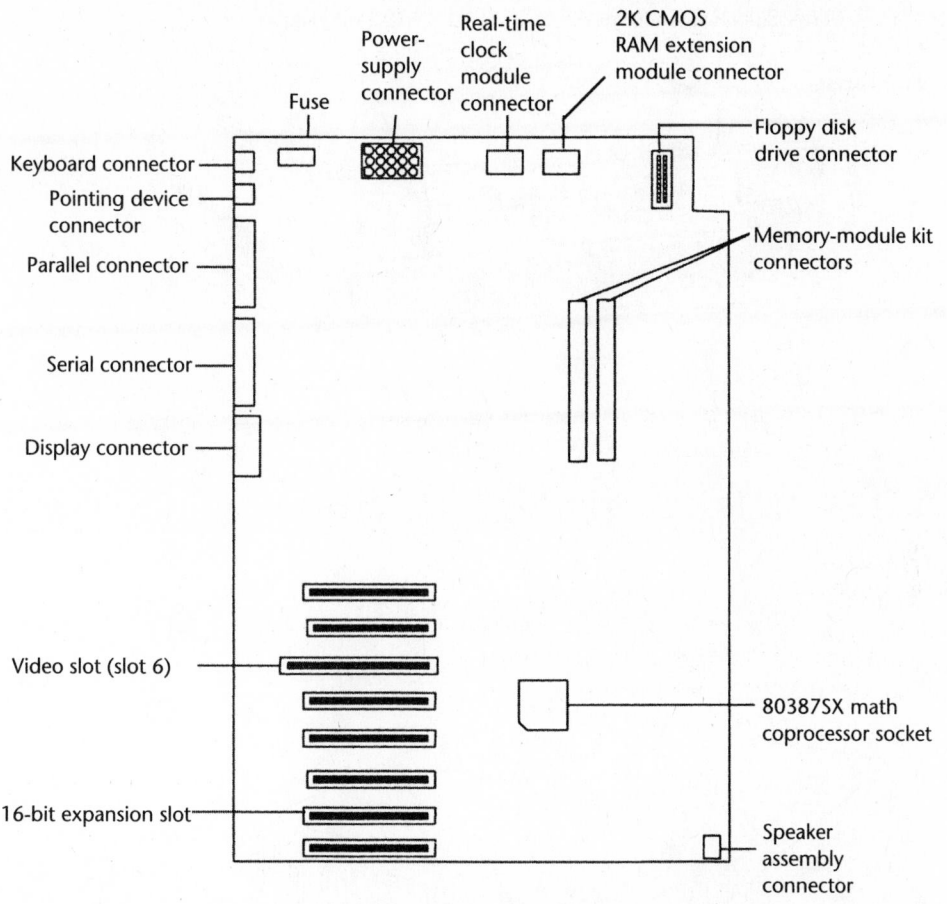

Fig. 4.31

PS/2 Model 65 SX system board.

Total/ available slots	STANDARD Video	KB	Date introduced	Date withdrawn
8/7	VGA	Enh	03/20/90	07/23/91
8/7	VGA	Enh	03/20/90	07/23/91
8/7	VGA	Enh	10/30/90	07/23/91

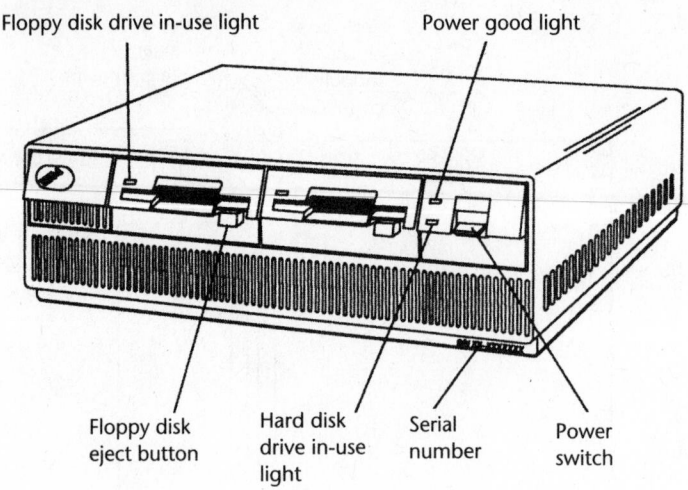

Floppy disk drive in-use light

Power good light

Floppy disk eject button

Hard disk drive in-use light

Serial number

Power switch

Fig. 4.32
PS/2 Model 70.

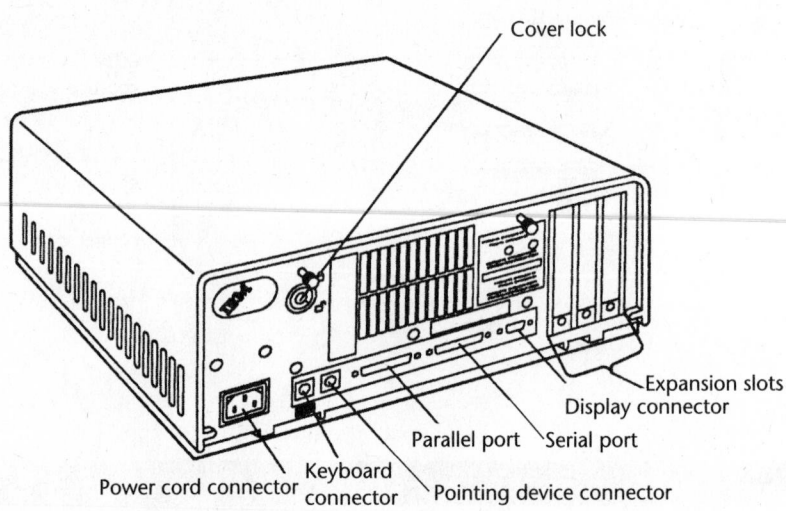

Cover lock

Expansion slots

Display connector

Parallel port   Serial port

Power cord connector

Keyboard connector

Pointing device connector

Fig. 4.33
PS/2 Model 70rear panel.

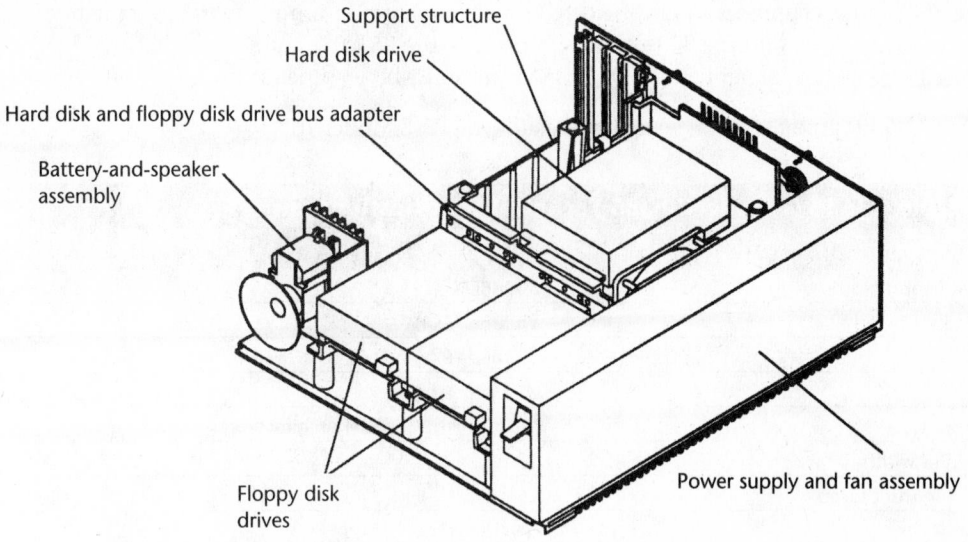

Support structure

Hard disk drive

Hard disk and floppy disk drive bus adapter

Battery-and-speaker
assembly

Floppy disk
drives

Power supply and fan assembly

Fig. 4.34
PS/2 Model 70 interior view.

Additional features of the Model 70 386 include one 16-bit and two 32-bit I/O slots. Because all the hard disks available with the Model 70 386 have integrated (embedded) controllers, no slot is lost to a disk controller card. The Model 70 386 also has a 132-watt, automatic voltage-sensing, universal power supply; a time-and-date clock with battery backup; an additional slot for a second 3 1/2-inch floppy disk drive; an optional 16 MHz, 20 MHz, or 25 MHz 80387 coprocessor; and the IBM Enhanced Keyboard. Figure 4.34 shows the interior view of the Model 70.

Several versions of the Model 70 386 are available. They differ mainly in clock speed, installed hard disk storage, and memory capabilities. Available system clock speeds are 16 MHz, 20 MHz, and 25 MHz, AND hard disks are available with 60M, 80M, 120M, and 160M of capacity. The 25 MHz models offer memory expansion to 8M on the system board and feature an upgradeable processor on a daughterboard (currently, only a single upgrade is available to a 25 MHz 80486DX processor).

The 25 MHz models have a few outstanding differences from the other models that give this system a higher than expected performance level. The 70 386-Axx models use an Intel 82385 cache controller chip, which manages 64K of extremely high-speed static memory. This memory is accessed at 0 wait states and uses a special algorithm to ensure an exceptionally high bit ratio for cache memory access. Because of this system's speed, this version of the Model 70 386 requires extremely fast (80ns) memory, which the other models do not need. Remember this requirement when you purchase additional memory for this system and when you make repairs.

The 80387 math coprocessor chip selected for each system unit must match the main processor in speed, and the 80387 chips (especially the 25 MHz chip) are expensive. These chips are no longer being sold by IBM and must be obtained from other sources.

Table 4.36 lists the technical specifications for the PS/2 Model 70 386.

Table 4.36 PS/2 Model 70 386 Technical Specifications	
System architecture	
Microprocessor	80386DX
Clock speed	16 MHz (Exx)
	20 MHz (0xx,1xx)
	25 MHz (Axx)
Bus type	MCA (Micro Channel Architecture)
Bus width	32-bit
Interrupt levels	16
Type	Level-sensitive
Shareable	Yes
DMA channels	15
DMA burst mode supported	Yes
Bus masters supported	15
Upgradeable processor complex	No
	Yes (Axx)
Memory	
Standard on system board	4M
Maximum on system board	6M
	8M (Axx)
Maximum total memory	16M
Memory speed and type	85ns dynamic RAM
	80ns dynamic RAM (Axx)
System board memory socket type	36-bit SIMM (single in-line memory module)
Number of memory module sockets	3 4 (Axx)
Number available in standard configuration	1 2 (Axx)
Memory used on system board	1M/2M 36-bit SIMMs
Paged memory logic	Yes
Memory cache controller	No Yes (Axx)
Internal/external cache	External
Standard memory cache size	64K

Memory

Cache memory speed and type	25ns static RAM
Wait states:	
System board	0-5 (Axx, 95 percent 0 wait states)
	0-2
Adapter	0-7 (Axx, 95 percent 0 wait states)
	0-4

Standard features

ROM size	128K
ROM shadowing	Yes
Optional math coprocessor	80387DX
Coprocessor speed	16 MHz (Exx) 20 MHz (0xx,1xx) 25 MHz (Axx)
Standard graphics	VGA (Video Graphics Array)
8-/16-/32-bit controller	8-bit
Bus master	No
Video RAM (VRAM)	256K
RS232C serial ports	1
UART chip used	NS16550A
Maximum speed (bits/second)	19,200 bps
FIFO mode enabled	Yes
Maximum number of ports	8
Pointing device (mouse) ports	1
Parallel printer ports	1
Bidirectional	Yes
Maximum number of ports	8
CMOS real-time clock (RTC)	Yes
CMOS RAM	64 bytes + 2K extension
Battery life	5 years
Replaceable	Yes

Disk storage

Internal disk and tape drive bays	3
Number 3 1/2-inch and 5 1/4-inch bays	3/0
Standard floppy drives	1×1.44M
Optional floppy drives:	
5 1/4-inch 360K	Optional
5 1/4-inch 1.2M	Optional
3 1/2-inch 720K	No

(continues)

II

Compatible Systems

Table 4.36 Continued

Disk Storage

3 1/2-inch 1.44M	Standard			
3 1/2-inch 2.88M	No			
Hard disk controller included:	IDE connector on Interposer Card			
IDE hard disks available:	60M/80M/120M/160M			
Drive form factor	3 1/2-inch			
Drive interface	IDE			
Drive capacity	60M	80M	120M	160M
Average access rate (ms)	27	17	23	16
Read-ahead cache	No	32K	No	32K
Encoding scheme	RLL	RLL	RLL	RLL
Cylinders	762	1021	920	1021
Heads	6	4	8	8
Sectors per track	26	39	32	39
Rotational speed (RPM)	3600	3600	3600	3600
Interleave factor	1:1	1:1	1:1	1:1
Data transfer rate (K/second)	780	1170	960	1170
Automatic head parking	Yes	Yes	Yes	Yes

Expansion slots

Total adapter slots	3
Number of long and short slots	3/0
Number of 8-/16-/32-bit slots	0/1/2
Number of slots with video ext.	1
Available slots	3

Keyboard specifications

101-key Enhanced Keyboard	Yes
Fast keyboard speed setting	Yes
Keyboard cable length	6 feet

Security features

Keylock:	
Locks cover	Yes
Locks keyboard	No
Keyboard password	Yes
Power-on password	Yes
Network server mode	Yes

Physical specifications

Footprint type	Desktop

Physical Specifications	
Dimensions:	
Height	5.5 inches
Width	14.2 inches
Depth	16.5 inches
Weight	21.0 lbs

Environmental specifications	
Power-supply output	132 watts
Worldwide (110/60,220/50)	Yes
Auto-sensing/switching	Yes
Maximum current:	
90-137 VAC	2.7 amps
180-265 VAC	1.4 amps
Operating range:	
Temperature	60-90 degrees F
Relative humidity	8-80 percent
Maximum operating altitude	7,000 feet
Heat (BTUs/hour)	751
Noise (average dB, operating, 1m)	40 dB
FCC classification	Class B

Figures 4.35, 4.36, and 4.37 show the components and layouts of the three different types of Model 70 motherboards.

Table 4.37 shows the primary specifications and costs of the various versions of PS/2 Model 70 386.

PS/2 Model 70 486

The IBM PS/2 Model 70 486, introduced June 20, 1989, is essentially a Model 70 386-Axx with the 486 25 MHz Power Platform upgrade. The 25 MHz 80486 32-bit microprocessor replaces the 386 processor module standard in the Model 70 386. The Model 70 496 is no different from a Model 70 386 with the Power Platform added later.

The Model 70 486 has been discontinued by IBM as of 09/11/91 and is no longer available. The 486 Power Platform, however, is still available for upgrading existing 25 MHz Model 70 386 systems.

The basic system features a 25 MHz 80486 32-bit microprocessor with a built-in 8K memory cache. With this processor and memory cache, this unit can perform approximately 100 percent faster than the 386 version. Also included is 4M of high-speed memory on the motherboard, expandable to 8M, with total memory expandable to 16M (with memory adapters). This system comes with a 1.44M, 3 1/2-inch floppy disk drive and either a 60M or 120M hard disk drive with integrated controller (IDE) as standard. Also standard are a serial port, a parallel port, a mouse port, and a VGA port.

II

Compatible Systems

Table 4.37 IBM PS/2 Model 70 386 Model Summary

Part number	CPU	MHz	PLANAR MEMORY Std.	Max.	STANDARD Floppy drive	Hard disk	Bus type
70 386							
8570-E61	386DX	16	2M	6M	1×1.44M	60M	MCA/32
8570-061	386DX	20	2M	6M	1×1.44M	60M	MCA/32
8570-081	386DX	20	4M	6M	1×1.44M	80M	MCA/32
8570-121	386DX	20	2M	6M	1×1.44M	120M	MCA/32
8570-161	386DX	20	4M	6M	1×1.44M	160M	MCA/32
8570-A61	386DX	25	2M	8M	1×1.44M	60M	MCA/32
8570-A81	386DX	25	4M	8M	1×1.44M	80M	MCA/32
8570-A21	386DX	25	2M	8M	1×1.44M	120M	MCA/32
8570-A16	386DX	25	4M	8M	1×1.44M	160M	MCA/32

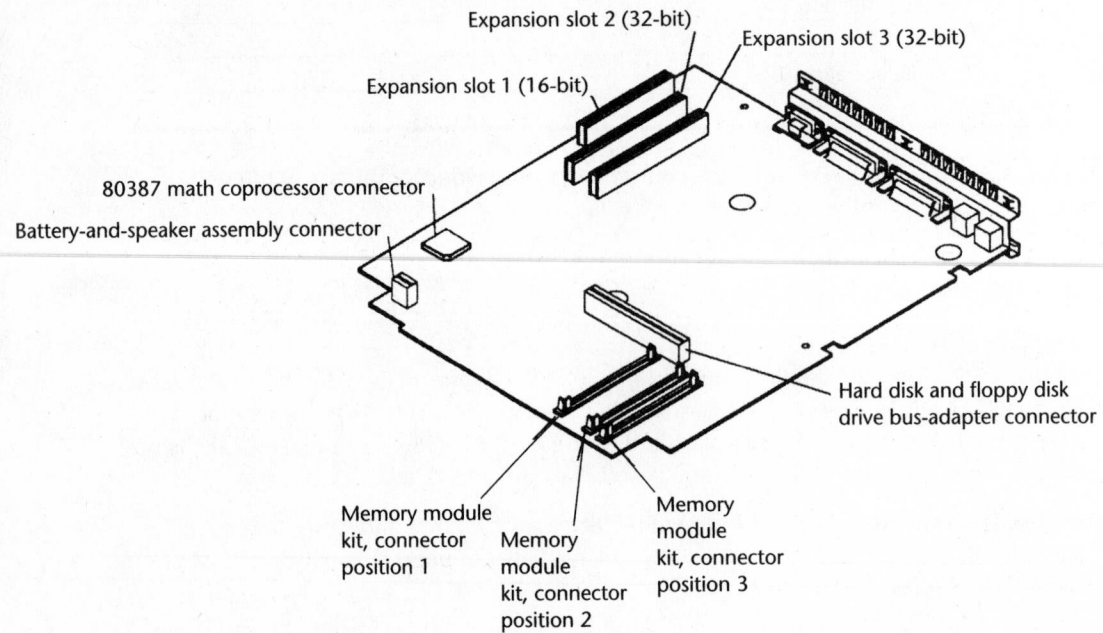

Fig. 4.35

PS/2 Model 70 386 system board (16 MHz and 20 MHz, type 1).

Total/ available slots	STANDARD Video	KB	Date introduced	Date withdrawn
3/3	VGA	Enh	06/07/88	07/23/91
3/3	VGA	Enh	09/26/89	09/11/91
3/3	VGA	Enh	06/11/91	—
3/3	VGA	Enh	09/26/89	09/11/91
3/3	VGA	Enh	06/11/91	—
3/3	VGA	Enh	09/26/89	09/11/91
3/3	VGA	Enh	06/11/91	01/17/92
3/3	VGA	Enh	09/26/89	09/11/91
3/3	VGA	Enh	06/11/91	—

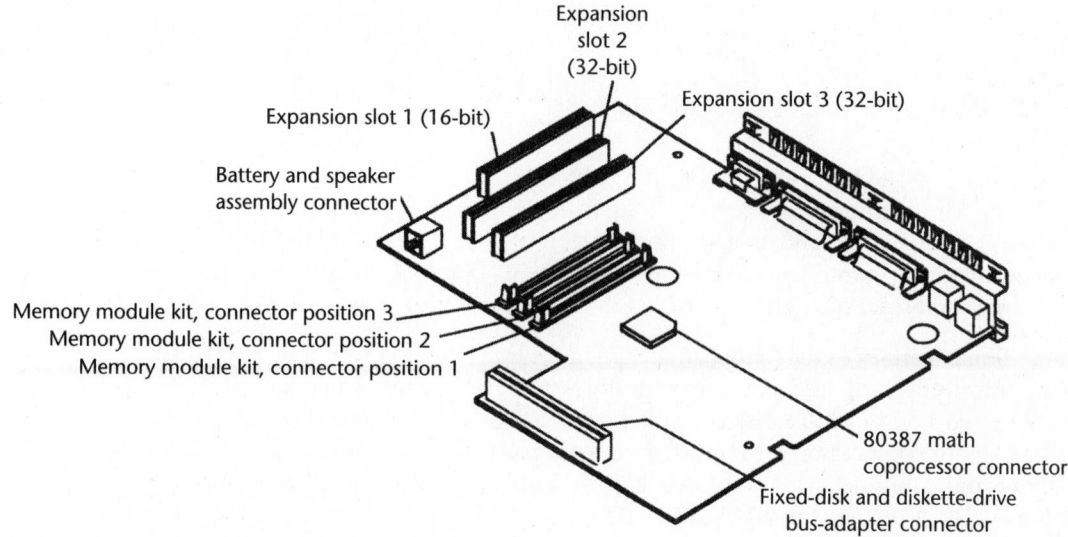

Fig. 4.36
PS/2 Model 70 386 system board (16 MHz and 20 MHz, type 2).

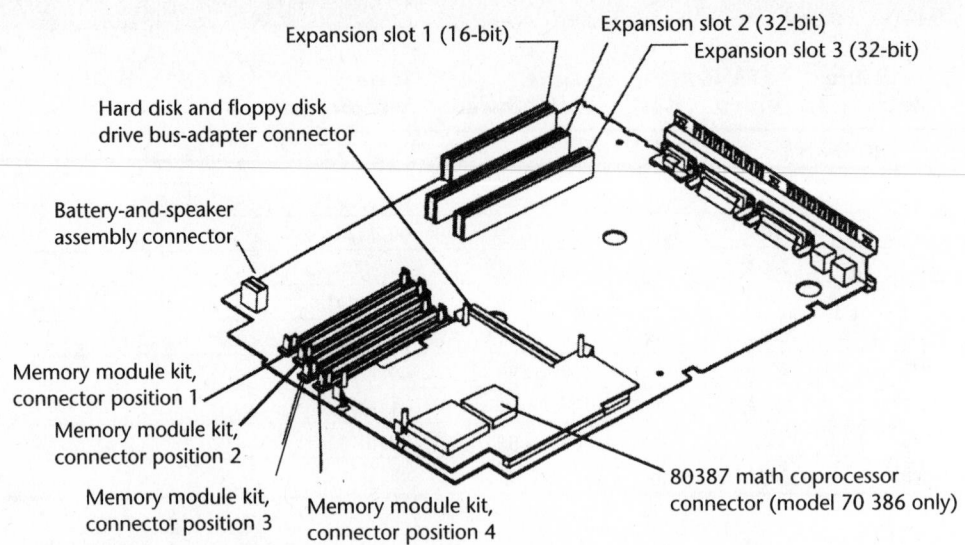

Expansion slot 1 (16-bit)

Expansion slot 2 (32-bit)

Expansion slot 3 (32-bit)

Hard disk and floppy disk
drive bus-adapter connector

Battery-and-speaker
assembly connector

Memory module kit,
connector position 1

Memory module kit,
connector position 2

Memory module kit,
connector position 3

Memory module kit,
connector position 4

80387 math coprocessor
connector (model 70 386 only)

Fig. 4.37
PS/2 Model 70 386 system board (25 MHz, type 3).

The Model 70 486 has two levels of BIOS, which total 128K: A Compatibility BIOS
(CBIOS) with memory addressability of up to 1M provides support for real-mode-based
application programs; and an additional version of BIOS, Advanced BIOS (ABIOS), provides support for protected-mode-based multitasking operating systems and has extended memory addressability of up to 16M.

Additional features of the Model 70 486 include one 16-bit and two 32-bit I/O slots.
Because all the hard disks available with the Model 70 have integrated (embedded) controllers, no slot is lost to a disk controller card. The Model 70 486 also has a 25 MHz
80387 math coprocessor; a 132-watt, automatic voltage-sensing, universal power supply;
a time-and-date clock with battery backup; an additional slot for a second 3 1/2-inch
floppy disk drive; and the IBM Enhanced Keyboard.

Table 4.38 lists the technical specifications for the PS/2 Model 70 486.

Table 4.38 PS/2 Model 70 486 Technical Specifications

System architecture

Microprocessor	80486
Clock speed	25 MHz
Bus type	MCA (Micro Channel Architecture)
Bus width	32-bit
Interrupt levels	16
Type	Level-sensitive
Shareable	Yes
DMA channels	15
DMA burst mode supported	Yes
Bus masters supported	15
486 burst mode enabled	No
Upgradeable processor complex	Included

Memory

Standard on system board	2M
Maximum on system board	8M
Maximum total memory	16M
Memory speed and type	80ns dynamic RAM
System board memory socket type	36-bit SIMM (single in-line memory module)
Number of memory module sockets	4
Number available in standard configuration	3
Memory used on system board	2M 36-bit SIMMs
Paged memory logic	Yes
Memory cache controller	Yes
Internal/external cache	Internal
Standard memory cache size	8K
Optional external memory cache	No
Wait states:	
System board	0-5 (95 percent 0 wait states)
Adapter	0-7

Standard features

ROM size	128K
ROM shadowing	Yes
Math coprocessor	Built-in
Coprocessor speed	25 MHz
Standard graphics	VGA
8-/16-/32-bit controller	8-bit

(continues)

Table 4.38 Continued				
Standard features				
Bus master	No			
Video RAM (VRAM)	256K			
RS232C serial ports	1			
UART chip used	NS16550A			
Maximum speed (bits/second)	19,200 bps			
FIFO mode enabled	Yes			
Maximum number of ports	8			
Pointing device (mouse) ports	1			
Parallel printer ports	1			
Bidirectional	Yes			
Maximum number of ports	8			
CMOS real-time clock (RTC)	Yes			
CMOS RAM	64 bytes + 2K extension			
Battery life	5 years			
Replaceable	Yes			
Disk storage				
Internal disk and tape drive bays	3			
Number of 3 1/2- and 5 1/4-inch bays	3/0			
Standard floppy drives	1×1.44M			
Optional floppy drives:				
5 1/4-inch 360K	Optional			
5 1/4-inch 1.2M	Optional			
3 1/2-inch 720K	No			
3 1/2-inch 1.44M	Standard			
3 1/2-inch 2.88M	No			
Hard disk controller included:	IDE connector on Interposer Card			
IDE hard disks available:	60M/80M/120M/160M			
Drive form factor	3 1/2-inch			
Drive interface	IDE			
Drive capacity	60M	80M	120M	160M
Average access rate (ms)	27	17	23	16
Read-ahead Cache	No	32K	No	32K
Encoding scheme	RLL	RLL	RLL	RLL
Cylinders	762	1021	920	1021
Heads	6	4	8	8
Sectors per track	26	39	32	39
Rotational speed (RPM)	3600	3600	3600	3600
Interleave factor	1:1	1:1	1:1	1:1
Data transfer rate (K/second)	780	1170	960	1170
Automatic head parking	Yes	Yes	Yes	Yes

Expansion slots

Total adapter slots	3
Number of long and short slots	3/0
Number of 8-/16-/32-bit slots	0/1/2
Number of slots with video ext.	1
Available slots	3

Keyboard specifications

101-key Enhanced Keyboard	Yes
Fast keyboard speed setting	Yes
Keyboard cable length	6 feet

Security features

Keylock:	
Locks cover	Yes
Locks keyboard	No
Keyboard password	Yes
Power-on password	Yes
Network server mode	Yes

Physical specifications

Footprint type	Desktop
Dimensions:	
Height	5.5 inches
Width	14.2 inches
Depth	16.5 inches
Weight	21.0 lbs

Environmental specifications

Power-supply output	132 watts
Worldwide (110/60,220/50)	Yes
Auto-sensing/switching	Yes
Maximum current:	
90-137 VAC	2.7 amps
180-265 VAC	1.4 amps
Operating range:	
Temperature	60-90 degrees F
Relative humidity	8-80 percent
Maximum operating altitude	7,000 feet
Heat (BTUs/hour)	751
Noise (Average dB, operating, 1m)	40 dB
FCC classification	Class B

II

Compatible Systems

Table 4.39 shows the primary specifications and costs of the various versions of PS/2 Model 70 486.

Table 4.39 IBM PS/2 Model 70 486 Model Summary

Part number	CPU	MHz	PLANAR MEMORY Std.	Max.	STANDARD Floppy drive	Hard disk	Bus type
70 486							
8570-B61	486DX	25	2M	8M	1×1.44M	60M	MCA/32
8570-B21	486DX	25	2M	8M	1×1.44M	120M	MCA/32

PS/2 Model P70 386

The PS/2 Model P70 386 (8573), introduced May 9, 1989, is a high-function, high-performance portable system designed to complement the PS/2 Model 70 386 desktop family of products. IBM has made the PS/2 Model P70 386 in 16 MHz and 20 MHz versions with 30M, 60M, and 120M hard disks. Effective July 23, 1991, IBM discontinued two versions of the Model P70 386: the 16 MHz model (031) and the 20 MHz, 60M disk model (061). The Model P70 386-121 (120M disk) continues to be sold. Figure 4.38 shows a front view of the Model P70.

The Model P70 386 includes MCA I/O slots, a VGA 16-grayscale plasma display, and a fully compatible PS/2 Enhanced Keyboard, all neatly integrated into a single package. It features an 80386DX processor, high-density memory technology, and a wide range of integrated features, supporting up to 16M of high-speed memory (4M standard, expandable up to 8M on system board), 120M or more disk storage, and an optional 80387 math coprocessor. Like most PS/2 systems, all models come standard with a 1.44M, 3 1/2-inch floppy disk drive, a pointing device port, a serial/asynchronous port, a parallel port, a VGA port, and an external storage device port. Figure 4.39 shows the rear panel view of the Model P70.

Exceptional features for a portable computer include the Model 70's two MCA expansion slots (one full and one half-length) and its ergonomic briefcase portable design. The expansion slots can be used for products such as the IBM PS/2 300/1200/2400 Internal Modem/A or P70 386 Token Ring Adapter. Figure 4.40 shows the interior view of the P70.

One exception to the norm is the external storage device port. The equivalent of the drive B internal floppy disk port, as found in the desktop Model 70, it permits attachment of externally powered devices, such as the IBM 360K external disk drive and some other manufacturers' backup devices. A cable (part number 23F2716) 35.5 centimeters or 14 inches long is available for attaching external drives. The cable features a Hoshiden Connector to attach to the P70 386 with an industry standard 37-pin D-shell connector that connects to the externally powered devices.

Total/ available slots	STANDARD Video	KB	Date introduced	Date withdrawn
3/3	VGA	Enh	09/26/89	09/11/91
3/3	VGA	Enh	06/20/89	09/11/91

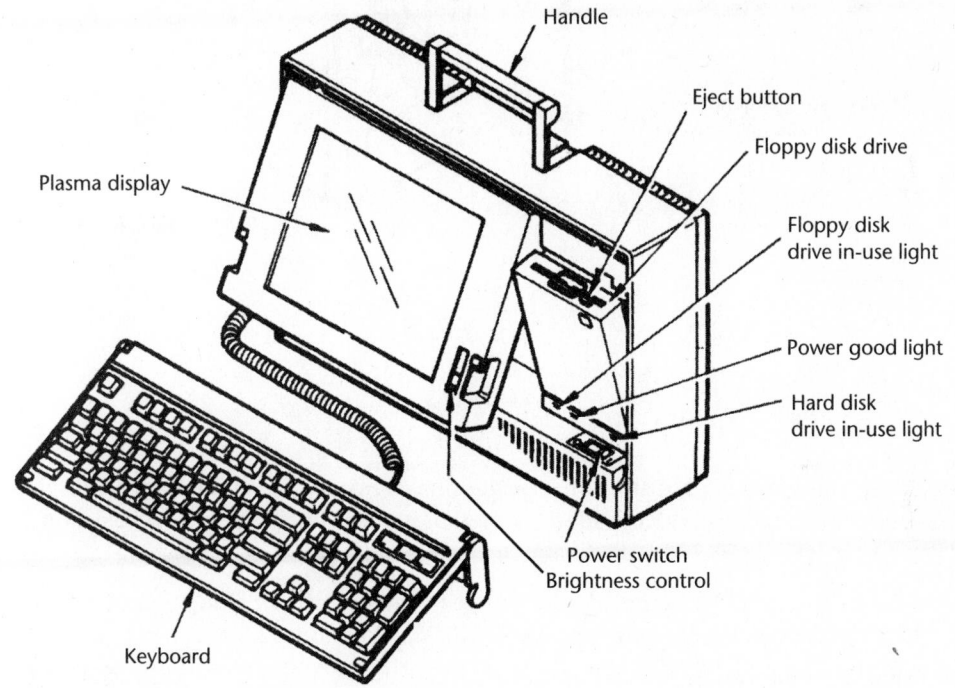

Fig. 4.38
PS/2 Model P70 386.

The VGA port supports all VGA graphics and text modes including 640 × 480 graphics, 320 × 200 graphics in 256 colors, and 720 × 400 text using any optional PS/2 VGA color display; and yet maintains compatibility with CGA and EGA modes. The gas plasma display normally shuts down when an external display is connected. You can override

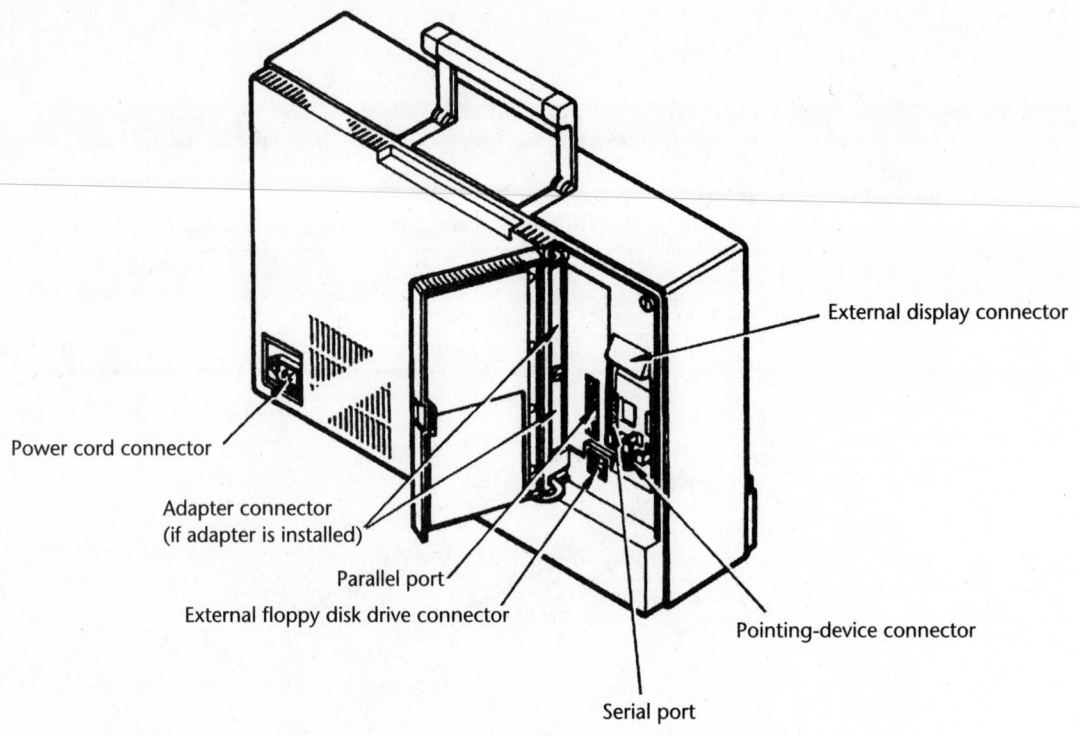

Fig. 4.39
PS/2 Model P70 386 rear panel view.

this feature and force both displays to operate simultaneously, with the external display in monochrome mode—which is ideal for presentations using large-screen projection devices.

In addition, the system is designed for tool-free installation and includes security features in BIOS. The Model P70 386 has two levels of BIOS, which total 128K: A Compatibility BIOS (CBIOS) with memory address-ability of up to 1M provides support for real-mode-based application programs; and an additional version of BIOS, Advanced BIOS (ABIOS), provides support for protected-mode-based multitasking operating systems and has extended memory addressability of up to 16M.

The P70 386 uses hard drives with integrated controllers (IDE). These drives plug directly into a special MCA IDE connector on the mother-board. All models use high-speed (85ns) memory, and have memory paging and ROM shadowing to improve performance. Several accessories are available for the system, including three different carrying cases, the external storage device cable, and a keyboard extension cable.

Table 4.40 lists the technical specifications for the PS/2 Model P70 386.

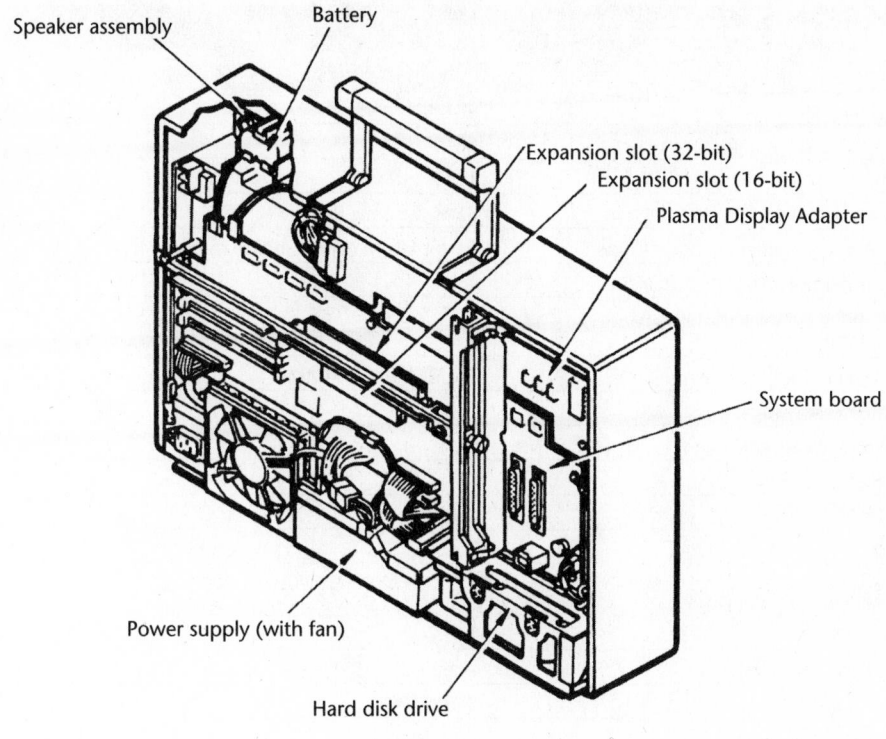

Speaker assembly   Battery

Expansion slot (32-bit)
Expansion slot (16-bit)
Plasma Display Adapter

System board

Power supply (with fan)

Hard disk drive

Fig. 4.40
PS/2 Model P70 386 interior view.

Table 4.40 PS/2 Model P70 386 Technical Specifications	
System architecture	
Microprocessor	80386DX
Clock speed	20 MHz
	16 MHz (031)
Bus type	MCA (Micro Channel Architecture)
Bus width	32-bit
Interrupt levels	16
Type	Level-sensitive
Shareable	Yes
DMA channels	15
DMA burst mode supported	Yes
Bus masters supported	15
Upgradeable processor complex	No

(continues)

Table 4.40 Continued

Memory

Standard on system board	4M
Maximum on system board	8M
Maximum total memory	16M
Memory speed and type	85ns dynamic RAM
System board memory socket type	36-bit SIMM (single in-line memory module)
Number of memory module sockets	4
Number available in standard configuration	2
Memory used on system board	1M/2M 36-bit SIMMs
Page memory logic	Yes
Memory cache controller	No
Wait states:	
System board	0-2
Adapter	0-4

Standard features

ROM size	128K
ROM shadowing	Yes
Optional math coprocessor	80387DX
Coprocessor speed	20 MHz
	16 MHz (031)
Standard graphics	VGA
8-/16-/32-bit controller	8-bit
Bus master	No
Video RAM (VRAM)	256K
Integrated display	Yes
Type	Gas plasma, orange
Size (diagonal measure)	10 inches
Gray-shades	16
RS232C serial ports	1
UART chip used	NS16550A
Maximum speed (bits/second)	19,200 bps
FIFO mode enabled	Yes
Maximum number of ports	8
Pointing device (mouse) ports	1
Parallel printer ports	1
Bidirectional	Yes
Maximum number of ports	8
CMOS real-time clock (RTC)	Yes

Standard features

CMOS RAM	64 bytes + 2K extension
Battery life	5 years
Replaceable	Yes

Disk storage

Internal disk and tape drive bays	2		
Number of 3 1/2-/5 1/4-inch bays	2/0		
Standard floppy drives	1×1.44M		
Optional floppy drives:			
5 1/4-inch 360K	Optional		
5 1/4-inch 1.2M	Optional		
3 1/2-inch 720K	No		
3 1/2-inch 1.44M	Standard		
3 1/2-inch 2.88M	No		
Auxiliary storage connector	Yes		
Drives supported	5 1/4-inch 360K		
Cable adapter	Optional		
Hard disk controller included:	MCA IDE connector on system board		
IDE hard disks available	30M/60M/120M		
Drive form factor	3 1/2-inch		
Drive interface	MCA IDE		
Drive capacity	30M	60M	120M
Average access rate (ms)	19	27	23
Encoding scheme	RLL	RLL	RLL
Cylinders	920	762	920
Heads	2	6	8
Sectors per track	32	26	32
Rotational speed (RPM)	3600	3600	3600
Interleave factor	1:1	1:1	1:1
Data transfer rate (K/second)	960	780	960
Automatic head parking	Yes	Yes	Yes

Expansion slots

Total adapter slots	2
Number of long and short slots	1/1
Number of 8-/16-/32-bit slots	0/1/1
Number of slots with video ext.	0
Available slots	2

Keyboard specifications

101-key Enhanced Keyboard	Yes

(continues)

Compatible Systems

Table 4.40 Continued

Keyboard specifications

Fast keyboard speed setting	Yes
Keyboard cable length	1.2 feet (14 inches)
Keyboard extension cable	Optional, 6 feet

Security features

Keylock:	
Locks cover	No
Locks keyboard	No
Keyboard password	Yes
Power-on password	Yes
Network server mode	Yes

Physical specifications

Footprint type	Portable
Dimensions:	
Height	12.0 inches
Width	18.3 inches
Depth	16.5 inches
Weight	20.8 lbs
Carrying handle	Yes
Carrying case	Optional, three styles available

Environmental specifications

Power-supply output	85 watts
Worldwide (110/60,220/50)	Yes
Auto-sensing/switching	Yes
Maximum current:	
90-137 VAC	2.4 amps
180-264 VAC	1.2 amps
Operating range:	
Temperature	50-95 degrees F
Relative humidity	8-80 percent
Maximum operating altitude	7,000 feet
Heat (BTUs/hour)	480
Noise (Average dB, operating, 1m)	39 dB
FCC classification	Class B

Figure 4.41 shows the components and layout of the Model P70 motherboard.

Table 4.41 shows the primary specifications and costs of the various versions of PS/2 Model P70 386. Table 4.42 shows accessories available from IBM for the PS/2 Model P70 386.

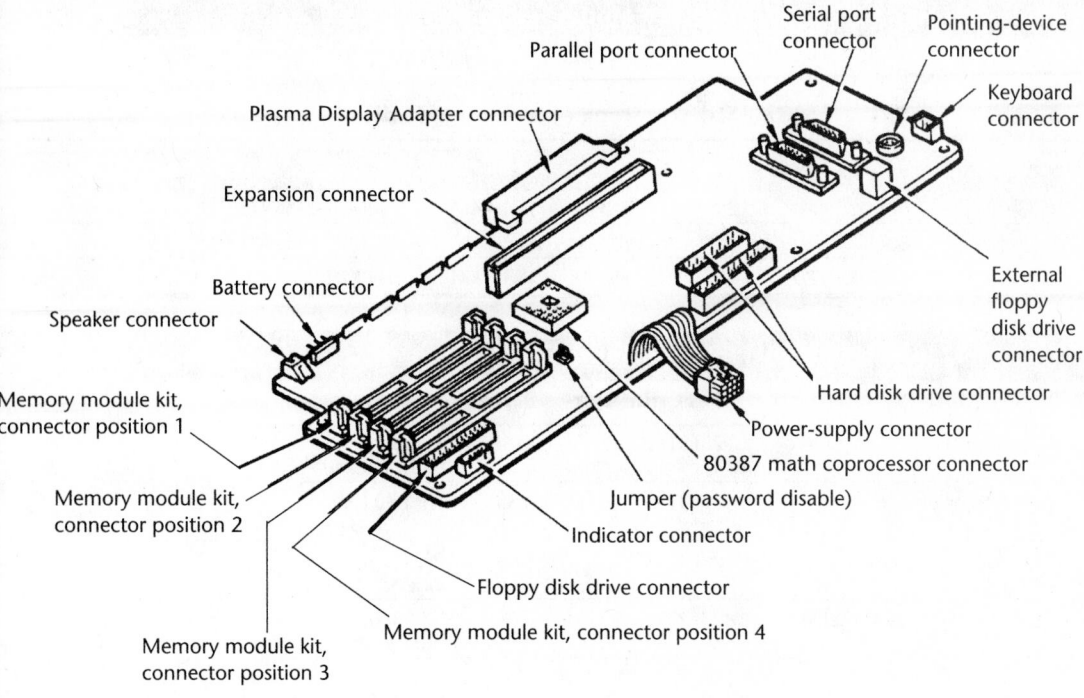

Fig. 4.41

PS/2 Model P70 386 system board.

PS/2 Model P75 486

The PS/2 Model P75 486, introduced November 12, 1990, is a high-end addition to IBM's portable computer family. The Model P75 486 features the powerful 486DX processor, operating at 33 MHz, and MCA slots. For several months after the introduction of this system, no other company had a portable that was as fast or as powerful. In fact, nearly every company that has tried to introduce a 33 MHz 486 portable has run into problems with the FCC in obtaining the proper Class B certification. This highlights one of the distinct advantages that IBM has with the Micro Channel Architecture: IBM will be able to make systems faster and faster, while keeping them within noise-emission guidelines set by the FCC, because of the superior electrical characteristics of the MCA bus over the ISA or EISA bus.

The PS/2 Model P75 486 enables applications that require portability to run on a system which rivals many desktop or even floor-standing tower systems in capacity. This system allows a portable application to use the processing power of the 486DX processor operating at 33 MHz, up to 16M of main storage, hard disk capacity to 400M, an external SCSI port, and four MCA adapter slots. Because of the built-in SCSI interface, internal hard disk drives can be easily upgraded to well over 1 gigabyte in capacity. This system has one of the largest disk storage capabilities for a portable system.

Table 4.41 IBM PS/2 Model P70 386 Model Summary

Part number	CPU	MHz	PLANAR MEMORY Std.	Max.	STANDARD Floppy drive	Hard disk	Bus type
P70 386							
8573-031	386DX	16	2M	8M	1×1.44M	30M	MCA/32
8573-061	386DX	20	4M	8M	1×1.44M	60M	MCA/32
8573-121	386DX	20	4M	8M	1×1.44M	120M	MCA/32

Table 4.42 IBM PS/2 Model P70 386 Special Accessories

Description	Part number	Price	Notes
Hartmann leather case	23F3192	$360	For P70 (not P75), pockets
Hartmann nylon case	23F3193	185	For P70 (not P75), pockets
Airline travel hard case	79F3205	299	Plastic, padded, wheels, storage
External storage device cable	23F2716	101	P70 360K, P75 360K/1.2M
Keyboard extension cable	79F3210	82	For P70/75, six-foot cable

The PS/2 Model P75 486 has the following features:

- 33 MHz 486DX processor on removable card

- 8M memory expandable to 16M

- Four slots (two full-length 32-bit, two half-length 16-bit)

- High-resolution eXtended Graphics Array (XGA) video port

- VGA 16-gray scale plasma display

- Choice of 160M or 400M disk drives

- Full-size PS/2 Enhanced Keyboard

- 3 1/2-inch 1.44M floppy disk drive

- External SCSI port

- AC operation (only)

- Maximum expansion

The PS/2 P75 486 offers power not previously available in a portable machine. It can be used as a network server or workstation for temporary offices at conventions, sporting events, and other temporary work locations. This system is ideal where a maximum system configuration must be carried along.

Total/ available slots	STANDARD Video	KB	Date introduced	Date withdrawn
2/2	VGA	Enh	03/20/90	07/23/91
2/2	VGA	Enh	05/09/89	07/23/91
2/2	VGA	Enh	05/09/89	—

The PS/2 P75 486 does not run on batteries and has no "low-power" devices that would limit performance and expandability. Due to the extreme power and integration of this unit, it currently ranks as one of IBM's most expensive PCs.

In addition to the powerful processor, the PS/2 P75 486 features a SCSI hard disk drive up to 400M as standard. With 3 1/2-inch SCSI drives becoming available in the gigabyte-capacity range and higher, it will be easy to upgrade this system to even larger-capacity storage.

The XGA graphics adapter built-in on the unit offers graphics resolution of 1,024 × 768. Because this device also is configured as a bus master, the performance is far beyond a standard VGA, even at VGA resolution. A device driver package is included with drivers for many popular applications and environments, such as OS/2 and Windows.

Several accessories are available, including the IBM PS/2 travel case (part number 79F3205). This hard case is constructed of molded plastic with easy-rolling wheels and an integrated, telescopic handle for pulling. The interior is padded and provides space for the P75 (or P70 386), cables, and a mouse. The case is designed to provide an easy, safe way to transport the system. It conforms to FAA luggage regulations, so it can be carried on board an aircraft and stored under the seat.

Also available is a keyboard extension cable. The keyboard extension cable (part number 79F3210) gives users the flexibility of placing the keyboard and the system unit farther apart for more comfort and convenience.

Table 4.43 lists the technical specifications for the PS/2 Model P75 486.

Table 4.43 PS/2 Model P75 486 Technical Specifications	
System architecture	
Microprocessor	80486DX
Clock speed	33 MHz
Bus type	MCA (Micro Channel Architecture)

(continues)

Table 4.43 Continued

System architecture

Bus width	32-bit
Interrupt levels	16
Type	Level-sensitive
Shareable	Yes
DMA channels	15
DMA burst mode supported	Yes
Bus masters supported	15
486 burst mode enabled	No
Upgradeable processor complex	Yes

Memory

Standard on system board	8M
Maximum on system board	16M
Maximum total memory	16M
Memory speed and type	70ns dynamic RAM
System board memory socket type	36-bit SIMM (single in-line memory module)
Number of memory-module sockets	4
Number available in standard configuration	2
Memory used on system board	2M/4M 36-bit SIMMs
Paged memory logic	Yes
Memory cache controller	Yes
Internal/external cache	Internal
Standard memory cache size	8K
Optional external memory cache	No
Wait states:	
System board	0-5 (95 percent 0 wait states)
Adapter	0-7

Standard features

ROM size	128K
ROM shadowing	Yes
Math coprocessor	Built-in to 486
Coprocessor speed	33 MHz
Standard graphics	XGA (eXtended Graphics Array)
8-/16-/32-bit controller	16/32-bit
Bus master	Yes
Video RAM (VRAM)	1M
Integrated display	Yes, VGA mode only
Type	Gas plasma, orange
Size (diagonal measure)	10 inches

Standard features

Grayshades	16
RS232C serial ports	1
UART chip used	NS16550A
Maximum speed (bits/second)	19,200 bps
FIFO mode enabled	Yes
Maximum number of ports	8
Pointing device (mouse) ports	1
Parallel printer ports	1
Bidirectional	Yes
Maximum number of ports	8
CMOS real-time clock (RTC)	Yes
CMOS RAM	64 bytes + 2K extension
Battery life	5 years
Replaceable	Yes

Disk storage

Internal disk and tape drive bays	2					
Number of 3 1/2- and 5 1/4-inch bays	2/0					
Standard floppy drives	1×1.44M					
Optional floppy drives:						
5 1/4-inch 360K	Optional					
5 1/4-inch 1.2M	Optional					
3 1/2-inch 720K	No					
3 1/2-inch 1.44M	Standard					
3 1/2-inch 2.88M	No					
Auxiliary storage connector	Yes					
Drives supported	5 1/4-inch 360K, 1.2M					
Cable adapter	Optional					
Hard disk controller included:	SCSI integrated on system board					
Bus master	Yes					
Devices supported per adapter	7					
SCSI hard disks available:	60M/80M/120M/160M/320M/400M					
Drive form factor	3 1/2-inch					
Drive interface	SCSI					
Drive capacity	60M	80M	120M	160M	320M	400M
Average access rate (ms)	23	17	23	16	12.5	11.5
Read-ahead cache	32K	32K	32K	32K	64K	128K
SCSI transfer mode	Async	Async	Async	Async	Sync	Sync
Encoding scheme	RLL	RLL	RLL	RLL	RLL	RLL
Cylinders	920	1021	920	1021	949	1201

(continues)

Table 4.43 Continued

Disk storage

Heads	4	4	8	8	14	14
Sectors per track	32	39	32	39	48	48
Rotational speed (RPM)	3600	3600	3600	3600	4318	4318
Interleave factor	1:1	1:1	1:1	1:1	1:1	1:1
Data transfer rate (K/second)	960	1170	960	1170	1727	1727
Automatic head parking	Yes	Yes	Yes	Yes	Yes	Yes

Expansion slots

Total adapter slots	4
Number of long and short slots	2/2
Number of 8-/16-/32-bit slots	0/2/2
Number of slots with video ext.	1
Available slots	4

Keyboard specifications

101-key Enhanced Keyboard	Yes
Fast keyboard speed setting	Yes
Keyboard cable length	1.2 feet (14 inches)
Keyboard extension cable	Optional, 6 feet

Security features

Keylock:	
Locks cover	No
Locks keyboard	No
Keyboard password	Yes
Power-on password	Yes
Network server mode	Yes

Table 4.44 IBM PS/2 Model P75 486 Model Summary

Part number	CPU	MHz	PLANAR MEMORY Std.	Max.	STANDARD Floppy drive	Hard disk	Bus type
P75 486							
8573-161	486DX	33	8M	16M	1×1.44M	160M	MCA/32
8573-401	486DX	33	8M	16M	1×1.44M	400M	MCA/32

Physical specifications

Footprint type	Portable
Dimensions:	
Height	12.0 inches
Width	18.3 inches
Depth	6.1 inches
Weight	22.1 lbs
Carrying handle	Yes
Carrying case	Optional hard-shell case

Environmental specifications

Power-supply output	120 watts
Worldwide (110/60,220/50)	Yes
Auto-sensing/switching	Yes
Maximum current:	
90-137 VAC	3.0 amps
180-264 VAC	1.5 amps
Operating range:	
Temperature	50-104 degrees F
Relative humidity	8-80 percent
Maximum operating altitude	7000 feet
Heat (BTUs/hour)	751
Noise (average dB, operating, 1m)	39 dB
FCC classification	Class B

Table 4.44 shows the primary specifications and costs of the various versions of PS/2 Model P75 486. Table 4.45 shows accessories available from IBM for the PS/2 Model P75 486.

Total/ available slots	STANDARD Video	KB	Date introduced	Date withdrawn
4/4	XGA	Enh	11/12/90	—
4/4	XGA	Enh	11/12/90	—

Table 4.45 IBM PS/2 Model P75 486 Special Accessories

Description	Part number	Price	Notes
Airline-travel hard case	79F3205	299	Plastic, padded, wheels, storage
Keyboard extension cable	79F3210	82	For P70/75, 6-foot cable
External storage device cable	23F2716	101	P70 360K, P75 360K/1.2M

PS/2 Model 80 386

IBM originally introduced the PS/2 Model 80 on April 2, 1987. Since then, many new models in the 80 family have been introduced and some have been discontinued. The Model 80 is a floor-standing, high-end system in the PS/2 family and includes MCA. Figure 4.42 shows a front view of the Model 80.

The basic Model 80 386 features a 16 MHz, 20 MHz, or 25 MHz 80386 microprocessor and 4M of high-speed (80ns) memory on the mother-board. Motherboard memory is expandable to 8M, depending on the model, and the total RAM can be expanded to 16M with memory adapters. This system comes standard with a 1.44M, 3 1/2-inch floppy disk drive and a wide variety of ST-506, ESDI, or SCSI hard disk drives ranging from 44M through 400M. Also standard are a serial port, a parallel port, a mouse port, and a VGA port. Figure 4.43 shows the rear panel view of the Model 80.

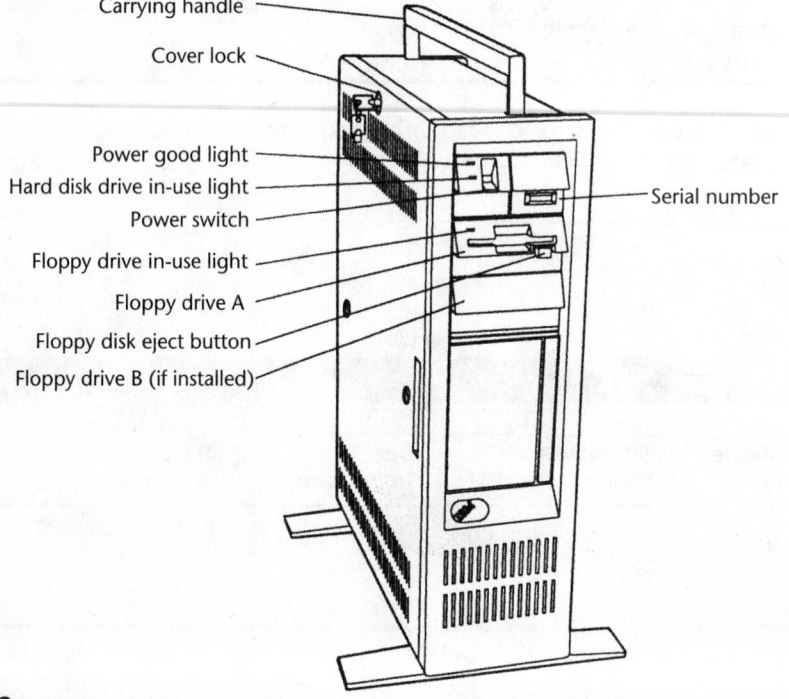

Fig. 4.42
PS/2 Model 80 386.

The 80386 32-bit microprocessor running at 16 MHz, 20 MHz, or 25 MHz coupled with the MCA and high-speed memory allows the Model 80 to perform three to four times faster than the IBM AT Model 339. The 80387 math coprocessor running at the system clock rate allows the Model 80 to perform math calculations four to five times faster than an IBM AT Model 339 with an 80287 math coprocessor.

The Model 80 386 has two levels of BIOS, which total 128K: A Compatibility BIOS (CBIOS) with memory addressability of up to 1M provides support for real-mode-based application programs; and an additional version of BIOS, Advanced BIOS (ABIOS), provides support for protected-mode-based multitasking operating systems and has extended memory addressability of up to 16M.

Additional features of the system unit include eight I/O bus slots, of which five are 16-bit slots and three are 16/32-bit slots. Each system includes a hard disk controller that occupies one 16-bit slot. This controller is either an ST-506/412, ESDI or SCSI controller. The Model 80 also has a 225-watt or 242-watt, automatic voltage-sensing, universal power supply with auto-restart; a time-and-date clock with battery backup;

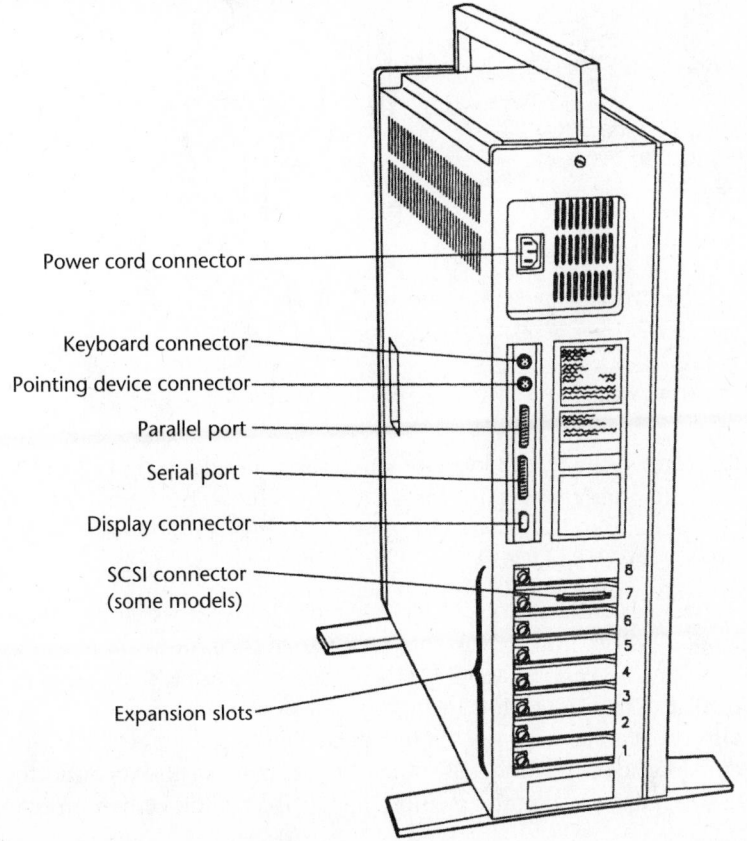

Fig. 4.43
PS/2 Model 80 386 rear panel view.

an additional position for a second 3 1/2-inch floppy disk drive; an additional position for a second full-height 5 1/4-inch hard disk; and the IBM Enhanced Keyboard. Figure 4.44 shows the interior view of the Model 80.

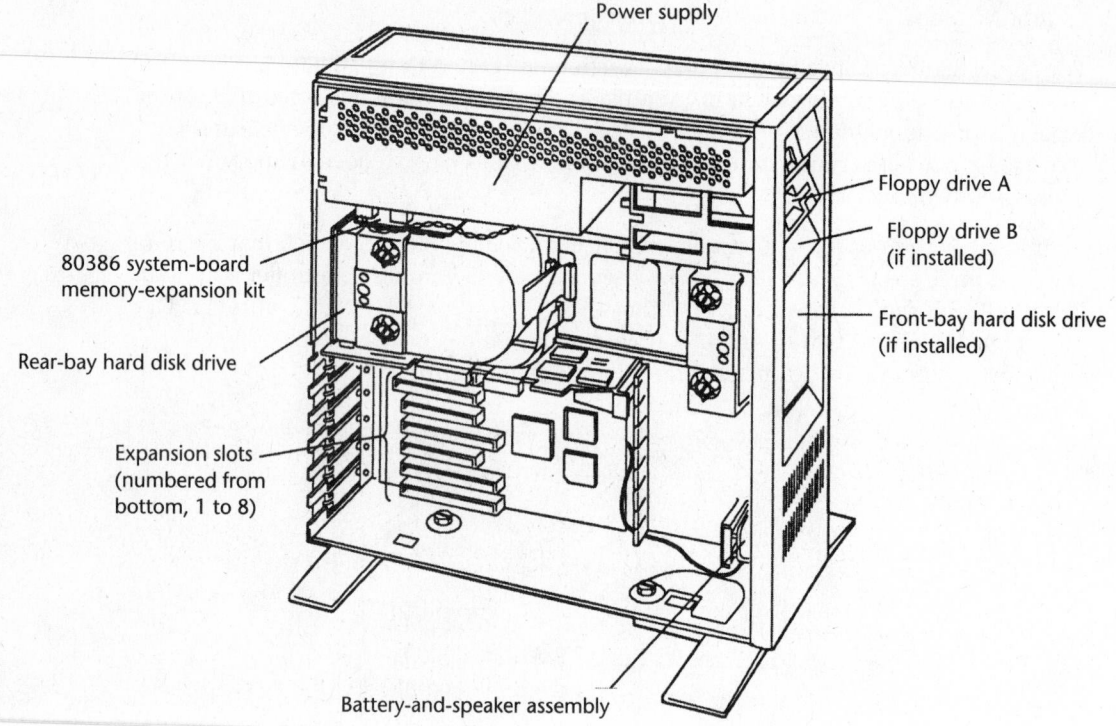

Power supply

Floppy drive A

Floppy drive B
(if installed)

80386 system-board
memory-expansion kit

Front-bay hard disk drive
(if installed)

Rear-bay hard disk drive

Expansion slots
(numbered from
bottom, 1 to 8)

Battery-and-speaker assembly

Fig. 4.44
PS/2 Model 80 386 interior view.

The auto-restart feature on the power supply enables the computer to restart automatically when AC power returns after a power decrease or outage. This feature enables the system to be programmed for unattended restart after power outages—a useful feature on a computer in a network file-server application.

Model 80 has a variety of configurations; three different Model 80 system boards are available. The motherboards differ primarily in the clock rate of the processor and the arrangement of the MCA slots. The 16 MHz and 20 MHz models have three 32-bit slots and five 16-bit MCA slots. One of the 16-bit slots includes a video extension connector. These mother-boards also allow a maximum of 4M to be installed using two nonstandard memory connectors. None of the Model 80 systems used standard SIMM connectors; they use a custom-designed card, making the memory upgrades available only from IBM.

The 25 MHz model differs from the others in that it has four 32-bit slots and four 16-bit slots, with two of the 16-bit slots having the video extension connector. These systems also incorporate a 64K static RAM cache on the motherboard, which essentially makes these systems run at 0 wait states. These motherboards support a maximum of 8M using two custom 4M memory cards plugged directly into the motherboard. Any additional memory beyond these maximums must be installed using an adapter card.

The hard disk drive interfaces also differentiate the different models. Three different disk interfaces and drive types were supplied with the Model 80. The 041 model used an ST-506 type controller that would handle up to two hard drives. The 071, 111, and 311 systems used an ESDI (Enhanced Small Device Interface) controller and drive. The ESDI controller would support up to two hard drives. The other (newer) models all include the IBM 16-bit MCA SCSI bus master adapter. This card provides an internal as well as external SCSI port for connecting devices. This card supports up to seven hard disks, and the system supports up to four of these cards. IBM has SCSI drives available from 60M through 400M to install in these systems. Also, because these drives are all in the 3 1/2-inch form factor (at least the ones from IBM), you can fit up to six of them inside the unit.

The 16 MHz systems also have a motherboard that always runs at 1 wait state, and does not offer ROM shadowing, in which the slower (150ns) ROM BIOS is copied into faster (80ns) motherboard memory chips. The ROM BIOS on this system board performs a ROM to RAM copy operation on start-up that uses 128K of the total 16M of RAM. This copy then is used for all subsequent ROM operations, and because the ROM now effectively resides in 80ns RAM, access to these routines is improved significantly. The chips then are re-addressed into the original BIOS locations and write protected. This means that you essentially have write-protected RAM acting as ROM, which can then run with fewer wait states. The 20 MHz systems incorporate a memory-paging scheme that reduces the number of wait states to 0 most of the time. All system board memory is accessed by a special paging scheme that allows for 0 wait state access to all 512 bytes within a single page. When access occurs outside the available page, you must perform a page swap requiring 2 wait states. Overall, this scheme allows for faster access to memory than a nonpaging, 1 wait state system. The 25 MHz systems incorporate a full-blown memory cache system that performs most operations in 25ns Static RAM. These systems are nearly always running at an apparent 0 wait states due to the efficiency of the cache.

Table 4.46 lists the technical specifications for the PS/2 Model 80 386.

Table 4.46 PS/2 Model 80 386 Technical Specifications	
System architecture	
Microprocessor	80386DX
Clock speed	16 MHz (041,071)
	20 MHz (081,111,121,161,311,321)
	25 MHz (Axx)
Bus type	MCA (Micro Channel Architecture)
Bus width	32-bit
Interrupt levels	16

(continues)

Compatible Systems

II

Table 4.46 Continued

System architecture

Type	Level-sensitive
Shareable	Yes
DMA channels	15
DMA burst mode supported	Yes
Bus masters supported	15
Upgradeable processor complex	No

Memory

Standard on system board	4M
Maximum on system board	4M
	8M (Axx)
Maximum total memory	16M
Memory speed and type	80ns dynamic RAM
System board memory socket type	Nonstandard memory card
Number of memory module sockets	2
Number available in standard configuration	1
Memory used on system board	1M/2M/4M card
Paged memory logic	Yes
	No (041,071)
Memory cache controller	No
	Yes (Axx)
Internal/external cache	External
Standard memory cache size	64K
Cache memory speed and type	25ns static RAM
Wait states:	
System board	0-5 (Axx, 95 percent 0 wait states)
	0-2 (081,111,121,161,311,321)
	1 (041,071)
Adapter	0-7 (Axx)
	0-4

Standard features

ROM size	128K
ROM shadowing	Yes
	No (041,071)
Optional math coprocessor	80387DX
Coprocessor speed	16 MHz (041,071)
	20 MHz (081,111,121,161,311,321)
	25 MHz (Axx)
Standard graphics	VGA (Video Graphics Array)

Standard features

8-/16-/32-bit controller	8-bit
Bus master	No
Video RAM (VRAM)	256K
RS232C serial ports	1
UART chip used	NS16550A
	NS16550 (041,071)
Maximum speed (bits/second)	19,200 bps
FIFO mode enabled	Yes
	No (041,071)
Maximum number of ports	8
Pointing device (mouse) ports	1
Parallel printer ports	1
Bidirectional	Yes
Maximum number of ports	8
CMOS real-time clock (RTC)	Yes
CMOS RAM	64 bytes + 2K extension
Battery life	5 years
Replaceable	Yes

Disk storage

Internal disk and tape drive bays	5 or 6 (reconfigurable)
	4 (041,071,111,311)
Number of 3 1/2-/5 1/4-inch bays	4/1 or 6/0 (reconfigurable)
	2/2 (041,071,111,311)
Floppy drives standard	1×1.44M
Optional floppy drives	
5 1/4-inch 360K	Optional
5 1/4-inch 1.2M	Optional
3 1/2-inch 720K	No
3 1/2-inch 1.44M	Standard
3 1/2-inch 2.88M	No
Hard disk controller included:	SCSI adapter (081,121,161,321,Axx)
	ESDI controller (071,111,311)
	ST-506 controller (041)
SCSI host adapter type	16-bit SCSI adapter
Bus master	Yes
Devices supported per adapter	7
Adapters supported per system	4
ST-506/ESDI hard disks available:	44M/70/115M/314M
Drive form factor	5 1/4-inch

(continues)

Table 4.46 Continued

Disk storage

Drive capacity	44M	44M	70M	115M	314M
Drive interface	ST-506	ST-506	ESDI	ESDI	ESDI
Average access rate (ms)	40	40	30	28	23
Encoding scheme	MFM	MFM	RLL	RLL	RLL
BIOS drive type	31	32	None	None	None
Cylinders	733	1023	583	915	1225
Heads	7	5	7	7	15
Sectors per track	17	17	36	36	34
Rotational speed (RPM)	3600	3600	3600	3600	3283
Interleave factor	1:1	1:1	1:1	1:1	1:1
Data transfer rate (K/second)	510	510	1080	1080	930
Automatic head parking	Yes	Yes	Yes	Yes	Yes

SCSI hard disks available:	60M/80M/120M/160M/320M/400M					
Drive form factor	3 1/2-inch					
Drive interface	SCSI					
Drive capacity	60M	80M	120M	160M	320M	400M
Average access rate (ms)	23	17	23	16	12.5	11.5
Read-ahead cache	32K	32K	32K	32K	64K	128K
SCSI transfer mode	Async	Async	Async	Async	Sync	Sync
Encoding scheme	RLL	RLL	RLL	RLL	RLL	RLL
Cylinders	920	1021	920	1021	949	1201
Heads	4	4	8	8	14	14
Sectors per track	32	39	32	39	48	48
Rotational speed (RPM)	3600	3600	3600	3600	4318	4318
Interleave factor	1:1	1:1	1:1	1:1	1:1	1:1
Data transfer rate (K/sec.)	960	1170	960	1170	1727	1727
Automatic head parking	Yes	Yes	Yes	Yes	Yes	Yes

Expansion slots

Total adapter slots	8
Number of long and short slots	8/0
Number of 8-/16-/32-bit slots	0/5/3
	0/4/4 (Axx)
Number of slots with video ext.	1
	2 (Axx)
Available slots	7
Keyboard specifications	
101-key Enhanced Keyboard	Yes
Fast keyboard speed setting	Yes
Keyboard cable length	10 feet
Security features	

Expansion slots	
Keylock:	
Locks cover	Yes
Locks keyboard	No
Keyboard password	Yes
Power-on password	Yes
Network server mode	Yes

Physical specifications	
Footprint type	Floor-standing
Dimensions:	
Height	23.5 inches
Width	6.5 inches
Depth	19.0 inches
Weight	45.3 lbs
	52.0 lbs (041,071,111,311)

Environmental specifications	
Power-supply output	242 watts
	225 watts (041,071,111,311)
Worldwide (110/60,220/50)	Yes
Auto-sensing/switching	Yes
Maximum current:	
90-137 volts AC	5.3 amps
180-265 volts AC	2.7 amps
Operating range:	
Temperature	60-90 degrees F
Relative humidity	8-80 percent
Maximum operating altitude	7,000 feet
Heat (BTUs/hour)	1390
	1245 (041,071,111,311)
Noise (average dB, operating, 1m)	40 dB
	46 dB (041,071,111,311)
FCC classification	Class B

Figures 4.45 and 4.46 show the components and layout of the Model 80 type 1 and type 2 motherboards.

Table 4.47 shows the primary specifications and costs of the various versions of PS/2 Model 80 386.

II

Compatible Systems

Table 4.47 IBM PS/2 Model 80 386 Model Summary

Part number	CPU	MHz	PLANAR MEMORY Std.	Max.	Floppy drive	STANDARD Hard disk	Bus type
80 386							
8580-041	386DX	16	1M	4M	1×1.44M	44M	MCA/32
8580-071	386DX	16	2M	4M	1×1.44M	70M	MCA/32
8580-081	386DX	20	4M	4M	1×1.44M	80M	MCA/32
8580-111	386DX	20	2M	4M	1×1.44M	115M	MCA/32
8580-121	386DX	20	2M	4M	1×1.44M	120M	MCA/32
8580-161	386DX	20	4M	4M	1×1.44M	160M	MCA/32
8580-311	386DX	20	2M	4M	1×1.44M	314M	MCA/32
8580-321	386DX	20	4M	4M	1×1.44M	320M	MCA/32
8580-A21	386DX	25	4M	8M	1×1.44M	120M	MCA/32
8580-A16	386DX	25	4M	8M	1×1.44M	160M	MCA/32
8580-A31	386DX	25	4M	8M	1×1.44M	320M	MCA/32

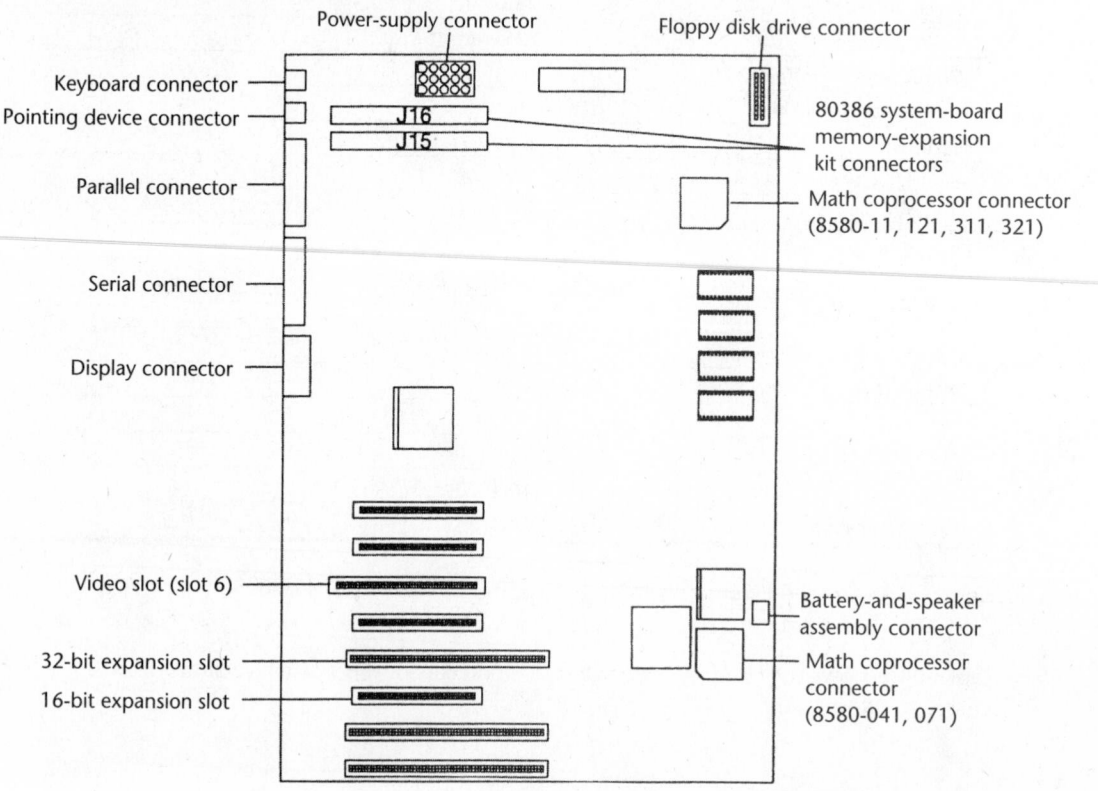

Fig. 4.45

PS/2 Model 80 386 system board (16 MHz and 20 MHz type 1).

Total/ available slots	STANDARD Video	KB	Date introduced	Date withdrawn
8/7	VGA	Enh	04/02/87	10/31/90
8/7	VGA	Enh	04/02/87	10/31/90
8/7	VGA	Enh	10/30/90	—
8/7	VGA	Enh	04/02/87	12/27/90
8/7	VGA	Enh	03/20/90	01/29/91
8/7	VGA	Enh	10/30/90	—
8/7	VGA	Enh	08/04/87	12/27/90
8/7	VGA	Enh	03/20/90	—
8/7	VGA	Enh	03/20/90	01/29/91
8/7	VGA	Enh	10/30/90	—
8/7	VGA	Enh	03/20/90	—

Compatible Systems

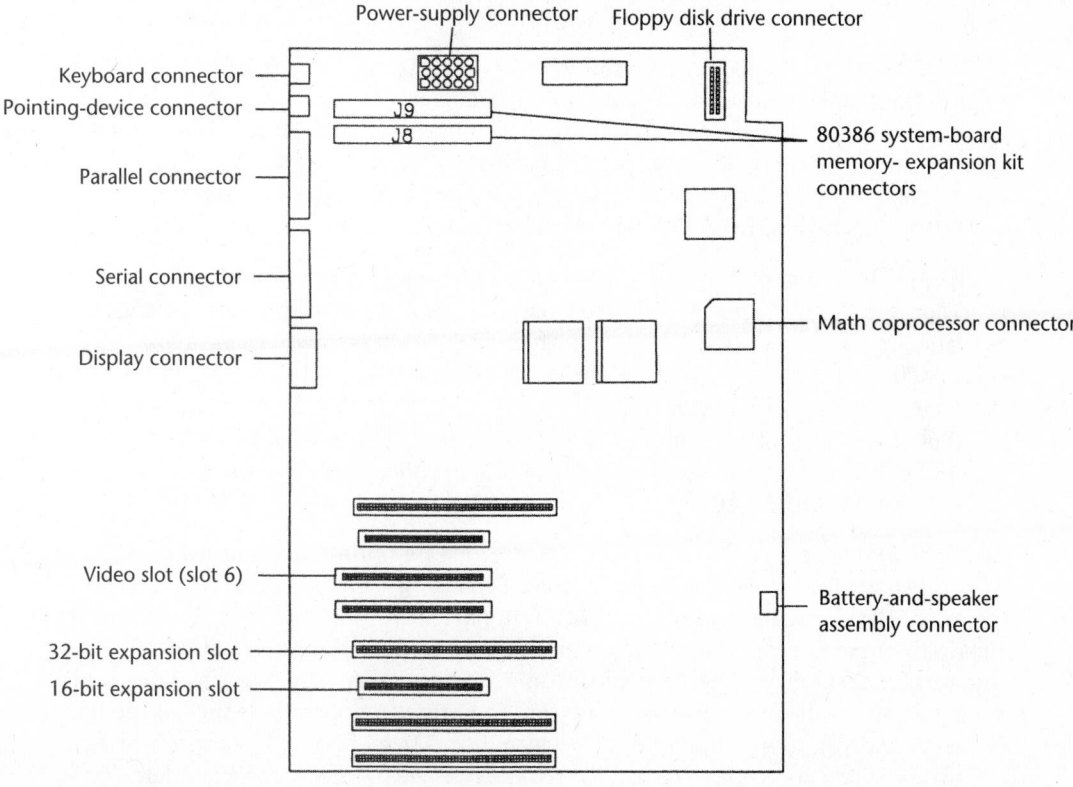

Fig. 4.46

PS/2 Model 80 386 system board (25 MHz type 2).

PS/2 Model 90 XP 486

The PS/2 Model 90 XP 486, introduced October 30, 1990, is a powerful and expandable MCA-based desktop system. Through an unusual design, the system's 32-bit 80486 processor is on a removable processor complex, allowing processor upgrade from the 25 MHz to the more powerful 33 MHz or 50 MHz system. This capability to upgrade can extend the life of the system as customer requirements for enhanced processor performance grow.

Highlights of the Model 90 include:

- Processor complex with 80486 20, 25, 33, or 50MHz processor

- 8M standard memory, expandable to 64M on the system board

- XGA graphics integrated on system board

- PS/2 SCSI 32-bit bus master adapter with cache

- Four internal storage device bays

- Four 32-bit Micro Channel expansion slots

- Two DMA serial ports and one DMA parallel port

- Selectable boot and disk loaded ROM BIOS

The PS/2 Model 90 XP 486 features the 20 MHz, 25 MHz, 33 MHz, or 50 MHz 80486 microprocessor. The processor includes an internal memory cache controller, an internal 8K memory cache, and an internal floating point processor unit. The PS/2 256K cache option provides additional memory cache capability beyond the 8K internal memory cache. The PS/2 256K cache option is supported on 486DX models of Model 90 and Model 95. This capability provides investment protection and flexibility for the user.

The Model 90 system provides four internal drive bays and four 32-bit MCA I/O slots (one slot is used for the IBM PS/2 Micro Channel SCSI Adapter with cache, leaving three available for expansion). The PS/2 Micro Channel SCSI adapter with cache allows up to seven SCSI devices to be attached to the Model 90. The Model 90 also supports an internal 5 1/4-inch floppy disk device. The 5 1/4-inch Slim High Disk Drive (part number 6451066) is an internal 5 1/4-inch, 1.2M floppy disk drive with electrical button eject. This drive does not require an attachment card or expansion slot for installation and is supported in Models 90 and 95.

The Model 90 memory subsystem has been designed for optimum performance with interleaved memory; it features parity memory checking for added reliability and data integrity. All system memory (up to 64M) is supported on the system board, eliminating the need for memory adapters in any of the expansion slots. Although the Model 90 supports a maximum of 64M of memory, only 16M of that is addressable by DMA. This effectively limits the use of memory past 16M to nonsystem operations such as caching, virtual memory, or other functions. The system board has a total of eight memory sockets, two of which are used by a pair of 2M SIMMs (single in-line memory modules) to provide the standard 4M of memory. Optional 2M, 4M, and 8M memory SIMMs (70ns, 80ns, and 85ns only) are supported in matched pairs to provide various memory configurations up to 64M. Although 80ns and 85ns memory SIMMs are supported, 70ns memory SIMMs provide optimum memory subsystem performance.

The eXtended Graphics Array (XGA), high-performance, 32-bit bus master video sub-system is a standard feature of the PS/2 Model 90 XP 486 system. The integrated XGA provides $1024 \times 768 \times 16$ colors or $640 \times 480 \times 256$ colors as standard and can be option-ally expanded to $1024 \times 768 \times 256$ colors with the addition of one PS/2 video memory expansion option. XGA supports all VGA modes and is optimized for use with window managers and other graphical user interfaces, allowing for highly interactive pop-up icons and pull-down menus. XGA also provides hardware support for 132-character text mode (using 8515 or 8514 display) and 16-bit direct color mode (64K colors at 640×480 resolution). MCA slot 3 of the PS/2 Model 90 XP 486 system contains a video feature bus connector that can be used to install a video adapter.

Other features of the Model 90 include the dual direct memory address (DMA) serial ports and a DMA parallel port included as standard. One of the serial port connectors is standard 25-pin D-shell, and the other connector is 9-pin D-shell. The 9-pin D-shell con-nector requires an adapter for attaching devices with 25-pin D-shell connectors. The DMA serial port provides support for speeds from 300 bits per second to 345.6K bits per second. It reduces processor loading and overhead when used in high-speed communica-tions and supports speeds up to 345.6K bits per second.

The Model 90 offers the selectable-boot feature. As part of the system CMOS setup pro-gram, the user can specify which drive should be booted from and in which order the boot process should try each drive (for example, boot first from drive A, then drive C, and load BASIC). This step enables the user to boot or load a program from the optional 5 1/4-inch internal floppy disk drive as if it were drive A.

Initial Microcode Load

One special feature that the Model 90 has is called Initial Microcode Load (IML). The Model 90 stores the BIOS, configuration programs, and diagnostics on the hard disk in a protected 3M system partition and loaded from the disk during a "pre-boot" process. (The system programs also are provided on the PS/2 Model 90 XP 486 Reference Disk.) The formatted capacity of the hard disk is reduced by 3M, and the total user-accessible capacity might vary slightly, based on operating environments. This partition is not affected when the drive is formatted using the DOS or OS/2 FORMAT command.

The Initial Microcode Load (IML) loads the BIOS program from the hard disk drive into system memory. This process makes updating the BIOS an easy task when the time comes. Rather than pulling and replacing ROM chips on the motherboard, all you have to do is obtain a newer copy of the reference floppy disk and restore the system programs using that disk. Updates are available from your dealer or directly from IBM.

For example, a problem has been noted with Model 90 systems that have more than 8M of memory. To fix the problem, you need the Model 90 Reference Disk Version 1.02 or higher. To obtain the latest version, call 1-800-426-7282, weekdays between 8 a.m. and 8 p.m., Eastern Standard time. Specify the floppy disk for IBM PS/2 Model 90 XP 486. In Canada, call 1-800-465-1234 weekdays between 8 a.m. and 4:30 p.m. Eastern Standard time. In Alaska, call (414) 633-8108. The update will be sent to you and is installed in a menu-driven fashion. Because IBM sets the standards in this industry, you probably will see other compatible vendors adopting this disk-based BIOS approach as well. The flexibility and ease of upgrading are welcome.

On October 17, 1991, IBM enhanced the PS/2 Model 90 XP family with new Intel 486SX 25MHz (0Hx) models. The new systems come equipped with a new 486SX 25MHz processor complex, which provides improved performance over the previous 25MHz 486DX processor—and at a lower price. The new processor complex provides improved Micro Channel performance, better bus arbitration, and enhancements to the memory controller, making it ideal for multitasking or operating in heavily loaded networked environments. An improved physical design with fewer parts provides for greater reliability. The new processor complex also incorporates a conventional math coprocessor socket. Because of the improved price and performance of the new 25 MHz systems, earlier models using the 486SX 20MHz (0Gx) and 486 25MHz (0Jx) processor complex are being withdrawn. Because the 486SX lacks the integrated math coprocessor unit, a socket for the addition of the optional 487SX Math coprocessor is provided. In addition, these entry-level models can be upgraded to the more powerful 486/33MHz or the 486/50MHz processors with the IBM PS/2 486/33 and 486/50 processor upgrade options.

Table 4.48 lists the technical specifications for the PS/2 Model 90 XP 486.

Table 4.48 PS/2 Model 90 XP 486 Technical Specifications	
System architecture	
Microprocessor and clock speed	80486SX 20 MHz (0Gx)
	80487SX 20 MHz
	80486SX 25 MHz (0Hx)
	80487SX 25 MHz
	80486DX 25 MHz (0Jx)
	80486DX 33 MHz (0Kx)
	80486DX 50 MHz
Bus type	MCA (Micro Channel Architecture)
Bus width	32-bit
Interrupt levels	16
Type	Level-sensitive
Shareable	Yes
DMA channels	15
DMA burst mode supported	Yes

System architecture

Bus masters supported	15
486 burst mode enabled	Yes
Upgradeable processor complex	Yes
Processor upgrades available	20 MHz 487SX
	25 MHz 486SX
	25 MHz 486DX
	33 MHz 486DX
	50 MHz 486DX

Memory

Standard on system board	4M (0Gx)
	8M (for all others)
Maximum on system board	64M
Maximum total memory	64M
Memory speed and type	70ns dynamic RAM
System board memory socket type	36-bit SIMM (single in-line memory module)
Number of memory module sockets	8
Number available in standard configuration	6 (0Gx)
	4 (for all others)
Memory used on system board	2M/4M/8M SIMMs
Memory interleaving	Yes
Paged memory logic	Yes
Memory cache controller	Yes
Internal/external cache	Internal
Standard memory cache size	8K
Optional external memory cache	No (0Gx, 0Hx)
	Yes
External cache size	256K
Cache memory speed and type	17ns static RAM
Wait states:	
System board	0-5 (95 percent 0 wait states)
Adapter	0-7

System features

ROM size	128K
ROM shadowing	Yes
BIOS extensions stored on disk	Yes
Setup and Diagnostics stored on disk	Yes
Optional math coprocessor	80487SX (0Gx)
	Built-in to 486DX
Coprocessor speed	20 MHz (0Gx)
	25 MHz (0Jx)

(continues)

Table 4.48 Continued

System features

	33 MHz (0Kx)
	50 MHz
Standard graphics	XGA (eXtended Graphics Array)
8-/16-/32-bit controller	32-bit
Bus master	Yes
Video RAM (VRAM)	512K
RS232C serial ports	2
UART chip used	Custom (compatible with NS16550A)
Maximum speed (bits/second)	345,600 bps
FIFO mode enabled	Yes
Supports DMA data transfer	Yes
Maximum number of ports	8
Pointing device (mouse) ports	1
Parallel printer ports	1
Bidirectional	Yes
Supports DMA data transfer	Yes
Maximum number of ports	8
CMOS real-time clock (RTC)	Yes
CMOS RAM	64 bytes + 2K extension
Battery life	5 years
Replaceable	Yes

Disk storage

Internal disk and tape drive bays	4
Number of 3 1/2-/5 1/4-inch bays	3/1
Selectable boot drive	Yes
Bootable drives	All physical drives
Standard floppy drives	1×1.44M
Optional floppy drives:	
5 1/4-inch 360K	Optional
5 1/4-inch 1.2M	Optional
3 1/2-inch 720K	No
3 1/2-inch 1.44M	Standard
3 1/2-inch 2.88M	No
Hard disk controller included:	32-bit SCSI adapter with 512K cache
Bus master	Yes
Devices supported per adapter	7
Adapters supported per system	4
SCSI hard disks available:	60M/80M/120M/160M/320M/400M
Drive form factor	3 1/2-inch
Drive interface	SCSI

Disk storage

Drive capacity	60M	80M	120M	160M	320M	400M
Average access rate (ms)	23	17	23	16	12.5	11.5
Read-ahead cache	32K	32K	32K	32K	64K	128K
SCSI transfer mode	Async	Async	Async	Async	Sync	Sync
Encoding scheme	RLL	RLL	RLL	RLL	RLL	RLL
Cylinders	920	1021	920	1021	949	1201
Heads	4	4	8	8	14	14
Sectors per track	32	39	32	39	48	48
Rotational speed (RPM)	3600	3600	3600	3600	4318	4318
Interleave factor	1:1	1:1	1:1	1:1	1:1	1:1
Data transfer rate (K/second)	960	1170	960	1170	1727	1727
Automatic head parking	Yes	Yes	Yes	Yes	Yes	Yes

Expansion slots

Total adapter slots	4
Number of long and short slots	4/0
Number of 8-/16-/32-bit slots	0/0/4
Number of slots with video ext.	1
Available slots	3

Keyboard specifications

101-key Enhanced Keyboard	Yes
Fast keyboard speed setting	Yes
Keyboard cable length	6 feet

Security features

Keylock:	
Locks cover	Yes
Locks keyboard	No
Keyboard password	Yes
Power-on password	Yes
Network server mode	Yes

Physical specifications

Footprint type	Desktop
Dimensions:	
Height	5.5 inches
Width	17.3 inches
Depth	16.9 inches
Weight	25.0 lbs

(continues)

II

Compatible Systems

Table 4.48 Continued	
Environmental specifications	
Power-supply output	194 watts
Worldwide (110/60,220/50)	Yes
Auto-sensing/switching	Yes
Maximum current:	
90-137 VAC	4.8 amps
180-264 VAC	2.4 amps
Operating range	
Temperature	50-95 degrees F
Relative humidity	8-80 percent
Maximum operating altitude	7,000 feet
Heat (BTUs/hour)	662
FCC classification	Class B

Table 4.49 shows the primary specifications and costs of the various versions of PS/2 Model 90 XP 486.

PS/2 Model 95 XP 486

The PS/2 Model 95 XP 486, introduced October 30, 1990, is a high-performance, highly expandable floor-standing system based on MCA. Like the Model 90, through an unusual design, this system's 32-bit 80486 processor is on a removable processor complex, allowing a processor upgrade from the 25 MHz to the more powerful 33 MHz or 50 MHz system. This capability to upgrade can extend the life of the system as customer requirements for enhanced processor performance grow.

Highlights of the Model 95 include:

- Processor complex with 80486 20, 25, 33, or 50MHz processor
- 8M standard memory, expandable to 64M on the system board
- Enhanced Performance XGA Display Adapter/A standard
- PS/2 SCSI 32-bit bus master adapter with cache
- Seven internal storage device bays
- Eight 32-bit Micro Channel expansion slots
- One DMA serial port and one DMA parallel port
- Selectable boot and disk loaded ROM BIOS

The PS/2 Model 95 XP 486 features the 20, 25, 33, or 50 MHz 80486 microprocessor. The processor includes an internal memory cache controller, an internal 8K memory cache, and an internal floating point processor unit. The PS/2 256K cache option provides additional memory cache capability beyond the 8K internal memory cache. The PS/2 256K cache option is supported on 486DX models of Model 90 and Model 95. This capability provides investment protection and flexibility for the user.

The system provides a total of seven storage device bays: Two can accommodate 5 1/4-inch half-high drives and the other five support 3 1/2-inch devices. Up to five high-speed SCSI hard disk drives can be installed internally, and a variety of other storage devices can be installed, such as CD-ROM drives, 5 1/4-inch floppy disk drives, and tape backup devices. The PS/2 Micro Channel SCSI adapter with cache allows as many as seven SCSI devices to be attached to the PS/2 Model 95. The PS/2 Model 95 also supports an internal 5 1/4-inch floppy disk device. The 5 1/4-inch Slim High Disk Drive (part number 6451066) is an internal 5 1/4-inch, 1.2M floppy disk drive with electrical button eject. This drive does not require an attachment card or expansion slot for installation and is supported in the Models 90 and 95.

The system provides eight 32-bit MCA slots: Two are used by the SCSI and XGA adapters, leaving six for other expansion adapters. A direct memory access (DMA) serial port and DMA parallel port are provided as standard. The Model 95 also features the capability of booting from any drive and an easy way to upgrade BIOS capability.

The Model 95 memory subsystem has been designed for optimum performance with interleaved memory; it features parity memory checking for added reliability and data integrity. All system memory (up to 64M) is supported on the system board, eliminating the need for memory adapters in any of the expansion slots. Although the Model 95 supports a maximum of 64M of memory, only 16M of that is addressable by DMA. This amount effectively limits the use of memory past 16M to nonsystem operations such as caching, virtual memory, or other functions. The system board has a total of eight memory sockets, two of which are used by a pair of 2M SIMMs (single in-line memory modules) to provide the basic standard 4M of memory. (Note that the amount of standard memory can vary according to the model from 4M to 8M.) Optional 2M, 4M, and 8M memory SIMMs (70ns, 80ns, and 85ns only) are supported in matched pairs to provide various memory configurations up to 64M. Although 80ns and 85ns memory SIMMs are supported, 70ns memory SIMMs provide optimum memory subsystem performance.

The Extended Graphics Array (XGA) Display Adapter/A with its high-performance 32-bit bus master video subsystem is a standard feature of the PS/2 Model 95 XP 486. The XGA adapter provides 1024 × 768 × 16 colors or 640 × 480 × 256 colors as standard and can be optionally expanded to 1024 × 768 × 256 colors with the addition of one PS/2 video memory expansion option. XGA supports all VGA modes and is optimized for use with window managers and other graphical user interfaces, allowing for highly interactive pop-up icons and pull-down menus. XGA also provides hardware support for 132-character text mode (using 8515 or 8514 display) and 16-bit direct color mode (64K colors at 640 × 480 resolution).

Other specific features of the Model 95 include a direct memory address (DMA) serial port and a DMA parallel port as standard. The DMA serial port provides support for

II

Compatible Systems

Table 4.49 PS/2 Model 90 XP 486 Model Summary

Part Number	CPU	MHz	PLANAR MEMORY Std.	Max.	STANDARD Floppy drive	Hard disk	Bus type
90 XP 486							
8590-0G5	486SX	20	4M	64M	1×1.44M	80M	MCA/32
8590-0G9	486SX	20	4M	64M	1×1.44M	160M	MCA/32
8590-0H5	486SX	25	4M	64M	1×1.44M	80M	MCA/32
8590-0H9	486SX	25	4M	64M	1×1.44M	160M	MCA/32
8590-0J5	486DX	25	8M	64M	1×1.44M	80M	MCA/32
8590-0J9	486DX	25	8M	64M	1×1.44M	160M	MCA/32
8590-0K9	486DX	33	8M	64M	1×1.44M	320M	MCA/32
8590-0KD	486DX	33	8M	64M	1×1.44M	320M	MCA/32
8590-0KF	486DX	33	8M	64M	1×1.44M	400M	MCA/32

speeds from 300 bits per second to 345.6K bits per second, which reduces processor loading and overhead when used in high-speed communications.

The Model 95 offers the selectable-boot feature. As part of the system CMOS setup program, the user can specify which drive should be booted from and in which order the boot process should try each drive (for example, boot first from A drive, then C drive, and load BASIC). This allows the user to boot or load a program from the optional 5 1/4-inch internal floppy disk drive as if it were drive A.

Initial Microcode Load

One special Model 95 feature is Initial Microcode Load (IML). The Model 95 stores the BIOS, configuration programs, and diagnostics on the hard disk in a protected 3M partition and loaded from the disk during a "pre-boot" process. (The system programs also are provided on the PS/2 Model 95 Reference Disk.) The formatted capacity of the hard disk is reduced by 3M, and the total user-accessible capacity might vary slightly, based on operating environments. This partition is not affected when the drive is formatted using the DOS or OS/2 FORMAT command.

The Initial Microcode Load (IML) loads the BIOS program from the hard disk drive into system memory. This step makes updating the BIOS an easy task when the time comes. Rather than pulling and replacing ROM chips on the motherboard, all you have to do is obtain a newer copy of the reference floppy disk and restore the system programs using that disk. Updates are available from your dealer or directly from IBM.

For example, a problem has been noted with Model 95 systems that have more than 8M of memory. To fix the problem, you need the Model 95 Reference Disk Version 1.02 or higher. To obtain the latest version, call 1-800-426-7282, weekdays between 8 a.m. and 8 p.m., Eastern Standard time. Specify the floppy disk for IBM PS/2 Model 90 XP 486. In Canada, call 1-800-465-1234 weekdays between 8 a.m. and 4:30 p.m. Eastern Standard time. In Alaska, call (414) 633-8108. The update will be sent to you and is installed in a

Total/available slots	STANDARD Video	KB	Date introduced	Date withdrawn
4/3	XGA	Enh	04/23/91	01/17/92
4/3	XGA	Enh	04/23/91	01/17/92
4/3	XGA	Enh	10/17/91	—
4/3	XGA	Enh	10/17/91	—
4/3	XGA	Enh	10/30/90	01/17/92
4/3	XGA	Enh	10/30/90	01/17/92
4/3	XGA	Enh	10/17/91	07/28/92
4/3	XGA	Enh	10/30/90	01/17/92
4/3	XGA	Enh	10/17/91	07/28/92

menu-driven fashion. Because IBM sets the standards in the computer industry, other IBM-compatible vendors probably will adopt this disk-based BIOS approach. The flexibility and ease of upgrading are welcome.

On October 17, 1991, IBM enhanced the PS/2 Model 95 XP family with new Intel 486SX 25 MHz (0Hx) models. The new systems come equipped with a new 486SX 25 MHz processor complex, which provides improved performance over the previous 25 MHz 486DX processor at a lower price. The new processor complex provides improved Micro Channel performance, better bus arbitration, and enhancements to the memory controller, making it ideal for multitasking or operating in heavily loaded networked environments. An improved physical design with fewer parts provides greater reliability. The new processor complex also incorporates a conventional math coprocessor socket. Because of the improved price and performance of the new 25 MHz systems, earlier models using the 486SX 20MHz (0Gx) and 486 25 MHz (0Jx) processor complex are being withdrawn. Because the 486SX lacks the integrated math coprocessor unit, a socket for the addition of the optional 487SX math coprocessor is provided. In addition, these entry-level models may be upgraded to the more powerful 486/33MHz or the 486/50MHz processors with the IBM PS/2 486/33 and 486/50 processor-upgrade options.

Table 4.50 lists the technical specifications for the PS/2 model 95XP 486.

Table 4.50 PS/2 Model 95 XP 486 Technical Specifications	
System architecture	
Microprocessor and clock speed	80486SX 20 MHz (0Gx)
	80487SX 20 MHz
	80486SX 25 MHz (0Hx)
	80487SX 25 MHz

(continues)

Compatible Systems

Table 4.50 Continued	
System architecture	
	80486DX 25 MHz (0Jx)
	80486DX 33 MHz (0Kx)
	80486DX 50 MHz
Bus type	MCA (Micro Channel Architecture)
Bus width	32-bit
Interrupt levels	16
Type	Level-sensitive
Shareable	Yes
DMA channels	15
DMA burst mode supported	Yes
Bus masters supported	15
486 burst mode enabled	Yes
Upgradeable processor complex	Yes
Processor upgrades available	20 MHz 487SX
	25 MHz 486DX
	33 MHz 486DX
	50 MHz 486DX
Memory	
Standard on system board	4M (0Gx)
	8M (for all others)
Maximum on system board	64M
Maximum total memory	64M
Memory speed and type	70ns dynamic RAM
System-board memory socket type	36-bit SIMM (single in-line memory module)
Number of memory module sockets	8
Number available in standard configuration	6 (0Gx)
	4 (for all others)
Memory used on system board	2M/4M/8M SIMMs
Memory interleaving	Yes
Paged memory logic	Yes
Memory cache controller	Yes
Internal/external cache	Internal
Standard memory cache size	8K
Optional external memory cache	No (0Gx, 0Hx)
	Yes (for all others)
External cache size	256K

Memory	
Cache memory speed and type	17ns static RAM
Wait states:	
System board	0-5 (95 percent 0 wait states)
Adapter	0-7

Standard features	
ROM size	128K
ROM shadowing	Yes
BIOS extensions stored on disk	Yes
Setup and Diagnostics stored on disk	Yes
Optional math coprocessor	80487SX (0Gx)
	Built-in to 486DX
Coprocessor speed	20 MHz (0Gx)
	25 MHz (0Jx)
	33 MHz (0Kx)
	50 MHz
Standard graphics	XGA (eXtended Graphics Array)
8-/16-/32-bit controller	32-bit
Bus master	Yes
Video RAM (VRAM)	512K
RS232C serial ports	2
UART chip used	Custom (compatible with NS16550A)
Maximum speed (bits/second)	345,600 bps
FIFO mode enabled	Yes
Supports DMA data transfer	Yes
Maximum number of ports	8
Pointing device (mouse) ports	1
Parallel printer ports	1
Bidirectional	Yes
Supports DMA data transfer	Yes
Maximum number of ports	8
CMOS real-time clock (RTC)	Yes
CMOS RAM	64 bytes + 2K extension
Battery life	5 years
Replaceable	Yes

Disk storage	
Internal disk and tape drive bays	7
Number of 3 1/2 and 5 1/4-inch bays	5/2
Selectable boot drive	Yes

Compatible Systems

(continues)

Table 4.50 Continued

Disk storage

Bootable drives	All physical drives
Standard floppy drives	1×1.44M
Optional floppy drives:	
5 1/4-inch 360K	Optional
5 1/4-inch 1.2M	Optional
3 1/2-inch 720K	No
3 1/2-inch 1.44M	Standard
3 1/2-inch 2.88M	No
Hard disk controller included:	32-bit SCSI adapter with 512K cache
Bus master	Yes
Devices supported per adapter	7
Adapters supported per system	4
SCSI hard disks available:	60M/80M/120M/160M/320M/400M
Drive form factor	3 1/2-inch
Drive interface	SCSI

Drive capacity	60M	80M	120M	160M	320M	400M
Average access rate (ms)	23	17	23	16	12.5	11.5
Read-ahead cache	32K	32K	32K	32K	64K	128K
SCSI transfer mode	Async	Async	Async	Async	Sync	Sync
Encoding scheme	RLL	RLL	RLL	RLL	RLL	RLL
Cylinders	920	1021	920	1021	949	1201
Heads	4	4	8	8	14	14
Sectors per track	32	39	32	39	48	48
Rotational speed (RPM)	3600	3600	3600	3600	4318	4318
Interleave factor	1:1	1:1	1:1	1:1	1:1	1:1
Data transfer rate (K/second)	960	1170	960	1170	1727	1727
Automatic head parking	Yes	Yes	Yes	Yes	Yes	Yes

Expansion slots

Total adapter slots	8
Number of long and short slots	8/0
Number of 8-/16-/32-bit slots	0/0/8
Number of slots with video ext.	2
Adapter form factor	IBM RISC system/6000
Available slots	6

Keyboard specifications	
101-key Enhanced Keyboard	Yes
Fast keyboard speed setting	Yes
Keyboard cable length	6 feet
Keylock:	
Locks cover	Yes
Locks keyboard	No
Keyboard password	Yes
Power-on password	Yes
Network server mode	Yes
Physical specifications	
Footprint type	Floor-standing
Dimensions:	
Height	19.8 inches
Width	8.0 inches
Depth	20.0 inches
Weight	51.0 lbs
Environmental specifications	
Power-supply output	329 watts
Worldwide (110/60,220/50)	Yes
Auto-sensing/switching	Yes
Maximum current:	
90-137 VAC	8.3 amps
180-264 VAC	4.7 amps
Operating range:	
Temperature	50-95 degrees F
Relative humidity	8-80 percent
Maximum operating altitude	7,000 feet
Heat (BTUs/hour)	1123
FCC classification	Class B

Table 4.51 shows the primary specifications and costs of the various versions of PS/2 Model 95 XP 486.

PS/2 BIOS Information

To uniquely identify each PS/2 system model through software, IBM encodes each system with a unique set of identifying information. By using this information and comparing it to a chart showing what versions have been available, you might be able to determine whether a system has an out-of-date ROM release that might be causing problems. A review of this information shows just how many different systems IBM has released.

Table 4.51 IBM PS/2 Model 95 XP 486 Model Summary

Part number	CPU	MHz	PLANAR MEMORY Std.	Max.	STANDARD Floppy drive	Hard disk	Bus type
95 XP 486							
8595-0G9	486SX	20	4M	64M	1×1.44M	160M	MCA/32
8595-0GF	486SX	20	4M	64M	1×1.44M	400M	MCA/32
8595-0H9	486SX	25	8M	64M	1×1.44M	160M	MCA/32
8595-0HF	486SX	25	8M	64M	1×1.44M	400M	MCA/32
8595-0J9	486DX	25	8M	64M	1×1.44M	160M	MCA/32
8595-0JD	486DX	25	8M	64M	1×1.44M	320M	MCA/32
8595-0JF	486DX	25	8M	64M	1×1.44M	400M	MCA/32
8595-0KD	486DX	33	8M	64M	1×1.44M	320M	MCA/32
8595-0KF	486DX	33	8M	64M	1×1.44M	400M	MCA/32

To identify one system from another, one item that many technicians use is the ROM BIOS date of creation. The date is stored in the ROM at absolute address FFFF:5. To see this date, you can use the DOS DEBUG program as follows:

1. Run the DEBUG program by typing the DEBUG command at the C: prompt:

   ```
   C:\>DEBUG
   ```

2. When the debug prompt (-) appears, type the following command and press Enter:

   ```
   -D FFFF:5 L 8
   ```

   This command instructs debug to dump the memory in segment FFFF and offset 5, for a length of 8 bytes.

3. Read the screen display, which looks something like the following line, showing the BIOS date, unless the compatible BIOS is nonstandard and does not store the date there:

   ```
   FFFF:0000      30 31 2F-31 38 2F 38 39     01/18/89
   ```

4. To exit DEBUG, press Q.

The screen will look something like this when you are done:

```
C:\>DEBUG
-D FFFF:5 L 8
FFFF:0000      30 31 2F-31 38 2F 38 39   01/18/89
-Q
```

Although many people use the BIOS date of creation to identify a system, IBM uses other information in addition to the version of BIOS to uniquely identify the system. IBM has

Total/ available slots	STANDARD Video	KB	Date introduced	Date withdrawn
8/6	XGA	Enh	04/23/91	01/17/92
8/6	XGA	Enh	04/23/91	01/17/92
8/6	XGA	Enh	10/17/91	—
8/6	XGA	Enh	10/17/91	—
8/6	XGA	Enh	10/30/90	01/17/92
8/6	XGA	Enh	10/30/90	01/17/92
8/6	XGA	Enh	04/23/91	01/17/92
8/6	XGA	Enh	10/30/90	01/17/92
8/6	XGA	Enh	04/23/91	—

given each PS/2 system a model ID byte (or model byte), a submodel byte, and a revision byte. With these three pieces of information, you can clearly identify any PS/2 system by booting the Reference Disk and executing the "Display Revision Levels" option at the main menu. The display that results looks something like this:

```
     Model Byte: F8
 Sub-Model Byte: 0B
       Revision: 00
```

The values are in hexadecimal because they represent raw byte values. Many diagnostics programs can locate this information for a given system because a standard way to retrieve the information involves executing an Int 15h instruction with the AH register set to C0, which returns a pointer to the location of the desired information.

You also can find out this information by using DEBUG. The first step in the procedure involves (A)ssembling at memory offset 100h a short program that will (MOV)e the value C0 into the AH register. Then execute (Int)errupt 15h, and (Int)errupt 3h. The Int 15 function C0 causes the ES and BX registers to contain the address of the System Configuration Parameters table. This table is in memory and contains information about how the system is configured and the model ID information you are looking for. The Int 3 is a breakpoint instruction that will cause the program to stop and display the register contents.

After the program is assembled in memory, the (G)o instruction tells DEBUG to run the program, which occurs until the Int 3 instruction is reached and causes the program to stop, gives DEBUG control of the system, and displays the current contents of the registers. The correct location of the System Configuration Table then is in the ES:BX registers. For my P70 system that would be E000:7CED, but the address will vary for other systems. When you run these steps, be sure to substitute whatever is reported on your

II

Compatible Systems

system in the ES and BX registers for the address in the (D)ump command. The "L A" part of the (D)ump command says that the (L)ength of data to dump is Ah (10) bytes. This includes the first two bytes of the table, which is a word indicating the length of the remaining portion of the table. Normally this word has a value of 0008h, which means that the remainder of the table is 8 bytes long.

To find out the model byte, submodel byte, and revision number of your system you can execute these steps using DOS DEBUG. You should notice that the address given in the (D)ump instruction will differ between systems. You must substitute whatever values are reported by the ES and BX registers:

```
C:\>DEBUG
-A 100
xxxx:0100 MOV AH,C0
xxxx:0102 INT 15
xxxx:0104 INT 3
xxxx:0105
-G

AX=00FF  BX=7CED  CX=0000  DX=0000  SP=FFEE  BP=0000  SI=0000  DI=0000
DS=269A  ES=E000  SS=269A  CS=269A  IP=0104    NV UP EI PL ZR NA PE NC
269A:0104 CC             INT    3
-D E000:7CED L A
E000:7CE0                                        08 00 F8           ...
E000:7CF0  0B 00 F6 40 00 00 00                             ...@...
-Q
```

Starting with the address reported in the ES:BX registers, the third, fourth, and fifth bytes listed after the (D)ump command are the model byte, sub-model byte, and revision number, respectively. In this case they are F8, 0B, and 00.

Table 4.52 is a relatively complete compilation of IBM BIOS ID information. Some systems have had BIOS changes during their life span. One piece of information this table provides is the total number of ST-506 drive types each BIOS supports. These types often are used when installing ST-506 or IDE hard disk drives. If the BIOS of your system is included in table 4.53, you can look up the IBM BIOS Hard Drive Table in this appendix and establish the exact drive types supported by your system.

Table 4.52 IBM ROM BIOS Model/Submodel/Revisions

System drive description	CPU	Clock speed	Bus type/ width	ROM BIOS date	ID byte	Sub-model byte	Rev	ST506 types
PC	8088	4.77 MHz	ISA/8	04/24/81	FF	—	—	—
PC	8088	4.77 MHz	ISA/8	10/19/81	FF	—	—	—
PC	8088	4.77 MHz	ISA/8	10/27/82	FF	—	—	—
PC-XT	8088	4.77 MHz	ISA/8	11/08/82	FE	—	—	—
PC-XT	8088	4.77 MHz	ISA/8	01/10/86	FB	00	01	—
PC-XT	8088	4.77 MHz	ISA/8	05/09/86	FB	00	02	—
PC*jr*	8088	4.77 MHz	ISA/8	06/01/83	FD	—	—	—
PC Convertible	80C88	4.77 MHz	ISA/8	09/13/85	F9	00	00	—
PS/2 25	8086	8 MHz	ISA/8	06/26/87	FA	01	00	26
PS/2 30	8086	8 MHz	ISA/8	09/02/86	FA	00	00	26
PS/2 30	8086	8 MHz	ISA/8	12/12/86	FA	00	01	26
PS/2 30	8086	8 MHz	ISA/8	02/05/87	FA	00	02	26
PC-AT	286	6 MHz	ISA/16	01/10/84	FC	—	—	15
PC-AT	286	6 MHz	ISA/16	06/10/85	FC	00	01	23
PC-AT	286	8 MHz	ISA/16	11/15/85	FC	01	00	23
PC-XT 286	286	6 MHz	ISA/16	04/21/86	FC	02	00	24
PS/1	286	10 MHz	ISA/16	12/01/89	FC	0B	00	44
PS/2 25 286	286	10 MHz	ISA/16	06/28/89	FC	09	02	37
PS/2 30 286	286	10 MHz	ISA/16	08/25/88	FC	09	00	37
PS/2 30 286	286	10 MHz	ISA/16	06/28/89	FC	09	02	37
PS/2 35 SX	386SX	20 MHz	ISA/16	03/15/91	F8	19	05	37
PS/2 35 SX	386SX	20 MHz	ISA/16	04/04/91	F8	19	06	37
PS/2 40 SX	386SX	20 MHz	ISA/16	03/15/91	F8	19	05	37
PS/2 40 SX	386SX	20 MHz	ISA/16	04/04/91	F8	19	06	37
PS/2 L40 SX	386SX	20 MHz	ISA/16	02/27/91	F8	23	02	37
PS/2 50	286	10 MHz	MCA/16	02/13/87	FC	04	00	32
PS/2 50	286	10 MHz	MCA/16	05/09/87	FC	04	01	32
PS/2 50Z	286	10 MHz	MCA/16	01/28/88	FC	04	02	33
PS/2 50Z	286	10 MHz	MCA/16	04/18/88	FC	04	03	33
PS/2 55 SX	386SX	16 MHz	MCA/16	11/02/88	F8	0C	00	33
PS/2 57 SX	386SX	20 MHz	MCA/16	07/03/91	F8	26	02	None
PS/2 60	286	10 MHz	MCA/16	02/13/87	FC	05	00	32
PS/2 65 SX	386SX	16 MHz	MCA/16	02/08/90	F8	1C	00	33
PS/2 70 386	386DX	16 MHz	MCA/32	01/29/88	F8	09	00	33

(continues)

Table 4.52 Continued

System drive description	CPU	Clock speed	Bus type/ width	ROM BIOS date	ID byte	Sub-model byte	Rev	ST506 types
PS/2 70 386	386DX	16 MHz	MCA/32	04/11/88	F8	09	02	33
PS/2 70 386	386DX	16 MHz	MCA/32	12/15/89	F8	09	04	33
PS/2 70 386	386DX	20 MHz	MCA/32	01/29/88	F8	04	00	33
PS/2 70 386	386DX	20 MHz	MCA/32	04/11/88	F8	04	02	33
PS/2 70 386	386DX	20 MHz	MCA/32	12/15/89	F8	04	04	33
PS/2 70 386	386DX	25 MHz	MCA/32	06/08/88	F8	0D	00	33
PS/2 70 386	386DX	25 MHz	MCA/32	02/20/89	F8	0D	01	33
PS/2 70 486	486DX	25 MHz	MCA/32	12/01/89	F8	0D	?	?
PS/2 70 486	486DX	25 MHz	MCA/32	09/29/89	F8	1B	00	?
PS/2 P70 386	386DX	16 MHz	MCA/32	?	F8	50	00	?
PS/2 P70 386	386DX	20 MHz	MCA/32	01/18/89	F8	0B	00	33
PS/2 P75 486	486DX	33 MHz	MCA/32	10/05/90	F8	52	00	33
PS/2 80 386	386DX	16 MHz	MCA/32	03/30/87	F8	00	00	32
PS/2 80 386	386DX	20 MHz	MCA/32	10/07/87	F8	01	00	32
PS/2 80 386	386DX	25 MHz	MCA/32	11/21/89	F8	80	01	?
PS/2 90 XP 486	486SX	20 MHz	MCA/32	?	F8	2D	00	?
PS/2 90 XP 486	487SX	20 MHz	MCA/32	?	F8	2F	00	?
PS/2 90 XP 486	486DX	25 MHz	MCA/32	?	F8	11	00	?
PS/2 90 XP 486	486DX	33 MHz	MCA/32	?	F8	13	00	?
PS/2 90 XP 486	486DX	50 MHz	MCA/32	?	F8	2B	00	?
PS/2 95 XP 486	486SX	20 MHz	MCA/32	?	F8	2C	00	?
PS/2 95 XP 486	487SX	20 MHz	MCA/32	?	F8	2E	00	?
PS/2 95 XP 486	486DX	25 MHz	MCA/32	?	F8	14	00	?
PS/2 95 XP 486	486DX	33 MHz	MCA/32	?	F8	16	00	?
PS/2 95 XP 486	486DX	50 MHz	MCA/32	?	F8	2A	00	?

The ID byte, submodel byte, and revision numbers are in hexadecimal.
— = This feature is not supported.
None = Only SCSI drives are supported.
?=No information available

Summary of IBM Hard Disk Drives

The tables in this section are a complete reference to all of the hard disk drives supplied by IBM in any XT, AT, or PS/2 system. This reference can be useful in determining which types of drives came with each system, and upgrades are possible.

You usually can easily install an upgraded drive of the same interface type in a given system. If I have a PS/2 Model 50Z that came with a 30M MCA IDE hard drive, for example, I easily can upgrade that system to any of the other MCA IDE drives that were available, such as the 120M or 160M units. Because the drives use the exact same interface, it would be a simple plug-in upgrade. Using this information, you can more easily "recycle" hard drives from systems that have since received upgrades.

Here are the standard and optional hard drives installed by IBM in its systems, grouped by interface

Table 4.53 IBM-Installed ST-506/412 Hard Drives Used in the XT, AT, and PS/2 Model 25

Drive form factor	5 1/4	5 1/4	5 1/4	5 1/4	3 1/2
Capacity	10MB	20MB	20MB	30MB	20MB
Physical/logical interface	ST506	ST506	ST506	ST506	ST506
Average access rate (ms)	85	65	40	40	38
Read-ahead cache (K)	—	—	—	—	—
Encoding scheme	MFM	MFM	MFM	MFM	RLL
BIOS drive type number	1	2	2	2	36
Cylinders	306	615	615	733	402
Heads	4	4	4	5	4
Sectors/track	17	17	17	17	26
Rotational speed (RPM)	3600	3600	3600	3600	3600
Standard interleave factor	6:1	3:1	3:1	3:1	3:1
Data transfer rate (K/second)	85	170	170	170	260
Automatic head parking	No	No	Yes	Yes	Yes

Table 4.54 IBM-Installed ST-506/412 Hard Drives Used in the XT, AT, and PS/2 Models 50, 60, and 80

Drive form factor	3 1/2	5 1/4	5 1/4
Capacity	20MB	44MB	44MB
Physical/logical interface	ST506	ST506	ST506
Average access rate (ms)	80	40	40
Read-ahead cache (K)	—	—	—
Encoding scheme	MFM	MFM	MFM
BIOS drive type number	30	31	32
Cylinders	611	732	1023
Heads	4	7	5
Sectors/track	17	17	17
Rotational speed (RPM)	3600	3600	3600
Standard interleave factor	1:1	1:1	1:1
Data transfer rate (K/second)	510	510	510
Automatic head parking	No	Yes	Yes

II

Compatible Systems

Table 4.55 IBM-Installed XT IDE Drives Used in the PS/2 Models 25, 30, 25 286 and 30 286

Drive form factor	3 1/2	3 1/2	3 1/2	3 1/2	3 1/2
Capacity	20MB	20MB	30MB	30MB	45MB
Physical interface	IDE	IDE	IDE	IDE	IDE
Logical interface	XT	XT	XT	XT	XT
Average access rate (ms)	80	27	27	19	32
Read-ahead cache (K)	—	—	—	—	—
Encoding scheme	MFM	RLL	RLL	RLL	RLL
BIOS drive type number	26	34	33	35	37
Cylinders	612	775	614	921	580
Heads	4	2	4	2	6
Sectors/track	17	27	25	33	26
Rotational speed (RPM)	3600	3600	3600	3600	3600
Standard interleave factor	2:1	3:1	3:1	4:1	3:1
Data transfer rate (K/second)	255	270	250	248	260
Automatic head parking	No	No	No	Yes	Yes

Table 4.56 IBM-Installed ATA IDE Drives Used in the PS/2 Models 35, 40, and L40

Drive form factor	2 1/2	3 1/2	3 1/2
Capacity	60MB	40MB	80MB
Physical interface	IDE	IDE	IDE
Logical interface	ATA	ATA	ATA
Average access rate (ms)	19	17	17
Read-ahead cache (K)	—	32K	32K
Encoding scheme	RLL	RLL	RLL
BIOS drive type number	—	—	—
Cylinders	822	1038	1021
Heads	4	2	4
Sectors/track	38	39	39
Rotational speed (RPM)	3600	3600	3600
Standard interleave factor	1:1	1:1	1:1
Data transfer rate (K/second)	1140	1170	1170
Automatic head parking	Yes	Yes	Yes

Table 4.57 IBM-Installed MCA IDE Drives Used in the PS/2 Models 50Z, 55, 70 386, and P70 386

Drive form factor	3 1/2	3 1/2	3 1/2	3 1/2	3 1/2	3 1/2	3 1/2	3 1/2
Capacity	30MB	30MB	30MB	40MB	60MB	80MB	120MB	160MB
Physical interface	IDE	IDE	IDE	IDE	IDE	IDE	IDE	IDE
Logical interface	ST506	ST506	ESDI	ESDI	ESDI	ESDI	ESDI	ESDI
Average access rate (ms)	39	27	19	17	27	17	23	16
Read-ahead cache (K)	—	—	—	32K	—	32K	—	32K
Encoding scheme	RLL	RLL	RLL	RLL	RLL	RLL	RLL	RLL
BIOS drive type number	33	33	—	—	—	—	—	—
Cylinders	614	614	920	1038	762	1021	920	1021
Heads	4	4	2	2	6	4	8	8
Sectors/track	25	25	32	39	26	39	32	39
Rotational speed (RPM)	3600	3600	3600	3600	3600	3600	3600	3600
Standard interleave factor	1:1	1:1	1:1	1:1	1:1	1:1	1:1	1:1
Data transfer rate (K/second)	750	750	960	1170	780	1170	960	1170
Automatic head parking	No	No	Yes	Yes	Yes	Yes	Yes	Yes

Table 4.58 IBM-Installed ESDI Drives Used in the PS/2 Models 60 and 80

Drive form factor	5 1/4	5 1/4	5 1/4
Capacity	70MB	115MB	314MB
Physical/logical interface	ESDI	ESDI	ESDI
Average access rate (ms)	30	28	23
Read-ahead cache (K)	—	—	—
Encoding scheme	RLL	RLL	RLL
BIOS drive type number	—	—	—
Cylinders	583	915	1225
Heads	7	7	15
Sectors/track	36	36	34
Rotational speed (RPM)	3600	3600	3283
Standard interleave factor	1:1	1:1	1:1
Data transfer rate (K/second)	1080	1080	930
Automatic head parking	Yes	Yes	Yes

Compatible Systems

Table 4.59 IBM-Installed SCSI Drives Used in the PS/2 Models 56, 57, 65, P75, 80, 90, and 95

Drive form factor	3 1/2	3 1/2	3 1/2	3 1/2	3 1/2	3 1/2
Capacity	60MB	80MB	120MB	160MB	320MB	400MB
Physical/logical interface	SCSI	SCSI	SCSI	SCSI	SCSI	SCSI
Average access rate (ms)	23	17	23	16	12.5	11.5
Read-ahead cache (K)	32K	32K	32K	32K	64K	128K
SCSI transfer mode	Async	Async	Async	Async	Sync	Sync
Encoding scheme	RLL	RLL	RLL	RLL	RLL	RLL
BIOS drive type number	—	—	—	—	—	—
Cylinders	920	1021	920	1021	949	1201
Heads	4	4	8	8	14	14
Sectors/track	32	39	32	39	48	48
Rotational speed (RPM)	3600	3600	3600	3600	4318	4318
Standard interleave factor	1:1	1:1	1:1	1:1	1:1	1:1
Data transfer rate (K/second)	960	1170	960	1170	1727	1727
Automatic head parking	Yes	Yes	Yes	Yes	Yes	Yes

Table 4.60 Standard PS/2 Accessories

Description	Part number	Price	Notes
PS/2 mouse	6450350	$101	2-button mouse
Trackpoint	1397040	95	Mouse/trackball
Dual serial adapter/A	6451013	231	For 50-95, NS16550, 9-pin plug
Serial/parallel adapter	6450215	161	25-40(not L40), NS16450, 9-pin
Floor stand	95F5606	45	Vertical mount for 35 LS/SX

Table 4.61 PS/2 Processor/Coprocessor Upgrades

Description	P/N	Price	Notes
16MHz 387SX Math Coprocessor	27F4676	84	For Model 55, 65
25MHz 486DX Power Platform	6450876	1,900.	70-Axx, trade in 386DX-25
25MHz 487SX Chip Upgrade	6451243	840.	90/95, CPU only
25MHz 486SX Processor Complex	6450759	665.	90/95, trade in 486SX-20
33MHz 486DX Processor Complex	6451094	985.	90/95, trade in 486SX-20
33MHz 486DX Processor Complex	6451094	935.	90/95, trade in 486SX-25
33MHz 486DX Processor Complex	6451094	935.	90/95, trade in 486DX-25
50MHz 486DX Processor Complex	6450757	3,255.	90/95, trade in 486SX-20
50MHz 486DX Processor Complex	6450757	3,200.	90/95, trade in 486SX-25
50MHz 486DX Processor Complex	6450757	3,200.	90/95, trade in 486DX-25
50MHz 486DX Processor Complex	6450757	2,800.	90/95, trade in 486DX-33

Description	P/N	Price	Notes
50MHz 486DX2 CPU only	32G3374	665.	90/95, CPU only
50MHz 486DX2 Proc. Complex	32G3491	1,335.	90/95, trade in 486SX-20
50MHz 486DX2 Proc. Complex	32G3491	935.	90/95, trade in 486DX-33
50MHz 486DX Enhanced Complex	6451269	4,880.	90/95, Trade in 486SX-20
50MHz 486DX Enhanced Complex	6451269	4,825.	90/95, Trade in 486SX-25
50MHz 486DX Enhanced Complex	6451269	4,825.	90/95, Trade in 486DX-25
50MHz 486DX Enhanced Complex	6451269	4,425.	90/95, Trade in 486DX-33
50MHz 486DX Enhanced Complex	6451269	2,295.	90/95, Trade in 486DX-50
50MHz 486DX Enhanced Complex	6451269	3,825.	90/95, Trade in 486DX2-50
50MHz 486DX Enhanced Complex	6451269	3,495.	90/95, Trade in 486DX2-66
66MHz 486DX2 CPU only	32G3690	899.	90/95, CPU only
66MHz 486DX2 Proc. Complex	32G3383	2,055.	90/95, trade in 486SX-20
66MHz 486DX2 Proc. Complex	32G3383	2,000.	90/95, trade in 486SX-25
66MHz 486DX2 Proc. Complex	32G3383	2,000.	90/95, trade in 486DX-25
66MHz 486DX2 Proc. Complex	32G3383	1,600.	90/95, trade in 486DX-33
66MHz 486DX2 Proc. Complex	32G3383	1,000.	90/95, trade in 486DX2-50
Processor Complex 256K Cache	6451095	1,595.	External Cache for 486DX

Table 4.62 PS/2 Memory Modules and Adapters

Description	Part number	Price	Notes
ISA 8-bit memory adapters			
Expanded memory adapter (XMA)	2685193	$1,395	2M RAM, LPT port, XT/AT/30
ISA bus 16-bit memory adapters			
0-12M multifunction adapter	30F5364	495	COM/LPT port, 30 286
All ChargeCard	34F2863	495	Memory manager for 25/30 286
3M expanded memory adapter	34F2864	1,830	ChargeCard, 0-12M card, 3M RAM
4M expanded memory kit	34F2866	1,285	ChargeCard, 4M system-board RAM
MCA bus 16-bit memory adapters			
1-8M 80286 memory optional/85ns	6450685	410	1M, EMS 4.0 for 50/55/60/65
2-8M 80286 memory optional/85ns	6450609	330	2M, EMS 4.0 for 50/55/60/65
MCA bus 32-bit adapters			
2-14M enhanced adapter/85ns	87F9856	480	2M, for 70/P70/80
4-14M enhanced adapter/85ns	87F9860	600	4M, for 70/P70/80

(continues)

II

Compatible Systems

Table 4.62 Continued

Description	Part number	Price	Notes
Memory module kits (SIMMs)			
25 system board memory/120ns	78X8955	40	128K kit (6 chips) for 25
512K memory module kit/120ns	30F5348	140	2-256K SIMMs for 30F5364/ 1497259, 25/30 286 system board
2M memory module kit/120ns	30F5360	250	2-1M SIMMs for 30F5364/ 1497259, 34F2866 25/30 286 system board
1M memory module kit/85ns	6450603	80	1M SIMM for 6450605/ 6450609, 6450685/ 34F3077/ 34F3011, 50Z/55/65/70 386 (Not Axx/Bxx)/P70 386
2M memory module kit/85ns	6450604	150	2M SIMM for 6450605/ 6450609, 6450685/ 34F3077/ 34F3011, 50Z/55/65/ 70 (Not Axx/Bxx)/P70 386
4M memory module kit/85ns	87F9977	290	4M SIMM for 35/40/55/65 34F3011/34F3077
2M memory module kit/80ns	6450608	150	2M SIMM for 35/40/70 -Axx/Bxx
8M memory module kit/80ns	6450129	590	8M SIMM for 35/40
2M memory module kit/70ns	6450902	160	2M SIMM for 57/90/95
4M memory module kit/70ns	6450128	295	4M SIMM for 57/P75/90/95
8M memory module kit/70ns	6450130	695	8M SIMM for 35/40/57/P75 /90/95
2M memory module kit/80ns	79F0999	215	2M CMOS SIMM for L40 (keyed)
4M memory module kit/80ns	79F1000	400	4M CMOS SIMM for L40 (keyed)
8M memory module kit/80ns	79F1001	785	8M CMOS SIMM for L40 (keyed)
1M system board kit/80ns	6450375	528	1M card for 80-041
2M system board kit/80ns	6450379	150	2M card for 80 (except Axx)
4M system board kit/80ns	6451060	280	4M card for 80-A21/A31

Table 4.63 PS/2 Floppy Drives, Adapters, and Cables

Description	Part number	Price	Notes
5 1/4-inch floppy drives			
5 1/4-inch external 360K drive	4869001	$489	For all PS/2s
5 1/4-inch external 1.2M drive	4869002	509	For 50-95, requires 6451007
5 1/4-inch internal 1.2M drive	6451006	365	For 60/65/80
5 1/4-inch internal 1.2M slim drive	6451066	310	For 35/40/57/90/95
3 1/2-inch floppy drives			
3 1/2-inch internal 720K drive	78X8956	180	For 25 S/N < 100,000
3 1/2-inch internal 720K 1/3-height drive	6451056	159	For 25 S/N > 100,000
3 1/2-inch internal 720K 1/3-height drive	6451027	159	For 30-001
3 1/2-inch internal 1.44M 1/3-height drive	6451063	263	For 25-006/G06
3 1/2-inch internal 1.44M drive	6450353	263	For 30-E01/50-80, not 55/P70 386
3 1/2-inch internal 1.44M slim drive	6451130	263	35/40/57, not L40, media-sense
3 1/2-inch internal 1.44M 1/3-height drive	6451072	263	50-95, not 55/P70/30-E01
3 1/2-inch internal 2.88M slim drive	6451106	325	35/40/57, not L40, media-sense
Floppy disk drive adapters			
5 1/4-inch external drive adapter	6450244	72	360K for 25-40, not L40
5 1/4-inch external drive adapter/A	6450245	72	360K for 50-80, not 55/P70 386
5 1/4-inch floppy disk drive adapter/A	6451007	216	For 1.2M/360K in 50-95
Cables and miscellaneous			
5 1/4-inch external 360K cable	6451033	21	For 30-001/021 external drive
5 1/4-inch external 360K cable	27F4245	18	For 30-Exx external drive
5 1/4-inch external drive adapter cable	6451124	40	For 35/40 and 4869001
External storage device cable	23F2716	101	P70 360K,P75 360K/1.2M
3 1/2-inch internal drive kit	6451037	30	Cable/Bezel for 6451353
3 1/2-inch internal 1/3-height drive kit	6451034	25	Cable/Bezel for 6451072
3 1/2-inch internal 1/3-height drive kit B	6451035	30	For 6451026 in 55 LS
Drive upgrade kit for 35 LS	6451127	45	For 6451130/6451106/6451066
IBM preformatted floppy disks			
5 1/4-inch 10 360K disks	6023450	44	Cardboard slipcase
5 1/4-inch 10 360K disks with case	6069769	45	Plastic library case/stand
5 1/4-inch 10 1.2M disks	6109660	54	Cardboard slipcase
5 1/4-inch 10 1.2M disks with case	6109661	55	Plastic library case/stand
3 1/2-inch 10 720K disks with case	6404088	33	Plastic library case/stand

(continues)

II

Compatible Systems

Table 4.63 PS/2 Continued

Description	Part number	Price	Notes
IBM performatted floppy disks			
3 1/2-inch 10 1.44M disks with case	6404083	49.50	Plastic library case/stand
3 1/2-inch 10 2.88M disks with case	72X6111	99	Plastic library case/stand

Table 4.64 PS/2 Hard Disks, Adapters and Cables

Description	Part number	Price	Notes
IDE hard disk drives			
20M 3 1/2-inch 80ms IDE drive	78X8958	$ 787	For 25
20M 3 1/2-inch 27ms IDE drive	6451075	787	For 25-xx6, Req 6451071
30M 3 1/2-inch 19ms IDE drive	6451076	695	For 25-xx6, Req 6451071
40M 3 1/2-inch 17ms IDE drive	6451047	290	For 55 LS
40M 3 1/2-inch 17ms IDE drive	6451073	290	For 35/40
80M 3 1/2-inch 17ms IDE drive	6451043	425	For 55 LS
80M 3 1/2-inch 17ms IDE drive	6451074	340	For 35/40
SCSI hard disk drives			
60M 3 1/2-inch 23ms, 32K cache	6451049	1,000	Async, 1.25M/sec Xfer rate
80M 3 1/2-inch 17ms, 32K cache	6451045	340	Async, 1.25M/sec Xfer rate
120M 3 1/2-inch 23ms, 32K cache	6451050	1,670	Async, 1.5M/sec Xfer rate
160M 3 1/2-inch 16ms, 32K cache	6451046	580	Async, 1.5M/sec Xfer rate
320M 3 1/2-inch 12.5ms, 64K cache	6451234	1,625	Sync, 2.0M/sec Xfer rate
400M 3 1/2-inch 11.5ms, 128K cache	6451235	1,835	Sync, 2.0M/sec Xfer rate
IG 3 1/2-inch 11ms, 256K cache	0451052	5,000	Sync, 2.0M/sec Xfer rate
SCSI host adapter			
SCSI Adapter/A	6451109	375	16-bit Bus Master
SCSI Adapter/A with 512K cache	6451133	750	32/16-bit Bus Master
SCSI external terminator	6451039	110	For Adapter with Cache
Cables and miscellaneous			
Fixed Disk Drive Kit A	6451071	65	Installation kit for 25-xx6
Fixed Disk Upgrade Kit/35	6451128	15	For 6451073/6451074 in 35 LS
SCSI Installation Kit A	6451053	90	For 3 1/2-inch drive in 60/65/80
Fixed Disk Drive Kit D	6451120	20	For 60/120M drives in 90/95
SCSI card to option cable	6451139	220	Includes terminator, replaces 6451041
SCSI option to option cable	6451042	90	Connect external options

Description	Part number	Price	Notes
CD-ROM drives			
Internal 600M CD-ROM drive	6451113	1,250	Requires SCSI adapter
External 600M CD-ROM drive	3510001	1,550	Requires SCSI adapter
CD-ROM installation kit/A	6450847	35	Install in 5 1/4-inch bay
3 1/2-inch 128M rewritable drive	6450162	1,795	Requires SCSI adapter
Optical drive kit A	6451126	29	For 6450162 in 60/80 (non-SCSI)
3 1/2-inch rewritable cartridge	38F8645	70	128M cartridge for 6450162
3 1/2-inch rewritable cartridge	38F8646	315	5-128M cartridges for 6450162
8mm tape backup drives and accessories			
2.3G internal SCSI drive	6451121	6,500	For 95/3511, requires SYTOS
2.3G external SCSI drive	6451121	6,915	Requires SCSI adapter and SYTOS
SCSI cable for external drive	31F4187	315	Connects tape drive to system
SCSI device-to-device cable	31F4186	78	Chains tape to other devices
8mm data cartridge	21F8595	29.25	Stores 2.3 gigabytes
8mm cleaning cartridge	21F8593	40	For cleaning heads
SYTOS plus V1.3 for DOS	04G3375	150	Data compression
SYTOS plus V1.3 for OS/2 PM	04G3374	195	Data compression, FAT/HPFS
SCSI expansion units			
3510 external SCSI storage unit	35100V0	360	1 half-height, 3 1/2-inch, 5 1/4-inch bay
3511 external SCSI storage unit	3511003	3,845	7 bays, 3 1/2/5 1/4-inch, 320M drive

Table 4.65 PS/2 Video Displays and Adapters

Description	Part number	Price	Notes
Analog displays			
8504 12-inch VGA Mono Display	8504001	$ 245	640×480
8507 19-inch XGA Mono Display	8507001	600	1024×768
8604 16-inch XGA Mono Display	8604001	850	1024×768
PS/1 Color Display Upgrade	1057108	699	Upgrade for mono systems
8512 14-inch Color Display	8512001	365	640×480, .41mm stripe
8513 12-inch VGA Color Display	8513001	665	640×480, .28mm dot, stand
8514 16-inch XGA Color Display	8514001	1,035	1024×768, .31mm dot, stand
8515 14-inch XGA Color Display	8515021	635	1024×768, .28mm dot, stand

II

Compatible Systems

(continues)

Table 4.65 Continued

Description	Part number	Price	Notes
Analog displays			
8518 14-inch VGA Color Display	8518001	535	640×480, .28mm dot, stand
8516 14-inch XGA Touch Screen	8516001	1,200	1024×768, .28mm dot, stand
Analog display adapters			
XGA Adapter/A	75X5887	210	1024×768, For 55-95 (Not 60/P70)
Video Memory Expansion Option	75X5889	60	512K Video RAM for XGA
8514/A Display Adapter	1887972	980	1024×768×16, for 50-80 (Not P70)
8514/A Memory Expansion Kit	1887989	283	1024×768×256 colors
Miscellaneous display accessories			
Display Stand for 8512	1501215	36	Tilt-swivel stand
TouchSelect for 12-inch displays	91F7951	670	Adds Touch screen to 8513
Privacy Filter for 8512	1053405	154	Prevents side view of display
Privacy Filter for 8513	1053401	154	Prevents side view of display
Privacy Filter for 8514	1053402	154	Prevents side view of display
Privacy Filter for 8515	1053403	154	Prevents side view of display

Table 4.66 PS/2 Network Adapters and Accessories

Description	Part number	Price	Notes
ISA bus Token Ring Network (TRN) adapters			
TRN Adapter II	25F9858	395	4Mbps for 25-40 (not L40)
TRN 16/4 Adapter	25F7367	895	16/4Mbps for 25-40 (not L40)
TRN 16/4 Trace & Performance	74F5121	1,220	16/4Mbps for 25-40 (not L40)
MCA bus Token Ring Network (TRN) adapters			
TRN Adapter/A (full-length)	69X8138	395	4Mbps, for 50-95
TRN Adapter/A (half-length)	39F9598	448	4Mbps for P70/75 (and 50-95)
TRN 16/4 Adapter/A	16F1133	895	16/4Mbps for 50-95
TRN 16/4 Adapter/A (half)	74F9410	895	16/4Mbps, 50-95, 80 percent faster
TRN 16/4 Trace & Perf./A	74F5130	1,220	16/4Mbps for 50-95
TRN 16/4 Busmaster Server/A	74F4140	1,030	16/4Mbps for 50-95 servers only

Description	Part number	Price	Notes
MCA bus EtherNet network adapters			
PS/2 EtherNet Adapter/A	6451091	575	10Mbps for 50-95, including boot ROM
Miscellaneous network adapter accessories			
TRN adapter cable	6339098	36	Connect card to LAN
TRN L-shaped connector cable	79F3229	50	For 74F9410 and P70/75
Miscellaneous network adapter accessories			
TRN 8230 4Mbps media filter	53F5551	55	For unshielded twisted pair
TRN Adapter II boot ROM	83X7839	99	EPROM for 25F9858
TRN Adapter/A boot ROM	83X8881	96	EPROM for 69X8138/ 39F9598
TRN 16/4 Adapter/A boot ROM	25X8887	99	EPROM for 25F7367/ 16F1133

Chapter Summary

This chapter has presented information about the PS/2 line of systems from IBM, including information about all the various PS/2 models and submodels, from low-end to high-end systems. The low-end PS/2 systems—the PS/2 Models 25, 30, PS/1, 25 286, 30 286, 35 SX, 40 SX, and L40 SX—are based closely on the original PC line and include the standard ISA-type of expansion slots. The higher-end PS/2 Models 50, 50Z, 55 SX, 57 SX, 60, 65 SX, 70 386, P70 386, P75, 80, 90, 95, and their respective submodels use the newer MCA slot design, which is dramatically different from the original ISA bus.

Chapter 5 examines IBM-compatible systems, including details on the available types of compatible systems and some of the criteria you might use to justify purchasing a particular IBM-compatible system over another IBM-compatible or an IBM system.

II

Compatible Systems

Chapter 5

IBM-Compatible Computers

The open architecture of IBM systems has allowed a variety of companies to introduce systems that are functionally identical to IBM's own. These non-IBM systems often do more than just run the same software; many are hardware copies of IBM systems and are virtually identical. Many exceed what IBM's own systems can do and offer higher performance, more features, or other benefits that the actual IBM systems lack. These non-IBM systems are usually called IBM compatibles or IBM clones. Because few systems actually duplicate IBM's own at the hardware level, the term *clone* is somewhat obsolete today. Most systems based on IBM designs are called *compatibles* because they are designed to work with the same basic software and peripheral components that IBM systems use. Although IBM does not control the PC marketplace as it once did, it still has the power to set new standards, and few companies can match IBM's engineering, design, or manufacturing capabilities. Today, however, a number of standards are being set by companies and organizations other than IBM. Even IBM has had to change to adapt to these standards, and make its systems compatible with everybody else's! Because of this development, many people have argued that the term "IBM compatible" is obsolete.

IBM has done its best to keep the rest of the PC marketplace on its toes. In some cases IBM introduced into the PC arena new standards that became technological hurdles for other manufacturers to leap. For example, the first major hurdle was IBM's Micro Channel Architecture. These MCA systems are much more difficult to copy than were the original ISA bus systems. Also, IBM is being stricter about what it allows as "cloning." Protecting massive amounts of development work and money poured into a new system is good business; and IBM is more rigidly enforcing its patents and license agreements with respect to MCA clones. Although every manufacturer that develops even an ISA or EISA system owes IBM licensing fees and royalties, IBM has been lax in enforcing payments, possibly fearing anti-trust actions. With Micro Channel, however, IBM seems to have increased its license enforcement.

Many people believe that anybody can make ISA or EISA systems free of charge, as though the designs are in the public domain; but, such is not the case. IBM holds in its portfolio many patents which ensure that anyone who develops an IBM-compatible

PC, no matter which bus it uses (even EISA), must license from IBM some of the technology for the system. The patents IBM holds for newer systems virtually guarantee that no compatible will be developed without such licensing. Several MCA-based compatibles exist, though not many, compared to the number of ISA or EISA systems. Tandy, NCR, Reply, Wang, and others sell PS/2 compatible systems with Micro Channel bus slots, but they are a very small part of the market compared to the majority of ISA and EISA bus systems.

IBM has introduced other standards that compatibles will have to follow. Perhaps the most prominent standard is the newer XGA video standard. IBM has licensed the XGA chipset technology to INMOS, a company that now can sell the chips to anyone who wants to make an XGA clone adapter. In essence, IBM is helping cloners develop their own XGA boards: IBM will benefit if the new standard is widely supported. Other standards include the IBM SCSI host adapters, which have complete real mode and protected mode BIOS support, and the 2.88M floppy drives that IBM introduced in the PS/2 Model 57. IBM even has introduced a custom version of the Intel 386SX processor, the 386SLC, which has features from the 486 design, including a built-in cache. This version has been licensed back to Intel, perhaps for others to purchase.

An interesting development is IBM's own entry into the "IBM compatible" market. IBM mounted an attack on several fronts, including introducing several lines of systems that cost much less than the premier PS/2 line. These new lines are as follows:

- PS/1
- PS/Valuepoint
- Ambra

The PS/1 is IBM's low-cost line sold through retail outlets and superstores. The PS/Valuepoint systems are virtually identical to the PS/1 systems, except that they offer greater expansion capabilities, higher performance versions, longer warranties, and are ordered, serviced, and supported directly through IBM. The Ambra systems are a high performance line designed to be sold directly through mail order to compete with other high-end mail order systems.

Another way that IBM is entering the compatible business is through motherboard and other component manufacturing. IBM recently became one of the largest clone motherboard makers in the world, having signed deals worth more than $350 million with several IBM compatible system manufacturers. IBM will be manufacturing and selling a variety of motherboards, disk drives, adapter cards, memory modules, and other components at competitive prices. This development means that some day you might purchase a vendor's IBM compatible system and find that it has many IBM-made components inside it! All of this is a part of the new IBM strategy to become more competitive in today's market.

This chapter examines compatibles from several points of view. The primary view is that of the system installer and repair person. Such a person has strict criteria for what makes a "good" compatible system. For a system even to be in the running, for example, it must come with proper and adequate documentation. A lack of documentation is the nemesis of any installer or repair person, and a system without documentation is not acceptable. From this same point of view, several other items are presented in this chapter for your consideration when you shop for a compatible system. What you learn here can and should be applied to the selection of any IBM or compatible system. These guidelines will direct you to a system that will be compatible, serviceable, and upgradeable for many years.

Examining Types of Compatibles

Although there are many brands, makes, and models of IBM and IBM-compatible systems, all systems can be separated into several types or categories. Any IBM or compatible system can be classified as one of two primary system types:

- PC XT compatible
- AT compatible

Any system that runs IBM software can be put in one of these categories. A COMPAQ Deskpro 486/66, for example, is really just another AT compatible—although, compared to the original IBM AT, the COMPAQ Deskpro 486/66 offers a great deal more performance. Even IBM's own systems can be classified as compatibles; the PS/2 Model 77, for example, is also compatible with the original AT, but again offers much more performance than the original AT. The XT class of system is virtually extinct, at least from a new system point of view. That is, there are few vendors selling systems that conform to the original PC or XT standards.

The distinction between the two types of systems comes primarily from the architectural differences in the microprocessors making up the systems. Intel processors have two basic modes of operation: real and protected. Systems that can run only in real mode are considered PC XT-compatible systems, and they are incapable of running the newer Windows and OS/2 operating systems. Systems that can run in protected mode will run Windows and OS/2 as well as DOS and are classified as AT-compatible systems.

AT compatibles that run the Micro Channel interface have different types of expansion adapters available, and are different from the viewpoint of the system installer, upgrader, or repair person. These systems are much easier to work on, have fewer components, are more reliable, and offer greater potential for performance. AT compatibles with 386 or greater processors have access to an additional mode, called *virtual 8086*, which allows multiple real-mode simulations not only to coexist in memory but also to process simultaneously in a true multitasking environment. These systems also offer an improved method for switching from real to protected mode, which Windows does frequently during operation. The 386- (or higher) based AT compatibles also offer improved memory-management capabilities that can be exploited by special memory-management software and operating systems.

Another, and totally different, method of categorizing systems is to separate clones from compatibles. A *clone* usually is defined as a system that is a virtual duplicate of one of IBM's systems: The system is the same physically and electronically, as well as being capable of running the same software as a given IBM system. For example, a clone of the IBM AT would use a motherboard that's electronically and physically compatible with the AT. The board has the same mounting-screw hole, standoff, slot connector, and keyboard connector locations as the IBM board. Such a board could be physically interchanged in a system with the IBM board, or vice versa. This capability would apply also to the power supply, disk drives, and perhaps even the chassis. Because of the wealth of physical replacement parts available to fit IBM systems, a clone of one of these systems will have access to the same wealth of parts. Clones, therefore, are easy to upgrade or repair at an extremely low cost.

A system that isn't a clone physically, but that will run the same software and even take the same plug-in cards as an IBM system, is defined as *compatible*. COMPAQ makes compatible systems that are not clones, for example. These systems use motherboards with completely different mounting hardware and connector locations than IBM, so physical interchangeability is impossible.

Some manufacturers go out of their way, in fact, to make their systems as physically incompatible as possible with any other system. Then replacement parts, repairs, and upgrades are virtually impossible to find—except, of course, from the original system manufacturer, at a significantly higher price than the equivalent part would cost to fit an IBM or clone system. For example, if the motherboard in your IBM AT (or AT Clone) dies, you can find any number of replacement boards to bolt to the AT chassis, with your choice of processors and clock speeds and at ridiculously low prices. If the motherboard dies in your COMPAQ Deskpro, you'll pay for a replacement available only from COMPAQ, and you have virtually no opportunity to select a board with a faster or better processor than the one that failed. In other words, upgrading one of these systems is almost out of the question.

With several million PS/2 systems sold, a market is developing for upgrades and replacement components for these systems as well. Although these systems will never be as popular as the AT-style systems, several companies are making parts for these systems.

No matter what the differences, there are certainly cases in which each system type is suitable for a particular need.

Learning the Levels of Compatibility

In developing a compatible computer, you can achieve a few basic levels of similarity to IBM systems. In order of increasing desirability, these are the levels of similarity:

- Operating-system level
- ROM BIOS level

- Hardware (register) level
  - Motherboard and CPU
  - Peripherals and I/O controllers
- Physical (dimensional) level

Compatibility at the Operating-System Level

For the most part, compatibles at only the first (operating system) level are the least desirable and have generally been shunned by the industry. The reason is that operating-system compatibles used licensed, highly customized versions of Microsoft's MS-DOS. These systems didn't run the IBM or standard Microsoft version of DOS. Today, these types of systems are but a fading memory, but this was a problem in the early to mid '80s. During that time, several systems had been developed that were compatible at only the operating-system level. A few examples were the DEC Rainbow 100, the Texas Instruments Professional, and the Tandy 2000. Compatibility at only the operating-system (OS) level definitely is not fashionable now, and most people would be well-advised to stay away from any of these older systems with this limitation.

Compatibility at the ROM BIOS Level

Most systems are compatible at the ROM level. The ROM BIOS interface in these systems appears, to software, to be exactly like the ROM BIOS of a particular IBM system. Generally, the same software that runs on a particular IBM system can run on this kind of system. The actual BIOS code differs from IBM's, but only in the area of the actual interface to the hardware.

This difference is necessary because compatibles operating at this level have hardware that differs from any particular IBM system. This feature generally doesn't cause problems unless you attempt to run actual BIOS code from an IBM system in this type of compatible. This situation rarely happens, though: Making a copy of IBM's ROM BIOS chips and placing them in the motherboard of a compatible system is not legal. The procedure wouldn't work anyway, unless that system truly was hardware compatible with the specific IBM system from which the ROM was copied. Systems that are compatible at this level usually run IBM DOS, unless the hardware is very different from the IBM standard. Software that runs on top of DOS remains unaffected unless, again, a special dependence on a different hardware feature exists.

A few systems could be considered compatible at the ROM BIOS level that are not actually hardware compatible, but they are few and far between. Perhaps one of the best examples is the Apple Macintosh systems. For some time, Apple engineers have been advertising their systems as "IBM Compatible." By "compatible," they mean that some software can be run on a Mac to allow it to emulate an IBM system. This emulation includes a compatible BIOS and DOS system, but of course the hardware remains distinctly different from any normal IBM compatible system. Using these software-based PC emulators, a Macintosh can actually run the majority of DOS-based software that runs on IBM compatible systems. But since the Mac is not hardware compatible, it will not run other operating systems like OS/2 or device-specific software that circumvents the BIOS and talks directly to the hardware.

Compatible Systems

With Windows and OS/2, compatibility at only this level is a problem. For example, when OS/2 is loaded it loads a copy of a ROM BIOS from disk. This copy is the *protected mode ROM BIOS*, or *Advanced BIOS (ABIOS)*. A system not truly hardware compatible won't run OS/2 or Windows because of direct access to the hardware.

Compatibility at the Hardware Level

To be a true hardware-level compatible, a system must match a particular IBM system at the basic motherboard hardware level. In other words, the system must use the same hardware interrupt request (IRQ) channels, direct memory access (DMA) channels, and I/O port addresses for the same purposes that IBM does, and the system must offer the same slot or bus interface—at the same clock rate—that IBM does. Most of today's systems offer this level of compatibility, which means that an adapter board that works in a particular IBM system unit will work also in a comparable unit of the compatible. ROM code should be much the same as IBM's; in some cases, you might be able to run IBM's own ROMs in a system such as this one.

Some differences in the hardware might make the system marginally compatible. The system and bus clock rate and the number of wait states inserted by the system during bus cycles, for example, can have a big effect on which peripherals work or don't work. Some systems offer customizable features such as bus speed and wait states. By changing these parameters, you may be able to increase the performance of the system compared to other compatibles, but some plug in boards may be affected. Resetting the motherboard bus to default speeds slows down the system but allows the boards in question to run without problems.

Most vendors who work with compatibles take a compatible approach, and make sure that important items like bus speed match the defined standards. Most systems today use a dual bus approach consisting of a traditional bus like ISA, EISA, or Micro Channel coupled with a processor direct Local Bus. The Local Bus can run at the full speed of the processor and can offer much higher performance than any of the standard busses. This approach allows standard adapters to function in the regular bus slots, and special high performance adapters and components to work on the processor direct local bus. Originally, these local bus boards were proprietary in design, but several standards (notably the Video Local or VL-Bus and Peripheral Connection Interface or PCI Bus) have evolved and allow for a variety of adapters to plug in.

Peripherals and I/O controllers are hardware-compatibility issues that usually are glossed over. Differences in these devices exist between the PC XT and AT types of systems. For example, in PC XT systems, IBM used a serial port (RS-232C) that incorporates a National Semiconductor 8250B Universal Asynchronous Receiver Transmitter (UART) device. In the AT, IBM used a newer chip by National Semiconductor: the 16450 UART. In many PS/2 systems, an NS 16550A chip is used. Mixing serial ports with these respective UARTs was never a problem under DOS, but under OS/2 you must have the 16450 or 16550 version in your AT. If you have the PC XT type of serial port with the 8250, serial communications of any kind either won't operate or will work unreliably under OS/2.

Similar problems exist with the hard disk controllers in AT systems. For the AT, IBM used a version of Western Digital 1002-WA2 or the later model 1003-WA2. These controllers have no on-board ROM BIOS and, instead, run from the BIOS interface built into the motherboard ROM. To successfully run OS/2 on your AT-compatible system, you must follow that standard. In other words, a hard disk controller with an on-board ROM BIOS that doesn't work in protected mode, or that isn't hardware-register-compatible with the Western Digital controllers, won't work for protected-mode environments such as OS/2 or Novell NetWare.

Finally, the graphics adapter can be a sensitive issue in a protected-mode environment. The reason is that every graphics adapter beyond the standard Color Graphics Adapter (CGA) has an on-board ROM BIOS interface. Because this on-board BIOS might not operate in protected mode, any protected-mode operating system then would load the correct drivers from disk to run the graphics board. Many users of some of the first EGA- and VGA-compatible cards found that their particular early-model EGA or—especially—early-model VGA adapters did not operate properly under Windows or OS/2. For standard types of adapters, such as serial ports, disk controllers, and graphics boards, the solution to this problem is to get boards that are truly hardware-register-compatible with the ones IBM has used, or be sure that the manufacturer provides the necessary Windows and OS/2 drivers. For other nonstandard types of peripherals that must work, such as tape drives or CD-ROM drives, you must get special drivers from the OEM of the particular unit.

Compatibility at the Physical (Dimensional) Level

The clone system is the final level of compatibility. Clone systems match the preceding levels of compatibility (operating system, ROM BIOS, and hardware), as well as the capability to interchange parts physically from IBM systems. As stated, this capability makes a system incredibly easy, as well as inexpensive, to maintain and upgrade. This level of compatibility ensures that the widest selection of upgrade components will be available.

Most users will want a compatible or clone that is at least truly hardware compatible and preferably physically compatible with one of IBM's systems. Having physical (usually called "form factor") compatibility means that you will be able to replace all of the major components in the system such as motherboards, power supplies, disk drives, and so forth, with readily available, "off-the-shelf" units. The cost of standard form factor components is also much less than nonstandard units because the market for them is bigger and more are sold. Having a form factor compatible system means that you will never go wanting for replacement parts or upgrades, even if the original manufacturer of the system is long gone.

Knowing What To Look For (Selection Criteria)

As a consultant, I often am asked to make a recommendation for a system purchase. Making these types of recommendations is one of the most frequent tasks a consultant performs. Many consultants charge a large fee for this advice. Unfortunately, most "consultants" don't have any rhyme or reason to their selections and instead base their choices solely on magazine reviews or, even worse, on some personal biases. To help eliminate this haphazard selection process, I have developed a checklist that will help you select a system. This list takes into consideration several important system aspects overlooked by most such checklists. The goal is to ensure that the selected system truly is compatible and has a long life of service and upgrades ahead.

Compatible-Selection Checklist

It helps to think like an engineer when you make your selection. Consider every aspect and detail of the systems in question. For example, you will want to consider all future uses and upgrades. Technical support at a professional (as opposed to a user) level is extremely important: What support will be provided? Is there documentation, and does it cover everything else?

You will also want to evaluate nonstandard parts and make sure that the OEM provides a spare-parts program that lets you purchase these parts when the system needs service. In addition, you should identify standard parts and their sources so that you can substitute parts where you want or need them, and establish avenues for purchase other than the OEM. It helps to identify the interfaces present at all connectors so that you can locate products that can plug into these connectors.

In short, a checklist is a good idea. Here is one for you to use in evaluating any IBM-compatible system. You might not have to meet every one of these criteria to consider a particular system, but if you miss more than a few of these checks, consider staying away from that system. The rest of this chapter discusses in detail the criteria in this checklist.

- What clock speed does the motherboard support (25 MHz, 33 MHz, and so on)? Is the clock speed switchable? Are all of the components and parts rated to run at the supported speeds?

- What bus does the motherboard support (ISA, EISA, MCA)? Are there any local bus slots? If so, what type (VL-Bus, PCI, proprietary)? How many total slots of each type are in the system, and how many are available in the standard configuration?

- Is the motherboard CPU upgradeable, if so to what level (DX2/Overdrive, Pentium Overdrive, full Pentium)? Is there a Zero Insertion Force (ZIF) socket for CPU upgrades? Does the system meet Intel cooling requirements for the possible CPU upgrades?

- Does the CPU have an internal (Level 1) cache? If so, how large is it? Does the motherboard have an external (Level 2) cache? If so, how large is it?

- What ROM BIOS does the motherboard use (AMI, Award, Phoenix, etc.)? Is the BIOS contained in an upgradable Flash ROM type chip?

- How much memory is included in the standard configuration? Is the memory in the form of SIMMs? If so, does the system use the more desirable 36-bit (72-pin) SIMMs? How much maximum memory will the system support?

- What other interfaces are present on the motherboard (Serial, Parallel, Video, Mouse, Floppy, IDE, SCSI, etc.)? Can they be disabled to allow for future expansion or repair via adapter cards?

- Is the power supply output ample enough for future expansion? What is the rated output? Are there spare power connectors available for disk drive upgrades?

- What types of floppy drives are supplied (1.44M or 2.88M 3 1/2-inch, 1.2M 5 1/4-inch)? Does the included floppy controller (and BIOS) support the newer ED 2.88M 3 1/2-inch drives? If both 3 1/2-inch and 5 1/4-inch drives are included, can you easily change or select which one is A or B?

- Does the system include a SCSI interface? If so, which OEM adapter is supplied (IBM, Future Domain, Adaptec, etc.)? Does it have support for DOS, OS/2 and Windows NT? What drivers are included?

- What type of hard disk is supplied (ATA-IDE, SCSI, ST-412, ESDI), and what is the capacity? How many drive bays are available for additional drives?

- Is a mouse included with the system? If so, what type (Motherboard, Serial, or Bus)?

- Is a Modem included with the system? If so, does it support V.32bis (14.4kbps) operation?

- What operating system is included (DOS, Windows, or OS/2) and what specific version is it?

- Are any diagnostics or utility software included?

- What applications software is bundled with the system? Is it installed on the hard disk only, or are diskettes included? Is complete documentation included? Is each application a full blown version, or are they limited in any way?

- What documentation is included with the system? Is a Technical Reference manual and/or Service manual available? If the system is assembled from other manufacturers components, is the OEM documentation for each of these components included?

- Is the system FCC approved, and if so does it meet the tougher class B standards?

- Are any proprietary or unique spare parts available directly from the manufacturer?

Where questions require a *yes* or *no* answer, *yes* is the desirable answer. Other questions in the list will give you a good idea of the features and capabilities of the system. If you can answer *yes* to all the appropriate questions, the system definitely is worth purchasing. Some systems, because of unique constraints, might not pass every check in the list. You must weigh any drawbacks in your consideration of such a system.

If you are buying a generic compatible system sold by an assembler rather than a manufacturer, be sure that the technical documentation is adequate. If the documentation is not adequate, then you will be at the mercy of the vendor when it comes to technical support. If possible, try to obtain technical support from the component (such as motherboard) manufacturers rather than the vendor or assembler.

Notice that these selection criteria will fully qualify many systems on the market. Most of the time you should purchase systems from better-known bigger-name companies. These systems might cost a little more than others that you have never heard of, but there is some safety in the more well-known brands. With well-known brands, the more systems sold the more likely problems will have been discovered by others and solved long before you get your system. Also, if service or support is needed, the larger vendors are more likely to be around in the long run.

Available Documentation

As mentioned earlier, extensive documentation is an important factor to consider when you're planning to buy a system. This section examines four forms of documentation: system documentation, technical-reference manuals, hardware-maintenance and service manuals, and advanced diagnostics software.

System Documentation. One of the most important things you want with your system is good documentation. Without it, repairing, upgrading, or troubleshooting will be nearly impossible. Many people are intimidated by the volume, technical nature, and cost of some of the documentation available for a system, but consider the purchase a necessary evil. This area separates the true manufacturers from the guy who slaps together motherboards and cases in a garage. Good documentation also keeps you from trying the two worst approaches when you have a question or problem: trial and error, or a computer dealer.

Of these approaches, many consider trial and error to be much more productive than calling your computer dealer. Some dealers, of course, are fully capable and can properly support a typical end user. Few dealers, however, want to become closely involved in your upgrade project, especially with a system purchased more than a year earlier, and no dealer will repair your system for free. Unless you want to waste innumerable hours with sometimes unresponsive technical-support departments or simply play a guessing game when you troubleshoot or upgrade your system, demand that certain technical-reference documents for your system be made available to you. In most cases, you will have to locate these documents as well as pay for them when you find them. Free reference documents rarely are included with the system, and in some cases can be difficult to obtain.

Technical-Reference Manuals. The technical-reference manual is the most important of all the manuals available for a system. You should refuse to purchase any system that does not have an appropriate technical-reference manual. Remember, many manufacturers include such information with the system as part of the standard documentation. You can also buy the manual long before you buy the system because the information in the manual is necessary for you to conduct a proper review of the system.

IBM and most other large, name brand manufacturers excel in this area. IBM system documentation sets a standard that is difficult for other manufacturers to follow. Having documentation as good as IBM's is not really necessary, but a basic technical-reference manual with detailed information is essential. You'll need this information in order to install certain floppy drives, hard drives, memory adapters and chips, communications adapters, and practically anything else. Expect to pay between $25 and $200 for a good technical-reference manual, unless of course it is provided free as part of the standard package. Contact the original equipment manufacturer (OEM) to obtain the manual for your system. Chapter 2 has more information about obtaining this documentation for IBM systems.

Hardware-Maintenance and Service Manuals. Service manuals are desirable for anyone who has to troubleshoot a system. This type of manual isn't an absolute necessity and, in fact, most manufacturers have none. Other manufacturers have service manuals but refuse to make them available to users, which might be OK because of the wealth of third-party diagnostics and repair utilities. In many cases, the actual IBM service documentation is satisfactory for use even with compatibles, since they are basically similar to one or more IBM systems.

Hardware-maintenance and service manuals from IBM contain several items such as the following:

- Jumper and switch settings for IBM systems

- A parts catalog for IBM systems

- Detailed diagnostic flowcharts

- Advanced diagnostics disks

The first two items don't do the owner of a compatible any good, but the last two items are valuable in almost all cases for IBM systems or compatibles. The diagnostic flowcharts, called *maintenance-analysis procedures* (MAPs) by IBM, are quite useful. These flowcharts are a list of step-by-step instructions for troubleshooting a failure down to the smallest plug-in part in a system. "Down to the smallest plug-in part" generally means down to the board level, but items such as memory are "troubleshot" down to the failed component.

MAPs are written in a manner that enables you to follow a logical progression. You check and test a cable before scrapping a controller card, for example, or test a controller card before tossing a disk drive, or check switch and jumper settings before even touching any hardware. Although someone with experience in troubleshooting and diagnosis may not use MAPs often, these flowcharts can be handy when all your own tried-and-true procedures have failed. MAPs are especially handy when the pressure is on and you're not thinking clearly.

Advanced diagnostics are included in hardware-maintenance and service manuals. The manual for the PC, XT, Portable, and AT comes with two diagnostics disks: one for PC-type systems and the other for AT-type systems. Supplements (updates) are available for newer systems not covered by the original diagnostics, such as the PS/2 Models 25 and 30. The updates include the proper diagnostics for these systems. Other updates are available for the XT-286, which comes with a new disk that replaces and supersedes the original AT disk supplied with the starter manual.

The hardware-maintenance and service manual for PS/2 Micro Channel systems comes with the same reference disk you received when you bought the system. You might not have realized that you already had the advanced diagnostics for these systems (only PS/2 Models 50 and higher, which have the MCA bus) without having to purchase the hardware-maintenance and service manual, as with the PC, XT, and AT. The Advanced Diagnostics for these systems are hidden on the reference disk and can be activated by a special "back door" command. This command becomes known to anyone who pays for the hardware-maintenance and service manual, in which the activation command is fully documented. The idea is to prevent an average user from knowing about and subsequently "wandering around in" the advanced diagnostics, because many of the disk tests can destroy data and should not be run by inexperienced people.

What is the command to activate the Advanced Diagnostics for the PS/2? Boot the reference disk, go to the main menu, and press Ctrl-A (for Advanced). The standard menu then is replaced by a new one: the Advanced Diagnostics menu. That's it. Even though you already have the diagnostics, you still might want to consider getting a copy of the manual; it contains valuable information.

Advanced Diagnostics Software. Advanced diagnostics software is a powerful set of routines that can inspect and test all major areas of the system and several minor ones. Additionally, any peripherals that are fully compatible with IBM's own can be tested by these diagnostics. The advanced diagnostics run on any system compatible at the hardware level with any IBM system. In fact, the Advanced Diagnostics software can be used as a sort of acid test for compatibility.

The diagnostics software can also test most add-on devices similar to those from IBM. For example, you can test the hard disk and controller as long as the interface is compatible with what IBM used. Graphics boards can be tested as though they were the specific IBM board that they replaced; examples of the IBM boards are the Color Graphics Adapter (CGA), Enhanced Graphics Adapter (EGA), and so on. I usually find that any hardware-compatible system passes at least the motherboard tests (they work even without an actual IBM ROM), memory tests, floppy controller and disk tests, and hard disk controller and drive tests. Non-IBM graphics boards usually fail the IBM tests, and most non-IBM communications boards such as terminal emulators and network adapters are not even recognized, even if they are in an IBM system unit.

In a later chapter, you can read about some aftermarket (non-OEM) advanced diagnostics. Many of these programs offer features and capabilities not provided by the manufacturer-specific diagnostics like IBM's.

System Software

The operating-system software for your computer is extremely important. The software is an essential part of the system because nothing can be done without it. The operating-system software should be considered equal in importance to the ROM BIOS code that runs the system because the operating system is in fact an extension of or replacement for the ROM BIOS. You might ask, "Why didn't they just put the entire DOS in ROM? And then, when I turn on the system, it will be ready to go." The answer is that an operating system is complicated and often changed. Would you want to take your system in for service every time a new DOS was introduced? Also, would you want to be restricted to using only one type of DOS? Of course not. Therefore, the system designers put in the system as little of an operating system as possible in the form of ROM chips or firmware. *Firmware* indicates a program burned into a ROM chip; software that is "hard" is called "firmware."

The importance of system software is easy to understand. Now, where do you get this software? Hopefully, you can get it from the company that makes your system. The original equipment manufacturer (OEM) of the system must supply this software because it is highly customized to the particular hardware design. Unfortunately, many lower-cost compatibles do not have OEM versions of any operating systems. And, a system with no real operating system can cause problems. Where do you get one? Where do you get upgrades to new versions? Will new versions be produced for other systems but not for yours? These tough questions are examined in this section.

DOS and Windows Compatibility. Asked which operating system they use, many people respond, "MS-DOS." Others might say that they use IBM DOS or Compaq DOS. Those who say that they use MS-DOS, however, might not be entirely correct. What is MS-DOS? And what, for instance, is the difference between MS-DOS and IBM DOS?

MS-DOS stands for *Microsoft Disk Operating System*, a collection of programs designed and produced by Microsoft and IBM in a special joint-development agreement. The programs are designed specifically to run on IBM and IBM-compatible systems. Microsoft owns the source code and sells licenses to various system OEMs, who then sell the programs as they are, or adapt the code to run on their systems. The OEMs then produce the documentation and provide all support for their specific version of DOS. Microsoft has not yet officially sold MS-DOS as a stand-alone retail product. They have offered DOS *upgrades* as a retail product, but only for systems that already have a version of DOS on them. Microsoft still stubbornly does not sell a bootable stand-alone version of DOS at the retail level (without a computer system, that is). Other companies who license DOS from Microsoft can distribute it in any way they choose. For example, IBM sells outright both standard and upgrade DOS versions, and they do not care whether you purchase a computer or not!

System Specific DOS Versions. Here is an analogy is from the automotive world: Most auto manufacturers produce a variety of different makes and models of automobiles based on exactly the same chassis. Suppose that I drive a 1994 Pontiac Firebird. If you ask me what type of car I drive, I could answer, "I drive a GM F-body automobile." The answer is correct, but not sufficiently detailed. True, the Firebird is an F-body (a GM Corporate designation), but so is the Chevrolet Camaro. You don't buy a pure or otherwise generic F-body car from General Motors; you buy either a Firebird or a Camaro. GM does not sell raw F-bodies to the public.

Rather, GM Corporate "sells" the bodies to the Pontiac and Chevrolet Motor Divisions, and they customize the autos to produce the final result. In 1994, Firebirds and Camaros were manufactured simultaneously by the same workers on the same assembly line at the F-body assembly plant in St. Therese, Canada,. The frames, engines, transmissions, brakes, axles, suspensions, and virtually all mechanical items are exactly the same between the two cars. The cars differ only in interior and exterior appearance items and trim. The same can be said for the '94 Mitsubishi 3000 GT and the Dodge Stealth, the Ford Explorer and Mazda Navajo, the Chevy Caprice and Buick Roadmaster, etc., all of which are virtually identical twins except for exterior sheet metal and ornamentation.

DOS is sold in much the same way: licensed by Microsoft and IBM to a particular computer-system manufacturer who then adapts the raw DOS source code to run properly on its own system. Because each manufacturer customizes DOS for its specific systems, you benefit the most by using the DOS from your system's manufacturer. Microsoft also produces a generic version, available as a retail product in the form of an upgrade, but you are better off to stick (if possible) with the DOS from your system's OEM. Compaq, for example, includes extra utilities specific to their systems with Compaq DOS.

The auto analogy helps to answer the second question, "What is the difference between MS-DOS and IBM DOS?" You can see that, as stated, the question can't be answered in definite terms. IBM DOS is a retail product that can be dissected and analyzed. MS-DOS, however, is a general term that applies to all the different DOS products produced from the same "assembly line" beginnings. The computer question is the same as the automotive question: "What is the difference between a GM F-body automobile and a Pontiac Firebird?" How do you answer? The Firebird is an F-body automobile, but not all F-bodies are Firebirds. Some end up as Camaros. Likewise, IBM DOS is an MS-DOS "flavor," but so are Compaq DOS, AT&T DOS, Zenith DOS, AST DOS, Toshiba DOS, NEC DOS, and so on.

A better question would be "What is the difference between the retail Microsoft DOS 6.0 Upgrade and the retail IBM DOS 6.1 Upgrade?" Well the answer to that is easy, the difference is ".1"! Seriously, these two DOS versions now differ in several ways, although both are essentially Microsoft DOS. In other words, IBM gets the DOS source code for their version direct from Microsoft. They then enhance it, fix bugs, and make any changes they want and finally market it as IBM DOS. The main differences between Microsoft and IBM versions center on the extra utility programs that come with the DOS, the help system, and documentation. IBM uses a different disk compression utility, backup utility, anti-virus utility, and other accessories than Microsoft does. Microsoft's version has an excellent on-line help system which is not found in IBM's version, however IBM supplies full documentation including a complete command reference while Microsoft only includes what could be best described as a "pamphlet" for documentation. IBM sells IBM

DOS not only for IBM systems but for any IBM compatible as well. Both IBM and Microsoft DOS are now supported by their respective companies on a variety of systems.

Although it may not be cost-effective, I have purchased both the Microsoft and IBM DOS upgrades. I normally use the IBM DOS as the base system, and then add in any of the utilities that Microsoft had which were left out of IBM's version such as the excellent on-line help system. Another reason I keep both versions around is that I have to support users with both versions.

Microsoft licenses DOS to many larger compatible system vendors who then produce their own specific version with unique utilities and features (Compaq DOS is an example). This does not suit the vendors of low cost, "assembled" type compatible systems. These vendors do not have the resources to license and develop their own DOS version. Microsoft has recognized this situation, and as of DOS V3.2, Microsoft has made special versions of MS-DOS just for generic compatibles called the Microsoft MS-DOS Packaged Product. A dealer can get this version from Microsoft on a small-quantity basis but must agree in writing to perform all the testing to verify that the version works correctly on his systems, provide all support to end users who purchase the product, and then sell it only with one of his tested computers. You supposedly cannot buy this generic MS-DOS without a computer system. Upgrades and bug fixes are handled by the seller. This generic version is not "tweaked" to run better on any certain system but rather is designed to run on IBM or 100 percent compatible systems. Any system not fully compatible with IBM still must use a specially customized version of DOS licensed from Microsoft and produced by the OEM. If the generic version does not work on a particular system for some reason, it is up to the system manufacturer to remedy the problem.

With the introduction of DOS V5.0 and later versions (including 6.0 and 6.2), Microsoft began selling DOS upgrades as a retail product directly to the public. It is interesting to note, however, that the upgrade product isn't bootable and works only on systems on which DOS already is running. Another interesting bit of information is that, technically, you still cannot purchase the complete generic version of DOS in a standard bootable form without a computer. The license agreements between compatible vendors who want to sell the MS-DOS Packaged Product remains the same.

Although Microsoft still does not have dealers selling standard DOS bootable copies as a stand-alone item through the retail channel, you rarely will encounter resistance in purchasing a generic copy of MS-DOS. It seems that many dealers are willing to sell DOS on the "gray market," perhaps without Microsoft's direct approval. I have purchased several copies of generic MS-DOS (full product, not just the upgrade) with no problems. Therefore it seems that virtually anyone can easily buy the generic version of MS-DOS.

In all honesty, you rarely will have problems with various compatibles running the pre-packaged "generic" Microsoft DOS or IBM DOS. I normally recommend running IBM DOS on compatibles because IBM offers better support than Microsoft. For example, IBM has an 800 number for DOS support while Microsoft has a 900 number! Also, IBM provides corrective service diskettes (patch disks) with updated versions of IBM DOS with bug fixes and corrections available for download from the IBM National Support Center BBS. Microsoft usually offers fewer fixes and makes them available on CompuServe. For

II

Compatible Systems

exampled, IBM had at least six different revisions of DOS 5.x out, while Microsoft only released a couple of fixed files over the life of DOS 5.x. Many of the fixes found in the later IBM DOS 5.x versions were never released by Microsoft. IBM also sells either the full blown DOS or the upgrade version as a retail product with no restrictions about purchasing it with a system.

OS/2 Compatibility. Although originally OS/2 was offered by several vendors including Microsoft, today only IBM sells OS/2. IBM has shown a commitment to make OS/2 run on as many compatible systems as possible and so far the results are very good. IBM has set up a test lab that certifies systems for OS/2 compatibility. If a system manufacturer wishes to have their system tested, they send it to IBM, where a battery of 18 different tests are run before the system is certified OS/2 compatible. If the system passes the tests, then the manufacturer or vendor can market the system as OS/2 compatible. This testing will give any potential purchaser of the system peace of mind.

Where possible, IBM has fixed incompatibilities within the software so that OS/2 would work on as many compatible systems as possible. Because of the number of systems tested, OS/2 now runs on the vast majority of systems on the market today with little or no problems. Some older systems may need hardware or BIOS updates, and some peripherals may not be supported, but generally the picture is much better than most people suspect.

If OS/2 compatibility is important to you, *make sure that your system is on the IBM compatibility list.* Also, for major system components like SCSI adapters or CD-ROM drives, make sure that your device is one of those supported by OS/2. A current list of supported computers and devices can be downloaded from IBM's National Support Bulletin board. The phone number for this board is listed in the vendor list found in the Appendix. Be sure that when purchasing a device like a SCSI adapter that the manufacturer either provides drivers for the device or that the drivers built-in to OS/2 will support it. Many popular adapters and devices have support already built-in to OS/2, eliminating the need for special external drivers.

Windows NT Compatibility. With Windows a big success and Windows NT just out, compatibility with Windows is of prime importance in a system today. Although virtually any system that runs DOS will run Windows, the NT version is another story. Windows NT places high demands on the hardware, and since it is a protected-mode operating system like OS/2, it carries with it protected-mode BIOS code for the system. This means that specific systems and hardware devices must be addressed through drivers, many of which are not yet available for specific devices.

If Windows NT is important to you, it is recommended that you ensure that any system you are going to purchase will be guaranteed to run NT. This tip would also apply to important system devices like SCSI adapters, CD-ROM drives, Tape drives, Video Adapters, etc. Make sure that all of these devices either work with the drivers built-in to NT, or they have separate drivers available to make them work.

ROM BIOS Compatibility. The issue of ROM BIOS compatibility is important. If the BIOS is not compatible, any number of problems can result. Several reputable companies that produce compatibles have developed their own proprietary ROM BIOS that works just like IBM's. These companies also frequently update their ROM code, to keep in step with the latest changes IBM has incorporated into its ROMs. Because IBM generally does not sell ROM upgrades or provide them for its systems unless the upgrade is absolutely necessary (IBM decides what is necessary), keeping current with an actual IBM system is more difficult than with most of the compatible systems on the market. Also, many of the compatibles' OEMs have designed ROMs that work specifically with additional features in their systems while effectively masking the effects of these improvements from any software that would "balk" at the differences.

OEMs. Many OEMs independently have developed their own compatible ROMs. Companies such as Compaq, Zenith, and AT&T have developed their own BIOS product, which has proven compatible with IBM's. These companies also offer upgrades to newer versions that often can offer more features and improvements or fix problems with the older versions. If you use a system with a proprietary ROM, make sure that it is from a larger company with a track record, and that will provide updates and fixes as necessary.

Several companies have specialized in the development of a compatible ROM BIOS product. The three major companies that come to mind in discussing ROM BIOS software are American Megatrends Inc. (AMI), Award Software, and Phoenix Software. Each company licenses its ROM BIOS to a motherboard manufacturer so that the manufacturer can worry about the hardware rather than the software. To obtain one of these ROMs for a motherboard, the OEM must answer many questions about the design of the system so that the proper BIOS can be either developed or selected from those already designed. Combining a ROM BIOS and a motherboard is not a haphazard task. No single, generic, compatible ROM exists, either. AMI, Award, and Phoenix ship to different manufacturers many variations of their BIOS code, each one custom-tailored to that specific system, much like DOS can be.

AMI. Although AMI customizes the ROM code for a particular system, it does not sell the ROM's source code to the OEM. An OEM must obtain each new release as it becomes available. Because many OEMs don't need or want every new version developed, they might skip several version changes before licensing a new one. The AMI BIOS is very popular and now is in a large number of systems. One special AMI feature is that it is the only third-party BIOS manufacturer to make its own motherboard as well. Knowing that both the motherboard and the BIOS originate from the same source gives me peace of mind.

The AMI BIOS has had a few problems with different keyboards and keyboard controller chips, and earlier versions also had some difficulty with certain IDE hard disk drives. To eliminate these types of problems, make sure that your BIOS is dated 4/9/90 or later, and has keyboard controller F or later. To locate this information, power-on the system and observe the character string on the lower left of the screen. This information will appear in two forms:

>   aaaa-bbbb-mmddyy-Kc

or

>   ee-ffff-bbbbbb-gggggggg-mmddyy-hhhhhhhh-c

The "aaaa-bbbb" and "ee-ffff-bbbbbb-gggggggg" codes indicate the motherboard manufacturer and model code. The "mmddyy" is the date code, which should be 040990 or later to prevent problems. The "c" is the keyboard controller revision, which should be F or later. You will possibly have keyboard lockups and problems running Windows or OS/2 if you do not have the latest keyboard controller chip.

The AMI BIOS has the standard features, including a built-in setup program activated by pressing the Del key in the first few seconds of booting up your computer. AMI offers user-definable hard disk types, essential for optimal use of many IDE or ESDI drives. A unique AMI BIOS feature is that, in addition to the setup, it has a built-in, menu-driven, diagnostics package, essentially the same as its stand-alone AMIDIAG product. Unfortunately, the diagnostics fall far short of ideal, and the Power-On Self Test seems to have suffered from the inclusion of the menu-driven diagnostics. Neither the POST nor the menu-driven diagnostics is capable of properly handling memory errors, for example, and the hard disk low-level formatter works only at the BIOS level rather than at the controller register level. These limitations often have prevented it from being capable of formatting severely damaged disks. I would rather have a "beefed-up" Power-On Self Test than menu-driven diagnostics.

You can be sure that because of the highly refined AMI diagnostics' popularity, nearly all problems have been worked out. Another AMI feature is that it offers a technical support BBS. You will find the phone number listed in the vendor list in the Appendix.

For updates to the AMI BIOS or keyboard controller, contact Washburn and Co. You will also find them listed in the vendor list in the Appendix.

Award. Award is unique among BIOS manufacturers because it sells its BIOS code to the OEM and allows the OEM to customize the BIOS. Of course, then the BIOS no longer is Award BIOS, but rather a highly customized version. AST uses this approach on its systems, as do other manufacturers, for total control over the BIOS code, without having to write the code from scratch. Although AMI or Phoenix customize the ROM code for a particular system, they do not sell the ROM's source code to the OEM. Some OEMs that seem to have developed their own ROM code started with a base of source code licensed to them by Award or some other company.

The Award BIOS has all the normal features you expect, including a built-in setup program activated by pressing Ctrl-Alt-Esc. This setup offers user-definable drive types, required in order to fully utilize IDE or ESDI hard disks. The Power-On Self Test is good, and Award runs a technical support BBS. The phone number for the BBS is listed in the vendor list in the Appendix.

In all, the Award BIOS is high quality, has minimal compatibility problems, and offers a high level of support.

Phoenix. The Phoenix BIOS for many years has been a standard of compatibility by which others are judged. It was one of the first third-party companies to legally reverse-engineer the IBM BIOS using a "clean room" approach. In this approach, a group of engineers studied the IBM BIOS and wrote a specification for how that BIOS should work and what features should be incorporated. This information then was passed to a second group of engineers who had never seen the IBM BIOS. They could then legally write a new BIOS to the specifications set forth by the first group. This work would then be unique and not a copy of IBM's BIOS; however, it would function the same way. This code has been refined over the years and has very few compatibility problems compared to some of the other BIOS vendors.

One recent development with Phoenix is the cross licensing of BIOS technology with IBM. Both Phoenix and IBM have introduced a new BIOS called Surepath that will be available in Compatible systems. What has essentially happened is that IBM is now selling their BIOS! Phoenix and IBM are trading BIOS technology, and making it available to others in the form of the Surepath BIOS. I have not yet seen any systems with this BIOS yet, but expect to over the next year or so.

The Phoenix BIOS excels in two areas that make it high on my list of recommendations. One is that the Power-On Self Test is excellent. The BIOS outputs an extensive set of beep codes that can be used to diagnose severe motherboard problems which would prevent normal operation of the system. In fact, this POST can isolate memory failures in Bank 0 right down to the individual chip with beep codes alone. The Phoenix BIOS also has an excellent setup program free from unnecessary frills, but that offers all of the features one would expect, such as user-definable drive types, and so on. The built-in setup is activated by typing either Ctrl-Alt-S or Ctrl-Alt-Esc, depending on the version of BIOS you have.

The second area in which Phoenix excels is in the documentation. Not only are the manuals that you get with the system detailed, but also Phoenix has written a set of BIOS technical-reference manuals that are a standard in the industry. The set consists of three books, titled *System BIOS for IBM PC/XT/AT Computers and Compatibles*, *CBIOS for IBM PS/2 Computers and Compatibles*, and *ABIOS for IBM PS/2 Computers and Compatibles*. Phoenix is one of few vendors who have done extensive research on the PS/2 BIOS and produce virtually all of the ROMs in the PS/2 Micro Channel clones on the market. In addition to being an excellent reference for the Phoenix BIOS, these books serve as an outstanding overall reference to anyone's IBM-compatible BIOS. Even if you never have a system with a Phoenix BIOS, I highly recommend these books, published by Addison-Wesley and available through most bookstores.

II

Compatible Systems

Phoenix is also one of the largest OEMs of Microsoft MS-DOS. Many owners of MS-DOS have the Phoenix OEM version. Phoenix licenses its DOS to other computer manufacturers so long as they use the Phoenix BIOS. Because of its close relationship with Microsoft, it has access to the DOS source code, which helps in eliminating compatibility problems.

Although Phoenix does not operate a technical support BBS by itself, their largest nationwide distributor does, which is Micro Firmware Inc. The BBS and voice phone numbers are listed in the vendor list in the Appendix.

Unless the ROM BIOS is a truly compatible, custom OEM version such as Compaq's, you might want to install in the system the ROM BIOS from one of the known quantities, such as that of AMI, Award, or Phoenix. These companies' products are established as ROM BIOS standards in the industry, and frequent updates and improvements ensure that a system containing these ROMs will have a long life of upgrades and service.

Conservative Design

For systems I recommend for business use, a principle of conservative design is important. Stay away from systems advertised to perform "impossible" feats of speed and performance or with features and prices simply too good to be true. Many of these systems use substandard components and often run at higher speeds than the components were designed to handle. These systems will have had limited testing and debugging and can have frustrating lockups, incompatibilities, and servicing problems.

If the expansion bus is running too fast or with inaccurate timing, many adapter cards don't run properly or at all in the system. If a system improperly runs the motherboard or CPU at speeds in excess of the rated capabilities of all of the components, you can have an unreliable, "flaky" system as a result. If a cheap power supply which has unstable or noisy output is used and runs at (or past) its limit, a system will experience a number of problems and failures. All these issues deal with the original design of the system. I believe in conservatism and a little overkill with these matters, which is part of the reason that my own systems, and those I recommend for others, run so well for so long.

Using Correct Speed-Rated Parts. Some compatible vendors use substandard parts in thier systems to save money. Since the CPU is one of the most expensive components on the motherboard, and many motherboards are sold to system assemblers without the CPU installed, it is tempting to the assembler to install a CPU rated for less than the actual operating speed. A system could be sold as a 33 MHz system, for example, but when you look "under the hood," you may find a CPU rated for only 25 MHz. The system does appear to work correctly, but for how long? If the company that manufactures the CPU chip installed in this system had tested the chip to run reliably at 33 MHz, it would have labeled the part accordingly. After all, the company could sell the chip for more money if it worked at the higher clock speed. When a chip is run at a speed higher than it is rated for, it will run hotter than it would normally. This may cause the chip to overheat occasionally, which would appear as random lockups, glitches, and frustration. I highly recommend you avoid systems whose operation speed exceeds the design of the respective parts.

This practice is easy to fall into since the faster rated chips cost more money, and Intel and other chip manufacturers usually rate their chips very conservatively. I have taken several 25MHz 486 processors and run them at 33MHz, and they seemed to work fine. What happens, though, is that when you run a chip past it's rated speed the chip becomes much hotter than it normally would. This can cause random lockups when the chip actually overheats. Some unscrupulous system vendors will place a heat sink on the "pushed" chip, which helps to prevent the overheating, but also prevents you from seeing that it is a substandard part! If the price of a system is too good to be true, ask before you buy: Are the parts really manufacturer-rated for the system speed?

To determine the rated speed of a CPU chip, look at the writing on the chip. Most of the time, the part number will end in a suffix of -xx where the xx is a number indicating the maximum speed. For example, a -66 indicates that the chip is rated for 66MHz operation. Table 5.1 provides a speed suffix decoding chart for the CPU chips you see in IBM-compatible systems.

Table 5.2 shows some of the different available Intel and Intel-compatible processors and the maximum speeds at which they are rated to run. As you can see, for a given processor, a variety of different speed versions are available.

Table 5.1 Speed Suffix Decoding Chart

CPU or NDP chip	Suffix	Maximum speed
8088/8086/8087	No marks	5 MHz
	-3	6 MHz
	-2	8 MHz
	-1	10 MHz
80286 or higher	-"x"	"x" MHz

Table 5.2 Intel and Intel-Compatible Microprocessor Clock Rates

Processor	Type	Available maximum speed ratings (MHz)												
		5	6	8	10	12	16	20	25	33	40	50	66	75	100
8086	CPU	X	X	X	X									
8088	CPU	X	X	X	X									
8087	NDP	X	X	X	X									
286	CPU	X	X	X	X	X	X							
287	NDP	X	X	X	X									
287 XL	NDP	X												

(continues)

Table 5.2 Continued

Processor	Type	Available maximum speedratings (MHz)													
		5	6	8	10	12	16	20	25	33	40	50	66	75	100
287 XLT	NDP	X													
386 DX	CPU	X	X	X	X	X									
387 DX	NDP	X	X	X	X	X									
386 SX	CPU	X	X	X											
387SX	NDP	X	X	X											
386 SL	CPU	X	X	X											
386 SLC	CPU	X													
486 SX	CPU	X	X	X											
487 SX	CPU+NDP	X	X	X	X	X									
486 SL	CPU	X	X	X											
486 SLC	CPU	X													
486 SLC2	CPU	X	X	X											
486 BL3	CPU	X	X												
486 DX	CPU+NDP	X	X	X	X										
486 DX2	CPU+NDP	X	X	X	X		X	X	X						
486 DX3	CPU+NDP	X	X												
Pentium	CPU+NDP	X	X												

CPU = Central processing unit
NDP = Numeric data processor (math coprocessor)
The DX2 (also called Overdrive) and SLC2 processors operate at double the clock rate of the system they are installed in, while the DX3 and BL3 processors operate at triple the system clock rate.

Slot Speed. For true compatibility and board exchangeability, you must know how fast a certain system runs the slots. Most high-speed compatibles using Industry Standard Architecture (ISA), otherwise known as the AT bus, employ a dual clock which ensures that the system slots for both PC XT or AT systems do not run the bus at a rate faster than 8 MHz or with less than 1 wait state. If the system can allow faster operation, you are free to try it. If the system bus cannot be slowed to this level, however, you will see that many adapter cards do not work in that system. Many memory cards are speed-sensitive, especially the expanded-memory types of boards. Also, most of the network adapters or other highly specialized communications adapters are speed-sensitive as well.

Note that because Micro Channel Architecture (MCA) or Extended Industry Standard Architecture (EISA) systems have strict timing definitions that must be adhered to as part of their respective standards, slot speed isn't an issue with these systems. Because of the standard definitions laid out for MCA and EISA, they also are free of many of the timing and other problems that have plagued various ISA systems in these areas.

Power-Supply Output. I always try to make sure that adequate power output is available from the power supply to run expansion devices added to the system. The power supply should supply sufficient airflow also to cool the system adequately. The system chassis lid or case might feel warm but should never feel hot to the touch. Most of the time, the power-output specification is stamped on the system's power supply or is listed in its technical-reference manual. Consult the technical manual for each disk drive you purchase, as well as for each adapter you intend to plug in, to see whether sufficient power is available to reliably run all these devices. Chapter 7, "Primary System Components," examines the consequences of overstressing the power supply.

Adhering to Standards. Check to see that certain standards are followed. IBM has declared specific uses for certain interrupt request (IRQ) lines, direct memory access (DMA) channels, and I/O ports. Be certain that the CMOS memory and real-time clock are set up the same way they are set up in the IBM units (that is, make sure that data is organized the same way and that the port locations are the same). Make sure that your system follows IBM standards. (An example of a system that did not follow these standards is the old AT&T 6300 system. This machine had severe compatibility problems with standard plug-in boards because of nonstandard use of interrupts and DMA channels. Locating items, therefore, such as disk controllers or other boards that worked properly in the system, was very difficult.) You usually can find this information in a system's technical-reference manual. Several charts in the Appendix describe these items and how they are allocated in an IBM system unit. Most systems today follow these standards and it is rare to find otherwise.

Support

Support from the system manufacturer is important. Some manufacturers rely solely on their vendors (dealers) to provide support, which isn't always a good idea because dealers rarely can provide true technical support. In addition to simply being able to ask technical questions, the source of support should include a spare-parts program and be able to exchange major components for rebuilt replacements. Most larger companies, such as IBM, HP, Toshiba, NEC, Gateway, and Dell, support their own products directly as well as through the dealer. Others don't support their products directly; any support you seek must be handled through your dealer or vendor.

Spare-Parts Availability. In any system, look for the availability of spare-parts. In other words, can you obtain any unique parts that make up a system? The parts can include motherboards, power supplies, proprietary adapter cards, special memory boards and chips, unique hardware, and cosmetic parts such as cases, front panels, and so on. In this regard, I like the way that *Popular Mechanics* magazine reviews an automobile. The end of the review is a list with the cost of most of the commonly replaced items on a car, such as brakes, front and rear body parts, alternators, and so on. The list provides much insight into comparing a low-cost foreign model (which has exorbitant parts and maintenance prices) with a domestic model (which has cheaper, more commonly available parts).

Because of the number of systems sold, many suppliers are available for these types of items for any of IBM's systems. You can buy a power supply or any type of drive or adapter at a low cost because of the competition. Other vendors prefer to lock you into high-cost custom parts, which you cannot find at a discount. For example, manufacturers such as Compaq and HP use motherboards and power supplies that are physically different from the IBM form factors used throughout the industry. You have to obtain replacement power supplies, motherboards, and often disk drives from these manufacturers. Some manufacturers will not even sell these parts directly to you, instead you have to go through a dealer.

IBM's PS/2 systems represent sort of a special case. These systems are definitely not form factor compatible with IBM's own earlier XT and AT systems, so parts initially were difficult to come by. In fact, usually they could only be obtained directly from IBM, and at a premium price. Since their introduction in 1987, IBM has sold well over 10 million PS/2 systems, which has created a tremendous demand for service parts. There are now many vendors selling both original IBM service and replacement parts as well as aftermarket parts for these systems. There are a multitude of upgrade components available from complete motherboards, to power supplies, to disk drives, and to any type of adapter card. In fact, with the modular construction of most of the PS/2 systems, they are extremely easy to upgrade compared to more conventional systems. One of the major breakthroughs in PS/2 upgrades and service is the advent of replacement upgrade motherboards. Reply Corp. (listed in the vendor list in the Appendix) manufactures and sells a variety of complete motherboard upgrades for several systems in the PS/2 line. Another company called Arco Electronics (also in the vendor list) makes a line of special upgrade IDE disk controllers and adapters that allow conventional ATA-IDE drives to be installed in the PS/2 systems. Other manufacturers such as IBM, Future Domain, and Adaptec make a variety of SCSI adapters for the PS/2 systems which allows for the attachment of a multitude of peripherals including hard disks, CD-ROM drives, Tape Backup drives, Optical drives, Scanners, Printers, etc. With all of the third-party support these systems now enjoy, it is fairly easy to support, service, and upgrade any of the IBM PS/2 systems.

In the end, purchasing a system with an ample supply of parts available and supported by the aftermarket pays off with a system that is easy to support, service, and upgrade in the long run. Unless you have special requirements, a "generic" form factor system is most recommended.

Exchanging Major Components. Most larger manufacturers offer a board-exchange policy. For expensive components such as the motherboard, you can trade in a defective component for a good one for much less money than in an outright purchase. You might want to consider this information when you look at other vendors' systems.

How To Buy a Compatible System

When purchasing a compatible system, there are some tips that will help prevent the purchase from being an exercise in frustration.

Pay by credit card if possible because if you end in dispute, your credit card company can go to bat for you and issue a credit until the dispute is resolved. In addition, many credit cards automatically double the manufacturer's warranty.

One of the decisions you will have to make is what type of system to purchase. Earlier in this chapter I gave some basic recommendations for what to look for in a compatible system. If you follow those guidelines you will end up with a system that should be adequately supported. Documentation is important, as is the use of known BIOS and component vendors. I also recommend looking for systems which are form factor compatible with the IBM AT, since replacement parts and upgrade components can then be obtained through many different sources. With a form factor compatible system, you will never be dependent on a single vendor or manufacturer for parts and service.

Another decision to make is where to purchase the system. There are traditional full-service computer dealers, computer superstore dealers, wholesale warehouse stores, consumer electronics stores, department stores, and mail order copmpanies. Each of these has benefits and drawbacks, but in most cases you should go where you can get the type of system you want at the best price.

Mail Order Purchasing. For many items I like to buy locally, so that I can check out the item in the store before I purchase it. This only works if it is an item that is normally kept in stock. If it is an item that must be ordered, normally they will only order it for you after you pay for the item or place a deposit. In these cases it is probably best to simply purchase the item by mail order, since you will not be getting much benefit out of purchasing locally.

Mail order purchasing has changed the computer industry significantly over the last few years. The rise of mail order system and peripheral vendors has all but wiped out the traditional computer dealer. It is no wonder, since these mail order vendors offer tremendous discounts on the items they sell, and usually have more items in stock for a quick delivery. Besides the simple fact that the prices are lower, purchasing through mail order saves money in other ways, since if you purchase from an out of state vendor, you will most likely not have to pay any sales tax on your order. System vendors such as Dell, Gateway, Northgate, and Zeos offer systems at prices that most conventional dealers simply cannot match. Companies such as IBM and Compaq who traditionally sold systems only through computer dealers are now selling through the mail to remain competitive.

Mail order purchasing can have it's drawbacks. One is that you simply cannot see or try the merchandise first. Many people would go to the traditional computer dealers to check out systems or peripherals to decide what they wanted, and then order the selected items through the mail. Although this practice is not completely ethical, it is simple human nature to try to get the best price. Another drawback to mail order purchasing is that you will have to pay for shipping. On a large or heavy item this can nearly equal what you might pay in sales tax on purchasing the item locally. Finally, returns of defective or incorrect merchandise can be costly and time-consuming. I know many individuals who have literally spent hundreds of dollars in phone and shipping charges trying to get a problem resolved on a system that was purchased through the mail. Often these charges are much more than any savings originally realized over more traditional purchases through a local store.

If you do decide to purchase through the mail, there are a couple of tips I can give you. Perhaps the most important is to use a credit card for all mail order purchases. Although there may be a service charge, the credit card company will be on your side if the merchandise you receive is damaged or incorrect, or in case you do not receive any merchandise at all! I know many individuals who have been burned by purchasing through mail order and paying by cash, check or money order. Once the vendor had their money, they could not get satisfaction and in some cases did not even get the items they ordered. Although most mail order vendors are honest, there have been a number of scams involving companies that purport to sell computer equipment through the mail and actually deliver nothing. By the time you realize what has happened, they have closed down and reopened somewhere else under a new name. Using a credit card will save you from losing money in situations like that.

Avoiding Pitfalls. If you are purchasing by mail order, it is best to deal with a company that has an 800 number for ordering and for questions about your order. Phone charges can add up, especially if the vendor is a long distance away, which is normally the case. If you have a choice between two vendors, and one is much closer than another, choose the closer one. It may save on phone charges if they do not have 800 numbers, and in some cases it has been necessary to actually visit the mail order company's location in person to get service and support especially where defective equipment is concerned. If you are having problems with service, it usually gets their attention when you show up at the door!

Here is a checklist of questions to ask any vendor before purchasing a system:

- Is there a money-back guarantee? What is the return and refund policy? What type of refund is available: store credit, cash, or exchange? Is there a restocking charge?

- How long is the warranty? Note that many vendors today are offering three-year warranties for their systems, but one-year seems to be most standard. Does the warranty cover both parts and labor? Who provides warranty service? Is maintenance performed on-site (at the customer's location) or only at the vendor's location? What is the service response time?

- What is the full price of the system including any hidden or additional charges such as shipping charges, credit card surcharges, taxes, or service charges?

- Is the item available for immediate shipment or is it on backorder? When will it be shipped?

- How long has the vendor been in business? How good is technical support? Is there a toll-free support line? 24 hours or limited hours? Is there a BBS (modem) telephone line for support?

These questions should provide you with some excellent guidelines to follow before purchasing from a vendor.

Dealing with Vendor Problems. Sometimes, no matter how much research you do beforehand, you can run into problems with a particular vendor. Remember when you are dealing with a mail order supplier that Federal Trade Commission rules apply. This means that there are certain rules and procedures that the vendor must adhere to. Some of these rules are as follows:

- Timeliness; the vendor must ship the order within 30 days of receiving it unless the advertisement states otherwise. If a delay will be experienced in shipment, the vendor must notify you in writing of a definite new shipment date and also offer you the chance to cancel the order with full refund. That notice must include a stamped or self-addressed envelope or card which allows you to indicate your choice. If you do not respond, the seller may rightfully assume you accept the delay. However, the vendor must either ship or cancel the original order within 30 days after the original shipping date that was promised.

- Refunds; any refunds for order cancellation must be made promptly. Even if you accept an indefinite delay, you have the right to cancel the original order at any time before the item is shipped. If you chose to cancel any order which has been paid by check or money order, the vendor must mail a refund within seven business days excluding weekends and holidays. Likewise if the order was paid for by credit card, the vendor must credit your account within one business cycle following your cancellation request. Store credits and other methods or offers of similar merchandise are not acceptable unless you agree. If the original item is not available, a substitute item, even if similar, is not acceptable unless the vendor has your consent.

When you first get the items you order from any company, keep the registration or warranty cards long enough to test the items first. This way you may be able to obtain a completely new replacement item instead of going through a normal warranty claim. Always keep all of the original cartons and packing material. Many vendors will require it in case of return, and it provides proper protection during shipping.

If you have problems with a mail order vendor, there are several avenues you can follow to obtain satisfaction. Any one of these will usually get the attention of the vendor and secure your satisfaction; combining several of these procedures will certainly get their attention!

One of the keys to obtaining satisfaction when dealing with a mail order vendor (or any vendor for that matter) is to document everything. This means recording the date and time of every call placed to the vendor, who you talked to, and the results of the conversation such as promised ship dates, etc. Keep a file with all paperwork from the vendor including any receipts, invoices, warranties, and shipping documents. Subsequently if you have problems with that vendor, and are unable to obtain satisfaction over the phone, you should inform them in writing about your problem (i.e. defective equipment) and desired course of action, such as a refund or replacement of the equipment. Include copies of any of the documentation you have collected, especially a copy of the invoice. Do not return any items to the vendor unless told when and how to do so. Most vendors have a formal return policy and require that you be given an RMA (Return Merchandise Authorization) number to place on the return. Keep a copy of any shipping receipts and/or packing slips. You may or may not be reimbursed for the return shipping charges depending on the policies of the vendor.

In most cases dealing directly with the vendor in this manner will result in your satisfaction, but sometimes further action will be required. The next step would be to report any violations of the previously mentioned FTC rules to the Federal Trade Commission. Your local telephone book will normally list a number and address for the FTC office in your area. Call the vendor and tell them that you will be reporting violations to the FTC, and if that does not get their attention, mail the vendor a copy of the letter you write to the FTC.

You might also try to contact the Better Business Bureau about your problems with the vendor. They will often try to mediate between you and the vendor and can often obtain results that you might not get otherwise. An even more powerful recourse is to contact the attorney general for the state in which you live as well as the state in which the vendor does business. This can be very effective especially if you send a copy of that letter to the vendor.

You have a final recourse available to you If the product you purchased was paid for with a credit card. You can contact the bank or credit card agency and have them cancel or withdraw payment to the vendor. This final way out is the main reason that you should always purchase mail order items with a credit card, no matter whether there is a surcharge or not. The risks otherwise are simply not worth it!

Dealing With an Orphaned System. Many PC vendors and manufacturers have gone out of business. One of the most common stories I hear is that somebody just bought some fancy new PC, and they find out that their vendor has vanished. Now how do they get support, spare parts, and service for these "orphaned" systems?

The answer is usually that you will have to service and support them yourself! This may not be as bad as it sounds, as there possibly are several things on your side. One thing to do is to take an inventory of the components in the system and contact the manufacturers of these components to find out the warranties that may be active. Many peripheral and component manufacturers offer warranties on their components such as motherboards, power supplies, and especially disk drives. A hard disk is one of the more expensive items in the system, and most hard disk manufacturers now offer five-year warranties on their drives. This means that even if the system vendor has gone out of business, you should be able to exchange a defective part like a hard disk with the original manufacturer of the component.

If you had purchased a PC that was form factor compatible with an IBM AT then you will never have any problems supporting or servicing the system. You will be able to purchase any part that goes in the system from the motherboard and power supply to the case and assembly hardware itself from a multitude of vendors. These types of systems are the easiest to support since they are so generic in nature.

On the other side of the coin would be a proprietary system like most portables or laptop computers. Since there is no standard for the form factor of laptop or portable motherboards, cases, or power supplies, these systems are difficult to service and maintain. When available, parts for these types of systems will be much more expensive than those for normal desktop systems because of the proprietary nature of the parts. If at all possible, make sure you buy laptop or portable systems from name brand vendors like IBM, Compaq, Toshiba, etc. This will insure that you will be able to service and support the system for a long while.

Building Your Own System

After reading most of this book, you will find that building your own system is something that you might want to try. Actually, It is more like assembling your own system than building it, since all you will be doing is purchasing ready made components and bolting them together.

Economics of Building Rather Than Buying. There are some advantages and drawbacks to this approach, and they may not be what you think. Some people want to assemble their own system in the interest of saving money. I can tell you from experience that you will generally not save money by building your own system! On the contrary, you will probably spend much more money to build your own system than if you purchased even name brand ready-made systems. The reason is that the bigger vendors simply get a much better discount on their parts than you do because you must purchase them one at a time. Also most ready-made systems will include many accessories such as modems, mice, multimedia equipment, and especially bundled software that you would be hard-pressed to duplicate for the same price on your own. You often get hundreds of dollars worth of bundled software alone, which can greatly offset the price of purchasing a system rather than building. Of course if you have no need or use for the bundled software, than getting it "free" with a ready-made system is not really an advantage for you.

There are really two main reasons to build your own system. The first is simply because it is probably the only way you can get precisely the configuration and type of system that you want. For example, you may want a particular brand or design of motherboard, a particular case style, certain adapter cards, disk drives, keyboard, etc. that are simply not sold as a ready-made combination by any vendor. This is especially true if you want the ultimate in performance or capabilities. You can choose each individual component in your system and build the best possible system for your own requirements.

The other reason to build your own system is for the learning experience! There is no other way to learn so much so quickly about all of the components that make up a typical PC than to try to buy these components individually and assemble the system yourself. Unfortunately one of the criteria for learning is that you inevitably will make mistakes! This may mean that you will end up purchasing several different components or options before you find the right one or the one that suits your needs. This can often be very expensive, but of course you are not building your own system to save money! Again, I must stress that you will spend much more money to build your own system than to purchase one ready made. I emphasize this because no matter how much I say it, people seem to get themselves involved in system building because they want to save money.

The more inexperienced you are with PC components, the more likely you will be spending additional money sending incorrect components back, and trying several different options before you find what you were looking for. If you have the stomach and budget, building your own system can be an incredible learning experience. As the saying goes—"Whatever doesn't kill you makes you stronger!" Building your own system can sometimes lead to all night long troubleshooting sessions, but the rewards and satisfaction of getting your own custom configuration to work are worth it.

Required Components for a Basic System. If you are going to build your own system, there are a few basic components you will need. The following section will examine some choices you have for these primary components.

The Case. Your system starts with the case. Choosing the correct case is primarily based on your needs in system configuration and future expandability. There are several different cases available for PC type systems, ranging from tiny desktop cases to large fileserver type tower cases. In order of size, here is a list of the popular style-compatible cases:

- Slim-Line Desktop Case

- Baby-AT Desktop Case

- AT Desktop Case

- Mini-Tower Case

- Tower Case

The Slim-Line case is just like it sounds—slim! The expansion cards used in these systems must be mounted sideways, and therefore cannot plug directly into the motherboard. These cases are characterized by having a special riser or "T" card that plugs into one of the motherboard slots, into which all of the normal expansion cards are then plugged. This configuration results in the expansion cards being mounted sideways in the case. The sideways mounting is somewhat clumsy and makes it relatively difficult to install and remove cards. For example, to install or remove a card in one of the lower sideways slots, you will generally have to remove all of the cards in the slots above. Since there is so little room in the case, cables always seem to be in the way, and it is very difficult to reach motherboard connectors, jumpers, and switches. Another problem with these cases is that they require a unique smaller power supply compared to the other case designs. In short, I do not recommend these cases unless you absolutely need the small footprint these systems have. I often use slim-line case systems in my troubleshooting seminars, for example, because they are easier and less costly to ship around. Unfortunately, they are more difficult for my students to work on!

The Baby AT case is actually a tall version of the original IBM XT case. The original XT would not support cards as tall as would fit into an AT system, so several manufacturers started making taller versions of the XT case and the name "Baby AT" was used to describe them. These cases are ideal for a small footprint desktop system since they allow conventional vertical expansion card placement and are fairly easy to work on. These cases can normally accept regular XT style or the larger AT style power supplies. Some will need the power supply to have an external switch instead of the built-in switch normally found on XT and AT supplies. The only shortcoming is that they usually have fewer drive bays than the larger cases. Even so, most Baby AT cases have at least three exposed drive bays and one or two additional internal bays as well. This is more than enough expansion for most people.

The AT case is basically a case that matches the dimensions of the original IBM AT. These are the full-size desktop cases and are characterized by having the standard vertical expansion card arrangement and a large number of drive bays. Many of the AT cases will have five externally accessible drive bays and possibly one or more internal bays as well. These cases are the most commonly available cases, and most compatible systems use them.

The Mini Tower case is basically an AT case designed for a sideways orientation. Some are as simple as an AT case turned sideways, while most relocate the externally accessible drive bays so that the drives are upright in the normal configuration. These cases take basically all of the same components that will fit in the standard AT cases including power supplies, except that the power supply normally must be configured with an external switch rather than the built-in switch normally used on standard AT supplies.

The Tower case is a larger version of the AT case which is also turned sideways. These cases are characterized by a large number of drive bays, both externally accessible and internal. They usually use the same components that fit into the standard AT desktop case, except that the power supply usually has a cable and external switch arrangement. For the ultimate in expandability, and especially for systems that need a large number of disk drives, the Tower case is ideal.

Power Supply. There are basically four different types of power supplies available for PC-compatible systems. The power supply you choose depends mostly on the type of case you want. The different types are:

- Slim Style
- PC/XT Style
- Baby AT Style
- AT/Tower Style

The following figures show the dimensions and shape of each of these different style power supplies.

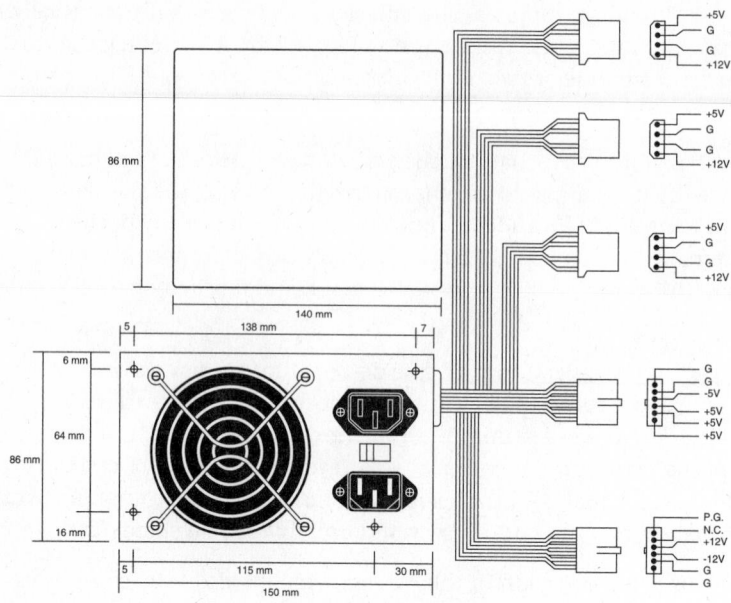

Fig. 5.1
Slim Style power supply.

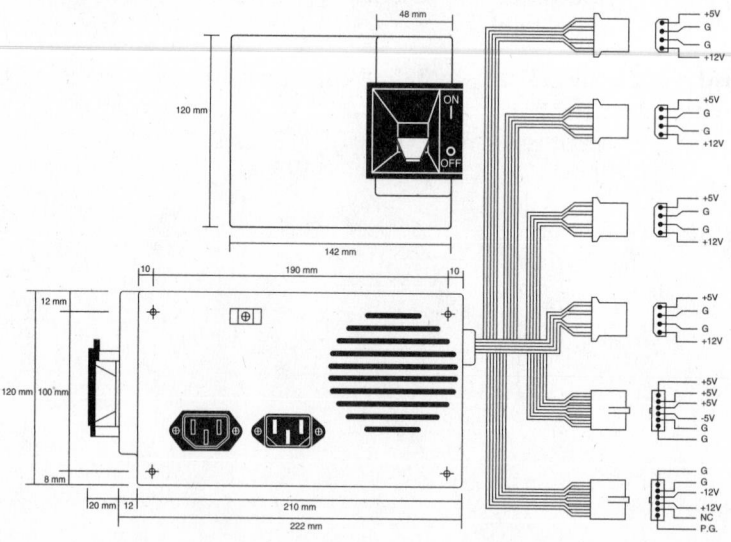

Fig. 5.2
PC/XT Style power supply.

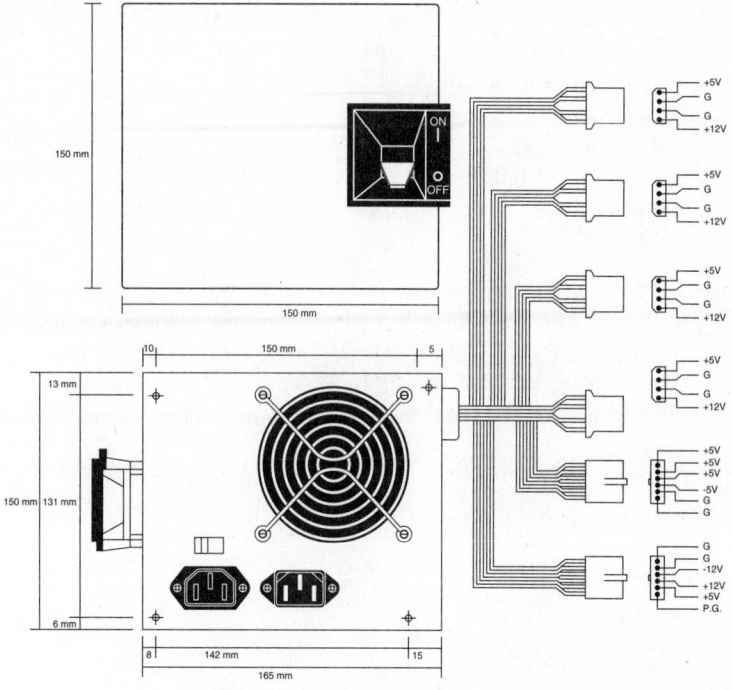

Fig. 5.3
Baby AT Style power supply.

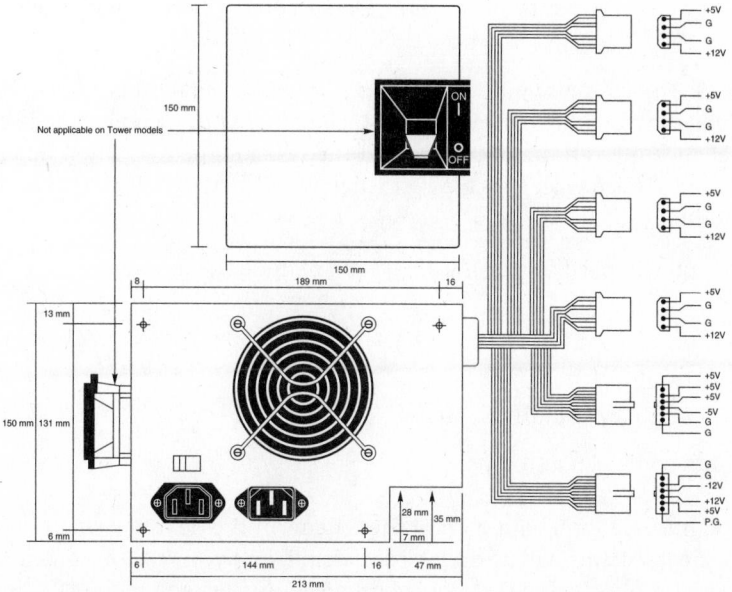

Fig. 5.4
AT/Tower Style power supply.

Each of these supplies are available in slightly different configurations and output levels. PC Power and Cooling and Astec are two manufacturers of power supplies that I recommend. PC Power and Cooling has the most complete line of power supplies from inexpensive lower output versions to high-end high-output models. They even have versions with built-in battery backup systems and special models with high-volume low-speed quiet fan assemblies. Their quiet models are especially welcome to people who can't take the fan noise that some emanates from supplies. You will find these vendors listed in the vendor list in the Appendix.

Motherboard. The motherboard is obviously the core of your system, and is one component that you do not want to take lightly. There are hundreds of versions available, with a variety of different CPUs, speeds, features, and options. Most of the questions I listed earlier for compatible systems should be applied to a motherboard purchase as well. Some general guidelines for what to look for would include the following:

- a minimum of a 486SX processor upgradeable to DX, DX2, or Pentium Overdrive

- external (Level 2) cache

- 36-Bit (72-pin) SIMM sockets for memory

- 33MHz speed capability

- either VL-Bus or PCI local bus slots

- name brand (AMI, Award, Phoenix, etc.) BIOS

There are many other possible options or features, but I would consider these to be a minimum set of requirements for the motherboard of any system you were going to build.

Other items. To finish off your system, you will need several other items. One of these would include the assembly hardware. This includes all of the screws, stand-offs, and other miscellaneous hardware needed to bolt the system together. Often times much of this should be included with the case you purchase. Sometimes stand-offs are included with the motherboard.

Other items you will need to finish your system include the following:

- a keyboard

- video adapter and display

- floppy controller and drives

- hard disk controller and drives

You will find information about each of these items in the next few chapters of this book. Each of these items will be discussed in detail, and you will see guidelines that should allow you to make the best possible choice for your requirements. These are critical parts of your system and you should take the time to carefully select the components you purchase for your system, especially the hard disk controller and drives. The hard disk drive and controller can easily cost as much or more than the motherboard, and have the greatest effect on system performance next to the motherboard itself. Be sure to read the appropriate sections of this book before making a decision on which of the multitude of these components you will purchase.

This section has given you some basic information and guidelines for assembling your own system. if you follow the recommendations carefully and do your research, you can end up putting together a system that is far superior than anything that you can purchase ready-made. The learning experience of assembling your own system is one that you will never forget, and will go a long way in furthering your PC education.

One last tip is that you will find an extensive listing of recommended vendors in the vendor list in the Appendix of this book. There are listings for suppliers and manufacturers of every single part needed to assemble a top quality system, from the case and motherboard to every card, drive, cable, and even the screws to bolt it all together. I consider the vendor list one of the most valuable resources in this book, and it should be especially useful to those assembling their own systems!

Chapter Summary

This chapter showed that there are several ways to break down the compatible marketplace. You saw that a system can be classified as an XT- or AT-class system, and as either a clone or a compatible system. The chapter examined the compatible marketplace from the point of view of a system installer or troubleshooter, keeping in mind that you can plan to upgrade a system later. The chapter provided a quick guide and checklist for what to look for in a compatible system that meets the needs of a business user, is serviceable for years to come, and has plenty of upgrade options.

II

Compatible Systems

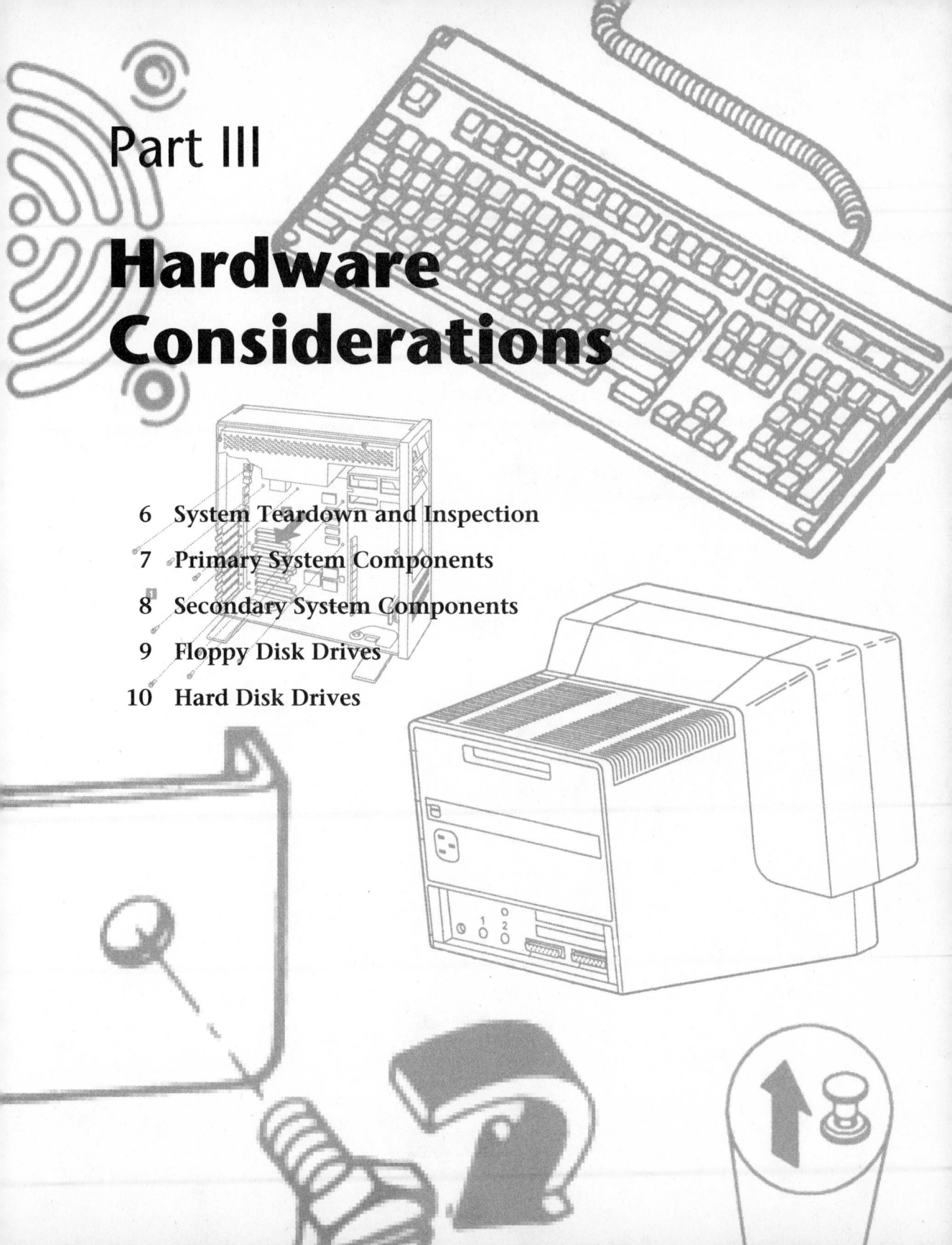

Part III

Hardware Considerations

Chapter 6

System Teardown and Inspection

This chapter examines procedures for tearing down and inspecting a system. It describes the types of tools required, the procedure for disassembling the system, and the various components that make up the system. A special section discusses some of the test equipment you can use, and another section covers some problems you might encounter with the hardware (screws, nuts, bolts, and so on).

Using the Proper Tools

To troubleshoot and repair PC systems properly, you need a few basic tools:

- Simple hand tools for basic disassembly and reassembly procedures

- Diagnostic software and hardware for testing system components

- Wrap plugs for diagnosing serial and parallel port problems

- Test and measurement devices (such as volt-ohm meters, or VOMs) that allow accurate measurement of voltage and resistance, and logic probes and pulsers that allow analysis and testing of digital circuits

- Chemicals (such as contact cleaners), component freeze sprays, and compressed air dusters for cleaning the system

In addition, you might also need soldering and desoldering tools for repairs that require removing or installing soldered devices. These basic tools are discussed in more detail in the following section. Diagnostic software and hardware is discussed in Chapter 13.

Hand Tools

After you work with PC systems, you will quickly learn that the tools required for nearly all service operations are very simple and inexpensive.

You can carry most of the required tools in a small pouch. Even a top-of-the-line "master mechanic's" set fits inside a briefcase-sized container. The cost of these tool kits ranges from about $20 (for a small-service kit) to $500 (for one of the briefcase-sized deluxe kits). Compare these costs to what may be necessary for an automotive technician. Most automotive service techs spend between $5,000 to $10,000 or more for the tools they need. Not only are the computer hand tools much less expensive, but also I can tell you from experience that you don't get nearly as dirty working on computers as you do when working on cars! I can say this with confidence because I am sort of a closet auto mechanic myself. Several years ago I even became a fully certified ASE (Automotive Service Excellence) master automotive technician, just to get the neat jacket patches. Now you know why most of my analogies are automobile related!

In this section you learn about the tools required to make up a set capable of basic, board-level service on PC systems. One of the best ways to start such a set of tools is with a small kit sold especially for servicing PCs.

The following list shows the basic tools you can find in one of the small "PC tool kits" sold for about $20:

> 3/16-inch nut driver
> 1/4-inch nut driver
> Small Phillips screwdriver
> Small flat-blade screwdriver
> Medium Phillips screwdriver
> Medium flat-blade screwdriver
> Chip extractor
> Chip inserter
> Tweezers
> Claw-type parts grabber
> T10 and T15 Torx drivers

You use nut drivers to remove the hexagonal-headed screws that secure the system-unit covers, adapter boards, disk drives, power supplies, and speakers in most systems. The nut drivers work much better than a conventional screwdriver.

Because some manufacturers have substituted slotted or Phillips head screws for the more standard hexagonal head screws, you can use the standard screwdrivers for these systems.

You use the chip-extraction and insertion tools to install or remove memory chips (or other, smaller chips) without bending any pins on the chip. Usually, you pry out larger chips, such as microprocessors or ROMs, with the small screwdriver. For very large square PGA (Pin Grid Array) devices like 386 and 486 processors, it is best to use a fork type pry tool that can distribute the force applied over more of the chip to prevent possible breakage. If these larger chips have been in the socket for a year or more, they can be very difficult to pry out.

The tweezers and parts grabber can be used to hold any small screws or jumper blocks that are difficult to hold in your hand. The parts grabber is especially useful when you drop a small part into the interior of a system; usually, you can remove the part without completely disassembling the system.

Finally, the Torx driver is a special, star-shaped driver that matches the special screws found in most COMPAQ systems and in many other systems as well.

Although this basic set is useful, you should supplement it with some other small hand tools, such as:

> Needlenose pliers
> Hemostats
> Wire cutter or wire stripper
> Metric nut drivers
> Tamper-proof Torx drivers
> Vise or clamp
> File
> Small flashlight

Pliers are useful for straightening pins on chips, applying or removing jumpers, crimping cables, or grabbing small parts.

Hemostats are especially useful for grabbing small components (such as jumpers).

The wire cutter or stripper obviously is useful in making or repairing cables or wiring.

The metric nut drivers can be used in many clone or compatible systems, as well as in the IBM PS/2 systems, which all use metric hardware.

You will need the tamper-proof Torx drivers to remove Torx screws with the tamper-resistant pin in the center of the screw. A tamper-proof Torx driver has a hole drilled into it to allow clearance for the pin.

You can use a vise for installing connectors on cables and for crimping cables to the shape you want, as well as for holding parts during delicate operations.

Finally, you can use the file for smoothing rough metal edges on cases and chassis, as well as for trimming the faceplates on disk drives for a perfect fit.

You can use the flashlight for lighting up system interiors, especially when the system is cramped and the room lighting is not good. I consider this an essential tool.

Another consideration for your tool kit is an Electrostatic Discharge (ESD) protection kit. These kits consist of a wrist strap with a grounding wire, and a specially conductive mat also with its own ground wire. Using a kit like this when working on a system will help to insure that you never accidentally zap any of the components with a static discharge.

The ESD kits and all the other tools listed in this section are available from a variety of tool vendors. Specialized Products Company and Jensen Tools are two of the more

III

Hardware Considerations

popular vendors of computer and electronic tools and service equipment. Their catalogs show an extensive selection of very high quality tools. These companies and several others are listed in the vendor list in the Appendix of this book. With a simple set of hand tools, you will be equipped for nearly every PC repair or installation situation. The total cost for these tools should be less than $150, which is not much considering the capabilities they give you.

Soldering and Unsoldering Tools

For certain situations, such as repairing a broken wire, reattaching a component to a circuit board, removing and installing chips that are not in a socket, or adding jumper wires or pins to a board, you must use a soldering iron to make the repair. Even if you do only board-level service, you will need a soldering iron in some situations.

You want a low-wattage iron, about 25 watts. Anything more than 30 watts generates too much heat and can damage the components on the board. Even with a low-wattage unit, you must limit the amount of heat to which you subject the board and its components. You can limit the amount of heat by using the soldering iron quickly and efficiently and by using the heat-sinking devices clipped to the leads of the device being soldered. A *heat sink* is a small, metal, clip-on device designed to absorb excessive heat before it reaches the component that the heat sink is protecting. In some cases, you can use a pair of hemostats as an effective heat sink while soldering a component.

To remove components originally soldered into place from a printed circuit board, you can use a soldering iron with a *solder sucker*. This device normally is constructed as a small tube with an air chamber and a plunger-and-spring arrangement. (I do not recommend the "squeeze bulb" type of solder sucker.) The unit is "cocked" when you press the spring-loaded plunger into the air chamber. To remove a device from a board, heat with the soldering iron the point at which one of the component leads joins the circuit board, from the underside of the board, until the solder melts. As soon as melting occurs, move the solder-sucker nozzle into position and press the actuator. This procedure allows the plunger to retract, and create a momentary suction that inhales the liquid solder from the connection and leaves the component lead dry in the hole.

Always do the heating and suctioning from the underside of a board, not from the component side. Repeat this action for every component lead joined to the circuit board. When you master this technique, you can remove a small chip, such as a 16-pin memory chip, in a minute or two with only a small likelihood of damage to the board or other components. Larger chips with many pins can be more difficult to remove and resolder without damaging other components or the circuit board.

If you intend to add soldering and unsoldering skills to your arsenal of abilities, you should practice. Take a useless circuit board and practice removing various components from the board. Then reinstall the components. When you are removing the components from the board, try to use the least amount of heat possible. Also, perform the solder-melting operations as quickly as possible and limit the time you apply the iron to the joint. Before you install any components, clean out the holes through which the leads must project and mount the component into place. Then apply the solder from the underside of the board, using as little heat and solder as possible. Attempt to produce joints as clean as the joints that the board manufacturer performed by machine. Soldered joints that do not look clean may keep the component from making a good connection with the rest of the circuit. You want the solder to melt completely but not overheat. If not enough heat is used, a cold-solder joint will be created and result in a poor connection.

> **Caution**
>
> Remember that you should not practice your new soldering skills on the motherboard of a system you are attempting to repair. Don't attempt to work on real boards until you are sure of your skills. I always keep a few junk boards around for soldering practice and experimentation.

No matter how good you get at soldering and desoldering, there are some jobs that are best left to the professionals. Because some components are surface-mounted to a circuit board and because some have very high pin densities, special tools (owned by the professionals) are required for soldering and desoldering. For example, I recently upgraded my IBM P75 portable system by replacing the 486DX-33 processor with a 486DX2-66 processor. This would normally be a simple procedure (especially if the system used a Zero Insertion Force or ZIF socket), but in this system the 168-pin 486DX chip was soldered into a special processor card in the system. To add to the difficulty, there were surface-mounted components on both sides (even the solder side) of the processor card. Well, needless to say, this was a very difficult job that required a special piece of equipment called a *hot air rework station*. This is a solder station that uses blasts of hot air to simultaneously solder or desolder all the pins of a chip at once. To perform this replacement job the components on the solder side were protected by a special heat resistant masking tape, and the hot air was directed at the 168-pins of the 486 chip while the chip was pulled out from the other side. Then the new chip was placed in the holes in the board, a special solder paste was applied to the pins, and the hot air was used again to simultaneously solder all 168 pins.

The use of professional equipment like this resulted in a perfect job that cannot be told apart from a factory original; it also resulted in a perfectly operating 66 MHz system. Attempting a job like this with a conventional soldering iron would have probably damaged the very expensive DX2 processor chip as well as the even more expensive multi-layer processor card.

Using Proper Test Equipment

In some cases you must use some very simple specialized devices to test a system board or component. This test equipment is not expensive or difficult to use, and using it can increase your troubleshooting capabilities. Inexpensive devices like Wrap plugs and a volt-ohm meter (VOM) are required gear for in-depth system testing. The wrap plugs allow the testing of serial and parallel ports and their attached cables. A VOM can serve many purposes, including checking for voltage signals at different points in a system, testing the output of the power supply, and checking for continuity in a circuit or cable. An outlet tester is another invaluable accessory that can check the electrical outlet for proper wiring. This is useful if you believe the problem lies outside of the computer system.

Logic probes and pulsers are not mandatory equipment, but by using them, you can improve your troubleshooting proficiency. Use the logic probe to check for the existence and status of digital signals at various points in a circuit. You use the logic pulser to inject signals into a circuit to evaluate the circuit's operation. Using these devices effectively requires more understanding of how the circuit operates.

Wrap Plugs (Loopback Connectors)

For diagnosing serial- and parallel-port problems, you need *wrap plugs* (also called *loopback connectors*), which are used to circulate (or wrap) signals. The plugs enable the serial or parallel port to send data to itself for diagnostic purposes. Several types of wrap plugs are available. You need one for the 25-pin serial port, one for the 9-pin serial port, and one for the 25-pin parallel port (see table 6.1). Many companies, including IBM, sell the plugs separately; IBM also sells a special version that includes all three types in one plug.

Table 6.1 Wrap Plug Types	
Description	**IBM Part Number**
Parallel-port wrap plug	8529228
Serial-port wrap plug, 25-pin	8529280
Serial-port wrap plug, 9-pin (AT)	8286126
Triconnector wrap plug	72X8546

The handy triconnector unit contains all the common plugs in one compact unit. The unit costs approximately $30 from IBM. Be aware that most professional diagnostic packages (especially the ones I recommend) include the three types of wrap plugs as part of the package, so you may not need to purchase them separately. If you're handy, you can even make your own wrap plugs for testing. I have included wiring diagrams for the three types of wrap plugs in the Appendix of this book.

Meters

Many troubleshooting procedures require that you measure voltage and resistance. You take these measurements by using a hand-held volt-ohm meter (VOM). The meters can be analog devices (using an actual meter) or digital-readout devices. The VOM has a pair of wires, called *test leads*, or *probes*. The test leads make the connections so that you can take readings. Depending on the meter's setting, the probes will measure electrical resistance, direct-current voltage (DCV), or alternating-current voltage (ACV).

Usually, each system-unit measurement setting has several ranges of operation. DC voltage, for example, usually can be read in several scales to a maximum of 200 millivolts,

2 volts, 20 volts, 200 volts, and 1,000 volts. Because computers use both +5 and +12 volts for various operations, you should use the 20-volt-maximum scale for making your measurements. Making these measurements on the 200-millivolt or 2-volt scales could "peg the meter" and possibly damage it because the voltage would be much higher than expected. Using the 200-volt or 1,000-volt scales works, but the readings at 5 volts and 12 volts are so small in proportion to the maximum that precision is low, and exact values are hard to read.

If you are taking a measurement and are unsure of the actual voltage, start at the highest scale and work your way down. Some better system-unit meters have an autoranging capability: The meter automatically selects the best range for any measurement. This type of meter is much easier to operate. You just set the meter to the type of reading you want, such as DC volts, and attach the probes to the signal source. The meter selects the correct voltage range and displays the value. Because of their design, these types of meters always have a digital display rather than a meter needle.

I prefer the small, digital meters. You can buy them for only slightly more than the analog style, and they're extremely accurate. Some are not much bigger than a cassette tape; they fit in a shirt pocket. Radio Shack sells a good unit (made for Radio Shack by Beckman) in the $30 price range, which is only a half-inch thick, weighs 3 1/2 ounces, and is digital and autoranging as well. This type of meter works well for most if not all PC troubleshooting and test uses.

You should be aware that many analog meters can be dangerous to digital circuits. These meters use a 9-volt battery to power the meter for resistance measurements. If you use this type of meter to measure resistance on some digital circuits, you can damage the electronics because you are essentially injecting 9 volts into the circuit. The digital meters universally run on 3 to 5 volts or less.

Logic Probes and Logic Pulsers

A logic probe can be useful in diagnosing problems with digital circuits. In a digital circuit, a signal is represented as either high (+5 volts) or low (0 volts). Because these signals might be present for only a short time (measured in millionths of a second), or might be oscillating or switching on and off rapidly, a simple voltmeter is useless. A logic probe is designed to display these signal conditions easily.

Logic probes are especially useful in troubleshooting a dead system. Using the probe, you can determine whether the basic clock circuitry is operating and whether other signals necessary to system operation are present. In some cases, a probe can help you also cross-check the signals at each pin on an IC chip. You can compare the signals present at each pin to what a known, good chip of the same type would show—a comparison helpful in isolating a failed component. Logic probes can be useful also in troubleshooting some disk drive problems by letting you test the signals present on the interface cable or drive-logic board.

A companion tool to the probe is the *logic pulser*. A pulser is designed to test circuit reaction by delivering into a circuit a logical high (+5 volt) pulse, usually lasting 1 1/2 to 10

III

Hardware Considerations

millionths of a second. Compare the reaction to that of a known functional circuit. This type of device normally is used much less frequently than a logic probe, but in some cases can be helpful in testing a circuit.

Outlet Testers

A very useful test tool is an *outlet tester*—a simple, inexpensive device sold in hardware stores—used to test electrical outlets. You simply plug in the outlet tester and three LEDs will light in various combinations indicating whether the outlet is wired correctly.

Although you may think that badly wired outlets are a rare problem, I have actually run into many installations where the outlets were wired incorrectly.

Most of the time it seems that the problems are with the ground wire. An improperly wired outlet can result in flaky system operations (such as random parity checks and lockups). With an improper ground circuit, currents can begin flowing on the electrical ground circuits in the system. Because the voltage on the ground circuits is used by the system as a comparator to determine whether bits are 0 or 1, data errors can erupt in the system. Once, while I was running one of my PC troubleshooting seminars, I came across a system that I literally could not approach without locking it up. When I walked by the system, the electrostatic field that was generated by my body interfered with the system, and the PC locked up with a "parity check" error message. The problem was that the hotel we were using was very old and had no grounded outlets in the room. The only way I could prevent the system from locking up was to run the class in my stocking feet, because my leather-soled shoes were generating the static charge.

Another symptom of bad ground wiring in electrical outlets is when you receive electrical shocks after you touch the case or chassis of the system. This situation indicates that voltages are flowing where they should not be flowing. It can also indicate that there are bad or improper grounds within the system itself. By using the simple outlet tester, you can quickly determine whether the outlet is at fault.

Chemicals

You can use chemicals to help clean, troubleshoot, and even repair a system. For the most basic function, cleaning components and electrical connectors and contacts, one of the most useful chemicals is 1,1,1 trichloroethane. This substance, sometimes sold as *carbo-chlor,* is a very effective cleaner. You can use it to clean electrical contacts and components, and it will not damage most plastics and board materials. In fact, carbo-chlor can be very useful for cleaning stains on the system case and keyboard. New replacements for tricholroethane are being offered by many electronic chemical supply companies because it is being regulated along with other CFCs (Chloroflourocarbons), such as Freon.

There is a unique type of contact enhancer and lubricant on the market called *Stabilant 22.* This chemical is applied to electrical contacts and acts to greatly enhance the connection as well as lubricate the contact point. It is much more effective than conventional contact cleaners or lubricants.

Stabilant 22 is actually a liquid polymer semiconductor that behaves like liquid metal and conducts electricity in the presence of an electrical current. It also serves to fill in the air gaps between the mating surfaces of two items in contact, which makes the surface area of the contact larger and keeps out oxygen and other contaminants that can oxidize and corrode the contact point.

Stabilant 22 is available in several forms. Stabilant 22 itself is the full-strength, concentrated version, while Stabilant 22a is a version diluted with isopropanol in a 4 to 1 ratio. An even more diluted 8 to 1 ratio version is sold in many high-end stereo and audio shops under the name *Tweek*. Just 15ml of Stabilant 22a sells for about $40, while a liter of the concentrate costs about $4000. As you can plainly see, Stabilant 22 is very expensive, but very little is required in an application, and nothing else has been found to be as effective in preserving electrical contacts. An application of Stabilant can provide protection for up to 16 years, according to the manufacturer, and is used by NASA on spacecraft electronics. Stabilant is manufactured and sold by D. W. Electrochemicals. You will find their address and phone number in the vendor list in the Appendix.

Stabilant is especially effective on I/O slot connectors, adapter card edge and pin connectors, disk drive connectors, power supply connectors, and virtually any connectors in the PC. In addition to enhancing the contact and preventing corrosion, an application of Stabilant will lubricate the contacts, making insertion and removal of the connector easier.

Compressed air often is used as an aid in system cleaning. Normally composed of Freon or carbon dioxide, compressed gas is used as a blower to remove dust and debris from a system or component. Be careful when you use these devices: Some of them can generate a tremendous static charge as the compressed gas leaves the nozzle of the can. Be sure that you are using the kind approved for cleaning or dusting off computer equipment, and consider wearing a static grounding strap as a precaution. Freon TF is known to generate these large static charges; Freon R12 is less severe. Of course, because both chemicals are damaging to the ozone layer, they are being phased out by most suppliers. Expect to see new versions of these compressed-air devices with carbon dioxide or some other less-harmful propellant.

Caution

If you use any chemical with the propellant Freon R12 (dichlorodifluoromethane), *do not expose the gas to an open flame or other heat source*. If you burn this substance, a highly toxic gas called *phosgene* is generated. Phosgene, used as a nerve gas in WWII, can be deadly.

Freon R12 is the substance used in most automobile air conditioner systems. Because of this, automobile service technicians are instructed *never* to smoke near air-conditioner systems. By 1995, the manufacture and use of R12 and many other CFCs will be either banned or strictly regulated by the government, and replacements will have to be found. For example, government regulations mandate that all new automobile air conditioning systems must change to to a non-ozone depleting chemical called *R-134a* by the start of 1995. The unfortunate side effect of this is that these newer replacement chemicals are much more expensive than the ones they replace.

III

Hardware Considerations

Related to compressed-air products are chemical-freeze sprays. These sprays are used to quickly cool down a suspected failing component to restore it to operation. These substances are not used to repair a device, but rather to confirm that you have found the failed device. Often, a component's failure is heat-related; cooling it temporarily restores it to normal operation. If the circuit begins operating normally, the device you are cooling is the suspect device.

A Word about Hardware

This section discusses some problems you might encounter with the hardware (screws, nuts, bolts, and so on) used in assembling a system.

Types of Hardware

One of the biggest aggravations you encounter in dealing with various systems on the market is the different hardware types and designs that hold the units together.

For example, most system hardware types use screws that can be driven with 1/4-inch or 3/16-inch hexagonal drivers. IBM used these screws in all original PC, XT, and AT systems, and most compatible systems use this standard hardware as well. Some manufacturers might use different hardware. COMPAQ, for example, uses Torx screws extensively in most of its systems. A Torx screw has a star-shaped hole driven by the correct-size Torx driver. These drivers carry size designations, such as T-8, T-9, T-10, T-15, T-20, T-25, T-30, and T-40. A variation on the Torx screw is the tamper-proof Torx screw, found in power supplies, displays, and other assemblies. These screws are identical to the regular Torx screws except that a pin sticks up exactly in the middle of the star-shaped hole in the screw. This pin prevents the standard Torx driver from entering the hole to grip the screw; a special tamper-proof driver with a corresponding hole for the pin is required. An alternative is to use a small chisel to knock out the pin in the screw. Usually, a device sealed with these types of screws is considered a complete, replaceable unit and rarely, if ever, needs to be opened.

The more standard, slotted-head and Phillips-head screws are used by many manufacturers as well. Using tools on these screws is relatively easy, but tools do not grip these fasteners as well as hexagonal-head or Torx screws, and the heads can be rounded off more easily than other types. Extremely cheap versions of these tools tend to lose bits of metal as they're turned with a driver, and these metal bits can fall onto the motherboard. Stay away from cheap fasteners whenever possible; the headaches from dealing with stripped screws aren't worth it.

English versus Metric

Another area of aggravation with hardware is that two types of thread systems are available: English and metric. IBM used mostly English-threaded fasteners in its original line of systems, but many other manufacturers used metric-threaded fasteners in their systems.

The difference between English and metric becomes especially apparent with disk drives. American-manufactured drives use English fasteners; drives made in Japan or Taiwan usually use metric fasteners. Whenever you replace a floppy drive in an early-model IBM unit, you encounter this problem. Try to buy the correct screws and any other hardware (such as brackets) with the drive because they might be difficult to find at a local hardware store. The OEM's drive manual has the correct data about a specific drive's hole locations and thread size.

Hard disks can use either English or metric fasteners. To find out what kind of fastener you have, check your hard drive directly or consult the documentation.

> **Caution**
>
> Some screws in a system might be length-critical, especially screws used to retain hard disk drives. You can destroy some hard disks by using a mounting screw that's too long. A screw that is too long can puncture or dent the sealed disk chamber when you install the drive and fully tighten the screw. When you install a new drive in a system, always make a trial fit of the hardware and see how far the screws can be inserted in the drive before they interfere with components on the drive. When in doubt, the drive manufacturer's OEM documentation will tell you precisely what screws are required, and how long they should be.

Disassembly Procedures

The process of physically disassembling and reassembling systems isn't difficult. Because of marketplace standardization, only a couple of different types and sizes of screws (with a few exceptions) are used to hold the systems together, and the physical arrangement of the major components is similar even among systems from different manufacturers. Also, not many individual components are in each system. This section breaks down the disassembly and reassembly procedure into these sections:

- Case or cover assembly
- Adapter boards
- Disk drives
- Power supply
- Motherboard

This section explains how to remove and install these components for several of the different system types. When it comes to assembly and disassembly, it is best to consider each system by the type of case it uses. For example, all systems with AT type cases are

III

Hardware Considerations

assembled and disassembled in much the same manner. Tower cases are basically AT type cases turned sideways, so the same basic instructions would apply there as well. Most of the slim-line and XT style cases are similar, and these systems are assembled and disassembled in much the same way as well. In the following section, disassembly and reassembly instructions are listed for several of the different case types, including standard IBM-compatible systems as well as several PS/2 systems.

Disassembly Preparation

Before you begin to disassemble any system, you should be aware of a couple of precautions. One is ESD protection. Another is recording the configuration of the system, both the physical aspects of the system (such as jumper or switch settings and cable orientations) and the logical configuration of the system (such as CMOS settings).

Electrostatic Discharge (ESD) Protection. When you work on the internal components of a system, you must take precautions to prevent accidental static discharges to the components. At any given time, your body can hold a large static voltage charge that can easily damage components in your systems. Before I ever put my hands into an open system, I first touch a grounded portion of the chassis (such as the power supply case). This touch equalizes the charge that both me and the device are carrying. Although some people would say that the charge is vented off to ground in this case, it really isn't, because the system should be unplugged. You see, I have never recommended working on a system with the cord plugged in because of the electrical hazard, as well as the simple fact that it is too easy to either power the system on at the wrong time or simply forget to turn it off. It is too easy to drop tools and other things into systems while they are powered on. When you drop items into systems, circuits can short out and get damaged. After once destroying an adapter card by accidentally plugging it in while the system was running, I decided that the only good way to insure that the system is really off is to unplug it.

I have been told by some people that if the system is not plugged in, the static charges cannot be vented off to ground. Although that is true, the problem with static is *not* whether a device carries a charge or not; it is whether that charge suddenly flows from one device to another through the delicate logic circuits. By touching the system chassis, or any other part of the system's ground circuit, you are equalizing the charge between you and the system, which will insure that no additional charge will pass from you to the IC chips. No matter what anybody says, you absolutely do not want the system plugged in.

A more sophisticated way to equalize the charges between you and any of the system components is to use the Electrostatic Discharge (ESD) protection kit mentioned earlier. These kits consist of a wrist strap and mat, with ground wires to attach them to the system chassis. Before you work on a system, place the mat next to or partially underneath the system unit. Then clip a ground wire to both the mat and the system's chassis, tying the grounds together. Then put on the wrist strap and attach that wire to a ground as well. Because the mat and system chassis are already wired together, you can attach the wrist-strap wire to either the system chassis or the mat itself. If you are using a wrist strap without a mat, then clip the wrist-strap wire to the system chassis. When you clip these wires to the chassis, be sure to use an area that is free from paint so that you can achieve good ground contact. This setup insures that any electrical charge is carried equally by you and any of the components in the system. This setup also prevents the sudden flow of static electricity, which can damage the circuits.

After you remove disk drives, adapter cards, and especially delicate items (such as the entire motherboard as well as SIMMs or processor chips), place them on the static mat. I see some people put the system unit on top of the mat, but it should be along the side of the mat so that you have room to lay out all of the components after you remove them. If you are going to remove the motherboard from a system, be sure to leave enough room on the mat for it.

If you do not have a static mat, then simply lay the removed circuits and devices on a clean desk or table surface. Always pick up loose adapter cards by the metal bracket used to secure the card to the system. This bracket is tied into the ground circuitry of the card. By touching the metal bracket first, you will prevent a discharge from damaging the components on the card. If the circuit board has no metal bracket (such as a mother-board), then carefully handle the board by the edges and try not to touch any of the components.

Caution

Some people have recommended that loose circuit boards and chips should be placed on sheets of aluminum foil. This procedure is absolutely *not recommended* and can actually result in an explosion. You see, many motherboards, adapter cards, and other circuit boards today have built-in lithium or nicad batteries. These batteries react violently when they are shorted out, which is exactly what you would be doing by laying such a board on a piece of aluminum foil. The batteries will quickly overheat and possibly explode like a large firecracker (with dangerous shrapnel). Because it is often not possible for you to know whether a board has a battery built into it somewhere, the simple warning is to *never* place any board on any conductive metal surface such as foil.

Recording Setup and Configuration. Before you power the system off for the last time to remove the case, there are several things you should find out about the system and record them. Many times, when working on a system, you will intentionally or accidentally wipe out the CMOS setup information. Most systems use a special battery-powered CMOS clock and data chip that are used to store the system configuration information. If the battery is disconnected, or if certain pins are accidentally shorted, you can discharge the CMOS memory and lose the setup. The CMOS memory in most systems is used to store simple things such as how many and what type of floppy drives are connected, how much memory is in the system, and the date and time. A critical piece of information is the hard disk type settings. Although you and the system can easily determine the other settings the next time you power the system on, the hard disk type information is another story. Most modern BIOS software can actually read the type information directly from most IDE and all SCSI drives. With older BIOS software, however, you have to explicitly tell the system what the parameters of the attached hard disk are. This

III

Hardware Considerations

means that you need to know the current settings for cylinders, heads, and sectors per track. Some BIOS software indicates the hard disk only by a *type* number, usually from 1 through 47. Be aware that most BIOS programs use type 47 as a *user-definable type,* which means that the cylinder, head, and sector counts for this type were manually entered and are not constant. These user-definable types are especially important to write down because this information may be very difficult to figure out later when you need to start up the system.

If you do not enter the correct hard disk type information in the CMOS setup program, you will not be able to access the data on the hard disk. I know of several people who have lost some or all of their data because they did not enter the correct type information when they reconfigured their system. If the type information is incorrect, you will most likely get a `Missing operating system` error message when you start the system and you won't be able to access the C drive. You may think that you can just figure out the parameters by looking up the particular hard disk in a table. For example, the table of popular hard disk drive parameters in the Appendix of this book has proven useful to me time and time again. Unfortunately, this only works if the original person setting up the system entered the correct parameters as well. I have encountered many systems where the hard disk parameters were not entered correctly, and the only way to regain access to the data was to determine and use the same incorrect parameters that were originally used. As you can see, you should always record the hard disk information from your setup program.

Most systems have the setup program built right into the ROM BIOS software itself. These built-in setup programs are activated by a hot key sequence such as Ctrl-Alt-Esc or Ctrl-Alt-S (if you have a Phoenix ROM). Other ROMs prompt you for the setup program every time the system boots, such as with the popular AMI BIOS. With the AMI, you simply press the Delete key when the prompt appears on-screen during a reboot.

When you get the setup program running, record all of the settings. The easiest way to do this is to print it out. If a printer is connected, press the Shift-Print Screen keys and a copy of the screen display will be sent to the printer. Some setup programs have several pages of information, so you should record the information on each page as well. Many setup programs, such as those in the AMI BIOS, allow for specialized control over the particular chipset used on the motherboard. These complicated settings can take up several screens of information; however, all the settings should be recorded. Most BIOS software will return all of these settings to a default state when the battery is removed, and you will lose any custom settings that were made.

MCA and EISA bus systems have a very sophisticated setup program that stores not only the motherboard configuration, but configurations for all the adapter cards as well. Fortunately, the setup programs on these systems can save the settings to a file on a floppy disk so that they can be restored later. To access the setup program for most of these systems, you will need the Setup or Reference Diskette for the particular system. Many of the new PS/2 systems store a complete copy of the Reference Diskette on the hard disk in a hidden partition. When these systems boot up, you will notice that the cursor jumps over to the right side of the screen for a few seconds. During this time, if you press Ctrl-Alt-Ins, the hidden setup programs will be executed.

Recording Physical Configuration. While you are disassembling a system, write down or record all the physical settings and configurations within the system. This includes jumper and switch settings, cable orientations and placement, ground wire locations, and even adapter board placement. Keep a notebook handy for recording these items, and write down all of the settings in the book. It is especially important to record all of the jumper and switch settings on every card you remove from the system as well as the motherboard itself. If you accidentally disturb these jumpers or switches, you will know how they were originally set. This is very important if you do not have all the documentation for the system handy; and, even if you do, there are often undocumented jumpers and switches that do not appear in the manuals but must be set a certain way for the item to function. It is very embarrassing, to say the least, if you take apart somebody's system and then cannot make it work again because you disturbed something. If you record these settings, you will save yourself the embarrassment.

You should also record all cable orientations. Most name brand systems use cables and connectors that are keyed so that they cannot be plugged in backwards, but most generic compatibles do not have this luxury. Because it is also possible to mix up hard disk and floppy cables, each cable should be marked or recorded according to what it was plugged into and the proper orientations. Ribbon cables will usually have a different colored wire (usually red, blue, or black) at one end that indicates pin 1. The devices that the cables are plugged into are also marked in some way to indicate the orientation of pin 1, and these should obviously match. Normally the circuit boards and disk drives will have the location of pin 1 silk screened on the board near the connector.

Although cable orientation and placement may seem like a very simple topic, some individuals find it difficult. I rarely get through an entire course in my PC troubleshooting seminars without several groups having cable connection problems. Fortunately, in most cases (except power cables), plugging any ribbon cable inside the system backwards rarely causes any permanent damage. Power and battery connections are a big exception to this, however, and plugging them in backwards will surely cause damage. In fact, plugging in the motherboard power connectors backwards or to the wrong plug location will put 12 volts where only 5 should be and can cause components on the board to explode violently. I know people with scars on their faces caused by shrapnel from exploding components. I always like to turn my face away from the system when I power it on for the first time. Plugging in the CMOS battery backwards can damage the CMOS chip itself, which is usually soldered into the motherboard, requiring replacement of the motherboard itself.

Finally, record other miscellaneous items such as the placement of any ground wires, adapter cards, or anything else you might have difficulty remembering later. Some configurations and setups are particular to which slots the adapter cards are located in, so you should put everything back exactly the way it was originally. This is especially true for any MCA or EISA bus systems.

Now that we have made the necessary preparations and taken the necessary precautions, we can actually begin working on the systems.

XT and Slim Line Case Systems

The procedure for disassembling the XT or Slim Line case systems offered by most manu-facturers is very simple. Only two tools are normally required: a 1/4-inch nut driver for the external screws holding the cover in place and a 3/16-inch nut driver for all other screws. I almost always prefer to use a nut driver, even though most of these screws have a Phillips-type slot embedded within the hexagonal head of the screw. The nut driver can get a much better grip on the screw, and you are much less likely to strip it out com-pared to using a Phillips screwdriver.

Removing the Cover. To remove the case cover:

1. Turn off the system and unplug the power cord from the system unit.

2. Turn the system unit around so that the rear of the unit is facing you, and locate the screws that hold the system-unit cover in place (see fig. 6.1).

3. Use the 1/4-inch nut driver to remove the cover screws.

4. Slide the cover toward the front of the system unit until it stops. Lift up the front of the cover and remove it from the chassis.

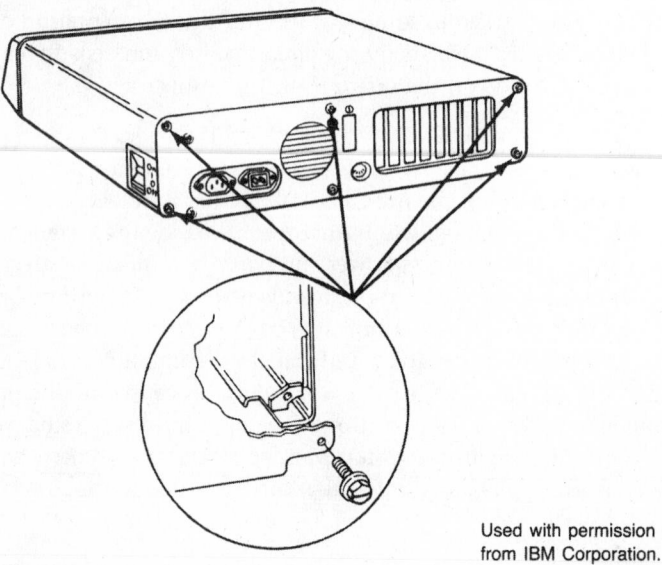

Used with permission
from IBM Corporation.

Fig. 6.1
The screws holding the XT-style case cover in place.

To remove all adapter boards from the system unit, first remove the system-unit cover, as described earlier. Then proceed as follows for each adapter:

1. Note which slot each adapter is in. If possible, make a diagram or drawing.

2. Use a nut driver or screwdriver to remove the screw holding the adapter in place (see fig. 6.2).

3. Note the position of any cable plugged into the adapter before removing it. In a correctly wired system, the colored stripe on one side of the ribbon cable always denotes pin number 1. The power connector is normally shaped (keyed) so that it can be inserted only the correct way, but be careful, some are not keyed in this manner.

4. Remove the adapter by lifting with even force at both ends.

5. Note the positions of any jumpers or switches on the adapter, especially when documentation for the adapter isn't available. Even when documentation is available, undocumented jumpers and switches often are used by manufacturers for special purposes, such as testing or unique configurations.

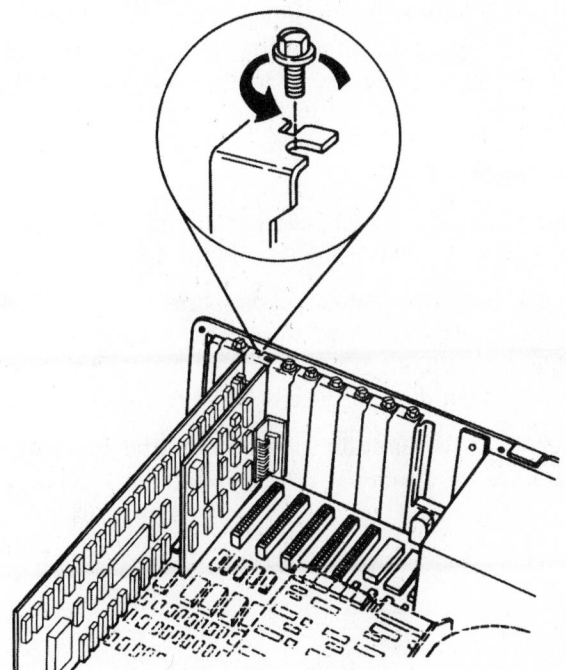

Used with permission from IBM Corporation.

Fig. 6.2
Removing the screw that holds the adapter in place.

III

Hardware Considerations

Jumpers and switches normally are named on the circuit board. SW1 and SW2 are used for switch 1 and switch 2, for example, and J1 and J2 are used for jumper 1 and jumper 2. If these jumpers or switches later are disturbed, you can return to the original configuration—as long as you noted it when the adapter was first removed. The best procedure usually is to make a diagram showing these features for a particular card.

Removing Disk Drives. Removing drives from XT or Slim Line cases is fairly easy. The procedures are similar for both floppy and hard disk drives.

Before you remove any hard disks from the system, they should be backed up. Older drives should have the heads parked as well, but almost all newer drives automatically park the heads when the power is off. Always handle the disk drives with care because data can be lost or the drive can be damaged from rough handling. Hard disks are discussed in more detail in Chapter 10.

First remove the cover and all adapters, as previously described. Then proceed as follows:

1. Some systems have drive-retaining screws on the bottom of the chassis. Lift up the front of the chassis so that the unit is standing with the rear of the chassis down and the disk drive facing straight up. Locate any drive-retaining screws in the bottom of the chassis and remove them. On IBM equipment, you will find these screws in the XT systems with hard disks or half-height floppy drives (see fig. 6.3). Sometimes the drive-retaining screws are shorter than others used in the system to prevent interference with the drive mechanism, circuitry, or HDA (Head Disk Assembly). If shorter screws are used to retain the disk drives, you must reinstall these screws in their original locations or use new screws of the correct length. A screw that is too long can damage the drive.

2. Set the chassis flat on the table and locate the drive-retaining screws on the outboard sides of the drive. Remove them (see fig. 6.4 and fig. 6.5).

3. Slide the disk drive forward about two inches and disconnect the power and signal cables from the drive (see fig. 6.6 and fig. 6.7). In a correctly wired system, the odd-colored stripe on one side of the ribbon cable always denotes pin number 1. The power connector is shaped so that it can be inserted only the correct way.

4. Slide the drive completely out of the unit. In some systems, the drives are removed by sliding them backwards into the interior of the system rather than out of a hole in the chassis.

   This connector is present only on double-sided drives.

   System/expansion board power connectors.

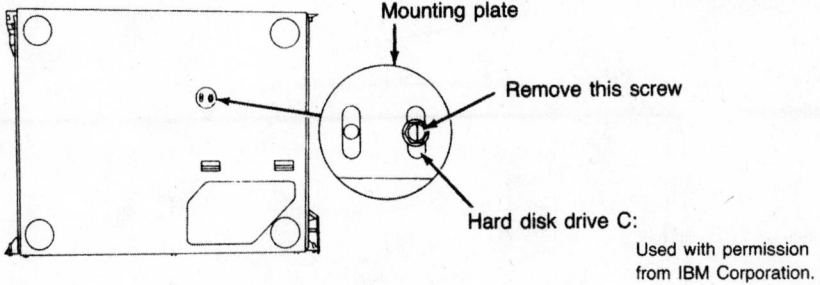

Mounting plate

Remove this screw

Hard disk drive C:

Used with permission
from IBM Corporation.

Fig. 6.3
Removing the retaining screws from the bottom of the chassis.

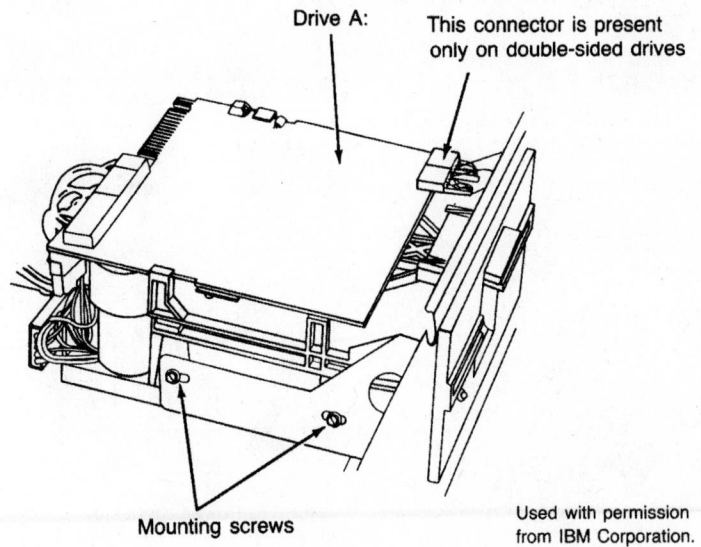

Drive A:

This connector is present
only on double-sided drives

Mounting screws

Used with permission
from IBM Corporation.

Fig. 6.4
Removing the retaining screws from the outboard sides of a floppy disk drive.

Removing the Power Supply. In XT or Slim Line case systems, the power supply is mounted in the system unit with four screws in the rear and usually two interlocking tabs on the bottom. Removing the power supply may require that you remove the disk drives before getting the power supply out. You will probably have to at least loosen the drives to slide them forward for clearance when you remove the supply.

III

Hardware Considerations

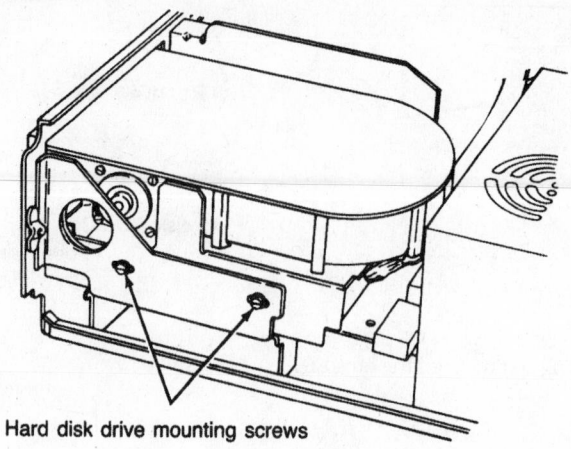

Hard disk drive mounting screws

Used with permission
from IBM Corporation.

Fig. 6.5
Removing the retaining screws from the outboard sides of the hard disk drive.

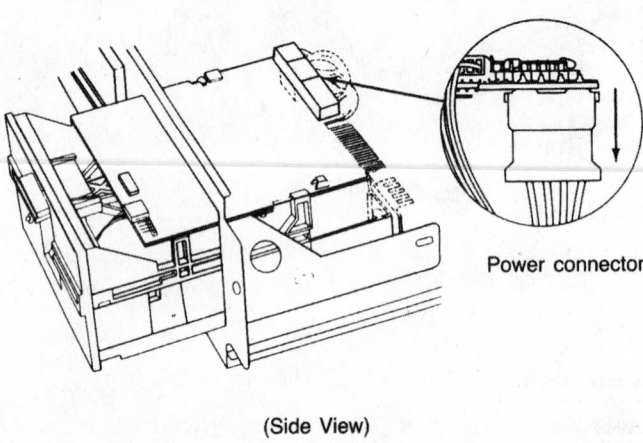

Power connector

(Side View)

Used with permission
from IBM Corporation.

Fig. 6.6
The power connector on a floppy disk drive.

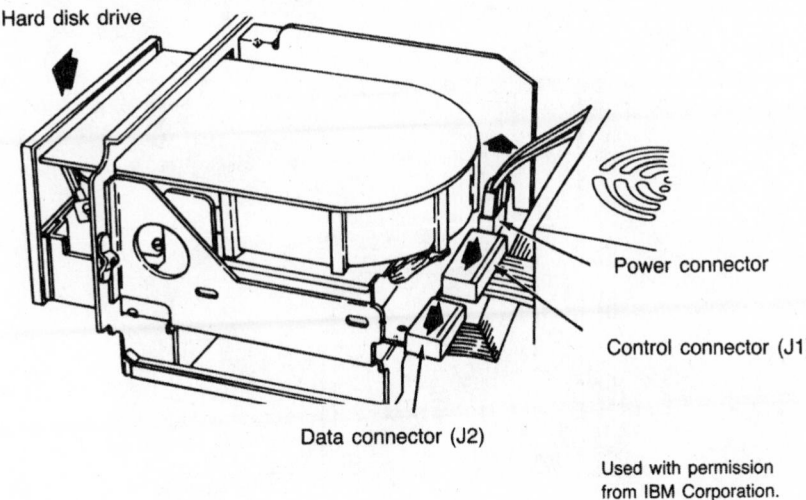

Used with permission
from IBM Corporation.

Fig. 6.7
Disconnecting the power and signal cables from the hard disk drive.

To remove the power supply, first remove the cover, all adapter boards, and the disk drives, as described earlier. If sufficient clearance exists, you might not have to remove the adapter boards and disk drives. Then proceed as follows:

1. Remove the four power-supply retaining screws from the rear of the system-unit chassis (see fig. 6.8).

2. Disconnect the cables from the power supply to the motherboard (see fig. 6.9). Disconnect the power cables from the power supply to the disk drives. Always grasp the connectors themselves; never pull on the wires.

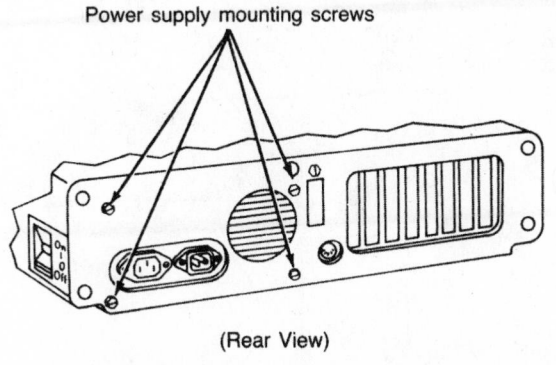

Used with permission
from IBM Corporation.

Fig. 6.8
Removing the power supply retaining screws from the rear of the chassis.

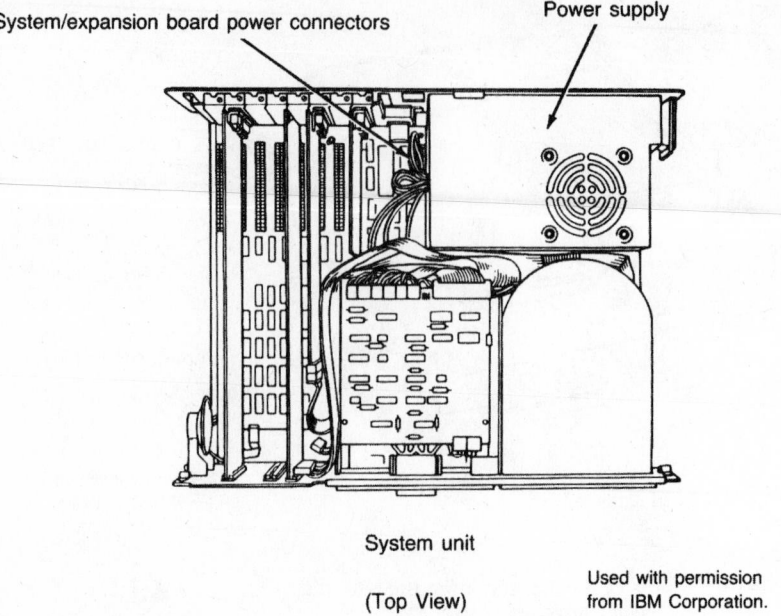

System/expansion board power connectors

Power supply

System unit

(Top View)

Used with permission
from IBM Corporation.

Fig. 6.9
Disconnecting the cables from the power supply to the motherboard.

3. Slide the power supply forward about a half-inch to disengage the interlocking tabs on the bottom of the unit. Lift the power supply out of the unit (see fig. 6.10).

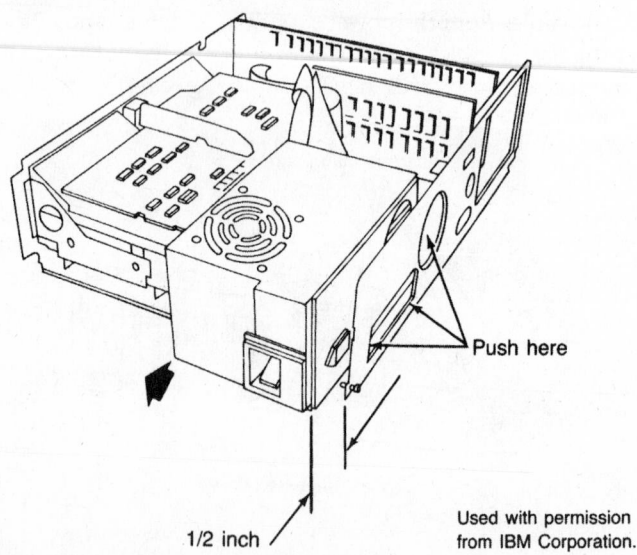

Push here

1/2 inch

Used with permission
from IBM Corporation.

Fig. 6.10
Sliding the power supply forward to disengage the interlocking tabs on the unit's bottom.

Removing the Motherboard. After all the adapter cards are removed from the unit, you can remove the system board, or *motherboard*. The motherboard in XT and Slim Line case systems is held in place by only a few screws and often several plastic standoffs. The standoffs are used to elevate the board from the metal chassis so that it does not touch the chassis and cause a short. The standoffs attatch to the motherboard through holes in the board and then slide into slots in the chassis. *These standoffs should remain with the motherboard.* You do not have to extract these standoffs from the motherboard to remove it; just remove the motherboard with the standoffs still attached. When you reinstall the motherboard, make sure that the standoffs slide properly in their slots. If one or more standoffs have not properly engaged the chassis, you might crack the motherboard when you tighten the screws or install adapter cards.

To remove the motherboard, first remove all adapter boards from the system unit, as described earlier. Then proceed as follows:

1. Disconnect from the motherboard all electrical connectors, including those for the keyboard, power supply, and speaker.

2. Locate and remove the motherboard retaining screws.

3. Slide the motherboard away from the power supply about a half-inch until the standoffs have disengaged from their mounting slots (see fig. 6.11).

4. Lift the motherboard up and out of the chassis.

AT/Tower Case Systems

Disassembling an AT or Tower case system normally requires only two tools: a 1/4-inch nut driver for the external screws holding the cover in place and a 3/16-inch nut driver for all the other screws.

Most of the procedures to disassemble an AT or Tower case system are exactly like those for the XT or Slimline case systems. One difference, however, is that many AT case systems use a different method for mounting the disk drives. Special rails are attached to the sides of the drives, and the drives slide into the system-unit chassis on these rails. Because the chassis has guide tracks for the rails, you can remove the drive from the front of the unit without having to access the side to remove any mounting screws. Normally the rails are made of plastic or fiberglass, but they can also be made of metal in some systems. To see a diagram that shows how most of these rails are constructed, refer to Chapter 9, "Floppy Disk Drives."

Removing the Cover. To remove the case cover:

1. Turn off the system and unplug the power cord from the system unit.

2. Turn the system unit around so that you're facing the rear of the unit. Locate the screws that hold the system-unit cover in place (see fig. 6.12).

3. Use the 1/4-inch nut driver to remove the cover screws.

4. Slide the cover toward the front of the system unit until it stops. Lift up the front of the cover and remove it from the chassis.

III

Hardware Considerations

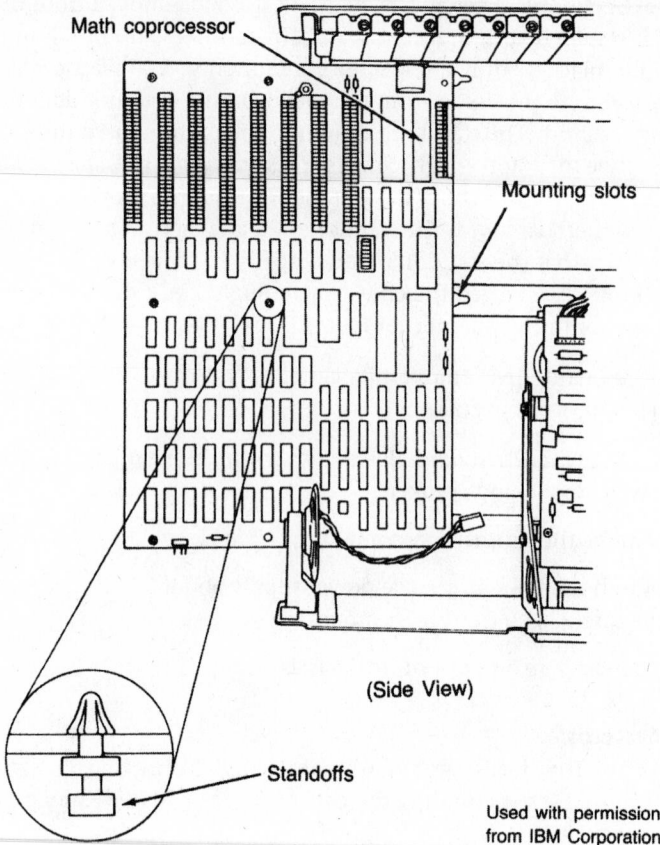

(Side View)

Used with permission
from IBM Corporation.

Fig. 6.11
Sliding the motherboard away from the power supply until standoffs disengage from mounting slots.

Removing Adapter Boards. To remove all the adapter boards from the system unit, first remove the system-unit cover, as described earlier. Then proceed as follows for each adapter:

1. Note which slot each adapter is in. If possible, make a diagram or drawing.

2. Use a nut driver or screwdriver to remove the screw holding the adapter in place (see fig. 6.12).

3. Note the positions of any cables plugged into the adapter before you remove them. In a correctly wired system, the colored stripe on one side of the ribbon cable always denotes pin number 1. Some connectors have keys that enable them to be inserted only the correct way.

4. Remove the adapter board by lifting with even force at both ends.

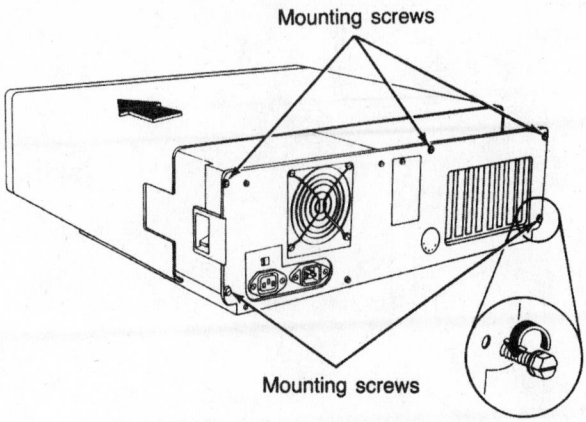

Mounting screws

Mounting screws

Used with permission
from IBM Corporation.

Fig. 6.12
Removing the screws holding the AT case cover in place.

5. Note the positions of all jumpers or switches on the adapter, especially when documentation for the adapter is not available. Even when documentation is available, undocumented jumpers and switches often are used by manufacturers for special purposes, such as testing or unique configurations. It's a good idea to know the existing settings in case they are disturbed.

Removing Disk Drives. Removing disk drives from AT case systems is very easy. The procedures are similar for both floppy and hard disk drives.

Always back up hard disks completely and park the heads before removing disks from the system. Most newer drives (IDE and SCSI) automatically park the heads when powered off. A backup is important because data can get lost or the drive can get damaged from rough handling.

To remove the drives from an AT case system, first remove the cover, as described earlier. Then proceed as follows:

1. Depending on whether the drive is a hard disk or floppy disk drive, it is retained by either a metal keeper bar with two screws or two small, L-shaped metal tabs that are each held in place by a single screw. Locate these screws and remove them, along with the tabs or keeper bar (see fig. 6.13 and fig. 6.14).

2. Slide the disk drive forward about two inches and disconnect it from the power cables, the signal and data cables, and the ground wire (see fig. 6.15 and fig. 6.16). In a correctly wired system, the colored stripe on one side of the ribbon cable always denotes pin number 1. The power connector is shaped so that it can be inserted only the correct way.

3. Slide the drive completely out of the unit. In some systems, the drives are removed by sliding them backwards into the interior of the system rather than out of a hole in the chassis.

III

Hardware Considerations

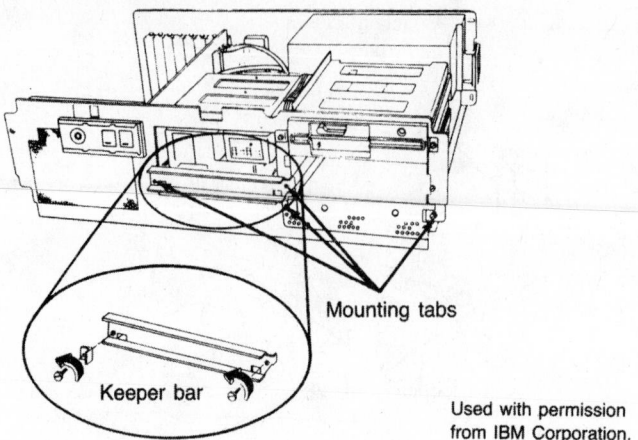

Fig. 6.13

Removing mounting tabs and the keeper bar on a hard disk drive.

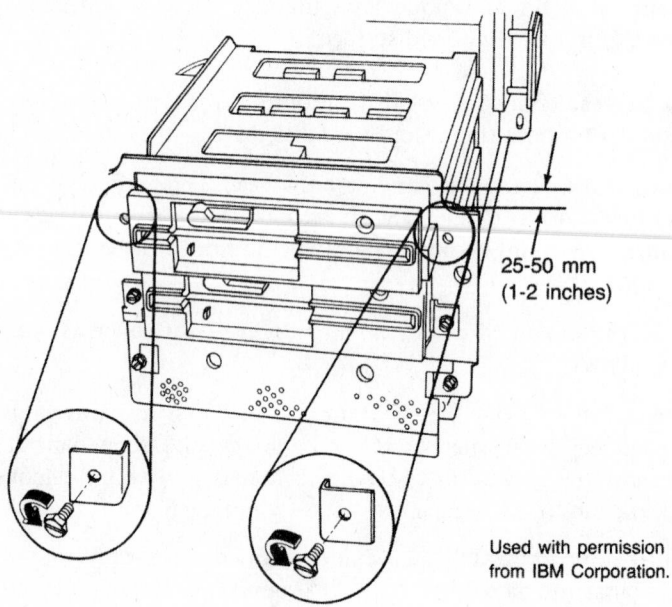

Fig. 6.14

Removing the mounting tabs on a floppy disk drive.

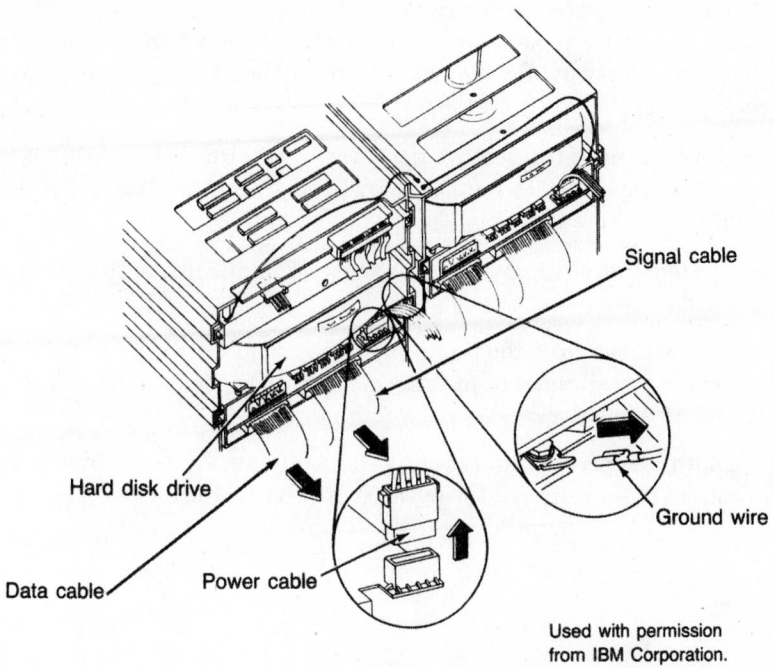

Signal cable

Hard disk drive

Data cable

Power cable

Ground wire

Used with permission
from IBM Corporation.

Fig. 6.15
Disconnecting the hard disk drive power cable, signal and data cables, and ground wire.

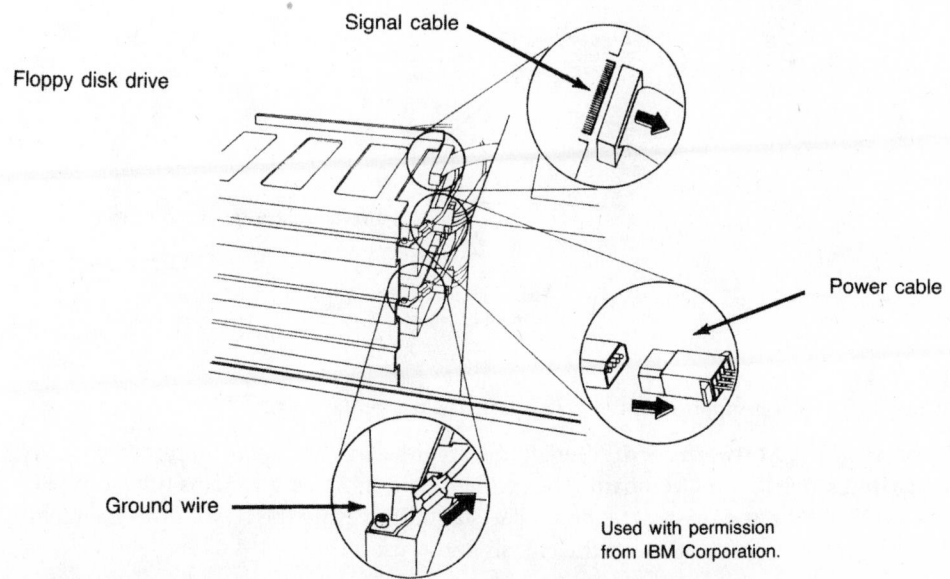

Signal cable

Floppy disk drive

Power cable

Ground wire

Used with permission
from IBM Corporation.

Fig. 6.16
Disconnecting the floppy disk drive power cable, signal cable, and ground wire.

III

Hardware Considerations

Removing the Power Supply. In AT case systems, the power supply is mounted in the system unit with four screws in the rear and usually two interlocking tabs on the bottom. Removing the power supply usually requires that you slide the disk drives forward for clearance when you remove the supply.

To remove the power supply, first remove the cover, loosen the disk drive mounting screws, and move the disk drive forward about two inches, as described earlier. Then proceed as follows:

1. Remove the four power-supply retaining screws from the rear of the system-unit chassis (see fig. 6.17).

2. Disconnect the cables from the power supply to the motherboard (see fig. 6.18). Disconnect the power cables from the power supply to the disk drive. Always grasp the connectors themselves; never pull on the wires.

3. Slide the power supply forward about a half-inch to disengage the interlocking tabs on the bottom of the unit. Lift the power supply out of the unit.

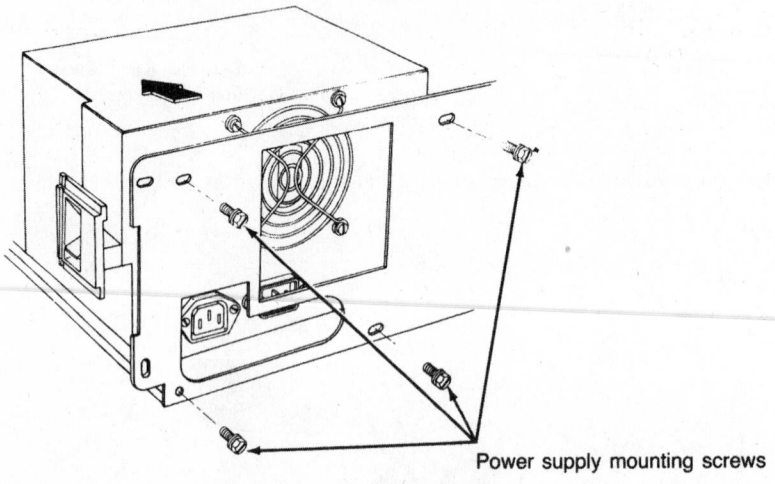

Power supply mounting screws

Used with permission
from IBM Corporation.

Fig. 6.17
Removing the power-supply retaining screws from the rear of the chassis.

Removing the Motherboard. After all the adapter cards are removed from the unit, you can remove the motherboard. The motherboard in AT case systems is held in place by several screws and plastic standoffs. The standoffs elevate the board from the metal chassis so that it does not touch the chassis and cause a short.

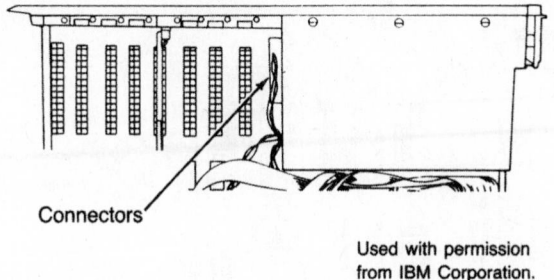

Connectors

Fig. 6.18
Disconnecting the cables from the power supply to the motherboard.

You should not separate the standoffs from the motherboard; remove the board and the standoffs as a unit. The standoffs slide into slots in the chassis. When you reinstall the motherboard, make sure that the standoffs are located properly in their slots. If one or more standoffs have not engaged the chassis properly, you might crack the motherboard when you tighten the screws or install adapter cards.

To remove the motherboard, first remove all adapter boards from the system unit, as described earlier. Then proceed as follows:

1. Disconnect from the motherboard all electrical connectors, including those for the keyboard, power supply, speaker, battery, and keylock.

2. Locate and remove the motherboard retaining screws.

3. Slide the motherboard away from the power supply about a half-inch until the standoffs have disengaged from their mounting slots (see fig. 6.19).

4. Lift the motherboard up and out of the chassis.

PS/2 Systems

The disassembly of IBMs PS/2 systems is incredibly easy. In fact, ease of disassembly and reassembly is one of the greatest features of these systems. In addition to being easy to service and repair, they were designed to be assembled primarily by robots and auto-mated machinery. This type of machinery does not handle conventional fasteners such as screws, nuts, and bolts very well. Most PS/2 systems therefore are assembled with a great deal of "snap together" technology. The screws that are used have a special self-centering design, in which the screw end is tapered so that it is self-guiding, to mate with the threads in the hole. Automated robotic machinery then can insert and tighten the screws more easily and accurately, and without stripping the threads. This approach to construction makes these systems not only easier to assemble by machine but also much easier for people to disassemble and reassemble.

If you can disassemble one style of PS/2 system, you will find that most others are disas-sembled in the same manner, especially systems that are physically similar or identical. Although a variety of PS/2 models exist, many of them are physically very similar. The three original, primary types of PS/2 chassis designs are the 30/30-286/55 SX, the 50/70,

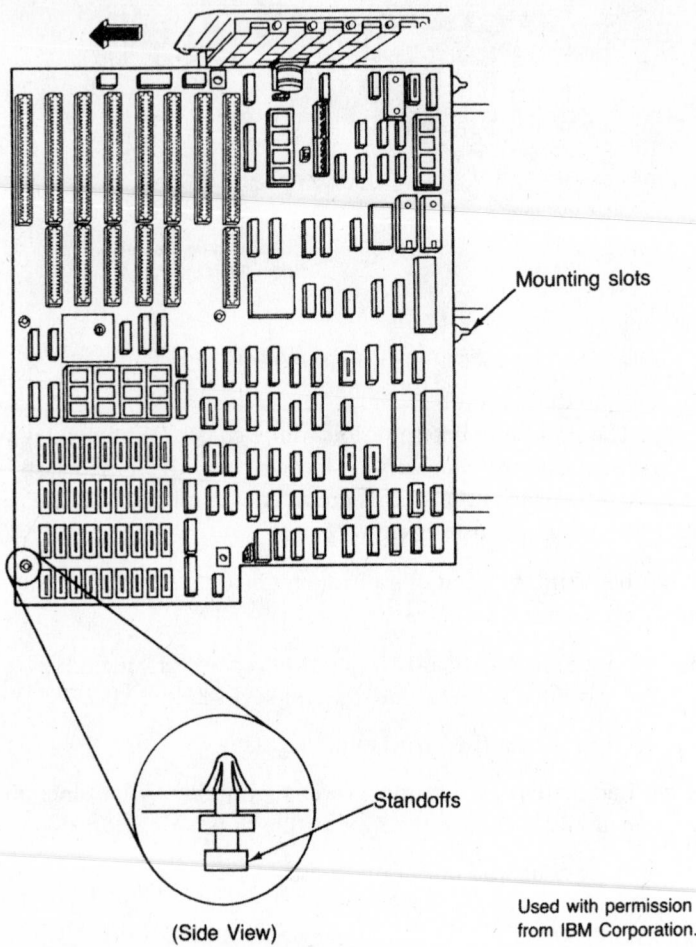

Mounting slots

Standoffs

Used with permission
from IBM Corporation.

(Side View)

Fig. 6.19

Disengaging standoffs from their mounting slots.

and the 60/65/80. Other designs, including the 90, 95, and 35/40/57/76/77, are similar in many ways to the three primary types. Models 25 and 25-286 are unique because of their built-in display. Here is a quick summary of the different PS/2 system chassis:

- Models 25 and 25-286 have a unique design with a built-in monitor.

- Models 30, 30-286, and 55 SX share a common chassis and mechanical design, although their circuit boards are different.

- The newer 35, 40, 56, 57, 76, and 77 systems are almost physically identical to each other. Many of these different models even share motherboards.

- Models 50, 50 Z, and 70 represent the "ultimate" in ease of disassembly and reassembly. These units have not a single cable in their default configuration and are snapped together almost entirely without conventional fasteners. Models 50 Z and 70 especially share many physical components and are difficult to tell apart from the outside.

■ Models 60, 65 SX, and 80 are full-size, floor-standing systems. These systems are virtually identical to each other from a physical standpoint and share most of their physical components, even though the motherboards are different.

■ The newer Model 90 is similar to the 50/70 systems in construction, but is unique in some ways. The newer Model 95 is similar to the 60/65/80 systems, but also differs in some ways.

The following section discusses, step-by-step, disassembly and reassembly procedures for the PS/2 systems. A section covers each of the three main system types. The disassembly procedures for the three primary designs can be applied to the other, similar PS/2 system designs as well.

Models 30, 30-286, and 55 SX

This section describes the disassembly procedures for the PS/2 Model 30, Model 30-286, and Model 55 SX. The systems are modular in nature, and most of the procedures are simple.

Removing the Cover. To remove the system-unit cover:

1. Park the hard disk.

2. Turn off the system and unplug the power cord from the wall socket.

3. Disconnect all external options.

4. If the keylock option is installed, make sure that the lock is in the unlocked position and the key removed.

5. Loosen all four screws located at the bottom corners on the sides of the system. Slide the cover back and lift it up and away.

6. Remove the rear cover that covers the system's back panel. You remove this cover by loosening the screw on each corner of the rear cover on the back of the system. Then pull the rear cover back and away from the system unit (see fig. 6.20).

Removing the 3 1/2-inch Floppy Disk Drive. The procedure for removing the floppy drive is very simple. Proceed as follows:

1. Remove the front cover (the bezel) from the drive by pushing down on the two plastic tabs on top of the bezel.

2. Pull the bezel off and away from the front of the system.

3. Disconnect the disk cabling by gently pulling the cable away from the drive.

4. Remove the plastic nails from each side of the drive bracket.

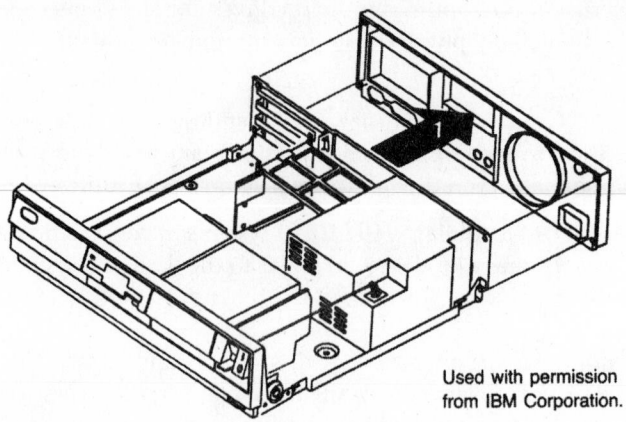

Used with permission
from IBM Corporation.

Fig. 6.20
Removing the rear cover (Models 30, 30-286, and 55 SX).

5. Press up on the plastic tab under the front of the drive.

6. Pull the drive forward out of the system (see fig. 6.21).

Removing the Fixed Disk Drive. Before removing the fixed disk, make sure that the heads have been parked. You can use the Reference Disk to perform this task. Simply boot the disk, and select the Move the computer option from the main menu. If this option is not present, IBM supplied your system with only self-parking drives; you park them by simply turning off the power. Even if the option is present, you still might have a self-parking drive (refer to Chapter 4 for more information). You can remove the drive by following these steps (which are similar to the steps for removing a floppy drive):

1. Remove the front cover (the bezel) from the drive by pushing down on the two plastic tabs on top of the bezel and pulling it off and away from the front of the system.

2. Disconnect the disk cabling by gently pulling the cable away from the drive.

3. Remove the plastic nails from each side of the drive bracket.

4. Press upward on the plastic tab under the front of the drive, and pull the drive forward out of the system.

Removing Adapters. To remove all adapter cards from the system unit, first remove the system-unit cover, as described earlier. Then proceed as follows for each adapter:

1. Remove the screw from the bracket retaining the card.

2. Slide the adapter sideways out of the system unit (see fig. 6.22).

If you add new options, their installation might require that you remove the plastic insert on the rear panel. Also, if you add a 3/4-length adapter, you must adjust the sliding support bracket to support the adapter properly.

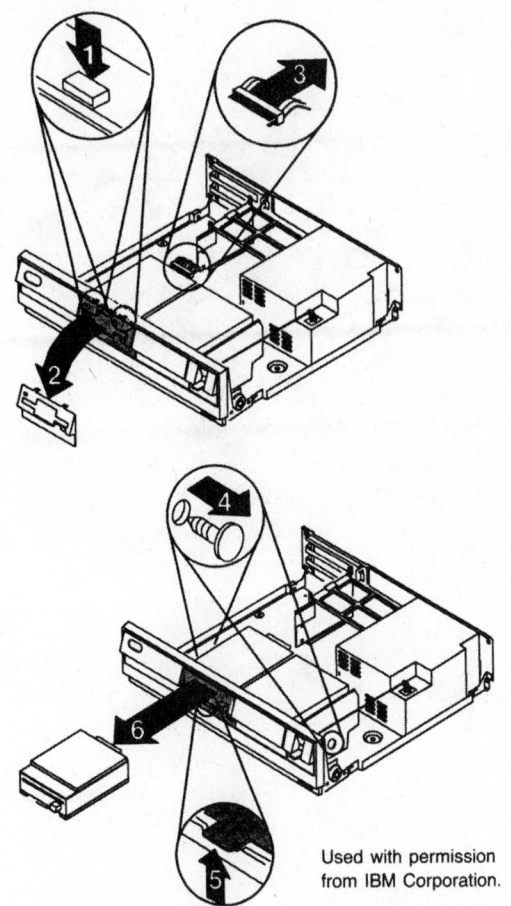

Used with permission
from IBM Corporation.

Fig. 6.21
Removing a 3 1/2-inch floppy disk drive (Models 30, 30-286, and 55 SX).

Removing the Bus Adapter. These systems have a bus adapter card that contains the slots. This adapter plugs into the motherboard. To remove the device, proceed as follows:

1. Push in on the two tabs on top of the bus adapter support.

2. Gently rotate the end of the support upward and disengage the tabs in the power supply.

3. Lift up and remove the bus adapter (see fig. 6.23).

Removing the Power Supply. When you remove the power supply, first remove the rear cover and the bus adapter support, as described earlier. Then proceed as follows:

1. Disconnect the power connector from the power supply to the motherboard by pulling the connector straight up.

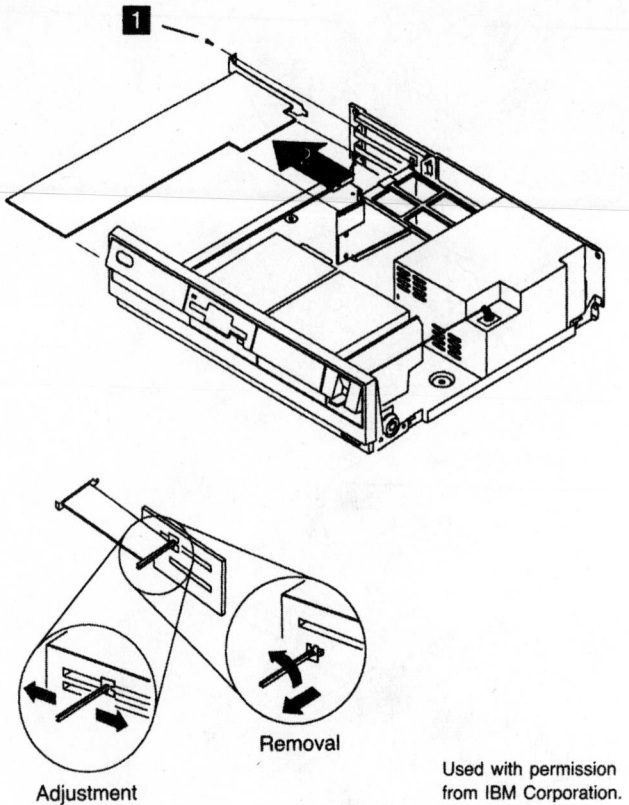

Fig. 6.22

Removing adapter cards (Models 30, 30-286, and 55 SX).

2. Disengage the power-switch link from the power supply.

3. Remove the three screws that secure the power supply to the system frame. The screws are at the back of the power supply.

4. Gently slide the power supply toward the front of the system to disengage the power supply from the base of the frame.

5. Lift the power supply up and away from the unit (see fig. 6.24).

Removing Single In-line Memory Modules (SIMMs). One benefit of using single in-line memory modules (SIMMs) is that they're easy to remove or install. When you remove memory modules, remember that because of physical interference you must remove the memory-module package closest to the disk drive bus-adapter slot before you remove the package closest to the edge of the motherboard. To remove a SIMM properly, follow this procedure:

1. Gently pull the tabs on each side of the SIMM socket outward.

2. Rotate or pull the SIMM up and out of the socket (see fig. 6.25).

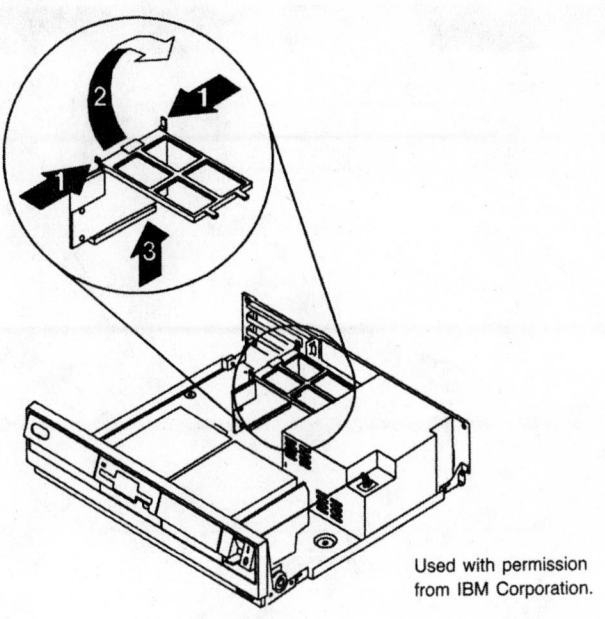

Used with permission
from IBM Corporation.

Fig. 6.23
Removing the bus adapter (Models 30, 30-286, and 55 SX).

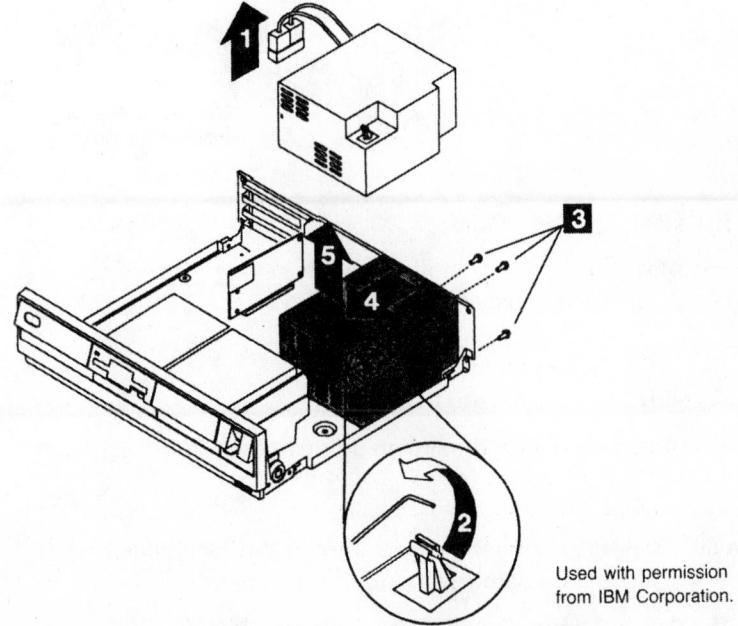

Used with permission
from IBM Corporation.

Fig. 6.24
Removing the power supply (Models 30, 30-286, and 55 SX).

III

Hardware Considerations

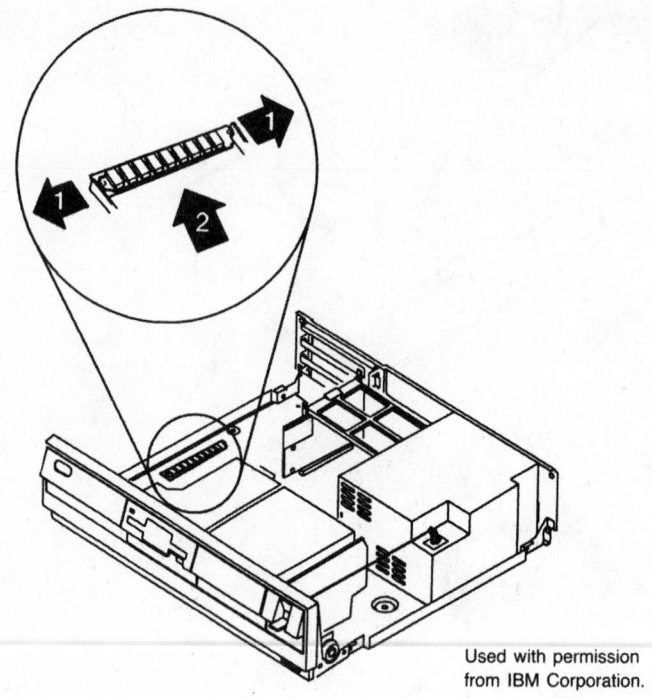

Used with permission
from IBM Corporation.

Fig. 6.25
Removing a SIMM (Models 30, 30-286, and 55 SX).

Removing the Motherboard. The motherboard is held in place by several screws, all of which must be taken out. Proceed as follows:

1. Remove all screws.

2. Carefully slide the motherboard to the left.

3. Lift the motherboard out of the system unit (see fig. 6.26).

Models 50, 50 Z, and 70

This section describes the disassembly procedures for the PS/2 Models 50, 50 Z, and 70. These systems are modular in nature, and most of the procedures are simple.

Removing the Cover. To remove the system-unit cover:

1. Park the hard disk. Nearly all these systems come with self-parking hard disks; only the 20M drive used in the Model 50 does not. Self-parking drives require no

manual parking operation. Because no parking program is necessary, the reference disks for the Model 70 do not have a head-parking program or menu selection.

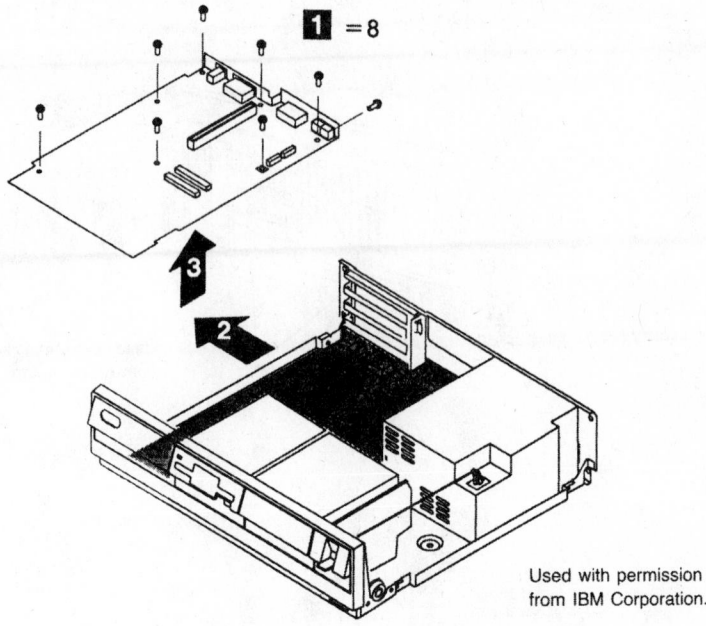

Used with permission from IBM Corporation.

Fig. 6.26
Removing the motherboard (Models 30, 30-286, and 55 SX).

2. Turn off the system and unplug the power cord from the wall socket.

3. Unlock the cover.

4. Loosen the two cover thumbscrews on the back of the system.

5. Slide the cover toward you and lift it off (see fig. 6.27).

Removing the Battery-and-Speaker Assembly. The battery and speaker are contained in a single assembly. To remove this assembly, follow these steps:

1. To avoid accidentally discharging the battery, remove the battery from its holder before removing the battery-and-speaker assembly: bend the tabs on the holder toward the rear and pull the battery straight up. Remember to install this assembly before replacing the battery.

2. Push the tab on the bottom of the speaker unit to disengage the speaker assembly from the support structure.

3. Lift the entire battery-and-speaker assembly up and out of the system (see fig. 6.28).

Removing the Fan Assembly. The fan assembly in Model 70 systems is an integral part of the power supply. In these systems, the fan is screwed directly to the power supply. You remove the fan by removing the power supply.

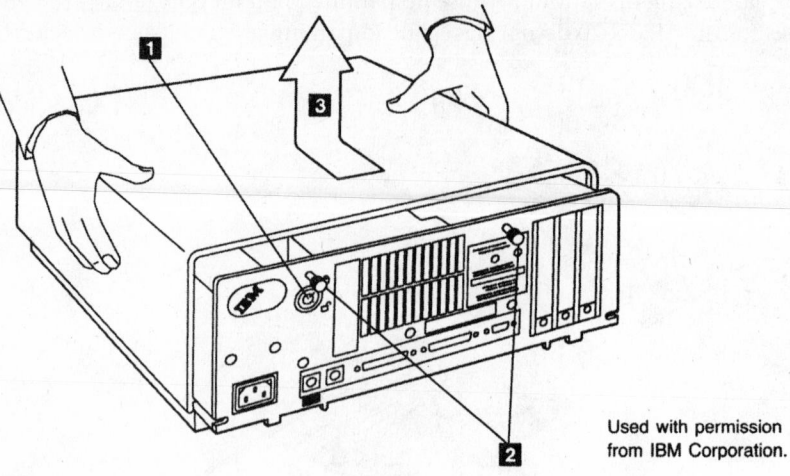

Used with permission
from IBM Corporation.

Fig. 6.27
Removing the cover (Models 50 and 70).

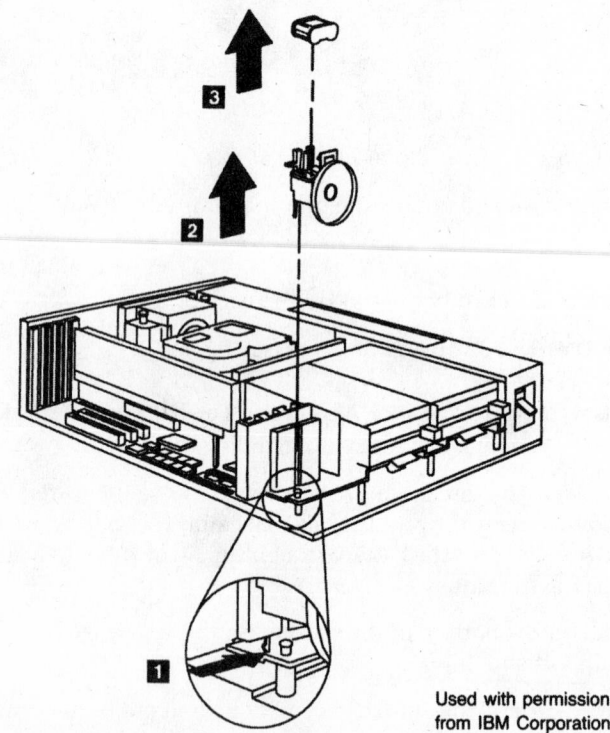

Used with permission
from IBM Corporation.

Fig. 6.28
Removing the battery-and-speaker assembly (Models 50 and 70).

In Model 50 systems, remove the fan assembly as follows:

1. Disengage the two plastic push-button tabs on either side of the fan assembly by prying them upward. If necessary, use the small pry tool located at the front, right corner of the system.

2. Pull the entire assembly up and out of the system (see fig. 6.29).

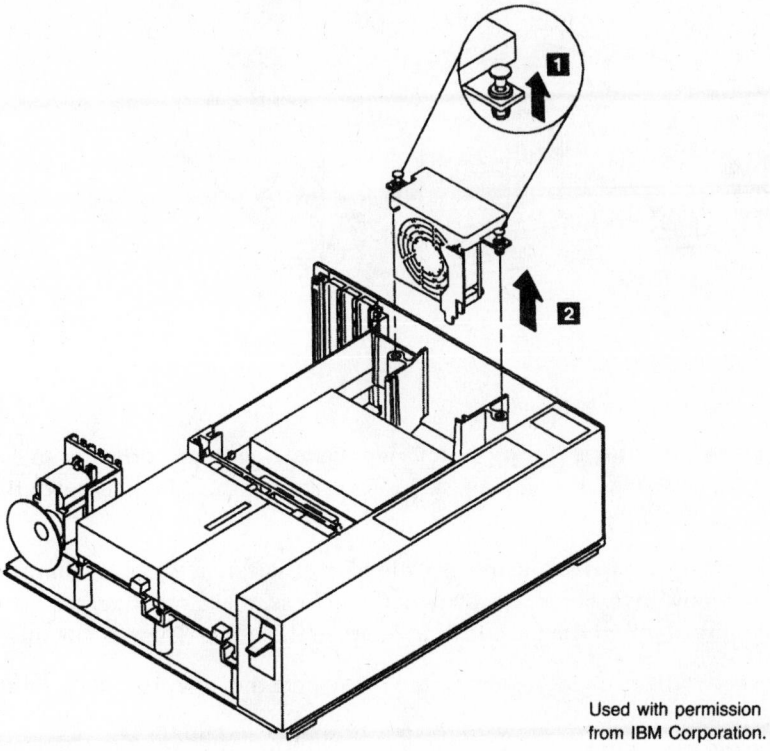

Used with permission
from IBM Corporation.

Fig. 6.29
Removing the fan assembly (Model 50).

Removing Adapters. An important part of removing adapter boards in these systems is to make a diagram of the adapter and cable locations.

You should put all adapters back in the same slot from which they were removed. Otherwise, the CMOS memory configuration must be run.

To remove the adapters, follow these steps:

1. Make sure that all cables are disconnected.

2. Loosen the retaining thumb screw at the base of the card bracket.

3. Grasp the option adapter and gently pull it up and out of the system unit (see fig. 6.30).

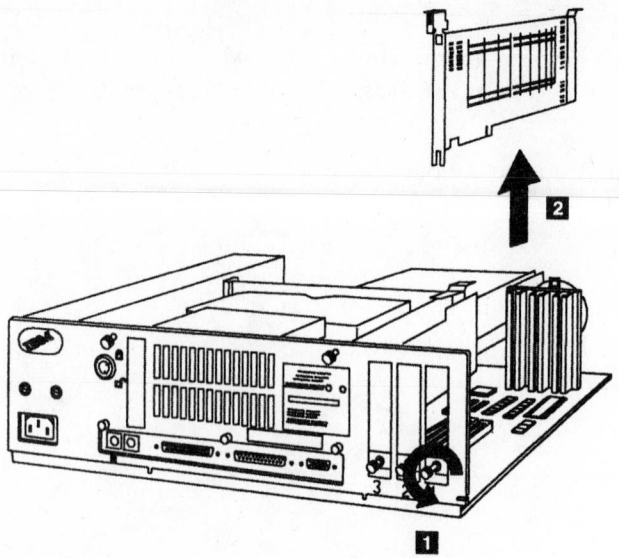

Used with permission
from IBM Corporation.

Fig. 6.30
Removing an adapter (Models 50 and 70).

Removing the 3 1/2-Inch Floppy Disk Drive. Removing floppy drives from 3 1/2-inch floppy disk drive systems is a simple task. Just push up on the tab underneath the floppy drive, and slide the drive out toward you.

Removing Fixed Disk Drives. Removing the hard disk from a system is almost as easy as removing a floppy drive. Before removing the hard disk, make sure that you've backed up all the information on the fixed disk and parked the heads. Then follow these steps:

1. Press down the two plastic tabs on the side where the power supply is located.

2. Slide the fixed disk drive toward the power supply and up.

3. Grasp the adapter at each end and gently pull the adapter up (see fig. 6.31).

Removing the Drive-Support Structure. To remove the support structure from the system unit, you first must remove these components:

    Cover
    Battery-and-speaker assembly
    Fan assembly
    Adapters
    Floppy disk drives
    Fixed disk drives

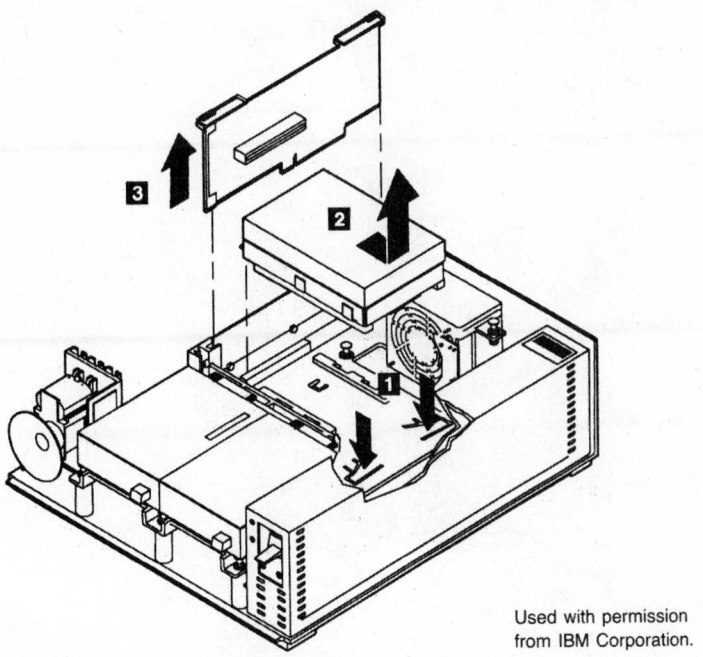

Used with permission
from IBM Corporation.

Fig. 6.31
Removing the fixed disk drive (Models 50 and 70).

After you have removed these items, pull up all six white, plastic, push-button lock tabs and lift the assembly up (see fig. 6.32). If necessary, use the small pry tool on the front, right side of the system to pry up the lock tabs.

Removing the Power Supply. To remove the power supply, follow these steps:

1. Remove the screw on the front, left side of the system.

2. Remove the two screws on the back of the power supply.

3. Slide the power supply to the right and then remove it from the system unit (see fig. 6.33).

Removing the Motherboard. To remove the motherboard from the system unit, you first must remove these components:

Cover
Battery-and-speaker assembly
Fan assembly
Adapters
Floppy disk drives
Fixed disk drives
Disk-support structure
Power supply

III

Hardware Considerations

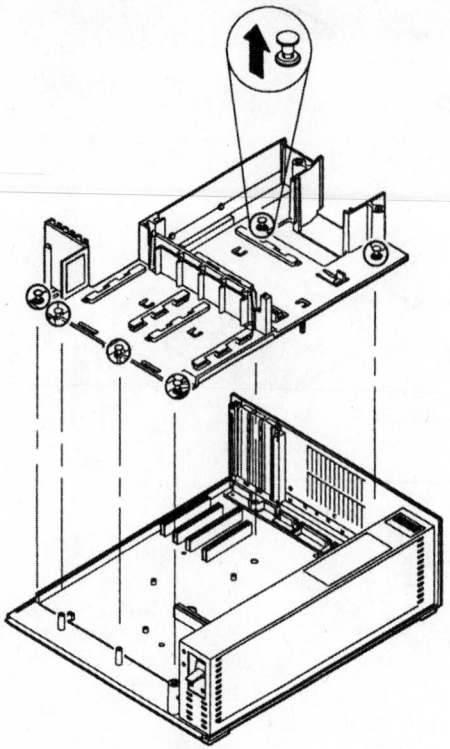

Used with permission
from IBM Corporation.

Fig. 6.32
Removing the drive-support structure (Models 50 and 70).

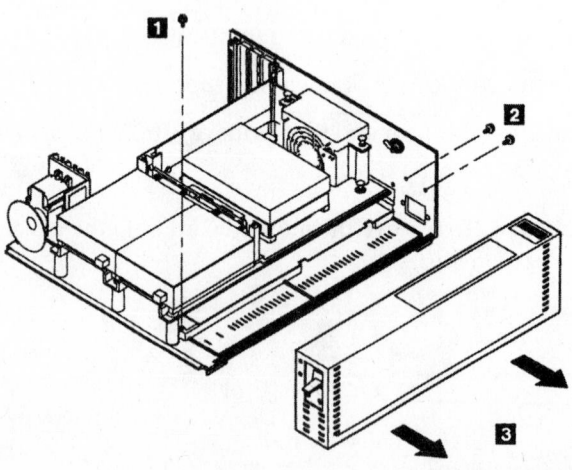

Used with permission
from IBM Corporation.

Fig. 6.33
Removing the power supply (Models 50 and 70).

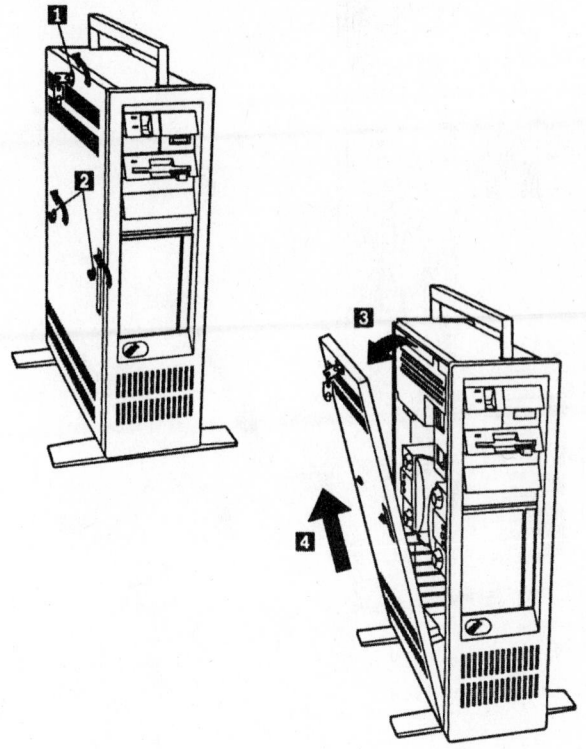

Used with permission
from IBM Corporation.

Fig. 6.36
Removing the cover (Models 60, 65 SX, and 80).

To remove the adapters, follow these steps:

1. Make sure that all cables are disconnected.

2. Loosen the retaining thumb screw at the base of the card bracket.

3. Grasp the option adapter and gently pull it up and out of the system unit (see fig. 6.37).

Removing the Battery-and-Speaker Assembly. The battery and speaker are contained in a single assembly. To remove this assembly, follow these steps:

1. To avoid accidentally discharging the battery, remove the battery from its holder before removing the battery-and-speaker assembly: bend the tabs on the holder toward the rear, and pull the battery straight up. Remember to install this assembly before replacing the battery.

2. Disconnect the battery-and-speaker assembly cable.

3. Push the tab on the bottom of the speaker unit to disengage the speaker assembly from the support structure (see fig. 6.38).

4. Lift the entire battery-and-speaker assembly up and out of the system.

III

Hardware Considerations

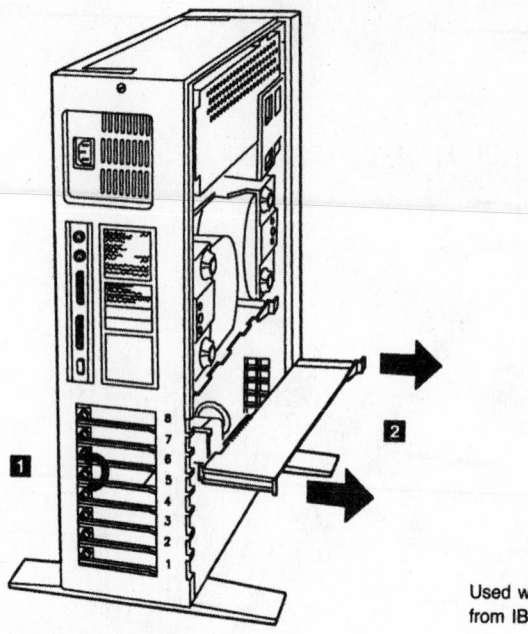

Used with permission
from IBM Corporation.

Fig. 6.37
Removing an adapter (Models 60, 65 SX, and 80).

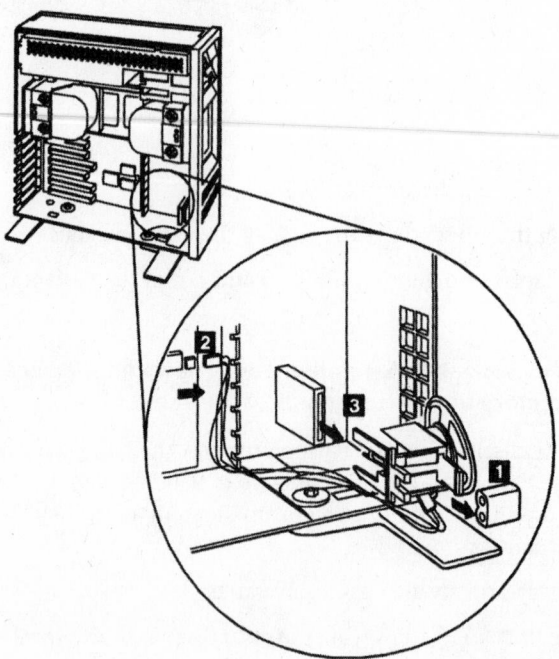

Used with permission
from IBM Corporation.

Fig. 6.38
Removing the battery-and-speaker assembly (Models 60, 65 SX, and 80).

Removing the Front Bezel. These models have a large front panel, or bezel, that you must remove to gain access to the floppy disk drives. The panel snaps off easily if you follow this procedure:

1. Grasp the bottom of the panel near the feet of the unit.

2. Pull out (see fig. 6.39). The bezel should snap off freely.

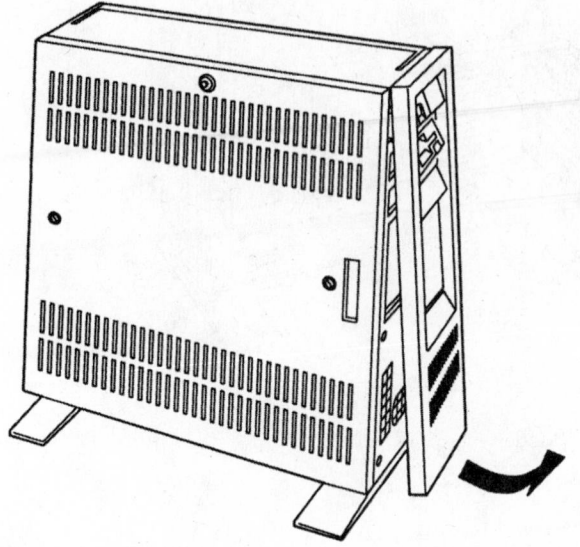

Used with permission
from IBM Corporation.

Fig. 6.39
Removing the bezel (Models 60, 65 SX, and 80).

Removing the Power Supply. To remove the power supply, you first must remove the cover and front bezel. Then follow these steps:

1. Disconnect all cables from the power supply.

2. Remove the three screws that retain the power supply. One screw is near the power switch, and the other two are near the back of the supply.

3. Lift the power supply out the side of the unit (see fig. 6.40).

Removing Floppy Disk Drives. The floppy drives are located next to the power supply. Removing floppy drives from these systems requires only these two steps:

1. Push the tab underneath the floppy drive up while you simultaneously press a tab on the rear of the drive sideways.

2. Slide the drive out the front of the unit (see fig. 6.41).

III

Hardware Considerations

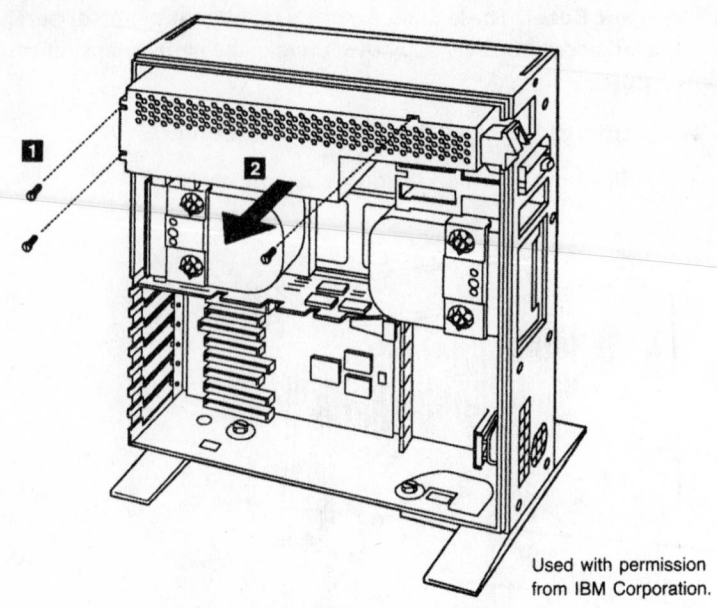

Used with permission
from IBM Corporation.

Fig. 6.40
Removing the power supply (Models 60, 65 SX, and 80).

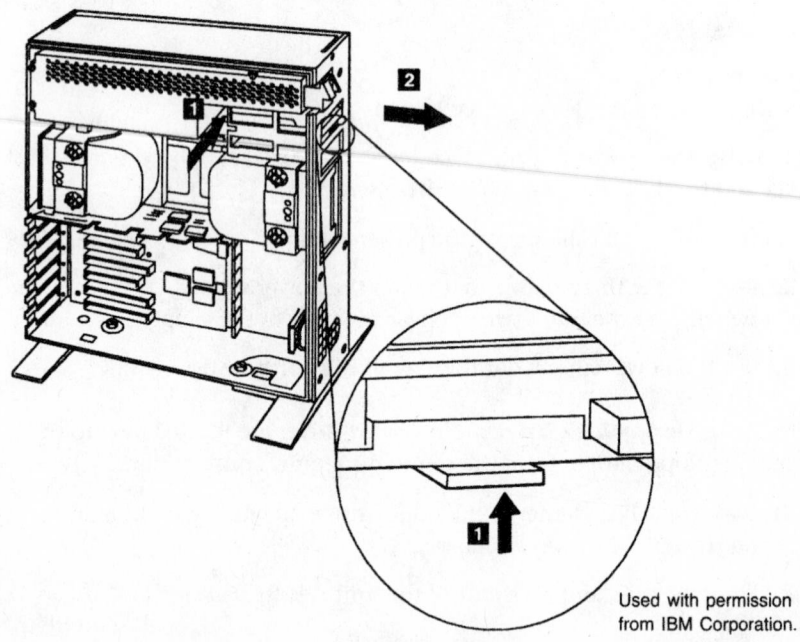

Used with permission
from IBM Corporation.

Fig. 6.41
Removing a disk drive (Models 60, 65 SX, and 80).

Removing the Floppy Disk Drive Cable Retainer. Floppy disk drive systems use a retainer to hold cables in place when the floppy drives are plugged in. To remove this cable retainer, follow these steps:

1. Press the tabs located on the side of the cable retainer.

2. Rotate the retainer out toward the back of the system unit.

3. Pull off the retainer (see fig. 6.42).

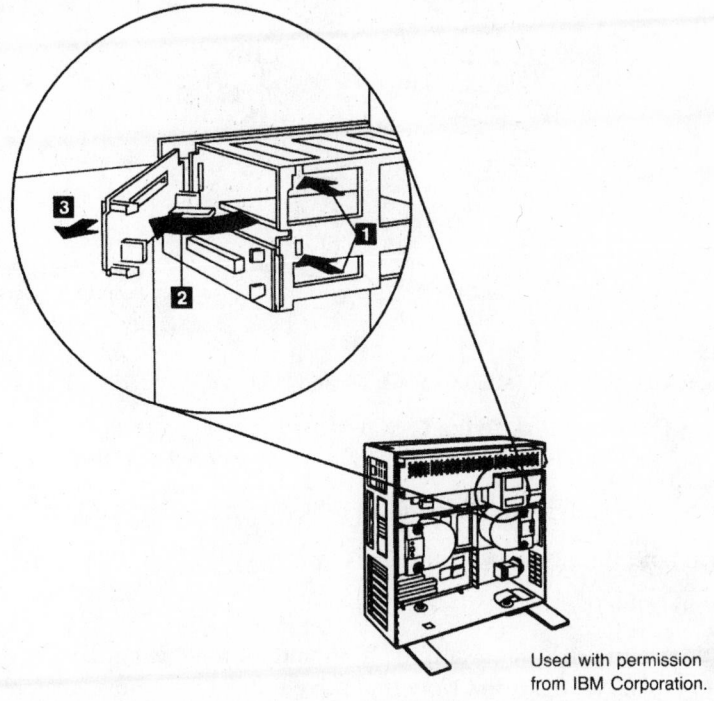

Used with permission
from IBM Corporation.

Fig. 6.42
Removing the disk drive cable retainer (Models 60, 65 SX and 80).

Removing the Fixed Disk Drive D. Make sure that you have a backup of the information on the drive before removing the disk. Then follow these steps:

1. Disconnect the ground wire and all cables from the fixed disk drive.

2. Turn both thumb screws counterclockwise.

3. Remove the front bezel.

4. Slide the fixed disk drive out the front of the system unit (see fig. 6.43). Note that drive D must be removed before drive C because of physical interference.

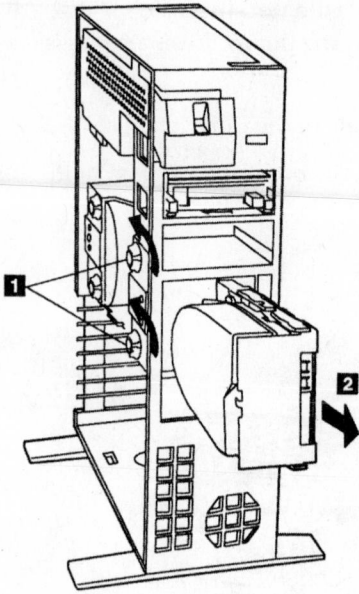

Used with permission
from IBM Corporation.

Fig. 6.43
Removing fixed disk drive D (Models 60, 65 SX, and 80).

Removing the Fixed Disk Drive C. Make sure that you have a backup of the information on the drive before removing the drive. Then proceed as follows:

1. Disconnect the ground wire and all cables from the fixed disk drive.

2. Turn both thumb screws counterclockwise.

3. Remove the front bezel.

4. Slide the drive a little toward the front and lift the fixed disk drive sideways out of the system (see fig. 6.44). Note that drive D must be removed before drive C because of physical interference.

Removing the Fixed Disk Drive-Support Structure. A large, metal hard disk drive support structure is used to clamp the hard disks in place. You must remove this structure in order to remove the motherboard. Follow these steps:

1. Remove the four screws located on the front portion of the structure.

2. Slide the structure forward and lift it up and sideways out of the system (see fig. 6.45).

Removing the Motherboard. To remove the motherboard from the system unit, you first must remove the cover, any adapters, the fixed disk drives, and the fixed disk support structure. With these components removed from the system unit, removal of the motherboard requires these three steps:

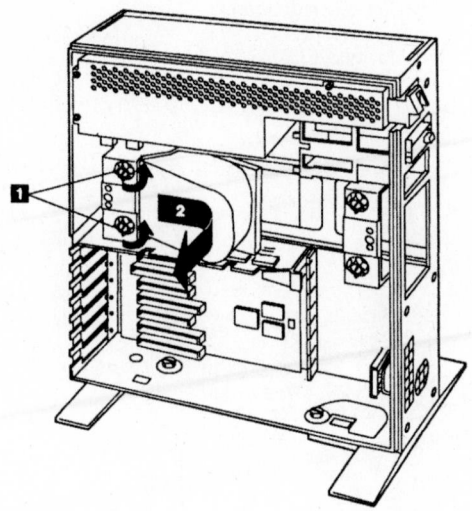

Used with permission
from IBM Corporation.

Fig. 6.44

Removing fixed disk drive C (Models 60, 65 SX, and 80).

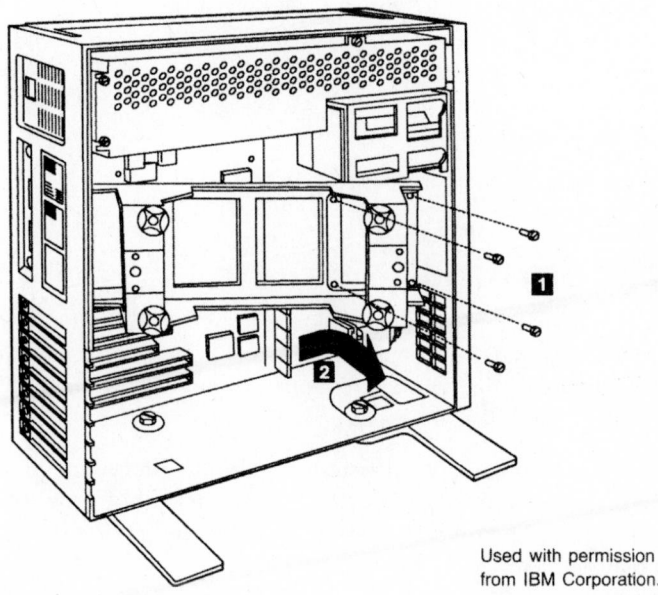

Used with permission
from IBM Corporation.

Fig. 6.45

Removing the fixed disk drive support structure (Models 60, 65 SX, and 80).

III

Hardware Considerations

1. Disconnect all cables from the motherboard.

2. Remove all eight retaining screws.

3. Gently lift the motherboard up and out of the system (see fig. 6.46).

Now that you've examined the procedures for disassembling a system, let's examine the different components that make up a system.

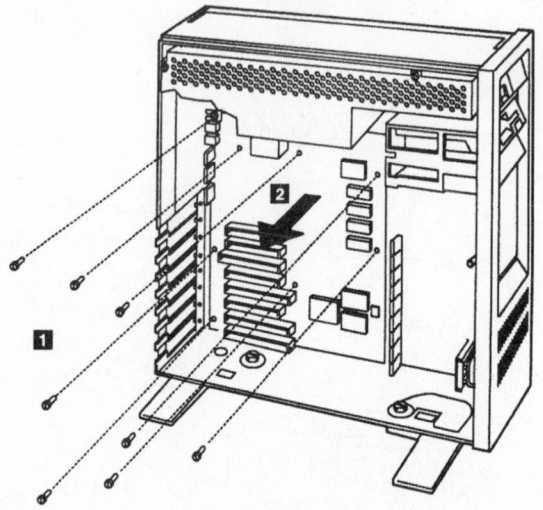

Used with permission from IBM Corporation.

Fig. 6.46
Removing the motherboard (Models 60, 65 SX, and 80).

Chapter Summary

This chapter has discussed the initial teardown and inspection of a system and looked at the types of tools required, from simple hand tools to meters for measuring voltage and resistance. It mentioned some of the problems you might encounter with the actual hardware (screws, nuts, bolts, and so on) in a system.

The chapter also has discussed the physical-disassembly procedure. Emphasis was made on the preliminary steps taken before and during disassembly, such as ESD protection and the recording of system setup information to insure that the system works properly again when reassembled.

Different disassembly procedures were discussed based on the type of case used for the system. Most systems built using a particular style case, such as the AT/Tower cases, are constructed in a similar fashion. After you have worked on a system with one particular type of case design, most others with the same type of case are almost identical.

Chapter 7

Primary System Components

This chapter studies the primary components that make up a typical system's base configuration. These components include:

- Motherboards
- Microprocessors
- Memory
- Slots
- Standard adapter boards
- Power supply
- Keyboards

Most systems are supplied with a system unit and a keyboard. The system unit includes a motherboard, which contains a microprocessor, usually some memory, and slots for expansion of the system. Many systems include one or more standard adapter boards in these slots, such as adapters for disk controllers or serial and parallel ports. At least one floppy disk drive typically is included as well. (For more on floppy disk drives, see Chapter 9.) The system unit also houses a power supply, which provides the correct voltage and current to run the system. The keyboard is an external device attached to the system unit by a cable. Knowing how all these components operate can help when you're trying to track down problems or repair systems.

These components constitute only the base configuration. You need additional devices to complete a system. Some systems, when purchased, don't include a display adapter board, a monitor, or ports for the connection of printers or modems. Systems often include only a minimum of memory, which you must expand before you can perform any serious computing. For example, a 486 might come with only 1M of memory, but you need a minimum of 4M to use Windows or OS/2.

The base configuration of some systems doesn't include a hard disk. Many new systems, however, do include a hard disk, serial and parallel ports, and a display adapter board and monitor. For more information about the peripherals used in a typical system, see Chapter 8.

Motherboards

Easily the most important component in a PC system is the main board or *motherboard*. The terminology can be confusing because IBM refers to the motherboard as a system board or *planar*. The terms *motherboard, system board,* and *planar* are interchangeable. The motherboards in the PS/2 family contain functionally the same components as the motherboards in the original PC family, but they also include components that support the increased functions in these systems. Not all systems have a motherboard in the true sense of the word. In some systems, the components found normally on a motherboard are located instead on an expansion adapter card plugged into a slot. In these systems, the board with the slots is called a backplane, *rather than* a motherboard. Systems using this type of construction are called *backplane systems*.

The motherboard system design and the backplane system design have both advantages and disadvantages. Most original personal computers were designed as backplanes in the late 1970's. Apple and IBM shifted the market to the now-traditional motherboard with a slot-type design because this type of system generally is cheaper to mass-produce than one with the backplane design. The advantage of a backplane system, however, is that you can upgrade it easily to a new processor and new level of performance by changing a single card. For example, you can upgrade a system with an 80286-based processor card to an 80386-based card just by changing the card. In a motherboard-design system, you must change the motherboard itself, a more formidable task.

Slightly different from a true backplane design is the processor-complex design, first used in some compatibles such as those from AST and ALR and now in the newer IBM PS/2 systems and systems from COMPAQ. In this design, the main processor and support chips are on a replaceable card, but the majority of system circuits are still on the motherboard. In effect, you have a modular motherboard design. You can replace the processor complex with a more powerful one for less money than a complete motherboard upgrade and usually for less money than if the entire motherboard circuitry were mounted on a replaceable card. Companies such as IBM and COMPAQ charge a high price for their upgrades, so you should consider this factor when you are deciding whether to purchase of one of these systems.

The processor-complex design has been used also in systems with the 486 processor. These systems offer processor-complex modules with a 20 MHz 486SX or 25 MHz, 33 MHz, or 50 MHz 486DX processor, or a clock-doubled DX2/50 or DX2/66 chip. Processor-complex designs provide a great deal of upgrade flexibility because you can move up to a faster, more powerful processor by changing only the processor module rather than installing a new motherboard. Such designs were especially popular just after the 486 chip was introduced. Some manufacturers sold processor-complex 386-based systems that later could be upgraded to a 486 by removing the processor module and plugging in a new one. However, such designs were quickly replaced by the Intel Overdrive socket, which enables you to remove the old CPU chip and plug in a new, more powerful chip.

The difference between modular CPU upgrades and backplane system designs has become somewhat confused. Intel, for example, sells the Inboard 386/AT board for the AT, which contains an 80386 processor and memory. You can justifiably call this board a *mothercard* because it replaces many functions of the motherboard into which it is plugged. The original motherboard now acts much like a backplane. Zenith and Kaypro are known for producing systems based on the backplane design, but most other manufacturers have followed IBM in producing typical motherboard-based systems.

A system usually has a motherboard designed specifically for it. The motherboard in the original IBM AT system, for example, was a new design produced especially for that system. After a motherboard is produced, however, it sometimes is revised during the life of a system. Beginning with systems sold during October 1985, for example, the AT motherboard design was changed to increase reliability and reduce manufacturing costs. The new design, called Type 2, was also found on the AT versions -319 and -339, where it increased the clock speed of the system to 8 MHz. For more information about speed, see the "Microprocessor Speed Ratings" section later in this chapter.

Be aware, then, that two apparently identical systems may have different physical motherboard designs or revisions, often depending on when the system was manufactured. The revisions sometimes are minor, as in the IBM XT, but can be major, as in the AT example cited in the preceding paragraph. (Chapters 3 and 4 discuss the changes IBM made in motherboards between the different model systems.) The same principle holds true for other manufacturers. For example, companies that design and build their own motherboards often implement changes within the same model as soon as new motherboard designs become available.

Sometimes a motherboard first designed for one IBM system is used in another IBM system. For example, the XT Type 1 motherboard used in the IBM Portable PC is used also in the PS/2 Models 25-286 and 30-286. Usually, however, different models are equipped with a different motherboard design. The differences among the models are primarily in configuration and optional accessories.

Newer systems seem to go through more motherboard revisions and redesigns than the older systems did. This is largely the result of increased automation in the design and assembly of systems. The powerful CAD CAM (computer-aided design and computer-aided manufacturing) systems make implementing a design change for new motherboards an easy task.

Microprocessors

The "brain" of the PC is the microprocessor, or central processing unit (CPU). The CPU performs the system's calculating and processing (except for special math-intensive processing on systems with a math coprocessing unit chip). The microprocessor is easily the most expensive chip in the system. All the IBM PC and PS/2 units and compatibles use microprocessors compatible with the Intel family of chips, although the microprocessor itself may have been manufactured or designed by various other companies—including IBM, Cyrix, and AMD.

The following sections cover the microprocessor chips used on personal computers since the first PC was introduced more than a decade ago. These sections provide a great deal of technical detail about these chips and explain why one type of CPU chip can do more work than another in a given period of time. First, however, you learn about two important components of the microprocessor: the data bus and the address bus.

Data Bus and Address Bus

One of the most common ways to describe a microprocessor is by the size of the processor's data bus and address bus. A *bus* is simply a series of connections to carry common signals. Imagine running a pair of wires from one end of a building to another. If you connect a 110-volt AC power generator to the two wires at any point and place outlets at convenient locations along the wires, you have constructed a "power bus." No matter which outlet you plug in to, you have access to the same "signal," which in this example is 110-volt AC power.

Any transmission medium with more than one outlet at each end can be called a bus. A typical computer system has several buses, and a typical microprocessor has two important buses for carrying data and memory-addressing information: the data bus and the address bus.

The microprocessor bus discussed most often is the *data bus,* the bundle of wires (or pins) used to send and receive data. The greater number of signals that can be sent at one time, the more data can be transmitted in a specified interval and, therefore, the faster the bus.

Table 7.1 Processor Specifications

Processor	Register size	Data bus	Address bus	Integral cache
8088	16-bit	8-bit	20-bit	No
8086	16-bit	16-bit	20-bit	No
286	16-bit	16-bit	24-bit	No
386SX	32-bit	16-bit	24-bit	No
386SL	32-bit	16-bit	24-bit	No
386SLC	32-bit	16-bit	24-bit	8K
386DX	32-bit	32-bit	32-bit	No
486SLC2	32-bit	16-bit	24-bit	16K
486SX	32-bit	32-bit	32-bit	8K
487SX	32-bit	32-bit	32-bit	8K
486DX	32-bit	32-bit	32-bit	8K
486DX2	32-bit	32-bit	32-bit	8K
586 (P5)	64-bit	64-bit	32-bit	Yes

Data in a computer is sent as digital information, consisting of a time interval in which a single wire carries 5 volts to signal a 1 data bit or 0 volts to signal a 0 data bit. The greater number of wires you have, the greater number of individual bits you can send in the same time interval. A chip such as the 80286, which has 16 wires for transmitting and receiving such data, has a 16-bit data bus. A 32-bit chip such as the 80386 has twice as many wires dedicated to simultaneous data transmission as a 16-bit chip and can send twice as much information in the same time interval as a 16-bit chip.

A good way to understand this flow of information is to consider a highway and the traffic it carries. If a highway has only one lane in each direction of travel, only one car at a time can move in a certain direction. If you want to have more traffic flow, you can add another lane and have twice as many cars pass in a specified time. You can think of an 8-bit chip as the single-lane highway because with this chip one byte flows at a time. (One byte equals eight individual bits.) The 16-bit chip, with two bytes flowing at a time, resembles a two-lane highway. To move a large amount of automobiles, you might have four lanes in each direction. This corresponds to a 32-bit data bus and the capability to move four bytes of information at a time.

Just as you can describe a highway by its lane width, you can describe a chip by the width of its data bus. When you read an advertisement describing a computer system as a 16-bit or 32-bit system, the ad usually is referring to the data bus of the CPU. This number provides a rough idea of the performance potential of the chip (and therefore the system).

Table 7.1 shows specifications, including the data-bus sizes, for the Intel family of micro-processors used in IBM and compatible PCs.

Not all the CPU chips are "pure," which sometimes confuses the data-bus issue. Some processors have an internal data bus (made up of data paths and of storage units called

Math coprocessor	Maximum memory	Number of transistors	Date introduced
No	1 MB	29,000	June 1979
No	1 MB	29,000	June 1978
No	16 MB	130,000	February 1982
No	16 MB	275,000	June 1988
No	16 MB	855,000	October 1990
No	4 GB	N/A	October 1991
No	16 MB	275,000	October 1985
No	4 GB	N/A	June 1992
No	4 GB	1,185,000	April 1991
Yes	4 GB	1,200,000	April 1991
Yes	4 GB	1,200,000	April 1989
Yes	4 GB	1,100,000	March 1992
Yes	4 GB	3,000,000	1993

registers) that is different from the external data bus. The 8088 and 80386SX are examples of this structure. Each chip has an internal data bus twice the width of the external bus. These designs sometimes are called *hybrid designs* and usually are low-cost versions of a "pure" chip. The 80386SX, for example, can pass data around internally with a full 32-bit register size; for communications with the outside world, however, the chip is restricted to a 16-bit-wide data path. This design enables a systems designer to build a lower-cost motherboard with a 16-bit bus design and still maintain full compatibility with the full 32-bit 80386.

The *address bus* is the set of wires carrying the addressing information used to describe the memory location to which the data is being sent or from which the data is being retrieved. As with the data bus, each wire in an address bus carries a single bit of information. This single bit is a single digit in the address. The more wires (digits) used in calculating these addresses, the greater the total number of address locations. The size (or width) of the address bus indicates the maximum amount of RAM that a chip can address.

The highway analogy can be used to show how the address bus fits in. If the data bus is the highway, and the size of the data bus is equivalent to the highway's width, the address bus relates to the house number or street address number. The size of the address bus is equivalent to the number of digits in the house address. If you live on a street where the address is limited to a two-digit number, no more than 100 distinct addresses (00 to 99) can exist for that street, using the IBM binary numbering system, which begins with zero. Add another digit, and the total number of available addresses increases to 1000 (000 to 999).

Remember that because a computer works in the binary numbering system, a two-digit number gives only four unique addresses (00, 01, 10, and 11), and a three-digit number provides only eight addresses (000 to 111). Examples are the 8086 and 8088 processors, each of which uses a 20-bit address bus with a maximum of 1,048,576 bytes (one megabyte) of address locations. Table 7.2 describes the memory-addressing capabilities of Intel microprocessors.

Table 7.2 Intel Microprocessor Memory-Addressing Capabilities					
Processor	**Address bus width**	**Memory addressing in:** bytes	**kilobytes**	**megabytes**	**gigabytes**
8088/8086	20 bits	1,048,576	1,024	1	—
286, 386SX, 386SL, 386SLC	24 bits	16,777,216	16,384	16	—
386DX, 486SX, 487SX, 486DX, Pentium (586)	32 bits	4,294,967,296	4,194,304	4,096	4

The data bus and address bus are independent, and chip designers can use whatever size they want for each. Usually, however, chips with larger data buses have larger address buses. The sizes of the buses can provide important information about a chip's relative power, measured in two important ways. The size of the data bus is an indication of the information-moving capability of the chip. The size of the address bus tells you how much memory the chip can handle.

Intel Microprocessors

IBM-compatible computers use microprocessors manufactured primarily by Intel. Some other companies, such as Cyrix and AMD, also manufacture CPU chips used in IBM-compatible computers, but these chips are fully Intel-compatible. IBM builds microprocessors for some of its own systems; they use the Intel designs and sometimes make modifications unique to the IBM version. IBM also markets its CPU chips to other system manufacturers.

To fully understand the capabilities of a system as well as perform any type of servicing, you must at least know the type of processor the system uses. If you need more information about a particular system, refer to the documentation that comes with the system.

8088 and 8086 Microprocessors. The original IBM PC used an Intel CPU chip called the 8088. The original 8088 CPU chip ran at 4.77 MHz. This means the computer's circuitry drove the CPU at a rate of 4,770,000 *ticks*, or computer heartbeats, per second. Each tick represents a small amount of work—the CPU executing an instruction or part of an instruction—rather than a period of elapsed time. The 8088 has an external data bus 8 bits wide, which means it can move 8 bits, or individual pieces, of information into memory at a time. But the 8088 is referred to as a 16-bit processor because it features internal 16-bit-wide registers and data paths. The 8088 also has a 20-bit address bus, which enables the system to have access to 1M of RAM. Using the 8088, a manufacturer could build a system that would run 16-bit software and have access to 1M of memory while keeping the cost in line with then-current 8-bit designs. Later, IBM used the 8088 chip in the PC/XT computer.

IBM used the 8088 to put together the original IBM PC 5150-001, which sold for $1,355 with 16K of RAM and no drives. A similarly configured Apple II system, the major competition for the original PC, cost around $1,600.

The 8088 eventually was redesigned to run at 8 MHz, nearly double the speed of the original PC. The speed at which the processor operates has a direct effect on the speed of program execution. Later sections in this chapter cover the speeds of the CPU chips that are successors to the 8088.

> ### Note
>
> The real mode of 80286 and higher CPU chips refers to the mode these advanced chips use to imitate the original 8088 chip in the first PC. Real mode is used by 80286 and higher CPU chips to run a single DOS program at a time, just as if systems based on these powerful chips were merely faster PCs. The additional modes of 80286 and higher CPU chips are covered in subsequent sections of this chapter.

III

Hardware Considerations

Sometimes computer users wonder why there is a *640K conventional memory barrier* if the 8088 chip can address 1M of memory. The conventional memory barrier exists because IBM reserved 384K of the upper portion of the 1024K (1M) address space of the 8088 for use by adapter cards and system BIOS (a computer program permanently "burned into" the ROM chips in the PC). The lower 640K is the conventional memory in which DOS and software applications execute.

In 1976, before Intel made the 8088 chip, they made a slightly faster chip named the *8086*. The 8086 was one of the first 16-bit chips on the market and addressed 1M of RAM. The design failed to catch on, however, because both the chip and a motherboard designed for the chip were costly. The cost was high because the system needed a 16-bit data bus, rather than the less expensive 8-bit bus. Systems available at that time were 8-bit and users apparently weren't willing to pay for the extra performance of the full 16-bit design. Therefore, Intel introduced the 8088 in 1978. Both the 8086 and the 8088 CPU chips are quite slow by today's standards.

IBM largely ignored the 8086 CPU chip until it manufactured the first PS/2 Models 25 and 30. Systems produced by many other manufacturers, such as the COMPAQ Deskpro and the AT&T 6300, had been using the 8086 for some time. The capability of the 8086 to communicate with the rest of the system at 16 bits gives it about a 20 percent throughput increase over an 8088 with an identical speed (in megahertz). This improvement is one reason IBM can claim that the 8 MHz 8086-based Model 30 is 2 1/2 times faster than the 4.77 MHz 8088-based PC or XT, even though 8 MHz is not more than twice the clock speed. This is the first indication of what a CPU chip with a wider data path can mean in terms of speed improvements.

80186 and 80188 Microprocessors. After Intel produced the 8086 and 8088 chips, it turned its sights toward producing a more powerful chip with an increased instruction set. Its first efforts along this line—the 80186 and 80188—were not a success. But incorporating system components onto the CPU chip was an important idea for Intel because it led to faster, better chips, such as the 80286.

The relationship between the 80186 and 80188 is the same as that of the 8086 and 8088; one is a slightly more advanced version of the other. Compared CPU to CPU, the 80186 is almost the same as the 8088, and has a full 16-bit design. The 80188 (like the 8088) is a hybrid chip that compromises the 16-bit design with an 8-bit external communications interface. The advantage of the 80186 and 80188 is that they combine on a single chip 15 to 20 of the 8086–8088 series system components, which can greatly reduce the number of components in a computer design. The 80186 and 80188 chips are used for highly intelligent peripheral adapter cards, such as network adapters.

Although the 80186 and 80188 did provide some new instructions and capabilities, not much was new compared to the improvements that came later in the 80286 and 80386 chips. The 80186 and 80188 chips were difficult for systems designers to use in the manufacture of a system compatible with the IBM PC. Slight differences in the instruction set caused problems when the 80186 and 80188 were supposed to emulate 8086 and 8088 chips. In addition to compatibility problems, the chips didn't offer much performance improvement over the earlier 8086 and 8088. In addition, the individual components the 80186 and 80188 chips were designed to replace had become inexpensive, which made the 80186 and 80188 chips less attractive.

286 Microprocessor. The Intel 80286 microprocessor did not suffer from the compatibility problems that had damned the 80186 and 80188. The 286 chip was introduced in 1981. The 80286 is the CPU behind the IBM AT. You also can find 80286 chips in IBM's original PS/2 Models 50 and 60 (later PS/2s contain 80386 or 80486 chips). Other computer makers manufactured what came to be known as *IBM clones*, many calling their systems AT or AT-class computers.

When IBM developed the AT, it selected the 80286 as the basis for the new system because the chip provided much compatibility with the 8088 used in the PC and the XT, which means that software written for those chips should run on the 80286. The 286 chip is many times faster than the 8088 used in the 8 MHz XT, and offered those who used PCs in business a major performance boost. The processing speed, or throughput, of the original AT (which ran at 6 MHz) was five times greater than the PC running at 4.77 MHz. 286 systems are faster than their predecessors because the 286 chip can handle up to 16 bits of data at a time. Another reason personal computing received a major boost from the 286 chip is *clock speed*. AT-type systems have been based on 6, 8, 10, 12, 16, and 20 MHz versions of the 286 chip.

The 286 chip has two modes of operation: real mode and protected mode. The two modes are distinct enough to make the 80286 resemble two different chips in one. In real mode, an 80286 acts essentially the same as an 8086 chip and is fully object-code compatible with the 8086 and 8088. (A processor with *object-code compatibility* can run programs written for another processor without modification and execute every system instruction in the same manner.)

In the protected mode of operation, the 80286 truly was something new. In this mode, a program designed to take advantage of the chip's capabilities "believes" it has access to 1 gigabyte of memory (including virtual memory). The 286 chip, however, can address only 16M of physical hardware memory. When a program calls for more memory than physically exists, the CPU swaps to disk some of the currently running code and enables the program to use the newly freed physical RAM. The program does not know about this swapping and instead acts as though 1 gigabyte of actual memory exists. V*irtual memory* is controlled by the operating system and the chip hardware.

A significant failing of the 286 chip is that it cannot switch from protected mode to real mode without a hardware reset (a warm reboot) of the system. (It can, however, switch from real mode to protected mode without resetting the system.) A major improvement of the 386 over the 286 is that software can switch the 386 from real mode to protected mode and vice versa.

When the 80286 chip was introduced, Intel said real mode was created so that much of the 8086- and 8088-based software could run with little or no modification until new software could be written to take advantage of the protected mode of the 286. However, as with later Intel processors, it was a long time before software took advantage of the capabilities of the 286 chip. For example, most 286 systems are used as if they were merely faster PCs. They are run in real mode most of the time because the programs were written for DOS, and DOS and DOS programs are limited to real mode. Unfortunately, much of the power of systems based on the 286 chip is unused. In real mode, an 80286 chip cannot perform any additional operations or use any extra features designed into the chip.

IBM and Microsoft together began the task of rewriting DOS to run both real and protected modes. The result was early versions of OS/2, which could run most old DOS programs just as they ran before, in real mode. In protected mode, OS/2 allowed true software multitasking and access to the entire 1 gigabyte of virtual or 16M physical address space provided by the 286. UNIX and XENIX also were written to take advantage of the 286 chip's protected mode. In terms of mass appeal, however, these operating systems were a limited success.

Little software that took advantage of the 286 chip was sold until Windows 3.0 offered Standard Mode for 286 compatibility, and by that time, the hottest selling chip was the 386.

Still, the 80286 was Intel's first attempt at producing a CPU chip that enabled *multitasking*, in which multiple programs run at the same time. The 286 is designed so that if one program locks up or fails, the entire system doesn't need a warm boot (reset) or cold boot (power off/on). Theoretically, what happens in one area of memory doesn't affect other programs. Before multitasked programs are "safe" from one another, however, the 286 chip (and subsequent chips) need an operating system that works cooperatively with the chip to provide such protection.

In a way, this leads back to OS/2, which could provide protection but never caught on in a big way for the 286. Although newer versions of OS/2 offer a graphical user interface similar to Windows, and on 386 systems OS/2 offers full 32-bit processing for software designed to take advantage of it, OS/2 is nowhere near replacing DOS as the operating system of choice on PCs and is nowhere near as popular as Windows. One reason is few OS/2 applications have been developed compared with the number of DOS and Windows programs.

Protected mode on a 286 enables multiple programs to run at one time only when those programs are specifically written for the operating system (or operating environment). For example, to run several programs at once on a 286 in Windows, each active program must be a Windows program (written specifically to run under only Windows).

Because of the virtual memory scheme of the 80286, the size of programs under operating systems such as OS/2 and UNIX can be extremely large. Even though the 286 does not address more than 16M of physical memory, the 286's virtual memory scheme enables programs to run as if 1 gigabyte of memory were available. But programs that require a lot of swapping run slowly, which is why software manufacturers usually indicate the amount of physical RAM needed to run their programs effectively. The more physical memory you install, the faster 286-based systems running OS/2 or UNIX will work.

Windows 3.0, which is not a true operating system because it uses DOS for its underpinnings, provides only poor protection on a 286. Unruly programs can still crash the entire system. Windows 3.1 does a better job of implementing protection on a 286, but is still far from perfect.

Although UNIX and XENIX provided some support for the 286 chip's protected mode, these operating systems found a following among a small group of extremely high-end computer users in primarily the sciences and business.

386 Microprocessor. The Intel 80386 caused quite a stir in the PC industry because of the vastly improved performance it brought to the personal computer. Compared with 8088 and 80286 systems, the 386 chip offers staggering performance in almost all areas of operation. The 80386 is a full 32-bit processor optimized for high-speed operation and multitasking operating systems. Intel introduced the chip in 1985, but it appeared in the first systems in late 1986 and early 1987. The COMPAQ Deskpro 386 and systems from several other manufacturers debuted the chip. Somewhat later, IBM used the chip in the PS/2 Model 80. Since then the chip has remained popular, notwithstanding the availability of systems based on the 486 and Pentium CPU chips. The reason for this success is due in part to the use of the chip in extremely small, lightweight, and powerful laptop and notebook computers.

The 386 can execute the real mode instructions of an 8086/8088, but in fewer clock cycles. The 386 also can switch to and from protected mode under software control without resetting the system, which makes it practical to use protected mode. In addition, the 386 has a new mode, called *virtual real mode*, which enables several real-mode sessions to run simultaneously under management software such as Windows 3.1 or OS/2 2.1. Other than raw speed, probably the most important feature of this chip is its available modes of operation, which are listed in the following:

- Real mode
- Protected mode
- Virtual real mode (sometimes called *virtual 86 mode*)

Real mode on a 386 chip, like on a 286 chip, is the 8086-compatible mode. In real mode, the 386 is essentially a much faster "turbo PC" with 640K of conventional memory, just like systems based on the 8088 chip. DOS and any software written to run under DOS require this mode to run.

The protected mode of the 386 is fully compatible with the protected mode of the 286. The protected mode for both these chips is often called their *native mode* of operation because these chips are designed for advanced operating systems such as OS/2 and Windows NT, which run in only protected mode. Intel extended the memory-addressing capabilities of 386 protected mode with a new memory management unit (MMU) that allows advanced memory paging and program switching. These features are extensions of the 286 type of MMU so the 386 remains fully compatible with the 286 at system-code level.

The 386 chip's virtual real mode is new. In virtual real mode, the processor can run with hardware memory protection while simulating an 8086's real mode operation. Multiple copies of DOS and other operating systems therefore can run simultaneously on this processor, each in a protected area of memory. If the programs in one segment crash, the rest of the system is protected. Software commands can "reboot" the blown partition.

In simple terms, a PC with a 386 has the capability to "become" multiple PCs under software control. With appropriate management software, the 386 chip can create several memory partitions, each containing the full services of DOS, and each of these partitions can function as if it were an individual stand-alone PC. These partitions are often called *virtual machines*. Under 386 virtual real mode with software such as Windows, several different DOS programs can be running at the same time as programs designed for Windows. Because the processor can service only a single application at a time by delivering a clock tick, Windows manages the amount of CPU time each program gets by using a system called *time slices*. Because the 386 chip is so fast and time slices are tiny fractions of a second, under Windows it appears that all applications are running simultaneously. OS/2 exploits the multitasking capabilities of the 386 chip even more than Windows. OS/2 2.x can simultaneously manage native OS/2 programs, DOS programs, and most Windows programs. These capabilities aren't possible with lesser processors, such as the 286.

The 386 exploits protected mode much more effectively than the 286. The 386 can switch to and from protected mode under software control without resetting the system. The 286 cannot switch from protected mode without a hardware reset.

There are numerous variations of the 386 chip, some less powerful and some less power hungry. The following sections cover the different members of the 386 chip family and their differences.

386DX Microprocessor. The 386DX chip was the first of the 386 family members to be introduced by Intel. The 386 is a full 32-bit processor, with 32-bit internal registers, a 32-bit internal data bus, and a 32-bit external data bus. The 386 contains 275,000 transistors in a VLSI (Very Large Scale Integration) circuit. The chip comes in a 132-pin package and draws approximately 400 milliamperes (ma), which is less power than even the 8086. The smaller power requirement of the 386 chip is due to the chip's construction from CMOS (Complementary Metallic Oxide Semiconductor) materials. The CMOS design enables devices to consume extremely low levels of power. The Intel 386 chip is available in clock speeds from 16 to 33 MHz.

The 386DX can address 4 gigabytes of physical memory. Its built-in virtual memory manager enables software designed to take advantage of enormous amounts of memory act as though a system has 64 terabytes of memory. (A terabyte is 1,099,511,627,776 bytes of memory.) Although most 386 systems are built to accept 64M or less in RAM chips on the motherboard, some high-end computer users do take advantage of the 386 chip's capacity for 4 gigabytes of physical memory, as well as its 64-terabyte virtual memory potential.

386SX Microprocessor. The 386SX, code-named the P9 chip during its development, was designed for systems designers looking for 386 capabilities with 286-system pricing. Like the 286, the 386SX is restricted to only 16 bits when communicating with other system components. Internally, however, the 386SX is identical to the DX chip; the 386SX can handle 32 bits of data at once (compared to the 8 bits handled by the original IBM PC). The 386SX uses a 24-bit memory-addressing scheme, like that of the 286, rather than the full 32-bit memory address bus of the standard 386. The 386SX, therefore, can address a maximum of 16M of physical memory rather than the 4 gigabytes of physical memory that the 386DX can address. The 386SX is available in clock speeds from 16 to 33 MHz.

The 386SX signaled the end of the 286 because of the 386SX chip's superior MMU and extra virtual 8086 mode. Using a software manager such as Windows or OS/2, the 386SX can run numerous DOS programs at one time. The capability to run 386-specific software is another important advantage of the 386SX over any 286 or older designs. For example, Windows 3.1 runs nearly as well on a 386SX as it does on a 386DX.

> ### Note
>
> One often-heard fallacy about the 386SX is that you can plug one into a 286 system and give the system 386 capabilities. This is not true. The 386SX chip is not pin-compatible with the 286 and does not plug into the same socket. But several upgrade products have been designed to adapt the chip to a 286 system. In terms of raw speed, there is little performance gain from converting a 286 system to a 386 CPU chip because 286 motherboards are built with a restricted 16-bit interface to memory and peripherals. A 16 MHz 386SX is not markedly faster than a 16 MHz 286, but it does offer improved memory-management capabilities on a motherboard designed for it and the capability to run 386-specific software.

386SL Microprocessor. Another variation on the 386 chip is the 386SL. This low-power CPU has the same capabilities as the 386SX, but it is designed for laptop systems where low power consumption is needed. The SL chips offer special power-management features that are important to systems that run on batteries. The SL chip offers several "sleep" modes that conserve power. These chips also include an extended architecture that includes a System Management Interrupt (SMI), which allows access to the power-management features. Also included in the SL chip is special support for LIM (Lotus Intel Microsoft) expanded memory functions and a cache controller. The cache controller is designed to control a 16K to 64K external processor cache. These extra functions account for the higher transistor count in the SL chips (855,000) compared with even the 386DX processor (275,000). The 386SL is available in 25 MHz clock speed.

Intel offers a companion to the 386SL chip for laptops called the *82360SL I/O subsystem*. The 82360SL provides many common peripheral functions, such as serial and parallel ports, a direct memory access (DMA) controller, an interrupt controller, and power-management logic for the 386SL processor. This one chip subsystem works with the processor to provide an ideal solution to the small size and low power consumption requirements of portable and laptop systems.

III

Hardware Considerations

386 Microprocessor Clones. Several manufacturers, including AMD, Cyrix, and Chips and Technologies, have developed their own versions of the Intel 386DX and SX processors. These 386-compatible chips are available in speeds up to 40 MHz; Intel produces 386 chips up to only 33 MHz. Intel will not offer a 386 chip faster than 33 MHz because that speed begins to tread on the performance domain of the slowest of its own 486 processors.

In general, these chips are fully function-compatible with the Intel processors, which means they run all software designed for the Intel 386. Many manufacturers choose these "cloned" 386 chips for their systems because they are faster and less expensive than an Intel 386 chip. (Intel developed its "Intel Inside" advertising campaign in hopes of enticing buyers with a promise of getting the real thing.)

486 Microprocessor. In the race for more speed, the Intel 486 was another major leap forward. If the clock speeds of a 386 and a 486 chip are equal, the 486 is about 75 percent faster. This has resulted in an unprecedented binge of hardware and software buying. Tens of millions of copies of Windows and millions of copies of OS/2 have been sold largely because the 486 finally made the Windows and OS/2 graphical user interface (GUI) a realistic option for those who work on their computers every day.

Before the 486, many people avoided GUIs because they didn't have the time to sit around waiting for the hourglass, which indicates the system is performing operations behind the scenes that can't be interrupted by the user. (It was said, only partly in jest, that you could turn on your system in the morning, start Windows or OS/2, then go make coffee for the office. By the time you got back to your computer, Windows or OS/2 might be finished loading so you could do some work.) The 486 changed that. Many believe that the 486 CPU chip spawned the widespread acceptance of GUIs.

The 486 chip's capability of handling the GUI has prompted the sales of a great deal of pricey hardware such as faster and larger hard drives, faster video display boards and larger monitors, faster and better printers, optical storage devices, CD-ROM drives, sound boards, and video capture boards. A happy occurrence prompted by all this spending is that hardware (and software) prices have been on a steep decline for some years.

Despite the release of its faster Pentium CPU chip, Intel has been cutting the price of the entire 486 line to entice the industry to shift over to the 486 as the mainstream system. The 486 chip is available in clock speeds from 20 MHz to 50 MHz, and in several variations including a *clock-doubled* version that internally doubles the clock speed of a 25 MHz or 33 MHz chip so it performs calculations much more quickly, an SX version that lacks some of the more important capabilities of the *real* 486, and some versions intended to save power on laptops and notebooks. The next sections of this chapter cover each of the variations on the basic 486 chip.

486DX Microprocessor. For a time after Intel introduced the 486, there was only one variation, the 486DX. Except in terms of raw speed, the 486 resembles a 386 with the addition of an internal math coprocessor chip. However, the faster clock speeds (20 MHz to 50 MHz) and other speed enhancements brought ready acceptance for this new chip. (The first 50 MHz chips had a flaw that caused the chip to gain a reputation as unreliable. But Intel quickly fixed the bug and, for a time, the 50 MHz DX chip was the fastest CPU chip available.)

The basic 80486 chip contains about 1.3 million transistors. Like the 386, the 486 can address 4 gigabytes of physical memory and manage as much as 64 terabytes of virtual memory. The 486 fully supports the three operating modes introduced in the 386: real mode, protected mode, and virtual real mode. In real mode, the 486 (like the 386) runs unmodified 8086-type software. In protected mode, the 486 (like the 386) offers sophisticated memory paging and program switching. In virtual real mode, the 486 (like the 386) can run multiple copies of DOS or other operating systems while simulating an 8086's real-mode operation. This means that under an operating system such as Windows or OS/2, programs can run simultaneously on this processor with hardware memory protection. If one program crashes, the rest of the system is protected, and the blown portion can be rebooted with software commands or by pressing Ctrl+Alt+Del (depending on the operating software).

Internal Cache for Improved Performance. The 486 has a built-in 8K processor cache and an integrated cache controller. This means the chip itself can hold 8K of information, and when it wants to read from memory, it first checks the internal cache. This reduces a traditional system bottleneck because system RAM is much slower than the CPU. Without the 8K cache, a 486 frequently would be forced to wait until system memory caught up. If the data the 486 chip wants is already in the 8K internal cache, the CPU does not have to wait. If the data is not in the cache, the CPU must fetch it from the the secondary processor cache or, on the least sophisticated system designs, from the system bus.

A *secondary processor cache* of up to 256K of extremely fast static RAM (SRAM) chips is used on most 486-based systems to further reduce the amount of time the CPU must spend waiting for data from system memory. The function of the secondary processor cache is similar to the 486 chip's onboard cache. The secondary processor cache holds information moving to the CPU, thereby reducing the time the CPU spends waiting and therefore increasing the time the CPU spends doing calculations. Fetching information from the secondary processor cache rather than system memory is much faster because of the extremely fast speeds of the SRAM chips (20 nanoseconds or less).

Built-In Math Coprocessor. The 80486DX has a built-in math coprocessor, unlike previous Intel CPU chips, which required you to add a math coprocessor if you needed faster calculations for complex mathematics. This 486 chip's internal math coprocessor is a duplicate of the external 386 math coprocessor. However, it delivers about twice the performance because its clock speed is identical to the main processor part of the chip and there is no motherboard circuitry to slow down communication between the math coprocessor and the main CPU.

486SX Microprocessor. As mentioned, the 386SX chip is functionally different than the 386DX, as well as less expensive to manufacture and less expensive for system designers to use in other machines. The 486SX chip, however, is something of a marketing quirk, rather than a difference in technology. To manufacture the 486SX, Intel must add

III

Hardware Considerations

a step that makes the chip more expensive to produce than the 486DX chip. To make the 486SX chip, Intel disables the math coprocessor chip functions in a fully functional 486DX chip. The 486SX chip does not make systems easier to design or less expensive to build, except for the lower price Intel charges for the chip.

The 486SX chip is produced merely to undercut the market for systems based on the 386 chip—in part because competition from 386 chips produced by AMD, Cyrix, and Chips and Technologies, had driven the prices down to the point where the 386 chip was barely profitable. Another factor is that CPU chip manufacturers other than Intel produce 386 chips with clock speeds up to 40 MHz. Intel had to undercut its own 486 prices to compete with these fast 386s, and the SX was the answer.

The 486SX chip is 40 percent faster than a 386 with the same clock speed. Intel markets the 486SX as the ideal chip for new computer buyers. As mentioned, Intel's prices for these and other 486 chips are competitive, and because of the high performance and built-in upgradability offered by the 486 line, this is where much of the industry has gone.

Unfortunately for Intel, other companies such as AMD, Cyrix, and Chips and Technologies, are also producing versions of the 486 chip. Cyrix markets a 486 chip that it states can be used as a direct replacement for a 386 chip in existing systems. Although the Cyrix chip lacks some important features of the Intel 486, it does give a 386-based system many of the benefits of the 486.

487 Microprocessor Upgrade. The 487 upgrade, or Overdrive, chip (which was advertised heavily by Intel when it introduced the 486SX chip) is not actually a math coprocessor upgrade. Rather, it is a fully functional 486DX chip. When plugged into the vacant CPU chip socket (the Overdrive socket) on a 486SX motherboard, the 487 upgrade disables the existing SX chip, takes over all the processing functions of the system, and adds the functionality of an internal math coprocessor chip.

The garish "Vacancy" sign in many Intel magazine advertisements is directed at those who purchased 486SX systems in an effort to get them to buy the fully functional replacement chip that will fit in their spare motherboard socket.

486SL Microprocessor. The 486SL chip, another member of the 486 family, is basically an SX constructed in a low-power design. The 486SL chip is designed to be installed in laptop or notebook systems that run on batteries, and features special power-management techniques such as sleep mode and clock throttling to reduce power consumption when necessary. For example, the hard drive can be stopped while the laptop or notebook system is not being used, and the CPU can switch to a very low power mode in which the major calculations have to do with keeping the system in a ready condition and determining when the user is resuming work.

486DX2 Processors. Intel has engineered an additional branch of the 486 family of chips called the *DX2* that greatly increase the performance of 486 systems without requiring the redesign of the system motherboard. Installing a DX2 chip in a computer motherboard is like adding a turbocharger to an already fast engine. The DX2 chips are based on the 25 MHz and 33 MHz 486DX chips. DX2 chips are called *clock-doubled* because the speed of the 25 MHz or 33 MHz DX chip is doubled internally so that it runs at 50 MHz or 66 MHz. For example, the DX2/50, based on the 25 MHz chip, operates internally at 50 MHz. Clock-doubled chips still continue to communicate with the rest of the system at the regular clock speed of the basic chip; for example, the DX2/50 communicates with other system components at 25 MHz.

When the DX2 accesses its internal registers, refers to a memory location already in its internal cache, or performs a floating-point operation, the chip works at the 50 MHz or 66 MHz rate. When the DX2 accesses system RAM or one of the other chips on the motherboard, the DX2's electrical signals move at the speed of the basic chip on which it is based (33 MHz for a 66 MHz DX2). The DX2 communicates with the RAM chips, the DMA controller chip, the 8259 programmable interrupt controller chip, keyboard-controller and adapter cards at the original chip speed (33 MHz for a 66 MHz DX2). While the DX2 is communicating with memory or one of the chips on the motherboard, it waits for the currently executing instruction to finish before it continues with the next instruction.

The two major types of DX2 chips (the DX2/66 and the DX2/50) are intended to be used in motherboards that were designed for 25 MHz or 33 MHz chips, with a minimum of changes to the motherboard and no need for redesign. The DX2/66 can replace the 33 MHz DX chip in existing motherboard designs, and the DX2/50 can replace the 25 MHz DX CPU chip in existing motherboard designs.

At this writing, the fastest 486 chip is the 66 MHz 486DX2. Until the introduction of the Pentium, the 486DX2/66 chip was the fastest processor made for the IBM-compatible computer for most computing tasks. The DX2/66 is about 30 percent faster than the 50 MHz 486DX chip and nearly twice as fast as the 33 MHz 486 chip on which the DX2/66 is based. A 486DX2/50 chip is somewhat slower for most computing tasks than a non-clock-doubled 486DX/50 chip.

Intel has announced it will make available a *clock-tripled* version of its 33 MHz DX chip, a DX3/99. The giant chip maker also is rumored to be developing a clock-doubled version of the 50 MHz version of its 486DX chip, a 486DX2/100.

DX2 chips are quite fast when used in existing motherboard designs. But DX2 chips perform even better in motherboards designed specifically for them with faster RAM chips and other circuitry. Sophisticated testing shows that on virtually all computing tasks, the 486DX2/66 not only runs much faster than a 486DX/33 but also significantly outperforms a 486DX/50, the fastest non-clock-doubled Intel chip until the Pentium. Testing shows that a DX2 CPU chip performs 60 percent to 75 percent faster than an equivalent non-clock-doubled CPU based on a typical mix of DOS software applications. Some computation-intensive applications (such as CAD/CAM software) perform even better on a DX2-equipped computer.

DX2 Overdrive Installation. Intel makes several flavors of the DX2 Overdrive chip, which can be used to give clock-doubled technology to SX and DX systems that include an Overdrive socket. In addition, as mentioned previously, 486SX systems with motherboards that include a so-called "487 math coprocessor" socket can be upgraded to a 486DX2 chip.

You must purchase the DX2 chip designed for your system: a 40 MHz DX2 if you have a 20 MHz SX, a 50 MHz DX2 if you have a 25 MHz SX or DX, or a 66 MHz DX2 if you have a 33 MHz DX or SX. You then must pry out your old CPU chip and install the DX2 in the same socket in which your old chip was installed.

Changing the CPU chip can be a daunting experience because if even one pin on an Overdrive 486 CPU chip is bent it is very difficult to straighten out the pin and install the chip. However, on most upgradable systems the old CPU chip is in what is called a Zero Insertion Force (ZIF) socket that makes the upgrade easy. You merely throw a lever, gently slide out the old CPU chip, slide in the new chip according to the chip's directions (being careful to properly align the chip), and push the lever back to its original position.

If your 486SX system is intended to be upgradable to the 487 chip, there is a vacant ZIF socket on the motherboard into which you plug the 487 upgrade chip.

Some motherboards are designed to be able to use different 486 chips interchangeably. On such a motherboard you can install your choice of 486DX/33, 486DX/50, or 486DX2/66 chips. Many of these system boards have ZIF sockets. To upgrade to a DX2/66 chip on such a motherboard, you remove the old CPU chip and install the new chip. You may also have to replace the oscillator, which is a simple upgrade.

Compatibility Problems. Compatibility problems related to the 486 are rare. Some software, particularly game programs, cannot be run as fast as the 486 attempts to run them. Systems with motherboard circuitry that can run the CPU chip at two (or on some motherboards, three) clock speeds have a "turbo button." When your computer is in turbo mode, the CPU is running at top speed. When you press the button to exit turbo mode, your computer runs at a slower speed. The turbo button is provided mostly for compatibility with software that cannot run at the high speeds of modern microprocessor chips.

Pentium Microprocessor. Intel's newest CPU chip, the Pentium (also called the 586 or P5), is different from other CPU chips in many ways. At least one of these differences is revolutionary. The Pentium features *twin data pipelines* that enable it to execute two instructions at the same time with software such as Windows NT. The 486 and all preceding chips can perform only a single instruction at a time. Intel calls the capability to execute two instructions at once *superscaler* technology. The use of such technology to perform more than one instruction at a time is termed *multithreading*.

Multithreading is considerably different from multitasking in operating platforms such as Windows or DESQview. When you use multitasking software to run more than one program at a time on CPUs capable of executing only one instruction at a time, the multitasking software switches your CPU's attention from one running program to another for a brief time, enabling each program in turn to do a small amount of work. This switching from one task to another occurs so quickly that both programs appear to operate at the same time. With multithreading, however, two programs can operate at the same time without the CPU switching from either one, or one program can perform two operations at the same time. To take advantage of the Pentium's capability to perform two simultaneous tasks, it must be run by operating software designed to capitalize on this capability: 32-bit operating systems such as Windows NT or OS/2 2.1.

With existing software, the Pentium running at 66 MHz does nearly twice the work as the fastest 486 (the 66 MHz DX2). In Intel demonstrations of the chip, graphics software runs so fast you might think you were watching television or a movie as the software erased and repainted the screen.

The Pentium was released to system designers in spring 1993. In its initial release, the Pentium offered clock speeds of 60 and 66 MHz, but Intel has said it expects to produce versions that run at or near 100 MHz. The Pentium contains 3.1 million transistors (double the 486). The Pentium has a 32-bit address bus width, giving it the same 4 gigabyte memory-addressing capabilities as the 386 and 486. But the Pentium uses new technology to expand the data path to 64 bits (compared to the 32-bit path of the 386 and 486 and the 16-bit path of the 286), which means it can move twice as much data into or out of the CPU when compared with a 486 of the same clock speed.

The Pentium has two internal 8K caches (compared with one in the 486), enabling the chip to hold multiple operations in memory and later send them to system memory in a single burst. The processor-cache controller circuitry is embedded in the CPU chip. The processor cache controller chip mirrors the information in normal RAM by keeping a copy of the memory locations in the cache. The Pentium cache system also can hold information to be written to memory when the load on the CPU and other system components is less. (The 486 makes all memory writes immediately.) This new cache technology results in less activity between the CPU and system memory. This is an important improvement because CPU access to system memory is a bottleneck on fast systems. The processor cache can hold noncontiguous memory locations (locations that are not adjacent to one another in system memory).

The Pentium's caches may seem small, but on the earlier 486, the CPU typically finds needed data in its internal cache about 90 percent of the time. The Pentium's improved caching system provides even better performance than available with a 486.

Systems based on the Pentium benefit greatly from *secondary processor caches*, which usually are made of extremely fast (20 nanoseconds or less), 256K to 512K static RAM (SRAM) chips. When the CPU fetches data that is not already available in its internal processor cache, wait states slow the CPU. But if the data is already in the secondary processor cache, the CPU can go ahead with its work without pausing for wait states.

The Pentium also employs new *branch prediction* technology, designed to find data in memory or on the hard drive that might be needed later, and a *prefetch buffer*, where branch prediction information is held and prepared for execution. The CPU obtains new information from the branch prediction unit in 256-bit bursts. The branch prediction unit also determines which of the Pentium's twin pipelines should carry each instruction.

The Pentium, like the 486, contains an internal math coprocessor. Pentium's *pipelined internal math coprocessor*, which handles floating-point math calculations with software designed to take advantage of it, can process data 64 bits at a time. The Pentium math coprocessor is estimated to be up to 10 times faster than the math coprocessor in the 486. In addition, the Pentium provides two units to handle integer math. (The math coprocessor handles only more complex calculations.) The 486 provides one integer math unit.

Pentium Overdrive Upgrade. Computer manufacturers are again looking toward the Overdrive concept so that they can give their customers a quick, easy upgrade path to the Pentium. Many manufacturers of 486DX2/66-based systems are adding a special *Pentium Overdrive* socket into which a special 238-pin version of the Pentium chip can be plugged. Although Intel itself designed the *Pentium Overdrive* socket and chip, the company is making efforts to lessen consumers' expectations of such chips, as well as warn consumers away from manufacturers of "cheap" Pentiums, who may simply use old 486 motherboards designs with a Pentium plugged into them.

Before a system can make the most of the Pentium CPU chip, its memory management system and a great deal of other important motherboard circuitry must be redesigned. Designing a system that contains a 486 CPU that can be swapped out for a Pentium, with a memory subsystem system able to deal optimally with the Pentium's faster performance, automatically means compromises in the design and operating efficiency of system memory and other subsystems. As of this writing, most upgradable 486DX2/66 system motherboards are not equipped with the complex new circuitry needed to take advantage of the several factors that make the Pentium twice as powerful when compared to the same clock speed 486: its 64-bit external data path, its twin onboard caches, and its built-in 64-bit math coprocessor. These Pentium Overdrive upgradable systems are unlikely to offer the same performance levels as a system specifically designed for the Pentium chip.

However, some manufacturers state that their upgradable 486DX2/66 systems are optimized for the Pentium Overdrive chip. For example, Zeos is offering a line of *Pentium Overdrive*-upgradable 486 DX2/66 computers the company says take full advantage of the Pentium Overdrive chip. If yesterday's modular systems are any kind of indicator, and they probably are, after you have installed the Pentium Overdrive in today's upgradable system, the system is unlikely to perform quite as well as a machine designed specifically for the Pentium. However, it is important to note that on virtually all systems in which these Pentium Overdrive chips are installed, the performance boost will be significant over the same system containing its original 486DX2/66 CPU chip.

Another factor to consider is that Pentium-upgradable systems from some manufacturers may cost somewhat more than other 486DX2/66-based systems, although this is not the case with initial offerings from Zeos. Computers optimized for a CPU upgrade are more complicated to develop and build than nonupgradable systems, and therefore can be more expensive to design and build. It will be no less so with computers upgraded from a 486 to a Pentium, if only because it is difficult to design the components of a computer with a CPU chip that has not yet been offered for sale—particularly when the system components must be designed to work at a variety of speeds with different CPU chips. As of this writing, the Pentium Overdrive chip has yet to be offered by Intel.

The Intel Pentium Overdrive chip probably will not be offered in all three speeds announced for the regular Pentium: 60 MHz, 66 MHz, and 100 MHz. Even if Intel does offer the chip in three speeds, it is unclear whether a Pentium Overdrive-equipped system will be able to handle any available Overdrive chip speed or only a particular speed of this chip (as 486 Overdrive-equipped computers do now). Also, an upgradable system probably will not be equipped with the Pentium-specific VESA-Standard Local Bus slots or the Intel Peripheral Component Interconnect (PCI) standard local bus, which should be important technology in speeding up the performance of hard drives and video subsystems. The VESA-Standard Local Bus and the IntelPCI are covered in Chapter 2.

The Pentium Overdrive chip will probably be expensive. The Pentium chip costs manufacturers roughly $1,000 apiece in volumes of 1,000 or more. How much manufacturers will increase the price before the Pentium Overdrive chip gets to you is unclear. Back in the days of 386-to-486 modular upgrades, some daughterboard upgrade modules cost nearly as much as the original computer. With the 386 to 486 modular systems, only the original manufacturer can supply the upgrade board. The Pentium Overdrive chip, however, probably will be available from many sources, including the chip suppliers who advertise in various magazines. If you choose an upgradable system, consider buying your Pentium Overdrive chip by mail order, because the price of the chip from mail order vendors should be considerably less than from Intel or a system manufacturer.

For companies that must purchase hundreds or thousands of computers, the Pentium Overdrive-upgradable systems should be a reasonable path to greater system performance, considering the prohibitively high cost of the initial offering of the more powerful Pentium-based systems. But an upgradable system should be considered only if you must purchase systems now. Systems fully optimized for the Pentium chip will decline in price, just as 486DX2/66 systems have, and these Pentium-optimized systems will be a better long-term investment than a 486 with a Pentium Overdrive socket.

IBM (Intel-Licensed) Microprocessors

For many years, IBM and Intel have had an agreement in which each time Intel introduces a new CPU chip, it shares with IBM the original mask, or design, of the chip. A *CPU chip mask* is the photographic blueprint of the processor and is used to etch the intricate signal pathways into a silicon chip. Using this mask, IBM may either produce the chip as Intel designed it or make modifications to the basic design. Currently, no other manufacturer has this type of relationship with Intel. The 386 chips produced by companies other than Intel and IBM are reverse-engineered without Intel's blessing.

Since the release of the 386 chip, IBM has produced its own variations of Intel chips. Some of these chips have few design changes, but others have major differences to make the chip faster, or less power hungry, or both. It is important to note that IBM has begun selling its CPU chips to other manufacturers. The following sections cover these IBM chips.

III

Hardware Considerations

386SLC Microprocessor. The IBM 386SLC is a low power consumption variation of the original 386SX. (It is pin-compatible with the 386SX.) This IBM-enhanced chip has some features of the 486, such as the internal 8K cache, and performs nearly as well as a 486SX for a much lower cost. IBM states that the SLC chip is as much as 80 percent faster than the standard 386SX chip, which means a 20 MHz 386SLC can outperform a 33 MHz 386DX system. The 386SLC chip requires a 5V power supply and can operate at clock speeds of 16, 20, and 25 MHz. This chip was first available in the PS/2 Model 57. It is now in several other PS/2 systems as well as other manufacturer's systems, particularly laptops and notebooks.

486SLC2 Microprocessor. The 486SLC2 is IBM's version of the 486SX chip designed by Intel. The 486SLC2 uses clock-doubled technology like the Intel 486DX2 chips and has an onboard cache of 16K. The 486SLC2 also incorporates low-voltage circuitry, which enables it to operate on 3.3V. This chip is used in mostly laptops and notebooks.

Blue Lightning Microprocessor. IBM has begun to market a CPU chip it calls the Blue Lightning, a clock-tripled 486 chip that runs at 99 MHz internally. Like the Intel DX2 chips, IBM's Blue Lightning communicates externally with system peripherals at 33 MHz. Internally, the Blue Lightning is the fastest 486 chip on the market, although Intel has announced a 486DX3/99 clock-tripled chip based on the 33 MHz 486DX and is said to be ready to market a DX2/100 clock-doubled chip based on the 50 MHz 486DX. IBM is marketing the chip as one-third faster for the same price as DX2/66. IBM also is marketing a 25/75 MHz version of the chip.

The Blue Lightning offers twice the internal cache of the 486DX2. The chips use half the power and two-thirds the voltage of the DX2, making them ideal for laptop and notebook computers. The Blue Lightning also has a "sleep" mode that enables the processor and other components to suspend active operation if the user is away from the system, which conserves battery power. The chip also is used on some non-IBM systems under license from IBM. Some industry analysts expect Blue Lightning to compete with the Pentium for use on laptop systems.

Intel-Compatible Microprocessors

As mentioned, several companies, including Cyrix, AMD, and Chips and Technologies, manufacture CPU chips used in IBM-compatible computers. These chips are fully Intel-compatible, which means they emulate every processor instruction in the Intel chips. Thus, any hardware or software that works on an Intel-based PC will work also on PCs made with these third-party CPU chips.

AMD, Cyrix, and Chips and Technologies have developed their own versions of the Intel 386DX and 386SX processors in speeds up to 40 MHz. These manufacturers also market their own versions of the 486 chip.

Cyrix, in a surprising turn of events to some industry analysts, markets a 486 chip that it states can be used as a direct replacement for a 386 chip in existing systems. Although the Cyrix chip lacks some important features of the Intel 486, it gives a 386-based system many of the benefits of the 486.

Math Coprocessor Chips

The next several sections cover the math coprocessor chip. Each central processing unit designed by Intel (and cloned by other companies) can use a math coprocessor chip, although the Pentium and 486 chips have a built-in math coprocessor. Coprocessors provide hardware for *floating-point math*, which would otherwise create an excessive drain on the main CPU. Math chips speed your computer's operation only when you are running software designed to take advantage of the coprocessor.

Math chips (as coprocessors sometimes are called) can perform high-level mathematical operations such as long division, trigonometric functions, roots, and logarithms at 10 to 100 times the speed of the corresponding main processor. Math chips are also more accurate in these calculations than the integer math units built into the primary CPU. The integer units built into the primary CPU work with real numbers, so they perform addition, subtraction, and multiplication. The primary CPU is designed to handle such computations; they are not off-loaded to the math chip.

The instruction set of the math chip is different from that in the primary CPU. A program must detect the existence of the coprocessor and then execute instructions written explicitly for that coprocessor. Otherwise, the math coprocessor chip draws power and does nothing else. Fortunately, most modern programs that can benefit from the use of the coprocessor can correctly detect and use the coprocessor. These programs are usually math-intensive programs such as spreadsheets, database applications, statistical programs, and some graphics programs such as computer-aided design (CAD) software. A word processor doesn't benefit from a math chip and, for this reason, doesn't use it. Table 7.3 summarizes the coprocessors available for the Intel family of microprocessors.

Table 7.3 Coprocessor Summary for Intel-Compatible Microprocessors

Microprocessor	Coprocessor
8086	8087
8088	8087
286	287
386SX	387SX
386SL	387SX
386SLC	387SX
386DX	387DX
486SX	487SX[*]
487SX	Built in[*]
486DX	Built in
Pentium	Built in

The 487SX chip is a fully capable 486 chip with the math coprocessor enabled. When you plug in a 487 chip, it disables the 486 chip and takes over all processing, including high-level math processing.

Within each 8087 group, the maximum speed of the math chips varies. A suffix digit after the main number, as shown in table 7.4, indicates the maximum speed at which a system can run a math chip.

Table 7.4 Maximum Math Chip Speeds	
Part	**Speed**
8087	5 MHz
8087-3	5 MHz
8087-2	8 MHz
8087-1	10 MHz
80287	6 MHz
80287-6	6 MHz
80287-8	8 MHz
80287-10	10 MHz
80387-16	16 MHz
80387-20	20 MHz
80387-33	33 MHz

The performance increase in programs that use the math chip can be dramatic—usually a geometric increase in speed. If the primary applications you use can take advantage of a math coprocessor, you should upgrade your system to include one.

Most systems, other than the Pentium or 486, are socketed for a coprocessor as an option but do not include it as standard equipment. A few systems on the market don't even have a socket for the coprocessor because of cost and size considerations. Usually, these systems are low-cost or portable systems such as older laptops, the IBM PS/1, or the PCjr. For more specific information about math coprocessors, see the discussions of the specific chips—8087, 287, 387, and 487SX—in the following sections. Table 7.5 shows some of the specifications of the various math coprocessors.

Table 7.5 Intel Math Coprocessor Specifications					
Name	**Power consumption**	**Case min. temp.**	**Case max. temp.**	**Number of transistors**	**Date introduced**
8087	3 watts	0° C	85° C	45,000	1980
287	3 watts	0° C	85° C	45,000	1982
287XL	1.5 watts	-65° C	110° C	40,000	1990
387SX	1.5 watts	0° C	85° C	120,000	1988
387DX	1.5 watts	-65° C	110° C	120,000	1987

Most often, you can find the CPU and math coprocessor installed in a particular system by checking the system documentation. The following section examines the Intel family of CPUs and math coprocessors in more detail.

8087 Coprocessor. Intel introduced the 8086 microprocessor in 1976. The math coprocessor paired to the chip, the 8087, was often called the *numeric data processor* (NDP), the *math coprocessor*, or simply *the math chip*. The 8087 is designed to perform high-level math operations at many times the speed and accuracy of the main processor. The primary advantage of using this chip is the increased execution speed in number-crunching programs such as a spreadsheet. Using the 8087 has several minor disadvantages, however, including software support, cost, power consumption, and heat production.

The primary disadvantage in installing the 8087 chip is that you notice an increase in speed only with programs written to use this coprocessor, and then not for all operations. Only math-intensive programs such as spreadsheets, statistical programs, CAD software, and engineering software support the chip. Even then, the effects vary with application to application, and support is limited to specific areas. For example, versions of Lotus 1-2-3 that support the coprocessor do not use the coprocessor for more common operations such as addition, subtraction, multiplication, and division. Applications that do not usually use the 8087 at all include word processing programs, telecommunications software, database programs, and presentation graphics programs.

To test the speed capabilities of the 8087 math coprocessor, two spreadsheets were created, each with 8,000 cells. The first spreadsheet used simple math tasks—addition, subtraction, multiplication, and division—split evenly among the 8,000 cells. The second spreadsheet used high-level math—including formulas that used SQRT, SIN, COS, and TAN calculations—throughout the 8,000 cells. The following table shows the recalculation times.

Spreadsheet	XT without 8087	XT with 8087
Sheet #1 (standard math)	21 seconds	21 seconds
Sheet #2 (high-level math)	195 seconds	21 seconds

The addition of an 8087 to a standard IBM XT did nothing for the spreadsheet containing only simple math, but calculated the spreadsheet containing high-level math in one-tenth the time. (This was also the time to calculate the spreadsheet containing only simple math on both systems.) If your spreadsheets consist of nothing but addition, subtraction, multiplication, and division calculations, before buying a math chip you need to know whether the particular spreadsheet program you use does take advantage of the math chip for simple calculations. Many newer programs have been designed to support the 8087 chip for these operations. Installing an 8087 can extend the useful life of the PC or XT because the chip closes some of the performance gaps between PC- or XT-type computers and AT-type computers. In short, the chip is an asset whenever the software supports it.

The 8087 chip is inexpensive, costing as little as $50. Remember to purchase the chip with the correct maximum-speed rating. The 8087 must be rated to run at the same rate of speed as the CPU or faster. The reason is that the main CPU and the coprocessor must run in synchronization. In an IBM XT, for example, the 8088 and the 8087 run at 4.77 MHz. Look in your system documentation to find the speed at which your system will run the math chip.

Math chips are quite power hungry because of the number of transistors included. A typical 8088 has only about 29,000 transistors, but the 8087 has about 45,000. (Nearly all the 45,000 transistors are dedicated to math functions, which is the reason that the 8087 can perform math so well.) This figure translates to nearly double the calculating horsepower, as well as double the electrical power drain. In a heavily loaded PC, the 8087 could be the straw that breaks the camel's back: the power supply might be insufficient for the increased load. The chip draws nearly one-half amp of current.

Another problem is the amount of heat generated: 3 watts. This heat level can raise the chip temperature to more than 150° Fahrenheit. (158° F is the approved maximum temperature for most 8087s.) For this reason, the chips are made of ceramic. The power and heat are not a problem in the XT or portable because these systems are built to handle it. The PC, however, usually requires a higher-watt power supply with a more powerful cooling fan to handle the load. Power supplies are covered later in this chapter.

80287 Coprocessor. Imagine that two company employees have computers. One user has an IBM XT, and another has a 6MHz AT. Both use Lotus 1-2-3 as their primary application. The AT user delights in being able to outcalculate the XT user by a factor of 3. The XT user purchases an 8087 math chip for $50 and installs it. The XT user then finds that the XT calculates many spreadsheets 10 times faster than before, or more than 3 times as fast as the AT. This frustrates the AT user, who thought that the AT was a faster system. The AT user, therefore, purchases an 80287 for $50 and discovers that the AT is merely equal in speed to the XT for many sheet recalculations. In a few situations, however, the XT may still outrun the AT.

Of course, the AT user wants to know why the 80287 chip did not make the AT "superior" to the XT by a significant margin for spreadsheet recalculations. (For "normal" processing, which does not use the math chip's high-level math functions, the AT still holds its performance edge.)

The answer is in the 80287 chip. For various design reasons, the 8087 chip has much more effect on the speed of the PC and XT than the 80287 has on the AT. The 80287, internally, is the same math chip as the 8087, although the pins used to plug them into the motherboard are different. Because the AT has a healthy power supply and generous, thermostatically controlled fan cooling, the heat and power problems mentioned when discussing the 8087 generally don't apply to the 287. But the 80287 and the 8087 operate internally as if they were identical.

Another reason is that the 80286 and its math chip are *asynchronous*, which means the chips run at different speeds. The 80287 math chip usually runs at two-thirds the speed of the CPU. In most systems, the 80286 internally divides the system clock by 2 to derive the processor clock. The 80287 internally divides the system clock frequency by 3. For this reason, most AT-type computers run the 80287 at one-third the system clock rate, which is also two-thirds the clock speed of the 80286. Because the 286 and 287 chips are asynchronous, the interface between the 286 and 287 chips is not as efficient as with the 8088 and 8087.

In summary, the 80287 and the 8087 chips perform about the same at equal clock rates. The original 80287 is not "better" than the 8087 in any real way, unlike the superiority of the 80286 to the 8086 or 8088. The performance gain in most AT systems from adding the coprocessor is much less substantial than the same type of upgrade for PC- or XT-type systems or for the 80386.

Some systems run the 80287 and the 8087 at the same speed. PS/2 Models 50, 50 Z, and 60 use circuitry that enables both the 80286 and 80287 to run at 10 MHz. The PS/2 Model 25-286 and 30-286, however, follow the standard AT-type design in which the 286 runs at 10 MHz and the 287 runs at 6.67 MHz.

You must consult the system documentation to find what speeds your system would run a 287 coprocessor, because the motherboard designers determine these specifications. Table 7.6 shows 80286 and 80287 clock speeds for most AT-type systems.

Table 7.6 80286 and 80287 Clock Speeds		
System clock	**80286 clock**	**80287 clock**
12.00	6.00	4.00
16.00	8.00	5.33
20.00	10.00	6.67
24.00	12.00	8.00
32.00	16.00	10.67

How can you improve this differential in performance gain? One way takes advantage of the fact that the 80286 and the 80287 run asynchronously. You can install an add-in board that uses its own clock signal to drive the 80287 chip, and therefore can drive the chip at any speed. Some companies have designed a simple speedup circuit that includes a crystal and an 8284 clock generator chip, all mounted on a special board, some of which are not much bigger than the 287 socket. This special board, called a *daughterboard*, is plugged into the 287 socket, and then the 287 is plugged in on top of the special board. Because such boards separate the crystal and clock generator from the motherboard circuitry, the daughterboard can run the 80287 at any speed you want, up to the maximum rating of the chip—8 MHz, 10 MHz, 12 MHz, or more—without affecting the rest of the system.

You could, for example, add one of these daughterboards to your old 6 MHz AT and run a 287 at 10 MHz. Without the daughterboard, the chip would run at only 4 MHz. The boards are available from many math coprocessor suppliers. Their use is highly recommended if you run math-intensive programs. Remember that this type of speedup cannot apply to systems that use 8087 or 80387 chips because these systems must run the math coprocessor at the same speed as the main CPU.

Intel has introduced new variations of the 80287 called the *287XL* and *287XLT*. (The original 287 has been discontinued, and only the 287XL and XLT are available today.) The XL version is designed as a replacement for the standard 287 math coprocessor.

The XLT version is functionally identical to the XL but has a plastic leadless chip carrier (PLCC) case, which is required by some laptop systems. These XL chips are redesigned and are patterned after the 387 instead of the 8087. The XL chips consume much less power than the original 287 chips because they are constructed with CMOS technology. The XL chips perform about 20 percent faster than the original 287 at any clock rate due to their improved design. The design improvements also extend to the instruction set, which includes 387 trigonometric functions not found in older 287 coprocessors. The XL chips are offered in only one speed rating—12.5 MHz. They can be run at lower speeds on slower systems. Unlike the 287 daughterboards, these chips do not speed up the clock speed of a math chip.

Many older diagnostics programs incorrectly identify the XL chips because they were designed after the 387 math chips. Some diagnostics simply indicate that the 287XL is a 387; other diagnostics may incorrectly show a problem with the math corprocessor if a 287XL is installed. Intel provides a special diagnostics program called *CHKCOP* (which stands for CHecK COProcessor) that can test all its math coprocessors. You can get this program on disk from Intel's customer support department or download it from the Intel BBS (503) 645-6275.

After considering all these issues, if you decide to invest in a 287 chip, note that only the XL or XLT versions are available now and that they are rated for up to 12.5 MHz operation. Adding the 287 to an AT is a good idea if the software you use supports the chip. You also should consider using one of the math coprocessor speedup daughterboards, which will run the newer XL chips at the maximum 12 MHz rating regardless of your system's clock speed. Otherwise, the benefits may not be enough to justify the cost.

80387 Coprocessor. Although the 80387 chips run asynchronously, systems are designed so that the chips run at the same clock speed as the main CPU. Unlike the 80287 coprocessor, which was merely an 8087 with different pins to plug into the AT motherboard, the 80387 coprocessor is a high-performance math chip designed specifically to work with the 386. All 387 chips use a low power consumption CMOS design. The 387 coprocessor has two basic designs: the 387DX coprocessor, which is designed to work with the 386DX processor, and the 387SX coprocessor, which is designed to work with the 386SX, SL, or SLC processors.

Originally, Intel offered several different speeds for the 387DX coprocessor. But when Intel designed the 33 MHz version, a smaller mask was required to reduce the lengths of the signal pathways in the chip. (A *mask* is the photographic blueprint of the processor and is used to etch the intricate signal pathways into a silicon chip.) Intel reduced the feature size from 1.5 to 1 micron. This action reduced the size of the silicon chip by 50 percent. In addition to reducing the size, other design improvements were engineered into the new mask, resulting in an improvement in processing efficiency of 20 percent. The 33 MHz version, therefore, would outperform other versions even at slower clock rates.

At the time, purchasing the 33 MHz version of the 387DX was a good idea (even for a 20 MHz 386 system), because the chip would run 20 percent faster than a 20 MHz 387.

In October 1990, however, Intel upgraded the entire 387DX line to the improved mask, resulting in a 20 percent performance boost across the board. You can easily identify these improved 387DX coprocessors by looking at the 10-digit code below the *387* part number. The older (slower) chips begin this line with the letter *S,* and the improved (faster) chips do not. More recently, Intel has discontinued all 387DX processors, except the 33 MHz version, which of course always used the new design. Remember that even though the chip is rated for 33 MHz, it runs at any lower speed.

The 387SX coprocessors are designed to work specifically with the 386SX, SL, or SLC processors. All versions of the 387SX use the improved mask design. When you are selecting a 387SX for your system, be sure that you purchase one rated at a speed equal to or higher than your CPU. Currently, 387SX chips are available from Intel at speeds up to 25 MHz.

> **Note**
>
> Because Intel lagged in originally developing the 387 coprocessor, some early 386 systems were designed with a socket for a 287 coprocessor. Performance levels associated with that union, however, leave much to be desired.

Installing a 387DX is easy, but you must be careful to orient the chip in its socket properly; otherwise, the chip will be destroyed. The most common cause for burned pins on the 387DX is incorrect installation. In many systems, the 387DX is oriented differently from other large chips. Carefully follow the manufacturer's installation instructions to avoid damaging the 387DX. Intel's warranty doesn't cover chips that are installed incorrectly.

Several manufacturers have developed their own versions of the Intel 387 coprocessors. Some are touted as being faster than the original Intel chips. The general compatibility record for these chips is very good. Intel has significantly reduced the prices on its own coprocessors, which means that these third-party chips are usually only a few dollars cheaper than the Intel version.

When the 387s were first introduced, the Intel 33 MHz 387DX chips listed for more than $2,000. Today, you can buy the chip from various suppliers for as little as $90. This cost is so low that many should consider this upgrade. If the software you run supports the chip, the performance gains can be very impressive.

Weitek Coprocessors. In 1981, several Intel engineers formed Weitek Corporation. Weitek has developed math coprocessors for a number of systems, including those based on Motorola processor designs. Intel originally contracted Weitek to develop a math coprocessor for the Intel 386 CPU because Intel was behind in its own development of the 387 math coprocessor. The result was the Weitek 1167, which was a custom math coprocessor that uses a proprietary Weitek instruction set that is incompatible with the Intel 387.

III

Hardware Considerations

The Weitek 1167 is not a single chip. It is a daughterboard consisting of several chip elements that plug into a special 112-pin Weitek socket. To use the Weitek processors, your system must have the required socket, which is incompatible with the 387 math coprocessor or 486SX processor enhancement sockets. The daughterboard includes a socket for an Intel 387 coprocessor so that both coprocessors can be installed in a system, allowing software that runs either Weitek or Intel math instructions to work.

The 1167 was replaced in April 1988 by a single chip version called the *3167*. Many computers, such as the COMPAQ 386, contain a special socket that enables you to use either a Weitek 3167 math coprocessor or an Intel 387DX. This socket has three rows of holes on all four sides. The inner two rows of pins are compatible with the Intel 387DX. If you want to install a 387DX in the special socket, however, you must use *extreme caution* to orient the chip correctly; otherwise, you could damage both the computer and the 387DX. Read your system documentation to determine the correct procedure for installing the 387DX in your computer. Some computers, such as the Tandy 4000, use the Weitek socket but *do not* support the 387DX. Contact your computer manufacturer or dealer for more specific information.

Unfortunately, even if you have the socket for the Weitek processor, your software probably does not support it. As mentioned, your software must contain programming code that makes use of the specific capabilities of a math coprocessor.

Weitek introduced the 4167 coprocessor chip for 486 systems in November 1989. To use the Weitek coprocessor, your system must have the required additional socket. Before purchasing one of the Weitek coprocessors, you should determine whether your software supports it and then contact the software company to determine whether the Weitek has a performance advantage over the Intel coprocessors.

80487 Upgrade. The Intel 80486 microprocessor was introduced in late 1989, and systems using this chip appeared during 1990. The 486DX integrated the math coprocessor right into the chip. The 486SX began life as a full-fledged 486DX chip, but Intel actually disabled the built-in math coprocessor before shipping. As part of this marketing scheme, Intel marketed what it termed a *487SX math coprocessor*. Motherboard manufacturers installed an Intel-designed socket for this so-called 487 chip. But in reality, this so-called 487SX math chip was a special 486DX chip (with the math coprocessor enabled). When you plugged it into your motherboard, it disabled the 486SX chip and gave you the functional equivalent of a full-fledged 486DX system.

Perhaps that somewhat strange marketing scheme is responsible for some of the confusion surrounding the Intel advertisements featuring a 486SX system with a neon "vacancy" sign pointing to an empty socket next to the CPU chip. Unfortunately, these ads do not transmit the message properly. Few people seem to understand that the socket next to the CPU in a 486SX system is not a math coprocessor socket but is instead an *Overdrive socket*.

On 486SX systems with an Overdrive socket, you can plug in a 486DX2 chip with the built-in math coprocessor enabled. In other words, the Overdrive chip, like the chip plugged into the so-called 487 math coprocessor socket, shuts down the original 486SX, and the new processor takes over, offering the functions of both a math coprocessor and a CPU. In addition, the Overdrive processor gives you the advantage of the clock-doubled, or DX2, technology.

The 486DX2 chips are based on a regular 486DX chip but double each chip's internal processing speed. The resulting chip performs its internal instructions at twice the original speed of the chip but communicates with the system at the old chip speeds. For example, a 66 MHz DX2 communicates with the system bus at 33 MHz while it performs internal computations at 66 MHz.

The internal math coprocessor in 486DX2 chips receive the benefit of the double-speed clock and perform much faster than the coprocessing functions in the 25 MHz and 33 MHz DX chips on which the DX2 is based. Perhaps the following list will help you differentiate between the 486SX, 486DX, and Overdrive chips:

486SX	486 with built-in math coprocessor disabled
486DX	486 with built-in math coprocessor enabled
486DX2/Overdrive	Clock-doubled 486 with built-in math coprocessor remaining enabled

If you have one of the original 486SX computers with a "math coprocessor" socket, you may be able to upgrade your system to a 486DX chip. You must purchase the DX2 chip designed for your system: a 40 MHz DX2 if you have a 20 MHz SX or a 50 MHz DX2 if you have a 25 MHz SX. You then have to pry out your old CPU chip and install the new DX2 in the socket in which your old SX chip was installed. A reputable chip supplier can help you determine whether such an upgrade will work on your system.

Overdrive processors can upgrade certain systems based on the 486DX/25 or 486DX/33 chips to clock-doubled technology. Such an upgrade requires an Overdrive socket. In addition, Intel produces clock-doubled 486DX2 chips intended to be used by systems designers in existing motherboard designs. DX2 chips are detailed in Chapter 4, "Improving Your PC's Processing Speed." Some 486 motherboards are designed to use various chip types interchangeably. For example, some motherboards enable you to use your choice of 486DX/33, 486DX/50, or 486DX2/66 chips. To upgrade to a DX2/66 chip on such a motherboard, you simply remove the old CPU chip and install the new one. Many such motherboards, as well as many motherboards with an Overdrive socket, provide Zero Insertion Force (ZIF) CPU sockets to make your upgrade easy. You merely throw a lever, gently slide out the old CPU, slide in the new one according to the directions that come with the chip, and push the lever back to its original position.

Microprocessor Speed Ratings

A common misunderstanding about microprocessors is their different speed ratings. This section covers microprocessor speed in general and then provides more specific information about Intel processors.

A computer system's clock speed is measured as a frequency, usually expressed as a number of cycles per second. A crystal oscillator controls clock speeds using a sliver of quartz in a small, tin container. As voltage is applied to the quartz, it begins to vibrate (oscillate) at a harmonic rate dictated by the shape and size of the crystal (sliver). The oscillations emanate from the crystal in the form of a current that alternates at the harmonic rate of the crystal. This alternating current is the clock signal. A typical computer system runs millions of these cycles per second, so speed is measured in megahertz (MHz). (One hertz is equal to one cycle per second.)

> **Note**
>
> The hertz was named for the German physicist Heinrich Rudolph Hertz. In 1885, he confirmed through experimentation the electromagnetic theory, which states that light is a form of electromagnetic radiation and is propagated as waves.

A single cycle is the smallest element of time for the microprocessor. Every action requires at least one cycle and usually multiple cycles. To transfer data to and from memory, for example, an 8086 chip needs four cycles plus wait states. (A *wait state* is a clock tick in which nothing happens to ensure that the microprocessor isn't getting ahead of the rest of the computer.) A 286 needs only two cycles plus wait states for the same transfer. For executing instructions, most processor instructions require 2 to 100 or more cycles to execute. One reason the 80386 is so fast is that it has an average instruction-execution time of 4.4 clock cycles. If two processors have the same cycling time, the processor that can execute instructions in fewer cycles is faster. For example, a 6 MHz 8086-based system is about half as fast as a 6 MHz 80286-based system, even though the clock rates are the same.

How can two different processors that run at the same clock rate perform differently, with one running "faster" than the other? The answer is simple: efficiency. Suppose that you are comparing two engines. An engine has a crankshaft revolution, called a cycle. This cycling time is measured in revolutions per minute (RPM). If two engines run the same maximum RPM, they should run the car at the same speed, right?

Wrong! Suppose that you're shopping for a fast sports car, and you decide to compare the Mazda Miata and the Chevrolet Corvette. You stop first at the Mazda dealership and look at the Miata. You ask the dealer, "What's the redline on the engine?" The dealer tells you that the Miata has a 4-cylinder engine that redlines at 6,500 RPM. You are impressed with the high RPM rating and you record the information. Then you see the Chevrolet dealer, who steers you toward a new Corvette model. You ask the same question about engine redline, and the dealer tells you that the Corvette has a V-8 engine that redlines at 5,700 RPM. You now figure that because the Mazda engine turns 6,500 RPM, it will propel that car much faster than the Corvette, whose engine can turn only 5,700 RPM.

Although a comparison of engine maximum RPM ratings shows the Miata to be faster than the Corvette, road tests show the opposite. The Corvette is the faster vehicle by a wide margin. You can see that comparing the performance of two vehicles based solely on engine redline is inaccurate. You would never make such a comparison because you know that many more factors than just engine redline are involved in determining vehicle speed and acceleration capability.

Unfortunately, we often make the same type of poor comparison in evaluating computers. Using engine RPM to compare how fast two cars can run is similar to using MHz to compare how fast two computers can run. A better specification to use when you are comparing the two vehicles would be engine horsepower, a measurement of the amount of work that each engine can perform. Then this would have to be adjusted for the weight of the vehicle, the coefficient of drag, drive-line gearing, parasitic losses, and so on. In effect, too many other variables are involved to make any simplistic paper comparison, even if you first picked a more meaningful specification to compare than engine redline. The best way to evaluate which of the two vehicles is faster is through road testing. In a computer, this would be equivalent to taking some of your software and running benchmarks, or comparative performance tests.

The big V-8 engine in the Corvette does more work in each crankshaft revolution (or cycle) than the 4-cylinder engine in the Mazda. In the same manner, an 80286 can perform much more work in a single CPU cycle than an 8088: it's simply more efficient. The 386 is even better; it is about four times more efficient than the 8088 in instruction execution. Whereas an 8088 requires nearly twenty cycles to execute the average processor instruction, the 386 chip requires only four cycles. Combine that with a higher clock rate and you know why a 16 MHz 386 system is about ten times faster than a 4.77 MHz 8088-based system. The 486 is about twice as efficient as the 386 due primarily to an on-chip memory cache. In essence, a 50 MHz 486 would perform approximately equal to a 100 MHz 386. As you can see, you must be careful in comparing MHz to MHz, because much more is involved in total system performance.

Another factor in CPU performance is clock speed. Clock speed is a function of a systems design and usually is controlled by an oscillator, which in turn is controlled by a quartz crystal. Typically, you divide the crystal-oscillation frequency by some amount to obtain the processor frequency. The divisor amount is determined by the original design of the processor (Intel), by related support chips, and by how the motherboard was designed to use these chips together as a system. For example, in IBM PC and XT systems, the main crystal frequency is 14.31818 MHz, which is divided by 3 by an 8284 clock generator chip to obtain a 4.77 MHz processor clock speed. In an IBM AT system, the crystal speeds are either 12.00 or 16.00 MHz, which is divided by 2 internally inside the 80286 for a 6.00 or 8.00 MHz processor clock speed, respectively.

If all other variables, such as the type of processor, number of wait states (empty cycles) added to memory accesses, and width of the data bus are equal, you can compare two systems by their respective clock rates. Be careful with this type of comparison, however, because certain variables, like the number of wait states, can greatly influence the speed of a system and cause the unit with the lower clock rate to run faster than you expect or cause a system with a numerically higher clock rate to run slower than it "should." The construction and design of the memory subsystem can have an enormous impact on a system's final execution speed.

In building a processor, a manufacturer tests it for operation at different speeds, temperatures, and pressures. After the processor is tested, it receives a stamp indicating the maximum safe speed at which the unit will operate under the wide variation of temperatures and pressures encountered in normal operation. The rating system usually is simple. For example, if you remove the lid of an IBM PS/2 Model 50, you can see markings on the processor that look like this:

  80286-10

This number indicates that the chip is an 80286 that runs at a maximum operating speed of 10 MHz. The chip is acceptable for any application in which the chip runs at 10 MHz or less. If the processor fails in a system such as the AT Model 339 or Model 319, both of which use an 80286-8, you can replace the processor with an 80286 rated at 8 MHz or higher. The 80286-6, rated at only 6 MHz, is not suitable as a replacement because its maximum speed rating is less than the 8 MHz at which the AT runs the chip.

Sometimes the markings don't indicate the speed. In the 8086, for example, a -3 translates to 6 MHz operation. Table 7.7 lists the available microprocessors and coprocessors and the manufacturer's markings and corresponding clock rates.

Table 7.7 Intel-Compatible Microprocessor Clock Rates

Processor	Type*	Available maximum speed ratings in MHz											
		5	6	8	10	12	16	20	25	33	40	50	66
8086	CPU	✔	✔	✔	✔								
8088	CPU	✔	✔	✔	✔								
8087	MCP	✔	✔	✔	✔								
286	CPU		✔	✔	✔	✔	✔	✔	✔				
287	MCP		✔	✔	✔	✔							
287 XL	MCP					✔							
287 XLT	MCP					✔							
386 DX	CPU						✔	✔	✔	✔	✔		
387 DX	MCP						✔	✔	✔	✔			
386 SX	CPU						✔	✔	✔				
387 SX	MCP						✔	✔	✔				
386 SL	CPU						✔	✔	✔				
386 SLC	CPU							✔					
486 SX	CPU						✔	✔	✔	✔			
487 SX	CPU+MCP									✔			
486 SLC2	CPU										✔		
486 SL	CPU							✔	✔	✔			
486 DX	CPU+MCP									✔		✔	✔
486 DX2	CPU+MCP										✔	✔	✔
586 (P5)	CPU+MCP											✔	✔

CPU = Central Processing Unit
MCP = Math Co-Processor
SL = SX processor, Low-power
SLC = SX processor, Low-power, Cached
SLC2 = SX processor, Low-power, Cached, double (2x clock) speed
DX2 = Overdrive (2x clock) processor

Note: The DX2/Overdrive processors will operate at double the clock rate of the system in which they are installed. In this table they are listed by the internally doubled speed. The 586 P5 chip will become generally available in 1993.

Sometimes a manufacturer will place the CPU under a heat sink, which prevents you from reading the rating printed on the chip. (A *heat sink* is a metal device that draws heat away from an electronic device.) Although having a heat sink is generally a good idea, Intel designs its chips to run at rated speed without a heat sink.

Testing Microprocessors

The processor is easily the most expensive chip in the system. Microprocessor manufacturers have specialized equipment designed to test their own processors, but you have to settle for a little less. The best microprocessor testing device to which you have access is a known, functional system. You then can use the diagnostics available from IBM and other systems manufacturers to test the motherboard and processor functions. Most systems mount processors in a socket for easy replacement.

Landmark offers specialized diagnostics software, called Service Diagnostics, to test various microprocessors. Special versions are available for each processor in the Intel family. If you don't want to purchase this kind of software, you can perform a "quick and dirty" microprocessor evaluation using the normal diagnostics program supplied with your system. Because the microprocessor is the brain in a system, most systems don't function with a defective one. If a system seems to have a dead motherboard, try replacing the microprocessor with one from a functioning motherboard that uses the same CPU chip. You might find that the processor in the original board is the culprit. If the system continues to "play dead," however, the problem is elsewhere.

Known Defective Chips. A few system problems are built in at the factory, although these bugs or design defects are rare. By learning to recognize one of these problems, you may avoid unnecessary repairs or replacements. This section describes several known defects in system processors.

Early 8088s. A bug in some early 8088 microprocessors allowed interrupts to occur after a program changed the stack segment register. (An interrupt usually is not allowed until the instruction after the one that changes the stack segment register.) This subtle bug might cause problems in older systems. Most programmers have adopted coding procedures that work around the bug, but you have no guarantee that these procedures are in all software. Another problem is that the bug might affect chip operation with an 8087 math coprocessor. Approximately 200,000 IBM PC units sold during 1981 and 1982 were manufactured with the defective chip.

Originally, in the 8087 math-coprocessor chip package, IBM always included an 8088 to be installed with the math chip. This practice led to rumors that the parts were somehow matched. The rumors were unfounded; IBM had just found an easy way to prevent machines using its 8087 chips from using the defective 8088. Because the cost of the chip was negligible, IBM included a bug-free 8088 and eliminated many potential service problems.

You can check the 8088 chip with diagnostics software, or you can identify a good or bad chip from its appearance. If you can open the unit to look at the 8088 chip, the manufacturer and copyright date printed on the chip provide clues to which version you have. An 8088 chip made by a manufacturer other than Intel is bug-free because Intel began licensing the chip mask to other manufacturers after the bug was corrected. If a chip was manufactured by Intel, older (defective) parts have a 1978 copyright date; newer (good) parts have 1978 and 1981 copyright dates, or some later year.

This marking on Intel 8088 chips indicates a chip with the interrupt bug:

```
8088
(c)INTEL 1978
```

The following markings on Intel 8088 chips indicate chips on which the bug is corrected:

```
8088
(c)INTEL '78 '81
```

```
8088
(c)INTEL '78 '83
```

Many diagnostics programs can identify the chip. You can also do it yourself with DEBUG, in DOS versions 2.0 and later. Just load DEBUG at the – prompt and enter the commands in the following example. The commands you enter are shown in boldface type. The DEBUG screen output is underlined. Note that XXXX indicates a segment address, which varies from system to system:

```
 -A 100
[XXXX:0100] MOV ES,AX
[XXXX:0102] INC AX
[XXXX:0103] NOP
[XXXX:0104
 -T
AX=0001 BX=0000 CX=0000 DX=0000 SP=FFEE BP=0000 SI=0000 DI=0000
DS=XXXX ES=0000 SS=XXXX CS=XXXX IP=0103 NV UP EI PL NZ NA PO NC
XXXX:0103 90    NOP
 -Q
```

The A 100 command tells DEBUG to assemble some instructions, of which three were then entered. The T command then executes a Trace, which should normally execute a single instruction, display the contents of the 8088's registers, and then stop. The Trace command usually executes only one instruction. However, when the instruction is MOV to a segment register, as in this case, the Trace command should execute the second instruction before interrupting the program. The third instruction is a dummy, no-operation instruction.

Look at the value shown by DEBUG for the register AX. If AX is equal to 0000, the microprocessor has a bug. If AX is 0001, the second instruction in the test was executed properly and the chip is good. If the second instruction is executed, it increments the value of the AX register by 1. In this example, after executing the Trace, AX equals 0001, which indicates a good chip.

> **Note**
>
> If you try this on 286 or higher systems, the test will fail! This test is valid only for 8088s.

If you have an 8087 and a 4.77 MHz 8088 dated '78, or an 8088 that fails this test, you can get a free replacement 8088. Contact Intel Customer Support for the replacement. Only 4.77 MHz 8088 chips may need to be upgraded. The 8088-2 and 8088-1 do not require replacement. You also can purchase a replacement 8088 for less than $10 from most chip houses. If you suspect that your chip is bad, a replacement is inexpensive insurance.

Early 80386s. Some early 16 MHz Intel 386DX processors had a small bug you might encounter in troubleshooting what seems to be a software problem. The bug, apparently in the chip's 32-bit multiply routine, manifests itself only when you're running true 32-bit code, in a program such as OS/2 2.X, UNIX/386, or Windows in Enhanced mode. Some specialized 386 memory-management software systems also might invoke this subtle bug, but 16-bit operating systems, such as DOS and OS/2 1.X, probably will not.

The bug usually causes the system to lock up. Diagnosing this problem can be difficult because the problem generally is intermittent and software-related. Running tests to find the bug is difficult; only Intel, with proper test equipment, can determine whether your chip has a bug. Some programs can diagnose the problem and identify a defective chip, but they cannot identify all defective chips. If a program indicates a bad chip, you certainly have a defective one; if the program passes the chip, you still might have a defective one.

Intel requested that its 386 customers return possibly defective chips for screening, but many vendors did not return them. Intel tested returned chips and replaced defective ones. The known defective chips later were sold to bargain liquidators or systems houses that wanted chips which would not run 32-bit code. The "known defective" chips were stamped with a *16-bit SW Only* logo, indicating that they were authorized to run only 16-bit software.

Chips that passed the test and all subsequent chips produced as bug-free were marked with a double sigma ($\Sigma\Sigma$) code, which indicates a good chip. 386DX chips not marked with either *16-bit SW Only* or the $\Sigma\,\Sigma$ designation have not been tested by Intel and might be defective. The following marking indicates that a chip has not yet been screened for the defect; it might be either good or bad. Return these chips to the system manufacturer, who then will return the chip for a free replacement.

```
80386-16
```

The following marking indicates that the chip has been tested and has the 32-bit multiply bug. The chip works with 16-bit software, such as DOS, but not with 32-bit, 386-specific software such as Windows/386.

```
80386-16
16-bit SW Only
```

The following mark on a chip indicates that it has been tested as defect-free. This chip fulfills all the capabilities promised for the 80386.

```
80386-16
ΣΣ
```

This problem was discovered and corrected before Intel officially added *DX* to the part number. So if you have a chip labeled as 80386DX or 386DX, it does not have this problem.

Another problem with the 386DX can be more specifically stated. When 386-based versions of XENIX or other UNIX implementations are run on a computer containing a 387DX math coprocessor, the computer will lock up under certain conditions. The problem won't occur in the DOS environment. For the lockup to occur, all of the following must happen simultaneously:

- Demand page virtual memory must be active
- A 387DX must be installed and in use
- DMA (direct memory access) must occur
- The 386 must be in a wait state

When all these conditions are true at the same instant, the 386DX ends up waiting for the 387DX and vice versa. Both processors will continue waiting for each other indefinitely. The problem is in certain versions in the 386DX, not in the 387DX math coprocessor.

Intel published this problem (Errata 21) immediately after it was discovered, to inform its OEM customers. At that point, it became the responsibility of each manufacturer to implement a fix in its hardware or software product. Some manufacturers, such as COMPAQ and IBM, responded accordingly by modifying their motherboards to prevent these lockups from occurring.

The Errata 21 problem is present only in the B Stepping version of the 386DX and not the later D Stepping version. You can easily identify the D Stepping version of the 386DX by the letters *DX* in the part number (for example, 386DX-20). If the chip is labeled with *DX* as part of the part number, the chip does not have this problem.

Other Processor Problems. Some other problems with processors and math coprocessors are worth noting. After removing a math coprocessor from an AT-type system, you must rerun your computer's SETUP program. Some AT-compatible SETUP programs do not properly unset the math coprocessor bit. If you receive a Power-On Self Test (POST) error message because the computer cannot find the math chip, you may have to temporarily unplug the battery from the system board. All SETUP information will be lost, so be sure to write down the hard drive type, floppy drive type, and memory and video configurations before unplugging the battery. This information is critical in correctly reconfiguring your computer.

Another strange problem occurs with some IBM PS/2 Model 80 systems when a 387DX is installed. With the following computers, you may hear crackling or beeping noises from the speaker while the computer is running:

- 8580 Model 111, with serial numbers below 6019000

- 8850 Model 311, with serial numbers below 6502022

If you are experiencing this problem, contact IBM service for a motherboard replacement.

Heat and Cooling Problems. Heat can be a problem in clock-doubled 486 chips and systems based on the Pentium chip. The Intel DX2/66 consumes about 40 percent more power than a 33 MHz 486DX and generates correspondingly more heat. The Pentium generates even more heat. If your system is based on the DX2 or Pentium chips, you must dissipate the extra thermal energy; the fan inside your computer case may not be able to handle the load.

To cool DX2 systems, for less than $20 you can buy a special attachment for the CPU chip called a *heat sink*, which draws heat away from the CPU chip. If you plan to buy a Pentium system, ensure that the manufacturer has dealt with the heat problem. In fact, the rumored reason for Intel's delay in releasing the 66 MHz Pentium chip is overheating problems. Some Pentium-based systems have two cooling fans in the case and a heat sink on the CPU chip. The three devices work together to keep the system cool. Other designers are using a special refrigerated cooling unit installed on or near the Pentium chip.

Memory

The CPU architecture dictates a computer's memory capacity. The 8088 and 8086, with 20 address lines, can use as much as 1M (1024K) of RAM. The 286 and 386SX CPUs have 24 address lines; they can keep track of as much as 16M of memory. The 386DX, 486, and Pentium CPUs have a full set of 32 address lines; they can keep track of a staggering 4 gigabytes of memory.

III

Hardware Considerations

When the 386DX, 486, and Pentium chips emulate the 8088 chip (as they do when running a single DOS program), they implement a hardware operating mode called real mode. Real mode is the same as the only mode on PC and XT systems. In *real mode,* all Intel processors—even the mighty Pentium—are restricted to using only 1M, and the motherboard design still reserves 384K of that amount. Only in protected mode can the 80286 or better chips use their maximum potential for memory addressing.

Motherboard Memory

As mentioned, Pentium-based systems can address as much as four gigabytes of memory. To put these memory-addressing capabilities into perspective, 4 gigabytes (4,096M) of memory costing $50 per megabyte for fast (70 nanoseconds or less) RAM chips would total more than $200,000 if purchased at the going rate for 1M SIMMs. Of course, you could probably negotiate a much better price with a chip vendor if you planned to buy 4 gigabytes of SIMMs.

Pentium-based systems are already racing toward the 4 gigabyte limit. Early Pentium-based systems, such as the Advanced Logic Research, Inc. (ALR) Evolution V-Q enable you to install as much as 1 gigabyte of RAM on the motherboard. How most system manufacturers will handle the issue of maximum installed RAM on Pentium-based systems is uncertain, but they can be expected to follow the lead set by ALR and other companies. Some 486DX-based systems enable you to install a maximum of 64M. Many 386s and some 486s enable you to install much less, some as little as 4M. Adding memory to such systems usually requires an add-on expansion board plugged into a special 32-bit expansion slot.

On many systems, accessing RAM chips installed directly on a motherboard is faster than accessing memory through an expansion slot. Even without considering this speed advantage, you have the advantage of saving slots. The more memory chips you can get on the motherboard, the fewer adapter slots you need to use. A system that does not have a memory expansion slot will face a large reduction in speed if you use a memory expansion board made for a standard 16-bit slot.

Some 386 and 486 motherboards don't fully use memory beyond 16M. On such systems, memory past 16M (if installed) can be used for video memory extensions, for ROM extensions, or as a scratchpad area for a program or adapter card. Some motherboards don't even address that memory. You can identify these by examining their documentation or contacting the manufacturer. Most 486 motherboards enable you to install a maximum of 64M on the motherboard.

Because the PC hardware design reserves the top 384K of the first megabyte of system memory for use by the system itself, you have access to 640K for your programs and data. The use of 384K by the system results in the 640K conventional memory limit. The amount of conventional memory you can actually use for programs depends on the memory used by device drivers (such as ANSI.SYS) and memory resident programs (such as MOUSE.COM) you load in your CONFIG.SYS and AUTOEXEC.BAT files. Device drivers and memory resident programs usually use conventional memory. For more on conventional memory, see Chapter 2.

RAM Chips. A *RAM chip* temporarily stores programs when they are running and the data being used by those programs. RAM chips are sometimes termed *volatile storage* because when you turn off your computer or there is an electrical outage, whatever is stored in RAM is lost unless you saved it to your hard drive. Because of the volatile nature of RAM, many computer users make it a habit to save their work frequently. (Some software applications can do timed backups automatically.)

Launching a computer program instructs DOS to bring an EXE or COM disk file into RAM and as long as they are running, computer programs reside in RAM. The CPU executes programmed instructions in RAM. RAM stores your keystrokes when you use a word processor. RAM stores numbers used in calculations. The CPU also stores results in RAM. Telling a program to save your data instructs the program to store RAM contents on your hard drive as a file.

If you decide to purchase more RAM, you will need the information on RAM chips and their speeds presented in the following sections to help ensure that you don't slow down your computer when you add memory.

Physical Storage and Organization. RAM chips can be physically integrated into the motherboard or adapter board in several forms. Older systems used individual memory chips, called *dual in-line pin* (DIP) chips, that were plugged into sockets or soldered directly to a board. Most modern systems use a memory package called a *single in-line memory module* (SIMM). These modules combine several chips on a small circuit board that is plugged into a retaining socket. A SIPP, or single in-line pin package, is similar to a SIMM, but it uses pins rather than edge connectors to connect to the motherboard.

Several types of memory chips have been used in PC system motherboards. Most of these chips are single-bit-wide chips, available in several capacities. The following is a list of available RAM chips and their capacities:

- *16K by 1 bit.* These devices, used in the original IBM PC with a Type 1 motherboard, have a small capacity compared with the current standard. You won't find much demand for these chips except from owners of original IBM PC systems.

- *64K by 1 bit.* These chips were used in the standard IBM PC Type 2 motherboard and in the XT Type 1 and 2 motherboards. Many memory adapters, such as the popular vintage-AST 6-pack boards, use these chips also.

- *128K by 1 bit.* These chips, used in the IBM AT Type 1 motherboard, often were a strange physical combination of two 64K chips stacked on top of one another and soldered together. True single-chip versions were used also for storing the parity bits in the IBM XT 286.

- *256K by 1 bit.* These chips once were popular in motherboards and memory cards. The IBM XT Type 2 and IBM AT Type 2 motherboards, as well as most compatible systems, use these chips.

- *1024K by 1 bit.* These 1M chips are very popular in systems today because of their low cost. These chips are often used in SIMMs because of their ease of installation and service. (See the section on SIMMs for more information.)

- *4096K by 1 Bit.* Four-megabit chips have gained popularity recently and now are used in many compatible motherboards and memory cards. They are used primarily in 4M and 8M SIMMs and generally are not sold as individual chips.

- *16,384K by 1 Bit.* Sixteen-megabit chips are new on the market. They will probably gain popularity in Pentium-based systems on which as much as 1 gigabyte can be installed on some systems. The use of these chips in SIMMs allows almost unbelievable memory capacities in very little physical space.

A typical memory chip resembles figure 7.1. Each marking on the chip is significant.

Fig. 7.1
The markings on a typical memory chip.

The -10 on the chip corresponds to its speed in nanoseconds (a 100-nanosecond rating). MB81256 is the chip's part number, which usually contains a clue about the chip's capacity. The key digits are 1256, which indicate that this chip is 1 bit wide, and has a depth of 256K. The 1 means that to make a full byte with parity, you need nine of these single-bit-wide chips. A chip with a part number KM4164B-10 indicates a 64K-by-1-bit chip at a speed of 100 nanoseconds. The following list matches common chips with their part numbers:

Part Number	Chip
4164	64K-by-1 bit
4264	64K-by-2 bits
4464	64K-by-4 bits
41128	128K-by-1 bit
42128	128K-by-2 bits
44128	128K-by-4 bits
41256	256K-by-1 bit
42256	256K-by-2 bits
44256	256K-by-4 bits

Chips wider than 1 bit are used to construct banks of less than 9, 18, or 36 chips (depending on the system architecture). For example, in the IBM XT 286, which is an AT-type 16-bit system, the last 128K bytes of memory on the motherboard consist of a bank with only six chips; four are 64K-by-4 bits wide, and two parity chips are 1 bit wide, storing 18 bits.

In figure 7.1, the F centered between two lines is the manufacturer's logo for Fujitsu Microelectronics. The 8609 indicates the date of manufacture (ninth week of 1986). Some manufacturers, however, use a Julian date code. To decode the chip further, contact a chip vendor. Many are happy to help.

When you know the depth, width, and speed rating of the chip, you can order a replacement. If the dates on the chips are consistent, you can probably use this information to identify a bad batch of chips.

Memory Banks. Memory chips (DIPs, SIMMs, and SIPPs) are organized in *banks,* or groups of nine chips, on motherboards and memory cards. You should know the memory bank layout and position on the motherboard and memory cards.

One reason to have this information is that to reduce the number of wait states on 486 systems these systems use interleaved memory speedup technology. Interleaved memory requires an even number of memory banks (at least 2 banks or a multiple of 2, never 1, 3, 5 or an odd number). You need to know the bank layout when adding memory to the system. In addition, memory diagnostics report error locations by bank and bit addresses, and you must use these numbers to locate the chip in your system.

The banks usually correspond to the data bus capacity of the system's microprocessor. Following is the width of an individual bank based on the type of PC:

- *8088* PC and XT memory banks are 9 bits wide: 8 data bits plus 1 parity bit

- *8086, 286,* and *386SX* memory banks are 18 bits wide: 16 bits plus 2 parity bits

- *386DX, 486,* and *Pentium* memory banks are 36 bits wide: 32 bits plus 4 parity bits

The IBM PC Type 2 and XT Type 1 motherboard contains four banks of memory labeled Bank 0, 1, 2, and 3. Each bank uses 9 64K-by-1-bit chips. The total number of chips present is 4 times 9, or 36 chips, organized as shown in figure 7.2.

This layout is used in several motherboards, including the Type 1 and 2 PC motherboards and the Type 1 and 2 XT motherboards. Most PC or XT clones also follow this scheme. Note that the parity chip is the leftmost chip in each bank on the XT motherboard.

In an AT-type system with a 286 or 386SX processor, memory is organized into larger banks of 18 chips or sometimes into two 9-bit SIMMs.

III

Hardware Considerations

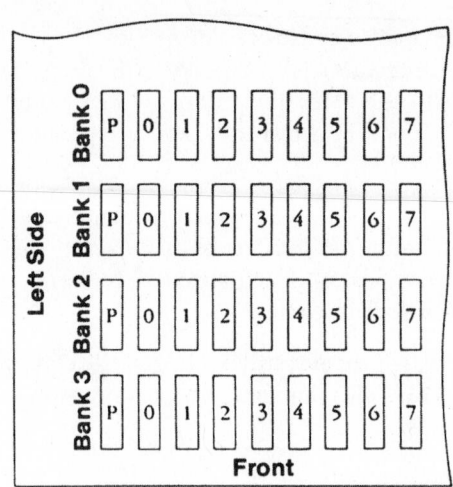

Fig. 7.2
Organization of memory on an IBM XT Type 1 motherboard showing 9-bit banks.

On the AT Type 2 motherboard, the chips in a single bank are organized into two vertical columns rather than horizontally in rows. The IBM AT Type 1 motherboard is different, with two banks of 18 chips laid out horizontally (two rows per bank). The first bank (Bank 0) is toward the front of the system, which is opposite the orientation in the PC and XT. The physical orientation used on a motherboard or memory card is arbitrary and determined by the board's designers. Documentation covering your system or card will come in very handy. You can determine the layout of a motherboard or adapter card through testing, but this takes time and may be difficult, particularly after you have a problem with a system.

One-bit-wide chips once were an almost a universal standard on PCs. Today, many systems use 2-bit-wide or 4-bit-wide chips.

Parity Checking. One standard IBM has set for the industry is that the memory chips in a bank of nine each handle one bit of data: 8 bits per character plus one extra bit called the *parity bit*. The parity bit enables memory-control circuitry to keep tabs on the other 8 bits, a built-in cross-check for the integrity of each byte in the system. If the circuitry detects an error, the computer stops and displays a message informing you of the malfunction. Some modern SIMMs have only three chips, however, with each chip handling 3 of the 9 bits.

IBM established the *odd parity* standard for error checking. The following explanation may help you understand what is meant by odd parity. As the 8 individual bits in a byte are stored in memory, a special chip called a *74LS280 parity generator/checker* on the motherboard (or memory card) evaluates the data bits by counting the number of 1s in the byte. If an even number of 1s are in the byte, the parity generator/checker chip creates a 1 and stores it as the ninth bit (parity bit) in the parity memory chip. That makes the total sum for all 9 bits an odd number. If the original sum of the 8 data bits is an odd number, the parity bit created is 0, keeping the 9-bit sum an odd number. The value of the parity bit is always chosen so that the sum of all 9 bits (8 data bits plus 1 parity bit) is an odd number. Remember that the 8 data bits in a byte are numbered 0 1 2 3 4 5 6 7. Here are some examples that may make it easier to understand:

Data bit number:	0 1 2 3 4 5 6 7	Parity
Parity bit value:	1 0 1 1 0 0 1 1	0

In this example, because the total number of data bits with a value of 1 is an odd number (5), the parity bit must have a value of 0 to ensure an odd sum for all 9 bits.

The following is another example:

Data bit number:	0 1 2 3 4 5 6 7	Parity
Parity bit value:	0 0 1 1 0 0 1 1	1

In this example, because the total number of data bits with a value of 1 is an even number (4), the parity bit must have a value of 1 to create an odd sum for all 9 bits.

When the system reads memory back from storage, it checks the parity information. If a (9-bit) byte has an even number of bits with a parity bit value of 1, that byte must have an error. The system cannot tell which bit has changed, or if only a single bit has changed. If three bits changed, for example, the byte still flags a parity-check error; if two bits have changed, however, the bad byte may pass unnoticed. The following examples show parity-check messages for three types of systems:

For the IBM PC:	PARITY CHECK X
For the IBM XT:	PARITY CHECK X YYYYY (Z)
For the IBM AT and late model XT:	PARITY CHECK X YYYYY

Where X is 1 or 2:

   1 = Error occurred on the motherboard

   2 = Error occurred in an expansion slot

YYYYY represents a number from 00000 through FFFFF that indicates, in hexadecimal notation, the byte in which the error has occurred.

Where *(Z)* is (S) or (E):

   (S) = Parity error occurred in the system unit

   (E) = Parity error occurred in the expansion chassis

III

Hardware Considerations

> **Note**
>
> An expansion chassis was an option IBM sold for the original PC and XT systems to add more expansion slots. This unit consisted of a backplane motherboard with eight slots, one of which contained a special extender/receiver card that was cabled to a similar extender/receiver card placed in the main system. Due to the extender/receiver cards in the main system and the expansion chassis, the net gain was six slots.

When a parity-check error is detected, the motherboard parity-checking circuits generate a *nonmaskable interrupt* (NMI), which halts processing and diverts the system's attention to the error. The NMI causes a routine in the ROM to be executed. The routine clears the screen and then displays a message in the upper left corner of the screen. The message differs depending on the type of computer system. On some older IBM systems, the ROM parity-check routine halts the CPU. In such a case, the system locks up, and you must perform a hardware reset or a power-off/power-on cycle to restart the system. Unfortunately, all unsaved work is lost in the process. (An NMI is a system warning that software cannot ignore.)

Most systems do not halt the CPU when a parity error is detected; instead, they offer you a choice of either rebooting the system or continuing as though nothing happened. Additionally, these systems may display the parity error message in a different format than IBM, although the information presented is basically the same. For example, many systems with a Phoenix BIOS display these messages:

```
Memory parity interrupt at YYYY:YYYY
Type (S)hut off NMI, Type (R)eboot, other keys to continue
```

or

```
I/O card parity interrupt at YYYY:YYYY
Type (S)hut off NMI, Type (R)eboot, other keys to continue
```

The first of these two messages indicates a motherboard parity error (Parity Check 1), and the second indicates an expansion-slot parity error (Parity Check 2). Notice that the address given for the memory error is in a segment:offset form rather than a straight linear address such as with IBM's message. The segment:offset address form still gives you the location of the error to a resolution of a single byte.

You have three ways to proceed after viewing this error message. You can press S, which shuts off parity checking and resumes system operation at the point where the parity check first occurred. Pressing R forces the system to reboot, losing any unsaved work. Pressing any other key causes the system to resume operation with further parity checking still enabled. If the problem recurs, it is likely to cause another parity-check interruption.

Although many systems enable you to continue processing after a parity error, and even allow for the disabling of further parity checking, continuing to use your system after a parity error is detected can be dangerous if misused. The idea behind letting you continue using either method is to give you time to save any unsaved work before you diagnose and service the computer, but be careful how you do this.

Caution

When you are notified of a memory parity error, remember that the parity check is telling you memory has been corrupted. Do you want to save potentially corrupted data over the good file from the *last* time you saved? Definitely not! Be sure that you save your work to a different file name. In addition, after a parity error, you should save only to a floppy disk if possible and avoid writing to the hard disk; there is a slight chance the hard drive could become corrupted if you save the contents of corrupted memory.

After saving your work, you should determine the cause of the parity error and repair the system. You may be tempted to use the S option to shut off further parity checking and simply continue using the system as if nothing were wrong. Doing so resembles unscrewing the oil pressure warning indicator bulb on a car with an oil leak so the oil pressure light won't bother you anymore.

IBM PS/2 systems have a slightly different way of communicating parity-check errors than the older IBM systems. To indicate motherboard parity errors, the message looks like this:

```
110
YYYYY
```

To indicate parity errors from an expansion slot, the message looks like this:

```
111
YYYYY
```

In these messages, *YYYYY* is the address of the parity error, as before. As with older IBM systems, the system is halted after these messages are displayed.

Single In-Line Memory Modules. For memory storage, most modern systems have adopted the single in-line memory module (SIMM) as an alternative to individual memory chips. These small boards plug into special connectors on a motherboard or memory card. The individual memory chips are soldered to the SIMM, so removing and replacing individual memory chips is impossible. Instead, you must replace the entire SIMM if any part of it fails. The SIMM is treated as though it were one large memory chip.

IBM compatibles have two main types of SIMMs—9 bits and 36 bits—with various capacities. The 9-bit SIMMs are smaller than the 36-bit versions. Chips may be on one or both sides. SIMMs for some non-IBM-compatible systems are slightly different. For example, Apple computers use either 8- or 32-bit SIMMs because Apple systems do not have parity-checked memory. You can use the IBM-compatible 9- or 36-bit SIMMs to replace the 8- or 32-bit SIMMs in Apple systems, but you cannot use 8- or 32-bit SIMMs in IBM-compatible systems. (If you service both IBM and Apple systems, you could simply stock only the IBM-compatible SIMMs because they can be used in either system.)

Figures 7.3 and 7.4 show typical 9-bit and 36-bit SIMMs, respectively. Note that the 9-bit SIMMs have 30 pins, and 36-bit SIMMs have 72 pins. The pins are numbered from left to right and are connected through to both sides of the module. Note that all dimensions are in both inches and millimeters (in parentheses).

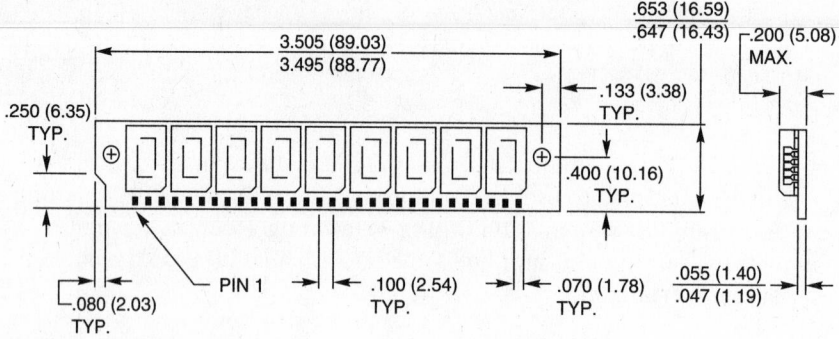

Fig. 7.3

A typical 9-bit (30-pin) SIMM.

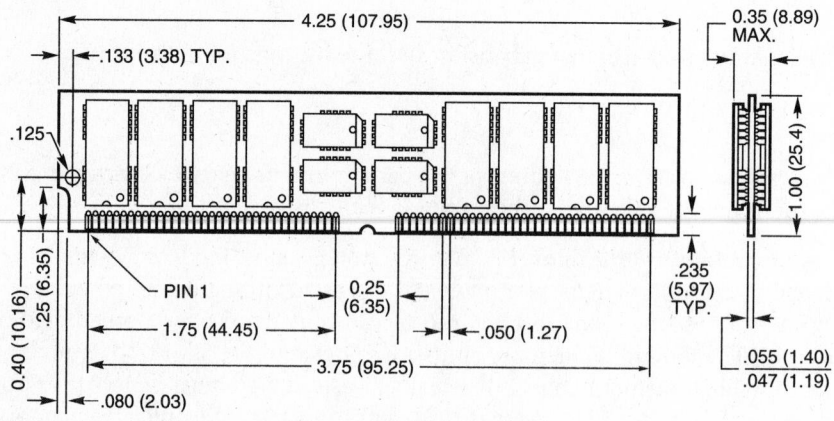

Fig. 7.4

A typical 36-bit (72-pin) SIMM.

A SIMM is extremely compact, considering the amount of memory it holds. SIMMs are available in several capacities, including the following:

9-bit SIMM capacities:
    256K
    1024K (1M)
    4096K (4M)

36-bit SIMM capacities:
>1024K (1M)
>2048K (2M)
>4096K (4M)
>8192K (8M)
>16,384K (16M)

Two main types of 9-bit SIMMs are available. Most systems use a *generic* type of SIMM, which has a standard pin configuration. IBM systems that use 9-bit SIMMs, starting with the XT-286 introduced in 1986, require a SIMM with different signals on five of the pins. These are known as *IBM-style* 9-bit SIMMs. You can modify a generic SIMM to work in the IBM systems and vice versa, but purchasing a SIMM with the correct pinouts is much easier. Be sure you identify to the SIMM vendor which type you want when you purchase 9-bit SIMMs.

The 36-bit SIMMs do not have different pinouts and are differentiated only by capacity and speed. The 36-bit SIMMs are ideal for 386 and higher systems because they comprise an entire bank of memory (32 data bits plus 4 parity bits). When you configure a system that uses a 36-bit SIMM, you can usually add or remove memory in single SIMM modules (except on systems that use interleaved memory schemes to reduce wait states). The 9-bit SIMMs are clumsy when used in a system with a 32-bit memory architecture because these SIMMs must be added or removed in quantities of four to make up a complete bank. A 386SX or a 286 system would require at least two 9-bit SIMMs for a single bank of memory.

> ### Note
>
> A *bank* is the smallest amount of memory that can be addressed by the processor at one time and usually corresponds to the data bus width of the processor.

Remember that many 486 systems (such as the PS/2 Models 90 and 95) use interleaved memory to reduce wait states. This requires a multiple of two 36-bit SIMMs because memory accesses are alternated between the SIMMs to improve performance. Interleaved memory is covered in Chapter 4, "Improving Your PC's Processing Speed."

SIMMs, like memory chips, have different speed ratings. The ratings vary from about 120ns for SIMMs used in older 286-based systems to 60ns or 70ns SIMMs used in fast 486 systems. Many systems based on the Pentium chip use even faster RAM chips. For more information on the speed of RAM chips, see the "RAM Chip Speed" section, which follows this section.

You cannot always replace a SIMM with a greater-capacity unit and expect it to work. For example, the IBM PS/2 Model 70-Axx and Bxx systems accept 36-bit SIMMs of 1M or 2M capacity, which are 80ns or faster. Although an 80ns 4M SIMM is available, it does not work in these systems. The PS/2 Model 55 SX and 65 SX, however, accept 1M, 2M, or 4M

III

Hardware Considerations

36-bit SIMMs. A larger-capacity SIMM works only if the motherboard has been designed to accept it in the first place. Consult your system documentation to determine the correct capacity and speed to use.

SIMMs were designed to eliminate chip creep, which plagues systems with memory chips installed in sockets. *Chip creep* occurs when a chip works its way out of its socket, caused by the normal thermal expansion and contraction from powering a system on and off. Eventually, chip creep leads to poor contact between the chip leads and the socket, and memory errors and problems begin.

The original solution for chip creep was to solder all the memory chips to the printed circuit board. This approach, however, was impractical. Memory chips fail more frequently than most other types of chips and soldering chips to the board made the units difficult to service.

The SIMM incorporates the best compromise between socketed and soldered chips. The chips are soldered to the SIMM, but you can replace the socketed SIMM module easily. In addition, the SIMM is held tight to the motherboard by a locking mechanism that does not work loose from contraction and expansion but is easy for you to loosen. This solution is a good one, but it can increase repair costs. You must replace what amounts to an entire bank rather than one defective chip.

For example, if you have a 486 with two 60ns 4M SIMMs and one goes bad, you could replace it for $165 or less from chip suppliers who advertise in the computer magazines. This is certainly more expensive than replacing a single 256K chip. Of course, 4M SIMMs are used only on systems that are not designed for single 256K chips; these systems have about ten times the memory and processing power of systems that might contain individual 256K chips. It would take 288 256K chips to equal the memory storage of two 4M SIMMs. Troubleshooting a problem with two RAM devices is much easier than troubleshooting 288 chips. In addition, two SIMMs are more reliable than 288 individual chips in sockets.

Nearly all systems on the market use SIMMs, including nearly all IBM PS/2 systems and many compatibles. Even Apple Macintosh systems use SIMMs. The SIMM is not a proprietary memory system but rather an industry-standard device. As mentioned, some SIMMs have different pinouts and specifications other than speed and capacity, so be sure that you obtain the correct SIMMs for your system.

RAM Chip Speed. Memory-chip speed is reported in nanoseconds (ns). (One *nanosecond* is the time that light takes to travel 11.72 inches.) PC memory speeds vary from about 20ns to 200ns. When you replace a failed memory module, you must install a module of the same type and speed as the failed module. You can substitute a chip with a different speed only if the speed of the replacement chip is equal to or faster than that of the failed chip.

Some people have had problems when "mixing" chips because they used a chip that did not meet the minimum required specifications (for example, refresh timing specifications) or was incompatible in pinout, depth, width, or design. Chip access time always can be less (that is, faster) as long as your chip is the correct type and meets all other specifications.

Substituting faster memory usually doesn't provide improved performance, because the system still operates the memory at the same speed. In systems not engineered with a great deal of "forgiveness" in the timing between memory and system, however, substituting faster memory chips might improve reliability. Faster RAM chips may improve your system performance also when the motherboard was designed for faster chips than the manufacturer installed. For example, if your motherboard was designed for 70ns chips, but the manufacturer installed cheaper 80ns RAM, you may get a slight performance boost from removing all the old RAM chips and installing faster ones. However, do not mix chip speeds by replacing only some 80ns chips with 70ns ones.

The same common symptoms result when the system memory has failed or is simply not fast enough for the system's timing. The usual symptoms are frequent parity-check errors or a system that does not operate at all. The POST also might report errors. If you're unsure of what chips to buy for your system, contact the system manufacturer or a reputable chip supplier.

System ROM. *ROM* (read-only memory) BIOS (basic input-output system) describes two things: the system *BIOS* and the *ROM* chip in which the BIOS is contained. The BIOS is a small, essential set of software programs that enables the computer to start itself (bootstrap or boot) automatically. The BIOS gets the CPU working with the rest of the system components before DOS or another operating system takes over. The ROM chip is read-only, or *nonvolatile*, memory. Therefore, its contents are not lost or changed when you turn off your computer or enter data (as the contents of RAM chips are lost). The ROM chip containing the BIOS is often referred to as simply the *BIOS chip,* the *system BIOS chip,* or *firmware.*

In addition to the basic input-output system, the ROM BIOS contains the power-on self test (POST), which checks many components of your system, including system RAM, before handing over control to DOS or another operating system. On IBM computers, the ROM BIOS also contains Cassette BASIC.

Over the years, the BIOS in various PC models has undergone changes almost always associated with either a new system or a new motherboard design for an existing system. There are several reasons for these changes. The introduction of the XT, for example, gave IBM a good opportunity to correct a few things in the system BIOS and also add necessary new features, such as automatic support for a hard disk. IBM retrofitted many of the same changes into the PC's BIOS at the same time.

Because an in-depth knowledge of the types of BIOS is something a programmer might find useful, IBM makes this information available in the technical-reference manuals sold for each system. A new ROM BIOS technical-reference manual covers all IBM systems in one book. Complete ROM BIOS listings (with comments) accompanied early IBM system documentation, but that information is not supplied for later IBMs.

III

Hardware Considerations

Even if you aren't a programmer, however, certain things about system BIOS are important to know. IBM has had more than 20 BIOS programs for the PC and PS/2 families. Sometimes a system has different versions of BIOS over the course of a system's availability. For example, there are at least three versions of BIOS for the PC, XT, and AT systems. Because a few important changes have been made in the software stored in BIOS, knowing which BIOS is in your system can be useful.

To determine which ROM BIOS module is installed in your system, first check your system documentation. If you have a 386 or later system, a few lines of text at the top of your screen during the POST probably identifies the manufacturer, BIOS revision number, and date of manufacture. The BIOS version you have also may be indicated by the manufacturer's name version number and date encoded in the chip.

On IBM systems, the ROM BIOS contains an identification byte (the second-to-last byte) that has the system type and a chip part number for reference. The value of the byte at location FFFFE (hexadecimal) corresponds to the system type, as shown in table 7.8.

Table 7.8 IBM ROM Versions

Date	System description	Revision number
04/24/81	PC	—
10/19/81	PC	—
10/27/82	PC	—
11/08/82	PC-XT	—
01/10/86	PC-XT	01
05/09/86	PC-XT	02
06/01/83	PCjr	—
09/13/85	PC convertible	00
06/26/87	PS/2 25	00
09/02/86	PS/2 30	00
12/12/86	PS/2 30	01
02/05/87	PS/2 30	02
01/10/84	PC-AT	—
06/10/85	PC-AT	01
11/15/85	PC-AT	00
04/21/86	PC-XT 286	00
12/01/89	PS/1	00
06/28/89	PS/2 25 286	02
09/02/86	PS/2 30	02
12/12/86	PS/2 30	01
08/25/88	PS/2 30 286	00
06/28/89	PS/2 30 286	02
03/15/91	PS/2 35 SX	05
04/04/91	PS/2 35 SX	06

Such programs should be used any time you receive a memory parity error message. Even if you do not receive error messages, if a previously sound system begins locking up or if strange characters appear on-screen you should run a good diagnostic program. Software diagnostics can help you spot trouble before a hardware problem destroys data.

Bus and System Resources

Closely related to system memory issues are bus and system resources such as interrupt request (IRQ) lines and Direct Memory Access (DMA) channels. Hardware devices and software programs use IRQ lines and DMA channels to access the system hardware directly rather than through DOS.

Chapter 2 describes these basic system resources as well as how to troubleshoot problems. Chapter 2 also suggests ways to use the Microsoft Diagnostics program and other diagnostic software to determine unused DMA channels and interrupts and the creation of a template showing free resources so you will not have IRQ and DMA channel problems when you install a new adapter board. In addition, Chapter 2 covers the use of memory managers to take advantage of Upper Memory Blocks (UMBs) to free up conventional memory.

The following sections cover input/output ports and provide troubleshooting tips when installing sound boards, SCSI host adapters, and other adapter boards.

I/O Ports. The computer's input/output ports enable you to attach a large number of important devices to your system to expand its capabilities. For example, a printer attached to one of your system's LPT (parallel) ports enables you to make a printout of the work on your system. A modem attached to one of your system's COM (serial) ports enables you to use the telephone lines to communicate with computers thousands of miles away. A scanner attached to an LPT port or a SCSI host adapter enables you to convert graphics or text into images and type you can use in the software installed on your computer.

Commonly Used COM Port Addresses. Most systems have at least two COM ports installed: COM1 and COM2. The basic architecture of the PC allows for as many as four COM ports, numbered 1 through 4. Theoretically, each of these COM ports can be used to attach devices such as a mouse or modem to your system.

However, depending on how you use the devices attached to your COM ports, you may not be able to use all four COM ports or you may not be able to use them at the same time. Each COM port needs access to an unused IRQ to gain access to the CPU. For example, a modem attached to COM1 on your system needs access to IRQ 4. If you also have a bus mouse adapter board configured for IRQ 4, the modem or the mouse or both may not work. In addition, if the memory address used by a COM port is already being used by another adapter board, you won't be able to use that COM port until you resolve the conflict. The following lists the IRQs and memory addresses commonly used by COM ports:

COM Port	IRQ	Base Address
COM1	4	03F8
COM2	3	02F8
COM3	4	03E8
COM4	3	02E8

As you can see from the list, the potential for a COM port conflict is designed into the IBM PC because COM1 and COM3 use the same IRQ, and COM2 and COM4 use the same IRQ. This means you cannot use COM1 at the same time as COM3, nor can you use COM2 at the same time as COM4.

When installing devices that use COM ports (or COM port IRQs) you must ensure that no two devices will be using the same IRQ at the same time. This can be a tricky issue. For example, if a mouse is configured for COM3 (and IRQ 4), you cannot use COM1 (which also uses IRQ4) for another device even if you do not plan to move the mouse or click its buttons. This is because the mouse driver, when it is installed in memory from CONFIG.SYS or AUTOEXEC.BAT, takes control of the IRQ for which it is configured. If another device attempts to use the IRQ used by the mouse, a conflict results that could destroy data or lock up your system.

8-bit ISA Interrupts. The 8-bit bus of the PC/XT-type system provides 8 interrupt request (IRQ) lines. This is a severe shortage given that these request lines are used not only by the modem and the mouse but also by other adapter boards and by the system itself. Installing several devices that need the services of system IRQs on a PC/XT-type system can be a study in frustration because the only way to resolve the interrupt shortage problem is to remove the adapter board you need the least.

16-bit ISA Interrupts. The 16-bit AT-type system has 15 interrupts, but the extra IRQs are of little help unless the adapter boards you plan to use enable you to configure them for unused IRQs. Some devices are hard-wired so that they can use only a particular IRQ. If you have a device that already uses that IRQ, you must resolve the conflict before installing the second adapter. If neither adapter enables you to reconfigure its IRQ usage, chances are you cannot use the two devices on the same system.

EISA Shared Interrupts. Extended Industry Standard Architecture (EISA) systems go a long way toward resolving the problem of IRQ conflicts because devices can share IRQs. Special circuitry on the EISA motherboard keeps track of the devices using each interrupt and keeps their signals separate. Such systems enable you to install a much wider array of adapter boards and hardware devices than possible on an 8- or 16-bit ISA system. Chapter 2 contains additional information about EISA systems.

MCA Shared Interrupts. Micro Channel Architecture (MCA) systems, like EISA systems, enable devices to share IRQs, so you can use adapter boards and other hardware devices that would conflict in 8- or 16-bit ISA system. Chapter 2 contains additional information about MCA systems.

LPT Ports. The basic IBM design for the PC enables you to have as many as three parallel (or LPT) ports. The base addresses and IRQ lines used by these three ports are shown in the following list:

LPT Port	Address	IRQ
LPT1	03BC	7
LPT2	0378	7
LPT3	0278	5 (optional)

If you have a device you want to connect to LPT3, you must configure the device so that it uses an available IRQ. You cannot use the IRQs assigned to the other LPT ports unless you do not intend to use these LPT ports. If you had intended to use LPT3 but not the lower-numbered ports, instead you should attach your device to the lowest available LPT port, making the IRQ that would be used by LPT3 available for additional devices. In other words, use LPT1 before LPT2 or LPT3.

Example Problem Configurations and Solutions. A number of devices you may want to install on a computer system require IRQ lines or DMA channels, which means a world of conflict could be waiting in the box the device comes in. As mentioned in Chapter 2, you can save yourself a lot of problems if you use MSD or another diagnostic software program to identify available (and unavailable) IRQ lines and DMA channels and create a template detailing these crucially important hardware communication channels. In addition, your template should show the upper memory addresses used by the adapter boards already on your system.

You can save yourself a lot of trouble also if you carefully read the documentation for a new adapter board before you attempt to install it. The documentation details the IRQ lines the board can use as well as its DMA channel requirements. In addition, the documentation will detail the adapter's upper memory needs for ROM and adapter RAM.

The following sections detail some of the conflicts you may encounter when installing today's most popular adapter boards. Although this is far from a comprehensive list of adapter boards, it serves as a guide to installing complex hardware with a minimum of hassle. Included are tips on sound boards, SCSI host adapters, and network adapters.

Sound Boards. Most sound boards require two kinds of hardware communication channels: one or more IRQ lines and exclusive access to a DMA channel. If you take the time to read your sound board's documentation and determine its communications channel needs, and compare those to the IRQ lines and DMA channels already in use on your system, and then set the jumpers or switches on the sound board to configure it for available channels, your installation will go quickly and smoothly.

One example of a potential sound board conflict is with the Pro Audio Spectrum 16 sound card. This card needs access to as many as two DMA channels—one for use by its own circuitry and the other for Sound Blaster compatibility—and as many as two IRQ lines. Before installing this board, you must determine not only how you plan to use the board (thus determining the IRQ lines and DMA channels you will need) but also the available IRQ lines and DMA channels that the board may be configured to use. The Pro Audio Spectrum 16 sound card is not singled out because there is something unusual about the card. Many high-end sound cards require a great deal of system resources.

SCSI Adapter Boards. SCSI adapter boards, like other advanced add-in devices for modern PCs, require a great deal of system resources. For example, SCSI host adapter boards may require an IRQ line, a DMA channel, or a large chunk of unused upper memory for its ROM and RAM uses.

Before installing a SCSI adapter, be sure to read the documentation for the card and check that any IRQ lines, DMA channels, and upper memory needed by the card are available. If the system resources needed for the card are already in use, use your system resource template to determine how you can free up the needed resources *before* you attempt to plug in the adapter card. In addition, don't forget to set the jumpers or switches detailed in the card's documentation and run any setup software required for the device.

Multiple COM Port Adapters. Because COM ports are required for so many peripherals that connect to the modern PC, and because the number of COM ports that can be used is strictly limited by the IRQ setup in the basic IBM system design, special COM port cards are available that enable you to assign a unique IRQ to each of the four COM ports on the card. For example, you might use such a card to leave COM1 and COM2 configured for IRQ 4 and IRQ3, respectively, but configure COM3 for IRQ 10 and COM4 for IRQ 11.

With a multiple COM port adapter card installed and properly configured for your system, you can have devices hooked to four different COM ports and all four devices can be functioning at the same time. For example, you can use a mouse, modem, plotter, and serial printer all at the same time.

The Power Supply

One of the most failure-prone components in computer systems is the power supply. You should know the function and limitations of a power supply, and its potential problems and their solutions. The following is an overview of the PC power supply.

The 200-watt (or greater) power supply in many 386-, 486-, and Pentium-based systems is designed to convert the 120-volt, 60 Hz AC current sent by the power company to your home or business into the 5-volt and 12-volt DC current that the computer can use. Usually, the digital electronic components and circuits in the system (motherboard, adapter cards, and disk drive logic boards) use the 5-volt power, and the motors (disk drive motors and the fan) use the 12-volt power. You must ensure a good, steady supply of both types of current so that the system can operate properly.

The power supply also ensures that the system doesn't run without proper power levels, in case there are times of reduced voltage to your area. The power supply completes internal checks and tests before allowing the system to start up. The power supply sends to the motherboard a special signal, called *Power Good*. If this signal is not present, the computer does not run. In addition, when the AC voltage dips and the power supply becomes overstressed or overheated, the Power Good signal goes down and forces a system reset or complete shutdown. If your system has ever seemed dead when the power switch is on and the fan and hard disks are running, you know the effects of losing the Power Good signal. IBM chose this conservative design with the view that if the power goes low or the supply is overheated or overstressed, causing output power to falter, the computer could be damaged if allowed to operate.

Most modern systems have an adequate power supply. Failure is normally caused not by overloading or a power surge, but by normal wear of power supply parts or thermal expansion and contraction caused by powering a system on and off. Most manufacturers have learned the hard way that a little overengineering in this area pays off.

Most power supplies are considered to be *universal*, or *worldwide*. They can operate with the 120-volt, 60-cycle current in the United States and the 220-volt, 50-cycle current used in Europe and many other parts of the world. Power supplies that can use either power frequency are termed *switching power supplies*. The units sense the current and then switch automatically. But others require you to use a switch on the back of the power supply.

The PS/2 P70, for example, runs on both 110- and 220-volt power; all you have to do is plug it in and the system automatically recognizes the incoming voltage and switches circuits accordingly. This is different from an older AT, which runs on both levels of power but requires you to flip a switch manually to select the proper circuits in the power supply.

Power-Supply Ratings. IBM provides charts with the technical specifications of each of its system-unit power supplies. The charts are in each system's technical-reference manual and often are on stickers on the power supply.

Tables 7.9 and 7.10 list power-supply specifications for IBM units. The input specifications are listed as voltages. The output specifications are listed as amps, at several voltage levels. IBM reports output wattage level as *specified output wattage*. You can convert amperage figures to output wattage by using this simple formula:

Wattage = voltage × amperage

Table 7.9 Power-Supply Specifications for PC Systems

	PC	PPC	XT	XT 286	AT
Input voltage range					
Minimum voltage	104	90	90	90	90
Maximum voltage	127	137	137	137	137
Universal (220V)	No	Yes	No	Yes	Yes
Switch/Automatic	—	Switch	—	Auto	Switch
Output amperage					
+5	7.00	11.20	15.00	20.00	19.80

(continues)

III

Hardware Considerations

Table 7.9 Continued

	PC	PPC	XT	XT 286	AT
–5	0.30	0.30	0.30	0.30	0.30
+12	2.00	4.40	4.20	4.20	7.30
–12	0.25	0.25	0.25	0.25	0.30
Calculated output wattage	63.5	113.3	129.9	154.9	191.7
Specified output wattage	63.5	114.0	130.0	157.0	192.0

Table 7.10 Power-Supply Specifications for PS/2 Systems

Model	Part number	Worldwide power	Manual/ auto	Output wattage
25	8525-xx1	Yes	Manual	90
	8525-xx4	Yes	Manual	115
30	8530-0xx	Yes	Auto	70
25 286	8525-xxx	Yes	Manual	124.5
30 286	8530-Exx	Yes	Manual	90
35 SX	8535-xxx	Yes	Auto	118
40 SX	8540-0xx	Yes	Manual	197
50	8550-0xx	Yes	Auto	94
55 SX	8555-xxx	Yes	Manual	90
57 SX	8557-0xx	Yes	Manual	197
60	8560-041	Yes	Auto	207
	8560-071	Yes	Auto	225
65 SX	8565-xxx	Yes	Auto	250
70 386	8570-xxx	Yes	Auto	132
70 486	8570-Bxx	Yes	Auto	132
P70 386	8573-xxx	Yes	Auto	85
P75 486	8573-xxx	Yes	Auto	120
80 386	8580-xxx	Yes	Auto	225
	8580-Axx	Yes	Auto	242
90 XP 486	8590-0xx	Yes	Auto	194
95 XP 486	8595-0xx	Yes	Auto	329

One way to see whether your system is capable of expansion is to calculate the levels of power drain in the different system components and then deduct the total from the maximum power supplied. This calculation might help you decide when to upgrade the power supply to a more capable unit.

Suppose, for example, that you examine some typical power-consumption figures for components in an IBM PC system unit. The PC comes with a 63 1/2-watt power supply.

The levels of power to be concerned about are the 5- and 12-volt levels. The PC power supply can provide 7.0 amps of 5-volt power and 2.0 amps of 12-volt power. The following calculation shows what happens when you subtract the amount of power necessary to run the different system components:

5-volt power	7.0 amps
Motherboard (full memory, 8087)	–4.0
Video adapter	–1.0
Two full-height floppy drives	–1.2 (0.6 each)
Multifunction (6-pack type) board	–1.0
Remaining power	–0.2
12-volt power	2.0 amps
Two full-height floppy drives	–0.9 (0.9 each)
Cooling fan	–0.25
Remaining power	0.85

As you can see, you're in trouble with this system. The 5-volt portion of the supply in this configuration is already overloaded, and only three slots are full and there is no hard disk. A typical full-height hard disk consumes 1.5 amps of 5-volt power, and a half-height drive draws 0.8 amps.

With 12-volt power, at least the basic configuration isn't overloaded. Suppose that you want to add a hard disk, however. A full-height drive draws about 4.0 amps of power for the first 5 to 10 seconds and then drops to a continuous draw of about 2.0 amps. A typical half-height drive draws about 2.2 amps of power during the first 5 to 10 seconds and then tapers off to about 0.9 amps of continuous draw. In this example, you might have enough 12-volt power for a small, half-height hard disk. Some of the newer 3 1/2-inch hard disks don't draw very much power because a disk drive's power draw is almost directly related to the drive's physical size. Some of the hard disks on a card operate on very low power also. For a typical PC system, however, even these units are too much to handle unless you're willing to replace the power supply with one that has more capacity.

In this example, you need an upgraded power supply, which you can purchase from many sources. Most users choose at least a 130-watt supply. The PC power and cooling unit described previously has 20.0 amps of 5-volt output and 8.0 amps of 12-volt output, nearly four times what's available in a standard IBM PC. Using this supply in a PC ensures that the system has enough power to drive nearly anything you can add to the unit.

Many people wait until an existing unit fails before they replace it with an upgraded version. If you're on a tight budget, this "if it ain't broke, don't fix it" attitude works. Power supplies, however, often do not just fail altogether; there are intermittent problems or they allow fluctuating power levels to reach the system, which results in unstable operation. You might be blaming system lockups on software bugs when the culprit is an

III

Hardware Considerations

overloaded power supply. If you've been running the system with your original power supply for a long time, because of normal wear and tear, you should expect some problems.

One thing to consider is that the figures most manufacturers report for maximum power output are full-duty-cycle figures, which means that these levels of power can be supplied continuously. A unit rated to continuously supply 200 watts of power, for example, supplies a greater amount of power for short periods of time. A supply usually can offer 50 percent greater output than the continuous figure indicates for as long as one minute. This cushion often is used to supply the necessary power to start spinning a hard disk. After the drive has spun to full speed, the power draw drops to a value in the system's continuous supply capabilities. Drawing anything over the rated continuous figure for a long time causes the power supply to run hot and fail early, and can prompt several nasty symptoms in the system.

When purchasing a new power supply, whether you are replacing a defective unit, or upgrading your power supply to solve an undersupply problem, you should make these calculations for your system:

- The output-level specifications for your power supply. These specifications are in your system's technical-reference manual. (The figures for IBM systems are in table 7.9.)

- The power-consumption figures for each type of component in the system. Most boards draw less than 1 amp; some boards, however, such as network adapters or internal modems, can draw even more. Disk drives are power hungry and draw both 5- and 12-volt power. Get the consumption figures for these types of products from the manufacturer or the system documentation. IBM has a technical-reference manual for options and adapters for IBM boards and disk drives. The original equipment manufacturer (OEM) manuals for your disk drives and adapter boards usually contain this type of information. If you do not have your system documentation, contact the manufacturer directly.

Troubleshooting Power-Supply Problems. A weak or inadequate power supply can put a damper on your ideas for system expansion. Some systems were designed with beefy power supplies, as if the designers were anticipating a great deal of system add-on or expansion components. Modern systems with 230-watt (or greater) power supplies were built in this manner. Some systems have inadequate power supplies from the start, however, and cannot accept the power-hungry options you might want to add.

In particular, the original PC's 63 1/2-watt supply is inadequate for all but the most basic system. Add a graphics board, a hard disk, an 8087 chip, and 640K of memory, and you will kill the system. The total power draw of all the items in the system determines the adequacy of the power supply.

Another problem with underengineered power supplies is that they run hot and force the system to do so as well. The repeated heating and cooling of solid-state components eventually causes a computer system to fail, and engineering principles dictate that the hotter a system's temperature, the shorter its life. Many people replace today's 200-watt power supplies with 250-watt or even 300-watt power supplies. On systems with a tower case (with their twin cooling fans and greater number of slots and expansion bays enabling you to install numerous devices such as sound boards, CD-ROM drives, and tape backup systems), many people choose 400-watt power supplies on the theory that it is better to have too much power-handling capacity than not enough.

> **Note**
>
> A bigger power supply does not increase the amount of voltage that flows to any individual adapter board or any other system component. The amount of voltage remains steady at 5 or 12 volts. A bigger power supply merely ensures that each system component has enough power, even when you add a lot of devices.

Power supplies used to be expensive. (Even the power supply for the original PC cost $344.) Now power supplies are an inexpensive replacement part. Power supply vendors advertising in Computer Shopper magazine advertise 150-watt power supplies for between $28 and $55 and 230-watt power supplies (for a tower case) for between $40 and $129. If you don't know which power supply to buy, check the computer magazines, which periodically cover these important devices. As with some other computer components, the power supply with the better warranty is likely to be the better equipment but is likely also to cost the most.

A debate about power continues among computer users who consider themselves technically astute (some call them "techies"). This debate concerns whether or not to turn off a system when you're not using it. Some argue you should *never* turn it off, not even overnight. That school says turning off your system wears out the hard drive and other peripherals more quickly and that you electrically "shock" the system each time you flip on system power. Others say it's a waste of electricity to leave the computer running when you're not using it, even for a few minutes.

The consensus among system designers and those who repair a lot of systems is that you should not turn a system on and off repeatedly during the day. After you have turned on the system in the morning, leave it running until you are sure you will not need it any more that day. Suppose you leave it running for 9 hours even though you use it for only 7 hours. By leaving the system running during the day, you waste a small amount of electricity, but you also prevent the system from heating and cooling too frequently, which can cause frequent expansion and contraction.

Such contraction and expansion can eventually cause many computer parts—even the motherboard—to fail. Too much expansion and contraction can cause socketed devices to work their way out of their sockets, for example, expansion and contraction can cause chip creep (loose chips on the motherboard). It can cause similar problems with connectors. Many "blown" power supplies are nothing more than a cracked or broken solder joint or a part that lost power when expansion and contraction worked the part loose from its circuitry.

III

Hardware Considerations

Repairing an individual problem caused by expansion and contraction usually is simple. But the process is cumulative, and recurring thermal stress causes the problem to return or a new one to surface. Starting the system at the beginning of the day and turning it off only at the end of the day seems a reasonable way to contribute to system longevity.

Note, however, that some system manufacturers think that powering a computer on and off each day wears it out much more quickly and do not even add an on/off button to their systems. Sometimes the monitor is turned off, but not the system. So the debate continues.

Some manufacturers, in an effort to keep people from turning their systems on and off numerous times during the day, and to save power, are building what are termed *green machines*, which switch themselves into a low power-consumption mode, sometimes called "sleep," when there is a period of inactivity.

Testing Power Supplies. If you suspect a power-supply problem, the simple measurements outlined in this section can help you determine whether the power supply is at fault. Because these measurements do not detect many intermittent or overload failures, you might have to use a spare power supply for long-term evaluation. If the symptoms and problems disappear with the replacement unit, you have found the source of your problem.

To test a power supply for proper output, check the voltage at the Power Good pin (P8-1 on IBM PC, XT, and AT supplies) for 2.4 to 5.4 Vdc. If the measurement is not in this range, the system never sees the Power Good signal and therefore never runs. In most cases, the supply is bad and must be replaced.

Continue by measuring the voltage ranges of the pins on the motherboard and drive power connectors. Refer to table 7.11. Note that the exact pin specifications and acceptable voltage ranges are for IBM PC, XT, AT, and most IBM-compatible power supplies. Some systems, such as the PS/2 machines from IBM, use a different type of connector and might accept different minimum and maximum voltages. Consult your system's technical-reference manual for this information.

Table 7.11 Power-Connector Measurements

Minimum voltage	Maximum voltage	PINS	
		-Leads	+Leads
Motherboard			
+4.8	+5.2	P8-5	P9-4
+4.5	+5.4	P9-3	P8-6
+11.5	+12.6	P9-1	P8-3
+10.8	+12.9	P8-4	P9-2
Disk Drive			
+4.8	+5.2	2	4
+11.5	+12.6	3	1

Replace the power supply if these voltages are incorrect. With older power supplies, they must have a proper load to function correctly. If you remove the supply from the system unit, set it on a workbench, plug it in, and power it on, the supply immediately shuts itself down. It does not run unless it is plugged into a motherboard and at least one disk drive. However, more modern power supplies often do work if you plug them in without a motherboard and drive connection.

Again, these measurements are from IBM's documentation; other systems may allow different ranges. On IBM-compatible systems, these ranges usually are acceptable:

For output rated at +-5 volts, from 4.5 to 5.4

For output rated at +-12 volts, from 10.8 to 12.9

The appendix has a detailed pin-out reference chart showing the proper voltage and signal at each power-supply connector. You can refer to this chart when you make power-supply voltage measurements.

The original AT systems were supplied with a huge load resistor mounted in place of the hard disk, which allowed the supply to operate properly even without a hard disk installed. If you are setting up a "diskless" system, make sure that you use a similar type of power load; otherwise, you will have problems with the supply and may even burn it out. You can construct the same type of load resistor originally used by IBM by connecting a 6-ohm, 30-watt sandbar resistor between pins 1 and 2 on the connector. This procedure puts a 2.5-amp load on the supply's 12-volt output, which enables it to run normally. You still should connect the other power connectors to a motherboard for a load on the 5-volt outputs.

Getting Replacement Units. Replacement power supplies are available from many manufacturers. When you buy a new power supply, you must replace it with one having the same shape, or *form factor*. For example, the power supply used in many tower cases is much larger than the power supplies used in smaller desktop units. Other differences include the screw-hole positions, the placement of the external power connectors, the placement of the fan, the number of internal adapter board connectors, and the type of on/off switch and its location.

Fortunately, most of the power supplies used in modern systems are one of a few designs, which means the right form factor, screw hole locations, and other physical design issues are not a major problem. You merely tell the power supply vendor the type of power supply and wattage you want.

These easily interchanged power supplies are the result of the massive market for replacement parts for IBM-compatible computers. This same market force enables you to plug a generic 1M SIMM into a slot on any IBM-compatible system designed for 1M SIMMs.

The user of a system with a nonstandard form-factor supply, however, doesn't have this choice and must get a replacement from the original manufacturer of the system—usually at a much higher price. PC and AT form-factor units sell for as little as $28, but proprietary units from some manufacturers cost as much as $400.

For example, in PS/2 systems, only the power supplies from the Models 60, 65, and 80 use the same form factor and are interchangeable. Other PS/2 systems have power supplies unique to the system. Several different output level power supplies have been available for these systems, including 207-, 225-, 242-, and 250-watt versions. The most powerful 250-watt unit was supplied originally for the Model 65 SX, although it fits in the other Model 60 or 80 systems. Several companies manufacture aftermarket supplies for the PS/2 systems, and various third-party companies repair and resell IBM PS/2 power supplies at prices greatly below the original IBM price.

COMPAQ systems are another example of compatible systems with proprietary power-supply designs. None of its systems use the same form-factor supply as the IBM systems, which means that COMPAQ usually is the only place you can get a replacement. To replace the power supply in a COMPAQ Deskpro system, for example, costs $395. An exception is PC Power and Cooling, which offers excellent replacement power supplies for the earlier COMPAQ Portable systems and for the Deskpro series. These replacement power supplies have higher-output power levels than the original supplies from COMPAQ and cost much less.

When *Popular Mechanics* magazine reviews an automobile, it always lists the replacement costs of the most failure-prone and replacement-prone components, from front bumpers to alternators to taillights. PC buyers often overlook this type of information and discover too late the consequences of buying a system made of nonstandard components.

Chapter Summary

This chapter covered many of the most important components of a personal computer, including the motherboard, the central processing unit (CPU) chip, the data bus and address bus, system memory, and the power supply. It also provided tips on the installation of adapter board and troubleshooting IRQ, DMA, and upper memory conflicts. In addition, this chapter provided tips on installing some of the hottest hardware on the market today: sound boards, SCSI adapters, and special COM port cards.

Chapter 8

Secondary System Components

When you equip an IBM or compatible computer, you can choose from a wide variety of display options, memory adapters, communications boards, and other components or peripherals. In this chapter, you learn about the features and drawbacks of the many additions you can make to your system.

Keyboards

One of the most basic system components is your keyboard. This section examines the keyboards available for IBM and compatible systems. IBM has had three different keyboard designs during the last few years:

- 83-key PC and XT keyboard

- 84-key AT keyboard

- 101-key Enhanced Keyboard

The Enhanced Keyboard has appeared in three different versions, but all three are the same electrically and can be interchanged. The three different versions are:

- Enhanced Keyboard without LED panel (lock indicators)

- Enhanced Keyboard with LED panel (lock indicators)

- Enhanced Keyboard (PS/2 logo)

The first two keyboards are the same cosmetically, but the second unit was designed for systems that support the full bidirectional capability needed to operate the LED panel that shows the status of the Caps Lock, Num Lock, and Scroll Lock keys. The third version is the same as the second, except for a logo on top that matches the PS/2 system logo. Electrically, these keyboards are the same, but the first one is missing a small add-on circuit board to control the lights. PC- or XT-type systems cannot operate these lights because they do not have the bidirectional interface necessary for light operation. If you use an XT and the IBM Enhanced Keyboard with the LED panel, the lights remain dark, unless the keyboard manufacturer has added circuitry internal to the keyboard that turns the LEDs on and off whenever you press the appropriate keys. In such a case, however, it is possible for the LEDs to get "out of sync" with the actual state of the toggles, which are maintained within the computer.

Any IBM keyboard can be ordered separately as a spare part. The newer Enhanced Keyboards come with an externally detachable keyboard that plugs into the keyboard port with a special connector, much like a telephone connector. The other end of the cable is one of two types:

- Earlier systems use a 5-pin DIN connector.

- PS/2 systems use a new, miniature, 6-pin DIN connector.

Because of the interchangeability of the newer Enhanced Keyboards, you can plug a 101-key unit from an XT into a PS/2 system simply by switching the cables. You also can plug the PS/2-style 101-key unit into any XT or AT system by switching cables. The PS/2-style cable is available in two different lengths. Because of the vastly superior "feel" of the IBM keyboards, I often equip compatible systems with these keyboards. In fact, IBM has spun off its keyboard and printer division (Lexmark), which is now selling keyboards on the open market to the compatible industry. Purchased from either Lexmark or from other third-parties, new IBM keyboards have sold for as low as $80 or less. Table 8.1 shows the part numbers of all the IBM keyboards and cables. These numbers can serve as a reference when you are seeking an IBM keyboard from IBM direct or from third-party companies.

The original 83/84-key keyboards are sold with a cable that has the larger, 5-pin DIN connector already attached. Enhanced Keyboards are always sold without a cable. You must order the proper cable as a separate item. Cables are available to connect the keyboards to either the older system units that use the larger DIN connector or to PS/2 systems (and many compatibles) that use the smaller mini-DIN connector.

PC and AT keyboards are different from each other. In addition to having different key layouts, the internal electronics are different. The 83-key keyboard uses an 8048 processor, and the other keyboards use a 6805 processor internally and an 8042 processor on the motherboard.

The 101-key keyboard was designed to replace both the 83-key and 84-key units, and theoretically replaces the earlier keyboards for any system. One problem, however, is that the individual system ROM BIOS might not be capable of operating the 101-key keyboard correctly. If this is the case, the 101-key keyboard does not work (as with all three ROM versions of the IBM PC), or only the new added keys (F11 and F12 function keys) do not work.

Table 8.1 IBM Keyboard and Cable Part Numbers

Description	Part Number
83-key U.S. keyboard assembly with cable	8529297
Cable assembly for 83-key unit	8529168
84-key U.S. keyboard assembly with cable	8286165
Cable assembly for 84-key unit	8286146
101-key U.S. keyboard without LED panel	1390290
101-key U.S. keyboard with LED panel	6447033
101-key U.S. keyboard (PS/2 logo)	1392090
6-foot Enhanced Keyboard cable (DIN plug)	6447051
6-foot Enhanced Keyboard cable (mini-DIN plug)	61X8898
6-foot Enhanced Keyboard cable (mini-DIN plug with additional shielding)	27F4984
10-foot Enhanced Keyboard cable (mini-DIN plug)	72X8537

You usually can tell whether your system has complete ROM BIOS support for the 101-key unit: when you plug in the keyboard and turn on the system unit, the Num Lock light automatically comes on and the numeric keypad portion of the keyboard is enabled. This method of detection isn't 100 percent accurate, but if the light goes on, your BIOS generally supports the keyboard. A notable exception is the IBM AT BIOS dated 06/10/85; it turns on the Num Lock light but still does not properly support the Enhanced Keyboard. Many users are irritated because the numeric keypad is automatically enabled when their system reboots. Some think that this is a function of the Enhanced Keyboard because they know that none of the earlier keyboards seemed to operate this way. Remember that this function isn't really a keyboard function—instead it's a function of the motherboard ROM BIOS, which identifies an enhanced 101-key unit and turns on the Num Lock as a "favor." Some compatible BIOS versions enable you to specify in the Setup routine whether the Num Lock should be activated when you boot your computer. In systems that cannot disable the automatic numeric keypad enable feature, I simply use one of the many public domain programs available for turning off the Num Lock function. Placing the program command to disable Num Lock in the AUTOEXEC.BAT file turns off the numeric keypad each time the system reboots.

Because of the processor in each keyboard, the keyboards are intelligent devices; they are computers in their own right, with their own built-in processor capable of running a self-test when they're turned on.

III

Hardware Considerations

83-Key PC and XT Keyboard

One of the most criticized components of the original PC and XT systems was the IBM keyboard; the 83-key keyboard has an awkward layout. The Shift keys are small and in the wrong place on the left side. The Enter key also is too small. These oversights were disturbing because IBM had produced the Selectric typewriter, perceived as a standard for keyboard layout. Figure 8.1 shows the layout of the original 83-key PC and XT keyboard.

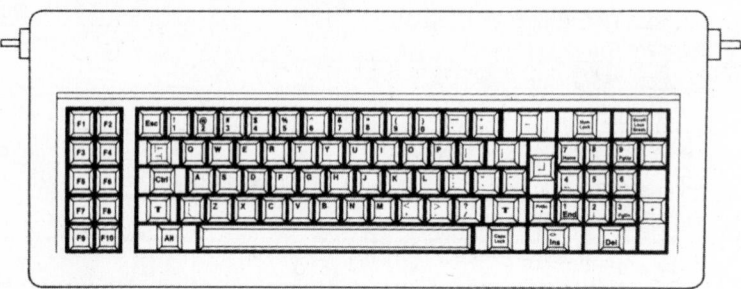

Fig. 8.1

PC and XT 83-key keyboard layout.

84-Key AT Keyboard

When the AT was introduced, it included a new keyboard—the 84-key unit (see fig. 8.2). This keyboard corrected many of the problems of the original PC and XT keyboards. The position and arrangement of the numeric keypad was modified. The Enter key was made much larger, like that of a Selectric typewriter. The Shift key positions and sizes were corrected. IBM also finally added LED indicators for the status of the Caps Lock, Scroll Lock, and Num Lock toggles.

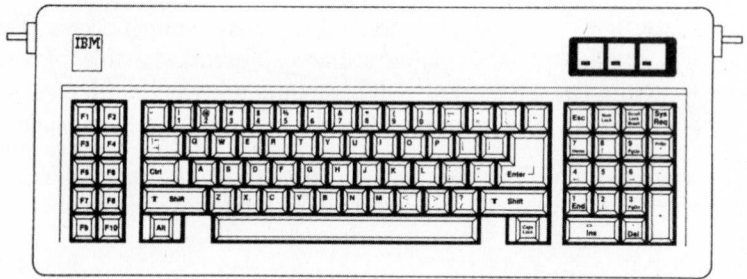

Fig. 8.2

AT 84-key keyboard layout.

Enhanced 101-Key

IBM then introduced the "corporate" Enhanced 101-key Keyboard for the newer XT and AT models (see fig. 8.3). I use the word "corporate" because this unit now is supplied with virtually every type of system and terminal IBM sells. This universal keyboard has a further improved layout over that of the 84-key unit, with perhaps the exception of the Enter key, which reverted to a smaller size. The 101-key Enhanced Keyboard was designed to conform to international regulations and specifications for keyboards. In fact, other companies such as DEC and TI had already been using designs similar to the IBM 101-key unit even earlier than IBM. These 101-key units came in versions with and without the status indicator LEDs, depending on whether the unit was sold with an XT or AT system.

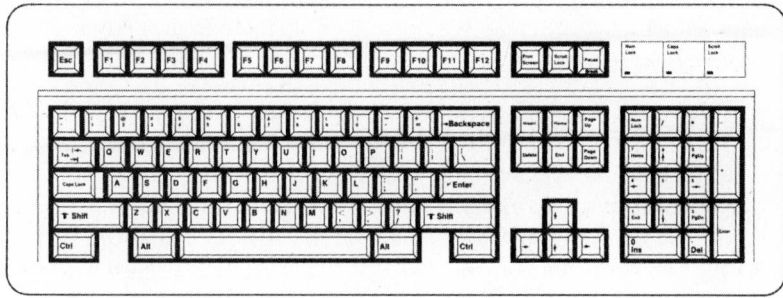

Fig. 8.3
101-key keyboard layout for the XT, AT, and PS/2.

The 101-key keyboard layout can be divided into four sections:

■ Typing area

■ Numeric keypad

■ Cursor and screen controls

■ Function keys

The 101-key arrangement is similar to the Selectric keyboard layout. The Tab, Caps Lock, Shift, Enter, and Backspace keys have a larger striking area and are located in the familiar Selectric locations. Ctrl and Alt keys are on each side of the space bar. The typing area and numeric keypad have home-row identifiers for touch typing.

The cursor- and screen-control keys have been separated from the numeric keypad, which is reserved for numeric input. (As with other PC keyboards, you can use the numeric keypad for cursor and screen control when the keyboard is not in Num Lock mode.) A division-sign key and an additional Enter key have been added to the numeric keypad.

The cursor-control keys are arranged in the inverted T format. The Insert, Delete, Home, End, Page Up, and Page Down keys, located above the dedicated cursor-control keys, are separated from the numeric keypad. The function keys, spaced in groups of four, are located across the top of the keyboard. The keyboard has two additional function keys: F11 and F12. The Esc key is isolated in the upper left corner of the keyboard. Dedicated Print Screen/Sys Req, Scroll Lock, and Pause/Break keys are provided for commonly used functions.

III

Hardware Considerations

One of the Enhanced Keyboard's many useful features is removable keycaps. With clear keycaps and paper inserts, you can customize the keyboard. Keyboard templates are available to provide specific operator instructions. IBM also provides a 9-foot cable for attaching the keyboard to the system unit.

The new keyboard probably will be on any desktop system IBM introduces for quite some time. If you want to change older systems to use the new keyboard, however, you may have problems with ROM BIOS support. IBM changed the ROM on the systems to support the new keyboard properly, and most compatible vendors have followed suit for newer systems. Older machines may require a ROM upgrade to properly use some of the features on the 101-key enhanced keyboards, such as the F11 and F12 keys.

In a somewhat informal test, I plugged the new keyboard into an earlier XT. The keyboard seemed to work well. None of the keys that didn't exist previously, such as F11 and F12, were operable, but the new arrow keys and the numeric keypad did work. The Enhanced Keyboard seems to work on XT or AT systems but will not function on the original PC systems. Many compatible versions of the 101-key Enhanced Keyboards have a manual XT-AT switch on the bottom, which may allow the keyboard to work in an original PC system. IBM sells its 101-key Enhanced Keyboard as a separate item for $275, but you can get this keyboard for as little as $80 or less from third-party companies, or maybe slightly more from Lexmark. Other manufacturers also offer enhanced keyboards that work on XT- and AT-type systems.

Cleaning a Keyboard

One of the best ways to maintain a keyboard in top condition is periodic cleaning. As preventive maintenance, you should vacuum the keyboard weekly. Or, you can use the canned compressed air available at electronics-supply houses. Before you dust a keyboard with the compressed air, turn the keyboard upside down so that particles of dirt and dust collected inside fall out.

On all the keyboards, each keycap is removable, which can be handy if a key sticks or acts erratically. For example, a common problem is a key that doesn't work every time you press it. This problem usually results from dirt collecting under the key. An excellent tool for removing keycaps on most any keyboard is the "U"-shaped chip-puller tool. You simply slip the hooked ends of the tool under the keycap, squeeze the ends together to grip the underside of the keycap, and lift up. IBM sells a tool specifically for removing keycaps from its keyboards, but the chip puller works better. After removing the cap, spray some compressed air into the space under the cap to dislodge the dirt. Then replace the cap and check the action of the key.

When you remove the keycaps, be careful not to remove the space bar on the original 83-key PC and 84-key AT-type keyboards. This bar is very difficult to reinstall. The newer 101-key units use a different wire support that is removed and replaced much more easily.

Spills also can be a problem. If you tip a soft drink or cup of coffee into a keyboard, you don't necessarily have a disaster. You should immediately (or as soon as possible) flush out the keyboard with distilled water. Partially disassemble the keyboard and use the water to wash the components. (See the following section for disassembly instructions.) If the spilled liquid has dried, let the keyboard soak in some of the water for a while. Then, when you're sure that the keyboard is clean, pour another gallon or so of distilled water over it and through the key switches to wash away any residual dirt. After the unit dries completely, it should be perfectly functional. You may be surprised to know that you can drench your keyboard with water, and it will not harm the components. Just make sure that you use distilled water, which is free from residue or mineral content. Also make sure that the keyboard is fully dry before you attempt to use it, or some of the components might short out: Water is a conductor of electricity.

Disassembly Procedures and Cautions

Repairing and cleaning a keyboard often requires that you take it apart. When you perform this task, you should know when to stop. An IBM keyboard generally has these four major parts:

- Cable
- Case
- Keypad assembly
- Keycaps

You easily can break down a keyboard to these major components and replace any of them, but don't disassemble the keypad assembly or you'll be showered with tiny springs, clips, and keycaps. Finding all these parts (several hundred of them) and piecing the unit back together is not a fun way to spend time. You also may not be able to assemble the keyboard as well as it was. Figure 8.4 shows a typical keyboard with the case opened.

Another problem is that you cannot purchase the smaller parts separately, such as contact clips and springs. The only way to obtain these parts is from another keyboard. If you ever have a keyboard that's beyond repair, keep it around for these parts. They might come in handy some day.

Most repair operations are limited to changing the cable or cleaning some component of the keyboard, from the cable contact ends to the key contact points. The keyboard cable takes quite a bit of abuse, and therefore can fail easily. The ends are stretched, tugged, pulled, and generally handled roughly. The cable uses strain reliefs, but you still might have problems with the connectors making proper contact at each end or even with wires that have broken inside the cable. You might want to carry a spare cable for every type of keyboard you have.

All keyboard cables plug into the keyboard and PC with connectors, and you can change the cables easily without having to splice wires or solder connections. With the earlier 83-key PC and 84-key AT keyboards, you must open the case to access the connector where the cable attaches. On the newer 101-key Enhanced Keyboards, the cable plugs into the keyboard from the outside of the case, using a modular jack and plug similar to a telephone jack. This design, one of the best features of this keyboard, also makes the keyboard universally usable on nearly any system except the original PC.

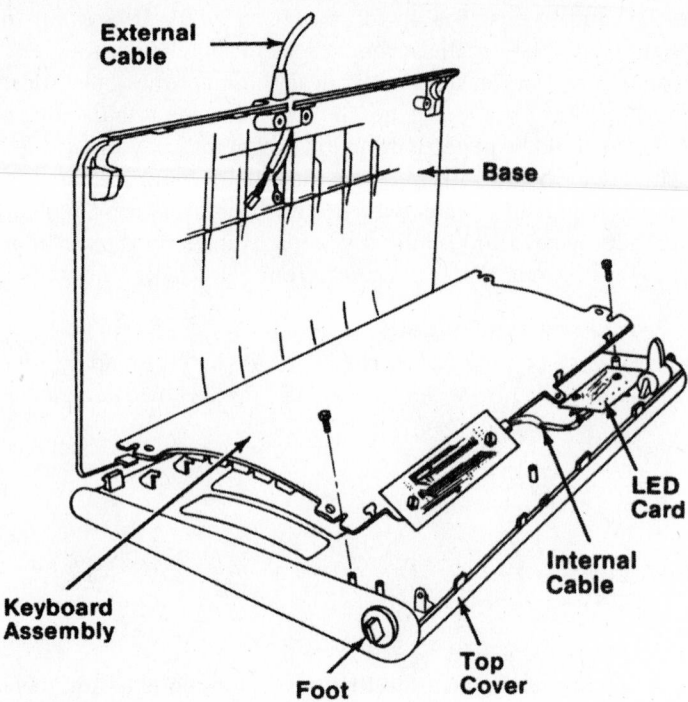

Fig. 8.4
Typical keyboard components.

The only feasible ways to repair a keyboard are to replace the cable and clean the individual keyswitch assemblies, the entire keypad, or the cable contact ends. Other than cleaning a keyboard, or replacing individual keycaps, the only thing you can do is replace the entire keypad assembly (virtually the entire keyboard) or the cable.

Mice

A mouse is one of the most common input devices used with computers today. In fact, certain user interfaces (such as Windows) virtually demand the use of a mouse. Because of this demand, it is common for a mouse to be sold with virtually every new system on the market.

Mice come in many shapes and sizes from many different manufacturers. The largest manufacturers of mice are Microsoft and Logitech. Although mice come in different varieties, their actual use and care differs very little. The mouse consists of three general parts:

- A housing, which you hold in your hand and move around on your desktop

- A cable

- A connector, which attaches to your computer

The *housing* is made of plastic and consists of very few moving parts. On top of the housing, where your fingers normally reside, are buttons. There may be any number of buttons, but typically in the PC world there are only two or three. On the bottom of the housing is a small rubber ball that rotates as you move the mouse across the tabletop. The movements of this rubber ball are translated into electrical signals that are transmitted to the computer across the cable.

The *cable* can be any length, but it is typically between four and six feet long. (If you have a choice on the length of cable to purchase, choose a longer one. The longer cable allows easier placement of the mouse in relation to your computer.)

The *connector* you use with your mouse depends on the type of interface you use. (The interfaces will be explained shortly.)

After the mouse is connected to your computer, it communicates with your system through the *device driver*. This device driver translates the electrical signals that are sent from the mouse into positional information and information that indicates the status of the buttons.

The following sections explain the different types of mouse interfaces and how you can care for the mice.

Types of Mouse Interfaces

You can connect mice to your computer in three different ways: with a serial interface, a bus interface, or through a mouse port.

Serial. The most popular method of connecting a mouse to an IBM-compatible computer is through a serial interface. As with other serial devices, the connector on the end of the mouse cable will be either a 9-pin or 25-pin male connector. You can use only a couple of pins in the DB-9 or DB-25 connectors for communications between the mouse and the device driver, but the mouse connector typically has all 9 or 25 pins present.

Because most PCs come with two serial ports, you can plug a mouse into either COM1 or COM2. The device driver, when initializing, searches the ports to determine which port the mouse is connected to.

Bus. A bus mouse is typically used in systems that do not have any available serial ports. For example, you may have a modem hooked to one serial port and a printer hooked to the other.

The name *bus mouse* is derived from the fact that the mouse requires a special interface board. This board occupies a slot in your computer and communicates with the device driver across the main motherboard bus. While the use of a bus mouse is transparent to the user (there is no operational difference between a bus mouse and other types of mice), many people view a bus mouse as less desirable than other types. This is because it occupies a computer board slot that may be needed for other peripherals.

Mouse Port. Some computers, primarily in the PS/2 line, include a special connector, dedicated for use by the mouse. This connector (known as a *mouse port*) is included with the motherboard. Connecting a mouse to the mouse port is perhaps the handiest method of connection, because you don't lose any interface slots or any serial ports.

III

Hardware Considerations

Mouse Troubleshooting

If you are experiencing problems with your mouse, there are only two general places you need to look—hardware or software. Because mice are basically very simple devices, looking at the hardware takes very little time. Detecting and correcting software problems can take a bit longer, however.

Hardware Problems. Several types of hardware problems may crop up when you are using a mouse. The most common problem is a dirty mouse, which is solved by doing some "mouse cleaning." The other problems, which are more difficult to solve, relate to interrupt conflicts.

Cleaning Your Mouse. If you notice that the mouse pointer moves across the screen in a jerky fashion, it may be time to clean your mouse. This jerkiness is caused because dirt and dust get trapped around the mouse's roller ball, thereby restricting its free movement.

From a hardware perspective, the mouse is a very simple device, and cleaning it is also very simple. The first step is to turn the mouse housing over so you can see the ball on the bottom. Notice that surrounding the ball is an access panel that you can open. There may even be some instructions that indicate how to open the panel. (Some off-brand mice may require you to remove some screws to get at the roller ball.) Remove the panel and you will see more of the roller ball, as well as the socket in which it rests.

If you turn the mouse back over, the rubber roller ball should fall out into your hand. Take a look at the ball. It may be gray or black, but it should have no visible dirt or other contamination. If it does, wash it in soapy water and dry it off.

Now take a look at the socket in which the roller ball normally rests. You will see two or three small wheels or bars against which the ball normally rolls. If you see dust or dirt on or around these wheels or bars, then you need to clean them. Do not use water to do this, however. Instead, use some compressed air to blow out the dirt and grime. Alternatively, you can use a cotton swab (such as a Q-Tip) soaked in rubbing alcohol. For stubborn dirt or dust, use a pair of tweezers or your fingernail. Remember, if any dirt or dust remains, then this impedes the movement of the roller ball and means the mouse won't work as it should.

Put the mouse back together by inserting the roller ball into the socket and then securely attaching the cover panel. The mouse should look just like it did before you removed the panel (except that it may be noticeably cleaner).

Interrupt Conflicts. Interrupts are internal signals used by your computer to indicate when something needs to happen. With a mouse, an interrupt is used whenever the mouse has information to send to the mouse driver. If there is a conflict, and the same interrupt used by the mouse is used by a different device, then the mouse will not work properly, or it may not work at all.

Interrupt conflicts will not normally occur if your system uses a mouse port, but they can occur with the other types of mouse interface. If you use a serial interface, interrupt conflicts will typically occur when you add a third and fourth serial port. This is because odd-numbered serial ports (1 & 3), as well as even-numbered serial ports (2 & 4), use the same interrupt. Thus, if your mouse is connected to COM2 and an internal modem uses COM4, then they both use the same interrupt, and you cannot use them at the same time. You may be able to use the mouse and the modem at the same time by moving them to a different serial port. For example, if your mouse uses COM1 and the modem still uses COM4, then you can use them both at once because odd and even ports use different interrupts.

If you are using a bus interface and suspect an interrupt problem, you can use a program such as Microsoft's MSD (supplied with Windows and DOS 6.0) to identify potential interrupt conflicts. After these conflicts are identified, you may need to change the interrupt address of one or more devices in your system so that everything will work together properly.

Software Problems. Software problems can be a little trickier than hardware problems. Software problems generally manifest themselves as the mouse "just not working." In such instances, check the driver and your software applications before assuming that the mouse itself has gone bad.

Driver Software. To function properly, the mouse requires the installation of a device driver. You can load this driver in your CONFIG.SYS file or in your AUTOEXEC.BAT file. If the driver is loaded in the CONFIG.SYS file, it is called MOUSE.SYS. If it is loaded in the AUTOEXEC.BAT file, it is called MOUSE.COM. (It is possible that your mouse drivers have different names, depending on who manufactured your mouse.)

Before you can load the driver, you must make sure that the proper command is in your CONFIG.SYS or AUTOEXEC.BAT file. If it is not, add the proper line, according to the information supplied with your mouse. For example, the proper command to load the mouse driver through the CONFIG.SYS file for a Microsoft mouse is as follows:

DEVICE=C:\MOUSE\MOUSE.SYS

The actual working of the command may vary, depending on whether you are loading the device into upper memory and where the device driver is located on your disk.

If the proper command is in place, and you still suspect that the driver is not loaded, watch your video screen as your system boots. At some point you should see a message from the mouse driver indicating that it is loaded. If, instead, you see a message indicating that the loading was not done, then you must determine why. For example, the driver may not be able to load because there is not enough memory available. After you determine why it is not loading, rectify the situation and make sure the driver loads.

It is also possible that some software requires a certain mouse device driver. For example, Microsoft is now up to mouse driver version numbers above 9.0. If you are using an older mouse driver, and your application software requires a newer mouse driver version, then the mouse will not work properly (or at all). In such a case, contact your vendor directly and request a mouse driver update. Often you can get these through the vendor's BBS or on CompuServe.

III

Hardware Considerations

Application Software. If your mouse will not work with a specific piece of application software, check the setup information or configuration section of the program. Make sure that you have indicated to the program (if necessary) that you are using a mouse. If that still doesn't work, and the mouse works with other software you are using, then contact the technical support department of the application software company.

Video Display Hardware

During the early years of the IBM PC and compatibles, the video system choice was simply color or monochrome. Since then, many adapter and display options have hit the market. A video subsystem consists of two main components: an adapter that plugs into an expansion slot or is built into the motherboard, and a video display or monitor that is compatible with the video adapter. This chapter explores the range of available IBM-compatible video adapters and the displays that work with them.

With the PS/2 systems, IBM developed new video standards that have completely overtaken the older display standards in popularity and support. Abiding by industry standards for video displays and adapters is extremely important. Many video systems are not supported by every program and system peripheral. Therefore, I usually avoid discussing proprietary standards because they offer the typical mainstream system user little more than incompatibility problems. So far only IBM has been able to define true video standards for the IBM-compatible industry, although others have made attempts. Sometimes even IBM has failed to have its video standards adopted throughout the industry.

The following IBM display systems are standards in today's industry:

MDA	Monochrome Display Adapter
CGA	Color Graphics Adapter
EGA	Enhanced Graphics Adapter
VGA	Video Graphics Array
XGA	eXtended Graphics Array

These adapters and video standards are supported by virtually every program that runs on IBM or compatible equipment. There are other systems that are developing into defacto standards, as well. For example, the super VGA (SVGA) offers different resolutions from different vendors, but the 1280 x 768 resolution is becoming a standard resolution for doing detailed work.

Obsolete Video Display Hardware

Although many types of display systems are considered standards, not all systems are considered viable standards for today's hardware and software. For example, the CGA will work, but it is unacceptable for running the graphics-intensive programs that many users rely on. The next several sections discuss the display adapters that are viewed as "obsolete" in today's market.

Monochrome Display Adapter (MDA) and Display

The simplest (and first available) display type is the IBM Monochrome Display and
Printer Adapter card. A character-only system, the display has no inherent graphics capabilities. The display was originally a top-selling option because it is fairly cost-effective.
As a bonus, the MDA also provides a printer interface that does not consume an extra
slot. The display is known for clarity and high resolution, making it ideal for businesses—especially businesses that use text-based word processing or spreadsheets.
Figure 8.5 shows the Monochrome Display Adapter pinouts.

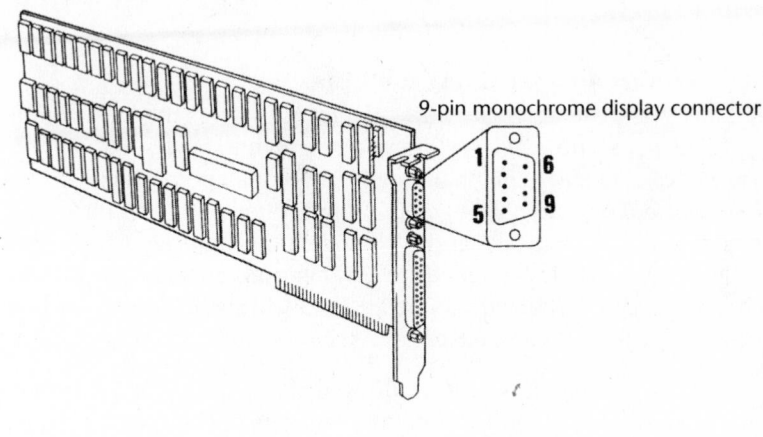

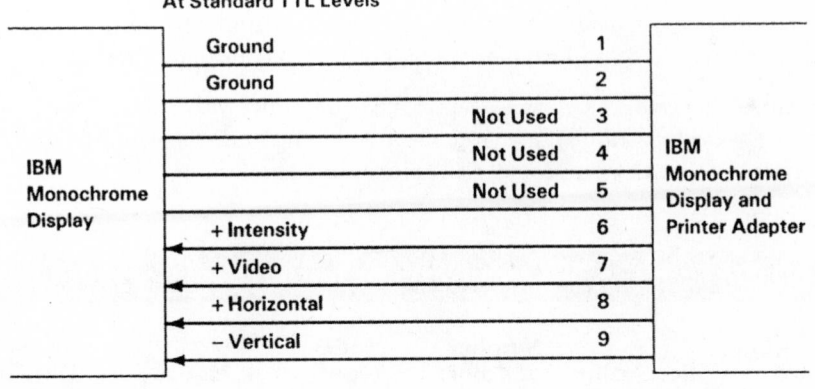

Fig. 8.5
Monochrome Display Adapter pinouts.

Because the monochrome display is a character-only display, you cannot run software
that requires graphics. Originally, that drawback only kept the user from playing games
on a monochrome display, but today even the most serious business software uses graphics and color to great advantage. With the 9-by-14 dots character box (matrix), the IBM
monochrome monitor displays attractive characters. Table 8.2 summarizes features of the
MDA's single mode or operation.

Table 8.2 IBM Monochrome Display Adapter (MDA) Specifications

Video Standard	Resolution	Number of Colors	Mode Type	BIOS Modes	Character Format
DA					
(08/12/81)	720 × 350	4	Text	07h	80 × 25

Colors refer different display attributes such as regular, highlight, reverse video, and underlined.

Color Graphics Adapter (CGA) and Display

For many years, the Color Graphics Adapter (CGA) was the most common display adapter, although now its capabilities leave much to be desired. This adapter has two basic modes of operation: alphanumeric (A/N) or all points addressable (APA). In A/N mode, the card operates in a 40-column by 25-line mode or an 80-column by 25-line mode with 16 colors. In APA and A/N modes, the character set is formed with a resolution of 8 × 8 pixels. In APA mode, two resolutions are available: a medium-resolution color mode (320 × 200) with four colors available, and a two-color high-resolution mode (640 × 200). Figures 8.6 and 8.7 show the pinouts for the Color Graphics Adapter.

Most of the monitors sold for the CGA were RGBs, not composite monitors. The color signal of a composite monitor contains a mixture of colors that must be decoded or separated. RGB monitors receive red, green, and blue separately and combine the colors in different proportions to generate other colors. RGB monitors offer better resolution than composite monitors and do a much better job of displaying 80-column text.

Most companies that sold a CGA-type adapter have long since discontinued the product. With many VGA cards costing under $100, recommending a CGA makes little sense. Table 8.3 gives the specifications for all CGA modes of operation.

Table 8.3 IBM Color Graphics Adapter (CGA) Specifications

Video Standard	Resolution	Number of Colors	Mode Type	BIOS Modes	Character Format
CGA					
(08/12/81)	320 × 200	16	Text	00/01h	40 × 25
	640 × 200	16	Text	02/03h	80 × 25
	160 × 200	16	APA	—	—
	320 × 200	4	APA	04/05h	40 × 25
	640 × 200	2	APA	06h	80 × 25

APA = All points addressable (graphics)
— = Not supported

Character Box	Scan Frequency Vertical (Hz)	Horizontal (KHz)	Scan Mode
9 × 14	50	18.432	Std

Enhanced Graphics Adapter (EGA) and Display

The IBM Enhanced Graphics Adapter, discontinued when the PS/2 systems were introduced, consisted of a graphics board, a graphics memory-expansion board, a graphics memory-module kit, and a high-resolution color monitor. The whole package originally cost about $1,800! The aftermarket gave IBM a great deal of competition in this area, and you could put together a similar system from non-IBM vendors for much less money.

One nice thing about the EGA was that you could build your system in modular steps. Because the card worked with any of the monitors IBM had at the time, you could use the card with the IBM Monochrome Display, the earlier IBM Color Display, or the new IBM Enhanced Color Display. With the EGA, the IBM color monitor displays 16 colors in 320 × 200 or 640 × 200 mode. With the EGA, the IBM monochrome monitor shows a resolution of 640 × 350 with a 9 × 14 character box (text mode). Figures 8.8 and 8.9 show you the pinouts and P-2 connector on the Enhanced Graphics Display Adapter.

With the EGA, the IBM Enhanced Color Display is capable of 640 × 350 with 16 colors. The character box for text is 8 × 14 compared to 8 × 8 for the earlier CGA board and monitor. The 8 × 8 character box can be used, however, to display 43 lines of text. Through software, the character box can be manipulated up to the size of 8 × 32. The 16 colors can be selected from a palette of 64.

Character Box	Scan Frequency Vertical (Hz)	Horizontal (KHz)	Scan Mode
8 × 8	60	15.75	Std
8 × 8	60	15.75	Std
—	60	15.75	Std
8 × 8	60	15.75	Std
8 × 8	60	15.75	Std

III

Hardware Considerations

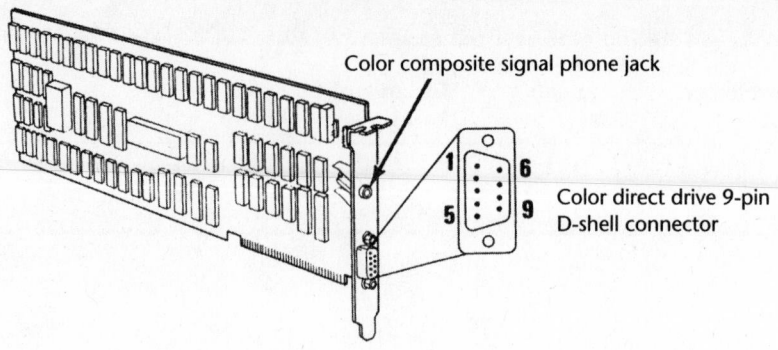

Color composite signal phone jack

Color direct drive 9-pin
D-shell connector

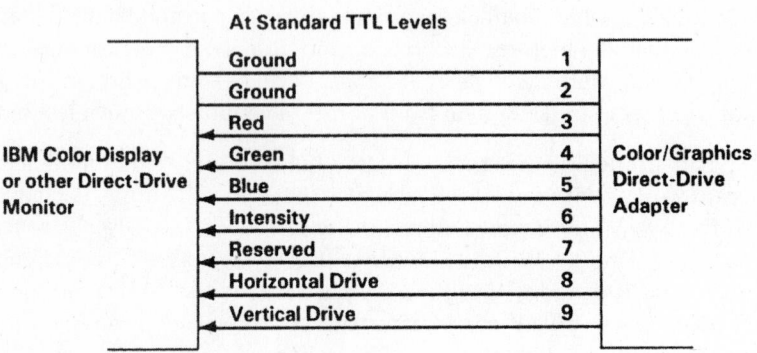

At Standard TTL Levels

IBM Color Display or other Direct-Drive Monitor		Color/Graphics Direct-Drive Adapter
Ground	1	
Ground	2	
Red	3	
Green	4	
Blue	5	
Intensity	6	
Reserved	7	
Horizontal Drive	8	
Vertical Drive	9	

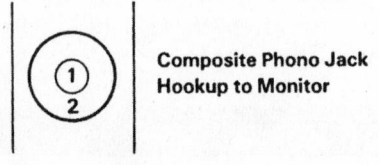

**Composite Phono Jack
Hookup to Monitor**

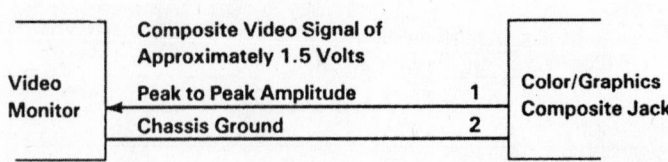

Video Monitor		Color/Graphics Composite Jack
Composite Video Signal of Approximately 1.5 Volts Peak to Peak Amplitude	1	
Chassis Ground	2	

Fig. 8.6
CGA display connector specifications.

P1 (4-pin Berg strip) for RF modulator   P2 (6-pin Berg strip) for light-pen connector

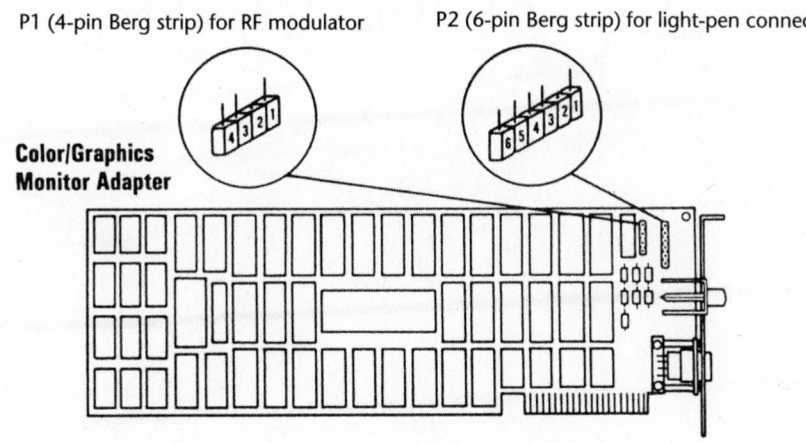

**Color/Graphics
Monitor Adapter**

| RF
Modulator | + 12 Volts | 1 | Color/Graphics
Monitor
Adapter |
|---|---|---|---|
| | (key) Not Used | 2 | |
| | Composite Video Output | 3 | |
| | Logic Ground | 4 | |

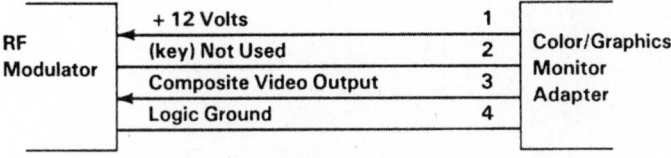

RF Modulator Interface

| Light
Pen | – Light Pen Input | 1 | Color/Graphics
Monitor
Adapter |
|---|---|---|---|
| | (key) Not Used | 2 | |
| | – Light Pen Switch | 3 | |
| | Chassis Ground | 4 | |
| | + 5 Volts | 5 | |
| | + 12 Volts | 6 | |

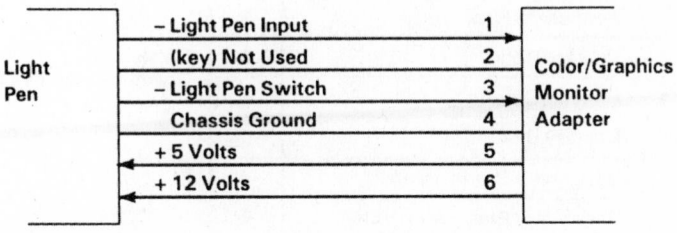

Light Pen Interface

Fig. 8.7
CGA RF modulator and light-pen connector specifications.

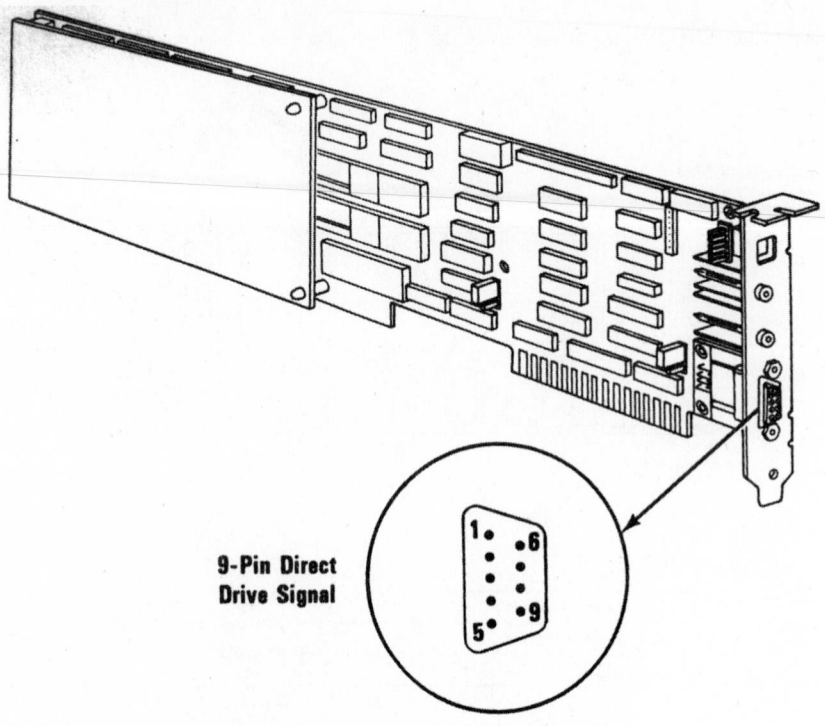

	Signal Name - Description	Pin	
	Ground	1	
	Secondary Red	2	
Direct	Primary Red	3	**Enhanced**
Drive			**Graphics Adapter**
Display	Primary Green	4	
	Primary Blue	5	
	Secondary Green/Intensity	6	
	Secondary Blue/Mono Video	7	
	Horizontal Retrace	8	
	Vertical Retrace	9	

Fig. 8.8
EGA display connector specifications.

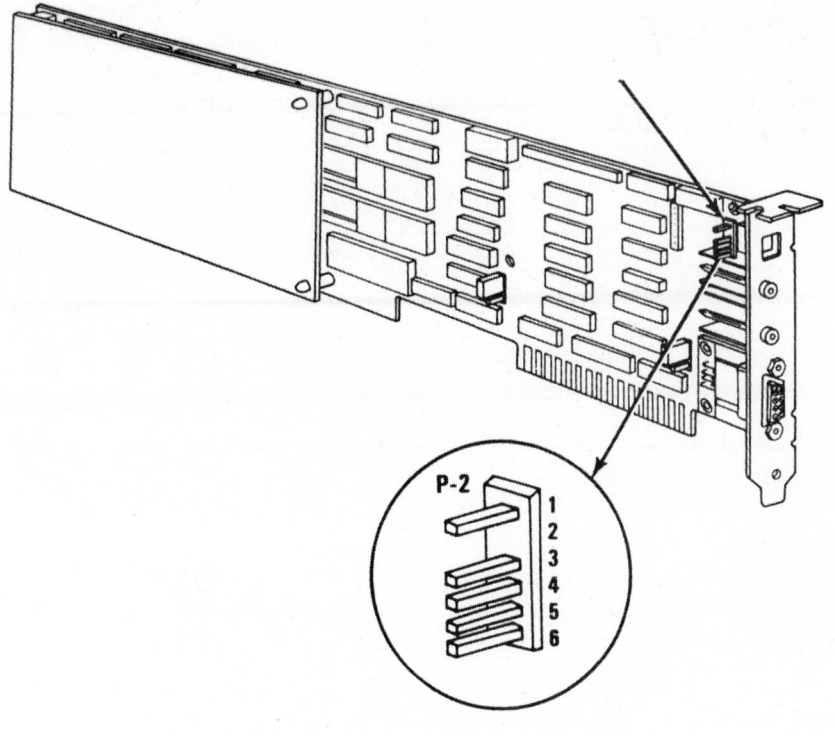

P-2 Connector		Pin	
	+Light Pen Input	1	
Light Pen Attachment	Not used	2	**Enhanced Graphics Adapter**
	+Light Pen Switch	3	
	Ground	4	
	+5 Volts	5	
	12 Volts	6	

Fig. 8.9

EGA light-pen connector specifications.

You can enlarge a RAM-resident, 256-member character set to 512 characters by using the IBM memory expansion card. A 1,024 character set is added with the IBM graphics memory-module kit. These character sets are loaded from programs.

All this memory fits in the unused space between the end of RAM user memory and the current display adapter memory. The EGA has a maximum 128K of memory that maps into the RAM space just above the 640K boundary. If you install more than 640K, you probably will lose the extra memory after installing the EGA. The graphics memory-expansion card adds 64K to the standard 64K for a total of 128K. The IBM graphics

Table 8.4 IBM Enhanced Graphics Adapter (EGA) Specifications

Video Standard	Resolution	Number of Colors	Mode Type	BIOS Modes	Character Format
EGA					
(09/10/84)	320 × 350	16	Text	00/01h	40 × 25
	640 × 350	16	Text	02/03h	80 × 25
	720 × 350	4	Text	07h	80 × 25
	320 × 200	16	APA	0Dh	40 × 25
	640 × 200	16	APA	0Eh	80 × 25
	640 × 350	4	APA	0Fh	80 × 25
	640 × 350	16	APA	10h	80 × 25

APA = All points addressable (graphics)

memory-module kit adds another 128K, for a total of 256K. This second 128K of memory is only on the card and does not consume any of the PC's memory space. Note that because almost every aftermarket EGA card came configured with the full 256K of memory, expansion options were not necessary.

The VGA system supersedes the EGA in many respects. The EGA had problems emulating the earlier CGA or MDA adapters, and some software that worked with the earlier cards would not run on the EGA until the programs were modified. Table 8.4 shows the modes supported by the EGA adapter.

Professional Color Display and Adapter

The Professional Graphics Display System is a video display product that IBM introduced in 1984. At $4,290, the system was too expensive to become a mainstream product. The system is composed of a Professional Graphics Monitor and a Professional Graphics Card Set. When fully expanded, this card set uses three slots in an XT or AT system, which is a high price to pay, but the features are impressive. The Professional Graphics Adapter

Table 8.5 IBM Professional Graphics Adapter (PGA) Specifications

Video Standard	Resolution	Number of Colors	Mode Type	BIOS Modes	Character Format
PGA					
(09/10/84)	320 × 200	16	Text	00/01	40 × 25
	640 × 200	16	Text	02/03	80 × 25
	320 × 200	4	APA	04/05	40 × 25
	640 × 200	2	APA	06	80 × 25
	640 × 480	256	APA	—	—

APA = All points addressable (graphics)
— = Not supported

Character Box	Scan Frequency Vertical (Hz)	Horizontal (KHz)	Scan Mode
8 × 14	60	21.85	Std
8 × 14	60	21.85	Std
9 × 14	50	18.432	Std
8 × 8	60	15.75	Std
8 × 8	60	15.75	Std
8 × 14	50	18.432	Std
8 × 14	60	21.85	Std

(PGA) offers three-dimensional rotation and clipping as a built-in hardware function. The adapter can run 60 frames per second of animation because the PGA uses a built-in dedicated microcomputer.

The Professional Graphics card and monitor were targeted toward the engineering and scientific areas rather than financial or business applications. This system was discontinued when the PS/2 was introduced and has been replaced by the VGA and other higher-resolution graphics standards for these newer systems. Table 8.5 shows all supported PGA modes.

VGA Adapters and Displays

When IBM introduced the PS/2 systems on April 2, 1987, they also introduced the Video Graphics Array display. On that day, in fact, IBM also introduced the lower-resolution MultiColor Graphics Array (MCGA) and higher-resolution 8514 adapters. The MCGA and 8514 adapters did not become standards like the VGA, and both were discontinued.

Character Box	Scan Frequency Vertical (Hz)	Horizontal (KHz)	Scan Mode
8 × 8	60	15.75	Std
8 × 8	60	15.75	Std
8 × 8	60	15.75	Std
8 × 8	60	15.75	Std
—	60	30.48	Std

Digital versus Analog Signals. Unlike earlier video standards that were digital, the VGA is an analog system. Why are the displays going from digital to analog, when most other electronic systems are going digital? Compact disc players (digital) have replaced most turntables (analog), while newer VCRs and camcorders have digital picture storage for smooth slow motion and freeze-frame capability. With digital televisions, you can watch several channels on a single screen by splitting the screen or placing a picture within another picture. With everything else going digital, why did IBM decide to change the video to analog? The answer is color.

Most personal computer displays introduced before the PS/2 were digital. This type of display generates different colors by firing the red, green, and blue (RGB) electron beams in an on-or-off mode. You can display up to 8 colors (2 to the third power). In the IBM displays and adapters, another signal—intensity—doubles the number of color combinations from 8 to 16 by displaying each color at one of two intensity levels. This digital display is easy to manufacture and offers simplicity with consistent color combinations from system to system. The real drawback of the digital display system is the limited number of possible colors.

In the PS/2 systems, IBM went to an analog display circuit. Analog displays work like the digital displays that use the RGB electron beams to construct various colors, but each color in the analog display system can be displayed at varying levels of intensity—64 levels in the case of the VGA. This versatility provides 262,144 possible colors (64 to the third power). To make realistic computer graphics, color is often more important than high resolution, because the human eye perceives a picture with more colors as more realistic. IBM moved graphics into an analog form to enhance the color capabilities.

MultiColor Graphics Array (MCGA). The MultiColor Graphics Array (MCGA) is a graphics adapter that has been integrated into the motherboard of the PS/2 Models 25 and 30. The MCGA supports all CGA modes when an IBM analog display is attached, but

Table 8.6 IBM MultiColor Graphics Array (MCGA) Specifications

Video Standard	Resolution	Number of Colors	Mode Type	BIOS Modes	Character Format
MCGA					
(04/02/87)	320 × 400	16	Text	00/01h	40 × 25
	640 × 400	16	Text	02/03h	80 × 25
	320 × 200	4	APA	04/05h	40 × 25
	640 × 200	2	APA	06h	80 × 25
	640 × 480	2	APA	11h	80 × 30
	320 × 200	256	APA	13h	40 × 25

APA = All points addressable (graphics)
DBL = Double scan

any previous IBM display is not compatible. In addition to providing existing CGA mode support, the MCGA includes four additional modes.

The MCGA uses as many as 64 shades of gray in converting color modes for display on monochrome displays so that those who prefer a monochrome display still can execute color-based applications.

Table 8.6 lists the MCGA display modes.

Video Graphics Array (VGA). PS/2 systems contain the primary display adapter circuits on the motherboard. The circuits are called the Video Graphics Array and are implemented by a single custom VLSI chip designed and manufactured by IBM. To adapt this new graphics standard to the earlier systems, IBM introduced the PS/2 Display Adapter. Also called a VGA card, this adapter contains the complete VGA circuit on a full-length adapter board with an 8-bit interface. IBM has since discontinued its VGA card, but many third-party units are available.

The VGA BIOS (basic input-output system) is the control software residing in the system ROM for controlling VGA circuits. With the BIOS, software can initiate commands and functions without having to manipulate the VGA directly. Programs become somewhat hardware-independent and can call a consistent set of commands and functions built into the system's ROM control software. Future implementations of the VGA will be different in hardware but will respond to the same BIOS calls and functions. New features will be added as a superset of the existing functions. The VGA, therefore, will be compatible with the earlier graphics and text BIOS functions that were built into the PC systems from the beginning. The VGA can run almost any software that was written originally for the MDA, CGA, or EGA.

In a perfect world, software programmers would write to the BIOS interface rather than directly to the hardware, and promote software interchanges between different types of hardware. More frequently, however, the programmer wants the software to perform

Character Box	Scan Frequency Vertical (Hz)	Horizontal (KHz)	Scan Mode
8 × 16	70	31.5	Std
8 × 16	70	31.5	Std
8 × 8	70	31.5	Dbl
8 × 8	70	31.5	Dbl
8 × 16	60	31.5	Std
8 × 8	70	31.5	Dbl

better and writes the program to control the hardware directly. The programmer achieves a higher-performance application dependent on the hardware to which it is first written. You have to make sure that your hardware is 100 percent compatible with the standard so that software written to a standard piece of hardware runs on your system. Note that just because a manufacturer claims this register level of compatibility does not mean that the product is 100 percent compatible or that all software runs as it would on a true IBM VGA. Most manufacturers have "cloned" the VGA system at the register level, which means that even applications which write directly to the video registers will function correctly. Also, the VGA circuits themselves emulate the older adapters even to the register level, and have an amazing level of compatibility with these earlier standards. This makes the VGA a truly universal standard.

The VGA displays up to 256 colors on-screen, from a palette of 262,144 (256K) colors. Because the VGA outputs an analog signal, you must have a monitor that accepts an analog input.

Color summing to 64 gray shades is done in the ROM BIOS for monochrome displays. The summing routine is initiated if the BIOS detects the monochrome display when the system is booted. This routine uses a formula that takes the desired color and rewrites the formula to involve all three color guns, producing varying intensities of gray. The color that would be displayed, for example, is converted into 30 percent red plus 59 percent green plus 11 percent blue to achieve the desired gray. Users who prefer a monochrome display, therefore, can execute color-based applications. Table 8.7 lists the VGA display modes.

Table 8.7 IBM Video Graphics Array (VGA) Specifications

Video Standard	Resolution	Number of Colors	Mode Type	BIOS Modes	Character Format
VGA					
(04/02/87)	360 × 400	16	Text	00/01h	40 × 25
	720 × 400	16	Text	02/03h	80 × 25
	320 × 200	4	APA	04/05h	40 × 25
	640 × 200	2	APA	06h	80 × 25
	720 × 400	16	Text	07h	80 × 25
	320 × 200	16	APA	0Dh	40 × 25
	640 × 200	16	APA	0Eh	80 × 25
	640 × 350	4	APA	0Fh	80 × 25
	640 × 350	16	APA	10h	80 × 25
	640 × 480	2	APA	11h	80 × 30
	640 × 480	16	APA	12h	80 × 30
	320 × 200	256	APA	13h	40 × 25

APA = All points addressable (graphics)
Del = Double scan

8514 Display Adapter

The PS/2 Display Adapter 8514/A offered higher resolution and more colors than the standard VGA. This adapter is designed to use the PS/2 Color Display 8514 and plugs into a Micro Channel slot in any PS/2 model so equipped. All operation modes of the built-in VGA continue to be available. An IBM Personal System/2 8514 memory-expansion kit is available for the IBM Display Adapter 8514/A. This kit gives increased color and gray-scale support.

The IBM Display Adapter 8514/A has these advantages:

- Hardware assistance for advanced text, image, and graphics functions
- New high-content display modes
- Increased color and monochrome capability
- Support for the new family of IBM displays
- MDA, CGA, EGA, and VGA modes available
- 256/256K colors and 64/64 gray scales with memory-expansion kit

To take full advantage of this adapter, the 8514 display should be used because it is matched to the capabilities of the adapter. Note that IBM has discontinued the 8514/A adapter and specifies the XGA in its place. The 8514 display continues to be sold because it works well with the newer XGA. Table 8.8 shows all 8514 modes.

Character Box	Scan Frequency Vertical (Hz)	Horizontal (KHz)	Scan Mode
9 × 16	70	31.5	Std
9 × 16	70	31.5	Std
8 × 8	70	31.5	Dbl
8 × 8	70	31.5	Dbl
9 × 16	70	31.5	Std
8 × 8	70	31.5	Dbl
8 × 8	70	31.5	Dbl
8 × 14	70	31.5	Std
8 × 14	70	31.5	Std
8 × 16	60	31.5	Std
8 × 16	60	31.5	Std
8 × 8	70	31.5	Dbl

Table 8.8 IBM 8514 Specifications

Video Standard	Resolution	Number of Colors	Mode Type	BIOS Modes	Character Format
8514					
(04/02/87)	1024 × 768	256	APA	H-0h	85 × 38
	640 × 480	256	APA	H-1h	80 × 34
	1024 × 768	256	APA	H-3h	146 × 51

APA = All points addressable (graphics)
IL = Interlaced

Super VGA (SVGA)

In recent years, many vendors have released video cards whose capabilities surpass those offered by the VGA adapter. These video cards fall into a category loosely known as *super VGA*. Unlike the types of display adapters discussed so far, you must remember that super VGA does not refer to a card that meets a particular specification, but to a group of cards with different capabilities. For example, one card may offer two resolutions (800 × 600 and 1024 × 768) which are greater than those achieved with a regular VGA, while another vendor may offer a card that provides those resolutions but also provides more color choices at each one. While these cards have different capabilities, they are nonetheless both classified as super VGA.

Because super VGA cards are a category rather than a specification, the market at this level has been fractured. To take advantage of the enhanced capabilities of each card, you need special drivers. For example, to use an Orchid card with Windows, you need Orchid drivers. You cannot use an Orchid driver with a different SVGA card; you can only use it with Orchid. This means that, unlike VGA cards, which can have a single driver that works with all VGA cards, regardless of the vendor, each SVGA card must have a corresponding driver for each application you will be using it with.

Physically, the SVGA cards look much like their VGA counterparts. They have the same connectors, including the feature adapter shown in figure 8.10. Because the technical specifications from different SVGA vendors vary tremendously, it is impossible to give a definitive technical overview in this book.

VESA SVGA Standards. Recognizing that it is virtually impossible to program for the many SVGA cards on the market, in October, 1989, the Video Electronics Standards Association (VESA) proposed a standard for a uniform programmer's interface for SVGA cards. This standard was called the *VESA BIOS Extension*. If a video card incorporated this standard, a program could easily determine the capabilities of the card and then access those capabilities.

The benefit of the VESA BIOS Extension is that a programmer would only need to worry about one routine or driver to support SVGA. Different cards from different manufacturers would all be accessible through the common VESA interface.

Character Box	Scan Frequency Vertical (Hz)	Horizontal (KHz)	Scan Mode
12 × 20	43.48	35.52	IL
8 × 14	60	31.5	Std
7 × 15	43.48	35.52	IL

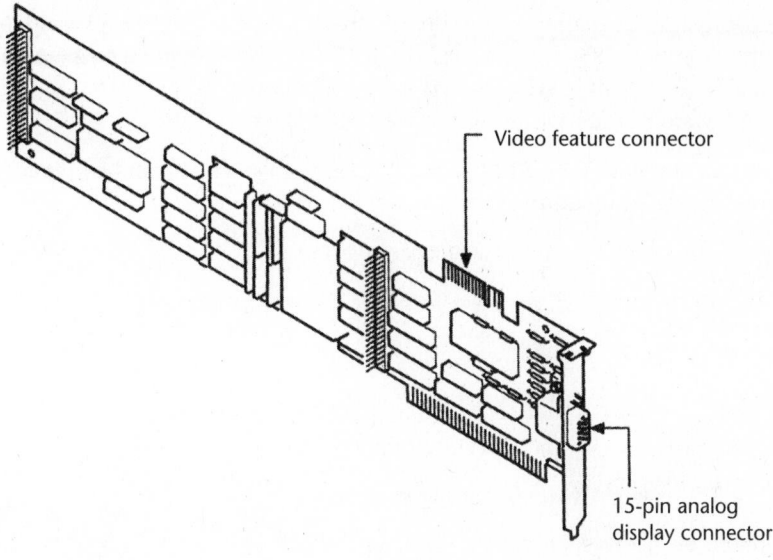

Video feature connector

15-pin analog display connector

Fig. 8.10
The IBM PS/2 Display Adapter (VGA card).

This concept, when first proposed, met with limited acceptance. Several major SVGA manufacturers started supplying the VESA BIOS Extension as a separate memory-resident program that you could load when you booted your computer. Over the years, other vendors started supplying the VESA BIOS Extension as an integral part of their SVGA BIOS. Obviously, from a user's perspective, support for VESA in BIOS is a better solution. You don't need to worry about loading a driver or other memory-resident program whenever you want to use a program that expects the VESA extensions to be present.

Today, most SVGA cards support the VESA BIOS Extensions in one way or another. When you shop for an SVGA card, make sure it supports the extensions in BIOS. Also, if you are interested in finding out more about programming for the VESA BIOS Extensions, check out the IBMPRO forum on CompuServe, or contact the Video Electronics Standards Association at 408-435-0333 for a copy of their VESA Programer's Toolkit.

III

Hardware Considerations

XGA and XGA/2

IBM announced the PS/2 XGA Display Adapter/A on October 30, 1990, and the XGA/2 in September, 1992. Both adapters are high-performance, 32-bit bus master adapters for Micro Channel-based systems. These video subsystems evolve from the VGA and provide greater resolution, more colors, and much better performance.

Combine a fast VGA, a graphics coprocessor, and bus mastering, and you have XGA. Being a bus master adapter means that the XGA can take control of the system as though it were the motherboard. In essence, a bus master is an adapter with its own processor that can execute operations independent of the motherboard. The XGA was introduced as the default graphics display platform with the Model 90 XP 486 and the Model 95 XP 486. In the desktop Model 90, the XGA is on the motherboard; in the Model 95 (a tower unit), it is located on a separate add-in board. This board, the XGA Display Adapter/A, is also available for other 386- and 486-based Micro Channel systems. The XGA adapter can be installed in any MCA systems that have 80386, 80386SX, or 80486 processors. These include systems such as the PS/2 models 55, 57, 65, 70, and 80.

The XGA comes standard with 512K of graphics memory, which can be upgraded to 1M with an optional video-memory expansion.

This list shows highlights of the XGA adapter features:

- 1024 × 768 with 256 colors (16 colors with standard memory)

- 640 × 480 with 256 colors

- DOS XGA adapter interface provides 8514/A compatibility

- Integrates a 16-bit compatible VGA

- Optimized for windowing operating systems

- Includes device drivers for DOS, OS/2, and Windows

- In addition to all VGA modes, the XGA offers several new modes of operation, shown in Table 8.9.

The 65,536 color mode provides almost photographic output. The 16-bit pixel is laid out as 5 bits of red, 6 bits of green, and 5 bits of blue (5-6-5), or in other words, 32 shades of blue, 64 shades of green, and 32 shades of blue. (The eye notices more variations in green than in red or blue.) One major drawback of the current XGA implementation is the interlacing that occurs in the higher-resolution modes. With interlacing, you can use a less expensive monitor, but the display updates more slowly, resulting in a slight flicker.

Table 8.9 XGA Unique Modes of Operation

Maximum Resolution	Maximum Colors	Required VRAM
1024 × 768	256 colors	1M
1024 × 768	16 colors	512K
640 × 480	65536 colors	1M
1024 × 768	64 gray shades	1M
1024 × 768	16 gray shades	512K
640 × 480	64 gray shades	512K

There are several ways the XGA/2 improves on the performance of the XGA. To begin with, the XGA/2 increases the number of colors supported at 1024 × 768 resolution to 64K. In addition, because of the circuitry on the XGA/2, it can process data at twice the speed of the XGA. The XGA/2 also works in noninterlaced mode, so it produces less flicker than the XGA.

Both the XGA and XGA/2 support all existing VGA and 8514/A video modes. A large number of popular applications have been developed to support the 8514/A high-resolution 1024 × 768 mode. These applications are written to the 8514/A Adapter interface, a software interface between the application and the 8514/A hardware. The XGA's extended graphics function maintains compatibility at the same level. Because of the power of the XGA and XGA/2, current VGA or 8514/A applications run much faster.

Much of the XGA and XGA/2's speed also can be attributed to its video RAM (VRAM), a type of dual-ported RAM designed for graphics-display systems. This memory can be accessed by both the processor on the graphics adapter as well as the system CPU simultaneously, allowing almost instant data transfer. The XGA VRAM is mapped into the system's address space. The VRAM normally is located in the top addresses of the 386's 4-gigabyte address space. Because no other cards normally use this area, conflicts should be rare. The adapters also have an 8K ROM BIOS extension that must be mapped somewhere in segments C000 or D000. Note that the motherboard implementation of the XGA does not require its own ROM because the motherboard BIOS contains all the necessary code.

Table 8.10 summarizes all the XGA modes.

Improving Video Speed

There are many efforts these days to improve the speed of video adapters. This is due to the complexity and sheer data of the high-resolution displays used by today's software. The improvements in video speed are centering along three fronts: the processor, the RAM, and the bus.

The Video Processor. There are three types of processors, or chip sets, that can be used in creating a video card. The chipset used is, for the most part, independent of which video specification (VGA, SVGA, or XGA) the adapter follows.

Table 8.10 IBM Extended Graphics Array (XGA) Specifications

Video Standard	Number Resolution	Mode of Colors	BIOS Type	Character Modes	Character Format
XGA					
(10/30/90)	360 × 400	16	Text	00/01h	40 × 25
	720 × 400	16	Text	02/03h	80 × 25
	320 × 200	4	APA	04/05h	40 × 25
	640 × 200	2	APA	06h	80 × 25
	720 × 400	16	Text	07h	80 × 25
	320 × 200	16	APA	0Dh	40 × 25
	640 × 200	16	APA	0Eh	80 × 25
	640 × 350	4	APA	0Fh	80 × 25
	640 × 350	16	APA	10h	80 × 25
	640 × 480	2	APA	11h	80 × 30
	640 × 480	16	APA	12h	80 × 30
	320 × 200	256	APA	13h	40 × 25
	1056 × 400	16	Text	14h	132 × 25
	1056 × 400	16	Text	14h	132 × 43
	1056 × 400	16	Text	14h	132 × 56
	1056 × 400	16	Text	14h	132 × 60
	1024 × 768	256	APA	H-0h	85 × 38
	640 × 480	65536	APA	H-1h	80 × 34
	1024 × 768	256	APA	H-2h	128 × 54
	1024 × 768	256	APA	H-3h	146 × 51

APA = All points addressable (graphics)
Dbl = Double scan
Il = Interlaced

The oldest technology used in creating a video adapter is known as *frame buffer technology*. In this scheme, the video card is responsible for displaying individual frames of an image. Each frame is maintained by the video card, but the computing necessary to create the frame comes from the CPU of your computer. This places a heavy burden on the CPU, which could be busy doing other program-related computing.

At the other end of the spectrum is a chip technology known as *coprocessing*. In this scheme, the video card includes its own processor, which performs all video-related computations. This frees the main CPU so it can do other tasks. Short of integrating video functions directly into the CPU, this chipset provides the fastest overall system throughput.

Between these two arrangements is a middle ground that uses a fixed-function accelerator chip. In this scheme, used in many of the graphics accelerator boards on the market

By and large, you should only be worried about the display size as it relates to the screen resolutions you are planning on using. Generally, the higher the resolution, the larger the display size you will want. For example, if you are operating at 640 × 480 resolution, then you should find a 14-inch monitor comfortable. At 1024 × 768, you will probably find that the display is too small for a 14-inch monitor and therefore prefer to use a larger one (such as a 21-inch monitor).

The actual display size you choose will ultimately depend on how comfortable you feel with the images displayed on your screen. It is best to test out different monitor sizes, if at all possible. This is most easily done at either a company that has a wide array of computer equipment or at your local computer dealer.

Screen Type. There are two general types of screens you can purchase. You may have already noticed that the typical display screen is curved, meaning that it bulges toward you in the middle of the screen. This is consistent with the vast majority of cathode ray tube (CRT) technology; it is the same as the tube on your television set.

There are many monitors that offer flat screen displays, which means that there is no bulge in the front of the screen. The advantage of this is that there is less glare and a better quality image produced. The disadvantage is that the technology required to produce flat screen displays is more expensive, resulting in higher prices for the monitors.

Dot Pitch. *Dot pitch* indicates the distance between the dots that make up the display. Smaller pitch values indicate sharper images. The original IBM PC color monitor had a dot pitch of 0.43 mm, which is considered poor by most any standard. The state-of-the-art displays marketed today have a dot pitch of 0.28 mm or less.

Scanning Frequencies. The scanning frequency of a monitor ties directly to the technology used to display information on-screen. In displays that use a CRT, the image is created by an electron gun shooting electrons at the screen. There are three electron guns, one for each of the primary red, green, and blue colors. The speed at which these electron guns move across the screen is called the *refresh rate,* or the *scanning frequency.* This is because each time the screen is scanned, it is refreshed.

The horizontal scan rate refers to the speed at which the electron guns can move across the screen. The vertical scan rate refers to the speed at which it moves down the screen. The higher the refresh rate, the better the image that can be reproduced. It is important that the scan rates expected by your monitor match those produced by your video card. If you have mismatched rates, you won't be able to see an image, and may actually damage your monitor.

Phosphor Types. Phosphor is the chemical that coats the inside of your picture tube. It glows when it is electrically charged, as occurs when it is struck by electrons from the electron guns in your CRT. This chemical has a quality called *persistence,* which indicates how long this glow will remain on-screen. You should have a good match between persistence and scanning frequency so that the image has less flicker (if the persistence is too low) and no ghosts (if the persistence is too high).

III

Hardware Considerations

Interlaced versus Noninterlaced. Interlacing is a process that was addressed when the XGA and XGA/2 cards were discussed. In an interlaced display, the video adapter displays alternate lines of the image. For example, if you are using the 640 × 480 display mode, there are 480 rows of pixels that must be displayed on-screen. In interlaced mode, the odd rows are displayed first and then the even ones. This results in a slightly slower refresh rate than a noninterlaced display, which displays all 480 rows consecutively.

The benefit of using an interlaced display is that the monitor can be a bit less expensive at higher resolutions. If you are looking for high-quality video, however, you will want to get a video adapter (and monitor) that support high-resolution, noninterlaced displays.

Multisync Monitors. Because of the wide variety of video adapter cards available on the market, display manufacturers have introduced a group of monitors referred to as *multisync*. This simply means that the monitor can detect the frequencies used by the adapter and can adjust accordingly. These monitors are much more forgiving than those that have a fixed frequency. They also tend to protect part of your video subsystem investment, because you can upgrade your video card with less worry about whether your monitor will work with it.

Most of the analog monitors produced today are, to one extent or another, multisync. Because there are literally hundreds of monitor manufacturers on the market (and thousands of monitor models), it is impractical to discuss technical aspects of each monitor model in detail. Suffice it to say that before investing in a monitor, you should check the technical specifications to make sure it meets your needs. If you are looking for a place to start, check out one of the reviews that appears in *PC Magazine* periodically about monitors and their quality. If you can't wait for a *PC Magazine* review, check out the monitors from any of the following vendors:

- IBM
- Mitsubishi
- NEC
- Sony

Each of these manufacturers has created monitors that set the standards by which other monitors can be judged. While you will typically pay a bit more for them, you will never be disappointed with their quality or the service you receive from the monitors.

Troubleshooting and Servicing Adapters and Displays

Solving most graphics adapter and monitor problems is fairly simple, although costly, because replacement of the adapter or display is the usual procedure. A defective or dysfunctional adapter or display is usually replaced as a single unit rather than repaired. Most of today's cards cost more to service than to replace, and the documentation required to service the adapters or displays properly is not always available. You cannot get schematic diagrams, parts lists, wiring diagrams, and so on, for most of the adapters or

Table 8.11 The Level 1 and Level 2 MPC Specifications

Component	Level 1 Specification	Level 2 Specification
CPU	386SX	25 MHz 486SX
RAM	2M	4M
Disk Drives	1.44M 3.5" floppy	1.44M 3.5" floppy
	30M hard drive	160M hard drive
CD-ROM	150K/sec transfer rate	300K/sec transfer rate
	1 sec or less seek time	400 ms or less seek time
	10,000 hours MTBF	10,000 hours MTBF
	Mode 1 capability	CD-ROM XA ready
		Multisession capable
	Subchannel Q	Subchannel Q
	CD-DA outputs	CD-DA outputs
	Front-panel volume control	Front-panel volume control
Audio Card	8-bit DAC and ADC	16-bit DAC and ADC
	Linear PCM sampling	Linear PCM sampling
	22 KHz sampling rate for DAC	44.1 KHz sampling rate for DAC
	11 KHz sampling rate for ADC	44.1 KHz sampling rate for ADC
		Stereo input and output
	Microphone input	Microphone input
	Synthesizer:	Synthesizer:
	Multivoice	Multivoice
	Multitimbral	Multitimbral
	6 melody/2 percussive	6 melody/2 percussive
	Mixer:	Mixer:
	3-channel input	3-channel input
	Stereo output	Stereo output
Video	VGA	VGA with 64K colors at 640 x 480
Input	101-key keyboard	101-key keyboard
	2-button mouse	2-button mouse
I/O	9600 bps serial port	9600 bps serial port
	Bidirectional parallel port	Bidirectional parallel port
	MIDI port	MIDI port
	Joystick port	Joystick port
System	Windows with Multimedia	Windows 3.1
		Extensions

Types of CD-ROM Drives. There are only a few types of CD-ROM drives on the market, but these come from a wide variety of manufacturers. When you are looking to add or upgrade your CD-ROM, you should examine each of the following areas:

- What interface do you require?

- Do you want an internal or external drive?

- Do you want audio capability?

- Do you want to use a carrier?

- What speed should the drive use?

- Do you need extended capabilities?

The answers to these questions will determine the type of drive you get. The following sections explore each of these areas.

CD-ROM Interfaces. There are generally two types of interfaces you can use with CD-ROM drives. The large majority of drives use SCSI interfaces. These are the same SCSI interfaces used for hard disk drives, which you learn about in Chapter 10, "Hard Disk Drives."

Other CD-ROM drives use proprietary interfaces. These interfaces typically come if you purchase the CD-ROM as part of a multimedia upgrade kit (such as the Sound Blaster) or as part of a special deal from some close-out vendor. *Remember that proprietary interfaces are typically developed for a specific purpose.* This means that although these interfaces can work great for that purpose, they may lack compatibility for other purposes.

To overcome the compatibility issue, stick with a relatively standard interface (such as SCSI). In this way, you can almost guarantee that your system will have as long a life as possible.

Internal vs. External Drives. Like regular hard drives, CD-ROM drives come in both internal and external models. The internal models are typically a bit cheaper, but they require you to take apart your computer to install them. (The external ones do not require you to take the computer apart if you already have a SCSI card installed; if one is not installed, you must still take your computer apart to install the interface card.) Internal models also require a free drive bay, which may be a sticky problem on some of the smaller PC cases.

External models, on the other hand, cost a bit more because of the casing and external power supply. They can often be plugged directly into a SCSI port on the back of your computer, which means they can be shared among several different computers, provided each one has a compatible interface.

The decision between internal and external is up to you. Unless you must use an external, however, it is usually more compact and neater if you use an internal drive.

Audio Capability. If you have handled CD-ROMs before, you already know that they are the same size and shape as the audio CDs that you play on your home stereo system. Both utilize the same recording technology, the only difference is how the information retrieved from the disc is processed. This processing requires different firmware chips within the actual CD-ROM drive.

Many CD-ROM drives are capable of both reading CD-ROMs and playing audio CDs. You can tell the difference by the presence of a headphone jack and audio knob on the front of the drive. If these exist, then you can play audio CDs. You will typically need special software to start the player and to skip to specific tracks, however. Most vendors will provide this with the purchase of the drive, although you can use the Windows Media Player accessory, as well.

CD-ROM Carriers. When you use your home CD player, you probably push a button that ejects a tray into which you place the audio CD. Push another button (or the same button again), and the tray retracts and the CD starts playing. Although you can find a few CD-ROM drive models that handle CD-ROMs in this same manner, most use a special carrier.

This carrier serves to hold and protect the disc. As far as I can determine, CD-ROM carriers are used because CD-ROM drives are typically used in a business environment where equipment is subject to harsher treatment or where the CD-ROM drive may be oriented vertically instead of horizontally. Otherwise, there is no real reason for the differences between the player and the drive.

Remember that only a few different models of CD-ROM drives don't use the special carriers. If you need one that uses the special carriers, you will limit your available choices quite a bit.

CD-ROM Drive and Transfer Speed. Like hard drives, CD-ROM drives have different data transfer speeds. These speeds are much slower than those in hard drives, however. When you are looking for a CD-ROM drive, remember that a guarantee that a CD-ROM is MPC compliant does not mean that you are purchasing the best available. The speeds provided in the MPC specifications are not the fastest available on the market. For example, the 1 second seek time, allowable in the spec, is fairly slow for CD-ROM drives. You should search for CD-ROMs that have access times under 300 ms.

Similarly, you will find that data transfer rates vary tremendously among different models of CD-ROM. You should look for the fastest transfer rate possible. Transfer rates above 300K/sec are beginning to be commonplace.

To help achieve higher transfer rates (jumping from 150K/sec to 300K/sec), you may want to consider double-speed CD-ROM drives. Part of the problem of holding back access rates and transfer times is the rotational speed of the disc within the drive. By doubling the speed at which the CD-ROM rotates, the overall speed and efficiency of the drive is improved. For example, with some disc drives, you can get transfer rates in excess of 600K/sec. Because these faster rates are a huge plus, you should not have to search far to find information about whether the drive is double-speed; it should be plainly featured in the sales information.

Extended Capabilities. Earlier you learned about the differences between CD-ROM and audio CDs, and how you can tell if a drive supports audio. Besides CD-ROM specifications, however, there have also been extended specifications written. These are known as CD-ROM XA (extended architecture). If possible, and if your budget will allow, you should purchase a CD-ROM that supports XA. Compliance with basic XA capabilities allows you to access images stored in Kodak's Photo CD format. If you purchase a system that has full XA compliance, you can access discs starting to appear in the CD-I (compact disc, interactive) format.

If you decide to purchase a drive that will read Photo CDs, make sure you get one that supports multisession discs. Many drives only support single-session discs, so make sure you read the fine print. This may mean the difference between accessing all the data on the disc and only being able to get to part of the data. *Session* is short for a recording session—that is, when the images were placed on the disc. Because Photo CD allows you to return the CD and store images from additional film on the disc, multisession capability is a big deal, so look for it.

Multimedia Sound Boards

Earlier you learned that the MPC specifications (both Level 1 and Level 2) require the addition of a sound card to your system. There are a large variety of sound cards on the market from which you can choose. Basically, however, the only choice you will need to make is whether the card provides 8-bit or 16-bit audio, and whether it works with the software you want to run.

The largest selling audio boards, and those that garner the highest percentage of awards, are the boards available from Creative Labs, Media Vision, and Turtle Beach Systems. The following sections should help you understand the differences between the 8-bit and 16-bit technology available.

8-Bit Cards. For the most part, 8-bit sound cards are compliant with Level 1 MPC specifications. The 8-bit boards that are on the market offer a wide range of capabilities and features, but have (lately) been eclipsed by the quality of the 16-bit audio boards discussed in the next section. Eight-bit audio cards were originally geared toward the recreational computer user (the game player), as indicated by the inclusion of a game port in many models of audio card. Only later did the use of these cards progress to the point where they were used to create multimedia presentations.

Creative Labs offers the Sound Blaster Pro, while Media Vision offers the Pro AudioSpectrum Plus. Both boards are compliant with the MPC Level 1 specification, and both exceed it in several areas. For example, the Sound Blaster Pro offers sampling rates up to 44.1 MHz, which is in excess of the specification.

The street prices of these boards are under $200, and you can get them as part of multimedia upgrade kits from both companies. (Multimedia upgrade kits are products that typically include a sound board, CD-ROM drive, and a variety of CD-ROM products.) Both boards are supported by thousands of software products, and will offer years of service. The board you purchase will probably boil down to which you can get at the best price.

16-Bit Cards. If you require compliance with the MPC Level 2 specification, or you are simply looking for the highest quality audio, you will want to acquire a 16-bit audio card. These boards provide a better sound quality due to the increased sampling size. In fact, the quality is the same as that of a CD audio, which also uses 16-bit sampling.

Another advantage of 16-bit sound cards is that they typically use sound creation technology beyond that of their 8-bit predecessors. For example, the 8-bit cards generally use FM synthesis to create instrument sounds. While the 16-bit cards also include FM synthesizers, they also often include sample table lookups—that is, they contain tables of actual instrument samples. The advantage is that when you play a grand piano, you are actually hearing the sounds made by a grand piano, not those that are approximated through FM synthesis.

The best-reviewed board in the 16-bit category is the MultiSound from Turtle Beach Systems. This board, which has a list price just under $1,000, is the Rolls Royce of sound boards. It consistently receives top honors in hardware reviews and comparisons. There are also 16-bit boards from Creative Labs (the Sound Blaster 16 ASP) and from Media Vision (the Pro AudioSpectrum 16). These boards, while sporting lower prices (around $350), do not have all the bells and whistles of the MultiSound. For example, you can add instrument sampling to the Sound Blaster 16 ASP by adding a WaveBlaster board, but that increases the total cost to near that of the MultiSound.

Because of the quality of the sound produced by the 16-bit boards, it is best to purchase one of them. It is doubtful that there will be much more improvement in actual sound quality in the future, because 16-bit sound sampling produces the truest and most vibrant sound available. Thus, your investment is secure for years to come.

External Speakers

It is possible to use headphones to listen to the sound from your audio card, but to get the full effect of a sound card, you need external speakers. This is particularly true if you want other people to view and hear your multimedia presentations. These speakers plug into a connector on the rear of the audio card. There are two types of speakers you can purchase—powered or unpowered. The powered speakers have their own power supply (they either plug in or require batteries), while unpowered speakers run off of whatever power comes from the audio card output.

For the best sound quality, you should look into powered speakers. These are more expensive, however, than the unpowered variety. A good set of powered speakers can easily go for more than $300 per pair, making this a costly investment. You can purchase unpowered speakers for as little as $19 per pair. If you are serious about the multimedia capabilities of your system, however, you will find the larger investment well worth it.

The least expensive speakers are the types you can find in any drug store as external speakers for a Walkman-type personal stereo. These are cheap speakers that do not offer rich, vibrant sound. Using this type of speaker with a good-quality 16-bit audio card is like skimping on gas, oil, and tires for your high-performance sports car. While you will get an idea of what sound is coming through your audio system, you will not be able to hear the full range of the true stereo output.

Speakers at the other end of the spectrum include high-quality units from veteran speaker manufacturers such as Altec-Lansing, Acoustic Research, Bose, and Sony. My personal favorite is the Powered Partner series from Acoustic Research. This series includes a speaker for almost any modest budget, between $100 and $500. The Powered Partner 570 has to be heard to be appreciated. With a good multimedia presentation, the sound will literally blow you away. To find good quality powered speakers, visit your local stereo store and discuss with them what you are looking for.

Regardless of whether you decide upon powered or unpowered speakers, you should make sure that the speakers you purchase are shielded. The natural tendency is to place one speaker on each side of your system's monitor; after all, this provides the best placement for sound. However, speakers contain magnets, and these magnets are strong enough to distort the image on your monitor. What happens is that the magnetic field from the speakers pulls the electron beam—used to paint the image on your monitor—so that it does not function normally. This effect is typically evidenced by rainbow colors near the edges of your monitor. To correct this you will need to move the speakers further from your monitor and have your monitor degaussed.

Shielded speakers, on the other hand, will not affect your monitor in this way. The magnetic field has been shielded so that your monitor is safe. Without shielding, the speakers will need to be placed several feet away from your monitor. If you need to place the speakers closer, shielding is an essential feature of any speakers you use. If you decide to purchase any of the higher-priced speaker sets (especially those made for computer use), shielding is always one of the speaker specifications.

Another way to get sound from your system is to hook up the output from your sound card to the auxiliary input on your home stereo system. The major drawback to this is that your computer must be near your stereo system. This drawback is offset, however, by the quality and control of the sound you will experience. In addition, you won't need to purchase additional speakers. Obviously, if you are taking your multimedia system on the road, this solution is not acceptable.

Example Sound Card Installation

The best selling sound card ever is the Sound Blaster. The term "Sound Blaster" has come to be a generic term that represents an entire family of audio cards, including the original Sound Blaster, the Sound Blaster 2.0, the Sound Blaster Pro, and most recently the Sound Blaster 16. Because these are the largest selling sound cards, it may be instructive to quickly look at how a Sound Blaster card is installed. The instructions provided in this section focus on these cards, but the techniques and general steps can be applied to installing virtually any sound card.

Please note that this discussion is not intended to take the place of the instructions provided with the audio card. Instead, it is designed to give you an idea of the overall procedure and to provide general information you may find helpful.

For the most part, installing an audio card is fairly quick and easy—that is, if you are comfortable with having the case off your computer and poking around the insides. To install an audio card, follow these steps:

1. Turn off and unplug your computer and all connected devices.

2. Remove the cables connected to the back of your computer.

3. Take off the computer cover, removing any screws as necessary.

4. Locate an empty slot into which the sound card will be placed. Note that the width of the slot should be the same as the width of the connector on the bottom of the audio card.

5. Remove any expansion slot cover at the rear of the slot you are going to use.

6. Chances are good that there are several dip switches or jumpers on your sound card that are used to set the interrupts, I/O addresses, and DMA addresses used by the card. Check the dip switch and jumper settings on the audio card to make sure the settings it uses do not interfere with the interrupts, I/O addresses, or DMA addresses used by other peripherals in your system. To ensure this, you will need to refer to your sound board documentation and the documentation supplied for each of the other cards in your system.

7. Insert the card in the slot you have chosen, securing it firmly with the screw removed from the expansion slot cover in step 5.

8. Replace the cover to your computer, and connect all the cables removed in step 2.

9. Plug in the speakers or headphone you plan on using with your sound card.

10. Try out the card using the diagnostic software provided with the audio card.

Troubleshooting Sound Card Problems

If you are going to have problems with your sound card, you will generally have them either when you first install it or when you install a different peripheral card. In either case, the problem can be traced to a conflict between the audio card and another card. For example, you may have a conflict between the interrupt used by the audio card and the interrupt used by a network adapter. In such a case, you must determine what the conflict is and then resolve it.

Remember that if you change the interrupts or I/O addresses used by your audio card, you must also change the software that uses the card. Most software that takes advantage of an audio card is written to use the default interrupts and I/O addresses for the audio card. If you change these, you must also reconfigure the software. Otherwise, the software will not be able to find the audio card. Symptoms may range from no sound to a hung system.

Another potential problem area is with your game port. Many sound cards include a game port that you can use to control a joystick. However, many systems already have a joystick controller. For example, the newer IDE hard drive controllers control not just the hard drive, but also your floppies, serial ports, parallel port, and the joystick. If you have two active joystick controllers, neither one will work reliably. You must first disable one of the controllers, and then the other will work properly.

III

Hardware Considerations

If you feel confident that there is no conflict between interrupts and I/O addresses in your system, run the diagnostic software supplied with your audio card. It may be able to determine a problem you could not find. If you still have no sound, make sure you have a good connection between the speaker cable and your sound card and the speaker cable and your speakers.

Keep in mind that your sound card cannot adequately drive large, unpowered speakers. For example, if you try to connect your home stereo speakers directly to the sound card, you probably won't hear anything. This is because the speakers require more power than the sound card can supply. You must either use smaller unpowered speakers, powered speakers, or use an amplifier between your sound card and speakers.

Memory Boards

In discussing memory and memory adapter boards, you should consider the following three types of memory:

- Conventional memory

- Extended memory

- Expanded memory

Memory differs in several ways, from where the memory is located to what processors can address what types of memory. Figure 8.11 shows the relative "locations" of the different types of memory in relation to the system logical memory map.

This map was constructed with an 80286-based system as a model. The 386 and 486 system map is basically the same, but the total amount of extended and conventional memory adds as much as 4 gigabytes. The 286 processor has a total of 16M of memory, including conventional and extended memories. These 16M provide all the memory addressable by the processor. Expanded memory lies completely out of the processor-addressable portion, except for the 64K window through which expanded memory is accessed. Expanded memory cannot be used for running applications programs, which explains why expanded memory is slower than conventional and extended memory.

Any system using an 8088 or 8086 processor, such as the original PC and XT or PS/2 Models 25 and 30, controls memory access through a 20-bit-wide address bus. An *address bus* is the numbering scheme used to uniquely identify all locations in random-access memory (RAM). The address bus width has an effect on how much RAM a system can address. With the 20-digit binary number used for addressing, these systems generate a total of 1M of memory locations. Any system using an 80286 uses a memory addressing system with 24 lines or digits. With this addressing system, a maximum of 16M of RAM is available. Any 386- or 486-based system uses a 32-bit memory addressing system that allows for a total of 4 gigabytes of RAM. This amount of processor-addressable memory equals the IBM 3090 Model 600 Sierra mainframe system that costs $10 million—not bad for a system that sits on or beside a desk. The memory-addressing capabilities of the various processors in native (protected) modes are listed in table 8.11.

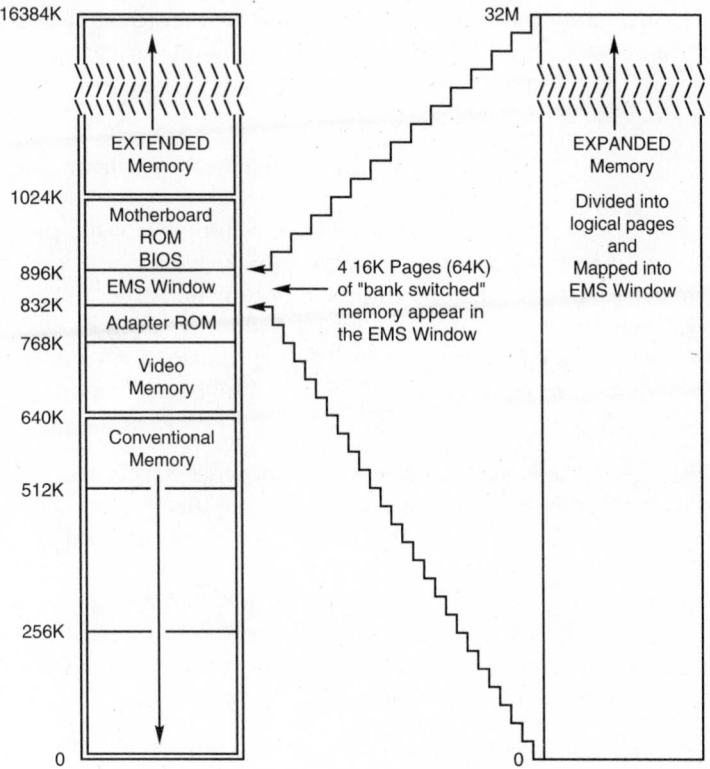

Fig. 8.11

The relationship between conventional, extended, and expanded memory.

These figures reflect only what is technically possible, not what is practical or immediately available. For example, because the Model 90 has eight 36-bit SIMM sockets, you could expand that system to 64M using 8M SIMMs. Any further memory would have to come from a card in a slot. Most systems are not nearly as gifted with memory-expansion capabilities as this, however, and the maximum you can fit in your system depends on many factors.

To put the memory-addressing capabilities of the 386 and 486 into perspective, 4 gigabytes of memory (4,096M) at a below market cost of $35 per megabyte for fast (70 nanoseconds or less) memory still would cost more than $143,000.

Microprocessor Operating Modes

When Intel designed the 80286 and 80386 microprocessors, the company wanted to add new features and retain compatibility with the large base of software that existed for the 8086 and 8088. Intel incorporated an 8086/8088 mode within the newer 286 and 386 processors. This combination is called *real mode*, or 8086/8088 compatibility mode. When the newer processors are in real mode, the emulation of the earlier 8086 is complete, including any limitations that apply to the earlier chip.

Protected mode is the native mode of the 286, 386, and 486. Protected mode enables these chips to perform as designed, with access to full memory-addressing capabilities, but is incompatible with software written for real mode. To run software written for real mode in protected mode entails rewriting the software.

When Intel designed the 286, the company included a method of instructing the chip to go from real mode to protected mode. It did not, however, include a method for getting the chip back into real mode because the whole idea of protection is to prevent rampant software from crashing the system. Now Windows, OS/2, and a whole host of DOS extenders and memory managers require the processor to switch often from protected to real mode. By switching the processor back into real mode, you can run a DOS application in an environment devoid of protection. The only documented way to switch from protected to real mode is to reset the chip by placing a high signal on the processor's reset pin.

When the chip is reset, the system reinitiates the boot process. Rebooting normally performs a power-on test of all memory and loads DOS from the first found disk drive. Rebooting wipes out anything running in the computer as if the operator used the Ctrl-Alt-Del combination. To get around this, operating systems such as OS/2 place a special flag value in the CMOS battery backed-up memory before performing the reset. This value is checked at boot time to see whether you are performing a real boot or a switch from protected mode. If a switch is indicated, normal booting procedures are skipped and the system is sent to a start-up code location.

While this reset operation is in progress, the system does not listen to hardware interrupts. Information coming in over a network adapter, communications port, keyboard, or other interrupt-driven device is lost. This operation resembles having to turn off the engine to shift your car from third to fourth gear. When the engine is off, you have no power steering or brakes, so you hope that no sudden curves are ahead.

The 386 or greater processors have an instruction to switch modes. Using this instruction, these processors can switch modes much faster than the 286.

Virtual 8086 mode is unique to the 386 and higher chips and enables the user to run several protected real mode sessions as one or more subtasks. This mode emulates an entire 8086 system within the 80386 chip. Multiple DOS programs can run as though they were running on a single-processor DOS system. Each virtual machine requires 1M of space for the simulation.

Conventional Memory

Conventional memory exists between 0 kilobytes and 1M (with 384K reserved and 640K usable) on any IBM or compatible system. Conventional memory is used by the Intel microprocessors in real mode. An operating system cannot use the full megabyte of conventional memory because the hardware uses 384K (for video RAM, adapter ROM and RAM, and the motherboard ROM BIOS), leaving 640K of conventional memory for use.

The maximum addressable memory for the IBM PC is 1M, not 640K. Addressable memory is all the memory that the processor can address regardless of function. Usable memory is the subset of addressable memory that operating systems and user programs occupy. When IBM introduced the PC in 1981, the company indicated that the unit could have only 256K because that was all the memory you could access with IBM memory boards installed. By 1983, IBM indicated that the maximum amount of usable memory could be 640K.

Addressing any memory above 640K is a problem because of the memory reserved for system operations. How much memory DOS has access to depends on how your system uses that reserved space and how the memory adapters are installed. You face the following limitations with DOS:

- DOS cannot address memory beyond 1,024K because DOS runs in real mode with a maximum of only 1,024K of addressable memory.

- DOS manages its own data and program code in contiguous memory, starting with the first byte in the system at address 00000h. The first obstruction (such as the video RAM) is the cap that prevents further memory from being managed. A program running under DOS, however, can store data in any addressable memory, including memory beyond the DOS range.

Because of these limitations, DOS handles programs that fit in the 1M workspace, minus any reserved memory after the video RAM. Table 8.12 shows the maximum usable DOS memory available in systems equipped with different video adapters.

Table 8.12 Maximum Usable DOS Memory

DOS memory	Video adapter
736K	Color Graphics Adapter (CGA)
704K	Monochrome Display Adapter (MDA)
640K	Enhanced Graphics Adapter (EGA)
640K	Video Graphics Array (VGA)
640K	eXtended Graphics Array (XGA)

The 8086/8088 addresses 1M of memory. From this memory, BIOS, the adapter board, and video memory are subtracted, leaving from 640K to 736K free for DOS and DOS-based applications. If you have a CGA or MDA video board and want to use this extra memory, you have to find a card that supports 640K as a starting address. One card that comes to mind is the discontinued Hicard. Other cards may support 640K as a starting address, but you probably can get only 704K—not 736K—because most memory boards use designs that allow expansion in 64K increments. I do not know of any board (except Hicard) that allows the system to fill the remaining 32K without overlaying the CGA video memory.

III

Hardware Considerations

Extended Memory

For even more memory expansion, you can install the more advanced 80286 or later chips that support larger amounts of memory. For example, the 80286 supports 16M of memory, and the 80386 or later supports up to 4 gigabytes of memory. The portion of memory beyond the first megabyte is called *extended memory*.

Extended memory is important for operating systems such as Windows or OS/2 that run in the protected mode of the higher-level processors. These operating systems take full advantage of all the extra memory.

Real-mode operation, which is required for DOS, does not support access to extended memory. If users need to transfer data to and from extended memory, they must switch the system from real to protected mode. Hardships encountered in using extended memory led to the development of expanded memory, and later to the development of mode-switching memory managers.

Expanded Memory

Expanded memory is not in the processors' direct address space. You can access expanded memory by *bank switching* (memory paging), a technique that provides small windows of memory (physical pages) through which blocks of expanded memory are traded with your base memory. A program places data elements in expanded memory as a type of cold storage until the data is needed. One problem with this method is that the program must keep track of every piece of data placed in expanded memory. When the program requires data that has been placed in expanded memory, the program must consult its own internal database to recall the correct memory page.

When large programs seemed to be running out of memory in the 640K workspace, several manufacturers sought ways to make more memory available. Lotus Development Corporation first designed expanded memory because most 1-2-3 users eventually ran out of memory in developing huge spreadsheets. (The Lotus program keeps all active data in memory.) Lotus, Intel, and Microsoft collaborated to devise the LIM Expanded Memory Standard (EMS).

The Expanded Memory Specification (EMS), created by Lotus, Intel, and Microsoft, describes a method in which four contiguous physical pages of 16K each (forming a block of 64K) can access up to 32M of expanded memory space through the Expanded Memory Manager (EMM). The page frame is located above 640K. Only video adapters, network cards, and similar devices are normally addressed between 640K and 1,024K.

Problems with LIM EMS are caused by several things. First, because expanded memory is not actual memory to the processor, nothing important can be placed there. Second, the memory window sits above the video RAM area, where DOS cannot manage programs and where storing program code is forbidden. Third, Lotus could not place spreadsheet numeric values in expanded memory because every time the user pressed the Recalc button, every value had to be recalled from the EMS. This process slows down the program, harming Lotus's reputation for fast recalculation times. Data stored in EMS memory is limited to items such as labels.

Because of the program's need to keep a database of what was placed in expanded memory, you still can run out of conventional memory long before the expanded memory is even half gone. Using all of the expanded memory is impossible.

The AST Enhanced Expanded Memory Standard (EEMS) and the IBM Expanded Memory Adapter (XMA) are two subtypes of expanded memory on the market. These different implementations are not fully compatible with each other.

The new version of the LIM EMS, Version 4.0, combines the features of all three standards—EEMS, XMA, and the original LIM EMS—into a newer unified standard. The AST and subsequent LIM 4.0 improvements included increased page size and a capability to position page windows anywhere in the memory map.

Despite some of the drawbacks, investing in an EMS board may be worthwhile. With the new specification in LIM 4.X, a breed of memory-management programs has appeared with the capacity to manage multiple programs in the conventional memory workspace. Aided by the improved paging in the new specification, these programs can move programs and datasets in and out of expanded memory. DESQview is one of the more popular programs with this capability and has a strong following. All 16-bit expanded memory boards can function also as conventional or extended memory boards; however, 8-bit cards can never run as extended memory. When you convert a system to run OS/2 or Windows, for example, you can reconfigure expanded memory boards to operate as extended memory boards. Remember that expanded memory is obsolete with OS/2 or Windows and not needed in any protected-mode system.

Systems with a 386 processor never need an expanded memory board because the 386 chip has advanced memory-management capabilities that enable you to use the 4 gigabytes of possible extended memory space as simulated expanded memory. This simulation is fast because the memory-management capability is built into the processor. With a 386-based system, you need only conventional and extended memory because the drivers that simulate the change of extended to expanded memory usually are supplied with the 80386 systems. COMPAQ, for example, supplies users with a disk containing the COMPAQ Expanded Memory Manager (CEMM). This type of driver is now part of the IBM and Microsoft DOS, under the name EMM386.EXE. (These emulators are for 80386-based systems only.)

Types of Memory Devices

You can break memory hardware down to its smallest removable component—the chip or the SIMM (single in-line memory module). In this section, you look at how to identify different memory chips and what effect the newer SIMMs have on the memory in your system. Most newer systems are installing memory in the SIMM format, which makes troubleshooting and diagnosing problems in memory much easier, and reduces labor in replacing these failed components. The real drawback to the SIMM is the cost.

Chips. At some point, you should be able to take a memory board out of a system, examine it, and identify the board's capacity by counting the installed chips. When you are repairing a memory board, you need this information to help locate the physical position of a defective memory chip, especially when you have an error's logical address location only.

Memory on a board usually is organized into banks of chips. A bank is the minimum amount of memory with which the processor communicates at one time. The size of a bank normally is determined by the width of the data bus on the system processor. Systems with an 8-bit processor data bus architecture will have banks that are 8 bits wide. Because most IBM-compatible systems use parity-checked memory, an additional bit is present for every 8 bits. A system with an 8-bit processor would have a memory bank that is 9 bits wide, systems with 16-bit processors would have banks 18 bits wide, and systems with 32-bit processors would have banks 36 bits wide. Because most chips are arranged as a memory column that is only 1 bit wide, a 9-bit bank would require 9 chips, an 18-bit bank would require 18 chips, and so on.

You should be able to identify how banks are placed on a given memory board or motherboard. Usually, some silk-screen writing on the board labels the banks as "Bank 0," "Bank 1," and so on. Each of the banks has 8 bits numbered 0 through 7, and an extra parity bit.

Examine a chip in one of the banks and look at the writing on the top. A typical memory chip resembles figure 8.12.

Fig. 8.12
Markings on a typical memory chip.

Each item on the chip means something. As mentioned in Chapter 7, the -10 corresponds to the speed of the chip in nanoseconds (a 100 nanosecond rating). MB81256 is the chip's part number, where you usually can find a clue about its capacity. The key digits are 1256, which indicates that this chip is 1 bit wide and has a depth of 256K. To make a full byte with parity, nine of these single-bit-wide chips are required. A chip with a part number KM4164B-10 indicates a 64K-by-1-bit chip at a speed of 100 nanoseconds. The following list of some common types of chips matches them with common part numbers:

4164	64K by 1 bit
4264	64K by 2 bits
4464	64K by 4 bits
41128	128K by 1 bit
42128	128K by 2 bits

44128	128K by 4 bits
41256	256K by 1 bit
42256	256K by 2 bits
44256	256K by 4 bits

Chips wider than 1 bit are used to construct banks of less than 9, 18, or 36 chips (depending on the system architecture). For example, in the IBM XT-286, which is an AT-type of 16-bit system, the last 128K bytes of memory on the motherboard consist of a bank with only 6 chips—4 that are 64K by 4 bits wide and 2 parity chips that are 1 bit wide, storing 18 bits.

In figure 8.12, the symbol centered between two lines is the manufacturer's logo, here for Fujitsu Microelectronics. A cross-reference showing manufacturer symbols is in the Appendix. The 8609 indicates the date of manufacture (ninth week of 1986), although some manufacturers use a Julian date code that looks different. To decode the chip further, contact the manufacturer for a data book or catalog.

With the depth, width, and speed rating of the chip, you can order a replacement. Knowing the date of a chip can sometimes help you identify a bad batch of chips if the dates are consistent.

SIMMs. Single in-line memory modules (SIMMs) are more reliable and easier to replace than standard memory chips. Because each SIMM contains entire bytes of memory rather than individual bits, determination of the physical fault domain in troubleshooting problems is simpler. You no longer have to narrow the problem to a particular failed bit within a byte. With a SIMM, figuring out the failed byte is enough to determine the physical fault domain. The higher memory densities achieved by SIMMs contribute to their use in smaller systems. They can be used also to place more memory on a single adapter card. Smaller MCA boards make SIMMs necessary for any PS/2 MCA applications because of the limited space for more memory and features. PS/2 system boards are available with 8M or more on a single adapter board, a density that could be achieved only with SIMMs. Over the past few years, the SIMM has replaced the individual memory module in new systems. Virtually any system you purchase today uses SIMMs.

SIMMs usually are constructed with 256K-bit, 1-megabit or 4-megabit chips. SIMMs also are available in different widths and depths. Chapter 7 has more information on different types of SIMMs. Make sure that you can identify the parts in your system so that you can order proper replacements. Many of today's high-memory-content boards are packed with SIMMs. You can purchase a single memory board today with up to 16 full megabytes. This purchase is the only memory board you need for many systems and brings most systems up to full-expansion capacity.

III

Hardware Considerations

Communications Ports and Devices

The basic communications ports in any PC system are the serial and parallel ports. The serial ports are used primarily for devices that must communicate bidirectionally with the system; such devices include modems, mice, scanners, digitizers, or any other device that "talks to" as well as receives information from the PC.

Parallel ports are used primarily for printers and operate normally as one-way ports, although sometimes they can be used bidirectionally. IBM sells a device and software called the Data Migration Facility, which is basically an adapter plug that enables two printer cables to be plugged into one another, and can be used to copy floppy disks from system to system. This device was designed to allow the transfer of data between systems that had different types of floppy drives.

Several companies also manufacture communications programs that perform high-speed transfers between PC systems using serial or parallel ports. For example, you may have a network adapter that plugs into the parallel port to enable your laptop to communicate with a network.

Finally, there are several products currently on the market that make untraditional use of the parallel port. For instance, you can purchase network adapters, floppy disk drives, or tape backup units that use the parallel port.

Serial Ports

The asynchronous serial interface is the primary system-to-system communications device. *Asynchronous* means that no synchronization or clocking signal is present, so characters may be sent with any arbitrary time spacing, as when a typist is providing the data.

Each character is framed by a standard start and stop signal. A single 0 bit, called the start bit, precedes each character to tell the receiving system that the next 8 bits constitute a byte of data. One or two stop bits follow the character to signal that the character has been sent. At the receiving end of the communication, characters are recognized by the start and stop signals instead of being recognized by the timing of their arrival. The asynchronous interface is character-oriented and has about 20 percent overhead for the extra information needed to identify each character.

Serial refers to data sent over one wire with each bit lining up in a series as they are sent. This type of communication is used over the phone system because this system provides one wire for data in each direction. Add-on serial ports for the PC are available from many manufacturers. You usually can find them on one of the available multifunction boards or on a board with at least a parallel port. IBM made single cards with only a serial or a parallel port, but these were not very popular. All IBM AT models that included a hard disk also came with an IBM serial/parallel port board, and all XT models with IBM hard disks came with a single serial port card in slot 8. Figure 8.13 shows the standard 9-pin AT-style serial port, and figure 8.14 shows the more conventional 25-pin version.

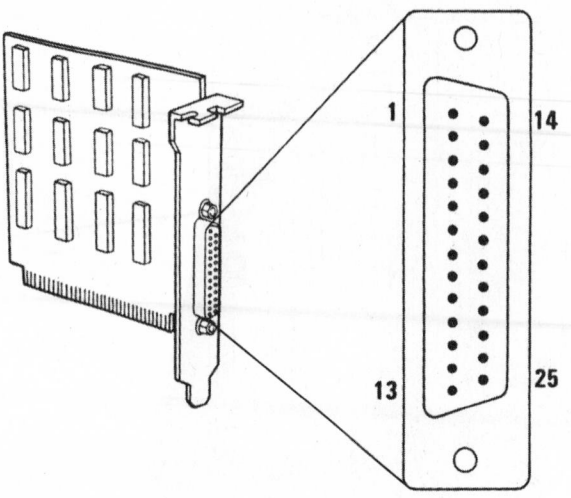

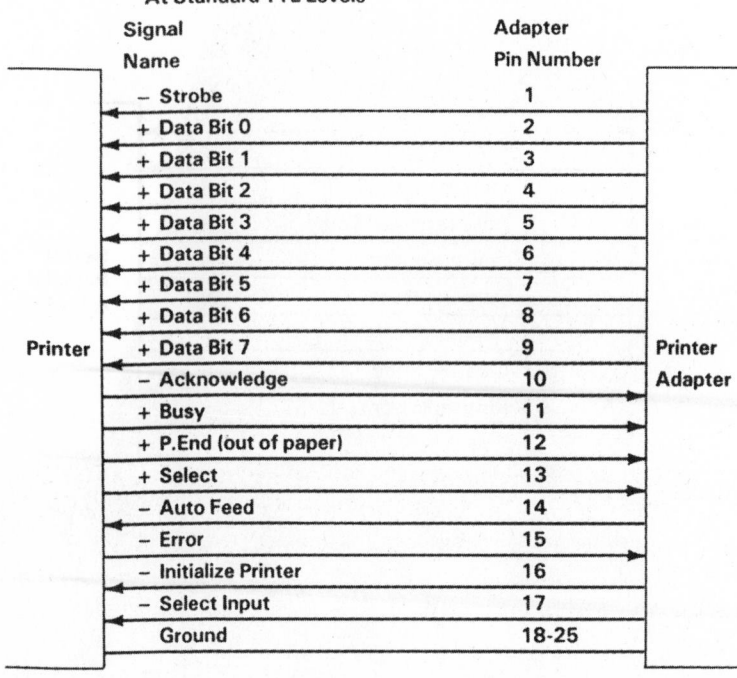

At Standard TTL Levels

	Signal Name	Adapter Pin Number	
	− Strobe	1	
	+ Data Bit 0	2	
	+ Data Bit 1	3	
	+ Data Bit 2	4	
	+ Data Bit 3	5	
	+ Data Bit 4	6	
	+ Data Bit 5	7	
	+ Data Bit 6	8	
Printer	+ Data Bit 7	9	Printer
	− Acknowledge	10	Adapter
	+ Busy	11	
	+ P.End (out of paper)	12	
	+ Select	13	
	− Auto Feed	14	
	− Error	15	
	− Initialize Printer	16	
	− Select Input	17	
	Ground	18-25	

Fig. 8.14

Standard 25-pin serial-port connector specifications.

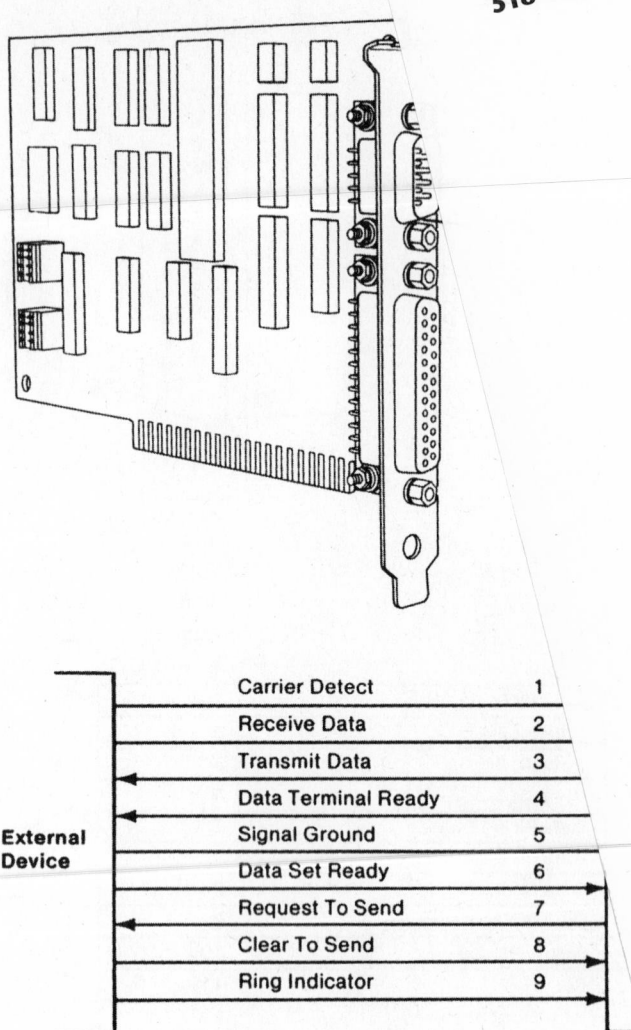

Fig. 8.13

AT-style 9-pin serial-port connector specifications.

Serial ports may connect to a variety of devices such as modems, plotters, printers, other computers, bar code readers, scales, and device control circuits. Basically, anything that needs a two-way connection to the PC uses the industry-standard Reference Standard number 232 revision c (RS-232c) serial port. This device enables data transfer between otherwise incompatible devices.

UART Chips. The heart of any serial port is the Universal Asynchronous Receiver/Transmitter (UART) chip. This chip completely controls breaking the native parallel data within the PC into serial format, and later converting serial data back into the parallel format.

There are several different types of UART chips on the market. The original PC and XT used the 8250 UART, which is still used in many low-price serial cards on the market. In the PC/AT (or other systems based on at least an 80286), the 16450 UART is used. The only difference between these chips is their suitability for high-speed communications. The 16450 is better suited for high-speed communications than the 8250; otherwise, both chips appear identical to most software.

The 16550 UART was the first serial chip used in the PS/2 line. This chip could function as the earlier 16450 and 8250 chips, but it also included a 16-byte buffer which aided in faster communications. Unfortunately, the 16550 also had a few bugs, particularly in the buffer area. These were corrected with the release of the 16550A UART, which is used in all high-performance serial ports.

Because the 16550A is a faster, more reliable chip than its predecessors, it is best to look for serial ports that use it. If you are in doubt about which chip you have in your system, you can use the Microsoft MSD program (provided with Windows or DOS 6) to determine the type of UART you have.

Most UART chips used by IBM are made by National Semiconductor. You also can identify the chips by looking for the largest chip on the serial port card and reading the numbers on that chip. Usually the chips are socketed, and replacing only the chip may be possible. Table 8.13 provides a complete list of UART chips that may be in your system.

> **Note**
>
> The interrupt bug referred to in table 8.13 is a spurious interrupt generated by the 8250 at the end of an access. The ROM BIOS code in the PC and XT has been written to work around this bug. If a chip without the bug is installed, random lockups may occur. The 16450 or 16550(A) chips do not have the interrupt bug, and the AT ROM BIOS was written without any of the bug workarounds in PC or XT systems.

III

Hardware Considerations

Table 8.13 UART Chips in PC or AT Systems

Chip	Description
8250	IBM used this original chip in the PC serial port card. The chip has several bugs, none of which is serious. The PC and XT ROM BIOS are written to anticipate at least one of the bugs. This chip was replaced by the 8250B.
8250A	Do not use the second version of the 8250 in any system. This upgraded chip fixes several bugs in the 8250, including one in the interrupt enable register, but because the PC and XT ROM BIOS expect the bug, this chip does not work properly with those systems. The 8250A should work in an AT system that does not expect the bug, but does not work adequately at 9600 bps.
8250B	The last version of the 8250 fixes bugs from the previous two versions. The interrupt enable bug in the original 8250, expected by the PC and XT ROM BIOS software, has been put back into this chip, making the 8250B the most desirable chip for any non-AT serial port application. The 8250B chip may work in an AT under DOS, but does not run properly at 9600 bps.
16450	IBM selected the higher-speed version of the 8250 for the AT. Because this chip has fixed the interrupt enable bug mentioned earlier, the 16450 does not operate properly in many PC or XT systems, because they expect this bug to be present. OS/2 requires this chip as a minimum, or the serial ports will not function properly. It also adds a scratch-pad register as the highest register. The 16450 is used primarily in AT systems because of its increase in throughput over the 8250B.
16550	This newer UART improves on the 16450. This chip cannot be used in a FIFO (first in, first out) buffering mode because of problems with the design, but it does enable a programmer to use multiple DMA channels and thus increase throughput on an AT or higher class computer system. I highly recommend replacing the 16550 UART with the 16550A.
16550A	This chip is a faster 16450 with a built-in 16-character Transmit and Receive FIFO (first in, first out) buffer that works. It also allows multiple DMA channel access. You should install this chip in your AT system serial port cards if you do any serious communications at 9600 bps or higher. If your communications program makes use of the FIFO, which most will today, it can greatly increase communications speed and eliminate lost characters and data at the higher speeds.

Various manufacturers make versions of the 16550A; National Semiconductor was the first. Its full part number for the 40-pin DIP is NS16550AN or NS16550AFN. Make sure that the part you get is the 16550A, and not the older 16550. You can contact any of the following distributors for the NS16550AN:

> Fry's Electronics
> Jameco Electronics

Serial-Port Configuration

Each time a character is received by a serial port, it has to get the attention of the computer by raising an Interrupt Request Line (IRQ). Eight-bit ISA bus systems have 8 of these lines, and systems with a 16-bit ISA bus have 16 lines. The 8259 interrupt controller chip usually handles these requests for attention. In a standard configuration, COM1 uses IRQ4, and COM2 uses IRQ3.

When a serial port is installed in a system, it must be configured to use specific I/O addresses (called ports), and interrupts (called IRQs for Interrupt ReQuest). The best plan is to follow the existing standards for how these devices should be set up. For configuring serial ports, you should use the addresses and interrupts as indicated in Table 8.14.

Table 8.14 Standard Serial I/O Port Addresses and Interrupts			
System	COMx	Port	IRQ
All	COM1	3F8h	IRQ4
All	COM2	2F8h	IRQ3
ISA bus	COM3	3E8h	IRQ4
ISA bus	COM4	2E8h	IRQ3
ISA bus	COM3	3E0h	IRQ4
ISA bus	COM4	2E0h	IRQ3
ISA bus	COM3	338h	IRQ4
ISA bus	COM4	238h	IRQ3
MCA bus	COM3	3220h	IRQ3
MCA bus	COM4	3228h	IRQ3
MCA bus	COM5	4220h	IRQ3
MCA bus	COM6	4228h	IRQ3
MCA bus	COM7	5220h	IRQ3
MCA bus	COM8	5228h	IRQ3

A problem can occur when the ROM BIOS logs in these ports. If the Power-On Self-Test (POST) does not find a 3F8 serial port but does find a 2F8, then the 2F8 serial port is mistakenly assigned to COM1. The reserved IRQ line for COM1 is IRQ4, but this serial port of 2F8 is using COM2's address, which means that it should be using IRQ3 instead of IRQ4. If you are trying to use BASIC or DOS for COM1 operations, therefore, the serial port or modem cannot work.

Another problem is that IBM never built BIOS support in its original ISA bus systems for COM3 and COM4. Therefore, the DOS MODE command cannot work with serial ports above COM2 because DOS gets its I/O information from the BIOS, which finds out what's installed where in your system during the POST. The POST in these older systems checks only for the first two installed ports. PS/2 systems have an improved BIOS that checks for as many as eight serial ports, although DOS is limited to handling only four of them.

To get around this problem, most communications software and some serial peripherals (such as mice) support higher COM ports by addressing them directly, rather than making DOS function calls. For example, the communications program PROCOMM supports the additional ports even if your BIOS or DOS does not. Of course, if your system or software does not support these extra ports or you need to redirect data using the MODE command, trouble arises.

III

Hardware Considerations

A couple of utilities enable you to append your COM port information to the BIOS, making the ports DOS-accessible. A program called Port Finder is one of the best, and is available in the "general hardware" data library of the IBMHW forum on CompuServe. Port Finder also can be obtained directly from the manufacturer at the following address:

    Port Finder

Port Finder activates the extra ports by giving the BIOS the addresses and providing utilities for swapping the addresses among the different ports. Address-swapping allows programs that don't support COM3 and COM4 to access them. Software that already directly addresses these additional ports usually is unaffected.

Extra ports, however, must use separate interrupts. If you are going to use two COM ports at one time, they should be on opposite interrupts. Using the standard port and interrupt configurations, the possibilities for simultaneous operation are as follows:

    COM1 (IRQ4) and COM2 (IRQ3)

    COM1 (IRQ4) and COM4 (IRQ3)

    COM2 (IRQ3) and COM3 (IRQ4)

    COM3 (IRQ4) and COM4 (IRQ3)

Divide your COM port inputs into these groups of two, pairing serial devices that won't be used simultaneously on the same interrupt, and devices that will be used at the same time on different interrupts. Note again that PS/2 Micro Channel Architecture systems are entirely exempt from these types of problems because they have a BIOS that looks for the additional ports, and because the MCA bus can share interrupts without conflicts.

To configure serial boards in ISA bus systems, you probably will have to set jumpers and switches. Because each board on the market is different, you always should consult the OEM manual for that particular card if you need to know how the card should or can be configured. IBM includes this information with each card's documentation. IBM also offers technical-reference options and adapters manuals as well as hardware-maintenance and service manuals, which also cover in detail all the jumper and switch settings for IBM adapter cards. Other manufacturers simply include with the card a manual that describes the card and includes the configuration information. The PS/2 MCA bus systems have an automatic or software-driven configuration that eliminates these configuration hassles.

Modem Standards

Bell Labs and the CCITT have set standards for modem protocols. Although the CCITT is actually a French term, it translates in English to the Consultative Committee on International Telephone and Telegraph. A protocol is a method by which two different entities agree to communicate. Bell Labs no longer sets new standards for modems, although several of its older standards are still used. Most modems built in the last few years conform to the CCITT standards. The CCITT is an international body of technical experts responsible for developing data communications standards for the world. The group falls under the organizational umbrella of the United Nations, and its members include representatives from major modem manufacturers, common carriers (such as AT&T), and governmental bodies.

The CCITT establishes communications standards and protocols in many areas, so one modem often adheres to several CCITT standards, depending on its various features and capabilities. Modem standards can be grouped into the following three areas:

- Modulation standards

    Bell 103

    Bell 212A

    CCITT V.21

    CCITT V.22bis

    CCITT V.29

    CCITT V.32

    CCITT V.32bis

- Error-correction standards

    CCITT V.42

- Data-compression standards

    V.42bis

Other standards have been developed by different companies, and not Bell Labs or the CCITT. These are sometimes called *proprietary standards,* even though most of these companies publish full specifications on their protocols so that other manufacturers can develop modems to work with them. The following list shows some of the proprietary standards that have become fairly popular.

Proprietary standards

    Modulation
        HST
        PEP
        DIS

    Error correction
        MNP 1-4
        Hayes V-series

    Data compression
        MNP 5
        CSP

Almost all modems today claim to be "Hayes compatible," which does not refer to any communication protocol, but instead to the commands required to operate the modem. Because almost every modem uses the Hayes command set, this compatibility is a given and should not really affect your decisions about modems.

Modulation Standards. Modems start with *modulation*, which is the electronic signaling method used by the modem (from modulator to demodulator). Modems must use the same modulation method to understand each other. Each data rate uses a different modulation method, and sometimes more than one method exists for a particular rate.

The three most popular modulation methods are frequency shift keying (FSK), phase shift keying (PSK), and quadrature amplitude modulation (QAM). FSK is a form of frequency modulation, otherwise known as FM. By causing and monitoring frequency changes in a signal sent over the phone line, two modems can send information. PSK is a form of phase modulation, in which the timing of the carrier signal wave is altered and the frequency stays the same. QAM is a modulation technique that combines phase changes with signal amplitude variations, resulting in a signal that can carry more information than the other methods.

Baud versus Bits Per Second (bps). Baud rate and the bit rate are often confused in discussions about modems. Baud rate is the rate at which a signal between two devices changes in one second. If a signal between two modems can change frequency or phase at a rate of 300 times per second, for example, that device is said to communicate at 300 baud. Sometimes a single modulation change is used to carry a single bit. In that case, 300 baud would also equal 300 bits per second (bps). If the modem could signal two bit values for each signal change, the bit-per-second rate would be twice the baud rate, or 600 bps at 300 baud. Most modems transmit several bits per baud, so that the actual baud rate is much slower than the bit-per-second rate. In fact, people usually use the term *baud* incorrectly. We normally are not interested in the raw baud rate but in the bit-per-second rate, which is the true gauge of communications speed.

Bell 103. Bell 103 is a U.S. and Canadian 300 bps modulation standard. It uses frequency shift keying (FSK) modulation at 300 baud to transmit one bit per baud. Most higher-speed modems will communicate using this protocol even though it is largely obsolete.

Bell 212A. Bell 212A is the U.S. and Canadian 1200 bps modulation standard. It uses differential phase shift keying (DPSK) at 600 baud to transmit two bits per baud.

V.21. V.21 is an international data-transmission standard for 300 bps communications similar to Bell 103. Because of some differences in the frequencies used, Bell 103 modems are not compatible with V.21 modems. This standard is used primarily outside of the United States.

V.22. V.22 is an international 1200 bps data-transmission standard. This standard is similar to the Bell 212A standard, but is incompatible in some areas, especially in answering a call. This standard was used primarily outside of the United States.

V.22bis. V.22bis is a data-transmission standard for 2400 bps communications. *Bis* is Latin for *second*, indicating that this data transmission is an improvement to or follows V.22. This data transmission is an international standard for 2400 bps and is used inside and outside the United States. V.22bis uses quadrature amplitude modulation (QAM) at 600 baud and transmits four bits per baud to·achieve 2400 bps.

V.23. V.23 is a split data-transmission standard, operating at 1200 bps in one direction and 75 bps in the reverse direction. Therefore, the modem is only "pseudo-full-duplex," meaning that it can transmit data in both directions simultaneously, but not at the maximum data rate. This standard was developed to lower the cost of 1200 bps modem technology, which was expensive in the early 1980s. This standard was used primarily in Europe.

V.29. V.29 is a data-transmission standard at 9600 bps, which defines a half duplex (one-way) modulation technique. This standard is generally used in Group III facsimile (FAX) transmissions, and only rarely in modems. Because V.29 is a half-duplex method, it is substantially easier to implement this high-speed standard than to implement a high-speed full-duplex standard. As a modem standard, V.29 has not been fully defined, so V.29 modems of different brands seldom can communicate with each other. This does not affect FAX machines, which have a fully defined standard.

V.32. V.32 is a full-duplex (two-way) data transmission standard at 9600 bps. It is a full modem standard, and also includes forward error-correcting and negotiation standards. V.32 uses TCQAM (trellis coded quadrature amplitude modulation) at 2400 baud to transmit 4 bits per baud, resulting in the 9600 bps transmission speed. The trellis coding is a special forward error-correction technique that creates an additional bit for each packet of 4. This extra check bit is used to allow on-the-fly error correction to take place at the other end. It also greatly increases the resistance of V.32 to noise on the line. In the past, V.32 has been expensive to implement because the technology it requires is complex. Because a one-way 9600-bps stream uses almost the entire bandwidth of the phone line, V.32 modems implement *echo cancellation*, meaning that they cancel out the overlapping signal that their own modems transmit and just listen to the other modems, signal. This procedure is complicated and costly. Recent advances in lower-cost chipsets make these modems inexpensive, so they are becoming the de facto 9600 bps standard.

V.32bis. V.32bis is a relatively new 14,400 bps extension to V.32. This protocol uses TCQAM modulation at 2400 baud to transmit 6 bits per baud, for an effective rate of 14,400 bits per second. The trellis coding makes the connection more reliable. This protocol is also a full-duplex modulation protocol, with fallback to V.32 if the phone line is impaired. Although this high-speed standard is newly developed, it is rapidly becoming the communications standard for dial-up lines because of its excellent performance and resistance to noise. I recommend the V.32bis-type modem.

V.32fast. V.32fast is a new standard being proposed to the CCITT. V.32fast will be an extension to V.32 and V.32bis but will offer a transmission speed of 28,800 bits per second. This standard, when approved, probably will be as advanced as modem communications ever gets. Looming on the horizon is that the phone system eventually will be

III

Hardware Considerations

digital. All further development on analog transmission schemes will end, and new digital modems will be developed. V.32fast will be the best and last of the analog protocols when it debuts.

Error-Correction Protocols. *Error correction* refers to a capability that some modems have to identify errors during a transmission, and to automatically resend data that appears to have been damaged in transit. For error correction to work, both modems must adhere to the same correction standard. Fortunately, most modem manufacturers follow the same error-correction standards.

V.42. V.42 is an error-correction protocol, with fallback to MNP 4. MNP stands for Microcom Networking Protocol (covered later in this chapter), and Version 4 is an error-correction protocol as well. Because the V.42 standard includes MNP compatibility through Class 4, all MNP 4 compatible modems can establish error-controlled connections with V.42 modems. This standard uses a protocol called LAPM (Link Access Procedure for Modems). LAPM, like MNP, copes with phone-line impairments by automatically retransmitting data corrupted during transmission, assuring that only error-free data passes through the modems. V.42 is considered to be better than MNP 4 because it offers about a 20 percent higher transfer rate due to more intelligent algorithms.

Data-Compression Standards. *Data compression* refers to a built-in capability in some modems to compress the data they're sending, thus saving time and money for long-distance modem users. Depending on the type of files that are sent, data can be compressed to 50 percent of its original size, effectively doubling the speed of the modem.

V.42bis. V.42bis is a CCITT data-compression standard similar to MNP Class 5, but providing about 35 percent better compression. V.42bis is not actually compatible with MNP Class 5, but nearly all V.42bis modems include the MNP 5 data-compression capability as well.

This protocol can sometimes quadruple throughput, depending on the compression technique used. This fact has led to some mildly false advertising: for example, a 2400-bps V.42bis modem might advertise "9600 bps throughput" by including V.42bis as well, but this would be possible in only extremely optimistic cases, such as in sending text files that are very loosely packed. In the same manner, many 9600-bps V.42bis makers now advertise "up to 38.4K bps throughput" by virtue of the compression. Just make sure that you see the truth behind such claims.

V.42bis is superior to MNP 5 because it analyzes the data first, and then determines whether compression would be useful. V.42bis only compresses data that needs compression. Files found on bulletin board systems are often compressed already (using ARC, PKZIP, and similar programs). Further attempts at compressing already compressed data can increase the size of the data and slow things down. MNP 5 always attempts to compress the data, which slows down throughput on previously compressed files. V.42bis, however, will compress only what will benefit from the compression.

To negotiate a standard connection using V.42bis, V.42 also must be present. Therefore, a modem with V.42bis data compression is assumed to include V.42 error correction. These two protocols combined result in an error-free connection that has the maximum data compression possible.

Proprietary Standards. In addition to the industry standard protocols for modulation, error correction, and data compression that are generally set forth or approved by the CCITT, several protocols in these areas were invented by various companies and included in their products without any official endorsement by the CCITT. Some of these protocols are quite popular and have become pseudo-standards of their own.

The most successful proprietary protocols are the MNP (Microcom Networking Protocols) that were developed by Microcom. These error-correction and data-compression protocols are widely supported by other modem manufacturers as well. Another company successful in establishing proprietary protocols as limited standards is USRobotics, with its HST (high speed technology) modulation protocols. Because of an aggressive marketing campaign with bulletin board system operators, it captured a large portion of the market with its products.

This section will examine these and other proprietary modem protocols.

HST. The HST is a 14400 and 9600 bps modified half-duplex proprietary modulation protocol used by USRobotics. Though common in bulletin board systems, the HST is probably destined for extinction within the next few years as V.32 modems become more competitive in price. HST modems run at 9600 bps or 14400 bps in one direction, and 300 or 450 bps in the other direction. This is an ideal protocol for interactive sessions. Because echo-cancellation circuitry is not required, costs are lower.

USRobotics also makes modems that use standard protocols as well as *dual standards*— modems that incorporate both V.32bis and HST protocols. This gives you the best of the standard and proprietary worlds and allows you to connect to virtually any other system at that system's maximum communications rate. I use and recommend the dual-standard modems.

DIS. The DIS is a 9600-bps proprietary modulation protocol by CompuCom, which uses dynamic impedance stabilization (DIS), with claimed superiority in noise rejection over V.32. Implementation appears to be very inexpensive, but like HST, only one company makes modems with the DIS standard. Because of the lower costs of V.32 and V.32bis, this proprietary standard will likely disappear.

MNP. MNP (Microcom Networking Protocol) offers end-to-end error correction, meaning that the modems are capable of detecting transmission errors and requesting retransmission of corrupted data. Some levels of MNP also provide data compression.

As MNP evolved, different classes of the standard were defined, describing the extent to which a given MNP implementation supports the protocol. Most current implementations support Classes 1 through 5. Higher classes usually are unique to modems manufactured by Microcom, Inc. because they are proprietary.

MNP generally is used for its error-correction capabilities, but MNP Classes 4 and 5 also provide performance increases, with Class 5 offering real-time data compression. The lower classes of MNP usually are not important to you as a modem user, but they are included for completeness in the following list:

■ MNP Class 1 (block mode) uses asynchronous, byte-oriented, half-duplex (one-way) transmission. This method provides about 70 percent efficiency and error correction only, so it's rarely used today.

■ MNP Class 2 (stream mode) uses asynchronous, byte-oriented, full-duplex (two-way) transmission. This class also provides error correction only. Because of protocol overhead (the time it takes to establish the protocol and operate it), throughput at Class 2 is only about 84 percent of that for a connection without MNP, delivering about 202 cps (characters per second) at 2400 bps (240 cps is the theoretical maximum). Class 2 is rarely used today.

■ MNP Class 3 incorporates Class 2, and is more efficient. It uses a synchronous, bit-oriented, full-duplex method. The improved procedure yields throughput about 108 percent of that of a modem without MNP, delivering about 254 cps at 2400 bps.

■ MNP Class 4 is a performance-enhancement class that uses Adaptive Packet Assembly and Optimized Data Phase techniques. Class 4 improves throughput and performance by about 5 percent, although actual increases depend on the type of call and connection, and can be as high as 25 to 50 percent.

■ MNP Class 5 is a data-compression protocol that uses a real-time adaptive algorithm. It can increase throughput up to 50 percent, but the actual performance of Class 5 depends on the type of data being sent. Raw text files allow the highest increase, although program files cannot be compressed as much and the increase is smaller. On precompressed data (files already compressed with ARC, PKZIP, and so on), MNP 5 *decreases* performance, and therefore is often disabled on BBS systems.

V-Series. The Hayes V-series is a proprietary error-correction protocol by Hayes that was used in some of its modems. Since the advent of lower-cost V.32 and V.32bis modems (even from Hayes), the V-series has all but become extinct. These modems used a modified V.29 protocol, sometimes called a ping-pong protocol because it has one high-speed channel and one low-speed channel that alternate back and forth.

CSP. The CSP (CompuCom Speed Protocol) is an error-correction and data-compression protocol available on CompuCom DIS modems.

FAXModem Standards. Facsimile technology is a science unto itself, although it has many similarities to data communications. These similarities have led to the combination of data and faxes into the same modem. You can now purchase a single board that will send and receive both data and fax; all of the major modem manufacturers have models that support this capability.

Over the years, the CCITT has set international standards for fax transmission. This has led to the grouping of faxes into one of four groups. Each group (I through IV) uses different technology and standards for transmitting and receiving faxes. Groups I and II are relatively slow and provide results that are unacceptable by today's standards. Group III is the standard in use today by virtually all fax machines, including those combined with modems. Whereas Groups I through III are analog in nature (similar to modems), Group IV is digital and designed for use with ISDN or other digital networks. Because the telephone system has not converted to a digital system yet, there are very few Group IV fax systems available.

If you are interested in detailed information on the technical fax specifications, you can contact either of two places:

Telecommunications Industry Association

or

Global Engineering Documents

Group III Fax. There are two general subdivisions within the Group III fax standard—Class 1 and Class 2. Many times you will hear about a FAXModem supporting Group III, Class 1 fax communications. This simply indicates the protocols which the board is able to send and receive. If your FAXModem does this, it can communicate with most of the other fax machines in the world. In FAXModems, the Class 1 specification is implemented by an additional group of modem commands that the modem translates and acts upon.

Earlier you learned about the V.29 modulation standard. As stated in that section, this standard is used for Group III fax transmissions.

Modem Recommendations. Today the cost of 9600 bps modems has dropped to where you can get one for just over $100. You can even find 14400 bps modems for under $200.

Today most modems come with multiple forms of error correction or data compression. Based on the discussions earlier in this chapter, you should search for the modem that offers the best combination of speed, error correction, and data compression. Probably the most universal modem is the USRobotics Courier HST Dual Standard, a high-speed modem that uses both the industry standard ultra-high speed V.32bis protocol and U.S. Robotics' own transmission standard as well. This modem also includes V.42bis, which enables throughput to hit 38.4K bps with the right data. The multiple protocols and standards in this modem make possible connections to almost any other modem at its full capability. You are limited only by the speed and protocols of the modem you are calling. This device's only drawback is its price (which has been coming down lately), but its flexibility makes it cost effective.

Secrets of Modem Negotiation. If you are curious about the complex negotiations that occur when two modems connect, two detailed descriptions of *modem handshaking* follow. The two examples of connections use V.22bis and V.32. These sequences may differ slightly depending on your modem, and can get more complicated when you combine different modem types into one box.

This information is not particularly useful, but I find it fascinating and valuable to have a deeper understanding of how amazing some of the technology that we take for granted really is.

Making a V.22bis connection between two modems involves the following sequence of events:

1. The answering modem detects a ring, goes off-hook, and waits for at least two seconds of *billing delay* (required by phone company rules so that no data passes before the network recognizes that the call has been connected).

2. The answering modem transmits an *answer tone* (described in CCITT Recommendation V.25, occurs at 2100 Hz, and lasts 3.3 ± 0.7 seconds). The answer tone tells manual-dial originators that they have reached a modem and can put their calling modem in data mode, and informs the network that data is going to be transferred so that echo suppressors in the network can be disabled. If the echo suppressors remain enabled, you cannot transmit in both directions at the same time. (The originating modem remains silent throughout this period.)

3. The answering modem goes silent for 75 ± 20 milliseconds (ms) to separate the answer tone from the that follow signals.

4. The answering modem transmits unscrambled binary 1s at 1200 bits per second (USB1), which cause the static, or hash sound, you hear after the answer tone. This sound is slightly higher in pitch than the answer tone because the signal's major components are at 2250 and 2550 Hz.

5. The originating modem detects the USB1 signal in 155 ± 10 ms, and remains silent for 456 ± 10 ms.

6. The originating modem transmits unscrambled double-digit 00s and 11s at 1200 bits (S1) for 100 ± 3 ms. A Bell 212 or V.22 modem does not transmit this S1 signal, and it is by the presence or absence of this single 100 ms signal that V.22bis knows whether to fall back to 1200 bps operation.

7. When the answering modem (which is still transmitting the USB1 signal) detects the S1 signal from the originator, it also sends 100 ms of S1 so that the originating modem knows that the answerer is capable of 2400 bps operation.

8. The originating modem then switches to sending scrambled binary 1s at 1200 bits (SB1). Scrambling has nothing to do with encryption or security, but is simply a method by which the signal is *whitened*, or randomized, to even out the power across the entire bandwidth. *White noise* is a term given by engineers to totally random noise patterns.

9. The answering modem switches to sending SB1 for 500 ms.

10. The answering modem switches to sending scrambled 1s at 2400 bps for 200 ms. After that, it is ready to pass data.

11. Six hundred ms after the originating modem hears SB1 from the answerer, it switches to sending scrambled 1s at 2400 bps. It does this for 200 ms, and then is ready to pass data.

The signals involved in a V.32 connection are more complicated than V.22bis because of the need to measure the total round-trip delay in the circuit so that the echo cancellers work. Making a V.32 connection involves the following sequence of events:

1. The answering modem detects a ring, goes off-hook, and waits two seconds (the billing delay).

2. The answering modem transmits a V.25 answer tone, but it is different from the previous example. The phase of signal is reversed every 450 ms, which sounds like little clicks in the signal. These phase reversals inform the network that the modems themselves are going to do echo cancellation, and that any echo cancellers in the network should be disabled so as not to interfere with the modems.

3. The originating V.32 modem does not wait for the end of the answer tone. After one second, it responds with an 1800 Hz tone, which in V.32 is known as signal AA. Sending this signal before the end of the answer tone allows the answering modem to know, very early, that it is talking to another V.32 modem.

4. When the answer tone ends (3.3 ± 0.7 seconds), if the answering modem heard signal AA, it proceeds to try to connect as V.32 immediately. If it did not hear AA, it first tries, for three seconds, to connect as a V.22bis modem (sends signal USB1 and waits for a response). If it does not get a response to USB1, it goes back to trying to connect as a V.32 modem because of the possibility that the calling V.32 modem didn't hear the answer tone, was manually dialed and switched to data mode late, or is an older V.32 model that does not respond to the answer tone.

5. To connect in V.32, the answering modem sends signal AC, which is 600 and 3000 Hz sent together, for at least 64 *symbol intervals* (1/2400 of a second). It then reverses the phase of the signal, making it into signal CA.

6. When the originating modem detects this phase reversal, in 64 ± 2 symbol intervals, it reverses the phase of its own signal, making AA into CC.

7. When the answer modem detects this phase reversal (in 64 ± 2 symbol intervals), it again reverses the phase of its signal, making CA back into AC. This exchange of phase reversals allows the modems to accurately time the total propagation (round trip) delay of the circuit so that the echo cancellers can be set to properly cancel signal echoes.

8. The modems go into a half-duplex exchange of training signals, to train the adaptive equalizers, test the quality of the phone line, and agree on the data rate to be used. The answering modem transmits first, from 650 to 3525 ms, and then goes silent.

9. The originating modem responds with a similar signal, but then leaves its signal on, while the answering modem responds one more time, establishing the final agreed-on data rate.

III

Hardware Considerations

10. Both modems then switch to sending scrambled binary 1 (marks) for at least 128 symbol intervals, and then are ready to pass data.

As you can see, these procedures are quite complicated; considering the quality of a normal dial-up line these days, it is amazing that these devices actually work! Although you do not need to understand these communications protocols to use a modem, you can get an idea of what you're hearing when the connection is being established.

Parallel Ports

A parallel port has eight lines for sending all the bits for one byte of data simultaneously across eight wires. This interface is fast and usually is reserved for printers rather than computer-to-computer communications. The only problem with parallel ports is that cables cannot be extended for any great length without amplifying the signal, or else errors will occur in the data.

Over the years, four types of parallel ports have evolved: Original, Type 1, Type 3, and Enhanced Parallel Port. The following sections discuss each of these types.

Original Unidirectional. The original IBM PC did not have different types of parallel ports available. The only one available was the parallel port used to send information from the computer to a device, such as a printer. This is not to say that bidirectional parallel ports were not available; indeed, they were common in other computers on the market and with hobbiest computers at the time.

The unidirectional nature of the original PC parallel port is consistent with its primary use—that is, sending data to a printer. There were times, however, when it was desirable to have a bidirectional port—for example, when you need feedback from a printer, which is common with PostScript printers. This could not be done with the original unidirectional ports.

Type 1 Bidirectional. With the introduction of the PS/2 in 1987, IBM introduced a bidirectional parallel port. This opened the way for true communications between the computer and the peripheral across the parallel port. This was done by defining a few of the previously unused pins in the parallel connector, and defining a status bit to indicate which direction information was traveling across the channel.

In IBM documentation, this original PS/2 port became known as a Type 1 parallel port. Other vendors also introduced third-party ports that were compatible with the Type 1 port; they were based on chips from Chips & Technologies, Inc. Unless you specifically configure the port for bidirectional use, however, the PS/2 Type 1 port functions the same as the original unidirectional port in the PC. This configuration is done with the configuration disk that accompanies the PS/2.

Type 3 DMA. With the introduction of the PS/2 Models 57, 90, and 95, IBM introduced the Type 3 parallel port. This port featured greater throughput by use of *direct memory access* (DMA) techniques. You may be wondering why IBM skipped from Type 1 to Type 3. In reality, they did not. There is a Type 2 parallel port, and it served as a predecessor to the Type 3. It is only slightly less capable, but was never widely used in any IBM systems.

The types of parallel ports described earlier all use the CPU to control operations. In these ports, the CPU sends one byte to the I/O addresses used by the port, test to see if it was sent, and then send the next. This process continues until all the information to be sent has been processed. The Type 3 port, however, allows you to define a block of memory that you want transmitted (perhaps a file stored in memory), and then allow the port controller to pace the sending of the information. This frees the CPU to perform other tasks, thereby increasing throughput.

You can also apply DMA techniques to receiving information through the parallel port. The information received is written directly to memory, where it can later be processed as the CPU is available.

Enhanced Parallel Port (EPP) Specification. This is a newer specification from Intel, sometimes referred to as the *Fast Mode parallel port*. While the IBM Type 3 port is designed to allow you to move large amounts of data without tying up the CPU, the Fast Mode port is aimed at quick bidirectional communication with intelligent peripherals. To do this, a Fast Mode port, when operating in that mode, redefines the parallel pins so they actually become bus control lines to augment communication and control between your system and the external device.

Parallel Port Configuration

Parallel-port configuration is not as complicated as it is for serial ports. Even the original IBM PC has BIOS support for three LPT ports, and DOS has always had this support as well. Table 8.15 shows the standard I/O address and interrupt settings for parallel port use.

Table 8.15 Parallel Interface I/O Port Addresses and Interrupts				
	LPTx		**I/O**	
System	**Std.**	**Alt**	**Port**	**IRQ**
8-bit ISA		LPT1	3BCh	IRQ7
8-bit ISA	LPT1	LPT2	378h	None
8-bit ISA	LPT2	LPT3	278h	None
16-bit ISA		LPT1	3BCh	IRQ7
16-bit ISA	LPT1	LPT2	378h	IRQ5
16-bit ISA	LPT2	LPT3	278h	None
All MCA	LPT1		3BCh	IRQ7
All MCA	LPT2		378h	IRQ7
All MCA	LPT3		278h	IRQ7

Because the BIOS and DOS have always provided three definitions for parallel ports, problems with older systems are infrequent. However, problems can arise from the lack of available interrupt-driven ports for the ISA bus systems. Normally an interrupt-driven port is not absolutely required for printing operations; in fact, many programs do not use the interrupt-driven capability. However, many programs do use the interrupt, such as network print programs and other types of background or spooler-type printer programs. Also, any high-speed laser-printer utility programs would often use the interrupt capabilities to allow for printing. If you use these types of applications on a port that is not interrupt driven, you see the printing slow to a crawl, if it works at all. The only solution is to use an interrupt-driven port. Note that because MCA bus PS/2 systems can share interrupts, they are completely exempt from this type of problem, and all parallel ports in these systems are interrupt driven on IRQ7.

To configure parallel ports in ISA bus systems, you probably will have to set jumpers and switches. Because each board on the market is different, you always should consult the OEM manual for that particular card if you need to know how the card should or can be configured. IBM includes this information with each card's documentation. IBM also offers technical-reference options and adapters manuals as well as hardware-maintenance and service manuals, which also cover in detail all the jumper and switch settings for IBM adapter cards. Other manufacturers simply include with the card a manual that describes the card and includes the configuration information. The PS/2 MCA bus systems have an automatic or software-driven configuration that eliminates these configuration hassles.

Parallel Port Devices. As already mentioned, the original IBM PC envisioned that the parallel port would only be used for communicating with a printer. Over the years, the number of devices that can be used with a parallel port has increased tremendously. You can now find everything from tape backup units to LAN adapters to CD-ROMs that connect through your parallel port.

Perhaps one of the most common uses for bidirectional parallel ports is to transfer data between your system and another, such as a laptop computer. If both systems utilize a Type 3 port, you can actually communicate at rates of up to 2M per second, which rivals the speed of some hard disk drives. This capability has led to an increase in software to serve this niche of the market. If you are interested in such software (and the parallel ports necessary to facilitate the software), you should refer to the reviews that periodically appear in sources such as PC Magazine.

Detecting Serial and Parallel Ports with DEBUG

If you cannot tell which ports (parallel and serial) the computer is using, check for the I/O ports by using DEBUG.

To use DEBUG, follow these steps :

1. Run DEBUG.

2. At the DEBUG prompt, type **D 40:0** and press Enter. This step displays the hexadecimal values of the active I/O port addresses, first serial and then parallel. Figure 8.15 shows a sample address.

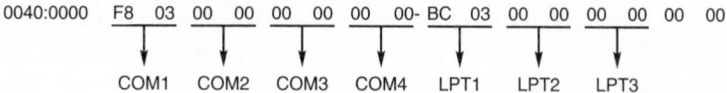

Fig. 8.15
DEBUG used to display installed serial and parallel port I/O port addresses.

The address for each port is shown in the corresponding position. Because addresses are stored as words, the byte values are swapped and should be read backward. This example indicates one serial port installed at 03F8 and one parallel port installed at 03BC.

3. To exit DEBUG, press Q and press Enter.

Testing Serial Ports

You can perform several tests on serial and parallel ports. The two most common types of tests involve software only, or both hardware and software. The software-only tests are done with diagnostic programs such as Microsoft's MSD, while the hardware and software tests involve using a wrap plug to perform loopback testing.

Microsoft Diagnostics (MSD). MSD is a diagnostic program supplied with MS-DOS 6 or Microsoft Windows. Early versions of the program were also shipped with some Microsoft applications such as Microsoft Word (for DOS).

To use MSD, switch to the directory in which it is located. This is not necessary, of course, if the directory containing the program is in your search path—which is often the case with the DOS 6- or Windows-provided versions of MSD. Then simply type **MSD** at the DOS prompt, and press Enter. Shortly you will see the MSD screen.

Select the option entitled Serial Ports by pressing S. Notice that you are provided information about what type of serial chip you have in your system, as well as information about what ports are available. If any of the ports are in use (for example, a mouse), that information is provided as well.

MSD is helpful in at least determining if your serial ports are responding. If MSD cannot determine the existence of a port, then it will not provide the report indicating the port exists. This sort of "look and see" test is the first action I usually take to determine why a port is not responding.

Advanced Diagnostics Using Loopback Testing. One of the most useful tests is the *loopback* test, which can be used to ensure the correct function of the serial port, as well as any attached cables. Loopback tests are basically internal (digital), or external (analog). Internal tests can be run by simply unplugging any cables from the port and executing the test via a diagnostics program.

The external loopback test is more effective. This test requires that a special loopback connector or wrap plug be attached to the port in question. When the test is run, the port is used to send data out to the loopback plug, which simply routes the data back into the port's receive pins so that the port is transmitting and receiving at the same

time. A loopback or wrap plug is nothing more than a cable doubled back on itself. Most diagnostics programs that run this type of test include the loopback plug, and if not, these types of plugs can be easily purchased or even built. See the Appendix in this book for the necessary diagrams to construct your own wrap plugs.

If you want to purchase a wrap plug, I recommend the IBM tri-connector wrap plug. IBM sells this triple plug, as well as individual wrap plugs under the following part numbers:

Description	IBM Part Number
Parallel-port wrap plug, 25-pin	8529280
Serial-port wrap plug, 9-pin (AT)	8286126
Tri-connector wrap plug	72X8546

As for the diagnostics software, IBM's own Advanced Diagnostics can be used to test serial ports. If you have a PS/2 system with Micro Channel Architecture, IBM has already given you the Advanced Diagnostics on the Reference disk that came with the system. To activate this normally hidden Advanced Diagnostics, press Ctrl-A at the Reference Disk's main menu. For IBM systems that are not MCA, the Advanced Diagnostics must be purchased.

For any system, you can use the serial port tests in the comprehensive diagnostics packages sold by several companies as a replacement for the IBM- (or other manufacturer) supplied Advanced Diagnostics. Programs such as Micro-Scope from Micro 2000, Service Diagnostics from Landmark, or QA-Plus FE from Diagsoft all have this type of test as part of their package. All include the necessary three wrap plugs as well. See the vendor list or Chapter 13, "System Diagnostics," for more information on these programs.

For testing serial ports, as well as any modems that are attached, I highly recommend an inexpensive ($19.95) program called the Modem Doctor. This comprehensive serial port and modem test program enables you to go beyond the simple loopback tests and test the complete communications system, including the cable and modem. The program is especially useful with the USRobotics modems or any other modem with a Hayes-compatible command structure. The program takes command of the modem and runs a variety of tests to determine whether it is functioning correctly. You can get the Modem Doctor at the following address:

>The Modem Doctor
>Hank Volpe

Testing Parallel Ports

Testing parallel ports is, in most cases, simpler than testing serial ports. The procedures you use are effectively the same as those used for serial ports, except that when you use the diagnostics software, you choose the obvious choices for parallel ports rather than serial ports.

Not only are the software tests similar, but the hardware tests require the proper plugs for the loopback tests on the parallel port. You can use the tri-connector wrap plug recommended earlier, or you can purchase an individual parallel port wrap plug. If you want the individual plug, ask for IBM part number 8529228.

Diagnosing Problems with Serial and Parallel Ports

To diagnose problems with serial and parallel ports, you need diagnostics software and a wrap plug for each type of port. The diagnostics software works with the wrap plugs to send signals through the port. The plug wraps around the port so that the same port receives the information it sent. This information is verified to ensure that the port works properly. For further information, see Chapter 14, "Hardware Troubleshooting Guide."

Many problems stem from using the wrong serial port card in a system. Most clone manufacturers are guilty of this practice in AT systems because the right card is more expensive. The big difference in serial ports is in the UART chip, described earlier in this chapter.

Some computers (particularly 4.77 MHz, 8088 machines) are not fast enough to support the higher communications speeds, especially 19200 or 38400 bps. Even if you have a faster system, if you are running a program that makes heavy use of extended memory, such as a RAM disk or a cache, you may lose characters. This problem occurs primarily on 286 machines. With some programs, such as VDisk, it helps to reduce the sector size or the number of sectors transferred at a time (transfer block size) helps.

Some terminate-and-stay-resident (TSR) programs interfere with communications programs. If you are having trouble with a communications program, try to reboot with no CONFIG.SYS or AUTOEXEC.BAT file, to eliminate the TSR programs. Then you can retest the system.

Chapter Summary

This chapter discussed and examined several main peripherals that work with your systems. Descriptions were given of the various types of peripherals, along with some recommendations. This chapter also has examined memory adapters and the available memory configurations. Finally, the chapter has looked at the serial and parallel communications ports on a system, with particular attention to modems.

III

Hardware Considerations

Chapter 9

Floppy Disk Drives

This chapter examines, in detail, floppy disk drives and disks. It explores how floppy disk drives and disks function, how DOS uses a disk, what types of disk drives and disks are available, and how to properly install and service drives and disks. You learn about all the types of drives available for today's personal computer systems; these drives include both the 5 1/4-inch and 3 1/2-inch drives in all different versions. The chapter discusses also the newer, Extra-high-Density (ED) 3 1/2-inch disks. Also discussed are several upgrade options including the addition of the 3 1/2-inch drives to the early PC-family systems, which enables them to be compatible with many newer systems, as well as upgrading newer systems to support the ED drives and disks.

Drive Components

This section describes the components that make up a typical floppy drive and examines how these components operate together to read and write data—the physical operation of the drive. All floppy drives, regardless of type, consist of several basic common components. To properly install and service a disk drive, you must be able to identify these components and understand their functions (see fig. 9.1).

Read/Write Heads

A floppy disk drive normally has two read/write heads, making the modern floppy disk drive a double-sided drive. A head exists for each side of the disk, and both heads are used for reading and writing on their respective disk sides. At one time, single-sided drives were available for PC systems (the original PC had such drives), but today single-sided drives are a fading memory (see fig. 9.2).

> **Note**
>
> Many people do not realize that the first head is the bottom one. Single-sided drives, in fact, use only the bottom head; the top head is replaced by a felt pressure pad. (see fig. 9.2) Another bit of disk trivia is that the top head (Head 1) is not directly over the bottom head—the top head is located either 4 or 8 tracks inward from the bottom head, depending on the drive type. Therefore, what we conventionally call "cylinders" should more accurately be called "cones."

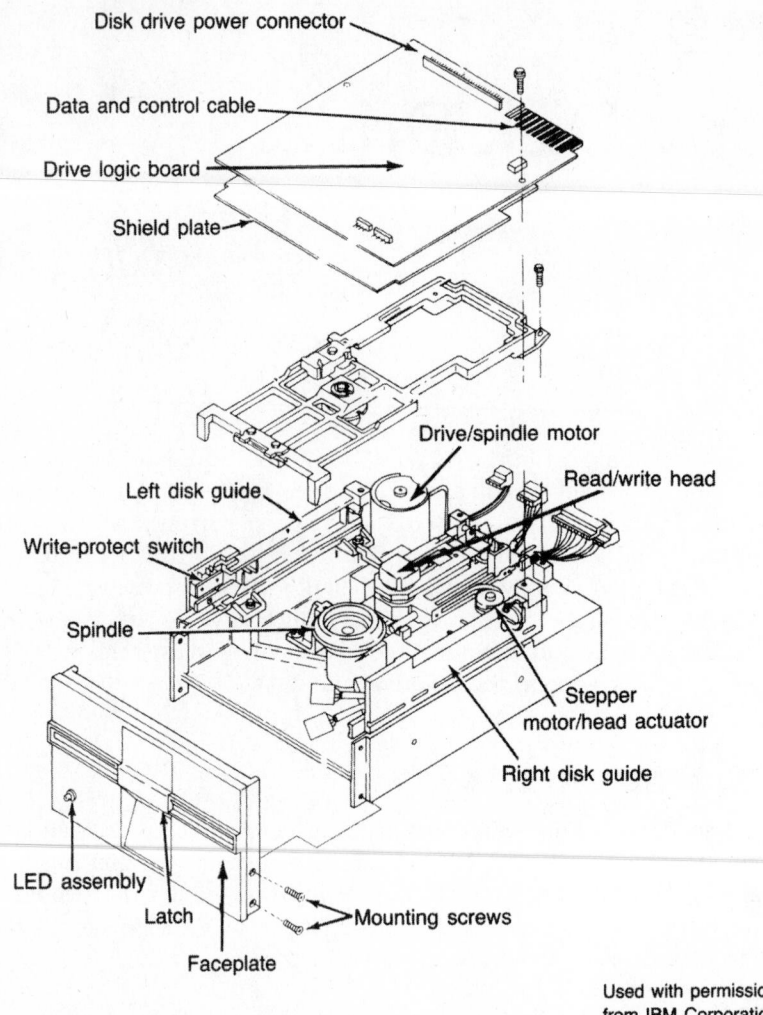

Disk drive power connector

Data and control cable

Drive logic board

Shield plate

Drive/spindle motor

Left disk guide

Read/write head

Write-protect switch

Spindle

Stepper motor/head actuator

Right disk guide

LED assembly

Latch

Mounting screws

Faceplate

Used with permission
from IBM Corporation.

Fig. 9.1
A typical full-height disk drive.

The head mechanism is moved by a motor called a *head actuator*. The heads can move in and out over the surface of the disk in a straight line to position themselves over various tracks. The heads move in and out tangentially to the tracks that they record on the disk. Because the top and bottom heads are mounted on the same rack, or mechanism, they move in unison and cannot move independently of each other. The heads are made of soft ferrous (iron) compounds with electromagnetic coils. Each head is a composite design, with a record head centered within two tunnel-erase heads in the same physical assembly (see fig. 9.3).

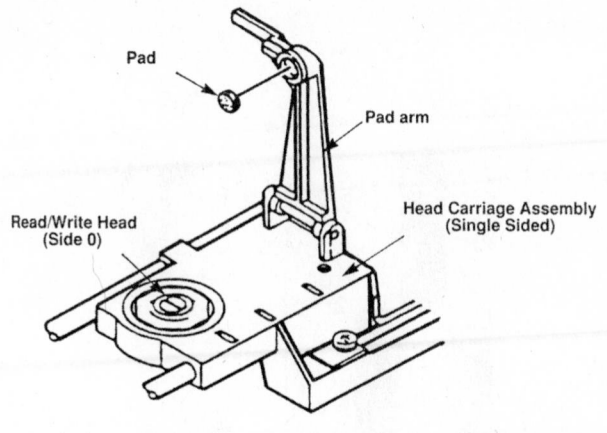

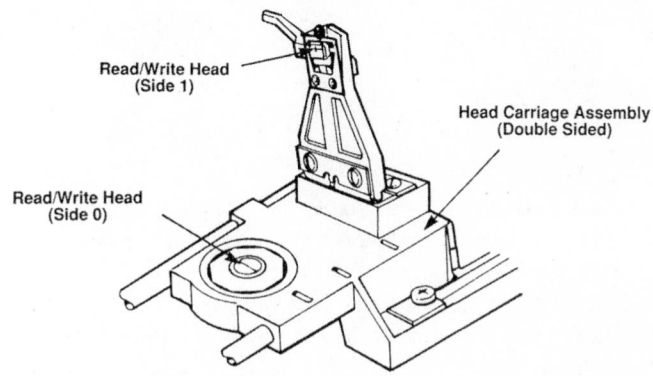

Fig. 9.2

Single- and Double-Sided drive head assemblies.

The recording method is called *tunnel erasure*; as the track is laid down, the trailing tunnel erase heads erase the outer bands of the track, trimming it cleanly on the disk. The heads force the data to be present only within a specified narrow "tunnel" on each track. This process prevents the signal from one track from being confused with the signals from adjacent tracks. If the signal were allowed to "taper off" to each side, problems would occur. The forcibly trimmed track prevents this problem.

Alignment is the placement of the heads with respect to the tracks they must read and write. Head alignment can be checked only against some sort of reference-standard disk recorded by a perfectly aligned machine. These types of disks are available, and you can use one to check your drive's alignment.

The two heads are spring-loaded and physically grip the disk with a small amount of pressure. This means that they are in direct contact with the disk surface while reading and writing to the disk. Because PC-Compatible floppy disk drives spin at only 300 or

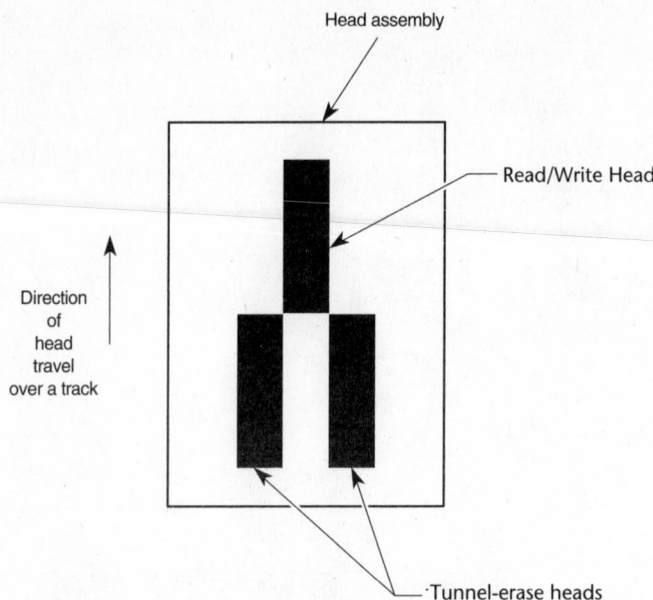

Head assembly

Read/Write Head

Direction
of
head
travel
over a track

Tunnel-erase heads

Fig. 9.3
Composite construction of a typical floppy drive head.

360 RPM, this pressure doesn't present an excessive friction problem. Some newer disks are specially coated with Teflon or other compounds to further reduce friction and enable the disk to slide more easily under the heads. Because of the contact between the heads and the disk, a buildup of the oxide material from the disk eventually forms on the heads. Periodically, the buildup can be cleaned off the heads as part of a preventive-maintenance or normal service program.

To read and write to the disk properly, the heads must be in direct contact with the media. Very small particles of loose oxide, dust, dirt, smoke, fingerprints or hair can cause problems with reading and writing the disk. Disk and drive manufacturer's tests have found that a spacing as little as .000032 inches (32 millionths of an inch) between the heads and the media can cause read/write errors. Figure 9.4 shows how some of these media contaminants can interfere with the proper contact between the heads and the media. Now you can see why it is important to handle disks carefully, and to avoid touching or contaminating the surface of the disk media in any way. The rigid jacket and protective shutter for the head access aperture on the 3 1/2-inch disks is excellent for preventing problems with media contamination. 5 1/4-inch disks do not have the same protective elements; therefore, more care must be exercised in their handling.

The Head Actuator
The *head actuator* is a mechanical motor device that causes the heads to move in and out over the surface of a disk. These mechanisms for floppy disk drives universally use a special kind of motor, a *stepper motor*, that moves in both directions an amount equal to or less than a single revolution. This type of motor does not spin around continuously;

rather, the motor normally moves only a partial revolution in each direction. Stepper motors move in fixed increments, or *detents*, and must stop at a particular detent position. Stepper motors are not infinitely variable in their positioning. Each increment of motion, or a multiple thereof, defines each track on the disk. The motor can be commanded by the disk controller to position itself according to any relative increment within the range of its travel. To position the heads at track 25, for example, the motor is commanded to go to the 25th detent position.

The stepper motor usually is linked to the head rack by a coiled, split steel band. The band winds and unwinds around the spindle of the stepper motor, translating the rotary motion into linear motion. Some drives use a worm gear arrangement rather than a band. With this type, the head assembly rests on a worm gear driven directly off the stepper motor shaft. Because this arrangement is more compact, you normally find worm gear actuators on the smaller 3 1/2-inch drives.

Most stepper motors used in floppy drives can step in specific increments that relate to the track spacing on the disk. Most 40-track drives have a motor that steps in increments of 3.6° (degrees). This means that each 3.6° of stepper motor rotation moves the heads from one track (or cylinder) to the next. Most 80-track drives have a stepper motor that moves in 1.8° increments, which is exactly half of what the 40-track drives use. Sometimes you will see this information actually printed or stamped right on the stepper motor itself, which can be a useful clue if you are trying to figure out what type of drive you have. 5 1/4-inch 360K drives are the only 40-track drives we have and would use the 3.6° increment stepper motor. All other drive types normally use the 1.8° stepper motor. On most drives, the stepper motor is a small cylindrical object near one of the corners of the drive.

A stepper motor usually has a full travel time of about 1/5 of a second—about 200 milliseconds. On average, a half-stroke is 100 milliseconds, and a one-third stroke is 66 milliseconds. The timing of a one-half or one-third stroke of the head-actuator mechanism often is used to determine the reported average-access time for a disk drive. *Average-access time* is the normal amount of time the heads spend moving at random from one track to another.

The Spindle Motor

The *spindle motor* spins the disk. The normal speed of rotation is either 300 or 360 RPM, depending on the type of drive. The 5 1/4-inch HD drive is the only drive that spins at 360 RPM; all others, including the 5 1/4-inch DD, 3 1/2-inch DD, 3 1/2-inch HD, and 3 1/2-inch ED drives, spin at 300 RPM. Most earlier drives used a mechanism on which the spindle motor physically turned the disk spindle with a belt, but all modern drives use a direct-drive system with no belts. The direct-drive systems are more reliable and less expensive to manufacture, as well as smaller in size. The earlier belt-driven systems did have more rotational torque available to turn a sticky disk, because of the torque multiplication factor of the belt system. Most newer direct-drive systems use an automatic torque-compensation capability that automatically sets the disk-rotation speed to a fixed 300 or 360 RPM and compensates with additional torque for sticky disks or less torque for slippery ones. This type of drive eliminates the need to adjust the rotational speed of the drive.

III

Hardware Considerations

Most newer direct-drive systems use this automatic-speed feature, but many earlier systems require that you periodically adjust the speed. Looking at the spindle provides you with one clue to the type of drive you have. If the spindle contains strobe marks for 50 Hz and 60 Hz strobe lights (fluorescent lights), the drive probably has an adjustment for speed somewhere on the drive. Drives without the strobe marks almost always include an automatic tachometer-control circuit that eliminates the need for adjustment. The technique for setting the speed involves operating the drive under fluorescent lighting and adjusting the rotational speed until the strobe marks appear motionless, much like the "wagon wheel effect" you see in old Western movies. The procedure is described later in this chapter, in the "Setting the Floppy Drive Speed Adjustment" section.

To locate the spindle-speed adjustment, you must consult the original equipment manufacturer's (OEM) manual for the drive. IBM provides the information for its drives in the *Technical Reference Options and Adapters* manual as well as in the hardware-maintenance reference manuals. Even if IBM had sold the drives, they most likely are manufactured by another company, such as Control Data Corporation (CDC), Tandon, YE-Data (C. Itoh), Alps Electric, or Mitsubishi. I recommend contacting these manufacturers about the original manuals for your drives.

Circuit Boards

A disk drive always incorporates one or more *logic* boards, circuit boards that contain the circuitry used to control the head actuator, read/write heads, spindle motor, disk sensors, and any other components on the drive. The logic board represents the drive's interface to the controller board in the system unit.

The standard interface used by all PC types of floppy disk drives is the Shugart Associates SA-400 interface. The interface, invented by Shugart in the 1970s, has been the basis of most floppy disk interfacing. The selection of this industry-standard interface is the reason that you can purchase "off the shelf" drives (raw, or bare, drives) that can plug directly into your controller. (Thanks, IBM, for sticking with industry-standard interfacing; it has been the foundation of the entire PC upgrade and repair industry!)

Some other computer companies making non-IBM-compatible systems (especially Apple, for example) have stayed away from industry standards in this and other areas, which can make tasks such as drive repair or upgrades a nightmare—unless, of course, you buy all your parts from them. For example, in both the Apple II series as well as the Mac, Apple has used nonstandard proprietary interfaces for the floppy drives.

The Mac uses an interface based on a proprietary chip called either the IWM (Integrated Woz Machine) or the SWIM (Super Woz Integrated Machine) chip, depending on which Mac you have. These interfaces are incompatible with the industry standard SA-400 interface used in IBM-compatible systems, which is based on the nonproprietary NEC PD765 chip. In fact, the Apple drives use an encoding scheme called GCR (group-coded recording), which is very different from the standard MFM (modified frequency modulation) used in most other systems. The GCR encoding scheme, in fact, cannot be performed by the NEC-type controller chips, which is why it is impossible for IBM-compatible systems to read Mac floppy disks. To Apple's credit, the Mac systems with the SWIM chip include drives that can read and write both GCR and MFM schemes, enabling these systems to read and write IBM floppy disks.

Unfortunately, because the electrical interface to the drive is proprietary, you still cannot easily (or cheaply) purchase these drives as bare units from a variety of manufacturers, as you can for IBM-compatible systems. IBM uses true industry standards in these and other areas, which is why the PC, XT, AT, and PS/2 systems, as well as most IBM-compatible vendors' systems, are so open to upgrade and repair.

Logic boards for a drive can fail and usually are difficult to obtain as a spare part. One board often costs more than replacing the entire drive. I recommend keeping failed or misaligned drives that might otherwise be discarded so that they can be used for their remaining good parts—such as logic boards. The parts can be used to restore a failing drive in a very cost-effective manner.

The Faceplate

The *faceplate*, or bezel, is the plastic piece that comprises the front of the drive. These pieces, usually removable, come in different colors and configurations.

Most drives use a bezel slightly wider than the drive. These types of drives must be installed from the front of a system because the faceplate is slightly wider than the hole in the system-unit case. Other drive faceplates are the same width as the drive's chassis; these drives can be installed from the rear—an advantage in some cases. In the later-version XT systems, for example, IBM uses this design in its drives so that two half-height drives can be bolted together as a unit and then slid in from the rear, to clear the mounting-bracket and screw hardware. On occasion, I have filed the edges of a drive faceplate to install the drive from the rear of a system, which made the installation much easier in some cases.

Connectors

Nearly all disk drives have at least two connectors: one for power to run the drive and the other to carry the control and data signals to and from the drive. These connectors are fairly standardized in the computer industry; a 4-pin in-line connector (called Mate-N-Lock, by AMP), in both a large and small style is used for power (see fig. 9.4), and a 34-pin connector in both edge and pin header designs are used for the data and control signals. 5 1/4-inch drives normally use the large style power connector and the 34-pin edge type connector, while most 3 1/2-inch drives use the smaller version of the power connector and the 34-pin header type logic connector. The drive controller and logic connectors and pinouts are detailed later in this chapter as well as in the Appendix.

Both the large and small power connectors from the power supply are female plugs. They plug into the male portion which is attached to the drive itself. One common problem with upgrading an older system with 3 1/2-inch drives is that your power supply will only have the large style connectors while the drive has the small style. An adapter cable is available from Radio Shack (Cat. No. 278-765) and other sources that will convert the large style power connector to the proper small style used on most 3 1/2-inch drives.

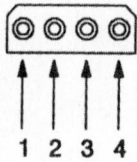

Fig. 9.4

A disk drive female power supply cable connector.

The following chart shows the definition of the pins on the drive power-cable connectors:

Large power connector	Small power connector	Signal	Wire color
Pin 1	Pin 4	+12 Vdc	Yellow
Pin 2	Pin 3	Ground	Black
Pin 3	Pin 2	Ground	Black
Pin 4	Pin 1	+5 Vdc	Red

Notice that the pin designations are reversed between the large and small style power connectors. Also, it is important to know that not all manufacturers follow the wire color coding properly. I have seen instances where all of the wires were a single color (for example, black), or where the wire colors were actually reversed from normal! For example, when I purchased one of the Radio Shack power connector adapter cables I just mentioned, the one I received had all of the wire colors backwards. This was not really a problem because the adapter cable was wired correctly from end to end, but it was disconcerting to see the red wire in the power supply connector attach to a yellow wire in the adapter (and vice versa).

Not all drives use the standard separate power and signal connectors. IBM, for example, uses either a single 34-pin or single 40-pin header connector for both power and floppy controller connections in most of the PS/2 systems. In some older PS/2 systems, for example, IBM used a special version of a Mitsubishi 3 1/2-inch 1.44M drive called the MF-355W-99, which has a single 40-pin power/signal connector. Some newer PS/2 systems use a Mitsubishi 3 1/2-inch 2.88M drive called the MF356C-799MA, which uses a single 34-pin header connector for both power and signal connections.

Most standard IBM clone or compatible systems use 3 1/2-inch drives with a 34-pin signal connector and a separate small style power connector. For older PC- or AT-type systems, many drive manufacturers also sell 3 1/2-inch drives that are installed in a 5 1/4-inch frame assembly and have a special adapter built-in that allows the larger power connector and standard edge type signal connectors to be used. Mitsubishi, for example, sold 1.44M drives as the MF-355B-82 (black faceplate) or MF-355B-88 (beige faceplate). These drives included an adapter that enables the standard large-style power connector and 34-pin edge type control and data connector to be used. Because no cable adapters are required and they install in a 5 1/4-inch half-height bay, these types of drives are ideal for upgrading earlier systems. Most 3 1/2-inch drive-upgrade kits sold today are similar and include the drive, appropriate adapters for the power and control and data cables, a 5 1/4-inch frame adapter and faceplate, and rails for AT installations. The frame adapter and faceplate enable the drive to be installed where a 5 1/4-inch half-height drive normally would go.

Drive-Configuration Devices

You must locate several items on a drive that you install in a system. These items control the configuration and operation of the drive and must be set correctly depending on which type of system the drive is installed in and exactly where in the system the drive is installed.

You must set or check these items during installation:

- Drive select jumper
- Terminating resistor
- Diskette Changeline jumper
- Media sensor jumper

You learn how to configure these items later in this chapter. In this section, you learn what functions these devices perform.

Drive Select Jumpers

Each drive in a controller and drive subsystem must have a unique drive number. The *drive select jumper* is set to indicate to the controller the number of a particular drive. The jumper indicates whether the specific drive should respond as drive 0 or 1 (A: or B:). Some idiosyncrasies can be found when you're setting this jumper in various systems, because of strange cable configurations or other differences. Most drives allow four different settings, labeled DS1, DS2, DS3, and DS4. Some drives start with 0, and thus the four settings are labeled DS0, DS1, DS2, and DS3. On some drives, these jumpers are not labeled. If they are not labeled, you have several resources available for information about how to set the drive: the OEM manual, your experience with other similar drives, or simply an educated guess. I recommend first checking the manual if it is available; if not, then perhaps you can rely on your past experiences and make an educated guess.

You might think that the first drive select position corresponds to A: and that the second position corresponds to B:, but in most cases you would be wrong. The configuration that seems correct is wrong because of some creative rewiring of the cable. IBM, for example, crosses the seven wires numbered 10 through 16 (the drive select, motor enable, and some ground lines) in the floppy interface cable between drives B: and A: to allow both drives to be jumpered the same way, as though they both were drive B:. This type of cable is shown later in this chapter.

When using a floppy cable with lines 10 through 16 twisted, you must set the DS jumper on both drives to the second (same) drive select position. This setup enabled dealers and installers to buy the drives pre-configured by IBM and to install them with a minimum of hassle. Sometimes this setup confuses people who attempt to install drives properly without knowing about the twisted-cabling system. With this type of cable design, to swap drive A: and B: positions you could simply swap the cable connections between the drives with no jumper setting changes required. You still will probably have to change the terminator resistor settings on the drives, however.

If the cable has a straight-through design, in which lines 10 through 16 are not twisted between the B: and A: connectors, you would then need to jumper the drives as you might have thought originally—that is, drive A: would be set to the first drive select position, and drive B: would be set to the second drive select position.

If you install a drive and it either does not respond or responds in unison with the other drive in the system in calling for drive A:, you probably have the drive select jumpers set incorrectly for your application. Check the DS jumpers on both drives as well as the cable for the proper setup.

Terminating Resistors

Any signal carrying electronic media or cable with multiple connections can be thought of as an electrical bus. In almost all cases, a bus must be terminated properly at each end with Terminating Resistors to allow signals to travel along the bus error-free. Terminating resistors are designed to absorb any signals that reach the end of a cabling system or bus so that no reflection of the signal echoes, or bounces, back down the line in the opposite direction. Engineers sometimes call this effect *signal ringing*. Simply put, noise and distortion can disrupt the original signal and prevent proper communications between the drive and controller. Another function of proper termination is to place the proper resistive load on the output drivers in the controller and drive.

Most floppy disk cabling systems have the controller positioned at one end of the cable, and a terminating resistor network is built-in to the controller to properly terminate that end of the bus. IBM and IBM clone or compatible systems use a floppy controller design that normally allows up to two drives on a single cable. To terminate the other end of the bus properly, a terminating resistor must be set, or enabled, on the drive at the end of the cable furthest from the controller. In most systems, this drive would also be the lowest-lettered drive (A:) of the pair. The drive that is plugged into the connector in the center of the cable must have the terminating resistor (or terminator) removed or disabled for proper operation.

Because a terminating resistor is already installed in the controller to terminate the cable at that end, we are concerned only about properly terminating the drive end. Sometimes a system will operate even with incorrect terminator installation or configuration, but the system might experience sporadic disk errors. Additionally, with the wrong signal load on the controller and drives, you run the risk of damaging them by causing excessive power output because of an improper resistive load.

AT-class systems use the DC signal to increase significantly the speed of the floppy inter-face. Because the AT can detect whether you have changed the disk, the AT can keep a copy of the disk's directory and file allocation table information in RAM buffers. On every subsequent disk access, the operations are much faster because the information does not have to be reread from the disk in every individual access. If the DC signal has been reset (has a value of 1), the AT knows that the disk has been changed and appropri-ately rereads the information from the disk.

You can observe the effects of the DC signal by trying a simple experiment. Boot DOS on an AT-class system and place in drive A: a formatted floppy disk with data on it. Drive A: can be any type of drive except 5 1/4-inch double-density, although the disk you use can be anything the drive will read, including a double-density 360K disk, if you want. Then type this command:

```
DIR A:
```

The disk drive lights up, and the directory is displayed. Note the amount of time spent reading the disk before the directory is displayed on-screen. Without touching the drive, enter the DIR A: command again, and watch the drive-access light and screen. Note again the amount of time that passes before the directory is displayed. The drive A: direc-tory should appear almost instantly the second time because virtually no time is spent actually reading the disk. The directory information was simply read back from RAM buffers or cache rather than read again from the disk. Now open and close the drive door, and keep the same disk in the drive. Type the DIR A: command again. The disk again takes some time reading the directory before displaying anything, because the AT "thinks" that you have changed the disk.

The PC and XT controllers (and systems) are not affected by the status of the DC signal. These systems "don't care" about signals on pin 34. The PC and XT systems always oper-ate under the assumption that the disk is changed before every access, and they reread the disk directory and file allocation table each time—one reason that these systems are slower in using the floppy disk drives.

A problem can occur when certain drives are installed in an AT system. As mentioned, some drives use pin 34 for a "Ready" signal. The RDY signal is sent when a disk is in-stalled and rotating in the drive. If you install a drive that has pin 34 set to send RDY, the AT "thinks" that it is continuously receiving a disk change signal, which will cause problems: Usually the drive fails with a "Drive not ready" error and is inoperable.

A different but related problem occurs if the drive is not sending the DC signal on pin 34 and it should. If an AT class system is told (through CMOS setup) that the drive is any other type than a 360K (which cannot ever send the DC signal), then the system expects the drive to send DC whenever a disk has been ejected. If the drive is not configured properly to send the signal, then the system will never recognize that a disk has been changed. Therefore, even if you do change the disk, the AT still acts as though the first disk is in the drive, and holds the first disk's directory and file allocation table informa-tion in RAM. This can be dangerous as the File Allocation Table (FAT) and directory information from the first disk can be partially written to any subsequent disks that are written to in the drive.

If you ever have seen an AT-class system with a floppy drive that shows "phantom directories" of the previously installed disk, even after you have changed or removed it, you have experienced this problem firsthand. The negative side effect is that all disks after the first one you place in this system are in extreme danger. You likely will overwrite the directories and file allocation tables of many disks with information from the first disk. Data recovery from such a catastrophe can require quite a bit of work with utility programs such as the Norton Utilities. These problems with Disk Change most often are traced to an incorrectly configured drive. Another possibility is that the disk-eject sensor mechanism no longer operates correctly. A temporary solution to the problem is to press the Ctrl-Break or Ctrl-C key combination every time you change a floppy disk in the drive. These commands cause DOS to flush the RAM buffers manually and reread the directory and file allocation table during the next disk access.

All drives except 5 1/4-inch double-density (360K) drives support the Disk Change signal. Therefore, if your system thinks that one of these drives is installed, the drive is expected to provide the signal. If the system thinks that the installed drive is a 360K drive, no signal is expected on pin 34.

To summarize, PC and XT systems are not affected by pin 34, but on AT systems, non-360K drives must have pin 34 set to send Disk Change. If the drive is a 360K drive and you want to install it in an AT, pin 34 must be disabled (usually preconfigured as such, or set by removing a jumper). Never set a 360K drive (or any other drive for that matter) to send a signal called Ready (RDY) on pin 34, because IBM-compatible systems cannot use this signal. The only reason that the Ready signal exists on some drives is that it happens to be a part of the standard Shugart SA-400 disk interface that was not adopted by IBM.

The Media Sensor Jumper

This configuration item exists only on the 3 1/2-inch 1.44M or 2.88M drives. The jumper selection, called the *media sensor (MS) jumper*, must be set to enable a special media sensor in the disk drive, which senses a media sensor hole found only in the 1.44M high-density (HD) and the 2.88M extra-high density (ED) floppy disks. The labeling of this jumper (or jumpers) varies greatly between different drives. In many drives, the jumpers are permanently set (enabled) and cannot be changed.

There are three types of configurations with regard to media sensing. They are:

- No Media Sense (sensor disabled or no sensor present)
- Passive Media Sense (sensor enabled)
- Active or Intelligent Media Sense (sensor supported by Controller/BIOS)

Most systems use a Passive Media Sensor arrangement. The passive media sensor setup enables the drive to determine the level of recording strength to use, and is required for most installations of these drives because of a bug in the design of the Western Digital hard disk and floppy controllers used by IBM in the AT systems. This bug prevents the controller from properly instructing the drive to switch to double-density mode when you write or format double-density disks. With the media sensor enabled, the drive no longer depends on the controller for density mode switching, and relies only on the drive's media sensor. Unless you are sure that your disk controller does not have this flaw, you must be sure that your HD drive includes a media sensor (some older or manufacturer specific drives do not), and that it is properly enabled. The 2.88M drives universally rely on media sensors to determine the proper mode of operation. The 2.88M drives, in fact, have two separate media sensors because the ED disks include a media sensor hole in a different position than the HD disks.

With only a few exceptions, high-density 3 1/2-inch drives installed in most IBM-compatible systems do not operate properly in double-density mode unless the drive has control over the write current (recording level) via an installed and enabled media sensor. Exceptions are found primarily in systems with floppy controllers integrated on the motherboard, including most older IBM PS/2 and Compaq systems as well as most laptop or notebook systems from other manufacturers. These systems have floppy controllers without the bug referred to earlier, and can correctly switch the mode of the drive without the aid of the media sensor. In these systems, it technically does not matter whether you enable the media sensor. If the media sensor is enabled, the drive mode is controlled by the disk you insert, as is the case with most IBM-compatible systems. If the media sensor is not enabled, the drive mode is controlled by the floppy controller, which in turn is controlled by DOS.

If a disk is already formatted (correctly), DOS reads the volume boot sector to determine the current disk format, and the controller then switches the drive to the appropriate mode. If the disk has not been formatted yet, DOS has no idea what type of disk it is, and the drive remains in its native HD or ED mode.

When you format a disk in systems without an enabled media sensor (such as most PS/2s), the mode of the drive depends entirely on the FORMAT command issued by the user, regardless of the type of disk inserted. For example, if you insert a DD disk into an HD drive in an IBM PS/2 Model 70 and format the disk by entering FORMAT A:, the disk is formatted as though it is an HD disk because you did not issue the correct parameters to cause the FORMAT command to specify a DD format. On a system with the media sensor enabled, this type of incorrect format would fail and you would see the Invalid media or Track 0 bad error message from FORMAT. In this case, the media sensor prevents an incorrect format from occurring on the disk, a safety feature most older IBM PS/2 systems lack.

Most of the newer PS/2 systems, including all of those that come standard with the 2.88M drives, have what is called an *active* or *intelligent* media sensor setup. This means that the sensor will not only detect what type of disk is in the drive and change modes appropriately, but the drive will also inform the controller (and the BIOS) about what type of disk is in the drive. Systems with an intelligent media sensor do not need to use the disk type parameters in the FORMAT command. In these systems, the FORMAT command will automatically "know" what type of disk is in the drive, and will format it properly. With an intelligent media sensor, you never have to know what the correct format parameters are for a particular type of disk, the system figures it out for you automatically! Many high-end systems such as the newer PS/2 systems as well as high-end Hewlett-Packard PCs have this type of intelligent media sensor arrangement.

The Floppy Disk Controller

The floppy disk controller consists of the circuitry either on a separate adapter card or integrated on the motherboard, which acts as the interface between the floppy drives and the system. Most PC- and XT- class systems used a separate controller card that occupied a slot in the system. The AT systems normally had the floppy controller and hard disk controller built into the same adapter card and also plugged into a slot. In most of the more modern systems built since then, the controller is integrated on the motherboard. In any case, the electrical interface to the drives has remained largely static, with only a few exceptions.

The original IBM PC and XT system floppy controller was a 3/4-length card that could drive as many as four floppy disk drives. Two drives could be connected to a cable plugged into a 34-pin edge connector on the card, and two more drives could be plugged into a cable connected to the 37-pin connector on the bracket of this card. These connectors and the pinouts for the controller are shown in figures 9.5 and 9.6.

The AT used a board made by Western Digital, which included both the floppy and hard disk controllers in a single adapter. The connector location and pinout for the floppy controller portion of this card is shown in figure 9.7. IBM used two variations of this controller during the life of the AT system. The first one was a full 4.8 inches high, which used all the vertical height possible in the AT case. This board was a variation of the Western Digital WD1002-WA2 controller, sold through distributors and dealers. The second-generation card was only 4.2 inches high, which enabled it to fit into the shorter case of the XT-286 as well as the taller AT cases. This card was equivalent to the Western Digital WD1003-WA2, also sold on the open market.

Disk Physical Specifications and Operation

PC Compatible systems now use one of as many as five standard types of floppy drives. Also, there are five types of disks that can be used in the drives. This section examines the physical specifications and operations of these drives and disks.

Drives and disks are in two classes: 5 1/4-inch and 3 1/2-inch. The physical dimensions and components of a typical 5 1/4-inch disk and a 3 1/2-inch disk are shown later in this chapter.

(34-pin keyed edge connector)

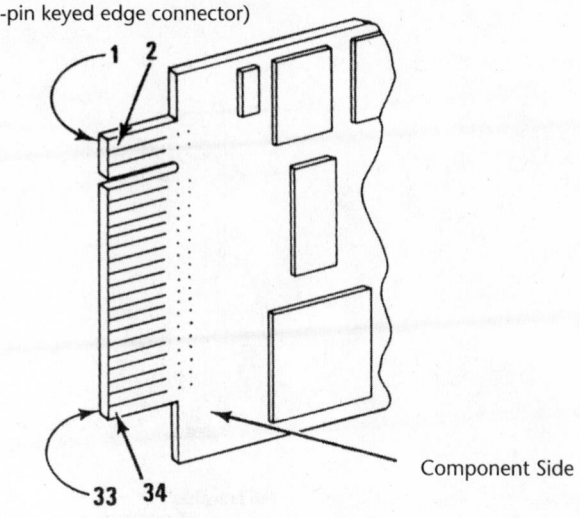

Component Side

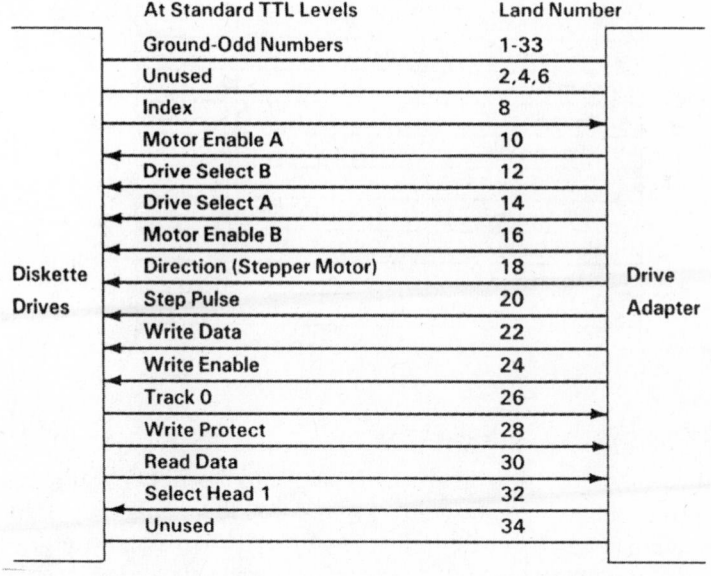

Fig. 9.5
A PC and XT floppy controller internal connector.

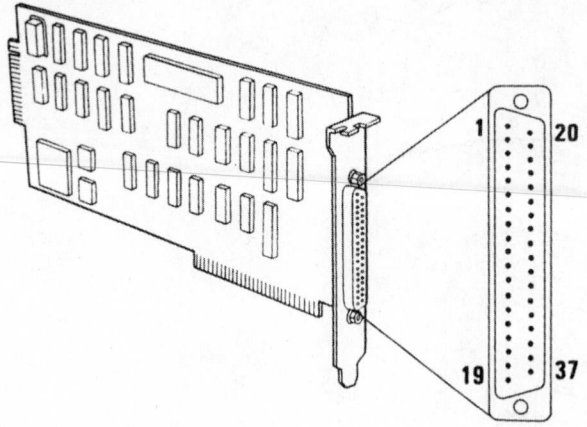

At Standard TTL Levels	Pin Number
Unused	1-5
Index	6
Motor Enable 1	7
Drive Select 2	8
Drive Select 1	9
Motor Enable 2	10
Direction (Stepper Motor)	11
Step Pulse	12
Write Data	13
Write Enable	14
Track 0	15
Write Protect	16
Read Data	17
Select Head 1	18
Ground	20-37

External Drives ... Drive Adapter

Fig. 9.6

A PC and XT floppy controller external connector.

The physical operation of a disk drive is fairly simple to describe. The disk rotates in the drive at either 300 or 360 RPM. Most drives spin at 300 RPM; only the 5 1/4-inch 1.2M drives spin at 360 RPM (even when reading or writing 360K disks). With the disk spinning, the heads can move in and out approximately one inch, and write either 40 or 80 tracks. The tracks are written on both sides of the disk and therefore sometimes are called *cylinders*. A single cylinder comprises the tracks on the top and bottom of the disk. The heads record by using a tunnel-erase procedure in which a track is written to a specified width, and then the edges of the track are erased to prevent interference with any adjacent tracks.

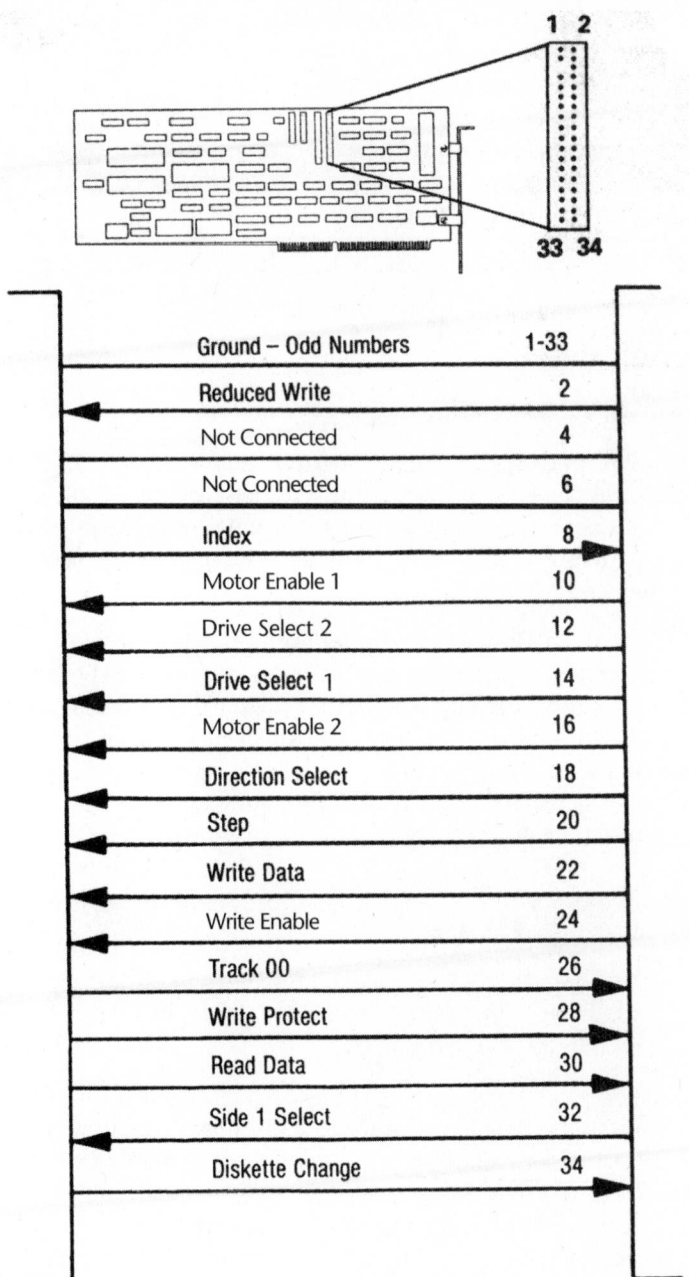

Fig. 9.7
An AT floppy controller connector.

The tracks are recorded at different widths for different drives. Table 9.1 shows the track widths in both millimeters and inches for the five types of floppy drives supported in PC systems.

Table 9.1 Floppy Drive Track-Width Specifications

Drive type	No. of tracks	Track width
5 1/4-inch 360K	40 per side	0.300 mm; 0.0118 in.
5 1/4-inch 1.2M	80 per side	0.155 mm; 0.0061 in.
3 1/2-inch 720K	80 per side	0.115 mm; 0.0045 in.
3 1/2-inch 1.44M	80 per side	0.115 mm; 0.0045 in.
3 1/2-inch 2.88M	80 per side	0.115 mm; 0.0045 in.

The differences in recorded track width can result in data-exchange problems between 5 1/4-inch drives. The 5 1/4-inch drives are affected because the double-density drives record a track width nearly twice that of the high-density drives. A problem occurs, therefore, if a high-density drive is used to update a double-density disk with previously recorded data on it.

Even in 360K mode, the high-density drive cannot completely overwrite the track left by an actual 360K drive. A problem occurs when the disk is returned to the person with the 360K drive: that drive reads the new data as embedded within the remains of the previously written track. Since the drive cannot distinguish either signal, an Abort, Retry, Ignore error message appears on-screen. The problem does not occur if a new disk (one that never has had data recorded on it) is first formatted in a 1.2M drive with the /4 option, which formats the disk as a 360K disk.

Note

You can also format a 360K disk in a 1.2M drive with the /N:9 /T:40 or /F:360 options, depending on the DOS version. The 1.2M drive then can be used to fill the brand-new and newly formatted 360K disk to its capacity, and every file will be readable on the 40-track, 360K drive.

I use this technique all the time to exchange data disks between AT systems that have only the 1.2M drive and between XT or PC systems that have only the 360K drive. The key is to start with either a new disk or one wiped clean magnetically by a bulk eraser or degaussing tool. Just reformatting the disk does not work by itself because formatting does not actually erase a disk; instead, it records data across the entire disk.

In addition to a track-width specification, there are specifications for the precise placement of tracks on a disk. A 5 1/4-inch DD disk has tracks placed precisely 1/48th of an inch apart. The outermost track on side 0 (the bottom of the disk) is the starting point for measurements, and this track (cylinder 0, head 0) has a radius of exactly 2.25 inches. Because Head 1 (the top of the disk) is offset by four tracks inward from Head 0, the radius of cylinder 0, Head 1 is 2.2500 inches - (1/48 * 4) = 2.1667 inches. Therefore, to calculate the exact track radius R in inches for any specified cylinder C and head position on a 360K disk, use these formulas:

For Head 0 (bottom): R = 2.2500 inches - C/48 inches

For Head 1 (top): R = 2.1667 inches - C/48 inches

That the tracks on top of the disk (Head 1) are offset toward the center of the disk from the tracks on the bottom of the disk (Head 0) might be surprising: in effect, the cylinders are cone shaped. Figure 9.8 shows the physical relationship between the top and bottom heads on a floppy drive. In this figure, both heads are positioned at the same cylinder. You can see that the top track of the cylinder is closer to the center of the disk than is the bottom track, resulting in cylinders that are shaped more like cones.

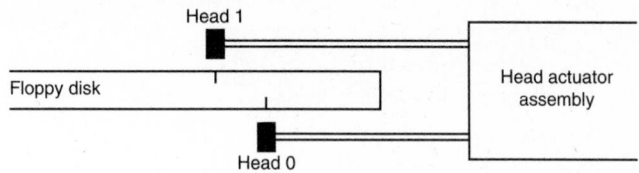

Fig. 9.8
Floppy disk drive head offset.

I first saw this track positioning in one of my data-recovery seminars. One of the experiments I perform in these courses is to stick a pin through a disk with data on it. The objective then is to recover as much data as possible from the disk. Normally, I can resolve the damage down to only a few unreadable sectors on either side of the disk and then easily recover all but these damaged sectors. As I was trying to determine the exact location of the hole by its cylinder, head, and sector coordinates, I noticed that I always had what seemed to be two groups of damaged sectors which were always located exactly 4 or 8 (depending on the type of disk) cylinders apart. Because I had stuck the pin straight through the disk, I realized that any offset had to be in the tracks themselves. I then removed the disk from its jacket to look more closely at the holes.

When I want to "see" the tracks on a disk, I use a special type of solution called Magnetic Developer, a fine-powdered iron suspended in a trichloroethane solution. When this developer, which dries very quickly, is sprayed on the disk, the iron particles align themselves directly over magnetized areas of the disk and show very graphically the exact physical appearance and location of the tracks and sectors on the disk. You can see every individual track and sector on the disk "develop" right before your eyes! With a magnifier or low powered microscope, I can locate the exact sectors and tracks damaged by the hole on either side of the disk. With this technique it was easy to see that the tracks on top of the disk start and end further toward the center of the disk. If you want to do similar experiments or simply "see" the magnetic image of your disks, you can obtain the Magnetic Developer solution from Sprague Magnetics (the address and phone number are in the vendor list in the Appendix of this book). By the way, after viewing this magnetic image, the disk "cookie" can be washed off with distilled water or pure trichloroethane, placed back into a new jacket, and reused!

The high-density 5 1/4-inch disk track dimensions are similar to the double-density disk, except that the tracks are spaced precisely 1/96th of an inch apart, and the top head (Head 1) is offset eight tracks inward from the bottom head (Head 0). The physical head offset between Head 0 and Head 1 is the same as DD disks because there are twice as many tracks in the same space as on a DD disk. The calculations for a given track radius R in inches for any cylinder C and head are as follows:

For Head 0 (bottom): R = 2.2500 inches - C/96 inches

For Head 1 (top): R = 2.1667 inches - C/96 inches

All the different 3 1/2-inch disks (DD, HD, ED) are dimensionally the same in track and cylinder spacing. The track and cylinder dimensions of these disks start with the radius of Cylinder 0, Head 0 (the bottom head outer track) defined as 39.5 millimeters. Tracks inward from this track are spaced precisely 0.1875 millimeters apart, and the top head (Head 1) is offset inward by eight tracks from Head 0. The radius, in millimeters, of the outer track on top of the disk (Cylinder 0, Head 1) therefore can be calculated as

39.5mm - (0.1875 * 8) = 38.0mm

Now you can calculate the radius R in millimeters of any specified cylinder C and head using these formulas:

For Head 0 (bottom): R = 39.5mm - (0.1875mm * C)

For Head 1 (top): R = 38.0mm - (0.1875mm * C)

An interesting note about the dimensions of the 3 1/2-inch disks is that the dimensional standards all are based in the metric system, unlike the 5 1/4-inch disks. I could have converted these numbers to their English equivalents for comparison with the 5 1/4-inch disk figures, but rounding would have sacrificed some accuracy in the numeric conversion. For example, many texts often give the track spacing for 3 1/2-inch disks as 135 TPI (tracks per inch). This figure is an imprecise result of metric-to-English conversion and rounding. The true spacing of 0.1875 mm between tracks converts to a more precise figure of 135.4667 TPI. The figures presented here are the specifications as governed by the ANSI standards X3.125 and X3.126 for 360K and 1.2M disks, and by Sony, Toshiba, and Accurite, which all were involved in specifying the 3 1/2-inch disk standards.

Disk Magnetic Properties

A subtle problem with the way a disk drive works magnetically is that the recording volume varies depending on the type of format you are trying to apply to a disk. The high-density formats use special disks that require a much higher volume level for the recording than do the double-density disks. My classes nearly always are either stumped or incorrect (unless they have read ahead in the book) when they answer this question: "Which type of disk is magnetically more sensitive: a 1.2M disk or a 360K disk?" If you answer that the 1.2M disk is more sensitive, you are wrong! The high-density disks are approximately half as sensitive magnetically as the double-density disks.

The high-density disks are called *high-coercivity disks* also because they require a magnetic field strength much higher than do the double-density disks. Magnetic field strength is measured in *oersteds*. The 360K floppy disks require only a 300-oersted field strength in order to record, and the high-density 1.2M disks require a 600-oersted field strength. Because the high-density disks need double the magnetic field strength for recording, you should not attempt to format a 1.2M high-density disk as though it were a 360K disk, or a 360K disk as though it were a 1.2M high-density disk.

The latter case in particular seems to appeal to people looking for an easy way to save money. They buy inexpensive 360K disks and format them in a 1.2M drive, to the full 1.2M capacity. Most of the time, this format seems to work, with perhaps a large amount of bad sectors; otherwise, most of the disk might seem usable. You should not store important data on this incorrectly formatted disk, however, because the data is recorded at twice the recommended strength and density. Eventually, the adjacent magnetic domains on the disk begin to affect each other and can cause each other to change polarity or weaken because of the proximity of these domains, and because the double-density disk is more sensitive to magnetic fields. This process is illustrated later in this chapter, in the "Media Coercivity and Thickness" section. Eventually, the disk begins to erase itself and deteriorates. The process might take weeks, months, or even longer, but the result is inevitable: a loss of the information stored on the disk.

Another problem results from this type of improper formatting: You can imprint the 360K disk magnetically with an image that is difficult to remove. The high-density format will have placed on the disk a recording at twice the strength it should have been. How do you remove this recording and correct the problem? If you attempt to reformat the disk in a 360K drive, the drive writes in a reduced write-current mode and in some cases cannot overwrite the higher-volume recorded image you mistakenly placed on the disk. If you attempt to reformat the disk in the high-density drive with the /4 (or equivalent) parameter, which indicates 360K mode, the high-density drive uses a reduced write-current setting and again cannot overwrite the recording.

You can correct the problem in several ways. You can throw away the disk and write it off as a learning experience, or you can use a bulk eraser or degaussing tool to demagnetize the disk. These devices can randomize all the magnetic domains on a disk and return it to an essentially factory-new condition. You can purchase a bulk-erasing device at electronic-supply stores for about $25.

The opposite problem with disk formatting is not as common, but some have tried it anyway: formatting a high-density disk with a double-density format. You should not (and normally cannot) format a 1.2M high-density disk to a 360K capacity. If you attempt to use one, the drive changes to reduced write-current mode and does not create a magnetic field strong enough to record on the "insensitive" 1.2M disk. The result in this case is normally an immediate error message from the FORMAT command: Invalid media or Track 0 bad—disk unusable. Fortunately, the system usually does not allow this particular mistake to be made.

The 3 1/2-inch drives don't have the same problems as the 5 1/4-inch drives—at least for data interchange. Because both the high-density and double-density drives write the same number of tracks and these tracks are always the same width, no problem occurs when one type of drive is used to overwrite data written by another type of drive. A system manufacturer therefore doesn't need to offer a double-density version of the 3 1/2-inch drive for systems equipped with the high-density or extra high-density drive. The HD and ED drives can perfectly emulate the operations of the 720K DD drive, and the ED drive can perfectly emulate the 1.44M HD drive.

The HD and ED drives can be trouble, however, for inexperienced users who try to format disks to incorrect capacities. Although an ED drive can read, write, and format DD, HD, and ED disks, a disk should be formatted and written at only its specified capacity. An ED disk therefore should be formatted only to 2.88M, and never to 1.44M or 720K. *You must always use a disk at its designated format capacity.* You are asking for serious problems if you place a 720K disk in the A: drive of a PS/2 Model 50, 60, 70, or 80 and enter FORMAT A:. This step causes a 1.44M format to be written on the 720K disk, which renders it unreliable at best and requires a bulk eraser to reformat it correctly. If you decide to use the resulting incorrectly formatted disk, you will have an eventual massive data loss.

This particular problem could have been averted if IBM had used media sensor drives in all PS/2 systems. Drives that use the disk media-sensor hole to control the drive mode are prevented from incorrectly formatting a disk. The hardware causes the FORMAT command to fail with an appropriate error message if you attempt to format the disk to an incorrect capacity.

By knowing how a drive works physically, you can eliminate most of these user "pilot error" problems and distinguish this kind of easily solved problem from a more serious hardware problem. You will be a much better user as well as a troubleshooter of a system if you truly understand how a drive works.

Logical Operation

Each type of drive can create disks with different numbers of sectors and tracks. This section examines how DOS sees a drive. It gives definitions of the drives according to DOS and the definitions of cylinders and clusters.

How DOS Uses a Disk. A technical understanding of the way DOS maintains information on your disks is not necessary to use a PC, but you will be a more informed user if you understand the general principles.

To DOS, data on your PC disks is organized in tracks and sectors. Tracks are narrow, concentric circles on a disk. Sectors are pie-shaped slices of the disk. DOS versions 1.0 and 1.1 read and write 5 1/4-inch double-density disks with 40 tracks (numbered 0 through 39) per side and 8 sectors (numbered 1 through 8) per track. DOS versions 2.0 and higher automatically increase the track density from 8 to 9 sectors, for greater capacity on the same disk. On an AT with a 1.2M disk drive, DOS V3.0 supports high-density 5 1/4-inch drives that format 15 sectors per track and 80 tracks per side; DOS V3.2 supports 3 1/2-inch drives that format 9 sectors per track and 80 tracks per side; DOS V3.3 supports 3 1/2-inch drives that format 18 sectors per track and 80 tracks per side. The distance between tracks and, therefore, the number of tracks on a disk is a built-in mechanical and electronic function of the drive. Tables 9.2 and 9.3 summarize the standard disk formats supported by DOS version 5.0 and higher.

Table 9.2 5 1/4-inch Floppy Disk Drive Formats

	Double-density/360K	High-density/1.2M
Bytes per Sector	512	512
Sectors per Track	9	15
Tracks per Side	40	80
Sides	2	2
Capacity (KBytes)	360	1,200
Capacity (Megabytes)	0.352	1.172
Capacity (Million Bytes)	0.369	1.229

Table 9.3 3 1/2-inch Floppy Disk Drive Formats

	Double Density 720K	High Density 1.44M	Extra-High Density 2.88M
Bytes per Sector	512	512	512
Sectors per Track	9	18	36
Tracks per Side	80	80	80
Sides	2	2	2
Capacity (K)	720	1,440	2,880
Capacity (M)	0.703	1.406	2.813
Capacity (MillionBytes)	0.737	1.475	2.949

You can calculate the capacity differences between different formats by multiplying the sectors per track by the number of tracks per side together with the constants of two sides and 512 bytes per sector. Note that the disk capacity can actually be expressed in three different ways. The most common method is to refer to the capacity of a floppy by the number of KBytes (1,024 bytes equals 1KB). This works fine for 360K and 720K disks, but is strange when applied to the 1.44M and 2.88M disks. As you can see, a 1.44M disk is really 1,440K, and not actually 1.44 Megabytes. Since a Megabyte is 1,024K, what we call a 1.44M disk is actually 1.406 Megabytes in capacity. Another way of expressing disk capacity is in Millions of Bytes. In that case, our 1.44M disk has 1.475 Million Bytes of capacity. To add to the confusion over capacity expression, both Megabyte and Millions of Bytes are abbreviated as "MB" or "M". There is no universally accepted standard for the definition of M or MB, so throughout this book I will try to be explicit.

III

Hardware Considerations

Like blank sheets of paper, new disks contain no information. Formatting a disk is similar to adding lines to the paper so that you can write straight across. Formatting puts on the disk the information DOS needs to maintain a directory and file table of contents. Using the /S (system) option in the FORMAT command resembles making the paper a title page. FORMAT places on the disk the portions of DOS required to boot the system.

DOS reserves the track nearest to the outside edge of a disk (track 0) almost entirely for its purposes. Track 0, Sector 1 contains the DOS Boot Record (DBR) or Boot Sector, the system needs in order to begin operation. The next few sectors contain the File Allocation Tables (FATs), which act as the disk "room reservation clerk" that keeps records of which clusters or allocation units (rooms) on the disk have file information and which are empty. Finally, the next few sectors contain the Root Directory, in which DOS stores information about the names and starting locations of the files on the disk; you see most of this information when you use the DIR command.

In computer-industry jargon, this process is "transparent to the user," which means that you don't have to (and generally cannot) decide where information is stored on disks. That this process is "transparent," however, doesn't necessarily mean that you shouldn't be aware of the decisions DOS makes for you.

When DOS writes data, it always begins by attempting to use the earliest available data sectors on the disk. Because the file might be larger than the particular block of available sectors that were selected, DOS then writes the remainder of the file in the next available block of free sectors. In this manner, files can become fragmented as they are written to fill a hole on the disk created by the deletion of some smaller file. The larger file completely fills the hole; then DOS continues to look for more free space across the disk, from the outermost tracks to the innermost tracks. The rest of the file is deposited in the next available free space.

This procedure continues until eventually all the files on your disk are intertwined. This situation is not really a problem for DOS because it was designed to manage files in this way. The problem is a physical one: Retrieving a fragmented file that occupies 50 or 100 separate places across the disk takes much longer than if the file were in one piece. Also, if the files were in one piece, recovering data in the case of a disaster would be much easier. You should consider unfragmenting a disk periodically simply because it can make recovery from a disk disaster much easier; many people, however, unfragment disks for the performance benefit in loading and saving files that are in one piece.

How do you unfragment a disk? IBM and MS-DOS 6.0 versions include a command called DEFRAG. This utility is actually a limited version of the Norton Utilities Speedisk program. It does not have some of the options of the more powerful Norton version and is not as fast, but it does work well in most cases. Earlier versions of DOS do not provide any easy method for unfragmenting a disk, although by backing up and restoring files, you can accomplish the goal. To unfragment a floppy disk for example, you can copy all the files one by one to an empty disk, delete the original files from the first disk, and then recopy the files. With a hard disk, you can back up all the files, reformat the disk, and restore the files. This procedure is time consuming, to say the least.

Because DOS versions earlier than 6.0 did not provide a good way to unfragment a disk, many software companies have produced utility programs that can easily unfragment disks in a clean and efficient manner. These programs can restore file contiguity without reformat and restore operations. My favorite for an extremely safe, easy, and *fast* unfragmenting program is the Vopt utility, by Golden Bow. In my opinion, no other unfragmenting utility even comes close to this amazing $50 package. Golden Bow's address and phone number are in the vendor list in the Appendix in this book.

Caution

These unfragmenting programs, inherently dangerous by nature, do not eliminate the need for a good backup program. Before using an unfragmenting program, make sure that you have a good backup. What shape do you think your disk would be in if the power failed during an unfragmenting session? Also, some programs have had bugs or have been incompatible with new releases of DOS.

Cylinders. The term *cylinder* usually is used in place of *track*. A cylinder is all the tracks that are under read/write heads on a drive at one time. For floppy drives, because a disk cannot have more than two sides and the drive has two heads, normally there are two tracks per cylinder. As you learn in Chapter 9, hard disks can have many disk platters, each with two (or more) heads, for many tracks per single cylinder.

Clusters or Allocation Units. A cluster is also called an *allocation unit* in DOS version 4.0 and higher. The term is appropriate because a single cluster is the smallest unit of the disk that DOS can allocate when it writes a file. A cluster or allocation unit consists of one or more sectors—usually two or more. Having more than one sector per cluster reduces the file-allocation table size and enables DOS to run faster because it has fewer individual allocation units of the disk with which to work. The tradeoff is in some wasted disk space. Because DOS can manage space only in the cluster size unit, every file consumes space on the disk in increments of one cluster. Table 9.4 lists the default cluster sizes used by DOS for different floppy disk formats. Hard disk cluster or allocation unit sizes are discussed in Chapter 9.

Table 9.4 DOS Default Cluster and Allocation Unit Sizes

Floppy Disk capacity	Cluster/Allocation	Unit size	FAT type
5 1/4-inch, 360K	2 sectors	1,024 bytes	12-bit
5 1/4-inch, 1.2M	1 sector	512 bytes	12-bit
3 1/2-inch, 720K	2 sectors	1,024 bytes	12-bit
3 1/2-inch, 1.44M	1 sector	512 bytes	12-bit
3 1/2-inch, 2.88M	2 sectors	1,024 bytes	12-bit

K = 1,024 bytes
M = 1,048,576 bytes

III

Hardware Considerations

The high-density disks normally have smaller cluster sizes, which seems strange because these disks have many more individual sectors than do double-density disks. The probable reason is that because these high-density disks are faster than their double-density counterparts, IBM and Microsoft thought that the decrease in wasted disk space cluster size and speed would be welcome. You learn later that the cluster size on hard disks can vary much more between different versions of DOS and different disk sizes. Table 9.5 shows the floppy disk logical parameters.

Types of Floppy Drives

Five types of standard floppy drives are available for an IBM-compatible system. The drives can be summarized most easily by their formatting specifications (refer to tables 9.2 and 9.3).

Most drive types can format multiple types of disks. For example, the 3 1/2-inch ED drive can format and write on any 3 1/2-inch disk. The 5 1/4-inch HD drive also can format and write on any 5 1/4-inch disk (although, as mentioned, sometimes track-width problems occur). This drive can even create some older obsolete formats, including single-sided disks and disks with eight sectors per track.

As you can see from table 9.5, the different disk capacities are determined by several parameters, some of which seem to remain constant on all drives, while others change from drive to drive. For example, all drives use 512-byte physical sectors, which remains true for hard disks as well. Notice, however, that DOS treats the sector size as though it could be a changeable parameter, although the BIOS does not.

Table 9.5 Floppy Disk Logical DOS-Format Parameters							
	Current Formats				**Obsolete Formats**		
Disk Size (inches)	3 1/2	3 1/2	3 1/2	5 1/4	5 1/4	5 1/4	5 1/4	5 1/4
Disk Capacity (Kilobytes)	2,880	1,440	720	1,200	360	320	180	160
Media Descriptor Byte	F0h	F0h	F9h	F9h	FDh	FFh	FCh	FEh
Sides (Heads)	2	2	2	2	2	2	1	1
Tracks per Side	80	80	80	80	40	40	40	40
Sectors per Track	36	18	9	15	9	8	9	8
Bytes per Sector	512	512	512	512	512	512	512	512
Sectors per Cluster	2	1	2	1	2	2	1	1
FAT Length (Sectors)	9	9	3	7	2	1	2	1
Number of FATs	2	2	2	2	2	2	2	2
Root Dir. Length (Sectors)	15	14	7	14	7	7	4	4
Maximum Root Entries	240	224	112	224	112	112	64	64
Total Sectors per Disk	5,760	2,880	1,440	2,400	720	640	360	320
Total Available Sectors	5,726	2,847	1,426	2,371	708	630	351	313
Total Available Clusters	2,863	2,847	713	2,371	354	315	351	313

Notice also that now all standard floppy drives are double sided. IBM has not shipped PC systems with single-sided drives since 1982; these drives are definitely considered obsolete. Also, IBM never has utilized any form of single-sided 3 1/2-inch drives, although that type of drive appeared in the first Apple Macintosh systems in 1984. IBM officially began selling and supporting 3 1/2-inch drives in 1986, and has used only double-sided versions of these drives.

The 360K 5 1/4-inch Drive

The 5 1/4-inch low-density drive is designed to create a standard-format disk with 360K capacity. Although I persistently call these low-density drives, the industry term is "double-density." I use "low-density" because I find the term "double-density" to be somewhat misleading, especially when I am trying to define these drives in juxtaposition to the high-density drives.

The term *double density* arose from the use of the term *single density* to indicate a type of drive that used frequency modulation (FM) encoding to store approximately 90 kilobytes on a disk. This type of obsolete drive never was used in any IBM-compatible systems, but was used in some older systems such as the original Osborne-1 portable computer. When drive manufacturers changed the drives to use Modified Frequency Modulation (MFM) encoding, they began using the term "double density" to indicate it, as well as the (approximately doubled) increase in recording capacity realized from this encoding method. All modern floppy disk drives use MFM encoding, including all types listed in this section. Encoding methods such as FM, MFM, and RLL variants are discussed in Chapter 10, "Hard Disk Drives."

The 360K 5 1/4-inch drive normally records 40 cylinders of two tracks each, with each cylinder numbered starting with 0 closest to the outside diameter of the floppy disk. Head position (or side) 0 is recorded on the underside of the floppy disk, and Head 1 records on the top of the disk surface. This drive normally divides each track into nine sectors, but it can optionally format only eight sectors per track to create a floppy disk compatible with DOS versions 1.1 or earlier. This type of format rarely (if ever) is used today.

The 360K 5 1/4-inch drives as supplied in the first IBM systems all were full-height units, which means that they were 3.25 inches tall. Full-height drives are obsolete now and have not been manufactured since 1986. Later units used by IBM and most compatible vendors have been the half-height units, which are only 1.6 inches tall. You can install two half-height drives in place of a single full-height unit. These drives, made by different manufacturers, are similar except for some cosmetic differences.

The 360K 5 1/4-inch drives spin at 300 RPM, which equals exactly 5 revolutions per second, or 200 milliseconds per revolution. All standard floppy controllers support a 1:1 interleave, in which each sector on a specific track is numbered (and read) consecutively. To read and write to a disk at full speed, a controller sends data at a rate of 250,000 bits per second. Because all low-density controllers can support this data rate, virtually any controller supports this type of drive, depending on ROM BIOS code that supports these drives.

All standard IBM-compatible systems include ROM BIOS support for these drives; therefore, you usually do not need special software or driver programs in order to use them. This statement might exclude some aftermarket (non-IBM) 360K drives for PS/2 systems that might require some type of driver in order to work. The IBM-offered units use the built-in ROM support to enable these drives to work. The only requirement usually is to run the Setup program for the machine to enable it to properly recognize these drives.

The 1.2M 5 1/4-inch Drive

The 1.2M high-density floppy drive first appeared in the IBM AT system introduced in August 1984. The drive required the use of a new type of disk to achieve the 1.2M format capacity, but it still could read and write (although not always reliably) the lower-density 360K disks.

The 1.2M 5 1/4-inch drive normally recorded 80 cylinders of two tracks each, starting with cylinder 0, at the outside of the disk. This situation differs from the low-density 5 1/4-inch drive in its capability to record twice as many cylinders in approximately the same space on the disk. This capability alone suggests that the recording capacity for a disk would double, but that is not all. Each track normally is recorded with 15 sectors of 512 bytes each, increasing the storage capacity even further. In fact, these drives store nearly four times the data of the 360K disks. The density increase for each track required the use of special disks with a modified media designed to handle this type of recording. Because these disks initially were expensive and difficult to obtain, many users attempted incorrectly to use the low-density disks in the 1.2M 5 1/4-inch drives and format them to the higher 1.2M-density format. This attempt results in data loss and unnecessary data-recovery operations.

A compatibility problem with the 360K drives stems from the 1.2M drive's capability to write twice as many cylinders in the same space as the 360K drives. The 1.2M drives position their heads over the same 40 cylinder positions used by the 360K drives through "double stepping," a procedure in which the heads are moved every two cylinders to arrive at the correct positions for reading and writing the 40 cylinders on the 360K disks. The problem is that because the 1.2M drive normally has to write 80 cylinders in the same space in which the 360K drive writes 40, the heads of the 1.2M units had to be made dimensionally smaller. These narrow heads can have problems overwriting tracks produced by a 360K drive that has a wider head, because the narrower heads on the 1.2M drive cannot "cover" the entire track area written by the 360K drive. This problem and possible solutions to it are discussed later in this chapter.

The 1.2M 5 1/4-inch drives spin at 360 RPM, or 6 revolutions per second, or 166.67 milliseconds per revolution. The drives spin at this rate no matter what type of disk is inserted—either low- or high-density. To send or receive 15 sectors (plus required overhead) six times per second, a controller must use a data-transmission rate of 500,000 bits per second (500 kilohertz, or KHz). All standard high- and low-density controllers support this data rate and, therefore, these drives. This support of course would depend also on proper ROM BIOS support of the controller in this mode of operation. When a standard 360K disk is running in a high-density drive, it also is spinning at 360 RPM; a data rate of 300,000 bits per second (300 KHz) therefore is required in order to work properly. All standard AT-style low- and high-density controllers support the 250 KHz, 300 KHz, and 500 KHz data rates. The 300 KHz rate is used only for high-density 5 1/4-inch drives reading or writing to low-density 5 1/4-inch disks.

Virtually all standard AT-style systems have a ROM BIOS that supports the controller's operation of the 1.2M drive, including the 300 KHz data rate.

The 720K 3 1/2-inch Drive

The 720K, 3 1/2-inch, double-density drives first appeared in an IBM system with the IBM Convertible laptop system introduced in 1986. In fact, all IBM systems introduced since that time have 3 1/2-inch drives as the standard supplied drives. This type of drive has been offered also by IBM as an internal or external drive for the AT or XT systems. Note that outside the IBM-compatible world, other computer-system vendors (Apple, Hewlett-Packard, and so on) offered 3 1/2-inch drives for their systems well before the IBM-compatible world caught on.

The 720K, 3 1/2-inch, double-density drive normally records 80 cylinders of two tracks each, with 9 sectors per track, resulting in the formatted capacity of 720 kilobytes. It is interesting to note that many disk manufacturers label these disks as 1.0-megabyte disks, which is true. The difference between the actual 1.0 megabyte of capacity and the usable 720K after formatting is that some space on each track is occupied by the header and trailer of each sector, the inter-sector gaps, and the index gap at the start of each track before the first sector. These spaces are not usable for data storage and account for the differences between the unformatted and formatted capacities. Most manufacturers report the unformatted capacities because they do not know on which type of system you will format the disk. Apple Macintosh systems, for example, can store 800K of data on the same disk because of a different formatting technique. Note also that the 720K of usable space does not account for the disk areas DOS reserves for managing the disk (boot sectors, FATs, directories, and so on) and that because of these areas, only 713K remains for file data storage.

IBM-compatible systems have used 720K, 3 1/2-inch, double-density drives primarily in XT-class systems because the drives operate from any low-density controller. The drives spin at 300 RPM, and therefore require only a 250 KHz data rate from the controller to operate properly. This data rate is the same as for the 360K disk drives, which means that any controller that would support a 360K drive would support also one of the 720K drives.

The only issue to consider in installing a 720K, 3 1/2-inch drive is whether the ROM BIOS offers the necessary support. An IBM system with a ROM BIOS date of 06/10/85 or later has built-in support for 720K drives and requires no driver in order to use them. If your system has an earlier ROM BIOS date, the DRIVER.SYS program from DOS V3.2 or higher—as well as the DRIVPARM config.sys command in some OEM DOS versions—is all you need in order to provide the necessary software support to operate these drives. Of course, a ROM BIOS upgrade to a later version negates the need for "funny" driver software, and is usually the preferred option when you add one of these drives to an older system.

III

Hardware Considerations

The 1.44M 3 1/2-inch Drive

The 3 1/2-inch, 1.44M, high-density drives first appeared from IBM in the PS/2 product line introduced in 1987. Although IBM has not officially offered this type of drive for any of its older systems, most compatible vendors started offering the drives as options in systems immediately after IBM introduced the PS/2 system.

The drives record 80 cylinders consisting of two tracks each with 18 sectors per track, resulting in the formatted capacity of 1.44 megabytes. Most disk manufacturers label these disks as 2.0-megabyte disks, and the difference between this unformatted capacity and the formatted usable result is lost during the format. Note that the 1,440K of total formatted capacity does not account for the areas DOS reserves for file management, leaving only 1423.5K of actual file-storage area.

These drives spin at 300 RPM, and in fact must spin at that speed to operate properly with your existing high- and low-density controllers. To utilize the 500 KHz data rate, the maximum from most standard high- and low-density floppy controllers, these drives could spin at only 300 RPM. If the drives spun at the faster 360 RPM rate of the 5 1/4-inch drives, they would have to reduce the total number of sectors per track to 15 or the controller could not keep up. In short, the 1.44M 3 1/2-inch drives store 1.2 times the data of the 5 1/4-inch 1.2M drives, and the 1.2M drives spin exactly 1.2 times faster than the 1.44M drives. The data rates used by both high-density drives are identical and compatible with the same controllers. In fact, because these 3 1/2-inch high-density drives can run at the 500 KHz data rate, a controller that can support a 1.2M 5 1/4-inch drive can support the 1.44M drives also. If you are using a low-density disk in the 3 1/2-inch high-density drive, the data rate is reduced to 250 KHz, and the disk capacity is 720K.

The primary issue in a particular system utilizing a 1.44M 3 1/2-inch drive is one of ROM BIOS support. An IBM system with a ROM BIOS date of 11/15/85 or later has built-in support for these drives, and no external driver support program is needed. You might need a generic AT setup program because IBM's setup program never offered the 1.44M drive as an option. Another problem relates to the controller and the way it signals the high-density drive to write to a low-density disk. The problem is discussed in detail in the following section.

The 2.88M 3 1/2-inch Drive

The new 2.88M drive was developed by Toshiba Corporation in the 1980s, and officially announced in 1987. Toshiba began production manufacturing of the drives and disks in 1989, and then several vendors began selling the drives as upgrades for systems. IBM officially adopted these drives for the PS/2 systems in 1991, and virtually all PS/2s sold since then have these drives as standard equipment. Since a 2.88M drive can fully read and write 1.44M and 720K disks, the change was an easy one. DOS version 5.0 or higher is required to support the 2.88M drives.

In order to support the 2.88M drive, modifications were required to the disk controller circuitry since these drives spin at the same 300 RPM but have an astonishing 36 sectors per track. Since all floppy disks are formatted with consecutively numbered sectors (1:1 interleave), these 36 sectors have to be read and written in the same time it takes a

1.44M drive to read and write 18 sectors. This requires that the controller support a much higher data transmission rate of 1 MHz (1 Million bits per second). Most of the older floppy controllers either found on an adapter card or built into the motherboard will support only the maximum of 500 KHz data rate used by the 1.44M drives. To upgrade to 2.88M drives would require that the controller be changed to one that supports the higher 1 MHz data rate.

An additional support issue is the ROM BIOS. The BIOS must have support for the controller and must have the ability to specify and accept the 2.88M drive as a CMOS setting. Newer motherboard BIOS sets from companies like Phoenix, AMI, and Award have support for the new Extra-high Density controllers.

In addition to the newer IBM PS/2 systems, most newer IBM clone and compatible systems now have built-in floppy controllers and ROM BIOS software that fully support the 2.88M drives. Adding or upgrading to a 2.88M drive in these systems is as easy as plugging the drive in and running the CMOS Setup program. For those systems who do not have this support built-in, this type of upgrade will be much more difficult. Several companies offer new controllers and BIOS upgrades as well as the 2.88M drives specifically for upgrading older systems.

Although the 2.88M drives themselves are not much more expensive than the 1.44M drives they replace, the disk media is currently still very expensive. Although you can purchase 1.44M disks for around (or under) one dollar each, the 2.88M disks can cost more than $5 per disk! As the drives become more generally available, the disk media prices should fall. The 1.44M and even 1.2M disk media was similarly very expensive when first introduced as well.

Handling Recording Problems with 1.44M 3 1/2-inch Drives

A serious problem awaits many users who use the 1.44M 3 1/2-inch drives: If the drive is installed improperly, any write or format operations performed incorrectly on 720K disks can end up trashing data on low-density disks. The problem is caused by the controller's inability to signal the high-density drive that a low-density recording will take place.

High-density disks require a higher write-current or signal strength when they record than do the low-density disks. A low-density drive can record at only the lower write-current, which is correct for the low-density disks; the high-density drive, however, needs to record at both high and low write-currents depending on which type of disk is inserted in the drive. If a signal is not sent to the high-density drive telling it to lower or reduce the write-current level, the drive stays in its normal high write-current default mode, even when it records on a low-density disk. The signal normally should be sent to the drive by the controller, but many controllers do not provide this signal properly for the 1.44M drives.

It seems that the Western Digital controller used by IBM would enable the reduced write-current (RWC) signal only if the controller also were sending data at the 300 KHz data rate, indicating the special case of a low-density disk in a high-density drive. The RWC signal is required to tell the high-density drive to lower the head-writing signal strength to be proper for the low-density disks. If the signal is not sent, the drive defaults to the higher write-current, which should be used for only high-density disks. If the controller were transmitting the 250 KHz data rate, the controller knows that the drive must be a low-density drive and therefore no RWC signal was necessary because the low-density drives can write only with reduced current.

This situation presented a serious problem for owners of 1.44M drives using 720K disks because the drives spin the disks at 300 RPM, and, in writing to a low-density disk, use the 250 KHz data rate-not the 300 KHz rate. This setup "fools" the controller into "thinking" that it is sending data to a low-density drive, which causes the controller to fail to send the required RWC signal. Without the RWC signal, the drive then records improperly on the disk, possibly trashing any data being written or any data already present. Because virtually all compatibles use controllers based on the design of the IBM AT floppy disk controller, most share the same problem as the IBM AT.

Drive and disk manufacturers devised the perfect solution for this problem, short of using a redesigned controller. They built into the drives a *media sensor*, which, when it is enabled, can override the controller's RWC signal (or lack of it) and properly change the head-current levels within the drive. Essentially, the drive chooses the write-current level independently from the controller when the media sensor is operational.

The sensor is a small, physical or optical sensor designed to feel, or "see," the small hole on the high-density 3 1/2-inch disks located opposite the write-enable hole. The extra hole on these high-density or extra-high density disks is the media sensor's cue that the full write-current should be used in recording. If an ED disk is detected, the ED drive enables the vertical recording heads. Low-density disks do not have these extra holes; therefore, when the sensor cannot see a media-sensor hole, it causes the drive to record in the proper reduced write-current mode for a double-density disk.

Some people, of course, foolishly attempt to override the function of these sensors by needlessly punching an extra hole in a low-density disk, to fool the drive's sensor into acting as though an actual high-density disk has been inserted. Several "con artist" companies have made a fast buck by selling media sensor hole-punchers to unwary or misinformed people. These disk-punch "hustlers" try to mislead you into believing that there is no difference between the low- and high-density disks except for the hole, and that punching the extra hole makes the low-density disk a legitimate high-density disk. This, of course, is absolutely untrue: The high-density disks are very different from low-density disks. The differences between the disks are explained in more detail later in this chapter.

Another reason that this hole-punching is needless is that if you want to record a high-density format on a low-density disk, you only have to remove the jumper from the drive that enables the media sensor. Removing the media sensor jumper still allows the drive to work properly for high-density disks writing at the full write-current level, but unfortunately also allows the higher write-current to be used on low-density disks as well because then the drive has no way of knowing the difference. If you really want to risk your data to low-density disks formatted as high-density disks, you can save yourself the cost of the $40 hole-punchers. Note that even if you attempt to format or record properly on a 720K disk, you still will be working at the higher write-current, and will risk trashing the disk.

Many systems, including the IBM PS/2 series, Compaq, Toshiba laptops, and many others with floppy controllers built in to the motherboard, do not need 1.44M drives with media sensors. Their controllers have been fixed to allow the RWC signal to be sent to the drive even when the controller is sending the 250 KHz data rate. This setup allows for proper operation no matter what type of disk or drive is used, as long as the user formats properly. Because these systems do not have a media sensor policing users, they easily can format low-density disks as though they were high-density disks regardless of what holes are on the disk. This has caused problems for users of the older PS/2 systems, where they have accidentally formatted 720K disks as 1.44M disks. When passed to a system that has an enabled media sensor, the system will refuse to read the disks at all because it is not correctly formatted. If you are having disk interchange problems, be sure that you are formatting your disks correctly.

The newer PS/2 and other high-end systems from other manufacturers (Hewlett-Packard, for example) use an active media sensor setup where the user no longer has to enter the correct FORMAT command parameters to format the disk. In these systems, the media sensor information is passed through the controller to the BIOS, which properly informs the FORMAT command about which disk is in the drive. With these systems, it is impossible for a user to accidentally format a disk incorrectly, and it eliminates the user from having to know anything about the different disk media types.

In summary, if you have a system with no media sensor or one that is disabled (such as the older PS/2 and Compaq systems), you can easily misformat your disks without punching any holes. I hope that you don't do this, of course—I am just stating that you can.

Handling Recording Problems with 1.2M and 360K Drives

The 5 1/4-inch drives have their own special problems. One major problem resulting in needless data destruction is that the tracks sometimes are recorded at different widths for different drives. These differences in recorded track width can result in problems with data exchange between different 5 1/4-inch drives.

As shown in table 9.1, the recorded track-width difference affects only the 5 1/4-inch drives because the 5 1/4-inch low-density drives record a track width more than twice that of the 5 1/4-inch high-density drives. This difference presents a problem if a high-density drive is used to update a low-density disk with previously recorded data on it. The high-density drive, even in 360K mode, cannot completely overwrite the track left by the 40-track drive. A problem occurs when the disk is returned to the person with the 360K drive, because that drive sees the new data as "embedded" within the remains of the previously written track. The 360K drive cannot distinguish either signal, and an Abort, Retry, Ignore error message results.

The way around this problem is to start with a brand-new disk that has never been formatted, and to format it in the 1.2M drive with the /4 (or equivalent) option. This procedure causes the 1.2M drive to place the proper 360K format on the disk. The 1.2M drive then can be used to fill the disk to its 360K capacity, and every file will be readable on the 40-track 360K drive because there were no previous wider data tracks to confuse the 360K drive. I use this trick all the time to exchange data disks between AT systems that have only a 1.2M drive and XT or PC systems that have only a 360K drive. The key is to start with a brand-new disk or a disk wiped clean magnetically by a bulk eraser. Simply reformatting the disk does not work because formatting actually writes data to the disk.

Note that because all the 3 1/2-inch drives write tracks of the same width, these drives have no disk-interchange problems related to track width.

Analyzing Floppy Disk Construction

The 5 1/4-inch and 3 1/2-inch disks each have unique construction and physical properties.

The flexible (or floppy) disk is contained within a plastic jacket. The 3 1/2-inch disks are covered by a more rigid jacket than are the 5 1/4-inch disks; the disks within the jackets, however, are virtually identical except, of course, for the size.

There are differences and similarities between these two different-size disks. Let's look at the physical properties and construction of each disk type.

When you look at a typical 5 1/4-inch floppy disk, you see several things (see fig. 9.9). Most prominent is the large, round hole in the center. When you close the disk drive's "door," a cone-shaped clamp grabs and centers the disk through the center hole. Many disks come with hub-ring reinforcements—thin, plastic rings like those used to reinforce three-ring notebook paper—intended to help the disk withstand the mechanical forces of the clamping mechanism. The high-density disks usually lack these reinforcements because the difficulty in accurately placing them on the disk means that they will cause alignment problems.

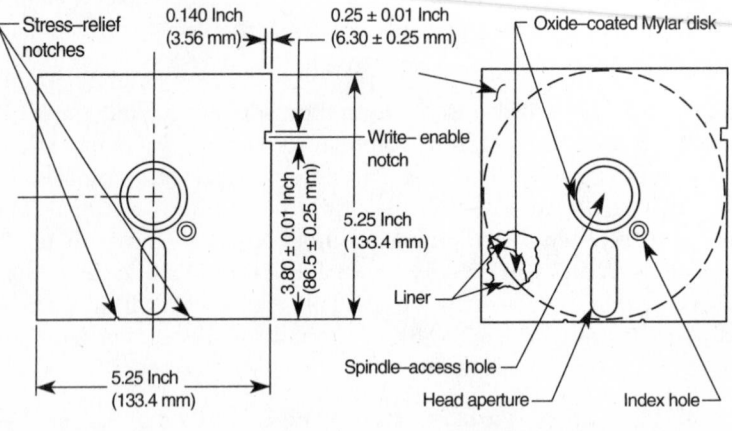

Courtesy of IBM Corporation

Fig. 9.9
Construction of a 5 1/4-inch floppy disk.

On the right side, just below the center of the hub hole, is a smaller, round hole called the *index hole*. If you carefully turn the disk within its protective jacket, you see a small hole in the disk. The drive uses the index hole as the starting point for all the sectors on the disk-sort of the "prime meridian" for the disk sectors. A disk with a single index hole is a *soft-sectored* disk; the software (operating system) decides the actual number of sectors on the disk. Some older equipment, such as Wang word processors, used hard-sectored disks, which had an index hole to demarcate individual sectors. Do not use hard-sectored disks in a PC.

Below the hub hole is a slot shaped somewhat like a long racetrack, through which you can see the disk surface. Through this *media-access hole*, the disk drive heads read and write information to the disk surface.

At the right side, about one inch from the top, is a rectangular punch from the side of the disk cover. If this *write-enable notch* is present, writing to the disk has been enabled. Disks without this notch (or with the notch taped over) are *write-protected* disks. The notch might not be on all disks, particularly those you have purchased with programs on them.

On the rear of the disk jacket, at the bottom, two very small, oval notches flank the head slot. The notches relieve stress on the disk and help prevent it from warping. The drive might use these notches also to assist in keeping the disk in the proper position in the drive.

Because the 3 1/2-inch disks use a much more rigid plastic case, which helps stabilize the disk, the disks can record at track and data densities greater than the 5 1/4-inch disks (see fig. 9.10). A metal shutter protects the media-access hole. The shutter is manipulated by the drive, and remains closed whenever the disk is not in a drive. The media then is insulated from the environment and from your fingers. The shutter also obviates the need for a disk jacket.

Rather than an index hole in the disk, the 3 1/2-inch disks use a metal center hub with an alignment hole. The drive "grasps" the metal hub, and the hole in the hub enables the drive to position the disk properly.

On the lower-left part of the disk is a hole with a plastic slider—the write-protect/-enable hole (refer to fig. 9.10). When the slider is positioned so that the hole is visible, the disk is write protected; the drive is prevented from recording on the disk. When the slider is positioned to cover the hole, writing is enabled and you can record on the disk. For more permanent write-protection, some commercial software programs are supplied on disks with the slider removed so that you cannot easily enable recording on the disk.

On the other (right) side of the disk from the write-protect hole, there might be in the disk jacket another hole called the *media-density-selector hole*. If this hole is present, the disk is constructed of a special medium and is therefore a high-density or extra-high-density disk. If the media-sensor hole is exactly opposite the write-protect hole, it indicates a 1.44M HD disk. If the media-sensor hole is located more toward the top of the disk (the metal shutter is at the top of the disk), it indicates an ED disk. No hole on the right side means that the disk is low-density. Most 3 1/2-inch drives have a media sensor that controls recording capability based on the existence or absence of these holes.

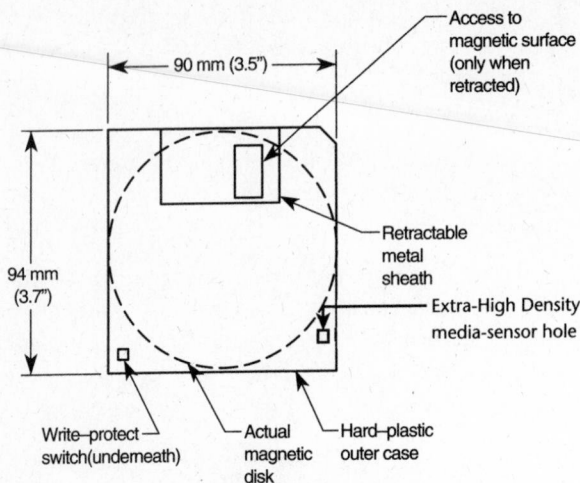

Fig. 9.10
Construction of a 3 1/2-inch floppy disk.

Both the 3 1/2-inch and 5 1/4-inch disks are constructed of the same basic materials. They use a plastic base (usually Mylar) coated with a magnetic compound. The compound is usually a ferric- (iron-) oxide-based compound for the standard density versions; a cobalt ferric compound usually is used in the higher-coercivity (higher-density) disks. A newly announced disk type, called *extended density*, uses a barium ferrite compound. The rigid jacket material on the 3 1/2-inch disks often causes people to believe incorrectly that these disks are some sort of "hard disk" and not really a floppy disk. The disk "cookie" inside the 3 1/2-inch case is just as floppy as the 5 1/4-inch variety.

Floppy Disk Types and Specifications

This section examines all the types of disks you can purchase for your system. Especially interesting are the technical specifications that can separate one type of disk from another. This section defines all the specifications used to describe a typical disk.

Single- and Double-Sided Disks. Whether a disk is single- or double-sided is really an issue only for the lower-density disks. Because no single-sided high-density drives are manufactured, no need exists for disks to match the drives. The original IBM PC had single-sided drives, but they were discontinued in 1982.

A single-sided disk is constructed of the same material as a double-sided disk. The only difference seems to be that only the single-sided disks are "certified" (whatever that means) on only one side, and the double-sided disks are certified on both sides. Because the single-sided disks are cheaper than the double-sided versions, many PC users quickly determined that they could save some money if they used the single-sided disks even in double-sided drives.

The reason that this reasoning can work is that it is economically impractical for disk manufacturers to make some disks with recording surfaces on one side and other disks with recording surfaces on both sides. Today's single-sided disks look, and usually behave, exactly the same as double-sided disks. The result of this—depending on the brand of disks you buy—is that you can generally format and use "single-sided" disks successfully in double-sided drives, at a savings in disk costs. Unfortunately, the savings now are so small that this practice is obsolete, if not risky.

The danger in this practice is that some manufacturers do not burnish, or polish, the unused (top) side to the same level of smoothness as the used (bottom) side. This practice can cause accelerated wear on the top head. In single-sided drives, because the top head was replaced by a soft, felt pad, the rougher top side caused no problems. For the cost, it is not worth using with the wrong disks. I recommend the conservative route: Spend the small amount of extra money for double-sided disks of the correct density, and you will rarely have to recover damaged data.

Density. *Density*, in simplest terms, is a measure of the amount of information that can be packed reliably into a specific area of a recording surface. The keyword here is *reliably*.

Disks have two types of densities: longitudinal density and linear density. *Longitudinal density* is indicated by how many tracks can be recorded on the disk, often expressed as a number of tracks per inch (TPI). *Linear density* is the capability of an individual track to store data, often indicated as a number of bits per inch (BPI). Unfortunately, both types of densities often are interchanged incorrectly in discussing different disks and drives. Table 9.6 provides a rundown of each available type of disk.

Table 9.6 Floppy Disk Media Specifications

	5 1/4-inch			3 1/2-inch		
	Double Density	Quad Density	High Density	Double Density	High Density	Extra-High Density
Media Parameters	(DD)	(QD)	(HD)	(DD)	(HD)	(ED)
Tracks Per Inch (TPI)	48	96	96	135	135	135
Bits Per Inch (BPI)	5,876	5,876	9,646	8,711	17,434	34,868
Media Formulation	Ferrite	Ferrite	Cobalt	Cobalt	Cobalt	Barium
Coercivity (Oersteds)	300	300	600	600	720	750
Thickness (Micro-In.)	100	100	50	70	40	100
Recording Polarity	Horiz.	Horiz.	Horiz.	Horiz	Horiz.	Vert.

It is notable that IBM skipped the quad-density disk type—that is, no IBM system has used a quad-density drive, or required quad-density disks. Don't purchase a quad-density disk unless you just want a better-quality double-density disk.

Both the quad- and double-density disks store the same linear data on each track. They use the same formula for the magnetic coating on the disk, but the quad-density versions represent a more rigorously tested, higher-quality disk. The high-density disks are entirely different, however. To store the increased linear density, an entirely different magnetic coating was required. In both the 5 1/4-inch and 3 1/2-inch high-density disks, a high-coercivity coating is used to allow the tremendous bit density for each track. A high-density disk never can be substituted for a double- or quad-density disk because the write-current must be different for these very different media formulations and thicknesses.

The extra-high density 3 1/2-inch disk in the chart is newly available in some systems. This type of disk, invented by Toshiba, is available from several other vendors as well. The extra-high density disks use a barium-ferrite compound to cover the disk with a thicker coating, which enables a vertical recording technique to be used. In vertical recording, the magnetic domains are recorded vertically rather than flat. The higher density results from their capability to be stacked much more closely together. These types of drives can read and write the other 3 1/2-inch disks because of their similar track dimensions on all formats.

Media Coercivity and Thickness. The *coercivity specification* of a disk refers to the magnetic-field strength required to make a proper recording on a disk. Coercivity, measured in oersteds, is a value indicating magnetic strength. A disk with a higher coercivity rating requires a stronger magnetic field to make a recording on that disk. With lower ratings, the disk can be recorded with a weaker magnetic field. In other words, *the lower the coercivity rating, the more sensitive the disk.*

Another factor is the thickness of the disk. The thinner the disk, the less influence a region of the disk has on another adjacent region. The thinner disks therefore can accept many more bits per inch without eventually degrading the recording.

When I ask someone whether the high-density disks are more sensitive or less sensitive than the double-density disks, the answer is almost always "more sensitive." But you can see that this is not true. The high-density disks are in fact as much as half as sensitive as the double-density disks. A high-density drive can record with a much higher volume level at the heads than can the standard double-density drive. For these high-density drives to record properly on a double-density disk, the drive must be capable of using a reduced write-current mode and enable it whenever the lower-density disks are installed. A big problem with users and floppy disks then can occur.

Most users do not like paying more for the high-density disks their drives can use. These users, in an attempt to save money, are tempted to use the lower-density disks as a substitute. Some users attempt to format the "regular" disk at the high-density capacity. This formatting is facilitated by DOS, which always attempts to format a disk to the maximum capacity of the drive's capabilities, unless specifically ordered otherwise through the use of proper parameters in the FORMAT command, or unless your system has an Active Media Sensor. If you use no parameters and simply enter FORMAT A:, however, the disk is formatted as though it were a high-density disk. Many users think that this procedure somehow is equivalent to using the single-sided disks in place of double-sided ones. I can assure you that this is not true—it is much worse. *Do not use double-density disks in place of high-density disks,* or you will experience severe problems and data loss from improper coercivity, media thickness, and write-current specifications.

The reasons for using the high-coercivity thin disks are simple. In designing the high-density drives, engineers found that the density of magnetic flux reversals caused adjacent flux reversals to begin to affect each other. The effect was that they started to cancel each other out, or cause shifts in the polarity of the domain. Data written at the high densities eventually began to erase itself. As an analogy, imagine a wooden track on which you place magnetic marbles, evenly spaced four inches apart in a specific pattern of magnetic polarity. At this distance, the magnetic forces from each marble are too weak to affect the adjacent marbles. Now imagine that the marbles must be placed only two inches apart. The magnetic attraction and repulsion forces now might start to work on the adjacent marbles so that they begin to rotate on their axis and thus change the direction of polarity and the data they represent.

You could eliminate the interaction of the magnetic domains by either spacing them further apart or making the domains "weaker," therefore reducing their sphere of influence. If the marbles were made half as strong magnetically as they were before, you could get them twice as close together without any interaction between them. This principle was behind the high-coercivity, thin media disks. Because they are weaker magnetically, they need a higher recording strength in order to store an image properly.

Try a simple experiment to verify this principle. Attempt to format a high-density disk in a low-density format. DOS responds with a `Track 0 bad`, `Disk unusable` message. The disk did not seem to accept a recording in low-density mode because the low-density recording is also low volume. The disk cannot make a recording on the disk, and therefore the `Track 0 bad` message is displayed.

It is unfortunate for users that the opposite attempt appears to work: that you can format a standard double-density disk as though it were a high-density disk and the FORMAT command or DOS does not seem to be affected. You might notice a large number of "bad sectors," but DOS allows the format to be completed anyway.

This situation is unfortunate for two reasons. First, you are recording on the (low-density) disk with a density that requires weak magnetic domains to eliminate interaction between the adjacent domains. A low-density disk unfortunately stores magnetic domains twice as strong as they should be, and eventually they interact. You will experience mysterious data losses on this disk over the next few days, weeks, or months.

Second, you have just placed a recording on this disk at twice the signal strength it should be. This "industrial strength" recording might not be removable by a normal disk drive, and the disk might be magnetically saturated. You might not ever be able to reformat it correctly as a double-density disk because a double-density reformat uses reduced write-current. The reduced write-current might not be capable of overwriting the high write-current signal that had been recorded incorrectly. The best way to remove this "burned in" recording then is to use a bulk eraser to renew the disk by removing all magnetic information. In most cases, however, a fresh format can overcome the magnetic image of the previous one, even if the write-current had been incorrect.

Do not use the wrong media for the format you are attempting to perform. You must use the correct type of disk. Note that the 3 1/2-inch disks have a perfect mechanism—the media sensor for deterring users. If you are sure that all your high-density 3 1/2-inch drives contain this sensor, set to function (by way of a jumper or switch), you are saved from your own ignorance. A drive with a media sensor sets the write-current and operating mode by the actual disk inserted. You are prevented from taking a 720K disk and attempting to cram 1.44 megabytes on it. Remember that IBM did not make using this sensor a requirement because it fixed the controller problem that necessitated it; therefore, incorrectly formatting a disk is easy on the PS/2 system. Also, if you want to format a low-density 3 1/2-inch disk incorrectly with a high-density format using an IBM PS/2 system, you don't need one of the "disk converters" or hole punchers.

Soft and Hard Sectors. Floppy disks are either *soft sectored* or *hard sectored*. A soft-sectored disk has only one index hole on the disk surface. Once every revolution, the hole is visible through the hole in the protective jacket, and the drive, controller, and DOS use the hole to establish the location and timing of the first sector on a track. Individual sectors are defined by the controller and the software that runs the controller, hence the term *soft sectored*. Hard-sectored disks have an index hole as well as a separate hole for each sector on the disk marking the beginning of that sector. Hard sectored disks are not used in IBM compatible PCs, but were used in some dedicated word processing systems and other proprietary computer systems. If you try to use a hard-sectored disk in a PC, the machine will get confused. Sometimes hard-sectored disks are not labeled specifically as hard-sectored, but rather specify "10 sectors" or "16 sectors." Because hard sectored disks are not used in IBM compatible systems, I have not seen these disks for sale in quite some time.

Formatting and Using High- and Low-Density Disks

This section describes how the different density capabilities of the high- and low-density drives sometimes can cause problems in formatting disks. You must always ensure that a disk initially is formatted to the density in which it was supposed to be run. In some cases, you should have a high-density drive format a low-density disk. You can perform this formatting with the correct format commands. The following section describes how to use DOS correctly so that your disks are formatted properly.

Reading and Writing 360K Disks in 1.2M Drives. Having 1.2M drives *read* or *write* to a 360K disk is a simple task. Just place a previously formatted 360K disk in the drive and use it normally. In other words, pretend that the drive is a 360K drive. Nothing special must be done. You can either read or write on the disk with absolutely no problems—yet.

You will have a problem if you decide to return the disk to a 360K drive and attempt to read it. Remember that the recorded track width of the 1.2M drive is half the track width of the 360K drive; therefore, if are any tracks have been *previously recorded by an actual 360K drive*, the tracks are twice as wide as the tracks recorded by the 1.2M drive. If you write to the disk with the 1.2M drive, you cannot overwrite the entire track width—only the center portion of it. When you return this disk to a 360K drive, the wider head system in the 360K drive then sees two signals on any overwritten tracks, and the new data is nestled within the image of the old data that could not be completely covered by the 1.2M drive. An immediate `Abort, Retry, Ignore` error from DOS usually is displayed for any updated portions of the disk.

To solve this problem easily, if you want to record data in an AT 1.2M drive and later read it properly in a 360K drive, make sure that you use *brand-new* disks for recording in the 1.2M drive. Because a new disk has no magnetic information on it, the smaller re-corded track width can be written on the 1.2M drive and read properly in the 360K drive: The more narrow track is written in "clean space." The 360K drive, therefore, no longer is confused by any "ghost images" of previously recorded wider tracks. Other than starting with a brand-new disk, your only other option is to use a disk erased by a bulk eraser. You cannot erase a disk by reformatting it if has been in use. Formatting records actual data on the disk, and causes the track-width problem. The new or bulk-erased disk in fact must be formatted by the 1.2M drive for this procedure to work again. Remember the simple rule: Any track recorded by a 360K drive *cannot be overwritten* by a 1.2M drive, even in the 360K format.

How do you format a 360K disk in a 1.2M drive? If you just execute the FORMAT command without parameters, DOS attempts to format the disk to its maximum capacity. Because the 1.2M drives have no media-sensing capability, DOS assumes that the disk capability is equal to the maximum capability of the drive, and attempts to create a 1.2M format on the disk. The write-current is increased also during a recording in this format, which is incompatible with the 360K media. To format the 360K disk correctly, there-fore, look at the alternative command examples in table 9.7.

Table 9.7 Proper Formatting of 5 1/4-inch 360K Disks in a 1.2M Drive

Command	DOS version						
	6.x	5.x	4.x	3.3	3.2	3.1	3.0
FORMAT d: /4	Yes	Yes	Yes	Yes	Yes	Yes	Yes
FORMAT d: /N:9 /T:40	Yes	Yes	Yes	Yes	Yes	No	No
FORMAT d: /F:360	Yes	Yes	Yes	No	No	No	No

d: = The drive to format
N = Number of sectors per track
T = Tracks per side
F = Format capacity

Note that DOS versions prior to 3.0 do not support 1.2M drives. Each example command accomplishes the same function, which is to place on a 360K disk a 40-track, 9-sector format using reduced write-current mode.

Reading and Writing 720K Disks in 1.44M and 2.88M Drives. The 3 1/2-inch drives do not have the same problems as the 5 1/4-inch disks—that is, at least not with data interchange. Because both the high- and low-density drives write the same number of tracks and are the same width, one type of drive can be used to overwrite data written by another type of drive. Because of this capability, IBM does not need to offer a low-density version of the 3 1/2-inch drives for the PS/2 systems. These systems (except Models 25 and 30) include only the HD or ED drives, which are capable of imitating perfectly the 720K drives in the Model 25 and Model 30. The high-density drives can be trouble, however, in the hands of an inexperienced (or cheapskate) user. You *must* be sure to use only the 1.44M high-density disks in the 1.44M format, and only the 720K disks in the 720K format. You will encounter serious problems if you stick a 720K disk in a drive in a PS/2 without a media sensor drive and enter the command FORMAT A:. If you decide to use the formatted disk anyway, massive data loss eventually will occur.

Problems with incorrect formatting could have been averted if IBM had universally used disk drives that included the media sensor. This special switch senses the unique hole found only on the right side of high-density disks. Drives that use this hole to control the status of reduced write-current never can format a disk incorrectly. The hardware saves you by causing the FORMAT command to end in failure with an appropriate error message if you attempt to format the disk incorrectly. All of the newer PS/2 systems from IBM include drives with an active media sensor that allows disks to be formatted correctly with no parameters on the format command. The information FORMAT needs about what type of disk is in the drive is supplied by the BIOS directly on these systems; no user supplied parameters are necessary.

The 1.44M drives and 720K drives do not have all the same problems as the 5 1/4-inch drives, primarily because all the 3 1/2-inch drives have the same recorded track width. The 1.44M or 2.88M drive has no problem recording 720K disks. For these reasons (and more), I applaud the industry move to the 3 1/2-inch drives. The sooner we stop using 5 1/4-inch disk drives, the better.

The only other problem with formatting, other than incorrectly selecting a drive without a media sensor or failing to enable it during the drive-installation procedure, is naive users attempting to format disks at a capacity for which they were not designed. *You must have a 720K (double-density) disk in order to write a 720K format; a 1.44M (high-density) disk in order to write a 1.44M format; and a 2.88M (extra-high-density) disk in order to write an extra-high-density format.* No ifs, ands, or buts. This chapter has explained already that this requirement stems from differences in the coercivity of the media and the levels of recording current used in writing the disks.

When you enter a standard format command with no parameters, DOS normally attempts to format the disk to the drive's maximum capacity as indicated by the BIOS. If you insert a 720K disk in a 1.44M drive, therefore, and enter the FORMAT command with no parameters, DOS attempts to create a 1.44M format on the disk. If the drive has a passive media sensor, the FORMAT command aborts with an error message. The media sensor does not communicate to DOS the correct information to format the disk—it just *prevents* incorrect formatting. You still must know the correct commands. If the system support active media sensing, no FORMAT command parameters are necessary, as the BIOS will supply the correct parameters based on the type of disk in the drive. Table 9.8 shows the correct FORMAT command and parameters to use in formatting a 720K disk in a 1.44M drive.

Reading and Writing 1.44M Disks in 2.88M Drives. The 2.88M extra-high-density (ED) drive used in some newer systems, such as virtually the entire PS/2 line, is a welcome addition to any system. This drive offers a capacity twice as great as the standard 1.44M HD drive, and also offers full backward compatibility with the 1.44M HD drive and the 720K DD drive.

The 2.88M ED drive uses a technique called *vertical recording* to achieve its great linear density of 36 sectors per track. This technique increases density by magnetizing the domains perpendicular to the recording surface. By essentially placing the magnetic domains on their ends and stacking them side by side, density increases enormously.

Table 9.8 Proper Formatting of 3 1/2-inch 720K Disks in a 1.44M or 2.88M Drive

Command	DOS version			
	6.x	5.x	4.x	3.3
FORMAT d: /N:9 /T:80	Yes	Yes	Yes	Yes
FORMAT d: /F:720	Yes	Yes	Yes	No

d: = The drive to format
N = Number of sectors per track
T = Tracks per side
F = Format capacity
Note that DOS versions before 3.3 do not support 1.44M drives, and versions before 5.0 do not support 2.88M drives.

The technology for producing heads that can perform a vertical or perpendicular recording has been around awhile. It is not the heads or even the drives that represent the major breakthrough in technology; rather, it is the medium that is special. Standard disks have magnetic particles shaped like tiny needles, which lie on the surface of the disk. Orienting these particles in a perpendicular manner to enable vertical recording is very difficult. The particles on a barium ferrite floppy disk are shaped like tiny, flat, hexagonal platelets that easily can be arranged to have their axis of magnetization perpendicular to the plane of recording. Although barium ferrite has been used as a material in the construction of permanent magnets, no one has been able to reduce the grain size of the platelets enough for high-density recordings.

Toshiba has perfected a glass-crystallization process for manufacturing the ultra fine platelets used in coating the barium ferrite disks. This technology, patented by Toshiba, is being licensed to a number of disk manufacturers, all of whom are producing barium ferrite disks using Toshiba's process. Toshiba also made certain modifications to the design of standard disk drive heads to enable them to read and write the new barium ferrite disks as well as standard cobalt or ferrite disks. This technology is used not only in floppy drives but also appears in a variety of tape drive formats.

III

Hardware Considerations

The disks are called 4MB disks in reference to their unformatted capacity. Actual formatted capacity is 2,880K, or 2.88M. Because of space lost in the formatting process, as well as space occupied by the volume boot sector, file-allocation tables, and root directory, the total usable storage space is 2,863K.

A number of manufacturers are making these drives, including Toshiba, Mitsubishi, Sony, and Panasonic. During the next few years, they should become more popular in higher-end systems.

Format Summary. This section is a short guide to the DOS FORMAT command. With newer DOS versions supporting more and different types of disk hardware, the once-simple FORMAT command has become more complex. Especially with the advent of DOS V5.0, the number of parameters and options available for the FORMAT command had increased dramatically. This section discusses the FORMAT command and these optional parameters. You will see a simple guide to proper formatting of disks, as well as a thorough description of the FORMAT command parameters and options.

Table 9.9 Proper Formatting of 3 1/2-inch 1.44M Disks in a 2.88M Drive

Command	DOS version 6.x	5.x
FORMAT d: /N:18 /T:80	Yes	Yes
FORMAT d: /F:1.44	Yes	Yes

d: = The drive to format
N = Number of sectors per track
T = Tracks per side
F = Format capacity
Note that DOS versions before 5.0 do not support the 2.88M drive. Also, most 2.88M installations have an active media sensor which will automatically format the disk correctly as determined by the media sensor. With active media sensing, the parameters indicating disk capacity are not necessary.

This chapter has emphasized that a specific disk must always be formatted to its designated capacity. Formatting a disk to a capacity different from what it was designed for results only in an eventual loss of data from the disk. Because all the higher-density drives can format all the lower-density disks of the same form factor, knowing when a particular command option is required can be pretty complicated.

The basic rule is that a drive always formats in its native mode unless specifically instructed otherwise through the FORMAT command parameters. Therefore, if you insert a 2.88M ED disk in a 2.88M ED A: drive, you then can format that disk by simply entering FORMAT A:—no optional parameters are necessary in that case. If you insert any other type of disk (DD or HD), however, you absolutely *must* enter the appropriate parameters in the FORMAT command to change the format mode from the default 2.88M mode to the mode appropriate for the inserted disk. Even though the drive might have a media sensor that can detect which type of disk is inserted in the drive, in most cases the sensor does not communicate to the controller or DOS, which does not know which disk it is. In effect, all the sensor does is forcibly control the drive write mode, and also forces the FORMAT command to fail if you do not enter the correct parameters for the inserted disk type.

Table 9.10 shows the proper format command for all possible variations in drive and disk types. It shows also which DOS versions support the various combinations of drives, disks, and FORMAT parameters.

To use this table, just look up the drive type and disk type you have. You then can see the proper FORMAT command parameters to use as well as the DOS versions that support the combination you want.

With the advent of DOS V5.0, the FORMAT command has received a number of new functions and capabilities, all expressed through two new parameters: /Q (Quickformat) and /U (Unconditional). Precisely describing the effect of these parameters on the FORMAT command is difficult, especially considering that they have different effects on hard disks and floppy disks. Table 9.11 summarizes the functions of these new parameters, and relates the new functions to the older versions of DOS.

Table 9.10 Proper Disk Formatting			
Drive type	**Disk type**	**DOS version**	**Proper format command**
5 1/4-inch 360K	DD 360K	DOS 2.0+	FORMAT d:
5 1/4-inch 1.2M	HD 1.2M	DOS 3.0+	FORMAT d:
5 1/4-inch 1.2M	DD 360K	DOS 3.0+	FORMAT d: /4
5 1/4-inch 1.2M	DD 360K	DOS 3.2+	FORMAT d: /N:9 /T:40
5 1/4-inch 1.2M	DD 360K	DOS 4.0+	FORMAT d: /F:360
3 1/2-inch 720K	DD 720K	DOS 3.2+	FORMAT d:
3 1/2-inch 1.44M	HD 1.44M	DOS 3.3+	FORMAT d:
3 1/2-inch 1.44M	DD 720K	DOS 3.3+	FORMAT d: /N:9 /T:80
3 1/2-inch 1.44M	DD 720K	DOS 4.0+	FORMAT d: /F:720
3 1/2-inch 2.88M	ED 2.88M	DOS 5.0+	FORMAT d:
3 1/2-inch 2.88M	HD 1.44M	DOS 5.0+	FORMAT d: /F:1.44
3 1/2-inch 2.88M	DD 720K	DOS 5.0+	FORMAT d: /F:720

+ = Includes all higher versions
d: = Specifies drive to format
DD = Double-Density
HD = High-Density
ED = Extra-high-Density

Table 9.11 DOS FORMAT Command Internal Operations

Hard Disk Format Operations:	DOS 2-4	DOS 5 and Higher				
FORMAT Command Parameters	Any	None	None	/Q	/U	/Q/U
Disk Previously Formatted?	-	Yes	No	Yes	Yes	Yes
Check DOS Boot Record	No	Yes	Yes	Yes	No	Yes
Save UNFORMAT Information	No	Yes	No	Yes	No	No
Read Verify (Scan) Disk	Yes	Yes	Yes	No	Yes	No
Overwrite DBR, FATs & Root Dir.	Yes	Yes	Yes	Yes	Yes	Yes
Overwrite Data Area	No	No	No	No	No	No
Floppy Disk Format Operations:						
FORMAT Command Parameters	Any	None	None	/Q	/U	/Q/U
Disk Previously Formatted?	-	Yes	No	Yes	Yes	Yes
Check DOS Boot Record	No	Yes	Yes	Yes	No	Yes
Save UNFORMAT Information	No	Yes	No	Yes	No	No
Read Verify (Scan) Disk	Yes	Yes	Yes	No	Yes	No
Overwrite DBR, FATs & Root Dir.	Yes	Yes	Yes	Yes	Yes	Yes
Overwrite Data Area	Yes	No	Yes	No	Yes	No

/Q = Quick Format   "-" = Does Not Matter   FAT = File Allocation Table
/U = Unconditional Format   DBR = Does Not Matter

From this table you should be able to discern the function of a specific FORMAT command relative to the use of the /Q and /U parameters. For example, suppose that you are using DOS V5.0 and you insert a brand-new 1.44M disk in a 1.44M drive A: on your system. If you enter the command FORMAT A: with no other parameters, what will happen? By looking at table 9.11, you can see that the default operation of the FORMAT command in this case would be the following:

■ Check the DOS Boot Record (DBR).

■ Perform a read verify (or scan) of the entire disk.

■ Overwrite the DBR, FATs, and the root directory.

■ Overwrite the entire data area of the disk.

These functions do not necessarily happen in this order; in fact, the last three items listed occur simultaneously as the format progresses. Now suppose that you write some files on this disk and reenter the same FORMAT A: command. As you can see from table 9.11, the functions of the FORMAT command are very different this time. The steps occur something like this:

1. Check the DOS Boot Record.

2. Save UNFORMAT information.

3. Perform a read verify (or scan) of the entire disk.

4. Overwrite the DBR, FATs, and the root directory.

The default operation of FORMAT on a disk that is already formatted has changed dramatically with DOS V5.0. The biggest differences between this and older versions of DOS is that DOS 5 and higher versions will (by default) save a backup copy of the disk's DOS Boot Record (sector), file-allocation tables, and root directory. This information, which is placed in a special format in sectors near the end of the disk, is designed to be utilized by the UNFORMAT command to restore these areas of the disk and therefore undo the work of the FORMAT command. In addition to saving this critical UNFORMAT information, the FORMAT command also defaults to *not* overwriting the data area of the disk; therefore, the UNFORMAT command can "restore" the disk data. The UNFORMAT does not actually restore the data—only the saved UNFORMAT information. The disk data is never lost. Older DOS versions do not check the disk to see whether it is formatted, and always overwrite the entire floppy disk.

The /Q parameter stands for Quickformat. The basic function of /Q, to eliminate the (sometimes lengthy) read verify scan for disk defects that otherwise would occur, can be performed only on a disk that already has been formatted. Any existing defect marks on the disk are preserved by using /Q. The net effect of /Q is to greatly speed up the formatting procedure for disks that were already formatted. It's a quick way to delete all the files from a disk quickly and efficiently.

The /U parameter stands for Unconditional. This parameter has two distinctly different effects depending on whether you are formatting a floppy disk or a hard disk. On a floppy disk, the /U parameter instructs the FORMAT command to overwrite the entire disk and skip saving UNFORMAT information because it would be useless anyway if the data were overwritten. On a hard disk, the purpose of /U is only to suppress saving UNFORMAT information. FORMAT on a hard disk *never* overwrites the data area of the disk, even with the /U parameter! If you have experience with the FORMAT command, you know that FORMAT never has overwritten data on a hard disk, no matter what version of IBM or MS-DOS you are using. (On some older OEM versions, such as Compaq and AT&T, DOS did overwrite the entire hard disk.)

When you combine the /Q and /U parameters, you get the fastest reformat possible. /Q prevents the scan for defects, which is the longest operation during formatting, and /U eliminates saving UNFORMAT information. The FORMAT command is restricted to simply erasing the DOS volume boot sector, FATs, and root directory, which it can do very quickly. In fact, a format using the /Q and /U parameters takes only a few seconds to complete no matter how large the disk.

For more information on the DOS FORMAT command, a master FORMAT command reference chart is in the Appendix of this book. This explicit chart explains what all the format parameters do, and even describes some useful undocumented parameters I discovered.

III

Hardware Considerations

Caring for and Handling Floppy Disks and Drives

Most computer users know the basics of disk care. Disks can be damaged or destroyed easily by:

- Touching the recording surface with your fingers or anything else

- Writing on a disk label with a ball-point pen or pencil

- Bending the disk

- Spilling coffee or other substances on the disk

- Overheating a disk (leaving it in the hot sun or near a radiator, for example)

- Exposing a disk to stray magnetic fields

Despite all these cautions, disks are rather hardy storage devices; I can't say that I have ever destroyed one by just writing on it with a pen, because I do so all the time. I am careful, however, not to press too hard, which can put a crease in the disk. Also, simply touching a disk does not necessarily ruin it but rather gets the disk and your drive head dirty with oil and dust. The danger to your disks comes from magnetic fields that, because they are unseen, can sometimes be found in places you never dreamed of.

For example, all color monitors (and color TV sets) have, around the face of the tube, a degaussing coil used to demagnetize the shadow mask inside when the monitor is turned on. The coil is connected to the AC line and controlled by a thermistor that passes a gigantic surge of power to the coil when the tube is powered on, which then tapers off as the tube warms up. The degaussing coil is designed to remove any stray magnetism from the shadow mask at the front area of the tube. Residual magnetism in this mask can bend the electron beams so that the picture appears to have strange colors or be out of focus.

If you keep your disks anywhere near (within one foot) of the front of the color monitor, you expose them to a strong magnetic field every time you turn on the monitor. Keeping disks in this area is not a good idea because the field is designed to demagnetize objects, and indeed works well for demagnetizing disks. The effect is cumulative and irreversible.

Another major disk destructor is the telephone. The mechanical ringer in a typical phone uses a powerful electromagnet to move the striker into the bell. The ringer circuit uses some 90 volts, and the electromagnetic fields have sufficient power to degauss a disk lying on the desk next to or partially underneath the phone. *Keep disks away from the telephone.* A telephone with an electronic ringer might not cause this type of damage to a disk, but be careful anyway.

Another source of powerful magnetic fields is an electric motor, found in vacuum cleaners, heaters or air conditioners, fans, electric pencil sharpeners, and so on. Do not place these devices near areas where you store disks.

Airport X-Ray Machines and Metal Detectors. People associate myths with things they cannot see, and we certainly cannot see data as it is stored on a disk, nor the magnetic fields that can alter the data.

One of my favorite myths to dispel is that the airport X-ray machine somehow damages disks. I have a great deal of experience in this area from having traveled around the country for the past 10 years or so with disks and portable computers in hand. I fly about 150,000 miles per year, and my portable computer equipment and disks have been through X-ray machines more than 100 times each year.

Most people commit a fatal mistake when they approach the airport X-ray machines with disks or computers: they don't pass the stuff through! Seriously, X-rays are in essence just a form of light, and disks and computers are just not affected by X-rays at anywhere near the levels found in these machines. What can damage your magnetic media is the *metal detector*. Time and time again, someone with magnetic media or a portable computer approaches the security check. They freeze and say, "Oh no, I have disks and a computer—they have to be hand inspected." The person then refuses to place the disk and computer on the X-ray belt, and either walks through the metal detector with disks and computer in hand or passes the items over to the security guard, in very close proximity to the metal detector. Metal detectors work by monitoring disruptions in a weak magnetic field. A metal object inserted in the field area causes the field's shape to change, which the detector observes. This principle, which is the reason that the detectors are sensitive to metal objects, can be dangerous to your disks; the X-ray machine, however, is the safest area through which to pass either your disk or computer.

The X-ray machine is not dangerous to magnetic media because it merely exposes the media to electromagnetic radiation at a particular (very high) frequency. Blue light is an example of electromagnetic radiation of a different frequency. The only difference between X-rays and blue light is in the frequency, or wavelength, of the emission.

Electromagnetic radiation is technically a form of wave energy characterized by oscillating electric and magnetic fields perpendicular to one another. An electromagnetic wave is produced by an oscillating electric charge. This wave is not the same thing as a magnetic field. When matter intercepts electromagnetic energy, the energy is converted to thermal, electrical, mechanical, or chemical energy, but not to a magnetic field. Simply put, an electromagnetic wave generates either heat or an electrical alternating current in an object through which the wave passes.

I have been electrically shocked, for example, by touching metal objects in the vicinity of a high-powered amateur-radio transmitter. Your microwave oven induces thermal (kinetic) or even electrical energy in objects because of the same principle. Although a microwave oven is designed to induce kinetic energy in an irradiated substance's molecules, most of you know that when you place conductive (metal) objects in the microwave, an alternating electrical current also is generated, and you might even see sparks. This activity is a generation of electrical or mechanical energy, not of a magnetic field. Because a disk is not a good conductor, the only noticeable effect a high-powered electromagnetic field has on a floppy disk is the generation of kinetic (or thermal) energy. In other words, the only way that X-rays, visible light, or other radiation in these areas of the electromagnetic spectrum can damage a disk is by heating it.

III

Hardware Considerations

Consider also that if electromagnetic radiation could truly magnetize a disk as a magnetic field can, all magnetic media (disks and tapes) in the world would be in danger. Much electromagnetic radiation is passing through you at this moment, and through all your disks and tapes as well. There is no danger of magnetic damage because the radiation's effect on an object is to impart electrical, thermal, mechanical, or chemical energy—*not to magnetize the object*. I am *not* saying that you cannot harm a disk with electromagnetic radiation, because you certainly can; the damage, however, is from the heating effects of the radiation.

You probably know what the sun's extremely powerful electromagnetic radiation can do to a disk. Just leave a disk lying in direct sunlight awhile and you can see the thermal effects of this radiation. A microwave oven would have basically the same cooking effect on a disk, only more intense! Seriously, at the levels of electromagnetic radiation to which we normally are exposed, or which are present in an airport X-ray machine, there is certainly no danger to your disks. The field strength is far too low to raise the temperature of the disk in any perceptible manner, and this radiation has no magnetic effect on a disk.

Some people worry about the effect of X-ray radiation on their system's EPROM (erasable programmable read-only memory) chips. This concern might actually be more valid than worrying about disk damage because EPROMs are erased by certain forms of electromagnetic radiation. In reality, however, you do not need to worry about this effect either. EPROMs are erased by direct exposure to very intense ultraviolet light. Specifically, to be erased, an EPROM must be exposed to a 12,000 uw/cm2 UV light source with a wavelength of 2537 angstroms for 15 to 20 minutes, and at a distance of one inch. Increasing the power of the light source or decreasing the distance from the source can shorten the erasure time to a few minutes. The airport X-ray machine is different by a factor of 10,000 in wavelength, and the field strength, duration, and distance from the emitter source are nowhere near what is necessary for EPROM erasure. Be aware that many circuit-board manufacturers use X-ray inspection on circuit boards (with components including EPROMs installed) to test and check quality control during manufacture.

I have conducted my own tests: I passed one disk through different airport X-ray machines for two years, averaging two or three passes a week. The same disk still remains intact with all the original files and data, and never has been reformatted. I have also several portable computers with hard disks installed; one of them has been through the X-ray machines safely every week for more than four years. I prefer to pass computers and disks through the X-ray machine because it offers the best shielding from the magnetic fields produced by the metal detector standing next to it. Doing so also significantly lowers the "hassle factor" with the security guards, because if I have it X-rayed, they usually do not require that I plug it in and turn it on.

In fact, to further put this issue to rest, a scientific study was performed and published by two scientists, one of whom designs X-ray tubes for a major manufacturer. Their study subjected 14 megabytes of data on several disks to varying doses of X-ray radiation up to seven times that used in airport baggage examination. They found that absolutely no data was altered, even after re-testing the disks after two years of storage! They concluded, as I have, that disks are simply unaffected by airport X-ray inspection.

Drive-Installation Procedures

The procedure for installing floppy drives is simple. You install the drive in two phases. The first phase is to configure the drive for the installation, and the second is to perform the physical installation. Of these two steps, the first one usually is the most difficult to perform, depending on your knowledge of disk interfacing and whether you have access to the correct OEM drive manuals.

Drive Configuration

Configuring a floppy drive consists of setting the jumpers and switches mounted on the drive to match the system in which the drive will be installed, as well as tailoring the function of the drive to the installer's requirements. Every drive has a stable of jumpers and switches, and many drives are different from each other. You will find no standards for what these jumpers and switches are called, where they should be located, or how they should be implemented. There are some general guidelines to follow, but to set up a specific drive correctly and know all the options available, you must have information from the drive's manufacturer, normally found in the original equipment manufacturer's (OEM) manual. The manual is a "must have" item when you purchase a disk drive.

Although additional options might be available, most drives have several configuration features that must be set properly for an installation. These standard options typically need attention during an installation procedure:

- Drive select jumper
- Terminating resistor
- Diskette Changeline or Ready jumper
- Media sensor jumper

Each configuration item was discussed in more detail earlier in this chapter. The following section describes how these items are to be set for various installations.

Floppy drives are connected by a cabling arrangement called a *daisy chain*. The name is descriptive because the cable is strung from controller to drive to drive in a single chain. All drives have a drive select (sometimes called DS) jumper that must be set to indicate a certain drive's physical drive number. The point at which the drive is connected on the cable does not matter; the DS jumper indicates how the drive should respond. Most drives allow four settings, but the controllers used in all PC systems support only two on a single daisy-chain cable. The PC and XT floppy controllers, for example, will support four drives but only on two separate cables—each one a daisy chain with a maximum of two drives.

Every drive on a particular cable must be set to have unique drive select settings. In a normal configuration, the drive you want to respond as the first drive (A:) is set to the first drive select position, and the drive you want to respond as the second drive (B:) is set to the second drive-select position. On some drives, the DS jumper positions are labeled 0, 1, 2, and 3; other drives use the numbers 1, 2, 3, and 4 to indicate the same positions. For some drives then, a setting of DS0 is drive A:. For others, however, DS1 indicates drive A:. Likewise, some drives use a setting of DS1 for drive B:, and others use a DS2 setting to indicate drive B:. On some drives, the jumpers on the drive circuit board are unlabeled! In this case, consult the drive's manual to find out the descriptions of each jumper setting on the drive. A typical daisy-chain drive cable with this included "twist" is connected as shown in figure 9.11.

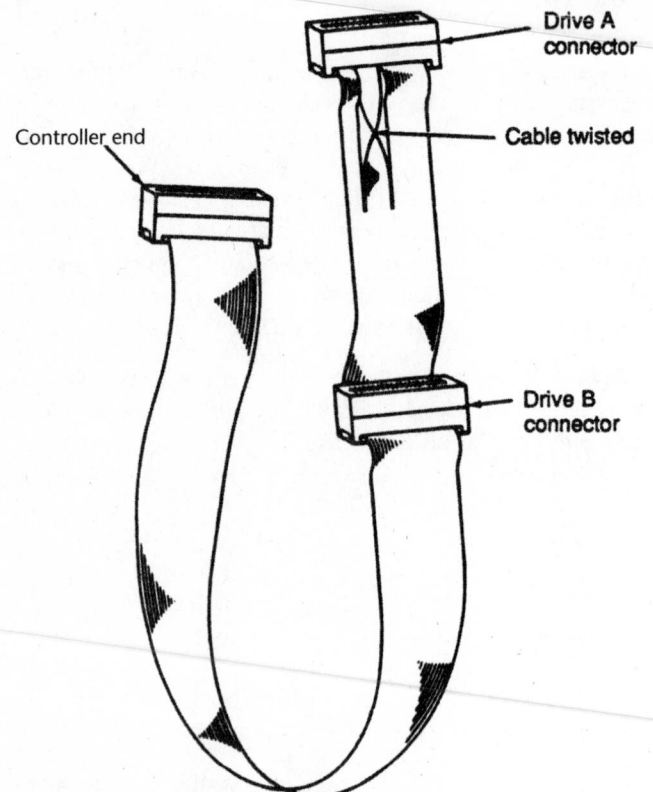

Fig. 9.11
A floppy controller cable showing the location of "the twist."

You should make sure that the DS settings for every drive on a single daisy-chain cable are different, or both drives will respond to the same signals. If you have incorrect DS settings, both drives respond simultaneously or neither drive responds at all.

The type of cable you use can confuse the drive select configuration. IBM puts in its cables a special twist that electrically changes the DS configuration of the drive plugged in after the twist. This twist causes a drive physically set to the first DS position (A:) to appear to the controller to be set to the second DS position (B:). If the first drive on the cable was before the twist in the cable and was set to the second DS position (B:), the controller would see a conflict. To the controller, both drives would appear to be set to the second DS position (B:), although physically they looked as though they were set differently. In essence, the system would think that two B: drives were installed. The adjustment for this problem is simple: When this type of cable is used, both drives should be set to the second DS position. The drive plugged in to the connector furthest from the controller, which is after the twist in the cable, then would have the physical second-DS-position setting appear to be changed to a first-DS-position setting. Then the system would see this drive as A:, and the drive plugged into the middle cable connector still would appear as B:.

An IBM-style floppy cable is a 34-pin cable with lines 10 through 16 sliced out and cross-wired (twisted) between the drive connectors. This twisting "cross-wires" the first and second drive-select and motor-enable signals, and therefore inverts the DS setting of the drive following the twist. All the drives in a system using this type of cable, therefore—whether you want them to be A: or B:—are physically jumpered the same way; installation and configuration are simplified because both floppies can be preset to the second DS position. Some drives used by IBM, in fact, have had the DS "jumper" setting permanently soldered into the drive logic board.

Most bare drives you purchase will have the DS jumper already set to the second position, which is correct for the majority of systems that use a cable with the twisted lines. Although this setting is correct for the majority of systems, if you are using a cable with no twist, you will have to alter this setting on at least one of the two drives. Some systems come with only a single floppy drive and no provisions for adding a second one. These types of systems often use a floppy cable with only one drive connector attached. This type of cable would not have any twisted lines, so how would you set up a drive plugged into this cable? Because there is no twist, the DS setting you make on the drive is exactly what the controller would see. You can attach only one drive, and it should appear to the system as A:—therefore, you would set the drive to the first DS position.

Most IBM-compatibles use a floppy cable with the twisted lines between the drive connectors. Drives plugged into this type of cable have their DS jumpers set to the second position. Drives on a single floppy cable or a cable with no twisted lines are set to the first DS position.

A terminating resistor should be placed (or enabled) in any drive plugged into the physical end of a cable. The function of this resistor is to prevent reflections or echoes of signals from reaching the end of the cable. All new drives will have this resistor installed by default. The terminating resistor should be removed or disabled for drives that are not the farthest away from the controller. Most 3 1/2-inch floppy drives use the distributed-termination technique, in which the installed terminating resistors are permanently installed, and are nonremovable and cannot be disabled. The resistor value in these drives is adjusted appropriately so that, in effect, the termination is distributed among both drives. When you mix 5 1/4-inch and 3 1/2-inch drives, you should enable or disable the terminators on the 5 1/4-inch drives appropriately, according to their position on the cable, and ignore the nonchangeable settings on the 3 1/2-inch drives.

In a typical cabling arrangement for two 5 1/4-inch floppies, for example, the terminating resistor is installed in drive A: (at the end of the cable), and this resistor is removed from the other floppy drive on the same cable (B:). The letter to which the drive responds is not important in relation to terminator settings; the important issue is that the drive at the end of the cable has the resistor installed and functioning and that other drives on the same cable have the resistor disabled or removed.

The terminating resistor usually looks like a memory chip; it might be white, blue, black, gray, or some other color, and memory chips usually are just black. IBM always labels the resistor with a T-RES sticker for easy identification. On some systems, the resistor is a built-in device enabled or disabled by a jumper or series of switches. If you have the removable type, be sure to store the resistor in a safe place because you might need it later. Figure 9.12 shows the location and appearance of the terminating resistor or switches on a typical floppy drive. Because most 3 1/2-inch drives have a form of automatic termination, there is no termination to configure; also, some 5 1/4-inch drives, such as Toshiba drives, have a permanently installed terminating resistor enabled or disabled by a jumper labeled TM.

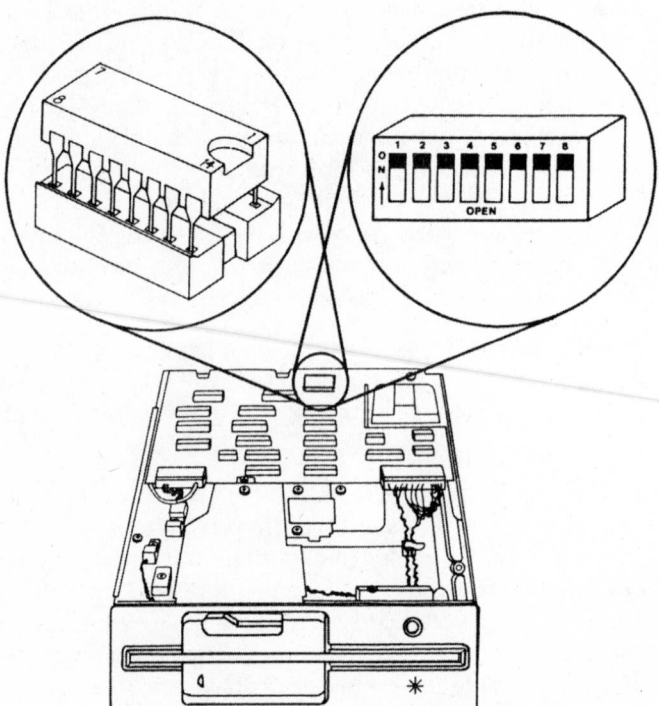

Fig. 9.12
A typical floppy drive terminating resistor, or termination switches.

Table 9.12 explains how a drive should be configured relative to the drive-select jumper and terminating resistor. You can use the table as a universal drive-select and terminating-resistor configuration chart that applies to all types of drives, including floppy disk drives and hard disks.

Table 9.12 Configuring Drive-Select Jumpers and Terminating Resistors				
Drive	**Twisted cable**		**Straight cable**	
A: drive (end connector)	DS = second	TR installed	DS = first	TR installed
B: drive (center connector)	DS = second	TR removed	DS = second	TR removed

DS = Drive select position
TR = Terminating resistor

The assumption in table 9.12 is that you always plug drive B: into the center connector on the cable and drive A: into the end connector. This arrangement might seem strange at first, but it is virtually required if you ever assemble a single-drive system. The logical first (A:) drive should be the end, or last, drive on the cable, and should be terminated. The twist in the cable is almost always between the two drive connectors on a cable and not between the controller and a drive.

Two other options might be available for you to set: the status of pin 34 on the drive's connector, and the function of a media-sensor feature. The guidelines for setting these options follow.

If the drive is a 5 1/4-inch 360K drive, set the status of pin 34 to Open (disconnected), regardless of the type of system in which you are installing the drive. The only other option normally found for pin 34 on 360K drives is Ready (RDY), which is incorrect. If you are using only a low-density controller, as in a PC or XT, pin 34 is ignored no matter what is sent on it. If the drive you are installing is a 5 1/4-inch 1.2M or 3 1/2-inch 720K, 1.44M, or 2.88M drive, be sure to set pin 34 to send the Disk Change (DC) signal. The basic rule is simple:

> For 360K drives only, pin 34 = Open (disconnected)

> For any other drive, pin 34 = Disk Change

The media-sensor setting is the easiest to describe. Only 1.44M and 2.88M drives have a media sensor. The best rule to follow is to set these drives so that the sensor is enabled; this step enables the sensor to control the drive's recording mode and, therefore, the drive's write-current level.

Physical Installation

When you physically install a drive, you plug in the drive (refer to Chapter 6). Here, your concerns are using the correct brackets and screws for the system and the correct drive you are installing.

III

Hardware Considerations

A special bracket usually is required whenever you install a half-height drive in place of an earlier full-height unit (see fig. 9.13). The brackets enable you to connect the two half-height drives together as a single full-height unit for installation. Remember also that nearly all floppy drives now use metric hardware; only the early, American-manufactured drives use the standard English threads.

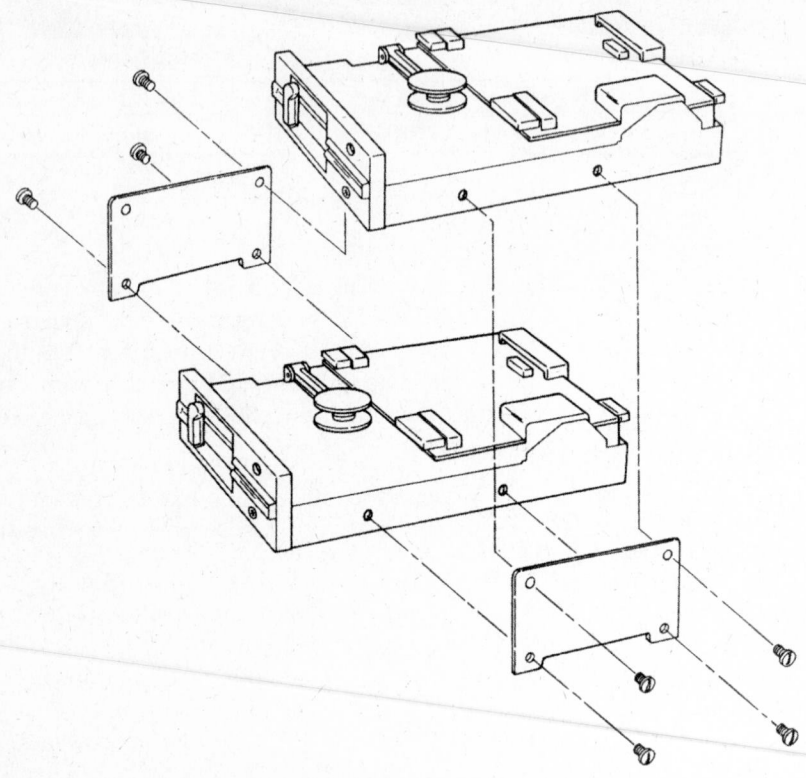

Fig. 9.13
Installing half-height drives in a full-height bay with adapter plates.

You can get these adapter plates from most vendors who sell drives, but sometimes they charge as much as $10 for basically a piece of sheet metal with four holes drilled in it! Several companies in the Appendix of this book specialize in cables, brackets, screw hardware, and other items useful in assembling systems or installing drives. I have also made up the template shown in figure 9.14, which will guide you if you want to make your own. I usually use a piece of galvanized sheet metal like that used in ventilation ductwork for the stock, which can be easily obtained at most hardware stores.

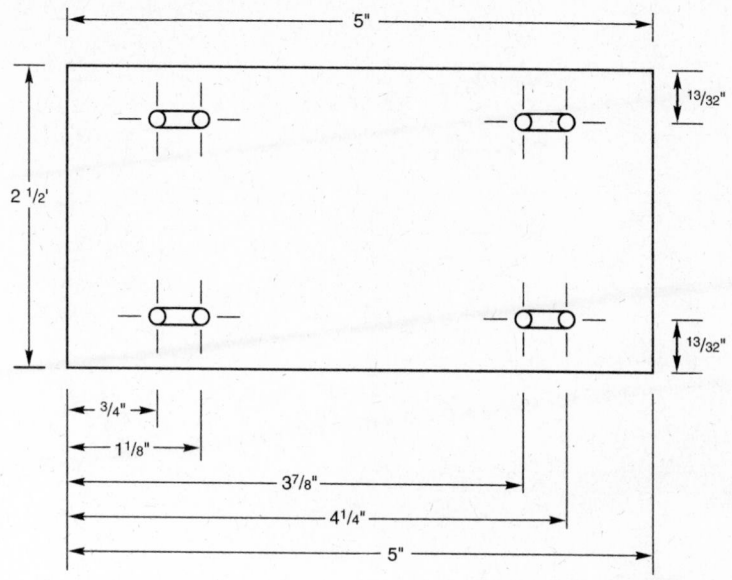

Fig. 9.14
The dimensions of a typical drive adapter plate.

Another piece of drive-installation paraphernalia you need are the rails used in installing disk drives in AT systems. Most IBM-compatible systems follow the IBM standard for rail design. Again, you can purchase these from some of the vendors listed in the Appendix in this book. If you want to construct your own, figure 9.15 shows the construction of a typical IBM-style drive rail. These rails can be made from metal, but usually are made from plastic. They probably can even be made from wood. Drives installed in an AT are grounded to the system chassis through a separate ground wire and tab, which is why the rails do not need to be made from a conductive material. I find it more cost effective to purchase the rails rather than make them.

As you might expect, Compaq uses a slightly different rail construction. The vendors mentioned in the Appendix who sell cables, brackets, and other installation accessories also carry the Compaq-style rails.

When you connect a drive, make sure that the power cable is installed properly. The cable normally is keyed so that it cannot be plugged in backward. Also, install the data and control cable. If no key is in this cable, which allows only a correct orientation, use the colored wire in the cable as a guide to the position of pin 1. This cable is oriented correctly when you plug it in so that the colored wire is plugged into the disk drive connector toward the cut-out notch in the drive edge connector.

III

Hardware Considerations

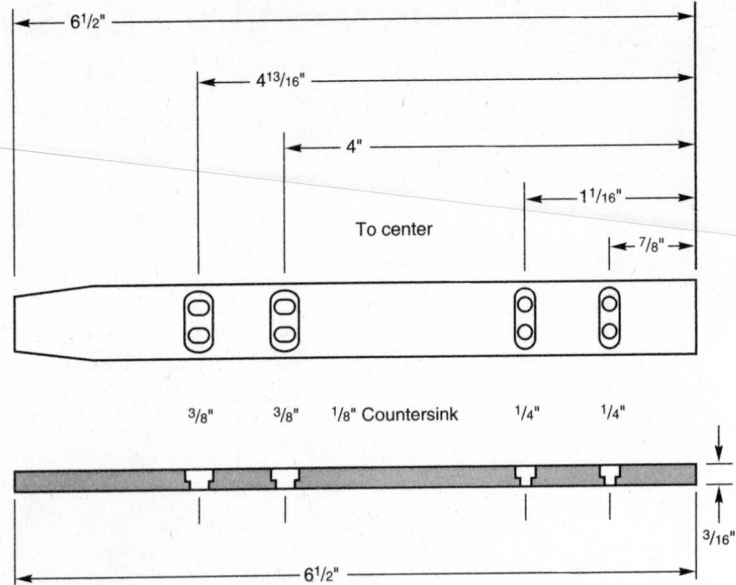

Fig. 9.15
A typical AT-drive mounting rail.

Floppy Drive Installation Summary

To install and set up a floppy drive properly, you must understand and set up primarily four different configuration items on the drive:

- Drive Select (DC) jumper setting

- Terminating Resistor (TR) enabled or disabled

- Send Disk Change (DC) or no signal on pin 34

- Enable Media Sensor

This section has explained the proper settings for these items in virtually any installation situation you might encounter.

For more information about configuring and installing a specific drive, you can use several resources. Obviously, this book contains much information about configuring and installing floppy disk drives—be sure that you have read it all! The best source of information about certain drives or controllers is the original equipment manufacturer's (OEM) documentation. These manuals tell you where all configuration items are located on the drive, what they look like, and how to set them. Unfortunately, most of the time you do not receive this detailed documentation when you purchase a drive or controller; instead, you must contact the OEM to obtain it.

Correcting Problems from Improper Drive Installation or Use

The majority of floppy drive problems I see are caused primarily by improper drive configuration, installation, or operation. Unfortunately, floppy drive configuration and installation is much more complicated than the average technician seems to realize. Even if you have had your drive "professionally" installed, it still might have been done incorrectly.

This section describes some of the most common problems that stem from improperly installing or configuring a drive. Also discussed are several problems that can occur from improperly using drives and disks. Solutions to these problems are presented also.

Handling the "Phantom Directory" (Disk Change)

One of the most common mistakes I have seen people make in installing a disk drive is incorrectly setting the signals sent by the drive on pin 34 of the cable to the controller. All drives *except* the 360K drive must be configured so that a Disk Change (DC) signal is sent along pin 34 to the controller.

If you have not enabled the DC signal when the system expects that it should have been, you might end up with trashed disks as a result. For example, a PC user with disk in hand might say to you, "Moments ago, this disk contained my document files, and now it seems as though my entire word processing program disk has mysteriously transferred to it. When I attempt to run the programs that now seem to be on this disk, they crash or lock up my system." Of course, in this case the disk has been damaged, and you will have to perform some data-recovery magic to recover the information for the user. My book *Que's Guide to Data Recovery* contains more information about data-recovery techniques. A good thing about this particular kind of problem is that recovering most—if not all—the information on the disk is entirely possible.

You also can observe this installation defect manifested in the "phantom directory" problem. For example, you place a disk with files on it in the A: drive of your AT-compatible system and enter the DIR A: command. The drive starts spinning, the access light on the drive comes on, and after a few seconds of activity, the disk directory scrolls up the screen. Everything seems to be running well. Then you remove the disk and insert in drive A: a different disk with different files on it and repeat the DIR A: command. This time, however, the drive barely (if at all) spins before the disk directory scrolls up the screen. When you look at the directory listing that has appeared, you discover in amazement that it is the same listing as on the first disk you removed from the drive.

You should understand that the disk you have inserted in the drive is in danger. If you write on this disk in any way, you will cause the file-allocation tables and root-directory sectors from the first disk (which are stored in your system's memory) to be copied over to the second disk, thereby "blowing away" the information on the second disk. Most AT-compatible systems with high- or low-density controllers utilize a floppy disk caching system that buffers the FATs and directories from the floppy disk that was last read in system RAM. Because this data is kept in memory, these areas of the disk do not have to be reread as frequently. This system greatly speeds access to the disk.

Opening the door lever or pressing the eject button on a drive normally sends the Disk Change signal to the controller, which in turn causes DOS to flush out the floppy cache. This action causes the next read of the disk drive to reread the FAT and directory areas. If this signal is not sent, the cache is not flushed when you change a disk, and the system acts as though the first disk still is present in the drive. Writing to this newly inserted disk writes not only the new data but also either a full or partial copy of the first disk's FAT and directory areas. Also, the data is written to what was considered free space on the first disk, which might not be free on the subsequent disk and results in damaged files and data.

There are several simple solutions to this problem. One is temporary; the other is permanent. For a quick, temporary solution, press Ctrl-Break or Ctrl-C immediately after changing any disk, to force DOS to flush manually the floppy I/O buffers. This method is exactly how the old CP/M operating system used to work. After pressing Ctrl-Break or Ctrl-C, the next disk access rereads the FAT and directory areas of the disk and places fresh copies in memory. In other words, you must be sure that every time you change a disk, the buffer gets flushed. Because these commands work only from the DOS prompt, you must not change a disk while working in an application.

A more permanent and correct solution to the problem is simple—just correct the drive installation. In my experience, incorrect installation is the root cause of this problem nine out of ten times. Remember this simple rule: *If a jumper block is on the disk drive labeled DC, you should install a jumper there.* If you are absolutely certain that the installation was correct—for instance, the drive has worked perfectly for some time, but then suddenly develops this problem—check the following list of items, all of which can prevent the Disk Change signal from being sent:

- Drive configuration/Setup. Make sure that the DC jumper is enabled, check CMOS Setup.
- Bad cable. Check for continuity on pin 34.
- Bad Disk Change sensor. Clean sensor or replace drive and retest.
- Bad drive logic board. Replace drive and retest.
- Bad controller. Replace controller and retest.
- Wrong DOS OEM version.

The last of these checklist items can stump you because the hardware seems to be functioning correctly. As a rule, you should use only the DOS supplied by the same OEM as the computer system on the system. For example, use IBM DOS on IBM systems, Compaq DOS on Compaq systems, Zenith DOS on Zenith systems, Toshiba DOS on Toshiba systems, Tandy DOS on Tandy systems, and so on. This problem is most noticeable with some laptop systems that apparently have a modified floppy controller design, such as some Toshiba laptops. On many of these systems, you *must* use the correct (Toshiba, for example) OEM version of DOS.

Handling Incorrect Media-Sensor Operation

Incorrect media-sensor operation occurs on only 1.44M or 2.88M, 3 1/2-inch, high-density drives, the only drives that have a media sensor. Again, this is largely a drive-configuration problem because the installer did not enable the sensor when it should have been enabled. You would think that the sensor would be set correctly when you purchase a drive, but that is not always the case. Never assume that a drive is preconfigured properly for your system. Remember that drive manufacturers sell drives for systems other than IBM-compatibles. Sometimes it is hard to remember that many other types of computers exist other than just IBMs or IBM clones.

If the media sensor is not operational, the controller likely will leave the drive in a state in which high write-current always is applied to the heads during write operations. This state is OK for high-density disks, but when low-density disks are used, random and sporadic read and write failures occur, usually ending with the DOS message Abort, Retry, Ignore, Fail?.

Another symptom of incorrect media-sensor operation would be generating double-density disks that seem eventually to lose data—maybe over a few weeks or months. This loss often can be traced back to an improperly configured media sensor on the drive. In some systems, the problem might be more obvious, such as not being capable of formatting or writing successfully on 720K disks. If your system can format a 720K disk to 1.44M without punching any extra holes in the disk, it is an immediate alert that the media sensor is not enabled.

Handling Problems Caused by Using Double-Density Disks at High Density

If you attempt to format a 5 1/4-inch, double-density disk at high-density format, you usually will hear several retries from the drive as DOS finds a large amount of bad sectors on the disk. When the format is completed, hundreds of kilobytes in bad sectors usually are reported. Most people would never use this disk. Because the 5 1/4-inch disks are so radically different from one another in terms of magnetic coercivity and media formulation, the double-density disks do not work well carrying a high-density format.

Problems are seen more often with the 3 1/2-inch disks because the double-density disks are not nearly as different from the high-density disks compared to the 5 1/4-inch versions, although they indeed are different. Because the 3 1/2-inch DD and HD disks differ less, however, a double-density, 3 1/2-inch disk usually accepts a high-density format with no bad sectors reported. This acceptance is unfortunate because it causes most users to feel that they are safe in using the disk for data storage.

A 3 1/2-inch, double-density disk with a 1.44M, high-density format initially seems to work with no problem. If you fill this type of double-density disk with 1.44M of data and store it on a shelf, you will notice that eventually the recording degrades and the data becomes unreadable. Several months might pass before you can detect the degradation, but then it is too late. From talking to hundreds of my clients, I have found that the average "half life" of such a recording is approximately six months from the time the data is written to the time that one or more files suddenly have unreadable sectors. In six months to a year, much of the rest of the disk rapidly degrades until all the data and files have extensive damage. The recording simply destroys itself during this time. I have substantiated this situation with my own testing and my clients' experiences. If the data is reread and rewritten periodically before any degradation is noticeable, then the recording can be "maintained" for longer periods of time before data is lost.

The technical reasons for this degradation were explained earlier in this chapter. In a sense, the disk eventually performs a self-erasure operation. Again, the time frame for damage seems to be approximately six months to a year from the time the data is written. I certainly expect my disks to hold data for more than six months; in fact, data written properly to your disks should be readable many, many years from now.

If you have been using double-density, 3 1/2-inch disks with high-density formats, you are asking for problems. Using these types of disks for backup, for instance, is highly inappropriate! Many people use double-density disks as high-density disks to save money. You should realize that high-density disks are not very expensive anymore; *data-recovery services, however, are very expensive*. I do not condone incorrectly formatting disks, and I certainly would not want anyone to use one of those ridiculous disk "hole punchers." There are good reasons that I rarely am in data-recovery situations with my own data; yet I have seen people seem to wipe out data and crash systems by just *breathing* near a PC!

If you have a disk that has been formatted improperly and is developing read problems, the first thing to do is DISKCOPY the disk immediately to another proper-density disk. Then you can survey the damage and make repairs to the new copy. Chapter 15 describes how to repair some simple problems with the FAT, directory, and other management areas of the disk. For a more detailed investigation into the subject of data recovery, see *Que's Guide to Data Recovery*.

Handling Track-Width Problems from Writing on 360K Disks with a 1.2M Drive

As discussed earlier in this chapter, the 5 1/4-inch, high-density drives usually write a narrower track than the 5 1/4-inch, double-density drives. Therefore, when you use a high-density drive to update a double-density disk originally formatted or written in a double-density drive, the wider tracks written by the double-density drive are not completely overwritten by the high-density drive. Of course, if the double-density disk is newly formatted and subsequently written in only a high-density drive (although at the proper 360K format), there is no problem with overwrites—that is, until you update the disk with a double-density (wide-track) drive and then update it again with a high-density (narrow-track) drive. In that case, you again have a wider track with a narrow-track update embedded within—but not completely covering—it.

You must remember *never* to use a high-density drive to write on a double-density disk that was previously written by a double-density drive. This procedure would make the disk unreadable by the double-density drive, but usually still readable by the high-density drive. In fact, the best way to recover information from a disk that has been incorrectly overwritten in this manner is to use a high-density disk drive to perform a DISKCOPY operation of the disk to a new, blank, never-formatted, low-density disk.

Handling Off-Center Disk Clamping

Clamping the disk off-center in the drive has to be absolutely the most frequently encountered cause of problems with floppy drives. In my worldwide troubleshooting seminars, we run the PC systems with the lid off for most of the course. Whenever someone has a problem reading or booting from a floppy disk, I look down at the top of the exposed disk drive on the system while it is spinning to see whether the disk has been clamped by the drive hub in an off-center position. *More often than not, that is the problem.* I know that the disk is clamped off-center because the disk wobbles while it rotates. Ejecting and reinserting the disk so that it is clamped properly usually makes the disk reading or booting problem disappear immediately. This step might solve the problem in most cases, but it is not much help if you have formatted or written a disk in an off-center position. In that case, all you can do is try to DISKCOPY the improperly written disk to another disk and attempt various data-recovery operations on both disks.

I have used a technique for inserting floppy disks that has eliminated this problem for me. After inserting a disk into a drive, I always take an extra half-second to wiggle the drive lever or door, first down, and then up, and then down again to clamp the disk rather than simply push the door or lever down once to clamp it. The reason is that the first partial closing of the lever serves to center the disk in its jacket so that the second motion allows the drive hub to clamp the disk properly in a centered position. If I were in charge of training for a large organization, I would make sure that all the basic PC starter classes taught proper disk handling, including insertion and on-center clamping in the drive.

Note that the 3 1/2-inch drives are virtually immune to this type of problem because of the different type of clamping and centering mechanisms they use. Some 5 1/4-inch drives have adopted a more reliable clamping mechanism similar to the 3 1/2-inch drives. Canon makes some of these new 5 1/4-inch drives, used by IBM and Compaq. The newest version used by IBM in some of its PS/2 systems is totally motorized. You merely slide the disk into the drive slot, and the drive grabs the disk and electrically pulls it in and centers it. These drives also include a motorized eject button.

Realigning Misaligned Drives

If your disk drives are misaligned, you will notice that other drives cannot read disks created in your drive, and you might not be able to read disks created in other drives. This situation can be dangerous if you allow it to progress unchecked. If the alignment is bad enough, you probably will notice it first in the inability to read original application-program disks, while still being able to read your own created disks. Chapter 13 discusses the Drive Probe program from Accurite for checking the alignment and operation of floppy drives.

To solve this problem, you can have the drive realigned. I usually don't recommend realigning drives because of the low cost of simply replacing the drive compared to aligning one. Also, an unforeseen circumstance catches many people off guard: You might find that your newly aligned drive might not be able to read all your backup or data disks created while the drive was out of alignment. If you replace the misaligned drive with a new one and keep the misaligned drive, you can use it for DISKCOPY purposes to transfer the data to newly formatted disks in the new drive.

Repairing Floppy Drives

Attitudes about repairing floppy drives have changed over the years primarily because of the decreasing cost of drives. When drives were more expensive, people often considered repairing the drives rather than replacing them. With the cost of drives decreasing every year, however, certain labor- or parts-intensive repair procedures have become almost as expensive as replacing the drive with a new one.

Because of the cost considerations, repairing floppy drives usually is limited to cleaning the drive and heads and lubricating the mechanical mechanisms. On drives that have a speed adjustment, adjusting the speed to within the proper operating range is common also. Note that most newer half-height drives and virtually all 3 1/2-inch drives do not have an adjustment for speed. These drives use a circuit that automatically sets the speed at the required level and compensates for variations with a feedback loop. If such an auto-taching drive is off in speed, the reason usually is that the circuit failed. Replacement of the drive usually is necessary.

Cleaning Floppy Drives

Sometimes read and write problems are caused by dirty drive heads. Cleaning a drive is easy. You can proceed in two ways. In one method, you use one of the simple head-cleaning kits available from computer- or office-supply stores. These devices are easy to operate and don't require the system unit to be open for access to the drive. The other method is the manual method: You use a cleaning swab with a liquid such as pure alcohol, Freon, or trichloroethane. With this method, you must open the system unit to expose the drive and, in many cases (especially in earlier full-height drives), also remove and partially disassemble the drive. The manual method can result in a better overall job, but usually the work required is not worth the difference.

The cleaning kits come in two styles: The wet type uses a liquid squirted on a cleaning disk to wash off the heads; the dry kit relies on abrasive material on the cleaning disk to remove head deposits. I recommend that you never use the dry drive-cleaning kits. Always use a wet system in which a liquid solution is applied to the cleaning disk. The dry disks can prematurely wear the heads if used improperly or too often; wet systems are very safe to use.

The manual drive-cleaning method requires that you have physical access to the heads, in order to swab them manually with a lint-free foam swab soaked in a cleaning solution. This method requires some level of expertise: Simply jabbing at the heads incorrectly with a cleaning swab might knock the drive heads out of alignment. You must use a careful in-and-out motion, and lightly swab the heads. No side-to-side motion (relative to the way the heads travel) should be used; this motion can snag a head and knock it out of alignment. Because of the difficulty and danger of this manual cleaning, for most applications I recommend a simple wet-disk cleaning kit because it is the easiest and safest method.

One question that comes up repeatedly in my seminars is "How often should you clean a disk drive?" Only you can answer that question. What type of environment is the system in? Do you smoke cigarettes near the system? If so, cleaning would be required more often. Usually, a safe rule of thumb is to clean drives about once a year if the system is in a clean office environment, in which no smoke or other particulate matter is in the air. In a heavy-smoking environment, you might have to clean every six months or perhaps even more often. In dirty industrial environments, you might have to clean every month or so. Your own experience is your guide in this matter. If DOS reports drive errors in the system by displaying the familiar DOS Abort, Retry, Ignore prompt, you should clean your drive to try to solve the problem. If cleaning does solve the problem, you probably should step up the interval between preventive-maintenance cleanings.

In some cases, you might want to place a (very small) amount of lubricant on the door mechanism or other mechanical contact points inside the drive. *Do not use oil.* I use a pure silicone lubricant. Oil collects dust rapidly after you apply it and usually causes the oiled mechanism to gum up later. Silicone does not attract dust in the same manner and can be used safely. Use very small amounts of silicone; do not drip or spray silicone inside the drive. You must ensure that the lubricant is applied only to the part that needs it. If the lubricant gets all over the inside of the drive, it may cause unnecessary problems.

Setting the Floppy Drive Speed Adjustment

Most older 5 1/4-inch floppy disk drives, especially full-height drives, have a small variable resistor used to adjust the drive's rotational speed. In particular, the Tandon and CDC full-height drives used by IBM in the PC and XT systems have this adjustment. The location of this variable resistor is described in the hardware-maintenance reference manuals IBM sells for these systems.

If you have a Tandon drive, you make the adjustment through a small, brass screw on a variable resistor mounted on the motor control board, attached to the rear of the drive (see fig. 9.16). The resistor is usually blue, and the screw is brass. To gauge the speed, you can use a program such as Drive Probe, by Accurite; IBM's Advanced Diagnostics, supplied with the hardware-maintenance and service manual; or even a purely mechanical method that relies on a fluorescent light to act as a strobe.

The software methods use a disk to evaluate the running speed of the drive. Usually, you turn the screw until the speed reads correctly (300 RPM) according to the program you use. The mechanical method requires you to remove the drive from the system and place it upside down on a bench. Sometimes the drive is set sideways on the power supply so that the drive's case is grounded. Then the underside of the drive is illuminated by a standard fluorescent light. The light acts as a strobe that flashes 60 times per second because of the cycling speed of the AC line current. On the bottom of the drive spindle are strobe marks for 50 Hz and 60 Hz (see fig. 9.17). Because 60 Hz power is used in the United States, you should use the 60 Hz marks. The 50 Hz marks are used for (50 cycle) European power. While the drive is running, turn the small screw until the strobe marks appear to be stationary, much like the "wagon wheel effect" you see in old western movies. When the marks are completely stationary as viewed under the light, the drive's rotation speed is correct.

III

Hardware Considerations

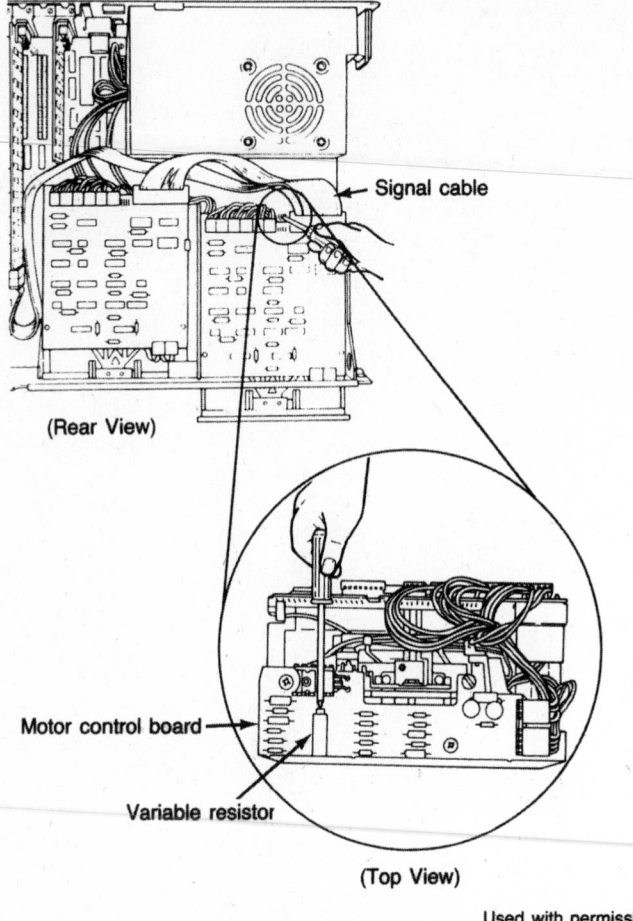

(Rear View)

Signal cable

Motor control board

Variable resistor

(Top View)

Used with permission
from IBM Corporation.

Fig. 9.16
The drive-speed adjustment for the Tandon TM-100 series drive.

With CDC drives, the adjustment resistor is mounted on the logic board, which is on top of the drive. The small, brass screw to the left of the board is the one you want. Other drives also might have an adjustment. The best way to tell whether a drive has a speed adjustment is to look for the telltale strobe marks on the spindle of the drive. If the marks are there, the drive probably has an adjustment; if the marks are not there, the drive probably has an automatic speed circuit and requires no adjustment. The OEM manual for the drive has information about all these adjustments (if any) and where you make them.

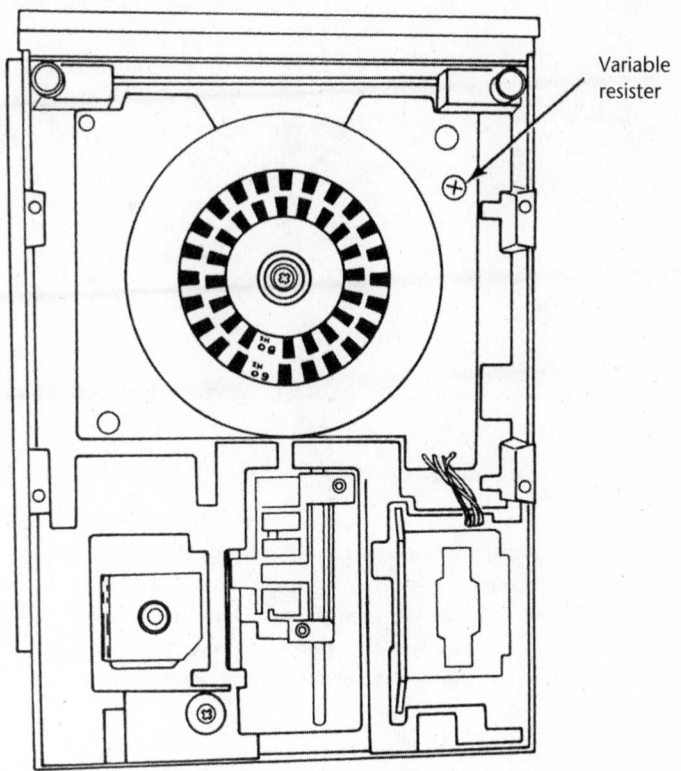

Variable
resister

Fig. 9.17
Strobe marks and speed adjustment on a typical half-height drive.

Aligning Floppy Disk Drives

Aligning disk drives is usually no longer done because of the high relative cost. To
align a drive properly requires access to an oscilloscope (for about $500), a special ana-
log-alignment disk ($75), and the OEM service manual for the drive; also, you must
spend half an hour to an hour aligning the drive. Compared to the $40 average cost of
most floppy drives today, an alignment seems like wasteful expenditure.

A new program, Drive Probe, by Accurite, uses special test disks called High-Resolution
Diagnostic (HRD) disks. These disks are as accurate as the analog alignment disks (AAD),
and eliminate the need for an oscilloscope to align a drive. You cannot use any program
that relies on the older Digital Diagnostic Disk (DDD) or Spiral format test disks because
they are not accurate enough to use to align a drive. The Drive Probe and HRD system
can make an alignment more cost-effective than before, but it is still a labor-intensive
operation. Figure 9.18 shows the main menu of the Accurite Drive Probe program, which
offers various functions, including fully automatic or manual drive testing.

III

Hardware Considerations

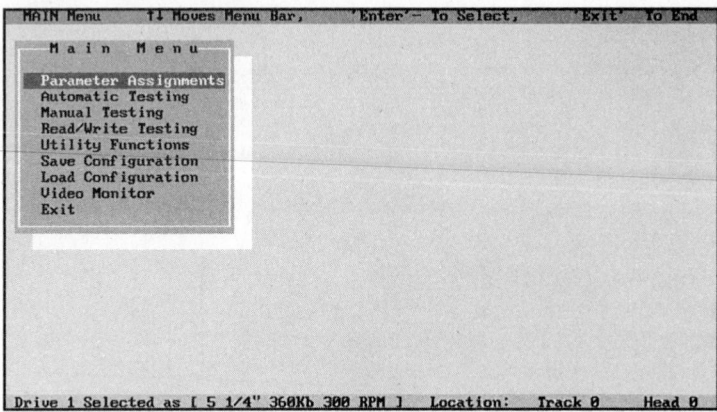

Fig. 9.18

The main menu screen from Accurite Drive Probe.

With the price of most types of floppy drives hovering at or below the $40 mark, aligning drives usually is not a cost-justified alternative to replacement. One exception exists. In a high-volume situation, drive alignment might pay off. Another alternative is to investigate local organizations that perform drive alignments, usually for $25 to $50. Weigh this cost against the replacement cost and age of the drive. Since you can purchase new 1.44M floppy drives for *as low as $35 or less,* alignment is no longer a viable option for most people.

Chapter Summary

This chapter has examined floppy drives and floppy media (disks) in great detail. One of the most important things to do when you're installing a drive in a system is to ensure that the drive is configured correctly. This chapter has discussed drive configuration also. With this information, installing drives correctly should be an easy task.

Many problems that confound floppy drive users, such as reading and writing double-density disks with high-density drives, were discussed in this chapter. It has discussed thoroughly the differences between high- and double-density drives and disks, and mentioned the consequences of using the wrong type of disk in the wrong drive. Simple drive servicing, such as cleaning and speed adjustment, were explained so that these operations can be performed in-house. After reading this chapter, you should know much about floppy drives. Chapter 10 discusses hard disk drives.

Chapter 10

Hard Disk Drives

To most users, the hard disk drive is the most important yet most mysterious part of a computer system. A *hard disk drive* is a sealed unit that holds the data in a system. When the hard disk fails, the consequences are usually very serious. To maintain, service, and expand a PC system properly, you must fully understand the hard disk unit.

Most computer users want to know how hard disk drives work, and what to do when a problem occurs. Few books about hard disks, however, cover the details necessary for PC technicians or sophisticated users. This chapter corrects the situation.

This chapter thoroughly describes the hard disk, from the drives to the cables and controllers that run them. In particular, it examines the construction and operation of a hard disk drive. You will learn about the different types of disk interfaces you can select, the shortcomings and strengths of working with each one, and the procedures for configuring, setting up, and installing drives. The chapter also shows you how to install and integrate a hard disk drive into a PC system.

Definition of a Hard Disk

A hard disk drive contains rigid, disc-shaped platters usually constructed of aluminum or glass. Unlike floppy disks, the platters cannot bend or flex, hence the term *hard disk*. In most hard disk drives, the platters cannot be removed; for that reason, IBM calls them *fixed disk drives*. Although there are removable-platter hard disk drives, their nonstandard nature, higher cost, and reliability problems make them unpopular.

Hard disk drives often are called *Winchester drives*. This term dates to the 1960s, when IBM developed a high-speed hard disk drive that had 30 megabytes of fixed-platter storage and 30 megabytes of removable platter storage. The drive had platters that spun at high speeds and heads that floated over the platters while they spun in a sealed environment. That drive, the *30-30 drive*, soon received the nickname "Winchester," after the famous Winchester 30-30 rifle. After that time, drives that used a high-speed spinning platter with a floating head also became known as Winchester drives. The term has no technical or scientific meaning; it is a slang term synonymous with *hard disk*.

Hard Drive Advancements

For the past 10 or more years hard disks have been used in PC systems and have undergone tremendous changes. Some of the most profound changes have been in hard disk storage. Following are some of the major changes:

- Maximum storage capacities have increased from 10M 5 1/4-inch full-height drives available in 1982 to 3G or more for drives in that form factor and well over 2G for small 3 1/5-inch half-height drives.

- Data transfer rates have increased from 102K per second for the original IBM XT in 1983 to nearly 10M per second for some of the fastest drives today.

- Average Seek times have decreased from over 85 milliseconds for the 10M XT hard disk in 1983 to less than 8 milliseconds for some of the fastest drives today.

- In 1982 a 10M drive cost more than $1,500 ($150 per megabyte). Today, hard drive cost has dropped to less than $1 per megabyte.

Areal density has been used as a primary technology growth rate indicator for the hard disk drive industry. Areal density is defined as the product of the linear bits per inch (BPI), measured along the length of the tracks around the disk, multiplied by the number of tracks per inch (TPI) measured radially on the disk. The results are expressed in units of Mb/sq-inch, and are used as a measure of efficiency in drive recording technology. Current high-end drives record at areal densities of about 160 Mb/sq-inch. Prototype models with densities as high as 1 Gb/sq-inch have been constructed, which allow for capacities of more than 1 Gigabyte on a single 3 1/5-inch platter. Areal density (and therefore drive capacity) has been doubling approximately every two to three years, and it is likely that disk drives will reach areal densities of 10 Gb/sq-inch before the year 2000. A drive built by using this technology would be capable of storing 1G of data on a single 1.3-in. platter, and the entire drive would be about the size of a large wristwatch. New media and head technologies such as ceramic or glass platters and fluid suspension are being developed to support these higher areal densities. Manufacturing drive heads and disks to operate at closer tolerances is the primary challenge in achieving higher densities.

It seems almost incredible that computer technology seems to improve by doubling performance or capacity every two to three years. If only other industries could match that growth and improvement rate!

Hard Disk Drive Operation

The basic physical operation of a hard disk drive is similar to that of a floppy disk drive: A hard drive uses spinning disks with heads that move over the disks and store data in tracks and sectors. In many other ways, however, hard disk drives are different from floppy disk drives.

Hard disks usually have multiple platters, each with two sides on which to store data. Most drives have at least two or three platters, which results in four or six sides, while some drives have up to 11 platters. The identically positioned tracks on each side of every platter together make up a *cylinder*. A hard disk drive has one head per platter side, and all the heads are mounted on a common carrier device, or *rack*. The heads are moved in and out across the disk in unison; they cannot move independently because they are mounted on the same rack.

Hard disks operate much faster than floppy drives. Most hard disks spin at 3,600 rpm, approximately 10 times faster than a floppy drive. Until recently, 3,600 rpm was pretty much a constant among hard drive manufacturers. Now, however, there are quite a few hard drives that spin even faster. One drive, for example, spins at 4,318 rpm, while others spin at 5,600, 6,400, or even 7,200 rpm. High rotational speed combined with a fast head-positioning mechanism and more sectors per track make one hard disk faster than another, and all of these things combine to make hard drives much faster than floppy drives at storing and retrieving data.

The heads in a hard disk do not (should not!) touch the platters during normal operation. When the heads are powered off, however, they land on the platters as they stop spinning. While the drive is on, a cushion of air keeps each head suspended a short distance above or below the platter. If the cushion is disturbed by a particle of dust or a shock, the head may come in contact with the platter spinning at full speed. When contact with the spinning platters is forceful enough to do damage, it is called a *head crash*, and the results may be anything from a few lost bytes of data to a totally trashed drive. Most drives have special lubricants on the platters and hardened surfaces that can withstand the daily "takeoffs and landings" as well as more severe abuse.

Because the platter assemblies are sealed from the environment and are non removable, they can have very high track densities. Many have 3,000 or more tracks per inch of media. Head Disk Assemblies (HDAs), which contain the platters, are assembled and sealed in clean rooms under absolutely sanitary conditions. Because few companies repair HDAs, the repair or replacement of items inside the sealed HDA can be expensive. Every hard disk ever made will eventually fail; the only questions are when will it fail?, and will your data be backed up?!

Many PC users think that hard disks are fragile, and generally they are one of the most fragile components in your PC. However, in my weekly PC Troubleshooting and Data Recovery seminars I have run various hard disks for days with the lids off, and have even removed and installed the covers while the drives were operating. Those drives continue to store data perfectly to this day with the lids either on or off. Of course, I don't recommend that you try this with your own drives, nor would I do it to my larger, more expensive drives.

The Ultimate Hard Disk Drive Analogy!

I'm sure you have heard the traditional analogy comparing the interaction of the head and media in a typical hard disk as being similar in scale to a 747 flying a few feet off of the ground at cruising speed (500+ mph). I've heard this analogy used over and over for years and have even used it myself many times in my seminars without really checking whether or not the analogy is technically accurate with respect to modern hard drives.

Without doing any calculations, there is one highly inaccurate aspect of the 747 analogy that has always bothered me, and that is the use of an airplane of any type to describe the head and platter interaction. This comparison implies that in a real hard drive the heads actually fly very low over the surface of the disk, but this is technically not true! The heads do not fly at all in the traditional aerodynamic sense; instead, they actually float on a cushion of air being dragged around by the platters. A much better analogy would use a hover craft instead of an airplane, as the action of a hover craft much more closely emulates the action of the heads in a hard disk drive. Like a hover craft, the drive heads rely somewhat on the shape of the bottom of the head to capture and control this cushion of air that keeps them floating over the disk. By nature, the cushion of air on which the heads float only forms close to the media, and is technically called an *air bearing* by the disk drive industry.

I thought it was time to come up with a new analogy that more correctly describes the physical scale of dimensions and speeds at which a hard disk operates today. I looked up the specifications on a hard disk drive, and then equally magnified and rescaled all of the dimensions involved to make the head floating height equal to 1 inch. For my example, I used a Seagate model ST-12550N Barracuda 2 drive, which is a 2G (formatted capacity) 3 1/5-inch SCSI-2 (Small Computer Systems Interface, pronounced "scuzzy") Drive. In fact, I intend to install this very drive in the P75 Portable on which I am writing this book, replacing the current 1.2G drive. The specifications of this drive, as found in the technical documentation, are as follows:

Table 10.1 Seagate ST-12550N Barracuda 2 2G 3 1/5-inch SCSI-2 Drive Specifications		
Specification	**Value**	**Unit of Measure**
Linear Density	52,187	Bits Per Inch (bpi)
Bit Spacing	19.16	micro-inches (u-in)
Track Density	3,047	Tracks Per Inch (tpi)
Track Spacing	328.19	micro-inches (u-in)
Total Tracks	2,707	tracks
Rotational Speed	7,200	Revolutions Per Minute (rpm)
Average Head Linear Speed	53.55	Miles Per Hour (mph)
Head Slider Length	0.08	inches
Head Slider Height	0.02	inches
Head Floating Height	5	micro-inches (u-in)
Average Seek Time	8	milliseconds (ms)

By interpreting these facts, you can see that in this particular drive the heads are about 0.08 inches long and 0.02 inches high. They float on a cushion of air about 5 micro-inches (millionths of an inch) away from the surface of the disk while traveling at an average speed of 53.55 mph (figuring an average track diameter of 2.5 inches). These heads read and write individual bits spaced only 19.16 micro-inches apart on tracks separated by only 328.19 micro-inches. The heads can move from one track to any other in only 8 milliseconds during an average seek operation.

Now to create the analogy, I simply magnified the scale to make the floating height equal 1 inch. Because 1 inch is 200,000 times greater than 5 micro-inches, everything else would also be scaled up the same amount. Are you ready?

The heads of this "typical" hard disk in operation magnified to such a scale would be equivalent to an object more than 1,300 feet long and 300 feet high (about the size of the Sears Tower lying sideways!) traveling at a speed of more than 10.7 million mph (!) at a distance of only 1 inch above the ground, reading data bits spaced a mere 3.83 inches apart on tracks separated by only 5.47 feet. Additionally, this enormous skyscraper-sized head would be able to move sideways to any track within a distance of 2.80 miles in an average of only 8 milliseconds, resulting in an average sideways velocity of about 1,402 miles per hour!

This information should give you a whole new appreciation for what a technological marvel the modern hard disk drive actually represents.

Magnetic Data Storage

Learning how magnetic data storage works will help you develop a feel for how your disk drives operate and can improve how you work with disk drives and disks.

Nearly all disk drives operate on magnetic principles. Purely optical disk drives are often used as a secondary form of storage, but the computer to which they are connected likely will always have a magnetic storage medium for primary disk storage. Because of the high performance and density capabilities of magnetic storage, optical disk drives and media will likely never totally replace magnetic storage in PC systems.

Magnetic drives such as floppy disk drives and hard disk drives operate by using *electromagnetism*. This basic principle of physics states that as an electric current flows through a conductor a magnetic field is generated around the conductor. This magnetic field then can influence magnetic material in the field. By reversing the direction of the flow of electric current, the magnetic field's polarity also is reversed. An electric motor operates by using electromagnetism to exert pushing and pulling forces on magnets attached to a rotating shaft.

Another effect of electromagnetism occurs when a conductor is passed through a changing magnetic field: an electrical current is generated. As the polarity of the magnetic field changes, so does the direction of the electric current flow. For example, an *alternator,* a type of electrical generator used in automobiles, operates by rotating electromagnets past coils of wire conductors in which large amounts of electrical current can be induced. This two-way operation of electromagnetism is how data can be recorded on a disk and read back later.

The read/write heads in your disk drives (both floppy and hard disks) are constructed basically as U-shaped pieces of conductive material. This U-shaped object is wrapped with coils of wire, through which an electric current can flow. When the disk drive logic passes a current through these coils, it generates a magnetic field in the drive head. By reversing the polarity of the electric current, the polarity of the field that is generated changes also. In essence, the heads are electromagnets whose voltage can be switched in polarity quickly.

When a magnetic field is generated in the head, the field jumps the gap at the end of the U-shaped head. Because a magnetic field passes through a conductor much more easily than through the air, the field bends outward through the media and actually uses the disk media directly underneath as the path of least resistance to get to the other side of the gap. As the field passes through the media directly under the gap, it polarizes the magnetic particles it is passing through so that they are aligned with the field. The field's polarity and therefore the polarity of the magnetic media is based on the direction of the flow of electric current through the coils.

The disk consists of some form of substrate material (such as mylar for floppy disks or aluminum or glass for hard disks) on which a layer of magnetizable material has been deposited. This material is usually a form of iron oxide with various other elements added. The polarities of the magnetic fields of the individual magnetic particles on an erased disk are normally in a state of random disarray. Because the fields of the individual particles point in different random directions, each tiny, magnetic field is canceled by one that points in the opposite direction, for a total effect of no observable or cumulative field polarity.

Particles in the area under the head gap are aligned in the same direction as the field emanating from the gap. When the individual magnetic domains are in alignment, they no longer cancel one another, and an observable magnetic field exists in that region of the disk. This local field is generated by the many magnetic particles that are now operating as a team to produce a detectable cumulative field of a unified direction. The term *flux* is applied to describe a magnetic field with a given direction.

As the disk surface rotates under the drive head, the head can lay a magnetic flux over a region of the disk. When the electrical current flow through the coils in the head is reversed, so is the magnetic field polarity in the head gap. This also causes the polarity of the flux being placed on the disk to reverse. The *flux reversal* or *flux transition* is a change in polarity of the alignment of magnetic particles in the disk surface.

A drive head places flux reversals on a disk to record data. For each data bit (or bits) written, a pattern of flux reversals is placed on the disk in specific areas known as *bit* or *transition cells*. A *bit cell* or *transition cell* is a specific area of the disk controlled by the time and rotational speed in which flux reversals are placed by a drive head. The particular pattern of flux reversals within the transition cells used to store a given data bit or bits is referred to as the *encoding method*. The drive logic or controller takes the data to be stored and encodes it as a series of flux reversals over a period of time according to the encoding method used. Popular encoding methods are known as Modified Frequency

Modulation (MFM) or Run Length Limited (RLL) encoding. All floppy disk drives use the MFM scheme. Hard disks use MFM or several variations of RLL encoding methods. These encoding methods are described in more detail later in this chapter.

During the write process, a voltage is applied to the head, and as the polarity of this voltage is changed, the polarity of the magnetic field being recorded also changes. The flux transitions are written exactly at the points where the recording polarity changes. It may seem strange, but during the read process, the heads do not output exactly the same signal that was written. Instead, the heads generate a voltage pulse or spike only whenever they cross a flux transition. When the transition is from positive to negative, then the pulse that would be detected is a negative voltage. When the transition changes from negative to positive, then the pulse would be a positive voltage spike. In essence, while reading the disk the head becomes a flux transition detector and outputs voltage pulses whenever it crosses a transition. Areas of no transition generate no pulse. Figure 10.1 shows the relationship between the read and write waveforms and the flux transitions recorded on a disk.

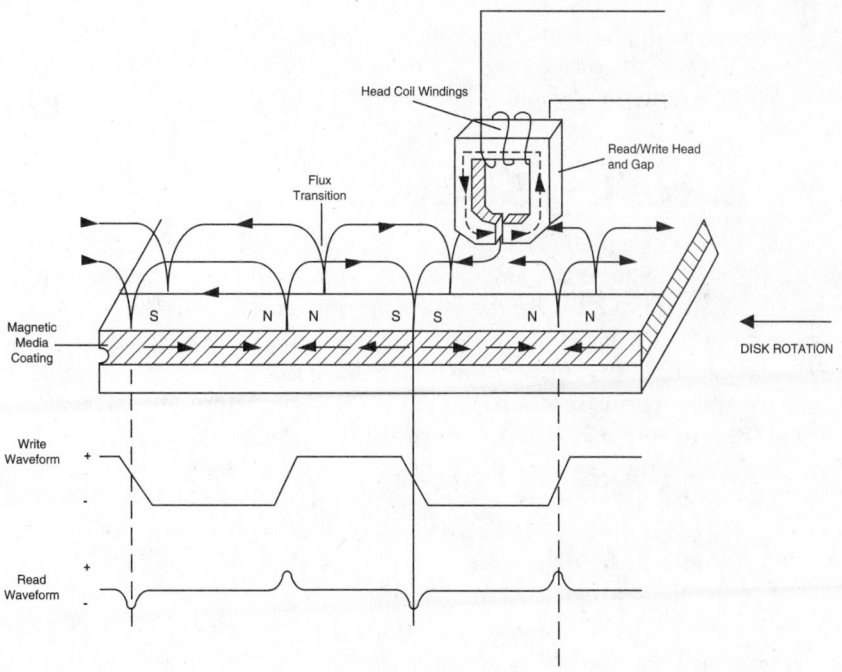

Fig. 10.1

Magnetic Write and Read processes

You can think of the write pattern as a square waveform that is either at a positive or negative voltage level and is continuously polarizing the disk media in one direction or another. Where the waveform transitions from positive to negative or vice versa, the magnetic flux on the disk also changes polarity. During a read, the head outputs a pulsed waveform, with the signal at zero volts unless a positive or negative pulse is being detected. Pulses only appear where there are flux transitions on the disk media. By knowing the clock timing used, the drive or controller circuitry can determine whether there is a pulse or no pulse within a given transition cell.

The electrical pulse currents generated in the head while it is passing over a disk in read mode are very weak and can contain significant noise. Sensitive electronics in the drive and controller assembly then can amplify the signal above the noise level and then decode the train of weak pulse currents back into data that is (theoretically) identical to the data originally recorded.

So as you can now see, disks are both recorded and read by using basic electromagnetic principles: Data is recorded on a disk by passing electrical currents through an electromagnet (the drive head) that generates a magnetic field stored on the disk. Data on a disk is read by passing the head back over the surface of the disk; and as the head encounters changes in the stored magnetic field, it generates a weak electrical current that indicates the presence or absence of flux transitions in the originally recorded signal.

Data Encoding Schemes

Magnetic media is essentially an analog storage medium, but the data you wish to store is digital information, that is, ones and zeros. When digital information is applied to a magnetic recording head, the head creates magnetic domains on the disk media with specific polarities. When a positive current is applied to the write head, the magnetic domains are polarized in one direction, and when a negative voltage is applied, they are polarized in the opposite direction. When the digital waveform that is recorded switches from a positive to a negative voltage, the polarity of the magnetic domains is reversed. During a readback, the head actually generates no voltage signal when a group of magnetic domains with the same polarity are encountered; however, a voltage pulse is generated everytime a switch in polarity is detected. These magnetic polarity switches are called *flux reversals*. Each flux reversal generates a voltage pulse in the read head, and it is these pulses that the drive detects when reading data. A read head will not generate the same waveform that was written; instead, it will generate a series of pulses, where each pulse appears where a magnetic flux transition has occurred.

To optimize the placement of pulses during magnetic storage, the raw digital input data is passed through a device called an Encoder/Decoder (Endec) which converts the raw binary information to a waveform that is more concerned with the optimum placement of the flux transitions (pulses). During a read operation, the Endec reverses the process and decodes the pulse train back into the original binary data. Over the years, several different schemes for encoding data in this manner have been developed, and some are better or more efficient than others.

In any consideration of binary information, the use of timing is important. When looking at a waveform, the timing of each voltage transition event is critical. If the timing is off, then a given voltage transition may be recognized at the wrong time, and bits may be either missed, added, or simply misinterpreted. To ensure that the timing is precise, both the transmitting and receiving devices must be in sync with each other. This can be accomplished by adding a separate line for timing, called a clock signal between the two devices. It can also be accomplished by combining the clock and data signals together and transmitting them on a single line. This combination of clock and data is exactly what is used in most magnetic data encoding schemes.

By adding the clock information you ensure the data to the timing accuracy in interpreting the individual bit cells between any two devices. A Bit Cell is a window in time inside of which a voltage transition will be placed to signify a bit. Clock timing is used to determine the start and end of each bit cell. Each bit cell is bounded by two clock cells where the clock transitions can be sent. There is a clock transition cell, then the data transition cell, and finally the clock transition cell for the data that follows. By sending the clock information along with the data, you assure that a long string of zero bits will not allow the clocks between the devices to get out of sync. Unfortunately, all of the transition cells used solely for clocking take up space on the media that could otherwise be used for data.

Because the number of flux transitions you can record on a particular media is limited by the disk media and head technology, disk drive engineers have been trying various ways of encoding the data into the minimum number of flux reversals as possible, taking into consideration that some flux reversals used solely for clocking are required. This allows maximum utilization of a given drive hardware technology. Although various encoding schemes have been tried, only a few are popular today. Over the years, these three basic types have been the most popular:

- Frequency Modulation (FM)
- Modified Frequency Modulation (MFM)
- Run Length Limited (RLL)

The following section examines these codes, discussing how they work, where they have been used, and any advantages or disadvantages that apply to each.

FM Encoding

One of the earliest techniques for encoding data for magnetic storage is called Frequency Modulation encoding. This encoding scheme is also sometimes called Single Density encoding, and was used in the earliest floppy disk drives that were installed in PC systems. For example, the original Osborne portable computer used these Single Density floppy drives, which stored about 80K of data on a single disk. Although popular up until the late '70s, FM encoding is no longer used today.

FM represents one of the simplest ways to encode zeros and ones on a magnetic surface. In each bit cell, a flux reversal is recorded to indicate a one bit, and no flux reversal is recorded to indicate a zero bit. With no other modifications, problems would occur if you were recording a long series of zeros, in which case no flux transitions would be recorded at all. With the absence of transitions for a long period of time, the controller could easily get out of sync with the drive, resulting in a possible misinterpretation of the data. To keep the devices in sync, a clock signal is written onto the drive along with the data. Using FM encoding, each bit actually requires two transition cells. A one bit is recorded as a clock flux reversal followed by a data flux reversal, which would simply look like two consecutive flux reversals to the drive. A zero bit is recorded using two transition cells also; however, only the clock cell has a flux reversal in it, while the data cell is empty (no reversal). Whether you are recording a one or a zero, the initial flux reversal represents the clock signal, while the second transition cell would carry a reversal only if the data was a one bit.

Although this method is simple and inexpensive, it has one major disadvantage. Each data bit requires two flux reversals, which reduces the potential disk capacity by half. Table 10.2 shows how each bit cell is encoded.

Table 10.2 FM Data to Flux Transition Encoding	
Data Bit Value	**Flux Encoding**
1	TT
0	TN

T = flux Transition
N = No flux transition

MFM Encoding

Modified Frequency Modulation encoding was devised to reduce the number of flux reversals used in the original FM encoding scheme and therefore pack more data on the disk. With MFM encoding, the use of the clock transition cells is minimized, leaving more room for the data. Clock transitions are only recorded if a zero bit is stored which is preceded by another zero bit. In all other cases a clock transition is not required. Because the use of the clock transitions has been minimized, the actual clock frequency can be doubled as compared to FM encoding, resulting in twice the number of data bits stored in the same number of flux transitions as with FM.

Because it is twice as efficient, MFM encoding has also been referred to as Double Density recording. MFM is still used on virtually all PC floppy drives today, and was used on nearly all PC hard disks for a number of years. Today, most hard disks use RLL (Run Length Limited) encoding which allows even greater efficiency than MFM.

Because MFM encoding places twice the number of data bits in the same number of flux reversals as FM, the clock speed of the data is doubled, so that the drive actually sees the same number of total flux reversals as with FM. This means that data is read and written at twice the speed with MFM encoding, even though the drive sees the flux reversals arriving at the same frequency as FM. This feature allows existing drive technology to store twice the data and deliver it twice as fast as was previously possible. The only caveat is that MFM encoding requires improved disk controller and drive circuitry because the timing of the flux reversals must be more precise than with FM. As it turned out, this was not difficult to achieve, and MFM encoding became the most popular encoding scheme in use for a long period of time.

When using MFM encoding, the data bit to flux reversal translation is shown in Table 10.3:

Table 10.3 MFM Data to Flux Transition Encoding	
Data Bit Value	**Flux Encoding**
1	NT
0 preceded by 0	TN
0 preceded by 1	NN

T = flux Transition
N = No flux transition

RLL Encoding

Today's most popular encoding scheme, called Run Length Limited, packs up to 50 percent more information on a given disk than even MFM, and three times as much information as FM. With RLL encoding, groups of bits are taken together as a unit, and combined to generate specific patterns of flux reversals. By combining the clock and data together in these patterns, the clock rate can be further increased while maintaining the same basic distance between the flux transitions on the disk. By optimizing the code to limit the minimum and maximum distance between two flux transitions, the clock rate (and therefore storage density) can be increased typically by three times over FM and 1.5 times over MFM encoding.

IBM invented RLL encoding and first used it in many of its mainframe disk drives. During the late 1980s the PC hard disk industry began using RLL encoding schemes as a way of increasing the storage capabilities of PC hard disks. Today, virtually every drive on the market uses one or another form of RLL encoding.

Instead of encoding a single bit, RLL normally encodes a group of data bits at a time. The term Run Length Limited is derived from the two primary specifications of these codes, which is the minimum number (the Run Length) and maximum number (the Run Limit) of transition cells allowed between two actual flux transitions. A number of schemes are actually possible by changing the Length and Limit parameters, but only two have achieved any real popularity. These two are known as RLL 2,7 and RLL 1,7. Even FM and MFM encoding can be expressed as a form of RLL. FM can also be referred to as RLL 0,1 because there can be as few as 0 and as many as 1 transition cell separating two flux transitions. MFM can also be referred to as RLL 1,3 because as few as 1 and as many as 3 transition cells can separate two flux transitions. Although these codes can be expressed in RLL form, it is not common to do so.

III

Hardware Considerations

RLL 2,7 was initially the most popular RLL variation because it offers a high density ratio (1.5 times that of MFM), with a transition detection window the same relative size as with MFM. This allows for a high storage density with fairly good reliability. With very high capacity drives, however, RLL 2,7 did not prove to be reliable enough. Most of today's highest capacity drives use RLL 1,7 encoding, which offers a density ratio of 1.27 times that of MFM, and a larger transition detection window relative to MFM. This means that compared to RLL 2,7 the storage density is a little less, but the reliability is much higher. Because of the larger relative window size within which a transition can be detected, RLL 1,7 is a more forgiving and more reliable code which is required when the media and head technology are being pushed to their limits. With the greater need for reliability in high capacity disk storage, it seems that RLL 1,7 will soon be the most popular code in use. There was another little-used RLL variation called RLL 3,9. This was sometimes referred to as ARLL (Advanced RLL), and allowed an even higher density ration than RLL 2,7. Unfortunately, reliability suffered too greatly with the RLL 3,9 scheme, and it was only used by a few controller companies who have all but disappeared.

It is difficult to understand how RLL codes work without looking at an example. Because RLL 2,7 is still the most popular form of RLL encoding, I will use it as an example. Even within a given RLL variation such as RLL 2,7 or 1,7 there are many different tables that can be constructed showing what groups of bits are encoded as what sets of flux transitions. Specifically with RLL 2,7 there are possibly thousands of different translation tables that could be constructed, but for my examples I will use the encoder/decoder (Endec) table used by IBM because it is the most popular variation you will find. Using the IBM conversion tables, specific groups of data bits 2, 3, and 4 bits long are translated into strings of flux transitions 4, 6, and 8 transition cells long respectively. The selected transitions coded for a particular bit sequence are designed to insure that flux transitions do not occur either too closely or too far apart.

It is necessary to limit how close two flux transitions can be because of the basically fixed resolution capabilities of the head and disk media. The requirements for limiting how far apart these transitions can be is to insure that the clocks in the devices remain in sync.

Table 10.4 shows the IBM developed encoding scheme for 2,7 RLL.

In studying this table, you may think that it would be impossible to encode a byte such as 00000001b because there are no combinations of data bit groups that fit this byte. This is not a problem, however, because the controller does not transmit individual bytes but instead sends whole sectors, making it possible to encode such a byte by simply including some of the bits in the following byte. The only real problem occurs with the last byte of a sector if additional bits are needed to complete the final group sequence. In these cases, the encoder/decoder (Endec) in the controller simply adds excess bits to the end of the last byte. These excess bits are subsequently truncated during any reads so that the last byte is always correctly decoded.

Encoding Scheme Comparisons

Figure 10.2 shows an example of the waveform written to store a capital "X" ASCII character on a hard disk drive by using three different encoding schemes.

Table 10.4 RLL 2,7 (IBM Endec) Data to Flux Transition Encoding

Data Bit Values	Flux Encoding
10	NTNN
11	TNNN
000	NNNTNN
010	TNNTNN
011	NNTNNN
0010	NNTNNTNN
0011	NNNNTNNN

T = flux Transition
N = No flux transition

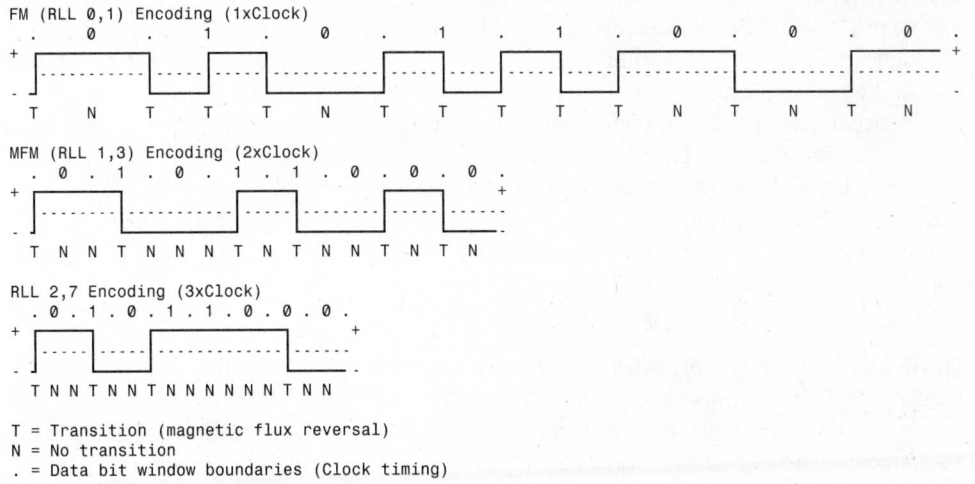

Fig. 10.2

ASCII "X" write waveforms using FM, MFM, and RLL 2,7 encoding.

In each of these encoding scheme examples, the top line shows the individual data bits (01011000b) in their bit cells separated in time by the clock signal, which is shown as a period ".". Below that line is the actual write waveform showing the positive and negative voltages as well as voltage transitions, which result in flux transitions being recorded. The bottom line shows the transition cells, with a "T" being used to represent a transition cell that contains a flux transition, while "N" is used to represent a transition cell that is empty (no flux transition).

The FM encoding example is easy to explain. Each bit cell has two transition cells, one for the clock information and one for the data itself. The clock transition cells all contain flux transitions, and the data transition cells contain a flux transition only if the data is a

1 bit. No transition at all is used to represent a 0 bit. Starting from the left, the first data bit is 0, which decodes as a flux transition pattern of "TN." The next bit is a 1, which decodes as "TT." The next bit is 0, which decodes as "TN," and so on. Using the FM encoding chart listed earlier, you can easily trace the FM encoding pattern to the end of the byte. Note that with FM encoding, you can see that it is possible for transitions to be written in adjacent transition cells, with no empty transition cells between them. This is called a minimum Run Length of 0. Also, the maximum number of empty transition cells between any two flux transitions is 1, which is why FM encoding can be referred to as RLL 0,1.

The MFM encoding scheme also has clock and data transition cells for each data bit to be recorded; however, as you can see, the clock transition cells only carry a flux transition when a 0 bit is stored that follows another 0 bit. Starting from the left, the first bit is a 0, and the previous bit is unknown (assume 0), so the flux transition pattern is "TN" for that bit. The next bit is a 1, which always decodes to a transition cell pattern of "NT." The next bit is 0, which was preceded by 1, so the pattern stored is "NN." Using the MFM encoding table listed earlier, you can easily trace the MFM encoding pattern to the end of the byte. You can see that the minimum and maximum number of transition cells between any two flux transitions is 1 and 3 respectively, hence MFM encoding can also be described as RLL 1,3. Notice that because half of the total transitions will be required compared to FM, the clock rate can be doubled, which results in the data taking up only half of the space. Also notice that even with the doubled clock rate, the minimum physical distance between any two flux transitions is exactly the same as with FM, meaning that the actual density of the write waveform is the same as with FM even though twice the data is being encoded.

The RLL 2,7 pattern is more difficult to see because it relies on encoding groups of bits rather than each bit individually. Starting from the left, the first group that matches the groups listed in the encoder/decoder (Endec) table are the first three bits 010. These bits are translated into a flux transition pattern of "TNNTNN." The next two bits "11" are translated as a group to "TNN," and the final group of "000" bits are translated to "NNNTNN." This completes the byte; as you can see in this example, no additional bits were needed to finish the last group. Notice that the minimum and maximum number of empty transition cells between any two flux transitions in this example are 2 and 6, although with a different example it would be possible to show a maximum of 7 empty transition cells. This is where the RLL 2,7 designation comes from. Because there are even fewer transitions recorded than with MFM, the clock rate can be further increased to three times that of FM or 1.5 times that of MFM, allowing more data to be stored in the same space on the disk. Notice, however, that the resulting write waveform itself looks exactly like a typical FM or MFM waveform as far as the number and separation of the flux transitions for a given physical portion of the disk. In other words the physical minimum and maximum distances between any two flux transitions remained the same with all three of these encoding scheme examples.

Another new feature found in high end drives involves the disk read circuitry. Read channel circuits using Partial-Response, Maximum-Likelihood (PRML) technology allows disk drive manufacturers to increase the amount of data that can be stored on a disk platter by up to 40 percent. PRML replaces the standard "detect one peak at a time" approach of traditional analog peak-detect read/write channels with digital signal processing. With digital signal processing, noise can be digitally filtered out, allowing flux change pulses to be placed closer together on the platter achieving greater densities.

I hope that the examinations of these different encoding schemes and how they work has taken some of the mystery out of how data is actually recorded on a drive. You can see that although schemes like MFM and RLL can store more data on a drive, the actual density of the flux transitions remains the same as far as the drive is concerned!

Sectors

A disk track is too large an area to manage effectively as a single storage unit. Many disk tracks can store 50,000 or more bytes of data, which would be very inefficient for storing small files. For that reason, a disk track is divided into several numbered divisions known as *sectors*. These sectors represent slices of the track.

Different types of disk drives and disks split tracks into different numbers of sectors, depending on the density of the tracks. For example, floppy disk formats use from 8 to 36 sectors per track; while hard disks usually store data at a higher density and can use from 17 to 100 or more sectors per track. Sectors created by standard formatting procedures on PC systems have a capacity of 512 bytes, but this capacity may change in the future.

Sectors are numbered on a track starting with 1, unlike the Heads or Cylinders, which are numbered starting with 0. For example, a 1.44M floppy disk contains 80 cylinders numbered from 0 to 79, two heads numbered 0 and 1, and each track on each cylinder has 18 sectors numbered from 1 to 18.

When a disk is formatted, additional areas are created on the disk for the disk controller to use for sector numbering and the identification of the start and end of each sector. These areas precede and follow each sector's data area, which accounts for the difference between a disk's unformatted and formatted capacities. For example, a 4.0M floppy disk (3 1/2-inch) has a capacity of 2.88M when it is formatted, and a 38M hard disk has a capacity of only 32M when it is formatted. All drives use some reserved space for managing the data that can be stored on the drive.

Although I have stated that each disk sector is 512 bytes in size, this statement is technically false. Each sector does allow for the storage of 512 bytes of data, but the data area is only a portion of the sector. Each sector on a disk typically occupies 571 bytes of the disk, of which only 512 bytes are usable for user data. The actual number of bytes required for the sector header and trailer can vary from drive to drive, but this figure is typical.

You may find it helpful to think of each sector as a page in a book. In a book, each page contains text, but the entire page is not filled with text. Rather, each page has top, bottom, left, and right margins. Information such as chapter titles (track and cylinder numbers) and page numbers (sector numbers) is placed in the margins. The "margin" areas of a sector are created and written to during the format process for the disk. Formatting also fills the data area of each sector with dummy values. After the disk is formatted, the data area can be altered by normal writing to the disk. The sector header and trailer information cannot be altered during normal write operations, unless you reformat the disk.

Each sector on a disk has a *prefix portion* or header that identifies the start of the sector and a sector number, and a *suffix portion* or trailer that contains a *checksum* (which helps ensure the integrity of the data contents). Each sector also contains 512 bytes of data. The data bytes normally are set to some specific value such as F6h (hex) when the disk is physically, or low-level, formatted. (Low-level formatting is explained in the following section.) In many cases, a specific pattern of bytes that are considered difficult to write is written so as to flush out any marginal sectors. In addition to the gaps within the sectors, there are gaps between sectors on each track, and gaps between tracks, none of which contains usable data space. The prefix, suffix, and gaps account for the lost space between the unformatted capacity of a disk and the formatted capacity.

Table 10.5 shows the format for each track and sector on a typical hard disk with 17 sectors per track.

This table refers to a hard disk track with 17 sectors. Although this capacity is typical, more advanced hard disks place as many as 100 or more sectors per track, and the specific formats of those sectors may vary slightly from the example.

Table 10.5 Typical MFM Disk Sector Format

Bytes	Name	Description
16	POST INDEX GAP	All 4Eh, at the track that begins after the Index mark
	Sector data format; repeated 17 times for an MFM encoded track	
13	ID VFO LOCK	All 00h to synch the VFO for the sector ID
1	SYNC BYTE	A1h to notify controller that data follows
1	ADDRESS MARK	FEh defining that ID field data follows
2	CYLINDER NUMBER	A value defining the Actuator position
1	HEAD NUMBER	A value defining the head selected
1	SECTOR NUMBER	A value defining the sector
2	CRC	Cyclic Redundancy Check to verify ID data
3	WRITE TURN-ON GAP	00h written by format to isolate the ID from DATA
13	DATA SYNC VFO LOCK	All 00h to synchronize the VFO for the DATA
1	SYNC BYTE	A1h to notify the controller that data follows
1	ADDRESS MARK	F8h defining that user DATA field follows
512	DATA	The area for user DATA

Bytes	Name	Description
2	CRC	Cyclic Redundance Check to verify DATA
3	WRITE TURN-OFF GAP	00h written by DATA update to isolate DATA
15	INTER-RECORD GAP	All 00h as a buffer for speed variation
693	PRE-INDEX GAP	All 4Eh, at track end before Index mark

571   Total bytes per sector
512   Data bytes per sector
10416 Total bytes per track
8704   Data bytes per track

As you can see, the usable space on each track is about 16 percent less than the unformatted capacity. This example is true for most disks, although some may vary slightly.

The Post Index Gap provides a head switching recovery period so that when switching from one track to another, sequential sectors may be read without waiting for an additional revolution of the disk. In some drives, when running 1:1 interleave controllers, this time is not enough and additional time may be added by skewing the sectors so that the arrival of the first sector is delayed.

The Sector ID data consists of the Cylinder, Head, and Sector number fields, as well as a CRC field to allow for verification of the ID data. Most controllers use bit 7 of the Head number field to mark the sector as bad during a Low Level Format or Surface Analysis. This is not absolute, some controllers may use other methods to indicate a marked bad sector, but usually the mark involves one of the ID fields.

The Write Turn on Gap follows the ID field CRC bytes and provides a pad to ensure a proper recording of the following user Data area as well as to allow full recovery of the ID CRC.

The user Data field consists of all 512 bytes of Data stored in the sector. This field is followed by a CRC field to verify the Data. While many controllers use two bytes of CRC here, the controller may implement a longer Error Correction Code (ECC) that requires more than two CRC bytes to store. The ECC data stored here provides the possibility of Data field read correction as well as read error detection. The correction/detection capabilities are dependent on the ECC code chosen and the controller implementation. A write turn off gap is a pad to allow the ECC (CRC) bytes to be fully recovered.

The Inter-Record Gap provides a means to accommodate variances in drive spindle speeds. A track may have been formatted while the disk is running slower than normal, then write updated with the disk running faster than normal. In such cases this gap prevents accidental overwriting of any information in the next sector. The actual size of this padding will vary depending on the disk rotational speed when the track was formatted and each time the Data Field is updated.

III

Hardware Considerations

The Pre-Index Gap allows for speed tolerance over the entire track. This gap will vary in actual size depending on the disk rotational speed variances and write frequency tolerance at the time of formatting.

All of this sector prefix information is extremely important because it contains the numbering information that defines the cylinder, head, and sector. All of this information except the Data Field, Data CRC bytes, and Write turn-off gap are written only during a low-level format. On a typical non-servo guided (stepper motor actuator) hard disk on which thermal gradients cause mistracking, the data updates that rewrite the 512-byte Data area and the CRC that follows may not be placed exactly in line with the sector header information. This situation eventually causes read or write failures of the Abort, Retry, Fail, Ignore variety. You can correct this problem by reformatting the disk, which rewrites the header and data information together at the current track positions. Then when you restore the data to the disk, the Data areas are written in alignment with the new sector headers.

Disk Formatting

You usually have two types of formats to consider:

- Physical, or *low-level*, format
- Logical, or *high-level*, format

When you format a floppy disk, the DOS FORMAT command performs both kinds of formats simultaneously. To format a hard disk, however, the operations must be done separately. Moreover, a hard disk requires a third step, between the two formats, in which the partitioning information is written to the disk. *Partitioning* is required because a hard disk is designed to be used with more than one operating system. Separating the physical format in a way that is always the same regardless of the operating system being used and regardless of the high-level format (which would be different for each operating system) makes possible the use of multiple operating systems on one hard drive. The partitioning step allows more than one type of operating system to use a single hard disk or a single DOS to use the disk as several volumes or logical drives. A volume or logical drive is anything that DOS assigns a drive letter.

Consequently, formatting a hard disk involves three steps:

1. Low-level format (LLF)

2. Partitioning

3. High-level format (HLF)

During a low-level format, the disk's tracks are divided into a specific number of sectors. The sector header and trailer information is recorded, as are inter-sector and inter-track gaps. Each sector's data area is filled with a dummy byte value or test pattern of values. For floppy disks, the number of sectors recorded on each track depends on the type of floppy disk and drive; for hard disks, the number of sectors per track depends on the drive and controller interface.

The original ST-506/412 MFM controllers always placed 17 sectors per track on a disk. ST-506/412 controllers with RLL encoding would increase the number of sectors on a drive to 25 or 26 sectors per track. ESDI drives can have anywhere from 32 or more sectors per track. IDE drives are drives with built-in controllers, and depending on exactly what type of controller design is built-in, the number of sectors per track can be anything from 17 to 100 or more. SCSI drives are essentially IDE drives with an added SCSI Bus Adapter circuit, meaning that they also have some type of controller built in, and like IDE, depending on what controller design was used, the number of sectors per track can be practically anything. Most IDE and SCSI drives use a technique called *Zoned Recording* that writes a variable number of sectors per track. The outermost tracks hold more sectors than the inner tracks, because they are longer. Because of limitations in the PC BIOS, these drives still have to act like they have a fixed number of sectors per track; this is handled by translation algorithms that are implemented in the controller.

Multiple Zone Recording

One way to increase the capacity of a hard drive is to format more sectors on the outer cylinders than on the inner ones. Because they have a larger circumference, the outer cylinders can easily hold more data. Drives without Zoned Recording store the same amount of data on every cylinder, even though the outer cylinders may be twice as long as the inner cylinders. This results in wasted storage capacity, because the disk media must be capable of storing data reliably at the same density as on the inner cylinders. With ST-506/412 and ESDI controllers, the number of sectors per track was unfortunately fixed and therefore drive capacity was limited by the density capability of the innermost (shortest) track.

In a Zoned Recording, the cylinders are split into groups called zones, with each successive zone having more and more sectors per track as you move out from the inner radius of the disk. All of the cylinders within a particular zone have the same number of sectors per track. The number of zones varies with specific drives, but most drives will have 10 or more individual zones.

Drives with separate controllers could not handle zoned recordings because there was no standard way to communicate information about the zones from the drive to the controller. With SCSI and IDE disks it became possible to format individual tracks with different numbers of sectors because they have the disk controller built-in. The built-in controllers on these drives can be made fully aware of the zoning used. These built-in controllers must then also translate the physical Cylinder, Head, and Sector numbers to logical Cylinder, Head, and Sector numbers so that the drive has the appearance of having the same number of sectors appear on each track. This is mainly because the PC BIOS was designed to handle a single number of sectors per track only. This means that zoned drives must always run by using a sector translation scheme.

The use of Zoned Recording has allowed drive manufacturers to increase the capacity of their hard drives by between 20 and 50 percent compared to a fixed sector per track arrangement. Nearly all IDE and SCSI drives today use Zoned Recording.

III

Hardware Considerations

Partitioning

Partitioning segments the drive into areas called partitions that can hold a particular operating system's file system. Right now the following common file systems are in use by PC operating systems today:

- FAT (File Allocation Table) — This is the standard file system used by DOS, OS/2, and Windows NT. FAT partitions support file names of 11 characters maximum (8 plus a 3-character extension), and a volume can be as large as 2G in size.

- HPFS (High Performance File System) — This is a Unix-style file system accessible only under OS/2 and Windows NT. DOS applications running under OS/2 or Windows NT can access files in HPFS partitions, but straight DOS cannot. File names can be 256 characters long, and the volume size is limited to 8G.

- NTFS (Windows NT File System) — This is a Unix-style file system currently accessible under Windows NT only; however, drivers should be available for OS/2 to access NTFS as well. DOS is unable to access these partitions, but DOS applications running under Windows NT can. File names can be 256 characters long, and the volume size is limited to 8G.

Of these three file systems, the FAT file system is still by far the most popular (and recommended). The main problem with the FAT file system is that disk space is used in groups of sectors called *Allocation Units* or *Clusters*. On large volumes, the larger cluster sizes required cause disk space to be inefficiently used. HPFS and NTFS always manage the disk space in sector increments, so there is no penalty of wasted disk space with large volumes. The FAT file system is still the most recommended because of compatibility. For example, few applications currently are compatible with the longer file names possible in the HPFS and NTFS file systems. All of the operating systems can access FAT volumes, and the file structures and data recovery procedures are well known. Data recovery can be difficult to impossible under the HPFS and NTFS systems; for those systems, good backups are imperative.

During partitioning, no matter what file system is specified, the partitioning software will write a special boot program and partition table to the first sector called the Master Boot Sector (MBS). Because the term *record* is sometimes used to mean *sector*, this can also be called the Master Boot Record (MBR).

High-Level Format

During the high-level format, the operating system (such as DOS, OS/2, or Windows NT) writes the structures necessary for managing files and data. FAT partitions have a Volume Boot Sector (VBS), a file allocation table (FAT), and a Root Directory on each formatted logical drive. These data structures (discussed in detail in Chapter 15) enable the operating system to manage the space on the disk, keep track of files, and even manage defective areas so that they do not cause problems.

High-level formatting is not really formatting: it is creating a table of contents for the disk. The low-level format is the real format, in which tracks and sectors are written on the disk. As mentioned, the single DOS FORMAT command can perform both low-level and high-level format operations on a floppy disk but performs only the high-level format for a hard disk. Hard disk low-level formats require a special utility usually supplied by the disk controller manufacturer.

Basic Hard Disk Drive Components

Many types of hard disks are on the market, but nearly all drives share the same basic physical components. Some differences may exist in the implementation of these components (and in the quality of materials used to make them), but the operational characteristics of most drives are similar. The components found in a typical hard disk drive (see fig. 10.3) are as follows:

- Disk platters

- Read/write heads

- Head actuator mechanism

- Spindle motor

- Logic board

- Cables and connectors

- Configuration items (such as jumpers or switches)

- Bezel (optional)

The platters, spindle motor, heads, and head actuator mechanisms usually are contained in a sealed chamber called the *Head Disk Assembly* (HDA). The HDA usually is treated as a single component; it is rarely ever opened. Other parts external to the drive's HDA, such as the logic boards, bezel, and other configuration or mounting hardware, can be disassembled from the drive.

Hard Disk Platters (Disks)

A typical hard disk has one or more platters, or disks. Hard disks for PC systems have been available in a number of form factors over the years. Normally the physical size of a drive is expressed as the size of the platters. The most common platter sizes used in types of PC hard disks in use today are as follows:

- 5 1/4-inch (Actually 130mm or 5.12 inches)

- 3 1/2-inch (Actually 95mm or 3.74 inches)

- 2 1/2-inch

- 1 1/8-inch

- 1 1/3-inch

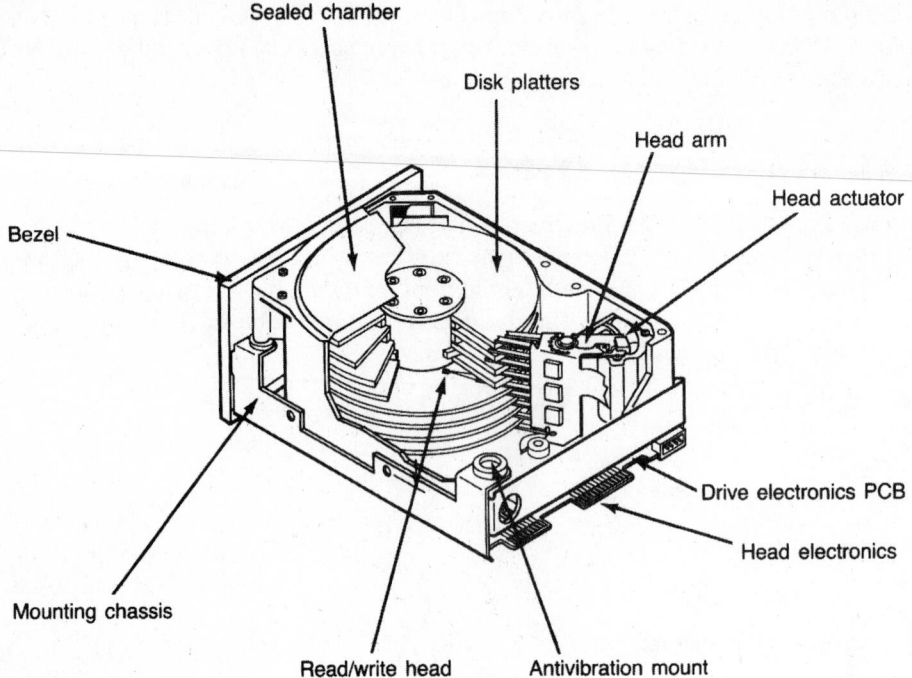

Sealed chamber

Disk platters

Head arm

Head actuator

Bezel

Drive electronics PCB

Head electronics

Mounting chassis

Read/write head   Antivibration mount

Fig. 10.3
Hard disk drive components.

There are larger hard drives with 8-inch, 14-inch, or even larger platters, but these drives typically have not been associated with PC systems. Currently the 3 1/2-inch drives are the most popular for desktop and some portable systems, while the 2 1/2-inch and smaller drives are very popular in portable systems. The 1 1/3-inch drives are the most recent to enter the market, and they are truly amazing. These drives are about the size of a large wristwatch, and can currently store 40M, with capacities of 100M or more not too far away. These 1 1/3-inch drives are expected to reach 1G capacity by the year 2000! Because of their small size, they are extremely rugged, and can withstand shocks of 100 times the force of gravity *while operating*, and double that when powered off.

Most hard drives have two or more platters, although some of the smaller drives have only one. The number of platters a drive can have is limited by the drive's physical size vertically. So far, the maximum number of platters I have seen in any 5 1/4-inch full-height drives is 11; and there are 3 1/2-inch drives with as many as 10 platters.

Each platter traditionally has been made from an aluminum metal alloy, for strength and light weight. With the desire for higher and higher densities and smaller drives, many drives now use platters made of glass or, more technically, a glass-ceramic composite. One such material being used is called MemCor, which is produced by the Dow Corning glass company. MemCor is composed of glass with ceramic implants, which resists cracking better than pure glass. Glass platters offer greater strength (rigidity) and can therefore be machined to one-half or less the thickness of conventional aluminum disks. Glass platters are also much more thermally stable than aluminum platters, which means that they do not change dimensions (expand or contract) very much with any changes in temperature. Several hard disks from companies like Seagate, Toshiba, Areal Technology, Maxtor, and Hewlett Packard are currently using glass or glass-ceramic platters. For most manufacturers, glass disks will be replacing the standard aluminum substrate over the next few years, especially in high performance 2 1/2- and 3 1/2-inch drives.

Recording Media

No matter what substrate is used, the platters are covered with a thin layer of a magnetically retentive substance called *media* in which magnetic information is stored. Two popular types of media are used on hard disk platters:

- Oxide media
- Thin Film media

Oxide media is made of various compounds containing iron oxide as the active ingredient. A magnetic layer is created by coating the aluminum platter with a syrup containing iron-oxide particles. This media is spread across the disk by spinning the platters at high speed and causing the material to flow from the center of the platter to the outside due to centrifugal force. This creates an even coating of media material on the platter. The surface is then cured and polished. Finally, a layer of material that protects and lubricates the surface is added and burnished smooth. Normally, the oxide media coating is about 30 millionths of an inch thick. If you could peer into a drive with oxide-media-coated platters, you would see that they are brownish or amber in color.

As drive densities increase, the media needs to be thinner and more perfectly formed. The capabilities of oxide coatings have been exceeded by most higher-capacity drives. Because oxide media is very soft, disks using this media are prone to head crash damage if the drive is jolted during operation. Most older drives, especially those sold as low-end models, have oxide media on the drive platters. Oxide media has been used since 1955, and remained popular because of its relatively low cost and ease of application. Today, there are very few drives left that still use oxide media.

Thin film media is thinner, harder, and more perfectly formed than oxide media. It was developed as a high-performance media to enable a new generation of drives to have lower head floating heights, which in turn made possible increases in drive density. Originally, thin film media was used only in higher-capacity or higher-quality drive systems but today virtually all drives have thin film media.

Thin film media is aptly named. The coating is much thinner than can be achieved by the oxide coating method. Thin film media is also known as *plated*, or *sputtered*, media because of the various processes used to get the thin film of media on the platters.

Thin film plated media is manufactured by placing the media material on the disk with an electroplating mechanism, much like chrome plating on the bumper of a car. The aluminum platter is immersed in a series of chemical baths that coat the platter with several layers of metallic film. The media layer is a cobalt alloy about 3 micro-inches (millionths of an inch) thick.

III

Hardware Considerations

Thin-film sputtered media is created by first coating the aluminum platters with a layer of nickel phosphorus and then applying the cobalt alloy magnetic material with a continuous vacuum deposition process called *sputtering*. During this process, magnetic layers as thin as 1 or 2 micro-inches are deposited on the disk, in a fashion similar to the way that silicon wafers are coated with metallic films in the semiconductor industry. The sputtering technique then is used again to lay down an extremely hard, 1 micro-inch protective carbon coating. The requirements of a near-perfect vacuum make sputtering the most expensive of the processes described here.

The surfaces of sputtered platters contain magnetic layers as thin as 1-millionth of an inch. Because this surface is also very smooth, the head can float closer to the disk surface than was previously possible. Floating heights as little as 3 micro-inches over the surface are possible. With the head closer, the density of the magnetic flux transitions can be increased to provide greater storage capacity. Additionally, the increased intensity of the magnetic field during a closer proximity read provides the higher signal amplitudes needed for good signal-to-noise performance.

Both the sputtering and plating processes result in a very thin, very hard film of media on the platters. Because the thin film media is so hard, it has a better chance of surviving contact with the heads at high speed. In fact, modern thin-film media is virtually uncrashable. Oxide coatings are scratched or damaged much more easily. If you could open a drive to peek at the platters, thin film media platters would look like the silver surface of a mirror.

The sputtering process results in the most perfect, thinnest, and hardest disk surface that can be commercially obtained. The sputtering process has largely replaced plating as the method of creating thin film media. Having a thin film media surface on a drive translates into increased storage capacity in a smaller area with fewer head crashes, and a drive that will provide many years of trouble-free use.

Read/Write Heads

A hard disk drive usually has one read/write head for each platter side, and these heads are connected, or "ganged," on a single movement mechanism. The heads therefore move in unison across the platters.

Mechanically, read/write heads are simple. Each head is on an actuator arm that is spring-loaded to force the head into a platter. Few people realize this, but each platter is actually "squeezed" by the heads above and below it. If you could open a drive safely and lift the top head with your finger, it would snap back into the platter when you released it. If you could pull down on one of the heads underneath a platter, the spring tension would cause it to snap back up into the platter when you released it. Figure 10.4 shows a typical hard disk head-actuator assembly from a voice coil drive.

When the drive is at rest, the heads are forced into direct contact with the platters by spring tension, but when the drive is spinning at full speed, air pressure develops underneath the heads and lifts them off the surface of the platter. On a drive spinning at full speed, the distance between the heads and the platter can be anywhere from 3 to 20 or more micro-inches. In the early 1960s, hard disk drive recording heads operated at floating heights as large as 200-300 micro-inches, while today's drive heads are designed to float as low as 3 to 5 micro-inches over the surface of the disk. To support higher densities in drives of the future, the physical separation between the head and disk is expected to be as little as .5 micro-inches by the end of the century.

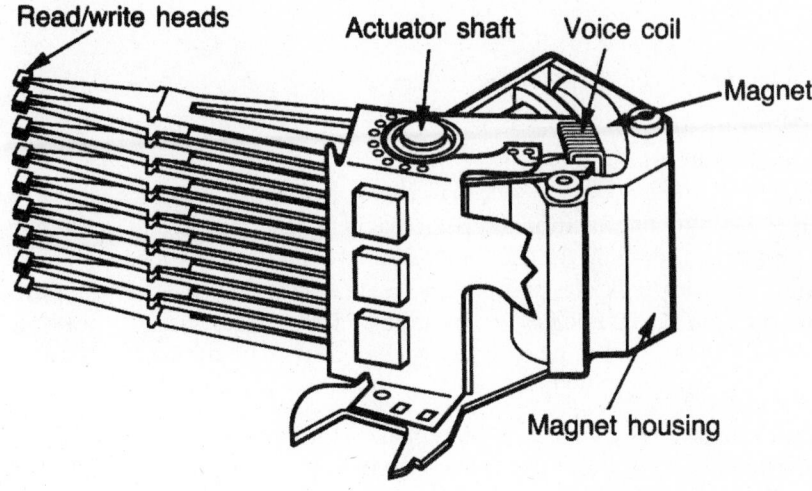

Fig. 10.4
Read/write heads and rotary voice coil actuator assembly.

Generally speaking, the older the drive and lower the capacity, the higher the heads float over the media. The small size of this gap is why the disk drive's Head Disk Assembly (HDA) should never be opened except in a clean room environment. Any particle of dust or dirt that gets into this mechanism could cause the heads to read improperly, or possibly even to strike the platters while at full speed. The latter event, may damage (scratch) the platter or the head.

To ensure the cleanliness of the interior of the drive, the HDA is assembled in a class 100 or better clean room. This specification is such that a cubic foot of air cannot contain more than one hundred particles up to 0.5 micron (19.7 micro-inch) in size. A single person breathing while standing motionless spews out 500 such particles in a single minute! These rooms contain special air-filtration systems that continuously evacuate and refresh the air. A drive's HDA should not be opened unless it is inside such a room.

Although it may seem expensive to maintain such an environment, there are many companies manufacturing table top or bench-sized clean rooms that sell for only a few thousand dollars. Some of these devices operate like a glove box, where the operator first inserts the drive and any tools required, then closes the box and turns on the filtration system. Inside the box, a clean room environment is maintained and through built-in gloves, a technician can work on the drive. Other clean room variations have the operator standing at a bench where a forced air curtain is used to maintain a clean environment on the bench top. The technician can walk in and out of the clean room field by simply walking through the air curtain. This air curtain is much like the curtain of air used in some stores and warehouses to prevent heat from escaping in the winter while leaving a passage wide open. Because the clean environment is very expensive to produce, few companies except those that manufacture the drives are prepared to service hard disk drives.

The following heads have been used in hard disk drives over the years:

- Ferrite

- Metal In Gap (MIG)

- Thin Film (TF)

- Magneto-Resistive (MR)

Ferrite. *Ferrite heads* are the traditional type of magnetic head design and evolved from the original IBM Winchester drive. They have an iron-oxide core wrapped with electromagnetic coils. A magnetic field is produced by energizing the coils; a field can be induced also by passing a magnetic field near the coils. This process gives the heads full read and write capability. Ferrite heads are larger and heavier than thin film heads and therefore require a larger floating height to prevent contact with the disk.

Many refinements have been made to the original (monolithic) ferrite head design. A type of ferrite head called a *composite ferrite head* has a smaller ferrite core bonded with glass in a ceramic housing. This design permits a smaller head gap, which allows higher track densities. These heads are less susceptible to stray magnetic fields than the older, monolithic design. Composite ferrite heads were popular in many low end drive designs during the 1980s such as the popular Seagate ST-225. As density demands grew, the competing MIG and thin film head designs were used in place of ferrite, which are virtually obsolete today. Ferrite heads are unable to write the higher coercivity media needed for high density designs, and have poor frequency response with higher noise levels. The main advantage of Ferrite heads is that they represent the cheapest type available.

Metal-In-Gap. *Metal-In-Gap* (MIG) heads are basically a specially enhanced version of the composite ferrite design. In MIG heads, a metal substance is sputtered into the recording gap on the trailing edge of the head. This material offers increased resistance to magnetic saturation, allowing a higher-density recording. MIG heads also produce a sharper gradient in the magnetic field for a more well-defined magnetic pulse. These heads enable the use of higher-coercivity thin film disks and can operate at lower floating heights.

Two versions of MIG heads are available: single-sided and double-sided. Single-sided MIG heads are designed with a layer of magnetic alloy placed along the trailing edge of the gap. Double-sided MIG designs apply the layer to both sides of the gap. The metal alloy is applied through a vacuum deposition process called sputtering. This alloy has twice the magnetization capability of raw ferrite and allows writing the higher coercivity thin film media needed at the higher densities. Double-sided MIG heads offer even higher coercivity capability than the single-sided designs. Because of these increases in capabilities through improved designs, MIG heads were for a time the most popular head used in all but the very high capacity drives.

Due to market pressures that have demanded higher and higher densities, MIG heads have been largely displaced in favor of thin film heads.

Thin Film. *Thin Film* (TF) heads are produced in much the same manner as a semiconductor chip: with a photo-lithographic process. In this manner, many thousands of heads can be made on a single circular wafer. This manufacturing process also results in a very small high quality product.

TF heads offer an extremely narrow and controlled head gap created by sputtering a hard aluminum material. Because this material completely encloses the gap, this area is very well protected, minimizing the chance of damage from contact with the media. The core is a combination of iron and nickel alloy two to four times more powerful magnetically than a ferrite head core.

Thin film heads produce a sharply defined magnetic pulse that allows extremely high densities to be written. Because thin heads do not have a conventional coil, they are more immune to variations in coil impedance. Thin film heads are small and lightweight, and can float at a much lower height than the Ferrite or MIG heads. Floating height has been reduced to as little as 2 micro-inches or less in some designs. Because the reduced height enables a much stronger signal to be picked up and transmitted between the head and platters, the signal-to-noise ratio increases, which improves accuracy. At the high track and linear densities in some drives, a standard ferrite head would not be able to pick out the data signal from the background noise. When thin film heads are used, their small size enables more platters to be stacked in a drive.

Until the past few years TF heads were considered relatively expensive compared to older technologies such as Ferrite and MIG. However, better manufacturing techniques as well as the requirements for higher densities have driven the market to TF heads. Their widespread use has also allowed these heads to become cost competitive if not cheaper than MIG heads.

Thin film heads are currently used in the majority of high capacity drives, especially in the smaller form factors. They have displaced MIG heads as the most popular head design being used in the majority of drives manufactured today. Enhancements to improve TF head efficiency are being pursued by the industry and are likely to allow thin film heads to remain popular for some time to come, especially in mainstream drives.

Magneto-Resistive. *Magneto-Resistive* (MR) heads are a relatively new technology, invented and pioneered by IBM. Magneto-Resistive heads are currently the most superior head design available, offering the highest performance available. Most 3 1/5-inch drives with capacities in excess of 1G are currently using MR heads, and as areal densities continue to increase the MR head will eventually become the head of choice for nearly all hard drives, displacing the popular MIG and TF head designs.

MR heads rely on the fact that the resistance of a conductor changes slightly when an external magnetic field is present. Rather than put out a voltage by passing through a magnetic field flux reversal as a normal head would, the MR head senses the flux reversal and changes resistance. A small current flows through the heads, and the change in resistance is measured by this sense current. This type of design enables the output to be three or more times more powerful than a thin film head during a read. In effect, MR heads are "power read" heads, acting more like a sensor than a generator.

MR head construction involves additional cost and complexity beyond that required for other types of heads, because a number of special features or steps must be added:

- Additional wires must be run to and from the head to carry the sense current

- Four to six more masking steps are required

- Because MR heads are so sensitive, they are very susceptible to stray magnetic fields and must be shielded

Because the MR principle can only read data and is not used for writing, MR heads are really two separate heads in one. A standard inductive thin film head is used for writing and a Magneto-Resistive head is used for reading. Because two separate heads are built into one assembly, each head can be optimized to its task. Ferrite, MIG, and thin film heads are known as single gap heads because the same gap is used for both reading and writing, while the MR head uses a separate gap for each operation. The problem with single gap heads is the gap length is always a compromise between what is best for reading versus what is best for writing. The read function needs a thin gap for higher resolution; while the write function needs a thicker gap for deeper flux penetration to switch the media. With the dual gap MR head the read and write gaps can be independently optimized for both functions. In MR heads, the write (thin film) gap writes a wider track than the read (Magneto-Resistive) gap reads. The read head then is less susceptible to picking up stray magnetic information from adjacent tracks.

Although MR heads have a lot of good qualities, they do have some disadvantages. The primary disadvantage is cost. This is actually not too limiting, however, because they are primarily used today in extremely high capacity drives where cost is not as much of a concern. Another disadvantage is that they are much more delicate than the other head designs. Handling MR heads during manufacturing requires more care due to their greater sensitivity to damage by ESD (Electro-Static Discharge). Finally, drives with MR heads require better shielding from stray magnetic fields that can more easily affect them compared to the other head designs. All in all, these drawbacks are minor compared to the advantages the MR heads offer.

Head Sliders

The term *slider* is used to describe the body of material that supports the actual drive head itself. The slider is what actually floats or slides over the surface of the disk carrying the head at the correct distance from the media for reading and writing. Most sliders are actually shaped similar to a Catamaran sailboat, with two outboard pods that float along the surface of the disk media, and a central "rudder" portion that actually carries the head and read/write gap.

The trend to smaller and smaller form factor drives has forced a requirement for smaller and smaller sliders as well. The typical Mini-Winchester slider design is about .160 × .126 × .034 inches in size. Most head manufacturers are now shifting to 50 percent smaller "nanosliders," which have dimensions of about .08 × .063 × .017 inches. The nanoslider is being used in both high-capacity as well as small-form factor drives. Smaller sliders also reduce the mass carried at the end of the head actuator arms, allowing for increased acceleration and deceleration leading to faster seek times. The smaller sliders also require less area for a landing zone thus increasing the usable area of the disk platters. The smaller slider contact area also reduces the slight wear on the media surface which occurs during normal startup and spindown of the drive platters.

Another feature of the newer nanoslider designs consists of specially modified surface patterns designed to maintain the same floating height over the disk surface whether the slider is over the inner or outer cylinders. Conventional sliders will increase or decrease their floating height considerably according to the velocity of the disk surface traveling underneath. When over the outer cylinders the velocity and floating height is higher. This is undesirable with newer drives using zone recording, where the same bit density is achieved on all of the cylinders. Because the same bit density is maintained throughout the drive, the head floating height should be relatively constant as well for maximum performance. Special textured surface patterns and manufacturing techniques allow the nanosliders to float at a much more consistent height, making them ideal for zone recorded drives.

Head Actuator Mechanisms

Possibly more important than the heads themselves is the mechanical system that moves them, called the *head actuator*. This mechanism moves the heads across the disk and positions them accurately over the desired cylinder. Many variations on head actuator mechanisms are in use, but they can all be categorized as one of two different basic types:

- Stepper motor actuators
- Voice coil actuators

The use of one or the other type of positioner has profound effects on a drive's performance and reliability. The effect is not limited to speed, but includes accuracy, sensitivity to temperature, position, vibration, and overall reliability. To put it bluntly, a drive equipped with a stepper motor actuator is much less reliable (by a large factor) than a drive equipped with a voice coil actuator.

The head actuator is the most important single specification in the drive. The type of head actuator mechanism in a drive tells you a great deal about the drive's performance and reliability characteristics. Table 10.6 shows the two types of hard disk drive head actuators and the affected performance parameters.

Table 10.6 Characteristics of Stepper Motor versus Voice Coil Drives

Characteristic	Stepper motor	Voice coil
Relative access speed	Slow	Fast
Temperature sensitive	Yes (very)	No
Positionally sensitive	Yes	No
Automatic head parking	Not usually	Yes
Preventive maintenance	Periodic format	None required
Relative reliability	Poor	Excellent

Generally, a stepper motor drive has a slow average access rating, is temperature-sensitive during read and write operations, is sensitive to the physical orientation during read and write operations, does not automatically park its heads over a save zone during power-down, and usually requires annual or biannual reformats to realign the sector data with the sector header information due to mistracking. Overall, stepper motor drives are vastly inferior to drives with voice coil actuators.

Some stepper motor drives feature automatic head parking at power-down. If you have a newer stepper motor drive, refer to the drive's technical-reference manual to determine whether your drive has this feature. (Other than removing the lid and watching as you power-off—which is definitely *not* recommended—the documentation is the only reliable way to tell.) Sometimes you can hear a noise after power-down, but that can be deceptive because some drives use a solenoid-activated spindle brake, which makes a noise as the drive is powered off and does not involve head parking.

Floppy disk drives position their heads using a stepper motor actuator. The accuracy of the stepper mechanism is suited to a floppy drive because the track densities are usually nowhere near those of a hard disk. Many of the less expensive, low-capacity hard disks also use a stepper motor system. Most hard disks with capacities of more than 40M have voice coil actuators, as do all drives I have seen with capacities of more than 100M. In IBM's product line, a drive of 40M or more is always a voice coil drive. On IBM systems with drives of less than 40M (usually 20M or 30M), both voice coil and stepper motor drives have been used.

This breakdown does not necessarily apply to other system manufacturers, but it is safe to say that hard disk drives with less than 80M capacity may have either type of actuator, and virtually all drives with greater than 80M capacities have voice coil actuators. The cost differential between voice coil drives and stepper motor drives of equal capacity is marginal today, so there is little reason not to use a voice coil drive anymore. Virtually no new stepper motor drives are being manufactured anymore.

Stepper Motor. A *stepper motor* is an electrical motor that can "step," or move from position to position, with mechanical detents. If you were to grip the spindle of one of these motors and spin it by hand, you would notice a clicking or buzzing. The sensation is much like that of the volume control on some stereo systems. Stepper motors cannot position themselves between step positions; they can stop at only the predetermined detent positions. The motors are small and can be square, cylindrical, or of a flat pancake design. They are outside the sealed HDA, although the spindle of the motor penetrates the HDA through a sealed hole. The stepper motor is located in one of the four corners of the hard disk drive and is usually easily visible.

Mechanical Links. The stepper motor is *mechanically linked* to the head rack by either a split-steel band coiled around the motor spindle or a rack-and-pinion gear mechanism. As the motor steps, each detent, or click-stop position, represents the movement of one track through the mechanical linkage. Some systems use several motor steps for each track. In positioning the heads, if the drive is told to move to track 100, the motor begins the stepping motion, proceeds to the 100th detent position, and stops, leaving the heads over the desired cylinder. The fatal flaw in this type of positioning system is that due to dimensional changes in the platter to head relationship over the life of a drive, the heads may not really be precisely placed over the cylinder location. This type of positioning system is called a blind system, because the heads have no true way of determining the exact placement of a given cylinder.

The most widely used stepper motor actuator systems use a *split metal band mechanism* to transmit the rotary stepping motion to the in-and-out motion of the head rack. The band is made of special alloys to limit thermal expansion and contraction as well as stretch. One end of the band is coiled around the spindle of the stepper motor, and the other is connected directly to the head rack. The band is inside the sealed HDA and is not visible from the outside of the drive.

Some drives use a *rack-and-pinion gear mechanism* to link the stepper motor to the head rack. This procedure involves a small pinion gear on the spindle of the stepper motor that moves a rack gear in and out. The rack gear is connected to the head rack, causing it to move. The rack-and-pinion mechanism is more durable than the split metal band mechanism and provides slightly greater physical and thermal stability. One problem, however, is *backlash*, the amount of play in the gears. Backlash increases as the gears wear, and eventually renders the mechanism useless.

Temperature Fluctuation Problems. Stepper motor mechanisms are affected by a variety of problems. The biggest problem is temperature. As the drive platters heat and cool, they expand and contract, respectively; the tracks then move in relation to a predetermined track position. The stepper mechanism does not allow the mechanism to move in increments of less than a single track to correct for these temperature-induced errors. The drive positions the heads to a particular cylinder according to a predetermined number of steps from the stepper motor, with no room for nuance.

The low-level formatting of the drive places the initial track and sector marks on the platters at the positions where the heads are currently located, as commanded by the stepper motor. If all subsequent reading and writing occur at the same temperature as the initial format, the heads always record precisely within the track and sector boundaries.

At different temperatures, however, the head position does not match the track position. When the platters are cold, the heads miss the track location because the platters have shrunk and the tracks have moved toward the center of the disk. When the platters are warmer than the formatted temperature, the platters will have grown larger, and the track positions are located outward. Gradually, as the drive is used, the data is written inside, on top of, and outside the track and sector marks. Eventually the drive fails to read one of these locations, and usually a DOS `Abort, Retry, Ignore` error message appears.

The temperature sensitivity of stepper motor drives may also cause the "Monday morning blues." When the system is powered up cold (on Monday, for example), a 1701, 1790, or 10490 Power-On Self Test (POST) error occurs. If you leave the system on for about 15 minutes, the drive can come up to operating temperature and the system then may boot normally. This problem sometimes occurs in reverse too, when the drive gets particularly warm, such as when a system is in direct sunlight, or in the afternoon when room temperature is highest. In that case, the symptom is a DOS error message with the familiar `Abort, Retry, Ignore` prompt.

Temperature-induced mistracking problems can be solved by reformatting the drive and restoring the data. Then the information is placed on the drive at the current head positions for each cylinder. Over time the mistracking recurs, necessitating another reformat-and-restore operation, which is a form of periodic preventive maintenance for stepper motor drives. An acceptable interval for this maintenance is once a year or perhaps twice a year if the drive is extremely temperature-sensitive.

Reformatting a hard drive, because it requires a complete backup-and-restore operation, is inconvenient and time consuming. To help with these periodic reformats, most low-level format programs offer a special reformat option that copies the data for a specific track to a spare location, reformats the track, and then copies the data back to the original track. When this type of format operation is finished, there is no need to restore your data because it already has been done for you.

Caution

Never use a so-called nondestructive format program without first making a complete backup. This type of program does wipe out the data as it operates. "Destructive-reconstructive" more accurately describes its operation. If there is a problem with the power, the system, or the program (maybe a bug that stops the program from finishing), all of the data will not be restored properly, and some tracks may be wiped clean. Although such programs save you from having to do the manual restore operation when the format is complete, they do not remove your obligation to perform a backup first.

Beware of programs whose advertising is filled with marketing hype and miracle claims for making a hard disk "better than new." One company even boasted in its advertisements that by using its program you will "Never have any problems" with your hard disk—an outrageous claim indeed! What the ads don't say is that any real low-level format program performs these same feats of "magic" without the misleading or exaggerated claims and unnecessary hype. Many of these nondestructive formatters will not be able to really format a large number of drives that are available today. Also, you should notice that annual or biannual formatting is not necessary with voice coil actuator drives because they do not exhibit these types of mistracking errors.

Voice Coil. A *Voice Coil Actuator* is found on all higher-quality hard disk drives, including most drives with capacities greater than 40M and virtually all drives with capacities exceeding 80M. Unlike the blind stepper motor positioning system, a voice coil actuator uses a feedback signal from the drive to accurately determine the head positions and adjust them if necessary. This allows for significantly greater performance, accuracy, and reliability than traditional stepper motor actuators.

A voice coil actuator works by pure electromagnetic force. The construction of this mechanism is similar to a typical audio speaker, which is where the voice coil term itself is derived. An audio speaker uses a stationary magnet surrounded by a voice coil connected to the speaker's paper cone. Energizing the coil causes the coil to move relative to the stationary magnet, which produces sound from the speaker cone. In a typical hard disk voice-coil system, the electromagnetic coil is attached to the end of the head rack, and is placed near a stationary magnet. There is no contact between the coil and the magnet; the coil moves by pure magnetic force. As the electromagnetic coils are energized, they attract or repulse the stationary magnet and move the head rack. Such systems are extremely quick and efficient, as well as usually much quieter than a system driven with a stepper motor.

Unlike a stepper motor, a voice coil actuator has no click stops, or detent positions. Instead, a special guidance system stops the head rack over a particular cylinder. Because it has no detents, the voice coil actuator can slide the heads in and out smoothly to any position desired, much like the slide on a trombone. Voice coil actuators use a guidance mechanism called a *servo* to tell the actuator where the heads are in relation to the cylinders, and to place them accurately at a desired position. Often you will hear these positioning systems termed as a *closed loop, servo-controlled mechanism. Closed loop* indicates that the index (or servo) signal is sent to the positioning electronics in a closed-loop system. This loop is sometimes called a *feedback loop,* Because the feedback from this information is used to accurately position the heads. *Servo-controlled* refers to this index or the servo information which is used to dictate or control head-positioning accuracy.

A voice coil actuator with servo control is not affected by temperature changes like a stepper motor is. When the temperature is cold and the platters have shrunk (or when the temperature is hot and the platters have expanded), the voice coil system compensates because it never positions to predetermined track positions. Rather, it searches for the specific track guided by the pre-written servo information and can position the head rack precisely over that track at the track's current position, regardless of the temperature. Because of the continuous feedback of servo information, the heads will adjust themselves to the current position of the track at all times. For example, as a drive warms up and the platters expand, the servo information will allow the heads to "follow" the track, this is why a voice coil actuator is often called a *track following* system.

Types of Voice Coil Actuators. There are two main types of voice-coil positioner mechanisms:

- Linear voice-coil actuators

- Rotary voice-coil actuators

The types differ only in the physical arrangement of the magnets and coils.

Linear actuators move the heads in and out over the platters in a straight line, much like a "tangential tracking" turntable. The coil moves in and out on a track surrounded by the stationary magnets. The primary advantage of the linear design is that it eliminates the head azimuth variations that occur with rotary positioning systems. Azimuth refers to the angular measurement of the head position relative to the tangent of a given cylinder. A linear actuator does not rotate the head as it moves from one cylinder to another, which eliminates this problem completely (see fig. 10.5).

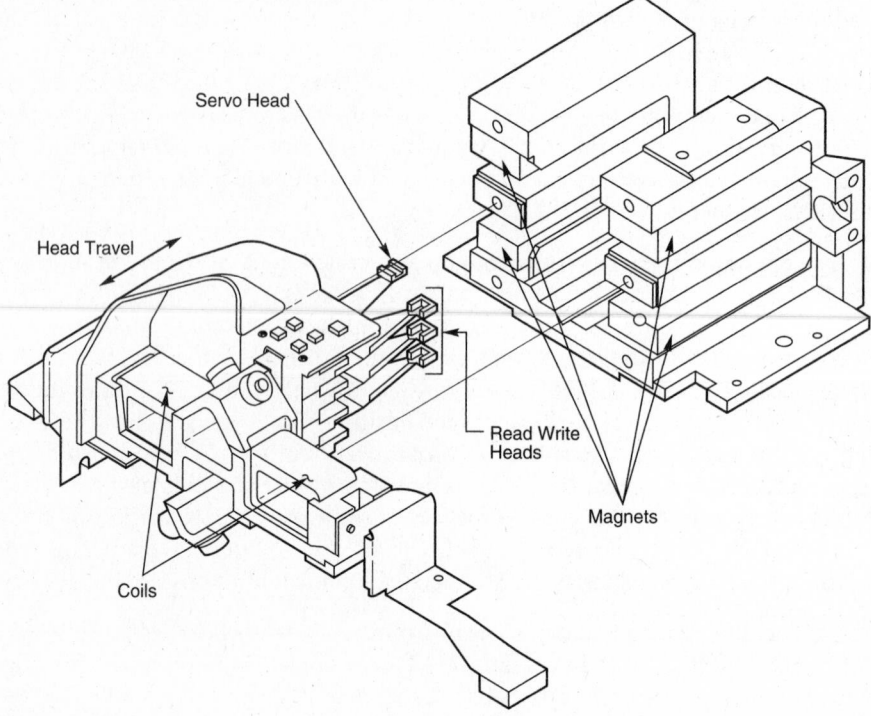

Fig. 10.5

A Linear Voice Coil Actuator

Although the linear actuator seems like a good design, they have one fatal flaw: they are way too heavy. As drive performance has increased, the desire for lightweight actuator mechanisms has become very important. The lighter the mechanism, the faster it can be accelerated and decelerated from one cylinder to another. Because they are much heavier than rotary actuators, the linear actuator was popular only for a short time and is virtually non-existent in drives manufactured today.

Rotary actuators also use stationary magnets and a moveable coil, but the coil is attached to the end of an actuator arm much like that of a record tonearm. As the coil is forced to move relative to the stationary magnet, it swings the head arms in and out over the surface of the disk. The primary advantage of this mechanism is light weight. This means that the heads can be accelerated and decelerated quickly, which results in fast average seek times. The disadvantage is that as the heads move from outer to inner cylinders, they are rotated slightly with respect to the tangent of the cylinders. This results in an azimuth error and is one reason that the area of the platter in which the cylinders are located is somewhat limited. By limiting the total motion of the actuator, the azimuth error can be contained to within reasonable specifications. Virtually all voice coil drives today use rotary actuator systems.

Servo Control Mechanisms. There have been three different servo mechanism designs used to control voice coil positioners over the years. These are as follows:

- Wedge Servo

- Embedded Servo

- Dedicated Servo

Each of these designs is slightly different, although they accomplish the same basic task: they allow the head positioner to continuously adjust position so that it is precisely placed over a given cylinder on the drive. These servo designs differ mainly in where the gray code information is actually written on the drive.

All servo mechanisms rely on special information only written to the disk when it is manufactured. This information is usually in the form of a special code called a *Gray Code*. A gray code is a special binary notational system in which any two adjacent numbers are represented by a code that differs in only one bit place or column position. In this manner, it is easy for the head to read the information and quickly determine its precise position. This guidance code can only be written when the drive is manufactured, and then is used over the life of the drive for accurate positional information.

The servo gray code is written at the time of manufacture by a special machine called a servo writer. This is basically a jig that mechanically moves the heads to a given reference position and then writes the servo information for that position. Many servowriters are themselves guided by a laser beam reference that calculates its own position by calculating distances in wavelengths of light. Because the servowriter must be able to move the heads mechanically, this process is done either with the lid of the drive off, or through special access ports on the HDA. After the servowriting is done, these ports are usually covered with sealing tape. You can often see these tape covered holes on the HDA, usually with warnings about voiding the warranty if the tape is removed. Because servowriting exposes the interior of the drive to the environment, it must be done in a clean room environment.

III

Hardware Considerations

A servowriter is an expensive piece of machinery, costing $50,000 or more, and often must be custom made for a particular make or model of drive. Some drive repair companies have servowriting capability, which means that they can rewrite the servo information on a drive if it becomes damaged. Lacking a servowriter, a drive with servo code damage must be sent back to the drive manufacturer to have the servo information rewritten. Fortunately, it is impossible to damage the servo information through any normal reading and writing to a hard disk. Drives are designed so that is not possible to overwrite the servo information, even when performing a low-level format on a drive. One myth that has been circulating (especially with respect to IDE drives) is that you can damage the servo information by improper low-level formatting. This is not true; an improper low-level format may compromise the performance of the drive, but the servo information is totally protected and cannot be overwritten.

The track-following capabilities of a servo controlled voice coil actuator totally eliminate the positioning errors that occur over time with stepper motor drives. Voice coil drives simply are not affected by things like thermal expansion and contraction of the platters. In fact, many of the voice coil drives today do a special thermal recalibration procedure at predetermined intervals while they are running. This usually involves seeking the heads from cylinder 0 to some other cylinder once for every head on the drive. As this sequence is happening, the control circuitry in the drive is monitoring how much the track positions have moved since the last time the sequence was performed and a thermal calibration adjustment is calculated and stored in the drive's memory. This information is then used every time the drive positions to insure the most accurate positioning possible. Most drives will do the thermal recalibration sequence every 5 minutes for the first half hour the drive is powered on and then once every 25 minutes after that. With some drives (like Quantum, for example), this thermal calibration sequence is very noticeable, as the drive basically stops what it is doing and you hear a rapid ticking sound that lasts for a second or so. Some people have thought that their drive was having a problem reading something and was perhaps doing read retries, but this is of course not true. Most of the newer intelligent drives (IDE and SCSI) employ this thermal recalibration procedure for the ultimate in positioning accuracy.

While you are on the subject of automatic drive functions, most of the drives that perform thermal recalibration sequences will also automatically perform a function called a *disk sweep.* This is an automatic head seek that occurs after the drive has been idle for a period of time (for example, nine minutes). The disk sweep function moves the heads to a random cylinder in the outer portion of the platters which is considered to be the high float height area because the head to platter velocity is highest. Then if the drive continues to remain idle for another time period, the heads are moved again to another cylinder in this area, and the process continues indefinitely as long as the drive is powered on. The disk sweep function is designed to prevent the head from remaining stationary over one cylinder on the drive, where friction between the head and platter will eventually dig a trench in the media! Although the heads are not in direct contact with the media, they are so close that the constant air pressure from the head floating over a single cylinder causes friction and excessive wear.

Wedge Servo. Some early servo controlled drives used a technique called a Wedge Servo. In these drives the gray code guidance information is contained in a "wedge" slice of the drive in each cylinder immediately preceding the index mark. The index mark indicates the beginning of each track, so the wedge servo information was written in the Pre Index Gap which is at the end of each track. This area is provided for speed tolerance and is normally not used by the controller. Figure 10.6 shows the servo wedge information on a drive.

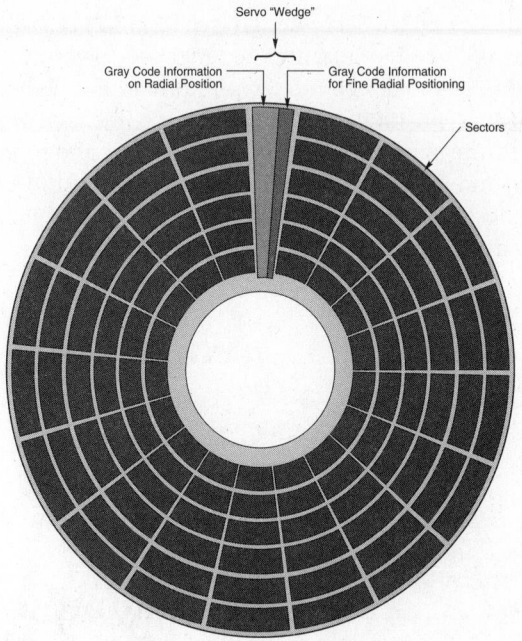

Fig. 10.6
A Wedge Servo.

Some controllers, like the Xebec 1210 that IBM used in the XT, had to be notified that the drive was using a wedge servo so that they could shorten the sector timing to allow for the wedge servo area. If they were not correctly configured, they would not work properly with such drives. Many users believed erroneously that the wedge servo information could accidentally be overwritten in such cases by an improper low-level format. This is not the case, however, as all drives using a wedge servo disable any write commands and take control of the head select lines whenever the heads are over the wedge area. This completely protects the servo from any possibility of being overwritten, no matter how hard you tried! If the controller tried to write over this area, the drive would prevent the write and the controller would be unable to complete the format. Most controllers simply do not write to the Pre Index Gap area and do not need to be specially configured for wedge servo drives.

III

Hardware Considerations

The only way that the servo information could normally be damaged is by a powerful external magnetic field or perhaps by a head crash or other catastrophe. In these cases the drive would have to be sent in for repair and reservicing.

One problem is that the servo information only appears once every revolution, which means that the drive often needed several revolutions before it could accurately determine and adjust the head position. Because of these problems, the wedge servo was never a real popular design, and it is no longer used in any drives today.

Embedded Servo. The Embedded Servo design (see fig. 10.7) is basically an enhancement of the wedge servo. Instead of placing the servo code before the beginning of each cylinder, in an embedded servo design the servo information is written before the start of each sector. This allows the positioner circuits to receive feedback many times in a single revolution, allowing the head positioning to be much faster and more precise. Another advantage is that each and every track on the drive has this positioning information so that each head can quickly and efficiently adjust position to compensate for any changes in the platter or head dimensions, especially due to thermal expansion or physical stress.

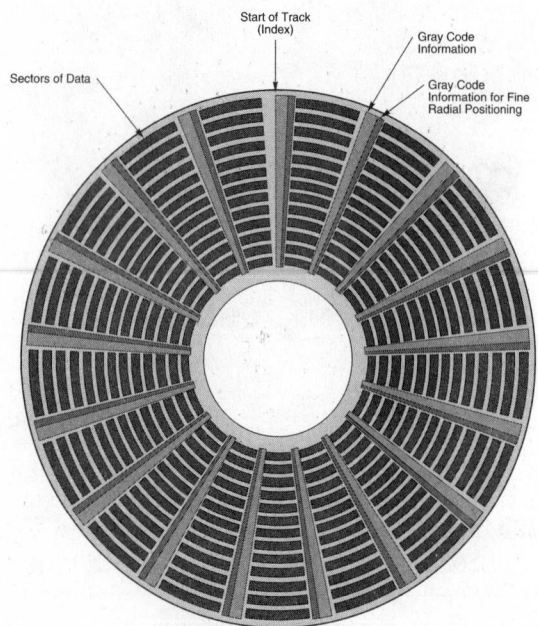

Fig. 10.7
An Embedded Servo.

Most drives today use an embedded servo to control the positioning system. Like the wedge servo, the embedded servo information is completely protected by the drive circuits, and any write operations are automatically blocked whenever the heads are over the servo information. Thus it is impossible to overwrite the servo information with a low-level format, as many have incorrectly believed.

Although it works much better than the wedge servo because the feedback servo information is available several times in a single disk revolution, a system which offered continuous servo feedback information would be better.

Dedicated Servo. A Dedicated Servo is a design where the servo information is written continuously throughout the entire track rather than just once per track or at the beginning of each sector. Unfortunately, if this were done to the entire drive, it would leave no room for data! For this reason a dedicated servo uses one side of one of the platters exclusively for the servo positioning information. The term *dedicated* comes from the fact that this platter side is completely dedicated to the servo information and cannot contain any data. While the dedicated servo design might seem wasteful, none of the other platter sides carry any servo information, and you end up losing about the same amount of total disk real estate as with the embedded servo.

When a dedicated servo drive is manufactured, one side of one platter is deducted from normal read/write usage; and on this platter are recorded a special set of gray code data that indicates proper track positions. Because the head sitting over this surface cannot be used for normal reading and writing, these marks can never be erased and the servo information is completely protected as with the other servo designs. No low level format or other procedure can possibly overwrite the servo information.

When the drive is commanded to move the heads to a specific cylinder, the internal drive electronics use the signals received by the servo head to determine the position of the heads. As the heads are moved, the track counters are read from the dedicated servo surface. When the requested track is detected under the servo head, the actuator is stopped. The servo electronics then fine-tune the position so that, before writing is allowed, the heads are positioned absolutely precisely over the desired cylinder. Although only one head is used for servo tracking, the other heads are attached to the same rigid rack, so if one head is over the desired cylinder, then all of the others will be as well.

One noticeable trait of dedicated servo drives is that they usually have an odd number of heads. For example, the Toshiba MK-538FB 1.2G drive I am currently saving this on has 8 platters but only 15 read/write heads. This is because the drive uses a dedicated servo positioning system, and the 16th head is the servo head. You will find that virtually all high end drives use a dedicated servo because such a design offers servo information continuously no matter where the heads are located. This offers the greatest possible positioning accuracy. Some drives even combine a dedicated servo with an embedded servo, but this type of hybrid design is more rare.

Automatic Head Parking. When a hard disk drive is powered off, the spring tension in each head arm pulls the heads into contact with the platters. The drive is designed to sustain thousands of takeoffs and landings, but it is wise to ensure that the landing occurs at a spot on the platter where there is no data. Some amount of abrasion occurs during the landing and takeoff process, which removes just a "micro puff" of the media; but if the drive is jarred during the landing or takeoff process, real damage can occur.

One benefit of using a voice coil actuator is *automatic head parking*. In a drive with a voice coil actuator, the heads are positioned and held by magnetic force. When power is removed from the drive, the magnetic field holding the heads stationary over a particular cylinder dissipates, enabling the head rack to skitter across the drive surface and potentially cause damage. In the voice coil design, therefore, the head rack is attached to a weak spring at one end and a head stop at the other end. When the system is powered on, the spring normally is overcome by the magnetic force of the positioner. When the drive is powered off, however, the spring gently drags the head rack to a park-and-lock position before the drive slows down and the heads land. On many drives you can actually hear the "ting, ting, ting" sound as the heads literally bounce-park themselves driven by this spring.

On a drive with a voice coil actuator, the parking mechanism is activated by simply turning off the system. There is no need to run a program to park or retract the heads. In case of a power outage, the heads even park themselves automatically. (The drives automatically unpark when the system is powered on.)

Some stepper motor drives (like the Seagate ST-251 series drives) do park their heads, but this is a rare function for stepper motor drives. Those that do usually use an ingenious system whereby the spindle motor is actually used as a generator after the power to the drive is turned off. The back EMF (Electro Motive Force) as it is called, is used to drive the stepper motor to park the heads.

Air Filters

Nearly all hard disk drives have two air filters. One is called the *recirculating filter*, while the other is called either a *barometric* or *breather filter*. These filters are permanently sealed inside the drive and are designed never to be changed for the life of the drive. This is unlike many older mainframe hard disks that had changeable filters. Many mainframe drives circulate air from outside the drive through a filter that must be changed periodically.

A hard disk on a PC system does not circulate air from inside to outside the HDA or vice versa. The recirculating filter which is permanently installed inside the HDA is designed to filter only the small particles of media scraped off the platters during head takeoffs and landings, and possibly any other small particles dislodged inside the drive. Because PC hard disk drives are permanently sealed and do not circulate outside air, they can run in extremely dirty environments.

The HDA in a hard disk is sealed, but not airtight. The HDA is vented through a barometric or breather filter element which allows for pressure equalization (breathing) between the inside and outside of the drive. It is for this reason that most hard drives are rated by the drive's manufacturer to run in a specific range of altitudes usually from -1,000 to +10,000 feet above sea level. In fact, some hard drives are not rated to exceed 7,000 feet while operating because the air pressure would be too low inside the drive to properly float the heads. As the environmental air pressure changes, air bleeds into or out of the drive so that internal and external pressures are identical. Although air does bleed through a vent, contamination is usually not a concern because the barometric filter on this vent is designed to filter out all particles larger than .3 microns (about 12 micro-inches) to meet the specifications for cleanliness inside the drive. You can see the vent holes on most drives which are covered internally by this breather filter. Some drives use even finer grade filter elements to keep out even smaller particles.

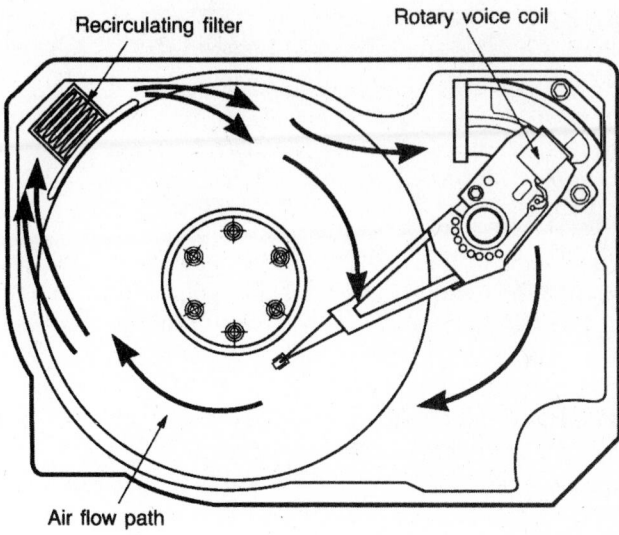

Fig. 10.8
Air circulation in a hard disk.

I recently got a laugh when I read an article in one of the better known computer magazines, which actually stated that not only were hard drives airtight, but also that the air was evacuated from the interior of the drive and the heads and platters ran in a vacuum! The person who wrote this obviously does not understand even the most basic principles of hard disk operation. Air is absolutely required inside the HDA to float the heads, and this cushion of air (sometimes called an air bearing) is the primary principle in Winchester hard disk design.

I was doing a seminar in Hawaii several years ago, and several of the students in the class were from the Mauna Kea astronomical observatory. They indicated that virtually all hard disks they had tried to use at the observatory site had failed quickly, if they worked at all. This was no surprise because the observatory sits on the 13,800-foot peak of the mountain, and at that altitude, even people don't function very well! At the time, it was suggested that they investigate solid state (RAM) disks, tape drives, or even floppy drives as their primary storage medium. Recently, IBM's Adstar division (they produce all IBM hard drives) has introduced a line of rugged 3 1/5-inch drives that are hermetically sealed (airtight), although they do have air inside the HDA. These drives can operate at any altitude, and can withstand extremes of shock and temperature. They are designed for military and industrial applications such as aircraft or wherever extremely harsh environments are encountered.

Hard Disk Temperature Acclimation

Although the HDA is sealed, it is not hermetically sealed, which means it is not airtight and there is air inside. To allow for pressure-equalization, hard drives have a filtered port to bleed air into or out of the HDA as necessary.

Caution

Airborne particulates such as cigarette smoke normally do not affect a PC hard disk drive because any air that bleeds into the hard drive is filtered before entering the drive. However, many other components in the system (such as floppy drives, keyboards, connectors, and sockets) will sustain damage from contaminants such as cigarette smoke.

This breathing also allows moisture to enter the drive, and after some duration of time, it must be assumed that the humidity inside any hard disk is similar to that of the outside environment. This humidity can become a serious problem if allowed to condense and especially if the drive is powered up with this condensation still present. Most hard disk manufacturers have specified procedures for acclimating a hard drive to a new environment where temperature and humidity have changed, especially when bringing a cold drive into a warmer environment where condensation can form. This should be of special concern to users of laptop or portable systems with hard disks. For example, if a portable system is left out in an automobile trunk in the winter, it could be catastrophic to bring it inside and power it up without allowing it to acclimate to the temperature inside.

The following text and chart are quoted from printing on the factory packaging which Control Data Corp. (later Imprimis and eventually Seagate) used to ship their hard drives:

"If you have just received or removed this unit from a climate with temperatures at or below 50°F (10°C) do not open this container until the following conditions are met, otherwise condensation could occur and damage to the device and/or media may result. Place this package in the operating environment for the time duration according to the temperature chart."

Table 10.7 Hard Disk Drive Environmental Acclimation Table

Previous Climate Temp.	Acclimation Time
+40°F (+4°C)	13 Hours
+30°F (-1°C)	15 Hours
+20°F (-7°C)	16 Hours
+10°F (-12°C)	17 Hours
0°F (-18°C)	18 Hours
-10°F (-23°C)	20 Hours
-20°F (-29°C)	22 Hours
-30°F (-34°C) or LESS	27 Hours

As you can see from this chart, a hard disk which has been stored in a colder than normal environment must be placed in the normal operating environment for a specified amount of time to allow for acclimation before powering on.

Spindle Motors

The motor that spins the platters is called the *spindle motor* because it is connected to the spindle around which the platters revolve. Spindle motors in hard disks are always connected directly; no belts or gears are used. The motors must be noise- and vibration-free; otherwise they transmit a "rumble" to the platters, which could disrupt reading and writing operations. The motors must also be precisely controlled for speed. The platters on hard disks revolve at speeds from 3,600 to 7,200 rpm or more, and the motor has a control circuit with a feedback loop to monitor and control this speed precisely. Because this speed control must be automatic, hard drives do not have a motor speed adjustment. Some diagnostics programs claim to measure hard drive rotational speed, but this is actually not possible. All these programs are doing is "guessing" at the rotational speed by the timing at which sectors arrive. There is actually no way for a program to measure hard disk rotational speed; this can only be done with sophisticated test equipment. Don't be alarmed if some diagnostic program tells you that your drive is spinning at a speed that is not correct; most likely the program is wrong, not the drive.

On most drives, the spindle motor is on the bottom of the drive, just underneath the sealed HDA. Many drives today, however, have the spindle motor built directly into the platter hub inside the HDA. With an internal hub spindle motor, the manufacturer can stack more platters in the drive because the spindle motor takes up no vertical space. This allows for more platters than would be possible if the motor were outside the HDA.

> **Note**
>
> Spindle motors, particularly on the larger form-factor drives, can consume a great deal of 12-volt power. Most drives require two to three times the normal operating power when the motor is first spinning the platters. This heavy draw lasts only a few seconds, or until the drive platters have reached operating speed. If you have more than one drive, you should try to sequence the start of the spindle motors so that the power supply does not receive such a large load from all of the drives at once. Most SCSI and IDE drives have a delayed spindle motor start feature.

Spindle Ground Strap

Most drives have a special grounding strap attached to a ground on the drive and resting on the center spindle of the platter spindle motor. This device is the single most likely cause of excessive drive noise.

The *grounding strap* usually is made of copper and often has a carbon or graphite button that contacts the motor or platter spindle. The grounding strap dissipates static generated by the platters as they spin through the air inside the HDA. If the platters generate static due to friction with the air, and no place exists for this electrical potential to bleed off, static may discharge through the heads or the internal bearings in the motor. When static discharges through the motor bearings, it can burn the lubricants inside the sealed bearings. If the static charge discharges through the read/write heads, they can be damaged or data will be corrupted. The grounding strap bleeds off this static buildup to prevent these problems.

Where the spindle of the motor contacts the carbon contact button (at the end of the ground strap) spinning at full speed, the button often wears, creating a flat spot. The flat spot causes the strap to vibrate and produce a high-pitched squealing or whining noise. The noise may come and go, depending on temperature and humidity. Sometimes, banging the side of the machine can jar the strap so that the noise changes or goes away, but this is not the way to fix the problem! *I am not suggesting that you bang on your system.* (Most people mistake this noise for something much more serious, such as a total drive-motor failure or bearing failure, which rarely occurs.) There are some ways to eliminate this noise.

If the spindle grounding strap vibrates and causes noise, you can remedy the situation in the following ways:

- Dampen the vibration of the strap by attaching some foam tape or rubber to it

- Lubricate the contact point

- Tear off the strap (not recommended!)

On some drives, the spindle motor strap is in an easily accessible position. On other drives, you have to partially disassemble the drive by removing the logic board or other external items to get to the strap.

Of these suggested solutions, the first one is the best. The best way to correct this problem is to glue or otherwise affix some rubber or foam to the strap. This procedure changes the harmonics of the strap and usually dampens vibrations. Most manufacturers now use this technique on newly manufactured drives. An easy way to do this is with some foam tape (place it on the back side of the ground strap).

You also can use a dab of silicone RTV (room-temperature vulcanizing) rubber or caulk on the back of the strap. If you try this, be sure to use the low-volatile (non-corrosive) silicone RTV sealer commonly sold at auto-parts stores. The non-corrosive silicone will be listed on the label as being safe for automotive oxygen sensors. This low-volatile silicone is free from corrosive acids that can damage the copper strap. It is also described as low odor because it does not have the vinegar odor usually associated with silicone RTV. Dab a small amount on the back side of the copper strap (do not interfere with the contact location), and the problem should be solved permanently.

Lubrication of the strap is also an acceptable, but often temporary, solution. You will want some sort of conducting lube, such as a graphite-based compound (the kind used on frozen car locks). Any conductive lubricant (moly or lithium) will work as long as it is conductive, but do not use standard oil or grease. Dab a small amount of lubricant on the end of a toothpick and place a small drop directly on the point of contact.

The last solution is not an acceptable one. Tearing off the strap eliminates the noise, but it has a number of other possible ramifications. Although the drive will work (silently) without it, an engineer placed the ground strap there for a reason. Imagine those un-grounded static charges leaving the platters through the heads, perhaps in the form of a spark—possibly even damaging the thin film heads. You should choose one of the other solutions.

The only reason I even mention this last solution is that several people have told me that tech-support staff members at some of the hard drive vendors, and even manufacturers, have told them to remove the strap. I do not recommend it.

Logic Boards

A disk drive, including a hard disk drive, has one or more logic boards mounted on it. The logic boards contain the electronics that control the drive's spindle and head actua-tor systems and present data to the controller in some agreed-on form. With some drives, the controller is located on the drive, which can save on a system's total chip count.

Many disk drive failures occur in the logic board and not in the mechanical assembly. (This statement does not seem logical, but it is true.) So you can repair many failed drives by replacing the logic board and not the entire drive. Replacing the logic board, more-over, lets you regain access to the data on the failed drive—something that replacing the entire drive precludes.

Logic boards can be removed or replaced because they plug into the drive. They usually are mounted with standard screw hardware. If a drive is failing and you have a spare, you may be able to verify a logic-board failure by taking the board off the known good drive and mounting it on the bad one. If your suspicions are confirmed, you can order a new logic board from the drive manufacturer. You may be able also to purchase a refurbished unit, or even trade in your old drive or logic board. The drive manufacturer will have details on what services it can offer. To reduce costs further, many third-party vendors also can supply replacement logic-board assemblies. These companies often charge much less than the drive manufacturers for the same components. (See the vendor list in the Appendix for vendors of drive components, including logic boards.)

Cables and Connectors

Most hard disk drives have several connectors for interfacing to the system, receiving power, and sometimes for grounding to the system chassis. Most drives have at least these three types of connectors:

- Interface connector(s)
- Power connector
- Optional Ground connector (tab)

Of these, the interface connectors are the most important because they carry the data and command signals from the system to and from the drive. In many drive interfaces, the drive interface cables can be connected in a daisy chain, or bus type configuration. Most interfaces support at least two drives, and SCSI supports up to seven in the chain.

III

Hardware Considerations

Some interfaces, like ST-506/412 or ESDI use a separate cable for data and control signals. These drives have two cables from the controller interface to the drive. SCSI and IDE drives usually have a single data and control connector. With these interfaces, the disk controller is built into the drive (see fig. 10.9).

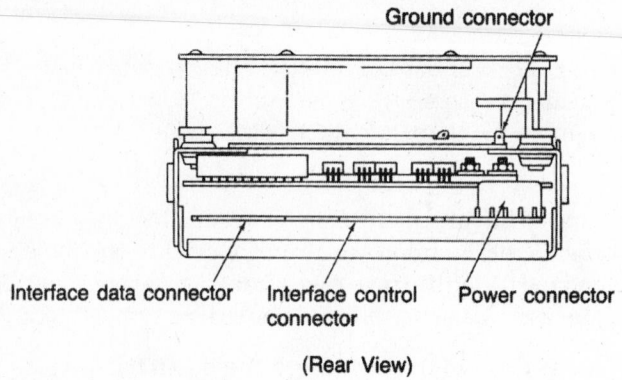

Ground connector

Interface data connector   Interface control connector   Power connector

(Rear View)

Fig. 10.9
Typical hard disk connections (ST-506/412 or ESDI shown).

The different interfaces and cable specifications are covered in the sections on each drive interface later in this chapter. You'll also find connector pinout specifications for virtually all drive interfaces and cable connections in the Appendix of this book.

The *power connector* is usually the same type as is used on floppy drives, and the same power-supply connector plugs into it. Most hard disk drives use both 5- and 12-volt power, although some of the smaller drives designed for portable applications use only 5-volt power. In most cases the 12-volt power runs the spindle motor and head actuator, and the 5-volt power runs the circuitry. Make sure that your power supply can adequately supply power for the hard disk drives installed in your PC system. Most hard drives draw quite a bit more power than a floppy drive.

Usually the 12-volt power consumption of a drive varies with the physical size of the unit. The larger the drive is and the more platters there are to spin, the more power is required. Also, the faster the drive spins the more power will be required as well. For example, most of the 3 1/5-inch drives on the market today use roughly one half to one fourth the power (in watts) of the full size 5 1/4-inch drives. Some of the very small (2 1/5, 1 1/8 or 1 1/3-inch) hard disks positively sip electrical power and actually use 1 watt or less!

Ensuring an adequate power supply is particularly important with some systems such as the original IBM AT. These systems have a power supply with three disk drive power connectors, labeled P10, P11, and P12. The three power connectors may seem equal, but the technical-reference manual for these systems indicates that 2.8 amps of 12-volt current is available on P10 and P11, and that only 1.0 amp of 12-volt current is available on P12. Because most full-height hard drives draw much more power than 1.0 amp, especially at start-up, the P12 connector can be used only by floppy drives or half-height hard drives. Some 5 1/4-inch drives draw as much as 4 amps of current during the first few seconds of start-up. These drives also can draw as much as 2.5 amps during normal operation.

Sometimes you can solve random boot-up failures by plugging the hard drive into a suitable power connector (P10 or P11 on the IBM AT). Most IBM-compatible PC systems have a power supply with four or more disk drive power connectors that provide equal power, but some use power supplies designed like the IBM AT.

A *grounding tab* provides a positive ground connection between the drive and the system's chassis. In a typical IBM PC or IBM XT system, because the hard disk drive is mounted directly to the chassis of the PC using screws, the ground wire is unnecessary. On AT-type systems from IBM and others, the drives are installed on plastic or fiberglass rails, which do not provide a proper ground. These systems must provide a grounding wire, plugged into the drive at this grounding tab. Failure to ground the drive may result in improper operation, intermittent failure, or general read and write errors.

Configuration Items

To configure a hard disk drive for installation in a system, usually several jumpers and possibly terminating resistors must be set or configured properly. These will vary from interface to interface, and often from drive to drive as well. A complete discussion of the configuration settings for each interface is described in the section for installing drives later in this chapter.

The Faceplate or Bezel

Most hard disk drives offer as an option a front faceplate, or *bezel* (see fig. 10.10). A bezel usually is supplied as an option for the drive rather than as a standard item.

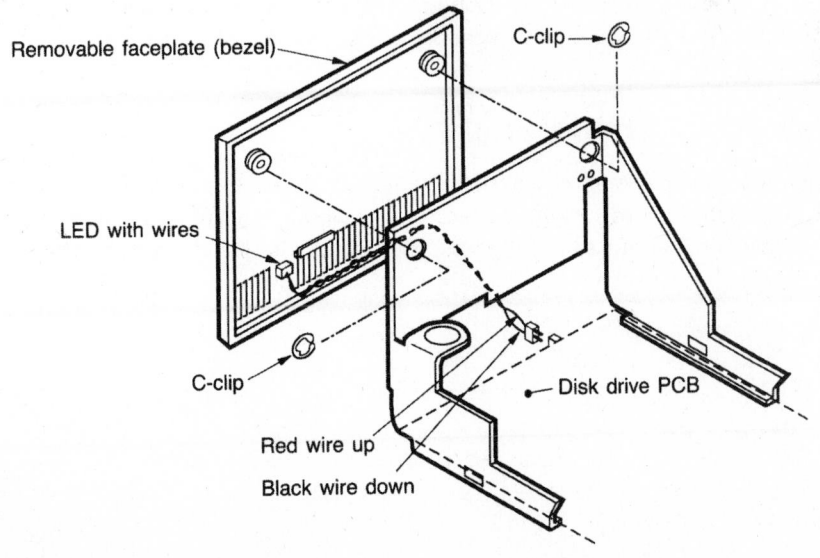

Fig. 10.10
A typical hard drive faceplate (bezel).

Bezels often come in several sizes and colors to match various PC systems. For standard full-height, 5 1/4-inch, form-factor drives, you have only one choice of bezel. For half-height drives, bezels come in half-height and full-height forms. Using a full-height bezel on a half-height drive enables a single drive to be installed in full height bays without leaving a hole in the front of the system. To add a second half-height drive, you may want to order the half-height bezels so that you can stack the old and new drives. There are many faceplate configurations for 3 1/2-inch drives, including bezels to fit 3 1/2-inch drive bays as well as 5 1/4-inch drive bays. You can even have a choice of colors (usually black, cream, or white).

Some bezels have a light-emitting diode that flickers when your hard disk is in use. The LED is mounted in the bezel; the wire hanging off the back of the LED plugs into the drive or sometimes the controller. In some drives, the LED is permanently mounted on the drive and the bezel has a clear or colored window so that you can see the LED flicker while the drive is accessed. One type of LED problem occurs with some AT type system hard disk installations: if the drive has an LED, the LED may remain on continuously as though it were a "power-on" light rather than an access light. This happens because the controller in the AT has a direct connection for the LED, thus altering the drive LED function. Some controllers have a jumper that enables the controller to run the drive in what is called *latched* or *unlatched* mode. Latched mode means that the drive is selected continuously, and the drive LED will remain lit; in unlatched mode (which you are more accustomed to), the LED lights only when the drive is accessed. Check to see whether your controller has this jumper, and you may be able to control how the LED operates.

In systems where the hard disk is hidden by the unit's cover, a bezel is not needed. In fact using a bezel may prevent the cover from sitting properly on the chassis, in which case it will have to be removed. If you are installing a drive that does not have a proper bezel, frame or rails to attach to the system, there are several vendors listed in the vendor list in the appendix who offer these accessories for a variety of drives.

Hard Disk Features

To make the best decision in purchasing a hard disk for your system or to understand what differentiates one brand of hard disk from another, you must consider many features. This section examines the following issues that you should consider when you evaluate drives:

- Actuator mechanism
- Media
- Head parking
- Reliability
- Speed
- Shock mounting
- Cost

Actuator Mechanism

A drive with high performance and reliability has two basic physical properties:

- Voice coil actuator mechanism

- Thin film media

Drives with stepper motor actuators should be used only when cost far outweighs other considerations. You should not use them in portable systems or systems that must operate under extremes of temperature, noise, or vibration. Don't use them where preventive maintenance cannot be provided, because they require periodic reformats to maintain data integrity. Finally, you should not use these drives in demanding situations, such as in a network file server. Drives with stepper motor actuators perform adequately in low-volume-usage systems, as long as you provide preventive maintenance at least annually or semiannually and the environment can be controlled. Fortunately, stepper motor drives are virtually out of production today; nearly all new drives use voice coil actuators.

Voice coil actuator drives should be used wherever possible, especially if any real demands are put on the drive. These drives are ideal for portable systems or systems that suffer extremes of temperature, noise, or vibration. They are ideal when a fast drive must be used. A voice coil drive requires little or no preventive maintenance, so the first low-level format is usually the only low-level format ever done. Less maintenance (no reformatting) enables this type of drive to be used for high-volume situations in which a single support person maintains many PC systems. Fortunately, virtually all drives manufactured today are voice coil drives, and they should be! Voice coil actuator technology is the only way to build a reliable, high performance, and low maintenance drive.

Head Parking

Head parking is an often misunderstood issue with hard disks. When a hard disk comes to a stop (actually before it completely stops), the heads land on the media. This contact occurs as the drive slows down, and with some drives the head skid distance before the platters completely stop may be many linear feet. This same skidding occurs when the drive is powered on and the platters begin to turn. With some drives, the heads land on whatever cylinder they were last positioned over—usually an area of the disk that contains data. Most drives today move the heads to a nondata area called the landing zone before the platters slow down enough for the heads to come into contact with them. This is referred to as *automatic head parking*. Drives that do not park their heads automatically can still be parked, but it requires the manual execution of a program to move the heads before the system is powered down.

Drives with voice coil actuators offer automatic head parking as a feature. These drives have a spring attached to the head. While the drive is running, an electric coil overcomes the spring tension and moves the head around the disk. When power is lost, the spring automatically pulls the head rack away from data areas of the disk to a special landing zone.

III

Hardware Considerations

Most stepper motor drives don't have an autoparking function; instead, they must be parked manually. To find out whether your drive autoparks, contact the drive manufacturer and ask for the technical or specification manual for the drive which will have the answer.

Some newer stepper drives do incorporate a parking mechanism. One example is the Seagate ST-251 series. This popular stepper drive autoparks the heads by using an ingenious system in which the drive spindle motor is used as a generator powering the stepper motor to park the heads. When the drive is powered off, you hear the stepper motor drive the heads to the landing zone. Seagate seems to be using this type of mechanism in many of their newer stepper motor drives as well.

Software is available to let you park the heads of drives that lack the automatic parking feature. The software is not quite as reliable as automatic parking because it does not park the heads if the power goes off unexpectedly. If your system requires a head parking program, it usually comes on the configuration or setup utility disk that goes with the system. For example, IBM supplied a head-parking routine on the diagnostics disk supplied with their original XT and AT systems, as well as on the Advanced Diagnostics disk supplied with the hardware-maintenance service manual. Boot these disks and select the option, "Prepare system for moving." This procedure invokes a program on the disk called SHIPDISK.COM. There are different SHIPDISK.COM files for XT and AT systems. The heads of all attached disks will be parked. Then shut down the system.

A sidenote: several years ago, IBM issued a warning to its dealers recommending that they not run SHIPDISK.COM from the DOS prompt. IBM said a slight chance exists that you can lose data because the program can accidentally write random data on the drive. The memo indicated that SHIPDISK.COM should be run only from the menu. Apparently the problem was that SHIPDISK.COM parks the disks and then executes a software interrupt to return to the diagnostics disk menu, and unpredictable things can happen (including stray disk writes) if the program was not run from the diagnostics disk menu.

For AT systems, in addition to the SHIPDISK program, IBM also supplied a separate program called SHUTDOWN.EXE, which is designed to be run from the DOS prompt. This program is on the AT diagnostics and advanced diagnostics disks. You can copy this program to the hard disk and enter the SHUTDOWN command at the DOS prompt. You will see a graphical picture of a switch, which turns off as the heads are parked. The program then halts the system, requiring a complete power-down. This program only works on AT type systems.

> **Note**
>
> It is usually not a good idea to run a hard disk parking program not designed for your system. Although no physical harm will occur, the heads may not actually be parked in the correct landing zone (many will improperly position the heads over Cylinder 0, the last place you want them).

If your hard drive is a stepper motor actuator drive without automatic parking, it should come with a parking program. If your system is from IBM, these programs come on the diagnostics and setup disks that came with the system. If you have a compatible, you also probably received such a program on your setup disk. Additionally, some public-domain programs will park a stepper motor hard disk.

Should you park the heads every time you shut down the drive? Some people think so, but IBM says that you do not have to park the heads on a drive unless you are moving the drive. My experiences are in line with IBM's recommendations, although a more fail-safe approach is to park the heads at every shutdown. Remember that voice coil drives park their heads automatically every time and require no manual parking operations. For stepper motor drives, I only park them if I am moving the unit, but there is nothing wrong with parking the heads at every shutdown. The procedure is simple and cannot hurt.

Reliability

When you shop for a drive, you may notice a feature called *the mean time between failures*, or MTBF, described in the brochures. MTBF figures usually range from 20,000 hours to 500,000 hours or more. I usually ignore these figures as they are usually just theoretical—not actual—statistical values. Most drives that boast these figures have not even been manufactured for that length of time. One year of 5-day workweeks with 8-hour days equals 2,080 hours of operation. If you never turn off your system for 365 days and run the full 24 hours per day, you operate your system 8,760 hours each year, then a drive with a 500,000-hour MTBF rating is supposed to last (on average) 57 years before failing. Obviously, that figure cannot be derived from actual statistics, because the particular drive has probably been on the market for less than a year.

Statistically, for the MTBF figures to have real weight, you must take a sample of drives and measure the failure rate for at least twice the rated figure and measure how many fail in that time. To be really accurate, you would have to wait until all the drives fail, and record the operating hours at each failure. Then you average the running time for all the test samples, which gives you the average time before a drive failure. For a reported MTBF of 500,000 hours (common today), the test sample should be run for at least 1 million hours (114 years) to be truly accurate, yet the drive carries this specification on the day it is introduced.

I have also seen manufacturers or vendors "play" with these numbers. For example, several years ago CDC rated a Wren II half-height drive at 20,000 hours MTBF (this drive was one of the most reliable in the world at the time), but I saw a reseller rate the same unit at 50,000 hours. Some of the worst drives I have used boasted high MTBF figures, and some of the best drives have lower ones. These figures do not necessarily translate to reliability in the field, and that is why I generally place little importance on them.

Performance

When you select a hard disk, an important feature to consider is the performance (speed) of the drive. Hard disks come in a wide range of performance capabilities. One of the best indicators of a drive's relative performance is the price. An old saying from the automobile racing industry is appropriate here: "Speed costs money. How fast do you want to go?"

You can measure the speed of a disk drive in two ways:

■ Average seek time

■ Transfer rate

Average seek time, normally measured in milliseconds, is the average amount of time it takes to move the heads from one cylinder to another a random distance away. One way to measure this specification is to run many random track-seek operations and divide the timed results by the number of seeks performed. This method provides an average time for a single seek. The standard way to measure average seek time used by many drive manufacturers involves measuring the time it takes the heads to move across one third of the total number of cylinders. Average seek time depends only on the drive; the type of interface or controller has little effect on this specification. (In some instances, the setup of the controller to the drive can affect seek times; this subject is discussed later.) This rating is a gauge of the capabilities of the head actuator.

Be careful with benchmarks that claim to measure drive seek performance. With most IDE and SCSI drives a scheme called sector translation is used, so any commands to the drive to move the heads to a specific cylinder do not actually cause the intended physical movement. This renders such benchmarks meaningless for these types of drives. SCSI drives also have an additional command overhead as the commands must first be sent to the drive over the SCSI bus. Even though they can have the fastest access times, because the command overhead is not factored in by most benchmarks, the benchmark programs will give poor performance figures for these drives. I don't put too much faith in the benchmarks, and the drive manufacturers have been very honest in reporting their true performance figures over the years. The bottom line is if you want to know the true seek performance of your drive, the most accurate way is to simply look it up in the drive specification manual.

A slightly different measurement, called average access time, involves another element, called latency. *Latency* is the average time (in milliseconds) it takes for a sector to be available after the heads have reached a track. On average, this figure is one-half the time it takes for a single rotation of the disk, which is 8.33 ms at 3,600 rpm. A drive that spins twice as fast would have one half the latency. A measurement of average access time is the sum of the average seek time and latency. This number provides the average amount of time required before a randomly requested sector can be accessed.

Latency is a factor in disk read and write performance. Decreasing the latency increases the speed of access to data or files, accomplished only by spinning the drive platters faster. One drive I have spins at 4,318 rpm, for a latency of 6.95 ms. Some drives spin at

7,200 rpm or faster, which results in an even shorter latency time of only 4.17 ms. In addition to increasing performance where real-world access to data is concerned, spinning the platters faster also increases the data-transfer rate after the heads have arrived at the desired sectors.

The transfer rate is probably more important to overall system performance than any other specification. *Transfer rate* is the rate at which the drive and controller can send data to the system. The transfer rate depends primarily on the drive's HDA and secondarily on the controller. Transfer rate used to be more bound by the limits of the controller, meaning that with older controllers, the drives they were connected to could often outperform them. This is where the concept of interleaving sectors came from. Interleaving refers to the ordering of the sectors so that they are not sequential, and which allows for a slow controller to keep up without missing the next sector. The next section will discuss interleaving in more detail, but for now, the point I am trying to make is that modern drives with integrated controllers are fully capable of keeping up with the raw drive transfer rate. In other words, they no longer have to interleave the sectors to slow down the data for the controller.

Another performance issue is the raw interface performance, which in IDE or SCSI drives is usually far higher than any of the drives themselves are able to sustain. Be careful when being quoted transfer specifications for the interface, because this may have little effect on what the drive can actually put out. The drive interface simply limits the maximum theoretical transfer rate, while the actual drive and controller present the real limits on performance.

In the older ST-506/412 interface drives you can sometimes double or triple the transfer rate by changing the controller alone, without changing the drive. This is because many of the older controllers could not support a 1:1 interleave. By changing the controller to one that does, the transfer rate will then be equal to what the drive is actually capable of.

To calculate the true transfer rate of a drive, you will need to know several important specifications. The two most important specifications you will need to know are the true rotational speed of the drive (in rpm), and the average number of physical sectors on each track. I say average because most drives today use a zoned recording technique that places different numbers of sectors on the inner and outer cylinders. The transfer rate on zone recorded drives will always be fastest in the outermost zone, where the sector per track count is highest. Also notice that many drives (especially zone recorded) are configured with sector translation, so that the BIOS reported number of sectors per track has little to do with physical reality. You need to know the true physical parameters rather than what the BIOS thinks. To determine the maximum transfer rate in Millions of bits per second (Mbps) knowing these figures, use the following formula:

> Maximum Data Transfer Rate (Mbps) = SPT * 512 bytes * RPM / 60 seconds / 1,000,000 bits

As an example, the ST-12551N 2GB 3.5-inch drive spins at 7,200 rpm and has an average of 81 sectors per track. This is figured as follows:

$$81 * 512 * 7200 / 60 / 1{,}000{,}000 = 4.98 \text{ Mbps}$$

Using this formula, you can calculate the true maximum sustained transfer rate of any drive.

Cache Programs and Caching Controllers

At the software level, disk cache programs, such as SMARTDRV or PCKwik, can have a major effect on disk drive performance. These cache programs hook into the BIOS hard drive interrupt and intercept the read and write calls to the disk BIOS from application programs and the device drivers of DOS.

When an application program wants to read data from a hard drive, the cache program intercepts the read request, passes the read request to the hard drive controller in the usual way, saves the data that was read in its cache buffer, and then passes the data back to the application program. Depending on the size of the cache buffer, numerous sectors are read into and saved in the buffer. When the application wants to read more data, the cache program again intercepts the request and examines its buffers to see if the data is still in the cache. If it is, the data is immediately passed back to the application without another hard drive operation. As you can imagine, this speeds up access tremendously and can greatly affect the disk drive performance measurements.

Most controllers now have some form of buffer or cache built in. This is a hardware buffer or cache and doesn't intercept or use any BIOS interrupts. Instead, the caching is performed at the hardware level and is invisible to normal performance measurement software. Track read-ahead buffers were originally included in controllers to allow for 1:1 interleave performance. Some controllers have simply increased the sizes of these read-ahead buffers, while others have added intelligence making them a cache instead of a simple buffer. Many IDE and SCSI drives have cache memory built directly into the drive. For example, the Toshiba MK-538FB 1.2G drive that I am currently saving this on has 512K of cache memory built in. Other drives have even more built-in cache, such as the Seagate Barracuda 2G drive with 1M of integral cache memory. I remember when 640K was a lot of memory—now tiny 3 1/5-inch hard disk drives have more than that built right in! These integral caches are part of the reason that most IDE and SCSI drives perform so well.

Although software and hardware caches can make a drive faster for routine transfer operations, a cache will not affect the true maximum transfer rate that can be sustained by the drive.

Interleave Selection

In a discussion of disk performance, the issue of interleave always comes up. Although traditionally this was more of a controller performance issue than a drive issue, most modern hard disks now have built-in controllers (IDE and SCSI) fully capable of taking the drive data as fast as the drive can send it. In other words, virtually all modern IDE and SCSI drives are formatted with no interleave (sometimes expressed as a 1:1 interleave ratio).

When a disk is low-level formatted, the sectors are assigned numbers. These numbers are written in the Sector ID fields in the sector header, and can only be written or updated by a low level format. With older drive interfaces that used discrete controllers like ST-506/412 or ESDI, you often had to calculate the best interleave value for the particular controller and system you were using so you could low-level format the drive and number the sectors so as to offer optimum performance. The following section describes the interleave ratio and how you can determine the best value for your system. Note that nearly all IDE and SCSI drives have interleave ratios fixed at 1:1 and built-in controllers that can handle this with no problem. In these drives there is no longer a need to calculate or specify an interleave ratio; however, knowing about interleaving can give you further insight into how these drives function.

Many older ST-506/412 controllers could not handle the sectors as quickly as the drive could send them. As an example, suppose you have a standard ST-5096/412 drive that has 17 sectors on each track and when you low level formatted the drive, you specified a 1:1 interleave, which is to say you numbered the sectors on each track consecutively.

Suppose you want to read some data from the drive. The controller commands the drive to position the heads to a specific track and read all 17 sectors from that track. The heads move and arrive at the desired track. The time it takes for the heads to move is called the seek time, and once the heads arrive at the desired track, you have to wait an average of one half a revolution of the disk for the first sector to arrive. This is called latency. After an average latency of one-half of a disk revolution, the sector numbered 1 arrives under the heads. While the disk continues to spin at 3,600 rpm (60 revolutions per second), the data is read from sector 1, and as the data is being transferred from the controller to the system board, the disk continues to spin. Finally the data is completely moved to the motherboard, and the controller is now ready for sector 2. Figure 10.11 shows what is happening.

But wait! There is a problem here. Because the disk continues to spin at such a high rate of speed, sector 2 passed under the head as the controller was working, and by the time the controller is ready again, the heads now are coming to the start of sector 3. However, because the controller needs to read sector 2 next, the controller must now wait for the disk to spin around a full revolution or until the start of sector 2 comes under the heads. After this additional disk revolution, sector 2 arrives under the heads and is read. While the controller is transferring the data from sector 2 to the motherboard, sector 3 passes under the heads. When the controller finally is ready to read sector 3, the heads are coming to the start of sector 4, so another complete revolution will be required and the controller will have to get sector 4 on the next go around. This scenario continues, with each new revolution allowing only one sector to be read and missing the next sector due to it coming under the heads before the controller is ready.

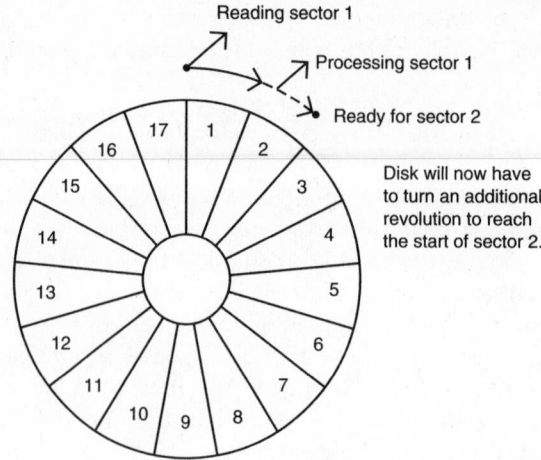

Fig. 10.11

A hard disk interleave ratio too low for the controller.

As you can see, the timing of this procedure is not working out very well. At this pace, 17 full revolutions of the disk will be required in order to read all 17 sectors. Because each revolution takes 1/60 of one second, it will take 17/60 of one second to read this track, almost one-third of a second—a very long time by computer standards.

Can this performance be improved? You notice that after reading a specific sector from the disk, the controller takes some time to transfer the sector data to the motherboard. The next sector that the controller can catch in this example is the second sector away from the first one. In other words, the controller seems to be capable of catching every second sector.

I hope that now you can imagine the perfect solution to this problem: simply *number* the sectors out of order. The new numbering scheme takes into account how fast the controller works; the sectors are numbered so that each time the controller is ready for the next sector, the sector coming under the heads is numbered as the next sector the controller will want to read. Figure 10.12 shows this new sector-numbering scheme.

The new numbering system eliminates the extra disk revolution previously required to pick up each sector. With the new scheme, the controller will read all 17 sectors on the disk in only two complete revolutions. Renumbering the sectors on the disk in this manner is called *interleaving*, normally expressed as a ratio. The interleave ratio in this example is 2 to 1 (also written as 2:1), which means that the next numbered sector is 2 sectors away from the preceding one, and if the controller is capable of handling this, then only 2 complete revolutions are needed to read an entire track. Thus reading the track takes only 2/60 of one second at the 2 to 1 interleave, rather than 17/60 of one second required to read the disk at the 1 to 1 interleave—an improvement of *800 percent* in data-transfer rate.

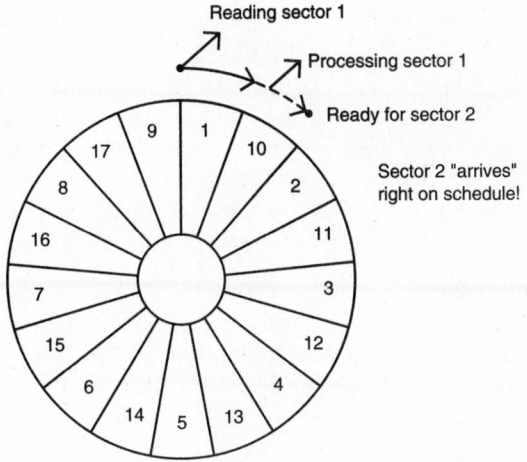

Fig. 10.12

A hard disk interleave ratio matching the controller's capabilities.

This example shows a system in which the ideal interleave is 2:1. I used this example because most controllers that came in older AT systems worked in exactly this manner. If you set one for a 1:1 interleave, you would likely make the drive eight times slower than it should be. This has changed with newer controller technology. Most disk controllers sold in the last couple of years are easily able to support a 1:1 interleave on any AT-class system, even the slowest 6 MHz 286 versions. If you are purchasing or upgrading a system today, I consider a disk subsystem with a 1:1 interleave controller to be a standard requirement. Fortunately, this is pretty much a non-issue because virtually all IDE or SCSI drives have controllers built-in to the drive that easily handle a 1:1 interleave, and all of these types of drives are pre-formatted at the factory in that manner. In many of these drives it is not even possible to change the interleave to any other value except 1:1.

The correct interleave for a system depends primarily on the controller, and secondarily on the speed of the system that the controller is plugged into. A controller and system that can handle a *consecutive sector interleave* (a 1 to 1 interleave) must transfer data as fast as the disk drive can present it; this used to be quite a feat, but is now commonplace.

Advances in controller technology have made a 1 to 1 interleave not only possible, but also affordable. Any 286 or faster system can easily handle the 1:1 interleave data transfer rate. The only types of systems that are truly too slow to effectively handle a 1 to 1 interleave are the original 4.77 MHz PC- and XT-type systems. Those systems have a maximum throughput to the slots of just under 400K per second, not fast enough to support a 1:1 interleave controller.

Now even with a 1:1 interleave, performance can vary significantly, and this is where the drive itself comes into play. A 1-to-1 interleave with a 17-sector disk is one thing, but with ESDI or SCSI drives spinning at 7,200 rpm and having 81 or more sectors per track, this results in *nearly 5M* of data transfer *each second*.

III

Hardware Considerations

The interleave used in standard-issue IBM XT systems with hard drives was 6 to 1; while in IBM AT systems, it was 3 to 1. The best interleave for these systems is actually one lower than what was setup as standard in each case: In other words, the best interleave for the Xebec 1210 controller in a 4.77 MHz IBM PC or IBM XT is 5 to 1, and the best interleave for the Western Digital 1002 and 1003 controllers in a 6 MHz or 8 MHz IBM AT system is 2 to 1. If you redo the low-level format on these systems to the lower interleave number, you gain about 20 to 30 percent in data-transfer performance, without changing any hardware and at no cost to you (except for some of your time).

Table 10.8 shows data transfer rates calculated from a variety of drives at a variety of different interleaves. The rows in this table each represent a particular drive and controller combination with respect to the speed of revolution and the number of sectors per track. In all but the lowest end setups, the interleave will be 1:1, but I listed the other interleaves to show what the effect would be if they were used.

Table 10.8 Data-Transfer Rates in K per second at various Interleaves, Spindle speeds, and Sector densities.

Speed (RPM)	Sectors /Track	1:1	2:1	Interleaves 3:1	4:1	5:1	6:1
3,600	17	510	255	170	128	102	85
3,600	25	750	375	250	188	150	125
3,600	26	780	390	260	195	156	130
3,600	27	810	405	270	203	162	135
3,600	32	960	480	320	240	192	160
3,600	33	990	495	330	248	198	165
3,600	34	1,020	510	340	255	204	170
3,600	35	1,050	525	350	263	210	175
3,600	36	1,080	540	360	270	216	180
3,600	37	1,110	555	370	278	222	185
3,600	38	1,140	570	380	285	228	190
3,600	39	1,170	585	390	293	234	195
4,500	50	1,875	938	625	469	375	313
3,600	81	2,430	1,215	810	608	486	405
4,500	70	2,625	1,313	875	656	525	438
5,400	70	3,150	1,575	1,050	788	630	525
6,300	90	4,725	2,363	1,575	1,181	945	788
7,200	81	4,860	2,430	1,620	1,215	972	810

Compare the 85K per second transfer rate of the original IBM XT drive and controller (3,600 rpm, 17 Sectors, and a 6:1 interleave standard), to the 4,860K per second transfer rate of the Seagate Barracuda 2 drive (7,200 rpm, 81 Sectors, and a 1:1 interleave). As you can see, you have come a long way in 10 years of disk and controller technology!

If you want to find out what the interleave of your drive is currently set to, I usually recommend the Norton Utilities for performing hard disk drive interleave testing. The Calibrate program included with the Norton Utilities can check and possibly even change the interleave on ST-506/412 interface drives through a "nondestructive" low-level format. Note that nondestructive in this case actually means that the format is done one track at a time, all the while backing up and restoring the data for the track. A full backup of the entire drive is still recommended beforehand, because if something goes wrong, one or more tracks can be wiped out.

Calibrate (and other utility programs like it) can only change the interleave on ST-506/412 and possibly some ESDI drives, and there can be problems even on drives they can handle. If you really want to change the interleave of a drive through a new low level format, I usually recommend whatever Low Level Format program the controller manufacturer specifies for the best possible job. With most modern drives (ESDI, IDE, or SCSI), it is not usually possible (nor is it desirable) to change the interleave with a generic Low Level Format program like Calibrate. With ESDI type drives, for example, you would normally need to use the controller's built-in (or supplied on disk) Low Level Format (LLF) program to reset the interleave (most ESDI controllers support 1:1, so there should be little reason to change). IDE and SCSI drives have the disk controller built-in, and most have the interleave permanently set (non-changeable) to the best possible choice, eliminating any reason to change. Virtually all modern drive/controller combinations today have a default 1:1 interleave anyway, so changing would not be beneficial.

Head and Cylinder Skewing

Most controllers today are capable of transferring data at a 1:1 sector interleave. This is especially true of controllers that are built-in to drive such as with IDE and SCSI drives. With a 1:1 interleave controller, the maximum data transfer rate can be maintained when reading and writing sectors to the disk. Although it would seem that there is no other way to further improve efficiency and transfer rate, many people overlook two other important factors similar to interleave. These are the Head and Cylinder skewing.

When a drive is reading (or writing) data sequentially, first all of the sectors on a given track are read, then the drive must electronically switch to the next head in the cylinder to continue the operation. If the sectors are not skewed from head to head within the cylinder, then there will be no delay after the last sector on one track and before the arrival of the first sector on the next track. Because all drives require some time (although small) to switch from one head to another, and the controller also adds some overhead to the operation, it is likely that by the time the drive is ready to read the sectors on the newly selected track the first sector will have already passed by. By skewing the sectors from one head to another, that is rotating their arrangement on the track so that the arrival of the first sector is delayed relative to the previous track, you can ensure that no extra disk revolutions will be required when switching heads. This will allow the highest possible transfer rate when head switching is involved.

In a similar fashion, it takes considerable time for the heads to move from one cylinder to another. If the sectors on one cylinder were not skewed from those on the previous adjacent cylinder, then it is likely that by the time the heads arrive the first sector will have already passed underneath them, requiring an additional revolution of the disk before reading the new cylinder can begin. By skewing the sectors from one cylinder to the next, you can account for the cylinder to cylinder head movement time and prevent any additional revolutions of the drive.

Head Skew

Head skew is defined as the offset in logical sector numbering between the same physical sectors on two tracks under adjacent heads of the same cylinder. The number of sectors being skewed when switching from head to head within a single cylinder is to compensate for head switching and controller overhead time. This allows continuous read or write operation across head boundaries without missing any disk revolutions, thus maximizing system performance.

In order to understand Head Skew, you first need to know the order in which tracks and sectors are read from a disk. If you imagine a single platter (two head) drive with 10 cylinders and 17 sectors per track, the first track that will be read on the entire drive is Cylinder 0, Head 0, Sector 1. Following that will be all of the remaining sectors on that first track (Cylinder 0, Head 0) until sector 17 is reached. After that, two things could take place: the heads could be moved so that the drive could continue reading the next track on the same side of the platter; or the other head could be selected, and you could read another track with no head movement at all. Because head movement takes much longer than electronically selecting another head, all drives will select all of the heads on a cylinder before moving the heads to the next cylinder. Thus the next sector to be read would be Cylinder 0, Head 1, Sector 1. Then all of the remaining sectors on that track are read (2 through 17), and then it is time to switch heads. This continues until the last sector on the last track is read, which in this example would be Cylinder 9, Head 1, Sector 17.

If you could take the tracks off of a cylinder in this example and lay them down on top of one another, it might look like this:

```
Cyl. 0, Head 0:    1- 2- 3- 4- 5- 6- 7- 8- 9-10-11-12-13-14-15-16-17

Cyl. 0, Head 1:    1- 2- 3- 4- 5- 6- 7- 8- 9-10-11-12-13-14-15-16-17
```

After reading all of the sectors on head 0, the controller switches heads to head 1 and continues the read (looping around to the beginning of the track). In this example, the sectors were not skewed at all between the heads, which means that the sectors are directly over and under one another in a given cylinder.

Now the platters in this example are spinning at 3,600 rpm, so one sector is passing beneath a head once every 980 millionths of a second! This is obviously a very small timing window. It takes some time for the head switch to occur (usually 15 millionths of a second) as well as some over head time for the controller to pass the head switch command. What this means is that by the time the head switch is complete and you are ready to read the new track, sector 1 has already gone by! This is a similar problem to interleaving where the interleave was too low. This forces the drive to wait while the platter spins around another revolution so it can begin to pick up the track starting with Sector 1.

This problem is easy to solve by offsetting the sector numbering on subsequent tracks from those that precede them sufficiently to account for the head switching and controller overhead time. That way, when Head 0 Sector 17 finishes and the head switches, Head 1 Sector 1 would be arriving right on time. The result would look something like this.

```
Cyl. 0, Head 0:     1- 2- 3- 4- 5- 6- 7- 8- 9-10-11-12-13-14-15-16-17

Cyl. 0, Head 1:    16-17- 1- 2- 3- 4- 5- 6- 7- 8- 9-10-11-12-13-14-15
```

Shifting the second track by two sectors gives us time to allow for the head switching overhead and is the equivalent to a Head Skew factor of 2. In normal use, a drive switches heads much more often than it switches physical cylinders, which makes Head Skew more important than Cylinder Skew. Throughput can rise dramatically when a proper head skew is in place. Different head skews can account for different transfer rates among drives that have the same number of sectors per track and the same interleave.

For example, a non-skewed MFM drive might have a transfer rate of 380K per second while the transfer rate of a drive with a head skew of 2 could rise to 425K per second. Notice that different controllers and drives have different amounts of overhead, so real world results will be different in each unique case. In most cases the head switch time is very small compared to the controller overhead. As with interleaving, it is better to be on the conservative side to avoid additional disk revolutions.

Cylinder Skew

Cylinder skew is defined as the offset in logical sector numbering between the same physical sectors on two adjacent tracks on two adjacent cylinders.

The number of sectors being skewed when switching tracks from one cylinder to the next is to compensate for track to track seek time. This allows continuous read or write operation across cylinder boundaries without missing any disk revolutions, thus maximizing system performance.

Cylinder skew is a larger numerical factor then head skew because there is more overhead. It takes much longer to move the heads from one cylinder to another than to simply switch heads. Also the controller overhead in changing cylinders is higher as well.

Here is a depiction of our example drive with a head skew factor of 2 but no cylinder skew.

```
Cyl. 0, Head 0:     1- 2- 3- 4- 5- 6- 7- 8- 9-10-11-12-13-14-15-16-17

Cyl. 0, Head 1:    16-17- 1- 2- 3- 4- 5- 6- 7- 8- 9-10-11-12-13-14-15

Cyl. 1, Head 0:     8- 9-10-11-12-13-14-15-16-17- 1- 2- 3- 4- 5- 6- 7
```

In this example the Cylinder Skew factor is 8. Shifting the sectors on the subsequent cylinder by eight sectors gives the drive and controller time to be ready for sector 1 on the next cylinder and eliminates an extra revolution of the disk.

Calculating Skew Factors

The correct head skew factor can be derived from the following information and formula:

Head Skew = (Head Switch Time/Rotational Period) x SPT + 2

In other words, the head switching time of a drive is divided by the time period for a single rotation. The result is multiplied by the number of sectors per track and then 2 is added for controller overhead. The result should then be rounded up to the next whole integer number (2.3 = 2, 2.5 = 3).

The correct cylinder skew factor can be derived from the following information and formula:

Cylinder Skew = (Track to Track Seek Time/Rotational Period) x SPT + 4

In other words, the track to track seek time of a drive is divided by the time period for a single rotation. The result is multiplied by the number of sectors per track and then 4 is added for controller overhead. Round up the result to an integer number (2.3 = 2, 2.5 = 3).

Here is an example using typical figures for an ESDI drive and controller. If the head switching time is 15us (micro-sec), the track to track seek is 3ms, the rotational period is 16.67ms (3,600 rpm), and the drive has 53 physical sectors per track, then:

Head Skew = (0.015/16.67) * 53 + 2 = 2 (rounded up)

Cylinder Skew = (3/16.67) * 53 + 4 = 14 (rounded up)

If you don't have the necessary information to make the calculations, contact the drive manufacturer for their recommendations. Otherwise you can make the calculations using conservative figures for the head switch and track to track access times. If you are unsure, just as with interleaving, it is better to be on the conservative side and minimize the possibility of additional rotations when reading sequential information on the drive. In most cases a default Head Skew of 2 and a Cylinder Skew of 16 will work well.

Because things like the controller overhead are variable factors that can vary from model to model, sometimes the only way to figure out the best value here is to experiment. You can try different skew values and then run data transfer rate tests to see which results in the highest performance. Be careful with these tests—many disk benchmark programs only transfer data from one track or one cylinder during testing, which totally eliminates the effect of skewing on the results. The best type of benchmark to use for this testing is one which reads and writes large files on the disk.

Most real (controller register level) low-level format programs can set skew factors. Those programs supplied by a particular controller or drive manufacturer are usually already optimized for their particular drives and controllers and may not offer you the ability to change the skew. One of the best general purpose register level formatters on the market that does give you this flexibility is the Disk Manager program by Ontrack. I highly recommend this program and you will find them listed in the vendor list in the Appendix.

I do not normally recommend programs like Norton Calibrate or Gibson Spinrite for re-interleaving drives because these programs only work through the BIOS INT 13h functions rather than directly with the disk controller hardware. Thus it is impossible for these programs to properly set skew factors, and using them may actually slow down a drive that already has optimum interleave and skew factors.

Note that most IDE and SCSI drives have their interleave and skew factors set to fully optimum values by the manufacturer. In most cases, you cannot even change these values, but in some cases you can, which would most likely result in slowing the drive down. This is the major reason that most IDE drive manufacturers recommend against low level formatting their drives. With some IDE drives, unless you use the right software, you might alter the optimum skew settings and slow down the drive. IDE drives that use Zoned Recording cannot ever have the interleave or skew factors changes, and as such they are fully protected. No matter how you try to format them, the interleave and skew factors cannot be altered. The same can be said for SCSI drives.

Shock Mounting

Most hard disks manufactured today have a *shock-mounted* HDA, which means that a rubber cushion is between the disk drive body and the mounting chassis. Some drives use more rubber than others, but for the most part, a shock mount is a shock mount. Some drives do not have a shock-isolated HDA due to physical or cost constraints. Be sure that the drive you are using has adequate shock isolation mounts for the HDA, especially if you are using the drive in a portable PC system or in a system in which environmental conditions are less favorable than in a normal office. I usually never recommend a drive that lacks at least some form of shock mounting.

Cost

The cost of a hard disk storage has recently fallen below the magic $1 per megabyte barrier. This means that you can purchase 2G drives for under $2,000, 1G drives for under $1,000, 500M drives for under $500, and so on. That places the value of the 10M drive I bought in 1983 at less than $10. Too bad I paid $1,800 for it at the time! Of course, the cost of drives continues to fall, and eventually even $1 per megabyte will seem expensive. Because of the low costs of disk storage today, there are not many drives even being manufactured anymore that are less than 200 megabytes, except perhaps the very small 1.3-inch or 1.8-inch drives for laptop systems.

III

Hardware Considerations

Capacity

Four figures are commonly used in advertising drive capacity:

- Unformatted capacity in millions of bytes (M)

- Formatted capacity in millions of bytes (M)

- Unformatted capacity in megabytes (Meg)

- Formatted capacity in megabytes (Meg)

With IDE and SCSI drives, most manufacturers now report only the formatted capacities, because these drives are delivered pre-formatted. Most of the time, you will see advertisements refer to the unformatted or formatted capacity in millions of bytes (M) because these figures are larger than the same capacity expressed in megabytes (Meg). This generates a lot of confusion when the user runs FDISK (which reports total drive capacity in Meg), and wonders where the missing space is. This ranks as one of the more common questions that I get in my seminars. Fortunately, the answer is easy; it only involves a little math to figure it out.

For example, here is a common question I get: "I just installed a new Western Digital AC2200 drive, billed as 212M. When I entered the drive parameters (989 Cylinders, 12 Heads, 35 Sectors per track), both the BIOS Setup routine and FDISK report the drive as only 203M. What happened to the other 9M?"

Well, the answer is only a few calculations away. By multiplying the drive specification parameters together, here is what you get:

Cylinders:	989
Heads:	12
Sectors per Track:	35
Bytes per Sector:	512
Total bytes:	212, 674, 560
Total Megabytes:	202.82

That figures to a capacity of 212.67M (million bytes) or 202.82 Megabytes. Drive manufacturers usually report drive capacity in millions of bytes, while your BIOS and FDISK will usually report the capacity in megabytes. 1M equals 1,048,576 bytes (or 1,024 K, where each K is 1,024 bytes). The bottom line is that this 212.67M drive is also a 202.82 Megabyte drive. One additional item to note about this drive is that it is a zone recorded drive and the actual physical parameters are different. Physically, this drive has 1,971 cylinders and 4 heads, however the total number of sectors on the drive (and therefore the capacity) is the same no matter how you translate the parameters.

Although Western Digital does not report the unformatted capacity of this particular drive, unformatted capacity usually works out to be about 19 percent larger than a drive's formatted capacity. As an example, the Seagate ST-12550N drive is advertised as having the following capacities:

Unformatted capacity:	2,572.00 M
Unformatted capacity:	2,452.85 Meg
Formatted capacity:	2,139.00 M
Formatted capacity:	2,039.91 Meg

Each of these four figures is a correct answer to the question: "What is the storage capacity of the drive?", but as you can see the numbers are very different. In fact there is even another number that could be used in this case. Taking the 2,039.91 Megabytes and dividing it by 1,024 gives the drive's capacity as 1.99G. So when you are comparing or discussing drive capacities, make sure that you are working in a consistent unit of measure, or your comparisons will be meaningless.

To eliminate confusion in capacity measurements. I am using what the industry regards as standard methods for indicating the unit of measure. M stands for million bytes (1,000,000 bytes), and Meg stands for Megabytes (1,048,576 bytes). Millions of bits are indicated by using a lower case "b" as in Mbps for million bits per second.

Specific Recommendations

If you're going to add a hard disk to a system today, there are a few recommendations I can give you. Starting with the actual physical hard disk itself, you should demand the following things in a hard disk drive to ensure that you're getting a quality unit:

- Voice Coil head actuator
- Thin Film media

For the drive interface, there are really only two types to consider today:

- IDE (Integrated Drive Electronics)
- SCSI (Small Computer System Interface)

Of these, I prefer SCSI because of the great expandability, the cross platform compatibility, high capacity, performance, and flexibility. IDE offers a very high performance solution, but expansion, compatibility, capacity, and flexibility are severely limited compared with SCSI.

Hard Disk Interfaces

There are a variety of different types of hard disk interfaces to choose from on the market today. As time has progressed, the number of choices has increased and many of the older designs are no longer viable in newer systems. You need to know about all of these interfaces, from the oldest to the newest designs, because you will encounter all of them in situations where upgrading or repairing systems is necessary.

III

Hardware Considerations

Each of the different interfaces have different cabling and configuration options, and the setup and format of drives will vary as well. There can be special problems when trying to install more than one drive of a particular interface type, or especially when mixing drives of different interface types in one system.

This section will cover the different hard disk drive interfaces completely, giving you all of the technical information you need to be able to deal with them in any way from troubleshooting, servicing, upgrading, and even mixing the different types.

This section examines the standard controllers and describes how you can work with these controllers, as well as replace them with much faster units. Also discussed are the different types of drive interfaces: ST-506/412, ESDI, IDE, and SCSI. Choosing among these interfaces is important because the choice also affects your disk drive purchases and the ultimate speed of the disk subsystem.

The primary job of the hard disk controller or interface is to transmit and receive data to and from the drive. The different interface types place limitations in how fast data can be moved from the drive to the system, and offer different levels of performance. It you are putting together a system where performance is a primary concern, you will need to know how these different interfaces affect performance, and what expectations you can have from them. Many of the statistics given in technical literature are not indicative of the real performance figures you will see in practice. I will separate the myths presented by some of these over-optimistic figures from the reality of what you will actually see.

In discussing disk drives, especially hard disk drives, the specification that seems to be focused on the most is the drive's reported average seek time—the (average) time it takes for the heads to be positioned from one track to another. Unfortunately, the importance of this specification often is overstated, especially in relation to other specifications such as the *data-transfer rate*.

The transfer rate of data between the drive and the system is more important than access time because most drives spend more time reading and writing information than simply moving the heads around. The speed with which a program or data file is loaded or read is affected most by the data-transfer rate. Specialized operations like sorting large files, which involve a lot of random access to individual records of the file (and therefore many seek operations), are helped greatly by a faster-seeking disk drive, so seeking performance is important in these cases, however most normal file load and save operations are most affected by the rate at which data can be read and written to and from the drive. The data-transfer rate depends on both the drive and the interface.

There are several different types of hard disk interfaces that have been used in PC systems over the years. These are as follows:

- ST-506/412
- ESDI
- IDE
- SCSI

Of these interfaces, only ST-506/412 and ESDI are what you could call true disk controller to drive interfaces. SCSI and IDE are system-level interfaces that usually incorporate a chipset based variation of one of the other two types of disk controller interfaces internally. For example, most SCSI and IDE drives incorporate internally the same basic controller circuitry as was found on separate ESDI controllers. The SCSI interface adds another layer of interface which attaches the controller to the system bus, while IDE is a direct bus attachment interface.

In data recovery, it helps to know the disk interface you are working with because many data-recovery problems involve drive setup and installation problems. Each interface requires a slightly different method of installation and drive configuration. If the installation or configuration is incorrect or accidentally altered by the system user, it may prevent access to data on a drive. Accordingly, anyone who wants to become proficient in data recovery must be an expert in installing and configuring various types of hard disks and controllers.

IBM's reliance on industry standard interfaces like those listed here was a boon for everybody in the IBM compatible industry. These standards allow a great deal of cross system and manufacturer compatibility. The use of these industry standard interfaces is what allows us to pick up a mail order catalog, purchase a hard disk for the lowest possible price compared to any other type of computer system, and be assured that it will work with our system. This "plug and play" capability results in affordable hard disk storage and a variety of options in capacities and speed.

The ST-506/412 Interface

The ST-506/412 interface was developed by Seagate Technologies around 1980. The interface originally appeared on the Seagate ST-506 drive, which was a 5M formatted (6M unformatted) drive in a full-height, 5 1/4-inch form factor. By today's standards, it is a tank! In 1981 Seagate introduced the ST-412 drive, which added a feature called *buffered seek* to the interface. This drive was a 10M formatted (12M unformatted) drive, which also qualifies as a tank by today's standards. The ST-412 was the first and later one of several drives that IBM selected for the XT. Since the original XT, Seagate has supplied drives for numerous IBM systems, including the AT and many PS/2 Models.

Most drive manufacturers who made hard disks for PC systems adopted the Seagate ST-506/412 standard, which helped to make this interface popular. One important feature is the interface's "plug and play" design. No custom cables or special modifications are needed for the drives, which means that virtually any ST-506/412 drive will work with any ST-506/412 controller. The only real compatibility issue with this interface was the level of BIOS support provided by the system.

When first introduced to the PC industry by IBM in 1983, ROM BIOS support for this hard disk interface was provided by a BIOS chip on the controller. The XT system BIOS had no inherent hard disk support. When the AT system was introduced, IBM placed the ST-506/412 interface support within the motherboard BIOS, and eliminated it from the controller. Since then, any system which is compatible with the IBM AT (which would include most systems on the market today) has an enhanced version of this very same

III

Hardware Considerations

support in the motherboard BIOS as well. Because this support was somewhat limited, especially in the older BIOS versions, many disk controller manufacturers also placed BIOS support for their controller directly on the controller itself. In some cases the controller BIOS and motherboard BIOS would be used together, in other cases you would disable the controller or motherboard BIOS and use one or the other. These issues will be discussed more completely later in this chapter when you read about configuring the system.

The ST-506/412 interface does not quite make the grade in today's high-performance PC systems. It was originally designed for a 5-megabyte drive, and I have not seen any drives larger than 152 megabytes (MFM encoding) or 233 megabytes (RLL encoding) available for this type of interface. Because the capacity, performance, and expandability of ST-506/412 are so limited, this interface is obsolete and generally unavailable in any new systems. However, there are many older systems out there that still use drives with this interface.

Encoding Schemes and Problems. As indicated earlier in this chapter, encoding schemes are used in communications for converting digital data bits into various tones for transmission over a telephone line. For disk drives, the digital bits are converted, or *encoded*, into a pattern of magnetic impulses, or *flux transitions* (also called flux reversals), which are written on the disk. These flux transitions are decoded later when the data is read from the disk. A device called an Endec (encoder/decoder) accomplishes the conversion to flux transitions for writing on the media and the subsequent reconversion back to digital data during read operations. The function of the Endec is very similar to that of a Modem (modulator/demodulator) in that digital data is converted to an analog waveform, which is then reconverted back to digital data. Sometimes the Endec is also called a *data separator*, because it is designed to separate data and clocking information from the flux transition pulse stream read from the disk.

One of the biggest problems with ST-506/412 was the fact that this Endec resided on the disk controller (rather than the drive), which resulted in the possibility for corruption of the analog data signal before it reached the media. This became especially pronounced when the ST-506/412 controllers switched to using RLL Endecs to store 50 percent more data to the drive. With the RLL encoding scheme, the actual density of magnetic flux transitions on the disk media remains the same as with MFM encoding, however the timing between the transitions must be measured much more precisely.

The original ST-506/412 controllers used MFM encoding, which is what the interface was originally designed for. A few years after it had been out, several controller manufacturers started using RLL Endec circuits in their controllers. These newer controllers were fully compatible with the ST-506/412 interface drives, however they could put 50% more data on them, and transfer it to and from the drive 50% faster than the older MFM variety controllers. Unfortunately, this caused many problems with the cheaper drives that were on the market at the time.

In RLL encoding, the intervals between flux changes are approximately the same as with MFM, however the actual timing between them is much more critical. This means that the transition cells in which signals must be recognized are much smaller and more precisely placed than with MFM. This means that RLL encoding places more stringent demands on the timing of the controller and drive electronics. With RLL encoding, accurately reading the timing of the flux changes is paramount. Additionally, because RLL encodes variable length groups of bits rather than single bits, a single error in one flux transition can corrupt anywhere from two to four bits of data. For these reasons, an RLL controller usually has a more sophisticated error-detection and error-correction routine than an MFM controller.

Most of the cheaper disk drives on the market did not have data channel circuits that were designed to be precise enough to handle RLL encoding without problems. RLL encoding is also much more susceptible to noise in the read signal, and the conventional oxide media coatings did not have a sufficient signal-to-noise ratio for reliable RLL encoding. This was often compounded by the fact that many drive of the time used stepper motor head positioning systems, which are notoriously inaccurate, further amplifying the signal-to-noise ratio problem.

At this time manufacturers starting "RLL Certifying" drives for use with RLL Endec controllers. This stamp of approval basically meant that the drive had passed tests and was designed to handle the precise timing requirements that RLL encoding required. In some cases the drive electronics were upgraded between a manufacturer's MFM and RLL drive versions, but essentially they are the same drive. In fact, if any improvements were made to the so called RLL certified drives, then these same upgrades were usually also applied to the MFM version. The bottom line is that other than improved precision, there is no real difference between an ST-506/412 drive that is sold as an MFM model from one sold as an RLL model. If you wanted to use a drive that was originally sold as an MFM model with an RLL controller, then I would suggest this only if the drive used a voice coil head actuator and thin film media. Virtually any ST-506/412 drive with these qualities is more than good enough to handle RLL encoding with no problems.

Using MFM encoding, a standard ST-506/412 format specifies that the drive will contain 17 sectors per track, with each sector containing 512 bytes of data. By changing to a controller that uses an RLL Endec, the number of sectors per track is raised to 25 or 26.

The real solution to reliability with RLL encoding was to place the Endec directly on the drive rather than on the controller. This reduces the susceptibility to noise and interference that can plague an ST-506/412 drive system running RLL encoding. ESDI, IDE, and SCSI drives all have the Endec (and often the entire controller) built-in to the drive by default. Because the Endec is attached to the drive without cables and with an extremely short electrical distance, the propensity for timing- and noise-induced errors is greatly reduced or eliminated. This is analogous to a local telephone call between the Endec and the disk platters. This local communication makes the ESDI, IDE, and SCSI interfaces much more reliable than the older ST-506/412 interface; they share none of the reliability problems that were once associated with RLL encoding over the ST-506/412 interface. Virtually all ESDI, IDE, and SCSI drives use RLL encoding today with tremendously increased reliability over even MFM ST-506/412 drives.

III

Hardware Considerations

ST-506/412 Configuration and Installation. The ST-506/412 interface (see figs. 10.13 and 10.14) is characterized by a two or three cable arrangement depending on whether one or two drives are connected. There is one 34-connector control cable which is daisy chained between up to two drives. The daisy-chain arrangement is much like that used for floppy drives. Each drive on the daisy chain is jumped to respond to a particular Drive Select (DS) line. In the controller implementation used in all PC systems, there are two available lines, called Drive Select 1 (DS1) and Drive Select 2 (DS2). Some drives will have support for as many as 4 DS lines, but only the first two are usable. Although it may appear as though you could string four drives on a single daisy-chain cable, the design of the PC system and controllers uses only the first two.

The control cable usually has lines 25 through 29 twisted between the drive D and C connectors. The first drive (drive C) is normally plugged into the last control cable connector at the end of the cable opposite from the controller, and a second drive (D) can be optionally installed in the middle control cable connector. The twist in the lines serves to reroute the Drive Select lines so that the drive plugged into the last cable position appears to the controller to be attached to Drive Select 1 even though the jumper on the drive is set for DS2. This is very similar to the arrangement used for floppy drives, where if the cable is twisted, then both drives must be set to the DS2 jumper position. If the cable does not have the twisted lines, then the drive at the end of the cable (C) must be set to DS1. Another configuration item is the terminating resistor, which must be installed on the drive at the end of the cable (C), and must be removed from the optional second drive (D) attached to the middle control cable connector. The controller has a permanently installed terminating resistor that does not ever have to be adjusted. Although the control cable is similar in function and appearance to the 34-pin cable for floppy drives, the cables are generally not interchangeable because different lines are twisted. While pins 25 through 29 are inverted on the hard disk control cable, pins 10 through 16 are inverted on the floppy cable, rendering them incompatible.

The other two cables are called *data cables*. These are 20-connector cables that each run from the controller to a single drive, as this cable is not daisy-chained. A two-drive system will therefore have one control cable from the controller to each of two drives in a daisy chain, plus two separate data cables, one for each drive. The controller has three connectors to support the two-drive maximum limit. As its name suggests, the data cable carries data to and from the drive.

If you're only using a single drive, then only the data cable connector closest to the control cable connector will be used, while the other is left unattached. Most ST-506/412 controllers also have an on-board floppy controller, which will also have a 34-pin connector for the floppy drives. Note that some of these combination controllers allow the floppy controller portion to be disabled, while others do not, which may cause a conflict if you have any other floppy controller in the system.

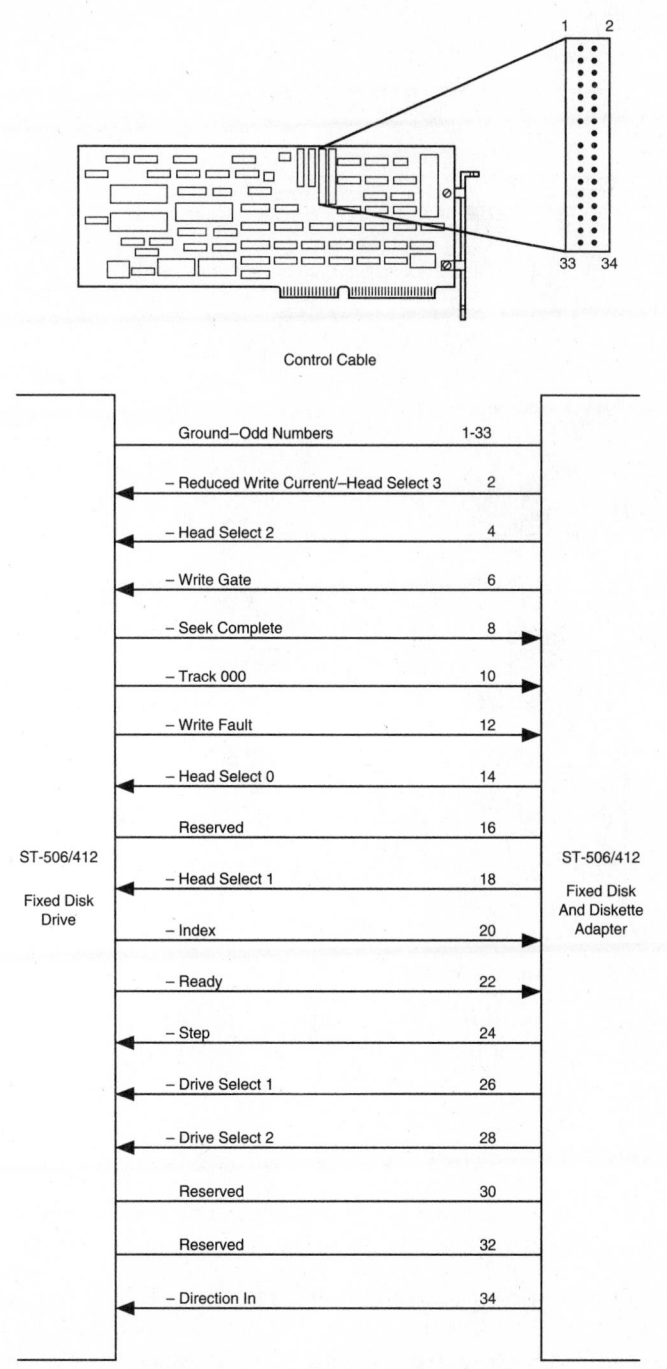

Control Cable

Ground–Odd Numbers	1-33	
– Reduced Write Current/–Head Select 3	2	
– Head Select 2	4	
– Write Gate	6	
– Seek Complete	8	
– Track 000	10	
– Write Fault	12	
– Head Select 0	14	
Reserved	16	
– Head Select 1	18	
– Index	20	
– Ready	22	
– Step	24	
– Drive Select 1	26	
– Drive Select 2	28	
Reserved	30	
Reserved	32	
– Direction In	34	

ST-506/412

Fixed Disk Drive

ST-506/412

Fixed Disk And Diskette Adapter

Fig. 10.13
ST-506/412 Controller Control Cable connector.

III

Hardware Considerations

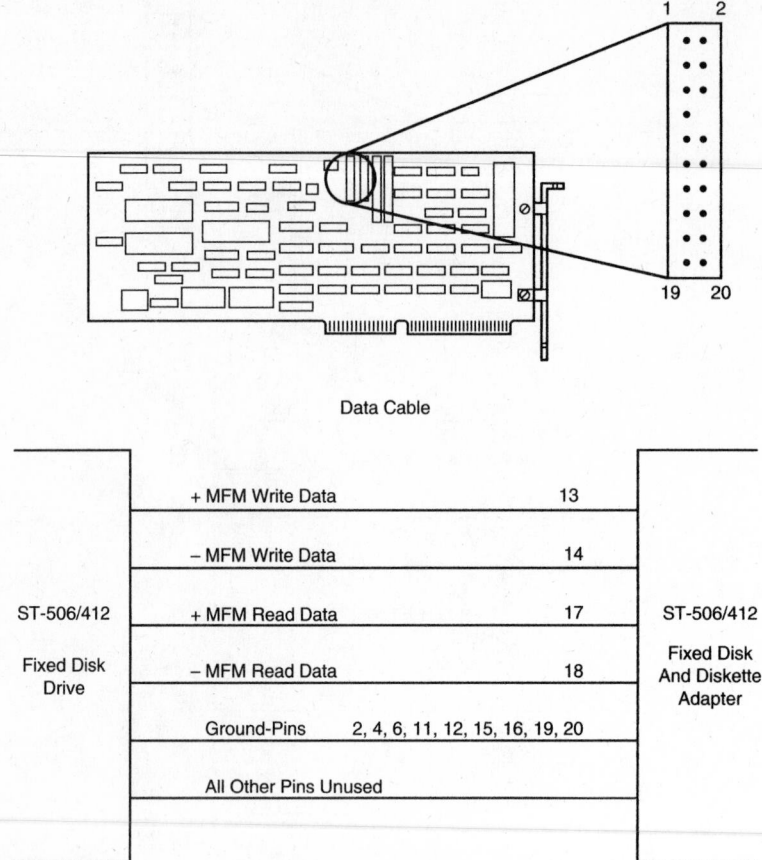

Data Cable

ST-506/412 Fixed Disk Drive		
+ MFM Write Data	13	ST-506/412 Fixed Disk And Diskette Adapter
− MFM Write Data	14	
+ MFM Read Data	17	
− MFM Read Data	18	
Ground-Pins 2, 4, 6, 11, 12, 15, 16, 19, 20		
All Other Pins Unused		

Fig. 10.14
ST-506/412 Controller Data Cable connectors.

ST-506/412 Drive Configuration. With ST-506/412 and ESDI drives you will have to configure these items on each of the drives:

■ Drive Select (DS) jumpers

■ Terminating Resistor

These configuration items are usually found near the rear of the drive on the disk drive logic board.

Drive Select Jumpers. The *Drive Select jumper* selects the Drive Select (DS) signal to which the drive should respond. The drive controller sends control signals on two DS lines, one for each drive. Because each drive must be set to respond to a different DS signal, this limits the number of drives per controller to two.

The DS jumpers must be set so that each drive responds to a different DS line from the controller (DS1 or DS2). If the 34-pin control cable has a twist in lines 25 through 29 then both drives should be set to DS2. If the control cable is a straight-through design (no twist), then the drive at the end of the cable opposite the controller (C) should be set to DS1, while a second drive attached to the middle control cable connector (D:) should be set to DS2. Notice that some drives label the DS jumpers starting with 0, such that DS1 would be labeled DS0, and DS2 would be labeled DS1.

Terminating Resistors. An ST-506/412 drive is always shipped from the factory with a terminating resistor installed. When you install these drives, you must ensure that the drive plugged into the end of the control cable daisy chain has this terminator installed. Additionally, this terminator must be removed (or disabled with a jumper in some cases) from the secondary drive installed in the center control cable connector.

The functions of the terminating resistor are the same as those discussed for floppy drives. The idea is to provide electrical signal termination so that the control signals to and from the drive and controller are not reflected back or echo along the cable. The terminating resistor provides the proper signal-to-noise ratio and the proper electrical load for the controller. Improper drive termination results in drives that do not function, or do so only with excessive problems. Improper termination may also damage the controller because of improper electrical loads.

Control and Data Cables. The control cable connects to the controller and daisy chains to the secondary and primary drives, while separate data cables (20-pin) run from the controller to each drive. The data cable connector closest to the control cable connector on the controller is used for the primary (C) drive.

When connecting cables, you should observe the proper pin-1 orientation from end to end. The ribbon cables will usually have the pin-1 line colored differently than the other lines. For example, in most ribbon cables, the pin-1 line will be red or blue while the rest of the cable is gray. You need to insure that this pin-1 line is plugged into pin-1 of the controller and drive connectors. Both the controller and drive should have the pin-1 position on each connector marked. Sometimes the mark is a number "1", other times it will be a dot or some other symbol silk-screened on the circuit board. The cable connectors at the controller end may be keyed, in which case pin-15 will be missing from the control cable connector on the controller connector and the corresponding hole will be plugged in the control cable. The data cable connectors will be missing pin-8 and the corresponding hole will also be plugged in the data cables. The edge connectors used at the drive end are also normally keyed to a notch in the drive connectors. The side of the connector with the notch cut out indicates the pin-1 orientation at the drive end.

Notice that the 34-pin control cable is very similar to the 34-pin control/data cable used for floppy drives, however they are usually not interchangeable. The ST-506/412 control cable has lines 25 through 29 twisted between the secondary and primary drive connectors, while the 34-pin floppy cable has lines 10 through 17 twisted. This renders them incompatible with each other and therefore noninterchangeable.

III

Hardware Considerations

Power Cables. To complete the required cable connections to the hard drive, you need a spare power connector. Some older power supplies have only two-drive power connectors. Several companies sell a *power splitter cable*, or Y cable, that can adapt one cable from the power supply so that it powers two drives. If you add a power splitter to a system, make sure that the power supply can handle the load of the additional drive or drives. If the original power supply is not adequate, purchase an after-market unit that can supply adequate power. Most better aftermarket supplies have four drive power connectors, eliminating the need for the splitter cables. Power splitter cables are available from several of the cable and accessory vendors listed in the vendor list in the Appendix as well as from electronic supply stores like Radio Shack.

Historical Notes. The following sections list some information on the original ST-506/412 controllers used in the PC environment. These were the controllers that IBM supplied in the XT and AT systems. At the time of introduction, these controllers set standards that, especially in the case of the AT controller, you still live with today. In fact the entire IDE interface standard is based on the controller IBM designed and used in the AT. All of the conventions and standards in the PC industry surrounding the hard disk interfaces you use today started with these controllers.

Original IBM 8-Bit Controllers

The first ST-506/412 controller standard sold for PC systems was the hard disk controller used in the original 10MB IBM XT. This was actually made for IBM by Xebec Corporation and was also sold under the Xebec name as the Xebec 1210 controller. The Xebec 1210 is an ST-506/412 controller that uses Modified Frequency Modulation (MFM) encoding to record data on a drive. This controller's ROM was produced by IBM and contains an 8K hard disk BIOS with an internal table that had entries for four different drives. Each of the drives was selected by jumpers on the controller, which were actually soldered in the early IBM units. If you purchased the controller from Xebec, you got a slightly different but completely compatible ROM, and the jumpers were not soldered so you could easily select one of the four BIOS table entries. Xebec also allowed system integrators to copy its ROM in order to modify the built-in drive tables for a specific drive.

Later IBM XT systems with a 20M hard disk still used the Xebec 1210, but it had a new 4K ROM that contained different drive tables, as well as the jumpers like those found on the one sold by Xebec. Xebec never sold an autoconfigure version of this controller, which would have made integrating different drives easier.

The Xebec 1210 is one of the slowest ST-506/412 controllers ever made, supporting at best a 5 to 1 interleave on a stock IBM PC or IBM XT system. If you use the IBM Advanced Diagnostics program for the IBM PC or IBM XT, the low-level formatter produces a standard 6 to 1 interleave, which results in a paltry 85K-per-second data-transfer rate. By changing the interleave to 5 to 1, you can wring 102K per second from this controller, still unbelievably slow by today's standards.

Xebec also made a Model 1220 that combined a hard disk and floppy disk controller, was hardware compatible with the 1210, and works with the IBM or standard Xebec ROM. The separate floppy controller could then be removed from the system, and you could save a slot.

I recommend replacing this controller with an autoconfigure controller whenever you get the chance. Most other controllers also are significantly faster than the Xebec.

Original IBM 16-bit Controllers

For the AT, IBM used two controllers made by Western Digital: the WD1002-WA2 and the WD1003A-WA2. The WD1003 is an upgraded WD1002 with a much lower chip count. The WD1003 was also shorter than the WD1002, to fit into the IBM XT 286.

The WD1002 is used in the IBM AT as a combination hard disk and floppy disk controller. The WD1002 and the WD1003 are standard ST-506/412 controllers that supply MFM encoding to the drive. Neither contains a ROM BIOS; instead, BIOS support is built in to the motherboard ROM. Both support a 2 to 1 interleave, even on a standard 6 MHz IBM AT system. The IBM Advanced Diagnostics low-level formatter can put down a 2 to 1 interleave, but the default is 3 to 1. Most users of these controllers can realize a performance gain if they simply reformat to the lower interleave.

The ESDI Interface

ESDI, or *Enhanced Small Device Interface*, is a specialized hard disk interface established as a standard in 1983 primarily by Maxtor Corporation. Maxtor led a consortium of drive manufacturers to adopt its proposed interface as a high-performance standard to succeed ST-506/412. ESDI was later adopted by the ANSI (American National Standards Institute) organization and published under the ANSI X3T9.2 Committee. The latest version of the ANSI ESDI document is known as X3.170a-1991. This and other ANSI standard documents can be obtained from ANSI themselves or Global Engineering Documents. These companies are listed in the Appendix.

Compared to ST-506/412, ESDI has provisions for increased reliability, such as building the Endec (Encoder/decoder) into the drive. ESDI is a very high speed interface, capable of a maximum 24-megabits-per-second transfer rate. Most drives running ESDI, however, are limited to a maximum of 10 or 15 megabits per second. Unfortunately, compatibility problems between different ESDI implementations combined with pressure from low cost high performance IDE interface drives have served obsolete the ESDI interface. Very few, if any, new systems today include ESDI drives, although it had become somewhat popular in high-end systems during the late '80s.

Enhanced commands enabled some ESDI controllers to read a drive's capacity parameters directly from the drive as well as to control defect mapping, but several manufacturers had different methods for writing this information on the drive. When you install an ESDI drive, in some cases the controller will automatically read the parameter and defect information directly from the drive; in other cases, however, you will still have to enter this information manually as with ST-506/412.

III

Hardware Considerations

The ESDI's enhanced defect mapping commands provide a standard way for the PC system to read a defect map from a drive, which means that the manufacturer's defect list can be written to the drive as a file. The defect list file then can be read by the controller and low-level format software, eliminating the need for the installer to type these entries from the keyboard and enabling the format program to update the defect list with new entries if it finds new defects during the low-level format or the surface analysis.

Most ESDI implementations have drives formatted to 32 sectors per track or higher (80 or more sectors per track are possible), many more sectors per track than the standard ST-506/412 implementation of 17 to 26 sectors per track. The greater density results in two or more times the data-transfer rate, with a 1 to 1 interleave. Almost without exception, ESDI controllers support a 1 to 1 interleave, which allows for more than a one megabyte-per-second or greater transfer rate.

Because ESDI is much like the ST-506/412 interface, it can replace that interface without affecting software in the system. Most ESDI controllers are register-compatible with the older ST-506/412 controllers, which enables OS/2 and other non-DOS operating systems to run with few or no problems. The ROM BIOS interface to ESDI is similar to the ST-506/412 standard, and many low-level disk utilities that run on one will run on the other. To take advantage of the ESDI defect mapping and other special features, however, use a low-level format and surface-analysis utility designed for ESDI (such as the ones usually built into the controller ROM BIOS and called by DEBUG).

Until the last year or so, most high-end systems from major manufacturers were equipped with ESDI controllers and drives. More recently, manufacturers have been dropping their ESDI systems for SCSI. The SCSI interface allows for much greater expandability, supports more types of devices than ESDI, and offers equal or greater performance. I no longer recommend that ESDI drives be installed in systems, unless you are upgrading a system that already has an ESDI controller.

Pinout diagrams of the ESDI connectors and cables can be found in the Appendix.

ESDI Drive Configuration. The ESDI interface was modeled after the ST-506/412 interface and shares virtually all of the same types of configuration items and procedures. The 34-pin control and 20-pin data cables are identical with those used in an ST-506/412 installation, and all of the configuration procedures with regards to Drive Select jumpers, twisted cables, and Terminating Resistors are the same as with ST-506/412.

Follow the configuration procedures for ST-506/412 drives when configuring ESDI drives. More information on the ESDI interface can be found in a previous section of this chapter.

The IDE Interface

Integrated Drive Electronics (IDE) is a generic term given to any drive with the disk controller integrated (built-in). The first drives with integrated controllers were Hardcards, although today there are a variety of different drive designs with integrated controllers. In a drive with IDE, the disk controller is integrated into the drive, and this combination drive/controller assembly usually plugs into a bus connector on the motherboard or on a bus adapter card. Combining the drive and controller greatly simplifies installation because there are no separate power or signal cables from the controller to the drive. Also, with the controller and the drive assembled as a unit, the number of total components is reduced, signal paths are shorter, and the electrical connections are more noise-resistant, resulting in a more reliable design than is possible using a separate controller connected to the drive by cables.

Placing the controller (including Endec) on the drive gives IDE drives an inherent reliability advantage over interfaces with separate controllers. Reliability is increased because the data encoding from digital to analog is done directly on the drive in a tight noise free environment. The timing-sensitive analog information does not have to travel along crude ribbon cables that are likely to pick up noise and insert propagation delays into the signals. This allows the clock rate of the encoder to be increased and also the storage density of the drive. Also, integrating the controller and drive gives the controller and drive engineers freedom from having to adhere to the strict standards imposed by the earlier interface standards. They can design essentially custom drive and controller implementations, because no other controller would ever have to be connected to the drive. This results in drive and controller combinations that can offer higher performance than previous stand-alone controller and drive setups. IDE drives are also sometimes called drives with *embedded controllers*.

The IDE connector on motherboards in many systems is nothing more than a "stripped down" bus slot. In ATA-IDE installations, these connectors contain a 40-pin subset of the 98 pins that would be available in a standard 16-bit ISA bus slot. The pins used are only the signal pins required by a standard type XT or AT hard disk controller. For example, because an AT style disk controller uses only interrupt line 14, the motherboard AT IDE connector supplies only that interrupt line; no other interrupt lines are needed. The XT IDE motherboard connector supplies interrupt line 5 because that is what an XT controller would use.

Many people who use systems with IDE connectors on the motherboard believe that a hard disk controller is built into their motherboard, but the controller is really in the drive. I do not know of any PC systems with hard disk controllers built into the motherboard.

When discussing IDE drives, usually the ATA-IDE variety is all that is mentioned, because it is so popular, however other forms of IDE drives do exist, based on other buses. For example, several PS/2 systems came with Micro Channel (MCA) IDE drives, which plug directly into a Micro Channel bus slot (through an angle adapter or Interposer card). An 8-bit ISA form of IDE exists also, but was never very popular. Most IBM-compatible systems with the ISA or EISA bus use AT-bus (16-bit) IDE drives. The ATA-IDE interface is by far the most popular type of drive interface available. A pinout chart showing the standard signals on the different IDE connectors (including ATA) is shown in the Appendix.

The primary advantage of IDE drives is cost. By eliminating the separate controller or host adapter and simplifying the cable connections, IDE drives cost much less than a standard controller-and-drive combination. They also have increased reliability because

III

Hardware Considerations

the controller is built into the drive. Therefore, the endec or *data separator* (the divisor between the digital and analog signals on the drive) keeps close to the media. Because the drive has a short analog signal path, it is less susceptible to external noise and interference.

Another advantage is performance. IDE drives are some of the highest performance drives that are available, but they are also some of the lowest. This apparent contradiction is a result of the fact that all IDE drives are different. You cannot make a blanket statement about performance with IDE drives because each one is unique. The high end models, however, do offer performance that is equal or superior to any other type of drive on the market for a single user single tasking operating system.

The biggest drawback to the IDE interface is capacity and expandability. IDE drives are not suited to bigger, high-performance systems requiring large-capacity, high-performance drives. Incompatibilities among different manufacturers' standards make it difficult to install more than one IDE drive on a system. Because the controller is mounted on the drive, to add a second drive you must disable its controller and have it use the controller on the first drive. This process can be difficult because of the many different kinds of controllers on the drives. In many cases, to add an IDE second drive you must use one from the same manufacturer as the first, for compatibility.

An additional drawback to IDE drives is that they are normally locked into a specific type of bus. You cannot easily move IDE drives of one type to a system that does not have the corresponding type of bus. Also, IDE drives are specific to IBM-compatible systems, and cannot be used in foreign environments such as the Apple Macintosh systems, UNIX systems, or other computing environments. Because of these drawbacks, I normally use SCSI drives myself, but for many situations IDE is the logical choice for others.

IDE Origins. Technically, the very first IDE drives were Hardcards. Companies like the Plus Development division of Quantum took small 3 1/5-inch drives (either ST-506/412 or ESDI) and attached them directly to a standard controller. The assembly was then plugged into a bus slot as if it were a normal disk controller. Unfortunately, the mounting of a heavy, vibrating hard disk in an expansion slot with nothing but a single screw to hold it in left a lot to be desired, not to mention the possibility of interference with adjacent cards due to the fact that many of these units were much thicker than a controller card alone.

Several companies got the idea that you could redesign the controller to replace the logic board assembly on a standard hard disk, and then mount it in a standard drive bay just like any other drive. Because the built-in controller in these drives still needed to plug directly into the expansion bus just like any other controller, a cable was run between the drive and one of the slots.

These connection problems were solved in different ways. COMPAQ was the first to incorporate a special bus adapter in their system to adapt the 98-pin AT bus edge connector on the motherboard to a smaller 40-pin header style connector that the drive would plug into. Forty pins were all that was needed, since it was known that a disk controller would never need more than 40 of the bus lines. In 1987, IBM developed their own MCA

IDE drives and connected them to the bus through a bus adapter device called an interposer card. These bus adapters (sometimes called paddle boards) only needed a few buffer chips, and did not require any real circuitry, since the drive based controller was designed to plug directly into the bus. Another 8-bit variation of IDE appeared in 8-bit ISA systems like the PS/2 Model 30. The XT IDE interface uses a 40-pin connector and cable similar to, but not compatible with the 16-bit version.

IDE Bus versions. There are three main types of IDE interfaces, with differences based on three different bus standards:

- AT Attachment (ATA) IDE (16-bit ISA)

- XT IDE (8-bit ISA)

- MCA IDE (16-bit Micro Channel)

The XT and ATA versions have both standardized on 40-pin connectors and cables, but the connectors have slightly different pinouts, rendering them incompatible with one another. MCA IDE uses a completely different 72-pin connector and is designed for MCA bus systems only.

In most cases you must use the type of IDE drive which matches your system bus. This means that XT IDE drives work only in XT-class 8-bit ISA slot systems, AT IDE drives work only in AT-class 16-bit ISA or EISA slot systems, and MCA IDE drives work only in Micro Channel systems (such as the IBM PS/2 Model 50 or higher). A company called Silicon Valley offers adapter cards for XT systems that will run ATA-IDE drives. Other companies like Arco Electronics and Sigma Data have IDE adapters for Micro Channel systems that allow ATA-IDE drives to be used on these systems. You can find these vendors in the vendor list in the Appendix. These adapters are very useful for XT or PS/2 systems, because there is a very limited selection of XT or MCA IDE drives, while the selection of ATA drives is virtually unlimited.

In most modern ISA and EISA systems, you will find an ATA connector on the motherboard. If your motherboard does not have one of these connectors and you wish to attach an AT IDE drive to your system, you can purchase an adapter card that changes your 98-pin slot connector into the 40-pin IDE connector. These adapter cards are nothing more than buffered cables; they are not really controllers. The controller is built into the drive. Some of them do offer additional features such as an on-board ROM BIOS or cache memory.

ATA-IDE. CDC, Western Digital, and COMPAQ actually created what could be called the first ATA type IDE interface drive and were the first to establish the 40-pin IDE connector pinout. The first ATA-IDE drives were 5 1/4-inch half-height CDC 40M units (I believe they had a green activity LED) with integrated WD controllers sold in the first Compaq 386 systems way back in '86. After that, COMPAQ helped to found a company called Conner Peripherals to supply them exclusively with IDE drives. Conner originally made drives only for COMPAQ, but later COMPAQ sold much of their ownership of Conner.

III

Hardware Considerations

Eventually, the 40-pin IDE connector and drive interface method was put before one of the ANSI standards committees, who in conjunction with drive manufacturers, ironed out some deficiencies, tightened up some loose ends, and published what is known as the CAM ATA (Common Access Method AT Attachment) interface. The CAM Committee was formed in October, 1988 and the first working document of the AT Attachment interface was introduced in March 1989. Before the CAM ATA standard many companies who followed CDC, such as Conner Peripherals, made proprietary changes to what had been done by CDC. This is why many older ATA drives are very difficult to integrate in a dual-drive setup with newer drives.

There are still some areas of the ATA standard left open for vendor-specific commands and functions. These vendor specific commands and functions are the biggest reason that it is so difficult to low-level format IDE drives. To work properly, the formatter you are using must usually know the specific vendor-unique commands to allow rewriting sector headers and for remapping defects. Unfortunately, these as well as other specific drive commands will differ from OEM to OEM, thus clouding the "standard" somewhat.

It is important to notice that only the ATA-IDE interface has been standardized on by the industry. The XT IDE and MCA IDE were never adopted as industry wide standards, and never became very popular. They are no longer in production, and I am aware of no new systems that come with these non-standard IDE interfaces.

The CAM ATA Specification. The ATA specification was first introduced in March of 1989 by the ANSI CAM committee. The current working draft version of this standard is X3T9.2/791D Rev 4a, and can be obtained from Global Engineering Documents, who is listed in the Appendix. This standard has gone a long way in helping to eliminate incompatibilities and problems with interfacing IDE drives to ISA and EISA systems. The ATA specification defines the signals on the 40-pin connector, the functions and timings of these signals, cable specifications, and so on. The following section lists some of the elements and functions defined by the CAM ATA specification.

Dual Drive Configurations. Dual-drive ATA installations can be problematic because each drive has its own controller and they must both function while being connected to the same bus. There has to be a way to insure that only one of the two controllers will respond to a command at a time.

The ATA standard provides the option of operating on the AT Bus with two drives in a daisy chained configuration. The primary drive (Drive 0) is also referred to as the Master, while the secondary drive (Drive 1) is normally referred to as the Slave. Control over the designation of a drive as Master or Slave may be made by setting a jumper or switch on the drive, or by use of a special line in the interface called the Cable Select (CSEL) pin.

When only one drive is installed, the controller responds to all commands from the system. When two drives (and therefore two controllers) are installed, all commands from the system are received by both controllers. Each controller must then be set up to respond only to commands for itself. In this situation, one of them must be designated as the Master and the other as the Slave. When the system sends a command for a specific drive, the controller on the other drive must remain silent while the selected controller and drive are functioning. Discrimination between the two controllers is handled by setting a special bit (the DRV bit) in the Drive/Head Register of a command block.

ATA I/O Connector. The ATA interface connector is defined as a 40-pin header type connector that should be keyed to prevent the possibility of installing it upside down. A key is provided by the removal of Pin 20, and the corresponding pin on the cable connector should be plugged so as to prevent a backwards installation. The use of keyed connectors and cables is highly recommended, because plugging an IDE cable in backwards can possibly damage both the drive and the bus adapter circuits, although I have done it many times myself with no smoked parts yet!

ATA I/O Cable. A 40-conductor ribbon cable is specified to carry signals between the bus adapter circuits and the drive (controller). To maximize signal integrity and eliminate potential timing and noise problems, the cable should not be longer than a maximum length of 0.46m (18 inches).

ATA Signals. The ATA interface signals and connector pinout are listed in the Appendix. Some of the most important signals are described in more detail here.

Pin 20 is used as a key pin for cable orientation and is not connected through in the interface. This pin should be missing from any ATA connectors, and the cable should have the pin-20 hole in the connector plugged off to prevent the cable from being plugged in backwards.

Pin 39 carries the Drive Active/Slave Present (-DASP) signal. This is a dual purpose signal that is time multiplexed. During power on initialization it is used to indicate whether a Slave drive is present on the interface. After that, each drive asserts the signal to indicate that it is active. Early drives were not able to multiplex these functions and required special jumper settings to work with other drives. Standardizing this function to allow for compatible dual-drive installations is one of the features of the ATA standard.

Pin 28 carries the Cable Select or Spindle Synchronization signal (CSEL or SPSYNC). This is a dual-purpose conductor; however, a given installation may only use one of the two functions. The CSEL (Cable Select) function is the most widely used, and is designed to control the designation of a drive as Master (Drive 0) or Slave (Drive 1) without requiring jumper settings on the drives. If a drive sees the CSEL as grounded, the drive is a Master, while if CSEL is open then the drive is a Slave. Special cabling can be installed to selectively ground CSEL. This is normally accomplished with a "Y" cable arrangement, with the IDE bus connector in the middle, and each drive at opposite ends of the cable. One leg of the "Y" has the CSEL line connected through (indicating a Master drive), while the other leg has the CSEL line opened (conductor interrupted or removed) making the drive at that end appear as the Slave.

ATA Commands. One of the best features of the ATA-IDE interface is the enhanced command set. The ATA-IDE interface was modeled after the WD1003 controller used by IBM in the original AT system. All ATA-IDE drives must support the original WD command set (8 commands) with no exceptions, which is why IDE drives are so easy to install in systems today. All IBM compatible systems have built-in ROM BIOS support for the WD1003, which means that essentially they support ATA-IDE as well.

In addition to supporting all of the WD1003 commands, the ATA specification has added numerous other commands to enhance performance and capabilities. These commands are an optional part of the ATA interface, but several of them are used by the majority of drives. Several of these are very important to the performance and use of ATA drives.

Perhaps the most important is the *Identify Drive* command. This command causes the drive to transmit a 512 byte block of data which details all kinds of information about the drive. Through this command, any program (including the system BIOS) can find out exactly what type of drive is connected, including the drive Manufacturer, Model number, operating parameters, and even the serial number of the drive. Many modern BIOSes use this information to automatically receive and enter the drive's parameters into CMOS memory, eliminating the need for the user to manually enter these parameters during system configuration. This helps to prevent mistakes that can later lead to data loss when the user no longer remembers what parameters he/she used during setup.

The Identify Drive data can tell you many things about your drive, including the following:

- Number of Cylinders in the recommended (default) translation mode.
- Number of Heads in the recommended (default) translation mode.
- Number of Sectors Per Track in the recommended (default) translation mode.
- Number of Cylinders in the current translation mode.
- Number of Heads in the current translation mode.
- Number of Sectors Per Track in the current translation mode.
- Manufacturer and Model Number.
- Firmware Revision.
- Serial Number.
- Buffer Type indicating sector buffering or caching capabilities.

There are a number of public domain programs that can execute this command to the drive and report the information on-screen. I use the IDEINFO program which can be downloaded from the IBM Hardware Special Interest Group (SIG) on CompuServe, or the IDEDIAG utility that can be downloaded from the Western Digital BBS. Phone numbers for these information services are listed in the vendor list in the Appendix. I find these programs especially useful when I am trying to install IDE drives and I need to know the correct parameters for a user-definable BIOS type. These programs get the information right from the drive itself.

Two other very important commands are the Read Multiple and Write Multiple commands. These allow multiple-sector data transfers and can result in incredible data-transfer rates, many times faster than single-sector PIO transfers, when combined with block mode Programmed I/O (PIO) capabilities on the system.

> ### Tip
>
> If you want the ultimate in IDE performance and installation ease, make sure that your motherboard BIOS goes beyond supporting just the WD1003 command set, and that it also supports block mode Programmed I/O (PIO) and the Identify Drive commands. This will allow your BIOS to execute data transfers to and from the IDE drive several times faster than normal, and will also ease installation and configuration because the BIOS will be able to "auto detect" the drive-parameter information. Block PIO and Auto Detection of the drive type are two features found in the latest versions of the AMI, MR, and Phoenix BIOS.

There are many other enhanced commands, including room for a drive manufacturer to implement what are called *vendor-unique commands*. A particular vendor often uses such commands for features unique to that vendor. Things like low-level formatting and defect management are often controlled with vendor-unique commands. This is why low-level format programs can be so specific to a particular manufacturer's IDE drives, and why many manufacturers make their own LLF programs available.

ATA-IDE Drive Categories. ATA-IDE drives can be divided into three main categories. These categories separate the drives by functionality, such as translation capabilities, and by design, which can affect things such as low-level formatting. The three drive types are:

- Nonintelligent ATA-IDE drives.

- Intelligent ATA-IDE drives.

- Intelligent Zone Recorded ATA-IDE drives.

The following sections describe these drive types.

Non-Intelligent IDE. As I stated earlier, the ATA standard requires that the built-in controller respond exactly as if it were a Western Digital WD1003 controller. Such a controller responds to a command set of eight total commands. Early IDE drives supported these commands and had few if any other options. These early drives were actually more like regular ST-506/412 or ESDI controllers bolted directly to the drive, rather than the more intelligent drives considered today as IDE.

These drives were not considered intelligent IDE drives. An intelligent drive is supposed to have several capabilities which these early IDE drives lacked. One is that they could not respond to any of the enhanced commands that were specified as (an optional) part of the ATA-IDE specification. This included the Identify Drive command among others. These drives also did not support sector translation, where the physical parameters could be altered to appear as any set of logical cylinders, heads, and sectors. Enhanced commands and sector-translation support are what makes an IDE drive an intelligent IDE drive; these features were lacking in the early IDE drives.

III

Hardware Considerations

These drives could be low-level formatted in the same manner as any normal ST-506/412 or ESDI drive. They were universally low-level formatted at the factory with factory-calculated optimum interleave (usually 1:1) and head and cylinder skew factors. Also, factory defects were recorded in a special area on the drive and no longer written on a sticker pasted to the exterior. Unfortunately, this meant that if you low-level formatted these drives in the field, you would most likely alter these settings (especially the skew factors) from what the factory had set as optimum, as well as wipe out the factory-written defect table. Some manufacturers released special low-level format routines that reformatted the drives while preserving these settings, but others did not make such programs available. Because they did not want you to overwrite the defect list, or potentially slow down the drive, most manufacturers stated that you should never low-level format their IDE drives.

This started a myth that you could somehow damage these drives or render them inoperable by attempting such a format, which is not truly the case. One rumor was that the servo information could be overwritten, which means that you would have to send the drive back to the manufacturer for re-servoing. This is also not true, as the servo information is completely protected and cannot be overwritten. The only consequences of an improper low-level format to these drives was the possible alteration of the skew factors and loss of the factory defect maps.

The Disk Manager program by Ontrack is the best special-purpose format utility to use on these drives because it is aware of these types of drives and can often restore the skew factors and preserve the defect information. If you are working with a drive that has already had the defect map overwritten, Disk Manager can do a very good surface analysis that marks off any of these areas it finds. Disk Manager allows you to specify the skew factors and to mark defects at the sector level so they will not cause problems later. Other general-purpose diagnostics that work especially well with IDE drives include the Microscope program by Micro 2000.

Intelligent IDE. Later IDE drives became known as intelligent IDE drives. These drives support enhanced ATA commands, such as the Identify Drive command, and sector-translation capabilities.

These drives can be configured two ways, either in raw physical mode or in translation mode. To configure the drive in raw physical mode, you simply enter the CMOS drive parameters during setup so that they exactly match the true physical parameters of the drive. For example, if the drive physically has 800 cylinders, 6 heads, and 50 sectors per track, these figures are what you enter during setup.

To configure the drive in translation mode, you simply enter any combination of cylinders, heads, and sectors such that they add up to equal to or less than the true number of sectors on the drive. In the example I just used, the drive has a total of 240,000 sectors (800*6*50). All I have to do is figure out another set of parameters that adds up to equal to or less than 240,000 sectors. The simplest way to do this is to cut the number of cylinders in half and double the number of heads. Thus the new drive parameters become 400 cylinders, 12 heads, and 50 sectors per track. This also adds up to 240,000 sectors and allows the drive to work in translation mode.

When these drives are in translation mode, a low-level format cannot alter the interleave and skew factors, nor can it overwrite the factory defect-mapping information; however, a low-level format program can still perform additional defect mapping or sector sparing while in this mode.

If the drive is in true physical mode, a low-level format rewrites the sector headers and modifies the head and cylinder skewing. If done incorrectly, this can be repaired by a proper low-level format program that allows you to set the correct head and cylinder skew. This can also be automatically accomplished by the drive manufacturer's own recommended low-level format program (if available) or by other programs, such as Disk Manager by Ontrack. When using Disk Manager, you have to enter the skew values manually, or the program uses predetermined defaults. To get the correct skew values, it is best to contact the drive manufacturer's technical support department. You can also calculate the skew values if the manufacturer cannot provide them.

To protect the skew factors and defect information on intelligent IDE drives, all you have to do with these intelligent drives is run them in translation mode. In translation mode, this information cannot be overwritten.

Intelligent Zone Recorded IDE. The last and most sophisticated IDE drives combine intelligence with *zoned recording*. With zoned recording, the drive has a variable number of sectors per track in several zones across the surface of the drive. Because the PC BIOS can only handle a fixed number of sectors on all tracks, these drives must always run in translation mode. Because these drives are always in translation mode, you can never alter the factory-set interleave and skew factors, nor can you wipe out the factory defect information. You can still low-level format these drives, however, and use such a format to map or spare out additional defective sectors that crop up during the life of the drive. To low-level format these intelligent zone-recorded drives, you need either a specific utility from the drive manufacturer, or one that is IDE-aware, like Disk Manager by Ontrack or Microscope by Micro 2000.

IDE Drive Configuration. IDE (Integrated Drive Electronics) drives can be both simple and troublesome to configure. Single-drive installations are usually very simple, with very few, if any, special jumper settings to worry about. Multiple-drive configurations, however, can often be a problem as jumpers have to be set on both drives, and the names, locations, and even functions of these jumpers can vary from drive to drive. Because the CAM ATA (Common Access Method AT Attachment) IDE specification was ironed out only after many companies had already been making and selling drives, many older IDE drives will have problems in dual-drive installations. This is especially true with drives from different manufacturers. In some cases, it may not be possible to have two particular drives function together at all. Fortunately, most of the newer drives do follow the CAM ATA specification, which clears up this area. Drives that do follow the specification have no problems in dual-drive installations.

Cable Configuration. The cable connection to IDE drives is usually very simple. There is a single 40-pin cable that normally has three pin-header style connectors on it. One of the connectors plugs into the IDE interface connector, and the two others plug into primary and secondary drives. The cable normally runs from the IDE connector to both drives in a daisy-chain arrangement. On one end, this cable plugs into the IDE interface connector, which is located on the motherboard in many systems, but may also be located on an IDE interface adapter card. The cable then connects to both the secondary (D) and primary (C) drives in succession, with the primary drive usually (but not always) at the other end of the cable, opposite the IDE interface connector. There are no terminating resistors to set with IDE drives; instead, a distributed termination circuit is built into all IDE drives. There is no requirement that the last drive on the cable be the primary drive, so you may actually find the primary or secondary drive at either connector. Jumpers on the drives themselves normally control whether a drive responds as primary or secondary.

You may see a different arrangement of cable connections in some IDE installations. There are some installations where the middle connector is plugged into the motherboard and then the primary and secondary drives are at opposite ends of the cable in a "Y" arrangement. If you see this, be careful; in some of these "Y" cable installations, the cable, rather than jumpers on the drives, actually controls which drive is primary and secondary. This is based off of a special signal on the IDE interface called CSEL (Cable SELect), which is on pin 28 of the interface. If the CSEL line is connected through from the drive to the IDE interface connector, the drive is automatically designated as primary. If the CSEL line is open between a drive and the IDE interface connector, that drive is automatically designated as secondary. With the "Y" cable approach, the IDE interface connector is in the middle of the cable, and a separate length of cable goes to each drive. Study this type of cable closely: if one of the ends of the "Y" has line 28 open (usually a hole in the cable through that wire), only the secondary drive can be plugged into that connector. HP Vectra PC systems use exactly this type of IDE cable arrangement. This type of setup eliminates the need to set jumpers on the IDE drives to configure them for primary or secondary operation, but can be troublesome if you do not know about it.

IDE Drive Jumper Settings. Configuring IDE drives can be simple, as is the case with most single-drive installations, or troublesome, especially when it comes to mixing two different drives on a single cable.

There are basically three different configurations for most IDE drives. These are the following:

- Single drive (master)
- Master (dual drive)
- Slave (dual drive)

Because each IDE drive brings with it its own controller, you must specifically tell one drive to be the master and the other to be the slave. There's no functional difference between the two except that the drive that's specified to be the slave will assert the DASP signal after a system reset, which informs the master that a slave drive is present in the system. The master drive then pays attention to the drive select line which is otherwise ignored. Telling a drive that it's the slave also usually causes it to delay its spinup for several seconds to allow the master to get going, which lessens the load on the system's power supply.

Until the ATA-IDE specification, there was no common implementation for drive configuration in use. Some drive companies even used different master/slave methods among their different models of drives. Because of these incompabilities, some drives work together only in a specific master/slave or slave/master order. This affects mostly older IDE drives that were introduced before the ATA specification.

Most drives that fully follow the ATA specification now only need one jumper (Master/Slave) for configuration. A few also need a Slave Present jumper as well. Table 10.9 shows the jumper settings required by most ATA-IDE drives.

Table 10.9 Jumper Settings for Most ATA-IDE-Compatible Drives			
Jumper Name	**Single Drive**	**Dual Drive Master**	**Dual Drive Slave**
Master (M/S)	On	On	Off
Slave Present (SP)	Off	On	Off

The Master jumper indicates that the drive is a master or slave. Some drives also require a Slave Present jumper, which is used only in a dual-drive setup, and then only installed on the master drive, which is somewhat confusing. This jumper lets the master know that a slave drive is also attached. With many ATA-IDE drives, the Master jumper is optional and may be left off. It does not hurt to install it in these cases, and it may eliminate confusion; so I recommend that you install the jumpers where listed here.

Conner Peripherals Drives. Because they were introduced before the ATA-IDE specification was formalized, Conner Peripherals drives are often different in configuration than many other brand drives. When mixing and matching IDE hard drives from different manufacturers, they are not always fully compatible with others. Table 10.10 shows the jumper settings that are correct for most Conner IDE drive installations.

Table 10.10 Jumper Settings for Conner Peripherals IDE Drives			
Jumper Name	**Single Drive**	**Dual Drive Master**	**Dual Drive Slave**
Master or Slave (C/D)	On	On	Off
Drive Slave Present (DSP)	Off	On	Off
Host Slave Present (HSP)	Off	Off	On
Drive Active (ACT)	On	On	Off

The C/D jumper is used to determine whether the drive is a master (drive C) or a slave (drive D). The drive is configured as master when this jumper is on. The DSP jumper indicates that a slave drive is present. The HSP jumper causes the drive to send the Slave Present signal to the master drive. The ACT jumper allows the master drive to signal when it is active.

III

Hardware Considerations

Some Conner drives are not set up to support the industry-standard CAM ATA (Common Access Method AT Attachment) interface by default. The problems show up when you attempt to connect another manufacturer's drive to some Conner drives in either a master or slave role. Fortunately many of these situations can be corrected by changing the configuration of the drive. There are two ways to do this. One is to use a special program to semipermanently change the mode of the drive. Conner has a special file available on their BBS called CAM-ISA.ZIP that contains a program which displays the current ISA/CAM setting and allows the setting to be changed. The change is actually stored in a feature byte in the firmware of the drive, and after this byte is changed, most other manufacturers' drives then work with the Conner drives. The program can also be used to reset the feature byte back to its original configuration, which is best when connecting to other Conner drives.

Some Conner drives also have a special jumper called ATA/ISA. This jumper should almost always be installed in the ATA position to enable compatibility with the ATA standard. If only Conner drives are being used, you can leave it in ISA mode. Some Conner drives also have a separate jumper (E1) that can delay startup of the drive to minimize the load on the power supply. This should be enabled on any drive configured as a slave. Most other drives automatically delay startup of the slave drive for a few seconds.

Most Conner drives also have a special 12-pin connector that is used to drive an optional LED (pin 1=LED +5v and pin 2=Ground), as well as to connect to special factory equipment for low-level formatting and configuration. A company called TCE (see the vendor list in the Appendix) sells a hardware and software product called "The Conner," which connects to this port and allows full factory-level initialization, formatting, and testing of Conner drives. I would consider this piece of gear essential to anybody who services or supports a large number of Conner Peripherals drives. Note that COMPAQ uses Conner drives in most of its systems.

For more information on any specific Conner drive, you can use the company's FaxBack system at (800) 4CONNER. Through this system, you can get drive information and jumper settings specific to Conner drives.

XT (8-bit) IDE. Many systems with XT ISA bus architecture used XT IDE hard drives. The IDE interface in these systems is usually built into the motherboard. The IBM PS/2 Model 25, 25-286, 30, and 30-286 systems used an 8-bit XT IDE interface. These 8-bit XT IDE drives are difficult to find because few manufacturers other than IBM, Western Digital, and Seagate made them; and none were available in capacities beyond 40M.

Note that the newer PS/1, PS/Valuepoint, and PS/2 systems with 16-bit ISA architecture all use ATA-IDE drives. Because nearly all hard disk manufacturers make a multitude of drives with the ATA-IDE interface, these systems are easy to upgrade or repair. ATA-IDE drives are available in capacities up to and beyond 1 gigabyte.

MCA IDE. The IBM PS/2 Models 50 and higher come with Micro Channel Architecture (MCA) bus slots. Although now most of these systems use SCSI drives, for some time IBM used a type of MCA IDE drive in these systems. This is a form of IDE interface, but is designed for the MCA bus and is not compatible with the more industry-standard

ATA-IDE interface. Few companies other than IBM and Western Digital make replacement MCA IDE drives for these systems. I recommend replacing these drives with either ATA-IDE drives using adapters from Arco Electronics or Sigma Data, or switching to SCSI drives instead. The IBM MCA IDE drives are expensive for the limited capacity they offer.

Introduction to SCSI

SCSI (pronounced "scuzzy") stands for *Small Computer System Interface*. This interface has its roots in SASI, the *Shugart Associates System Interface*. SCSI is not a disk interface, but a system-level interface. It is not a type of controller, but instead is a bus that supports as many as eight separate devices. One of these devices is a *host adapter* and functions as the gateway between the SCSI bus and the PC system bus. The SCSI bus itself does not talk directly with devices like hard disks, but instead talks to the controller that is built into the drive.

A single SCSI bus can support as many as 8 *physical units*, usually called SCSI IDs. One of these is the adapter card in your PC; the other 7 can be other peripherals. You could have hard disks, tape drives, CD-ROM drives, a graphics scanner, or other devices (up to 7 in total) attached to a single SCSI host adapter. Most systems support up to 4 host adapters, each with 7 devices for a total of 28 devices!

When you purchase a SCSI hard disk, you usually are purchasing the drive, controller, and SCSI adapter in one circuit. This type of drive usually is called an *embedded SCSI drive*; the SCSI interface is built into the drive. Most SCSI hard drives are actually IDE drives with SCSI bus adapter circuits added. You do not need to know what type of controller is inside the SCSI drive, because your system cannot talk directly to the controller, as though it were plugged into the system bus like a standard controller. Instead, communications go through the SCSI host adapter installed in the system bus. You can access the drive only with the SCSI protocols.

Apple originally rallied around SCSI as an inexpensive way out of the bind it put itself in with the Macintosh. When the engineers at Apple realized the problem in making the Macintosh a closed system (with no slots), they decided that the easiest way to gain expandability was to build a SCSI port into the system, which is how external peripherals can be added to the slotless Macs. Because PC systems always have been expandable, the push toward SCSI has not been as urgent. With eight bus slots supporting different devices and controllers in IBM and IBM-compatible systems, it seemed as if SCSI was not needed.

SCSI is now becoming popular in the IBM-based computer world because of the great expandability it offers and the number of devices available with built-in SCSI. One thing that stalled acceptance of SCSI in the PC marketplace was the lack of a real standard: the SCSI standard has been designed primarily by a committee. No single manufacturer has led the way, at least in the IBM arena; each has its own interpretation of how SCSI should be implemented, particularly at the host adapter level.

SCSI is a standard, in much the same way that RS-232 is a standard. The SCSI standard (like the RS-232 standard) defines only the hardware connections, not the driver specifications required to communicate with the devices. Software ties the SCSI subsystem into your PC, but unfortunately most of the driver programs work only for a specific device and a specific host adapter. For example, a graphics scanner comes with its own SCSI host adapter to connect to the system, and a CD-ROM drive comes with another (different) SCSI host adapter and driver software that works only with that SCSI adapter. On a system with those two SCSI adapters, you would need a third SCSI host adapter to run SCSI hard disk drives because the host adapters supplied by the scanner and CD-ROM companies do not include a built-in, self-booting BIOS that supports hard disk drives. SCSI has become somewhat of a mess in the IBM world because of the lack of a host adapter standard, a software interface standard, and standard ROM BIOS support for hard disk drives attached to the SCSI bus. Fortunately, there are some simple recommendations that can keep you from living this compatibility nightmare!

The lack of capability to run hard disks off the SCSI bus and to boot from these drives and use a variety of operating systems is a problem that results from the lack of an interface standard. The standard IBM XT and AT ROM BIOS software was designed to talk to ST-506/412 hard disk controllers. The software easily was modified to work with ESDI because ESDI controllers are similar to ST-506/412 controllers at the register level. (This similarity at the register level enabled manufacturers to easily design self-booting, ROM-BIOS-supported ESDI drives.) The same can be said of IDE, which completely emulates the WD1003 ST-506/412 controller interface and works perfectly with the existing BIOS as well. SCSI is so different from these other standard disk interfaces that a new set of ROM BIOS routines is necessary to support the system so that it can self-boot. The newer IBM PS/2 systems that come with SCSI drives include this support built into the motherboard BIOS or as an extension BIOS on the SCSI host adapter.

Companies such as Adaptec and Future Domain have produced SCSI cards with built-in ROM BIOS support for several years, but these BIOS routines were limited to running the drives under DOS only. The BIOS would not run in the AT-protected mode, and other operating systems included drivers for only the standard ST-506/412 and ESDI controllers. Thus, running SCSI was impossible under many non-DOS operating systems. This has changed significantly because IBM is now supporting many third-party SCSI host adapters in OS/2, especially those from Adaptec and Future Domain. For compatibility reasons, I usually recommend using SCSI adapters from these two companies, or any others which are fully hardware compatible with the Adaptec or Future Domain adapters.

Because of the lead taken by Apple in developing systems software (operating systems and ROM) support for SCSI, peripherals connect to Apple systems in fairly standard ways. Until recently, this kind of standard-setting leadership was lacking for SCSI in the IBM world. This changed on March 20, 1990, however, because IBM introduced several "standard" SCSI adapters and peripherals for the IBM PS/2 systems, with complete ROM BIOS and full operating system support.

IBM has standardized on SCSI for nearly all of its high-end systems. In these systems, a SCSI host adapter card is in one of the slots, or the system has a SCSI host adapter built into the motherboard. This seems to be similar in appearance to the IDE interface because a single cable runs from the motherboard to the SCSI drive, but SCSI supports as many as seven different devices (some of which may not be hard disks); IDE supports only two devices, which must be either a hard disk or a tape drive. PS/2 systems with SCSI drives are easily upgradeable because virtually any third-party SCSI drive will plug in and function.

The example set by IBM is now causing others to supply systems with either SCSI host adapters or SCSI interfaces integrated into the motherboards, as well. As SCSI becomes more and more popular in the PC world, the SCSI peripheral integration will be easier due to better operating systems and device driver support.

ANSI SCSI standards. The SCSI standard defines the physical and electrical parameters of a parallel I/O bus used to interconnect computers and peripheral devices in a a daisy chained manner. Devices such as disk drives, tape drives, CD-ROM drives, and others are supported. Since the original SCSI standard (ANSI X3.131-1986) was approved in 1986, two new revisions, called SCSI-2 and SCSI-3, have been in development.

The SCSI interface is defined as a standard by ANSI (American National Standards Institute), an organization which approves and publishes standards. The X3 Task Group operates as an ASC (Accredited Standards Committee) under ANSI to develop Information Processing System standards. X3T9 is the I/O Interfaces group, and X3T9.2 specifically is in charge of low-level interfaces, such as SCSI and ATA-IDE (among others). The original SCSI-1 standard was published by the X3T9 ANSI group in 1986 and is officially published by ANSI as X3.131-1986.

One problem with the original SCSI-1 document was that many of the commands and features were optional, and there was little or no guarantee that a particular peripheral would support the expected commands. This caused the industry as a whole to define a set of 18 basic SCSI commands called the Common Command Set (CCS), which would become the minimum set of commands supported by all peripherals. This Common Command Set became the basis for what is now the SCSI-2 specification.

In addition to formal support for the CCS, SCSI-2 provided additional definitions for commands to access CD-ROM drives (and their sound abilities), tape drives, removable drives, optical drives, and several other peripherals. In addition, an optional higher speed called FAST SCSI-2 and a 16-bit version called WIDE SCSI-2 were defined as well. Another feature of SCSI-2 is command queuing, which allows a device to accept multiple commands and execute them in the order the device deems most efficient. This is most beneficial when using a multitasking operating system that can send several requests at once on the SCSI bus.

The X3T9 group originally approved the SCSI-2 standard in August 1990 as X3.131-1990; however, the document was recalled in December 1990 for changes before final ANSI publication. Final approval has not been made yet for the SCSI-2 document, although it has changed little from the original 1990 release. Most call the unfinished SCSI-2 document as ANSI X3.131-199X where the "X" will eventually be filled in with the year of approval. The last known revision goes under the working document name of X3T9.2/ 375R Rev 10k and is available from Global Engineering Documents, listed in the Appendix. Approval of this specification is expected very shortly.

III

Hardware Considerations

Most companies indicate that their host adapters follow the ANSI X3.131-1986 standard; however, most also comply fully with the 1990 (SCSI-2) standard as well, because they support the CCS and other SCSI-2 mandatory features.

Other optional parts of the SCSI-2 specification includes a fast synchronous mode that doubles the standard synchronous transfer rate from 5 to 10 megabytes per second (mbps). This Fast SCSI transfer mode can also be combined with 16-bit Wide or 32-bit Wide SCSI for transfer rates of up to 40 mbps. Currently, there are no 32-bit peripherals to speak of, and only a few 16-bit Wide SCSI devices and host adapters exist. Most SCSI implementations are 8-bit standard SCSI or Fast SCSI.

Table 10.11 shows the maximum transfer rates for the SCSI bus at various speeds and widths. Also listed is the cable type required for the specific transfer width.

> **Note**
>
> The A cable is the standard 50-pin SCSI cable, while the P and Q cables are 68-pin cables designed for 16-bit and 32-bit Wide SCSI. For 32-bit SCSI, both P and Q cables must be used together. Pinouts for these cable connections are listed in the Appendix.

Table 10.11 SCSI Data Transfer Rates

Bus Width	Std. SCSI	Fast SCSI	Cable Type
8-bit	5 mbps	10 mbps	A
16-bit	10 mbps	20 mbps	P
32-bit	20 mbps	40 mbps	P&Q

So-called SCSI-1 adapters have no problems with SCSI-2 peripherals; however, you can't take advantage of FAST transfers, WIDE transfers, although the extra commands defined in SCSI-2 can be sent using a SCSI-1 controller. For example, I am running a Toshiba MK-538FB 1.2G Fast SCSI-2 drive with my IBM SCSI Host Adapter, and it runs fine. Most adapters are similar in that they are actually SCSI-2 compatible, even if they advertise only SCSI-1 support. This is because no one can say they truly follow the SCSI-2 standard because it has not reached final publication yet. On the other hand, many other companies have been advertising SCSI-2 devices for some time, because in reality it has been published in prerelease form for several years.

SCSI Hard Disk Evolution and Construction. SCSI is not a disk interface, but a bus that supports SCSI bus interface adapters connected to disk and other device controllers. The first SCSI drives for PCs were simply standard ST-506/412 or ESDI drives with a separate SCSI bus interface adapter (sometimes called a "bridge controller") which converted the ST-506/412 or ESDI interfaces to SCSI. This was originally in the form of a secondary logic board, and the whole assembly was often mounted in an external case.

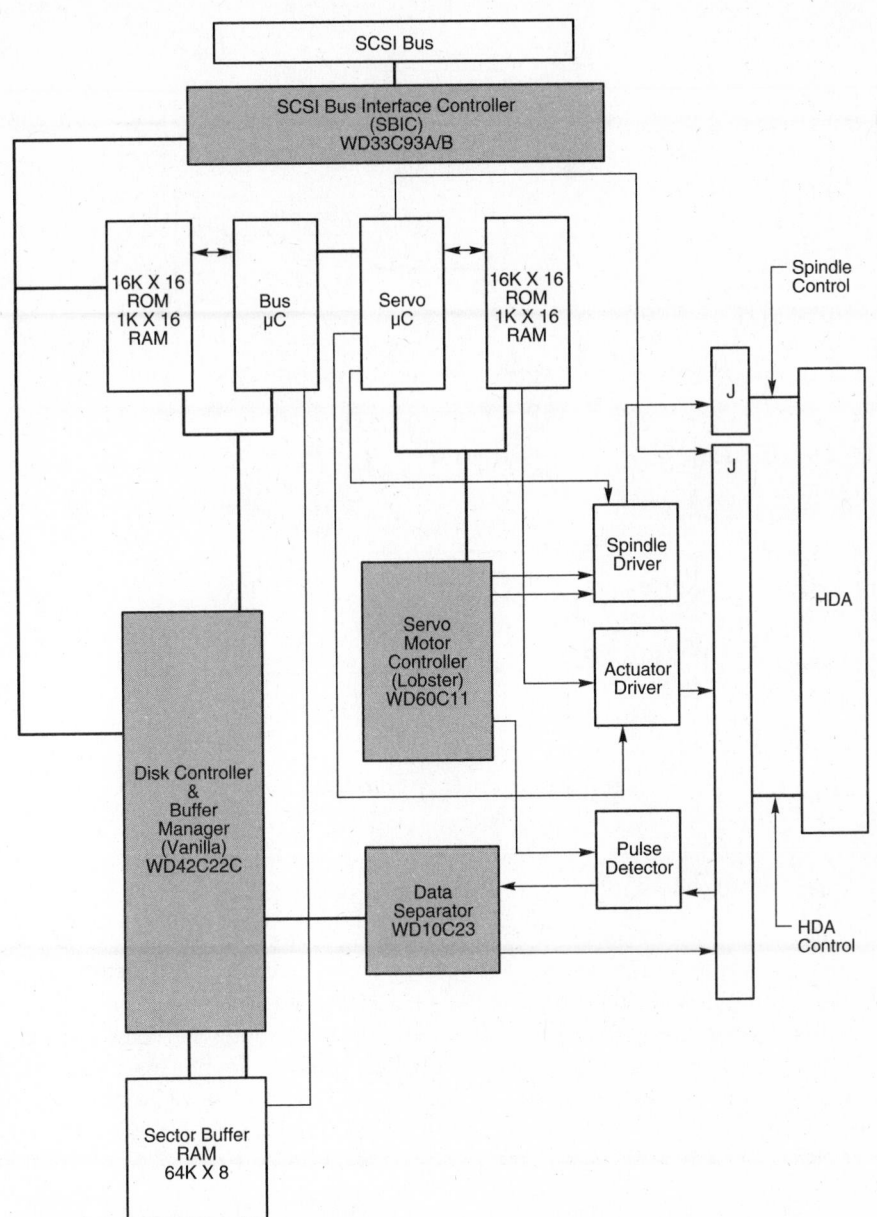

Fig. 10.16

Western Digital WD-SP4200 200M SCSI drive logic board block diagram.

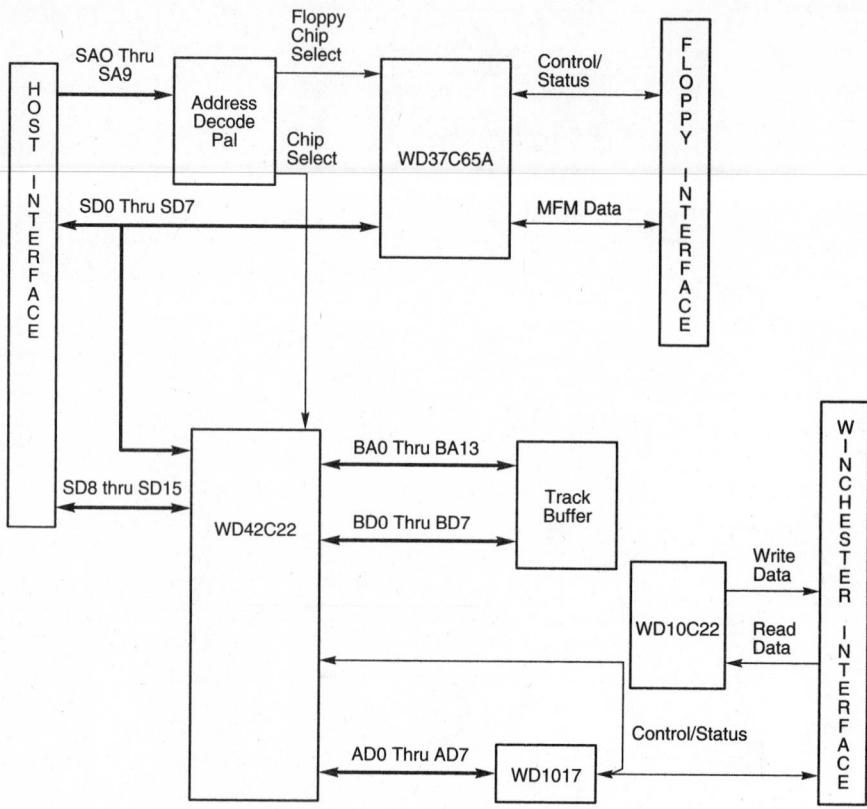

Fig. 10.17

Western Digital WD1006V-MM1 ST-506/412 disk controller block diagram.

You can clearly see that the main LSI chip on board is the same WD42C22 disk control-ler chip that was found in the IDE and SCSI drives. Here is what the WD technical refer-ence literature says about that chip: "The WD42C22 integrates a high performance, low cost Winchester controller's architecture. The WD42C22 integrates the central elements of a Winchester controller subsystem such as the host interface, buffer manager, disk formatter/controller, encoder/decoder, CRC/ECC (Cyclic Redundancy Check/Error Cor-rection Code) generator/checker, and drive interface into a single 84-pin PQFP (Plastic Quad Flat Pack) device."

This type of virtually identical design between ATA-IDE and SCSI drives is not unique to Western Digital. Most drive manufacturers design their ATA-IDE and SCSI drives the same way, often using these very same Western Digital chips as well as disk controller and SCSI bus interface chips from other manufacturers. You should now be able to un-derstand also that most SCSI drives are simply "regular" ATA-IDE drives with the SCSI bus logic added. This fact will come up again when discussing SCSI versus IDE perfor-mance issues.

In another example, I have several IBM 320M and 400M embedded SCSI-2 hard disks, and each of these drives has on board a WD-10C00 Programmable Disk Controller in the form of a 68-pin PLCC (Plastic Leaded Chip Carrier) chip. The WD technical literature states "This chip supports ST412, ESDI, SMD, and Optical interfaces. It has 27-Mbit/sec maximum transfer rate and an internal, fully programmable 48- or 32-bit ECC, 16-bit CRC-CCITT or external user defined ECC polynomial, fully programmable sector sizes and 1.25 micron low power CMOS design." In addition, these particular embedded SCSI drives also include the 33C93 SCSI Bus Interface Controller chip used in the other SCSI drive I mentioned previously. Again, there is a distinctly separate disk controller, and the SCSI interface is added on.

So again, what we have in most embedded SCSI drives is a built-in disk controller (usually based on previous ST-506/412 or ESDI designs), and then additional logic to interface that controller to the SCSI bus (a built-in bridge controller if you like). Now think about this from a performance standpoint. If virtually all SCSI drives are really ATA-IDE drives with a SCSI Bus Interface controller chip added, what conclusions can you draw? First, no drive can perform sustained data transfers faster than the data can actually be read off the disk platters. In other words, the HDA (Head Disk Assembly) limits performance to whatever it is capable of. Drives can transmit data in short bursts at very high speeds because they often have built-in cache or read-ahead buffers which store data. Many of the newer high-performance SCSI and ATA-IDE drives have 1M or more of cache memory on board! No matter how big or intelligent the cache is, however, sustained data transfer will still be limited by the HDA.

Data from the HDA must pass through the disk controller circuits, which are virtually identical between similar SCSI and ATA-IDE drives. In the ATA-IDE drive, this data is then presented directly to the system bus. In the SCSI drive, however, the data must pass through a SCSI Bus Interface adapter on the drive, travel the SCSI bus itself, and then pass through another SCSI Bus Interface controller in the SCSI host adapter card in your system. All of the extra path a SCSI transfer must take of course slows it down with respect to the much more direct ATA-IDE transfer.

The conventional wisdom has been that SCSI is always much faster than IDE, but unfortunately this is usually wrong! This incorrect conclusion was originally derived by looking at the raw SCSI and ISA bus performance capabilities. An 8-bit Fast SCSI-2 bus can transfer data at 10 million bytes per second, whereas the 16-bit ISA bus used directly by IDE drives can transfer data anywhere from 2 to 8 million bytes per second. Based on these raw transfer rates, it seems that SCSI is faster, but the raw transfer rate of the bus is not the limiting factor; instead, the actual HDA and disk controller circuitry place the limits on performance. Another point to remember is that unless you are using a VL-Bus, EISA, or 32-bit MCA SCSI adapter, the SCSI data transfer speeds will be limited by the host bus performance as well as the drive performance.

Single-Ended or Differential SCSI. "Normal" SCSI is also called "single-ended" SCSI. For each signal that needs to be sent across the bus, there exists a wire to carry it. With differential SCSI, for each signal that needs to be sent across the bus, there exists a pair of wires to carry it. The first in this pair carries the same type of signal the single-ended

SCSI carries. The second in this pair, however, carries the logical inversion of the signal. The receiving device takes the difference of the pair (thus the name differential), which makes it less susceptible to noise and allows for greater cable length. Because of this, differential SCSI can be used with cable lengths of up to 25 meters, whereas single-ended SCSI limits are 6 meters for standard SCSI, or only 3 meters for Fast SCSI.

You cannot mix single-ended and differential devices on a single SCSI bus, the results would be catastrophic. That is to say, you would probably see smoke! Because the cables and connectors are the same, this mistake is entirely possible to make. This is usually not a problem because there are very few differential SCSI implementations out there. Especially with SCSI in the PC environment, single-ended is about all you will ever see. If, however, you happen to come upon a peripheral that you believe might be differential, there are a few ways to tell. One is by looking for a special symbol on the unit. The industry has adopted different universal symbols for single-ended and differential SCSI. Figure 10.18 shows these symbols.

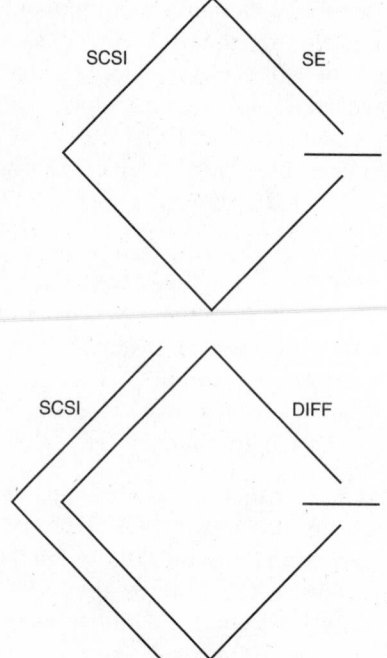

Fig. 10.18
Single-ended and differential SCSI universal symbols.

If you do not see such symbols, you can tell whether you have a differential device by using an ohm meter to check the resistance between pins 21 and 22 on the device connector. On a single-ended system, they should both be tied together and also tied to ground. On a differential device, they should be open or have a significant resistance between them. Again, this should not be a problem generally because virtually all devices used in the PC environment are single-ended.

SCSI-1 and SCSI-2. The SCSI-2 specification is basically an improved version of SCSI-1 with some parts of the specification tightened up and several new features and options added. Normally, SCSI-1 and SCSI-2 devices are compatible; however, the additional features found in SCSI-2 will be ignored by SCSI-1 devices.

Some of the changes in SCSI-2 are very minor. For example, SCSI-1 allowed SCSI bus parity to be optional; in SCSI-2, parity must be implemented. Another requirement is that initiator devices, such as host adapters, must provide terminator power to the interface, which most did already.

SCSI-2 also has several optional features such as the following:

- Fast SCSI
- Wide SCSI
- New Commands
- Command queuing
- High-density cable connectors
- Improved active termination

None of these features are absolutely required, but are optional under the SCSI-2 specification. For example, if you connect a standard SCSI host adapter to a Fast SCSI drive, the interface will work, but only at standard SCSI speeds.

Fast SCSI. Fast SCSI refers to a high-speed, synchronous transfer capability. Fast SCSI achieves a 10 megabyte per second transfer rate on the standard 8-bit SCSI cabling. When combined with a 16-bit or 32-bit Wide SCSI interface, this results in 20 or 40M per second.

Wide SCSI. Wide SCSI allows for parallel data transfer at bus widths of 16 and 32 bits. These wider connections required new cable designs. The standard 50-conductor, 8-bit cable is called the A-cable. SCSI-2 originally defined a special 68-conductor B-cable that was supposed to be used in conjunction with the A-cable for wide transfers, but this has been totally ignored by the industry in favor of a newer 68-conductor P-cable that was introduced as part of the SCSI-3 specification. The P-cable superseded the A-B-cable combination because the P-cable can be used alone (without the A cable) for 16-bit Wide SCSI.

32-bit Wide SCSI has not found popularity, and probably never will in the PC environment. Theoretically, 32-bit SCSI implementations would require two cables: a 68-conductor P-cable and a 68-conductor Q-cable.

Termination. The single-ended SCSI bus depends on very tight termination tolerances to function reliably. Unfortunately, the original 132-Ohm passive termination defined in the SCSI-1 document was not designed for use at the higher synchronous speeds now possible. These passive terminators can allow signal reflections to cause errors when

III

Hardware Considerations

transfer rates increase or when more devices are added to the bus. In SCSI-2, an active (voltage regulated) terminator has been defined that lowers termination impedance to 110 ohms and improves system integrity.

Command Queuing. In SCSI-1, an initiator device such as a host adapter was limited to sending one command per device. With SCSI-2, the host adapter can send as many as 256 commands to a single device, which will store them and process them internally before responding on the SCSI bus. The target device can even resequence the commands to allow for the most efficient execution or performance possible. This is especially useful in multitasking environments like OS/2 or Windows NT, which can really take advantage of this feature.

New Commands. SCSI-2 first took the Common Command Set that was being used throughout the industry and made it an official part of the standard. The CCS was mainly designed for disk drives, and did not include specific commands designed for other types of devices. SCSI-2 has reworked many of the old commands, and several new commands have been added. Complete new command sets have been added for CD-ROMs, optical drives, scanners, communications devices, and media changers (jukeboxes).

SCSI-3. Even though the SCSI-2 specification is not yet completely finalized (although it has remained stable for some time), the SCSI-3 specification is already being worked on. SCSI-3 will have everything that SCSI-2 has and definitely will add new commands, features, and implementations. For example, SCSI-3 will provide support for up to 32 devices on the bus instead of only 8.

One of the most exciting things about SCSI-3 is the proposed Serial SCSI, a scheme that will possibly use only a six-conductor cable and be able to transfer data at up to 100M per second! The switch to serial instead of parallel is to control propagation delay, noise, and termination problems that have plagued SCSI-2, as well as to greatly simplify the cable connection. Serial SCSI will be able to transfer more data over 6 wires than 32-bit Fast Wide SCSI-2 can over 128 wires! The intention is that Serial SCSI be implemented on the motherboard of future systems, which will give them incredible expansion and performance capabilities.

Although Serial SCSI may not make the older host adapters and cables obsolete overnight, it does make future cabling possibilities even more of a puzzle. Serial SCSI offers the possibility of longer cable lengths, less electromagnetic interference, and easier connections on laptops, notebooks, and docking stations. Expect SCSI-3 to offer almost pain-free installations with automatic SCSI ID setup and termination schemes.

SCSI Cables and Connectors. The SCSI standards are very specific when it comes to cables and connectors. The most common connectors specified in this standard are the 50-position, unshielded pin-header connector for internal SCSI connections, and the 50-position, shielded Centronics latch-style connectors for external connections. The shielded Centronics-style connector is also called "Alternative 2" in the official specification. Passive or Active termination (Active is preferred) are specified for both the single-ended and differential buses. The 50-conductor bus configuration has been defined as the A-cable in the SCSI-2 standard.

The SCSI-2 revision added a high-density, 50-position D-shell connector option for the A-cable connectors. This connector is now called Alternative 1. The Alternative 2 Centronics latch-style connector remained unchanged from SCSI-1. A 68-conductor B-cable specification was added to the SCSI-2 standard and provided for 16- and 32-bit data transfers; however, it had to be used in parallel with an A-cable. The industry did not widely accept the B-cable option, and it has been dropped from the SCSI-3 standard. To replace the ill-fated B-cable, a new 68-conductor P-cable was developed as a part of the SCSI-3 specification. Shielded and unshielded high-density D-shell connectors are specified for both the A-cable and P-cable. The shielded high-density connectors use a squeeze-to-release latch rather than the wire latch on the Centronics-style connectors. Active termination for single-ended buses is specified, providing a high level of signal integrity.

SCSI Bus Termination. All buses need to be electrically terminated at each end, and the SCSI bus is no exception. Improper termination is still one of the most common problems with SCSI installations. There are three different types of terminators typically available for the SCSI bus:

- Passive
- Active (called Alternative 2)
- Forced Perfect Termination (FPT)

Typical passive terminators (a network of resistors) allow signal fluctuations in relation to the terminator power signal on the bus. Usually, passive terminating resistors suffice over short distances, like 2–3 feet, but for longer distances active termination is a real advantage. Active termination is absolutely required with Fast SCSI.

An active terminator actually has one or more voltage regulators to produce the termination voltage, rather than resistor voltage dividers. This helps to ensure that the SCSI signals are always terminated to the correct voltage level. The SCSI-2 specification recommends active termination on both ends of the bus and requires active termination whenever Fast or Wide SCSI devices are used. A variation on active termination, called Forced Perfect Termination, is available. Forced Perfect Termination is an even better form of active termination where diode clamps are added to eliminate signal over and undershoot. The "trick" is that instead of clamping to +5 and ground, they clamp to the output of two regulated voltages. This allows the clamping diodes to eliminate signal overshoot and undershoot, especially at higher signaling speeds and over longer distances.

Several companies make high-quality terminators for the SCSI bus, including Methode's Data Mate division and Aeronix. Both of these companies make a variety of terminators, but Aeronics is well known for very high quality FPT versions that are especially suited to problem configurations with long cable runs, multiple external devices, or other situations where higher signal integrity is needed. One of the best investments you can make in any SCSI installation is in high-quality cables and terminators.

III

Hardware Considerations

SCSI Drive Configuration. SCSI drives are not too difficult to configure, especially when compared to IDE drives. The SCSI standard controls how the drives must be set up. There are basically two or three items to set when configuring SCSI drives:

■ SCSI ID setting (0–7)

■ Terminating resistors

SCSI ID Setting. The SCSI ID setting is very simple. There can be up to 8 total SCSI devices on a single SCSI bus, and each must have a unique SCSI ID address. The host adapter will take one address, and up to 7 SCSI peripherals will take the others. Most SCSI host adapters are factory set to ID 7, which is the highest priority ID. All other devices must have unique IDs that do not conflict with one another. Some host adapters will only boot from a hard disk set to a specific ID. In my system, for example, the IBM SCSI Host Adapter requires the boot drive to be set to ID 6. Newer IBM host adapters and systems allow you to boot from a hard disk at any SCSI ID. Older Adaptec host adapters required the boot hard disk to be ID 0, whereas newer ones can boot from any ID.

Setting the ID usually involves changing jumpers on the drive itself. If the drive is installed in an external chassis, the chassis may have an ID selector switch that is accessible at the rear. This makes ID selection a simple matter of pressing a button or rotating a wheel until the desired ID number appears. If no external selector is present, you must open up the external device chassis and set the ID via the jumpers on the drive.

Three jumpers are required to set the SCSI ID, and the particular ID selected is actually derived from the binary representation of the jumpers themselves. For example, setting off all three ID jumpers results in a binary number of 000b, which translates to an ID of 0. In this manner, a binary setting of 001b equals ID 1, 010b equals 2, 011b equals 3, and so forth. Notice that as I write these values, I append a lowercase *b* to indicate binary numbers. Unfortunately, the jumpers can appear either forwards or backwards on the drive, depending how the manufacturer set them up. To keep things simple, I have recorded all the different ID jumper settings in tables 10.12 and 10.13. One table is for drives that order the jumpers with the *most significant bit* (MSB) to the left, and the other is for drives with the jumpers ordered such that the MSB is to the right.

Termination. SCSI Termination is very simple. Termination is required at both ends of the bus, with no exceptions. If the host adapter is at one end of the bus, it must have termination enabled. If the host adapter is in the middle of the bus, and both internal and external bus links are present, the host adapter must have its termination disabled and the devices at each end of the bus must have terminators installed. Several different types of terminators are available, varying in quality and in the physical form they take. For more information on these different types, see the SCSI interface section in this chapter.

Table 10.12 SCSI ID Jumper Settings with the Most Significant Bit to the Left

SCSI ID	Jumper settings		
0	0	0	0
1	0	0	1
2	0	1	0
3	0	1	1
4	1	0	0
5	1	0	1
6	1	1	0
7	1	1	1

Note: 1 = Jumper On; 0 = Jumper Off

Table 10.13 SCSI ID Jumper Settings with the Most Significant Bit to the Right

SCSI ID	Jumper settings		
0	0	0	0
1	1	0	0
2	0	1	0
3	1	1	0
4	0	0	1
5	1	0	1
6	0	1	1
7	1	1	1

Note: 1 = Jumper On; 0 = Jumper Off

The rules are simple: use the best terminators possible and make sure that only the ends of the SCSI bus are terminated. The majority of problems I see with SCSI installations are due to improper termination. Some devices have built-in termination resistors that are enabled or disabled through a jumper or by physically removing them. Other devices do not have terminating resistors built-in and instead rely on external terminator modules for termination.

When installing an external SCSI device, you will usually find the device in a storage enclosure with both input and output SCSI connectors. This is to enable you to use the device in a daisy chain. If the enclosure is at the end of the SCSI bus, an external termi-nator module will most likely have to be plugged into the second (outgoing) SCSI port. This provides proper termination at that end of the bus (see fig. 10.19).

III

Hardware Considerations

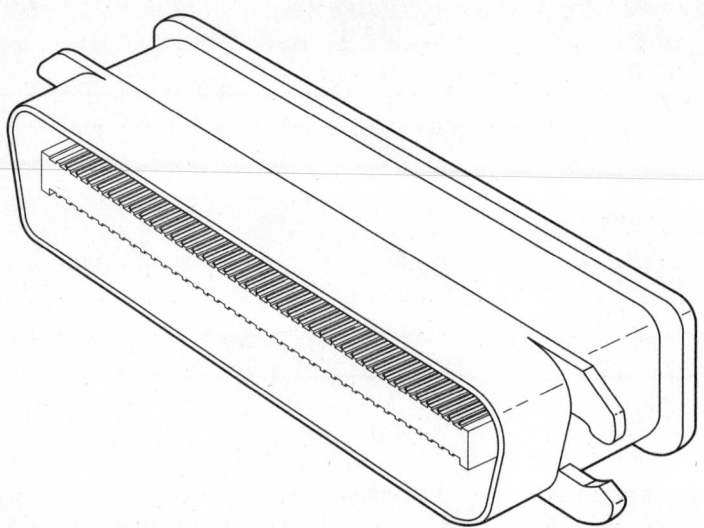

Fig. 10.19

External SCSI device terminator.

External terminator modules are available in a variety of connector configurations, including pass-through designs, which are needed if only one port is available. Pass-through terminators are also commonly used in internal installations where the device does not have it's own terminating resistors built in. Many hard drives use pass-through terminators for internal installations to save space on the logic board assembly (see fig. 10.20).

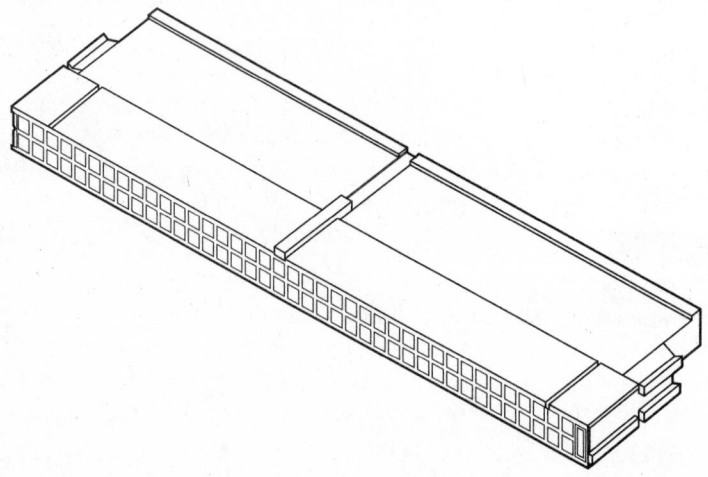

Fig. 10.20

Internal pin-header connector pass-through SCSI terminator.

The pass-through models are required where a device is at the end of the bus and only one SCSI connector is available.

Remember to stick with high-quality active or forced-perfect terminators at each end of the bus, and you will eliminate most common termination problems.

Other Settings. There may be other configuration items on a SCSI drive that you can set via jumpers. Some of the most common additional settings you will find are:

- Start on Command (delayed start)
- SCSI Parity
- Terminator Power
- Synchronous Negotiation

The following sections describe these configuration items.

Start on Command (Delayed Start). If you have more than one drive installed in a system, it is wise to set them up so that all of the drives do not start to spin immediately upon powering up the system. A hard disk drive can consume three or four times more power during the first few seconds after power on than during normal running operation. The motor requires this additional power to get the platters spinning quickly; if several drives are drawing all of this power at once, the power supply may be overloaded, which can cause the system to hang or have intermittent startup problems. Nearly all SCSI drives provide a way to have the drive delay spinning so that this problem does not occur. When most SCSI host adapters initialize the SCSI bus, they send out a command called "Start Unit" to each of the ID addresses in succession. By setting a jumper on the hard disk, you can prevent it from spinning until it receives this Start Unit command from the host adapter. Because the host adapter sends this command to all of the IDs in succession from the highest priority (ID 7) to the lowest (ID 0), the higher priority drives can be made to start first, with each lower priority drive spinning up sequentially in order. Because some host adapters do not send the Start Unit command, some drives may have the ability to simply delay spin-up for a fixed number of seconds rather than wait for a command that will never arrive.

If drives are installed in external chassis with separate power supplies, there is no need to implement the delayed start function. This function is best applied to internal drives that must be run from the same power supply that also runs the system. For internal installations, I recommend setting Start on Command (delayed start) even if you have only one SCSI drive. Even with one drive, this will ease the load on the power supply by spinning the drive up after the rest of the system has full power. This is especially good for portable systems or other systems where power-supply capacity is limited.

SCSI Parity. SCSI Parity is a limited form of error checking that helps to ensure that all data transfers are reliable. Virtually all host adapters support SCSI parity checking, so this option should universally be enabled on every device. The only reason it exists as an option is because some older host adapters will not work with SCSI parity, so the parity can be turned off.

Terminator Power. The terminators on each end of the SCSI bus require power from at least one of the devices on the bus. In most cases the host adapter will supply this terminator power, but may not in some cases. For example, parallel port SCSI host adapters typically do not supply terminator power. It does not cause problems if more than one device supplies terminator power, so it is usually recommended for simplicity's sake to configure all devices to supply this power. If no device supplies terminator power, the bus will not be terminated correctly and will not function properly.

SCSI Synchronous Negotiation. The SCSI bus can run in two modes, *asynchronous* (default) and *synchronous*. The bus actually switches modes during transfers through a protocol called *synchronous negotiation*. Before data is transferred across the SCSI bus, the sending device (called the *initiator*) and the receiving device (called the *target*) negotiate how the transfer will take place. If both devices support synchronous transfers, they will discover this through the negotiation, and the transfer will then take place at the faster synchronous rate. Unfortunately, some older devices do not respond to a request for synchronous transfer and can actually be disabled when such a request is made. For this reason, both host adapters and devices that support synchronous negotiation will often have a jumper that can be used to disable this negotiation so it can work together with older devices. By default, all devices today should support synchronous negotiation and this function should be left as enabled.

SCSI Drivers. Each SCSI peripheral you add to your SCSI bus (other than hard disk drives) will require an external driver to make the device work. Hard disks are accepted because driver support for them is normally provided as a part of the SCSI host adapter BIOS. These external drivers are not only specific to a particular device, but to the host adapter, as well. Recently, two types of standard host adapter interface drivers that greatly reduce this problem have become popular. By having a standard host adapter driver to write to, peripheral makers can more quickly get new drivers done that support their devices and then talk to the universal host adapter driver. This eliminates the dependence on one particular type of host adapter.

These primary or universal drivers link the host adapter and the operating system.

The Advanced SCSI Programming Interface (ASPI) is currently the most popular universal driver, with most peripheral makers writing their drivers to talk to ASPI. The A in ASPI originally stood for Adaptec, the company that introduced it, but they changed the Adaptec designation to Advanced when they sought to license the interface to other companies. Now many SCSI device vendors have licensed the right to use ASPI with their products. DOS does not support ASPI directly, but does when an ASPI driver is loaded. OS/2 2.1 and higher provide automatic ASPI support for a number of different SCSI host adapters.

Future Domain and NCR have created another interface driver called the Common Access Method (CAM). CAM is an ANSI-approved protocol that allows several host adapters to be controlled from a single driver. In addition to ASPI, OS/2 2.1 and higher currently offers support for CAM. Future Domain also provides a CAM-to-ASPI converter free as part of the utilities that go with their host adapters.

SCSI Configuration Tips. When installing a chain of devices on a single SCSI bus, things can get complicated very quickly. Here are some tips for getting your setup to function quickly and efficiently.

Start by adding one device at a time. Rather than plug numerous peripherals into a single SCSI card and then try to configure them all at once, install the host adapter and a single hard disk to start with. Then you can continue installing devices one at a time, checking to see that everything works before moving on.

Keep good documentation. When you add a SCSI peripheral, write down the SCSI ID address as well as any other switch and jumper settings, such as SCSI Parity, Terminator Power, and Remote Start. For the host adapter, record the BIOS addresses, interrupt, DMA channel, and I/O port addresses used by the adapter, as well as any other jumper or configuration settings such as termination that might be important to know later.

Use proper Termination. Each end of the bus must be terminated, preferably with active or Forced Perfect (FPT) terminators. If you are using any Fast SCSI-2 devices, you must use active terminators rather than the cheaper passive types. Even with standard (slow) SCSI devices, active termination is highly recommended. If you have only internal or external devices on the bus, the host adapter and last device on the chain should be terminated. If you have external and internal devices on the chain, you will generally terminate the first and last of these devices, but not the SCSI host adapter itself (which is in the middle of the bus).

Use high-quality shielded SCSI cables. Make sure your cable connectors match your devices, as there are several different connector styles possible. Use high-quality shielded cables, and observe the SCSI bus length limitations. Use cables designed for SCSI use, and if possible, stick to the same brand of cable throughout a single SCSI bus. Different brands of cables have different impedance values, which can sometimes cause problems, especially in longer or high-speed SCSI implementations.

Following these simple tips will help to minimize the occurrence of any problems, and will leave you with a trouble free SCSI installation.

IDE versus SCSI

When comparing the performance and capabilities of IDE (Integrated Drive Electronics) and SCSI (Small Computer System Interface) interfaced drives, there are several factors that need to be considered. These two types of drives are the most popular for use in PC systems today, and often a single manufacturer will even have identical drives available in both interfaces. Deciding which of these is best for your system is a difficult decision that depends on many factors.

In most specific cases, you will often find that an IDE drive outperforms an equivalent SCSI drive at a given task or benchmark, and IDE drives usually cost less than SCSI drives thus offering a better value. However, there are instances where SCSI has significant performance and value advantages over IDE, as well.

III

Hardware Considerations

Performance. ATA-IDE drives are currently used in the majority of PC configurations on the market today. This is based on the low cost of an IDE drive implementation combined with the high-performance capabilities. In comparing any given IDE and SCSI drive for performance, you have to look specifically at the capabilities of the particular HDAs (Head Disk Assemblies) that are involved.

In order to minimize the variables in this type of comparison, it is easiest to compare IDE and SCSI drives from the same manufacturer that also uses the identical HDA. You will find that in most cases, a drive manufacturer makes a given drive available in both IDE and SCSI forms. As an example, Seagate makes the ST-3600A (ATA-IDE) and ST-3600N (Fast SCSI-2) drives which both use identical HDAs and differ only in the logic board. The IDE version has a logic board with a built-in disk controller and a direct AT Bus interface. The SCSI version has the same built-in disk controller and bus interface circuits, but also has a SCSI Bus Interface Controller (SBIC) chip. The SBIC chip is a SCSI adapter that places the drive on the SCSI bus. What you will find in essence is that virtually all SCSI drives are actually IDE drives with the SBIC chip added.

The HDAs in these example drives are capable of transferring data at a sustained rate of between 2.38 and 4M per second. Because the SCSI version always has the additional overhead of the SCSI bus to go through, you will find in almost all cases that the directly attached IDE version will perform faster.

IDE Advantages and Limitations. IDE drives have much less command overhead for a given sector transfer than SCSI drives. In addition to the drive to controller command overhead that both IDE and SCSI must perform, a SCSI transfer also involves negotiation for the SCSI bus, selecting the target drive, requesting data, terminating the transfer over the bus, and finally converting the logical data addresses to the physical cylinder, head, and sector addresses that are required.

This gives IDE an advantage for sequential transfers, as would be done by a single-tasking operating system. With a multitasking system that can take advantage of the extra intelligence of the SCSI bus, SCSI can have the performance advantage.

SCSI Advantages. SCSI drives offer significant architectural advantages over IDE and other drives. Because each SCSI drive has its own embedded disk controller that can function independently from the system CPU, it is possible for the computer to issue simultaneous commands to every drive in the system. Each drive can store these commands in a queue and then perform the commands simultaneously with other drives in the system. The data could be fully buffered on the drive and transferred at high speed over the shared SCSI bus when a time slot was available.

Although IDE drives also each have their own controller, they do not operate simultaneously, and command queuing is not supported. In effect, the dual controllers in a dual drive IDE installation only work one at a time so as not to step on each other.

Although SCSI drives do require an additional cost host adapter card, more and more PCs require tape backup, CD-ROM, or optical drive support, and thus must still be configured with a SCSI host bus adapter. This means that the incremental cost of supporting SCSI drives is virtually nil, because the SCSI host bus adapter is shared with other devices like tape and optical drives. In addition, all major operating systems today include software support for a large range of SCSI devices.

What are the limitations of IDE?

- IDE does not support overlapped, multitasked I/O.
- IDE does not support command queuing.
- IDE does not support bus mastering.
- No more than two IDE drives can be supported without multiple IDE adapters.
- IDE drives are normally limited to 504M per drive without an enhanced BIOS.
- IDE does not normally support other devices like tape or optical drives.

As you can see, SCSI has many advantages over IDE, especially where expansion is concerned and also with regard to support for multitasking operating systems.

Recommended Aftermarket Controllers and Host Adapters

Many companies manufacture disk controllers for IBM and IBM-compatible systems. Many newer systems include IDE drives, which have the controller built in and offer a high level of performance at a low cost. Other systems are using SCSI drives because of the inherent flexibility of the SCSI bus to support many drives and other peripherals.

I recommend IDE drives for most standard installations because the connections are so simple and the drives are inexpensive for the power. SCSI drive systems are recommended for higher end systems, or when upgradability and flexibility are most important.

Silicon Valley makes a line of IDE adapters that are excellent for systems without the special IDE connector on the motherboard. It also has a special adapter that enables you to put AT IDE drives in 8-bit XT systems, which few other cards do. Arco Electronics and Sigma Data make IDE adapters that allow ATA IDE drives to be installed in PS/2 MCA bus systems. They even have unique versions for the Model 50z and 70 that replace the interposer card, therefore using no MCA slots in the system. All of these companies are listed in the vendor list in the Appendix.

Recommended SCSI Host Adapters. For SCSI host adapters, I recommend IBM for MCA cards, and Adaptec or Future Domain for ISA or EISA bus cards. All these adapters work well and come complete with the necessary formatting and operating software. OS/2 has built-in support for IBM and Adaptec SCSI adapters. This support is a consideration in many cases because it eliminates having to deal with external drivers.

Examples of a new breed of SCSI adapter on the market include the Adaptec AHA-1540C and 1542C. The 1542 has a built-in floppy controller, whereas the 1540 does not. These adapters are most notable for their easy installation and use. Virtually all functions on the card can be configured and set through software. No more digging through manuals looking for interrupt, DMA, I/O port, or other jumper settings. Everything is controlled by software and saved in a flash memory module on the card. Here is a brief look at some of the features of this card:

- Complete configuration utility built into the adapter's ROM

- Software configurable IRQ, ROM addresses, DMA, I/O port addresses SCSI Parity, SCSI ID, and more

- Software selectable termination; no resistors to pull out!

- Enhanced BIOS support for up to eight 7.88-gigabyte drives

- No drivers required for more than two hard disks

- Enables drive spin-up on a per drive basis

- Boots from any SCSI ID

- The 1542C model (see fig. 10.21) includes an Intel 82077 floppy controller chip (which supports 2.88M drives); however, 2.88M BIOS support must also be provided by your motherboard BIOS.

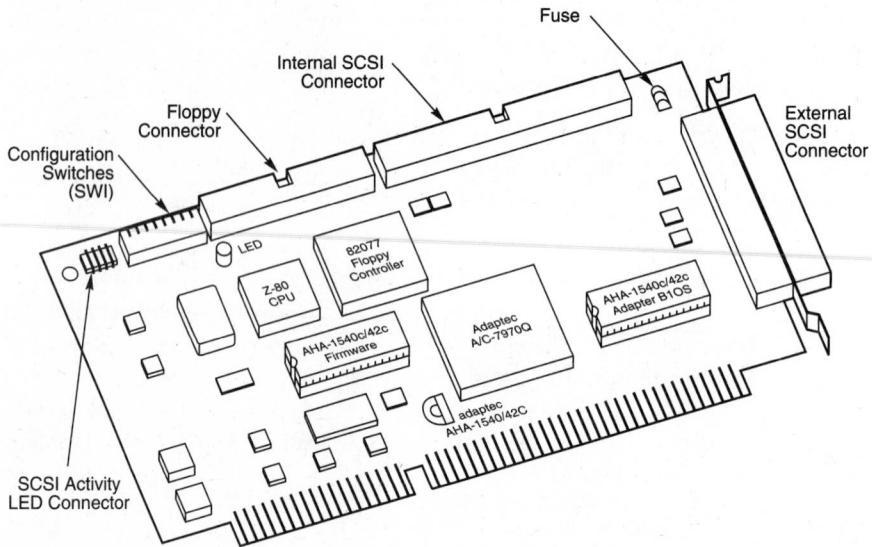

Fig. 10.21
An Adaptec AHA-1542C SCSI host adapter.

All in all, this is one of the easiest SCSI adapters to install that I have worked with. Most peripheral manufacturers write drivers for Adaptec's cards first, so you will not have too many compatibility or driver support problems with any Adaptec card.

As a tip, if you are using the older AHA-1542B SCSI host adapter, the current ROM revision available is version 3.20, which adds Enhanced BIOS support for multiple drives up to 7.88 gigabytes with no drivers.

Future Domain also makes SCSI cards that are well supported throughout the industry. If compatibility is important, you can't go wrong with either the Adaptec or Future Domain cards.

IBM SCSI Adapters. IBM has shipped several different types of SCSI adapters since first introducing PC SCSI in 1990. Basically, they have offered three types of adapters:

- 16-bit SCSI MCA adapter

- 32-bit SCSI MCA adapter with cache

- 16-bit Fast SCSI ISA adapter

The IBM host adapters (especially the MCA versions) are among the easiest to install and configure in the industry. Much of this comes from the Micro Channel architecture itself, which eliminates the need to worry about interrupts, DMA channels, I/O port addresses, and even BIOS addresses. By virtue of MCA, these adapters are virtually self configuring.

The only real problem they have is with drivers. They all have built-in support for hard disk drives, but no drivers are included for any other devices. This is important to know if you decide to attach external peripherals to these cards, because you will need drivers to make the peripherals work.

IBM only makes DOS drivers available for the peripherals they sell, but IBM OS/2 amazingly includes SCSI drivers not only for numerous IBM and non-IBM peripherals, but also for non-IBM SCSI host adapters. If you cannot use OS/2, one way around the driver support problem is to use the same peripherals that IBM sells, in which case you can get the drivers from IBM to support them. For example, IBM sells a CD-ROM drive that actually incorporates a Toshiba mechanism. By purchasing a Toshiba CD-ROM drive, I can make it work by simply using the drivers that IBM supplies with their (Toshiba) CD-ROM drive. IBM makes their drivers available free for the downloading on the IBM NSC BBS (the phone number is in the Vendor list in the Appendix). I am also using a Hewlett-Packard DAT (Digital Audio Tape) drive for backup, because that is the same mechanism that IBM sells in their own DAT drive. Again, I get the drivers from IBM. This does not always work, however. For example, I would like to attach a Hewlett-Packard Scanner to my IBM host adapter, but neither HP nor IBM (or anybody else so far) makes drivers to run the scanner with the IBM card. My only choice is to use a different SCSI card to run the scanner—not a very good alternative in my estimation.

The 16- and 32-bit MCA adapters have both been available in two versions. The original version of the 16-bit (noncached) MCA adapter was known as FRU (Field Replacement Unit) # 15F6561 and was recalled for a defect. The replacement was labeled FRU # 85f0002. Some of the earlier cards were reworked and returned to the field without having the new FRU # applied over the old one. These repaired adapters can be identified by two yellow wires running from the upper to the lower side of the module labeled ZM10. If you have the original version of this card, it is important that you get the replacement (IBM should replace it free) because the original card could cause random lockups and data corruption.

The original 32-bit cached MCA adapter did not have such a serious problem that required replacement, but it was updated over the years with improved functionality. The original SCSI adapter with cache will not support drive capacities greater than 1gigabyte. If you install a drive larger than 1G, the drive will work, but only the first 1G will be recognized.

A new version of this card was issued that had an improved BIOS which supports drives up to 8G. The way you can tell which SCSI adapter with cache you have is by physically inspecting the adapter. The new adapter comes with an orange terminating resistor on the end of the card, similar to the noncached adapter. If you do not have both internal and external devices installed, this orange resistor should be located on the adapter. If you do have both internal and external devices, the resistor should be removed, and there will be an empty socket on the adapter where the resistor was originally located. The new SCSI adapter with cache is sold under the part number 6451133 and known as FRU # 85F0063. If you have the original SCSI adapter with cache, then you will not have an orange resistor on the card, nor will you have an empty socket where the resistor is supposed to go. The original adapter does not implement termination on the card itself.

One tip I have is that it is not widely known that you can upgrade the cache on the IBM SCSI Adapter with Cache from the standard 512K to 2M by simply replacing the 256K (9-bit) SIMMs with 1M SIMMs. The only caveat is that you must use the IBM-style 9-bit SIMMs, which have a slightly different pinout than so-called industry standard 9-bit SIMMs. I have done this to my IBM SCSI card, and there is as much as a 10-percent improvement in throughput.

IBM sells a Fast SCSI-2 adapter for their ISA bus systems, which is actually made for them by Future Domain. This adapter is sold for use in the ISA bus systems such as PS/1 and PS/Valuepoints. Because of support by Future Domain, this adapter actually has many more drivers available for it than the MCA adapters, making it very easy to add a variety of peripherals under DOS as well as OS/2. This adapter also supports Fast SCSI transfers, while the original MCA IBM adapters do not.

Hard Disk Installation Procedures

This section describes the installation of a typical hard disk and its integration in a particular PC system. To install a hard drive in an IBM-compatible system, you must perform several procedures:

- Configure the drive
- Configure the controller or interface
- Physically install the drive
- Configure the system
- Low-level format the drive (not required or optional with IDE and SCSI)
- Partition the drive
- High-level format the drive

Drive configuration was already discussed with each different interface type. Consult the section that covers the particular type of drive you are installing for complete configuration information. The following sections describe each of the other steps. The steps are simple to execute and, if done properly, result in the successful installation of a bootable hard disk. Special attention is given to issues of reliability and data integrity, to ensure that the installation is long-lasting and trouble-free.

To begin the setup procedure, you have to know several details about the hard disk drive, controller or host adapter, and system ROM BIOS, as well as most of the other devices in the system. This information is usually contained in the various OEM manuals that come with these devices. Make sure that when you purchase these things, the vendor includes these manuals. (Many vendors do not include the manuals unless you specifically ask for them.) For most equipment sold today, you will get enough documentation from the vendor or reseller of the equipment to allow you to proceed. If you are like me, however, and want all of the technical documentation on the device possible, you will want to contact the original manufacturer of the device and order the technical specification manual from them. For example, if you purchase an IBM-compatible system that comes with a Western Digital IDE hard disk, you will probably get some limited information put together on the drive by the seller; however, this will not contain nearly the same amount of information as the actual Western Digital technical specification manual would have. To get this documentation, you will have to call Western Digital and order it. The same goes for any of the other components in most clones that are assembled rather than actually manufactured. I find the OEM technical manuals to be essential in obtaining the highest level of technical support possible.

Controller Configuration

Configuring a disk controller involves setting the different system resources that the controller will require. Some controllers have these resources fixed, which means they cannot be altered. Other controllers provide jumpers, switches, or even software that allows you to reconfigure or change the resources used. Controllers with adjustable resource settings can often be used in conjunction with other controllers in a system, while controllers with fixed resources usually can not coexist with others.

All hard disk controllers or SCSI host adapters will require one or more of these system resources:

- ROM addresses
- Interrupt Request Channel (IRQ)
- DMA channel (DRQ)
- I/O port addresses

Not all adapters use every one of these resources, but some use them all. In most cases, these resources must be configured so that they are unique and cannot be shared among several adapters. For example, if a disk controller is using I/O port addresses from 1F0–1F7h, no other device in the system can use those addresses.

A conflict in resource usage often results in all adapters involved not functioning. In the case of disk controllers, the controller will not function and disk access will be impossible or corrupted. You will need to identify which boards in the system have overlapping resources and change the configuration of one or more of them so that the conflict is eliminated. Before installing a board, you should know the resources the board will require and make sure that these resources are not being used by any other boards.

In most systems, this is a manual procedure requiring you to know exactly what this and every other adapter in the system is using, but with MCA and EISA systems, this is all under software control. MCA and EISA systems can automatically determine whether two adapters use the same resource and change the configuration to eliminate the conflict. This only works on EISA systems if you have all EISA 32-bit adapters. EISA systems also may have standard ISA adapters, which cannot be configured in this manner. MCA systems are universally self-configuring and are the easiest systems for the average user to configure.

For most systems, you need the documentation for each and every adapter in the system to ensure that there are no conflicts and to find out how to reconfigure a card to eliminate a conflict. Software such as Infospotter by Renasonce or MSD (Microsoft Diagnostics) can help when documentation is not available or is limited. Programs cannot usually identify direct conflicts, but if you install one board at a time, they can identify what addresses or resources a given board is using. MSD comes free with Windows and MS-DOS 6.x, and the excellent Infospotter program is available from Renasonce (see the vendor list in the Appendix).

Many system resources simply cannot be identified by software alone. A company called Allied Microcomputer manufactures a card called the Trapcard II, which can be used to monitor interrupt and DMA channels. This board is very helpful in identifying which of these resources are used in your system. They are listed in the vendor list in the Appendix.

ROM Addresses

Many disk controllers or SCSI host adapters require an on-board BIOS to function. An on-board BIOS can provide many functions including:

- Low-level formatting
- Drive type (parameter) control
- Adapter configuration
- Support for nonstandard I/O port addresses and interrupts

If a hard disk controller can be supported by the motherboard BIOS, then an on-board BIOS is not needed, and in fact is undesirable because it uses memory in the upper memory area (UMA). Fortunately, the on-board BIOS can usually be disabled if it is not required.

Only controllers that meet certain standards can run off of the motherboard BIOS, including ST-506/412 controllers, ESDI controllers, and IDE bus adapters. These standards include the use of I/O port addresses 170-17Fh and Interrupt 14. If you are installing a controller that uses other I/O port addresses or interrupt settings (such as when adding a second controller to a system), then the motherboard BIOS will not be able to support it, and an on-board BIOS will be required. XT controllers universally need an on-board BIOS because the motherboard BIOS has no hard disk support whatsoever.

SCSI adapters do not normally emulate the WD1003 type disk interface and almost always require an on-board BIOS to provide disk driver functions. This on-board BIOS will support any of the adapter's settings, and in most cases multiple SCSI host adapters can all use the BIOS of the first adapter, in which case the BIOS on all but the first can be disabled.

If an on-board BIOS is required and enabled, it will use specific memory address space in the UMA. The UMA is the top 384K in the first megabyte of system memory. The UMA is divided into three areas of two 64K segments each, with the first and last areas used by the video adapter circuits and the motherboard BIOS, respectively. Segments C000h and D000h are specifically reserved for use by adapter ROMs such as those found on disk controllers or SCSI host adapters.

You need to ensure that any adapters using space in these segments do not overlap with other adapters using this space. No two adapters can share this memory space. Most adapters have jumpers, switches, or even software which can adjust the configuration of the board and change the addresses which are used to avoid conflict.

Interrupt Request Channel (IRQ)

All disk controllers or SCSI host adapters require an interrupt line to gain the system's attention. They invoke a hardware interrupt to gain timely access to the system for data transfers and control. The original 8-bit ISA systems have only eight different interrupt levels, with interrupts 2 through 7 available to any adapters. AT bus (16-bit ISA), EISA, MCA, systems have 16 different interrupt levels, with 3–7, 9–12, and 14–15 available to any adapter cards. IRQs 10–12 and 14–15 are 16-bit interrupts available to 16- or 32-bit adapters only. Tables 10.14 and 10.15 show the normally used and normally available interrupts in ISA, EISA, MCA, and 8-bit ISA systems. For each interrupt, the default usage and whether or not the interrupt is available in a bus slot is listed.

Some of the interrupts are simply not available in slots at all, they are reserved for use by the indicated system function only. Any interrupt that is listed as in use by an item not installed in your system would be available. For example, if your system does not have a motherboard mouse port, IRQ 12 would be available; if your system does not have a second serial port, IRQ 3 would be available.

You must discover what interrupts are currently in use and available in a system, and then configure any new cards to use the available interrupts only. In a standard configuration, the hard disk controller uses interrupt (IRQ) 14. Any secondary controllers have to use other interrupts. The suggested interrupt for a secondary controller is IRQ 15. Any controllers that do not use IRQ 14 must have an on-board BIOS for them to function. The motherboard BIOS only supports disk controllers at IRQ 14.

Table 10.14 ISA, EISA, and MCA Default Interrupt Assignments

IRQ	Function	Bus Slot
0	System Timer	No
1	Keyboard Controller	No
2	Second IRQ Controller	No
8	Real-Time Clock	No
9	Available (Redirected IRQ 2)	Yes (8-bit)
10	Available	Yes (16-bit)
11	Available	Yes (16-bit)
12	Motherboard Mouse Port	Yes (16-bit)
13	Math Coprocessor	No
14	Hard Disk Controller	Yes (16-bit)
15	Available	Yes (16-bit)
3	Serial Port 2 (COM2:)	Yes (8-bit)
4	Serial Port 1 (COM1:)	Yes (8-bit)
5	Parallel Port 2 (LPT2:)	Yes (8-bit)
6	Floppy Disk Controller	Yes (8-bit)
7	Parallel Port 1 (LPT1:)	Yes (8-bit)

Table 10.15 XT-Bus (8-Bit ISA) Default Interrupt Assignments

IRQ	Function	Bus Slot
0	System Timer	No
1	Keyboard Controller	No
2	Available	No
3	Serial Port 2 (COM2:)	Yes (8-bit)
4	Serial Port 1 (COM1:)	Yes (8-bit)
5	Hard Disk Controller	Yes (8-bit)
6	Floppy Disk Controller	Yes (8-bit)
7	Parallel Port 1 (LPT1:)	Yes (8-bit)

Most adapters come preconfigured for IRQ 14, which is fine if it is the only disk adapter in the system. Many SCSI host adapters like the Adaptec 1540/1542C come configured to one of the other available 16-bit interrupts because they will never be run off of the motherboard BIOS. XT (8-bit) controllers normally use IRQ 5.

DMA Channel

Direct Memory Access (DMA) is a technique for transferring blocks of data directly into system memory without the complete attention of the main processor. The motherboard has DMA control circuits that orchestrate and govern DMA transfers. In the original 8-bit XT bus, DMA was the highest performance transfer method, and XT hard disk controllers universally used DMA channel 3 for high-speed transfers.

In AT bus (16-bit ISA) systems, most 16-bit disk controllers and SCSI host adapters do not use a DMA channel. This is partly because the performance of the AT bus DMA circuitry turned out to be very poor, so most adapters use a technique called Programmed I/O (PIO), which simply sends bytes of data through the I/O ports. PIO transfers ended up being faster than DMA transfers in most cases, especially if the motherboard BIOS and device support block mode PIO, such as with the new IDE drives. If an adapter does not use DMA, you can assume that PIO is used as the data transfer method and no DMA channel is required.

Some adapters have found a way around the poor performance of the ISA bus by becoming what is known as a *bus master*. A bus master device actually takes control over the bus and can override the DMA controller circuitry on the motherboard to perform fast DMA transfers. These transfers can exceed the performance of a PIO transfer (even block mode PIO), so you will find that many of the highest performing controllers have bus master capabilities. With bus master adapters, you have to select a DMA channel for them to use. In an 8-bit ISA bus, normally only DMA channel 1 is available; however, in a 16-bit ISA bus, DMA channels 0–1, 3, and 5–7 are available. DMA channels 5–7 are 16-bit channels that most high performance bus master adapters would desire to use. XT disk controllers always use DMA channel 3. Tables 10.16 and 10.17 show the normally used and normally available DMA channels in ISA, EISA, MCA, and 8-bit ISA systems. For each DMA channel, the default usage is listed and whether the DMA Channel is available in a bus slot.

Table 10.16 ISA, EISA, and MCA Default DMA Channel Assignments

DMA	Function	Bus Slot
0	Available	Yes (16-bit)
1	Available	Yes (8-bit)
2	Floppy Disk Controller	Yes (8-bit)
3	Available	Yes (8-bit)
4	First DMA Controller	No
5	Available	Yes (16-bit)
6	Available	Yes (16-bit)
7	Available	Yes (16-bit)

Table 10.17 XT-Bus (8-Bit ISA) Default DMA Channel Assignments

DMA	Function	Bus Slot
0	Dynamic RAM Refresh	No
1	Available	Yes (8-bit)
2	Floppy Disk Controller	Yes (8-bit)
3	Hard Disk Controller	Yes (8-bit)

III

Hardware Considerations

Some of the DMA Channels are simply not available in slots at all; they are reserved for use by the indicated system function only. Any DMA channel that is listed as in use by an item not installed in your system would be available. For example, if your 8-bit ISA bus system does not have a hard disk controller, DMA channel 3 is available.

MCA and EISA bus systems have additional DMA capabilities that support even faster transfers without the problems in performance associated with nonbus master cards. The MCA and EISA buses also provide even better support for bus master devices which offer even higher performance.

To configure an adapter that requires a DMA channel, you must first find out what DMA channels are currently used and available in your system. Unless you have an MCA or EISA system, software techniques for showing this are very limited. Most programs that claim to be able to discover what DMA channels are currently used are only reporting what any standard configuration would be. With standard ISA systems, the only way to know for sure is to look up the documentation for each adapter, or use a special hardware device that monitors DMA transfers. Allied Electronics makes a card called the Trapcard II, which monitors IRQ and DMA lines and can tell you for certain which are used and which are not. This is an inexpensive card that plugs into a slot and monitors the bus, with LEDs that indicate which resources are being used. Allied is listed in the vendor list in the Appendix.

After determining what DMA channels are free, you can set your adapter to any of those free channels. DMA conflicts usually result in improper operation or corrupted data transfers, so you will usually know quickly if you have made a mistake.

MCA and EISA systems automatically set up the boards so that there are no DMA conflicts. This only works fully in EISA systems if you have all EISA 32-bit adapters installed.

I/O Port Addresses

I/O port addresses are like mailboxes where data and commands are sent to and from an adapter. These addresses are different than memory addresses. I/O ports must be used exclusively and cannot be shared among different adapters. Each adapter usually uses a group of sequential port addresses for communication with the bus.

The standard I/O port addresses used by disk controllers are 1F0–1F7h. These are the only addresses supported by the motherboard BIOS, so if you have a disk controller at any other port address, then it must have an on-board BIOS. Obviously, if you are adding a secondary controller to a system, it must use different I/O addresses and must also have an on-board BIOS. Most controllers use 170–177h as secondary I/O addresses, which would be used if another disk controller was already in the system, however any I/O addresses that are free may be used.

It is rare to have I/O port conflicts unless you are installing multiple disk controllers in a system. In that case, each controller will need different I/O port address settings so as not to conflict with the others. To determine what I/O ports are currently in use, you normally will have to refer to the documentation that comes with each device in your system. It is not normally possible for software to identify all used I/O port addresses, unless you have a Micro Channel or EISA system. Port conflicts usually result in each of the devices in conflict not functioning or functioning improperly.

Physical Installation

The physical installation of a hard disk is much the same as for a floppy drive. You must have the correct screws, brackets, and faceplates for the specific drive and system before you can install the drive.

IBM AT systems require plastic rails that are secured to the sides of the drives so that they can slide into the proper place in the system. COMPAQ uses a different type of rail. When you purchase a drive, the vendor usually includes the IBM-type rails, so be sure to specify whether you need the special COMPAQ type. IBM PC-type and XT-type systems do not need rails but may need a bracket to enable double-stacking of half-height drives. Several companies in the vendor list specialize in drive-mounting brackets, cables, and other hardware accessories (see fig. 10.22).

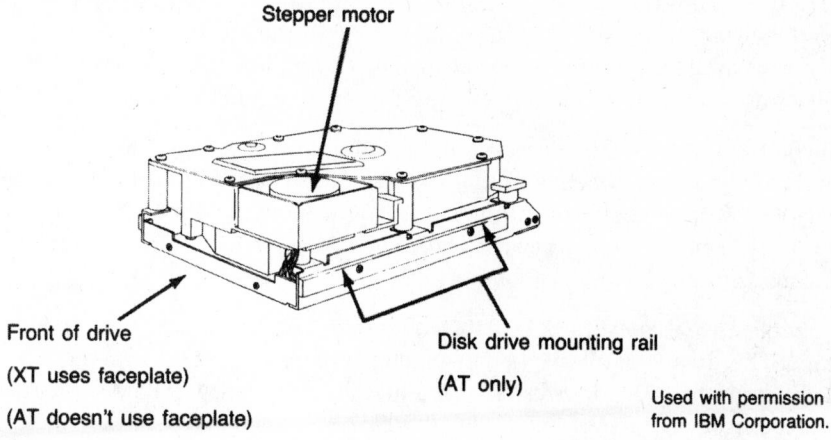

Stepper motor

Front of drive

(XT uses faceplate)

(AT doesn't use faceplate)

Disk drive mounting rail

(AT only)

Used with permission from IBM Corporation.

Fig. 10.22
A full-height hard disk with AT mounting rails.

There are different faceplate, or bezel options; make sure that you have the correct bezel for your application. Some systems, for example, do not need a faceplate; if a faceplate is on the drive, it must be removed. If you are installing a half-height drive in a full-height bay, you may need a blank half-height bezel to fill the hole, or you may want to order a half-height drive with a full-height bezel so that no hole is created. There are several vendors listed in the vendor list in the Appendix that sell a variety of drive mounting kits, hardware, rails, adapters, and cables.

System Configuration

With the drive physically installed, you can begin configuring the system to the drive. You have to tell the system about the drive so that the system can boot from it when it is powered on. How you set and store this information depends on the type of drive and system you have. Standard setup procedures are used for most hard disks except SCSI drives. SCSI drives normally follow a custom setup procedure that varies depending on which host adapter you are using. If you have SCSI drives, follow the instructions included with the host adapter to configure the drives.

AT Class System Setup Program and Drive Types

If the system is an AT type and you are using the motherboard BIOS to support the hard disks, you will need to know some information about the BIOS, such as what drives are supported in the hard drive table. Many BIOS versions now have user definable drive types which allow you to enter any set of parameters required to match your drive. For IDE drives, many new BIOS versions have automatic typing which interrogates the drive to and automatically enters the parameter information returned by the drive. This eliminates errors or confusion in parameter selection.

Normally you will find the information about the drive table in the technical manuals provided with the motherboard or the BIOS. The Appendix includes a list of drive types for many different BIOS versions. For other systems not listed, you can find this information in the system's technical reference manual. Often the BIOS setup program will show you all of the available selections on-screen, allowing you to select the best choice interactively. This eliminates the need to look up this information.

When you have collected the necessary information, the next step is to tell the system the kind of drive that is attached so that the system can boot from the drive (eventually). This chapter discusses the installation of an example drive in both an XT-type and an AT-type of system. The same drive is installed on both systems. With knowledge of drive interfacing, you can install just about any drive in any system.

The example drive is a Maxtor XT-1140, which is an ST-506/412 drive designed for MFM encoding. This drive is a full-height 5 1/4-inch platter drive that fits into any 5 1/4-inch, full-height drive bay. The drive capacity is 140M unformatted, 119.85M formatted using MFM encoding, or 183.31M formatted with RLL 2,7 encoding. You can use the drive in a system with an ST-506/412 interface controller. In it's day it was a fairly high-performance drive (as far as ST-506/412 drives go anyway), with an advertised 27ms seek time. This drive is a voice coil drive with thin film media, and it has eight platters with 15 read/write heads and one dedicated servo head.

First, you need to read the drive manual and locate the required information. In this example from the drive manual, I find the following drive parameter information:

- 918 cylinders

- 15 heads

- 17 or 26 Sectors per Track (MFM or RLL encoding)

- No write precompensation required

- 2 to 3100µs head step pulse timing acceptable

- 2 to 13µs head step pulse timing optimum

- 7 defective tracks:

  Cyl 188 Head 7

  Cyl 217 Head 5

  Cyl 218 Head 5

  Cyl 219 Head 5

  Cyl 601 Head 13

  Cyl 798 Head 10

  Cyl 835 Head 5

To install this Maxtor XT-1140 in an IBM AT, I could simply use the original IBM AT controller (Western Digital WD1003A-WA2); however, I would have to live with the slow 2:1 interleave this controller provides. A better choice would be to upgrade the controller with a Data Technology Corporation DTC7287 controller. Not only will this controller support a 1:1 interleave, but it also has an RLL Endec, which will increase the storage capacity of the drive by 50 percent compared to the original MFM encoding controller. Because this drive is a high-quality voice coil actuated drive with thin film media, it should work well with RLL encoding. This controller also has an optional on-board ROM that can be used to set the drive type if the motherboard does not have a matching or user definable type. The on-board ROM (if enabled) also has a low-level format program. For most systems, you set the drive type by looking up the drive information in the table of types located in the system ROM. You match the drive parameters to one of the table entries in the system ROM, or set the parameters using the user definable drive type.

The required information for installing the DTC7287 controller is as follows:

- Interrupt Request Channel (IRQ) = 14

- I/O ports = 1F0 to 1F7

- Step pulse rate = 35µs (selected by BIOS)

- Best interleave = 1 to 1

This controller uses Programmed I/O (PIO) transfers and does not require a DMA channel for the hard disk controller portion. Because this controller also contains a floppy controller, some additional information specific to the floppy controller portion of the card is required:

- Interrupt Request Channel (IRQ) = 6

- DMA channel (DRQ) = 2

- I/O ports = 3F0 to 3F7

You need some of this information to ensure that the card is uniquely configured compared with other cards in the system. The system cannot have other cards using the same IRQ, DMA, ROM, or I/O ports as this card. Keep this information for future reference, and cross-check for conflicts when other cards are added to the system. The step pulse rates and interleave information are all you need to complete the setup.

As mentioned, the Maxtor XT-1140 manual states that drive-seek performance degrades if step pulses are sent at intervals greater than 13µs. Unfortunately, the IBM AT ROM BIOS hard-codes this specification to 35µs, which slows the drive's performance. In my experience, a drive that runs 25ms seeks with the proper step pulse rate, but an average of 29ms seeks with the slower step pulse rate selected in the IBM AT. If you want to bother with patching the AT ROM BIOS, you can change the controller's step pulse rate to 16µs, which would probably pick up a few milliseconds of average seek time. The instructions for making this patch are in Chapter 12, in the section "Upgrading the ROM BIOS." I made this modification to my own system to see whether it could be done, and I learned a lot in the process, but the results are not really worth the trouble!

After you find the information about the drive and controller, you need to match the drive's parameters to one of the drive table entries in the motherboard ROM. ROM drive tables for IBM and many other compatible systems are in the Appendix. It also includes a detailed listing of a large number of hard disk drives with parameter specifications. The information in the Appendix has saved me several times when the original manuals were nowhere to be found.

With the drive tables and drive information in hand, try to find a table entry that matches on heads, cylinders, and write precompensation starting cylinder. If you do not find an exact match on any of these values, use a type that has fewer cylinders and heads than your drive. (You cannot use a type that has more.) Remember that many compatible ROMs, such as those from Phoenix, Award, and AMI, have a user-definable drive type that enables you to support any drive parameters you want by simply typing them in during setup.

Because the Maxtor XT-1140 drive has 918 cylinders and 15 heads, type 9 with 900 cylinders, and 15 heads is the best match in an IBM AT—if you are running an MFM controller, that is. All the types in an original AT BIOS have 17 sectors per track, but the drive will actually have 26 sectors per track with RLL encoding. If the BIOS has a user-definable type entry (the original AT does not), you are home-free; simply select the user-definable type and enter the exact parameters, including the correct number of sectors per track. If you select or define a type that indicates more cylinders, heads, or sectors than your drive has, you probably will see 1790 or 1791 Power-On Self Test (POST) error codes. These error codes indicate a "fixed disk 0 (or disk 1) read error," which most likely means that your selection is improper. If you are installing an Intelligent IDE drive, it will translate the parameters you enter, which means they will work as long as they do not add up to more total sectors than the drive actually has.

The Maxtor XT-1140 drive requires no write precompensation. Type 9 in the original AT BIOS indicates a precompensation start cylinder of 65535, the largest number that can be stored with 16 bits; this essentially means that write precompensation will never be done, because you will never reach an actual cylinder number that high. For entries that have a value of 0 for the Write Precompensation figure, write precompensation is performed on all cylinders (starting with 0).

The "landing cylinder" designation is superfluous because this drive automatically parks and locks its heads at power-down, although it would be used if you ever ran a correctly written head parking program.

Because there is no acceptable type in the original AT BIOS, and there is no user-definable type either, this controller has an on-board BIOS that can override the motherboard BIOS and provide the drive-type information to the system. In this case, the motherboard BIOS is set to type 1, and the on-board controller BIOS takes over. To run the format program in the on-board BIOS, you use the DOS DEBUG program to point to the starting address of the BIOS format routine.

IBM AT Drive-Type Tables

Rather than use a ROM on the controller card to support the card and drive tables, IBM incorporated the hard disk ROM BIOS as part of the main system ROM that resides on the motherboard. This ROM contains a hard disk table with at least 15 entries. Later AT ROMs have tables with 23 entries. The XT 286 (really a late-model AT) has a table with 24 entries, and some PS/1 and PS/2 systems have as many as 44 entries. In each of these tables, entry 15 is reserved and not usable. The tables are downward-compatible in the newer systems. For example, the PS/2 Model 80-111 has 32 table entries in its ROM, and the entries in the earlier systems match exactly on the specifications. Drive type 9, for example, is the same in all these systems, from the earliest AT to the newest PS/2 systems. Compatible systems are not consistent in regard to drive tables. The Appendix lists a number of hard disk drive tables for different compatible systems.

Table 10.18 lists the entries in the IBM motherboard ROM BIOS hard disk parameter table for AT or PS/2 systems using ST-506/412 (standard or IDE) controllers.

Type tables for compatible BIOS versions are listed in the Appendix. Most IBM systems do not have every entry in this table. The maximum usable type number varies for each specific ROM version. The maximum usable type for each IBM ROM is indicated in table 10.19.

Type	Cyls	Heads	WPC	Ctrl	LZ	S/T	Meg	MB
1	306	4	128	00h	305	17	10.16	10.65
2	615	4	300	00h	615	17	20.42	21.41
3	615	6	300	00h	615	17	30.63	32.12
4	940	8	512	00h	940	17	62.42	65.45
5	940	6	512	00h	940	17	46.82	49.09
6	615	4	65535	00h	615	17	20.42	21.41

Table 10.18 IBM AT and PS/2 Hard Disk Drive Types

(continues)

III

Hardware Considerations

Table 10.18 Continued

Type	Cyls	Heads	WPC	Ctrl	LZ	S/T	Meg	MB
7	462	8	256	00h	511	17	30.68	32.17
8	733	5	65535	00h	733	17	30.42	31.90
9	900	15	65535	08h	901	17	12.06	117.50
10	820	3	65535	00h	820	17	20.42	21.41
11	855	5	65535	00h	855	17	35.49	37.21
12	855	7	65535	00h	855	17	49.68	52.09
13	306	8	128	00h	319	17	20.32	21.31
14	733	7	65535	00h	733	17	42.59	44.66
15	0	0	0	00h	0	0	0	0
16	612	4	0	00h	663	17	20.32	21.31
17	977	5	300	00h	977	17	40.55	42.52
18	977	7	65535	00h	977	17	56.77	59.53
19	1024	7	512	00h	1023	17	59.50	62.39
20	733	5	300	00h	732	17	30.42	31.90
21	733	7	300	00h	732	17	42.59	44.66
22	733	5	300	00h	733	17	30.42	31.90
23	306	4	0	00h	336	17	10.16	10.65
24	612	4	305	00h	663	17	20.32	21.31
25	306	4	65535	00h	340	17	10.16	10.65
26	612	4	65535	00h	670	17	20.32	21.31
27	698	7	300	20h	732	17	40.56	42.53
28	976	5	488	20h	977	17	40.51	42.48
29	306	4	0	00h	340	17	10.16	10.65
30	611	4	306	20h	663	17	20.29	21.27
31	732	7	300	20h	732	17	42.53	44.60
32	1023	5	65535	20h	1023	17	42.46	44.52
33	614	4	65535	20h	663	25	29.98	31.44
34	775	2	65535	20h	900	27	20.43	21.43
35	921	2	65535	20h	1000	33	29.68	31.12
36	402	4	65535	20h	460	26	20.41	21.41
37	580	6	65535	20h	640	26	44.18	46.33
38	845	2	65535	20h	1023	36	29.71	31.15
39	769	3	65535	20h	1023	36	40.55	42.52
40	531	4	65535	20h	532	39	40.45	42.41
41	577	2	65535	20h	1023	36	20.29	21.27
42	654	2	65535	20h	674	32	20.44	21.43
43	923	5	65535	20h	1023	36	81.12	85.06
44	531	8	65535	20h	532	39	80.89	84.82

Type	Cyls	Heads	WPC	Ctrl	LZ	S/T	Meg	MB
45	0	0	0	00h	0	0	0.00	0.00
46	0	0	0	00h	0	0	0.00	0.00
47	0	0	0	00h	0	0	0.00	0.00

Type = Drive type number
Cyls = Total number of cylinders
Heads = Total number of heads
WPC = Write precompensation starting cylinder
Ctrl = Control byte, values as follows:
    Bit 0   01h, not used (XT=drive step rate)
    Bit 1   02h, not used (XT=drive step rate)
    Bit 2   04h, not used (XT=drive step rate)
    Bit 3   08h, more than 8 heads
    Bit 4   10h, not used (XT=embedded servo)
    Bit 5   20h, OEM defect map at (Cyls + 1)
    Bit 6   40h, disable disk retries
    Bit 7   80h, disable disk retries
LZ = Landing zone cylinder for head parking
S/T = Number of sectors per track
Meg = Drive capacity in megabytes
MB = Drive capacity in millions of bytes
Table entry 15 is reserved as a CMOS pointer to indicate that the actual type is greater than 15.

Type tables for compatible BIOS versions are listed in the Appendix. Most IBM systems do not have every entry in this table. The maximum usable type for each IBM ROM is indicated in table 10.19.

Table 10.19 Number of Drive Types in Various IBM BIOS Versions					
System Description	ROM BIOS date	ID byte	Sub-model byte	Revision	No. of ST-506 /412 drive types
PS/2 25	06/26/87	FA	01	00	26
PS/2 30	09/02/86	FA	00	00	26
PS/2 30	12/12/86	FA	00	01	26
PS/2 30	02/05/87	FA	00	02	26
PC-AT	01/10/84	FC	N/A	N/A	15
PC-AT	06/10/85	FC	00	01	23
PC-AT	11/15/85	FC	01	00	23
PC-XT 286	04/21/86	FC	02	00	24
PS/1	12/01/89	FC	0B	00	44
PS/2 25-286	06/28/89	FC	09	02	37
PS/2 30-286	08/25/88	FC	09	00	37

(continues)

III

Hardware Considerations

Table 10.19 Continued					
System Description	**ROM BIOS date**	**ID byte**	**Sub-model byte**	**Revision**	**No. of ST-506 /412 drive types**
PS/2 30-286	06/28/89	FC	09	02	37
PS/2 35 SX	03/15/91	F8	19	05	37
PS/2 35 SX	04/04/91	F8	19	06	37
PS/2 40 SX	03/15/91	F8	19	05	37
PS/2 40 SX	04/04/91	F8	19	06	37
PS/2 L40 SX	02/27/91	F8	23	02	37
PS/2 50	02/13/87	FC	04	00	32
PS/2 50	05/09/87	FC	04	01	32
PS/2 50 Z	01/28/88	FC	04	02	33
PS/2 50 Z	04/18/88	FC	04	03	33
PS/2 55 SX	11/02/88	F8	0C	00	33
PS/2 60	02/13/87	FC	05	00	32
PS/2 65 SX	02/08/90	F8	1C	00	33
PS/2 70 386	01/29/88	F8	09	00	33
PS/2 70 386	04/11/88	F8	09	02	33
PS/2 70 386	12/15/89	F8	09	04	33
PS/2 70 386	01/29/88	F8	04	00	33
PS/2 70 386	04/11/88	F8	04	02	33
PS/2 70 386	12/15/89	F8	04	04	33
PS/2 70 386	06/08/88	F8	0D	00	33
PS/2 70 386	02/20/89	F8	0D	01	33
PS/2 P70 386	01/18/89	F8	0B	00	33
PS/2 80 386	03/30/87	F8	00	00	32
PS/2 80 386	10/07/87	F8	01	00	32

Numbers in ID byte, Submodel byte, and Revision columns are in hexadecimal.

If you have a compatible, this table will probably be inaccurate for any of the entries past type 15. (Most compatibles follow the IBM table for at least the first 15 entries.) A number of compatible system drive tables are in the Appendix at the back of this book, including tables for a number of different compatible systems from COMPAQ to Zenith.

Most IBM PS/2 systems are supplied with hard disk drives that have the defect map written as data on the cylinder that is one cylinder beyond the highest reported cylinder. This special data is read by the IBM PS/2 Advanced Diagnostics low-level format program, which automates the entry of the defect list and eliminates the chance for human error (as long as you use only the IBM PS/2 Advanced Diagnostics program for hard disk low-level formatting).

This drive table information does not apply to IBM, ESDI, or SCSI hard disk controllers, host adapters, and drives. Because ESDI and SCSI controllers and host adapters query the drive directly for the required parameters, no table entry selection is necessary. The table for ST-506/412 drives, however, is still in the ROM BIOS of most PS/2 systems, even if the model came standard with the ESDI or SCSI disk subsystem.

Most compatibles have enhanced the motherboard ROM BIOS tables in three ways:

- *Additional types.* The first thing they did was to add more drive types to the table. Because the table had room for 47 or more entries, many compatible BIOS versions simply filled out all of the entries with values matching the most popular drives on the market, making drive installations generally easier. IBM tables were often short of the maximum number of possible entries.

- *User-definable drive types.* Most compatibles then added a user-definable type, which took unused areas of the CMOS memory and used them to store all of the drive parameter information. This was an excellent solution because then you could type in parameters during setup that matched any drive on the market. The only draw-back was that if the CMOS battery died or the saved values were corrupted in some way, the information would have to be reentered exactly as it was before to regain access to the drive. Many people did not write down the parameters they used, or used improper parameters that caused them problems.

- *Automatic Detection.* Most of the newer BIOS versions now include a feature that is specific to IDE drives. Because most IDE drives are intelligent and will respond to a command called Identify Drive, the BIOS sends this command to the drive, which then responds with the correct parameters. This feature completely eliminates the need to type in the parameters, as the BIOS will accept what the drive tells it.

Most of the newer compatible BIOS versions actually have both the user definable type feature as well as the automatic determination for IDE drives.

Drive Table Alteration

Some drives do not match the table entries well. One way around the table match problem is to purchase drives that match your tables. This solution can be limiting, however, especially if you have the earlier ROM-equipped systems. Most IBM-compatible systems have table entries all the way to type 47, but IBM AT systems stop much lower than that.

ROM Patching

A second way around the drive-table limitation is to patch the correct entries for the desired drive and reburn your own ROMs. This solution is illegal commercially and therefore is limited to "hacker" status, which means that you can do it to your own system but that you cannot legally sell patched IBM ROMs. For those so inclined, instructions for patching the BIOS are included in Chapter 12.

ROM Replacement

A third way around the drive-table limits is to purchase and install a new ROM BIOS. A Phoenix ROM BIOS set, for example, costs about $50. These ROMs include a user-definable drive type setting, which is the most elegant solution to this problem. A new set of ROMs probably will give you additional features that you did not have originally, such as a built-in Setup program, support for HD or ED 3 1/2-inch floppy drives, and Enhanced Keyboard support.

RLL / ESDI System Configuration

RLL and ESDI drives are usually not represented at all in the internal drive tables of older BIOS versions, and consequently, the controllers for these drives often have onboard a ROM BIOS which either contains its own internal list of choices for the interface or else provides the ability to dynamically configure (define) the controller to the specific geometry of the drive.

If you have a motherboard BIOS with a user-defined drive type (recommended), then you can simply enter the correct parameters and the drive will be supported. Remember to write down the parameters you use as if you lose them, you can lose access to the drive if they are not re-entered properly. When using a user-definable type, you can disable the controller BIOS.

IDE System Configuration

Intelligent IDE drives can use the geometry that represents their true physical parameters, or else they can translate to other drive geometries that are equal to or less than the total number of sectors. Simply select a type or enter a user-definable type that is less than or equal to the total capacity of the drive, and they should work.

SCSI System Configuration

Almost all SCSI drives use DRIVE TYPE 0 or NONE, as the host adapter BIOS and the drive communicate together to establish the drive geometry. The low-level formatting routines are usually accessed on the host adapter through DEBUG or are found on disk in the form of a configuration, setup, and format program. All SCSI drives are low-level formatted at the factory.

XT Type System Drive Configuration

XT type systems typically store the drive setup or type information in ROM. The IBM XT uses a controller with a ROM that contains the hard disk controller BIOS (basic input-output system) and a table of four drive types indicating the supported drives. You set jumpers or switches on that controller to indicate which of the four drives you are installing. XT systems lack the CMOS memory and setup methods used by AT class systems.

Because the on-board BIOS in IBM's original XT controllers only supported four drives, most aftermarket controllers rapidly evolved into having an autoconfigure capability. This is essentially equivalent to the user definable type in most later compatible AT BIOS versions. This allowed you to dynamically configure the controller and drive by entering parameters through the controller BIOS configuration routine. These parameters were often stored in a hidden sector on the drive and were loaded each time the system was powered on. This technique was used because XT class systems do not have CMOS memory in which to store information like this.

XT Class System Drive Selection

IBM XT hard disk controllers have used two different ROMs over the years, but they each have only four entry tables, which means that only four different drives can be supported by a single ROM. Thus, virtually every time you want to add a different type of hard disk to an IBM XT, you must reburn the ROM with the correct values for the new drive. You can try to anticipate future upgrades and burn in the values for those drives as well.

A new generation of controllers for the IBM PC and IBM XT alleviates the problem with the IBM XT disk controller. These new controllers request the type of drive being connected and store the information in a specially reserved track on the drive. Every time the system is booted, the information is read from that location and the system has the correct drive type. Thus, a drive table with an infinite number of entries is possible. Regardless of the parameters for your drive, the system can support it because this "autoconfigure ROM" is built into the controller. No matter what type of disk drive you select, make sure that your controller is an *autoconfigure type*; it eliminates problems with table entries that do not match your drives.

Tables 10.20 and 10.21 list the ROM BIOS drive parameters in IBM XT (Xebec 1210) hard disk controllers.

> **Note**
>
> *MB* and *Meg* sometimes are used interchangeably, but this is not exactly correct. MB is one million bytes, or 1,000,000 bytes. Meg (or M) is one megabyte, which is equal to 1,048,576 bytes. (1 megabyte = 1 kilobyte times 1 kilobyte, and 1 kilobyte = 1024 bytes. Thus, 1 megabyte = 1024 times 1024 = 1,048,576.)

To select one of the drive table entries in the IBM XT controllers (Xebec 1210), you would set the drive table selection jumper (Jumper W5). The following table shows how these jumpers should be set to select a particular table entry. For example, to select table entry 2 for drive 0 (C:), you would set the jumper Off at position 1 and On at position 2.

Table 10.20 IBM 10M Hard Disk Controller (Xebec 1210) Drive Parameter Tables

Entry	Type	Cyls	Heads	WPC	Ctrl	LZ	S/T	Meg	MB
0	_	306	2	0	00h	00h	00h	5.08	5.33
1	_	375	8	0	05h	00h	00h	24.90	26.11
2	_	306	6	256	05h	00h	00h	15.24	15.98
3	_	306	4	0	05h	00h	00h	10.16	10.65

III

Hardware Considerations

Table 10.21 IBM 20M Hard Disk Controller (Xebec 1210) Drive Parameter Tables									
Entry	**Type**	**Cyls**	**Heads**	**WPC**	**Ctrl**	**LZ**	**S/T**	**Meg**	**MB**
0	1	306	4	0	05h	305	17	10.16	10.65
1	16	612	4	0	05h	663	17	20.32	21.31
2	2	615	4	300	05h	615	17	20.42	21.41
3	13	306	8	128	05h	319	17	20.32	21.31

Entry = Controller table position
Type = Drive type number
Cyls = Total number of cylinders
Heads = Total number of heads
WPC = Write precompensation starting cylinder
Ctrl = Control byte, values as follows:
    Bit 0   01h, drive step rate
    Bit 1   02h, drive step rate
    Bit 2   04h, drive step rate
    Bit 3   08h, more than eight heads
    Bit 4   10h, embedded servo drive
    Bit 5   20h, OEM defect map at (Cyls + 1)
    Bit 6   40h, disable ECC retries
    Bit 7   80h, disable disk access retries
Xebec 1210 Drive Step Rate Coding (Control Byte bits 0-3)
    00h, 3-millisecond step rate
    04h, 200-microsecond buffered step
    05h, 70-microsecond buffered step
    06h, 30-microsecond buffered step
    07h, 15-microsecond buffered step
LZ = Landing zone cylinder for head parking
S/T = Number of sectors per track
Meg = Drive capacity in megabytes
MB = Drive capacity in millions of bytes
The Landing Zone field and Sectors per Track fields are not used in the 10M (original) controller and contain 00h values for each entry.

Table 10.22 IBM XT Controller (Xebec 1210) Drive Table Jumper (W5) Settings				
Drive 0 Table Entry	**1**	**2**	**3**	**4**
Jumper 1	On	On	Off	Off
Jumper 2	On	Off	On	Off
Jumper 3	On	On	Off	Off
Jumper 4	On	Off	On	Off

Autoconfigure Controllers

To install the example drive in an IBM XT, I could use the original IBM XT controller (Xebec 1210), but the built-in tables in that controller do not match my drive. I would have to download the ROM to disk and patch it to contain the correct drive-table values.

If you can wield the DOS DEBUG program and have access to an EPROM burner, you can patch the correct table into one of the existing four table positions on the controller, and the controller will operate correctly with the drive. (I used this procedure on my vintage 1983 XT controller. The system works fine, but its best interleave is 5 to 1.)

Faster autoconfigure ROM controllers are available at such low prices that a better alternative is to purchase one. This example describes the installation of a Scientific Micro Systems Omti 5520A-10 controller, which has complete autoconfigure capability and supports a 2-to-1 interleave in the IBM PC and XT. Although this controller is no longer available, Data Technology Corporation (DTC) makes a DTC5150XL controller that offers even more features. The installation and configuration of all autoconfigure controllers are very similar. DTC also makes a DTC5160XL controller that is an RLL version of the previous controller. These controllers support co-residency, which means that they can be added to a system which already has an existing controller. These controllers can be installed with no hassle, run three times faster than the old Xebec controller, and cost less than $100. (Times have changed—an original Xebec 1210 cost me $795 in 1983.)

The next set of required information for the example installation follows:

- Interrupt Request Channel (IRQ) = 5

- DMA channel (DRQ) = 3

- ROM locations used = C8000 to C9FFF

- I/O ports = 320 to 32F

- Autoconfigure start location = C8006

- Step pulse rates = 10, 25, 50, 70, 200, and 3000μs

- Best interleave = 2 to 1 (4.77 MHz XT)

You need some of this information to ensure that the card is uniquely configured compared with other cards in the system. The system cannot have another card using the same IRQ, DMA, ROM, or I/O ports as this card. Keep this information for future reference, and cross-check for conflicts when you add other cards to the system. The autoconfigure start location, step pulse rates, and interleave information is necessary for completing the drive setup.

The next step is to activate the controller's built-in autoconfigure routine. When you do so, an autoconfigure controller prompts you for information about the drive (otherwise found in ROM tables), and then records the information directly on the drive in an area reserved by the controller on the first track. The advantage of the autoconfigure controller is that when you change drives, the controller can adapt. You never have to patch ROM-based tables with an EPROM burner because this drive stores them dynamically on the drive. After the routine is completed, the controller reads this information every time the system is powered up, and "knows" how to boot from the drive.

III

Hardware Considerations

One potential problem with storing the parameters on the drive is that if they are accidentally overwritten, the drive is inaccessible. For this reason, you must be careful with any program that performs a low-level format on the drive. Most nondestructive formatters, such as the Norton Utilities Calibrate program, refuse to reformat the first track of any drive, to avoid overwriting any of this special autoconfigure data.

To run the autoconfigure routine, follow these steps:

1. Boot DOS 3.3 or higher.

2. Run the DOS DEBUG program.

3. At the DEBUG prompt, enter the information to tell DEBUG to move the system instruction pointer to the autoconfigure ROM start location. For this specific controller, you enter:

    G=C800:6

Because autoconfigure controllers from different manufacturers have different starting locations for the ROM BIOS format routine built into the controller, look in the manual to find the starting location for the specific controller you are installing. Table 10.23 provides the controller BIOS low-level format addresses used with DEBUG for several popular controller brands.

Table 10.23 Controller BIOS Low-Level Format Addresses	
Controller Manufacturer	**Low-Level Format Address**
Western Digital	g=XXXX:5
DTC	g=XXXX:5
Adaptec	g=XXXX:CCC
Seagate	g=XXXX:5
SMS-OMTI	g=XXXX:6

Replace the "XXXX" value with the starting segment address of the ROM as configured in the controller. Most controller ROMs can be configured for a variety of starting addresses in segments C000h and D000h. Most controllers will have C800 or D800h as starting segment addresses, but you will have to consult the controller documentation and controller jumper settings to be sure.

After you enter the last DEBUG instruction, the autoconfigure routine asks several questions about the drive and controller: how many heads and cylinders the drive has, what the starting write precompensation cylinder is, and how fast the step pulses should be sent. Use the information you gathered about the drive and controller to answer these questions.

In the example, you would indicate that the controller should pulse the drive with step pulses spaced 10µs apart. To establish this figure, look at the range of spacing the drive will accept, compare it to what the controller can send, and select the fastest rate that both can agree on. This procedure is similar to configuring a serial printer and serial port for 9600 bps transmission. Why not go as fast as the hardware will allow? The Maxtor XT-1140 manual states that drive seek performance on this particular drive degrades if step pulses are sent at intervals greater than 13µs. Setting this specification to a setting that is optimum for your drive can really "tweak" a drive's seek performance.

The autoconfigure program also asks you to specify the desired interleave. An interleave of 2 to 1 is the best value for the example controller in a 4.77 MHz IBM PC or IBM XT system. This interleave value was determined by a simple trial-and-error testing session in which the disk was formatted at various interleaves, from 6 to 1 (the IBM XT default) down to 1 to 1. The transfer rate improved with each lower interleave until 1 to 1, at which point the transfer rate slowed by more than 800 percent. At 1 to 1, this controller cannot keep up with the rate at which the next sector comes under the heads; it requires 17 full revolutions of the disk to read a track, compared with 2 revolutions to read a track at a 2-to-1 interleave.

Finally, the autoconfigure program asks whether the drive has defects and gives you the opportunity to enter them. The example drive has seven defects (printed on a sticker on top of the drive as well as included on a printed sheet). Entering this information causes the low-level format program to specially mark these tracks with invalid checksum figures, ensuring that these locations are never read or written to. Later, when DOS is used to high-level format the disk, the DOS format program will be unable to read these locations and will mark the file allocation table with information so that the locations will never be utilized. If you do not enter these locations properly, data or program files could use these defective tracks and become corrupted. Always mark these locations.

With the controller used for this example, the low-level format is part of the autoconfigure routine. After you answer the questions, the drive is low-level formatted, the defects are marked, and a scan is made for defects that were marked improperly or became bad after the manufacturer's original tests. Finally, the autoconfigure information is written to a specially reserved track on the disk. When this process is completed, the drive is ready for DOS installation.

Formatting and Software Installation

Proper setup and formatting are critical to a drive's performance and reliability. This section describes the procedures used to format a hard disk drive correctly. Use these procedures when you install a new drive in a system or immediately after you recover data from a hard disk that has been exhibiting problems.

Three major steps complete the formatting process for a hard disk drive subsystem:

- Low-level format
- Partitioning
- High-level format

Considerations before Low-Level Formatting

In a low-level format (LLF), which is a real format, the tracks and sectors of the disk are outlined and written. During the LLF, data is written across the entire disk. An improper low-level format results in lost data and many read and write failures. You need to consider several things before initiating a low-level format.

Data Backup. Low-level formatting is the primary standard repair procedure for hard disk drives that are having problems. Because data values are copied to the drive at every possible location during an LLF, necessary data-recovery operations must be performed *before* an LLF operation.

> **Caution**
>
> After an LLF has been performed, you cannot recover any information previously written to the drive.

Because a LLF will overwrite all of the data on a drive, it is a good way to erase an entire drive if you are trying to insure that nobody will be able to get the data from it. Government standards for this type of procedure actually require the data to be overwritten several times with different patters, but for most intents and purposes, if the drive is overwritten once, nobody will be able to read any data that was on it.

System Temperature. Sector header and trailer information is written or updated only during the LLF operation. During normal read and write activity, only the 512 bytes plus the CRC (Cyclic Redundancy Check) bytes in the trailer are written in a sector. Temperature-induced dimensional changes in the drive platters during read and write operations can become a problem.

When a 5 1/4-inch platter drive is low-level formatted five minutes after power up at a relatively cold platter temperature of 70 degrees F, the sector headers and trailers and the 512-byte dummy data values are written to each track on each platter at specific locations. Suppose that you save a file on a drive that has been running for several hours and at a platter temperature of 140 degrees F. The data areas of only several sectors are updated. But with the drive platters as much as 70 degrees warmer than when the drive was formatted, each aluminum drive platter will have expanded in size by 2.5-thousandths of an inch (taking into account the coefficient of linear thermal expansion of aluminum). Each track therefore would have moved outward a distance of approximately 1.25-thousandths of an inch. Most 5 1/4-inch hard disks have track densities between 500 and 1000 tracks per inch, with distances of only 1- to 2-thousandths of an inch between adjacent tracks. As a result, the thermal expansion of a typical 5 1/4-inch hard disk platter could cause the tracks to migrate from one-half to more than one full track of distance underneath the heads. If the drive head movement mechanism does not compensate for these thermally induced dimensional changes in the platters, severe mistracking results.

When this happens, the data areas in each sector that have been updated at the higher temperature fail to line up with the sector header and trailer information. If the sector header and trailer information cannot be read properly, DOS usually issues an error message like this one:

```
Sector not found reading drive A
Abort, Retry, Ignore, Fail?
```

The data is misaligned with the sector boundaries on those tracks. This thermal effect can work in reverse also: If the drive is formatted and written to while it is extremely hot, it may not read properly while cold because of dimensional changes in the platters. This problem occurs with drives that have the "Monday morning blues," in which they spin but cannot read data properly when they are first powered on, especially after being off for an extended period of time (over a weekend, for example). If you leave the power to the system on for some time so that the drive can warm up, the system then may boot and run normally. If this happens, the next step is to back up the drive completely and initiate a new low-level format at the proper operating temperature (described next). This procedure enables the drive to work normally again until temperature-induced mistracking becomes great enough to cause the problem again.

Knowing that temperature fluctuations can cause mistracking, you should understand the reason for the following basic rules for disk use:

- Leave the system's power on for at least 30 minutes before performing a low-level format on its hard disk. This step ensures that the platters are at a normal operating temperature and have dimensionally stabilized.

- If possible, allow a system some time to warm up after power up before storing any data on the hard disk. This is not required for voice coil drives.

If you have a cheap stepper motor drive that consistently exhibits temperature-related mistracking problems, you may want to consider running the drive constantly. Doing so would extend its trouble-free life span significantly because the temperature and dimensions of the platters would stay relatively constant.

These kinds of temperature-fluctuation problems are more of a problem with drives that have open-loop stepper motor actuators (which offer no thermal compensation) than with the closed-loop voice coil actuators (which follow temperature-induced track migration and compensate completely, resulting in no tracking errors even with large changes in platter dimensions).

Modern voice coil actuator drives do not exhibit these dimensional instabilities due to thermal expansion and contraction of the platters because they have a track-following servo mechanism. As the tracks move, the positioner automatically compensates. Many of these drives undergo a noticeable thermal compensation sequence every five minutes or so for the first 30 minutes after first being powered on, and then usually every 30 minutes after that. During these thermal compensation routines, you will hear the heads move back and forth to measure and compensate for platter dimensional changes.

Drive Operating Position. Another consideration before formatting a drive is ensuring that the drive is formatted in the operating position it will have when it is installed in the system. Gravity can place different loads on the head actuator that can cause mistracking if the drive changes between a vertical and a horizontal position. This effect is minimized or even completely eliminated in most voice coil drives, but it cannot hurt.

Additionally, drives that are not properly shock mounted (such as the Seagate ST 2xx series) should be formatted only when they are installed in the system because the installation screws exert twisting forces on the drive's Head Disk Assembly (HDA), which can cause mistracking. If you format the drive with the mounting screws installed tightly, it may not read with the screws out, and vice versa. Be careful not to over tighten the mounting screws because doing so can stress the HDA. This is usually not a problem if the drive's HDA is isolated from the frame by rubber bushings.

In summary, for a proper low-level format, the drive should be

- At a normal operating temperature.

- In a normal operating position.

- Mounted in the host system (if the drive HDA is not shock-mounted or isolated from the drive frame by rubber bushings).

Because many different makes and models of controllers differ in how they write data to a drive, especially with respect to the encoding scheme, it is best to format the drive using the same make and model of controller as the controller that will be used in the host system. Some brands of controllers work exactly alike, however, so this is not an absolute requirement even if the interface is the same. This is, of course, not a problem with IDE or SCSI drives because the controller is built into the drive. Usually, if the controller establishes the drive type using its own on-board ROM rather than the system Setup program, it will be incompatible with other controllers.

Low-Level Format. Of these procedures, the low-level format is most important to ensure trouble-free operation of the drive. It is the most critical of the operations and must be done correctly in order for the drive to work properly. The low-level format includes several subprocedures:

- Scanning for existing defect mapping

- Selecting the interleave

- Formatting and marking (or re-marking) manufacturer defects

- Running a surface analysis

On some systems, such as the IBM PS/2, these sub procedures are performed automatically by the system's low-level format program and require no user intervention. On others, you must take the initiative.

To perform the drive defect mapping, to select an interleave, and to complete a surface analysis of the drive, you need information about the drive, the controller, and possibly the system. This information usually is provided in separate manuals or documents for each item; therefore, be sure that you get the complete documentation for your drive and controller products when you purchase them. The specific information required depends on the type of system, controller, and low-level format program used.

Defect Mapping. Before formatting the disk, you need to know whether the drive has defects that have to be mapped out. Most drives come with a list of defects discovered by the manufacturer during the drive's final quality-control testing. These defects must be marked so that they are not used later to store programs or data.

Defect mapping is one of the most critical aspects of low-level formatting. To understand the defect-mapping procedures, you first must understand what happens when a defect is mapped on a drive.

The manufacturer's defect list usually indicates defects by cylinder and track. When this information is entered, the low-level format program marks these tracks with invalid checksum figures in the header of each of the sectors, which ensures that nothing can read or write to these locations. When DOS does a high-level format of the disk, the DOS FORMAT program cannot read these locations and marks the involved clusters in the file allocation table (FAT) so that they will never be used.

The list of defects the manufacturer gives you is probably more extensive than what a program could determine from your system because the manufacturer's test equipment is far more sensitive than a regular disk controller. Do not expect a format program to automatically find the defects; you will probably have to enter them manually. An exception to this is the new IBM PS/2 systems, in which the defect list is encoded in a special area of the drive not accessible by normal software. The IBM PS/2 low-level format program (included on the Reference disk that comes with IBM PS/2 systems) reads this special map, thereby eliminating the need to enter these locations manually.

Most new drives are not low-level formatted by the manufacturer. Even if you bought a drive that had been low-level formatted, you would not know the temperature and the operating position of the drive when it was formatted. For best results, perform your own low-level format on a drive after you receive it. If you bought a system with a drive already installed by the manufacturer or dealer, they probably did a low-level format for you. To be safe, however, you might want to do a new low-level format in the system's new environment.

Although an *actual defect* is technically different from a *marked defect*, they should correspond to one another if the drive is formatted properly. For example, I can enter the location of a good track into the low-level format program as a defective track. The low-level format program then corrupts the checksum values for each of the sectors on that track, rendering them unreadable and unwriteable. When the DOS FORMAT program encounters that track, it finds it unreadable and marks the clusters occupying that track as bad in the FAT. After that, as the drive is used, DOS ensures that no data is ever written to that track. The drive stays in that condition until I redo the low-level format of that track, indicate that the track is not to be marked defective, and redo the high-level format that no longer will find the track unreadable and therefore allow those clusters to be used. In general, unless an area is marked as defective in the low-level format, it will not be found by the high-level format and DOS will use it for data storage.

Defect mapping becomes a problem when someone formats a hard disk and fails to enter the manufacturer's defect list, which contains actual defect locations, so that the low-level format can establish these tracks or sectors as marked defects. Letting a defect go unmarked will cost you data when the area is used to store a file that subsequently cannot be retrieved. Unfortunately, the low-level format program does not automatically find and mark any areas that are defective on a disk. The manufacturer defect list is produced by very sensitive test equipment that tests the drive at an analog level. Most manufacturers indicate areas as defective even if they are just marginal. The problem is that a marginal area today may be totally unreadable in the future. You should avoid any area suspected as being defective by entering the location during the low-level format so that the area is marked; then DOS is forced to avoid the area.

Currently Marked Defects Scan. Most low-level format programs have the capability to perform a scan for previously marked defects on a drive. Some programs call this operation a defect scan; IBM calls it Read Verify in the IBM Advanced Diagnostics. This type of operation is nondestructive and reports by cylinder and head position all track locations marked bad. Do not mistake this for a true scan for defective tracks on a disk, which is a destructive operation normally called a surface analysis (discussed later, in the "Surface Analysis" section).

If a drive was previously low-level formatted, you should scan the disk for previously marked defects before running a fresh low-level format, for two reasons:

- *Ensure that the previous low-level format correctly marked all manufacturer-listed defects.* Compare the report of the defect scan to the manufacturer's list, and note discrepancies. Any defects on the manufacturer's list but not found by the defect scan were not marked properly.

- *Look for tracks that are marked as defective but are not on the manufacturer's list.* These tracks may have been added by a previously run surface-analysis program, in which case they should be retained, or they may result from typographical errors in marking the manufacturer's defect on the part of the previous formatter. One of my drive's manufacturer's list showed Cylinder 514 Head 14 as defective. A defect scan, however, showed that track as good but Cylinder 814 Head 14 marked as bad. Because the latter location was not on the manufacturer's list and the transcription of a 5 to an 8 would be an easy mistake to make, I concluded that a typographical error was the cause and reformatted the drive, marking Cylinder 514 Head 14 as bad, and enabling Cylinder 814 Head 14 to be formatted as a good track, thus "unmarking" it.

If you run a surface analysis and encounter defects in addition to those on the manufacturer's list, you can do one of two things. If the drive is under warranty, consider returning it. If the drive is out of warranty, grab a pen and write on the defect list sticker, adding the bad tracks discovered by the surface-analysis program. (The IBM PS/2 low-level formatter built into the Reference disk automatically performs a surface analysis immediately after the low-level format; if it discovers additional defects, it adds them automatically to the defect list recorded on the drive.) Adding new defects to the sticker in this manner means that these areas are not forgotten when the drive is subsequently reformatted.

Manufacturer's Defect List. The manufacturer tests a new hard disk using sophisticated analog test instruments that perform an extensive analysis of the surface of the platters. This kind of testing can indicate the functionality of an area of the disk with great accuracy, precisely measuring information such as the signal-to-noise ratio and recording accuracy.

Some manufacturers have more demanding standards than others about what they consider defects. Many people are bothered by the fact that when they purchase a new drive, it comes with a list of defective locations. Some even demand that the seller install a defect-free drive. The seller can satisfy this request by substituting a drive made by a company with less stringent quality control, but the drive will be of poorer quality. The manufacturer who produces drives with more listed defects usually has a higher-quality product because the number of listed defects depends on the level of quality control. What constitutes a defect depends on who is interpreting the test results.

To mark the manufacturer defects listed on the drive, consult the documentation that goes with your low-level format program. For most drives, the manufacturer's defect list shows the defects by cylinder and head; other lists locate the defect down to the bit that is bad on the track, starting with the index location.

Caution

Make sure that all manufacturer's defects have been entered before proceeding with the low-level format.

Some systems automatically mark the manufacturer's defects, using a special defect file recorded on the drive by the manufacturer. For such a system, you need a special low-level format program that knows how to find and read this file. Automatic defect-map entry is standard for IBM PS/2 systems and for most ESDI and all SCSI systems. Consult the drive or controller vendor for the proper low-level format program and defect-handling procedures for your drive.

Note

Do not mark defective clusters on the disk with a data-recovery utility such as Norton, Mace, or PC Tools because they cannot mark the sectors or tracks at the low-level format level. The bad cluster marks they make are stored only in the FAT and are erased during the next high-level format operation.

III

Hardware Considerations

Surface Analysis. A *defect scan* is a scan for marked defects; a *surface analysis* is a scan for actual defects. A surface analysis ignores tracks already marked defective by a low-level format and tests the unmarked tracks. The surface analysis program writes 512 bytes to each sector on the good tracks, reads the sectors back, and compares the data read to what was written. If the data does not verify, the program (like a low-level format) marks the track bad by corrupting the checksum values for each of the sectors on that track. A proper surface analysis is like a low-level format program in that it should bypass DOS and the BIOS so that it can turn off controller retry operations and also to see when ECC (Error Correction Code) is invoked to correct soft errors.

Surface-analysis programs are destructive: they write over every sector, except those already marked bad. A surface-analysis program should be run immediately after a low-level format, to determine whether defects have appeared in addition to the manufacturer's defects entered during the low-level format. A defect scan after the low-level format and the surface analysis shows the cumulative tracks marked bad by both programs.

If the manufacturer's defect list has been lost, you can use the surface-analysis program to indicate which tracks are bad, but this program can never duplicate the accuracy or sensitivity of the original manufacturer testing.

For example, if a spot in the sector were performing to 51 percent of capacity, it would be good enough to pass in a PC surface analysis. The next day, due to variances in the drive and electronics, that same spot might perform at only 49 percent of capacity, failing a surface analysis. If you must use a surface analysis as your only source of defect information for a drive, be sure to use the option of increasing the number of times each track will be tested, and run the program over an evening or weekend for a higher probability of catching an elusive or intermittent bad track.

Some low-level format and surface-analysis programs have hype-filled advertisements that make misleading and even false claims of performance and capability. Some programs even "unmark" defects that have been purposely marked by the initial, properly done low-level format according to the manufacturer's supplied list of defects, because the program determines that the area in question is not defective. (This is unbelievable!) If the drive is a good one, no surface-analysis program can possibly find all the defects on the manufacturer's list. Only factory testing at the analog level could indicate these defects because most manufacturers include even slightly marginal areas on their list.

For example, I have a 40-megabyte drive that has 27 manufacturer defects on the bad-track list; this drive is probably the highest quality 40-megabyte unit sold. Most cheaper 40-megabyte drives would have five or fewer defects on the bad-track list. I have run virtually every surface-analysis program on this drive, and none could find more than five of the 27 defects. This of course means that higher quality drives are subjected to more stringent testing that will flag more questionable areas. Do not judge a drive by the number of defects listed by the manufacturer, unless you are sure that the manufacturers perform tests at the same threshold levels.

I do not normally run a surface analysis after low-level formatting, for several reasons:

- Compared to formatting, surface analysis takes a long time. Most surface-analysis programs take two to five times longer than a low-level format to complete. A low-level format of a 120M drive takes about 15 minutes, and a surface analysis of the same drive takes an hour or more. Moreover, if you increase the accuracy of the surface analysis by allowing multiple passes or multiple patterns, the surface analysis takes even longer.

- With high-quality drives, I never find defects beyond what the manufacturer specified. In fact, the surface-analysis programs do not even find all the manufacturer's defects if I do not enter them manually. Because the high-quality (voice coil) drives that I use have been tested by the manufacturer to a greater degree than a program can perform on my system, I simply mark all the defects from the manufacturer's list in the low-level format and am done with it. If I were using low-quality (stepper motor) drives or installing a used and out-of-warranty drive, I would consider performing the surface analysis after the low-level format.

Defect-Free Drives. Although some manufacturers claim that the drives they sell or install are defect-free, this is not really true. The defects are mapped out and replaced by spare sectors and tracks. This type of defect mapping, usually called *sector sparing*, insulates the operating system from having to handle the defects. IDE and SCSI drives universally use sector sparing to hide defects, so they all seem defect free.

When you finish the low-level format and surface analysis of a hard disk in non-IDE or non-SCSI installations, several areas on the disk have been marked defective by corrupting the checksum values in the sector headers on the indicated tracks. When the high-level format scans the disk, it locates the defective sectors by failing to read them during the defect scan portion of the high-level format operation. The clusters or allocation units that contain these unreadable sectors are then marked bad in the FAT. When the CHKDSK command is executed, you get a report of how many of these bad clusters are on the disk. The CHKDSK report looks like this (although yours will have different numbers):

```
Volume DRIVE C     created 06-02-1993 9:14p
Volume Serial Number is 3311-1CD3

117116928 bytes total disk space
    73728 bytes in 3 hidden files
   593920 bytes in 268 directories
106430464 bytes in 4068 user files
   143360 bytes in bad sectors
  9875456 bytes available on disk

     2048 bytes in each allocation unit
    57186 total allocation units on disk
     4822 available allocation units on disk

   655360 total bytes memory
   561216 bytes free
```

The 143360 bytes in bad sectors are really only 70 clusters, or allocation units, because each allocation unit contains 2048 bytes.

When I did the low-level format of this disk, I had entered 14 defects, which caused 14 tracks to be corrupted. This disk has 17 sectors per track; therefore, 238 total sectors (17 sectors times 14 tracks) have been corrupted by the low-level format program. Therefore, 121856 total bytes have been marked bad (238 sectors times 512 bytes per sector).

This number does not agree with the total reported by CHKDSK because DOS must mark entire allocation units, not individual sectors. Each allocation unit is made up of four sectors (2,048 bytes) on this disk. Therefore,

> 1 track = 17 sectors = 4 allocation units plus 1 extra sector

DOS must mark a whole allocation unit as bad in the file allocation tables even if only one sector in the unit is bad; therefore, DOS marks five allocation units as bad for each marked track. In bytes, this becomes

> 5 allocation units = 20 sectors = 10,240 bytes (20 sectors times 512 bytes)

Therefore, 10,240 bytes are marked as bad in the FAT for each track marked in the low-level format. And 10,240 bytes per track marked bad times 14 total marked tracks equals 143,360 total bytes marked bad.

From these calculations, you can see that all of the correct defect mapping is in place. The bytes in bad sectors will never be used by files, so they will never bother you. This number should not change over the life of the drive, unless new defects are entered in a subsequent low-level format or surface-analysis program.

The relationship between CHKDSK results and disk defects is not as clear with all drives and controllers. For example, I have an IBM PS/2 Model 70-121 that has a 120M IBM drive with an MCA IDE drive with an embedded ESDI controller. (The controller is built into the drive.) I formatted this drive using IBM Advanced Diagnostics for the IBM PS/2 (included free with the system). After finishing the high-level format, I ran CHKDSK and it reported no bad sectors. Could this be true? Not really. In fact, this drive has more than 140 defects, and all have been correctly marked. How could that be? If the defects were marked, the high-level format should have been unable to read those locations, and CHKDSK would have reported the xxxxxx bytes in bad sectors message. The answer lies in how the drive and controller operate together.

IBM advertises this drive as having 32 sectors per track and 920 cylinders with eight heads, but it actually has 33 sectors per track or a spare sector on every track. When a defect location is given to the low-level format program, it removes the defective sector from use by not numbering it as one of the 32 sectors on that track. Then the program gives the spare sector the number that the defective one would have been given, and the defective sector becomes the spare. Through this technique, the disk can have up to one defect for every track on the drive (7,360 total) without losing capacity. Moreover, entire spare tracks are available on several spare cylinders past 920; if more than one sector on a track is defective, those extra tracks can be used. The disk has enough spare sectors and tracks to accommodate all possible defects.

Sector sparing is standard on all intelligent IDE and all SCSI drives. It is also an option on many ESDI controllers. This is why IDE and SCSI drives never seem to have any bytes in bad sectors. Of course they do, but they are replaced with good sectors from the spare sector pool.

Why Low-Level Format? Even though it is generally not necessary or even recommended to low-level format IDE or SCSI drives, there are a few good reasons to consider a low-level format. One is simply that a low-level format will wipe out all of the data on a drive, ensuring that others will not be able to read or recover it. This is useful if you are selling a system and do not want your data to be readable by the purchaser. Another reason for wiping all of the data from a drive is to remove corrupted or non-DOS operating system partitions, and even virus infections. The best reason, however, is for defect management. As you may have noticed, most ATA-IDE drives appear to have no "bytes in bad sectors" under CHKDSK or any other software.

Any defects that were present on the drive after manufacturing were reallocated by the factory low-level format. Essentially, any known bad sectors are replaced by spare sectors stored in different parts of the drive. If any new defects occur, such as from a minor head/platter contact or drive mishandling, a proper IDE-aware, low-level format program will be able to map the new bad sectors to other spares, thus hiding them and restoring the drive to what appears to be defect-free status.

Because the IDE (ATA) specification is an extension of the IBM/WD ST-506/412 controller interface, the specification includes several new CCB commands that were not a part of the original INT 13h/CCB support. Some of these new CCB commands are vendor-specific and unique to each IDE drive manufacturer. Some manufacturers use these special CCB commands for things such as rewriting the sector headers to flag bad sectors, which in essence means LLF. When using these commands, the drive controller can rewrite the sector headers and data areas and then carefully step over any servo information (if the drive uses an embedded servo).

IDE drives CAN be low-level formatted, although some drives require special vendor-specific commands to enable certain low-level formatting features and defect management options. Seagate, Western Digital, Maxtor, IBM, and others make specific low-level format and spare-sector defect management software specific to their respective IDE drives. Conner drives are unique in that to actually low-level format them, you need a special hardware device that attaches to a diagnostic port connector on the Conner IDE drive. There is a company called TCE (see the vendor list in the Appendix) that sells such a device for $99. Coincidentally, it is called "The Conner" and includes software and the special adapter device that allows true low-level formatting (including rewriting all sectors and sector headers as well as complete spare sector defect management) at the factory level.

Other companies have developed more general purpose low-level format software that will recognize the particular IDE drive and use the correct vendor-specific commands for the low-level format and defect mapping. The best of these is Ontrack's Disk Manager software. A general-purpose diagnostic program that also supports IDE drive formatting is the MicroScope package by Micro 2000.

Intelligent IDE drives must be in nontranslating or "native" mode in order for you to low-level format them. Zone-recorded drives can only do a partial low-level format, where the defect map is updated and new defective sectors can be marked or spared; the sector headers are usually only partially rewritten, and only for the purpose of defect mapping. In any case, you are writing to some of the sector headers in one form, and physical (sector level) defect mapping and sector sparing can be performed. This is by any standard definition a LLF.

On an embedded servo drive, all the servo data for a track is recorded at the same time by a specialized (usually laser-guided) servowriter. This servo information is used to continuously update the head position during drive function so the drive automatically compensates for thermal effects. This means all of the individual servo bursts are inline on the track. Because the servo controls head position, there is no appreciable head-to-sector drift as there could be on a non-servo drive.

This is why even though it is possible to "low-level format" embedded servo drives, it is rarely necessary. The only purpose for a low-level format on an embedded servo drive is to perform additional physical (sector) level defect mapping or sector sparing for the purposes of managing defects that occur after manufacture. Because there is no drift, once a sector is found to contain a flaw, it should remain permanently marked bad, as a physical flaw cannot be repaired by reformatting.

Most IDE drives have three to four spare sectors for each physical cylinder of the drive. These hundreds of spare sectors are more than enough to accommodate the original and any subsequent defects. If more than that are required, the drive likely has serious physical problems that cannot be fixed by software!

Software for Low-Level Formatting. You often can choose from several types of low-level format programs, but no single low-level format program works on all drives or all systems. Because low-level format programs must operate very closely with the controller, they are often specific to a controller or controller type. Therefore, ask the controller manufacturer for the formatting software it recommends.

If the controller manufacturer supplies a low-level format program (usually in the controller's ROM), use its program because it is the one most specifically designed for your system and controller. The manufacturer's program can take advantage of special defect-mapping features, for example. A different format program might not only fail to use a manufacturer-written defect map but also overwrite and destroy it.

IBM supplies a low-level format program for its PS/2 systems. With Models 50 and higher, the program is included in the Advanced Diagnostics portion of the Reference disk that comes with the system. With system models lower than 50, users can purchase the Advanced Diagnostics program separately.

For a general-purpose ST-506/412, ESDI, or IDE low-level format program, I recommend the Disk Manager program by Ontrack. For the ST-506/412 interface only, I recommend the IBM Advanced Diagnostics or the HDtest program by Jim Bracking, a user-supported product found on many electronic bulletin boards, including CompuServe. (These companies are listed in the vendor list at the back of this book.) For SCSI systems and systems on which the other recommended programs do not work, you will normally use the format program supplied with the SCSI host adapter.

Low-Level Format Software. There are several ways a program can LLF (low-level format) a drive. The simplest is to call the BIOS using INT 13h functions such as the INT 13h, function 05h (Format Track) command. The BIOS then converts this command into what is called a CCB (Command Control Block) Command, which is a block of bytes sent out the proper I/O ports directly to the disk controller. In this example, the BIOS would take the INT 13h, 05h and convert it to a CCB 50h (Format Track) command which would be sent out the Command Register Port (I/O address 1F7h for ST-506/412 or IDE). When the controller receives the CCB Format Track command, it may actually format the track, or may instead simply fill the data areas of each sector on the track with a predetermined pattern.

The best way to low-level format a drive is to bypass the ROM BIOS and send the CCB commands directly to the controller. Probably the greatest benefit in sending commands directly to the drive controller is in being able to correctly flag defective sectors via the CCB Format Track command, including the ability to perform sector sparing. This is why IDE drives that are properly low-level formatted will never show any bad sectors.

By using the CCB commands, you also gain the ability to read the Command Status and Error registers, which allow you to detect things like ECC-corrected data that is masked by DOS INT 13h. You also have the ability to detect whether a sector had already been marked bad by the manufacturer or a previous LLF, and you can maintain those marks in any subsequent Format Track commands, thereby preserving the defect list. I do not recommend unmarking a sector (returning it as "good"), especially where the manufacturer had previously marked it.

With CCB commands, you can read and write sector(s) with automatic retries, as well as with ECC turned off. This is essential for any good surface-analysis or LLF program and is why I recommend programs that use the CCB hardware interface rather than the DOS INT 13h interface.

Advanced Diagnostics Formatters. The standard low-level format program for IBM systems is the Advanced Diagnostics program. For the IBM PS/2 Models 50 and above, this formatting software is provided on the Reference disk included with the system. To get this software for other IBM PS/2 systems (lower than the 50), you must purchase the hardware-maintenance service manuals, which cost several hundred dollars.

To access the Advanced Diagnostics portion of the Reference disk, you press Ctrl-A (for Advanced) at the Reference disk main menu. The "secret" advanced diagnostics will

III

Hardware Considerations

appear. IBM does not document this feature in the regular system documentation, because it does not want the average user "wandering around" in this software. The Ctrl-A procedure is documented in the service manuals.

The IBM PS/2 low-level format programs are excellent, and are the only low-level format programs you should use on these systems. Only the IBM format tools know to find, use, and update the IBM-written defect map.

For standard IBM AT or IBM XT systems, the Advanced Diagnostics low-level format program is fine at formatting and testing hard disks and has the standard features associated with this type of program. However, the AT version does not allow an interleave selection of 1 to 1; this may not be a problem for most, but it renders the program useless if you upgrade to a controller that can handle a 1 to 1 interleave.

The IBM PC/XT version allows only a 6-to-1 interleave selection, which renders it useless on most IBM PC and IBM XT systems because most controllers can handle between 2-to-1 and 5-to-1 interleaves. Using the IBM XT formatting program results in a very slow system. An additional problem with the IBM PC/XT version is that it does not allow the entry of the manufacturer's defect list, an unforgivable oversight that makes the IBM PC/XT low-level format program definitely *not* recommended. Fortunately, most PC- or XT-type system users use aftermarket autoconfigure-type controllers that come with a proper built-in ROM-based formatter.

Ontrack Disk Manager. For AT-type systems and other systems with controllers that do not have an autoconfigure routine, the Disk Manager program from Ontrack is excellent. It is probably the most sophisticated hard disk format tool available and has many capabilities that make it a desirable addition to your toolbox.

Disk Manager is a true register-level format program that goes around the BIOS and manipulates the disk controller directly. This direct controller access gives it powerful capabilities that are simply not possible in programs that work through the BIOS.

Some of these advanced features include the ability to set head and cylinder skew factors. Disk Manager can also detect intermittent (soft) errors much better than most other programs because it can turn off the automatic retries that most controllers will perform. It can also tell when ECC (Error Correction Code) has been used to correct data, indicating that an error had occurred, as well as manipulate the bytes directly that are used for ECC. Disk Manager has also been written to handle most IDE drives and uses vendor-specific commands to unlock the ability to do a true low-level format on IDE drives.

All of these capabilities and more make Disk Manager one of the most powerful and capable low-level format programs available. Ontrack also has an excellent package of hard disk diagnostic and data recovery utilities called Dos Utils. Anybody who has to support, maintain, troubleshoot, repair, or upgrade PCs needs a powerful disk formatter like Disk Manager.

HDtest. HDtest is an excellent BIOS-level format program. It will function on virtually any drive that has an INT 13h ROM BIOS interface, which includes most drives. It does not have some of the capabilities of true register-level format programs, but can be used where the additional capabilities of a register-level program are not required. For example, you can use it to do a quick wipe of all of the data on a drive, no matter what the interface or controller type is. It is also good for BIOS-level read and write testing and has proven especially useful in verifying the functions of disk interface BIOS code.

HDtest, by Jim Bracking, is a user-supported software program. This program is distributed through electronic bulletin boards and public-domain software libraries. You can also obtain the program from the Public Software Library (see the vendor listing in the Appendix). It costs $35, but you can try it for free.

HDtest has an easy-to-use interface and pull-down menu system. The program offers all functions normally associated with a standard low-level format program and some extras:

- Normal formatting

- Defect mapping

- Surface analysis

- Interleave test

- Nondestructive low-level reformat

- Hard disk tests (duplicate of the IBM Advanced Diagnostics hard disk tests), including tests for drive seek, head selection, error detection and correction, and a read/write/verify of the diagnostics cylinder (This program can also run low-level ROM BIOS commands to the controller.)

HDtest includes most of what you would want in a generic low-level format program and hard disk diagnostics utility. Its real limitation is that it works only through the BIOS and cannot perform functions that a true register-level format program can. In some cases, it will be unable to format a drive that a register-level program could. Only register-level programs can perform defect mapping in most IDE and SCSI environments.

SCSI Low-Level Format Software. If you are using a SCSI drive, you must use the low-level format program provided by the manufacturer of the SCSI host adapter. The design of these devices varies enough that a register-level program can work only if it is tailored to the individual controller. Fortunately, all SCSI host adapters include such format software either in the host adapter's BIOS or in a separate disk-based program.

The interface to the SCSI drive is through the host adapter. SCSI is a standard, but there are no true standards for what a host adapter is supposed to look like. This means that any formatting or configuration software will be specific to a particular host adapter. For example, IBM supplies formatting and defect-management software that works with the IBM PS/2 SCSI host adapters directly on the PS/2 Reference disk. That software performs everything that needs to be done to a SCSI hard disk connected to an IBM host adapter.

III

Hardware Considerations

IBM has defined a standard interface to its adapter through an INT 13h and INT 4Bh BIOS interface in a ROM installed on the card. The IBM adapters also include a special ABIOS (Advanced BIOS) interface that runs in the processor's protected mode of operation (for use under protected-mode operating systems such as OS/2).

Other SCSI host adapters will often include the complete setup, configuration, and formatting software in the host adapter's on-board ROM BIOS. Most also include an INT 13h interface in the BIOS, as well. The best example of this is the Adaptec 1540/1542C adapters, which include software in ROM that completely configures the card and all attached SCSI devices.

SCSI format and configuration software is keyed to the host adapter and is not specific in any way to the particular SCSI hard disk drive you are using.

IDE Low-Level Format Software. IDE-drive manufacturers have defined extensions to the standard Western Digital 1002/1003 AT interface, which was further standardized for IDE drives as the CAM (Common Access Method) ATA (AT Adapter) interface. The CAM ATA specification provides for "vendor-unique" commands, which are manufacturers' proprietary extensions to the standard. To prevent improper low-level formatting, many of these IDE drives have special codes that must be sent to the drive to unlock the format routines. These codes vary among manufacturers. If possible, you should obtain low-level format and defect-management software from the drive manufacturer, which will usually be specific to their own products.

The custom nature of the ATA interface drives is the source of some myths about IDE. Many people say, for example, that you cannot perform a low-level format on an IDE drive, and that if you try, you will wreck the drive! This statement is untrue! What can happen is that in some drives, you may be able to set new head and sector skew factors that are not optimum for the drive as the manufacturer had originally set, and you may also be able to overwrite the defect-map information. This is not good, but the drive can still be used with no problems provided a proper surface analysis is also done.

Most ATA-IDE drives are protected from any alteration to the skew factors or defect map erasure because they are in a translated mode. Zone-recorded drives are always in translation mode and are fully protected. Most ATA drives have a custom command set that must be used in the format process; the standard format commands defined by the ATA specification usually do not work, especially with intelligent or zone-recorded IDE drives. Without the proper manufacturer-specific format commands, you will not be able to perform the defect management in the manufacturer-specified method, where often bad sectors can be spared.

Currently, these manufacturers offer specific low-level format and defect-management software for their own IDE drives:

- Seagate
- Western Digital
- Maxtor
- IBM

These utilities are available for downloading on the various BBSs run by these companies. The numbers can be found in the vendor list in the Appendix.

Conner Peripherals drives are unique in that they cannot be low-level formatted through the standard interface, but must be formatted by a device that attaches to a special diagnostics and setup port on the drive. You will see this as 12-pin connector on Conner drives. A company called TCE sells an inexpensive device that attaches your PC to this port through a serial port in your system and includes special software that can perform sophisticated test, formatting, and surface-analysis operations. The product, called The Conner, is sold by TCE, which is listed in the vendor list in the Appendix.

For other drives, I recommend Disk Manager by Ontrack as well as the MicroScope program by Micro 2000. These programs can format most IDE drives because they know the manufacturer-specific IDE format commands and routines. They can also perform defect mapping and surface-analysis procedures.

Nondestructive Formatters. General-purpose, BIOS-level nondestructive formatters like Calibrate or Spinrite are not recommended in most situations where a real low-level format (LLF) is required. These programs have several limitations and problems that limit their effectiveness, and in some cases they can even cause problems with the way defects are handled on a drive. These programs attempt to do a track-by-track LLF using BIOS functions, while backing up and restoring the track data as they go. These programs do not actually perform a complete LLF because they do not even try to LLF the first track (Cyl 0, Hd 0) due to problems with some controller types that store hidden information on the first track. These programs also do not perform defect mapping in the proper way that a standard LLF program does, and they can even remove the carefully applied sector header defect marks that are applied during a proper LLF. This will potentially allow data to be stored in sectors that were originally marked defective and may actually void the manufacturer's warranty on some drives. Another problem is that these programs will only work on drives that are already formatted and can format only drives which are formattable through BIOS functions.

A true LLF program will bypass the system BIOS and send commands directly to the disk controller hardware. For this reason, many LLF programs are specific to the disk controller hardware they are designed for. It is virtually impossible to have a single format program that will run on all different types of controllers. Many hard drives have been incorrectly diagnosed as defective because the wrong format program was used, and it did not operate properly.

As an example case history, I was helping a user with an IBM PS/2 Model 30, which uses an 8-bit IDE interface 20M drive. This drive was having serious problems reading and writing files. To start with, CHKDSK showed about 40 kilobytes in bad sectors, and several programs would not load because they were corrupted. Files could not be copied to the drive without getting Data error writing drive C: messages. Also, the system was having problems with booting; sometimes it would boot fine, and other times it wouldn't boot at all, failing with a Non-System disk or disk error message.

Before contacting me, he had first run Spinrite II Version 2.0, using the deepest (level 4) pattern testing and formatting. This operation had taken an incredible 72 hours to complete, and it ended up marking more than 4 megabytes of the drive as bytes in bad sectors! Spinrite also indicated bad sectors in cylinders 00 and 01 in the FAT and root directory areas. After Spinrite was finished, he had tried running FDISK to repartition the drive from scratch, but FDISK crashed with the error message No space to create a DOS partition. At this point, FDISK had also trashed the existing partition table, but fortunately he was wise and had made a partition table backup and stored it on a floppy disk with the MIRROR /PARTN command. He then recovered this partition table backup with the UNFORMAT /PARTN command, which reads the backup file from the floppy and uses it to restore the partition data.

At this point, even though Spinrite had marked out more than 4 megabytes of the disk as bad during a 72-hour test, he still could not load any additional software on the drive without getting write error messages from DOS. At this point, many people would have considered the drive defective and replaced it with a new one. Fortunately, he called me instead.

I decided that what was needed was to low-level format the drive, but this time using a real LLF program that bypassed the BIOS routines and worked directly with the disk controller hardware registers.

IBM publishes a Hardware Maintenance Service package for the PS/2 Model 30 (about $60) that includes a troubleshooting pamphlet and a special Advanced Diagnostics disk. All Micro Channel based PS/2 systems come with a free Advanced Diagnostics disk, but with most of the ISA-bus systems, you have to purchase the disk separately. The IBM NSC (National Support Center) BBS also has many of these disks available free for the downloading (see the vendor list in the Appendix for the phone number), but the Model 30 disk was unfortunately not available through the BBS.

Using the IBM Advanced Diagnostics, I had him run an unconditional format and then a surface analysis, which together took less than an hour. During the surface analysis, only a single sector was marked bad on the entire drive. After the format and surface analysis were complete, he ran FDISK (which worked perfectly this time) and, by accepting the defaults, partitioned the entire drive as a primary DOS partition and marked it as active. Then the drive was formatted with DOS 5.0, which picked up the sector flagged bad during the surface analysis and marked the cluster containing the flagged sector as bad in the FAT. When the DOS format was complete, he ran CHKDSK and it showed only 2,048 bytes in bad sectors (equal to the single cluster marked bad in the FAT).

The user of the system was then able to reinstall all the original software that had been on the drive with no problems or glitches, and the drive has been working flawlessly ever since. So what is the moral of the story? Perhaps the most important one is that you should not replace a hard disk unless you have tried to format it with a real register-level, low-level format program. I have little use for "partial" low-level format programs and recommend that when a real format is needed, you use a program that works directly with the controller hardware registers. When in doubt, contact the manufacturer of the controller or drive and find out whether the manufacturer has or can recommend something specific that you should use. If they don't have their own special programs, most controller and drive manufacturers recommend the Disk Manager program from Ontrack for real low-level formatting. I also highly recommend the Ontrack software, and you will find it listed in the Appendix.

Drive Partitioning

Partitioning a hard disk is the act of defining areas of the disk for an operating system to use as a volume. To DOS, a volume is an area of a disk denoted as a drive letter; for example, drive C: is volume C:, drive D: is volume D:, and so on. Some people think that you have to partition a disk only if you are going to divide it into more than one volume. This is a misunderstanding; a disk must be partitioned even if it will be the single volume C:.

When a disk is partitioned, a master partition boot sector is written at cylinder 0, head 0, sector 1—the first sector on the hard disk. This sector contains data describing the partitions by their starting and ending cylinder, head, and sector locations. The partition table also indicates to the ROM BIOS which of the partitions is bootable, and thus where to look for an operating system to load. A single hard disk can have from 1 to 24 partitions. This number includes all the hard drives installed in the system, which means that you can have as many as 24 separate hard disks with one partition each, a single hard disk with 24 partitions, or a combination of disks and partitions such that the total number of partitions is no more than 24. If you have more than 24 drives or partitions, DOS does not recognize them, although other operating systems may. What limits DOS is that a letter is used to name a volume, and the Roman alphabet ends with Z, the 24th volume when you begin with C.

FDISK

The DOS FDISK program is the accepted standard for partitioning hard disks. Partitioning prepares the boot sector of the disk such that the DOS FORMAT program can operate correctly, and enables different operating systems to coexist on a single hard disk.

If a disk is set up with two or more partitions, FDISK shows only two total DOS partitions, the *primary partition* and the *extended partition*. The extended partition is then divided into *logical DOS volumes*, which are partitions themselves. FDISK gives a false impression of how the partitioning is done. FDISK reports that a disk divided as C:, D:, E:, and F: is set up as two partitions, with a primary partition having a volume designator of C: and a single extended partition, with logical DOS volumes D:, E:, and F:. But in the real structure of the disk, each logical DOS volume is a separate partition with an extended partition boot sector describing it. Each drive volume constitutes a separate partition on the disk, and the partitions point to one another in a daisy-chain arrangement.

Different versions of DOS have had different partitioning capabilities:

- DOS 1.x had no support whatsoever for hard disk drives.

- DOS 2.0 was the first version of DOS that included hard disk support, and this included the ability to partition a drive as a single volume with a maximum partition size of 16M. DOS versions 2.x support only 16-megabyte maximum partitions due to limitations of the 12-bit FAT system. A 12-bit FAT can manage a maximum of only 4,096 total clusters on a disk. The limit of 16 megabytes does not come from the FAT, but from the high-level DOS FORMAT command, which aborts with an `Invalid media or Track 0 bad - disk unusable` error message if the partition is larger than 16 megabytes. On a disk that has no bad sectors beyond the first 16 megabytes of the disk, you can ignore the error message and continue the setup of the disk with the SYS command. If the disk has defects beyond 16 megabytes, they are not properly marked in the FAT. Most vendors supplied modified high-level format programs enabling partitions of up to 32 megabytes to be formatted properly. Unfortunately, then each cluster or minimum allocation unit on the disk is 8,192 bytes (8K) because of the 12-bit FAT.

■ DOS 3.0 increased the maximum partition and therefore volume size to 32M, but could still only support a single partition for DOS (assigned the C: volume designator). The size limit is 32 megabytes due to the limit of 65,536 total sectors in a partition.

■ DOS 3.3 introduced the concept of extended partitions, which allows DOS to see the drive as multiple volumes (drive letters). The extended partition logical DOS volumes are actually partitions themselves. In the organization of the disk, the primary partition is assigned drive letter C, and the extended partitions are assigned letters sequentially from D through Z. Each drive letter (which is a volume or partition) can be assigned only as much as 32 megabytes of disk space.

■ DOS 4.0 increased the size of a single DOS partition or volume to 2 gigabytes. FDISK was modified to allocate disk space in megabytes, rather than in individual cylinders as with previous versions of DOS. IBM DOS FDISK could handle up to eight physical hard disk drives.

■ DOS 5.0 had no changes to partitioning capabilities, but MS-DOS could by then universally handle up to eight physical hard drives (IBM had this in DOS 4.x).

■ DOS 6.0 and later versions have no changes to partitioning capabilities, although both Microsoft and IBM have added disk compression software to DOS that create additional compressed volumes.

The minimum size for a partition for any version of DOS is one cylinder; however, FDISK in DOS 4 or higher allocates partitions in megabytes, meaning that the minimum size partition it will create is 1 megabyte. DOS 4.x and any higher versions allow individual partitions or volumes to be as large as 2 gigabytes, whereas versions of DOS earlier than 4.0 have a maximum partition size of 32 megabytes.

The current DOS limits of eight physical hard disks with a maximum of 24 total volumes between them, and up to two gigabytes per volume do not seem too restrictive for most people.

FDISK Undocumented Functions. FDISK is a very powerful program, and in DOS 5.0 and higher, it gained some additional capabilities. Unfortunately, these capabilities were never documented in the DOS manual and still remain undocumented even in DOS 6.x.

The most important undocumented parameter in FDISK is the /MBR (Master Boot Record) parameter. This causes FDISK to rewrite the Master Boot Sector code area, leaving the partition tables intact. Be aware that it can overwrite the partition tables if the two signature bytes at the end of the sector (55AAh) are damaged, but this is highly unlikely. In fact, if these signature bytes were damaged, you would know because the system would not boot and would act as though there were no partitions at all. The /MBR parameter seems to be tailor made for eliminating boot-sector virus programs that infect the Master Partition Boot Sector (Cylinder 0, Head 0, Sector 1) of a hard disk. To use this feature, you simply enter

```
FDISK /MBR
```

FDISK will then rewrite the boot sector code, leaving the partition tables intact. This should not cause any problems on a normally functioning system, but just in case, I recommend backing up the partition-table information to floppy disk before trying it. That can be done with the command

```
MIRROR /PARTN
```

This uses the MIRROR command to store partition-table information in a file called PARTNSAV.FIL, which should be stored on a floppy disk for safe keeping. To restore the complete partition-table information, including all of the Master and Extended Partition Boot Sectors, you use the UNFORMAT command as follows:

```
UNFORMAT /PARTN
```

This causes the UNFORMAT command to ask for the floppy disk containing the PARTNSAV.FIL file and then restore it back to the hard disk.

FDISK also has three other undocumented parameters: /PRI:, /EXT:, and /LOG:. These parameters can be used to have FDISK create Master and Extended partitions as well as Logical DOS volumes in the Extended partition directly from the command line rather than by using the FDISK menus. This was designed so that you can run FDISK in a batch file to partition drives automatically. Some system vendors probably use these parameters (if they know about them, that is) when setting up system on the production line. Other than that, they have little use for a normal user and in fact may be dangerous.

Other Partitioning Software. Since DOS 4.0 first became available, there has been little need for aftermarket disk partitioning utilities, except in special cases. If a system is having problems that cause you to consider using a partitioning utility, I recommend that you upgrade to a newer version of DOS instead. Using nonstandard partitioning programs to partition your disk places the data in these partitions in jeopardy and makes recovery of data lost in these partitions extremely difficult.

The reason that disk partitioning utilities other than FDISK even existed is that the maximum partition size in older DOS versions was restricted (16 megabytes for DOS 2.x and 32 megabytes for DOS 3.x). These limits are bothersome for people with physical hard disks much larger than 32 megabytes because they have to divide the hard disk into many partitions to use all the disk. Versions of DOS prior to 3.3 cannot even create more than a single DOS-accessible partition on a hard disk. If you have a 120-megabyte hard disk and are using DOS 3.2 or earlier versions, you can access only 32 megabytes of that disk as a C: partition. To overcome this limitation, several software companies created enhanced partitioning programs you can use rather than FDISK. These programs create multiple partitions and partitions larger than 32 megabytes on a disk recognizable by DOS. These partitioning programs include a high-level format program because the FORMAT program in DOS 3.3 or earlier versions can format partitions only up to 32 megabytes.

Disk Manager by Ontrack, Speedstor by Storage Dimensions, and Vfeature Deluxe by Golden Bow are among the best known of the partitioning utilities. They also include low-level format capabilities, so they can be used as a single tool to set up a hard disk. They even include disk driver software that provides the capability to override the physical type selections in the system ROM BIOS, enabling a system to use all of a disk, even though the drive-type table in the system ROM BIOS does not have an entry that exactly matches the hard disk.

These nonstandard partitioning and formatting programs were given away by many drive vendors and integrators, which makes some purchasers of such products feel that they must use these drivers to operate the drive. In most cases, there are better alternatives; nonstandard disk partitioning and formatting can cause more problems than it solves.

For example, Seagate shipped Ontrack Disk Manager with its drives larger than 32M. One purpose of the program is to perform low-level formatting of the drive, which Disk Manager does well, and I recommend it highly for this function. If possible, however, you should avoid the partitioning and high-level formatting functions and stick with FDISK and FORMAT.

When you use a program other than standard FDISK and FORMAT to partition and high-level (DOS) format a drive, the drive is set up in a nonstandard way, different from pure DOS. This difference can cause trouble with utilities including disk cache programs, disk test and interleave check programs, and data recovery or retrieval programs written to function with a standard DOS disk structure. In many situations that a standard format would avoid, a nonstandard disk format can cause data loss and also make data recovery impossible.

> **Caution**
>
> You should only use standard DOS FDISK and FORMAT to partition or high-level format your hard disks. If you use aftermarket partitioning software to create a nonstandard disk system, some programs that bypass DOS for disk access will not understand the disk properly and may write in the wrong place. Windows is an example of a program that bypasses DOS when you turn on Use 32-bit Disk Access in the Control Panel.

It is especially dangerous to use these partitioning programs to override your ROM BIOS disk-table settings. Consider the following disaster scenario:

Suppose that you have a Seagate ST-4096 hard disk, which has 1024 cylinders and nine heads, and requires that your controller never perform a data write modification called *write precompensation* to cylinders of the disk. Some drives require this precompensation on the inner cylinders to compensate for "peak shifting" that takes place because of the higher density of data on the (smaller size) inner cylinders. The ST-4096 internally compensates for this effect and therefore needs no precompensation from the controller.

Now suppose that you install this drive in an IBM AT that does not have a ROM BIOS drive table that exactly matches the drive. The best matching type you can select is type 18, which enables you to use only 977 cylinders and seven heads, or 56.77 megabytes of what should be a 76.5-megabyte hard disk. If your IBM AT is one of the older ones with a ROM BIOS dated 01/10/84, the situation is worse because its drive-table ends with type 14. In that case, you would have to select type 12 as the best match, giving you access to 855 cylinders and seven heads, or only 49.68 megabytes of a 76.5-megabyte drive. ROM BIOS drive tables are listed in the Appendix of this book for reference. Most IBM-compatibles have a more complete drive-type table and would have an exact table match for this drive, allowing the full 76.5 megabytes to be used with no problems. For example, in most compatibles with a Phoenix ROM BIOS, you would select type 35, which would support the drive entirely.

Now suppose that, not content with using only 57 or 50 megabytes of this 76.5-megabyte drive, you invoke the "SuperPartition" aftermarket partitioning program that came with the drive and use it to low-level format the drive. Then you use the aftermarket program to override the type 18 or type 12 settings in the drive table. The program instructs you to set up a very small C: partition (of only 1 megabyte) and then partitions the remaining 75.5 megabytes of the disk as D:. This partitioning overrides the DOS 3.3 32-megabyte partition limitation. (If you had an IBM-compatible system that did not require the drive-type override, you would still need to use the aftermarket partitioner to create partitions larger than the DOS 3.3 standard 32 megabytes.) Following that, you use the partitioner to high-level format the C: and D: partitions because the DOS high-level format in DOS 3.3 works only on volumes of 32 megabytes or less.

Most aftermarket partitioners create a special driver file they install in the CONFIG.SYS file through the DEVICE command. After the system boots from the C: partition and loads the device driver, the 75.5-megabyte D: partition is completely accessible.

Along comes an innocent user of the system who always boots from her own DOS floppy disk. After booting from the floppy, she tries to log into the D: partition. No matter what version of DOS this user boots from on the floppy disk, the D: partition seems to have vanished. An attempt to log in to that partition results in an `Invalid drive specification` error message. No standard version of DOS can recognize that specially created D: partition if the device driver is not loaded.

III

Hardware Considerations

An attempt by this user to recover data on this drive with a utility program such as Norton or PC Tools results in failure because these programs interpret the drive as having 977 cylinders and seven heads (type 18), or 855 cylinders and seven heads (type 12). In fact, when these programs attempt to correct what seems to be partition-table damage, data will be corrupted in the vanished D: partition.

Thinking that there may be a physical problem with the disk, the innocent user boots and runs the Advanced Diagnostics software to test the hard disk. Because Advanced Diagnostics incorporates its own special boot code and does not use standard DOS, it does not examine partitioning but goes to the ROM BIOS drive-type table to determine the capacity of the hard disk. It sees the unit as having only 977 or 855 cylinders, indicated by the type 18 or 12 settings, as well as only seven heads. The user then runs the Advanced Diagnostics hard disk tests, which use the last cylinder of the disk as a test cylinder for diagnostics read and write tests. This cylinder is subsequently overwritten by the diagnostics tests, which all pass because there is no physical problem with the drive.

This innocent user has just wiped out the D: drive data that happened to be on cylinder 976 in the type 18 setup or cylinder 854 in the type 12 setup. Had the drive been partitioned by FDISK, the last cylinder indicated by the ROM BIOS drive table would have been left out of any partitions, reserved so that diagnostics tests could be performed on the drive without damaging data.

Beyond the kind of disaster scenario just described, other potential problems can be caused by nonstandard disk partitioning and formatting, such as the following:

- Problems when using the 32-bit Disk Access feature provided by Windows, which bypasses the BIOS for faster disk access in 386 Enhanced Mode

- Data loss by using OS/2, UNIX, XENIX, Novell Advanced NetWare, or other non-DOS operating systems that do not recognize the disk or the nonstandard partitions

- Difficulty upgrading a system from one DOS version to another

- Difficulty installing a different operating system, such as OS/2, on the hard disk

- Data loss by using a low-level format utility to run an interleave test (The test area for the interleave test is the diagnostics cylinder, which contains data on disks formatted with Disk Manager.)

- Data loss by accidentally deleting or overwriting the driver file and causing the D: partition to disappear after the next boot

- Data-recovery difficulty or failure because nonstandard partitions do not follow the rules and guidelines set by Microsoft and IBM, and there is no documentation on their structure. The sizes and locations of the FATs and root directory are not standard, and the detailed reference charts in this book (which are valid for an FDISK-created partition) are inaccurate for nonstandard partitions.

I could continue, but I think you get the idea. If these utility programs are used only for low-level formatting, they do not cause problems. It is the drive-type override, partitioning, and high-level format operations that cause difficulty. If you consider data integrity important and want to be able to perform data recovery, follow these disk support and partitioning rules:

■ Every hard disk must be properly supported by system ROM BIOS, with no software overrides. If the system does not have a drive table that supports the full capacity of the drive, either accept the table's limit, upgrade to a new ROM BIOS (preferably with a user-definable drive type setting), or use a disk controller with an on-board ROM BIOS for drive support.

■ Use only FDISK to partition a hard disk. If you want partitions larger than 32M, use DOS 4.0 or later versions.

High-Level (Operating System) Format

The final step in the software preparation of a hard disk is the DOS high-level format. The primary function of the high-level format is to create a FAT and a directory system on the disk so that DOS can manage files.

Usually, you do the high-level format with the standard DOS FORMAT program, using the following syntax:

```
FORMAT C: /S /V
```

This step high-level formats drive C: (or volume C: in a multivolume drive), places the hidden operating system files on the first part of this partition, and prompts for the entry of a volume label to be stored on the disk at completion.

The high-level format program performs the following functions and procedures in the order listed:

1. Scans the disk (read only) for tracks and sectors marked bad during the low-level format. Notes these tracks as unreadable.

2. Returns the drive heads to the first cylinder of the partition, and at cylinder 0, head 1, sector 1, writes a DOS volume boot sector.

3. Writes a file allocation table (FAT) at head 1, sector 2. Immediately after this FAT, it writes a second copy of the FAT. These FATs are essentially blank except for bad cluster marks noting areas of the disk found unreadable during the marked defect scan.

4. Writes a blank root directory.

5. If the /S parameter is specified, copies the system files (IBMBIO.COM and IBMDOS.COM or IO.SYS and MSDOS.SYS depending on which DOS you run), and COMMAND.COM files to the disk (in that order).

6. If the /V parameter is specified, prompts the user for a volume label, which is written as the fourth file entry in the root directory.

Now DOS can use the disk for storing and retrieving files, and the disk is a bootable disk.

During the first phase of the high-level format, a marked defect scan is performed. Defects marked by the low-level format operation show up during this scan as unreadable tracks or sectors. When the high-level format encounters one of these areas, it automatically performs up to five retries to read these tracks or sectors. If the unreadable area was marked by the low-level format, the read fails on all attempts.

After five retries, the DOS FORMAT program gives up on this track or sector and moves to the next. Areas unreadable after the initial read and the five retries are noted as bad clusters in the FAT. DOS 3.3 and earlier versions can mark only entire tracks bad in the FAT, even if only one sector was marked in the low-level format. DOS 4.0 and higher versions individually check each cluster on the track and recover those that do not involve the low-level marked-bad sectors. Because most low-level format programs mark all the sectors on a track as bad rather than the individual sector containing the defect, the result using either DOS 3.3 or 4.0 is the same: all clusters involving sectors on that track are marked bad in the FAT.

> **Note**
>
> Some low-level format programs mark only the individual sector that is bad on a track, rather than the entire track. For example, this is true of the IBM PS/2 low-level formatters on the IBM PS/2 Advanced Diagnostics or Reference disks. In this case, high-level formatting with DOS 4.0 or higher versions results in fewer lost bytes in bad sectors because only the clusters containing the marked bad sectors are marked bad in the FAT. DOS 4.0 and higher display the `Attempting to recover allocation unit x` message, where x is the number of the cluster, in an attempt to determine whether a single cluster or all the clusters on the track should be marked bad in the FAT.

If the controller and low-level format program together support sector and track sparing, the high-level format finds the entire disk defect-free, because all the defective sectors have been exchanged for spare good ones.

If a disk has been low-level formatted correctly, the number of bytes in bad sectors is the same before and after the high-level format. If the number does change after redoing a high-level format (reporting fewer bytes or none), the low-level format was not done correctly. Probably the manufacturer's defects were not marked, or Norton, Mace, PC Tools, or a similar utility was used to mark defective clusters on the disk. The utilities cannot mark the sectors or tracks at the low-level format level; the bad cluster marks they make are stored only in the FAT and erased during the next high-level format operation. Defect marks made in the low-level format consistently show as bad bytes in the high-level format, no matter how many times you run it.

Only a low-level format or a surface analysis tool can correctly mark defects on a disk; anything else makes only temporary bad cluster marks in the FAT. This kind of marking may be acceptable temporarily, but when additional bad areas are found on a disk, you should run a new low-level format of the disk and either mark the area manually or run a surface analysis to place a more permanent mark on the disk.

Disk Hardware and Software Limitations

By studying the capabilities of the different disk interfaces, as well as the ROM BIOS and Operating Systems, it is possible to determine what limits there are on disk storage. The following sections detail the limits under the different interfaces and operating systems.

Disk Interface Capacity Limitations

Different disk interfaces have different limitations on the theoretical maximum drive capacities they may support. These limitations are due to variations in the way that each interface operates at the hardware level. It is important to note that even though a particular interface may allow access to a given amount of disk real estate, the BIOS and DOS are usually much more limiting, and end up being the true limits for system disk capacity.

ST-506/412, ESDI and IDE

To determine the capacity limits for the ST-506/412, ESDI, or IDE interface, we first need to determine the limits on the maximum number of cylinders, heads, and sectors per track. These are found by looking at the size of the registers that hold this data in the controller. All of these interfaces have the same controller register specifications, so the capacity limits calculated here apply to all of them. As you will see, the interface capacity limits are quite high. The drive parameter limits are as follows:

Cylinders (16-bits) = 65,536

Heads (4 bits) = 16

Sectors (8-bits) = 256

This calculates to a maximum theoretical drive size of:

65,536 Cyls * 16 Hds * 256 Secs * 512 Bytes = 137,438,953,472 Bytes (128G)

This maximum capacity of 128 gigabytes is unfortunately limited by the BIOS. There are two different BIOS types with regards to disk size limitations. The standard BIOS built into most systems is limited to 1,024 cylinders, 16 heads, and 63 sectors per track. If the BIOS is an enhanced version, it will be limited to 1,024 cylinders, 256 heads, and 63 sectors per track. Combining the BIOS and interface limits results in the following maximum capacities (assuming 512 byte sectors):

Limit w/ Std. BIOS: 1,024 Cyls * 16 Hds * 63 Secs = 528,482,304 Bytes (504M)

Limit w/ Enh. BIOS: 1,024 Cyls * 256 Hds * 63 Secs = 8,455,716,864 Bytes (7.88G)

If you did not have enhanced BIOS support in your motherboard, you could add an IDE bus adapter that has an on-board enhanced BIOS. To get around such BIOS problems, some IDE drive implementations over 528 million bytes split the drive to act as two physical units. In this case, the drive would appear on the IDE bus connector as both Master and Slave and could only be used as two 504 megabyte maximum sized drives.

SCSI

According to the SCSI specification, drives are not addressed by cylinders, heads, and sectors, but instead by what is called a Logical Block Address (LBA). This is a sector number, where all of the sectors on the drive are numbered sequentially from start to finish. The LBA is specified by a 32-bit number and, with 512-byte sectors, results in the following limitation:

4,294,967,296 LBAs (sectors) * 512 Bytes = 2,199,023,255,552 Bytes (2,048G or 2 terabytes)

As you can see, SCSI drive capacity limits are extremely high. However, because the SCSI drive must appear to the BIOS as a given number of cylinders, heads, and sectors per track, the BIOS will limit SCSI capacity. Virtually all SCSI adapters have an enhanced type BIOS, which supports a maximum drive capacity as follows (assuming 512 byte sectors):

SCSI w/ Enh. BIOS: 1,024 Cyls * 256 Hds * 63 Secs = 8,455,716,864 Bytes (7.88G)

If you did not have enhanced BIOS support in your SCSI adapter or motherboard, in some cases there will be an external driver for your adapter that you can load to provide this support.

Most systems will support up to four SCSI host adapters, each with up to seven hard disk drives for a total of 28 physically installed drives.

ROM BIOS Capacity Limitations

In addition to the capacity limit of 504 megabytes, the standard ROM BIOS is limited to supporting only two hard disk drives. The enhanced BIOS is limited to 128 drives maximum. Most SCSI and IDE adapters get around the two drive standard BIOS limits by incorporating an enhanced BIOS on board that takes over the disk interface.

Operating System Capacity Limitations

IBM and Microsoft officially say that DOS 5 and up support up to eight physical hard disks. IBM says that OS/2 1.30.1 or higher (including 2.x) supports up to 24 physical hard disks, and because OS/2 includes DOS, that would imply that DOS under OS/2 would support 24 physical drives as well. OS/2 HPFS (High Performance File System) also supports a maximum partition size of 8GB and a maximum single file size of 2G, whereas DOS and OS/2 FAT partitions have a maximum size of 2G and a maximum single file size of 2G, also. As you have seen, BIOS limitations currently limit the maximum physical hard disk size to about 7.88G (or about 8.46 million bytes).

DoubleSpace Capacity Limitations

The current version of Microsoft's DoubleSpace disk compression software limits the maximum size of a compressed volume to 512M. Because a nearly 2:1 compression ratio is achieved, it is not recommend to use DoubleSpace to compress a drive larger than 256M. The DoubleSpace-compressed volume actually exists as a hidden file on your regular hard disk. DoubleSpace maintains its own FAT and directory structure within the hidden volume, making data recovery of any file inside one of these volumes difficult to impossible.

As an aside, I do not use DoubleSpace myself and generally recommend against most forms of data compression done at the software level, with the exception of perhaps using the shareware PKZIP program to compress (zip) files that are not used often. In my opinion, the only reliable data compression is that which is built into the hardware and is transparent. With hard disk real estate equal to or less than $1 per megabyte, I find it much more cost effective to purchase more disk real estate than to purchase and use clumsy, slow, and often dangerous software-compression schemes. About the only situation in which I would recommend using DoubleSpace (or anything else like it) would be for a laptop system where larger hard disks might be unavailable. If you must use some form of compression, I recommend Stacker by Stac Electronics, which seems to be the most reliable and time-tested compression program on the market. They also have a version for OS/2, which DoubleSpace does not support.

Disk compression will eventually be built right into the hardware. Already there are tape drives that offer built-in disk compression hardware. When it is implemented in this fashion, the compression is totally transparent to any applications or operating software. This means no funny drivers or special programs are required; the device simply stores more information transparently. Eventually these compression chips will be implemented in hard disks. Until then, be careful when you use any of the software compression schemes because they can be troublesome and problems often result in lost data.

Hard Disk Drive Troubleshooting and Repair

If a hard disk drive has a problem inside its sealed HDA (Head Disk Assembly), repairing the drive is usually not feasible. If the failure is in the logic board, that assembly can be replaced with a new or rebuilt assembly easily and for a much lower cost than replacing the entire drive.

Most hard disk problems are not really hardware problems; instead, they are "soft" problems, in which a new low-level format and defect mapping session can solve the problem. Soft problems are characterized by a drive that sounds normal but gives various read and write errors.

III

Hardware Considerations

"Hard" problems are mechanical, such as when the drive sounds as if it contains loose marbles. Constant scraping and grinding noises from the drive, with no reading or writing capability, also qualifies as a hard error. In these cases, it is unlikely that a low-level format will put the drives back into service. If a hardware problem is indicated, first replace the logic board assembly. You can do this repair yourself and, if successful, you can recover the data from the drive.

If replacing the logic assembly does not solve the problem, contact the manufacturer or a specialized repair shop that has clean room facilities for hard disk repair. See the vendor list in the Appendix for a list of drive manufacturers and companies that specialize in hard disk drive repair.

The cost of HDA repair may be more than half the cost of a new drive, so you may want to consider replacing rather than repairing the drive. If the failed drive is an inexpensive 20-megabyte or 30-megabyte stepper motor drive, the better option is to purchase something better. If the drive is a larger voice coil drive, however, it is usually more economical to repair rather than replace the drive because the replacement cost is much higher.

17xx, 104xx, 210xxxx Hardware Error Codes

When there is a failure in the hard disk subsystem at power on, the Power-On Self Test (POST) finds the problem and reports it with an error message. The 17xx, 104xx, and 210xxxx errors during the POST or while running the Advanced Diagnostics indicate problems with hard disks, controllers, or cables. The 17xx codes apply to ST-506/412 interface drives and controllers; 104xx errors apply to ESDI drives and controllers; and 210xxxx errors apply to SCSI drives and host adapters.

A breakdown of these error messages and their meanings are shown in Table 10.24.

Table 10.24 Hard Disk and Controller Diagnostic Error Codes

ST-506/412 Drive and Controller Error Codes

1701	Fixed disk general POST error
1702	Drive/controller time-out error
1703	Drive seek error
1704	Controller failed
1705	Drive sector not found error
1706	Write fault error
1707	Drive track 0 error
1708	Head select error
1709	Error Correction Code (ECC) error
1710	Sector buffer overrun
1711	Bad address mark
1712	Internal controller diagnostics failure
1713	Data compare error
1714	Drive not ready

ST-506/412 Drive and Controller Error Codes

1715	Track 0 indicator failure
1716	Diagnostics cylinder errors
1717	Surface read errors
1718	Hard drive type error
1720	Bad diagnostics cylinder
1726	Data compare error
1730	Controller error
1731	Controller error
1732	Controller error
1733	BIOS undefined error return
1735	Bad command error
1736	Data corrected error
1737	Bad track error
1738	Bad sector error
1739	Bad initialization error
1740	Bad sense error
1750	Drive verify failure
1751	Drive read failure
1752	Drive write failure
1753	Drive random read test failure
1754	Drive seek test failure
1755	Controller failure
1756	Controller Error Correction Code (ECC) test failure
1757	Controller head select failure
1780	Seek failure; drive 0
1781	Seek failure; drive 1
1782	Controller test failure
1790	Diagnostic cylinder read error; drive 0
1791	Diagnostic cylinder read error; drive 1

ESDI Drive and Controller Error Codes

10450	Read/write test failed
10451	Read verify test failed
10452	Seek test failed
10453	Wrong device type indicated
10454	Controller test failed sector buffer test
10455	Controller failure
10456	Controller diagnostic command failure
10461	Drive format error
10462	Controller head select error

(continues)

III

Hardware Considerations

Table 10.24 Continued

ESDI Drive and Controller Error Codes

10463	Drive read/write sector error
10464	Drive primary defect map unreadable
10465	Controller; Error Correction Code (ECC) 8-bit error
10466	Controller; Error Correction Code (ECC) 9-bit error
10467	Drive soft seek error
10468	Drive hard seek error
10469	Drive soft seek error count exceeded
10470	Controller attachment diagnostic error
10471	Controller wrap mode interface error
10472	Controller wrap mode drive select error
10473	Read verify test errors
10480	Seek failure; drive 0
10481	Seek failure; drive 1
10482	Controller transfer acknowledge error
10483	Controller reset failure
10484	Controller; head select 3 error
10485	Controller; head select 2 error
10486	Controller; head select 1 error
10487	Controller; head select 0 error
10488	Controller; read gate - command complete 2 error
10489	Controller; write gate - command complete 1 error
10490	Diagnostic area read error; drive 0
10491	Diagnostic area read error; drive 1
10499	Controller failure

SCSI Drive and Host Adapter Error Codes

096xxxx	SCSI adapter with cache (32-bit) errors
112xxxx	SCSI adapter (16-bit without cache) errors
113xxxx	System board SCSI adapter (16-bit) errors
210xxxx	SCSI fixed disk errors

For SCSI Errors:
First x in xxxx is SCSI ID number.
Second x in xxxx is logical unit number (usually 0).
Third x in xxxx is Host Adapter slot number.
Fourth x in xxxx is a letter code indicating drive capacity.
A complete list of all IBM SCSI error codes can be found in the Appendix.

Most of the time a seek failure indicates that the drive is not responding to the controller. This failure is usually caused by one of the following:

- Incorrect drive-select jumper setting

- Loose, damaged, or backward control cable

- Loose or bad power cable

- Stiction between drive heads and platters

- Bad power supply

If a diagnostics cylinder read error occurs, the most likely problems are these:

- Incorrect drive-type setting

- Loose, damaged, or backward data cable

- Temperature-induced mistracking

Correcting most of these problems is obvious. For example, if the drive-select jumper setting is incorrect, correct it. If a cable is loose, tighten it. If the power supply is bad, replace it. You get the idea.

If the problem is temperature related, the drive will usually read data acceptably at the same temperature at which it was written. Let the drive warm up for a while and then attempt to reboot it, or let the drive cool and reread the disk if the drive has overheated.

The stiction problem may not have an obvious solution; the next section addresses this problem.

Drive Spin Failure (Stiction)

Other than a faulty power-supply cable connection or a faulty power supply, stiction is the primary cause of a hard disk drive not spinning. *Stiction* (static friction) is a condition in which the drive heads are stuck to the platters in a way that the platter motor cannot overcome the sticking force and spin the drive up for operation. This situation happens more frequently than you might imagine.

The heads stick to the platters in the same way two very smooth pieces of glass might stick together. It is especially noticeable if the drive has been off for a week or more. It also seems more noticeable if the drive is operated under very hot conditions and then shut down. In the latter case, the excessive heat buildup in the drive softens the lubricant coating on the platter surface; after the drive is powered off, the platters cool rapidly and contract around the heads, which have settled in this lubricant coating. Drives with more platters and heads are more prone to this problem than drives with fewer ones.

To solve this problem, you must spin the platters with enough force to rip the heads loose from the platters. Usually this is accomplished by twisting the drive violently in the same plane as the platters, using the platter's inertia to overcome the sticking force.

III

Hardware Considerations

The heavy platters tend to remain stationary while you twist the drive and essentially make the heads move around the platters.

Another technique is to spin the spindle motor manually, which rotates the platters inside the drive. To do this, you may have to remove the circuit board from the bottom of the drive to get to the spindle motor. In other cases, you can insert a thin wooden stick into the gap between the bottom of the drive and the circuit board and push on the spindle motor drum with the stick. You will probably feel heavy resistance to rotation, and then the platters will suddenly move free as the heads are unstuck. Many drives today have spindle motors located inside the platter hub area which is totally enclosed within the HDA. You will not be able to spin these platters by hand unless you open up the HDA, which is recommended only in situations where nothing else has worked. In most cases, simply twisting the whole drive in the same plane as the platters will use the inertia of the platters to jerk the heads free from their stuck position.

Another problem that can cause the appearance of stiction is a stuck spindle motor (platter) brake. Many drives use a solenoid-actuated spindle motor brake (see fig. 10.23) to stop the platters rapidly when the drive is powered off. This is designed to minimize the distance that the heads skid on the platter surface when the drive is powered down. When the brake solenoid fails, it does not release the spindle motor and can give the exact same symptoms as stiction. Because this device is almost always external to the HDA, it can usually be easily removed if it fails, allowing the drive to spin freely. Because every drive is designed differently, consult the drive manual to see whether your drive has such a spindle braking system and where it is located. Of course, long-term reliability may be affected because the heads will now skid for a much longer distance when the drive is powered off, accelerating wear of the heads and media.

After you free the platters, reapply the power, and the drive should spin up normally. I have solved stiction problems many times using these methods, and have never lost data as long as I could get the drive to spin. If you cannot make the drive spin, you certainly will not be able to recover any data from it.

A majority of drive failures are in the logic board, which also contains motor control circuits in most drives, as well. This means that a no spin situation can be caused by a defective logic board. Unless you have a spare drive with the same type of logic board to swap with, it is difficult to know whether the logic board is truly at fault. Some drive manufacturers and repair depots will sell logic boards individually, but I usually find it easier to simply purchase another (duplicate) entire drive. It is often cheaper to purchase a used drive exactly like the one that failed rather than a single part like a logic board. This used drive can then be cannibalized for parts to restore the failed drive to operation. This is not designed to be a cost-effective way to repair a drive, but it will allow you to possibly recover the data from the failed drive, which is usually worth much more than the drive itself. Most good data recovery operations have a variety of functioning used drives available to them to be cannibalized for parts in recovering data from failed drives.

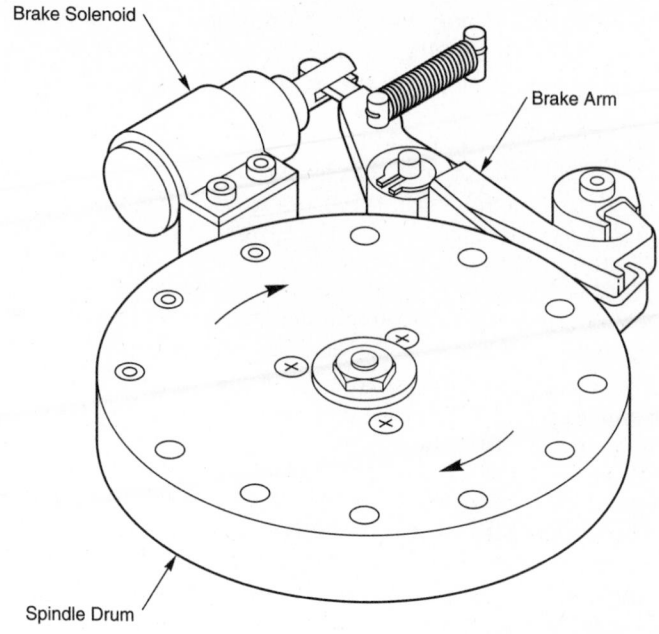

Fig. 10.23

A typical spindle motor solenoid and brake assembly.

In some cases, I have had to resort to opening the HDA to forcibly spin the platters by hand to recover data. In many cases, this worked to free up the platters and start the drive operating, after which I was able to close up the HDA and back up all of the data on the drive. If you are nervous about handling your drive in this manner, consult a professional drive repair facility.

I know that the impression everybody normally has is that opening a drive will destroy or damage it in some way (head crash?), especially considering the extremely close proximity that the heads float above (or below) the disk platters. I can say from experience, however, that most hard drives are much sturdier than people think. Not only have I opened up many functioning hard drives, but I have operated them exposed in this manner for extended periods of time, all the while reliably reading and writing data. In fact, I have several drives that I regularly use in my PC Troubleshooting and Data Recovery seminars which I have been operating with the lids off practically every week for several years now with no lost data. Even more amazing is that I often use them to perform torture demonstrations where I literally bend the HDA with my bare hands while the drive is reading files. This instantly causes the file read operation to fail due to the heads being forced away from their proper track positions. When I release the bending force, the heads return to normal track position and the files can then be read with no problem!

Although I use these seminar demonstrations to get people's attention, these "lid off" techniques have helped me at times in extreme data recovery situations. Of course, I am obligated to state the standard "don't try this at home" warning!

Logic Board Failures

A disk drive, including a hard disk drive, has one or more logic boards mounted on it. These boards contain the electronics that control the drive's spindle and head actuator systems and present data to the controller. Some drives have built-in controllers.

Logic boards on hard disks fail more often than the mechanical components. Most professional data-recovery companies stock a number of functional logic boards for popular drives. When a drive comes in for recovery, data-recovery professionals check the drive for problems such as installation or configuration errors, temperature mistracking, and stiction. If these are not the problem, they replace the logic board on the drive with a known good unit. Often the drive then works normally, and data can be read from it.

The logic boards on most hard disks can be removed and replaced easily; they simply plug into the drive and are usually mounted with standard screw hardware. If a drive is failing, and you have a spare of the same type, you might be able to verify a logic board failure by removing the board from a known good drive and mounting it on the bad one. Then if your suspicions are confirmed, in some cases you can order a new logic board from the drive's manufacturer. Be prepared for sticker shock; parts like this may cost more than replacing the entire drive with a new or refurbished unit. A less-expensive option is buying a refurbished unit, or trading in the old board. (The drive manufacturer will have details on these options.) Purchasing a new logic board may not always be cost-effective, but borrowing one from a drive that works is one of the only ways to verify that the logic board has failed, and may be the only way to recover all the data from the problem drive.

Chapter Summary

This chapter has examined hard disks and controllers and explored the physical and logical operations of the disk. You learned about configuring, installing, and trouble-shooting hard disks and controllers. Now you can use this information to upgrade an existing system with a new hard disk, or troubleshoot and repair an existing configuration. A properly designed and installed hard disk system will give you fewer problems than a haphazardly installed system. Most problems are related to software, installation, or formatting, so you can use the information in this chapter to restore many failing drives to normal operation.

The next chapter continues your tour through the system and focuses on other peripherals, such as video subsystems and communications adapters.

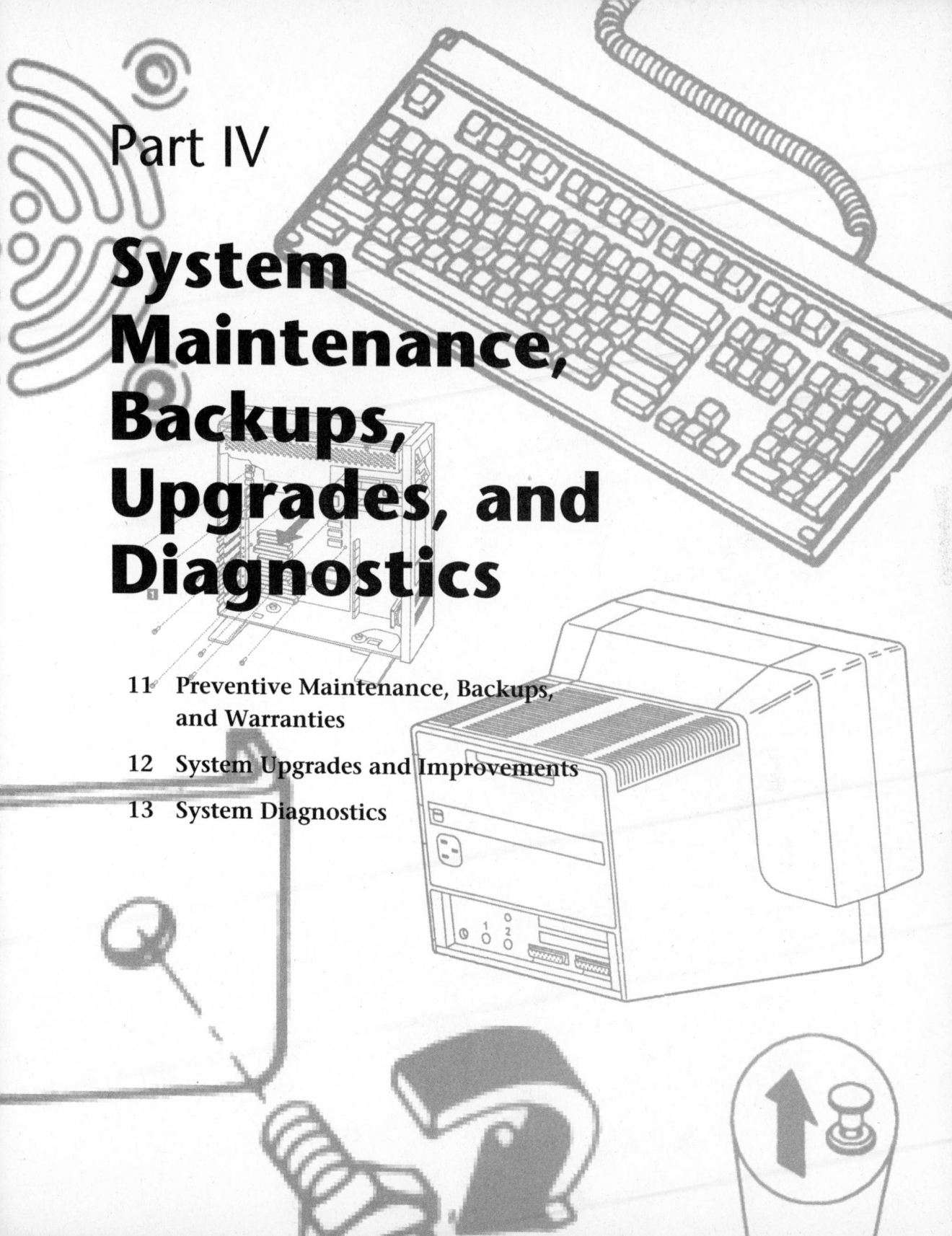

Part IV

System Maintenance, Backups, Upgrades, and Diagnostics

Chapter 11
Preventive Maintenance, Backups, and Warranties

Preventive maintenance is the key to obtaining years of trouble-free service from your computer system. A properly administered preventive maintenance program pays for itself by reducing problem behavior, data loss, component failure, and ensuring a long life for your system. In several cases, I have repaired an ailing system with nothing more than a preventive maintenance session. Preventive maintenance also increases your systems resale value because it will look and run better. This chapter describes preventive maintenance procedures and how often you should perform them.

You will also learn the importance of creating backup files of data and the various backup procedures available. A sad reality in the computer repair and servicing world is that hardware can always be repaired or replaced, but data cannot. Most hard disk troubleshooting and service procedures, for example, require that a low-level format be done. This low-level format overwrites any data on the disk.

In Chapter 15, "Software Troubleshooting Guide," simple techniques are explained for recovering data from a damaged disk or disk drive. These procedures, however, are not perfect.

Because data recovery depends a great deal on the type and severity of damage and the expertise of the recovery specialist, data-recovery services are very expensive. Most recovery services charge a premium for these services and offer no guarantees that the data will be completely recovered. Backing up your system as discussed in this chapter is the only guarantee you have of seeing your data again.

Most of the discussion of backing up systems in this chapter is limited to professional solutions that require special hardware and software. Backup solutions that employ floppy disk drives, such as the DOS backup software, are insufficient and too costly in most cases for hard disk backups. It would take 1,456 1.44M floppy disks, for example, to backup the 2G hard disk in my portable system! That would cost more than $1,000 in disks, not to mention the time involved. A tape system can put 4G to 8G on a single $15 tape.

Finally, the last section in this chapter discusses the standard warranties and optional service contracts available for many systems. Although most of this book is written for people who want to perform their own maintenance and repair service, taking advantage of a good factory warranty that provides service for free definitely is prudent. Some larger computer companies, such as IBM, offer attractive service contracts that, in some cases, are cost-justified over self service. These types of options are examined in the final section.

Developing a Preventive Maintenance Program

Developing a preventive maintenance program is important to everyone who uses or manages personal computer systems. Two types of preventive maintenance procedures exist: active and passive.

Active preventive maintenance includes steps you apply to a system that promote a longer, trouble-free life. This type of preventive maintenance primarily involves periodic cleaning of the system and its components. This section describes several active preventive maintenance procedures, including cleaning and lubricating all major components, reseating chips and connectors, and reformatting hard disks.

Passive preventive maintenance includes steps you can take to protect a system from the environment, such as using power-protection devices; ensuring a clean, temperature-controlled environment; and preventing excessive vibration. In other words, passive preventive maintenance means treating your system well. This section also describes passive preventive maintenance procedures.

Active Preventive Maintenance Procedures

How often you should implement active preventive maintenance procedures depends on the system's environment and the quality of the system's components. If your system is in a dirty environment, such as a machine shop floor or a gas station service area, you might need to clean your system every three months or less. For normal office environments, cleaning a system every one to two years is usually fine. However, if you open your system after one year and find dust bunnies inside, you should probably shorten the cleaning interval.

Another active preventive maintenance technique discussed in this section is reformatting hard disks. Low-level reformatting restores the track and sector marks to their proper locations and forces you to back up and restore all data on the drive. Not all drives require this procedure, but if you are using drives with a stepper-motor head actuator, periodic reformatting is highly recommended. Most drives with a voice-coil head actuators run indefinitely without reformatting due to their track following servo mechanisms which prevent temperature induced mistracking.

Other hard disk preventive maintenance procedures include making periodic backups of critical areas such as Boot Sectors, File Allocation Tables, and Directory structures on the disk.

Cleaning a System. One of the most important operations in a good preventive maintenance program is regular and thorough cleaning of the system. Dust buildup on the internal components can lead to several problems. One is that the dust acts as a thermal insulator, which prevents proper system cooling. Excessive heat shortens the life of system components and adds to the thermal stress problem caused by wider temperature changes between power-on and power-off states. Additionally, the dust may contain conductive elements that can cause partial short circuits in a system. Other elements in the dust and dirt accelerate corrosion of electrical contacts and cause improper connections. In all, the removal of any layer of dust and debris from within a computer system benefits that system in the long run.

All IBM and IBM-compatible systems use a forced-air cooling system that allows for even cooling inside the system. A fan is mounted in, on, or near the power supply and pushes air outside. This setup depressurizes the interior of the system relative to the outside air. The lower pressure inside the system causes outside air to be drawn into openings in the system chassis and cover. This draw-through, or depressurization, system is the most efficient cooling system that can be designed without an air filter. Air filters typically are not used with depressurization systems because there is no easy way to limit air intake to a single port that can be covered by a filter.

Some industrial computers from IBM and other companies use a forced-air system that uses the fan to pressurize, rather than depressurize, the case. This system forces air to exhaust from any holes in the chassis and case or cover. The key to the pressurization system is that all air intake for the system is at a single location—the fan. The air flowing into the system therefore can be filtered, by simply integrating a filter assembly into the fan housing. The filter must be cleaned or changed periodically. Because the interior of the case is pressurized relative to the outside air, airborne contaminants are not drawn into the system even though it may not be sealed. Any air entering the system must pass through the fan and filter housing, which removes the contaminants. Pressurization cooling systems are used primarily in industrial computer models designed for extremely harsh environments.

Most systems you have contact with are depressurization systems. Mounting any sort of air filter on these types of systems is impossible because air enters the system from too many sources. With any cooling system in which incoming air is not filtered, dust and other chemical matter in the environment is drawn in and builds up inside the computer. This buildup can cause severe problems if left unchecked.

One problem that can develop is overheating. The buildup of dust acts as a heat insulator, which prevents the system from cooling properly. Some of the components in a modern PC can generate an enormous amount of heat that must be dissipated for the component to function. The dust also might contain chemicals that conduct electricity. These chemicals can cause minor current shorts and create electrical signal paths where none should exist. The chemicals also cause rapid corrosion of cable connectors, socket-installed components, and areas where boards plug into slots. All of which can cause intermittent system problems and erratic operation.

> **Tip**
>
> Cigarette smoke contains chemicals that can conduct electricity and cause corrosion of computer parts. The smoke residue can infiltrate the entire system, causing corrosion and contamination of electrical contacts and sensitive components such as floppy drive read/write heads and optical drive lens assemblies. You should avoid smoking near computer equipment and encourage your company to develop and enforce a similar policy.

Floppy disk drives are particularly vulnerable to the effects of dirt and dust. Floppy drives are a large hole within the system through which air continuously flows. Therefore, they accumulate a large amount of dust and chemical buildup within a short time. Hard disk drives do not present quite the same problem. Because the head disk assembly (HDA) in a hard disk is a sealed unit with a single barometric vent, no dust or dirt can enter without passing through the barometric vent filter. This filter insures that contaminating dust or particles cannot enter the interior of the HDA. Thus, cleaning a hard disk requires simply blowing the dust and dirt off from outside the drive. No internal cleaning is required.

Disassembly and Cleaning Tools. To properly clean the system and all the boards inside requires certain supplies and tools. In addition to the tools required to disassemble the unit (see Chapter 6, "System Teardown and Inspection"), you should have these items:

- Contact cleaning solution
- Canned air
- A small brush
- Lint-free foam cleaning swabs
- Antistatic wrist-grounding strap

You might also want to acquire these optional items:

- Foam tape
- Low-volatile room-temperature vulcanizing (RTV) sealer
- Silicone type lubricant
- Computer vacuum cleaner

These simple cleaning tools and chemical solutions will allow you to perform most common preventive maintenance tasks.

Chemicals. There are several different types of cleaning solutions you can use with computers and electronic assemblies. Most fall into several categories. These are:

- Standard Cleaners

■ Contact Cleaner/Lubricants

■ Dusters

> **Tip**
>
> The makeup of many of the chemicals used for cleaning electronic components has been changing because many of the chemicals originally used are now considered environmentally unsafe. They have been attributed to damaging the Earth's ozone layer, a natural protective barrier in the stratosphere, which prevents harmful Ultraviolet (UV-B) radiation from reaching Earth. Chlorine atoms from ChloroFluoro Carbons (CFCs) and Chlorinated Solvents attach themselves to ozone molecules and destroy them. Many of these chemicals are now strictly regulated by Federal and International agencies in an effort to preserve the ozone layer. Most of the companies that produce chemicals used for system cleaning and maintenance have had to introduce environmentally safe replacements. The only drawback is that many of these safer chemicals cost more and usually do not work as well as those they replace.

There are many specific chemicals used in cleaning and dusting solutions, but five types are of particular interest. The EPA has classified ozone damaging chemicals into two classes, called Class I and Class II. Chemicals that fall into these two classes have their usage regulated. Other chemicals are non-regulated. Class I chemicals include:

■ Chlorofluorocarbons (CFCs)

■ Chlorinated Solvents

Class I chemicals can only be sold for use in professional service and not to consumers. A new law that went into effect on May 15, 1993, requires that the containers for Class I chemicals be labeled with a warning that the product "Contains substances which harm public health and the environment by destroying ozone in the atmosphere." Additionally, electronics manufacturers and other industries must also apply a similar warning label to any products that use Class I chemicals in the production process. This means that any circuit board or computer that is manufactured with CFCs will have this label!

The most popular Class I chemicals are the various forms of Freon, which are CFCs. A very popular cleaning solution called 1,1,1 Trichloroethane is a chlorinated solvent and is also strictly regulated. Up until the last year or so, virtually all computer or electronic cleaning solutions contained one or both of these chemicals. While you can still purchase them, regulations have made them more difficult to find and more expensive because production is limited.

Class II chemicals include Hydrochlorofluorocarbons (HCFCs). These are not as strictly regulated as Class I chemicals because they have a lower ozone depletion potential. Many cleaning solutions have switched to HCFCs, because they do not require the restrictive labeling required by Class I chemicals and are not as harmful. Most HCFCs have only one tenth the ozone damaging potential of CFCs.

Other non-regulated chemicals include Volatile Organic Compounds (VOCs) and Hydrofluorocarbons (HFCs). These chemicals do not damage the ozone layer but actually contribute to ozone production, which, unfortunately, appears in the form of smog or ground level pollution. Pure Isopropyl Alcohol is an example of a VOC that is commonly used in electronic part and contact cleaning. HFCs are used as a replacement for CFCs since the HFCs do not damage the ozone layer.

The EPA has developed a method to measure the ozone damaging capability of a chemical. The Ozone Depletion Potential (ODP) of a chemical solution is the sum of the depletion potentials of each of the chemicals used in the solution by weight. The ODP of Freon R12 (Automotive Air Conditioning Freon), is 1.0 on this scale. Most modern CFC replacement chemicals have an ODP rating of 0.0 to 0.1, as opposed to those using CFCs and Chlorinated Solvents which usually have ODP ratings of .75 or higher.

Standard Cleaners. Standard cleaning solutions are available in a variety of types and configurations. You can use pure isopropyl alcohol, acetone, Freon, Trichloroethane, or a variety of other chemicals. Most are now leaning to the alcohol, acetone, or others that do not cause ozone depletion and which comply with government regulations and environmental safety. You should be sure that your cleaning solution is designed to clean computers or electronic assemblies. In most cases this means that the solution should be chemically pure and free from contaminants or other unwanted substances. You should not, for example, use drugstore rubbing alcohol for cleaning electronic parts or contacts because it is not pure and could contain water or perfumes. The material must be moisture-free and residue-free. The solutions should be in liquid form, not a spray. Sprays can be wasteful and you almost never spray the solution directly on components. Instead, wet a foam or chamois swab used for wiping the component. These electronic-component cleaning solutions are available at any good electronics parts stores.

Contact Cleaner/Lubricants. These are very similar to the standard cleaners but include a lubricating component. The lubricant eases the force required when plugging and unplugging cables and connectors, which reduces strain on the devices. The lubricant coating also acts as a conductive protectant that insulates the contacts from corrosion. These chemicals can greatly prolong the life of a system by preventing intermittent contacts in the future.

Contact cleaner/lubricants are especially effective on I/O slot connectors, adapter card edge and pin connectors, disk drive connectors, power supply connectors, and virtually any connectors in the PC.

In Chapter 6, "System Teardown and Inspection," a contact enhancer and lubricant called Stabilant 22 is mentioned. It is more effective than conventional contact cleaners or lubricants. This chemical is available in several forms. Stabilant 22 is the full-strength concentrated version, while Stabilant 22a is a version diluted with isopropyl alcohol in a 4 to 1 ratio. An even more diluted 8 to 1 ratio version is sold in many high-end stereo and audio shops under the name "Tweek." Just 15ml of Stabilant 22a sells for about $40, while a liter of the concentrate costs about $4,000. While Stabilant 22 is expensive, very little is required and an application can provide protection for a long time. Stabilant is manufactured by D. W. Electrochemicals, which is listed in the vendor list in the Appendix.

Dusters. Compressed gas often is used as an aid in system cleaning. The compressed gas is used as a blower to remove dust and debris from a system or component. Originally, these dusters used CFCs such as Freon, while modern dusters now use HFCs or carbon dioxide, neither of which is damaging to the ozone layer. Be careful when you use these devices because some of them can generate a static charge when the compressed gas leaves the nozzle of the can. Be sure that you are using the kind approved for cleaning or dusting off computer equipment, and consider wearing a static grounding strap as a precaution. The type of compressed-air cans used for cleaning camera equipment can sometimes differ from the type used for cleaning static sensitive computer components.

Most older computer-grade canned gas dusters consisted of dichlorodifluoromethane (Freon R12), the same chemical used in many automotive air-conditioning systems built until 1995, when a ban of the manufacture and use of R12 takes place. In 1992 many automobile manufacturers began switching to an ozone safe chemical called R134a. Manufacturing of R12 will cease by 1995, and the regulations placed on its use have forced companies to use other products such as carbon dioxide for compressed gas dusters. In addition to the environmental concerns about depleting the ozone layer, Freon can be dangerous if exposed to an open flame.

> **Caution**
>
> If you use any chemical with the propellant Freon R12 (dichlorodifluoromethane), *do not expose the gas to an open flame or other heat source.* If you burn this substance, a highly toxic gas called *phosgene* is generated. Phosgene, used as a nerve gas in World War II, can be deadly.

Related to compressed-air products are chemical-freeze sprays. These sprays are used to quickly cool down a suspected failing component, which often temporarily restores it to operation. These substances are not used to repair a device but to confirm that you have found a failed device. Often, a components failure is heat-related and cooling it temporarily restores it to function. If the circuit begins operating normally, the device you are cooling is the suspect device.

Vacuum Cleaners. Some people prefer to use a vacuum cleaner instead of canned gas dusters for cleaning a system. Canned gas is usually better for cleaning in small areas. A vacuum cleaner is more useful when you are cleaning a system loaded with dust and dirt. You can use the vacuum cleaner to suck out dust and debris instead of blowing them on other components, which sometimes happens with canned air. For outbound servicing (when you are going to the location of the equipment instead of the equipment coming to you), canned air is easier to carry in a toolkit than a small vacuum cleaner.

Brushes and swabs. A small brush (makeup, photographic, or paint) can be used to carefully loosen accumulated dirt and dust before spraying with canned air or using the vacuum cleaner. Be careful about generating static electricity. In most cases the brushes should not be used directly on circuit boards but instead on the case interior and other parts like fan blades, air vents, and keyboards. Wear a grounded wrist strap if you are brushing on or near any circuit boards, and brush slowly and lightly to prevent static discharges from occurring.

Cleaning swabs are used for wiping off electrical contacts and connectors, disk drive heads, and other sensitive areas. The swabs should be made of foam or synthetic chamois material, which does not leave lint or dust residue. Unfortunately, proper foam or chamois cleaning swabs are more expensive than the typical cotton swabs. Do not use cotton swabs because they leave cotton fibers on everything they touch. Cotton fibers are conductive in some situations and can remain on drive heads, which can scratch disks. The foam or chamois swabs can be purchased at most electronics-supply stores.

One item to avoid is an eraser for cleaning contacts. Many people (including myself) have recommended using a soft pencil type eraser for cleaning circuit board contacts. Testing has proven this to be bad advice for several reasons. One is that any such abrasive wiping on electrical contacts generates friction and an electrostatic discharge (ESD). This ESD can be damaging to boards and components, especially with newer low voltage devices made using CMOS (Complimentary Metal Oxide Semiconductor) technology. These devices are especially static sensitive, and cleaning the contacts without a proper liquid solution is not recommended. Also the eraser will wear off the gold coating on many contacts, exposing the tin contact underneath, which will rapidly corrode when exposed to air. Some companies sell pre-moistened contact cleaning pads that are soaked in a proper contact cleaner and lubricant. These are safe to wipe on conductor and contacts with no likelihood of ESD damage or abrasion of the gold plating.

Foam Tape or RTV sealer. Hard disks usually use a small copper strap to ground the spindle of the disk assembly to the logic board, thus bleeding off any static charge carried by the spinning disk platters. Unfortunately, this strap often can begin to harmonize, or vibrate, and result in an annoying squealing or whining noise. (Sometimes the noise is similar to fingernails dragged across a chalkboard.)

To eliminate the source of irritation, you can stop the strap from vibrating by weighting it with one of two easy methods. One method is to use a piece of foam tape cut to match the size of the strap and stuck to the straps back side. Another way to dampen the vibration is to apply a low-volatile RTV sealer. You apply this silicone-type rubber to the back of the grounding strap. After it hardens to a rubber-like material, the sealer stops the vibrations that produce the annoying squeal. You can buy the RTV sealer from an automotive-supply house.

I prefer using the foam tape rather than the RTV because it is easier and neater to apply. If you use the RTV, be sure that it is the low-volatile type, which does not generate acid when it cures. This acid produces the vinegar smell common to the standard RTV sealer, and can be highly corrosive to the strap and anything else it contacts. The low-volatile RTV also eliminates the bad vinegar smell. You can purchase the foam tape at most electronics-supply houses, where it often is sold for attaching alarm switches to doors or windows. The low-volatile RTV is available from most auto-supply stores. To be sure that you buy low-volatile RTV, look for the packaging to state specifically that the product is either a low-volatile type or is compatible with automobile oxygen sensors.

Silicone Lubricants. Silicone lubricants are used to lubricate the door mechanisms on floppy disk drives, and any other part of the system that may require clean, non-oily lubrication. Other items you can lubricate are the disk drive head slider rails or even printer-head slider rails, which allow for smooth operation.

Using silicone instead of conventional oils is important because silicone does not gum up and collect dust and other debris. Always use the silicone sparingly. Do not spray it anywhere near the equipment as it tends to migrate and will end up where it doesn't belong (such as on drive heads, etc.). Instead, apply a small amount to a toothpick or foam swab and dab the silicone on the components where needed. You can use a lint-free cleaning stick soaked in silicone lubricant to lubricate the metal print-head rails in a printer.

Remember that some of the cleaning operations described in this section might generate a static charge. You may want to use a static grounding strap in cases in which static levels are high to ensure that you do not damage any boards as you work with them.

Obtaining Required Tools and Accessories. Most cleaning chemicals and tools can be obtained from a number of electronics supply houses, or even the local Radio Shack. A company called Chemtronics specializes in chemicals for the computer and electronics industry. These and other companies who supply tools, chemicals, and other computer and electronic cleaning supplies are listed in the vendor list in the Appendix. With all these items on hand, you should be equipped for most preventive maintenance operations.

Disassembling and Cleaning Procedures. To properly clean your system, it must at least be partially disassembled. Some people go as far as removing the motherboard. Removing the motherboard results in the best possible access to other areas of the system but in the interest of saving time, you probably need to disassemble the system only to where the motherboard is completely visible.

All plug-in adapter cards must be removed, along with the disk drives. Although you can clean the heads of a floppy drive with a cleaning disk without opening the system units cover, you probably will want to do more thorough cleaning. In addition to the heads, you also should clean and lubricate the door mechanism and clean any logic boards and connectors on the drive. This procedure usually requires removing the drive.

Next, do the same procedure with a hard disk: clean the logic boards and connectors, as well as lubricate the grounding strap. To do so, you must remove the hard disk assembly. As a precaution, be sure it is backed up before removal.

Reseating Socketed Chips. A primary preventive maintenance function is to undo the effects of chip creep. As your system heats and cools, it expands and contracts, and the physical expansion and contraction causes components plugged into sockets to gradually work their way out of those sockets. This process is called *chip creep*. To correct its effects, you must find all socketed components in the system and make sure that they are properly reseated.

In most systems, all the memory chips are socketed or are installed in socketed SIMMs (Single Inline Memory Modules). SIMM devices are retained securely in their sockets by a positive latching mechanism and cannot creep out. Memory SIPP (Single Inline Pin Package) devices (SIMMs with pins rather than contacts) are not retained by a latching mechanism and therefore can creep out of their sockets. Standard socketed memory chips are prime candidates for chip creep. Most other logic components are soldered in. You can also expect to find the ROM chips, the main processor or CPU, and the math coprocessor in sockets. In most systems, these items are the only components that are socketed; all others are soldered in.

Exceptions, however, might exist. A socketed component in one system might not be socketed in another—even if both are from the same manufacturer. Sometimes this difference results from a parts-availability problem when the boards are manufactured. Rather than halt the assembly line when a part is not available, the manufacturer adds a socket instead of the component. When the component becomes available, it is plugged in and the board is finished. Many newer systems place the CPU in a Zero Insertion Force (ZIF) socket, which has a lever that can release the grip of the socket on the chip. In most cases there is very little creep with a ZIF socket.

To make sure that all components are fully seated in their sockets, place your hand on the underside of the board and then apply downward pressure with your thumb (from the top) on the chip to be seated. For larger chips, seat the chip carefully in two movements, and press separately on each end of the chip with your thumb to be sure that the chip is fully seated. (The processor and math coprocessor chips can usually be seated in this manner.) In most cases, you hear a crunching sound as the chip makes its way back into the socket. Because of the great force sometimes required to reseat the chips, this operation is difficult if you do not remove the board.

For motherboards, forcibly seating chips can be dangerous if you do not directly support the board from the underside with your hand. Enough pressure on the board can cause it to bow or bend in the chassis, and the pressure can crack it before seating takes place. The plastic standoffs that separate and hold the board up from the metal chassis are spaced too far apart to properly support the board under this kind of stress. Try this operation only if you can remove and support the board adequately from underneath.

You may be surprised to know that, even if you fully seat each chip, they might need reseating again within a year. The creep usually is noticeable within a year or less.

Cleaning Boards. After reseating any socketed devices that may have creeped out of their sockets, the next step is to clean the boards and all connectors in the system. For this step, the cleaning solutions and the lint-free swabs described earlier are needed.

First, clean the dust and debris off the board and then clean any connectors on the board. To clean the boards, it is usually best to use a vacuum cleaner designed for electronic assemblies and circuit boards or a duster can of compressed gas. The dusters are especially effective at blasting any dust and dirt off the boards.

Also blow any dust out of the power supply, especially around the fan intake and exhaust areas. You do not need to disassemble the power supply to do this, just use a duster can and blast the compressed air into the supply through the fan exhaust port. This will blow the dust out of the supply and clean off the fan blades and grille which will help with system airflow.

Caution

Be careful with electrostatic discharge (ESD), which can damage components, when cleaning electronic components. Take extra precautions in the dead of winter in an extremely dry, high-static environment. There are antistatic sprays and treatments that you can apply to the work area to reduce the likelihood of ESD damage.

An antistatic wrist-grounding strap is recommended. This should be connected to a ground on the card or board you are wiping. This strap ensures that no electrical discharge occurs between you and the board. An alternative method is to keep a finger or thumb on the ground of the motherboard or card as you wipe it off. It is easier to insure proper grounding while the motherboard is still installed in the chassis, so it might be a good idea not to remove it.

Cleaning Connectors and Contacts. Cleaning the connectors and contacts in a system promotes reliable connections between devices. On a motherboard, you will want to clean the slot connectors, power-supply connectors, keyboard connector, and speaker connector. For most plug-in cards, you will want to clean the edge connectors that plug into slots on the motherboard as well as any other connectors, such as external ones mounted on the card bracket.

Submerge the lint-free swabs in the liquid cleaning solution. If you are using the spray, hold the swab away from the system and spray a small amount on the foam end until the solution starts to drip. Then, use the soaked foam swab to wipe the connectors on the boards. Pre-soaked wipes are the easiest to use. Simply wipe them along the contacts to remove any accumulated dirt and leave a protective coating behind.

On the motherboard, pay special attention to the slot connectors. Be liberal with the liquid; resoak the foam swab repeatedly, and vigorously clean the connectors. Don't worry if some of the liquid drips on the surface of the motherboard. These solutions are entirely safe for the whole board and will not damage the components.

Use the solution to wash the dirt off the gold contacts in the slot connectors, and then douse any other connectors on the board. Clean the keyboard connector, the grounding positions where screws ground the board to the system chassis, power-supply connectors, speaker connectors, battery connectors, and so on.

If you are cleaning a plug-in board, pay special attention to the edge connector that mates with the slot connector on the motherboard. When people handle plug-in cards, they often touch the gold contacts on these connectors. Touching the gold contacts coats them with oils and debris, which prevents proper contact with the slot connector when the board is installed. Make sure that these gold contacts are free of all finger oils and residue. It is a good idea to use one of the contact cleaners that has a conductive lubricant, which both allows connections to be made with less force, and also protects the contacts from corrosion.

> **Caution**
>
> Many people use a common pink eraser to rub the edge connectors clean. I do not recommend this procedure, for two reasons. One, the eraser eventually removes some of the gold and leaves the tin solder or copper underneath exposed. Without the gold, the contact corrodes rapidly and requires frequent cleaning. The second reason to avoid cleaning with the eraser is that the rubbing action can generate a static charge. This charge can harm any component on the board. Rather than use an eraser, use the liquid solution and swab method described earlier.

You also will want to use the swab and solution to clean the ends of ribbon cables or other types of cables or connectors in a system. Clean the floppy drive cables and connectors, the hard disk cables and connectors, and any others you find. Don't forget to clean off the edge connectors that are on the disk drive logic boards as well as the power connectors to the drives.

Cleaning Floppy Drives. Because Chapter 8 explains the procedure for cleaning floppy drives, the information is not repeated here. The basic idea is to use a canned gas duster to dust off the interior of the drive, use the silicone lubricant on whatever items need lubrication, and follow up with a head cleaning, either manually with a foam swab or most likely with a chemical soaked cleaning disk.

For hard disks, take this opportunity to dampen or lubricate the grounding strap if you have a noise problem as described earlier. Dampening is the recommended solution because if you lubricate this point, the lubricant eventually dries up and the squeal can come back. Because the dampening is usually a more permanent fix for this sort of problem, I recommend it whenever possible. Most newer hard disks have this dampening material applied at the factory and are not likely to generate noise like older drives.

Cleaning the Keyboard and Mouse. Keyboards and Mice are notorious for picking up dirt and garbage. If you have ever opened up an older keyboard, you often will be amazed at the junk you will find in there.

To prevent problems, it is a good idea to periodically clean out the keyboard with a vacuum cleaner. An alternative method is to turn the keyboard upside down and shoot it with a can of compressed gas. This will blow out the dirt and debris that has accumulated inside the keyboard and possibly prevent future problems with sticking keys or dirty keyswitches.

If a particular key is stuck or making intermittent contact, then you can soak or spray that switch with contact cleaner. The best way to do this is to first remove the keycap and then spray the cleaner into the switch. This usually does not require complete disassembly of the keyboard. Periodic vacuuming or compressed gas cleaning will prevent more serious problems with sticking keys and keyswitches.

Most mice are easily cleaned. In most cases there is a twist off locking retainer that keeps the mouse ball retained in the body of the mouse. By removing the retainer, the ball will drop out. After removing the ball, you should clean it with one of the electronic cleaners. I would recommend a pure cleaner instead of a contact cleaner with lubricant because you do not want any lubricant on the mouse ball. Then you should clean off the rollers in the body of the mouse with the cleaner and some swabs.

Periodic cleaning of a mouse in this manner will eliminate or prevent skipping or erratic movement that can be frustrating. I also recommend a mouse pad for most ball type mice because the pad will prevent the mouse ball from picking up debris from your desk.

Mice often need frequent cleaning before they start sticking and jumping, which can be frustrating. If you never want to clean a mouse again, I suggest you look into the Honeywell mouse. These mice have a revolutionary new design that uses two external wheels rather than the conventional ball and roller system. The wheels work directly on the desk surface and are unaffected by dirt and dust. Because the body of the mouse is sealed, dirt and dust cannot enter it and gum up the positional sensors. I find this mouse excellent to use with my portable system becasue it works well on any surface. This mouse is virtually immune to the sticking and jumping that plagues ball and roller designs and never needs to be cleaned, so it is less frustrating than conventional mice.

Hard Disk Maintenance. There are certain preventive maintenance procedures that will protect your data and insure that your hard disk works efficiently. Some of these procedures will actually minimize wear and tear on your drive, which will prolong its life. Additionally, a high level of data protection can be implemented by performing some simple commands periodically. These commands provide methods for backing up (and possibly later restoring) critical areas of the hard disk that, if damaged, would disable access to all your files.

Defragmenting Files. Over time, as you delete and save files to a hard disk, the files become fragmented. This means that they are split into many non-contiguous areas on the disk. One of the best ways to protect both your hard disk and the data on it is to periodically defragment the files on the disk. This serves two purposes. One is that by insuring that all of the files are stored in contiguous sectors on the disk, head movement and drive wear and tear will be minimized. This has the added benefit of improving the speed at which files will be retrieved from the drive by reducing the head thrashing that occurs every time a fragmented file is accessed.

The second major benefit, and in my estimation the more important of the two, is that in the case of a disaster where the File Allocation Tables (FATs) and Root Directory are severely damaged, the data on the drive can usually be recovered very easily if the files were contiguous. On the other hand, if the files are split up in many pieces across the drive, it is virtually impossible to figure out which pieces belong to which files without an intact File Allocation Table (FAT) and directory system. For the purposes of data integrity and protection, I recommend defragmenting your hard disk drives on a weekly basis, or immediately after you perform any major backup.

There are three main functions found in most defragmenting programs. These are:

- File Defragmentation
- File Packing (Free Space Consolidation)
- File Sorting

The defragmentation is the basic function but most other programs also add the file packing function. Packing the files is optional on some programs because it usually takes additional time to perform. This function packs the files at the beginning of the disk so that all of the free space is consolidated at the end of the disk. This feature minimizes future file fragmentation by eliminating any empty holes on the disk. Because all of the free space is consolidated into one large area, any new files written to the disk will be able to be written in a contiguous manner with no fragmentation necessary.

The last function, file sorting, is not usually necessary and is performed as an option by many defragmenting programs. This function adds a tremendous amount of time to the operation, and has little or no effect on the speed at which information is accessed. It can be somewhat beneficial for disaster recovery purposes because you will have an idea of which files came before or after other files if a disaster occurs. These benefits would be minimal compared to having the files be contiguous no matter what their order. Not all defragmenting programs offer file sorting and the extra time it takes is probably not worth any benefits you will receive. There are other programs which will sort the order that files are listed in directories, which is a quick and easy operation compared to sorting the file ordering the disk.

There are several programs available that can defragment the files on a hard disk but the one available to most people would be the DEFRAG program built into DOS 6.x. This is a reduced function version of the SPEEDISK program, which is a part of the Symantec Norton Utilities. If you have the Norton Utilities, by all means use SPEEDISK instead of DEFRAG. The DOS DEFRAG program offers all three functions including defragmenting, packing, and sorting. The SPEEDISK program performs these operations faster and with more efficient use of memory. Many of these programs will have problems on very large disks, and SPEEDISK will work on drives as large as 2G (the maximum DOS volume size), while DEFRAG is limited to disks of about 512M or less due to memory constraints.

There are several aftermarket defragmenting programs that are more powerful or faster than the DOS DEFRAG program. They include:

- SPEEDISK by Symantec (Norton Utilities)
- Power Disk by PC-KWIK
- Optune by Gazelle
- VOPT by Golden Bow

All of these are highly recommended and usually perform much better than the DEFRAG program in DOS. The Power Disk, Optune, and VOPT programs are also much faster than DEFRAG. The VOPT program is the simplest and quickest of these. It is a command line program not a menu driven program like the others and does not offer a sort capability while all the others do. What it does offer is the ultimate in speed and efficiency in defragmenting and packing files. Currently, most of these programs will work on drives up to 1G while some will handle drives of up to 2G. These programs are being updated constantly, so contact the manufacturer for more detailed specifications if you are interested. Each of these manufacturers is listed in the vendor list in the Appendix.

No matter which program you end up using, defragmenting and packing your disk helps to reduce drive wear and tear by minimizing the amount of work required to load files. It also greatly increases the chances for data recovery in the case of serious corruption in the File Allocation Tables (FATs) and directories on the disk.

Backing Up the FAT and Directory System. There are several areas on a formatted disk that the operating system uses to manage the files stored on the disk. These areas are extremely critical because if they are damaged, all access to the drive volume may be compromised or completely disabled. In some cases, these critical areas can be rebuilt using known data recovery procedures and tools but the easiest and best way to recover from damage to these areas is to simply have a backup of them to restore.

The critical areas of a hard disk file system are:

- Master (Partition) Boot Record (MBR)
- Extended (Partition) Boot Record (EBR)
- DOS Boot Record (DBR)
- File Allocation Tables (FATs)
- Root Directory

These areas are stored on the disk in the order listed, except that each volume will start with an MBR or EBR but not both. Unlike complete file backups of the entire hard disk, a backup of these system areas is relatively quick and easy. This is because these areas are very small in comparison to the remainder of the drive and normally occupy a fixed amount of space on the disk. For example, the MBR, EBRs, and DBRs are only one sector long each, while the two FATs used on each volume cannot exceed 512 sectors (256K), and the Root Directory is limited to 32 sectors (15K). This means that even for the largest hard disk drive, these areas will not consume more than about 300K of space.

The boot record (sector) areas do not change during day-to-day usage of the disk. These areas will change only if you reformat, repartition, or change operating system versions. Because they are relatively constant, it makes good sense to back these areas up to a file on a floppy disk for later restore if necessary.

Each normal disk volume will have two File Allocation Tables and a single Root Directory. These areas change constantly as files are written and deleted from the disk. A backup of these areas is only good for temporary purposes and can be useful when trying to undelete files. Because of this, these backups are often written on the hard disk in a special hidden file near the end of the disk. Other recovery or restoration programs can then look for this special file and use the information within it to rebuild the FATs or directory system. Often this type of backup is very useful in a situation where files need to be undeleted.

DOS 5.0 provided the MIRROR command for backups of all of these areas. MIRROR has two functions: it can backup the boot sector areas on the hard disk to a file on a floppy disk as well as backup the FAT and directory areas to the end of the hard disk as a special hidden file that recovery programs can find. To use MIRROR to backup the boot sectors to a floppy disk, execute the command as follows:

```
MIRROR /PARTN
```

This will create a special file called PARTNSAV.FIL on a floppy disk you designate. This file contains an image of all of the boot sectors across all of the DOS accessible partitions on your hard disk. This information can later be restored by the UNFORMAT command as follows:

```
UNFORMAT /PARTN
```

The UNFORMAT program will ask for the disk containing the PARTNSAV.FIL file and restore the boot sector information to the hard disk.

MIRROR can also be used to backup the FATs and Directory structure to a special hidden file on the disk by simply executing the command with no parameters at all:

```
MIRROR
```

By executing the command in this manner, a special file called MIRROR.FIL as well as a hidden file called MIRRORSAV.FIL will be created in the root directory, and a copy of the FAT and Directory structures will be copied into some free space at the end of the drive. The actual FAT and Directory data is not stored in a normal file with a file name but is instead written to empty sectors at the end of the drive. These sectors will eventually be overwritten, which is why it is a good idea to run the MIRROR command frequently. The second time you run it, it will actually create a second backup and retain the first. Every subsequent run will retain the previous one as a secondary backup. It is a good idea to put the MIRROR command in your AUTOEXEC.BAT file so that these critical areas of the disk are backed up every time your system boots. Usually, MIRROR only takes a few seconds to perform its backup functions so there will be little delay in booting.

To restore the FAT and Directory area backups, you would use the UNFORMAT program, also with no parameters. This program will then search the disk for the MIRROR backups and prompt you for a possible restore. Be careful in restoring these areas as they may be out of sync somewhat with the actual files on your disk. You should always run MIRROR after defragmenting your drive because the defragmenting process moves many files on the disk, making the MIRROR backup obsolete.

There is one unfortunate problem with the MIRROR program; both Microsoft and IBM removed it from DOS 6. Fortunately, you can retain your copy of MIRROR from DOS 5, or you can download the DOS 6 supplemental disk from the MSDOS forum on CompuServe. This package will provide you with a number of utilities left out of DOS 6 but the MIRROR command is the most useful. You can also order this disk directly from Microsoft for $5 using an order form in the back of the DOS 6 manual from Microsoft.

Many other data recovery programs offer the ability to backup these areas on the disk. The Norton Utilities by Symantec is one of the best and most well known data recovery packages on the market. It offers this capability and does a much better job than DOS alone. Norton uses an IMAGE command instead of MIRROR, and also has a special program called RESCUE that creates a rescue disk with not only the boot sector areas on it, but copies of your AUTOEXEC.BAT and CONFIG.SYS files, the DOS system files, and the CMOS RAM data from your system. Also included on the rescue disk are copies of the appropriate Norton Utilities programs that can be used to restore these areas.

Checking for Virus Programs. Both Microsoft and IBM now provide standard anti-virus software in DOS 6.x. The Microsoft Anti-Virus program is actually a reduced function version of the Central Point Anti-Virus software. IBM has written a package called the IBM Anti-Virus program. There are also many aftermarket utility packages that will scan for and remove virus programs. One of the best known is the McAfee Associates SCANV program, which is also one of the easiest to run because it is a command line utility. The McAfee program is also distributed through BBS systems and is often site licensed to large companies.

No matter which of these programs you use, it is a good idea to perform a scan for virus programs periodically, especially before making hard disk backups. This will help to insure that you catch any potential virus problem before it spreads and becomes a major hassle.

Reformatting a Hard Disk. Periodically reformatting a hard disk is an operation often overlooked as part of a preventive maintenance plan. Reformatting serves two purposes. On non-servo controlled drives (stepper motor head actuators) the low-level format rewrites the sector header information in alignment with current head positions, which can drift in stepper motor head-actuator drives because of temperature- and stress-induced dimensional changes between the platters and heads. If these alignment variations continue unchecked, they eventually will cause read and write errors. Note that this reformatting operation applies to stepper motor head-actuator drives only and not to voice-coil drives, which maintain their positional accuracy due to the closed loop servo control mechanism that guides the heads.

The second function of a low-level format is to locate and mark or spare out any new defective sectors. This can be accomplished during the low-level format and also by a subsequent surface analysis.

Reformatting a hard disk lays down new track and sector ID marks and boundaries, re-marks the manufacturers defects, and performs a surface scan for new defects that might have developed since the last format. With Zone Recorded drives, only the defect mapping and surface analysis are performed. The sector headers are usually not completely rewritten. Temperature variations, case flexing, and physical positioning can add up to eventual read and write errors in a stepper-motor-actuated hard disk. This type of failure sometimes appears as a gradually increasing number of disk retries and other read and write problems. You also might notice difficulties when you boot the disk for the first time each day or if the system has been turned off for some time. The cause of these problems is a mistracking between where the data has actually written on the drive and where the track and sector ID marks are located. If the drive is used in a variety of temperatures and environmental conditions, dimensional changes between the heads and platters can cause the data to be written at various improper offsets from the desired track locations.

The reformatting procedure for hard disks is the equivalent of aligning a floppy drive. For hard disks, however, the concern is not for the actual locations of each track, but that the drive heads are positioned accurately to the same track location each time. Because of the inherent problems in tracking with stepper motor drives and the lack of a track-following system, mistracking errors accumulate and eventually cause a failure to read or write a particular location. To correct this problem, you must lay down a new set of track and sector ID marks that correspond as closely as possible to the position from which the heads actually read and write data. To do this (with stepper motor drives), you must perform a low-level format.

To make the new format effective, you must do it at the drives full operating temperature and with the drive in its final mounted position. If the drive runs on its side when it is installed, the format must be done in that position.

For inexpensive drives that lack a proper shock-mounting system (such as the Seagate ST-225, -238, -251, or any ST-2XX drive), make sure that the drive is completely installed before beginning low-level formatting. When you attach the mounting screws to these drives, you are placing screws almost directly into the Head Disk Assembly (HDA), which can cause the HDA to bend or warp slightly depending on how much you tighten the screws. Turn the screws just until they are snug. Do not over tighten them, or your drive might fail if the screws ever loosen and the HDA stress is relaxed. Screws that are too tight can cause continuous read and write problems from stress in the HDA. Having this type of drive completely installed when you are formatting places the HDA under the same physical stress and distortion that it will be under when data is read and written, which makes the format much more accurate.

The frequency with which you should reformat a hard disk depends primarily on the types of drives you have. If the drives are inexpensive stepper motor types (the Seagate ST-2XX series, for example) you probably should reformat the drives once a year. People who must support large numbers of these cheaper drives become known as hard disk reformatting specialists. A joke in the industry is that some of these drives require winter and summer formats because of temperature sensitivity. This joke, unfortunately, can be somewhat truthful in some cases.

High-quality voice coil drives usually are formatted only once, either at the factory, as in the case of most IDE or SCSI drives, or by the installer, as is the case with most other types of hard disks. With these drives, a reformat is only performed when the drive begins to exhibit problems reading or writing any sectors on the disk. This might appear in the form of DOS Abort, Retry, Fail, Ignore error messages, or other read or write errors. Upon encountering difficulty with any sectors on the disk, it should be fully backed up and then a reformat performed. In this case, the reformat and subsequent surface analysis will locate and mark off or spare out the marginal sectors, thus restoring the drive to proper operation.

As mentioned earlier, voice coil drives do not require reformatting the hard disk as do stepper motor drives. Voice coil drives do not usually develop difficulties with *hysteresis*, a measurement of how accurately a drive can repeatedly locate to a specified position. Hysteresis is measured by commanding a drive to position itself at a particular cylinder and later (at a different temperature), commanding the drive to position itself at the same cylinder. The voice coil drive always positions itself at the same position relative to the disk platter because of the track-following servo guide head. The stepper motor drive, however, is fooled by temperature and other environmental or physical stress changes because it is essentially a *blind* positioning system.

Refer to Chapter 10 (Hard Disk Drives), which describes hard disk formatting procedures, for more information about the proper tools and procedures for reformatting the different types of hard disk drives.

Passive Preventive Maintenance Procedures

Passive preventive maintenance involves taking care of the system in an external smanner: basically, providing the best possible environment—both physical as well as electrical—for the system to operate in. Physical concerns are conditions such as ambient temperature, thermal stress from power cycling, dust and smoke contamination, and disturbances such as shock and vibration. Electrical concerns are items such as electrostatic discharge (ESD), power-line noise and radio-frequency interference. Each of these environmental concerns is discussed in this section.

Examining the Operating Environment. Oddly enough, one of the most overlooked aspects of microcomputer preventive maintenance is protecting the hardware—and the sizable financial investment it represents—from environmental abuse. Computers are relatively forgiving, and they generally are safe in an environment that is comfortable for people. Computers, however, often are treated with no more respect than desktop calculators. The result of this type of abuse is many system failures.

Before you acquire a system, prepare a proper location for your new system, free of airborne contaminants such as smoke or other pollution. Do not place your system in front of a window: The system should not be exposed to direct sunlight or temperature variations. The environmental temperature should be as constant as possible. Power should be provided through properly grounded outlets, and should be stable and free from electrical noise and interference. Keep your system away from radio transmitters or other sources of radio frequency energy. This section examines these issues in more detail.

Heating and Cooling. Thermal expansion and contraction from temperature changes place stress on a computer system. Therefore, keeping the temperature in your office or room relatively constant is important to the successful operation of your computer system.

Temperature variations can lead to serious problems. You might encounter excessive chip creep, for example. If extreme variations occur over a short period, signal traces on circuit boards can crack and separate, solder joints can break, and contacts in the system undergo accelerated corrosion. Solid-state components such as chips can be damaged also, and a host of other problems can develop.

Temperature variations can play havoc with hard disk drives also. Writing to a disk at different ambient temperatures can, on some drives, cause data to be written at different locations relative to the track centers. Read and write problems then might accelerate later.

To ensure that your system operates in the correct ambient temperature, you first must determine your system's specified functional range. Most manufacturers provide data about the correct operating temperature range for their systems. Two temperature specifications might be available, one indicating allowable temperatures during operation and another indicating allowable temperatures under non-operating conditions. IBM, for example, indicates the following temperature ranges as acceptable for most of its systems:

System on: 60 to 90 degrees Fahrenheit

System off: 50 to 110 degrees Fahrenheit

For the safety of the disk and the data it contains, avoid rapid changes in ambient temperatures. If rapid temperature changes occur—for example, when a new drive is shipped to a location during the winter and then brought indoors—let the drive acclimate to room temperature before turning it on. In extreme cases, condensation forms on the platters inside the drive Head Disk Assembly—disastrous for the drive if you turn it on before the condensation can evaporate. Most drive manufacturers specify a timetable to use as a guide in acclimating a drive to room temperature before operating it. You usually must wait several hours to a day before a drive is ready to use after it has been shipped or stored in a cold environment.

Most office environments provide a stable temperature in which to operate a computer system, but some do not. Be sure to give some consideration to the placement of your equipment.

Power Cycling (On/Off). As you have just learned, the temperature variations a system encounters greatly stress the system's physical components. The largest temperature variations a system encounters, however, are those that occur during system warm-up when you initially turn it on. Turning on (also called powering on) a cold system subjects it to the greatest possible internal temperature variations. For these reasons, limiting the number of power-on cycles a system is exposed to greatly improves its life and reliability.

If you want a system to have the longest, most trouble-free life possible, you should limit the temperature variations in its environment. You can limit the extreme temperature cycling in two simple ways during a cold start-up: leave the system off all the time or leave it on all the time. Of these two possibilities, of course, you want to choose the latter option. Leaving the power on is the best way I know to promote system reliability. If your only concern is system longevity, then the simple recommendation would be to keep the system unit powered on (or off!) continuously. In the real world, however there are more variables to consider, such as the cost of electricity, the potential fire hazard of unattended running equipment, and other concerns as well.

If you think about the way light bulbs typically fail, you can begin to understand that thermal cycling can be dangerous. Light bulbs burn out most often when you first turn them on, because the filament must endure incredible thermal stresses as it changes temperature—in less than one second—from ambient to several thousands of degrees. A bulb that remains on continuously lasts longer than one that is turned on and off repeatedly.

Some people argue that the reason you should leave a computer system on continuously is to prevent the electrical shock from the inrush of power when you start up a system. The cause of failure in a low-voltage solid-state circuit repeatedly powered on and off, however, is not inrushing electrons, but rather physical stresses caused by thermal expansion and contraction of the components. Component engineers agree, and tests prove, that a device left on continuously outlasts one that is powered on and off repeatedly.

Where problems can occur immediately at power-on is in the power supply. The start-up current draw for the system and for any motor during the first few seconds of operation is very high compared to the normal operating-current draw. Because the current must come from the power supply, the supply has an extremely demanding load to carry for the first few seconds of operation, especially if several disk drives will be started. Motors have an extremely high power-on current draw. This demand often overloads a marginal circuit or component in the supply and causes it to burn or break with a snap. I have seen several power supplies die the instant a system was powered up. To enable your equipment to have the longest possible life, try to keep the temperature of solid-state components relatively constant, and limit the number of start-ups on the power supply. The only way I know to do so is to leave the system on.

Although it sounds as though I am recommending that you leave all of your computer equipment on 24 hours a day, seven days a week, I no longer recommend this type of operation. A couple of concerns have tempered my urge to leave everything running continuously. One is that an unattended operating system represents a fire hazard. I have seen monitors start themselves on fire after internally shorting, and systems whose cooling fans have frozen, enabling the power supply and entire system to overheat. I do not leave any system running in an unattended building. Another problem is wasted electrical power. Many companies have adopted austerity programs that involve turning lights and other items off when not in use. The power consumption of some of todays high-powered systems and accessories is not trivial. Also, an unattended operating system is more of a security risk than one that is powered off and locked.

Realities—such as the fire hazard of unattended systems running during night or weekend hours, security problems, and power-consumption issues—might prevent you from leaving your system on all the time. Therefore, you must compromise. Power on the system only one time daily. Don't power the system on and off several times every day. This good advice is often ignored, especially when several users share systems. Each user powers on the system to perform work on the PC and then powers off the system. These systems tend to have many more problems with component failures.

If you are concerned about running your hard disk continuously, let me dispel your fears. Running your hard disk continuously might be the best thing you can do for your drive. Leaving the drive powered on is the best method for reducing read and write failures caused by temperature changes. If you are using extremely inexpensive drives with stepper motor actuators, leaving the drive on greatly improves reliability and increases the time between low-level formats caused by mistracking. A drives bearings and motors also function longer if you reduce the power-on temperature cycling. You might have had a disk that didn't boot after you turned the drive off for a prolonged period (over the weekend, for example) and you fixed the problem with a subsequent low-level format, but you most likely wouldn't have had the problem if you had left your drive on.

If you are in a building with a programmable thermostat, you have another reason to be concerned about temperatures and disk drives. Some buildings have thermostats programmed to turn off the heat overnight or over the weekend. These thermostats are programmed also to quickly raise the temperature just before business hours every day. In Chicago, for example, outside temperatures in the winter can dip to 20 degrees below 0 (not including a wind-chill factor). An office buildings interior temperature can drop as low as 50 degrees during the weekend. When you arrive Monday morning, the heat has been on for only an hour or so, but the hard disk platters might have not yet reached even 60 degrees when you turn on the system unit. During the first 20 minutes of operation, the disk platters rapidly rise in temperature to 120 degrees or more. If you have an inexpensive stepper motor hard disk and begin writing to the disk at these low temperatures, you are setting yourself up for trouble. Again, many systems with these cheap drives don't even boot properly under these circumstances and must be warmed up before they even boot DOS.

> ### Tip
>
> If you do not leave a system on continuously, at least give it 15 minutes or more to warm up before writing to the hard disk. Power up the system and go get a cup of coffee, read the paper, or do some other task. This practice does wonders for the reliability of the data on your disk, especially cheaper units.

If you do leave your system on for long periods of time, make sure that the screen is blank or displays a random image if the system is not in use. The phosphor on the picture tube can burn if a stationary image is left on-screen continuously. Higher-persistence phosphor monochrome screens are most susceptible, and the color displays with low-persistence phosphors are the least susceptible. If you ever have seen a monochrome display with the image of some program permanently burned in—even with the display off—you know what I mean. Look at the monitors that display flight information at the airport—they usually show the effects of phosphor burn.

Screen savers or blankers will either blank the screen completely or display some sort of moving random image to prevent burn in. This can be accomplished by either a manual or automatic procedure as follows:

■ Manual: Turn the brightness and contrast levels all the way down, or even power the display off completely. This technique is effective but it is a manual method; you must remember to do it.

■ Automatic: There are many types of programs that can cause the screen to blank or display random images automatically at a pre-determined interval. Screen savers are built in to most Graphical User Interfaces (GUIs) such as Windows and OS/2. These can easily be enabled and you can also specify the time delay before they activate. If you run under plain DOS, there are a number of public domain as well as commercial screen saver programs that can be used. These programs usually run as terminate-and-stay-resident (TSR) programs. The program watches the clock as well as the keyboard and mouse ports. If several minutes pass with nothing typed at the keyboard or no mouse movement, the program activates and either shuts off all signals to the display or creates an image that moves around on the screen to prevent burn in.

Static Electricity. Static electricity can cause numerous problems within a system. The problems usually appear during the winter months when humidity is low or in extremely dry climates where the humidity is low year-round. In these cases, you might need to take special precautions to ensure that the system functions properly.

Static discharges outside a system-unit chassis are rarely a source of permanent problems within the system. The usual effect of a static discharge to the case, keyboard, or even in close proximity to a system, is a parity check (memory) error or a locked-up system. In some cases, I have been able to cause parity checks or system lockups by simply walking past a system. Most static-sensitivity problems such as this one are caused by improper grounding of the system power. Be sure that you always use a three-prong, grounded power cord plugged into a properly grounded outlet. If you are unsure about the outlet, you can buy an outlet tester at most electronics-supply or hardware stores for only a few dollars.

Whenever you open a system unit or handle circuits removed from the system, you must be much more careful with static. You can damage permanently a component with a static discharge if the charge is not routed to a ground. I usually recommend handling boards and adapters first by a grounding point such as the bracket to minimize the potential for static damage.

An easy way to prevent static problems is with good power-line grounding, which is extremely important for computer equipment. A poorly designed power-line grounding system is one of the primary causes of poor computer design. The best way to prevent static damage is to prevent the static charge from getting into the computer in the first place. The chassis ground in a properly designed system serves as a static guard for the computer, which redirects the static charge safely to ground. For this ground to be complete, therefore, the system must be plugged into a properly grounded three-wire outlet.

If the static problem is extreme, you can resort to other measures. One is to use a grounded static mat underneath the computer. Touch the mat first before you touch the computer, to ensure that any static charges are routed to ground and away from the system units internal parts. If problems still persist, you might want to check out the electrical building ground. I have seen installations in which three-wire outlets exist but are not grounded properly. You can use an outlet tester to be sure that the outlet is wired properly.

Power-Line Noise. To run properly, a computer system requires a steady supply of clean noise-free power. In some installations, however, the power line serving the computer serves heavy equipment also, and the voltage variations resulting from the on-off cycling of this equipment can cause problems for the computer. Certain types of equipment on the same power line also can cause voltage *spikes*—short transient signals of sometimes 1,000 volts or more—that can physically damage a computer. Although these spikes are rare, they can be crippling. Even a dedicated electrical circuit used only by a single computer can experience spikes and transients, depending on the quality of the power supplied to the building or circuit.

During the site-preparation phase of a system installation, you should be aware of these factors to ensure a steady supply of clean power:

- If possible, the computer system should be on its own circuit with its own circuit breaker. This setup does not guarantee freedom from interference but it helps.

- The circuit should be checked for a good, low-resistance ground, proper line voltage, freedom from interference, and freedom from brownouts (voltage dips).

- A three-wire circuit is a must but some people substitute grounding-plug adapters to adapt a grounded plug to a two-wire socket. This setup is not recommended; the ground is there for a reason.

- Power-line noise problems increase with the resistance of the circuit, which is a function of wire size and length. To decrease resistance, therefore, avoid extension cords unless absolutely necessary, and then use only heavy-duty extension cords.

- Inevitably, you will want to plug in other equipment later. Plan ahead to avoid temptations to use too many items on a single outlet. If possible, provide a separate power circuit for noncomputer-related accessories.

Air conditioners, coffee makers, copy machines, laser printers, space heaters, vacuum cleaners, and power tools are some of the worst corrupters of a PC systems power. Any of these items can draw an excessive amount of current and play havoc with a PC system on the same electrical circuit. I've seen offices in which all the computers begin to crash at about 9:05 a.m. daily, which is when all the coffee makers are turned on!

Also, try to ensure that copy machines and laser printers do not share a circuit with other computer equipment. These devices draw a large amount of power.

Another major problem in some companies is partitioned offices. Many of these partitions are prewired with their own electrical outlets and are plugged into one another in a sort of power-line daisy chain, similar to chaining power strips together. I pity the person in the cubicle at the end of the electrical daisy chain, who will have very flaky power!

As a real-world example of too many devices sharing a single circuit, I can describe several instances in which a personal computer had a repeating parity check problem.

All efforts to repair the system had been unsuccessful. The reported error locations from the parity check message also were inconsistent, which normally indicates a problem with power. The problem could have been the power supply in the system unit or the external power supplied from the wall outlet. This problem was solved one day as I stood watching the system. The parity check message was displayed at the same instant some-one two cubicles away turned on a copy machine. Placing the computers on a separate line solved the problem.

By following the guidelines in this section, you can create the proper power environment for your systems and help to ensure trouble-free operation.

Radio-Frequency Interference. Radio-frequency interference (RFI) is easily overlooked as a problem factor. The interference is caused by any source of radio transmissions near a computer system. Living next door to a 50,000-watt commercial radio station is one sure way to get RFI problems, but less powerful transmitters cause problems too. I know of many instances in which portable radio-telephones have caused sporadic random keystrokes to appear, as though an invisible entity were typing on the keyboard. I also have seen RFI cause a system to lock up. Solutions to RFI problems are more difficult to state because every case must be handled differently. Sometimes, reorienting a system unit eliminates the problem because radio signals can be directional in nature. At other times, you must invest in specially shielded cables for cables outside the system unit, such as the keyboard cable.

One type of solution to an RFI noise problem with cables is to pass the cable through a *toroidal iron core*, a doughnut-shaped piece of iron placed around a cable to suppress both the reception and transmission of electromagnetic interference (EMI). If you can isolate an RFI noise problem in a particular cable, you often can solve the problem by passing the cable through a toroidal core. Because the cable must pass through the center hole of the core, it often is difficult, if not impossible, to add a toroid to a cable that already has end connectors installed.

Radio Shack sells a special snap-together toroid designed specifically to be added to cables already in use. This toroid looks like a thick-walled tube that has been sliced in half. You just lay the cable in the center of one of the halves, and snap the other half over the first. This type of construction makes it easy to add the noise-suppression features of a toroid to virtually any existing cable.

IBM also makes a special 6-foot long PS/2 keyboard cable with a built-in toroid core (part number 27F4984) that can greatly reduce interference problems. This cable has the smaller 6-pin DIN (PS/2 style) connector at the system end and the standard SDL (Shielded Data Link) connector at the keyboard end; it costs about $40.

The best, if not the easiest, way to eliminate the problem probably is to correct it at the source. You likely won't convince the commercial radio station near your office to shut down but if you are dealing with a small radio transmitter that is generating RFI, some-times you can add to the transmitter a filter that suppresses spurious emissions. Unfortu-nately, problems sometimes persist until the transmitter is either switched off or moved some distance away from the affected computer.

Note that your own computer systems can be a source of RFI. Computer equipment must meet one of these two classifications to be certified and salable, according to the FCC (Federal Communications Commission): Class A or Class B. The Class A specification applies to computing devices sold for use in commercial, business, and industrial environments. Class B indicates that the equipment has passed more stringent tests and can be used in residential environments, in addition to any environments allowed under Class A.

The FCC does not really police users or purchasers of computer equipment so much as it polices the equipment manufacturers or vendors. Therefore, if you are using a Class A-rated system in your home, you don't need to worry about radio police showing up at your door. If, however, you are making or selling PCs that meet one of these conditions:

- Marketed through retail or direct-mail outlets

- Sold to the general public rather than commercial users only

- Operates on battery or 120-volt AC electrical power

You must obtain a Class B certification for these systems. Notice that a system has to fit each of these three categories to be considered a personal computer and be subject to the stricter Class B rules. Notice also that the FCC considers all portable computer systems as meeting Class B standards because their portability makes them likely to be used in a residential setting.

The FCC standards for Class A and Class B certification governs two kinds of emissions: conductive emissions, radiated from the computer system into the power cord, and radio-frequency emissions, radiated from the computer system into space. Table 11.1 shows the conductive and radio-frequency emissions limitations to be eligible for both Class A and Class B ratings.

Table 11.1 FCC Class A and Class B Emission Limitations

Conductive Emissions: Frequency	Maximum signal level (mv) Class A	Class B
0.45 to 1.705MHz	1000	250
1.705 to 30.0MHz	3000	250

Radiated Emissions: Frequency	Maximum field strength (uv/M) Class A (10M)	Class B (3M)
30 to 88MHz	90	100
88 to 216MHz	150	150
217 to 960MHz	210	200
960MHz and up	300	500

MHz = Megahertz
10M = Measured at 10 meters
3M = Measured at 3 meters
mv = Millivolts
uv/M = Microvolts per meter

Notice that although some of the specific numbers listed for Class A seem lower than those required for Class B, you must consider that field-strength measurements normally decline under the inverse square law: The strength of the signal decreases as the square of the distance from the source. A rating of 100 microvolts per meter at 3 meters, therefore, would be approximately equal to a rating of about 9 microvolts per meter at 10 meters. This calculation just means that the limits to pass Class B certification are much tougher than they look, and certainly are much tougher than Class A limits. Additionally, Class A certification is tested and verified entirely by the manufacturer; Class B certification requires a sample of the equipment to be sent to the FCC for testing.

IBM and most other responsible manufacturers ensure that all systems they sell meet the stricter Class B designations. One of the primary reasons for the Micro Channel Architecture design was to meet, and also greatly exceed these FCC classifications. IBM knew that as computing clock speeds go up, so do the radio emissions. As clock rates of 66, 75, and 100 MHz and higher become more common (and they will soon), IBM will have a distinct advantage over manufacturers still using the AT or EISA bus designs because vendors using ISA or EISA bus designs will have to invest in more expensive chassis and case shielding to combat the emission problem, IBM and other Micro Channel clones will gain a distinct manufacturing cost advantage.

Dust and Pollutants. Dirt, smoke, dust, and other pollutants are bad for your system. The power-supply fan carries airborne particles through your system, and they collect inside. If your system is used in an extremely harsh environment, you might want to investigate some of the industrial systems on the market designed for harsh conditions. IBM used to sell industrial-model XT and AT systems but discontinued them after introducing the PS/2. IBM has licensed several third-party companies to produce industrial versions of PS/2 systems.

Compatible vendors also have industrial systems; many companies make special *hardened* versions of their systems for harsh environments. Industrial systems usually use a different cooling system from the one used in a regular PC. A large cooling fan is used to pressurize the case rather than depressurize it, as most systems do. The air pumped into the case passes through a filter unit that must be cleaned and changed periodically. The system is pressurized so that no contaminated air can flow into it; air flows only outward. The only way air can enter is through the fan and filter system.

These systems also might have special keyboards impervious to liquids and dirt. Some flat-membrane keyboards are difficult to type on, but are extremely rugged; others resemble the standard types of keyboards, but have a thin, plastic membrane that covers all the keys. You can add this membrane to normal types of keyboards to seal them from the environment.

A new breed of humidifier can cause problems with computer equipment. This type of humidifier uses ultrasonics to generate a mist of water sprayed into the air. The extra humidity helps cure problems with static electricity resulting from a dry climate, but the airborne water contaminants can cause many problems. If you use one of these systems, you might notice a white ash-like deposit forming on components. The deposit is the result of abrasive and corrosive minerals suspended in the vaporized water. If these deposits collect on the disk drive heads, they will ruin the heads and scratch disks.

The only safe way to run one of these ultrasonic humidifiers is with pure distilled water. If you use a humidifier, be sure it does not generate these deposits.

If you do your best to keep the environment for your computer equipment clean, your system will run better and last longer. Also, you will not have to open your unit as often for complete preventive maintenance cleaning.

Using Power-Protection Systems

Power-protection systems do just what the name implies: They protect your equipment from the effects of power surges and power failures. In particular, power surges and spikes can damage computer equipment, and a loss of power can result in lost data. In this section, you learn about the four primary types of power-protection devices available and under what circumstances you should use them.

Before considering any further levels of power protection, you should know that the power supply in your system (if your system is well-made) already affords you a substantial amount of protection. The power supplies in IBM equipment are designed to provide protection from higher-than-normal voltages and currents, and provide a limited amount of power-line noise filtering. Some of the inexpensive aftermarket power supplies probably do not have this sort of protection, so be careful if you have an inexpensive clone system. In those cases, protecting your system further might be wise.

IBM's PS/2 power supplies will stay within operating specifications and continue to run a system if any of these power line disturbances occur:

- Voltage drop to 80 volts for up to 2 seconds

- Voltage drop to 70 volts for up to .5 seconds

- Voltage surge of up to 143 volts for up to 1 second

IBM also states that neither their power supplies nor systems will be damaged by the following occurrences:

- Full power outage

- Any voltage drop (brownout)

- A spike of up to 2,500 volts

Because of the high quality power supply design that IBM uses, they state in their documentation that external surge suppressors are not needed for PS/2 systems. Most other high quality name brand manufacturers also use high quality power supply designs. Companies like Astec, PC Power and Cooling, and others make very high quality units.

To verify the levels of protection built in to the existing power supply in a computer system, an independent laboratory subjected several unprotected PC systems to various spikes and surges up to *6,000 volts*—considered the maximum level of surge that can be transmitted to a system by an electrical outlet. Any higher voltage would cause the power to arc to ground within the outlet itself. Note that none of the systems sustained permanent damage in these tests; the worst thing that happened was that some of the systems rebooted or shut down if the surge was more than 2,000 volts. Each system restarted when the power switch was toggled after a shutdown.

I do not use any real form of power protection on my systems, and they have survived near-direct lightning strikes and powerful surges. The most recent incident, only 50 feet from my office, was a direct lightning strike to a brick chimney that *blew the top of the chimney apart.* None of my systems (which were running at the time) was damaged in any way from this incident; they just shut themselves down. I was able to restart each system by toggling the power switches. An alarm system located in the same office, however, was destroyed by this strike. I am not saying that lightning strikes or even much milder spikes and surges cannot damage computer systems—another nearby lightning strike did destroy a modem and serial adapter installed in one of my systems. I was just lucky that the destruction did not include the motherboard.

This discussion points out an important oversight in some power-protection strategies: you may elect to protect your systems from electrical power disturbances, but do not forget to provide similar protection also from spikes and surges on the phone line.

The automatic shutdown of a computer during power disturbances is a built-in function of most high-quality power supplies. You can reset the power supply by flipping the power switch from on to off and back on again. Some power supplies, such as those in most of the PS/2 systems, have an *auto-restart function.* This type of power supply acts the same as others in a massive surge or spike situation: it shuts down the system. The difference is that after normal power resumes, the power supply waits for a specified delay of three to six seconds and then resets itself and powers the system back up. Because no manual switch resetting is required, this feature is desirable in systems functioning as a network file server or in a system in a remote location.

The first time I witnessed a large surge cause an immediate shutdown of all my systems, I was extremely surprised. All the systems were silent, but the monitor and modem lights were still on. My first thought was that everything was blown, but a simple toggle of each system-unit power switch caused the power supplies to reset, and the units powered up with no problem. Since that first time, this type of shutdown has happened to me several times, always without further problems.

The following types of power-protection devices are explained in the sections that follow:

- Surge suppressors
- Line conditioners
- Standby power supplies (SPS)
- Uninterruptible power supplies (UPS)

Surge Suppressors (Protectors)

The simplest form of power protection is any of the commercially available surge protectors; that is, devices inserted between the system and the power line. These devices, which cost between $20 and $200, can absorb the high-voltage transients produced by nearby lightning strikes and power equipment. Some surge protectors can be effective for certain types of power problems, but they offer only very limited protection.

Surge protectors use several devices, usually metal-oxide varistors (MOVs), that can clamp and shunt away all voltages above a certain level. MOVs are designed to accept voltages as high as 6,000 volts and divert any power above 200 volts to ground. MOVs can handle normal surges, but powerful surges such as a direct lightning strike can blow right through them. MOVs are not designed to handle a very high level of power, and self-destruct while shunting a large surge. These devices therefore cease to function after either a single large surge or a series of smaller ones. The real problem is that you cannot easily tell when they no longer are functional; the only way to test them is to subject the MOVs to a surge, which destroys them. Therefore, you never really know if your so-called surge protector is protecting your system.

Some surge protectors have status lights that let you know when a surge large enough to blow the MOVs has occurred. A surge suppressor without this status indicator light is useless because you never know when it has stopped protecting.

Underwriters Laboratories has produced an excellent standard that governs surge suppressors, called UL 1449. Any surge suppressor that meets this standard is a very good one, and definitely offers an additional line of protection beyond what the power supply in your PC already does. The only types of surge suppressors worth buying, therefore, should have two features: conformance to the UL 1449 standard and a status light indicating when the MOVs are blown. Units that meet the UL 1449 specification say so on the packaging or directly on the unit. If this standard is not mentioned, it does not conform, and you should avoid it.

Another good feature to have in a surge suppressor is a built-in circuit breaker that can be reset rather than a fuse. The breaker protects your system if the system or a peripheral develops a short. These better surge suppressors usually cost about $40.

Phone Line Surge Protectors

In addition to protecting the power lines, it is critical to provide protection to your systems from any phone lines that are connected. If you are using a modem or fax board which is plugged into the phone system, any surges or spikes that travel the phone line can potentially damage your system. In many areas, the phone lines are especially susceptible to lightning strikes, which is the largest cause of fried modems and any computer equipment attached to them.

Several companies manufacture or sell simple surge protectors that plug between your modem and the phone line. These inexpensive devices can be purchased from most electronics supply houses. Most of the cable and communication products vendors listed in the Appendix sell these phone line surge protectors.

Line Conditioners

In addition to high-voltage and current conditions, other problems can occur with incoming power. The voltage might dip below the level needed to run the system and result in a brownout. Other forms of electrical noise other than simple voltage surges or spikes might be on the power line, such as radio-frequency interference or electrical noise caused by motors or other inductive loads.

Remember two things when you wire together digital devices (such as computers and their peripherals). A wire is an antenna and has a voltage induced in it by nearby electromagnetic fields, which can come from other wires, telephones, CRTs, motors, fluorescent fixtures, static discharge, and, of course, radio transmitters. Digital circuitry also responds with surprising efficiency to noise of even a volt or two, making those induced voltages particularly troublesome. The wiring in your building can act as an antenna and pick up all kinds of noise and disturbances. A line conditioner can handle many of these types of problems.

A line conditioner is designed to remedy a variety of problems. It filters the power, bridges brownouts, suppresses high-voltage and current conditions, and generally acts as a buffer between the power line and the system. A line conditioner does the job of a surge suppressor, and much more. It is more of an active device functioning continuously rather than a passive device that activates only when a surge is present. A line conditioner provides true power conditioning and can handle myriad problems. It contains transformers, capacitors, and other circuitry that temporarily can bridge a brownout or low-voltage situation. These units usually cost several hundreds of dollars, depending on the power-handling capacity of the unit.

Backup Power

The next level of power protection includes backup power-protection devices. These units can provide power in case of a complete blackout, which provides the time needed for an orderly system shutdown. Two types are available: the standby power supply (SPS) and the uninterruptible power supply (UPS). The UPS is a special device because it does much more than just provide backup power; it is also the best kind of line conditioner you can buy.

Standby Power Supplies (SPS). A standby power supply is known as an *off-line device*: It functions only when normal power is disrupted. An SPS system uses a special circuit that can sense the AC line current. If the sensor detects a loss of power on the line, the system quickly switches over to a standby battery and power inverter. The power inverter converts the battery power to 110-volt AC power, which then is supplied to the system.

SPS systems do work, but sometimes a problem occurs with the switch to battery power. If the switch is not fast enough, the computer system unit shuts down or reboots anyway, which defeats the purpose of having the backup power supply. A truly outstanding SPS adds to the circuit a *ferroresonant transformer*, a large transformer with the capability to store a small amount of power and deliver it during the switch time. Having this device is similar to having on the power line a buffer that you add to an SPS to give it almost truly uninterruptible capability.

SPS units also may or may not have internal line conditioning of their own; most cheaper units place your system directly on the regular power line under normal circumstances and offer no conditioning. The addition of a ferroresonant transformer to an SPS gives it additional regulation and protection capabilities due to the buffer effect of the transformer. SPS devices without the ferroresonant transformer still require the use of a line conditioner for full protection. SPS systems usually cost from $200 to several thousands of dollars, depending on the quality and power-output capacity.

Uninterruptible Power Supplies (UPS). Perhaps the best overall solution to any power problem is to provide a power source that is both conditioned and that also cannot be interrupted—which describes an uninterruptible power supply. UPSs are known as on-line systems because they continuously function and supply power to your computer systems. Because some companies advertise ferroresonant SPS devices as though they were UPS devices, many now use the term *true UPS* to describe a truly on-line system. A true UPS system is constructed much the same as an SPS system; however, because you always are operating from the battery, there is no switching circuit.

In a true UPS, your system always operates from the battery, with a voltage inverter to convert from 12 volts DC to 110 volts AC. You essentially have your own private power system that generates power independently of the AC line. A battery charger connected to the line or wall current keeps the battery charged at a rate equal to or greater than the rate at which power is consumed.

When power is disconnected, the true UPS continues functioning undisturbed because the battery-charging function is all that is lost. Because you already were running off the battery, no switch takes place and no power disruption is possible. The battery then begins discharging at a rate dictated by the amount of load your system places on the unit, which (based on the size of the battery) gives you plenty of time to execute an orderly system shutdown. Based on an appropriately scaled storage battery, the UPS functions continuously, generating power and preventing unpleasant surprises. When the line power returns, the battery charger begins recharging the battery, again with no interruption.

UPS cost is a direct function of both the length of time it can continue to provide power after a line current failure, and how much power it can provide; therefore, purchasing a UPS that gives you enough power to run your system and peripherals as well as enough time to close files and provide an orderly shutdown would be sufficient. In most PC applications, this solution is the most cost-effective because the batteries and charger portion of the system must be much larger than the SPS type of device, and will be more costly.

Many SPS systems are advertised as though they were true UPS systems. The giveaway is the units switch time. If a specification for switch time exists, the unit cannot be a true UPS because UPS units never switch. Understand, however, that a good SPS with a ferroresonant transformer can virtually equal the performance of a true UPS at a lower cost.

Because of a UPSs almost total isolation from the line current, it is unmatched as a line conditioner and surge suppressor. The best UPS systems add a ferroresonant transformer for even greater power conditioning and protection capability. This type of UPS is the best form of power protection available. The price, however, can be very high. A true UPS costs from $1 to $2 per watt of power supplied. To find out just how much power your system requires, look at the UL sticker on the back of the unit. This sticker lists the maximum power draw in watts, or sometimes in just volts and amperes. If only voltage and amperage are listed, multiply the two figures to calculate a wattage figure.

As an example, the back of an IBM PC AT Model 339 indicates that the system can require as much as 110 volts at a maximum current draw of 5 amps. The maximum power this AT can draw is about 550 watts. This wattage is for a system with every slot full, two hard disks and one floppy—in other words, the maximum possible level of expansion. The system should never draw any more power than that; if it does, a 5-ampere fuse in the power supply blows. This type of system normally draws an average 300 watts; to be safe when you make calculations for UPS capacity, however, be conservative and use the 550-watt figure. Adding a monitor that draws 100 watts brings the total to 650 watts or more. To run two fully loaded AT systems, you need an 1100-watt UPS. Dont forget two monitors, each drawing 100 watts; the total, therefore, is 1300 watts. Using the $1 to $2 per watt figure, a UPS of at least that capacity or greater will cost from $1300 to $2600 dollars—expensive, but unfortunately what the best level of protection costs. Most companies can justify this type of expense for only a critical-use PC, such as a network file server.

In addition to the total available output power (wattage), several other factors can differentiate one UPS from another. The addition of a ferroresonant transformer improves a units power conditioning and buffering capabilities. Good units have also an inverter that produces a true sine wave output; the cheaper ones may generate a square wave. A square wave is an approximation of a sine wave with abrupt up-and-down voltage transitions. The abrupt transitions of a square wave signal are not compatible with some computer equipment power supplies. Be sure that the UPS you purchase produces a signal compatible with your computer equipment. Every unit has a specification for how long it can sustain output at the rated level. If your systems draw less than the rated level, you have some additional time. Be careful, though: Most UPS systems are not designed for you to sit and compute for hours through an electrical blackout. They are designed to provide power to whatever is needed, to remain operating long enough to allow for an orderly shutdown. You pay a large amount for units that provide power for more than 15 minutes or so.

There are many sources of power protection equipment, but two of the best are Best Power and Tripp Lite. These companies sell a variety of UPS, SPS, line, and surge protectors. They are listed in the vendor list in the Appendix.

Using Data-Backup Systems

Making a backup of important data on a computer system is one thing that many users fail to do. A backup is similar to insurance: You need it only when you are in big trouble! Because of the cost in not only dollars, but also in time and effort, many users do not have adequate backup—which is not a problem until the day you have a catastrophe and suddenly find yourself without your important data or files. This section discusses several forms of backup hardware and software that can make the job both easier and faster, and—hopefully—cause more users to do it.

Backup is something a service technician should be aware of. After I repair a system that has suffered some kind of disk crash, I can guarantee that the disk subsystem will be completely functional. I cannot guarantee, however, that the original files are on the disks; in fact, the drive may have to be replaced. Without a backup, the system can be physically repaired, but the original data may be lost forever.

Nothing destroys someone's faith in computer technology faster than telling them that the last year or more of work (in the form of disk files) no longer exists. When I visit a customer site to do some troubleshooting or repair, I always tell my clients to back up the system before I arrive. They may be reluctant to do so at first, but it is better than paying a technician by the hour to do it. A backup must be done before I operate on a system, because I do not want to be liable if something goes wrong and data is damaged or lost. If the system is so dysfunctional that a backup cannot be performed, I make sure that the client knows that the service technician is not responsible for the data.

A good general rule is never to let a backup interval be longer than what you are willing to lose some day. You always can reload or even repurchase copies of software programs that might have been lost, but you cannot buy back your own data. Because of the extremely high value of data compared to the system itself, I have recommended for some time that service technicians become familiar with data-recovery principles and procedures. Being able to perform this valuable service gives you a fantastic edge over technicians who can only fix or replace the hardware.

Backup Policies. All users and managers of computer systems should develop a plan for regular disk backups. I recommend that one person in an office have the responsibility for performing these backups so that the job is not left undone.

A backup interval should be selected based on the amount of activity on the system. Some users find that daily backups are required, and others find that a weekly arrangement is more suitable. Backups rarely must be scheduled at more than weekly intervals. Some users settle on a mixed plan: perform weekly disk backups and daily backups of only the changed files.

The procedures for backing up and for dealing with copy protection are explained in the following sections.

Backup Procedures. You should back up to removable media such as cartridge or tape, which you remove from a system and store in a safe place. Backups performed on nonremovable media, such as another hard disk, are much more vulnerable to damage, theft, or fire; also, having multiple backups is much more expensive.

Because of the relatively low cost of hard disks, some users unfortunately install two hard disks and back up one to the other. Worse, some users split a single disk into two partitions and back up one partition to the other. These backups are false backups. If the system were subjected to a massive electrical surge or failure, the contents of both drives could be lost. If the system were stolen, again, both backups would be lost. Finally, if the system were physically damaged, such as in a fire or other mishap, both the data and the backup would be lost. These are good reasons that it is important to back up to removable media.

Perform your backups on a rotating schedule. I recommend using a tape-backup system with at least three tapes per drive, in which you back up data to the first tape the first week. The second week, you use a second tape. That way, if the second tape has been damaged, you can use the preceding week's backup tape to restore data. The third week, you should use still another tape and place the first tape in a different physical location as protection against damage from fire, flood, theft, or another disaster.

The fourth week, you begin to rotate each tape so that the first (off-site) tape is used again for backup, and the second tape is moved off-site. This system always has two progressively older backups on-site, with the third backup off-site to provide for disaster insurance. Only removable media can provide this type of flexibility, and tape is one of the best forms of removable media for backup.

Dealing with Copy Protection. One thing standing in the way of proper backups of some of your software is copy protection, a system in which the original disk the software is on is modified so that it cannot be copied exactly by your system. When the programs on the disk are run, they look for this unique feature to determine whether the original disk is in the system. Some software makers force you to use master copies of their programs by using this technique to require that the original disks be placed in the floppy drive for validation even though the system might have the software loaded on the hard disk.

Some forms of copy protection load the software on a hard disk only from an original disk, and modify the hard disk loaded version so that it runs only if it remains on the system in a specified set of sectors. If the program ever is moved on the disk, it fails to operate. Because these requirements make the software highly prone to failure, copy protection has no place on software used in a business environment.

My personal response to copy protection is to refuse to use, buy, or recommend any software from a company engaged in this practice. With rare exceptions, I simply do not buy copy-protected software. Unprotected alternatives always are available for whatever type of program you want. You might even discover that the unprotected alternative is a better program. If you don't make the software-purchasing decisions in your organization, however, you may have little choice in this matter.

Experienced computer users know that you never should use original disks when you install or configure software. After I purchase a new program, I first make a copy and store the original disks. In fact, I use the original disks solely for making additional backup copies. Following this procedure protects me if I make a mistake in installing or using the software. Because of the need for backup and the fact that copy protection essentially prevents proper backup, a solution has been devised.

When you must use a piece of protected software, you can purchase special programs that enable you to back up and even remove the protection from most copy-protected programs on the market. Two such programs are CopyWrite, by Quaid Software Ltd., and Copy II PC, by Central Point Software. These programs cost about $50 and are absolutely necessary when you are forced to deal with copy-protected software.

Note that no matter what a software license agreement says, you have a legal right to back up your software; this right is guaranteed under U.S. copyright law. Do not let a software license agreement bamboozle you into believing otherwise.

The best way to fight copy protection is with your wallet. Most companies respond to this economic pressure; many of them have responded by removing the protection from their programs. Fortunately, because of this economic pressure by influential users, the scourge of copy protection has been almost eliminated from the business-software marketplace. Only a few remaining programs have this unfortunate defect; I hope that the protection will be eradicated from them as well.

Backup Software. In considering how to back up your system, you should be aware of both the hardware and software options available. This section first explores the software-only options; that is, using either what you get with DOS, or some more-powerful aftermarket software to back up using a floppy drive. You will learn that the aftermarket software usually offers many features and capabilities that the standard DOS BACKUP program does not have. After discussing software alternatives, this section looks at complete, dedicated hardware and software backup systems. Using specialized hardware is the best way to have an easy, effective, and safe way of backing up your system.

The DOS BACKUP Command. The most basic backup software you can use are the DOS commands BACKUP and RESTORE. Since their introduction in Version 2.0 of DOS, and up to Version 3.3, these commands have frustrated users with their bugs and other problems. The versions supplied with DOS V4.0 and higher have been greatly improved, but they still do not offer what many aftermarket products offer. Because of the way BACKUP and RESTORE use the floppy drive as the hardware device, you can use this software only for backing up systems with low-capacity hard drives.

New Backup Software With DOS 6.x. Both Microsoft and IBM have included new backup software with their respective versions of DOS 6.x. These programs far outstrip the capabilities of the original BACKUP command and are much easier and safer to use.

In MS-DOS, Microsoft supplies a limited version of the Norton Backup software called MSBACKUP. This program is a full featured menu driven program that is designed to backup to floppy drives only. It is very easy to use, and represents a great leap from the older BACKUP and RESTORE commands. Since it is really a restricted version of the Norton Backup program by Symantec, you can easily upgrade to the more full featured Norton Backup program and still retain compatibility with all of your existing backups.

IBM went a different route in PC DOS and supplies an only slightly limited version of the Central Point Backup program called CPBACKUP. This offers a great deal more functionality than the MSBACKUP program supplied by Microsoft. CPBACKUP can backup to a

have capacities anywhere from 60M, at the low end, to 525M or more at the high end.

■ *DC-2000 cartridges.* Also invented by 3M, this cartridge is one of the most popular media for backup purposes. This tape is 2.415x3.188x0.570 inches in LxWxD, with a heavy metal base plate. Although early versions held only 20M, the most common ones now hold 80M or more. A variety of capacities result from the different tape formats available.

■ *4mm DAT (digital audio tape) cartridges.* At first glance, this cartridge looks like a regular audiocassette but is slightly smaller. These cartridges come in several recording formats. The most widely used is digital data storage, or DDS for short. Another format, DataDAT, is also available. The recording technology is similar to digital audio tape decks and is done in a Helical-Scan format; it is licensed by Sony (the original DAT developer). DAT tapes can hold as much as 1.3 gigabytes (1 gigabyte = 1,024M).

■ *8mm cartridges.* These cartridges, which use the 8mm videotape developed by Sony for camcorders, comprise one of the highest-capacity backup systems available. Most units store 2.3G but larger-capacity units are available. The recording is done physically as a Helical-Scan, the same method used in a video recorder.

The DC-600 drives now store from 60M to 525M or more, depending on the format and quality of tape used. The DC-2000 media stores only 40M to 80M or more per tape and might be suitable for low-end (such as home) use. Because the larger-capacity 4mm and 8mm units store more than 1 or 2G on a tape, they are ideal for network server applications. These large-capacity units can cost from $1,500 to $6,000 or more, depending on the features included and—of course—where you buy it.

Make sure that the system is capable of handling your largest drive either directly or through the use of multiple tapes. With this unit, you can change tapes in the middle of a backup session to accommodate greater capacities; because this method is inconvenient and requires an operator, however, you eliminate unattended, overnight backups. For network applications or large storage requirements, or anything else for which you need top performance and the most reliable backup, you should select DC-600 or the 4mm or 8mm rather than the DC-2000 media.

I recommend only tape systems that use these media because they offer the greatest value per dollar, are the most reliable, and hold a large amount of data. Stay away from devices that use the 3M DC-1000 tapes, Phillips audio tapes, or VHS VCR tape systems. These systems often are slow, error prone, and inconvenient to use; some do not handle larger capacities, and they are not standard.

Interfaces for Tape Backup Systems. Of the three primary hardware-interface standards, virtually all professional backup systems use the QIC-02 (for Quarter-Inch Committee 02) or SCSI (for *Small Computer Systems Interface*), and more recently, the parallel port interface. Some low-end systems use the Shugart Associates 400 (SA-400) interface, which is the standard floppy controller. The interface you select controls the backup speed, whether an adapter card and slot are required, and the reliability and capacity of the unit.

In the PC and XT systems with their 4-drive floppy controllers, you can use the extra connector on the back of the existing floppy controller for some tape-backup units. This connector saves the use of a slot in these systems. Unfortunately, the AT systems require some sort of multiplexer card to enable sharing one of the internal floppy ports or another complete floppy controller so that these systems can work.

I don't recommend these floppy interface systems in general because they are slow, and the floppy controller lacks any form of error-detection and -correction capability, which can make the backups unreliable. A system using the SA-400 interface has a maximum data rate of 2M per minute, less than half the QIC-02 or SCSI interfaces. These floppy interface systems are suitable for home computer users on a tight budget but should not be used in business or professional environments. Another problem is that the interface limits the capacity to 40M, and you might have to format the tapes before using them.

The QIC-02 interface, designed specifically for tape-backup products, represents an industry standard. Many companies offer products that use this interface. The QIC-02 can back up at a rate of 5M per minute. The interface usually is a short adapter card that requires a free slot in the system. You can buy these adapters separately and enable many systems to use the same externally mounted drive. A free slot is required, however, and might not be available with a regular PC.

Perhaps the best hardware interface is the Small Computer Systems Interface (SCSI), which enables your PC to back up at high data rates. The data throughput of the SCSI interface is either 5MB or 10MB per minute for standard and fast 8-bit SCSI respectively. There are currently no tape drives or hard disks that can sustain this rate of transfer, so the performance is dictated by the drives rather than the SCSI interface. Because of the high speed of the SCSI interface relative to the tape and hard disk drives, when faster media and drives are available, SCSI can easily take advantage of the greater speed.

The SCSI interface is supplied as a SCSI host adapter card that plugs into the system unit and can connect to the tape drive. The SCSI host adapter requires an expansion slot, but it can connect to other devices such as hard disk drives or tape drives with embedded SCSI interfaces. The use of a single host adapter for as many as six hard disk drives and one tape unit is a strong case in favor of SCSI as a general disk and tape interface. The only real problem with SCSI is that you will need drivers which support both your particular tape drive as well as your particular host adapter. Most tape drivers support host adapters that have ASPI (Advanced SCSI Programming Interface) or CAM (Common Access Method) drivers. In other words, you will need the ASPI or CAM driver for your host adapter, and a tape driver that connects to ASPI or CAM for your tape drive. Although there can sometimes be problems getting the correct drivers for a particular system, SCSI is still the highest performance and most flexible interface for tape backup systems.

Another interface gaining wide acceptance is the parallel port. It is used for more than just printers, as several companies have introduced versions of their backup hardware and software systems that use the parallel port to connect to your system. The parallel port offers a high speed data transfer interface with easy configuration and cabling. Unlike serial ports, there is usually no confusion as to how the cables are wired for parallel port connections.

Several companies, like MicroSolutions and Colorado, offer complete external backup systems including all hardware, software, and cables needed to connect to the parallel port of any system. These types of backup systems offer independence from a particular type of system, which is especially useful in a mixed machine or mixed bus environment.

Other companies, like Trantor, offer parallel port SCSI adapters, to which you can connect any SCSI device including hard disk, CD-ROM, tape backup, scanners, etc. If you are out of slots or desire to set up an external backup system that will attach to and backup several systems, then I recommend using one of these parallel to SCSI adapters like the Trantor MiniSCSI Plus. Using a parallel port SCSI adapter and one of the higher performance DAT tape drives, you can set up a highly capable external backup system that can function on virtually any machine.

Tape Backup Drivers and Software. Now you need to consider the software that will run the tape system. Some manufacturers have written their own software, which is proprietary and used only by that manufacturer. In other words, even though you might be using a tape unit with the same media and interface, if the software is different you cannot interchange data between the units. One type of software does not recognize the data formats of another proprietary software system. Other tape software packages are designed to run on a variety of tape hardware rather than a single manufacturer's system. There are several hardware independant backup software packages that support a variety of tape drives such as SyTOS Sytron tape operating system) by Sytron, Novaback by Novastor, and Central Point Backup by Central Point. All of these products work with a number of different tape drives. SyTOS is somewhat of an industry standard because it is endorsed (and sold) by IBM and many other vendors, as well as having versions that work on all major PC operating systems.

SyTOS has been selected by IBM as the standard software for its units. Because of market pressures to be compatible with IBM, Compaq and other system and tape-drive vendors are offering SyTOS with their tape systems. Because two systems that use the same media, interface, and software can read and write each other's tapes, you can have data interchangeability among different tape-unit manufacturers. You should consider using a system that runs SyTOS software for those reasons. Of course, the proprietary software is generally just as good, if not better. You can exchange data tapes only with other users of the same systems.

All software should be capable of certain basic operations. Make sure that your software does what you want, and consider buying only software that has these features:

- Can back up an entire DOS partition (full volume backup)

- Can back up any or all files individually (file-by-file backup)

- Allows a selective file-by-file restore from a volume backup as well as a file-by-file backup

- Can combine several backups on a single tape

- Can run the software as commands from DOS BATCH files

- Works under a network

Also, make sure that the backup system has these features:

- Can span a large drive on multiple tapes

- Can be completely verified

If the software you are considering does not have any of these essential features, look for another system.

Physical Location: Internal or External. Physical location of the tape-backup units is a simple factor often not considered in detail. I almost never recommend any tape-backup unit mounted internally in a system unit. I recommend that you buy a tape unit externally mounted in its own chassis and one that connects to the system unit through a cable and connectors.

Tape units are relatively expensive, and I never want to tie up a backup unit for only one system. The amount of time that just one system spends using the unit makes this proposition wasteful. With an external unit, many systems can share the backup unit. I just equip every system unit with the required interface, if they aren't already equipped. Extra QIC-02 cards are available for about $100 each, and SCSI host adapters are about $200. Note that many systems now include a SCSI host adapter as part of the mother-board, or as a card already installed. I already share my system among more than five computers and will continue adding systems to the backup pool. In some companies, the backup unit is mounted on a wheeled cart so that workers easily can move it from computer to computer.

If you have only one system or if all your data is stored in a single file-server system, you might have a legitimate argument for using an internal tape drive. You might wish that you had an external system, however, on the day a new system arrives, or when the server is down and you have to get a new one up and running.

Recommended Backup System. Although there are a variety of backup systems available, I recommend units from any manufacturer that meets these requirements:

Type of media: DC-2000, DC-600, 4mm DAT, or 8mm

Hardware interface: QIC-02, Parallel Port, or SCSI

My preferences lean towards the 4mm DAT drives because of their high capacity (4G plus with built in data compression) and relatively high performance. Also, the media cost is very low, around $15 per cartridge. DAT devices almost always use a SCSI interface, which means you would need a SCSI host adapter installed in the system. This could be either a standard type of SCSI host adapter in a slot (or integrated into the motherboard of some systems), or for a lower cost portable solution, you could run the SCSI DAT drive from a parallel port with one of the parallel to SCSI adapters like those from Trantor. The parallel port adapters make it easy to use a single external DAT drive to backup a variety of systems.

Purchasing Warranty and Service Contracts

Extended warranties are a recent trend in the computer industry. With the current fierce competition among hardware vendors, a good warranty is one way for a specific manufacturer to stand out from the crowd. Although most companies offer a one-year warranty on their systems, others offer longer warranty periods, such as two years or more.

In addition to extended-length warranties, some manufacturers offer free or nearly free on-site service during the warranty period. Many highly competitive mail-order outfits offer service such as this for little or no extra cost. Even IBM has succumbed to market pressure to lower service costs, and has an option for converting the standard 1-year warranty into a full blown, on-site service contract for only $40. This same option can be extended to cover monitors and printers for only a small additional cost.

> ### Tip
>
> IBM and other companies are beginning to offer extended-length warranties and free or low-cost on-site service. IBM has a somewhat unknown option to upgrade the standard 1-year warranties on its PS/2 systems into a full-blown, on-site service contract. Under this option, you can upgrade the standard Customer Carry-in Repair warranty to an IBM On-site Repair warranty for only $40 for the first year.
>
> If you have only the carry-in warranty, as its name implies you must carry in your computer to a depot for service; with the on-site warranty, the service technician comes to you. One car trip to a service center costs me more than $40 in wasted gasoline and time. I gladly pay the fee to have the service technician come to see me. Be sure to ask for this option when you buy your system. If your dealer is unfamiliar with it, ask that your order include IBM feature code #9805.

In most normal cases, service contracts are not worth the price. In the retail computer environment, a service contract is often a way for a dealer or vendor to add income to a sale. Most annual service contracts add 10 to 15 percent of the cost of the system. A service contract for a $5,000 system, for example, *costs $500 to $750 per year*. Salespeople in most organizations are trained to vigorously sell service contracts. Much like in the automobile sales business, these contracts are largely unnecessary except in special situations.

The high prices of service contracts also might affect the quality of service you receive. Technicians could try to make their work seem more complex than it actually is to make you believe that the contracts price is justified. For example, a service technician might replace your hard disk or entire motherboard with a spare when all you need is low-level formatting for the hard disk or a simple fix for the motherboard such as a single memory chip. A defective drive, for example, probably is just returned to the shop for low-level formatting. Eventually, it ends up in somebody else's system. Replacing a part is faster and leaves the impression that your expensive service contract is worth the price because you get a new part. You might be much less impressed with your expensive service contract if the service people visit, do a simple troubleshooting procedure, and then replace a single $2 memory chip or spend 15 minutes reformatting the hard disk.

With some basic troubleshooting skills, some simple tools, and a few spare parts, you can eliminate the need for most of these expensive service contracts. Unfortunately, some companies practice deceptive servicing procedures to justify the expensive service contracts they offer. Users are made to believe that these types of component failures are the norm, and they have a mistaken impression about the overall reliability of today's systems.

> **Tip**
>
> If you have many systems, you can justify carrying a spare-parts inventory, which can also elimi-
> nate the need for a service contract. For less than what a service contract costs for five to ten
> systems, you often can buy a complete spare system each year. Protecting yourself with extra
> equipment rather than service contracts is practical if you have more than ten computers of the
> same make or model. For extremely time-sensitive applications, you might be wise to buy a second
> system along with the primary unit—such as in a network file-server application. Only you can
> make the appropriate cost-justification analysis to decide whether you need a service contract or a
> spare system.

In some instances, buying a service contract can be justified and beneficial. If you have a system that must function at all times and is so expensive that you cannot buy a complete spare system, or for a system in a remote location far away from a centralized service operation, you might be wise to invest in a good service contract that provides timely repairs. Before contracting for service, you should consider your options carefully. These sources either supply or authorize service contracts:

- Manufacturers
- Dealers or vendors
- Third parties

Although most users take the manufacturer or dealer service, sometimes a third-party tries harder to close the deal; for example, it sometimes includes all the equipment installed, even aftermarket items the dealers or manufacturers don't offer. In other cases, a manufacturer might not have its own service organization; instead, it makes a deal with a major third-party nationwide service company to provide authorized service.

After you select an organization, several levels of service often are available. Starting with the most expensive, these levels of service typically include:

- Four-hour on-site response
- Next-day on-site response

- Courier service (a service company picks up and returns a unit)
- Carry-in, or depot, service

The actual menu varies from manufacturer to manufacturer. For example, IBM offers only a full 24-hours-a-day, 7-days-a-week, on-site service contract. IBM claims that a technician is dispatched usually within four hours of your call. For older systems, but not the PS/2, IBM also offers a courier or carry-in service contract. Warranty work, normally a customer carry-in depot arrangement, can be upgraded to a full on-site contract for only $40. After the first-year $40 contract upgrade expires, you can continue the full on-site service contract for standard rates. Table 11.2 lists the rates for IBM service contracts after the warranty has expired.

Table 11.2 PS/2 Service-Contract Fees after Warranty for Annual IBM On-site Repair (IOR) Service

PS/2 model	Contract	PS/2 model	Contract
8525-x01/x02	$95	8570-0x1/1x1	$450
8525-x04/x05	$110	8570-Axx	$595
8525-x06/x36	$210	8570-Bx1	$645
8530-001	$190	8573-031/061	$385
8530-002	$140	8573-121	$385
8530-021	$190	8573-161	$750
8530-E01/E21	$190	8573-401	$850
8530-E31/E41	$190	8580-041	$360
8535-all	$260	8580-071	$425
8540-all	$400	8580-081	$550
8543-044	$430	8580-111/121	$500
8550-021	$220	8580-161	$600
8550-031/061	$220	8580-311	$575
8555-0x1	$260	8580-321	$605
8555-LT0/LE0	$260	8580-A21	$675
8557-045/049	$400	8580-A16/A31	$785
8560-041	$310	8590-0G5/0G9	$800
8560-071	$345	8590-0J5/0J9	$850
8565-061	$425	8590-0KD	$950
8565-121	$475	8595-0G9/0GF	$1,400
8565-321	$550	8595-0Jx	$1,450
8570-E61	$415	8595-0Kx	$1,550

If you have bought a service contract in the past, these prices might surprise you. With the PS/2 systems, IBM has rewritten the rules for PC servicing. The same type of on-site annual contract for an earlier 20M AT system, for example, costs nearly $600 annually, compared with $220 for the PS/2 Model 50. Smaller third-party service companies are having difficulty competing with these newer prices. IBM claims that the PS/2 systems are five times more reliable than the earlier systems, and the service-contract pricing is about one-third what the earlier systems cost. If the claims of additional reliability are true, IBM is doing well even with lower pricing. If the claims are not true (which is unlikely), then IBM would be losing money on their service contracts.

> ### Tip
>
> In summary, for most standard systems, a service contract beyond what is included with the original warranty is probably a waste of money. For other systems that have not yet achieved commodity status, or for systems that must be up and running at all times, you might want to investigate a service-contract option, even though you might be fully qualified and capable of servicing the system.
>
> The PS/2 systems are a somewhat special case; they have low-priced, on-site warranty upgrades and fairly inexpensive service contracts compared to the costs of the systems. Remember, however, that you can buy most, if not all, parts for these systems from non-IBM sources; also, third-party companies that specialize in difficult items such as motherboards and power supplies can repair these items. Only after carefully weighing every option and cost involved can you decide how your systems should be serviced.

Chapter Summary

This chapter has presented the steps you can take to ensure proper operation of your system. It has examined active and passive preventive maintenance—the key to a system that gives many years of trouble-free service. You have learned about the procedures involved in preventive maintenance and the frequency with which these procedures should be performed.

Backup was discussed as a way to be prepared when things go wrong. The only guarantee for being able to retrieve data is to back it up. In this chapter, you also have learned about backup options.

Finally, you have learned about the commonly available warranty and service contracts provided by computer manufacturers. Sometimes the contracts can save you from worrying about tough-to-service systems or systems whose parts are largely unavailable on short notice

Chapter 12

System Upgrades and Improvements

IBM and IBM-compatible systems are easy to upgrade and improve not only because of support from IBM, but also because of the huge industry that has grown up around the IBM-compatible computer standard. For example, third-party manufacturers not only produce a wide range of complete IBM-compatible systems, but they also make virtually every component for what is known as "IBM clones." IBM uses many third-party components in its own systems as well. Because of the third-party support, a wide range of options is available for upgrading a system to achieve increased performance or expanded capabilities.

You can extend the life of older systems by adding functions and features that match the newest systems on the market. You also can add new components to a modern system to squeeze cutting-edge performance out of what is already a premium system. In this chapter, you learn about these types of system upgrades:

- Increasing system memory
- Upgrading a ROM BIOS
- Increasing disk storage
- Increasing system speed
- Improving a video subsystem
- Upgrading to a new version of DOS

> **Caution**
>
> You must be careful not to overdo system upgrades. Sometimes people throw far too much money and materials into a "junk" system. For example, upgrading a typical PC- or XT-class system into a 386 AT-class system is not practical cost-wise. Keep track of the cost of your upgrades. Changes to an existing system can become so expensive that purchasing a new system becomes the better choice. By making extensive changes in a system, you also risk creating a "Frankenstein" system with strange quirks and eccentric, if not flaky, operation. This type of system might be acceptable as a "toy" for your personal use but is not recommended for a system used in a business environment. In business, there's no room for a marginally functional system.

Upgrading by Increasing System Memory

Adding memory to a system is one of the more useful upgrades you can perform, and one of the least expensive, especially when you consider the increased capabilities of DOS, Windows, and OS/2 when given more memory with which to work. You can add three primary types of memory to a system: conventional, extended, and expanded. (These types of memory are described in detail in Chapter 7.) *Conventional memory* is the memory within the first megabyte of a system's memory that can be used by DOS or application software. Conventional memory is accessible in the native mode of the 8088 processor and in the 80286 and higher processor's real mode of operation. *Extended memory* is any memory after the first megabyte and normally extends to the 16th or 4,096th megabyte of memory. *Expanded memory* is accessed by the processor in chunks that are "bank switched" in and out of the processor's view. Expanded memory is slow and clumsy for the system to use and is generally considered obsolete by today's standards. 386 and higher systems can create expanded memory from extended memory, so normally you only physically add extended memory to a system . Extended memory is also directly usable by DOS, Windows, and OS/2, and expanded memory is not.

This section discusses adding memory, including selecting and installing memory chips and testing the results of the installation.

Conventional Memory

Today, most systems are sold with the full 640K of usable conventional memory installed. If your system does not have the full compliment of 640K conventional memory, you can add additional extended or expanded memory only after filling the 640K conventional memory amount.

Extended Memory

PC or XT systems cannot use extended memory because the 8088/8086 processors in PC or XT systems cannot run in protected mode. Expanded memory, however, can enhance some of the capabilities—but generally not the speed—of these computer systems. With AT-class systems, you can install both extended and expanded memory. Extended memory is more useful than expanded memory. Windows and OS/2 can take full advantage of the 16M of available conventional- and extended-memory space. The need or desire for expanded memory in AT systems is virtually nonexistent because it must be implemented in a slow and clumsy way. Fortunately, you easily can change almost any AT-type, 16-bit expanded memory board from expanded to extended memory by reconfiguring the adapter switches.

Expanded Memory

IBM and Microsoft have added limited expanded-memory support to DOS starting with DOS 4.0. Expanded memory requires specialized hardware to implement the bank-switching techniques, so for PC and XT systems you must purchase a special type of memory adapter with built-in switching capability. If you decide to add one or more of these expanded-memory adapters to a PC- or XT-type system, be sure that the adapter meets Expanded Memory Specification 4.0 (EMS 4.0) or higher standards in the hardware and the software. Many older expanded-memory adapters meet only the inferior EMS 3.x standards in hardware even though the software driver might comply with EMS 4.x. The major difference between the 3.x and 4.x EMS designs is that the newer 4.x versions provide a larger, variable-size paging area that can occupy a larger range of memory areas within the system memory map.

Because they use advanced AT chipsets, some 286 AT-class systems can use extended memory to emulate expanded memory. If your 286 systems have this capability, check your system documentation for more information. An enhanced Setup program usually controls this capability.

Upgrade Strategies

Adding expanded memory to PC- or XT-type systems is not a good idea mainly because an expanded memory board with a couple of megabytes of expanded memory installed can cost more than the entire system is worth (especially when you consider that this memory does not function for Windows and that a PC- or XT-class system cannot run OS/2). Instead, purchase a more powerful system—for example, an inexpensive 486SX—with greater expansion capabilities.

If you decide to upgrade to a more powerful computer system, you cannot normally salvage the memory from a PC or XT system. The 8-bit memory boards are useless in AT or Micro Channel systems, and the speed of the memory chips usually is inadequate for newer systems. Many new systems use high-speed SIMM modules rather than chips. A pile of 150-nanosecond, 64K or 256K chips is useless if your next system is a high-speed system that uses SIMMs or memory devices faster than 80 nanoseconds. Be sure to weigh carefully your future needs for computing speed and a multitasking operating system (OS/2, for example) with the amount of money you spend to upgrade current equipment.

Motherboard Memory

This section discusses *motherboard memory*—the memory actually installed on the motherboard—rather than the memory that resides on adapter boards. The first part of this section presents recommendations for selecting and installing chips. The last part has instructions for modifying an IBM XT Type 1 motherboard. This modification enables a full 640K of memory to be placed on the motherboard, to eliminate the need for memory-expansion boards. IBM's more recent XT Type 2 motherboards already include this modification.

Selecting and Installing Memory Chips or SIMMs

If you are upgrading a motherboard by adding memory, follow the manufacturer's guidelines about which memory chips or modules to purchase. For example, as detailed in Chapter 7, memory comes in various form factors. These include individual chips known as DIP (Dual Inline Pin) memory chips, SIMMs (Single Inline Memory Modules), and SIPPs (Single Inline Pin Package). The following describes each chip or module type:

DIP—Dual Inline Pin chips are roughly the size of a piece of Dentyne chewing gum with pins—about 1/10th inch apart—protruding downward from the edges.

SIMMs—Single Inline Memory Modules are like small circuit boards with chips soldered on them. Different numbers of chips can be mounted on the SIMM, and the chips can be mounted on one or both sides of the SIMM. A SIMM has a row of contacts on one edge of the board. The contacts can be tin or gold plated. The SIMMs are retained in the system by special sockets with a positive latching mechanism that locks the SIMM in place. SIMM connectors use a high force wiping contact that is extremely resistant to corrosion.

SIMMs are available in two types: 30-pin and 72-pin. The 30-pin modules come in 9-bit form with parity or 8-bit form for systems that lack parity checking. The 72-pin SIMMs are 36-bits wide with parity (32 data bits and 4 parity bits), or 32-bits wide without parity. Note that the 9-bit and 36-bit SIMMs with parity can always be used in systems that lack parity checking, and the non-parity SIMMs cannot be used in normal systems that require parity bits. Systems that lack parity checking for memory are not recommended.

SIPP—Single Inline Pin Packages are really SIMMs with pins rather than contacts. The pins are designed to be installed in a long connector socket that is much cheaper than the standard SIMM socket. SIPPs are inferior to SIMMs because they lack the positive latching mechanism that retains the module, and the connector lacks the high force wiping contacts that resist corrosion. SIPP modules are not are not recommended because of their inferiority over standard SIMMs.

For more information on the form factor of RAM chips, see Chapter 7, "Primary System Components."

RAM Chip Type (Capacity). Individual RAM chips come in different capacities. The capacity determines the number of data bits that can be stored in a chip of a particular size. For example, RAM chips for the original IBM PC stored 16 kilobits of data. This RAM chip is the smallest used on any IBM-compatible system. The RAM chips for the original version of the IBM XT stored 64 kilobits of data. The standard chip for 386-based systems is the 1 megabit chip (usually found in SIMMs). 4 or 16 megabit chips (again on SIMMs) are common on 486 and greater systems today.

Before you add RAM to a system (or replace defective RAM chips), you must determine the exact memory chips required for your system. Your system documentation contains this information. If you do not have the documentation, you should obtain it as quickly as possible. If you are stuck with replacing a defective RAM chip and do not have the system documentation, you can determine the correct chip for your system by inspecting the chips that are already installed. To help you with your inspection, check with the system manufacturer's technical support operation, or a chip vendor. Each chip has markings that indicate the chip capacity and its speed. For example, the markings on individual 1 megabit chips produced by various companies are listed here:

Markings	Manufacturer
TMS4C1024N/DJ	Texas Instruments
HM511000AP/AJP/AZP	Hitachi
MB81C1000P/PJ/PSZ	Fujitsu

If you do not have the documentation for your system, and the manufacturer does not offer technical support, open up your system case and carefully write down the markings that appear on your memory chips. Then contact a local computer store or mail-order chip vendor for help in determining the proper RAM chips for your system. Adding the wrong RAM chips to a system can make it as unreliable as leaving a defective chip on the motherboard and trying to use the system in that condition.

RAM Chip Speed. RAM chips also come in various speeds, for example 120ns (nanosecond) chips are used on older systems and 60 or 70ns chips on fast 486- and Pentium-based systems.

The motherboard manufacturer determines the correct speed of the memory chips installed on each system. For example, IBM specifies different speed memory for different systems. Table 12.1 lists the required RAM chip speeds and wait states for IBM motherboards.

Table 12.1 IBM Motherboard memory timing

System	CPU	Clock speed (MHz)	Wait states	Memory-access time (ns)	Notes
PC	8088	4.77	1	200	
XT	8088	4.77	1	200	
AT	286	6	1	150	
AT	286	8	1	150	
XT-286	286	6	0	150	Zero wait

(continues)

Table 12.1 Continued

System	CPU	Clock speed (MHz)	Wait states	Memory-access time (ns)	Notes
PS/1	286	10	1	120	
25	8086	8	0	150	Zero wait
30	8086	8	0	150	Zero wait
25-286	286	10	1	120	
30-286	286	10	1	120	
35 SX	386SX	20	0-2	85	Paged memory
40 SX	386SX	20	0-2	85	Paged memory
L40	386SX	20	0-2	80	Paged memory
50	286	10	1	150	
50Z	286	10	0	85	Zero wait
55 SX	386SX	16	0-2	100	Paged memory
57 SX	386SX	20	0-2	70	Paged memory
60	286	10	1	150	
65	386SX	16	0-2	100	Paged memory
70	386DX	16	0-2	85	Paged memory
70	386DX	20	0-2	85	Paged memory
70	386DX	25	0-5	80	External 64K cache
70	486DX	25	0-5	80	Internal 8K cache
P70	386DX	16	0-2	85	Paged memory
P70	386DX	20	0-2	85	Paged memory
P75	486DX	33	0-5	70	Internal 8K cache
80	386DX	16	0-2	80	Paged memory
80	386DX	20	0-2	80	Paged memory
80	386DX	25	0-5	80	External 64K cache
90	486SX	20	0-5	70	Interleaved memory, internal 8K cache
90	486SX	25	0-5	70	Interleaved memory, internal 8K cache
90	486DX	25	0-5	70	Interleaved memory, internal 8K cache, optional external 256K cache
90	486DX	33	0-5	70	Interleaved memory, internal 8K cache, optional external 256K cache

System	CPU	Clock speed (MHz)	Wait states	Memory-access time (ns)	Notes
90	486DX	50	0-5	70	Interleaved memory, internal 8K cache, optional external 256K cache
95	486SX	20	0-5	70	Interleaved memory, internal 8K cache
95	486SX	25	0-5	70	Interleaved memory, internal 8K cache
95	486DX	25	0-5	70	Interleaved memory, internal 8K cache, optional external 256K cache
95	486DX	33	0-5	70	Interleaved memory, internal 8K cache, optional external 256K cache
95	486DX	50	0-5	70	Interleaved memory, internal 8K cache, optional external 256K cache

In some cases, you can have slower-speed memory on an adapter than is tolerated by the system on the motherboard. Many systems run the expansion slots at a fixed slower speed—8 MHz for most ISA bus systems—so that installed adapters function properly. The PS/2 system memory adapters might be able to run more slowly than main memory because of the Micro Channel Architecture (MCA) interface's higher level of controls and capabilities. The MCA's asynchronous design enables adapters to remain independent of the processor's speed and request additional wait states as required to accommodate the slower adapters. (A wait state is an idle cycle in which the processor and system essentially wait for a component, such as memory, to "catch up.")

All the memory adapters that IBM offers for the PS/2 50 and 60, for example, use 120ns memory chips. These adapters also are specified for the Model 50Z, which normally runs with no wait states and requires 85ns memory on the motherboard. If these slower 120ns memory adapters are used in the Model 50Z, they cause the MCA in the 50Z to insert a wait state when the adapter memory is accessed by the system. Only the motherboard memory, therefore, runs with 0 wait states. Several third-party board manufacturers offer special 0-wait-state boards for the 50Z, which require faster access memory than 120ns.

In some systems, the motherboard memory speed can be controlled. Systems with adjustable wait-state settings enable you to choose optimal performance by purchasing the proper high-speed memory or to choose lower performance by purchasing cheaper memory. Many compatibles offer a wait-state jumper or configuration option, which controls whether the motherboard runs with wait states. To run with zero wait states may require faster access speed memory. Other systems can configure themselves dynamically to the memory installed. The PS/2 Model 90 and 95 system boards check the speeds of the SIMMs installed on the system board and adjust the number of wait states accordingly. Most other PS/2 systems simply check the speed of SIMMs installed on the system board and flag an error condition if the minimum speed requirements are not met.

Systems that use 36-bit SIMMs can detect both the speed and capacity of the installed SIMMs through four special contacts called *presence detect pins*. The motherboard can use these pins to determine the installed SIMM's rated speed and capacity in much the same way that many cameras can tell what speed film you have loaded by "reading" a series of contacts on the film canister. In the Model 90 and Model 95, if the SIMM is slower than 70ns, the system adds wait states so that the rest of the memory can keep up. In other systems, such as the Model 70, if memory slower than the required 80 or 85ns is installed, a 225 POST error message appears. If you look this error code up in the IBM error code list in the appendix of this book, it says Wrong-speed memory on system board.

This error message means that the installed memory is too slow for the system.

Systems with 16 MHz or higher clock speeds require extremely fast memory to keep up with the processor. In fact, the speeds that are required are so excessive that standard Dynamic RAM is not even available and faster (more expensive) Static RAM must be used. One alternative, adding wait states to reduce the memory-speed requirements, greatly decreases performance—not what you want in a fast system. Some special memory-architecture schemes have been devised to reduce the number of wait states required, boost over-all system performance, and keep costs down. The following list shows the most commonly used architecture schemes that increase memory performance:

- Paged memory
- Memory caching
- Interleaved memory

Paged memory is a simple scheme for improving memory performance that divides memory into pages from 512 bytes to a few kilobytes long. The paging circuitry then enables memory locations within a page to be accessed with zero wait states. If the desired memory location is outside the current page, one or more wait states are added while the system selects the new page. Paged memory has become common in higher-end 286 systems as well as in many 386 systems. For example, many PS/2 systems, like the Model 70 and Model 80, use paged memory to increase performance and enable slower 80 or 85ns memory to be used.

Interleaved memory offers greater performance than paged memory. This higher-performance scheme combines two banks of memory into one, organized as even and odd bytes. With this combination, an access cycle can begin in the second bank while the first is already processing a previous access, and vice versa. By alternating access to even and odd banks, you can request data from one bank and, while the request is pending, the system can move to the next bank to process another request. The first request becomes available while the second request is still pending, and so on. By interleaving access to memory in this manner, a system can effectively double memory-access performance without using faster memory chips. Many of the highest-performance systems use interleaved memory to achieve increased performance. Some systems that offer interleaved memory can use the interleaving function only if you install banks in matched capacity pairs. That usually means adding two 36-bit SIMMs of equal capacity at a time. If you add only a single bank or add two banks of different capacity, the system still functions, but memory interleaving is disabled and you pay a considerable performance penalty. Consult your system's technical-reference manual for more information.

Secondary Processor Cache. Memory caching is the most popular and usually the most effective scheme for improving memory performance. This technique relies on a small amount (8K to 256K) of raw, high-speed memory fast enough to keep up with the processor with zero wait states. This small bank of cache memory often is rated at *15 nanoseconds or less* in access speed. Because this rate is faster than normal Dynamic RAM components can handle, a special type of memory component, called Static RAM (SRAM), is used. Static RAM devices do not need the constant refresh signals required by Dynamic RAM devices. This feature, combined with other design properties, results in extremely fast access times and very high costs.

Although SRAM chips are expensive, only a small number of SRAM chips are required in a caching scheme. SRAM is used by a special cache controller circuit that stores frequently accessed RAM locations and also is preloaded with the RAM values that the cache controller expects to be accessed next. The cache acts as an intelligent buffer between the CPU and slower Dynamic RAM.

A *cache hit* means that the particular data the CPU wanted was available in the cache RAM and that there are no additional wait states to retrieve this data. A *cache miss* means that the data the CPU wanted had not been loaded into the cache RAM, and that wait states must be inserted while the data is retrieved. A good cache controller has a hit ratio of 95 percent or more (the system runs with zero wait states 95 percent of the time). The net effect is that the system acts as though nearly all the memory is 15ns or less in speed, although most of the memory is really much slower and therefore much less costly.

Systems based on the 486SX, SL, DX, and processors include a cache controller and 8K of internal cache RAM in the CPU, that makes them much faster than earlier systems. Systems with 386SX or DX processors must use an external cache controller with externally provided cache RAM. The 386SL provides a built-in cache controller, and the IBM-designed 386SLC incorporates virtually the same cache controller and 8K of built-in cache RAM as the 486 processors. IBM therefore can claim an 80 percent performance increase over the regular 386SX or DX chips for systems that use the 386SLC processor.

The amount of secondary processor cache RAM a system has does not automatically indicate a given level of performance increase. You may find that the system with the least cache RAM can outperform a system with a greater amount of cache RAM. It depends on the efficiency of the cache controller and the system design. For example, a cache integrated into a CPU can far outperform an external cache. A CPU internal cache is called a primary or Level 1 (L1) cache, and an external cache is called a secondary or Level 2 (L2) cache.

For example, adding the 256K L2 cache RAM option to a PS/2 Model 90 or 95 with a 486DX processor offers only a small increase in performance relative to the 8K of L1 cache memory already built in to the 486 CPU chip because the L1 cache integrated into the CPU can outperform an external (L2) cache. Also, adding cache RAM does not result in a proportional increase in performance. I have an older clone 386SX system that has 16K of L2 cache on the motherboard, with sockets for an additional 16K. Even with the meager 16K of L2 cache, this system is 20 percent faster than another 386DX system I have that runs at exactly the same clock rate but that has no cache. I added the additional 16K of L2 cache to the 386SX system and could barely measure another 5 percent increase in performance. With cache, clearly a little goes a long way.

To get maximum system performance and reliability, the best recommendation when you add chips or SIMMs to a motherboard is to use memory rated at the speeds recommended by the manufacturer. Faster memory will likely work in the system, but it creates no performance benefit and so is a waste of money. The minimum access-time specification for motherboard memory in a specific system is in the technical-reference manual for the system. For IBM-compatible systems that lack proper documentation, you can refer to Table 12.1 as a guide because most compatibles follow IBM's requirements. Because of the variety of system designs on the market, you should try to acquire the proper documentation from the manufacturer.

For many systems (such as COMPAQ) with proprietary local bus memory-expansion connectors, you must purchase all memory-expansion boards from that company. Similarly, IBM used proprietary memory connectors in the PS/2 Model 80 systems. For other industry-standard systems that use non-proprietary memory expansion, such as the IBM PC, XT, and AT, and most IBM-compatible systems, as well as most PS/2 systems, you can purchase from hundreds of vendors memory expansion boards that plug into the standard bus slots. Unfortunately, any memory expansion that plugs into a standard bus slot runs at bus speed rather than at the full system speed. For this reason most systems today provide standard SIMM connector sockets directly on the motherboard so the memory can be plugged directly into the system's local bus. Using memory adapter cards in these systems only slows them down. Other systems use proprietary local bus connectors for memory expansion adapters, which can cause additional problems and expense when you have to add or service memory.

Adapter Boards

In some cases, you can have slower-speed memory on an adapter board than is tolerated by the system on the motherboard. Many systems run memory expansion slots at a fixed slower speed—8 MHz for most ISA bus systems—so that installed adapters function properly. The PS/2 system memory adapters might be able to run more slowly than main memory because of the Micro Channel Architecture (MCA) interface's higher level of controls and capabilities. The MCA's asynchronous design enables adapters to remain independent of the processor's speed and request additional wait states as required to accommodate the slower adapters.

All the memory adapters that IBM offers for the PS/2 50 and 60, for example, use 120ns memory chips. These adapters also are specified for the Model 50Z, which normally runs with no wait states and requires 85ns memory on the motherboard. If these slower 120ns memory adapters are used in a Model 50Z, they cause the Micro Channel Architecture in the 50Z to insert a wait state when the adapter memory is accessed by the system. Only the motherboard memory, therefore, runs with 0 wait states. Several third-party board manufacturers offer special 0-wait-state boards for the 50Z, that require faster access memory than 120ns.

Memory Installation

This section discusses installing memory chips. Specifically it covers installing new RAM chips or memory modules. It also covers the problems you are most likely to encounter and how to avoid them. It also provides information on configuring your system to use new memory.

When you install or remove memory, these are the three problems you most likely will encounter:

- Electrostatic discharge
- Broken or bent pins
- Incorrect switch and jumper settings

To prevent electrostatic discharge (ESD) when you install sensitive memory chips or boards, do not wear synthetic clothes or leather-soled shoes. Remove any static charge you are carrying by touching the system chassis before you begin, or—better yet—wear a good commercial grounding strap on your wrist. These straps consist of a conductive wristband grounded at the other end by clipping a wire to the system chassis, usually with an alligator clip.

Caution

Be sure to use a properly designed commercial wrist strap; *do not make one yourself*. Commercial units have a one-megohm resistor that acts as protection if you accidentally touch live power. The resistor ensures that you do not become "the path of least resistance" to ground and become electrocuted. An improperly designed wrist strap can cause the power to conduct through you to the ground, which might possibly kill you.

Broken or bent leads are another potential problem associated with installing individual memory chips (DIPs) or SIPP modules. Sometimes the pins on new chips are bent in a V-shape, making them difficult to align with the socket holes. If you notice this problem on a DIP chip, place the chip on its side on a table and press gently to bend the pins so that they are at a 90-degree angle to the chip. With a SIPP module, you might want to use needlenose pliers to carefully straighten the pins so they protrude directly downward from the edge of the module with an equal amount of space between each pin. Then, install the chips in the sockets one at a time.

> **Caution**
>
> Straightening the pins on a DIP chip or SIPP module is not difficult work, but if you are not careful you can easily break off one of the pins, rendering the chip or memory module useless. Use great care when straightening the bent pins on any memory chip or module. Chip-insertion and pin-straightening devices are available to make sure that the pins are straight and aligned with the socket holes; using one of these inexpensive tools can save you a great deal of time.

When you install an individual chip or a memory module you must place it in the socket with proper orientation. When dealing with individual chips, take a close look at the top of the chip (the side with the manufacturer's markings) Each chip has a U-shaped notch that matches a similar mark on the socket. If the socket is not marked, you should use other chips as a guide. The orientation of the notch indicates the location of Pin 1 on the chip. Aligning this notch correctly with the others on the board ensures that you do not install the chip backward. Gently set each chip into a socket, ensuring every pin is properly aligned with the connector into which it fits, and push the chip in firmly with both thumbs until the chip is fully seated.

SIMM memory is oriented by a notch on one side of the module that is not present on the other side. You see that the socket has a protrusion that must fit into this notched area on one side of the SIMM. This makes it impossible to install a SIMM backward unless you physically break the connector. SIPP modules are not so fortunate, because they do not plug into a keyed socket. You have to orient them properly. The system documentation can be helpful if there are no marks on the motherboard to guide you. You also can use existing SIPP modules as a guide.

Before installing memory, be sure that the system power is off. Remove the PC cover and any installed cards. SIMMs snap easily into place, but chips can be more difficult to install. A chip-installation tool is not required, but it can make inserting the chips into sockets much easier. For removing chips, use a chip extractor or small screwdriver. Never try removing a RAM chip with your fingers because you can bend the chip's pins or poke a hole in your finger with one of the pins. You remove SIMMs by releasing the locking tabs and either pulling or rolling them out of their sockets.

After adding memory chips, and putting the system back together, you might have to alter motherboard switches or jumper settings. The PC includes two switch blocks with eight individual switches per block. Switch positions 1 through 4 of a PC's second switch block must be set to reflect the total installed memory. The XT has only one switch block, set to reflect the number of memory banks installed on the system board but not the expansion-card memory. The Appendix of this book provides more detailed information about the PC and XT motherboard switch settings.

IBM AT and PS/2 systems have no switches or jumpers for memory. Rather, you must run a setup program to inform the system of the total amount of memory installed. IBM-compatible AT-type systems usually have a setup program built into the system ROM-BIOS, and you must run this program after installing new memory to properly configure the system.

Most memory-expansion cards also have switches or jumpers that must be set. You often must set two items when you configure a memory card. The first, a starting address for the memory on the card, usually enables the memory on the card to begin using the system memory addresses higher than those used by any existing memory. The second setting is for the total amount of memory installed on the card.

Because of the PS/2's influence in the market, many memory boards as well as other types of adapter cards are made without switches. Instead, these boards have a configuration program used to set up the card. The configuration is stored in a special nonvolatile memory device contained on the card; after the settings are set, the card can remember the settings permanently. The Intel Above Board 286 and Plus versions, for example, have this switchless setup and configuration capability. Following a menu-driven configuration program is much easier than flipping tiny switches or setting jumpers located on a card. Another benefit of software configuration is that you don't even have to open up the system to reconfigure a card.

After properly configuring your system to work with the additional memory, you should run a memory-diagnostics program to ensure the proper operation of the new memory. At least two—and sometimes three—memory-diagnostic programs are available for all systems. In order of accuracy, these programs are

- POST (Power-On Self Test)
- User diagnostics disk
- Advanced diagnostics disk
- Aftermarket diagnostics software

The POST is used every time you power up the system; you can press Ctrl+A at the opening menu to access the advanced diagnostics on the reference disk.

PS/2 systems include the user diagnostics and advanced diagnostics programs on one reference disk. The disk ensures that PS/2 owners have all three memory-test programs.

Owners of standard PC systems receive (in the guide-to-operations manual) a diagnostics disk that has a good memory test. PC owners should purchase the advanced diagnostics disk as part of the hardware-maintenance service manual package. If you have purchased this package, you should use the advanced diagnostics program.

Many additional diagnostics programs are available from aftermarket utility software companies. I have listed several companies in the vendor list in the appendix that have excellent diagnostics and test software for testing memory and other components in a system. These programs are especially useful when the manufacturer of the system does not provide their own diagnostics.

Installing 640K on an XT Motherboard

This section describes how to install 640K of RAM on the system board in an IBM XT and an IBM Portable. The upgrade essentially changes what IBM calls an XT Type 1 motherboard into a Type 2 motherboard.

The upgrade consists of installing two banks of 256K chips and two banks of 64K chips on the motherboard, and then enabling the memory chips by adding a multiplexer/decoder chip to an empty socket provided for it, and a jumper wire. The jumper wire enables an existing memory decoder chip (U44) to enable the additional memory. These modifications are relatively easy to perform and can be done with no soldering.

A memory chip address is selected by two signals called *row-address select* (RAS) and *column-address select* (CAS). These signals determine where a value in a chip is located. The signals are modified by installing the jumper as indicated in these instructions so that the first two banks can be addressed four times deeper than they were originally, thus using the additional address locations in the 256K chips rather than in the original 64K chips.

To install 640K on an IBM XT motherboard, you must obtain the following parts from a chip vendor or electronics supply store (see the vendor list for sources):

- Eighteen 256K-by-1-bit 200-nanosecond (or faster) memory chips

- One 74LS158 (multiplexer/decoder) chip

- A small length of thin (30-gauge) jumper or wire-wrapping wire

After you have these parts, follow these steps:

1. Remove the motherboard (as explained in Chapter 6).

2. Plug the 74LS158 chip into the socket labeled U84.

   All motherboard components are identified by an alphanumeric value. The letter usually indicates the type of component, and the number indicates a sequential component ID number for that type of component. The coding can differ among manufacturers, but most use this lettering scheme:

U	Integrated circuit
Q	Transistor
C	Capacitor
R	Resistor

Because of the variety of motherboard designs on the market, ordering a BIOS upgrade often is more difficult than it sounds initially. If you have a name-brand system with a well-known design, the process can be simple. For many lesser-known compatible systems, however, you must provide the BIOS vendor with information about the system, such as the type of manufacturer's chipset the motherboard uses.

For most BIOS upgrades, you must obtain the following information:

- The make and model of the system unit

- The type of CPU; for example, 286, 386DX, 386SX, 486DX, 486SX, and so on

- The make and version of the existing BIOS

- The part number of the existing ROM chips (you might have to peel back the label to read this information)

- The make, model, or part numbers of integrated motherboard chip-sets, if used— for example, Chips & Technologies, SUNTAC, VLSI, OPTI, and others.

An *integrated chipset* is a group of chips on the original AT motherboard that perform the functions of up to hundreds of discrete chips. Many chipsets offer customizable features, available only if you have the correct BIOS. Most differences between systems today lie in the variety of integrated chipsets now used to manufacture PCs and the special initialization required to operate these chips. Even IBM uses third-party integrated chipsets from VLSI in PS/2 ISA-bus systems such as Models 30-286, 35 SX, and 40 SX.

The BIOS also must support variations in keyboard-controller programming and the way nonstandard features such as speed switching are handled. For example, a computer using the Chips & Technologies NEAT chipset must have a BIOS specifically made for it. The BIOS must properly initialize the NEAT chipset registers; otherwise, the machine does not even boot. The BIOS also must have support for this chipset's special features. Each one of the 20 or more popular chipsets for 286, 386, 486, and 586 machines requires specific BIOS support for proper operation. A generic BIOS might boot some systems, but certain features, such as shifting to and from protected mode or speed switching, might not be possible without the correct BIOS.

Keyboard Controller Chips

Besides the main system ROM, AT-class computers also have a keyboard controller or keyboard ROM, which is a keyboard controller microprocessor with its own built-in ROM. The keyboard controller is usually an Intel 8042 microcontroller, which incorporates a microprocessor, RAM, ROM, and I/O ports. The keyboard controller usually is a 40-pin chip, often with a label that has a copyright notice identifying the BIOS code programmed into the chip.

The keyboard controller controls the reset and A20 lines and deciphers the keyboard scan codes. The A20 line is used in extended memory and other protected-mode operations. On many systems, one of the unused ports is used to select the CPU clock speed. Because of the tie-in with the keyboard controller and protected-mode operation, many problems with the keyboard controllers become evident when you use either Windows or OS/2. If you experience lockups or keyboard problems with either Windows or OS/2 software, or with any software that runs in protected mode, such as Lotus 1-2-3 Release 3.x, get a replacement from your BIOS vendor or system-board vendor.

IBM systems do not need a replacement of the keyboard controller for upgrade purposes. (Replacement is difficult because the chip normally is soldered in.) Most manufacturers of IBM-compatible systems install the keyboard controller chip in a socket so that you easily can upgrade or replace it. If you upgrade the BIOS in your system, often the BIOS vendor includes a compatible keyboard controller as well. You usually do not have to buy the controller unless your old keyboard controller has a problem with the new BIOS.

BIOS Manufacturers and Vendors

Several BIOS manufacturers have developed ROM-BIOS software to use in upgrading IBM or IBM-compatible systems. These companies are the largest manufacturers of ROM-BIOS software:

- Phoenix

- American Megatrends International (AMI)

- Microid Research (MR)

- Award

Phoenix pioneered the IBM-compatible BIOS and the legal means to develop a product fully compatible with IBM's BIOS without infringing on the corporation's copyright. Phoenix first introduced many new features, such as user-defined hard drive types and 1.44M drive support. The Phoenix BIOS has a very good Power-On Self Test. This thorough POST presents a complete set of failure codes for diagnosing problems, especially the ones that occur when a system seems dead. The Appendix of this book has a complete list of Phoenix BIOS POST error codes.

The Phoenix BIOS documentation, a complete three-volume reference package, is one of its most useful features. It includes *System BIOS for IBM PC/XT/AT Computers and Compatibles*, *CBIOS for IBM PS/2 Computers and Compatibles*, and *ABIOS for IBM PS/2 Computers and Compatibles*. I recommend these excellent reference works, published by Addison-Wesley, even if you do not have the Phoenix BIOS (although some of its specific information does not apply to other systems).

The BIOS produced by AMI is very popular, and surpasses even Phoenix in new systems installations. The AMI BIOS offers a less comprehensive Power-On Self Test than does Phoenix, but it has an extensive diagnostics program in ROM. You can even purchase the program separately, as AMIDIAG. The in-ROM version, however, lacks the capability to test memory—crucial if the failure is in the first bank. On the other hand, the BIOS is very compatible, available for a number of different chipsets and motherboards, and has been handled responsibly from a support level. When problems have occurred, AMI has fixed them, earning this program full compatibility with OS/2, and other difficult environments.

Because AMI manufactures its own motherboards, it has a distinct advantage over other BIOS companies. Knowing that the motherboard and BIOS are made by the same source means that any interaction problems between the BIOS and motherboard likely can be resolved quickly by the single vendor with no shifting of blame for the problem to another party. I recommend buying AMI's motherboards because you generally don't have to worry about compatibility problems between the AMI BIOS and AMI motherboard. Even if problems occur, AMI corrects them.

Microid Research is newer than some of the other BIOS manufacturers, but their BIOS has proven to be very compatible. The MR BIOS as it is called, supports a number of different CPU and motherboard chipset combinations. The MR BIOS offers one of the easiest and most informative setup programs that really helps explain the options available. Some of you know that setting the advanced chipset functions is not always intuitive with the other BIOS vendors. In short, I recommend you look at the MR BIOS if you are considering a BIOS upgrade, or if you are configuring bare motherboards from scratch.

Award, the third-largest manufacturer of BIOS software, has made a name for itself with many system vendors because it licenses the BIOS code to them for further modification. AST, for example, purchased the rights to the Award BIOS for its own systems and now can modify the BIOS internally as though it had created the BIOS from scratch. In a sense, AST could develop its own custom BIOS using the Award code as a base, or starting point. Award also provides precustomized BIOS code for manufacturers. Although Award's BIOS is not yet as popular as the Phoenix and AMI BIOS, it is very popular, and compatibility even in tough environments such as OS/2 is ensured.

If you want to replace or upgrade your BIOS, you can obtain replacement chips directly from the BIOS manufacturer or from these recommended distributors:

- *Micro Firmware, Inc.* Micro Firmware has an extensive line of Phoenix BIOS upgrades, with more than 50 common 8088, 286, 386, and 486 versions. This company develops BIOS upgrades for specific hardware platforms, even when the original motherboard manufacturer is no longer in business or Many other BIOS vendors sell BIOS, developed by Micro Firmware, for specific platforms.

- *Washburn & Company Distributors.* This licensed AMI distributor deals exclusively with AMI BIOS upgrades. Washburn has complete AMI motherboard and BIOS packages. A primary distributor for AMI, Washburn has great expertise in dealing with BIOS upgrade problems. It also sells Second Nature, a disk drive support product that might eliminate the need for a BIOS if all you want is additional hard disk or floppy drive support.

- *Microid Research.* They manufacture and sell their own MR BIOS direct and offer technical support as well.

Alternatives to Upgrading the BIOS

Some companies, especially those who purchase only IBM systems, are timid about removing the BIOS and replacing it with a BIOS made by a company other than IBM. If you are leery of removing your system BIOS, another solution is available: You can purchase an accessory ROM to augment—rather than replace—your existing BIOS.

Second Nature is one of the best of these products. An accessory ROM for IBM and compatibles, it adds the following important features to a system:

- Greatly expanded BIOS hard disk parameter table

- Support for 720K and 1.44M drives

No software drivers or other memory-resident programs are used when Second Nature is installed. The hard disk parameters supplied by Second Nature overlay existing drive parameters that are already in your system ROM BIOS. Second Nature, compatible with all popular operating systems—including DOS, Windows and OS/2—also has a built-in, low-level format-and-verify utility.

Most AT-type computers have four 28-pin ROM sockets, two of which normally are occupied by the existing ROM BIOS chips. If there are no additional empty sockets (such as in the IBM XT-286 or some early IBM ATs) or if your computer cannot load accessory ROMS in the E000 memory segment (as with Sperry, Leading Edge, and some other AT clones), you can buy an optional card to install the Second Nature ROMs in any 8- or 16-bit slot. For more information about this product, contact Washburn & Company Distributors (see the vendor list in the appendix of this book).

Special ROM BIOS Related Problems

Some known problems exist in certain ROM-BIOS versions as well as in some systems sold during the past few years. Several of these problems have the potential to affect a large number of individuals because either the problem is severe or a large number of systems have the problem. This section describes some of the more important known BIOS- and system-interaction problems, and provides solutions for the problems as well.

If you use an AT&T 6300 system, you will want to use BIOS Version 1.43, the most recent one made for the system. This version solves many problems with older 6300 systems, and enables support of a 720K floppy disk drive. You can order BIOS Version 1.43 (for about $35) from the AT&T National Parts Sales Center (see the vendor list in the appendix) under part number 105203780.

Some systems with the AMI BIOS have had problems with IDE hard disk drives. IDE (Integrated Drive Electronics) drives have been touted as being fully port-compatible with existing ST-506/412 (MFM or RLL) and ESDI drives. Some IDE drives, however, take somewhat longer than they should after certain commands to present valid data at their ports. In late 1989, AMI had received many reports of problems with IDE drives, especially Conner and Toshiba drives. Because of these timing problems, AMI BIOS versions dated earlier than April 9, 1990 (04/09/90) are not recommended for use with IDE drives, and data loss can result if earlier versions are used. You might experience Drive C not ready errors with certain IDE drives, such as those from Conner Peripherals. If you have a computer with an IDE drive and an AMI BIOS dated earlier than 04/09/90, you should get a newer BIOS from the system vendor.

To be sure that you have the correct AMI BIOS version, look for this figure in the lower left corner of the screen when you boot your computer:

```
xxxx-zzzz-040990-Kr
```

The 040990 indicates a BIOS date of April 9, 1990, the minimum version to use. Older versions are OK only if you are *not* using IDE drives. The xxxx-zzzz indicates the BIOS type code and an OEM (original equipment manufacturer) ID number. For AMI-manu-factured motherboards, for example, the BIOS type code is DAMI-(model code). The r indicates the keyboard controller chip revision level, which should be revision F or later to avoid problems.

Modifying Your Existing BIOS

If you have access to the correct tools and knowledge, you can perform some interesting modifications or upgrades to your system by altering your existing ROM BIOS. This sec-tion discusses several modifications I have performed on my own systems. These modifi-cations have worked *for me*, and I am not necessarily recommending that anyone else perform them. If nothing else, the research and development of these modifications has taught me much about the way some things work in an IBM-compatible system, and I know that many of you are interested in some of this information.

> **Note**
>
> These types of modifications are for those readers who are either especially technically astute or extremely adventurous and are not recommended for everyone, especially those for whom system reliability is of crucial importance. However, even for readers of this book who do not attempt these operations on their system, the following information should prove interesting.

EPROM Programming Equipment. Some interesting modifications or upgrades and even repairs can be accomplished with a system by using an EPROM programmer, or "burner," as it is sometimes called. EPROM stands for Erasable Programmable Read-Only Memory, a type of chip that can have a program "burned," or fused, into it by way of an EPROM programmer device. These devices cost anywhere from about $100 to several thousands of dollars, depending on the capabilities of the device. Most cheaper EPROM programmers are more than adequate for burning PC ROMs. Both JDR Microdevices and Jameco Electronics sell EPROM programmers; I use and recommend one from Androm-eda Research (see the vendor list). They either connect to a slot or use the standard serial or parallel ports for communications. The Andromeda Research EPROM burner connects to a system parallel port that gives it flexibility and performance not found in most other units. To erase an EPROM, you also need an EPROM eraser, an inexpensive device ($30 to $100) that exposes the EPROM chip to intense ultraviolet light for about three to five minutes. I recommend and use a simple unit from DataRace (see the vendor list in the appendix).

With an EPROM programmer, you can modify or customize your system ROM BIOS, as well as the ROMs found on many expansion cards. You can also add hard drives to the drive table, change sign-on or error messages, or make specific changes to increase performance or otherwise customize your system. The ability to alter ROMs gives you an extra level of capability in both upgrading and repairing systems. Note that you can use an EPROM programmer to work with ROMs from other types of computer systems as well; I have even altered the ROMs that contain the programs and data tables for the Electronic Control Module (ECM) found in several different General Motors automobiles, allowing me total control over things like turbocharger boost settings, engine temperature and electric fan calibrations, vehicle speed governors, torque converter clutch operation, and even fuel injector and spark advance curves. If you are interested in these ECM PROM modifications, I have posted a detailed description of them in a file you can download from the CARS forum on CompuServe.

Backing Up Your BIOS. One often-overlooked benefit of an EPROM programmer is that you can essentially "back up" your ROMs in case they are later damaged. Many hardware vendors, such as IBM, do not offer ROM upgrades for their systems, and the only way to repair a motherboard or card with a damaged ROM is to burn a new copy from a backup. The backup can be in the form of another EPROM chip with the original program burned in, or even in the form of a disk file. I keep files containing images of the ROMs in each of my motherboards and expansion cards in case I have to burn a new copy to repair one of my systems.

To create a disk file copy of your motherboard ROM BIOS, you can either place the ROM in an EPROM programmer and use the function provided by the device to read the EPROM into a disk file, or you can use the DOS DEBUG program to read your ROM BIOS from memory and transfer it to disk as a file. To use DEBUG in this manner, follow these instructions:

```
C:\>DEBUG              ;Run DEBUG
-N SEG-F.ROM           ;Name the file
-R BX                  ;Change BX register (high-order file size)
BX 0000                ; from 0
:1                     ;   to 1 (indicates 64K file)
-M F000:0 FFFF CS:0    ;Move BIOS data to current code segment
-W 0                   ;Write file from offset 0 in code segment
Writing 10000 bytes    ;   10000h = 64K
-Q                     ;Quit DEBUG
```

These instructions save the entire 64K segment range from F000:0000 to 000:FFFF as a file by first setting up the name and size of the file to be saved, and then moving (essentially copying) the ROM BIOS code to the current code segment when DEBUG was loaded. The data then can be written to the disk. IBM AT systems and most compatibles have only 64K of BIOS, but PS/2 systems from IBM normally have a full 128K of BIOS code that resides in both segment E000 and F000. For these systems, repeat the procedure using E000:0 as the starting address in the Move command (rather than F000:0) and, of course, a different file name in the Name command. One important quirk of this procedure is that the commands should be entered in the order indicated here. In particular, the Name command must precede the Move command, or else some of the data at the beginning of the current code segment area is trashed.

You also can use this routine to "back up" any adapter-board ROMs installed in your system. For example, to back up the ROM on the IBM SCSI adapter with cache, installed in my system, a similar DEBUG session works. You must know the ROM's starting address and ending address or length to continue. My SCSI adapter ROM is located at D400:0 and is 16K (4000h bytes) long, which means it ends at D400:3FFF. To save this ROM as a file, execute these instructions:

```
C:\>DEBUG                    ;Run DEBUG
-N SCSI.ROM                  ;Name the file
-R CX                        ;Change CX register (low-order file size)
CX 0000                      ;  from 0
:4000                        ;  to 4000 (indicates 16K file)
-M D400:0 3FFF CS:0          ;Move BIOS data to current code segment
-W 0                         ;Write file from offset 0 in code segment
Writing 04000 bytes          ;  4000h = 16K
-Q                           ;Quit DEBUG
```

Most EPROM programmers are supplied with software that runs in your PC and enables you to control the unit. Functions available include the capability to read a ROM and save it as a disk file or write a ROM from a disk file, and the capability to copy or test ROMs. The software also should be able to split a file into even and odd addresses for 16- or 32-bit systems, as well as combine two split files into one. Another requirement is the capability to calculate the proper checksum byte (usually the last byte) in the ROM so that diagnostics passes it. All the programmers mentioned have these functions and more.

Removing the POST Speed Check. One problem in the IBM AT and XT-286 systems is that the clock speed is checked during the Power-On Self Test (POST). Checking the clock speed is probably a good idea, but it causes problems if you want to take advantage of the socketed clock crystal in these systems for a cheap and easy speedup. Most IBM-compatibles do not have this speed check, and can run at different clock rates with usually no modifications to the BIOS required.

In IBM systems, the Verify Speed/Refresh Clock Rates test checks the system refresh rate (clock speed) to ensure that it is 6 or 8 MHz, depending on which IBM system you have. A marginally faster or slower rate causes the test to fail, and results in a POST error of one long and one short beep followed by a halt (HLT) instruction.

This test occurs at POST checkpoint 11h, which is sent to the manufacturer's test port 80h. A failure of this test as indicated by one of the POST-card products that read this port can be identified by reading 11h as the last value sent to the manufacturer's test port. To eliminate the test, and enable a higher than normal clock rate, you must patch the instruction at the proper location from a 73h (JAE - Jump if Above or Equal) to an EBh (JMP - Jump unconditionally); this patch causes the test for an abnormally high refresh rate (resulting in a low test value) to pass through the JAE instruction. When this instruction is changed to a JMP instruction, the test never passes through and falls into the error routine no matter how fast the rate.

Note that the test for a slow refresh rate is still intact, and fails if the clock is below 6 or 8 MHz, depending on the system. The JAE instruction occurs at F000:05BC in IBM AT systems with the 06/10/85 or 11/15/85 ROM BIOS versions, or at F000:05C0 in an XT-286 system. The original AT system with the 01/10/84 BIOS *does not have this test*. By creating a new set of chips with this value changed with an EPROM programmer, you can eliminate this speed check and enable faster clock rates to go unstopped.

Modifying ROM BIOS Hard Disk Drive Parameter Tables. Probably the most common change made to a BIOS is to add or change drives in existing hard drive tables. For example, I have added two new drive types to one of my systems, Types 25 and 26, which have these parameters:

Type	Cylinders	Heads	WPC	Ctrl	LZ	S/T	Meg	MB
25	918	15	65535	08h	918	17	114.30	119.85
26	918	15	65535	08h	918	26	174.81	183.31

See Chapter 10 for more information about these parameters. In my old AT system, these table entries originally were unused (zeros), as are the remainder of types from 27 through 47. By burning a new set of ROMs with these two new completed entries, I can use my Maxtor XT-1140 drive to maximum capacity with either an MFM controller (as type 25) or an RLL controller (as type 26). This setup precludes the need for a controller BIOS to override the motherboard table values, and saves me some memory in the C000 or D000 segments, where a hard disk controller ROM normally would otherwise reside. It also makes my system more standard. If you are interested in performing this modification, get the *IBM AT Technical Reference Manual*, which documents the position and format of the drive tables in the BIOS.

Changing the Hard Disk Controller Head Step Rate. Another more complicated modification that can be performed is to increase the stepping rate of the hard disk controller. The first edition of this book briefly mentioned this modification, and someone wrote to me expressing an interest in it. This edition explains the precise nature of this modification and what is being changed, to give you greater insight into how the BIOS and disk controller work together. The performance gain, in fact, is relatively slight; I see the change as a learning experience more than anything else.

The Western Digital AT Controllers (1002/1003/1006) used by IBM in the original AT system, as well as other compatible controllers, such as those from DTC (Data Technology Corporation) and Adaptec, have a default head-stepping rate of 35μsec (micro-seconds). The fastest usable step rate is 16µsec—more than twice as fast. Most ST-506/412 hard disks have optimum stepping rates as low as 10µsec. By decreasing the rate to 16µsec, you can improve the seeking performance of the drive, resulting in an improvement of several milliseconds or more during an average seek. Because the standard rate is so slow compared to the optimum rate, many ST-506/412 drives, especially fast-seeking drives, do not perform to their manufacturer-rated seek performance unless the step rate from the controller is optimized in this manner.

There are two ways to decrease the step rate to 16µsec. The easiest and best way is to simply set a jumper on the controller card; not all cards, however, support this option. In fact, only one of the many Western Digital ST-506/412 controllers—the WD1003-WAH (ST-506/412 MFM, no floppy support)—supports this option. None of the other WD cards for the AT enables changing the step rate by way of a jumper. Adaptec, on the other hand, has a jumper to select the step rate on all its AT ST-506/412 controllers. Other than Adaptec's cards, most cards do not have a jumper and require other means of changing the step rate.

The second method of changing the step rate is universal, and works with virtually all AT bus ST-506/412 controllers, regardless of whether they are MFM or RLL or support floppy drives. This change is completed by changing two bytes in the ROM BIOS hard disk support code, which alters the way two specific commands are sent to the controller card.

First, let's discuss a little background on how the BIOS and controller operate. When DOS reads or writes data to or from a hard disk, it accesses the disk through the ROM BIOS. Specifically, DOS uses the Int 13h (h = hexadecimal) functions provided in the BIOS. Int 13h functions are commands incorporated into the BIOS of an AT system that enable DOS (or any other software) to perform specific commands in relation to the drive. These Int 13h commands then are translated into direct controller register level commands by the BIOS. The direct controller commands are called command control block (CCB) commands because each command must be presented to the controller in the form of a 7-byte command block with the command byte itself as the last (seventh) one. The other six bytes contain information such as the number of sectors on which to operate, as well as the cylinder and head positions where the command operates.

Sixteen different Int 13h commands are available for hard disks in the IBM AT BIOS. Some of these commands perform functions that do not involve accessing the controller or drive, such as the Get Disk Type BIOS command. Most other commands, however, are translated by the BIOS into the required code to send one of eight total CCB commands to the controller. Table 12.2 shows the Int 13h BIOS commands, and the specific CCB command the BIOS executes in the process.

Table 12.2 Int 13h AT Hard Disk BIOS and AT Controller Command Control Block (CCB) Commands

BIOS command	Description	CCB command	Description
00h	Reset Disk System	91h 10h	Set Parameters Recalibrate
01h	Get Status of Last Operation	—	—
02h	Read Sectors	20h	Read Sector
03h	Write Sectors	30h	Write Sector
04h	Verify Sectors	40h	Read Verify
05h	Format Track	50h	Format Track
08h	Read Drive Parameters	—	—
09h	Initialize Drive Characteristics	91h	Set Parameters
0Ah	Read Long	22h	Read Sector
0Bh	Write Long	32h	Write Sector
0Ch	Seek	70h	Seek
0Dh	Alternate Hard Disk Reset	10h	Recalibrate
10h	Test for Drive Ready	—	—
11h	Recalibrate Drive	10h	Recalibrate
14h	Controller Internal Diagnostic	80h	Diagnose
15h	Get Disk Type	—	—

Although only eight CCB commands are specific to the standard Western Digital (or compatible) AT hard disk controller, there are variations on some of the commands. Each CCB command consists of a single byte, with the most significant four bits (bits 4-7) of the byte indicating the actual command, and the least significant four bits (bits 0-3) indicating various command options. For two of the CCB commands, the option bits indicate and, in fact, set the step rate for the controller. By changing these bits, you also change the default step rate.

Table 12.3 shows the eight standard CCB commands:

Table 12.3 WD1002/WD1003/WD1006 AT Hard Disk Controller Command Control Block (CCB) Commands

CCB command	Description
10h-1Fh	Recalibrate
20h-23h	Read Sector
30h-33h	Write Sector
40h-41h	Read Verify
50h	Format Track
70h-7Fh	Seek
80h	Diagnose
91h	Set Parameters

In each of these commands, the CCB command byte is sent to the controller as the seventh byte of the total command block. The primary value is the first one listed in the chart. By setting the option bits, the command function can be altered. For example, the Read Sector command is 20h. By adding +1h to the command byte (making it 21h), automatic retries in case of errors are disabled. This step prevents the controller from automatically rereading the sector as many as 19 additional times in some cases; instead, the error is reported immediately. For error-correction code (ECC) errors, the controller simply attempts an immediate ECC correction, rather than rereading the sector as many as eight times in attempting to get a good read before making the ECC correction. You can disable retries only for the Read Sector, Write Sector, and Read Verify commands. This capability is useful especially during low-level formatting, surface analyzing, or even just Read Verify testing on the drive, because any errors are reported more accurately without automatic retrying taking place.

You can set another option for only the Read Sector and Write Sector commands. This option includes the ECC bytes, an additional four bytes of data past the data area of the sector; it makes the sector read or write include a total of 516 bytes rather than the normal 512. To set the "long" option, add +2h to the Read Sector or Write Sector CCB byte value. For example, to change the standard Read Sector command (20h) to include the ECC bytes, you add +2h, which results in a CCB command byte value of 22h. The option to include the ECC bytes during a read or write is especially useful in testing the ECC circuitry on the controller by specifically writing incorrect values and then reading them back to see the ECC in action.

For the Read Sector and Write Sector CCB commands, you can combine the disable-retries option with the long option by adding the two options together (+1h and +2h = +3h), resulting in a CCB command byte value of 23h (Read Sector) or 33h (Write Sector).

The last two commands, Recalibrate and Seek, have options that can be set through the option bits. For these two commands only, the option bits are used to set the stepping rate for subsequent seek commands to the drive. By adding a value from 1h through Fh to the CCB command byte for the Recalibrate or Seek commands, you can change the step rate from the default of 35µsec to something else. The following chart shows the different step rates possible by adding the step option to these commands:

Step option	Step rate (µsec)
0h	35
1h	500
2h	1000
3h	1500
4h	2000
5h	2500
6h	3000
7h	3500
8h	4000

(continues)

Step option	Step rate (μsec)
9h	4500
Ah	5000
Bh	5500
Ch	6000
Dh	6500
Eh	3.2
Fh	16

In this case, you want to add Fh to change the step rate from the default of 35μsec to 16μsec. Notice that the other possible values are much too slow (from 500 to 6500μsec), and that the 3.2μsec rate is much too fast for most drives. To change the Recalibrate and Seek commands to use the 16μsec step rate, you must patch the BIOS, changing the 10h and 70h to 1Fh and 7Fh, respectively. You essentially are patching the code executed when an Int 13h, Function 11h (Recalibrate Drive) or Function 0Ch (Seek) BIOS command is executed. These BIOS routines contain the code that sends the 10h (Recalibrate) or 70h (Seek) CCB commands to the controllers. Because the other BIOS routines that also execute the CCB Recalibrate command do so by calling the same Int 13h Function 11h code, only one patch is required to change all instances of the CCB Recalibrate command.

Because these two commands can be in different positions in different BIOS, the following code shows you how to find them using the DOS DEBUG command:

```
C:\>DEBUG                      ;Run DEBUG
-S F000:0 L 0 C6 46 FE 10      ;Search ROM for Recalibrate command
F000:30CF                      ; Found it!
-S F000:0 L 0 C6 46 FE 70      ;Search ROM for Seek command
F000:309A                      ; Found it!
-Q                             ;Quit
```

The first Search command locates the code sent to the controller for a CCB Recalibrate command, and the second Search locates the Seek command. The 10h (Recalibrate) command is at F000:30D2h in this example because the address returned by the Search command points to the beginning of the search string, not to the end. Remember to add 3 to each location returned for the actual location of the 10h or 70h command. For example, the 70h byte is at F000:309Dh. These "found" locations vary from system to system; this example used an IBM AT Model 339 with an 11/15/85 BIOS. Therefore, you can change these bytes to 1Fh and 7Fh, respectively. You must have an EPROM programmer to record these changes in another set of chips.

This section has examined some simple changes you can make to a ROM-BIOS with the help of an EPROM programmer. The steps involved in modifying or burning the ROMs were not described because these instructions normally are included with the programmer device you purchase.

Flash BIOS. Flash ROM is a type of EEPROM chip that is found in a number of systems today. EEPROM stands for Electrically Erasable Programmable Read Only Memory, and is a type of ROM chip that can be erased and reprogrammed directly in the system without using ultraviolet light and an EPROM programmer device. Using Flash ROM enables a manufacturer to send out ROM upgrades on disk, that can then be loaded into the Flash ROM chip on the motherboard without physically having to remove and replace the chip. This saves time and money for both the system manufacturer and end user as well.

Normally the Flash ROM in a system is write-protected, and the protection must be disabled before an update can be performed. This is usually accomplished through a jumper or switch that controls the lock on the ROM update. Without the lock, any program that knows the right instructions can rewrite the ROM in your system—not a comforting thought! Without the write protection, it is conceivable that virus programs could even be written that copy themselves directly into the ROM BIOS code in your system! Fortunately, I have not seen an implementation of Flash that did not have write protection capability.

Most manufacturers who use the Flash BIOS system notify their customers when the BIOS for a particular system line has been upgraded. Usually the cost to purchase the upgrade is nominal (and it might be free if your system is new enough).

IML System Partition BIOS. IBM uses a scheme similar to a Flash ROM called Initial Microcode Load (IML). This is a technique in which the BIOS code is installed on the hard disk in a special hidden System Partition, and is loaded every time the system is powered up. Of course the system still has a core BIOS on the motherboard, but all it does is locate and load updated BIOS code from the System Partition.

This technique allows IBM to distribute ROM updates on disk, which are then installed on the System Partition. The IML BIOS is loaded every time the system is reset or powered on. Along with the system BIOS code, the System Partition contains a complete copy of the Reference Diskette, which allows the option of running the setup and system configuration software at any time during a reboot operation. This eliminates the need for booting off of the Reference Diskette to reconfigure the system, and gives the impression that the entire Reference Diskette is contained in "ROM."

One drawback to this technique is that the BIOS code is installed on the (SCSI) hard disk, and the system cannot function properly without the properly set up hard disk connected. You can always boot from the Reference Diskette floppy should the hard disk fail or become disconnected, but you cannot boot from a standard floppy disk.

Upgrading Disk Drives

The interfacing of a system to the different types of floppy and hard disk drives can be a problem sometimes because of the differences in controllers and support software. This section discusses adding floppy disk and hard disk drives to a system.

Upgrading a Floppy Disk Drive. To add floppy drives to an existing system, you must connect them to a controller board. Virtually every PC, XT, or AT comes equipped with at least one floppy disk controller. The controllers and system BIOS routines support different drives. The floppy drive types commonly installed on PCs are listed here:

5 1/4-inch double-density (DD) drive (360K)

5 1/4-inch high-density (HD) drive (1.2M)

3 1/2-inch double-density (DD) drive (720K)

3 1/2-inch high-density (HD) drive (1.44M)

3 1/2-inch extra-high-density (ED) drive (2.88M)

With 5 1/4-inch drives, you need to be concerned about the track-width differences. The 360K drives write wider tracks than 1.2M drives. You must be careful when writing 360K diskettes in a 1.2M drive if they have previously been written on by a 360K drive because of these track width differences. However, all 3 1/2-inch drives write the same track width and you need not be concerned about problems related to track width.

Because the ED or HD drives can read and write DD disks as well, a system with as few as two drives—one 5 1/4-inch HD drive and one 3 1/2-inch ED drive—can read and write any disk format. When you upgrade, therefore, you should add these higher-density drives whenever possible.

DOS versions 3.3 or higher support both double-density and high-density drives. DOS versions 5.0 and higher support the newer ED 3 1/2-inch drives. DOS versions earlier than 3.3 support fewer drives and probably should not be used anymore. Table 12.4 lists the floppy disk support provided in each DOS version.

Table 12.4 DOS Version Floppy Disk Format Support

	DOS versions						
Supported disk formats	**1.0**	**1.1**	**2.0**	**3.0**	**3.2**	**3.3**	**5.0**
5 1/4-inch DD (160K)	✔	✔	✔	✔	✔	✔	✔
5 1/4-inch DD (180K)			✔	✔	✔	✔	✔
5 1/4-inch DD (320K)		✔	✔	✔	✔	✔	✔
5 1/4-inch DD (360K)			✔	✔	✔	✔	✔
5 1/4-inch HD (1.2M)				✔	✔	✔	✔
3 1/2-inch DD (720K)					✔	✔	✔
3 1/2-inch HD (1.44M)						✔	✔
3 1/2-inch ED (2.88M)							✔

Along with DOS support, the floppy drive controller is another issue of concern. Standard controllers in PC and XT systems support only double-density drives. To save money, consider adding only the double-density versions of the 5 1/4-inch and 3 1/2-inch drives to PC- or XT-type systems because they require no special controllers, cables, or software. DOS provides everything you need in the DRIVER.SYS driver file, which can be used to support the 3 1/2-inch 720K drive in systems without built-in ROM support for that drive.

The HD drives use a higher data rate (500 KHz) than do the DD drives (250 KHz). To use these higher-density drives, you must have a controller and software capable of supporting the higher data rate. Because the newer extra-high-density (ED) drives require a 1 MHz data rate, faster than most current controllers are capable of, you may need a controller upgrade to run those drives.

To use 1.2M or 1.44M drives in PC or XT systems, you must purchase a controller and software that can handle the high- or extra-high-density formats. Because the AT floppy controller already supports the 500 KHz data rate required by the 1.2M or 1.44M high-capacity drives, no additional controller is necessary. To upgrade your system with a newer 2.88M drive, however, you must have a new controller that supports the 1 MHz data rate.

The final issue to consider when you upgrade a floppy disk drive is BIOS support. Many older systems do not have BIOS support for the newer floppy disk drives. Therefore, even if you have the correct drive, controller, and DOS version, you still cannot use the drive correctly unless your BIOS supports it. Table 12.5 shows the IBM BIOS versions and the floppy disk drives they support.

Table 12.5 IBM BIOS Floppy Drive Support

Floppy BIOS support System description	ROM BIOS date	ID byte	Submodel byte	Revision	5 1/4 DD	5 1/4 HD	3 1/2 DD	3 1/2 HD	ED
PC	04/24/81	FF	—	—	✓				
PC	10/19/81	FF	—	—	✓				
PC	10/27/82	FF	—	—	✓				
PC-XT	11/08/82	FE	—	—	✓				
PC-XT	01/10/86	FB	00	01	✓		✓		
PC-XT	05/09/86	FB	00	02	✓		✓		
PS/2 25	06/26/87	FA	01	00	✓		✓		
PS/2 30	09/02/86	FA	00	00	✓		✓		
PS/2 30	12/12/86	FA	00	01	✓		✓		
PS/2 30	02/05/87	FA	00	02	✓		✓		
PC-AT	01/10/84	FC	—	—	✓		✓		
PC-AT	06/10/85	FC	00	01	✓	✓	✓		
PC-AT	11/15/85	FC	01	00	✓	✓	✓	✓	
PC-XT 286	04/21/86	FC	02	00	✓	✓	✓	✓	
PS/1	12/01/89	FC	0B	00	✓	✓	✓	✓	
PS/2 25-286	06/28/89	FC	09	02	✓	✓	✓		

(continues)

Table 12.5 Continued

Floppy BIOS support System description	ROM BIOS date	ID byte	Submodel byte	Revision	5 1/4 DD	5 1/4 HD	3 1/2 DD	3 1/2 HD	ED
PS/2 30-286	08/25/88	FC	09	00	✓	✓	✓	✓	
PS/2 30-286	06/28/89	FC	09	02	✓	✓	✓	✓	
PS/2 35 SX	03/15/91	F8	19	05	✓	✓	✓	✓	✓
PS/2 35 SX	04/04/91	F8	19	06	✓	✓	✓	✓	✓
PS/2 40 SX	03/15/91	F8	19	05	✓	✓	✓	✓	✓
PS/2 40 SX	04/04/91	F8	19	06	✓	✓	✓	✓	✓
PS/2 L40 SX	02/27/91	F8	23	02	✓	✓	✓	✓	
PS/2 50	02/13/87	FC	04	00	✓	✓	✓	✓	
PS/2 50	05/09/87	FC	04	01	✓	✓	✓	✓	
PS/2 50Z	01/28/88	FC	04	02	✓	✓	✓	✓	
PS/2 50Z	04/18/88	FC	04	03	✓	✓	✓	✓	
PS/2 55 SX	11/02/88	F8	0C	00	✓	✓	✓	✓	
PS/2 57 SX	07/03/91	F8	26	02	✓	✓	✓	✓	✓
PS/2 60	02/13/87	FC	05	00	✓		✓	✓	
PS/2 65 SX	02/08/90	F8	1C	00	✓		✓	✓	
PS/2 70 386	01/29/88	F8	09	00	✓	✓	✓	✓	
PS/2 70 386	04/11/88	F8	09	02	✓	✓	✓	✓	
PS/2 70 386	12/15/89	F8	09	04	✓	✓	✓	✓	
PS/2 70 386	01/29/88	F8	04	00	✓	✓	✓	✓	
PS/2 70 386	04/11/88	F8	04	02	✓	✓	✓	✓	
PS/2 70 386	12/15/89	F8	04	04	✓	✓	✓	✓	
PS/2 70 386	06/08/88	F8	0D	00	✓	✓	✓	✓	
PS/2 70 386	02/20/89	F8	0D	01	✓	✓	✓	✓	
PS/2 70 486	12/01/89	F8	0D	?	✓	✓	✓	✓	
PS/2 70 486	09/29/89	F8	1B	00	✓	✓	✓	✓	
PS/2 P70 386	?	F8	50	00	✓	✓	✓	✓	
PS/2 P70 386	01/18/89	F8	0B	00	✓	✓	✓	✓	
PS/2 P75 486	?	F8	52	00	✓	✓	✓	✓	✓
PS/2 80 386	03/30/87	F8	00	00	✓	✓	✓	✓	
PS/2 80 386	10/07/87	F8	01	00	✓	✓	✓	✓	
PS/2 80 386	11/21/89	F8	80	01	✓	✓	✓	✓	
PS/2 90 XP 486	?	F8	2D	00	✓	✓	✓	✓	✓
PS/2 90 XP 486	?	F8	2F	00	✓	✓			
PS/2 90 XP 486	?	F8	11	00	✓	✓			
PS/2 90 XP 486	?	F8	13	00	✓	✓			
PS/2 90 XP 486	?	F8	2B	00	✓	✓			
PS/2 95 XP 486	?	F8	2C	00	✓	✓	✓		

| **Floppy BIOS support** | | | | | 5 1/4 | | 3 1/2 | | |
System description	ROM BIOS date	ID byte	Submodel byte	Revision	DD	HD	DD	HD	ED
PS/2 95 XP 486	?	F8	2E	00	✔	✔			
PS/2 95 XP 486	?	F8	14	00	✔	✔			
PS/2 95 XP 486	?	F8	16	00	✔	✔			
PS/2 95 XP 486	?	F8	2A	00	4	4			

The ID byte, submodel byte, and revision numbers are in hexadecimal form.

Table 12.5 shows that the original PC-AT (01/10/84) BIOS supports only the 5 1/4-inch drives, and that the second revision (06/10/85) adds the 720K drive support. The final AT BIOS (11/15/85) supports the 1.44M drive as well. Some of this information is undocumented by IBM; in fact, IBM states that the AT never supported the 1.44M drives. However, 1.44M drives have been installed on hundreds of AT systems with a BIOS date of 11/15/85.

If your BIOS does not support a 720K drive, DOS can add support for a 720K drive by adding a DRIVPARM command in CONFIG.SYS. You also can load DRIVER.SYS by way of a command similar to DRIVPARM, for DOS versions that do not support the DRIVPARM command. For example, to support a 3 1/2-inch floppy disk drive on an older system without this support, you can use the following commands:

For a PC/XT-class system:

DRIVPARM=/D:1 /F:2 /I

For an AT-class system:

DRIVPARM=/D:1 /F:2 /I /C

The /D parameter indicates which physical drive unit is being specified; in this case, 1 equals B:. The /F parameter indicates a 720K drive format. The /I parameter indicates that this drive is not supported in the BIOS. The /C parameter indicates that the drive has Disk Changeline support: the drive can alert the controller that the disk has been changed. Because the PC/XT controllers do not support a disk change, you cannot use /C with those systems. As an alternative, especially if you are using versions of DOS 4.0 or earlier (which lack the DRIVPARM command), you can use DRIVER.SYS instead. The following example assumes your DOS files are in C:\DOS

For a PC/XT-class system:

DEVICE=C:\DOS\DRIVER.SYS /D:2 /F:2

For an AT-class system:

DEVICE=C:\DOS\DRIVER.SYS /D:2 /F:2 /C

Deciding whether to use DRIVPARM or DRIVER.SYS can be confusing for those who are new to personal computers. For example, the parameters for DRIVPARM and DRIVER.SYS are identical and their use has much the same effect. The primary difference in using DRIVPARM or DRIVER.SYS comes after you boot your machine.

Using DRIVPARM, the B: drive has the new, correct parameters, and functions as a normal 720K drive, as though your BIOS fully supported the drive. If you place a disk in the new drive and enter FORMAT B:, the drive properly formats the disk as a 720K disk without additional parameters.

However, it is not so simple if you use DRIVER.SYS. The new Drive B: acts as though it was a 360K drive; that is, if you execute a FORMAT B: command, DOS formats the 3 1/2-inch disk to 360K. This situation takes place because DRIVER.SYS creates a new drive letter to represent the 720K format of the new drive (one drive letter higher than your last hard disk partition letter) as a substitute letter for B. This new drive, which on a system with a C: drive is D:, operates properly as a 720K drive. When you execute the command FORMAT D:, the B: drive operates in 720K mode.

The solution to this floppy drive alphabet soup is to use DRIVPARM if your DOS version supports it. The first IBM DOS version to support DRIVPARM is 5.0. MS-DOS versions (and original equipment manufacturer versions) as early as 3.2 support the command.

DRIVPARM and DRIVER.SYS work only for adding 720K support to a system that does not have that support for the BIOS. The DRIVPARM and DRIVER.SYS commands do not work for adding 1.44M or 2.88M support to a system that lacks that support in the BIOS, even though the DOS manual seems to indicate that they work. In these cases, you must either purchase a third-party driver program or upgrade your BIOS to support the new drive. A BIOS upgrade is the recommended route to adding support for 1.44M or 2.88M drives.

PC and XT controllers can connect two floppy drives internally, through the supplied cable, and to two drives externally, through a cable you can purchase. The AT controller supports two floppy drives and two hard disks. If you add large-capacity floppy drives to a PC or XT system, you must have a new controller card and driver programs that operate with the card to support high-density drives. Numerous vendors offer these special controllers and software drivers, as well as complete kits for installing 360K, 720K, 1.44M, and even 2.88M drives in any PC, XT, or AT system.

Adding a High-Density Floppy Drive to an XT System

Adding high-density floppy drives (1.2M or 1.44M) to an XT-class (8088) machine can be a problem. Some people incorrectly believe that a new motherboard BIOS is necessary. It's not, because the XT BIOS and system hardware does not support high-density floppy drive operation.

Special high-density floppy controllers for XTs are available. These controllers, however, include their own ROM BIOS extension that provides the BIOS-level support tailored for their specific controller. The main BIOS normally has nothing to do with supporting a high-density drive on an XT.

In some cases, the BIOS extension on an XT high-density controller might not work properly with some motherboard BIOS versions; ask the controller manufacturer for verification. You know that the controller BIOS is having problems when you see phantom-directory problems—that is, problems with the controller recognizing the Disk Change signal. If you have this problem, contact the manufacturer of the controller. The manufacturer can recommend a solution, such as changing the BIOS on the controller card or installing a new motherboard BIOS. Of course, an incorrectly configured drive or bad cable also can cause these problems. Be sure to check your installation thoroughly.

Adding a Hard Disk to a System

When you add hard disks to a system, purchase the entire package from one company unless you are familiar with disk drive interfacing. Because certain interfaces have emerged as industry standards, it is possible to take the "plug and play" approach to selecting hard drives and interface cards. But for a novice to upgrading and repairing PCs, this can be a confusing process. The key is that your hard drive and your disk controller or interface card must be matched perfectly so that they work together in your system.

For example, older ESDI drives and controllers often experience significant compatibility problems unless the drive and the controller card are matched. Nearly all SCSI hard drives work with any SCSI host adapter, but to get the maximum performance from the drive and adapter combination you should ensure that they offer the same type of SCSI interface. For example, there is Standard SCSI, Fast SCSI, and Fast/Wide SCSI. The Fast and Fast/Wide versions are sometimes called SCSI-2, but not all drives or adapters advertised as SCSI-2 support Fast or Fast/Wide connections. Consult Chapter 10, "Hard Disk Drives," for more information about the SCSI interface and hard disks.

IDE drives are simple to install if they are the only drive in the system. Complications arise when you are attempting to use two IDE drives on one cable, or install an IDE drive in a system that also uses some other type of drive. Because the IDE specification was pretty loose until 1990, many older IDE drives have problems sharing a cable with the newer, more standard drives. If you are installing multiple IDE drives, or installing IDE drives to co-exist with other types of drives (ST-506/412, ESDI, or SCSI) in a single system, they you may encounter some problems. Some problems can be solved by using special IDE adapters that incorporate an on-board BIOS driver for support. Other problems such as installing two different manufacturer's drives on a single cable can require experimentation with master/slave jumpers and other jumper settings on the drive. In many cases you have to contact the respective drive manufacturers who can help you with the multiple drive configuration.

Differences between SCSI, IDE, ESDI, and old-style ST-506/412 interface can complicate the process of upgrading your hard drive. To learn more about different hard disk installations, be sure to familiarize yourself with the information in Chapter 10.

Speeding Up a System

This section examines ways to increase a system's speed. For example, a common and easy way to increase a system's calculating performance is to add a math coprocessor. Products advertised to make your system run faster are discussed also in this section, along with indications of their relative performance gains.

Another type of performance improvement involves increasing the system clock rate, changing the processor for another type, or both. The idea of replacing the processor with a faster one can extend to replacing the entire motherboard. In this case, you do not really upgrade your system—you change it entirely. This "extreme" upgrade is not always recommended. This section also examines the cost benefit of these upgrades.

Math Coprocessors

Adding a math coprocessor is an easy way to upgrade a system's performance with minimum effort. Be sure that the software you use supports these chips; they lighten your wallet only when they are specifically recognized and supported by software. Depending on how your motherboard is designed and the type of main processor you have, you can add the appropriate math coprocessor chip.

These chips are rated for different speeds of operation. Be sure that the chip you purchase is designed to operate at the clock rate at which the system runs the math chip. Be careful with static discharges when you handle these chips; the chips are delicate and expensive. For detailed information about math coprocessors, refer to Chapter 7.

A math coprocessor upgrade does not speed up all system operations, or even all math operations. For example, I created a sample Lotus spreadsheet consisting of 10,000 cells of multiplication, division, addition, and subtraction. It showed no improvement in speed in a system with a math coprocessor compared to a system without one. The overhead to have these math operations transferred to the coprocessor, executed, and returned is not worth the additional speed gained; most software packages that support the coprocessor do not use it for addition, subtraction, multiplication, or division operations.

Because of the transfer overhead, Lotus software does not use the math coprocessor for simple mathematical operations; rather, Lotus software calculates these kinds of instructions on the main processor. High-level math—such as exponentiation, trigonometry functions, and logarithms—are executed on the math coprocessor for an approximate tenfold increase in speed. As an upgrade, a math coprocessor is a very selective speed improvement. A math coprocessor works with software written specifically to recognize the coprocessor and only in limited areas within a program. A spreadsheet does not increase speed in all operations throughout a system.

To install a math coprocessor, follow these steps:

1. Turn off the system power.

2. Remove the system-unit cover assembly.

NEC V20 and V30 chip. A simple way to increase the performance of an 8088- or 8086-based system is to use the more efficient alternative processors produced by NEC— the NEC V20 and the NEC V30. These processors are plugged into the system as direct replacements for the original processors. The NEC unit selected varies according to the original processor type in the system. The processors are exchanged as follows:

Original processor	Replacement processor
Intel 8088	NEC V20
Intel 8086	NEC V30

These NEC chips were created several years ago when Intel could not meet the demand for the production of 8088 and 8086 chips. Intel licensed other manufacturers to make these chips. NEC, one of the manufacturers, was given the chip mask specifications for the Intel chips and complete access to the Intel processors' source code. NEC then created a new processor that mimics the Intel units but that is more efficient in several instructions. Intel has attempted to restrain NEC from manufacturing and importing these devices, but they remain available.

One problem with the NEC processor upgrades is that they are not 100 percent compatible with Intel units. The IBM PS/2 Models 25 and 30 cannot use the NEC chips, for example, and some of the special disk-duplicating programs that back up copy-protected disks do not work when the NEC chips are installed. In addition, the performance gain of upgrading to these chips is as little as 5 percent.

Because of the very small performance gain and the potential for both incompatibility and legal problems, business users probably should avoid purchasing NEC chips. You might want to consider this upgrade for a home or experimental system, however, because of its low cost. The following provides information about each of the NEC processor upgrades for the 8088 chip.

The original processor in an IBM XT is a 4.77 MHz 8088. The replacement, the NEC V20, is rated to run at 8 MHz but these chips operate properly on systems rated for the slower speed. The operating speed of the chip is controlled by the motherboard clock circuitry. The V30 chip works only on systems designed for the Intel 8086.

To install the NEC processor replacement, locate the 8088 or 8086 processor on the motherboard, remove the processor, and plug the NEC device into place. NEC chips are available for about $15 to $25, depending on the chip, the speed rating, and the retailer.

This processor upgrade is very inexpensive (about $15) and easy to install, but the speed increase is so small that it is difficult to detect. You should test-run applications and time different operations with a stopwatch to determine any time savings from using the new chip. The normal increase in performance is about 5 to 10 percent of the former speed. If an operation originally took 10 seconds to complete, the same operation takes 9 to 9 1/2 seconds with the new NEC chip. However, a 5 percent performance increase for only $15 is not bad.

Increasing the System Clock Rate. Another option for speeding up your PC or XT system is to increase the processor's clock rate. This type of upgrade is difficult to implement for PC or XT systems because the clock crystal cannot be easily altered or replaced. The crystal is soldered, not socketed, in place, and the crystal is multiplexed—that is, it is used for other functions besides running the system clock.

The crystal in an IBM XT, for example, is a 14.31818 MHz unit whose frequency is divided by 3 by the timer circuits to generate the 4.77 MHz system clock. This 14.31818 MHz crystal frequency also is on the system bus (slot) connectors at Pin B30. (This signal is one of the PC bus specifications.) Many cards, such as video boards, depend on this oscillator signal to be present for their operation. The oscillator signal is divided by 4 to obtain a 3.58 MHz signal used to drive circuits in the Color Graphics Adapter. An upgrade that attempts to increase the clock rate of the main processor, therefore, probably would interfere with the original crystal and its subset function of generating a 14.31818 MHz oscillator signal for the system bus.

Several years ago, some devices sold for PC and XT systems could increase the clock rate for the main processor without interfering with other circuits on the motherboard. These devices have been unavailable for some time. A much better alternative is to install an in-circuit emulator (ICE) board or a processor-enhancement card that has a 286 or 386 processor on board, or by replacing the entire motherboard.

In-Circuit Emulator (ICE) Boards. You can upgrade your PC/XT system with an In-Circuit Emulator (ICE) board that serves as an entire replacement for the 8086 or 8088 CPU chip. An ICE board plugs into one of the system's expansion slots and has a cable that plugs into the microprocessor socket from which the CPU chip has been removed. The ICE board has a 286 or 386 processor running at a high clock rate, as well as high-speed, 16- or 32-bit memory on board. The ICE board takes over the system as though it were a new processor. These boards are a relatively economical system upgrade given that they provide a tremendous performance boost.

Another feature of some of the better ICE boards is that you can install your original 8086 or 8088 processor on the ICE board. For compatibility and reliability testing, you can then use the original processor to run the system.

To install an ICE board, follow these steps:

1. Remove the main processor from the motherboard. In some units, you install the processor on the speedup board. Other units require that you store the original processor for safekeeping.

2. Plug the speedup board into an open slot, preferably next to the processor socket.

3. Run a cable from the board to the processor socket, and plug in the cable.

The installation is complete. These units have their own on-board memory, a full complement of 640K, or a small amount of cache memory. The high-speed memory is directly accessible by the 80286 or 80386 processor on the speedup board. Your system memory still is used on some of these units.

Most of these boards do not convert a PC or XT into an AT-type system with the capability to address 16M of memory and run OS/2 or perform other AT functions, but they give a PC or XT system the speed of an AT system.

Replacing the PC/XT Motherboard. Another way of increasing system speed is to replace the original PC/XT motherboard. Replacing motherboards can convert a PC-type system into an AT design, but you must replace many other items to complete the procedure. By the time you complete and pay for this conversion, you probably could buy a complete AT-compatible system and leave your PC/XT alone. You also could sell the PC or XT system and use the money for options on the new AT, or donate it to charity and take the tax break. Because of the cost, complexity, and numerous compatibility problems with other system components and accessories, motherboard replacement should be considered on PC/XT-type systems only in special cases, and then when money is no object.

Complete motherboard replacements consist of placing a complete AT-type motherboard of 286, 386, or 486-based design in your original PC/XT case. The replacement motherboard usually has 16-bit ISA—or even 32-bit EISA—slots. The original AT motherboard was much larger than the PC or XT motherboards. Normally, you cannot find a full-size AT-style motherboard to fit a PC case because the PC has openings for only five slots in the back of the case, and the slot spacing is different from that of an XT or AT system. Replacement AT-type motherboards that fit an XT case usually are called "baby AT" designs.

Installing a replacement motherboard is relatively difficult, but only because you must disassemble the entire system to replace the motherboard and then reassemble the system. It is important when undertaking this kind of a task that you mark all data and control cables, to remind yourself which cables work with which device. It also is a good idea to mark the power connectors, particularly those that plug into the motherboard itself (usually marked P8 and P9), to help you remember the orientation of these connectors. If you install the motherboard power connectors backward you may ruin the new motherboard.

The idea of replacing the motherboard sounds attractive at first, especially when you see the low prices on some of the replacement motherboards. But problems occur when you reassemble the rest of your old system. For example, are you going to use that XT hard disk controller in what is now an AT system? If you do, you get XT hard drive performance on a fast AT system. This list shows some additional issues and problems you encounter when you create a "hybrid" system that is part AT and part XT:

■ You must tell the Setup program that no hard disks are installed so that your XT controller's built-in ROM BIOS can operate the card properly.

■ The XT controller uses Interrupt 5, which conflicts with a second parallel port (LPT2:) in the AT.

■ Your XT floppy controller does not support the high-density drives required to boot and run OS/2 and other software.

- For proper AT and OS/2 operation, you must change all your serial ports to those with a 16450 or 16550A UART chip.

- Any memory you already have in the XT system probably does not work properly in an AT, including both chips and complete memory cards.

Replacing the motherboard has other disadvantages over the ICE board upgrade discussed in preceding sections. The biggest disadvantage is that you have many more items to replace or upgrade after replacing the motherboard; many peripherals and components used in XT systems, that continue to work just fine after you install an ICE board, are not suitable for an AT-type system.

Another disadvantage is that you are losing your original system; if you encounter a compatibility that prompts you to switch back to your old system configuration, it means removal of the new motherboard and reinstallation of the old. No "switch" can enable you to use your old processor until you work out conflicts or other compatibility problems, as in some ICE board designs.

286 Systems. Upgrading AT-class systems is much simpler than upgrading PC- or XT-type systems because you have fewer alternatives to consider. Also, the motherboard replacement upgrade in an AT system works well because you start and end with an AT-class system. You do not have to change other system components such as disk controllers, drives, serial ports, memory, keyboards, and so on.

AT-type systems have primarily three levels of upgrade. The following lists these three levels of upgrade:

- Increase the clock rate of the CPU by replacing the crystal oscillator with a faster one.

- Replace the existing processor with an In-Circuit Emulator (ICE) board.

- Replace the motherboard with one containing a more powerful processor.

These upgrades are described in the following sections.

Increasing an AT System's Clock Rate. The IBM decision to socket the clock crystal in the PC AT met with much interest and speculation when the machine first appeared. The ability to easily unplug and replace the crystal is the key factor in attempting to increase an AT's clock rate. By increasing the speed of the system beyond what it was originally designed for can result in a somewhat unstable system. A lot depends on how far you want to push.

Increasing system speed from 6 MHz to 8 MHz, or from 8 MHz to 10 MHz, is relatively conservative, and usually enables the system to operate without problems. Attempting to increase the system beyond this amount, however, can result in erratic or flaky system operation. The type of upgrade described in this section is what I call a "hacker" upgrade—suitable for people who want to experiment with their systems, but probably unsuitable for people with a system used in a business environment.

Because the crystal is not multiplexed as it is in PC or XT systems (it does not perform functions other than regulating the system clock speed), replacing it does not disturb other areas of the system. The oscillator signal required for Pin B30 in the expansion-bus connectors is generated independently by a 14.31818 MHz crystal that is separate from the main clock crystal on the motherboard. To minimize radio interference, the bus oscillator crystal is under a large, square piece of metal shielding. Because the two oscillators are separate, you can replace the processor clock crystal with a faster one and not interfere with the rest of the system. Upgrading an AT system's clock crystal is inexpensive because you don't have to supply any additional clock circuitry.

The main system clock crystal is in a 1/2-inch-by-3/8-inch silver housing that plugs into the socket near the 80286 chip, behind the center opening for the hard disk. To remove the crystal, you insert a small screwdriver between the crystal and the socket, push the crystal out of the socket, and lift the crystal up and out of the retaining clip. You can insert a faster crystal to increase the operating speed of the 80286 CPU chip driven at half the crystal's speed.

For a few dollars, you can buy a 16 MHz replacement crystal and plug it into the system in place of the original 12 MHz crystal used in the original AT Models 068 and 099. Remember that because the 80286 internally divides the system-clock crystal frequency by 2, it runs at half the crystal speed. The system then runs at 8 MHz, a 30 percent improvement in processing speed. If the 16 MHz crystal works and your system runs well at 8 MHz, you can try different crystals of increasing speeds to see how far your system can go. Some systems tolerate running at speeds as high as 10 MHz, depending on several factors. You know that you have exceeded your system's capabilities if it locks up or otherwise experiences erratic operation. If your system doesn't run at a certain speed, just reinstall the last crystal that worked properly.

The type of crystal used by IBM in the AT has a large case and thick, gold-plated leads that may differ from what you find at your local electronic-parts store. The standard crystal IBM used is a series mode, AT-cut, fundamental crystal with an HC-25/U case, and .01 percent frequency tolerance. *AT-cut* refers to the angle at which the quartz inside the crystal is sliced, and has nothing to do with AT-type computers. Any good crystal vendor should be able to supply this type of crystal.

Installing Faster RAM in an AT. If you want to try for more speed than your system seems to allow, you can experiment further to increase the maximum running speed by replacing system memory with higher-speed RAM chips. The standard-speed chip in most AT systems is 150 nanoseconds. If you replace all the memory with 120- or 100-nanosecond chips, you might be able to take the extra step to 10 MHz or more.

However, this upgrade is ineffective, and is a waste of money. The one instance in which replacing your system memory with faster RAM chips is likely to result in a faster system is if the system manufacturer installed slow RAM on a motherboard that is rated for fast RAM. For example, if a system rated for 80ns RAM chips had 150ns chips installed in the factory, you could probably get a significant performance boost by installing 80ns chips. But remember, you have to replace all the RAM chips on the motherboard if you decide to try this upgrade.

Replacing an AT's CPU Chip. You can replace the processor on a slower AT with one rated to run at higher speeds. For example, replace the 80286-6 with an 80286-10 or 80286-12. This upgrade also requires the installation of a clock crystal of greater frequency than the one used by your 6MHz 80286 chip. Don't forget that the math coprocessor, if you have one, also might have to be replaced with a faster chip.

This simple crystal swap works only in the original AT models with ROM BIOS dated 01/01/84. You cannot change the crystal speed of systems with 06/10/85 or 11/15/85 ROM BIOS dates, or the POST detects the crystal change and automatically fails the motherboard test. You hear the audio code for motherboard failure: one long and one short beep. Fortunately, this failure is only temporary. When you reinstall the original crystal, the system works OK. The failed POST results from intentional changes IBM made to the POST routines in later ROM versions.

If you want to swap CPU chips and clock chips on systems with BIOS dated later than 01/01/84, the simplest way around the POST speed check is to replace the IBM ROM BIOS with a BIOS from Phoenix, AMI, or Award. Or you can remove the test from the IBM BIOS by changing the ROM BIOS code and reprogramming a new chip as detailed in the section of this chapter titled "Removing the POST Speed Check."

Several years ago, some companies had developed variable-speed devices that throttle the system up and down by twisting a knob. These devices also could monitor the system-reset line to detect a reboot operation, and automatically kicked the system into low gear until the POST was passed, thus working around the speed test. These devices unfortunately cost much more than a simple crystal change, and have for the most part been discontinued.

386 and 486 Processor Upgrade Boards For AT Systems. Various manufacturers have produced modular-design AT-type computers, designed to enable you to replace a small daughtercard containing the processor. In this processor-complex design, the main processor and support chips reside on a replaceable card, with the majority of system circuits still on the motherboard. In effect, you have a modular motherboard design. Usually at considerable expense, this processor card can be replaced with one containing a more powerful processor. Some of these modular systems enable you to replace your 286 chip with a 386. Others enable you to upgrade all the way to a 486, providing you with a lengthy upgrade path.

If you have a processor complex AT motherboard design, contact the manufacturer of the system to determine the cost of an upgrade.

In-Circuit Emulator Boards for ATs are not as diverse or complicated as the (ICE) boards for PC/XT type systems. AT upgrade boards normally act as direct processor replacements: They plug into the processor socket and do not take up a slot like ICE boards. You install these processor upgrade boards by removing the 286 chip and installing an upgrade module in the 286 socket. Processor upgrade boards are available that use the 386SX, 386DX, 486SX, or 486DX chips running at various clock speeds. Some 386-based boards have sockets for math coprocessor chips.

Because some of these upgrade boards have had compatibility problems with the original IBM AT BIOS, most are supplied with a set of aftermarket BIOS chips as well. In many cases, these new BIOS chips also amount to an upgrade, because the new BIOS gives you enhancements discussed earlier in this chapter, including enhanced hard disk drive support and floppy drive support.

Several processor upgrade boards are on the market, including quality offerings from Intel, Kingston, and Sigma Data (addresses and phone numbers for these companies are in the vendor list in the appendix of this book).

These processor-upgrade modules are a relatively simple and effective way to double the performance of older AT computers.

Replacing the AT Motherboard. You can choose from many motherboard replacements for AT systems, most of which use 486 processors, and some of which include Zero Insertion Force (ZIF) Overdrive sockets that accept the Pentium Overdrive chip when it is released. Motherboard upgrades for an AT system do not share the same problems as in upgrading an XT in this manner because you do not have to worry about changing other system components to be compatible with the new motherboard. In general, because you are both starting and ending with an AT-class system, you do not have to worry about changing the existing disk controller, memory, serial ports, floppy controller, or floppy drives because they are already AT devices.

Be sure that the board you purchase has the correct screw holes for mounting in the existing chassis. Most AT replacement motherboards include both AT and XT form-factor mounting holes, to enable the boards to be mounted in a variety of system chassis. Some higher-performance upgrade motherboards work only in an AT chassis because they exploit the full AT motherboard form factor, and are designed specifically for only the larger AT case.

For a list of recommendations for what to look for in a motherboard, see Chapter 5.

386 Systems. The modular-design AT-type computer became most popular when the 486 was first introduced and 386 buyers, who often did not want to pay the high price of a 486 during the first months it was available, still wanted an upgrade path to the more powerful processor chip. As with 286-based modular systems, on a processor-complex 386 the CPU chip and some support circuitry are placed on a separate card that plugs into the motherboard.

As with 286-based modular systems, replacing the 386 CPU card with one equipped with a 486 chip can be quite expensive. Contact the manufacturer of the system to determine the cost of an upgrade.

Various manufacturers provide upgrades for 386-based systems. Among the most common are plug-in boards containing a 486SX or 486DX chip. This plug-in card usually requires you to unplug the 386 from the motherboard and plug in a card containing the new processor and support circuitry. Some upgrade cards also require you to plug an adapter board into one of your system slots with a cable running to the replacement CPU chip card. The cost of these upgrade cards varies depending on the manufacturer.

In addition, CPU and math chip manufacturer Cyrix produces what the company terms a 486 chip that plugs directly into a 386 CPU socket. The Cyrix 486 chip, marketed by various companies, is quite inexpensive (roughly $200) and, although it does not give 386-based computers all the speed of a 486, it does considerably increase the 386's speed.

486 Systems. Upgrades for 486-based systems are so diverse it almost takes a scorecard to keep up with them. Within the family of 486 chips, upgrades include a wide range of chips, which, more than anything, reflects a desire on the part of computer buyers to remain, somehow, on the cutting edge of technology in an age when the fastest computer chip changes every couple of years. Upgrades for 486-based systems include these options:

- 486SX to 486DX (by way of the so-called 487 upgrade)

- 486SX to 486DX (through direct CPU chip replacement)

- Slow clock-speed 486 to a faster 486 (for example, a 25MHz to a 50MHz)

- Normally clocked CPU chip to the clock-doubled (DX2 chips) chip

- Normally clocked CPU or clock-doubled CPU to clock-tripled CPU

- 486 to Pentium (by way of the Pentium Overdrive chip)

Sorting out all these chips and chip designation numbers is quite difficult for someone who has better things to do than read computer magazines all day. But the following provides some general guidelines on CPU upgrades for 486-based systems.

486SX to 486DX. Generally speaking, a system based on the 486SX chip can be upgraded in two ways. The most common way to upgrade a 486SX-based system is by filling the empty CPU socket known as the Overdrive Socket with a 487 upgrade. As detailed in Chapter 7, the 487 upgrade is a fully functional 486 chip (with math coprocessor functions intact) which, when plugged into the Overdrive socket, disables the original SX chip. The second route, supported on some 486SX-based systems but not all, involves removing the 486SX chip and replacing it with a 486DX chip. Before the second choice is available, the motherboard must have been designed to accept not only the 486SX but also the 486DX. Upgrading these motherboards may also require you to replace the system clock chip. For information on the compatibility of these two upgrade options with your system, contact the manufacturer.

Slow Clock-Speed 486 to a Faster 486. Some 486 motherboards enable you to replace a slower clock-speed 486 CPU chip with a faster 486 chip. For example, these motherboards can support an upgrade from a 25 MHz 486DX chip to a 50 MHz 486DX chip. Manufacturers often do not advertise that their motherboards support this upgrade, but many computer makers use motherboards that accept various speed 486 chips because it is less expensive to purchase a single motherboard design that supports all the chips the manufacturer plans to use, rather than various CPU-speed-specific motherboard designs.

For information on whether your system supports a direct upgrade from a slower clock-speed 486 CPU to a faster chip, you should consult your system documentation. If the motherboard manual discusses configuring for various speed CPU chips, chances are it is possible for you to upgrade to the fastest CPU the motherboard supports. It is important to note that this type of upgrade also may require replacement of your system clock chip and ROM-BIOS chip. If this kind of upgrade appeals to you, contact your motherboard manufacturer to find out what is involved in swapping CPU chips. When it comes time to purchase a new CPU chip, be sure to shop around. Mail order chip vendors sell the same Intel CPU chips as system manufacturers, so shopping solely based on price is a good idea.

Normally-Clocked CPU Chip to Clock-Doubled (DX2 chips) Chip. The most common route to greater speed and power with a 486-based system is upgrading from a normally-clocked CPU chip, for example upgrading a 33MHz DX to 66MHz DX2. Intel designed the DX2 line of chips, which operate externally at the original 25MHz or 33MHz chip speed but internally run at twice the speed, so that these chips would work in existing motherboard designs. The DX2 chip greatly speeds up 486-based systems.

As mentioned in the previous section, the motherboards on many computer systems accept various speed 486 chips, so a direct replacement of the CPU with its clock-doubled version is possible. However, upgrading a DX-based system to a DX2 chip is not always "plug and play." Replacing the existing CPU chip with its internally faster twin also can require you to replace the system clock chip and ROM-BIOS chips. But usually this is not necessary because externally the CPU continues to communicate with system circuitry at the speed of the original CPU chip. This upgrade is not possible on some motherboards because the motherboard design does not support it.

Many manufacturers of systems that support upgrading from a normally-clocked 486 chip to a fast 486DX2 include a special CPU chip socket on the motherboard. This socket, called a Zero Insertion Force (ZIF) socket, enables you to easily remove the old CPU chip and replace it with a faster one. Some manufacturers even allow you to trade in your old 486 CPU chip on the faster one.

486SX, DX, or DX/2 to Clock-Tripled 486. The clock-tripled 486 CPU chip is another attempt to squeeze greater and greater speed out of existing motherboard designs. For example, IBM is marketing the fastest 486 chip on the market—a 99MHz clock-tripled 486 CPU chip called "Blue Lightning." Like the Intel DX2 chips, Blue Lightning communicates externally with system peripherals at 33MHz. But internally, Blue Lightning runs at 99MHz. IBM is marketing the chip as 1/3 faster for the same price as DX2-66. The company also is marketing a 25/75 MHz version of the chip. IBM's chip offers twice the internal cache of Intel's 486DX2, helping to make this chip efficient at high speeds.

Some industry analysts expect Blue Lightning to compete with the Pentium for use on laptop systems. The Blue Lightning uses only half the power and 2/3 the voltage of a DX2, making it ideal for laptop and notebook computers. Blue Lightning also conserves battery power with a "sleep mode" that enables the processor and other components to suspend active operation if the computer is idle for a certain time. Blue Lightning also is used on some non-IBM systems.

Intel has announced what is being called the 486DX3-99, a clock-tripled chip based on the 33 MHz DX 486. Intel also is considering marketing a DX2/100 clock-doubled chip based on the 50 MHz 486 DX.

The clock-tripled CPU chips, although they are most likely to be used in new mid-price desktop systems and high-end notebooks and laptops, could find an application as an upgrade for systems based on normally-clocked and clock-doubled CPU chips, and some 486SX systems, particularly those with ZIF sockets. Some systems would require a new clock chip and ROM-BIOS for the upgrade. Using this upgrade path may not be possible on some systems because of motherboard design limitations.

Upgrading to a clock-tripled chip should be attempted only by a technically aware computer user. If you want to make this kind of upgrade, consult some of the more trustworthy computer magazines before purchasing the chip. It will be helpful to know the pros and cons of this upgrade as they become known.

486 to Pentium. For some time, now, the hottest marketing tool for 486 system manufacturers has been the Pentium Upgrade socket, a ZIF socket specifically designed to accept the Pentium Overdrive chip, which has yet to be released by Intel. Nearly every computer manufacturer is marketing systems with the promise that you can buy a 486 now and upgrade to a Pentium later. This upgrade is likely to be simple plug-and-play on systems designed for it. You should be able to flip the lever on the ZIF socket, gently slide out the old CPU chip, and, after properly orienting and inserting the new Pentium, enjoy the benefits of greatly enhanced system performance.

Compatibility problems of this upgrade, if any, are not known at of the time of this writing. However, many system manufacturers are relying heavily on the Pentium Overdrive being easier than any previous CPU upgrade.

Adding High-Performance Video

Adding a high-resolution video adapter and monitor is a great way to breathe some life into a system. This type of upgrade, however, can be expensive. High-resolution, color-graphics monitors cost between $500 and several thousand dollars, depending primarily on the resolution and size of the monitor. Video adapters usually cost less than monitors, anywhere from well under $100 to $500 or more, but some of today's cutting-edge video adapters are quite costly. For detailed information on video cards and monitors, please refer to Chapter 8, "Secondary System Components."

At the core of the decision to upgrade your monitor and display adapter is how you plan to use your system. For example, if you use primarily DOS-based text-mode applications you probably do not need one of today's large-screen edge-to-edge monitors or the high-end video adapters that drive them. However, if you use a graphical user interface such as Windows or OS/2, you find that a large screen monitor and a fast video card are near-necessities. Nothing in life seems so slow as scrolling through a lengthy document in a Windows word processor using a common VGA adapter. The adapter card just cannot keep up with the incredible number of pixels it takes to repaint a Windows screen. A problem with running Windows at normal VGA resolution (640x480), is that you have to constantly scroll from side-to-side in a document to read each line. In VGA resolution, word processors can display only about 4/5 the width of a page.

The hottest video adapters for Windows and other GUIs are VESA-Standard Local Bus (VLB) video cards. These cards plug into a special VESA slot in motherboards designed with them, and are capable of boosting video output to an incredible degree. The Diamond Viper, for example, one of the fastest of the Windows local bus video adapters, can paint as many as 43 million pixels per second onto your screen in real world uses of the card (of course, the company advertises that the card is even faster). Other companies also make extremely fast VLB adapters.

If your system doesn't have a VLB slot, you can speed up Windows and other GUIs by adding a graphics accelerator card to your ISA-based system. The Orchid Fahrenheit VA card is capable of painting 14 million pixels per second onto your screen in real world uses (even greater performance is claimed by the manufacturer). Numerous other companies market graphics accelerator cards designed to speed up your video in popular GUIs.

As mentioned previously, running a GUI in 640x480 (VGA) resolution can be a problem that not only makes work harder, but makes you less productive. Scrolling from side to side in a word processor to just read an entire line of a document, for example, is hardly a performance enhancement. In fact it's the kind of thing that can make the workday seem as if it will never end.

Today's 17-inch high-resolution monitors enable you to run your system in Super VGA mode (800x600 resolution), which allows you to view an entire line of a document without scrolling back and forth (as well as viewing more lines of the page).

Modern video adapters and high-resolution monitors not only make your work go more quickly, they also enable you to work with graphic images containing millions of colors. Although not everyone needs the capabilities to view photographic images on their monitor, many computer users do make use of this capability.

Adding a Hardware Reset Switch

A switch that applies a full reset to your system keeps power moving to the system and rescues you from a system lockup. A reset switch saves much time and some of the wear and tear on your unit from using the power switch as a reset button. Of course, IBM and most compatible vendors have built reset circuitry into the motherboard, and have added reset switches to the front of the computer case. But if you don't already have a reset switch, the following section teaches you how to add one. The hardest part of adding a reset switch to your system is figuring out where to mount it.

Adding a reset button is possible on any system, including all IBM systems, because it has a power supply that provides a Power Good signal. On most IBM-compatible computers, the Power Good signal is on the connector that plugs into the rearmost power-supply connectors. In PC and XT systems, this signal traces through the motherboard to the 8284a chip at Pin 11. When the line is shorted to ground and returned to normal, the 8284a (82284 in an AT) clock-timer chip generates a reset signal on Pin 10. The reset signal is sent to the 8088 at Pin 21, and the boot process begins. In other systems with different processors and timer chips, for example, AT or PS/2 systems, the Power Good signal also initiates a reset if the signal is grounded and returned to normal, although the wiring details vary.

In all IBM-compatible systems, when the CPU is reset, it begins to execute code at memory location F000:FFF0, known as the power-up reset vector. An immediate jump instruction at this location sends the CPU's instruction pointer to the start location for the particular system ROM. The system then begins the POST. The processor and DMA chips are tested first, but before initiating the full POST memory test, the memory location 0000:0472 is compared to the value 1234h. If they are equal, a *warm* start is indicated and the POST memory tests are skipped. If any other value is there, a *cold* start forces all memory to be tested.

This procedure is the basis of an effective reset switch. By setting the flag value at memory location 0000:0472, you can have the system perform either a cold or warm start when you press a reset button. The type of reset, a hardware reset, "unfreezes" a locked-up machine, unlike the Ctrl-Alt-Del software reset command.

To add a reset switch, you need these parts:

- Six inches of thin (about 20-gauge) insulated wire

- A single-pole, normally open, momentary-contact push-button switch

The idea behind installing a reset switch is to run a momentary-contact switch parallel with the Power Good line and ground. To do so, follow these steps:

1. Remove from the motherboard the power-supply connector containing the Power Good signal.

   Look in your technical-reference manual to make sure that you have the right connector and can identify the signal wire containing the Power Good signal. Sometimes this information also is on a sticker attached to the power supply.

2. Poke the stripped end of a wire into the hole in the power-supply connector in which the Power Good signal is carried.

3. Plug the connector, with the wire inserted, back into the motherboard.

4. Run the other end of the wire under one of the screws that secures the motherboard. The screw serves as a ground.

5. Cut the wire in the middle, bare the ends, and attach the stripped wire ends to the normally open, single-pole, momentary-contact push-button switch.

6. Run the wire and the switch outside the case.

You should now have a functioning reset button. You can mount the switch to an available place in the unit, such as an empty card bracket, in which you can drill a small hole to accept the switch.

A simple button and wire are sufficient for adding a reset switch, but as a safety precaution you can place a 1/4-watt resistor with a value between 1K ohms and 2.7K ohms in-line with the wire from the Power Good line to the switch. The reason for adding the resistor is that the Power Good signal is provided by a PNP transistor inside the power supply with its emitter connected to the +5 volt signal. Without the resistor, shorting the Power Good signal to ground for a long period can burn out the transistor.

When you press the switch, you initiate the boot sequence. The boot process that occurs (warm or cold) depends on the status of memory location 0000:0472. The value at this location is 0000h when you first power up the system and until you press Ctrl-Alt-Del for the first time. If the last boot operation was a cold boot (an initial power-on), every subsequent time you press the reset button a cold boot occurs. After you press Ctrl-Alt-Del once to initiate a manual warm-boot sequence, every subsequent time you press the reset button you initiate a warm boot that skips the memory tests. To eliminate the need to press Ctrl-Alt-Del after you start the system every day to "set" the reset button for subsequent warm boot operations, you can enter a program using DEBUG that produces a WARMSET.COM program to run in your AUTOEXEC.BAT file. This simple program quickly sets the memory flag to indicate that a warm boot should be initiated when the reset switch is pressed.

To create WARMSET.COM, be sure that you have the DEBUG program available in the path, and enter these commands at the DOS prompt:

```
C:\>DEBUG
-N WARMSET.COM
-A 100
xxxx:0100 MOV AX,0040
xxxx:0103 MOV DS,AX
xxxx:0105 MOV WORD PTR [0072],1234
xxxx:010B INT 20
xxxx:010D
-R CX
CX 0000
:D
-W
Writing 0000D bytes
-Q
```

Unlike the Ctrl-Alt-Del combination, the hardware reset cannot be ignored by your system no matter how locked up the system is.

The Phoenix BIOS sets the warm-boot flag during every boot sequence, regardless of whether it's warm or cold. Immediately after power-up, therefore, the flag is zero, which causes the standard POST test to run. Immediately after the POST, the Phoenix BIOS sets the flag for a warm boot, because many compatibles that use the Phoenix BIOS have a reset button already integrated into the system. The reset button works in the same way as the button you can construct. Because of the warm boot flag's automatic setting, a warm boot occurs every time you press the reset button no matter what the previous boot was. If you want a cold boot to occur (including POST), you can create a COLDSET.COM program also using DEBUG.

To create COLDSET.COM, enter these commands:

```
C:\>DEBUG
-N COLDSET.COM
-A 100
xxxx:0100 MOV AX,0040
xxxx:0103 MOV DS,AX
xxxx:0105 MOV WORD PTR [0072],0000
xxxx:010B INT 20
xxxx:010D
-R CX
CX 0000
:D
-W
Writing 0000D bytes
-Q
```

This procedure causes a reset button to initiate a cold boot with POST tests no matter which BIOS you have. An interesting variation on these programs is to produce two additional companion programs called WARMBOOT.COM and COLDBOOT.COM. As their names indicate, they go one step farther than the WARMSET.COM and COLDSET.COM programs: They not only set the flag but also cause an immediate boot. You might wonder why you would need that operation when you can just press Ctrl-Alt-Del or turn the power off and on to reboot the system? The answer is that with these programs you can initiate the boot you want from a batch file with no operator intervention.

I use the WARMBOOT.COM program in batch files that copy new CONFIG.SYS files to my root directory, and then reboot the system automatically to initiate the new configuration. For example, one batch file copies a CONFIG.SYS file, which loads local area network (LAN) drivers as well as a new AUTOEXEC.BAT file to the root directory of the C: drive. The AUTOEXEC.BAT file has commands that automatically log on to the network. In seconds, my network is up and running, and I am automatically logged in, with only one command. You probably can come up with other uses for these programs.

To create WARMBOOT.COM, enter these commands:

```
C:\>DEBUG
-N WARMBOOT.COM
-A 100
xxxx:0100 MOV AX,0040
xxxx:0103 MOV DS,AX
```

```
xxxx:0105 MOV WORD PTR [0072],1234
xxxx:010B JMP FFFF:0
xxxx:0110
-R CX
CX 0000
:10
-W
Writing 00010 bytes
-Q
```

To create COLDBOOT.COM, enter these commands:

```
C:\>DEBUG
-N COLDBOOT.COM
-A 100
xxxx:0100 MOV AX,0040
xxxx:0103 MOV DS,AX
xxxx:0105 MOV WORD PTR [0072],0000
xxxx:010B JMP FFFF:0
xxxx:0110
-R CX
CX 0000
:10
-W
Writing 00010 bytes
-Q
```

Whether or not you have a reset button, the WARMBOOT.COM and COLDBOOT.COM programs can be useful.

Upgrading the DOS Version

An upgrade many users overlook is an upgrade to a new version of an operating system. You can complicate a DOS upgrade by using different OEM versions of DOS, but normally you should not have to reformat your hard disk when you upgrade from one version of DOS to another. If you are using nonstandard drivers or other non-DOS support programs, you might have to format the disk or use Norton Utilities or some other low-level utility to modify the disk's boot sector and root directory. This modification enables the SYS command in the new version to operate properly.

You can perform an operating-system upgrade in several ways. One is to use the automatic installation and upgrade facility built in to DOS. The automatic DOS upgrade and installation utility that comes with DOS 6.0 works well. If you want to upgrade on your own, following the set of simple instructions in the next section completes the upgrade in a relatively short amount of time.

To repartition your hard disk at the same time you are upgrading to a new DOS version, you must back up your entire hard disk, repartition and reformat it, and then restore all your original files. Then you can install the new version of DOS over your original (restored) version. Depending on the type of backup hardware you use, this procedure can be somewhat time-consuming.

Upgrading DOS the Easy Way

To perform a DOS-version upgrade the easy way, follow these steps:

1. Boot the new DOS version from drive A:.

2. Transfer the system files to C: with this command:

    SYS C:

3. Locate the DOS disk with the REPLACE program, insert it in drive A:, and execute this command:

    COPY REPLACE.* C:

4. Use this command to replace all DOS transient files on C: with new versions in all subdirectories and enable read-only files to be overwritten:

    C:REPLACE A:*.* C: /S /R

> ### Caution
>
> This command replaces any file on the C: drive with a file of the same name on the DOS disks, no matter where on the C: drive the file is located. Any files on C: that have the same name as any of the DOS files on A: therefore are overwritten by this command.

5. Change the disk in drive A: to the second DOS floppy disk, and repeat the preceding step until you have inserted all the DOS floppy disks.

6. Place the DOS boot disk back in drive A:.

7. Add any new DOS transient files to the C:\DOS directory with this command (if you have a C:\DOS directory already in place on the hard disk):

    C:REPLACE A:*.* C:\DOS /A

8. Replace the boot disk with the second DOS floppy disk, and repeat the preceding step until you have inserted all DOS floppy disks.

When you are finished, the system is capable of booting the new DOS version from the hard disk. This method ensures that all previous DOS files are overwritten by new versions, no matter in which subdirectories they are located.

If you use a directory other than C:\DOS to store your DOS program files, replace C:\DOS in the preceding steps with that directory. If you have problems with the SYS command, your original installation probably has a problem, which must be repaired before you can proceed. Note that the SYS commands in DOS 4.0 and higher versions are more tolerant of different configurations on the destination drive. If you have problems, I recommend *Que's Guide to Data Recovery* for additional information on this subject.

Upgrading DOS the Hard Way

You must use the more difficult method of upgrading a DOS version to take advantage of newer DOS-version disk formatting capabilities. A common use for this method is upgrading from DOS 3.3 to 5.0, with a hard disk larger than 32 megabytes in capacity. Because DOS V3.3 could create disk partitions a maximum of only 32M in capacity, the disk must be currently partitioned into several volumes. Because DOS V5.0 allows partitions as large as 2 gigabytes, it's a good idea to use the upgrade as an opportunity to condense the multiple partitions into one partition that matches the total capacity of the drive.

This method requires first backing up the data on all the partitions because the existing partitions must be destroyed and re-created as a single partition.

To perform a DOS-version upgrade using the full backup, format, and restore method, follow these steps:

1. Boot the system from the original (older) version of DOS.

2. Execute a complete backup of all partitions using the backup method of your choice.

3. Boot the new version of DOS.

4. Use the new DOS FDISK command to remove the existing DOS partition or partitions.

5. Use the new DOS FDISK to create the new partition or partitions.

6. Perform a high-level format and install the new DOS system files with this command:

   FORMAT C: /S

7. Restore the previous partition backups to the new partition, but do not restore the original system files (IBMBIO.COM and IBMDOS.COM). Your restore program should have a way to enable you to selectively ignore certain files like this. BACKUP and RESTORE in DOS V3.3 and higher always ignore the system files.

8. Locate the new DOS disk with the REPLACE program, insert it in drive A:, and execute this command:

   COPY REPLACE.EXE C:

9. Use this command to replace all DOS transient files on C: with new versions in all subdirectories and enable read-only files to be overwritten:

   REPLACE A:*.* C: /S /R

Caution

This command replaces any file on the C: drive with a file of the same name on the DOS disks, no matter where on C: the file is located. Any files on C: that have the same name as any of the DOS files on A: therefore are overwritten by this command.

10. Place the second DOS floppy disk in drive A:, and repeat the preceding step until you have inserted all DOS floppy disks.

11. Place the boot disk back in drive A:.

12. Add new DOS transient files to the C:\DOS directory with this command:

REPLACE A:*.* C:\DOS /A

13. Replace the boot disk with the second DOS floppy disk, and repeat the preceding step until you have inserted all DOS floppy disks.

When you are finished, the system is capable of booting the new DOS version from the hard disk. If you store program files in a directory other than C:\DOS, replace C:\DOS with that directory. This method ensures that all previous DOS files are overwritten by new versions.

Backup procedures make this method very difficult unless you have a good backup system. You also must determine how to prevent your backup system from restoring the system files.

If you are using the DOS V3.3 or higher BACKUP and RESTORE commands, preventing the system files from being overwritten is much more simple. Because RESTORE never can restore the files IBMBIO.COM, IBMDOS.COM, and COMMAND.COM, the chances of overwriting them are eliminated.

You must use the new DOS version's FDISK command to remove and especially create the partitions in order for the newer DOS version's partitioning capabilities to become available. One variation on this method is to substitute a low-level format operation on the hard disk for step 4 of this procedure. One advantage of not repeating the low-level format is that any existing non-DOS partitions survive; with a low-level format, nothing is left on the disk. An advantage to the low-level format is that it rewrites the sectors and tracks, which might be a good idea for some older hard disks.

Chapter Summary

This chapter has examined many types of system upgrades, including the upgrade of the system's most important chip, the central processing unit. It also covered adding system memory, expanding hard drive storage and adding floppy drives, ways to speed up a system, improving the video subsystem, adding a reset switch, and upgrading to a new version of DOS. You should now have some insight on ways to make your system faster and, therefore, more useful, as well as some useful recommendations on how to avoid upgrade pitfalls others have endured.

Upgrading a system can be a cost-effective way to keep up with the rest of the computing community and to extend the life of your system. By upgrading, however, you also can create a "Frankenstein" system with compatibility problems before realizing how much money you have poured into the system. It is important to learn when to say *no* to more upgrades and to recognize when it is time to buy a new system.

Chapter 13

System Diagnostics

This chapter describes the three levels of diagnostic software (POST, system, and advanced) and describes how you can get the most from them. IBM's audio codes, error codes, and their descriptions also are listed. This chapter also examines aftermarket diagnostics and public-domain diagnostic software.

Diagnostics Software

IBM-compatible PCs, as well as the IBM PC, XT, AT, and PS/2, have several types of diagnostic-software procedures available to assist users in identifying many problems that can occur with a computer's components. These programs can do most of the work in determining which PC component is defective. Three programs that can help you locate a problem are available; each program is more complex and powerful than the preceding one. The diagnostic programs include these three items:

- *POST*: The Power-On Self Test operates whenever a PC is powered up (switched on).

- *General diagnostics software*: IBM's general diagnostic software (on the diagnostics disk) and its accompanying problem—determination procedures—outlined in the guide-to-operations manual for each system. Many IBM-compatible systems come with their own manufacturer's version of this diagnostic software.

- *Advanced diagnostics*: The IBM Advanced Diagnostics (provided on the Advanced Diagnostics disk with OS/2 systems and optional for PC/XT and AT-type systems) and procedures provided in the hardware-maintenance service manual. This level of diagnostic software is not supplied with most IBM-compatible systems; however, this chapter covers software utilities such as Symantic's Norton Utilities 7. The chapter also covers software from numerous other companies, which provides detailed diagnostics of IBM-compatible PC systems.

Many computer operators use the first and last of these software systems to test and troubleshoot most systems.

The IBM Advanced Diagnostics disk is included with the hardware-maintenance service manual, and it—along with the accompanying hardware-maintenance reference and assorted updates to both manuals—costs more than $400. Although this price might seem expensive, anyone supporting more than just a single PC system quickly can recoup the expense in labor costs saved and avoid the trouble of carry-in service. The Appendix includes a catalog of these manuals.

Although the IBM service manuals are expensive, they are complete and represent the definitive work on the subject. Unlike many companies, IBM provides truly in-depth system documentation. Indeed, this documentation is one of the primary reasons for the success of the IBM systems as the industry standard.

The Power-On Self Test (POST)

When IBM first began shipping the IBM PC in 1981, it included safety features that had never been seen in a personal computer. These features were the POST and parity-checked memory. The parity-checking feature is explained in the section of Chapter 7 titled, "Memory." The following provides much more detail on the POST, a series of program routines, buried in the motherboard ROM firmware, that tests all the main system components at power-on time. This program series causes the delay when you turn on an IBM-compatible system; the program is executed before the system loads the operating system.

What Is Tested?

Whenever you start up your computer, the computer automatically performs a series of tests that check various components—the primary components—in your system. Items such as the CPU, ROM, motherboard support circuitry, memory, and major peripherals (such as an expansion chassis) are tested. These tests are brief and not very thorough compared with other available disk-based diagnostics. The POST process provides error or warning messages whenever a faulty component is encountered. Although the diagnostics performed by the system POST are not always very thorough, they are the first line of defense, especially in handling severe motherboard problems. If the POST encounters a problem severe enough to keep the system from operating properly, it halts bootup of the system and produces an error message that often leads you directly to the cause of the problem. Such POST-detected problems are sometimes called *fatal errors*. The POST tests normally provide three types of output messages: audio codes, display-screen messages, and hexadecimal numeric codes to an I/O port address.

POST Audio Error Codes

POST audio error codes usually are audio codes consisting of variations of beeps that identify the faulty component. If your computer is functioning normally, you hear one short beep when the system is started up. If a problem is detected, a different series of audio codes is sounded. These BIOS-dependent codes can vary among different BIOS manufacturers. The audio codes and corresponding problem areas as indicated by an IBM BIOS are listed in table 13.1.

Table 13.1 IBM BIOS POST Audio Codes and Fault Domains

Audio code	Sound graph	Fault domain
1 short beep	.	Normal POST—system OK
2 short beeps	..	POST error—error code
No beep		Power supply, system board
Continuous beep	———	Power supply, system board
Repeating short beeps	......	Power supply, system board
One long, one short beep	–.	System board
One long, two short beeps	–..	Display adapter (MDA, CGA)
One long, three short beeps	–...	Enhanced Graphics Adapter (EGA)
Three long beeps	– – –	3270 keyboard card

The Appendix in this book lists the audio POST codes for the AMI BIOS and Phoenix BIOS, both of which have a much more detailed set of audio response codes than IBMs— much more helpful in diagnosing problems with a system motherboard. In particular, the Phoenix BIOS POST is so well done that many times I do not need to use any other diagnostics to isolate a problem—the BIOS has done it for me. The sophisticated POST procedure is one of the reasons I like the Phoenix BIOS.

POST Display Error Codes

On the XT, AT, PS/2, and most compatibles, the POST also displays system memory as it is tested. The last number displayed is the amount of memory that tested properly—for example, 640K OK. This number should agree with the total amount of memory installed in your system, including conventional and extended memory. For example, on a system with 32M of memory, the POST displays 32768KB OK. The RAM on an expanded memory card is not tested by the POST and does not count in the numbers reported. However, if you are using an expanded memory driver such as EMM386.EXE or Quarterdeck's QEMM to configure extended memory as expanded, the POST executes before this driver is loaded so that all installed memory is counted. If the POST memory test stops short of the expected total, then the number displayed often indicates how far into the systems memory a memory error lies. This number alone is a valuable troubleshooting aid.

If an error is detected during the POST procedures, an error message is displayed. These messages usually are in the form of a numeric code is several digits long; for example, 1790-Disk 0 Error. The information in the hardware-maintenance service manual identifies the malfunctioning component. I have researched all available IBM documentation and have included an abbreviated list of the error codes in this chapter, as well as a complete and extended list in the Appendix. By looking in the error-code chart in the Appendix, you can see that a 1790 error code indicates a read error on the diagnostics cylinder for hard disk drive 0.

I/O Port POST Codes

A less-well-known feature of the POST is that at the beginning of each POST, the BIOS sends test codes to a special I/O port address. These POST codes can be read only by a special adapter card plugged into one of the system slots. These cards originally were designed to be used by the system manufacturers for burn-in testing of the motherboard during system manufacturing, without the need for a video display adapter or display. Several companies now make these cards available to technicians. Micro 2000, Landmark, JDR Microdevices, Data Depot, Ultra-X and MicroSystems Development (MSD) are just a few of the manufacturers of these POST cards.

When one of these adapter cards is plugged into a slot, during the POST you see two-digit hexadecimal numbers flash on a display on the card. If the system stops unexpectedly or hangs, you can just look at the two-digit display on the card for the code indicating the test in progress during the hang. This step usually identifies the failed part. A complete list of these POST codes is in the Appendix in this book; the list covers several different manufacturer's BIOS, including IBM, AMI, Award, and Phoenix.

Most BIOS on the market in systems with an ISA or EISA bus output the POST codes to I/O port address 80h. Compaq is different: its systems send codes to port 84h. IBM PS/2 models with ISA bus slots, such as the Model 25 and 30, send codes to port 90h. Some EISA systems send codes to port 300h (most EISA systems also send the same codes to 80h). IBM MCA bus systems universally send codes to port 680h. With all these different addresses, you should be sure that the card you purchase will read the port addresses you need.

Several cards read only port address 80h. This port address is certainly the most commonly used, and works in most situations, but the cards do not work in Compaq systems, some EISA systems, and IBM PS/2 systems. A POST card designed specifically for the PS/2 MCA bus needs to read only port address 680h because the card cannot be used in ISA or EISA bus systems anyway.

To read a port address, a card needs to have only an 8-bit design; it does not have to have a 16-bit or 32-bit POST card. The two normal types of POST cards are those that plug into the 8-bit connector which is a part of the ISA or EISA bus, and those that plug into the MCA bus. Some companies, such as Ultra-X, offer both types of POST cards—one for MCA bus systems and one for ISA/EISA bus systems. Micro 2000 does not offer a separate card; rather, it includes with its POST Probe card a unique slot adapter that enables it to work in MCA bus systems as well as in ISA and EISA systems. Most other companies offer only ISA/EISA POST cards and have ignored the MCA bus.

Notice that because the EISA bus includes the ISA bus as a subset, and only the 8-bit portion of the ISA bus is needed to even read the required port addresses, it is unnecessary to have a separate card specific to EISA bus systems. Beware, however, that at least one manufacturer sells a separate EISA card that it claims is designed specifically for the EISA bus. As long as an ISA card is properly designed to latch the correct port addresses, there is no reason for it not to function perfectly in both ISA and EISA bus systems. There is absolutely no need for a separate (and expensive) EISA card.

POST-code cards are invaluable in diagnosing systems where the power supply comes on (you can hear the fan) but the motherboard seems dead. Just pop the card into a slot, and observe the code on the cards display. Then look up the code in a list corresponding to the specific BIOS on the motherboard. These cards also can be very helpful with tough problems such as a memory-bit failure in Bank 0, which does not allow error codes to be displayed on a CRT in most EGA or VGA systems.

POST-code cards can help also to troubleshoot other problems that occur so early in the POST tests that no error messages can be displayed. The only problem is that each manufacturers BIOS runs different tests in a different sequence, and even outputs different code numbers for the same tests. Therefore, without the proper documentation specific to the BIOS on the motherboard you are testing, the numbers shown on the POST card are meaningless! An important feature that separates the many POST cards on the market is that some provide extensive documentation of different BIOS, and others do not.

The documentation supplied with the Micro 2000, Landmark, Data Depot, and Ultra-X cards offers excellent information covering a wide variety of different BIOS manufacturers' codes. One company, MicroSystems Development (MSD) supplies its POST Card documentation both in printed form and on a disk with a built-in POST Code lookup program. This method is unique and desirable especially if you carry a laptop or portable system with you when you troubleshoot. The JDR Microdevices card offers less than most of the others in the way of documentation, but is also the least expensive card by a wide margin. Another thing that distinguishes the JDR card is that it is designed to be left in a system permanently. The two-digit display can be moved to the back bracket of the card so that it can be read outside the system. There is also a connector for an external two-digit display. The other cards have the display on the card only, which is impossible to read unless you open the system case.

Some cards have additional features worth mentioning. The Micro 2000 card (called the POST Probe) includes a built-in logic probe for testing signals on the major motherboard components. The POST Probe includes a series of individually separate LED readouts for several important bus signals as well as power-supply voltage levels. The separate LEDs enable these bus signals to be monitored simultaneously. Sometimes you can help to determine the cause of a failure by noting which bus LED is lit at a certain time. The power-supply LEDs verify the output of the +5, -5, +12, and -12 volt signals from the supply. Another feature is meter-probe attachment points on which you can easily connect a voltmeter to the card for more accurate measurements.

The basic card functions in all ISA bus and EISA bus systems because of its capability to monitor any port addresses mentioned earlier in this section. As mentioned, this card includes a unique adapter that enables it to function in MCA bus systems as well. This card is the only one that functions in every system on the market. The extensive documentation not only covers the expected POST codes for different BIOS versions but also includes a detailed reference to the bus signals monitored by the card. A reference in the documentation enables even novices to use the included logic probe for some more-sophisticated motherboard tests. This card offers more features than others on the market.

The Data Depot Pocket POST is a unique card that includes an LED for monitoring bus signals. It can monitor a single signal at a time, which is selected by a jumper. The card includes LEDs for testing all the power-supply voltage levels, and includes attachment points for a voltmeter as well. The Pocket POST is designed for ISA and EISA bus systems, and can connect to any port addresses used in these systems for POST codes. As its name suggests, the card is small compared to most others, and therefore is easy to carry around. The entire package, including the comprehensive manual, fits in a standard (included) floppy disk case.

Ultra-X has two cards: the Quick-POST PC for ISA/EISA bus systems, and the Quick-POST PS/2 for MCA bus systems. Because the Quick-POST cards monitor only one port address each—80h for the PC card and 680h for the PS/2 card—the ISA/EISA version is less flexible than some others. The included documentation is excellent and covers a variety of BIOS versions. Both cards also include LEDs used to monitor the power-supply voltages.

As mentioned, the MicroSystems Development (MSD) card is unique because of its documentation on disk. A printed manual is supplied also. This POST Code Master is capable of monitoring either port address 80h or 84h. It also includes voltage-test LEDS for checking the power supply.

A second type of diagnostics card goes beyond the function of a basic POST-code card. In addition to monitoring POST codes, these cards include an on-board ROM chip that contains a more sophisticated diagnostics program than normally is in the motherboard ROM BIOS alone. Several cards that offer this function are the Kickstart II card, by Landmark, and the RACER II card, by Ultra-X. These cards not only monitor POST codes but also have a diagnostics program of their own in on-board ROM. Because of the extra expense of having these programs and other options on-board, the cards are more expensive than the standard POST-code cards.

The idea of a higher-level diagnostics card is valid, but I normally do not recommend it because the standard POST-code cards provide 95 percent of the capabilities of these cards with no BIOS conflicts or other problems. Beyond the standard POST card functions, I usually rely on disk-based diagnostics for further tests that are more thorough than the tests on these cards. To eliminate conflicts with ROMs on other cards, in many cases other adapters must be removed from the system to execute the tests. Although these cards are quite capable, and function as a basic POST-code card if necessary, I find it more valuable to spend the extra money on a disk-based diagnostics program and stick to the basic POST-code cards. This way, I get the most functionality for my money.

System Diagnostics Disk

Every IBM computer comes with a guide-to-operations (GTO) or Quick Reference manual. The GTO manual is in a reddish purple binder; it includes a diagnostics disk to assist you in identifying problems your computer might have. PS/2 computers are supplied with a much smaller quick-reference guide that includes a reference disk. The disk contains both the regular and advanced diagnostics, as well as the normal SETUP program.

The diagnostics disk and corresponding manual provide step-by-step instructions for you to test the various parts of your computer system, including the system unit and many installed options, such as the expansion unit, keyboard, display, and printer. Unfortunately, these diagnostics are at customer level and are lacking in many respects. The tests cannot be run individually; you must always run them all together, and many of the better tests have been deleted. These diagnostics are a crippled version of the much more powerful advanced diagnostics IBM sells. Many compatible-system vendors do not segregate the diagnostics software like IBM does; many include an advanced-type diagnostics disk free with the system. For example, AST includes free with every system its diagnostics program, called ASTute. This program is similar to the IBM advanced diagnostics.

You must boot from the IBM diagnostics disk to run the program because a special version of DOS resides on the diagnostics disk. The DOS version suppresses the system parity checking during the boot process. Disabling parity checking might enable a defective system to limp through the diagnostics, whereas normally the system continually locks up with the parity-check message. After the disk is loaded, the main diagnostics menu is displayed. The opening menu looks something like this:

```
The IBM Personal Computer
DIAGNOSTICS
Version 2.06
Copyright IBM Corp. 1981,1986

SELECT AN OPTION

0 - SYSTEM CHECKOUT
1 - FORMAT DISKETTE
2 - COPY DISKETTE
3 - PREPARE SYSTEM FOR MOVING
4 - SETUP
9 - END DIAGNOSTICS

SELECT THE ACTION DESIRED
?
```

Options 0, 1, and 2 on the IBM diagnostics screen are part of the diagnostics procedures. These options, as well as options 3, 4 and 9, are detailed in the following:

Option 0: Used for general testing. When this option is selected, the diagnostics software loads from the disk various modules that perform a presence test to see whether the device to which the module corresponds is in the system. The option presents a list of installed devices and you are asked whether the list is correct.

Option 1: Used to format a disk with a special format used by the diagnostic program when it is running tests on your system. The format is different from a normal DOS format, and should not be used to format disks for normal use under DOS. This option is designed to create a special scratch disk used by the diagnostics for testing purposes. Among other things, there are differences in the construction of the boot sector of diagnostics scratch disk and a normal DOS disk.

Option 2: Used to copy a disk. This routine is the same as the DISKCOPY command in normal DOS. Option 2 creates a mirror-image copy of a disk. This routine was designed to copy the diagnostics disk because the original disk should be placed in a safe location and not used for testing purposes. The diagnostics disk was designed to be used to boot your system (the disk includes system files that enable the computer to boot without the presence of DOS). You use this option to make backups of your master diagnostics disk so that you can use the copies for actual testing purposes. The diagnostics disks can be copied by any other means as well because they are not copy-protected. IBM never has protected the regular or advanced diagnostics, which enables you to make proper backups and keep the master disks safe.

Option 3: Used to park, or secure, the heads on a hard disk so that the system unit can be moved safely without damaging the disk or its contents.

Option 4: Present only on the AT version of the diagnostics. This option is used on the AT to identify installed options when you first set up your system.

Option 9: Used to quit the diagnostics software and restart your system. You must remove the diagnostics disk from your floppy drive.

For several reasons, this list does not always match the system configuration. The only items listed are those that have diagnostic software modules on the disk. The diagnostics (or advanced diagnostics) disks do not incorporate the testing modules for certain devices. For example, the diagnostics cannot test an IBM Token Ring network adapter in your system. IBM provides a separate diagnostics program on its own disk for this adapter.

Most standard devices should show up on the list, however, even if the particular device was not made by IBM. Your hard disk controller should show up, as should your video board, serial and parallel ports, conventional and extended memory, floppy drives, and the motherboard. If you purchase a newer type of expansion item, such as a VGA graphics card, the diagnostics might instead identify this board as an EGA board, if the VGA module is not present on the disk. Because modules are not available for most expanded-memory boards, those boards almost never appear on the list, with the exception of IBMs XMA card. Nonstandard communications boards (boards containing other than normal serial or parallel ports) normally are not seen either.

If an installed device shows up because it is installed in the system, and you know that the diagnostics software normally would find it but doesn't, then the device is configured incorrectly or has a serious problem. Signify that the list is incorrect by answering No when you are asked whether the installed device list is correct. Then add the item to the list. If an item appears that is not installed, use the same procedure to remove the item from the list. This list represents all the tests that can be run. The only way you can test an item is to have it appear on this list.

After going through the installed-devices list, you see another menu, similar to this one:

```
0 - RUN TESTS ONE TIME
1 - RUN TESTS MULTIPLE TIMES
2 - LOG UTILITIES
3 - END SYSTEM CHECKOUT
```

Option 0 normally is selected to test one or all of the items in the system. Option 1 enables you to test any (or all) of these items repetitively as many times as you want, or forever. The forever option is handy because it enables you to run the diagnostics for an item continuously overnight or over a weekend to find particularly troublesome problems. This method can be an easy way to flesh out an intermittent problem. To record errors that occur while you're not present, you first select Option 2, which can be used to set up an error log. The log records the date, time, and error message to a floppy disk or printer so that you can review them at a later time.

If an error occurs while these tests are running, a numerical error message appears along with the date and time. These numbers, listed in this chapter and in the Appendix in this book, follow the same conventions as the numbers displayed by the POST, and are the same numbers in some cases. The diagnostic tests usually are much more powerful than the tests run in the POST.

Although the diagnostics do an excellent job of identifying specific problem areas or problem components, they provide limited assistance in telling you how to correct the source of the errors. Little documentation is provided with these diagnostics and, in fact, the information most often provided is `Have your system unit (or problem device) serviced`. These diagnostics are a crippled version of the real diagnostics, which are part of the hardware-maintenance service manual. You should be using the Advanced Diagnostics; they are the diagnostics to which the remainder of this book refers.

Advanced Diagnostics Programs

For technician-level diagnostics, IBM sells the hardware-maintenance service manuals, which include the Advanced Diagnostics disks. These disks contain the real diagnostics programs and, combined with the hardware-maintenance service manuals, represent the de facto standard diagnostics information and software for IBM and compatible systems. These programs produce error messages in the form of numbers. The number codes used are the same as those used in the POST and general-diagnostics software. The meaning of the numbers is consistent across all IBM diagnostic programs. This section explores the Advanced Diagnostics and lists most of the known error-code meanings. IBM constantly adds to this error-code list as it introduces new equipment.

Using Advanced Diagnostics

If you have a PS/2 system with the MCA (Micro Channel Architecture) bus slots (models produced later than the Models 25-to-40), you already have IBM's Advanced Diagnostics for these systems, even if you don't know it. To access these diagnostics, boot the PS/2 Reference Disk. When the main menu is displayed, press Ctrl-A (for Advanced). The menu switches and displays the menu for advanced diagnostics. Non-MCA systems, such as the PS/2 25-to-40 systems, come with a Starter Disk, equivalent to the Setup and Diagnostics Disk that came with the original AT system. This Starter Disk includes the Setup program and a limited diagnostics version that lacks many functions found in the advanced diagnostics. To get the advanced diagnostics for these systems, you must purchase the initial PS/2 *Hardware Maintenance and Service* (HMS) *Manual*, which includes the advanced diagnostics disks for Models 25, 30, and 30-286. If you want the diagnostics for later systems, such as Models 35 or 40, you must purchase the respective update package for the PS/2 HMS manual. These updates usually cost about $30.

Hiding advanced diagnostics from average users is probably a good idea. For example, an inexperienced user can do great damage by using this disk's option of low-level formatting the hard disk. The remainder of the contents of the PS/2 book are skimpy because not many parts are found in the average PS/2 system, and they are easy to repair. The PS/2 book often seems to end a troubleshooting session with this advice: Replace the system board. Although I recommend the hardware-maintenance and service manuals, if all you are looking for is the advanced-diagnostics software (and you have a PS/2 system with the MCA bus), you already have it, saving you $268!

Still, if you really want in-depth information about your system, you can purchase the IBM *Hardware Maintenance Service Manual* (for about $235). This single book covers earlier systems, including the PC, XT, and AT. Updates cover the XT-286 and PS/2 Models 25 and 30. The real PS/2 systems have their own separate version of this book, called *PS/2 Hardware Maintenance and Service*. This book costs $268 and includes spare copies of the standard reference disks. The newer versions of the PS/2 book now cover also all PS/2 systems, those with ISA (Industry Standard Architecture) as well as MCA (Micro Channel Architecture) slots.

Although the guide-to-operations manual is good only for identifying a problem component, the HMS manual provides information for you to more accurately isolate and repair the failure of any field-replaceable unit (FRU).

The HMS manual includes an Advanced Diagnostics disk and accompanying maintenance-analysis procedures (MAPs), which are instructions that help you to isolate and identify problem components. To run the advanced diagnostics tests, follow the procedures detailed in this section.

After booting the Advanced Diagnostics disk for your particular system (PC or AT), a menu similar to this one appears:

```
The IBM Personal Computer
ADVANCED DIAGNOSTICS
Version 2.07
Copyright IBM Corp. 1981,1986

ROS P/N: 78X7462
ROS DATE: 04/21/86

SELECT AN OPTION

0 - SYSTEM CHECKOUT
1 - FORMAT DISKETTE
2 - COPY DISKETTE
3 - PREPARE SYSTEM FOR MOVING
4 - SETUP
9 - END DIAGNOSTICS

SELECT THE ACTION DESIRED

?
```

IV

System Maintenance

The advanced diagnostics disks show the date of the ROM as well as the IBM part number for the particular chips in your system. The screen shows this information near the top as ROS (read-only software). The 04/21/86 date identifies the version of the ROM in this example. If you look up this date in the table in Chapter 7, "Primary System Components," which shows ROM identification information for IBMs systems, you see that the date indicates an IBM XT Model 286. The part number, read directly from the ROM, is academic information because IBM does not sell the ROM chips separately—only with a complete motherboard swap.

After you select Option 0, which invokes the diagnostic routines, each module on the disk loads and executes a presence test to determine whether the applicable piece of hardware is truly in the system. In this example, the result looks like this:

```
THE INSTALLED DEVICES ARE

1  - SYSTEM BOARD
2  - 2688KB MEMORY
3  - KEYBOARD
6  - 2 DISKETTE DRIVE(S) AND ADAPTER
7  - MATH COPROCESSOR
9  - SERIAL/PARALLEL ADAPTER
9  - - PARALLEL PORT
11 - SERIAL/PARALLEL ADAPTER
11 - - SERIAL PORT
17 - 1 FIXED DISK DRIVE(S) AND ADAPTER
74 - PERSONAL SYSTEM/2 DISPLAY ADAPTER

IS THE LIST CORRECT (Y/N)

?
```

You then answer Yes or No depending on the accuracy of the list. Remember that not everything appears on this list. An IBM Token Ring network adapter does not appear, for example, and never appears on this list because no software module designed for that option is present on the disk. The following list contains all the items that could appear on the list (as of Version 2.07 of these diagnostics). This list is different for other versions.

```
1  SYSTEM BOARD
2  MEMORY
3  KEYBOARD
4  MONOCHROME & PRINTER ADAPTER
5  COLOR/GRAPHICS MONITOR ADAPTER
6  DISKETTE DRIVE(S)
7  MATH COPROCESSOR
9  SERIAL/PARALLEL ADAPTER - PARALLEL PORT
```

```
10  ALTERNATE SERIAL/PARALLEL ADAPTER - PARALLEL PORT
11  SERIAL/PARALLEL ADAPTER - SERIAL PORT
12  ALTERNATE SERIAL/PARALLEL ADAPTER - SERIAL PORT
13  GAME CONTROL ADAPTER
14  MATRIX PRINTER
15  SDLC COMMUNICATIONS ADAPTER
17  FIXED DISK DRIVE(S) AND ADAPTER
20  BSC COMMUNICATIONS ADAPTER
21  ALT BSC COMMUNICATIONS ADAPTER
22  CLUSTER ADAPTER(S)
24  ENHANCED GRAPHICS ADAPTER
29  COLOR PRINTER
30  PC NETWORK ADAPTER
31  ALT. PC NETWORK ADAPTER
36  GPIB ADAPTER(S)
38  DATA ACQUISITION ADAPTER(S)
39  PROFESSIONAL GRAPHICS CONTROLLER
71  VOICE COMMUNICATIONS ADAPTER
73  3.5" EXTERNAL DISKETTE DRIVE AND ADAPTER
74  PERSONAL SYSTEM/2 DISPLAY ADAPTER
85  EXPANDED MEMORY ADAPTER - 2 MB -
89  MUSIC FEATURE CARD(S)
```

After certifying that the list is correct, or adding or deleting items as necessary to make it correct, you might begin testing each item listed.

The tests performed by the Advanced Diagnostics disk are far more detailed and precise than the tests on the general diagnostics disk in the GTO. In addition to identifying the problem component, the advanced diagnostics further attempt to identify the specific malfunctioning part of the device.

After a problem is identified, the HMS manual provides detailed instructions for performing adjustments, preventive maintenance, and removal and replacement of the affected part. To help you, comprehensive hardware and design information is available, including parts lists that specify replacement-part numbers and internal design specifications.

Examining Error Codes

Nearly all the personal computer error codes for the POST, general diagnostics, and advanced diagnostics are represented by the display of the device number followed by two digits other than 00. A display of the device number plus 00 indicates successful completion of a test. This listing is a compilation from various sources including technical-reference manuals, hardware-maintenance service manuals, and hardware-maintenance reference manuals.

If a designation such as 2xx is indicated in the chart, error codes that begin with the first character or characters listed and with any character in place of x indicate errors in the device listed. For example, 7xx indicates math coprocessor errors, which also means that any displayed error codes from 700 to 799 (except 700, which means all is well) indicates that the math coprocessor is bad (or is having problems). Table 13.2 lists the error codes and their descriptions.

Table 13.2 Personal Computer Error Codes

Code	Description
1xx	System Board errors
2xx	Memory (RAM) errors
3xx	Keyboard errors
4xx	Monochrome Display Adapter (MDA) errors
4xx	PS/2 System Board Parallel Port errors
5xx	Color Graphics Adapter (CGA) errors
6xx	Floppy Drive/Controller errors
7xx	Math Coprocessor errors
9xx	Parallel Printer adapter errors
10xx	Alternate Parallel Printer Adapter errors
11xx	Primary Async Communications (serial port COM1:) errors
12xx	Alternate Async Communications (serial COM2:, COM3: and COM4:)
13xx	Game Control Adapter errors
14xx	Matrix Printer errors
15xx	Synchronous Data Link Control (SDLC) Communications Adapter errors
16xx	Display Station Emulation Adapter (DSEA) errors (5520, 525x)
17xx	ST-506/412 Fixed Disk and Controller errors
18xx	I/O Expansion Unit errors
19xx	3270 PC Attachment Card errors
20xx	Binary Synchronous Communications (BSC) Adapter errors
21xx	Alternate Binary Synchronous Communications (BSC) Adapter errors
22xx	Cluster Adapter errors
23xx	Plasma Monitor Adapter errors
24xx	Enhanced Graphics Adapter (EGA) errors
24xx	PS/2 System Board Video Graphics Array (VGA) errors
25xx	Alternate Enhanced Graphics Adapter (EGA) errors
26xx	XT or AT/370 370-M (Memory) and 370-P (Processor) Adapter errors
27xx	XT or AT/370 3277-EM (Emulation) Adapter errors
28xx	3278/79 Emulation Adapter or 3270 Connection Adapter errors
29xx	Color/Graphics Printer errors
30xx	Primary PC Network Adapter errors
31xx	Secondary PC Network Adapter errors
32xx	3270 PC or AT Display and Programmed Symbols Adapter errors
33xx	Compact Printer errors
35xx	Enhanced Display Station Emulation Adapter (EDSEA) errors
36xx	General Purpose Interface Bus (GPIB) Adapter errors
38xx	Data Acquisition Adapter errors
39xx	Professional Graphics Adapter (PGA) errors
44xx	5278 Display Attachment Unit and 5279 Display errors

(continues)

Table 13.2 Continued

Code	Description
45xx	IEEE Interface Adapter (IEEE-488) errors
46xx	A Real-Time Interface Coprocessor (ARTIC) Multiport/2 Adapter errors
48xx	Internal Modem errors
49xx	Alternate Internal Modem errors
50xx	PC Convertible LCD errors
51xx	PC Convertible Portable Printer errors
56xx	Financial Communication System errors
70xx	Phoenix BIOS/Chip Set Unique Error Codes
71xx	Voice Communications Adapter (VCA) errors
73xx	3 1/2-inch External Diskette Drive errors
74xx	IBM PS/2 Display Adapter (VGA card) errors
74xx	8514/A Display Adapter errors
76xx	4216 PagePrinter Adapter errors
84xx	PS/2 Speech Adapter errors
85xx	2Mb XMA Memory Adapter or Expanded Memory Adapter/A errors
86xx	PS/2 Pointing Device (Mouse) errors
89xx	Musical Instrument Digital Interface (MIDI) Adapter errors
91xx	IBM 3363 Write-Once Read Multiple (WORM) Optical Drive/Adapter errors
096xxxx	SCSI Adapter with Cache (32-bit) errors
100xx	Multiprotocol Adapter/A errors
101xx	300/1200bps Internal Modem/A
104xx	ESDI Fixed Disk or Adapter errors
107xx	5 1/4-inch External Diskette Drive or Adapter errors
112xxxx	SCSI Adapter (16-bit w/o Cache) errors
113xxxx	System Board SCSI Adapter (16-bit) errors
129xx	Model 70 Processor Board errors; Type 3 (25MHz) System Board
149xx	P70/P75 Plasma Display and Adapter errors
165xx	6157 Streaming Tape Drive or Tape Attachment Adapter errors
166xx	Primary Token Ring Network Adapter errors
167xx	Alternate Token Ring Network Adapter errors
180xx	PS/2 Wizard Adapter errors
194xx	80286 Memory Expansion Option Memory Module errors
208xxxx	Unknown SCSI Device errors
209xxxx	SCSI Removable Disk errors
210xxxx	SCSI Fixed Disk errors
211xxxx	SCSI Tape Drive errors
212xxxx	SCSI Printer errors
213xxxx	SCSI Processor errors
214xxxx	SCSI Write-Once Read Multiple (WORM) Drive errors

Code	Description
215xxxx	SCSI CD-ROM Drive errors
216xxxx	SCSI Scanner errors
217xxxx	SCSI Optical Memory errors
218xxxx	SCSI Jukebox Changer errors
219xxxx	SCSI Communications errors

I have compiled in the Appendix in this book a detailed list of every IBM error code I have encountered. Also listed are charts I have developed concerning SCSI errors. The SCSI interface has introduced a whole new set of error codes because of the large number and variety of devices that can be attached.

Aftermarket Diagnostics Programs

One way to determine whether a system is fully IBM-compatible is to see whether it will run IBM's advanced diagnostics. IBMs diagnostics programs work just fine on fully-compatible PCs produced by other manufacturers. Some system manufacturers offer their own diagnostics. Zenith, AT&T and Tandy, for example, offer their own versions of service manuals and diagnostics programs for their systems. Some other system manufacturers include a version of a 3rd-party diagnostic utilities package when you purchase their systems.

Many third-party diagnostics utilities are available for IBM and compatible systems. Specific programs are available also to test memory, floppy drives, hard disks, video boards, and most other areas of the system. Although some of these utility packages should be considered essential in any toolkit, many fall short of the level needed by professional-level troubleshooters. Many products, geared more toward end users, lack the accuracy, features, and capabilities needed by technically proficient people who are serious about troubleshooting. I have tested virtually all diagnostics packages available; two stand out from all the others: Micro-Scope, by Micro 2000, and Service Diagnostics, by Landmark.

These two programs offer several advantages over the IBM diagnostics. Micro-Scope and Service Diagnostics usually are better at determining where a problem lies within a system, especially in IBM-compatible systems. Serial- and parallel-port loopback connectors, or wrap plugs, are included in these packages. The plugs are required in order to properly diagnose and test serial and parallel ports. (IBM charges extra for these plugs.)

Both programs can be run in batch mode, which enables a series of tests to be run from the command line without operator intervention. You then can set up automated test suites, which can be especially useful in burning in a system or executing the same tests on many systems.

These programs test all types of memory including conventional (base) memory, extended memory, and expanded memory. Failures can be identified down to the individual chip (bank and bit) level.

Like IBM's diagnostics, neither program is copy-protected. Most software manufacturers long ago eliminated any form of copy protection from their software, but a few diagnostics packages still have this intolerable feature. (I try not to purchase any program that cannot be backed up easily, especially one as essential as a diagnostics program.)

Both of these recommended diagnostics programs have outstanding individual features. The remainder of this section describes the advantages of these two programs.

Micro-Scope

The Micro-Scope package is one of only a few diagnostics packages that is truly PS/2 aware. Micro-Scope not only helps you troubleshoot PS/2 systems, but also does some things that even IBM advanced diagnostics cannot do: for example, it can format industry-standard ESDI hard disk drives attached to the IBM PS/2 ESDI controller. When you attach an ESDI drive to the IBM ESDI controller, the BIOS on the controller queries the drive for its capacity and defect map information. IBM apparently chose a proprietary format for this information on its drives; if the controller cannot read the information, you cannot set up the drive nor format it by using the PS/2 Reference Diskette.

Although IBM used an ESDI controller in its PS/2 system, you could not get just any ESDI drive to work on that system. Some drive manufacturers produced special PS/2 versions of their drives that had this information on them. Another way around the problem was to use an aftermarket ESDI controller in place of the IBM controller so that you could use the IBM ESDI drive as well as any other industry-standard ESDI drive. With this method, however, you could not use the Reference Disk format program anymore because it works only with IBM's controller. Micro-Scope can solve many of these problems because it can format an industry-standard ESDI drive attached to the IBM ESDI controller and save you from having to purchase an aftermarket controller or a special drive when you add drives to these systems.

Micro-Scope has also a hardware interrupt and I/O port address check feature that is more accurate than the same feature in other software. It enables you to accurately identify the interrupt or I/O port address a certain adapter or hardware device in your system is using—a valuable capability in solving conflicts between adapters. Some user-level diagnostics programs have this feature, but the information they report can be grossly inaccurate, and they often miss items installed in the system. Micro-Scope goes around DOS and the BIOS; because the program has its own operating system and its tests bypass the ROM BIOS when necessary, it can eliminate the masking that occurs with these elements in the way. For this reason, the program also is useful for technicians who support PCs that run under non-DOS environments such as UNIX or on Novell file servers. For convenience, you can install Micro-Scope on a hard disk and run it under regular DOS.

Finally, Micro 2000 offers excellent telephone technical support. Its operators do much more than explain how to operate the software—they help you with real troubleshooting problems. This information is augmented by good documentation and on-line help built in to the software so that, in many cases, you don't have to refer to the manual.

Service Diagnostics

The Landmark Service Diagnostics program also has several features that distinguish it from other packages. These features are described in this section.

The Service Diagnostics program is an excellent, all-around, comprehensive diagnostics package. The program has been around for awhile and has evolved to include nearly any test a troubleshooter could want. Service Diagnostics is known for its excellent memory tests, which are extremely thorough and accurate; it also gives you much control over the type of test to run. For example, you can optionally turn parity checking on or off during the tests, a feature not found in other programs. All memory errors are reported to the individual-bit level.

The Service Diagnostics program also has specific test routines for each different micro-processor that might be in a PC compatible system. In other words, it detects the type of processor in your system, and tests it by using specific routines designed for the processor. You can override the processor detection and specify the processor you have. The program can recognize and test specific Intel-based systems using 8088, 8086, 286, 386, and 486 CPUs. Also, Service Diagnostics specifically recognizes and tests Harris 80C88 and AMD 386 chips, as well as Intel, Cyrix, and IIT math coprocessors. The program also tests for several known bugs in 386 and 486 systems that have been known to cause problems in some systems.

Another Service Diagnostics feature is its floppy disk alignment diagnostics, which enable you to check the alignment of both 3 1/2-inch and 5 1/4-inch drives through the use of an included Digital Diagnostics Diskette (DDD). These disks are accurate to a resolution of 500µ inches (micro-inches = millionths of an inch), accurate enough for checking alignment but not accurate enough for use in aligning a drive. For performing drive alignment, the program has a menu of analog-alignment aids, designed to be used in conjunction with a more-accurate Analog Alignment Disk (AAD) and an oscilloscope.

The Service Diagnostics progam has an excellent hard disk, low-level format program for ST-506/412 drives. You can specify not only the interleave, but also the skew factor. *Skew* is the offset of sectors from one track to the next to allow for head-switching time. This process is possible because the low-level format routines in the Service Diagnostics work at the controller register level: the program bypasses DOS and the BIOS and interacts directly with the controller hardware. The program formats most ESDI drives but cannot be used on SCSI or IDE drives.

A printer-test feature in the Service Diagnostics program enables test patterns to be sent to different printers. You can quickly verify the functionality of the port, cable, and printer in one simple operation.

I recommend diagnostics programs that accommodate the special features of IBM's PS/2 systems; Service Diagnostics meets this test. It has a separate stand-alone PS/2 version of the software designed specifically for PS/2 systems. This version recognizes PS/2 hardware differences and works correctly with the unique PS/2 CMOS RAM for adapter setup and configuration.

A useful feature in limited situations is the inclusion of diagnostics in ROM chips. The ROM POST can be plugged into the BIOS-chip sockets on a PC, XT, AT, or IBM-compatible motherboard to test a system that otherwise does not function. These BIOS diagnostics do not function on all systems, but they can be useful on an IBM PC, XT, or AT, or a fully-compatible system.

The Service Diagnostics package includes excellent documentation that describes not only how to operate the software, but also how the software routines work. Landmark offers good technical support for its products. The Service Diagnostics program is available in three primary kits: the PC, XT, AT Kit with ROM POST modules sells for $595; the PS/2 Complete Kit costs $495, and a Super Kit includes everything for $895. You can also buy special lower-cost software modules that cover specific types of systems. The price starts at about $195 per module, depending on the versions and how many modules you need.

Both the Micro-Scope and Service Diagnostics packages are excellent; I highly recommend both of them. They each have strengths in some areas, and having a second opinion in some cases is a good idea when you are troubleshooting. Although somewhat expensive for casual troubleshooters, these professional-level programs will save you money in the long run with increased accuracy and capabilities in troubleshooting and servicing your systems.

QAPlus/FE

QAPlus/FE by Diagsoft is one of the most advanced and comprehensive sets of diagnostics you can buy for 386, 486, or Pentium-based computers, including PS/2s. Its testing is extremely thorough and its menu-based interface makes it downright easy to use, even for someone who is not particularly well-versed in diagnosing problems with personal computers. QAPlus/FE also includes some of most accurate system benchmarks you can get, which can be used to find out if that new system you are thinking of buying is really all that much faster than the one you already have. What's more important, QAPlus/FE comes on bootable 3 1/2- and 5 1/4-inch disks that (regardless of whether your operating system is DOS, OS/2 or Unix) can be used to start your system when problems are so severe your system hardware cannot even find the hard drive. You also can install QAPlus/FE on your hard drive if you are using DOS 3.2 or later.

A watered-down version of QAPlus ships with systems built by various manufacturers, but QAPlus/FE makes this version, and many other diagnostic packages, seem like an old west sheriff armed with a squirt gun.

QAPlus/FE can be used to test your motherboard, system RAM (conventional, extended, and expanded), video adapter, hard drive, floppy drives, CD-ROM drive, mouse, keyboard, printer, and parallel and serial ports (the QAPlus/FE package includes loopback plugs for full testing of these ports). It also provides exhaustive information on your system configuration, including the hardware installed on your system, its CPU, and the total amount of RAM installed on your system. It provides full interrupt mapping, crucial when installing new adapter boards and other hardware devices, and gives you a full picture of the device drivers and memory resident programs loaded in CONFIG.SYS and AUTOEXEC.BAT, as well as other information about DOS and system memory use.

QAPlus/FE also includes various other utilities, some more likely to appeal to the serious PC troubleshooter than to the average PC user. These special capabilities include a CMOS editor that can be used to change system date and time, as well as the hard drive type, installed memory size and other CMOS information, a COM port debugger, a hard drive test and low-level formatting utility, a floppy drive test utility, a configuration file editor that can be used to edit AUTOEXEC.BAT, CONFIG.SYS, a remote system communication host program that enables service people with the full remote package to operate your computer via modem, as well as other text files. An optional module enables you to tweak the speed of your floppy drives, but this option is not for the average PC user because its price is higher than the cost of a new floppy drive.

Unlike some diagnostics programs, QAPlus/FE has a system *burn-in* capability, meaning it can be used to run your system non-stop under a full-load of computations and hardware activity for the purpose of determining whether any system component is likely to fail in real life use. Many people use a burn-in utility when they receive a new system, and just before the warranty runs out. A true system burn-in usually lasts 48-72 hours, or even longer, and the amount of time QAPlus/FE can burn-in a system is user-configurable by setting the number of times the selected tests are to be run.

The package is quite expensive (it lists at $349.95, and even mail order is more expensive than most of the good-quality diagnostic packages). But if you need serious diagnostic software, QAPlus/FE is some of the best.

Checkit Pro

Touchstone Software Corp.'s Checkit Pro, although less expensive than QAPlus/FE (as little as $85 mail order) offers an excellent suite of testing capabilities, including tests of the system CPU, conventional, extended and expanded memory, hard and floppy drives, video card and monitor (including VESA-Standard cards and monitors, mouse, and keyboard).

Checkit Pro also provides limited benchmarking capabilities, but gives detailed information about your system hardware such as the following: total installed memory, hard drive type and size, current memory allocation (including upper memory usage), IRQ availability and usage, modem/faxmodem speed, and a variety of other tests important to someone troubleshooting a PC. Checkit Pro includes a text editing module that opens automatically to CONFIG.SYS and AUTOEXEC.BAT. If you use Windows, Checkit Pro's Windows option makes it easy to edit your Windows SYSTEM.INI and WIN.INI files.

Checkit Pro cannot run a system burn-in, as can QAPlus/FE. But some of the testing done by Checkit Pro is uncommon for diagnostic utility packages (for example, its ability to test modem/faxmodem settings). Still, Checkit Pro lacks important features such as easy-to-use listing of available DMA channels, which is crucial if you are trying to install a sound card and other hardware devices.

All things considered, especially its very attractive price, Checkit Pro is an outstanding value. Many people would do well to get this inexpensive and widely available package rather than another package that offered only a little more functionality for a lot more money.

Norton Diagnostics

When you consider that Norton Diagnostics (NDIAGS) comes with the Norton Utilities version 7.0, and that Norton Utilities is already an essential collection of system data safeguarding, troubleshooting, testing, and repairing utilities, NDIAGS probably is the best value in diagnostic programs.

If you already have a version of Norton Utilities earlier than 7.0, get the upgrade. If you don't already have Norton Utilities, you'll want to strongly consider this package of utilities, not only for NDIAGS, but also for enhancements to other utilities such as the Stacker 3.1-ready Speedisk, Disk Doctor, and Calibrate. These three hard drive utilities basically represent the state of the art in hard drive diagnostics and software-level repair. SYSINFO still handles the benchmarking for the Norton Utilities, and it does as good a job as any other package on the market.

NDIAGS adds diagnostic capabilities that previously were not provided by the Norton Utilities, including comprehensive information about the overall hardware configuration of your system—the CPU, system BIOS, math coprocessor, video adapter, keyboard and mouse type, hard and floppy drive types, amount of installed memory (including extended and expanded), bus type (ISA, EISA, or MCA), and the number of serial and parallel ports. Unlike QAPlus/FE, loopback plugs do not come in the box for NDIAGS, but a coupon is included that enables you to get loopback plugs free.

NDIAGS also thoroughly tests the major system components and enables you to check minor details such as the NumLock, CapsLock, and ScrollLock LEDs on your keyboard. NDIAGS also provides an on-screen grid you can use to center the image on your monitor and to test for various kinds of distortion that may indicate a faulty monitor. The Norton Utilities 7.0, as mentioned previously, is available inexpensively for registered users of a previous version, and can be purchased for $100 or less.

Disk Diagnostics

Several excellent programs are available for testing floppy and hard drives. For example, Norton Utilities and QAPlus/FE both test hard and floppy drives, and are thorough. The following section of this chapter discusses some of the best disk diagnostic and testing programs on the market and what they can do for you.

Disk Doctor and Calibrate

Disk Doctor and Calibrate are two of the modules included with the Norton Utilities version 7.0. Together, these two utilities provide exhaustive testing of a hard drive. Disk Doctor tests the ability of the drive to work with the system in which it is installed, including the drive's boot sector, file allocation tables (FAT), file structure, and data areas. Calibrate, which is used for the most intensive testing of the data area of a drive, also tests the hard drive controller electronics.

Calibrate also can be used to perform deep-pattern testing of IDE, SCSI, and ST-506/412-interface drives, writing literally millions of bytes of data to every sector of the drive to see whether it can properly retain data, moving data if the sector where it is stored is flawed, and marking the sector as bad in the FAT.

Calibrate can perform a non-destructive low-level format of ST-506/412 drives, which means that the data stored on the drive is not destroyed as it is when you use the controller BIOS to perform a low-level format on these drives. Often, in performing deep-pattern testing and low-level formatting of ST-506/412 drives, Calibrate can refresh, or remagnetize bad sectors and return them to service so they can safely be used again for data storage. Calibrate also can be used to test for the optimal interleave on ST-506/412 drives and nondestructively change the format if system performance would benefit.

> **Note**
>
> Calibrate, and other hard drive repair utilities, cannot be used to low-level format an IDE or SCSI drive. These devices are low-level formatted at the factory and this procedure cannot be repeated in the field by an end-user.

NDIAGS Floppy Disk Tests

The Norton Diagnostics, or NDIAGS, performs a wide variety of tests on floppy drives, including random and sequential read tests, rotation tests, speed tests, disk change tests, and write protect tests.

QAPlus/FE Disk Tests

QAPlus/FE tests most IDE, SCSI, and ST-506/412-interface drives. The QAPlus/FE "Look for Bad Tracks" option scans an entire drive for defective tracks (rather than bad sectors). The operation of QAPlus/FE is somewhat complex, however, because it logs any bad tracks to a log file. You then must run the "Remap Bad Sectors" option to mark these tracks as bad in the FAT.

The QAPlus/FE floppy drive tests leave something to be desired. The floppy drive test option executes some read/write, disk change, and head movement tests, but does not measure rotation or drive speed. To get those capabilities, you have to buy an additional module, QAFloppy, which also includes a special high-resolution diagnostics test disk that enables you to adjust drive alignment without an oscilloscope. Frankly, if you choose QAPlus/FE as your diagnostics package you can live without the QAFloppy module unless you have to service a large number of PCs.

Drive Probe

Many programs on the market evaluate the condition of floppy disk drives by using a disk created or formatted on the same drive. A program that uses this technique cannot make a proper evaluation of a disk drive's alignment. A specially created disk produced by a tested and calibrated machine is required. This type of disk can be used as a reference standard by which to judge a drive. Accurite, the primary manufacturer of such reference standard floppy disks, helps specify floppy disk industry standards. Accurite produces the following three main types of reference standard disks used for testing drive function and alignment:

- Digital Diagnostic Diskette (DDD)

- High-Resolution Diagnostic Diskette (HRD)

- Analog Alignment Diskette (AAD)

The DDD disk, introduced in 1982, enables you to test drive alignment by using only software; no oscilloscope or special tools are needed. This disk is accurate to only 500μ-inches (millionths of an inch), good enough for a rough *test* of drive alignment but not nearly enough to use for *aligning* a drive.

The HRD disk, introduced in 1989, represents a breakthrough in floppy disk drive testing and alignment. The disk is accurate to within 50μ-inches (millionths of an inch), accurate enough to use not only for precise testing of floppy drives, but also for aligning drives. With software that uses this HRD disk, you can align a floppy drive by using no special tools or oscilloscope. Other than the program and the HRD disk, you need only an IBM-compatible system to which to connect the drive. This product has lowered significantly the cost of aligning a drive and has eliminated a lot of hassling with special test equipment.

The AAD disk has been the standard for drive alignment for many years. The disks, accurate to within 50μ inches (millionths of an inch), require that you use special test gear, such as an oscilloscope, to read the disk. These disks have no computer-readable data, only precisely placed analog tracks. Until HRD disks were available, using AADs was the only way to align drives properly.

The Accurite program Drive Probe is designed to work with the HRD disks (also from Accurite). Drive Probe is *the* most accurate and capable floppy disk testing program on the market, thanks to the use of HRD disks. Until other programs utilize the HRD disks for testing, Drive Probe is my software of choice for floppy disk testing. Because the Drive Probe software also acts as a disk exerciser, for use with AAD disks and an oscilloscope, you can move the heads to specific tracks for controlled testing.

Shareware and Public-Domain Diagnostics

Many excellent Shareware and public domain diagnostic programs are available, including programs for diagnosing problems with memory, hard disks, floppy disks, monitors and video adapters, and virtually any other part of the system. These programs can be excellent for users who would rather not spend the money on programs like Norton Utilities or QAPlus/FE.

Shareware is commercial-quality programs distributed under a *try now, pay later* concept. The authors of Shareware programs depend on honest users to pay for the Shareware they use (generally only a few dollars). Public domain software has been released by the author to be used by anyone without the payment of a fee of any kind to the author.

This software is distrubuted mostly via electronic bulletin board systems (BBS). To obtain software from a BBS, you download it by using a modem. However, there also are companies that distribute Shareware on disk, and one of them stands out: the Public Software Library. This organization, started as an outgrowth of a Houston computer users' group, has acquired the best single collection of public-domain and user-supported software. What makes this company extraordinary is that all the software is tested before entering the library. Bugged programs usually don't make it in the front door, which eliminates virus or Trojan-horse programs that damage a system. All the programs are the latest available versions, and earlier versions are purged from the library. Many other companies don't think twice about sending you a disk full of old programs.

The programs in this library are not sold, but are just distributed. The authors are aware of how these programs are distributed, and no excessive fees are charged for the disk and copying services. This truly legitimate company has program authors' approval to distribute software in this manner. All disks are guaranteed, unlike many comparable organizations that seem bent on making as much money as they can.

DOS Diagnostics Software

Since the introduction of Windows 3.1, and now with DOS 6.0, Microsoft is including its system diagnostics program, which is limited in comparison with the bells and whistles of Norton Utilities or QAPlus/FE. But MSD provides quick answers to system configuration problems such as interrupt request line (IRQ) conflicts and memory address problems.

In addition, MSD provides basic information about the system BIOS, CPU chip type, video adapter, network (if any), the mouse, installed disk drives (including CD-ROM drives), parallel and serial ports, the DOS version, and the device drivers and memory resident programs loaded in CONFIG.SYS and AUTOEXEC.BAT. MSD is installed in the Windows 3.1 and DOS 6.0 directories automatically if you have this software.

Windows Diagnostic Software

With the startling success of Windows 3.0 and 3.1, software utility manufacturers have raced to fill what was perceived as a shortage of diagnostic programs that will run under Windows. The results have been mixed. But some good utility packages have emerged.

For example, the Norton Desktop for Windows, which many users think of first as a replacement for Program Manager, includes the following: benchmarks that measure your CPU performance and your system's Windows performance; SYSINFO, an excellent system hardware information program; and details on your drives, available IRQs, memory, video adapter, printer, and other system information.

Another excellent Windows diagnostic program is WinSleuth Gold, which benchmarks your system and performs extremely thorough testing of your system hardware. It also details your drives, memory, video adapter, printer, and other system components. But a real treasure is its ability to tell you not only the IRQs available when Windows is running, but also available direct memory access (DMA) channels. Although numerous

DOS-based utility packages provide this information, few do so in Windows. And WinSleuth Gold can save you literally hours of scratching your head while trying to configure a sound board or other adapter to run in Windows.

Chapter Summary

This chapter has examined the diagnostic software utilities you can use as a valuable aid in diagnosing and troubleshooting a system. The chapter described the three levels of diagnostic software (POST, system, and advanced) and describes how you can get the most from the POST each time your system boots. Also included in this chapter was detailed information about IBM error codes. The chapter also included a reference chart showing the meanings of some of these codes.

In addition, this chapter covered diagnostic and benchmarking utility packages such as IBM's system diagnostics and advanced diagnostics, as well as Norton Utilities, Norton Desktop for Windows, QAPlus/FE, Checkit Pro, and WinSleuth Gold. Each of these packages, although taking different approaches to troubleshooting a PC, provides specialized diagnostics for particular areas of the system, such as system memory, hard drives, floppy drives, COM ports, parallel ports, video adapters, keyboards, the mouse, and other components.

Finally, this chapter included a discussion of diagnostic utilities distributed as Shareware or released into the public domain. Shareware and public domain software are a rich source of fantastic utilities that are relatively inexpensive, or free for the downloading.

Chapter 14

Hardware Troubleshooting Guide

By now, you have a good understanding of how things work and how they should be installed. The information in this chapter is what you need for troubleshooting various system components. To be a good troubleshooter, you should understand a system better than average computer users.

The procedures listed here are not meant to replace the hardware-maintenance service manuals your system manufacturer provides; they are designed to augment that information. These procedures are simple and concise, and they can be applied to almost any IBM or compatible system.

This chapter also lists the items that fail most often in a system and recommends the items you should carry in inventory as spare parts.

Getting Started with Troubleshooting

When you troubleshoot a system, approach the task with a clear mind and a relaxed attitude. If you get overexcited or panic, you will make determining the problem much more difficult.

Don't start taking apart the system unit right away. First, sit back and think about the problem. Make notes and record any observations. Your notes can be valuable, especially for difficult problems. Don't throw away the notes after the problem is solved, either, because they can be valuable for a recurring problem also. You should develop a systematic approach to determining what the problem is.

Here are some basic troubleshooting rules of thumb:

1. Check the installation and configuration. Usually, if I have just assembled a system and it doesn't work properly, it's my fault. I might have set a jumper incorrectly, plugged a cable in backward (or left it unplugged), or left out some other small detail.

2. *Check the installation and configuration again.* Even when I am sure that it's correct, I still make mistakes. Double-check everything.

3. If you still have a problem, work your way through the system item by item, from those most likely to cause the problem to those least likely to cause the problem. Because power supplies often cause problems, for example, you should check the power supply before many other devices. Cables can cause many problems, and usually are easy to test. *Always check the cables before replacing any attached devices.* An improper low-level format can cause hard disk problems, so check that possibility before you assume that the disk is bad.

4. A variation of the preceding rule is to work your way through the system from the simplest, least expensive, and easiest-to-replace item to the most complex, most expensive, and hardest-to-replace item. This rule is just common sense. Check cables before adapter cards, for example, and check adapter cards before disk drives. *Check everything else before you check the motherboard.*

5. Check the environment, including incoming power, ambient temperature fluctuations, humidity, static electricity, and airborne contaminants. Environmental influences can cause many problems, and these problems can be the most difficult to track down. (How can you see temperature or humidity variations?)

6. Keep system documentation and manuals nearby. Write your own documentation for your systems and include anything you put into your system. Document the interrupt and DMA channel settings, port usage, memory usage, which slots the adapter cards are installed in, which kinds of memory chips you used in the system, and so forth. This documentation can save you from much unnecessary labor.

Keep these simple rules in mind, and your troubleshooting sessions can be enjoyable challenges.

Handling Intermittent Problems

The bane of any troubleshooter is the intermittent problem. Often you must rely on a report from a user who cannot describe the symptom in an accurate, precise manner. You must interpret the user's description and guess at what really happened. You might think that you have fixed the problem, only to discover that it occurs again.

If you can, get the system user to write down when the problem occurs and the exact symptoms. Make sure they include information about how long the system was on before the problem occurred (this is helpful in determining if a problem is heat related). Before you begin disassembling the system, try to re-create the problem. When you have witnessed the intermittent problem, run the diagnostics software.

One of the best resources in the case of an intermittent failure is the advanced diagnostics software. This software can execute a test in endless-loop mode, which can be set to run all night or over a weekend. Another weapon commonly used to track down these types of problems is heat. You can use a hair dryer to warm up the motherboard and other electronics to help the failure along. You must be careful not to do any real damage, and I almost hesitate to mention it. Only experience and practice can give you a feel for just how hot you should make a board and when enough is enough.

Sometimes the opposite approach can work too. When a system is exhibiting a problem, you can spray on the suspected component some component cooler or Freon, which chills it. If the components failure is heat-related, this chilling often restores its operation.

Static electricity and other external environmental influences often can cause what seems to be an intermittent problem. Noting the state of the surrounding environment when the problems are occurring is important. Pay attention to time too. Sometimes strange time patterns can help you discover that a problem is related to an external influence, such as turning on large motors at the same time every day.

Keep these tips in mind the next time you have an intermittent problem, and you may find it easier to handle.

Troubleshooting Flowcharts

V

Troubleshooting Guide

Attempting to find a city in an unfamiliar state is made easy by the use of a road map. In the same vein, a map or flowchart can help you find a problem with a computer system. Knowing the appropriate path can get you to your destination for repairing the system with the least amount of detours. This section shows you the paths to follow to solve problems most successfully.

The Power Supply

If you suspect a power-supply problem, the simple measurements outlined in this section can help you determine whether the power supply is at fault. Because these measurements do not detect many intermittent or overload failures, you might have to use a spare power supply for long-term evaluation. If the symptoms and problems disappear with the replacement unit, you have found the source of your problem.

To test a power supply for proper output, check the voltage at the Power Good pin (P8-1 on IBM PC-XT-AT supplies) for 2.4 to 5.4 vdc. If the measurement is not within this range, the system never sees the Power Good signal and therefore never runs. In most cases, the supply is bad and must be replaced.

Continue by measuring the voltage ranges of the pins on the motherboard and drive power connectors (see table 14.1 and table 14.2). Note that the exact pin specifications and acceptable voltage ranges are for IBM PC-XT-AT power supplies as well as for most IBM-compatibles. Some systems, such as the PS/2 machines from IBM, use a different type of connector, and might accept different minimum and maximum voltages. Consult your systems technical-reference manual for this information.

Table 14.1 Motherboard Power-Connector Measurements

		PINS	
Minimum voltage	Maximum voltage	-Leads	+Leads
+4.8	+5.2	P8-5	P9-4
+4.5	+5.4	P9-3	P8-6
+11.5	+12.6	P9-1	P8-3
+10.8	+12.9	P8-4	P9-2

Table 14.2 Disk Drive Power-Connector Measurements

		PINS	
Minimum voltage	Maximum voltage	-Leads	+Leads
+4.8	+5.2	2	4
+11.5	+12.6	3	1

Replace the power supply if these voltages are incorrect. All these measurements must be made with the power supply installed in a system, and the system must be running. Again, these measurements are from IBM's documentation; other systems may allow different ranges to function. Most of the time on IBM-compatible systems, these ranges are acceptable:

> For output rated at +-5 volts, from 4.5 to 5.4.
> For output rated at +-12 volts, from 10.8 to 12.9.

The Appendix of this book has a detailed pin-out reference chart showing the proper voltage and signal at each power-supply connector. You can use this chart for reference when you make power-supply voltage measurements.

The types of power supplies used in these systems are called *switching* power supplies. These supplies always must have a proper load in order to function correctly. If you remove the supply from the system unit, set it on a workbench, plug it in, and power it on, the supply immediately shuts itself down. It does not run unless it's plugged into a motherboard and at least one disk drive.

The original AT systems were supplied with a huge load resistor mounted in place of the hard disk, which allowed the supply to operate properly even without a hard disk installed. If you are setting up a diskless system, make sure that you use a similar type of power load or you will have problems with the supply and possibly even burn it out. You can construct the same type of load resistor originally used by IBM by connecting a 6-ohm, 30-watt sandbar resistor between pins 1 and 2 on the connector. This procedure puts a 2.5-amp load on the supply's 12-volt output, which enables it to run normally. You still should connect the other power connectors to a motherboard for a load on the 5-volt outputs.

The System Board

A motherboard failure can be difficult to detect. In many cases, the system is simply nonfunctional. If the system is nonfunctional or partially functional and you suspect a motherboard failure, these troubleshooting procedures can be helpful:

■ Check all connectors to ensure that they are plugged in correctly.

■ Confirm that the wall outlet is a working outlet.

■ Look for foreign objects such as screws you might have dropped on the motherboard, and make sure that the board is clean.

■ Confirm that all system-board switch settings are correct.

■ Run the advanced diagnostics system-board test.

■ Check for error codes, displayed as follows:

1xx	System board errors
101	System board error; interrupt failure
102	System board error; timer failure
103	System board error; timer-interrupt failure
104	System board error; protected-mode failure
105	System board error; 8042 keyboard controller command failure
106	System board error; converting logic test
107	System board error; hot non-maskable interrupt (NMI) test
108	System board error; timer bus test
109	System board error; memory-select error
110	PS/2 system board parity-check error (PARITY CHECK 1)
111	PS/2 I/O channel (bus) parity-check error (PARITY CHECK 2)
112	PS/2 Micro Channel arbitration error; watchdog time-out
113	PS/2 Micro Channel arbitration error; DMA arbitration time-out
114	PS/2 external ROM checksum error
115	Cache parity error
121	Unexpected hardware interrupts occurred
131	PC system board cassette-port wrap test failure
131	Direct memory access (DMA) compatibility registers error
132	Direct memory access (DMA) extended registers error
133	Direct memory access (DMA) verify logic error
134	Direct memory access (DMA) arbitration logic error
151	PC Convertible; real-time clock RAM failed
151	Battery or CMOS RAM failure
152	PC Convertible; real-time clock failed
152	Real-time clock or CMOS RAM failure
160	PS/2 system board ID not recognized
161	CMOS configuration empty (dead battery)

(continues)

162	CMOS checksum error
163	CMOS error; date and time not set
164	Memory size error; CMOS setting does not match memory
165	PS/2 Micro Channel adapter ID and CMOS mismatch
166	PS/2 Micro Channel adapter time-out error
167	PS/2 CMOS clock not updating
168	CMOS configuration error; math coprocessor
170	PC Convertible LCD not in use when suspended
171	PC Convertible base 128K checksum failure
172	PC Convertible diskette active when suspended
173	PC Convertible real-time clock RAM verification error
174	PC Convertible LCD configuration changed
175	PC Convertible LCD alternate mode failed
194	System board memory error
199	User indicated INSTALLED DEVICES list is not correct

The Appendix in this book contains an extensive listing of POST (Power-On Self Test) and diagnostics error codes.

Next, check the supply voltage for 2.4 to 5.2 vdc between pins 1 and 5 (ground) at the system board. Turn off the power and remove all option adapters from the system board. Check in table 14.3 for the resistance values at the motherboard power connectors.

Table 14.3 Pin Minimums

-Lead	+Lead	Resistance
5	3	17 ohms
6	4	17 ohms
7	9	17 ohms
8	10	0.8 ohms
8	11	0.8 ohms
8	12	0.8 ohms

Improper resistance readings might indicate that the motherboard is defective, particularly if the resistance is below the minimums indicated. If the voltage measurements aren't within the parameters specified, the power supply might be defective.

Many IBM-compatible motherboards might not exhibit these same resistance characteristics. A better way to test systems that seem dead is to use one of the POST-code adapter cards. These cards show the manufacturer POST codes sent by the ROM BIOS to a special manufacturing-test I/O port address. These boards are described in more detail in Chapter 13, "System Diagnostics." Also, the Appendix lists POST codes for IBM and most other popular BIOS manufacturers. By using one of these cards plugged into a slot and reading the resulting code on the card's two-digit hex display, you often can accurately determine the cause of the system failure. Of course, if the cause is a component on the motherboard such as a DMA controller or other soldered IC chip, replacing the motherboard might be more prudent than repairing it.

Many boards use large-scale integrated chip sets that combine several functions in one chip. These chip sets, often surface mounted, are impossible to replace with conventional soldering tools; instead, special surface-mount rework solder equipment is needed. Also, obtaining a replacement part might prove very difficult, if not impossible, even if you can remove the bad one.

I remember one particularly difficult problem I was having with a system. I replaced a card in the system, tested it out (before putting the cover back on the system unit), and everything worked great. When it was time to put everything back together, I tightened all the screws, put on the cover, plugged in the printer, modem, video, and power cables, and turned the system back on. It didn't work. This was frustrating, especially since it had worked only moments earlier. I knew that the only thing I had done was to tighten the screws, so I tried loosening them. I learned that if I loosened the motherboard mounting screws by one-half turn, the system worked perfectly. It seems that tightening them applied just enough torque to the board that a hairline manufacturing crack (invisible to the naked eye) was widened to the point where a critical circuit was disrupted. As long as the pressure of the screw was not applied, the system was fine. The lesson learned is that you will want to check *everything* (including the smallest of screws) before replacing the actual motherboard.

The Battery

A defective battery usually is indicated during the POST with a 161 error. Other symptoms include your system being unable to maintain the date and time with the power off, or the inability to retain CMOS settings. The simplest way to determine whether a battery is defective is to replace it. Otherwise, first rerun the SETUP program; if this step doesn't correct the problem, disconnect the battery from the system board. The battery voltage between pins 1 and 4 on the battery connector should be at least 6.0 vdc. Replace the battery if it doesn't meet the correct voltage specifications.

> **Tip**
>
> Try lithium batteries rather than the cheaper alkaline batteries when you replace the batteries in a system. If you shop prudently, you should be able to buy the standard, AT-style, 6-volt lithium battery for between $6 to $12. The alkaline batteries, although they're cheaper, do not last as long. Never use conventional batteries, because they might leak acid on the motherboard.

Many newer systems do not use a standard type of battery. Rather, they use a special module developed by Dallas Semiconductor. These Dallas modules are the Dallas DS-1287 or DS-1387 Real-Time Clock modules. They combine the clock and CMOS circuitry with a built-in battery. The modules look like large, square IC chips, and usually are imprinted with the Dallas name and logo, which looks like an alarm clock. The battery in these modules is supposed to be good for more than ten years in the absence of power, and even longer if the system is running. Essentially, these units should outlast the computers in which they are installed.

If the Dallas modules require replacement, you can get new modules for about $14 if you purchase directly from Dallas, or about $30 if you buy the same chip from IBM or COMPAQ. The nice thing about replacing these modules is that you are replacing the entire clock and CMOS circuit along with the battery. If the CMOS chip was damaged on a normal motherboard without the Dallas module, you would have to desolder the defective chip and solder in a replacement. The Dallas modules are installed in sockets in most systems, like those from IBM and COMPAQ. You should keep a few of these modules around as spares, in case of CMOS configuration problems.

The Keyboard

Keyboard errors sometimes can be difficult to detect. To troubleshoot the keyboard and cable assembly, power on and observe the POST. Write down the 3xx error if you received one.

If your 3xx error is preceded by a two-digit hexadecimal number, this number is the scan code of a failing or stuck keyswitch. A complete set of scan-code-to-key-symbol reference charts is in the Appendix of this book. These charts tell you to which key the scan code refers. By removing the keycap of the offending key and cleaning the switch, you often can solve the problem. The scan-code reference charts in the Appendix cover all the keyboard types, including the original 83-key PC/XT keyboard, the 84-key AT keyboard, and the 101/102-key enhanced style keyboard.

Next, turn off the power and disconnect the keyboard. Then, turn on the power and check the voltage at the system-board keyboard connector for the specifications in table 14.4.

Table 14.4 Keyboard Connector Specifications	
Pin	**Voltage**
1	+2.0 to +5.5
2	+4.8 to +5.5
3	+2.0 to +5.5
4	Ground
5	+2.0 to +5.5

If your measurements don't match these voltages, the motherboard might be defective. Otherwise, the keyboard cable or keyboard might be defective. Keyboard-connector pinout reference charts are included in the Appendix of this book. These charts can help you test a cable or identify the functions of the pins on the keyboard connectors on the motherboard, keyboard, and each end of the keyboard cable. If you suspect the cable as a problem, the easiest thing to do is replace the keyboard cable with a known good one and run the Advanced Diagnostics keyboard test.

A list of diagnostics keyboard error codes is displayed as follows:

3xx	Keyboard errors
301	Keyboard reset or stuck-key failure (XX 301, XX = scan code in hex)
302	System-unit keylock is locked
302	User indicated keyboard test error
303	Keyboard or system-board error; keyboard controller failure
304	Keyboard or system-board error; keyboard clock high
305	Keyboard +5v error; PS/2 keyboard fuse (on system board) error
341	Keyboard error
342	Keyboard cable error
343	Keyboard LED card or cable failure
365	Keyboard LED card or cable failure
366	Keyboard interface cable failure
367	Keyboard LED card or cable failure

The Video Adapter

If you suspect problems with the video board, make sure the switch settings on the motherboard and video card are correct, and turn on the power. Listen for audio response during the POST (one long and two short beeps indicate a video failure).

If the adapter is supported, run the Advanced Diagnostics video adapter test for the particular adapter you want to test. Adapters that aren't supported always fail the tests even though they might be good. Error codes are displayed as follows:

4xx	Monochrome Display Adapter (MDA)/parallel port errors
401	Monochrome memory, horizontal sync frequency, or video-test failure
401	PS/2 system board parallel-port failure
408	User indicated display-attributes failure
416	User indicated character-set failure
424	User indicated 80x25 mode failure
432	Parallel-port test failure; Monochrome Display Adapter

5xx	Color Graphics Adapter (CGA) errors
501	CGA memory, horizontal sync frequency, or video-test failure
503	CGA adapter controller failure
508	User indicated display-attribute failure
516	User indicated character-set failure
524	User indicated 80x25 mode failure
532	User indicated 40x25 mode failure

(continues)

540	User indicated 320x200 graphics mode failure
548	User indicated 640x200 graphics mode failure
556	User indicated light-pen test failed
564	User indicated paging-test failed

24xx	**Enhanced Graphics Adapter (EGA) errors**
24xx	**PS/2 system board Video Graphics Array (VGA) errors**
2401	Video-adapter test failure
2402	Video-display error
2408	User indicated display-attribute test failed
2409	Video-display error
2410	Video-adapter error
2416	User indicated character-set test failed
2424	User indicated 80x25 mode failure
2432	User indicated 40x25 mode failure
2440	User indicated 320x200 graphics mode failure
2448	User indicated 640x200 graphics mode failure
2456	User indicated light-pen test failure
2464	User indicated paging-test failure

25xx	**Alternate Enhanced Graphics Adapter (EGA) errors**
2501	Video-adapter test failure
2502	Video-display error
2508	User indicated display-attribute test failed
2509	Video-display error
2510	Video-adapter error
2516	User indicated character-set test failed
2524	User indicated 80x25 mode failure
2532	User indicated 40x25 mode failure
2540	User indicated 320x200 graphics mode failure
2548	User indicated 640x200 graphics mode failure
2556	User indicated light-pen test failure
2564	User indicated paging-test failure

39xx	**Professional Graphics Adapter (PGA) errors**
3901	PGA test failure
3902	ROM1 self-test failure
3903	ROM2 self-test failure
3904	RAM self-test failure
3905	Cold Start Cycle power error
3906	Data error in communications RAM
3907	Address error in communications RAM
3908	Bad data reading or writing 6845-like register

3909	Bad data in lower E0h bytes reading or writing 6845-like registers
3910	Graphics controller display-bank output-latches error
3911	Basic clock error
3912	Command-control error
3913	Vertical sync scanner error
3914	Horizontal sync scanner error
3915	Intech error
3916	Look-up table address error
3917	Look-up table red RAM chip error
3918	Look-up table green RAM chip error
3919	Look-up table blue RAM chip error
3920	Look-up table data latch error
3921	Horizontal-display error
3922	Vertical-display error
3923	Light-pen error
3924	Unexpected error
3925	Emulator-addressing error
3926	Emulator data-latch error
3927	Base for error codes 3928-3930 (emulator RAM)
3928	Emulator RAM error
3929	Emulator RAM error
3930	Emulator RAM error
3931	Emulator horizontal- or vertical-display problem
3932	Emulator cursor-position error
3933	Emulator attribute-display problem
3934	Emulator cursor-display error
3935	Fundamental emulation RAM problem
3936	Emulation character-set problem
3937	Emulation graphics-display error
3938	Emulation character-display problem
3939	Emulation bank-select error
3940	Adapter RAM U2 error
3941	Adapter RAM U4 error
3942	Adapter RAM U6 error
3943	Adapter RAM U8 error
3944	Adapter RAM U10 error
3945	Adapter RAM U1 error
3946	Adapter RAM U3 error
3947	Adapter RAM U5 error
3948	Adapter RAM U7 error
3949	Adapter RAM U9 error
3950	Adapter RAM U12 error

V

Troubleshooting Guide

(continues)

3951	Adapter RAM U14 error
3952	Adapter RAM U16 error
3953	Adapter RAM U18 error
3954	Adapter RAM U20 error
3955	Adapter RAM U11 error
3956	Adapter RAM U13 error
3957	Adapter RAM U15 error
3958	Adapter RAM U17 error
3959	Adapter RAM U19 error
3960	Adapter RAM U22 error
3961	Adapter RAM U24 error
3962	Adapter RAM U26 error
3963	Adapter RAM U28 error
3964	Adapter RAM U30 error
3965	Adapter RAM U21 error
3966	Adapter RAM U23 error
3967	Adapter RAM U25 error
3968	Adapter RAM U27 error
3969	Adapter RAM U29 error
3970	Adapter RAM U32 error
3971	Adapter RAM U34 error
3972	Adapter RAM U36 error
3973	Adapter RAM U38 error
3974	Adapter RAM U40 error
3975	Adapter RAM U31 error
3976	Adapter RAM U33 error
3977	Adapter RAM U35 error
3978	Adapter RAM U37 error
3979	Adapter RAM U39 error
3980	Graphics controller RAM-timing error
3981	Graphics controller read/write latch error
3982	Shift register bus output-latches error
3983	Addressing error (vertical column of memory; U2 at top)
3984	Addressing error (vertical column of memory; U4 at top)
3985	Addressing error (vertical column of memory; U6 at top)
3986	Addressing error (vertical column of memory; U8 at top)
3987	Addressing error (vertical column of memory; U10 at top)
3988	Base for error codes 3989-3991 (horizontal bank-latch errors)
3989	Horizontal bank-latch errors
3990	Horizontal bank-latch errors
3991	Horizontal bank-latch errors
3992	RAG/CAG graphics controller error

3993	Multiple write modes, nibble mask errors
3994	Row nibble (display RAM) error
3995	Graphics controller addressing error

50xx	**PC Convertible LCD errors**
5001	LCD display buffer failure
5002	LCD font buffer failure
5003	LCD controller failure
5004	User indicated PEL/drive test failed
5008	User indicated display-attribute test failed
5016	User indicated character-set test failed
5020	User indicated alternate character-set test failure
5024	User indicated 80x25 mode test failure
5032	User indicated 40x25 mode test failure
5040	User indicated 320x200 graphics test failure
5048	User indicated 640x200 graphics test failure
5064	User indicated paging-test failure

74xx	**IBM PS/2 Display Adapter (VGA card) errors**
	74xx 8514/A Display Adapter errors
7426	8514 display error
7440	8514/A memory module 31 error
7441	8514/A memory module 30 error
7442	8514/A memory module 29 error
7443	8514/A memory module 28 error
7444	8514/A memory module 22 error
7445	8514/A memory module 21 error
7446	8514/A memory module 18 error
7447	8514/A memory module 17 error
7448	8514/A memory module 32 error
7449	8514/A memory module 14 error
7450	8514/A memory module 13 error
7451	8514/A memory module 12 error
7452	8514/A memory module 06 error
7453	8514/A memory module 05 error
7454	8514/A memory module 02 error
7455	8514/A memory module 01 error
7460	8514/A memory module 16 error
7461	8514/A memory module 27 error
7462	8514/A memory module 26 error
7463	8514/A memory module 25 error
7464	8514/A memory module 24 error

V

Troubleshooting Guide

(continues)

7465	8514/A memory module 23 error
7466	8514/A memory module 20 error
7467	8514/A memory module 19 error
7468	8514/A memory module 15 error
7469	8514/A memory module 11 error
7470	8514/A memory module 10 error
7471	8514/A memory module 09 error
7472	8514/A memory module 08 error
7473	8514/A memory module 07 error
7474	8514/A memory module 04 error
7475	8514/A memory module 03 error

149xx	**P70/P75 Plasma Display and Adapter errors**
14901	Plasma Display Adapter failure
14902	Plasma Display Adapter failure
14922	Plasma Display failure
14932	External Display failure

The Fixed Disk Drive

Problems with hard disks are indicated by 17xx errors. If you suspect any problems with a drive, controller, or cable, you can substitute equipment that you know works properly.

Check for proper configuration of drives (drive-select jumpers and terminating resistors). Turn off the power. Power on and boot the advanced diagnostics (or a similar program). Run the fixed disk drive and adapter tests. Error codes indicating various problems are displayed as follows:

17xx	**ST-506/412 fixed disk and controller errors**
1701	Fixed disk general POST error
1702	Drive or controller time-out error
1703	Drive-seek error
1704	Controller failed
1705	Drive sector not found error
1706	Write-fault error
1707	Drive track 0 error
1708	Head-select error
1709	Error correction code (ECC) error
1710	Sector-buffer overrun
1711	Bad address mark
1712	Internal controller diagnostics failure
1713	Data-compare error
1714	Drive not ready
1715	Track 0 indicator failure

1716	Diagnostics cylinder errors
1717	Surface-read errors
1718	Hard drive type error
1720	Bad diagnostics cylinder
1726	Data-compare error
1730	Controller error
1731	Controller error
1732	Controller error
1733	BIOS undefined error return
1735	Bad command error
1736	Data-corrected error
1737	Bad track error
1738	Bad sector error
1739	Bad initialization error
1740	Bad sense error
1750	Drive verify failure
1751	Drive read failure
1752	Drive write failure
1753	Drive random-read test failure
1754	Drive-seek test failure
1755	Controller failure
1756	Controller error-correction code (ECC) test failure
1757	Controller head-select failure
1780	Seek failure; drive 0
1781	Seek failure; drive 1
1782	Controller test failure
1790	Diagnostic cylinder read error; drive 0
1791	Diagnostic cylinder read error; drive 1

104xx	**ESDI fixed disk or adapter errors**
10450	Read/write test failed
10451	Read verify test failed
10452	Seek test failed
10453	Wrong device type indicated
10454	Controller test failed sector-buffer test
10455	Controller failure
10456	Controller diagnostic command failure
10461	Drive format error
10462	Controller head-select error
10463	Drive read/write sector error
10464	Drive primary defect map unreadable
10465	Controller; error correction code (ECC) 8-bit error

(continues)

10466	Controller; error correction code (ECC) 9-bit error
10467	Drive soft-seek error
10468	Drive hard-seek error
10469	Drive soft-seek error count exceeded
10470	Controller-attachment diagnostic error
10471	Controller wrap mode interface error
10472	Controller wrap mode drive-select error
10473	Read verify test error
10480	Seek failure; drive 0
10481	Seek failure; drive 1
10482	Controller test failure
10482	Controller transfer-acknowledge error
10483	Controller reset failure
10484	Controller; head select 3 error
10485	Controller; head select 2 error
10486	Controller; head select 1 error
10487	Controller; head select 0 error
10488	Controller; read gate—command complete 2 error
10489	Controller; write gate—command complete 1 error
10490	Diagnostic area read error; drive 0
10491	Diagnostic area read error; drive 1
10499	Controller failure

SCSI device errors

096xxxx	SCSI adapter with cache (32-bit) errors
112xxxx	SCSI adapter (16-bit without cache) errors
113xxxx	System board SCSI adapter (16-bit) errors
208xxxx	Unknown SCSI device errors
209xxxx	SCSI removable disk errors
210xxxx	SCSI fixed disk errors
211xxxx	SCSI tape drive errors
212xxxx	SCSI printer errors
213xxxx	SCSI processor errors
214xxxx	SCSI Write-Once Read Mostly (WORM) drive errors
215xxxx	SCSI CD-ROM drive errors
216xxxx	SCSI scanner errors
217xxxx	SCSI optical-memory errors
218xxxx	SCSI jukebox-changer errors
219xxxx	SCSI communications errors

Check the cables to make sure that they aren't defective, and measure voltages at the drive power connector as indicated in the section "The Power Supply" earlier in this chapter.

If you are sure that the power supply is not the cause, you can attempt to replace the logic board on the drive with one from another unit. This procedure might restore the drive to operation and also enable the data to be read. If preserving the data is not important, you might attempt a low-level format without replacing the logic board. Often, intermittent hard disk read and write or boot-up problems can be caused by a drive whose low-level format has become unstable.

The Floppy Disk Drive

If you suspect that the floppy drives are defective, make sure that the problem isn't in the floppy disk being used. A number of problems can stem from improperly inserting and clamping the floppy disk in the drive. Before you continue, remove and carefully reinsert the floppy disk to be sure that it is not the problem. If the drive receives power separately from the computer, make sure that nothing is wrong with the power outlet. Be sure that all cables and connectors are plugged in correctly. Check to see that all drives are configured properly (drive-select jumpers, terminating resistors, pin 34, and media sensor) and then run the advanced diagnostics disk drive and adapter tests. Error codes are displayed as follows:

6xx	Floppy drive and controller errors
601	Floppy drive and controller Power-On Self Test failure
602	Diskette boot sector is not valid
603	Diskette size error
606	Diskette verify test failure
607	Write-protect error
608	Drive command error
610	Diskette initialization failure; track 0 bad
611	Drive time-out error
612	Controller chip (NEC) error
613	Direct memory access (DMA) error
614	Direct memory access (DMA) boundary-overrun error
615	Drive index timing error
616	Drive speed error
621	Drive seek error
622	Drive Cyclic Redundancy Check (CRC) error
623	Sector Not Found error
624	Address mark error
625	Controller chip (NEC) seek error
626	Diskette data-compare error
627	Diskette change error
628	Diskette removed

(continues)

630	Index stuck high; drive A:
631	Index stuck low; drive A:
632	Track 0 stuck off; drive A:
633	Track 0 stuck on; drive A:
640	Index stuck high; drive B:
641	Index stuck low; drive B:
642	Track 0 stuck off; drive B:
643	Track 0 stuck on; drive B:
645	No index pulse
646	Drive track 0 detection failed
647	No transitions on read data line
648	Format test failed
649	Incorrect media type in drive
650	Drive-speed error
651	Format failure
652	Verify failure
653	Read failure
654	Write failure
655	Controller error
656	Drive failure
657	Write-protect stuck; protected
658	Changeline stuck; changed
659	Write-protect stuck; unprotected
660	Changeline stuck; unchanged
73xx	**3 1/2-inch external diskette drive errors**
7301	Diskette drive or adapter test failure
7306	Disk Changeline failure
7307	Diskette is write-protected
7308	Drive-command error
7310	Diskette initialization failure; track 0 bad
7311	Drive time-out error
7312	Controller chip (NEC) error
7313	Direct memory access (DMA) error
7314	Direct memory access (DMA) boundary overrun
7315	Drive index timing error
7316	Drive-speed error
7321	Drive-seek error
7322	Drive Cyclic Redundancy Check (CRC) error
7323	Sector not found error
7324	Address mark error
7325	Controller chip (NEC) seek error
107xx	5 1/4-inch external diskette drive or adapter errors

Check the voltages at the power connector for the floppy drives, as indicated in the section "The Power Supply" earlier in this chapter.

Test the drive for correct rotational speed using diagnostics, and adjust the speed if the drive allows a speed adjustment. Most floppy disk drives made since 1986 have no speed adjustment. Rather, these drives automatically adjust themselves to the correct speed. If a nonadjustable drive is off-speed, it must be replaced. If you use a program such as the Accurite Drive Probe, you can check the alignment of the drive.

Make sure that the cable and connectors are good, and check the cables for continuity. If the power-connector voltages don't measure as they should, the power supply might be bad.

Serial- and Parallel-Port Tests

To test serial- or parallel-port cards, run the advanced-diagnostics communications adapter tests. Most tests require that you attach a loopback connector (also called a wrap plug) to the port, to allow the port to transmit and receive signals simultaneously for test purposes. Pinout charts for all forms of serial and parallel connectors are in the Appendix of this book. Also included are wiring diagrams for serial and parallel wrap plugs if you want to make your own rather than purchase them.

The diagnostics tests display error codes as follows:

9xx	**Parallel printer adapter errors**
901	Printer adapter data-register latch error
902	Printer adapter control-register latch error
903	Printer adapter register-address decode error
904	Printer adapter address decode error
910	Status line(s) wrap connector error
911	Status line bit 8 wrap error
912	Status line bit 7 wrap error
913	Status line bit 6 wrap error
914	Status line bit 5 wrap error
915	Status line bit 4 wrap error
916	Printer adapter interrupt wrap error
917	Unexpected printer-adapter interrupt
92x	Feature-register error

10xx	**Alternate parallel printer adapter errors**
1001	Printer adapter data register latch error
1002	Printer adapter control register latch error
1003	Printer adapter register address decode error
1004	Printer adapter address decode error
1010	Status line(s) wrap connector error
1011	Status line bit 8 wrap error

(continues)

1012	Status line bit 7 wrap error
1013	Status line bit 6 wrap error
1014	Status line bit 5 wrap error
1015	Status line bit 4 wrap error
1016	Printer adapter interrupt wrap error
1017	Unexpected printer-adapter interrupt
102x	Feature-register error

11xx	**Primary Async communications (serial port COM1:) errors**
1101	16450/16550 chip error
1101	PC Convertible internal modem 8250 baud generator test failed
1102	Card-selected feedback error
1102	PC Convertible internal modem test failed
1103	Port 102h register test failure
1103	PC Convertible internal modem dial-tone test 1 failed
1104	PC Convertible internal modem dial-tone test 2 failed
1106	Serial option cannot be put to sleep
1107	Cable error
1108	Interrupt request (IRQ) 3 error
1109	Interrupt request (IRQ) 4 error
1110	16450/16550 chip register failure
1111	Internal wrap test of 16450/16550 chip modem-control-line failure
1112	External wrap test of 16450/16550 chip modem-control-line failure
1113	16450/16550 chip transmit error
1114	16450/16550 chip receive error
1115	16450/16550 chip receive error; data not equal to transmit data
1116	16450/16550 chip interrupt function error
1117	16450/16550 chip baud-rate test failure
1118	16450/16550 chip receive external data wrap test failure
1119	16550 chip first-in first-out (FIFO) buffer failure
1120	Interrupt enable register error; all bits cannot be set
1121	Interrupt enable register error; all bits cannot be reset
1122	Interrupt pending; stuck on
1123	Interrupt ID register; stuck on
1124	Modem control register error; all bits cannot be set
1125	Modem control register error; all bits cannot be reset
1126	Modem status register error; all bits cannot be set
1127	Modem status register error; all bits cannot be reset
1128	Interrupt ID error
1129	Cannot force overrun error
1130	No modem-status interrupt
1131	Invalid interrupt pending

1132	No data ready
1133	No data available interrupt
1134	No transmit holding interrupt
1135	No interrupts
1136	No received line status interrupt
1137	No receive data available
1138	Transmit holding register not empty
1139	No modem-status interrupt
1140	Transmit holding register not empty
1141	No interrupts
1142	No interrupt 4
1143	No interrupt 3
1144	No data transferred
1145	Maximum baud-rate error
1146	Minimum baud-rate error
1148	Time-out error
1149	Invalid data returned
1150	Modem status register error
1151	No data set ready and Delta data set ready
1152	No data set ready
1153	No Delta data set ready
1154	Modem status register not clear
1155	No clear to send and Delta clear to send
1156	No clear to send
1157	No Delta clear to send

12xx	**Alternate Async communications (serial COM2:, COM3:, and COM4:) errors**
1201	16450/16550 chip error
1202	Card-selected feedback error
1203	Port 102h register test failure
1206	Serial option cannot be put to sleep
1207	Cable error
1208	Interrupt request (IRQ) 3 error
1209	Interrupt request (IRQ) 4 error
1210	16450/16550 chip register failure
1211	Internal wrap test of 16450/16550 chip modem control line failure
1212	External wrap test of 16450/16550 chip modem control line failure
1213	16450/16550 chip transmit error
1214	16450/16550 chip receive error
1215	16450/16550 chip receive error; data not equal to transmit data
1216	16450/16550 chip interrupt function error

(continues)

V

Troubleshooting Guide

1217	16450/16550 chip baud rate test failure
1218	16450/16550 chip receive external data wrap test failure
1219	16550 chip first-in first-out (FIFO) buffer failure
1220	Interrupt enable register error; all bits cannot be set
1221	Interrupt enable register error; all bits cannot be reset
1222	Interrupt pending; stuck on
1223	Interrupt ID register; stuck on
1224	Modem control register error; all bits cannot be set
1225	Modem control register error; all bits cannot be reset
1226	Modem status register error; all bits cannot be set
1227	Modem status register error; all bits cannot be reset
1228	Interrupt ID error
1229	Cannot force overrun error
1230	No modem-status interrupt
1231	Invalid interrupt pending
1232	No data ready
1233	No data available interrupt
1234	No transmit holding interrupt
1235	No interrupts
1236	No received line status interrupt
1237	No receive data available
1238	Transmit holding register not empty
1239	No modem-status interrupt
1240	Transmit holding register not empty
1241	No interrupts
1242	No interrupt 4
1243	No interrupt 3
1244	No data transferred
1245	Maximum baud rate error
1246	Minimum baud rate error
1248	Time-out error
1249	Invalid data returned
1250	Modem status register error
1251	No data set ready and Delta data set ready
1252	No data set ready
1253	No Delta data set ready
1254	Modem-status register not clear
1255	No clear to send and Delta clear to send
1256	No clear to send
1257	No Delta clear to send

For serial ports only, check for a voltage reading of -10.8 to -12.9 vdc between pins 4 and 8 (ground) and the system-board power connector. If the voltage measurement isn't within the range specified, the power supply might be defective.

The Speaker

To verify the operation of the speaker in the system unit, turn off the power. Set your meter to Ohms X1 Scale. Disconnect the speaker from the system board. Check the continuity of the speaker. If the speaker doesn't have continuity, it is defective and should be replaced.

Common Failures

Of all possible problems that can occur with a computer, some are more common than others. This section reviews some of a computer's most common failures.

Items with a High Failure Rate

The most common failures in a PC are mechanical—disk drives (floppy and hard disk) and power supplies. These items can and do fail, sometimes with no warning. Memory devices also fail periodically.

The power supply is a very failure-prone item, especially in the IBM PC in which an underrated unit was used. I usually replace the PC power supply when I upgrade a PC because most upgrades (such as hard disks) use much power—more than is available in the original supply. Having too much power supply is better than not enough.

These system components are most likely to fail:

> Power supply
> Hard disk low-level format
> Floppy drive
> Hard disk controller
> Hard disk
> Memory chips

Floppy Drive Failure

Only two floppy disk drive problems can be fixed quickly: the drive speed and dirty drives. If you have other problems with a floppy disk drive, you probably have to replace the drive with a new or rebuilt unit. Because floppy disk drives are relatively inexpensive, spending a lot of time trying to fix them doesn't make sense.

Adjusting the speed of a floppy disk drive is easy if the drive is an older unit that is adjustable. You usually can do so by turning a screw on the motor-control logic board while watching the results with one of the many floppy disk testing programs available.

If you have many drives to be repaired or aligned, you should locate a service company that specializes in disk drive service and alignments. Most service companies will align a floppy drive for $25 to $50. This cost must be weighed against the replacement cost.

I have purchased new high-density drives for as low as $59, so I'm not sure that I would spend almost that much to align an old drive. If you want to have your drives aligned, see the vendor list in the Appendix of this book for a list of some companies that perform this service.

Cleaning disk drives is normally part of a preventive maintenance program, but it might have been neglected. Always remember to clean a problem drive before deciding to replace it. Because some of the disk-based cleaners are abrasive to the drive heads, always use the wet-type cleaners—they are gentler on the heads.

Recommended Spare Components and Parts

I recommend carrying spares for these items:

> Cables of all types
> Power supplies
> Memory chips
> Floppy disk drives
> Floppy drive controllers
> Batteries

If the system is very important and must be up all the time, you should add a couple more items to the spares list:

> Hard disk drives and controllers
> Keyboards

With these items on hand, you are prepared for 90 percent of all system failures and problems.

Last-Ditch Fixes

When all else fails when you are troubleshooting a problem, a foolproof method exists for diagnosing the problem.

Locate a system identical to the failing one. The closer the match, the better. The duplicate system should be the same type, and from the same manufacturer if possible. Also, if possible, it should have the same adapter boards installed and be configured exactly the same way.

Verify that the duplicate system runs correctly and does not exhibit the symptoms of the failing unit. Begin placing items from the spare unit into the malfunctioning unit one by one, and test after replacing each item. First replace each cable, for example, using the spare systems cables. Progress to each adapter card, disk drive, power supply, motherboard, and so on.

You will know when you have found the problem part when the malfunctioning unit begins to work.

Fortunately, this brute force method is rarely required, but in a pinch, it works. This method requires little thought, and it's a method anyone can use. Keep it in mind when you are under pressure to fix a system.

Chapter Summary

This chapter has covered hardware troubleshooting techniques in detail. You have received some basic tips for good troubleshooting. The body of this chapter has covered specific component troubleshooting, giving you the procedures, measurements, and observations you should make to determine the location of a system fault. The last part of this chapter has focused on failure-prone items and how to handle certain troublesome situations.

V

Troubleshooting Guide

Chapter 15

Software Troubleshooting Guide

This chapter focuses on the problems that occur in PC systems because of faulty or incompatible software. First, it describes the structure of DOS and how DOS works with hardware in a functioning system. Topics of particular interest are

- DOS file structure

- DOS disk organization

- DOS programs for data and disk recovery (their capabilities and dangers)

Additionally, the chapter examines two other important software-related issues: using memory-resident software (and dealing with the problems it can cause) and distinguishing a software problem from a hardware problem.

Understanding the Disk Operating System (DOS)

Information about DOS may seem out of place in a book about hardware upgrade and repair, but if you ignore DOS and other software when you troubleshoot a system, you can miss a number of problems. The best system troubleshooters and diagnosticians know the entire system—hardware and software.

This book cannot discuss DOS in depth, but if you need to read more about it, Que Corporation publishes some good books on the subject (*Using MS DOS 6*, for example).

This section describes the basics of DOS: where it fits into the PC system architecture, what its components are, and what happens when a system boots (starts up). Understanding the booting process can be helpful when you're diagnosing start-up problems. This section also explains DOS configuration—an area in which many people experience problems—and the file formats DOS uses, as well as how DOS manages information on a disk.

Operating-System Basics

DOS is just one component in the total system architecture. A PC system has a distinct hierarchy of software that controls the system at all times. Even when you are operating within an application program such as 1-2-3 or another high-level application software, several other layers of programs are always executing underneath. Usually the layers can be defined distinctly, but sometimes the boundaries are vague.

Communications generally occur only between adjoining layers in the architecture, but this rule is not absolute. Many programs ignore the services provided by the layer directly beneath them and eliminate the middleman by skipping one or more layers. An example is a program that ignores the DOS and ROM BIOS video routines and communicates directly with the hardware in the interest of the highest possible screen performance. Although the high-performance goal is admirable, many operating environments (such as OS/2 and Windows) no longer allow direct access to the hardware. Programs that do not play by the rules must be rewritten to run in these new environments.

At the lowest level of the system hierarchy is the hardware. By placing various bytes of information at certain ports or locations within a systems memory structure, you can control virtually anything connected to the CPU. Maintaining control at the hardware level is difficult; doing so requires a complete and accurate knowledge of the system architecture. The level of detail required of the software operating at this level is the most intense. Commands to the system at this level are in *machine language* (binary groups of information applied directly to the microprocessor). Machine-language instructions are limited in their function: You must use many of them to perform even the smallest amount of useful work. The large number of instructions required is not really a problem because these instructions are executed extremely rapidly, wasting few system resources.

Programmers can write programs consisting of machine-language instructions, but generally they use a tool—an *assembler*—to ease the process. They write programs using an *editor,* and then use the assembler to convert the editor's output to pure machine language. Assembler commands are still very low level, and using them effectively requires that programmers be extremely knowledgeable. No one (in his or her right mind) writes directly in machine code anymore; assembly language is the lowest level of programming environment typically used today. Even assembly language, however, is losing favor among programmers because of the amount of knowledge and work required to complete even simple tasks and because of its lack of portability between different kinds of systems.

When you start a PC system, a series of machine-code programs assume control: They are the ROM BIOS. This set of programs, always present in a system, talks (in machine code) to the hardware. The BIOS accepts or interprets commands supplied by programs above it in the system hierarchy and translates them to machine-code commands that then are passed on to the microprocessor. Commands at this level typically are called *interrupts* or *services.* A programmer generally can use nearly any language to supply these instructions to the BIOS. A complete list of these services is supplied in the IBM *BIOS Interface Technical Reference Manual.*

DOS itself is made up of several components. It attaches to the BIOS, and part of DOS actually becomes an extension of the BIOS, providing more interrupts and services for other programs to use. DOS provides for communication with the ROM BIOS in PCs and with higher-level software (such as applications). Because DOS gives the programmer interrupts and services to use in addition to those provided by the ROM BIOS, a lot of reinventing the wheel in programming routines is eliminated. For example, DOS provides an extremely rich set of functions that can open, close, find, delete, create, rename, and perform other file-handling tasks. When programmers want to include some of these functions in their programs, they can rely on DOS to do most of the work.

This standard set of functions that applications use to read from and write data to disks makes data-recovery operations possible. Imagine how tough writing programs and using computers would be if every application program had to implement its own custom disk interface, with a proprietary directory and file-retrieval system. Every application would require its own special disks. Fortunately, DOS provides a standard set of documented file-storage and -retrieval provisions that all software can use; as a result, you can make some sense out of what you find on a typical disk.

Another primary function of DOS is to load and run other programs. As it performs that function, DOS is the *shell* within which another program can be executed. DOS provides the functions and environment required by other software—including operating environments such as GEM and Windows—to run on PC systems in a standard way.

The System ROM BIOS

Think of the system ROM BIOS as a form of compatibility glue that sits between the hardware and an operating system. Why is it that IBM can sell the same DOS to run on the original IBM PC *and* on the PS/2 Model 90 XP 486—two very different hardware platforms? If DOS were written to talk directly to the hardware on all systems, it would be a very hardware-specific program. Instead, IBM developed a set of standard services and functions each system should be capable of performing and coded them as programs in the ROM BIOS. Each system then gets a completely custom ROM BIOS that talks directly to the hardware in the system and knows exactly how to perform each specific function on that hardware only.

This convention enables operating systems to be written to what amounts to a standard interface that can be made available on many different types of hardware. Any applications written to the operating-system standard interface can run on that system. Figure 15.1 shows that two very different hardware platforms can each have a custom ROM BIOS that talks directly to the hardware and still provides a standard interface to an operating system.

The two different hardware platforms described in figure 15.1 can run not only the exact same version of DOS, but also the same applications programs because of the standard interfaces provided by the ROM BIOS and DOS. Keep in mind, however, that the actual ROM BIOS code differs among the specific machines and that it is not usually possible therefore to run a ROM BIOS designed for one system in a different system. ROM BIOS upgrades must come from a source that has an intimate understanding of the specific motherboard on which the chip will be placed because the ROM must be custom written for that particular hardware.

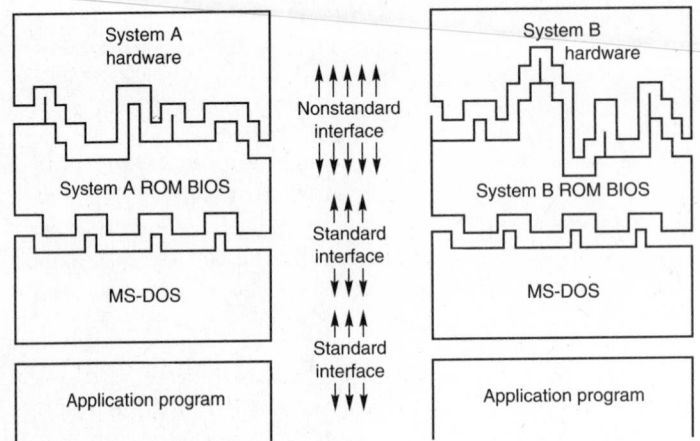

Fig. 15.1

A representation of the software layers in an IBM-compatible system.

The portion of DOS shown in figure 15.1 is the system portion, or core, of DOS. This core is found physically as the two system files on any bootable DOS disk. These hidden system files will usually have one of two sets of names, IBMBIO.COM and IBMDOS.COM (used in IBM and COMPAQ DOS), or IO.SYS and MSDOS.SYS (used in MS-DOS and versions of DOS licensed from Microsoft by original equipment manufacturers (OEMs). These files must be the first and second files listed in the directory on a bootable DOS disk.

Figure 15.1 represents a simplified view of the system. In reality, some subtle but important differences exist. Ideally, application programs are insulated from the hardware by the ROM BIOS and DOS, but in reality many programmers write portions of their programs to talk directly to the hardware, circumventing DOS and the ROM BIOS. A program therefore might work only on specific hardware, even if the proper DOS and ROM BIOS interfaces are present in other hardware.

Programs designed to go directly to the hardware are written that way mainly to increase performance. For example, many programs directly access the video hardware to improve screen-update performance. These applications often have install programs that require you to specify exactly what hardware is present in your system so that the program can load the correct hardware-dependent routines into the application.

Additionally, some utility programs absolutely must talk directly to the hardware to perform their function. For example, a low-level format program must talk directly to the hard disk controller hardware to perform the low-level format of the disk. Such programs are very specific to a certain controller or controller type. Another type of system-specific utility, the driver programs, enables extended memory to function as expanded memory on an 80386-based system. These drivers work by accessing the 80386 directly and utilizing specific features of the chip.

Another way that reality might differ from the simple view is that DOS itself will communicate directly with the hardware. In fact, much of the IBMBIO.COM file consists of low-level drivers designed to supplant and supersede ROM BIOS code in the system. People who own both IBM systems and compatibles might wonder why IBM never seems to have ROM BIOS upgrades to correct bugs and problems with its systems, although for vendors of most compatible systems, a ROM upgrade is at least a semiannual occurrence. The reason is simple: IBM distributes its ROM patches and upgrades in DOS. When IBM DOS loads, it determines the system type and ID information from the ROM, and loads different routines depending on which version of ROM it finds. For example, at least four different hard disk code sections are in IBM DOS, but only one is loaded for a specific system.

I have taken a single DOS boot disk with only the system files (COMMAND.COM and CHKDSK.COM) on it, and booted the disk on both an XT and an AT system, each one with an identical 640K of memory. After loading DOS, CHKDSK reported different amounts of free memory, which showed that DOS had taken up different amounts of memory in the two systems. This is due to the different code routines loaded, based on the ROM ID information. In essence, DOS, the ROM BIOS, and the hardware are much more closely related than most people realize.

DOS Components

DOS consists of two primary components: the input/output (I/O) system and the shell. The I/O system consists of the underlying programs that reside in memory while the system is running; these programs are loaded first when DOS boots. The I/O system is stored in the form of two files that are hidden on a bootable DOS disk. The files are called IBMBIO.COM and IBMDOS.COM on an IBM DOS disk, but might go by other names for other manufacturers' versions of DOS. For example, IO.SYS and MSDOS.SYS are the MS-DOS file names. No matter what the exact names are, the function of these two files is basically the same for all versions of DOS. However, each individual system's ROM-BIOS looks for the system files by name, and often will not recognize them by another name, one reason that the OEM version of DOS you use must be the correct one for your system.

The user-interface program, or shell, is stored in the COMMAND.COM file, which also is loaded during a normal DOS boot-up. The shell is the portion of DOS that provides the DOS prompt and that normally communicates with the user of the system.

The following sections examine the DOS I/O system and shell in more detail, to help you properly identify and solve problems that are DOS problems rather than hardware problems. Also included is a discussion on how DOS allocates disk file space.

V

Troubleshooting Guide

DOS File Space Allocation

DOS allocates disk space for a file on demand (space is not preallocated). The space is allocated one *cluster* (or allocation unit) at a time. A cluster is always one or more sectors. (For more information about sectors, refer to Chapter 10.)

The clusters are arranged on a disk to minimize head movement for multi-sided media. DOS allocates all the space on a disk cylinder before moving to the next cylinder. It does this by using the sectors under the first head, then all the sectors under the next head, and so on until all sectors of all heads of the cylinder are used. The next sector used is sector 1 of head 0 on the next cylinder. (You will find more information on floppy disks and drives in Chapter 8 and on hard disks in Chapter 9.)

DOS version 2.X uses a simple algorithm when it allocates file space on a disk. Every time a program requests disk space, DOS scans from the beginning of the FAT until it finds a free cluster in which to deposit a portion of the file; then the search continues for the next cluster of free space, until all of the file is written. This algorithm, called the First Available Cluster algorithm, causes any erased file near the beginning of the disk to be overwritten during the next write operation, because those clusters would be the first available to the next write operation. This system prevents recovery of that file and promotes file fragmentation because the first available cluster found is used regardless of whether the entire file can be written there. DOS simply continues searching for free clusters in which to deposit the remainder of the file. The algorithm used by DOS 2.X therefore often prevents unerasing files after new data has been written to a disk, as well as promotes file fragmentation as the disk is used.

The algorithm used for file allocation in DOS 3.0 and later versions is called the Next Available Cluster algorithm. In this algorithm, the search for available clusters in which to write a file starts not at the beginning of the disk, but rather from where the last write occurred. Therefore, the disk space freed by erasing a file is not necessarily reused immediately. Rather, DOS maintains a Last Written Cluster pointer indicating the last written cluster and begins its search from that point. This pointer is maintained in system RAM and is lost when the system is reset or rebooted, or when a disk is changed in a floppy drive.

In working with 360K drives, all versions of DOS always use the First Available Cluster algorithm because the Last Written Cluster pointer cannot be maintained for floppy disk drives that do not report a disk change (DC) signal to the controller, and because 360K drives do not supply the DC signal. With 360K floppy drives, therefore, DOS always assumes that the disk could have been changed, which flushes any buffers and resets the Last Written Cluster pointer.

The Next Available Cluster algorithm in DOS 3.0 and later versions is faster than the First Available Cluster algorithm and helps minimize fragmentation. Sometimes this type of algorithm is called elevator seeking because write operations occur at higher and higher clusters until the end of the disk area is reached. At that time the pointer is reset, and writes work their way from the beginning of the disk again.

Files still end up becoming fragmented using the new algorithm, because the pointer is reset after a reboot, a disk change operation, or when the end of the disk is reached. Nevertheless, a great benefit of the newer method is that it makes unerasing files more likely to succeed even if the disk has been written to since the erasure, because the file just erased is not likely to be the target of the next write operation. In fact, it might be some time before the clusters occupied by the erased file are reused.

Even when a file is overwritten under DOS 3.0 and later versions, the clusters occupied by the file are not actually reused in the overwrite. For example, if I accidentally save on a disk a file using the same name as an important file that already exists, the existing file clusters are marked as available, and the new file (with the same name) is written to the disk in other clusters. It is possible, therefore, that the original copy of the file can still be retrieved. I can continue this procedure by saving another copy of the file with the same name, and each file copy is saved to higher-numbered clusters, and each earlier version overwritten might still be recoverable on the disk. This process can continue until the system is rebooted or reset, or until the end of the available space is reached. Then the pointer is set to the first cluster, and previous file data is overwritten.

Because DOS always uses the first available directory entry when it saves or creates a file, the overwritten or deleted files whose data is still recoverable on the disk no longer appear in a directory listing. No commercial quick unerase or other unerase utilities therefore can find any record of the erased or overwritten file on the disk—true, of course, because these programs look only in the directory for a record of an erased file. Some newer undelete programs have a memory-resident delete tracking function which in essence maintains a separate directory listing from DOS. Unless an unerase program has a memory-resident delete tracking function, and that function has been activated before the deletion, no program will be able to recall the files overwritten in the directory entry.

Because unerase programs do not look at the FAT, or at the data clusters themselves (unless they use delete tracking), they see no record of the files' existence. By scanning the free clusters on the disk one by one using a disk editor tool, you can locate the data from the overwritten or erased file and manually rebuild the FAT and directory entries. This procedure enables you to recover erased files even though files have been written to the disk since the erasure took place. This type of powerful unerase operation and FAT and directory rebuilding are discussed in the problem-solving chapters of this book.

The I/O System

This section briefly describes the two files that make up the I/O system: IBMBIO.COM and IBMDOS.COM.

IBMBIO.COM (or IO.SYS). IBMBIO.COM is one of the hidden files that the CHKDSK command reports on any system (bootable) disk. This file contains the low-level programs that interact directly with devices on the system and the ROM BIOS. IBMBIO.COM usually is customized by the particular original equipment manufacturer (OEM) of the system to match perfectly with that OEM's ROM BIOS. The file contains low-level drivers loaded in accord with a particular ROM BIOS, based on the ROM ID information, as well as on a system initialization routine. During boot-up, the DOS volume boot sector loads the file into low memory and gives it control of the system (see the section DOS Volume Boot Sectors later in this chapter). All of the file except the system initializer portion remains in memory during normal system operation.

The name used for the file that performs the functions just described varies among versions of DOS from different OEMs. Many versions of DOS, including Microsoft's MS-DOS, use IO.SYS as the name of this file. Some other manufacturers call the file MIO.SYS, and Toshiba calls it TBIOS.SYS. Using different names for this file is not normally a problem, until you try to upgrade from one OEM version of DOS to a different OEM version. If the different OEMs have used different names for this file, the SYS command might fail with the error message No room for system on destination. Today most OEMs use the standard IBMBIO.COM name for this file to eliminate problems in upgrading and otherwise remain standard.

For a disk to be bootable, IBMBIO.COM or its equivalent must be listed as the first file in the directory of the disk and must occupy at least the first cluster on the disk (cluster number 2). The remainder of the file might be placed in clusters anywhere across the rest of the disk (versions 3 and higher). The file normally is marked with hidden, system, and read-only attributes, and placed on a disk by the FORMAT command or the SYS command.

IBMDOS.COM (or MSDOS.SYS). IBMDOS.COM, the core of DOS, contains the DOS disk handling programs. The routines present in this file make up the DOS disk and device handling programs. IBMDOS.COM is loaded into low memory at system boot-up by the DOS volume boot sector and remains resident in memory during normal system operation.

The IBMDOS.COM program collection is less likely to be customized by an OEM but still might be present on a system by a different name than IBMDOS.COM. The most common alternative name, MSDOS.SYS, is used by Microsoft's MS-DOS and some OEM versions of DOS. Another name is TDOS.SYS (used by Toshiba). Most OEMs today stick to the IBM convention to eliminate problems in upgrading from one DOS version to another.

IBMDOS.COM or its equivalent must be listed as the second entry in the root directory of any bootable disk. This file usually is marked with hidden, system, and read-only attributes, and is normally placed on a disk by the FORMAT command or the SYS command. There are no special requirements for the physical positioning of this file on a disk.

Potential DOS Upgrade Problems. You already know that the DOS system files have special placement requirements on a hard disk. Sometimes these special requirements cause problems when you are upgrading from one version of DOS to another.

If you have attempted to upgrade a PC system from one version of DOS to another, you know that you use the DOS SYS command to replace old system files with new ones. The SYS command copies the existing system files (stored on a bootable disk with hidden, system, and read-only attributes) to the disk in the correct position and with the correct names and attributes. The COPY command does not copy hidden or system files (nor would it place the system files in the required positions on the destination disk if their other attributes had been altered so that they could be copied using COPY).

In addition to transferring the two hidden system files from one disk to another, SYS also updates the DOS volume boot sector on the destination disk so that it is correct for the new version of DOS. Common usage of the SYS command is as follows:

SYS C: (for drive C) or

SYS A: (to make a floppy in drive A bootable)

The syntax of the command is as follows:

SYS[d:][path]d:

In this command line, *d:/path* specifies an optional source drive and path for the system files. If the source drive specification is omitted, the boot drive is used as the source drive. This parameter is supported in DOS 4.0 and later versions only. Versions of DOS older than 4.0 automatically look for system files on the default drive (not on the boot drive). The **d** in the syntax specifies the drive to which you want to transfer the system files.

When the SYS command is executed, you usually are greeted by one of two messages:

    System transferred

or

    No room for system on destination disk

If a disk has data on it before you try to write the system files to it, the SYS command from DOS versions 3.3 and earlier probably will fail because they are not capable of moving other files out of the way. The SYS command in DOS 4.0 and higher versions rarely fail because they can and do move files out of the way.

Some users think that the cause of the No room message on a system which has an older version of DOS is that the system files in any newer version of DOS are always larger than the previous version, and that the new version files cannot fit into the space allocated for older versions. Such users believe that the command fails because this space cannot be provided at the beginning without moving other data away. This belief is wrong. The SYS command fails in these cases because you are trying to install a version of DOS that has different file names than the names already on the disk. There is no normal reason for the SYS command to fail when you update the system files on a disk that already has them.

Although the belief that larger system files cannot replace smaller ones might be popular, it is wrong for DOS 3.0 and later versions. The system files can be placed virtually anywhere on the disk, except that the first clusters of the disk must contain the file IBMBIO.COM (or its equivalent). After that requirement has been met, the

IBMDOS.COM file might be fragmented and placed just about anywhere on the disk, and the SYS command implements it with no problems whatsoever. In version 3.3 or later, even the IBMBIO.COM file can be fragmented and spread all over the disk, as long as the first cluster of the file occupies the first cluster of the disk (cluster 2). The only other requirement is that the names IBMBIO.COM and IBMDOS.COM (or their equivalents) must use the first and second directory entries.

DOS 4.0 and Later Versions. Under DOS 4.0 and later versions, the SYS command is much more powerful than under previous versions. Because the system files must use the first two entries in the root directory of the disk as well as the first cluster (cluster 2) of the disk, the DOS 4.0 and later versions' SYS command moves any files that occupy the first two entries but that do not match the new system file names to other available entries in the root directory; the SYS command also moves the portion of any foreign file occupying the first cluster to other clusters on the disk. Whereas the SYS command in older versions of DOS would fail, and require a user to make adjustments to the disk, the DOS 4.0 and later versions' SYS command automatically make the required adjustments. For example, even if you are updating a Phoenix DOS 3.3 disk to IBM DOS 4.0, the IBM DOS SYS command relocates the Phoenix IO.SYS and MSDOS.SYS files so that the new IBMBIO.COM and IBMDOS.COM files can occupy the correct locations in the root directory as well as on the disk.

DOS 5.0 and 6.0. The SYS command in DOS Versions 5.0 and 6.0 go one step further: They replace old system files with the new ones. Even if the old system files had other names, DOS 5.0 and higher ensure that they are overwritten by the new system files. If you are updating a disk on which the old system file names match the new ones, the SYS command of any version of DOS will overwrite the old system files with the new ones with no moving of files necessary. With the enhanced SYS command in DOS 4.0 and later versions, it is difficult to make a DOS upgrade fail.

DOS 3.3. The DOS 3.3 SYS command does not move other files out of the way (as SYS does in DOS 4.0 and later versions); therefore, you must ensure that the first two root directory entries are either free or contain names that match the new system file names. As in DOS 4.0 and later versions, the first cluster on the disk must contain the first portion of IBMBIO.COM; unlike DOS 4.0 and later versions, however, the SYS command under DOS 3.3 does not move any files for you. Necessary manual adjustments, such as clearing the first two directory entries or relocating a file that occupies the first cluster on the disk, must be done with whatever utility programs you have available. The DOS 3.3 system files can be fragmented and occupy various areas of the disk.

SYS under DOS 3.3 does not automatically handle updating from one version of DOS to a version that has different system file names. In that case, because the system file names are not the same, the new system files do not overwrite the old ones. If you are making this kind of system change, use a directory editing tool to change the names of the current system files to match the new names so that the system file overwrite can occur.

DOS 3.2. DOS 3.2 or earlier requires that the entire IBMBIO.COM file be contiguous starting with cluster 2 (the first cluster) on the disk. The other system file

(IBMDOS.COM) can be fragmented or placed anywhere on the disk; it does not have to follow the first system file physically on the disk.

DOS 2.X. DOS 2.X requires that both system files (IBMBIO.COM and IBMDOS.COM) occupy contiguous clusters on the disk starting with the first cluster (cluster 2). The DOS 2.1 system files are slightly larger than the DOS 2.0 files in actual bytes of size, but the size change is not enough to require additional clusters on the disk. A SYS change from DOS 2.0 to DOS 2.1 therefore is successful in most cases.

Upgrading DOS from the Same OEM. Updating from one version of DOS to a later version from the same OEM by simply using the SYS command has never been a problem. I have verified this with IBM DOS. I installed IBM DOS 2.0 on a system with a hard disk through the normal FORMAT /S command. I copied all the subsequent DOS-transient programs into a \DOS subdirectory on the disk. Then I updated the hard disk, in succession, to IBM DOS 2.1, 3.0, 3.1, 3.2, 3.3, 4.0, and 5.0, using nothing more than the SYS and COPY (or XCOPY or REPLACE) commands. Between each version change, I verified that the hard disk would boot the new version of DOS with no problems. Based on this experiment, I have concluded that you never would have to use the FORMAT command to update one DOS version to a later version, as long as both versions are from the same OEM. I also verified the same operations on a floppy disk. Starting with a bootable floppy disk created by IBM DOS 2.0, I used SYS and COPY to update that disk to all subsequent versions of DOS through 5.0 without ever reformatting it. After each version change, the floppy disk was bootable with no problems.

You should be able to update a bootable hard disk or floppy disk easily from one DOS version to another without reformatting the disk. If you are having problems, you probably are attempting to upgrade to a version of DOS that uses different names for the system files than those used by the existing DOS, which means that you are moving from a DOS made by one OEM to a DOS made by a different company. If you are having trouble and this is not the case, carefully examine the list of requirements at the beginning of this section. Your problem must be that one of those requirements is not being met.

Downgrading DOS. One important and often overlooked function of the SYS command is its capability to update the DOS volume boot sector of a disk on which it is writing system files. Later versions of SYS are more complete than earlier versions in the way they perform this update; therefore, using SYS to go from a later version of DOS to an earlier version is sometimes difficult. For example, you cannot use SYS to install DOS 2.1 on a disk that currently boots DOS 3.0 and later versions. Changing from DOS 4.0 or DOS 5.0 to DOS 3.3 usually works, if the partition is less than or equal to 32 megabytes in capacity. You probably will never see a problem with a later version of SYS updating a DOS volume boot sector created by an earlier version, but earlier versions might leave something out when they attempt to change back from a later version. Fortunately, few people ever attempt to install a lower version of DOS over a higher version.

The Shell or Command Processor (COMMAND.COM). The DOS command processor COMMAND.COM is the portion of DOS with which users normally interact.

The commands can be categorized by function, but IBM DOS divides them into two types by how they are made available: *resident* or *transient.*

Resident Commands. *Resident commands* are built into COMMAND.COM and are available whenever the DOS prompt is present. They are generally the simpler, frequently used commands such as CLS and DIR. Resident commands execute rapidly because the instructions for them are already loaded into memory. They are *memory-resident.*

When you look up the definition of a command in the DOS manual, you will find an indication of whether the command is resident or transient. You then can determine what is required to execute that command. A simple rule is that, at a DOS prompt, all resident commands are instantly available for execution, with no loading of the program from disk required. Resident commands are also sometimes termed *internal.* Commands run from a program on disk are termed *external*, or *transient*, and also are often called *utilities.*

Transient Commands. *Transient commands* are not resident in the computer's memory, and the instructions to execute the command must be located on a disk. Because the instructions are loaded into memory only for execution and then are overwritten in memory after they are used, they are called *transient commands.* Most DOS commands are transient; otherwise, the memory requirements for DOS would be astronomical. Transient commands are used less frequently than resident commands and take longer to execute because they must be found and loaded before they can be run.

Most executable files operate like transient DOS commands. The instructions to execute the command must be located on a disk. The instructions are loaded into memory only for execution and are overwritten in memory after the program is no longer being used.

DOS Command File-Search Procedure. DOS looks only in specific places for the instructions for a transient command, or a software application's executable file. The instructions that represent the command or program are in files on one or more disk drives. Files that contain execution instructions have one of three specific extensions to indicate to DOS that they are program files: .COM (command files), .EXE (executable files), or .BAT (batch files). .COM and .EXE files are machine-code programs; .BAT files contain a series of commands and instructions using the DOS batch facilities. The places in which DOS will look for these files is controlled by the current directory and the PATH command.

In other words, if you type several characters, like WIN, at the DOS prompt and press the Enter key, DOS attempts to find and run a program named WIN. DOS performs a two- or three-level search for program instructions (the file). The first step in looking for command instructions is to see whether the command is a resident one and, if so, run it from the program code already loaded. If the command is not resident, DOS looks in the current directory for .COM, .EXE, and .BAT files, in that order, and loads and executes the first file it finds with the specified name. If the command is not resident and not in the current directory, DOS looks in all the directories specified in the DOS PATH setting (which the user can control); DOS searches for the file within each directory in the extension order just indicated. Finally, if DOS fails to locate the required instructions, it displays the error message Bad command or filename. This error message might be misleading because the command instructions usually are missing from the search areas rather than actually being bad.

Suppose that, at the DOS prompt, I type the command XYZ and press Enter. This command sends DOS on a search for the XYZ programs instructions. If DOS is successful, the program will start running within seconds. If DOS cannot find the proper instructions, an error message is displayed. Here is what happens:

1. DOS checks internally to see whether it can find the XYZ command as one of the resident commands whose instructions are already loaded. It finds no XYZ command as resident.

2. DOS looks next in the current directory on the current drive for files named XYZ.COM, then for files named XYZ.EXE, and finally for files named XYZ.BAT. I had logged on to drive C:, and the current directory was \ (the root directory); therefore, DOS did not find the files in the current directory.

3. DOS looks to see whether a PATH has been specified. If not, the search ends here. In this scenario, I do have a PATH that was specified when my system was started, so DOS checks every directory listed in that PATH for the first file it can find named XYZ.COM, XYZ.EXE, or XYZ.BAT (in that order). My PATH lists several directories, but DOS does not find an appropriate file in any of them.

4. The search ends, and DOS gives me the message Bad command or filename.

For this search-and-load procedure to be successful, I must ensure that the desired program or command file exists in the current directory on the current drive, or I must set my DOS PATH to point to the drive and directory in which the program does exist. This is why the PATH is so powerful in DOS.

A common practice is to place all simple command files or utility programs in one directory and set the PATH to point to that directory. Then each of those programs (commands) is instantly available by simply typing its name, just as though it were resident.

This practice works well only for single-load programs such as commands and other utilities. Major applications software often consists of many individual files and might have problems if they are called up from a remote directory or drive using the DOS PATH. The reason is that when the application looks for its overlay and accessory files, the DOS PATH setting has no effect.

On a hard disk system, users typically install all transient commands and utilities in subdirectories and ensure that the PATH points to those directories. The path literally is a list of directories and subdirectories in the AUTOEXEC.BAT file that tells DOS where to search for files when these files are not in the same directory you are when you enter a command. The system then functions as though all the commands were resident because

Troubleshooting Guide

V

DOS finds the necessary files without further thought or effort on the part of the user. A path on such a hard drive may look like this:

```
PATH=C:\DOS;C:\BAT;C:\UTILS;
```

It is important to know that when DOS loads each time you power up your system, it looks for two such text files. The first text file DOS looks for is CONFIG.SYS, which also can be edited by the system user. This file loads device drivers like ANSI.SYS. The following is an example of a common CONFIG.SYS file:

```
FILES=30

BUFFERS=17

SHELL=C:\DOS\COMMAND.COM C:\DOS /E:512 /P

LASTDRIVE=G

DEVICE=C:\DOS\ANSI.SYS
```

The second text file DOS looks for each time you power up your system is AUTOEXEC.BAT, which sets the PATH and loads memory resident programs and performs other system configuration tasks like creating a C:\> prompt. A typical AUTOEXEC.BAT file might look like the following:

```
PROMPT $P$G
PATH=C:\DOS;C:\BAT;C:\UTILS;
C:\MOUSE\MOUSE.COM
```

The PATH normally cannot exceed 128 characters in length (including colons, semicolons and back-slashes). As a result of that limitation, you cannot have a PATH that contains all your directories if the directory names exceed 128 characters. For more information on the AUTOEXEC.BAT and CONFIG.SYS files, consult Que's *Using DOS 6* or *Using IBM PC DOS 6.1*.

You can completely short-circuit the DOS command search procedure by simply entering at the command prompt the complete path to the file. For example, rather than include C:\DOS in the PATH and enter this command:

```
C:\>CHKDSK
```

you can enter the full name of the program:

```
C:\>C:\DOS\CHKDSK.COM
```

The latter command immediately locates and loads the CHKDSK program with no search through the current directory or PATH setting. This method of calling up a program speeds the location and execution of the program and works especially well to increase the speed of DOS batch-file execution.

A few major software applications have problems if they are called up from a remote directory or drive using the DOS PATH. Such an application often is made up of many individual files, including overlay and accessory files. Problems can occur when an application expects you to run it from its own directory by making that directory current and then running the program's COM or EXE file. Such applications look for their own files in the current directory. If you did not change to the application's directory, since the program does not look for its files by checking the path, the program does not find its own files. The path entry in AUTOEXEC.BAT has no effect.

Such applications can be called up through batch files or aided by programs that "force-feed" a path-type setting to the programs; the software then works as though files are "here" even when they are in some other directory. The best utility for this purpose is the APPEND command in DOS 3.0 and later versions. For information on the use of the APPEND command see Que's *Using MS-DOS 6*.

The Boot Process

The term *boot* comes from the term bootstrap and describes the method by which the PC becomes operational. Just as you pull on a large boot by the small strap attached to the back, a PC can load a large operating-system program by first loading a small program that then can pull in the operating system. A chain of events begins with the application of power and finally results in an operating computer system with software loaded and running. Each event is called by the event before it and initiates the event after it.

Tracing the system-boot process might help you find the location of a problem, if you examine the error messages the system displays when the problem occurs. If you can see an error message displayed only by a particular program, you can be sure that the program in question was at least loaded and partially running. Combine this information with the knowledge of the boot sequence, and you can at least tell how far along the system's start-up procedure is. You usually want to look at whatever files or disk areas were being accessed during the failure in the boot process. Error messages displayed during the boot process as well as those displayed during normal system operation can be hard to decipher, but the first step in decoding an error message is to know where the message came from—what program actually sent or displayed the message. These programs are capable of displaying error messages during the boot process:

- Motherboard ROM BIOS

- Adapter card ROM BIOS extensions

- Master-partition boot sector

- DOS volume boot sector

- System files (IBMBIO.COM and IBMDOS.COM)

- Device drivers (loaded through CONFIG.SYS)

- Shell program (COMMAND.COM)

- Programs run by AUTOEXEC.BAT

This section examines the system start-up sequence and provides a detailed account of many of the error messages that might occur during this process.

How DOS Loads and Starts

If you have a problem with your system during start-up and you can determine where in this sequence of events your system has stalled, you know what events have occurred and you probably can eliminate each of them as a cause of the problem. The following steps occur in a typical system start-up:

1. You switch on electrical power to the system.

2. The power supply performs a self-test. When all voltages and current levels are acceptable, the supply indicates that the power is stable and sends the Power Good signal to the motherboard. The time from switch-on to Power Good is normally between .1 and .5 seconds.

3. The microprocessor timer chip receives the Power Good signal, which causes it to stop generating a reset signal to the microprocessor.

4. The microprocessor begins executing the ROM BIOS code, starting at memory address FFFF:0000. Because this location is only 16 bytes from the very end of the available ROM space, it contains a JMP (jump) instruction to the actual ROM BIOS starting address.

5. The ROM BIOS performs a test of the central hardware to verify basic system functionality. Any errors that occur are indicated by audio codes because the video system has not yet been initialized.

6. The BIOS performs a video ROM scan of memory locations C000:0000 through C780:0000, looking for video adapter ROM BIOS programs contained on a video adapter card plugged into a slot. If a video ROM BIOS is found, it is tested by a checksum procedure. If it passes the checksum test, the ROM is executed, the video ROM code initializes the video adapter, and a cursor appears on-screen. If the checksum test fails, this message appears:

   ```
   C000 ROM Error
   ```

7. If the BIOS finds no video adapter ROM, it uses the motherboard ROM video drivers to initialize the video-display hardware, and a cursor appears on-screen.

8. The motherboard ROM BIOS scans memory locations C800:0000 through DF80:0000 in 2K increments for any other ROMs located on any other adapter cards. If any ROMs are found, they are checksum-tested and executed. These adapter ROMs can alter existing BIOS routines as well as establish new ones.

9. Failure of a checksum test for any of these ROM modules causes this message to appear:

   ```
   XXXX ROM Error
   ```

10. The address XXXX indicates the segment address of the failed ROM module.

11. The ROM BIOS checks the word value at memory location 0000:0472 to see whether this start is a cold start or a warm start. A word value of 1234h in this location is a flag that indicates a warm start, which causes the memory-test portion of the POST (Power-On Self Test) to be skipped. Any other word value in this location indicates a cold start and full POST.

12. If this is a cold start, the POST executes. Any errors found during the POST are reported by a combination of audio and displayed error messages. Successful completion of the POST is indicated by a single beep.

13. The ROM BIOS searches for a DOS volume boot sector at cylinder 0, head 0, sector 1 (the very first sector) on the A: drive. This sector is loaded into memory at 0000:7C00 and tested. If a disk is in the drive but the sector cannot be read, or if no disk is present, the BIOS continues with the next step.

14. If the first byte of the DOS volume boot sector loaded from the floppy disk in A: is less than 06h, or if the first byte is greater than or equal to 06h, and the first nine words contain the same data pattern, this error message appears and the system stops:

    ```
    602-Diskette Boot Record Error
    ```

15. If the disk was prepared with FORMAT or SYS using DOS 3.3 or an earlier version and the specified system files are not the first two files in the directory, or if a problem was encountered loading them, this message appears:

    ```
    Non-System disk or disk error

    Replace and strike any key when ready
    ```

16. If the disk was prepared with FORMAT or SYS using DOS 3.3 or an earlier version and the boot sector is corrupt, you might see this message:

    ```
    Disk Boot failure
    ```

17. If the disk was prepared with FORMAT or SYS using DOS 4.0 and later versions and the specified system files are not the first two files in the directory, or if a problem was encountered loading them or the boot sector is corrupt, this message appears:

    ```
    Non-System disk or disk error

    Replace and press any key when ready
    ```

18. If no DOS volume boot sector can be read from drive A:, the BIOS looks for a master-partition boot sector at cylinder 0, head 0, sector 1 (the very first sector) of the first fixed disk. If this sector is found, it is loaded into memory address 0000:7C00 and tested for a signature.

19. If the last two (signature) bytes of the master-partition boot sector are not equal to 55AAh, software interrupt 18h (Int 18h) is invoked on most systems. On an IBM PS/2 system, a special character-graphics message is displayed that depicts inserting a floppy disk in drive A: and pressing the F1 key. For non-PS/2 systems made by IBM, an Int 18h executes the ROM BIOS-based Cassette BASIC Interpreter. On any other IBM-compatible system, a message indicating some type of boot error is displayed. For example, systems with Phoenix AT ROM BIOS display this message:

    ```
    No boot device available -

    strike F1 to retry boot, F2 for setup utility
    ```

20. The master partition boot-sector program searches its partition table for an entry with a system-indicator byte indicating an extended partition. If the program finds such an entry, it loads the extended-partition boot sector at the location indicated. The extended-partition boot sector also has a table that is searched for another extended partition. If another extended-partition entry is found, that extended-partition boot sector is loaded from the location indicated, and the search continues until either no more extended partitions are indicated or the maximum number of 24 total partitions has been reached.

21. The master-partition boot sector searches its partition table for a boot-indicator byte marking an active partition.

22. On an IBM system, if none of the partitions is marked active (bootable), ROM BIOS-based Cassette BASIC is invoked. On most IBM-compatible systems, some type of disk error message is displayed.

23. If any boot indicator in the master-partition boot record table is invalid, or if more than one indicates an active partition, this message is displayed, and the system stops:

    ```
    Invalid partition table
    ```

24. If an active partition is found in the master-partition boot sector, the volume boot sector from the active partition is loaded and tested.

25. If the DOS volume boot sector cannot be read successfully from the active partition within five retries due to read errors, this message appears and the system stops:

    ```
    Error loading operating system
    ```

26. The hard disk DOS volume boot sector is tested for a signature. If the DOS volume boot sector does not contain a valid signature of 55AAh as the last two bytes in the sector, this message appears and the system stops:

    ```
    Missing operating system
    ```

27. The volume boot sector is executed as a program. This program checks the root directory to ensure that the first two files are IBMBIO.COM and IBMDOS.COM. If these files are present, they are loaded.

28. If the disk was prepared with FORMAT or SYS using DOS 3.3 or an earlier version and the specified system files are not the first two files in the directory, or if a problem was encountered loading them, this message appears:

```
Non-System disk or disk error

Replace and strike any key when ready
```

29. If the disk was prepared with FORMAT or SYS using DOS 3.3 or an earlier version and the boot sector is corrupt, you might see this message:

```
Disk Boot failure
```

30. If the disk was prepared with FORMAT or SYS using DOS 4.0 or a later version and the specified system files are not the first two files in the directory, or if a problem was encountered loading them or the boot sector is corrupt, this message appears:

```
Non-System disk or disk error

Replace and press any key when ready
```

31. If no problems have occurred, the DOS volume boot sector executes IBMBIO.COM.

32. The initialization code in IBMBIO.COM copies itself into the highest region of contiguous DOS memory and transfers control to the copy. The initialization code copy then relocates IBMDOS over the portion of IBMBIO in low memory that contains the initialization code, because the initialization code no longer needs to be in that location.

33. The initialization code executes IBMDOS, which initializes the base device drivers, determines equipment status, resets the disk system, resets and initializes attached devices, and sets the system default parameters.

34. The full DOS filing system is active, and the IBMBIO initialization code is given back control.

35. The IBMBIO initialization code reads CONFIG.SYS four times.

36. During the first read, all the statements except DEVICE, INSTALL, and SHELL are read and processed in a predetermined order.

Thus, the order of appearance for statements other than DEVICE, INSTALL, and SHELL in CONFIG.SYS is of no significance.

37. During the second read, DEVICE statements are processed in the order in which they appear, and any device driver files named are loaded and executed.

38. During the third read, INSTALL statements are processed in the order in which they appear, and the programs named are loaded and executed.

39. During the fourth and final read, the SHELL statement is processed and loads the specified command processor with the specified parameters. If the CONFIG.SYS file contains no SHELL statement, the default \COMMAND.COM processor is loaded with default parameters. Loading the command processor overwrites the initialization code in memory (because the job of the initialization code is finished).

40. If AUTOEXEC.BAT is present, COMMAND.COM loads and runs AUTOEXEC.BAT. After the commands in AUTOEXEC.BAT have been executed, the DOS prompt appears (unless the AUTOEXEC.BAT calls an application program or shell of some kind, in which case the user might operate the system without ever seeing a DOS prompt).

41. If no AUTOEXEC.BAT is present, COMMAND.COM executes the internal DATE and TIME commands, displays a copyright message, and displays the DOS prompt.

These steps are the ones an IBM AT system performs, and most IBM-compatible systems closely emulate them. Some minor variations from this scenario are possible, such as those introduced by other ROM programs in the various adapters that might be plugged into a slot. Also, depending on the exact ROM BIOS programs involved, some of the error messages and sequences might vary. Generally, however, a computer follows this chain of events in "coming to life."

You can modify the system start-up procedures by altering the CONFIG.SYS and AUTOEXEC.BAT files. These files control the configuration of DOS and allow special start-up programs to be executed every time the system starts. The *User's Guide and Reference* that comes with DOS 5 has an excellent section on DOS configuration.

DOS Floppy Disk Formats

Since the debut of DOS version 1.0, the number of floppy disk formats supported by DOS has increased. Fortunately, newer versions of DOS from a particular OEM can always read from and write to earlier versions disks. Table 15.1 lists all the formats supported under DOS 6.0.

File Management

DOS uses several elements and structures to store and retrieve information on a disk. These elements and structures enable DOS to communicate properly with the ROM BIOS as well as application programs to process file storage and retrieval requests. Understanding these structures and how they interact will help you to troubleshoot and even repair these structures.

Interfacing to Disk Drives

DOS uses a combination of disk management components to make files accessible. These components differ slightly between floppies and hard disks and between disks of different sizes. They determine how a disk appears to DOS and to applications software. Each component used to describe the disk system fits as a layer into the complete system. Each layer communicates with the layer above and below it. When all of the components work together, an application can access the disk to find and store data.

Table 15.1 Floppy Disk Format Specifications

Disk size (inches) Disk capacity (K)	Current Formats			Obsolete Formats				
	3 1/2 2880	3 1/2 1440	3 1/2 720	5 1/4 1200	5 1/4 360	5 1/4 320	5 1/4 180	5 1/4 160
Media descriptor byte	F0h	F0h	F9h	F9h	FDh	FFh	FCh	FEh
Sides (heads)	2	2	2	2	2	2	1	1
Tracks per side	80	80	80	80	40	40	40	40
Sectors per track	36	18	9	15	9	8	9	8
Bytes per sector	512	512	512	512	512	512	512	512
Sectors per cluster	2	1	2	1	2	2	1	1
FAT length (sectors)	9	9	3	7	2	1	2	1
Number of FATs	2	2	2	2	2	2	2	2
Root directory length (Sectors)	15	14	7	14	7	7	4	4
Maximum root entries	240	224	112	224	112	112	64	64
Total sectors / disk	5760	2880	1440	2400	720	640	360	320
Total available sectors	5726	2847	1426	2371	708	630	351	313
Total available clusters	2863	2847	713	2371	354	315	35	

The four primary layers of interface between an application program running on a system and any disks attached to the system consist of software routines that can perform various functions, usually to communicate with the adjacent layers. These layers are shown in this list:

- DOS Interrupt 21h (Int 21h) routines

- DOS Interrupt 25/26h (Int 25/26h) routines

- ROM BIOS disk Interrupt 13h (Int 13h) routines

- Disk controller I/O port commands

Each layer accepts various commands, performs different functions, and generates results. These interfaces are available for both floppy disk drives and hard disks, although the floppy disk and hard disk Int 13h routines differ widely. The floppy disk controllers and hard disk controllers are very different as well, but all of the layers perform the same functions for both floppy disks and hard disks.

Interrupt 21h

The DOS Int 21h routines exist at the highest level and provide the most functionality with the least amount of work. For example, if an application program needs to create a subdirectory on a disk, it can call Int 21h, Function 39h. This function performs all operations necessary to create a subdirectory on the disk, including updating the appropriate directory and FAT sectors. The only information this function needs is the name of the subdirectory to create. DOS Int 21h would do much more work by using one of the lower-level access methods to create a subdirectory on the disk. Most applications programs you run access the disk through this level of interface.

Interrupt 25h and Int 26h

The DOS Int 25h and Int 26h routines provide much lower-level access to the disk than the Int 21h routines. Int 25h reads only specified sectors from a disk, and Int 26h only writes specified sectors to a disk. If you were to write a program that used these functions to create a subdirectory on a disk, the work required would be much greater than that required by the Int 21h method. For example, your program would have to perform all these tasks:

- Calculate exactly which directory and FAT sectors need to be updated

- Use Int 25h to read these sectors

- Modify the sectors appropriately to contain the new subdirectory information

- Use Int 26h to write the sectors back out

The number of steps would be even greater considering the difficulty in determining exactly what sectors have to be modified. According to Int 25/26h, the entire DOS-addressable area of the disk consists of sectors numbered sequentially from 0. A program designed to access the disk using Int 25h and Int 26h must know the location of everything by this sector number. A program designed this way might have to be modified to handle disks with different numbers of sectors or different directory and FAT sizes and locations. Because of all the overhead required to get the job done, most programmers would not choose to access the disk in this manner, and instead would use the higher-level Int 21h—which does all of the work automatically.

Only disk- and sector-editing programs typically access a disk drive at the Int 25h and Int 26h level. Programs that work at this level of access can edit only areas of a disk that have been defined to DOS as a logical volume (drive letter). For example, DEBUG can read sectors from and write sectors to disks with this level of access.

Interrupt 13h

The next lower level of communications with drives, the ROM BIOS Int 13h routines, usually are found in ROM chips on the motherboard or on an adapter card in a slot; however, an Int 13h handler also can be implemented by using a device driver loaded at boot time. Because DOS requires Int 13h access to boot from a drive (and a device driver cannot be loaded until after boot-up), only drives with ROM BIOS-based Int 13h support can become bootable. Int 13h routines need to talk directly to the controller using the I/O ports on the controller. Therefore, the Int 13h code is very controller-specific.

If you design your own custom disk controller device, you need to write an IBM-compatible Int 13h handler package and install it on the card using a ROM BIOS that will be linked into the system at boot time. To use Int 13h routines, a program must use exact cylinder, head, and sector coordinates to specify sectors to read and write.

Accordingly, any program designed to work at this level must be intimately familiar with the parameters of the specific disk on the system on which it is designed to run. Int 13h functions exist to read the disk parameters, format tracks, read and write sectors, park heads, and reset the drive.

A low-level format program for ST-506/412 drives needs to work with disks at the Int 13h level or lower. Most ST-506/412 controller format programs work with access at the Int 13h level, because virtually any operation a format program would need is available through the Int 13h interface. This is not true, however, for other types of controllers (such as IDE, SCSI or ESDI), for which defect mapping and other operations differ considerably from the ST-506/412 types. Controllers that must perform special operations during a low-level format, such as defining disk parameters to override the motherboard ROM BIOS drive tables, would not work with any formatter that used only the standard Int 13h interface. For these reasons, most controllers require a custom formatter designed to bypass the Int 13h interface. Most general-purpose, low-level reformat programs that perform a nondestructive format (such as Norton Calibrate and SpinRite II) access the controller through the Int 13h interface (rather than going direct) and therefore cannot be used for an initial low-level format; the initial low-level format must be done by a controller-specific utility.

Few high-powered disk utility programs, other than some basic formatting software, can talk to the disk at the Int 13h level. The Kolod Research hTEST/hFORMAT utilities also can communicate at the Int 13h level, as can the DOS FDISK program. The Norton DISKEDIT and NU programs can communicate with a disk at the Int 13h level when these programs are in their absolute sector mode; they are two of the few utilities that can do so. These programs are important because they can be used for the worst data-recovery situations, in which the partition tables have been corrupted. Because the partition tables as well as any non-DOS partitions exist outside the area of a disk that is defined by DOS, only programs that work at the Int 13h level can access them. Most utility programs for data recovery, such as the Mace Utilities MUSE program, work only at the DOS Int 25/26h level, which makes them useless for accessing areas of a disk outside of DOSs domain.

Disk Controller I/O Port Commands

In the lowest level of interface, programs talk directly to the disk controller in the controller's own specific native language. To do this, a program must send controller commands through the I/O ports to which the controller responds. These commands are specific to the particular controller and sometimes differ even among controllers of the same type, such as different ESDI controllers. The ROM BIOS in the system must be designed specifically for the controller because the ROM BIOS talks to the controller at this I/O port level. Most manufacturer-type low-level format programs also need to talk to the controller directly, because the higher-level Int 13h interface does not provide enough specific features for many of the custom ST-506/412 or ESDI and SCSI controllers on the market.

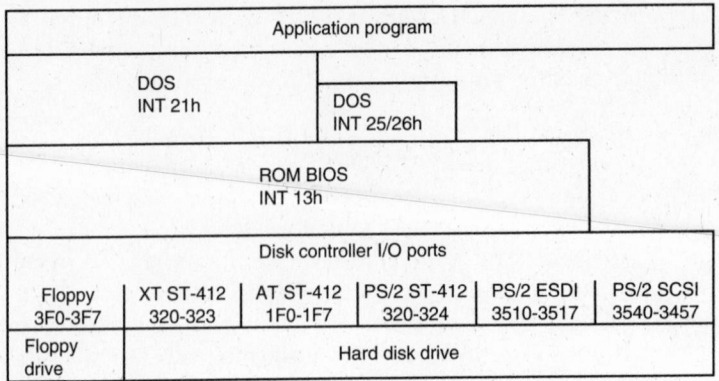

Fig. 15.2

Shows the relative relationships between the various interface levels.

Figure 15.2 shows that most application programs work through the Int 21h interface, which passes commands to the ROM BIOS as Int 13h commands; these commands then are converted into direct controller commands by the ROM BIOS. The controller executes the commands and returns the results through the layers until the desired information reaches the application. This process enables applications to be written without worrying about such low-level system details, leaving such details up to DOS and the ROM BIOS. It also enables applications to run on widely different types of hardware, as long as the correct ROM BIOS and DOS support is in place.

Any software can bypass any level of interface and communicate with the level below it, but doing so requires much more work. The lowest level of interface available is direct communication with the controller using I/O port commands. As figure 15.2 shows, each different type of controller has different I/O port locations as well as differences among the commands presented at the various ports, and only the controller can talk directly to the disk drive.

If not for the ROM BIOS Int 13h interface, a unique DOS would have to be written for each available type of hard and floppy disk drive and disk. Instead, DOS communicates with the ROM BIOS using standard Int 13h function calls translated by the Int 13h interface into commands for the specific hardware. Because of the standard ROM BIOS interface, DOS can be written relatively independently of specific disk hardware and can support many different types of drives and controllers.

DOS Structures

To manage files on a disk and enable all applications programs to see a consistent disk interface no matter what type of disk is used, DOS uses several structures. The following list shows all the structures and areas that DOS defines and uses to manage a disk, in roughly the order in which they are encountered on a disk:

- Master- and extended-partition boot sectors

- DOS volume boot sector

- Root directory

- File allocation tables (FAT)

- Clusters (allocation units)

- Data area

- Diagnostic read-and-write cylinder

A hard disk has all of these DOS disk-management structures allocated, and a floppy disk has all but the master- and extended-partition boot sectors and the diagnostic cylinder. These structures are created by the DOS FDISK program, which has no application on a floppy disk because floppy disks cannot be partitioned. Figure 15.3 is a simple diagram showing the relative locations of these DOS disk management structures on the 32M hard disk in an IBM AT Model 339.

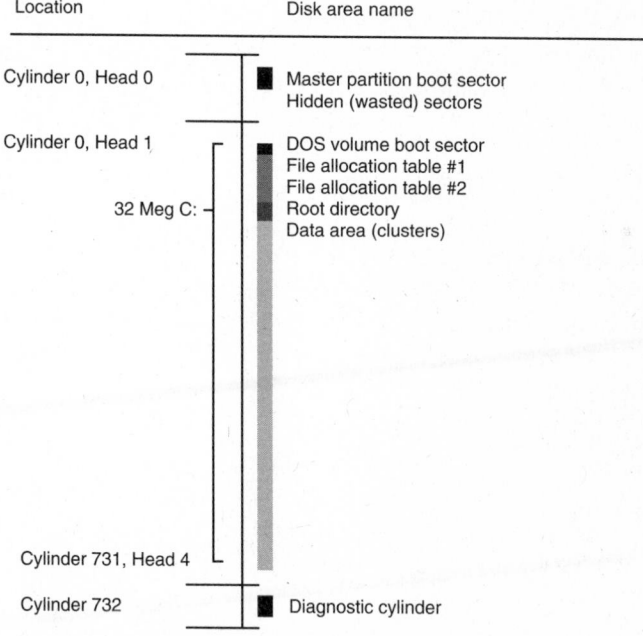

Fig. 15.3

DOS disk-management structures on an IBM AT Model 339 32M hard disk.

Each disk area has a purpose and function. If one of these special areas is damaged, serious consequences can result. Damage to one of these sensitive structures usually causes a domino effect, and limits access to other areas of the disk or causes further problems in using the disk. For example, DOS cannot read and write files if the FAT is damaged or corrupted. You therefore should understand these data structures well enough to be able to repair them when necessary. Rebuilding these special tables and areas of the disk is essential to the art of data recovery.

Master-Partition Boot Sectors

To share a hard disk among different operating systems, the disk might be logically divided into one to four master partitions. Each operating system, including DOS (through versions 3.2), might own only one partition. DOS 3.3 and later versions introduced the extended DOS partition, which allows multiple DOS partitions on the same hard disk. With the DOS FDISK program, you can select the size of each partition. The partition information is kept in several partition boot sectors on the disk, with the main table embedded in the master-partition boot sector. The master-partition boot sector is always located in the first sector of the entire disk (cylinder 0, head 0, sector 1). The extended-partition boot sectors are located at the beginning of each extended-partition volume.

Each DOS partition contains a DOS volume boot sector as its first sector. With the DOS FDISK utility, you might designate a single partition as active (or bootable). The master-partition boot sector causes the active partitions volume boot sector to receive control when the system is started or reset. Additional master disk partitions can be set up for Novell NetWare, and for OS/2 HPFS, PCIX (UNIX), XENIX, CP/M-86, or other operating systems. Any of these foreign operating-system partitions cannot be accessible under DOS, nor can any DOS partitions normally be accessible under other operating systems. (OS/2 and DOS share FAT partitions, but high-performance file system (HPFS) partitions are exclusive to OS/2.)

A hard disk must be partitioned to be accessible by an operating system. You must partition a disk even if you want to create only a single partition.

DOS Volume Boot Sectors

The *volume boot sector* is the first sector on any area of a drive that is addressed as a volume (or logical DOS disk). On a floppy disk, for example, this sector would be the first one on the floppy disk because DOS recognizes the floppy disk as a volume with no partitioning required. On a hard disk, the volume boot sector or sectors are located as the first sector within any disk area allocated as a nonextended partition, or any area recognizable as a DOS volume.

This special sector resembles the master-partition boot sector in that it contains a program as well as some special data tables. The first volume boot sector on a disk is loaded by the system ROM BIOS for floppies or by the master-partition boot sector on a hard disk. This program is given control; it performs some tests and then attempts to load the first DOS system file (IBMBIO.COM). The volume boot sector is transparent to a running DOS system; it is outside the data area of the disk on which files are stored.

You create a volume boot sector with the DOS FORMAT command (high-level format). Hard disks have a volume boot sector at the beginning of every DOS logical drive area allocated on the disk, in both the primary and extended partitions. Although all the logical drives will contain the program area as well as a data table area, only the program code from the volume boot sector in the active partition on a hard disk is executed.

The others are simply read by the DOS system files during boot-up to obtain their data table and determine the volume parameters.

The volume boot sector contains program code and data. The single data table in this sector is called the *media parameter block* or *disk parameter block*. DOS needs the information it contains to verify the capacity of a disk volume as well as the location of important features such as the FAT. The format of this data is very specific. Errors can cause problems with booting from a disk or with accessing a disk. Some non-IBM OEM versions of DOS have not adhered to the standards set by IBM for the format of this data, which can cause interchange problems with disks formatted by different versions of DOS. The later versions can be more particular, so if you suspect that boot sector differences are causing inability to access a disk, you can use a utility program such as DOS DEBUG or Norton Utilities to copy a boot sector from the newer version of DOS to a disk formatted by the older version. This step should enable the new version of DOS to read the older disk and should not interfere with the less-particular older version. This has never been a problem in using different DOS versions from the same OEM but might occur in mixing different OEM versions.

Root Directory

A *directory* is a simple database containing information about the files stored on a disk. Each record in this database is 32 bytes long, and there are no delimiters or separating characters between the fields or records. A directory stores almost all the information that DOS knows about a file: name, attribute, time and date of creation, size, and where the beginning of the file is located on the disk. (The information a directory does *not* contain about a file is where the file continues on the disk and whether the file is contiguous or fragmented. The FAT contains that information.)

Two basic types of directories exist: the *root directory* and *subdirectories*. They differ primarily in how many there can be and in where they can be located. Any given volume can have only one root directory, and the root directory is always stored on a disk in a fixed location immediately following the two FAT copies. Root directories vary in size because of the varying types and capacities of disks, but the root directory of a given disk is fixed. After a root directory is created, it has a fixed length and cannot be extended to hold more entries. Normally a hard disk volume has a root directory with room for 512 total entries. Subdirectories are stored as files in the data area of the disk and therefore have no fixed length limits.

Every directory, whether it is the root directory or a subdirectory, is organized in the same way. A directory is a small database with a fixed record length of 32 bytes. Entries in the database store important information about individual files and how files are named on a disk. The directory information is linked to the FAT by the starting cluster entry. In fact, if no file on a disk were longer than one single cluster, the FAT would be unnecessary. The directory stores all the information needed by DOS to manage the file, with the exception of all of the clusters that the file occupies other than the first one. The FAT stores the remaining information about other clusters the file uses.

To trace a file on a disk, you start with the directory entry to get the information about the starting cluster of the file and its size. Then you go to the file allocation table. From there, you can follow the chain of clusters the file occupies until you reach the end of the file.

File Allocation Tables (FATs)

The file allocation table (FAT) is a table of number entries describing how each cluster is allocated on the disk. The data area of the disk has a single entry for each cluster. Sectors in the nondata area on the disk are outside the range of the disk controlled by the FAT. The sectors involved in any of the boot sectors, file allocation table, and root directory are outside the range of sectors controlled by the FAT.

The FAT does not manage every data sector specifically, but rather allocates space in groups of sectors called *clusters* or *allocation units*. A cluster is one or more sectors designated by DOS as allocation units of storage. The smallest space a file can use on a disk is one cluster; all files use space on the disk in integer cluster units. If a file is one byte larger than one cluster, two clusters are used. DOS determines the size of a cluster when the disk is high-level-formatted by the DOS FORMAT command.

You might find it useful to think about the FAT as a sort of spreadsheet that controls the cluster use of the disk. Each cell in the spreadsheet corresponds to a single cluster on the disk; the number stored in that cell is a sort of code telling whether the cluster is used by a file, and if so where the next cluster of the file is located.

The numbers stored in the FAT are hexadecimal numbers that are either 12 or 16 bits long. The 16-bit FAT numbers are easy to follow because they take an even two bytes of space and can be edited fairly easily. The 12-bit numbers are 1 1/2 bytes long, which presents a problem when most disk sector editors show data in byte units. To edit the FAT, you must do some hex/binary math to convert the displayed byte units to FAT numbers. Fortunately (unless you are using the DOS DEBUG program), most of the available tools and utility programs have a FAT-editing mode that automatically converts the numbers for you. Most of them also show the FAT numbers in decimal form, which most people find easier to handle.

The DOS FDISK program determines whether a 12-bit or 16-bit FAT is placed on a disk, even though the FAT is written during the high-level format (FORMAT). All floppy disks use a 12-bit FAT, but hard disks can use either. On hard disk volumes with more than 16 megabytes (32,768 sectors), DOS creates a 16-bit FAT; otherwise, DOS creates a 12-bit FAT.

DOS keeps two copies of the FAT. Each one occupies contiguous sectors on the disk, and the second FAT copy immediately follows the first. Unfortunately, DOS uses the second FAT copy only if sectors in the first FAT copy become unreadable. If the first FAT copy is corrupted, which is a much more common problem, DOS does not use the second FAT copy. Even the DOS CHKDSK command does not check or verify the second FAT copy. Moreover, whenever DOS updates the first FAT, large portions of the first FAT automatically are copied to the second FAT. If, therefore, the first copy was corrupted and then subsequently updated by DOS, a large portion of the first FAT would be copied over the second FAT copy, damaging it in the process. After the update, the second copy is usually a mirror image of the first one, complete with any corruption. Two FATs rarely stay out of sync for very long. When they are out of sync and DOS writes to the disk and causes the first FAT to be updated, it also causes the second FAT to be overwritten by the first FAT. Because of all this, the usefulness of the second copy of the FAT is limited to manual repair operations, and even then it is useful only if the problem is caught immediately, before DOS has a chance to update the disk.

Clusters (Allocation Units)

The term *cluster* has been changed to *allocation unit* in DOS 4.0. The newer term is appropriate because a single cluster is the smallest unit of the disk that DOS can handle when it writes or reads a file. A cluster is equal to one or more sectors, and although a cluster can be a single sector, it is usually more than one. Having more than one sector per cluster reduces the size and processing overhead of the FAT and enables DOS to run faster because it has fewer individual units of the disk to manage. The trade-off is in wasted disk space. Because DOS can manage space only in full cluster units, every file consumes space on the disk in increments of one cluster.

The following table shows default cluster sizes used by DOS for the various disk formats:

Drive type	Default cluster size
5 1/4-inch 360K	2 sectors (1,024 bytes)
5 1/4-inch 1.2M	1 sector (512 bytes)
3 1/4-inch 720K	2 sectors (1,024 bytes)
3 1/4-inch 1.44M	1 sector (512 bytes)
3 1/4-inch 2.88M	2 sectors (1,024 bytes)

It seems strange that the high-density disks, which have many more individual sectors than low-density disks, sometimes have smaller cluster sizes. The larger the FAT, the more entries DOS must manage, and the slower DOS seems to function. This sluggishness is due to the excessive overhead required to manage all of the individual clusters; the more clusters to be managed, the slower things become. The trade-off is in the minimum cluster size.

Smaller clusters generate less *slack* (space wasted between the actual end of each file and the end of the cluster). With larger clusters, the wasted space grows larger. High-density floppy drives are faster than their low-density counterparts, so perhaps IBM and Microsoft determined that the decrease in cluster size balances the drive's faster operation and offsets the use of a larger FAT.

For hard disks, the cluster size can vary greatly among different versions of DOS and different disk sizes. The following table shows the cluster sizes IBM and most other OEM versions of DOS will select for a particular volume size:

Hard disk volume size	Default cluster size	FAT type
0M to less than 16M	8 sectors or 4,096 bytes	12-bit
16M through 128M	4 sectors or 2,048 bytes	16-bit
Over 128M through 256M	8 sectors or 4,096 bytes	16-bit
Over 256M through 512M	16 sectors or 8,192 bytes	16-bit
Over 512M through 1,024M	32 sectors or 16,384 bytes	16-bit
Over 1,024M through 2,048M	64 sectors or 32,768 bytes	16-bit

In most cases, these cluster sizes, selected by the DOS FORMAT command, are the minimum possible for a given partition size. Therefore, 8K clusters are the smallest possible for a partition size of greater than 256M. Although most non-IBM OEM versions of DOS work like the IBM version, some versions might use cluster sizes different from what this table indicates. For example, COMPAQ DOS 3.31 shifts to larger cluster sizes much earlier than IBM DOS does. COMPAQ DOS shifts to 4K clusters at 64M partitions, 8K clusters at 128M partitions, and 16K clusters at 256M partitions. A 305M partition that uses 8K clusters under IBM DOS has clusters of 16K under COMPAQ DOS 3.31.

The effect of these larger cluster sizes on disk use can be substantial. A drive containing about 5,000 files, with average slack of one-half of the last cluster used for each file, wastes about 20 megabytes [5000*(.5*8)K] of file space on a disk set up with IBM DOS or MS-DOS. Using COMPAQ DOS 3.31, this wasted space doubles to 40 megabytes for the same 5,000 files. Someone using a system with COMPAQ DOS 3.31 could back up, repartition, and reformat with IBM DOS, and after restoring all 5,000 files, gain 20 megabytes of free disk space.

The reason that COMPAQ DOS 3.31 does not use the most efficient (or smallest) cluster size possible for a given partition size is that its makers were interested in improving the performance of the system at the expense of great amounts of disk space. Larger cluster sizes get you a smaller FAT, with fewer numbers to manage; DOS overhead is reduced when files are stored and retrieved, which makes the system seem faster. For example, the CHKDSK command would run much faster on a disk with a smaller FAT. Unfortunately, the trade-off for speed here is a tremendous loss of space on the disk. (COMPAQ DOS 4.0 and 5.0 use IBM DOS and MS-DOS conventions.)

The Data Area

The data area of a disk is the area that follows the boot sector, file allocation tables, and root directory on any volume. This area is managed by the FAT and the root directory. DOS divides it into allocation units that are sometimes called clusters. These clusters are where normal files are stored on a volume.

Diagnostic Read-and-Write Cylinder

The FDISK partitioning program always reserves the last cylinder of a hard disk for use as a special diagnostic read-and-write test cylinder. That this cylinder is reserved is one reason FDISK always reports fewer total cylinders than the drive manufacturer states are available. DOS (or any other operating system) does not use this cylinder for any normal purpose, because it lies outside the partitioned area of the disk.

On systems with IDE, SCSI, or ESDI disk interfaces, the drive and controller might allocate additional area past the logical end of the drive for a bad-track table and spare sectors for replacing bad ones. This situation may account for additional discrepancies between FDISK and the drive manufacturer.

The diagnostics area enables diagnostics software such as the manufacturer-supplied Advanced Diagnostics disk to perform read-and-write tests on a hard disk without corrupting any user data. Low-level format programs for hard disks often use this cylinder as a scratch-pad area for running interleave tests or preserving data during nondestructive formats. This cylinder is also sometimes used as a head landing or parking cylinder on hard disks that do not have an automatic-parking facility.

Known Bugs in DOS

Few things are more frustrating than finding out that software you depend on every day has bugs. It's even worse when DOS does. Every version of DOS ever produced has had bugs, and users must learn to anticipate them. Some problems are never resolved; you must live with them.

Sometimes the problems are severe enough, however, that Microsoft, IBM and other OEM distributors of DOS issue a patch disk that corrects the problems. If you use IBM DOS, you can request patches from an IBM dealer. With MS-DOS, you can request a patch by calling the technical support number in the front of your DOS manual. Or, if you have a modem, you can download patches from the Microsoft Download Service (206-936-6735). The section titled, "MS-DOS 5.0 Bugs and Patches" contains more information on calling the Microsoft Download Service.

If you have IBM PC DOS, check with your system vendor periodically to find out whether patches are available. You do not have to go to the dealer from which you purchased PC DOS; any dealer must provide the patches for free when you show you have a legal license for PC DOS. The proof-of-license page from the PC DOS 4.0 manual satisfies as a license check. If you ask a dealer who does not know about these patches, or who does not provide them for some reason, try another dealer. PC DOS is a warranted product, and the patches are part of the warranty service.

The following list details IBM patches for PC DOS 3.3, PC DOS 4.0, and IBM DOS 5.0. These versions have official IBM-produced patch disks that are available at no cost from your nearest IBM dealer.

PC DOS 3.3 Bugs and Patches

The PC DOS 3.3 official patches and fixes from IBM originally were issued by IBM's National Support Center on September 9, 1987. A second update, issued October 24, 1987, superseded the first update. These disks fix two general problems with DOS 3.3:

- BACKUP did not work properly in backing up a large number of subdirectories in a given directory. A new version of BACKUP was created to resolve this problem.

■ Systems that had slow serial printers with small input buffers sometimes displayed a false Out Of Paper error message when attempting to print. A new program, I17.COM, resolves this problem.

In addition to the two general problems resolved by this patch, IBM PS/2 systems had a particular problem between their ROM BIOS and DOS 3.3; a special DASDDRVR.SYS driver was provided on the patch disk to fix these BIOS problems. The versions of DASDDRVR.SYS supplied on the DOS 3.3 patch disks have been superseded by later versions supplied elsewhere; DASDDRVR.SYS was placed on the IBM PS/2 Reference disks for more widespread distribution, and you can obtain it directly from IBM on a special system-update floppy disk. This driver and the problems it can correct are discussed later in this chapter, in the section "PS/2 BIOS Update."

PC DOS 4.0 and 4.01 Bugs and Patches

Six different versions of IBM DOS 4.0 have been issued, counting the first version and the five patch disks subsequently released. The disks are not called patch disks anymore; they are called *corrective service disks* (CSDs). Each level of CSD contains all the previous-level CSDs. The first CSD issued for PC DOS 4.0 (UR22624) contained a series of problem fixes that later were incorporated into the standard-release version of DOS Version 4.01. Several newer CSDs have been released since Version 4.01 appeared. Unfortunately, these more recent updates have not been integrated into the commercially packaged DOS. The only way to obtain these fixes is to obtain the CSDs from your dealer.

If you purchase DOS 4.1 from an IBM dealer today, you get the equivalent of DOS 4.0 plus CSD UR22624. You have to ask the dealer for the current CSDs to have the corrected version of the latest release. Any truly responsible dealer automatically includes the latest CSDs with a DOS purchase; but, in my experience, a few dealers do not, and many do not even have the CSDs on hand.

The VER command in any level of DOS 4.x always shows 4.00, which causes much confusion about which level of CSD fixes are installed on a specific system. To eliminate this confusion and allow for the correct identification of installed patches, the CSD UR29015 and later levels introduce to DOS 4.x a new command: SYSLEVEL. This command is resident in COMMAND.COM and is designed to identify conclusively to the user the level of corrections installed. On a system running PC DOS 4.X with CSD UR35284 installed, the SYSLEVEL command reports:

```
DOS Version: 4.00 U.S. Date: 06/17/88

CSD Version: UR35284 U.S. Date: 09/20/91
```

The following list notes each of the IBM DOS 4.0 Corrective Service Diskettes (CSDs) and when they first became available:

CSD	Date available
UR22624	08/15/88 (this equals 4.01)
UR24270	03/27/89
UR25066	05/10/89
UR29015	03/20/90
UR31300	06/29/90
UR35284	09/20/91

These CSDs are valid only for the IBM version of DOS—PC DOS 4.0. Microsoft and OEM versions of DOS may not have corresponding patches. Some OEMs provide patches or corrections in different ways, and some may not even offer them. Because most OEMs release their versions of DOS after IBM, other manufacturers have had a chance to incorporate fixes in their standard version and may not need to provide patches. If you have a version of DOS by a manufacturer other than Microsoft or IBM, contact its source to find out which patch corrections have been applied to your version of DOS. With a system that can run standard MS-DOS, you can get patches from Microsoft. If you have an IBM, you must rely on a reputable dealer to get the latest version of DOS.

MS-DOS 4

Microsoft released its version of DOS 4 after IBM had fixed most of the bugs in PC DOS 4.0. Yet MS-DOS 4.01 introduced some bugs of its own. A patch for MS-DOS 4.x is available for download from the Microsoft Download Service or by calling Microsoft technical service. The patch disk for MS-DOS 4.0x is available on the Microsoft Download service as PD0255.EXE.

> **Note**
>
> If you have a non-IBM computer purchased in the past few years, it very likely uses standard MS-DOS, rather than a version modified by your system vendor. When MS-DOS 5.0 was introduced, many computer manufacturers who had previously used nonstandard versions of DOS began using the version released to the public by Microsoft. MS-DOS 5.0 represented the first time Microsoft marketed any DOS version directly to the public, and many manufacturers switched because they did not want to risk being incompatible. Exceptions, however, include Compaq and Zenith and other manufacturers who continue to supply their own versions of DOS. If you have such a system you must use the OEM version. With the release of MS-DOS 6.0, Microsoft continued selling direct to the public.

IBM DOS 5.0 Bugs and Patches

With the release of its DOS version 5.0, IBM changed the product name from PC DOS to IBM DOS (Version 6.0 of IBM's DOS has been changed back to PC DOS). IBM DOS Version 5.0 has a CSD that fixes a couple of problems. The most significant is a defect in the XCOPY command that causes it to fail sometimes when it uses the /E or /S switches. The following list notes the IBM DOS 5.0 CSDs and indicates when they first became available:

CSD	Date available
UR35423	08/91
UR35748	10/91
UR35834	11/91
UR36603	02/92
UR37387	09/92

Problems fixed by these patch disks are shown in this list:

CSD	Item	Problem
UR35423	XCOPY	Wrong output when using /E and /S switches
UR35423	QBASIC	Enables QBASIC and QEDIT compatibility
UR35748	SYS	Corrupted hard file after installing UR35423
UR35834	DOSSHELL	DOSSHELL takes 27 seconds to load
UR35834	MEUTOINI	4.0 .MEU to 5.0 .INI conversion incomplete
UR35834	MEM	MEM switch hangs system with PC3270
UR35834	IBMBIO	L40SX will not SUSPEND or RESUME
UR35834	DOSSHELL	Can't edit Dialog Box if length is maximum
UR35834	EMM386	Int 19H fails with EMM386 and DOS=HIGH
UR35834	FORMAT	FORMAT on unpartitioned drive; rc = 0
UR35834	REPLACE	REPLACE /a returns error
UR35834	XCOPY	XCOPY /s incorrectly sets error level
UR35834	GRAPHICS	PrtScr of graphics display produces garbage
UR35834	DOSSHELL	DOSSHELL.INI corrupted from CTRL-ALT-DEL
UR35834	BACKUP	BACKUP calls wrong FORMAT.COM from OS/2
UR35834	MIRROR	MIRROR doesn't enable Interrupts correctly
UR35834	BACKUP	BACKUP /a backs up too large a file
UR36603	EDIT	Alt ### key combo doesn't work in EDIT
UR36603	MIRROR	MIRROR fails with /T switch and DOS=UMB
UR36603	IBMBIO	L40SX will not SUSPEND or RESUME if DOS=LOW
UR36603	BACKUP	BACKUP fails to backup all files
UR36603	QBASIC	QBASIC help msgs missing in nls versions
UR36603	CHKDSK	CHKDSK Data loss when sectors per FAT>256
UR36603	EMM386	DMA transfer may not function on EISA systems
UR36603	RECOVER	RECOVER can corrupt disks with 12bit FAT
UR36603	RECOVER	RECOVER may not adjust file size correctly
UR36603	DOSSHELL	DOSSHELL incorrectly copies certain file sizes
UR36603	DOSSWAP	Task Swapper destroys CX register
UR36603	DOSSWAP	Task Swapper does not swap EMS memory
UR36603	DOSSWAP	Task Swapper incorrectly swaps large XMS memory
UR36603	DOSSWAP	DOSSHELL overwrites an interrupt vector

CSD	Item	Problem
UR36603	DOSSWAP	DOSSHELL random skip of swapping application memory
UR36603	DOSSHELL	DOSSHELL uses environment var to set 2nd swap path
UR37387	RESTORE	RESTORE fails to display backup files
UR37387	IBMDOS	FASTOPEN causes bad FAT message
UR37387	KEYB	Pause key doesn't work on PS/2 25 and 30
UR37387	IBMDOS	Unmapped network drive returns error
UR37387	MODE	MODE and offline printer across net hangs
UR37387	IBMDOS	RAMDRIVE errors with certain combinations
UR37387	DOSSHELL	Unattended start mode - lose keyboard with DOSSHELL
UR37387	COMMAND	Error with greater than 1GB free space
UR37387	IBMDOS	INT 27 returns no data after file create
UR37387	IBMBIO	L40SX loses time during suspend
UR37387	DOSSHELL	CTRL+ESC hangs when returning to DOSSHELL
UR37387	IBMDOS	Extended File Open returns incorrect code
UR37387	HIMEM	Device driver fails to load
UR37387	HIMEM	HIMEM incorrectly indentifies memory on EISA
UR37387	UNDELETE	Doesn't work if partition is a multiple of 128MB
UR37387	UNDELETE	Doesn't handle foreign characters correctly
UR37387	BACKUP	Restore does not ask for 2nd diskette
UR37387	KEYBOARD	Keyboard changes for Latin II countries
UR37387	MEM	Finland MEM/C displays invalid characters
UR37387	DOSSHELL	INT 33 DOSSHELL re-entry problem with BASIC
UR37387	MODE	MODE LPT1:,,P reports Bad mode
UR37387	BACKUP	Occasionally get Cannot Restore File error

MS-DOS 5.0 Bugs and Patches

As mentioned earlier, the Microsoft Download Service DOS files listing includes fixes for MS-DOS Versions 4.0 and 5.0. When you call the Microsoft Download Service, you are asked to enter your name and city and to choose a password. Choose a password you will not forget because once you realize how simple it is to always have the most current bug fixes for MS-DOS, you will want to call back. After you have entered your name and a password the following screen is displayed:

```
***************************************
****Microsoft Download Service****
****       Main Menu       ****
[I]nstructions on Using This Service
[D]ownload File
[F]ile Index

[W]indows 3.1 Driver Library Update
[N]ew Files & Complete file listing
```

```
[M]icrosoft Information
[A]lter User Settings
[U]tilities - Comments
[L]ength of Call
[E]xit ... Logoff the System
[H]elp - System Instructions
Command:
```

At the command prompt choose **f** (for file) to display the following screen:

```
*****************************************
****  File Sections Available  ****
*****************************************
[1] Windows and MS-DOS
[2] Word, Excel and Multiplan
[3] PowerPoint, Publisher and Project
[4] LAN Manager and Microsoft Mail
[5] Languages and Windows SDK
[6] Works and Flight Simulator
[7] MS FOX, MS Access & MS Money
[8] MS Video for Windows

[F]ile Search

[-]Previous Menu
[M]ain Menu

[L]ength of Call
[E]xit ... Logoff the System

Command:
```

Choose **1** (for Windows and MS-DOS) to display the following screen:

```
Windows and MS-DOS Files
[1] Windows for Workgroups Appnotes
[2] Windows 3.1 Driver Library
[3] Windows 3.1 Application Notes
[4] Windows 3.1 Resource Kit
[5] Windows 3.0 Driver Library-SDL
[6] Windows 3.0 Application Notes
[7] Windows 3.0 Resource Kit
[8] MS DOS Files

[-]Previous Menu
[M]ain Menu

[L]ength of Call
[E]xit ... Logoff the System

Command:
```

Choose **8** (for MS-DOS files).

MS-DOS 5.0 fixes available on the Microsoft Download Service are:

PD0445.EXE	Replacement DOSSWAP.EXE
PD0455.EXE	ADAPTEC.SYS Driver (for adaptec drives)
PD0488.EXE	8514.VID Video Driver for MS-DOS 5.0 Shell
PD0489.EXE	MS-DOS Messages Reference
PD0495.EXE	PRINTFIX.COM patch for PRINT problems
PD0646.EXE	Updated CHKDSK.EXE and UNDELETE.EXE
PD0315.EXE	BACKUP/RESTORE Supplemental Utilities

MS-DOS 6.0 and IBM PC DOS 6.1

As of this writing, there had been one bug fix for MS-DOS version 6.0—a new version of SmartDrive, which fixes a problem on some systems when Smartdrive is used at the same time as DoubleSpace. The fix can be used if you have experienced cross-linked files you think are related to upgrading to DOS 6.0. You can download the file, named PD0805.EXE, from the Microsoft Download Service. The Microsoft Download Services also enables you (free of charge) to download the MS-DOS 6.0 Supplemental Disk. This supplemental disk contains utilities that are helpful to the handicapped. The disk also contains new versions of various utilities that were part of DOS 5.0 but not included on the DOS 6.0 upgrade disks, including MIRROR, EDLIN, ASSIGN, JOIN, BACKUP (MSBACKUP is a new menu-based backup program included with DOS 6), COMP, PRINTER.SYS, the DVORAK keyboard. Also available is a utility to fix a problem using the Shift key in Quick Basic 1.1. named PD0415.EXE.

> **Note**
>
> If you received the MS-DOS 6.0 Supplemental Disk from Microsoft on 720K or 360K diskettes and had problems installing the files from these disks, you need replacements. To replace your low-density disks, contact Microsoft. They will send you one new 720K disk or two 360K disks. Microsoft says its first release of the MS-DOS 6.0 Supplemental Disk on low-density diskettes was faulty.

In addition, numerous technical papers on setting up and running MS-DOS 6.0 are available on the download service. They include:

File name	Subject
PD0456.TXT	Running MS-DOS in the High Memory Area
PD0457.TXT	HIMEM.SYS "ERROR: Unable to Control A20 Line"
PD0459.TXT	EMM386.EXE: No Expanded Memory Available

(continues)

V

Troubleshooting Guide

PD0460.TXT	Running Both Extended and Expanded Memory

File name	Subject
PD0462.TXT	Mouse Doesn't Work with MS-DOS Shell
PD0463.TXT	Using the Setver Command
PD0465.TXT	Problems Formatting or Reading a Floppy Disk
PD0470.TXT	System Fails When You Are Using EMM.386
PD0471.TXT	Explanation of the WINA20.386 File
PD0473.TXT	Installing MS-DOS from Drive B
PD0474.TXT	Windows 3.0 Doesn't Run in 386 Enhanced Mode
PD0476.TXT	IBM PS/1 Fails After MS-DOS Is Installed
PD0477.TXT	Setup Stops Before Completing Upgrade to MS
PD0743.TXT	MS-DOS 6.0 Installation and Partition Q&A
PD0744.TXT	MS-DOS 6.0 General Installation Q&A
PD0745.TXT	DoubleSpace Questions and Answers
PD0746.TXT	MemMaker Questions and Answers
PD0747.TXT	MS-DOS 6.0 Configuration Q&A
PD0748.TXT	Backup and Miscellaneous Q&A
PD0771.TXT	Repartitioning Your Hard Disk to Upgrade to MS-DOS 6.0
PD0785.TXT	Upgrading DR DOS to MS-DOS 6

A utility used to automatically convert Stacker drives to MS-DOS 6.0 DoubleSpace drives is not available from the download service. To obtain this utility, you must send the coupon from your DOS 6.0 manual, along with $10, to Microsoft. For more information, contact Microsoft's Sales and Service department at 1-800-228-7007.

IBM has not yet released any patches for its PC DOS 6.1, which was released in late summer of 1993. If you experience problems with this new version of DOS, call IBM technical support or consult an IBM dealer near you. It need not be the same IBM dealer from whom you purchased your system or your old version of DOS.

PS/2 BIOS Update (DASDDRVR.SYS)

The DASDDRVR.SYS (direct-access storage device driver) file is a set of software patches that fix various ROM BIOS bugs in several models of the IBM PS/2. DASDDRVR.SYS is required for specific PS/2 systems using IBM's PC DOS Versions 3.30 or later, to correct several bugs in the IBM PS/2 ROM BIOS. Before IBM's PC DOS 4.00 was released, conflicting information indicated that PC DOS 4.00 would include the updates to correct the PS/2 ROM BIOS problems fixed by DASDDRVR.SYS under PC DOS 3.30. This information was not accurate, however. In fact, an IBM PS/2 system needs DASDDRVR.SYS with IBM DOS 5.00 (or any higher version of DOS) even with the most current corrective service disk (CSD) update.

The PS/2 needs the DASDDRVR.SYS fixes only in the DOS environment. Some users assume, therefore, that the PS/2 problems with DOS are DOS bugs; they are not. The DASDDRVR.SYS program is provided on the PS/2 Reference disk (included with every

PS/2 system) and is available separately on a special PS/2 system update disk. The disks contain the device driver program (DASDDRVR.SYS) and an installation program.

The PS/2 ROM BIOS bugs in the following list are fixed by DASDDRVR.SYS (the problem numbers are shown in table 12.2, and more detailed information is provided later in this section):

1. Failures occur in reading some 720K program floppy disks (Models 8530, 8550, 8560, and 8580).

2. Intermittent Not ready or General failure error messages appear (Models 8550, 8560, and 8580).

3. 3 1/2-inch floppy disk format fails when user tries to format more than one floppy disk (Models 8550, 8560, and 8580).

4. Combined 301 and 8602 error messages appear at power-on or after power interruption (Models 8550 and 8560).

5. System clock loses time, or combined 162 and 163 errors appear during system initialization (Models 8550 and 8560).

6. User is unable to install Power-On Password program with DASDDRVR.SYS installed (Models 8550, 8560, and 8580).

7. Devices attached to COM2:, COM3:, or COM4: are not detected (Model 8530).

8. Devices that use Interrupt Request level 2 (IRQ2) fail (Model 8530).

9. 3 1/2-inch floppy disk format fails when user tries to format more than one floppy disk (Model 8570).

10. System performance degradation occurs from processor-intensive devices (Models 8550, 8555, and 8560).

11. Error occurs in a microcode routine that enhances long-term reliability of 60/120M disk drives (Models 8550, 8555, 8570, and 8573).

12. Time and date errors occur when user resets the time or date. Intermittent date changes occur when the system is restarted by pressing Ctrl-Alt-Del (Model 8530).

If you are an IBM PS/2-system user running PC DOS 3.3 or higher and experiencing any of these problems, load the DASDDRVR.SYS file. The problems are system-specific, and DASDDRVR.SYS fixes the problems for only the systems listed. IBM requires its dealers to distribute the System Update disk containing DASDDRVR.SYS to anyone who requests it. Neither the dealer nor the customer pays a fee for the System Update disk. You also can obtain copies directly from IBM by calling (800) IBM-PCTB (800-426-7282) and ordering the PS/2 System Update disk.

Check table 15.2 for detailed descriptions of each of these problems and for the specific systems affected. Models not listed for a particular problem do not need DASDDRVR.SYS, and no benefit results from installing it.

V

Troubleshooting Guide

Table 15.2 DASDDRVR.SYS Version Summary

Version	File size	Problems fixed	Source
1.10	648 bytes	1-3	DOS 3.3 Fix Disk (08/24/87)
1.20	698 bytes	1-5	Reference Disk, DOS 3.3 Fix Disk (09/09/87)
1.30	734 bytes	1-6	Reference Disk
1.56	1170 bytes	1-10	Reference Disk (03/90), System Update Disk 1.01 (part number 64F1500)
1.56	3068 bytes	1-12	Reference Disk (xx/xx), System Update Disk 1.02 (part number 04G3288)

The first three problem fixes originally were provided by the DASDDRVR.SYS version 1.10 file supplied on the first PC DOS 3.3 fix disk. Fixes for problems 4 and 5 were added in DASDDRVR.SYS version 1.20, included on all IBM PS/2 Reference disks (30-286, 50/60, and 70/80), Version 1.02 or later, as well as on an updated version of the PC DOS 3.3 fix disk. The fix for problem 6 was added in DASDDRVR.SYS Version 1.30, included on all 50/60 and 70/80 Reference Disks, Version 1.03 or later. Fixes for problems 7 through 10 were added to DASDDRVR.SYS Version 1.56, included on all IBM PS/2 Reference Disks dated March 1990 or later. This version of DASDDRVR.SYS also was available separately, on the IBM PS/2 System Update disk Version 1.01. The latest DASDDRVR.SYS (also called Version 1.56, but dated January 1991) can be found on newer reference disks or on the IBM PS/2 System Update disk Version 1.02.

By using the DASDDRVR.SYS driver file, IBM can correct specific ROM BIOS problems and bugs without having to issue a new set of ROM chips for a specific system. Using this file eliminates service time or expense in fixing simple problems, but causes the inconvenience of having to load the driver. The driver does not consume memory, nor does it remain in memory (as does a typical driver or memory-resident program); it either performs functions on boot only and then terminates, or overlays existing code or tables in memory, thereby consuming no additional space. Because DASDDRVR.SYS checks the exact ROM BIOS by model, submodel, and revision, it performs functions only on those for which it is designed. If it detects a BIOS that does not need fixing, the program terminates without doing anything. You can load DASDDRVR.SYS on any system; it functions only on systems for which it is designed.

Because a system BIOS occasionally needs revising or updating, IBM used disk-based BIOS programs for most newer PS/2 systems. The Models 57, P75, 90, and 95, in fact, load the system BIOS from the hard disk every time the system is powered up, during a procedure called *initial microcode load* (IML). You can get a ROM upgrade for these systems by obtaining a new Reference disk and loading the new IML file on the hard disk. This system makes DASDDRVR.SYS or other such patches obsolete.

Installing DASDDRVR.SYS. To install DASDDRVR.SYS, you must update the CONFIG.SYS file with the following entry and restart the system:

DEVICE=*[d:\path\]*DASDDRVR.SYS

The drive and path values must match the location and name of the DASDDRVR.SYS file on your system.

Detailed Problem Descriptions. This section gives a detailed description of the problems corrected by the most current release of DASDDRVR.SYS and indicates for which systems the corrections are necessary.

1. Failures occur in reading some 720K program disks.

> *IBM PS/2 systems affected:*
>
>> Model 30 286 8530-E01, -E21
>>
>> Model 50 8550-021
>>
>> Model 60 8560-041, -071
>>
>> Model 80 8580-041, -071

Intermittent read failures on some 720K original application software disks. Example: Not ready reading drive A: appears when a user attempts to install an application program. Attempting to perform DIR or COPY commands from the floppy disk also produces the error message.

2. Intermittent Not ready or General failure error messages are displayed.

> *IBM PS/2 systems affected:*
>
>> Model 50 8550-021
>>
>> Model 60 8560-041, -071
>>
>> Model 80 8580-041, -071

A very intermittent problem with a floppy disk drive Not ready or a fixed disk General failure message. This problem can be aggravated by certain programming practices that mask off interrupts for long periods. The update ensures that interrupts are unmasked on each disk or floppy disk request.

3. A 3 1/2-inch floppy disk format fails when the user tries to format more than one floppy disk.

> *IBM PS/2 systems affected:*
>
>> Model 50 8550-021
>>
>> Model 60 8560-041, -071
>>
>> Model 80 8580-041, -071

The DOS FORMAT command fails when a user tries to format multiple 3 1/2-inch floppy disks. The failure appears as an Invalid media or Track 0 bad--disk unusable message when the user replies Yes to the prompt Format another (Y/N)? after the format of the first floppy disk is complete. The error message appears when the

Troubleshooting Guide

user tries to format the second disk. If a system is booted from a floppy disk, the problem does not occur. This problem occurs only with DOS 3.3, not with later versions.

4. Combined 301 and 8602 error messages at power-on or after power interruption.

IBM PS/2 systems affected:

Model 50 8550-021

Model 60 8560-041, -071

When power is interrupted momentarily or a system is otherwise switched on and off quickly, a 301 (keyboard) and 8602 (pointing device) error message may appear during the Power-On Self Test (POST). This error occurs because the system powers-on before the keyboard is ready. The problem is more likely to occur if the system was reset previously by pressing Ctrl-Alt-Del.

5. System clock loses time or combined 162 and 163 errors during system initialization.

IBM PS/2 systems affected:

Model 50 8550-021

Model 60 8560-041, -071

Intermittent 162 (CMOS checksum or configuration) and 163 (Clock not updating) Power-On Self Test (POST) errors occur. Various time-of-day problems on specified IBM PS/2 Model 50 systems; for example, the user turns on the machine in the morning and finds the time set to the same time the machine was turned off the day before.

6. User is unable to install Power-On Password program with DASDDRVR.SYS installed.

IBM PS/2 systems affected:

Model 50 8550-021

Model 60 8560-041, -071

Model 80 8580-041, -071

When a user tries to install the Power-On Password feature with DASDDRVR.SYS Version 1.3 or earlier installed, a message appears which says (incorrectly) that a password already exists. The user also may be prompted for a password (on warm boot), even though password security has not been implemented.

7. Devices attached to COM2:, COM3:, or COM4: are not detected.

IBM PS/2 systems affected:

Model 30 286 8530-E01, -E21

8. Devices that use Interrupt Request level 2 (IRQ2) fail.

> *IBM PS/2 systems affected:*
>
>> Model 30 286 8530-E01, -E21

9. A 3 1/2-inch disk format fails when user tries to format more than one disk.

> *IBM PS/2 systems affected:*
>
>> Model 70 8570-Axx (all)
>>
>> Model 80 8580-Axx (all)

The DOS FORMAT command fails when the user tries to format multiple 3 1/2-inch disks. The failure appears as an `Invalid media or Track 0 bad -- disk unusable` message when the user replies Yes to the prompt `Format another (Y/N)?` after the format of the first disk is complete. The error message appears when the user tries to format the second disk. If the system is booted from a floppy disk, the problem does not occur.

10. System performance degradation occurs from processor-intensive devices.

> *IBM PS/2 systems affected:*
>
>> Model 50 8550-021, -031, -061
>>
>> Model 55 SX 8555-031, -061
>>
>> Model 60 8560-041, -071

11. Error occurs in a microcode routine that enhances long-term reliability of 60/120M disk drives.

> *IBM PS/2 systems affected:*
>
>> Model 50 8550-061
>>
>> Model 55 SX 8555-061
>>
>> Model 70 8570-061, -121, -A61, -A21, -B61, -B21
>>
>> Model P70 8573-061, -121

12. Time and date errors occur when the user resets the time or date. Intermittent date changes occur when the system is restarted by pressing Ctrl-Alt-Del.

> *IBM PS/2 systems affected:*
>
>> Model 30 8530 (all)

OS/2 versions 1.2 and earlier contained these BIOS fixes in the form of a .BIO file for each specific BIOS needing corrections. These files were automatically loaded by OS/2 at boot time, depending on the specific system on which it was being loaded.

V

Troubleshooting Guide

OS/2 Versions 1.3 and later contain the fixes directly in-line in the system files, not as separate files. When a system running one of these OS/2 versions is booted, OS/2 determines the model, submodel, and revision bytes for the particular BIOS under which it is running. Based on this information, OS/2 determines the correct .BIO file to load or the correct in-line code to run. For example, the IBM PS/2 55SX BIOS is Model F8, Submodel 0C, Revision 00, which causes IBM OS/2 Version 1.2 to load the file F80C00.BIO automatically during boot-up. OS/2 Versions 1.3 or later use this information to run the proper fix code contained in the system files. This procedure enables execution of only those BIOS fixes necessary for this particular system.

Any symptom described as being resolved by the DASDDRVR.SYS update may have other causes. If you install the DASDDRVR.SYS update and continue to have problems, consider the errors valid and follow normal troubleshooting procedures to find the causes.

Disk and Data Recovery

The CHKDSK, RECOVER, and DEBUG commands are the DOS damaged-disk recovery team. These commands are crude and their actions sometimes are drastic, but at times they are all that is available or needed. RECOVER is best known for its function as a data-recovery program, and CHKDSK usually is used for inspection of the file structure. Many users are unaware that CHKDSK can implement repairs to a damaged file structure. DEBUG, a crude, manually controlled program, can help in the case of a disk disaster, if you know exactly what you are doing.

The CHKDSK Command

The useful and powerful DOS CHKDSK command also is generally misunderstood. To casual users, the primary function of CHKDSK seems to be providing a disk space-allocation report for a given volume and a memory-allocation report. CHKDSK does those things, but its primary value is in discovering, defining, and repairing problems with the DOS directory and FAT system on a disk volume. In handling data-recovery problems, CHKDSK is a valuable tool, although it is crude and simplistic compared to some of the aftermarket utilities that perform similar functions.

The output of the CHKDSK command run on a typical hard disk is as follows:

```
Volume 1GB_SCSI    created 12-12-1993 3:51a
Volume Serial Number is 2F6E-0AD8

1,201,274,880 bytes total disk space
      163,840 bytes in 3 hidden files
   14,188,544 bytes in 433 directories
  665,518,080 bytes in 8,040 user files
  521,404,416 bytes available on disk

       32,768 bytes in each allocation unit
       36,660 total allocation units on disk
       15,912 available allocation units on disk

      655,360 total bytes memory
      632,736 bytes free
```

A little-known CHKDSK function is reporting a specified file's (or files') level of fragmentation. CHKDSK also can produce a list of all files (including hidden and system files) on a particular volume, similar to a super DIR command. By far, the most important CHKDSK capabilities are its detection and correction of problems with the DOS file-management system.

The name of the CHKDSK program is misleading: It seems to be a contraction of CHECK DISK. The program does not actually check a disk, or even the files on a disk, for integrity. CHKDSK cannot even truly show how many bad sectors are on a disk, much less locate and mark them. The real function of CHKDSK is to inspect the directories and FATs to see whether they correspond with each other or contain discrepancies. CHKDSK does not detect (and does not report on) damage in a file; it checks only the FAT and directory areas (the table of contents) of a disk. Rather than CHKDSK, the command should have been called CKDIRFAT (for CHECK DIRECTORY FAT) because its most important job is to verify that the FATs and directories correspond with one another. The name of the program gives no indication of the programs capability to repair problems with the directory and FAT structures.

CHKDSK also can test files for contiguity. Files loaded into contiguous tracks and sectors of a disk or floppy disk naturally are more efficient. Files spread over wide areas of the disk make access operations take longer. DOS always knows the location of all of a file's fragments by using the pointer numbers in the file allocation table (FAT). These pointers are data that direct DOS to the next segment of the file. Sometimes, for various reasons, these pointers might be lost or corrupted and leave DOS incapable of locating some portion of a file. Using CHKDSK can alert you to this condition and even let you reclaim the unused file space for use by another file.

CHKDSK Command Syntax

The syntax of the CHKDSK command is as follows:

```
CHKDSK [d:\path\] [filename] [/F] [/V]
```

The *d:* specifies the disk volume to analyze. The *path* and *filename* options specify files to check for fragmentation in addition to the volume analysis. Wild cards are allowed in the file-name specification, to include as many as all of the files in a specified directory for fragmentation analysis. One flaw with the fragmentation analysis is that it does not check for fragmentation across directory boundaries, only within a specified directory.

The switch /F (Fix) enables CHKDSK to perform repairs if it finds problems with the directories and FATs. If /F is not specified, the program is prevented from writing to the disk and all repairs were not really performed.

The switch /V (Verbose) causes the program to list all the entries in all the directories on a disk and give detailed information in some cases when errors are encountered.

The drive, path, and file specifiers are optional. If no parameters are given for the command, CHKDSK processes the default volume or drive and does not check files for contiguity. If you specify [path] and [filename] parameters, CHKDSK checks all specified files to see whether they are stored contiguously on the disk. One of two messages is displayed as a result:

```
All specified file(s) are contiguous
```

or

```
[filename] Contains xxx non-contiguous blocks
```

The second message is displayed for each file that is fragmented on the disk and displays the number of fragments the file is in. A *fragmented file* is one that is scattered around the disk in pieces rather than existing in one contiguous area of the disk. Fragmented files are slower to load than contiguous files, which reduces disk performance. Fragmented files are also much more difficult to recover if a problem with the FAT or directory on the disk occurs.

Utility programs that can defragment files are discussed in Chapter 10. But if you have only DOS, you have several possible ways to accomplish a full defragmentation. To defragment files on a floppy disk, you can format a new floppy disk and COPY or XCOPY all the files from the fragmented disk to the replacement. For a hard disk, you must completely BACKUP, FORMAT, and then RESTORE the disk. This procedure on a hard disk is time-consuming and dangerous, which is why so many defragmenting utilities have been developed.

CHKDSK Limitations

In several instances, CHKDSK operates only partially or not at all. CHKDSK does not process volumes or portions of volumes that have been created as follows:

- SUBST command volumes

- ASSIGN command volumes

- JOIN command subdirectories

- Network volumes

SUBST Problems. The SUBST command creates a virtual volume, which is actually an existing volumes subdirectory using another volume specifier (drive letter) as an alias. To analyze the files in a subdirectory created with SUBST, you must give the TRUENAME or actual path name to the files. TRUENAME is an undocumented command in DOS 4.0 and later versions that shows the actual path name for a SUBSTed volume.

You also can use the SUBST command to find out the TRUENAME of a particular volume. Suppose that you use SUBST to create volume E: from the C:\AUTO\SPECS directory:

```
C:\>SUBST E: C:\AUTO\SPECS
```

After entering the following two commands to change to the E: volume and execute a CHKDSK of the volume and files there, you see the resulting error message:

```
C:\>E:

E:\>CHKDSK *.*

Cannot CHKDSK a SUBSTed or ASSIGNed drive
```

To run CHKDSK on the files on this virtual volume E:, you must find the actual path the volume represents. You can do so by entering the SUBST command (with no parameters):

```
E:\>SUBST

E: => C:\AUTO\SPECS
```

You can also find the actual path with the undocumented TRUENAME command (in DOS 4.0 and later versions only).

```
E:\>TRUENAME E:

C:\AUTO\SPECS
```

After finding the path to the files, you can issue the appropriate CHKDSK command to check the volume and files:

```
E:\>CHKDSK C:\AUTO\SPECS\*.*

Volume 1GB_SCSI     created 12-12-1993 3:51a
Volume Serial Number is 2F6E-0AD8

1,201,274,880 bytes total disk space
      163,840 bytes in 3 hidden files
   14,188,544 bytes in 433 directories
  665,518,080 bytes in 8,040 user files
  521,404,416 bytes available on disk

       32,768 bytes in each allocation unit
       36,660 total allocation units on disk
       15,912 available allocation units on disk

      655,360 total bytes memory
      632,736 bytes free

All specified file(s) are contiguous
```

ASSIGN Problems. Similarly, CHKDSK does not process a disk drive that has been altered by the ASSIGN command. For example, if you have given the command ASSIGN A=B, you cannot analyze drive A: unless you first unassign the disk drive with the ASSIGN command, that is, ASSIGN A=A.

JOIN Problems. CHKDSK does not process a directory-tree section created by the JOIN command (which JOINs a physical disk volume to another disk volume as a subdirectory), nor does it process the actual JOINed physical drive, because such a drive is an Invalid drive specification, according to DOS. On volumes on which you have used the JOIN command, CHKDSK processes the actual portion of the volume and then displays this warning error message:

```
Directory is joined

tree past this point not processed
```

This message indicates that the command cannot process the directory on which you have used JOIN. CHKDSK then continues processing the rest of the volume and outputs the requested volume information.

Network Problems. CHKDSK does not process a networked (shared) disk on either the server or workstation side. In other words, at the file server, you cannot use CHKDSK on any volume that has any portion of itself accessible to remote network stations. At any network station, you can run CHKDSK only on volumes physically attached to that specific station and not on any volume accessed through the network software. If you attempt to run CHKDSK from a server or a workstation on a volume shared on a network, you see this error message:

```
Cannot CHKDSK a network drive
```

If you want to run CHKDSK on the volume, you must go to the specific PC on which the volume physically exists and suspend or disable any sharing of the volume during the CHKDSK.

CHKDSK Command Output

CHKDSK normally displays this information about a disk volume:

- Volume name and creation date

- Volume serial number

- Number of bytes in total disk space

- Number of files and bytes in hidden files

- Number of files and bytes in directories

- Number of files and bytes in user files

- Number of bytes in bad sectors (unallocated clusters)

- Number of bytes available on disk

- Number of bytes in total memory (RAM)

- Number of bytes in free memory

- Error messages if disk errors are encountered

By using optional parameters, CHKDSK also can show the following:

- Names and number of fragments in noncontiguous files

- Names of all directories and files on disk

If a volume name or volume serial number does not exist on a particular volume, that information is not displayed. If no clusters are marked as bad in the volume's FAT, CHKDSK returns no display of bytes in bad sectors.

As an example, suppose that a disk was formatted under DOS 6.2 with this command:

```
C:\>FORMAT A: /F:720 /U /S /V:floppy_disk
```

The output of the FORMAT command will look like this:

```
Insert new diskette for drive A:
and press ENTER when ready...

Formatting 720K
Format complete.
System transferred


        730,112 bytes total disk space
        135,168 bytes used by system
        594,944 bytes available on disk

          1,024 bytes in each allocation unit.
            581 allocation units available on disk.

Volume Serial Number is 266D-1DDC

Format another (Y/N)?
```

The status report at the end of the FORMAT operation is similar to the output of the CHKDSK command. The output of the CHKDSK command when run on this disk would appear as follows:

```
C:\>CHKDSK A:

Volume FLOPPY_DISK created 01-16-1994 10:18p
Volume Serial Number is 266D-1DDC

        730,112 bytes total disk space
         79,872 bytes in 2 hidden files
         55,296 bytes in 1 user files
        594,944 bytes available on disk

          1,024 bytes in each allocation unit
            713 total allocation units on disk
            581 available allocation units on disk

        655,360 total bytes memory
        632,736 bytes free
```

In this case, CHKDSK shows the volume name and serial number information because the FORMAT command placed a volume label on the disk with the /V: parameter, and FORMAT under DOS 4.0 and later versions automatically places the volume serial number on a disk. Note that three total files are on the disk, two of which have the HIDDEN attribute. DOS versions earlier than 5.0 will report the Volume Label "FLOPPY_DISK" as a third hidden file. To see the names of the hidden files, you can execute the CHKDSK command with the /V parameter:

```
C:\>CHKDSK A: /V

Volume FLOPPY_DISK created 01-16-1994 10:18p
Volume Serial Number is 266D-1DDC
Directory A:\
A:\IO.SYS
A:\MSDOS.SYS
A:\COMMAND.COM

    730,112 bytes total disk space
     79,872 bytes in 2 hidden files
     55,296 bytes in 1 user files
    594,944 bytes available on disk

      1,024 bytes in each allocation unit
        713 total allocation units on disk
        581 available allocation units on disk

    655,360 total bytes memory
    632,736 bytes free
```

With the /V parameter, CHKDSK lists the names of all directories and files across the entire disk, which in this example is only three total files. CHKDSK does not identify which of the files are hidden, it simply lists them all. Note that the DIR command in DOS versions 5.0 and higher can specifically show hidden files with the /AH parameter. The DOS System files are the first two files on a bootable disk, and normally have HIDDEN, SYSTEM, and READ-ONLY attributes. After listing how many bytes are used by the hidden and normal files, CHKDSK lists how much total space is available on the disk.

If you are using DOS 4.0 or a later version, CHKDSK also tells you the size of each allocation unit (or cluster), the total number of allocation units present, and the number not currently being used.

Finally, CHKDSK counts the total amount of conventional memory or DOS-usable RAM (in this case, 640K or 655,360 bytes) and displays the number of bytes of memory currently unused or free. This information tells you the size of the largest executable program you can run.

CHKDSK under DOS versions 3.3 and earlier does not recognize the IBM PS/2 Extended BIOS Data Area (which uses the highest 1K of addresses in contiguous conventional memory) and therefore reports only 639K, or 654,336, bytes of total memory. For most IBM PS/2 systems with 640K of contiguous memory addressed before the video wall, the Extended BIOS Data Area occupies the 640th K. DOS 4.0 and later versions provide the correct 640K report.

During the FORMAT of the disk in the example, the FORMAT program did not find any unreadable sectors. Therefore, no clusters were marked in the FAT as bad or unusable, and CHKDSK did not display the *xxxxxxxx* Bytes in bad sectors message. Even if the disk had developed bad sectors since the FORMAT operation, CHKDSK still would not display any bytes in bad sectors because it does not test for and count bad sectors: CHKDSK reads the FAT and reports on whether the FAT says that there are any bad sectors. CHKDSK does not really count sectors; it counts clusters (allocation units) because that is how the FAT system operates.

Although bytes in bad sectors sounds like a problem or error message, it is not. The report is simply stating that a certain number of clusters are marked as bad in the FAT and that DOS therefore will never use those clusters. Because nearly all hard disks are manufactured and sold with defective areas, this message is not uncommon. In fact, the higher-quality hard disks on the market tend to have more bad sectors than the lower-quality drives, based on the manufacturer defect list shipped with the drive (indicating all the known defective spots). Many of the newest controllers allow for sector and track sparing, in which the defects are mapped out of the DOS-readable area so that DOS never has to handle them. This procedure is almost standard in drives that have embedded controllers, such as IDE (Integrated Drive Electronics) or SCSI (Small Computer Systems Interface) drives.

Suppose that I use a utility program to mark two clusters (150 and 151, for example) as bad in the FAT of the 720K floppy disk I formatted earlier. CHKDSK then reports this information:

```
Volume FLOPPY_DISK created 01-16-1994 10:18p
Volume Serial Number is 266D-1DDC

    730,112 bytes total disk space
     79,872 bytes in 2 hidden files
     55,296 bytes in 1 user files
      2,048 bytes in bad sectors
    592,896 bytes available on disk

      1,024 bytes in each allocation unit
        713 total allocation units on disk
        579 available allocation units on disk

    655,360 total bytes memory
    632,736 bytes free
```

CHKDSK reports 2,048 bytes in bad sectors, which corresponds exactly to the two clusters I just marked as bad. These clusters, of course, are perfectly good—I simply marked them as bad in the FAT. Using disk-editor utility programs such as those supplied with the Norton or Mace Utilities, you can alter the FAT in almost any way you want.

CHKDSK Operation

Although bytes in bad sectors does not constitute an error or problem, CHKDSK reports problems on a disk volume with a variety of error messages. When CHKDSK discovers an error in the FAT or directory system, it reports the error with one of several descriptive messages that vary to fit the specific error. Sometimes the messages are cryptic or misleading. CHKDSK does not specify how an error should be handled; it does not tell you whether CHKDSK can repair the problem or whether you must use some other utility, and what the consequences of the error and the repair will be. Neither does CHKDSK tell you what caused the problem or how to avoid repeating the problem.

The primary function of CHKDSK is to compare the directory and FAT to determine whether they agree with one another—whether all the data in the directory for files (such as the starting cluster and size information) corresponds to what is in the FAT (such as chains of clusters with end-of-chain indicators). CHKDSK also checks subdirectory file entries, as well as the special . and .. entries that tie the subdirectory system together.

The second function of CHKDSK is to implement repairs to the disk structure. CHKDSK patches the disk so that the directory and FAT are in alignment and agreement. From a repair standpoint, understanding CHKDSK is relatively easy. CHKDSK almost always modifies the directories on a disk to correspond to what is found in the FAT. In only a couple of special cases does CHKDSK modify the FAT; when it does, the FAT modifications are always the same type of simple change.

Think of CHKDSK's repair capability as a directory patcher. Because CHKDSK cannot repair most types of FAT damage effectively, it simply modifies the disk directories to match whatever problems are found in the FAT.

CHKDSK is not a very smart repair program and often can do more damage repairing the disk than if it had left the disk alone. In many cases, the information in the directories is correct and can be used (by some other utility) to help repair the FAT tables. If you have run CHKDSK with the /F parameter, however, the original directory information no longer exists, and a good FAT repair is impossible. You therefore should never run CHKDSK with the /F parameter without first running it in read-only mode (without the /F parameter) to determine whether and to what extent damage exists.

Only after carefully examining the disk damage and determining how CHKDSK would fix the problems do you run CHKDSK with the /F parameter. If you do not specify the /F parameter when you run CHKDSK, the program is prevented from making corrections to the disk. Rather, it performs repairs in a mock fashion. This limitation is a safety feature because you do not want CHKDSK to take action until you have examined the problem. After deciding whether CHKDSK will make the correct assumptions about the damage, you might want to run it with the /F parameter.

Sometimes people place a CHKDSK /F command in their AUTOEXEC.BAT file—*a very dangerous practice*. If a system's disk directories and FAT system become damaged, attempting to load a program whose directory and FAT entries are damaged might lock the system. If, after you reboot, CHKDSK is fixing the problem because it is in the AUTOEXEC.BAT, it can irreparably damage the file structure of the disk. In many cases, CHKDSK ends up causing more damage than originally existed, and no easy way exists to undo the CHKDSK repair. Because CHKDSK is a simple utility that makes often-faulty assumptions in repairing a disk, you must run it with great care when you specify the /F parameter.

Problems reported by CHKDSK are usually problems with the software and not the hardware. You rarely see a case in which lost clusters, allocation errors, or cross-linked files reported by CHKDSK were caused directly by a hardware fault, although it is certainly possible. The cause is usually a defective program or a program that was stopped before it could close files or purge buffers. A hardware fault certainly can stop a program before it can close files, but many people think that these error messages signify fault with the disk hardware—almost never the case.

I recommend running CHKDSK at least once a day on a hard disk system because it is important to find out about file-structure errors as soon as possible. Accordingly, placing a CHKDSK command in your AUTOEXEC.BAT file is a good idea, but do not use the /F parameter. Also run CHKDSK whenever you suspect that directory or FAT damage might have occurred. For example, whenever a program terminates abnormally or a system crashes for some reason, I run CHKDSK to see whether any file system damage has occurred.

Common Errors

All CHKDSK can do is compare the directory and FAT structures to see whether they support or comply with one another; as a result, CHKDSK can detect only certain kinds of problems. When CHKDSK discovers discrepancies between the directory and the FAT structures, they almost always fall into one of the following categories. (These errors are the most common ones you will see with CHKDSK.)

- Lost allocation units
- Allocation errors
- Cross-linked files
- Invalid allocation units

The RECOVER Command

The DOS RECOVER command is designed to mark clusters as bad in the FAT when the clusters cannot be read properly. When a file cannot be read because of a problem with a sector on the disk going bad, the RECOVER command can mark the FAT so that those clusters are not used by another file. Used improperly, this program is highly dangerous.

Many users think that RECOVER is used to recover a file or the data within the file in question. What really happens is that only the portion of the file before the defect is recovered and remains after the RECOVER command operates on it. RECOVER marks the defective portion as bad in the FAT, and returns to available status all the data after the defect. Always make a copy of the file to be recovered before using RECOVER, because the copy command can get all the information, including that after the location of the defect.

Suppose that you are using a word processing program. You start the program and tell it to load a file called DOCUMENT.TXT. The hard disk has developed a defect in a sector used by this file, and in the middle of loading it, you see this message appear on-screen:

```
Sector not found error reading drive C
Abort, Retry, Ignore, Fail?
```

V

Troubleshooting Guide

You might be able to read the file on a retry, so try several times. If you can load the file by retrying, save the loaded version as a file with a different name, to preserve the data in the file. You still have to repair the structure of the disk, to prevent the space from being used again.

After ten retries or so, if you still cannot read the file, the data will be more difficult to recover. This operation has two phases:

- Preserve as much of the data in the file as possible.

- Mark the FAT so that the bad sectors or clusters of the disk are not used again.

Preserving Data

To recover the data from a file, use the DOS COPY command to make a copy of the file with a different name; for example, if the file you are recovering has the name DOCUMENT.TXT and you want the copy to be named DOCUMENT.NEW, you enter the following at the DOS prompt:

COPY *document.txt document.new*

In the middle of the copy, you see the Sector not found error message again. The key to this operation is to answer with the (I)gnore option. Then the bad sectors are ignored, and the copy operation can continue to the end of the file. This procedure produces a copy of the file with all of the file intact, up to the error location and after the error location. The bad sectors appear as gibberish or garbage in the new copied file, but the entire copy is readable. Use your word processor to load the new copy and remove or retype the garbled sectors. If this file were a binary file (such as a part of a program), you probably would have to consider the whole thing a total loss because you generally do not have the option of retyping the bytes that make up a program file. Your only hope then is to replace the file from a backup. This step completes phase one, which has recovered as much of the data as possible. Now you go to phase two, in which you mark the disk so that these areas will not be used again.

Marking Bad Sectors

You mark bad sectors on a disk with the RECOVER command. After making the attempted recovery of the data, you can use the following RECOVER command at the DOS prompt to mark the sectors as bad in the FAT:

RECOVER *document.txt*

In this case, the output of the RECOVER command looks like this:

```
Press any key to begin recovery of the file(s) on drive C:
XXXXX of YYYYY bytes recovered
```

The DOCUMENT.TXT file still is on the disk after this operation, but it has been truncated at the location of the error. Any sectors the RECOVER command could not read are marked as bad sectors in the FAT and will show up the next time you run CHKDSK. You might want to run CHKDSK before and after running RECOVER, to see the effect of the additional bad sectors.

After using RECOVER, delete the DOCUMENT.TXT file because you have already created a copy of it that contains as much good data as possible.

This step completes phase two—and the entire operation. You now have a new file that contains as much of the original file as possible, and the disk FAT is marked so that the defective location will not be a bother.

Caution

Be very careful when you use RECOVER. Used improperly, it can do much damage to your files and the FAT. If you enter the RECOVER command without a file name for it to work on, the program assumes that you want every file on the disk recovered, and operates on every file and subdirectory on the disk; it converts all subdirectories to files, and places all file names in the root directory and gives them new names (FILE0000.REC, FILE0001.REC, and so on). This process essentially wipes out the file system on the entire disk. *Do not use RECOVER without providing a file name for it to work on.* This program is so dangerous when you misuse it that you should consider immediately deleting it from your hard disk, to prevent anyone from invoking it accidentally.

When you get the Sector not found error reading drive C:, rather than using the DOS RECOVER command, use the Norton Disk Doctor, or a similar utility, to repair the problem. If the error is on a floppy disk, use Norton's DiskTool before you use Disk Doctor. DiskTool is designed to help you recover data from a defective floppy disk. Disk Doctor and DiskTool preserve as much of the data in the file as possible, and afterward mark the FAT so that the bad sectors or clusters of the disk are not used again. These Norton Utilities also save UNDO information, making it possible for you to reverse any data recovery operation.

The DEBUG Program

The DOS DEBUG program is a powerful debugging tool for programmers who develop programs in assembly language. The following list shows some of the things you can do with DEBUG:

- Display data from any memory location.

- Display or alter the contents of the CPU registers.

- Display the assembly source code of programs.

- Enter data directly into any memory location.

- Input from a port.

- Move blocks of data between memory locations.

- Output to a port.

- Perform hexadecimal addition and subtraction.

V

Troubleshooting Guide

- Read disk sectors into memory.

- Trace the execution of a program.

- Write disk sectors from memory.

- Write short assembly language programs.

To use the DEBUG program, make sure that DEBUG.COM is in the current directory or in the current DOS PATH. The following is the DEBUG command syntax:

DEBUG *[d:][path][filename][arglist]*

Entering DEBUG alone at the DOS prompt launches DEBUG. The d\path option represents the drive and directory where the file you want to DEBUG is located. The *filename* entry represents the file you want to DEBUG and when you want to use DEBUG to work on a file, the filename is mandatory. The *arglist* entry represents parameters and switches that will be passed to a program being DEBUGged and can be used only if the file name is present.

Once DEBUG has been executed, its prompt is displayed (the DEBUG prompt is a hyphen). At the DEBUG hyphen prompt you can enter a DEBUG command.

Because more powerful programs are available for debugging and assembling code, the most common use for DEBUG is patching assembly language programs to correct problems, change an existing program feature, or patch disk sectors.

DEBUG Commands and Parameters

The documentation for DEBUG no longer is provided in the standard DOS manual. If you are serious about using DEBUG, you should purchase the *DOS Technical Reference Manual*, which contains the information you need to use this program. Many third-party books also provide documentation of the DEBUG commands and parameters.

As a quick reference to the DEBUG program, the following is a brief description of each command.

A address assembles macro assembler statements directly into memory.

C range address compares the contents of two blocks of memory.

D address or *D range* displays the contents of a portion of memory.

E address displays bytes sequentially and enables them to be modified.

E address list replaces the contents of one or more bytes, starting at the specified address, with values contained in the list.

F range list fills the memory locations in the range with the values specified.

G processes the program you are debugging without breakpoints.

G =address processes instructions beginning at the address specified.

G =address address processes instructions beginning at the address specified. This command stops the processing of the program when the instruction at the specified address is reached (breakpoint), and displays the registers, flags, and the next instruction to be processed. As many as ten breakpoints can be listed.

H value value adds the two hexadecimal values and then subtracts the second from the first. It displays the sum and the difference on one line.

I portaddress inputs and displays (in hexadecimal) one byte from the specified port.

L address loads a file.

L address drive sector sector loads data from the disk specified by drive and places the data in memory beginning at the specified address.

M range address moves the contents of the memory locations specified by range to the locations beginning at the address specified.

N filename defines file specifications or other parameters required by the program being debugged.

O portaddress byte sends the byte to the specified output port.

P =address value causes the processing of a subroutine call, a loop instruction, an interrupt, or a repeat-string instruction to stop at the next instruction.

Q ends the DEBUG program.

R displays the contents of all registers and flags and the next instruction to be processed.

R F displays all flags.

R registername displays the contents of a register.

S range list searches the range for the characters in the list.

T =address value processes one or more instructions starting with the instructions at CS:IP, or at =address if it is specified. This command also displays the contents of all registers and flags after each instruction is processed.

U address unassembles instructions (translates the contents of memory into assembler-like statements) and displays their addresses and hexadecimal values, together with assembler-like statements.

W address enables you to use the WRITE command without specifying parameters or by specifying only the address parameter.

W address drive sector sector writes data to disk beginning at a specified address.

XA count allocates a specified number of expanded-memory pages to a handle.

XD handle deallocates a handle.

Troubleshooting Guide

XM lpage ppage handle maps an EMS logical page to an EMS physical page from an EMS handle.

XS displays the status of expanded memory.

Changing Disks and Files

DEBUG can be used to modify sectors on a disk. Suppose that you use this DEBUG command:

```
-L 100 1 0 1
```

This command loads into the current segment at an offset of 100h, sectors from drive B:\ (1), starting with sector 0 (the DOS volume boot sector), for a total of 1 or more sectors.

You then could write this sector to a file on drive C:\ by using these commands:

```
-N C:\B BOOT.SEC

-R CX

CX 0000

:200

-W

Writing 0200 bytes

-Q
```

The Name command sets up the name of the file to read or write.

The Register command enables you to inspect and change the contents of registers. The CX register contains the low-order bytes indicating the size of the file to load or save, and the BX register contains the high-order bytes. You would not need to set the BX register to anything but 0 unless the file was to be more than 65535 (64K) bytes in size. Setting the CX register to 200 indicates a file size of 200h, or 512 bytes.

The Write command saves 512 bytes of memory, starting at the default address of offset 100, to the file indicated in the Name command.

After quitting the program, your C:\ drive will have a file called B BOOT.SEC that contains an image of the DOS volume boot sector on drive B:\.

Memory Resident-Software Conflicts

One area that gives many users trouble is a type of memory-resident software called *popup utilities*. This software loads itself into memory and stays there, waiting for an activation key (usually a keystroke combination).

The problem with popup utilities is that they often conflict with each other, as well as with applications programs and even DOS. Popup utilities can cause many types of problems. Sometimes the problems appear consistently, and at other times they are intermittent. Some computer users do not like to use popup utilities unless absolutely necessary because of its potential for problems.

Other memory resident programs, such as MOUSE.COM, are usually loaded in AUTOEXEC.BAT. These memory resident programs usually do not cause the kind of conflicts that popup utilities do, mainly because popup utilities are constantly monitoring the keyboard for the hotkey that activates them (and popup utilities are known to barge into memory addresses being used by other programs in order to monitor the keyboard, or to activate). Memory resident programs like MOUSE.COM are merely installed in memory, do not poll the keyboard for a hotkey and generally they do not clash with the memory addresses used by other programs.

Device drivers loaded in CONFIG.SYS are another form of memory-resident software, and can cause many problems.

If you are experiencing problems that you have traced to any of the three types of memory-resident programs, a common way to correct the problem is to eliminate the conflicting program. Another possibility is to change the order in which device drivers and memory resident programs are loaded into system memory. Some programs must be loaded first, and others must be loaded last. Sometimes this order preference is indicated in the documentation for the programs, but often it is discovered through trial and error.

Unfortunately, conflicts between memory-resident programs are likely to be around as long as DOS is used. The light at the end of the tunnel is operating systems like Windows NT 3.1 and OS/2. The problem with DOS is that it establishes no real rules for how resident programs must interact with each other and the rest of the system. Windows NT and OS/2 are built on the concept of many programs being resident in memory at one time, and all multitasking. These operating systems should put an end to the problem of resident programs conflicting with each other.

Hardware Problems versus Software Problems

One of the most aggravating situations in computer repair is opening up a system and troubleshooting all the hardware just to find that the cause of the problem is a software program, not the hardware. Many people have spent large sums of money on replacement hardware such as motherboards, disk drives, adapter boards, cables, and so on, all on the premise that the hardware was causing problems, when software was actually the culprit. To eliminate these aggravating, sometimes embarrassing, and often expensive situations, you must be able to distinguish a hardware problem from a software problem.

V

Troubleshooting Guide

Fortunately, making this distinction can be relatively simple. Software problems often are caused by device drivers and memory resident programs loaded in CONFIG.SYS and AUTOEXEC.BAT on many systems. One of the first things to do when you begin having problems with your system is to boot the system from a DOS disk that has no CONFIG.SYS or AUTOEXEC.BAT configuration files on it. Then test for the problem. If it has disappeared, the cause was probably something in one or both of those files. To find the problem, begin restoring device drivers and memory resident programs to CONFIG.SYS and AUTOEXEC.BAT one at a time (starting with CONFIG.SYS). For example, add one program back to CONFIG.SYS, reboot your system, and then determine if the problem has reappeared. Once you discover the device driver or memory resident program that is causing the problem, you might be able to solve the problem by editing CONFIG.SYS and AUTOEXEC.BAT to change the order in which device drivers and memory resident programs are loaded, or you might have to eliminate the problem device driver or memory resident program.

DOS can cause other problems, such as bugs or incompatibilities with certain hardware items. For example, DOS 3.2 does not support the 1.44M floppy drive format; therefore, using DOS 3.2 on a system equipped with a 1.44M floppy drive might lead you to believe (incorrectly) that the drive is bad. Be sure that you are using the correct version of DOS and that support is provided for your hardware. Find out whether your version of DOS has any official patches available; sometimes a problem you are experiencing might be one that many others have had, and IBM or Microsoft might have released a fix disk that takes care of the problem. For example, many PS/2 users have a floppy formatting problem under DOS 3.3. They get a track 0 bad message after answering Yes to the Format another diskette message. This problem was solved by a special driver file on the DOS 3.3 patch disk.

If you are having a problem related to a piece of application software, a word processor or spreadsheet, for example, contact the company that produces the software and explain the problem. If the software has a bug, the company might have a patched or fixed version available, or it might be able to help you operate the software in a different way to solve the problem.

Chapter Summary

This chapter has examined the software side of your system. Often when a system has a problem, the problem is in the software and is not hardware-related. The chapter has examined DOS and showed how DOS organizes information on a disk. You have learned about the CHKDSK, RECOVER, and DEBUG commands to see how DOS can help you with data and disk recovery. Finally, the chapter has described memory-resident software and some of the problems it can cause, and has given you an idea of how to distinguish a software problem from a hardware problem.

Chapter 16

A Final Word

The contents of this book cover most of the components of an IBM-compatible personal computer system. In this book, you discovered how all the components operate and interact and how these components should be set up and installed. You saw the ways that components fail and learned the symptoms of these failures. You reviewed the steps in diagnosing and troubleshooting the major components in a system so that you can locate and replace a failing component. You also learned about upgrades for components, including what upgrades are available, the benefits of an upgrade, and how to obtain and perform the actual upgrade. Because failing components so often are technically obsolete, it is often desirable to combine repair and upgrade procedures to replace a failing part with an upgraded or higher performance part.

The information I have presented in this book represents years of practical experience with IBM and IBM-compatible systems. Much research and investigation have gone into each section. This information has saved companies many thousands of dollars. By reading this book, you also have taken advantage of this wealth of information, and may already have saved you and your company time, energy, and most important, money!

Bringing microcomputer service and support in-house is one of the best ways to save money. Eliminating service contracts for most systems and reducing down-time are just two of the benefits of applying the information presented in this book. As I have indicated many times in this book, you can also save a lot of money on component purchases by eliminating the middleman and purchasing the components directly from distributors or manufacturers. The vendor list in the Appendix provides the best of these sources for you to contact. If you intend to build your own systems, the vendor list will be most useful; I've found that this list is the most often used part of the book. Many people are unable to make direct purchases, however, because doing so requires a new level of understanding of the components involved. Also, many of the vendors are unable to provide support for beginning users. I hope that this book has given you the deeper level of knowledge and understanding you need so that you can purchase the components you want directly from the vendors who manufacture and distribute them.

I have used many sources to gather the information in this book, starting with my own real world experiences. I also have taught this information to thousands of people in seminars presented by my company, Mueller Technical Research. During these seminars, I am often asked where more of this type of information can be obtained and whether I have any "secrets" for acquiring this knowledge. Well, I won't keep any secrets! I can freely share the following four key sources of information that can help you become a verifiable expert in PC upgrading and repairing:

- Manuals
- Machines
- Modems
- Magazines

Manuals

Manuals are the single most important source of computer information. Unfortunately, manuals also are one of the most frequently overlooked sources of information. Much of my knowledge came from poring over technical-reference manuals and other Original Equipment Manufacturer's (OEM) manuals. I would not even consider purchasing a system that does not have a detailed technical-reference manual available. This statement applies also to system components—whether it's a floppy drive, hard disk, power supply, motherboard, or memory card. I have to have a detailed reference manual to help me understand what future upgrades are possible and to provide valuable insight into the proper installation, use, and support of a product.

A simple analogy explains the importance of manuals, as well as other issues concerning repair and maintenance of a system. Compare your business use of computers to a taxicab company. The company has to purchase automobiles to use as cabs. The owners purchase not one car but an entire fleet of cars. Do you think that they would purchase a fleet of automobiles based solely on reliability, performance, or even gas-mileage statistics? Would they neglect to consider on-going maintenance and service of these automobiles? Would they purchase a fleet of cars that could be serviced only by the original manufacturer and for which parts could not be obtained easily? Do you think that they would buy a car that did not have available a detailed service and repair manual? Would they buy an automobile for which parts were scarce and that was supported by a sparse dealer network with few service and parts outlets, making long waits for parts and service inevitable? The answer (of course) to all these questions is No, No, No!

You can see why most taxicab companies as well as police departments use "standard" automobiles such as the Chevrolet Caprice or Ford Crown Victoria. If ever there were "generic" cars, these models would qualify. Dealers and parts and documentation for these particular models are everywhere, and they share parts with many other automobiles as well, making them easy to service and maintain.

Doesn't your business (especially if it is large) use what amounts to a "fleet" of computers? If so, then why don't you think of this fleet as the cars of the cab company, which would go out of business quickly if these cars could not be kept running smoothly and inexpensively. Now you know why the Checker Marathon automobile used to be so popular with cab companies: its design barely changed over the span of its availability. In many ways, the standard XT and AT compatible systems are like the venerable Checker Marathon. You can get technical information by the shelf-full for these systems. You can get parts and upgrade material from so many sources that anything you need is always immediately available and at a discounted price. I'm not saying that you should standardize on using older XT or AT systems, just that there is a case for standardizing on systems that follow the "generic" physical design of the XT or AT, but use newer internal components. This results in systems that are completely modern in performance and capabilities, and which are easily supported, repaired, and upgraded.

Even the PS/2 systems now are capable of being considered in this light because their installed base exceeds 10 million units. Many third parties now have replacement and upgrade motherboards, power supplies, and disk drives for these systems. You can purchase everything from upgraded motherboards to disk drives, memory, video adapters, power supplies and just about any other component in the system. Because PS/2 systems are easy to disassemble, the upgrade procedure also is usually very easy, even if you are replacing the motherboard.

It's amazing that people purchase computers that have no technical documentation and no spare-parts program, or parts available only through dealers, or that use nonstandard form-factor components, and so on. The upgrade, repair, and maintenance of a company's computer systems always seem to take a back seat to performance and style.

In addition to the system OEM manuals, I like to collect documentation from the different Original Equipment Manufacturers that make the components used in various systems. For example, I recently worked with Gateway and Hewlett-Packard systems, both of which use Epson floppy drives. The OEM documentation for these systems did not include detailed information on the Epson floppy drives, so I called Epson and ordered the specification manual for these drives. I also ordered the specification manuals for several other drives used in these systems, including Western Digital and Quantum hard disks. I now have information on these drives, which covers jumper settings, service and repair information, and other technical specifications not provided otherwise. I recommend that you inventory each major component of your system by manufacturer and model number. If you don't have the specification or technical reference manuals for these components, call the manufacturers (the vendor list in the Appendix will help), and ask for them. You'll be amazed at the wealth of information you can get.

If you're looking for more general purpose documentation, especially on operating systems or applications software, try Que Corporation, which specializes in this type of computer book. In particular, I recommend *Killer PC Utilities*, and *Que's Guide to Data Recovery*. These books combine basic hardware information with more extensive software and operating system coverage. Microsoft and IBM also publish books of interest to computer enthusiasts and technicians. For example, Microsoft sells the *DOS Resource Kit*, and IBM sells the *DOS Technical Reference Manual*. The Microsoft kit consists of a command reference book (Microsoft left the command reference out of the DOS 6 documentation), and a very useful disk of utilities that both Microsoft and IBM left out of DOS 6 and 6.1. Que also publishes the *IBM OS/2 Technical Reference* library (IBM calls them "Red Books," because the covers originally were red), which is recommended for anybody using OS/2. IBM has several other technical reference manuals for use with IBM-compatible systems. A detailed list of these manuals is included in the Appendix of this book.

Machines

Machines refers to the systems themselves. Machines are one of my best sources of information. For example, suppose that I need to answer the question, "Will the XYZ SCSI host adapter work with the ABC tape drive?" The answer is as simple as plugging everything in and pressing the switch. (Simple to talk about, that is.) Seriously, experimenting with and observing running systems are some of the best learning tools at your disposal. I recommend that you try everything; rarely will anything you try harm the equipment. Harming valuable data is definitely possible, if not likely, however, so make regular backups as insurance. People sometimes are reluctant to experiment with systems that cost a lot of money, but much can be learned through direct tests and studies of the system.

Support people in larger companies have access to quantities of hardware and software I can only dream about. Some larger companies have "toy stores," where they regularly purchase equipment solely for evaluation and testing. Dealers and manufacturers also have access to an enormous variety of equipment. If you are in this position, take advantage of this access to equipment, and learn from this resource. When new systems are purchased, take notes on their construction and components.

Every time I encounter a system I have not previously worked with, I immediately open it up and start taking notes. I want to know the make and model of all the internal components, such as disk drives, power supplies, and motherboards. As far as motherboards, I like to record the numbers of the primary IC chips on the board, such as the processor (of course), integrated chip sets, floppy controller chips, keyboard controller chips, video chipsets, and any other major chips on the board. By knowing which chip set your system uses, you can often infer other capabilities of the system, such as enhanced setup or configuration capabilities. I like to know which BIOS version is in the system, and I even make a copy of the BIOS on-disk for backup and further study purposes. I want to know the hard drive tables from the BIOS, and any other particulars involved in setting up and installing a system. Write down the type of battery a system uses so that you can obtain spares. Note any unique brackets or construction techniques such as specialized hardware (Torx screws, for example) so that you can be prepared for servicing the system later.

This discussion brings up a pet peeve of mine. Nothing burns me up as much as reading a "review" of computer systems in a major magazine, in which reviewers test systems and produce benchmark and performance results for, let's say, the hard disks or video displays in a system. Then, they do not open up the machines and tell me (and the world) exactly which components the manufacturer of the system is using! I want to know *exactly* which disk controller, hard drive, BIOS, motherboard, video adapter, and so on are found in each system. Without this information, their review and benchmark tests are useless to me. Then they run a test of disk performance between two systems with the same disk controller and drives and say (with a straight face) that the one that came out a few milliseconds ahead of the other wins the test. With the statistical variation that normally occurs in any manufactured components, these results are meaningless. The point is perhaps to be very careful of what you trust in a normal magazine review. If it tells me exactly which components were tested, then I can draw my own conclusions and even make comparisons to other systems not included in that review. The (now defunct) *PC Tech Journal* magazine always did *excellent* reviews, and told readers what components were in the systems it tested. The review test data then was much more accurate and informative because it could be properly interpreted.

Modems

Modems refers to the use of public- and private-information utilities, which are a modem and a phone call away. With a modem, you can tie into everything from local electronic bulletin board systems (BBSs), vendor boards, and major information networks such as CompuServe. Many hardware and software companies offer technical support and even software upgrades over their own semi-public bulletin boards. The public-access information networks such as CompuServe and other BBS systems include computer enthusiasts and technical-support people from various organizations, as well as experts in virtually all areas of computer hardware and software. Bulletin boards are a great way to have questions answered and to collect useful utility and help programs that can make your job much easier. The world of public-domain and user-supported software awaits, as well as more technical information and related experiences than you can imagine.

The vendor list in the Appendix includes not only the name, address, and voice phone number for the company, but also the BBS numbers where available. If you need more information on a vendor's products, or need technical support, try using the vendor's BBS. Many companies run a BBS to provide updated software or driver files so that you can download them quickly and easily. One of the best examples of a BBS is the IBM National Support Center (NSC). This BBS not only provides information on all of IBM's products, but also serves as the source for Corrective Service disk patches to DOS, OS/2, and other IBM software. Also provided are fully downloadable copies of the reference and setup disks needed to configure IBM hardware. This BBS is the ideal way to get the latest versions of these disks directly from IBM at no charge. When a vendor provides a BBS service, I consider that service a major advantage in comparison to other vendors who do not provide such a service. Using vendor BBSs have saved me money and countless hours of time.

Many companies that provide a BBS do so through a public access utility, such as CompuServe, rather than running their own BBS. The CompuServe Information Service (CIS) is a public information access utility with an extensive network of dial-in nodes that allows you to log on to its cluster of mainframe systems (based in Ohio) from virtually anywhere in the world through a local telephone call. Among CompuServe's

V

Troubleshooting Guide

resources are special interest groups (SIGs), sponsored by most of the major software and hardware companies, as well as enthusiasts of all types. Some interesting discussions take place in the SIGs. CompuServe, combined with a local electronic bulletin board or two, can greatly supplement the information you gather from other sources. In fact, CompuServe electronic mail is probably the most efficient method of reaching me. My CompuServe ID is 73145,1566, and if you have questions or just a comment or useful information you think I might be interested in, please send me a message. Because of the extra steps in processing, my standard mail can get backed up and it can take me awhile to answer a regular postal letter; electronic mail, however, involves fewer steps for me to send, and always seems to have a higher priority.

Magazines

The last source of information, *magazines*, is one of the best sources of up-to-date reviews and technical data. Featured are "bug fixes," problem alerts, and general industry news. Keeping a printed book up to date with the latest events in the computer industry is extremely difficult or impossible. Things move so fast that the magazines themselves barely keep pace. I subscribe to most of the major computer magazines and am hard-pressed to pick one as the best. They all are important to me, and each one provides different information or the same information with a different angle or twist. Although the reviews sometimes leave me wanting, the magazines still are a valuable way to at least hear about products, most of which I never would have known about without the magazines' reports and advertisements. Most computer magazines now are on CD-ROM, which can ease the frantic search for a specific piece of information you remember reading about. If CD-ROM versions are too much for your needs, you can access and search most major magazines on CompuServe. This capability is valuable when you want to research everything you can about a specific subject.

One of the best kept secrets in the computer industry is the excellent trade magazines that offer free subscriptions. Although many of these magazines are directed toward the wholesale end of the industry, I like to subscribe to them. Some of my favorites magazines include the following:

- *The Processor*
- *Computer Hotline*
- *Computer Reseller News*
- *Electronic Buyer's News*
- *Electronic Engineering Times*
- *Computer Design*
- *Electronic Products*
- *Test and Measurement World*
- *Service News*

These magazines offer free subscriptions to anyone who qualifies. Aimed at people in the computer and electronics industries, these magazines offer a much greater depth and breadth of technical and industry information compared to the more "public" magazines that most people are familiar with. You'll find these and other recommended magazines in the vendor list in the Appendix of this book.

The Appendix

The *Appendix* provides a collection of technical information, tables, charts, and lists especially useful to people in a computer support, troubleshooting, service, or upgrading role. Whether you're looking for the meaning of a word in the Glossary, seeking the address and phone number of a company or vendor in the Vendor List, or searching for something as technical as determining the pinout of the ISA bus connector, you'll most likely find the information in the Appendix.

The Appendix started out as a brief collection of information, but has grown into a complete reference. No other book currently on the market contains such a complete and informative reference, which is one reason why so many large companies and educational institutions have standardized on this book for their technicians and students.

In Conclusion

I hope that *Upgrading and Repairing PCs*, 3rd Edition, is beneficial to you and I hope that you have enjoyed reading it as much as I have enjoyed writing it. If you have questions about this book, or if you have ideas for future versions, I can be reached at the following address:

Scott Mueller
Mueller Technical Research
21718 Mayfield Lane
Barrington, IL 60010-9733
(708)726-0709
(708)726-0710 FAX
73145,1566 - CompuServe ID

I am especially interested in any ideas you have for new topics and information to be included in future releases of this book. If you want a response through the mail, please include a self-addressed stamped envelope.

Thank you again for reading this book, and a special thanks to those people who have been loyal readers since the first edition came out in 1989.

Sincerely,

Scott Mueller

V

Troubleshooting Guide

Appendix

This appendix has a great deal of useful information, primarily reference information, designed not to be read but to be looked up. This type of information can be very useful in troubleshooting or upgrading sessions, but usually is spread out among many sources. In this third edition of *Upgrading and Repairing PCs*, even more information has been added to the appendix, including information I have needed during the course of normal PC troubleshooting, servicing, or upgrading.

The information in this appendix is in the form of many reference charts and tables—in particular, information about the default interrupt, DMA channel, I/O port, and memory use of the primary system and most standard options. This information is invaluable if you install new boards or upgrade a system in any way and can be important when you troubleshoot a conflict between two devices.

This appendix has information about various system connectors—from the serial and parallel ports to the power-supply connections. Diagrams for making serial and parallel wrap (test) plugs are shown also.

Tables indicate the hard disk drive tables in the two versions of the IBM XT hard disk controller, as well as all versions of the IBM AT and PS/2 system ROM BIOS to date. Many compatible BIOS drive tables also are included. This information is necessary when you add a hard disk to systems using these components.

One of the most useful tables in this appendix is a concise listing of the IBM diagnostics error codes. These codes can be generated by the POST and by the disk-based diagnostics programs. These error codes are not documented by IBM in tabular form; this compilation is the result of poring over hardware-maintenance service, technical-reference, and other manuals that IBM produces. Some of the codes come from reading the commented ROM listings in the technical-reference manuals. This information can be very useful in deciphering the codes quickly and efficiently, without having to look through a stack of books.

This appendix also has a listing of all the available IBM technical manuals and a description of all the documentation available. The included listing has part-number and pricing information as well as information useful in ordering this documentation.

Although all of this information comes from a wide range of sources, most of it comes from the technical-reference manuals and hardware-maintenance service manuals available for various systems from IBM and other manufacturers. These documents are invaluable if you want to pursue this topic more extensively.

ASCII Character Code Charts

Figures A.1 through A.3 list ASCII control, standard, and extended character values. Figure A.4 shows the IBM extended ASCII line-drawing characters in an easy-to-use format. I frequently use these extended ASCII line-drawing characters for visual enhancement in documents I create.

ASCII Control Codes:

DEC	HEX	CHAR	NAME		CONTROL CODE
0	00		Ctrl-@	NUL	Null
1	01	☺	Ctrl-A	SOH	Start of Heading
2	02	●	Ctrl-B	STX	Start of Text
3	03	♥	Ctrl-C	ETX	End of Text
4	04	♦	Ctrl-D	EOT	End of Transmit
5	05	♣	Ctrl-E	ENQ	Enquiry
6	06	♠	Ctrl-F	ACK	Acknowledge
7	07	•	Ctrl-G	BEL	Bell
8	08	□	Ctrl-H	BS	Back Space
9	09	○	Ctrl-I	HT	Horizontal Tab
10	0A	■	Ctrl-J	LF	Line Feed
11	0B	♂	Ctrl-K	VT	Vertical Tab
12	0C	♀	Ctrl-L	FF	Form Feed
13	0D	♪	Ctrl-M	CR	Carriage Return
14	0E	♫	Ctrl-N	SO	Shift Out
15	0F	☼	Ctrl-O	SI	Shift In
16	10	►	Ctrl-P	DLE	Data Line Escape
17	11	◄	Ctrl-Q	DC1	Device Control 1
18	12	↕	Ctrl-R	DC2	Device Control 2
19	13	‼	Ctrl-S	DC3	Device Control 3
20	14	¶	Ctrl-T	DC4	Device Control 4
21	15	§	Ctrl-U	NAK	Negative Acknowledge
22	16	▬	Ctrl-V	SYN	Synchronous Idle
23	17	↨	Ctrl-W	ETB	End of Transmit Block
24	18	↑	Ctrl-X	CAN	Cancel
25	19	↓	Ctrl-Y	EM	End of Medium
26	1A	→	Ctrl-Z	SUB	Substitute
27	1B	←	Ctrl-[	ESC	Escape
28	1C	∟	Ctrl-\	FS	File Separator
29	1D	↔	Ctrl-]	GS	Group Separator
30	1E	▲	Ctrl-^	RS	Record Separator
31	1F	▼	Ctrl-_	US	Unit Separator

Fig. A.1

ASCII control codes.

Standard ASCII Characters (Including Control Codes):

DEC	HEX	CHAR	DEC	HEX	CHAR	DEC	HEX	CHAR	DEC	HEX	CHAR
0	0		32	20		64	40	@	96	60	`
1	1	☺	33	21	!	65	41	A	97	61	a
2	2	●	34	22	"	66	42	B	98	62	b
3	3	♥	35	23	#	67	43	C	99	63	c
4	4	♦	36	24	$	68	44	D	100	64	d
5	5	♣	37	25	%	69	45	E	101	65	e
6	6	♠	38	26	&	70	46	F	102	66	f
7	7	•	39	27	'	71	47	G	103	67	g
8	8	□	40	28	(	72	48	H	104	68	h
9	9	○	41	29	)	73	49	I	105	69	i
10	A	■	42	2A	*	74	4A	J	106	6A	j
11	B	♂	43	2B	+	75	4B	K	107	6B	k
12	C	♀	44	2C	,	76	4C	L	108	6C	l
13	D	♪	45	2D	-	77	4D	M	109	6D	m
14	E	♫	46	2E	.	78	4E	N	110	6E	n
15	F	☼	47	2F	/	79	4F	O	111	6F	o
16	10	►	48	30	0	80	50	P	112	70	p
17	11	◄	49	31	1	81	51	Q	113	71	q
18	12	↕	50	32	2	82	52	R	114	72	r
19	13	‼	51	33	3	83	53	S	115	73	s
20	14	¶	52	34	4	84	54	T	116	74	t
21	15	§	53	35	5	85	55	U	117	75	u
22	16	▬	54	36	6	86	56	V	118	76	v
23	17	↨	55	37	7	87	57	W	119	77	w
24	18	↑	56	38	8	88	58	X	120	78	x
25	19	↓	57	39	9	89	59	Y	121	79	y
26	1A	→	58	3A	:	90	5A	Z	122	7A	z
27	1B	←	59	3B	;	91	5B	[	123	7B	{
28	1C	∟	60	3C	<	92	5C	\	124	7C		
29	1D	↔	61	3D	=	93	5D	]	125	7D	}
30	1E	▲	62	3E	>	94	5E	^	126	7E	~
31	1F	▼	63	3F	?	95	5F	_	127	7F	⌂

Fig. A.2

Standard ASCII characters (including control codes).

Extended ASCII Characters:

DEC	HEX	CHAR	DEC	HEX	CHAR	DEC	HEX	CHAR	DEC	HEX	CHAR
128	80	Ç	160	A0	á	192	C0	└	224	E0	α
129	81	ü	161	A1	í	193	C1	┴	225	E1	β
130	82	é	162	A2	ó	194	C2	┬	226	E2	Γ
131	83	â	163	A3	ú	195	C3	├	227	E3	π
132	84	ä	164	A4	ñ	196	C4	─	228	E4	Σ
133	85	à	165	A5	Ñ	197	C5	┼	229	E5	σ
134	86	å	166	A6	ª	198	C6	╞	230	E6	µ
135	87	ç	167	A7	º	199	C7	╟	231	E7	τ
136	88	ê	168	A8	¿	200	C8	╚	232	E8	Φ
137	89	ë	169	A9	⌐	201	C9	╔	233	E9	Θ
138	8A	è	170	AA	¬	202	CA	╩	234	EA	Ω
139	8B	ï	171	AB	½	203	CB	╦	235	EB	δ
140	8C	î	172	AC	¼	204	CC	╠	236	EC	∞
141	8D	ì	173	AD	¡	205	CD	═	237	ED	φ
142	8E	Ä	174	AE	«	206	CE	╬	238	EE	ε
143	8F	Å	175	AF	»	207	CF	╧	239	EF	∩
144	90	É	176	B0	░	208	D0	╨	240	F0	≡
145	91	æ	177	B1	▒	209	D1	╤	241	F1	±
146	92	Æ	178	B2	▓	210	D2	╥	242	F2	≥
147	93	ô	179	B3	│	211	D3	╙	243	F3	≤
148	94	ö	180	B4	┤	212	D4	╘	244	F4	⌠
149	95	ò	181	B5	╡	213	D5	╒	245	F5	⌡
150	96	û	182	B6	╢	214	D6	╓	246	F6	÷
151	97	ù	183	B7	╖	215	D7	╫	247	F7	≈
152	98	ÿ	184	B8	╕	216	D8	╪	248	F8	°
153	99	Ö	185	B9	╣	217	D9	┘	249	F9	·
154	9A	Ü	186	BA	║	218	DA	┌	250	FA	·
155	9B	¢	187	BB	╗	219	DB	█	251	FB	√
156	9C	£	188	BC	╝	220	DC	▄	252	FC	ⁿ
157	9D	¥	189	BD	╜	221	DD	▌	253	FD	²
158	9E	₧	190	BE	╛	222	DE	▐	254	FE	■
159	9F	ƒ	191	BF	┐	223	DF	▀	255	FF	

Fig. A.3

Extended ASCII characters.

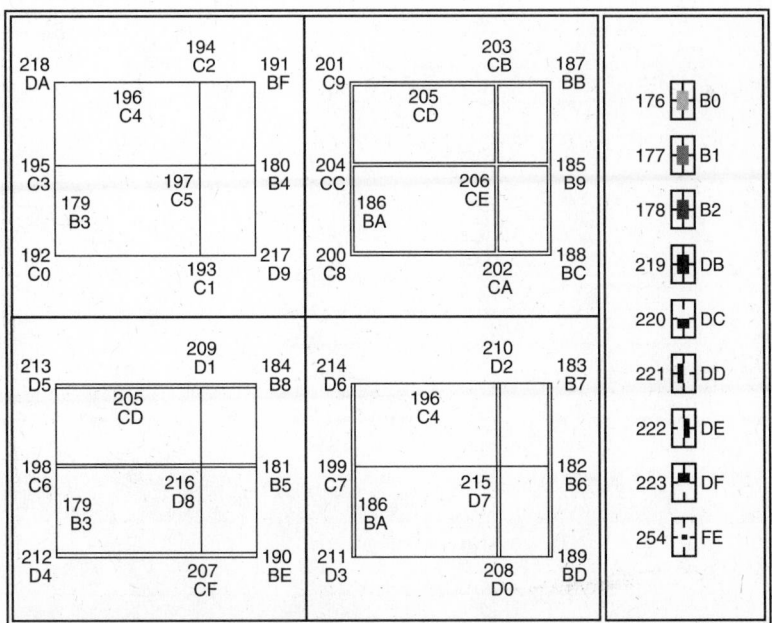

Fig. A.4

Extended ASCII line-drawing characters.

DOS Information

Tables A.1 through A.3 show all the resident, batch, and transient DOS commands and in which DOS version they are supported. If you are responsible for providing technical support, you should know what DOS commands are available to the users at the other end of the phone. These tables identify which commands are supported in any version of DOS released to date.

Table A.1 Resident DOS Commands

Command name	DOS Version number										
	1.0	1.1	2.0	2.1	3.0	3.1	3.2	3.3	4.x	5.x	6.x
CD/CHDIR			X	X	X	X	X	X	X	X	X
CHCP									X	X	X
CLS			X	X	X	X	X	X	X	X	X
COPY	X	X	X	X	X	X	X	X	X	X	X
CTTY			X	X	X	X	X	X	X	X	X
DATE	X	X	X	X	X	X	X	X	X	X	X
DEL/ERASE	X	X	X	X	X	X	X	X	X	X	X
DIR	X	X	X	X	X	X	X	X	X	X	X
EXIT					X	X	X	X	X	X	X
EXPAND										X	X
LOADHI/LH										X	X
MD/MKDIR			X	X	X	X	X	X	X	X	X
PATH			X	X	X	X	X	X	X	X	X
PROMPT			X	X	X	X	X	X	X	X	X
RD/RMDIR			X	X	X	X	X	X	X	X	X
REN/RENAME	X	X	X	X	X	X	X	X	X	X	X
SET			X	X	X	X	X	X	X	X	X
TIME	X	X	X	X	X	X	X	X	X	X	X
TYPE	X	X	X	X	X	X	X	X	X	X	X
VER					X	X	X	X	X	X	X
VERIFY			X	X	X	X	X	X	X	X	X
VOL			X	X	X	X	X	X	X	X	X

Table A.2 DOS Batch File Commands

Command name	DOS Version number										
	1.0	1.1	2.0	2.1	3.0	3.1	3.2	3.3	4.x	5.x	6.x
CALL								X	X	X	X
ECHO	X	X	X	X	X	X	X	X	X	X	X
FOR	X	X	X	X	X	X	X	X	X	X	X
GOTO	X	X	X	X	X	X	X	X	X	X	X

Command name	DOS Version number										
	1.0	1.1	2.0	2.1	3.0	3.1	3.2	3.3	4.x	5.x	6.x
IF	X	X	X	X	X	X	X	X	X	X	X
PAUSE	X	X	X	X	X	X	X	X	X	X	X
REM	X	X	X	X	X	X	X	X	X	X	X
SHIFT	X	X	X	X	X	X	X	X	X	X	X

Table A.3 Transient DOS Commands

Command name	DOS Version number										
	1.0	1.1	2.0	2.1	3.0	3.1	3.2	3.3	4.x	5.x	6.x
APPEND								X	X	X	X
ASSIGN			X	X	X	X	X	X	X	X	X
ATTRIB					X	X	X	X	X	X	X
BACKUP			X	X	X	X	X	X	X	X	X
BASIC	X	X	X	X	X	X	X	X	X	X	X
BASICA	X	X	X	X	X	X	X	X	X	X	X
CHCP								X	X	X	X
CHKDSK	X	X	X	X	X	X	X	X	X	X	X
COMMAND			X	X	X	X	X	X	X	X	X
COMP	X	X	X	X	X	X	X	X	X	X	X
DEBUG	X	X	X	X	X	X	X	X	X	X	X
DISKCOMP	X	X	X	X	X	X	X	X	X	X	X
DISKCOPY	X	X	X	X	X	X	X	X	X	X	X
DOSKEY										X	X
DOSSHELL									X	X	X
EDIT										X	X
EDLIN	X	X	X	X	X	X	X	X	X	X	X
EMM386										X	X
EXE2BIN			X	X	X	X	X			X	X
FASTOPEN								X	X	X	X
FC										X	X
FDISK			X	X	X	X	X	X	X	X	X
FIND			X	X	X	X	X	X	X	X	X
FORMAT	X	X	X	X	X	X	X	X	X	X	X
GRAFTABL			X	X	X	X	X	X	X	X	X
GRAPHICS			X	X	X	X	X	X	X	X	X
HELP										X	
JOIN					X	X	X	X	X	X	X
KEYB								X	X	X	X
KEYBFR					X	X	X				

(continues)

Table A.3 Continued

Command name	DOS Version number										
	1.0	1.1	2.0	2.1	3.0	3.1	3.2	3.3	4.x	5.x	6.x
KEYBGR					X	X	X				
KEYBIT					X	X	X				
KEYBSP					X	X	X				
KEYBUK					X	X	X				
LABEL					X	X	X	X	X	X	X
LIB	X	X	X	X	X	X	X				
LINK	X	X	X	X	X	X	X				
MEM									X	X	X
MIRROR										X	X
MODE	X	X	X	X	X	X	X	X	X	X	X
MORE			X	X	X	X	X	X	X	X	X
NLSFUNC								X	X	X	X
PRINT			X	X	X	X	X	X	X	X	X
QBASIC										X	
RECOVER			X	X	X	X	X	X	X	X	X
REPLACE					X	X	X	X	X	X	X
RESTORE			X	X	X	X	X	X	X	X	X
SETVER										X	X
SHARE					X	X	X	X	X	X	X
SORT			X	X	X	X	X	X	X	X	X
SUBST					X	X	X	X	X	X	X
SYS	X	X	X	X	X	X	X	X	X	X	X
TREE			X	X	X	X	X	X	X	X	X
UNDELETE										X	X
UNFORMAT										X	X
XCOPY								X	X	X	X

LIB, LINK, and EXE2BIN are included with the DOS technical-reference manual for DOS versions 3.3 and higher. EXE2BIN is included with DOS V5.0.

IBM DOS 4.xx Versions

DOS 4.xx has had many revisions since being introduced in mid-1988. Since the first release, IBM has released different Corrective Service Diskettes (CSDs), which fix a variety of problems with DOS V4. Each CSD is cumulative, which means that the later ones include all previous fixes. Note that these fixes are for IBM DOS and not for any other manufacturer's version.

IBM typically provides much more support in the way of fixes and updates than any other manufacturer. Microsoft, for example, never implemented any of the fixes in the fourth through seventh releases of IBM DOS. This is the reason that I always run IBM DOS, even on clone systems.

Table A.4 shows a summary of the different IBM DOS 4.xx releases and specific information about the system files and shell so that you can identify the release you are using. To obtain the latest Corrective Service Diskettes (CSD) that update you to the latest release, contact your dealer—the fixes are free.

Table A.4 IBM DOS 4.xx Releases					
File name	**Size**	**Date**	**Version**	**SYSLEVEL**	**Comments**
IBMBIO.COM	32810	06/17/88	4.00	—	Original release
IBMDOS.COM	35984	06/17/88			
COMMAND.COM	37637	06/17/88			
IBMBIO.COM	32816	08/03/88	4.01	CSD UR22624	EMS fixes
IBMDOS.COM	36000	08/03/88			
COMMAND.COM	37637	06/17/88			
IBMBIO.COM	32816	08/03/88	4.01	CSD UR24270	Date change fixed
IBMDOS.COM	36000	11/11/88			
COMMAND.COM	37652	11/11/88			
IBMBIO.COM	33910	04/06/89	4.01	CSD UR25066	Death disk fixed
IBMDOS.COM	37136	04/06/89			
COMMAND.COM	37652	11/11/88			
IBMBIO.COM	34660	03/20/90	4.01	CSD UR29015	SCSI support added
IBMDOS.COM	37248	02/20/90			
COMMAND.COM	37765	03/20/90			
IBMBIO.COM	34660	04/27/90	4.01	CSD UR31300	HPFS compatibility
IBMDOS.COM	37264	05/21/90			
COMMAND.COM	37765	06/29/90			
IBMBIO.COM	34692	04/08/91	4.01	CSD UR35280	HPFS and CHKDSK
IBMDOS.COM	37280	11/30/90			
COMMAND.COM	37762	09/27/91			

IBM DOS 5.xx Versions

DOS 5.xx has had several different revisions since being introduced in mid-1991. Since the first release, IBM has released various Corrective Service Diskettes (CDSs), which fix a variety of problems with DOS 5. Each CSD is cumulative, which means that the later ones include all previous fixes. You should note that these fixes are for IBM DOS and not any other manufacturer's version. IBM typically provides much more support in the way of fixes and updates than any other manufacturer. Microsoft, for example, does not have a CSD type program for DOS 5, and has not (as of this writing) released equivalent fixes to IBM's third and fourth releases. Note that IBM now supports the installation of DOS 5 on clone systems and has a special utility, the Upgrade Installation Enhancement Utility (UIEU), that facilitates the installation of IBM DOS over previous versions of MS-DOS.

Table A.5 shows a summary of the different IBM DOS 5.xx releases and specific information about the system files and shell so that you can identify the release you are using. To obtain the latest Corrective Service Diskettes (CSD) that update you to the latest release, contact your dealer—the fixes are free.

Table A.5 IBM DOS 5.xx Releases

File name	Size	Date	Version	SYSLEVEL	Comments
IBMBIO.COM	33430	05/09/91	5.00	—	Original release
IBMDOS.COM	37378	05/09/91			
COMMAND.COM	47987	05/09/91			
IBMBIO.COM	33430	05/09/91	5.00	CSD UR35423	XCOPY fixed
IBMDOS.COM	37378	05/09/91			QEDIT fixed
COMMAND.COM	48005	08/16/91			
IBMBIO.COM	33430	05/09/91	5.00	CSD UR35748	SYS fixed
IBMDOS.COM	37378	05/09/91			
COMMAND.COM	48006	10/25/91			
IBMBIO.COM	33446	11/29/91	5.00	CSD UR35834	EMM386, FORMAT,
IBMDOS.COM	37378	11/29/91			BACKUP, fixed
COMMAND.COM	48006	11/29/91			
IBMBIO.COM	33446	02/28/92	5.00.1	CSD UR36603	Many fixes,
IBMDOS.COM	37378	11/29/91	Rev. A		Clone support,
COMMAND.COM	48006	02/28/92			New retail version
IBMBIO.COM	33446	05/29/92	5.00.1	CSD UR37387	RESTORE,
IBMDOS.COM	37362	05/29/92	Rev.1		UNDELETE fixed,
COMMAND.COM	48042	09/11/92			>1G HD fixed
IBMBIO.COM	33718	09/01/92	5.02	—	New retail version,
IBMDOS.COM	37362	09/01/92	Rev. 0		Several new
COMMAND.COM	47990	09/01/92			commands added

MS and IBM DOS 6.xx Versions

There have been several different versions of DOS 6.x from both Microsoft and IBM. The original release of MS DOS 6.0 came from Microsoft. One of the features included in MS DOS 6.0 was the new DoubleSpace disk compression (see table A.6). Unfortunately DoubleSpace had some problems with certain system configurations and hardware types. In the meantime, IBM had taken DOS 6.0 from Microsoft and updated it to fix several small problems, removed the disk compression, and sold it as IBM DOS 6.1. IBM also selected a different type of compression program and wanted to test it completely to avoid problems like DoubleSpace. The early copies of IBM DOS 6.1 came without the compression software, however a coupon was included which was good for a free copy later. The later versions of IBM's DOS 6.1 (now called PC DOS 6.1) included the compression software. Also included in the updated 6.1 release were enhanced PCMCIA commands. Microsoft later released MS DOS 6.2 as a free upgrade for MS 6.0 users. The new 6.2 version had fixes to several programs and especially fixes to the DoubleSpace compression.

Table A.6 IBM and Microsoft DOS 6.xx Releases

File name	Size	Date	Version	SYSLEVEL	Comments
IO.SYS	40470	03/10/93	MS	—	Original Microsoft
MSDOS.SYS	38138	03/10/93	6.00		release
COMMAND.COM	52925	03/10/93	Rev. A		
IBMBIO.COM	40694	06/29/93	IBM	—	Original IBM
IBMDOS.COM	38138	06/29/93	6.10		release. Has fixes
COMMAND.COM	52589	06/29/93	Rev. 0		over MS version
IBMBIO.COM	40964	09/30/93	PC	—	SuperStor/DS
IBMDOS.COM	38138	09/30/93	6.10		compression,
COMMAND.COM	52797	09/30/93	Rev. 0		enhanced PCMCIA
IO.SYS	40566	09/30/93	MS	—	DoubleSpace fixes
MSDOS.SYS	38138	09/30/93	6.20		Enhanced cleanboot
COMMAND.COM	54619	09/30/93	Rev. A		and data recovery

DOS Formatting Information

With the DOS FORMAT command, you can perform low- and high-level formatting of floppy disks and high-level format hard disks. The following syntax is used with the FORMAT command:

FORMAT d: [/V[:label]] [/Q] [/U] [/F:size] [/B | /S]

FORMAT d: [/V[:label]] [/Q] [/U] [/T:tracks /N:sectors] [/B | /S]

FORMAT d: [/V[:label]] [/Q] [/U] [/1] [/4] [/B | /S]

FORMAT d: [/Q] [/U] [/1] [/4] [/8] [/B | /S]

Table A.7 is a concise and detailed list of all of the parameters associated with the DOS FORMAT command, including all parameters new to DOS 5. Also included are several undocumented parameters you may never have seen before.

Table A.7 FORMAT Command (Undocumented Features)

Standard parameters	
/Q	Performs a Quick format
/U	Performs an Unconditional format

(continues)

Table A.7 Continued

Standard parameters

/S	Copies the DOS system files (IBMBIO.COM or IO.SYS and IBMDOS.COM or MSDOS.SYS) and COMMAND.COM from the boot drive to the new disk
/V[:label]	Creates a volume label on the new disk. The label can be as long as 11 characters.
/F:nnnn	Specifies the format of the floppy disk. For 5 1/4-inch drives, the size can be 160K, 180K, 320K, 360K, or 1.2M. For 3 1/2-inch drives, valid sizes are 720K, 1.44M, and 2.88M.
/4	Formats a 5 1/4-inch, 360K, double-sided, double-density floppy disk in a high-density 1.2M drive
/T:nnnn	Specifies the number of tracks (1 to 1,024) per side on the disk to format
/N:nn	Specifies the number of sectors (1 to 64) per track on the disk to format

Obsolete (but still functional) parameters

/1	Formats single-sided disks (5 1/4-inch only)
/8	Formats eight sectors per track (5 1/4-inch only)
/B	Creates dummy system files and reserves room for a DOS version SYS command to copy actual files later

Undocumented parameters (floppy disks only)

/H	Skips the message Insert new diskette for drive d: and strike ENTER when ready
/BACKUP	Skips the message Insert new diskette for drive d: and press ENTER when ready
/SELECT	Skips the message Insert new diskette for drive d: and press ENTER when ready. Also suppresses the disk space report, the Format another (Y/N)? message, and any error messages.
/AUTOTEST	Skips the Insert new diskette for drive d: and press ENTER when ready message. Also suppresses the disk space report, the Format another (Y/N)? message, any error messages, and the Volume label (11 characters, ENTER for none)? message.

Notes

/S	Looks for system files on the default drive in V3.3 or earlier versions; the boot drive is searched in V4.0 and later versions, and COMMAND.COM is copied in V5.0 and later versions
/V	Is assumed in 4.0 and later versions if /V:label is not specified; DOS 3.3 and earlier versions do not support the :label specification with /V
/F	Supported in 4.0 and later versions
/T and /N	/N defaults to 9 in DOS 3.3. No defaults are assumed in 4.0 and later versions; therefore, if one of the parameters is specified, the other must be specified as well
/H	Supported in V3.3 only
/BACKUP, /SELECT, and /AUTOTEST	Supported in V4.0 and later versions

Table A.8 shows the correct FORMAT command parameters to use when you are formatting low-density floppy disks in high-density drives. This table considers all possible permutations of floppy disk types, drive types, and DOS versions.

Table A.8 Formatting Low-Density Floppy Disks in High-Density Drives

DOS version	Drive type	Floppy disk type	Format command
DOS 3.0+	5 1/4-inch, 1.2M	DD 360K	FORMAT d: /4
DOS 3.2+	5 1/4-inch, 1.2M	DD 360K	FORMAT d: /N:9 /T:40
DOS 4.0+	5 1/4-inch, 1.2M	DD 360K	FORMAT d: /F:360
DOS 3.3+	3 1/2-inch, 1.44M	DD 720K	FORMAT d: /N:9 /T:80
DOS 4.0+	3 1/2-inch, 1.44M	DD 720K	FORMAT d: /F:720
DOS 5.0+	3 1/2-inch, 2.88M	HD 1.44M	FORMAT d: /F:1.44
DOS 5.0+	3 1/2-inch, 2.88M	DD 720K	FORMAT d: /F:720

+ = Includes all higher versions
d: = Specifies the drive to format
DD = Double density
HD = High density

Table A.9 shows the default cluster (allocation unit) size selected by DOS for all possible floppy disk formats and hard disk partition sizes.

Table A.9 DOS Disk Default Cluster (Allocation Unit) Sizes

Disk or volume size	Cluster/allocation unit size	FAT type
5 1/4-inch 360K	2 sectors, or 1,024 bytes	12-bit
5 1/4-inch 1.2M	1 sectors, or 512 bytes	12-bit
3 1/2-inch 720K	2 sectors, or 1,024 bytes	12-bit
3 1/2-inch 1.44M	1 sectors, or 512 bytes	12-bit
3 1/2-inch 2.88M	2 sectors, or 1,024 bytes	12-bit
0M < Volume < 16M	8 sectors, or 4,096 bytes	12-bit
16M <= Volume <= 128M	4 sectors, or 2,048 bytes	16-bit
128M < Volume <= 256M	8 sectors, or 4,096 bytes	16-bit
256M < Volume <= 512M	16 sectors, or 8,192 bytes	16-bit
512M < Volume <= 1,024M	32 sectors, or 16,384 bytes	16-bit
1,024M < Volume <= 2,048M	64 sectors, or 32,768 bytes	16-bit

K = 1,024 bytes
M = 1,048,576 bytes

DOS Error Messages

Table A.10 DOS Extended Error Codes

Hex Code	Dec Code	Description
01h	1	Invalid function number
02h	2	File not found
03h	3	Path not found
04h	4	Too many open files (no handles left)
05h	5	Access denied
06h	6	Invalid handle
07h	7	Memory control blocks destroyed
08h	8	Insufficient memory
09h	9	Invalid memory block address
0Ah	10	Invalid environment
0Bh	11	Invalid format
0Ch	12	Invalid access code
0Dh	13	Invalid data
0Eh	14	Reserved
0Fh	15	Invalid drive was specified
10h	16	Attempt to write on write-protected disk
11h	17	Not same device
12h	18	No more files
13h	19	Attempt to write-protect disk
14h	20	Unknown unit
15h	21	Drive not ready
16h	22	Unkown command
17h	23	Cyclic Redundancy Check (CRC) error
18h	24	Bad request structure length
19h	25	Seek error
1Ah	26	Unknown media type
1Bh	27	Sector not found
1Ch	28	Printer out of paper
1Dh	29	Write fault
1Eh	30	Read fault
1Fh	31	General failure
20h	32	Sharing violation
21h	33	Lock violation
22h	34	Invalid disk change
23h	35	FCB unavailable
24h	36	Sharing buffer overflow
25h	37	Reserved by DOS 5.0

Hex Code	Dec Code	Description
26h	38	Unable to complete file operation
27h - 31h	39 - 49	Reserved by DOS 5.0
32h	50	Network request not supported
33h	51	Remote computer not listening
34h	52	Duplicate name on network
35h	53	Network path not found
36h	54	Network busy
37h	55	Network device no longer exists
38h	56	NETBIOS command limit exceeded
39h	57	System error; NETBIOS error
3Ah	58	Incorrect response from network
3Bh	59	Unexpected network error
3Ch	60	Incompatible remote adapter
3Dh	61	Print queue full
3Eh	62	Not enough space for print file
3Fh	63	Print file was cancelled
40h	64	Network name was deleted
41h	65	Access denied
42h	66	Network device type incorrect
43h	67	Network name not found
44h	68	Network name limit exceeded
45h	69	NETBIOS session limit exceeded
46h	70	Sharing temporarily paused
47h	71	Network request not accepted
48h	72	Print or disk redirection is paused
49h - 4Fh	73 - 79	Reserved
50h	80	File exists
51h	81	Reserved
52h	82	Cannot make directory entry
53h	83	Fail on Interrupt 24
54h	84	Too many redirections
55h	85	Duplicate redirection
56h	86	Invalid password
57h	87	Invalid parameter
58h	88	Network data fault
59h	89	Function not supported by network
5Ah	90	Required system component not installed

Table A.11 DOS Parse Error Codes

Code	Description
1	Too many paramters
2	Required parameter missing
3	Invalid switch
4	Invalid keyword
6	Parameter value not in allowed range
7	Parameter value not allowed
8	Parameter value not allowed
9	Parameter format not correct
10	Invalid parameter
11	Invalid parameter combination

Troubleshooting Error Codes

The following sections list a variety of system error codes. Included are manufacturer test POST codes, display POST error codes, and advanced diagnostics error codes. This section includes also a detailed list of SCSI interface error codes, which can be very helpful in troubleshooting SCSI devices.

ROM BIOS Port 80h Power-On Self Test (POST) Codes

When the ROM BIOS is performing the Power-On Self Test, in most systems the results of these tests are sent to I/O Port 80h so that they can be monitored by a special diagnostics card. These tests sometimes are called *manufacturing tests* because they were designed into the system for testing systems on the assembly line without a video display attached. The POST-code cards have a 2-digit hexadecimal display used to report the number of the currently executing test routine. Before executing each test, a hexadecimal numeric code is sent to the port, and then the test is run. If the test fails and locks up the machine, the hexadecimal code of the last test being executed remains on the cards display.

Many tests are executed in a system before the video display card is enabled, especially if the display is EGA or VGA. Therefore, many errors can occur that would lock up the system before the system could possibly display an error code through the video system. To most normal troubleshooting procedures, a system with this type of problem (such as a memory failure in Bank 0) would appear completely dead. By using one of the commercially available POST-code cards, however, you can correctly diagnose the problem.

These codes are completely BIOS dependent because the card does nothing but display the codes sent to it. Some BIOSes have better Power-On Self Test procedures and therefore send more informative codes. Some BIOS versions also send audio codes that can be used to help diagnose such problems. The Phoenix BIOS, for example, sends the most informative set of audio codes, which eliminates the need for a Port 80h POST card. Tables A.12, A.13, and A.14 list the Port 80h codes and audio codes sent by a number of different BIOS manufacturers and versions.

AMI BIOS Audio and Port 80h Error Codes

Table A.12 AMI BIOS Audio POST Codes

Beep code	Fatal errors
1 short	DRAM refresh failure
2 short	Parity circuit failure
3 short	Base 64K RAM failure
4 short	System timer failure
5 short	Processor failure
6 short	Keyboard controller Gate A20 error
7 short	Virtual mode exception error
8 short	Display memory R/W test failure
9 short	ROM BIOS checksum failure

Beep code	Nonfatal errors
1 long, 3 short	Conventional/extended memory failure
1 long, 8 short	Display/retrace test failed

Table A.13 AMI 286 BIOS Plus Port 80h POST Codes

Checkpoint	Meaning
01h	NMI disabled and 286 register test about to start
02h	286 register test over
03h	ROM checksum OK
04h	8259 initialization OK
05h	CMOS pending interrupt disabled
06h	Video disabled and system timer counting OK
07h	CH-2 of 8253 test OK
08h	CH-2 of delta count test OK
09h	CH-1 delta count test OK
0Ah	CH-0 delta count test OK
0Bh	Parity status cleared
0Ch	Refresh and system timer OK
0Dh	Refresh link toggling OK
0Eh	Refresh period On/Off 50% OK
10h	Confirmed refresh On and about to start 64K memory
11h	Address line test OK
12h	64K base memory test OK
13h	Interrupt vectors initialized
14h	8042 keyboard controller test OK

(continues)

Table A.13 Continued

Checkpoint	Meaning
15h	CMOS read/write test OK
16h	CMOS checksum/battery check OK
17h	Monochrome mode set OK
18h	Color mode set OK
19h	About to look for optional video ROM
1Ah	Optional video ROM control OK
1Bh	Display memory R/W test OK
1Ch	Display memory R/W test for alternate display OK
1Dh	Video retrace check OK
1Eh	Global equipment byte set for video OK
1Fh	Mode set call for Mono/Color OK
20h	Video test OK
21h	Video display OK
22h	Power-on message display OK
30h	Virtual mode memory test about to begin
31h	Virtual mode memory test started
32h	Processor in virtual mode
33h	Memory address line test in progress
34h	Memory address line test in progress
35h	Memory below 1M calculated
36h	Memory size computation OK
37h	Memory test in progress
38h	Memory initialization over below 1M
39h	Memory initialization over above 1M
3Ah	Display memory size
3Bh	About to start below 1M memory test
3Ch	Memory test below 1M OK
3Dh	Memory test above 1M OK
3Eh	About to go to real mode (shutdown)
3Fh	Shutdown successful and entered in real mode
40h	About to disable gate A-20 address line
41h	Gate A-20 line disabled successfully
42h	About to start DMA controller test
4Eh	Address line test OK
4Fh	Processor in real mode after shutdown
50h	DMA page register test OK
51h	DMA unit-1 base register test about to start
52h	DMA unit-1 channel OK, about to begin CH-2

Checkpoint	Meaning
53h	DMA CH-2 base register test OK
54h	About to test f/f latch for unit-1
55h	f/f latch test both unit OK
56h	DMA unit 1 and 2 programmed OK
57h	8259 initialization over
58h	8259 mask register check OK
59h	Master 8259 mask register OK, about to start slave
5Ah	About to check timer and keyboard interrupt level
5Bh	Timer interrupt OK
5Ch	About to test keyboard interrupt
5Dh	ERROR! timer/keyboard interrupt not in proper level
5Eh	8259 interrupt controller error
5Fh	8259 interrupt controller test OK
70h	Start of keyboard test
71h	Keyboard BAT test OK
72h	Keyboard test OK
73h	Keyboard global data initialization OK
74h	Floppy setup about to start
75h	Floppy setup OK
76h	Hard disk setup about to start
77h	Hard disk setup OK
79h	About to initialize timer data area
7Ah	Verify CMOS battery power
7Bh	CMOS battery verification done
7Dh	About to analyze diagnostics test result for memory
7Eh	CMOS memory size update OK
7Fh	About to check optional ROM C000:0.
80h	Keyboard sensed to enable SETUP
81h	Optional ROM control OK
82h	Printer global data initialization OK
83h	RS-232 global data initialization OK
84h	80287 check/test OK
85h	About to display soft error message
86h	About to give control to system ROM E000.0
87h	System ROM E000.0 check over
00h	Control given to Int 19, boot loader

Table A.14 AMI Color BIOS Port 80h POST Codes

Port 80h code	Test description
01h	Processor register test about to start, and NMI to be disabled
02h	NMI is disabled; power-on delay starting
03h	Power-on delay complete; any initialization before keyboard BAT is in progress
04h	Any initialization before keyboard BAT is complete; reading keyboard SYS bit to check soft reset/power-on
05h	Soft reset/power-on determined; going to enable ROM (that is, disable shadow RAM/cache if any)
06h	ROM enabled; calculating ROM BIOS checksum and waiting for KB controller input buffer to be free
07h	ROM BIOS checksum passed, KB controller I/B free; going to issue BAT command to keyboard controller
08h	BAT command to keyboard controller issued; going to verify BAT command
09h	Keyboard controller BAT result verified; keyboard command byte to be written next
0Ah	Keyboard-command byte code issued; going to write command byte data
0Bh	Keyboard controller command byte written; going to issue Pin-23,24 blocking/ unblocking command
0Ch	Pin-23,24 of keyboard controller blocked/unblocked; NOP command of keyboard controller to be issued next
0Dh	NOP command processing done; CMOS shutdown register test to be done next
0Eh	CMOS shutdown register R/W test passed; going to calculate CMOS checksum and update DIAG byte
0Fh	CMOS checksum calculation done and DIAG byte written; CMOS initialization to begin (If INIT CMOS IN EVERY BOOT is set.)
10h	CMOS initialization done (if any); CMOS status register about to initialize for date and time
11h	CMOS status register initialized; going to disable DMA and interrupt controllers
12h	DMA controller #1,#2, interrupt controller #1,#2 disabled; about to disable video display and init port-B
13h	Video display is disabled and port-B initialized; chipset init/auto memory detection to begin
14h	Chipset initialization/auto memory detection over; 8254 timer test about to start
15h	CH-2 timer test halfway; 8254 CH-2 timer test to be complete
16h	Ch-2 timer test over; 8254 CH-1 timer test to be complete
17h	CH-1 timer test over; 8254 CH-0 timer test to be complete
18h	CH-0 timer test over; about to start memory refresh
19h	Memory refresh started; memory refresh test to be done next
1Ah	Memory refresh line is toggling; going to check 15 micro-second On/Off time
1Bh	Memory refresh period 30 micro-second test complete; base 64K memory test about to start
20h	Base 64K memory test started; address line test to be done next
21h	Address line test passed; going to do toggle parity

Port 80h code	Test description
22h	Toggle parity over; going for sequential data R/W test
23h	Base 64K sequential data R/W test passed; any setup before interrupt vector initialization about to start
24h	Setup required before vector initialization complete; interrupt vector initialization about to begin
25h	Interrupt vector initialization done; going to read I/O port of 8042 for turbo switch (if any)
26h	I/O port of 8042 is read; going to initialize global data for turbo switch
27h	Global data initialization is over; any initialization after interrupt vector to be done next
28h	Initialization after interrupt vector is complete; going for monochrome mode setting
29h	Monochrome mode setting is done; going for color mode setting
2Ah	Color mode setting is done; about to go for toggle parity before optional ROM test
2Bh	Toggle parity over; about to give control for any setup required before optional video ROM check
2Ch	Processing before video ROM control is done; about to look for optional video ROM and give control
2Dh	Optional video ROM control is done; about to give control to do any processing after video ROM returns control
2Eh	Return from processing after the video ROM control; if EGA/VGA not found, then do display memory R/W test
2Fh	EGA/VGA not found; display memory R/W test about to begin
30h	Display memory R/W test passed; about to look for the retrace checking
31h	Display memory R/W test or retrace checking failed; about to do alternate display memory R/W test
32h	Alternate display memory R/W test passed; about to look for the alternate display retrace checking
33h	Video display checking over; verification of display type with switch setting and actual card to begin
34h	Verification of display adapter done; display mode to be set next
35h	Display mode set complete; BIOS ROM data area about to be checked
36h	BIOS ROM data area check over; going to set cursor for power-on message
37h	Cursor setting for power-on message ID complete; going to display the power-on message
38h	Power-on message display complete; going to read new cursor position
39h	New cursor position read and saved; going to display the reference string
3Ah	Reference string display is over; going to display the Hit <Esc> message
3Bh	Hit <Esc> message displayed; virtual mode memory test about to start
40h	Preparation for virtual mode test started; going to verify from video memory
41h	Returned after verifying from display memory; going to prepare the descriptor tables

(continues)

Table A.14 Continued

Port 80h code	Test description
42h	Descriptor tables prepared; going to enter virtual mode for memory test
43h	Entered in virtual mode; going to enable interrupts for diagnostics mode
44h	Interrupts enabled (if diagnostics switch is on); going to initialize data to check memory wrap-around at 0:0
45h	Data initialized; going to check for memory wrap-around at 0:0 and find total system memory size
46h	Memory wrap-around test done; memory-size calculation over; about to go for writing patterns to test memory
47h	Pattern to be test-written in extended memory; going to write patterns in base 640K memory
48h	Patterns written in base memory; going to determine amount of memory below 1M memory
49h	Amount of memory below 1M found and verified; going to determine amount of memory above 1M memory
4Ah	Amount of memory above 1M found and verified; going for BIOS ROM data area check
4Bh	BIOS ROM data area check over; going to check <Esc> and clear memory below 1M for soft reset
4Ch	Memory below 1M cleared (Soft Reset); going to clear memory above 1M
4Dh	Memory above 1M cleared (Soft Reset); going to save the memory size
4Eh	Memory test started (No Soft Reset); about to display the first 64K memory test
4Fh	Memory size display started; will be updated during memory test; going for sequential and random memory test
50h	Memory test below 1M complete; going to adjust memory size for relocation and shadow
51h	Memory size adjusted due to relocation/shadow; memory test above 1M to follow
52h	Memory test above 1M complete; going to prepare to go back to real mode
53h	CPU registers are saved including memory size; going to enter in real mode
54h	Shutdown successful, CPU in real mode; going to restore registers saved during preparation for shutdown
55h	Registers restored; going to disable Gate A20 address line
56h	A20 address line disable successful; BIOS ROM data area about to be checked
57h	BIOS ROM data area check halfway; BIOS ROM data area check to be complete
58h	BIOS ROM data area check over; going to clear Hit <ESC> message
59h	Hit <ESC> message cleared; <WAIT...> message displayed; about to start DMA and interrupt controller test
60h	DMA page-register test passed; about to verify from display memory
61h	Display memory verification over; about to go for DMA #1 base register test
62h	DMA #1 base register test passed; about to go for DMA #2 base register test
63h	DMA #2 base register test passed; about to go for BIOS ROM data area check
64h	BIOS ROM data area check halfway; BIOS ROM data area check to be complete

Port 80h code	Test description
'65h	BIOS ROM data area check over; about to program DMA unit 1 and 2
66h	DMA unit 1 and 2 programming over; about to initialize 8259 interrupt controller
67h	8259 initialization over; about to start keyboard test
80h	Keyboard test started, clearing output buffer, checking for stuck key; about to issue keyboard reset command
81h	Keyboard reset error/stuck key found; about to issue keyboard controller interface test command
82h	Keyboard controller interface test over; about to write command byte and initialize circular buffer
83h	Command byte written, global data initialization done; about to check for lock-key
84h	Lock-key checking over; about to check for memory-size mismatch with CMOS
85h	Memory size check done; about to display soft error and check for password or bypass setup
86h	Password checked; about to do programming before setup
87h	Programming before setup complete; going to CMOS setup program
88h	Returned from CMOS setup program and screen is cleared; about to do programming after setup
89h	Programming after setup complete; going to display power-on screen message
8Ah	First screen message displayed; about to display <WAIT...> message
8Bh	<WAIT...> message displayed; about to do main and video BIOS shadow
8Ch	Main and video BIOS shadow successful; Setup options programming after CMOS setup about to start
8Dh	Setup options are programmed, mouse check and initialization to be done next
8Eh	Mouse check and initialization complete; going for hard disk, floppy reset
8Fh	Floppy check returns that floppy is to be initialized; floppy setup to follow
90h	Floppy setup is over; test for hard disk presence to be done
91h	Hard disk presence test over; hard disk setup to follow
92h	Hard disk setup complete; about to go for BIOS ROM data area check
93h	BIOS ROM data area check halfway; BIOS ROM data area check to be complete
94h	BIOS ROM data area check over; going to set base and extended memory size
95h	Memory size adjusted due to mouse and hard disk type 47 support; going to verify display memory
96h	Returned after verifying display memory; going to do initialization before C800 optional ROM control
97h	Any initialization before C800 optional ROM control is over; optional ROM check and control to be done next
98h	Optional ROM control is done; about to give control to do any required processing after optional ROM returns control
99h	Any initialization required after optional ROM test over; going to set up timer data area and printer base address
9Ah	Return after setting timer and printer base address; going to set the RS-232 base address

(continues)

Table A.14 Continued	
Port 80h code	**Test description**
9Bh	Returned after RS-232 base address; going to do any initialization before coprocessor test
9Ch	Required initialization before coprocessor is over; going to initialize the coprocessor next
9Dh	Coprocessor initialized; going to do any initialization after coprocessor test
9Eh	Initialization after coprocessor test is complete; going to check extended keyboard, keyboard ID, and Num Lock
9Fh	Extended keyboard check is done, ID flag set, Num Lock on/off; keyboard ID command to be issued
A0h	Keyboard ID command issued; keyboard ID flag to be reset
A1h	Keyboard ID flag reset; cache memory test to follow
A2h	Cache memory test over; going to display any soft errors
A3h	Soft error display complete; going to set the keyboard typematic rate
A4h	Keyboard typematic rate set; going to program memory wait states
A5h	Memory wait states programming over; screen to be cleared next
A6h	Screen cleared; going to enable parity and NMI
A7h	NMI and parity enabled; going to do any initialization required before giving control to optional ROM at E000
A8h	Initialization before E000 ROM control over; E000 ROM to get control next
A9h	Returned from E000 ROM control; going to do any initialization required after E000 optional ROM control
AAh	Initialization after E000 optional ROM control is over; going to display the system configuration
00h	System configuration is displayed; going to give control to Int 19h boot loader

Award BIOS Port 80h POST Codes

Table A.15 provides information on the majority of Award POST codes displayed during the POST sequence. These POST codes are output to I/O port address 80h. Although this chart specifically lists all the POST codes output by the Award Modular BIOS, Version 3.1, the codes are valid also for these Award Modular BIOS types:

PC/XT Version 3.0 and greater
AT Version 3.02 and greater

Not all these POST codes apply to all of the BIOS types. Note that the POST tests do not necessarily execute in the numeric order shown:

The POST sequence may vary depending on the BIOS.

Table A.15 Award BIOS Port 80h POST Codes

Port 80h code	Code meaning
01h	Processor Test 1. Processor status verification. Tests the following processor-status flags; carry, zero, sign, and overflow. The BIOS sets each flag, verifies that they are set, and turns each flag off and verifies that it is off. Failure of a flag causes a fatal error.
02h	Determine POST Type. This test determines whether the status of the system is manufacturing or normal. The status can be set by a physical jumper on some motherboards. If the status is normal, the POST continues through and, assuming no errors, boot is attempted. If manufacturing POST is installed, POST is run in continuous loop, and boot is not attempted.
03h	8042 Keyboard Controller. Tests controller by sending TEST_KBRD command (AAh) and verifying that controller reads command.
04h	8042 Keyboard Controller. Verifies that keyboard controller returned AAh, sent in test 3.
05h	Get Manufacturing Status. The last test in the manufacturing cycle. If test 2 found the status to be manufacturing, this POST triggers a reset and POSTs 1 through 5 are repeated continuously.
06h	Initialize Chips. POST 06h performs these functions: disables color and mono video, disables parity circuits, disables DMA (8237) chips, resets math coprocessor, initializes timer 1 (8255), clears DMA chip, clears all page registers, and clears CMOS shutdown byte.
07h	Processor Test 2. Reads, writes, and verifies all CPU registers except SS, SP, and BP with data pattern FF and 00.
08h	Initialize CMOS Timer. Updates timer cycle normally.
09h	EPROM Checksum. Checksums EPROM; test failed if sum not equal to 0. Also checksums sign-on message.
0Ah	Initialize Video Interface. Initializes video controller register 6845 to the following: 80 characters per row 25 rows per screen 8/14 scan lines per row for mono/color First scan line of cursor 6/11 Last scan line of cursor 7/12 Reset display offset to 0
0Bh	Test Timer (8254) Channel 0. These three timer tests verify that the 8254 timer chip is functioning properly.
0Ch	Test Timer (8254) Channel 1.
0Dh	Test Timer (8254) Channel 2.
0Eh	Test CMOS Shutdown Byte. Uses a walking bit algorithm to check interface to CMOS circuit.
0Fh	Test Extended CMOS. On motherboards with chipsets that support extended CMOS configurations, such as Chips & Technologies, the BIOS tables of CMOS information are used to configure the chip set. These chip sets have an extended storage mechanism that enables the user to save a desired system configuration after the power is turned off. A checksum is used to verify the validity of the extended storage and, if valid, permit the information to be loaded into extended CMOS RAM.

(continues)

Table A.15 Continued

Port 80h code	Code meaning
10h	Test DMA Channel 0. These three functions initialize the DMA (direct memory access) chip and then test the chip using an AA, 55, FF, 00 pattern. Port addresses are used to check the address circuit to DMA page registers.
11h	DMA Channel 1.
12h	DMA Page Registers.
13h	Keyboard Controller. Tests keyboard controller interface.
14h	Test Memory Refresh. RAM must be refreshed periodically to keep the memory from decaying. This function ensures that the memory-refresh function is working properly.
15h	First 64K of System Memory. An extensive parity test is performed on the first 64K of system memory. This memory is used by the BIOS.
16h	Interrupt Vector Table. Sets up and loads interrupt vector tables in memory for use by the 8259 PIC chip.
17h	Video I/O Operations. This function initializes the video, either CGA, MDA, EGA, or VGA. If a CGA or MDA adapter is installed, the video is initialized by the system BIOS. If the system BIOS detects an EGA or VGA adapter, the option ROM BIOS installed on the video adapter is used to initialize and set up the video.
18h	Video Memory. Tests memory for CGA and MDA video boards. This test is not performed by the system BIOS on EGA or VGA video adapters—the boards own EGA or VGA BIOS ensures that it is functioning properly.
19h	Test 8259 Mask Bits - Channel 1. These two tests verify 8259 masked interrupts by alternately turning the interrupt lines off and on. Unsuccessful completion generates a fatal error.
1Ah	8259 Mask Bits - Channel 2.
1Bh	CMOS Battery Level. Verifies that the battery status bit is set to 1. A 0 value can indicate a bad battery or some other problem, such as bad CMOS.
1Ch	CMOS Checksum. This function tests the CMOS checksum data (located at 2Eh, and 2Fh) and extended CMOS checksum, if present, to be sure that they are valid.
1Dh	Configuration from CMOS. If the CMOS checksum is good, the values are used to configure the system.
1Eh	System Memory. The system memory size is determined by writing to addresses from 0K to 640K, starting at 0 and continuing until an address does not respond. Memory size value then is compared to the CMOS value to ensure that they are the same. If they are different, a flag is set, and, at the end of POST an error message is displayed.
1Fh	Found System Memory. Tests memory from 64K to the top of the memory found by writing the pattern FFAA and 5500, and then reading the pattern back, byte by byte, and verifying that it is correct.
20h	Stuck 8259 Interrupt Bits. These three tests verify the functionality of the 8259 interrupt controller.
21h	Stuck NMI Bits (Parity or I/O Channel Check).
22h	8259 Function.

Port 80h code	Code meaning
23h	Protected Mode. Verifies protected mode: 8086 virtual mode as well as 8086 page mode. Protected mode ensures that any data about to be written to extended memory (above 1M) is checked to ensure that it is suitable for storage there.
24h	Extended Memory. This function sizes memory above 1M by writing to addresses starting at 1M and continuing to 16M on 286 and 386SX systems, and to 64M on 386 systems until there is no response. This process determines the total extended memory, which is compared with CMOS to ensure that the values are the same. If the values are different, a flag is set and at the end of POST an error message is displayed.
25h	Found Extended Memory. This function tests extended memory using virtual 8086 paging mode and writing an FFFF, AA55, 0000 pattern.
26h	Protected Mode Exceptions. This function tests other aspects of protected mode operations.
27h	Cache Control or Shadow RAM. Tests for shadow RAM and cache controller (386 and 486 only) functionality. Systems with CGA and MDA adapters indicate that video shadow RAM is enabled, even though there is no BIOS ROM to shadow (this is normal).
28h	8242. Optional Intel 8242/8248 keyboard controller detection and support.
29h	Reserved.
2Ah	Initialize Keyboard. Initializes keyboard controller.
2Bh	Floppy Drive and Controller. Initializes floppy disk drive controller and any drives present.
2Ch	Detect and Initialize Serial Ports. Initializes any serial ports present.
2Dh	Detect and Initialize Parallel Ports. Initializes any parallel ports present.
2Eh	Initialize Hard Drive and Controller. Initializes hard drive controller and any drives present.
2Fh	Detect and Initialize Math Coprocessor. Initializes math coprocessor.
30h	Reserved.
31h	Detect and Initialize Option ROMs. Initializes any option ROMs present from C800h to EFFFh.
3Bh	Initialize Secondary Cache with OPTi chipset. Initializes secondary cache controller for systems based on the OPTi chipset (486 only).
CAh	Micronics Cache Initialization. Detects and initializes Micronics cache controller if present.
CCh	NMI Handler Shutdown. Detects untrapped Non-Maskable Interrupts during boot.
EEh	Unexpected Processor Exception.
FFh	Boot Attempt. When the POST is complete, if all the system components and peripherals are initialized, and if no error flags were set (such as memory size error), then the system attempts to boot.

Phoenix BIOS Audio and Port 80h POST Codes

Table A.16 is a list of POST fatal errors that may be reported by the Phoenix BIOS. Table A.17 is a list of nonfatal errors. Fatal errors halt the system and prevent any further processing from occurring; nonfatal errors are less severe.

Table A.16 Phoenix BIOS Fatal System-Board Errors

Beep code	Code at Port 80h	Description
None	01h	CPU register test in progress
1-1-3	02h	CMOS write/read failure
1-1-4	03h	ROM BIOS checksum failure
1-2-1	04h	Programmable interval timer failure
1-2-2	05h	DMA initialization failure
1-2-3	06h	DMA page register write/read failure
1-3-1	08h	RAM refresh verification failure
None	09h	First 64K RAM test in progress
1-3-3	0Ah	First 64K RAM chip or data line failure, multibit
1-3-4	0Bh	First 64K RAM odd/even logic failure
1-4-1	0Ch	Address line failure first 64K RAM
1-4-2	0Dh	Parity failure first 64K RAM
2-1-1	10h	Bit 0 first 64K RAM failure
2-1-2	11h	Bit 1 first 64K RAM failure
2-1-3	12h	Bit 2 first 64K RAM failure
2-1-4	13h	Bit 3 first 64K RAM failure
2-2-1	14h	Bit 4 first 64K RAM failure
2-2-2	15h	Bit 5 first 64K RAM failure
2-2-3	16h	Bit 6 first 64K RAM failure
2-2-4	17h	Bit 7 first 64K RAM failure
2-3-1	18h	Bit 8 first 64K RAM failure
2-3-2	19h	Bit 9 first 64K RAM failure
2-3-3	1Ah	Bit 10 first 64K RAM failure
2-3-4	1Bh	Bit 11 first 64K RAM failure
2-4-1	1Ch	Bit 12 first 64K RAM failure
2-4-2	1Dh	Bit 13 first 64K RAM failure
2-4-3	1Eh	Bit 14 first 64K RAM failure
2-4-4	1Fh	Bit 15 first 64K RAM failure
3-1-1	20h	Slave DMA register failure
3-1-2	21h	Master DMA register failure
3-1-3	22h	Master interrupt mask register failure
3-1-4	23h	Slave interrupt mask register failure
None	25h	Interrupt vector loading in progress
3-2-4	27h	Keyboard controller test failure
None	28h	CMOS power failure/checksum calculation in progress
None	29h	Screen configuration validation in progress
3-3-4	2Bh	Screen initialization failure
3-4-1	2Ch	Screen retrace failure
3-4-2	2Dh	Search for video ROM in progress

Beep code	Code at Port 80h	Description
None	2Eh	Screen running with video ROM
None	30h	Screen operable
None	31h	Monochrome monitor operable
None	32h	Color monitor (40 column) operable
None	33h	Color monitor (80 column) operable

Table A.17 Nonfatal System-Board Errors

Beep code	Code at Port 80h	Description
4-2-1	34h	Timer tick interrupt test in progress or failure
4-2-2	35h	Shutdown test in progress or failure
4-2-3	36h	Gate A20 failure
4-2-4	37h	Unexpected interrupt in protected mode
4-3-1	38h	RAM test in progress or address failure > FFFFh
4-3-3	3Ah	Interval timer Channel 2 test or failure
4-3-4	3Bh	Time-of-day clock test or failure
4-4-1	3Ch	Serial port test or failure
4-4-2	3Dh	Parallel port test or failure
4-4-3	3Eh	Math coprocessor test or failure
low 1-1-2	41h	System-board select failure
low 1-1-3	42h	Extended CMOS RAM failure

low *means that a lower-pitched beep precedes the other tones.*

Hewlett-Packard POST and Diagnostics Error Codes

Table A.18 Hewlett-Packard 386/N & 486/N POST Error Codes

Code	Description
000F	Microprocessor test error. Check CPU and system board.
001x	ROM BIOS memory error. Check ROM BIOS and system board.
008x	Memory error in address range C000-C7FF. Check system board video ROM and/or video adapter.
009x, 00Ax, 00Bx	Memory error in address range C800-DFFF. Check Adapter ROMs.
00C0	Memory error in address range E000-EFFF. Check Adapters or System Board LAN Boot ROM.
011x	CMOS register test error, Real Time Clock (RTC) is not working correctly.
0120, 0130	CMOS Real Time Clock (RTC) failed or corrupted. Check Battery.
0240	CMOS system configuration information corrupted by power failure. Check Battery.
0250	CMOS system configuration information does not match system. Run Setup, Check Battery.

(continues)

Table A.18 Continued

Code	Description
0241, 0280	CMOS power failure, check Battery.
02C0, 02C1	EEPROM master configuration information corrupted or not set correctly. Check system board configuration switches. If the fifth switch (Clear EEPROM) is ON, set it to the OFF position, reset the system, and run Setup to reenter the system configuration.
030x, 0311, 0312, 03E0, 03E1, 03E2, 03E3, 03E4, 03EC	Keyboard/mouse controller failed to respond to a command. Check system board.
034x, 035x	Keyboard failed to respond during keyboard test. Check Keyboard cable, Keyboard, system board.
03E5, 03E6, 03E7, 03E8, 03E9, 03EA, 03EB	Mouse test failure, check mouse and cable.
0401	Protected Mode switch failure, check system board.
0503, 0505	Serial Port failure or Configuration error. Check setup and system board.
0543, 0545	Parallel port failure or Configuration error. Check setup and system board.
0506, 0546	Serial or Parallel port conflict, check configuration.
06xx	Stuck Key failure, xx = the Scan Code of the stuck key.
0800	System board LAN Boot ROM conflict. Check memory address configurations.
0801	Cannot find LAN Boot ROM declared in Setup, check configuration, Boot ROM.
110x, 1200, 1201	System timer failure, check the system board.
20xA	SIMM size mismatch, interleaved memory disabled, check SIMM installation in the affected bank or banks as identified below: 201A = A 205A = A,C 209A = A,D 20DA = A,C,D 202A = B 206A = B,C 20AA = B,D 20EA = B,C,D 203A = A,B 207A = A,B,C 20BA = A,B,D 20FA = A,B,C,D 204A = C 208A = D 20CA = C,D
21xx, 22xx	DMA channel failure, check system board.
4F01, 4F02, 4F03,	SIMM memory error, check the defective SIMM
4F04, 4F05, 4F06, 4F07, 4F08	as identified below: 4F01 = Bank A, slot 1 4F05 = Bank C, slot 1 4F02 = Bank A, slot 2 4F06 = Bank C, slot 2 4F03 = Bank B, slot 1 4F07 = Bank D, slot 1 4F04 = Bank B, slot 2 4F08 = Bank D, slot 2
61xx	Memory Address Line failure, check SIMMs and system board.
63xx	Memory Parity Error, check Memory and system board.
6500	ROM BIOS Shadowing error, check system memory, ROM BIOS.
6510	Video ROM Shadowing error, check system memory, Video ROM BIOS.
6520	LAN Option ROM Shadowing error, check system memory, LAN Option ROM.
65A0, 65B0, 65C0, 65D0, 65E0, 65F0	ROM BIOS Shadowing error, memory segment failure, check system memory in the segment indicated by the third digit, A = A000, B = B000, C = C000, D = D000, E = E000, F = F000.

Code	Description
66xx	ROM BIOS Shadowing error, check configuration or ROM checksum.
7xxx	Interrupt failure, check system board.
8003, 8006	Hard drive configuration error, parameters do not match drive, check configuration and cabling.
8004, 8007	CMOS hard disk configuration error, check drive and battery.
800D, 8010, 8012, 8020, 8021, 8038, 803C, 8040, 8045	Hard Disk Controller timeout (12 seconds without responding), check drive and controller.
800E	Hard Disk Boot failure, check cables, disk drive failure.
800F	Hard Disk CMOS configuration does not match drive.
8011, 8013, 8030, 8039, 803A, 803B, 8041, 8042, 8043, 8044, 8049, 804B, 8310, 8311, 8313	Hard Drive does not respond to commands, check drive, controller and cables.
8048, 804A	System failed to identify installed hard disk drive, check setup and cables.
8050	System failed to identify installed hard disk controller, check configuration.
8400	Hard disk drive boot sector was corrupted or could not be loaded, check drive partitions.
9x00, 9x01, 9x02,	Floppy drive error, check drives and cables.
9x03, 9x04, 9x05, 9x06, 9x07, 9x08,9x09	Drive "x" not responding, where: $X = 0$ for drive 0 $X = 1$ for drive 1 $X = 2$ for drive 2 $X = 3$ for drive 3 Check cables and drives.
9x10, 9x0A	CMOS floppy configuration error, where: $X = 0$ for drive 0 $X = 1$ for drive 1 $X = 2$ for drive 2 $X = 3$ for drive 3
A00x	Math Coprocessor error, check coprocessor and system board.
B300	Memory cache controller error.
Exxx	Memory adapter error, check adapters or SIMMs.

Table A.19 Hewlett-Packard 486/U POST Error Codes

Code	Description
00Ax, 00Bx, 00Cx, 00Dx	Adapter ROM (Read-Only Memory) checksum error, check configuration.
008x	Video ROM (Read-Only-Memory) checksum error, check video ROM or adapter.
009x	Adapter ROM (Read-Only-Memory) checksum error in addresses between C8000h and CFFFFh, check configuration and adapter.

(continues)

Table A.19 Continued	
Code	**Description**
0111x, 0120	CMOS Real Time Clock is not updating, check battery and system board.
0130	CMOS Real Time Clock has invalid time and or date. Reset date and time.
0240, 0241	CMOS memory information is incorrect, check the clear configuration switch on the system board, it should be OFF.
0250	CMOS configuration does not match installed devices.
0280, 0282	CMOS configuration information has been corrupted.
02C0	EEPROM memory has not been set or was corrupted.
0301, 0302, 0303, 0305, 0306, 0307, 0311, 0312, 03E0, 03E1, 03E2, 03E3, 03E4, 03E5, 03EE,03EC	System board Keyboard/mouse controller did not respond.
0342, 0343, 0344, 0345, 0346, 0350, 0351	System board keyboard/mouse controller self-test failure, check keyboard controller.
0352, 0353	Keyboard not responding to POST tests, check cable, keyboard controller.
0354	Keyboard self test failure, check Keyboard.
03E6, 03E7, 03E8, 03E9	Mouse interface test failure, check mouse, cable or keyboard/mouse controller.
03EA, 03EB	Keyboard/Mouse reset failure, check mouse and cable.
0401	Gate A20 failure, check Keyboard/mouse controller (8042) on system board or the system board itself.
0503, 0505	Serial port error or conflict, check system board or adapters.
0543, 0545	Parallel port or configuration failure, check configuration, system board or adapters.
06xx	Keyboard stuck key failure, xx = Scan code (hex) of the key.
1100, 1101	System timer failure, check system board.
1300	Floppy controller conflict, check configuration.
13x1	Adapter communications error, x = slot containing adapter (i.e., 1351=slot 5).
13x2	CMOS indicates a slot is empty, but a board is installed, x = slot.
13x3	CMOS indicates a slot contains a board with no readable identification, but a board with a readable identification is present, x = slot.
13x4	CMOS Configuration information does not match the board in slot x, where x = slot.
13x5	CMOS Configuration information is incomplete.
2002	SIMM not detected, check SIMMs and system board.
2003, 2005, 2007	Incorrect SIMM configuration, for example, when you have 2M and 8M memory modules installed at the same time, the 8M modules must be in the first sockets.
21xx, 22xx	DMA (Direct Memory Access) controller is not functioning correctly, check system board.
4F0x	SIMM error, x = SIMM socket for example, 4F02=socket 2.

Code	Description
61xx	Memory addressing error, check installed SIMMs.
62F0	Memory Parity error, check SIMMs or system board.
62F1	Memory Controller error, check system board.
6300	Adapter RAM error, check installed adapters and memory.
6500	System board ROM BIOS Shadowing error, check system board and setup for conflicts.
6510	Video ROM Shadowing error, check system board or video adapter.
6520	Adapter ROM Shadowing error, check system board adapters and memory.
65C0, 65D0, 65E0	Reserved memory for shadowing failed tests. Segment indicated by third digit, for example 65D0 = segment D000h.
70xx, 71xx, 7400, 7500	Interrupt controller failure, check system board and adapters.
8003, 8103	Hard disk configuration (number of sectors) is not correct.
8004, 8104	CMOS hard disk parameters are not correct, where 8004 = drive C, and 8104 = drive D.
8005, 8105	CMOS hard disk parameters not supported, where 8005 = drive C, and 8105 = drive D.
8x06	BIOS shadow RAM on your system board must be functioning if you have either a hard disk drive type 33 or type 34 installed.
8007, 8107	The number of hard disk drive cylinders specified for your type 33 or type 34 hard disk drive is not correct, where 8007 = drive C, and 8107 = drive D.
800D, 8010, 800E, 800F	Hard drive controller not responding, check controller or cables.
8011	Hard disk test failure.
8012, 8013	Hard disk controller test failure.
8020, 8120	Hard drive not ready, where 8020 = drive C, mm and 8120, hard drive D.
8021, 8121	Unable to communicate with Hard Disk controller, where 8021 = drive C and 8121 = drive D is at fault.
8028	Hard disk controller is configured for drive splitting, but splitting is not supported or is not functioning, check configuration.
8030, 8130	Identify drive failure, 8030 = drive C, and 8130 = drive D is at fault.
	Manager in the EISA Configuration Utility.
8038, 8138, 803A, 813A, 803B, 813B	Hard Disk (Recalibrate) error, where 8039, 803A, 803C = hard disk or controller for drive C, and 8139, 8013A, or 813C = drive D or its controller is at fault.
8040, 8140, 8041, 8141, 8042, 8142, 8043, 8143, 8044, 8144, 8045, 8145.	Hard Disk (Read Verify) command failure, where 804x = hard disk drive or controller for C, and 814x = hard drive or controller for D.
8048, 8148, 804A, 814A	Hard Disk (Drive Identify) command failure, where 804x = drive C, and 814x = drive D.
8049, 8149, 804B, 814B	Hard Disk (Set Multiple Mode) command failure, where 804x = drive C, and 814x = drive D.
8400	No boot sector (or corrupted boot sector) on hard disk.

(continues)

Table A.19 Continued

Code	Description
900A, 910A, 920A	CMOS floppy configuration does not match actual drives installed, where 900A = drive A, 910A = drive B, and 920A = a third floppy drive.
9000, 9100, 9200, 9001, 9101, 9201	Floppy controller communication error, where 90xx = drive A, 91xx = drive B, and 92xx = a third floppy drive.
9002, 9102, 9202	Floppy drive (Seek) error, where 90xx = drive A, 91xx = drive B, and 9202 = a third floppy drive.
9003, 9103, 9203	Floppy drive (Recalibrate) error, where 90xx = drive A, 9103 = drive B, and 9203 = a third floppy drive.
9005, 9105, 9205	Floppy drive (Reset) error, where 9005 = drive A, 9105 = drive as B, and 9205 = a third floppy drive.
9008, 9108, 9208	Floppy drive command error, where 9008 = drive A, 9108 = drive B, and 9208 = a third floppy drive.
9009, 9109, 9209	Floppy drive track zero error, where 9009 = drive A, 9109 = drive B, and 9209 = a third floppy drive.
A001, A002, A003, A004, A005, A006, A007, A008, A009, A00A, A00B, A00C, A00D, A00E	Math coprocessor failure.
B300	CPU Level 2 cache failure.
Exxx	Memory board failure (non-HP)

IBM POST and Diagnostics Display Error Codes

When an IBM or compatible system is first powered on, the system runs a Power-On Self Test (POST). If errors are encountered during the POST, the errors are displayed in the form of a code number and possibly some additional text. When you are running the IBM Advanced Diagnostics, which you can purchase from IBM or which is included on many of the PS/2 Reference Diskettes, similar codes are displayed if errors are encountered during the tests. IBM has developed a system in which the first part of the error code indicates the device the error involves, and the last part indicates the exact error meaning. One of the biggest problems with these error codes is that IBM does not publish a complete list of the errors in any single publication; instead, it details specific error codes in many different publications. I have researched these codes for many years; tables C.9 and C.10 represent all the codes I have found meanings for. These codes have been selected from a number of sources, including all of IBMs technical-reference and hardware-maintenance and service manuals.

When diagnostics are run, any code ending in 00 indicates that the particular test has passed. For example, an error code of 1700 indicates that the hard disk diagnostics tests have passed.

After completing the Power-On Self Test (POST), an audio code indicates either a normal condition or that one of several errors has occurred. Table A.20 lists the audio codes for IBM systems, and table A.21 lists the IBM POST and diagnostics error codes.

Table A.20 IBM POST Audio Error Codes

Audio code	Sound graph	Fault domain
1 short beep	·	Normal POST - system OK
2 short beeps	· ·	POST error - error code on CRT
No beep		Power supply, system board
Continuous beep	———	Power supply, system board
Repeating short beeps	· · · · · ·	Power supply, system board
1 long, 1 short beep	— ·	System board
1 long, 2 short beeps	— · ·	Display adapter (MDA, CGA)
1 long, 3 short beeps	— ·	Enhanced Graphics Adapter (EGA)
3 long beeps	— — —	3270 keyboard card

Table A.21 IBM POST and Diagnostics Error-Code List

Code	Description
1xx	System-board errors
101	System-board interrupt failure (Unexpected interrupt)
102	System-board timer failure
102	PS/2; real-time clock (RTC)/64 byte CMOS RAM test failure
103	System-board timer interrupt failure
103	PS/2; 2K CMOS RAM extension test failure
104	System-board protected mode failure
105	System-board 8042 Keyboard Controller command failure
106	System-board converting logic test failure
107	System-board Non-Maskable Interrupt (NMI) test failure, Hot NMI
108	System-board timer bus test failure
109	System-board memory select error, Low MB chip select test failed
110	PS/2 system-board parity check error (PARITY CHECK 1)
111	PS/2 I/O channel (bus) parity check error (PARITY CHECK 2)
112	PS/2 Micro Channel Arbitration error; watchdog time-out (NMI error)
113	PS/2 Micro Channel Arbitration error; DMA arbitration time-out (NMI error)
114	PS/2 external ROM checksum error
115	Cache parity error, ROM checksum error or DMA error
116	System board port read/write failure
118	System board parity or L2-cache error during previous power-on
119	"E" Step level 82077 (floppy controller) and 2.88M drive installed (not supported)
120	Microprocessor self test error
121	256K ROM checksum error (second 128K bank)
121	Unexpected hardware interrupts occurred
131	PC system-board Cassette port wrap test failure

(continues)

Table A.21 Continued

Code	Description
131	Direct memory access (DMA) compatibility registers error
132	Direct memory access (DMA) extended registers error
133	Direct memory access (DMA) verify logic error
134	Direct memory access (DMA) arbitration logic error
151	Battery or CMOS RAM failure
152	Real-time clock or CMOS RAM failure
160	PS/2 system-board ID not recognized
161	CMOS configuration empty (dead battery)
162	CMOS checksum error or adapter ID mismatch
163	CMOS error; date and time not set (Clock not updating)
164	Memory size error; CMOS setting does not match memory
165	PS/2 Micro Channel adapter ID and CMOS mismatch
166	PS/2 Micro Channel adapter time-out error, Card busy
167	PS/2 CMOS clock not updating
168	CMOS configuration error; math coprocessor
169	System board and processor card configuration mismatch, run Setup.
170	ASCII setup conflict error
170	PC Convertible; LCD not in use when suspended
171	Rolling-bit-test failure on CMOS shutdown address byte
171	PC Convertible; base 128K checksum failure
172	Rolling-bit-test failure on NVRAM diagnostic byte
172	PC Convertible; diskette active when suspended
173	Bad CMOS/NVRAM checksum
173	PC Convertible; real-time clock RAM verification error
174	Bad configuration
174	PC Convertible; LCD configuration changed
175	Bad EEPROM CRC #1
175	PC Convertible; LCD alternate mode failed
176	Tamper evident
177	Bad PAP (Privileged-Access Password) CRC
177	Bad EEPROM
178	Bad EEPROM
179	NVRAM error log full
180x	Sub Address data error, x = Slot number which caused the error
181	Unsupported configurations
182	Privileged-access switch (JMP2) is not in the write-enable position
183	PAP is needed to boot from the system programs
183	Privileged-access password required
184	Bad Power On Password checksum - Erase it

Code	Description
615	Drive index timing error
616	Drive speed error
621	Drive seek error
622	Drive cyclic redundancy check (CRC) error
623	Sector not found error
624	Address mark error
625	Controller chip (NEC) seek error
626	Diskette data compare error
627	Diskette change error
628	Diskette removed
630	Index stuck high; Drive A:
631	Index stuck low; Drive A:
632	Track 0 stuck off; Drive A:
633	Track 0 stuck on; Drive A:
640	Index stuck high; Drive B:
641	Index stuck low; Drive B:
642	Track 0 stuck off; Drive B:
643	Track 0 stuck on; Drive B:
645	No index pulse
646	Drive track 0 detection failed
647	No transitions on read data line
648	Format test failed
649	Incorrect media type in drive
650	Drive speed error
651	Format failure
652	Verify failure
653	Read failure
654	Write failure
655	Controller error
656	Drive failure
657	Write protect stuck protected
658	Changeline stuck changed
659	Write protect stuck unprotected
660	Changeline stuck unchanged
7xx	Math Coprocessor errors
701	Math coprocessor presence/initialization error
702	Exception errors test failure
703	Rounding test failure
704	Arithmetic test 1 failure

(continues)

Table A.21 Continued	
Code	**Description**
705	Arithmetic test 2 failure
706	Arithmetic test 3 (80387 only) failure
707	Combination test failure
708	Integer load/store test failure
709	Equivalent expressions errors
710	Exception (interrupt) errors
711	Save state (FSAVE) errors
712	Protected mode test failure
713	Special test (voltage/temperature sensitivity) failure
9xx	Parallel Printer Adapter errors
901	Printer adapter data register latch error
902	Printer adapter control register latch error
903	Printer adapter register address decode error
904	Printer adapter address decode error
910	Status line(s) wrap connector error
911	Status line bit 8 wrap error
912	Status line bit 7 wrap error
913	Status line bit 6 wrap error
914	Status line bit 5 wrap error
915	Status line bit 4 wrap error
916	Printer adapter interrupt wrap error
917	Unexpected printer adapter interrupt
92x	Feature register error
10xx	Alternate Parallel Printer Adapter errors
1001	Printer adapter data register latch error
1002	Printer adapter control register latch error
1003	Printer adapter register address decode error
1004	Printer adapter address decode error
1010	Status line(s) wrap connector error
1011	Status line bit 8 wrap error
1012	Status line bit 7 wrap error
1013	Status line bit 6 wrap error
1014	Status line bit 5 wrap error
1015	Status line bit 4 wrap error
1016	Printer adapter interrupt wrap error
1017	Unexpected printer adapter interrupt
102x	Feature register error
11xx	Primary Async Communications (serial COM1:) errors
1101	16450/16550 chip error, Serial port A error

Code	Description
1102	Card selected feedback error
1102	PC Convertible internal modem test failed
1103	Port 102h register test failure
1103	PC Convertible internal modem dial tone test 1 failed
1104	PC Convertible internal modem dial tone test 2 failed
1106	Serial option cannot be put to sleep
1107	Cable error
1108	Interrupt request (IRQ) 3 error
1109	Interrupt request (IRQ) 4 error
1110	16450/16550 chip register failure
1111	Internal wrap test of 16450/16550 chip modem control line failure
1112	External wrap test of 16450/16550 chip modem control line failure
1113	16450/16550 chip transmit error
1114	16450/16550 chip receive error
1115	16450/16550 chip receive error; data not equal to transmit data
1116	16450/16550 chip interrupt function error
1117	16450/16550 chip baud rate test failure
1118	16450/16550 chip receive external data wrap test failure
1119	16550 chip first-in first-out (FIFO) buffer failure
1120	Interrupt enable register error; all bits cannot be set
1121	Interrupt enable register error; all bits cannot be reset
1122	Interrupt pending; stuck on
1123	Interrupt ID register; stuck on
1124	Modem control register error; all bits cannot be set
1125	Modem control register error; all bits cannot be reset
1126	Modem status register error; all bits cannot be set
1127	Modem status register error; all bits cannot be reset
1128	Interrupt ID error
1129	Cannot force overrun error
1130	No modem status interrupt
1131	Invalid interrupt pending
1132	No data ready
1133	No data available interrupt
1134	No transmit holding interrupt
1135	No interrupts
1136	No received sine status interrupt
1137	No receive data available
1138	Transmit holding register not empty
1139	No modem status interrupt

(continues)

Table A.21 Continued	
Code	**Description**
1140	Transmit holding register not empty
1141	No interrupts
1142	No interrupt 4
1143	No interrupt 3
1144	No data transferred
1145	Maximum baud rate error
1146	Minimum baud rate error
1148	Time-out error
1149	Invalid data returned
1150	Modem status register error
1151	No data set ready and delta data set ready
1152	No data set ready
1153	No delta data set ready
1154	Modem status register not clear
1155	No clear to send and delta clear to send
1156	No clear to send
1157	No delta clear to send
12xx	Alternate Async Communications (Serial COM2:, COM3:, and COM4:) errors
1201	16450/16550 chip error
1202	Card selected feedback error
1203	Port 102h register test failure
1206	Serial option cannot be put to sleep
1207	Cable error
1208	Interrupt request (IRQ) 3 error
1209	Interrupt request (IRQ) 4 error
1210	16450/16550 chip register failure
1211	Internal wrap test of 16450/16550 chip modem control line failure
1212	External wrap test of 16450/16550 chip modem control line failure
1213	16450/16550 chip transmit error
1214	16450/16550 chip receive error
1215	16450/16550 chip receive error; data not equal to transmit data
1216	16450/16550 chip interrupt function error
1217	16450/16550 chip baud rate test failure
1218	16450/16550 chip receive external data wrap test failure
1219	16550 chip first-in first-out (FIFO) buffer failure
1220	Interrupt enable register error; all bits cannot be set
1221	Interrupt enable register error; all bits cannot be reset
1222	Interrupt pending; stuck on
1223	Interrupt ID register; stuck on

Code	Description
1224	Modem control register error; all bits cannot be set
1225	Modem control register error; all bits cannot be reset
1226	Modem status register error; all bits cannot be set
1227	Modem Status Register error; all bits cannot be reset
1228	Interrupt ID error
1229	Cannot force overrun error
1230	No modem status interrupt
1231	Invalid interrupt pending
1232	No data ready
1233	No data available interrupt
1234	No transmit holding interrupt
1235	No interrupts
1236	No received sine status interrupt
1237	No receive data available
1238	Transmit holding register not empty
1239	No modem status interrupt
1240	Transmit holding register not empty
1241	No interrupts
1242	No interrupt 4
1243	No interrupt 3
1244	No data transferred
1245	Maximum baud rate error
1246	Minimum baud rate error
1248	Time-out error
1249	Invalid data returned
1250	Modem status register error
1251	No data set ready and delta data set ready
1252	No data set ready
1253	No delta data set ready
1254	Modem status register not clear
1255	No clear to send and delta clear to send
1256	No clear to send
1257	No delta clear to send
13xx	Game Control Adapter errors
1301	Game control adapter test failure
1302	Joystick test failure
14xx	Matrix Printer errors
1401	Printer test failure
1402	Printer not ready error

(continues)

Table A.21 Continued	
Code	**Description**
1403	Printer no-paper error
1404	System-board time-out
1405	Parallel adapter failure
1406	Printer presence test failed
15xx	Synchronous Data Link Control (SDLC) communications adapter errors
1501	SDLC adapter test failure
1510	8255 Port B failure
1511	8255 Port A failure
1512	8255 Port C failure
1513	8253 Timer #1 did not reach terminal count
1514	8253 Timer #1 stuck on
1515	8253 Timer #0 did not reach terminal count
1516	8253 Timer #0 stuck on
1517	8253 Timer #2 did not reach terminal count
1518	8253 Timer #2 stuck on
1519	8273 Port B error
1520	8273 Port A error
1521	8273 command/read time-out
1522	Interrupt Level 4 failure
1523	Ring Indicate stuck on
1524	Receive Clock stuck on
1525	Transmit Clock stuck on
1526	Test Indicate stuck on
1527	Ring Indicate not on
1528	Receive Clock not on
1529	Transmit Clock not on
1530	Test Indicate not on
1531	Data Set Ready not on
1532	Carrier Detect not on
1533	Clear to Send not on
1534	Data Set Ready stuck on
1535	Carrier Detect stuck on
1536	Clear to Send stuck on
1537	Interrupt level 3 failure
1538	Receive interrupt results error
1539	Wrap data compare error
1540	Direct memory access channel 1 error
1541	Direct memory access channel 1 error
1542	8273 error checking or status reporting error

Code	Description
1547	Stray Interrupt level 4
1548	Stray Interrupt level 3
1549	Interrupt presentation sequence time-out
16xx	Display Station Emulation Adapter (DSEA) errors (5520, 525x)
1604	DSEA or Twinaxial network error
1608	DSEA or Twinaxial network error
1624	DSEA error
1634	DSEA error
1644	DSEA error
1652	DSEA error
1654	DSEA error
1658	DSEA error
1662	DSEA interrupt level error
1664	DSEA error
1668	DSEA interrupt level error
1669	DSEA diagnostics error; use 3.0 or higher
1674	DSEA diagnostics error; use 3.0 or higher
1674	DSEA station address error
1684	DSEA device address error
1688	DSEA device address error
17xx	ST-506/412 Fixed Disk and Controller errors
1701	Fixed disk general POST error
1702	Drive/controller time-out error
1703	Drive seek error
1704	Controller failed
1705	Drive sector not found error
1706	Write fault error
1707	Drive track 0 error
1708	Head select error
1709	Error-correction code (ECC) error
1710	Sector buffer overrun
1711	Bad address mark
1712	Internal controller diagnostics failure
1713	Data compare error
1714	Drive not ready
1715	Track 0 indicator failure
1716	Diagnostics cylinder errors
1717	Surface read errors
1718	Hard drive type error

(continues)

Table A.21 Continued	
Code	**Description**
1720	Bad diagnostics cylinder
1726	Data compare error
1730	Controller error
1731	Controller error
1732	Controller error
1733	BIOS Undefined error return
1735	Bad command error
1736	Data corrected error
1737	Bad track error
1738	Bad sector error
1739	Bad initialization error
1740	Bad sense error
1750	Drive verify failure
1751	Drive read failure
1752	Drive write failure
1753	Drive random read test failure
1754	Drive seek test failure
1755	Controller failure
1756	Controller error-correction code (ECC) test failure
1757	Controller head select failure
1780	Seek failure; drive 0
1781	Seek failure; drive 1
1782	Controller test failure
1790	Diagnostic cylinder read error; drive 0
1791	Diagnostic cylinder read error; drive 1
18xx	I/O Expansion Unit errors
1801	I/O expansion unit POST failure
1810	Enable/disable failure
1811	Extender card wrap test failure; disabled
1812	High-order address lines failure; disabled
1813	Wait state failure; disabled
1814	Enable/disable could not be set on
1815	Wait state failure; disabled
1816	Extender card wrap test failure; enabled
1817	High-order address lines failure; enabled
1818	Disable not functioning
1819	Wait request switch not set correctly
1820	Receiver card wrap test failure
1821	Receiver high order address lines failure

Code	Description
19xx	3270 PC Attachment Card errors
20xx	Binary Synchronous Communications (BSC) Adapter errors
2001	BSC adapter test failure
2010	8255 Port A failure
2011	8255 Port B failure
2012	8255 Port C failure
2013	8253 Timer #1 did not reach terminal count
2014	8253 Timer #1 stuck on
2015	8253 Timer 2 did not reach terminal count
2016	8253 Timer #2 output stuck on
2017	8251 data set ready failed to come on
2018	8251 clear to send not sensed
2019	8251 data SET ready stuck on
2020	8251 clear to send stuck on
2021	8251 hardware reset failure
2022	8251 software reset failure
2023	8251 software error reset failure
2024	8251 transmit ready did not come on
2025	8251 receive ready did not come on
2026	8251 could not force overrun error status
2027	Interrupt failure; no timer interrupt
2028	Interrupt failure; transmit, replace card or planar
2029	Interrupt failure; transmit, replace card
2030	Interrupt failure; receive, replace card or planar
2031	Interrupt failure; receive, replace card
2033	Ring indicate stuck on
2034	Receive clock stuck on
2035	Transmit clock stuck on
2036	Test indicate stuck on
2037	Ring indicate stuck on
2038	Receive clock not on
2039	Transmit clock not on
2040	Test indicate not on
2041	Data set ready not on
2042	Carrier detect not on
2043	Clear to send not on
2044	Data set ready stuck on
2045	Carrier detect stuck on
2046	Clear to send stuck on

(continues)

Table A.21 Continued	
Code	**Description**
2047	Unexpected transmit interrupt
2048	Unexpected receive interrupt
2049	Transmit data did not equal receive data
2050	8251 detected overrun error
2051	Lost data set ready during data wrap
2052	Receive time-out during data wrap
21xx	Alternate Binary Synchronous Communications (BSC) Adapter errors
2101	BSC adapter test failure
2110	8255 Port A failure
2111	8255 Port B failure
2112	8255 Port C failure
2113	8253 Timer #1 did not reach terminal count
2114	8253 Timer #1 stuck on
2115	8253 Timer #2 did not reach terminal count
2116	8253 Timer #2 output stuck on
2117	8251 Data set ready failed to come on
2118	8251 Clear to send not sensed
2119	8251 Data set ready stuck on
2120	8251 Clear to send stuck on
2121	8251 Hardware reset failure
2122	8251 Software reset failure
2123	8251 Software error reset failure
2124	8251 Transmit ready did not come on
2125	8251 Receive ready did not come on
2126	8251 could not force overrun error status
2127	Interrupt failure; no timer interrupt
2128	Interrupt failure; transmit, replace card or planar
2129	Interrupt failure; transmit, replace card
2130	Interrupt failure; receive, replace card or planar
2131	Interrupt failure; receive, replace card
2133	Ring indicate stuck on
2134	Receive clock stuck on
2135	Transmit clock stuck on
2136	Test indicate stuck on
2137	Ring indicate stuck on
2138	Receive clock not on
2139	Transmit clock not on
2140	Test indicate not on
2141	Data set ready not on

Code	Description
2142	Carrier detect not on
2143	Clear to send not on
2144	Data set ready stuck on
2145	Carrier detect stuck on
2146	Clear to send stuck on
2147	Unexpected transmit interrupt
2148	Unexpected receive interrupt
2149	Transmit data did not equal receive data
2150	8251 detected overrun error
2151	Lost data set ready during data wrap
2152	Receive time-out during data wrap
22xx	Cluster Adapter errors
23xx	Plasma Monitor Adapter errors
24xx	Enhanced Graphics Adapter (EGA) or Video Graphics Array (VGA) errors
2401	Video adapter test failure
2402	· Video display error
2408	User indicated display attribute test failed
2409	Video display error
2410	Video adapter error; video port error
2416	User indicated character set test failed
2424	User indicated 80525 mode failure
2432	User indicated 40525 mode failure
2440	User indicated 3205200 graphics mode failure
2448	User indicated 6405200 graphics mode failure
2456	User indicated light-pen test failure
2464	User indicated paging test failure
25xx	Alternate Enhanced Graphics Adapter (EGA) errors
2501	Video adapter test failure
2502	Video display error
2508	User indicated display attribute test failed
2509	Video display error
2510	Video adapter error
2516	User indicated character set test failed
2524	User indicated 80525 mode failure
2532	User indicated 40525 mode failure
2540	User indicated 3205200 graphics mode failure
2548	User indicated 6405200 graphics mode failure
2556	User indicated light-pen test failure
2564	User indicated paging test failure

(continues)

Table A.21 Continued

Code	Description
26xx	XT or AT/370 370-M (memory) and 370-P (processor) adapter errors
2601	370-M (memory) adapter error
2655	370-M (memory) adapter error
2657	370-M (memory) adapter error
2668	370-M (memory) adapter error
2672	370-M (memory) adapter error
2673	370-P (processor) adapter error
2674	370-P (processor) adapter error
2677	370-P (processor) adapter error
2680	370-P (processor) adapter error
2681	370-M (memory) adapter error
2682	370-P (processor) adapter error
2694	370-P (processor) adapter error
2697	370-P (processor) adapter error
2698	XT or AT/370 diagnostic diskette error
27xx	XT or AT/370 3277-EM (emulation) adapter errors
2701	3277-EM adapter error
2702	3277-EM adapter error
2703	3277-EM adapter error
28xx	3278/79 Emulation Adapter or 3270 Connection Adapter errors
29xx	Color/Graphics Printer errors
30xx	Primary PC Network Adapter errors
3001	Processor test failure
3002	ROM checksum test failure
3003	Unit ID PROM test failure
3004	RAM test failure
3005	Host interface controller test failure
3006	±12v test failure
3007	Digital loopback test failure
3008	Host detected host interface controller failure
3009	Sync failure and no Go bit
3010	Host interface controller test OK and no Go bit
3011	Go bit and no command 41
3012	Card not present
3013	Digital failure; fall through
3015	Analog failure
3041	Hot carrier; not this card
3042	Hot carrier; this card!
31xx	Secondary PC Network Adapter errors

Code	Description
3101	Processor test failure
3102	ROM checksum test failure
3103	Unit ID PROM test failure
3104	RAM test failure
3105	Host interface controller test failure
3106	± 12v test failure
3107	Digital loopback test failure
3108	Host detected host interface controller failure
3109	Sync failure and no Go bit
3110	Host interface controller test OK and no Go bit
3111	Go bit and no command 41
3112	Card not present
3113	Digital failure; fall through
3115	Analog failure
3141	Hot carrier; not this card
3142	Hot carrier; this card!
32xx	3270 PC or AT Display and Programmed Symbols Adapter errors
33xx	Compact Printer errors
35xx	Enhanced Display Station Emulation Adapter (EDSEA) errors
3504	Adapter connected to Twinaxial cable during off-line test
3508	Workstation address error
3509	Diagnostic program failure
3540	Workstation address invalid
3588	Adapter address switch error
3599	Diagnostic program failure
36xx	General-Purpose Interface Bus (GPIB) adapter errors
3601	Adapter test failure
3602	Serial poll mode register write error
3603	Adapter address error
3610	Adapter listen error
3611	Adapter talk error
3612	Adapter control error
3613	Adapter standby error
3614	Adapter Asynchronous control error
3615	Adapter Asynchronous control error
3616	Adapter error; cannot pass control
3617	Adapter error; cannot address to listen
3618	Adapter error; cannot un-address to listen
3619	Adapter error; cannot address to talk

(continues)

Table A.21 Continued	
Code	**Description**
3620	Adapter error; cannot un-address to talk
3621	Adapter error; cannot address to listen with extended addressing
3622	Adapter error; cannot un-address to listen with extended addressing
3623	Adapter error; cannot address to talk with extended addressing
3624	Adapter error; cannot un-address to talk with extended addressing
3625	Write to self error
3626	Generate handshake error
3627	Cannot detect Device Clear message error
3628	Cannot detect Selected Device Clear message error
3629	Cannot detect end with end of identify
3630	Cannot detect end of transmission with end of identify
3631	Cannot detect end with 0-bit end of string
3632	Cannot detect end with 7-bit end of string
3633	Cannot detect group execute trigger
3634	Mode 3 addressing error
3635	Cannot recognize undefined command
3636	Cannot detect remote, remote changed, lockout, or lockout changed
3637	Cannot clear remote or lockout
3638	Cannot detect service request
3639	Cannot conduct serial poll
3640	Cannot conduct parallel poll
3650	Adapter error; direct memory access (DMA) to 7210
3651	Data error; error on direct memory access (DMA) to 7210
3652	Adapter error; direct memory access (DMA) from 7210
3653	Data error on direct memory access (DMA) from 7210
3658	Uninvoked interrupt received
3659	Cannot interrupt on address status changed
3660	Cannot interrupt on address status changed
3661	Cannot interrupt on command output
3662	Cannot interrupt on data out
3663	Cannot interrupt on data in
3664	Cannot interrupt on error
3665	Cannot interrupt on device clear
3666	Cannot interrupt on end
3667	Cannot interrupt on device execute trigger
3668	Cannot interrupt on address pass through
3669	Cannot interrupt on command pass through
3670	Cannot interrupt on remote changed
3671	Cannot interrupt on lockout changed

Code	Description
3672	Cannot interrupt on service request in
3673	Cannot interrupt on terminal count on direct memory access to 7210
3674	Cannot interrupt on terminal count on direct memory access from 7210
3675	Spurious direct memory access terminal-count interrupt
3697	Illegal direct memory access configuration setting detected
3698	Illegal interrupt level setting detected
37xx	System board SCSI controller error
38xx	Data acquisition adapter errors
3801	Adapter test failure
3810	Timer read test failure
3811	Timer interrupt test failure
3812	Delay, binary input 13 test failure
3813	Rate, binary input 13 test failure
3814	Binary output 14, interrupt status - interrupt request test failure
3815	Binary output 0, count-in test failure
3816	Binary input strobe, count-out test failure
3817	Binary output 0, binary output clear to send test failure
3818	Binary output 1, binary input 0 test failure
3819	Binary output 2, binary input 1 test failure
3820	Binary output 3, binary input 2 test failure
3821	Binary output 4, binary input 3 test failure
3822	Binary output 5, binary input 4 test failure
3823	Binary output 6, binary input 5 test failure
3824	Binary output 7, binary input 6 test failure
3825	Binary output 8, binary input 7 test failure
3826	Binary output 9, binary input 8 test failure
3827	Binary output 10, binary input 9 test failure
3828	Binary output 11, binary input 10 test failure
3829	Binary output 12, binary input 11 test failure
3830	Binary output 13, binary input 12 test failure
3831	Binary output 15, analog input CE test failure
3832	Binary output strobe, binary output GATE test failure
3833	Binary input clear to send, binary input HOLD test failure
3834	Analog input command output, binary input 15 test failure
3835	Counter interrupt test failure
3836	Counter read test failure
3837	Analog output 0 ranges test failure
3838	Analog output 1 ranges test failure
3839	Analog input 0 values test failure

(continues)

Table A.21 Continued	
Code	**Description**
3840	Analog input 1 values test failure
3841	Analog input 2 values test failure
3842	Analog input 3 values test failure
3843	Analog input interrupt test failure
3844	Analog input 23 address or value test failure
39xx	Professional Graphics Adapter (PGA) errors
3901	PGA test failure
3902	ROM1 self-test failure
3903	ROM2 self-test failure
3904	RAM self-test failure
3905	Cold start cycle power error
3906	Data error in communications RAM
3907	Address error in communications RAM
3908	Bad data reading/writing 6845-like register
3909	Bad data in lower E0h bytes reading/writing 6845-like registers
3910	Graphics controller display bank output latches error
3911	Basic clock error
3912	Command control error
3913	Vertical sync scanner error
3914	Horizontal sync scanner error
3915	Intech error
3916	Look-up table address error
3917	Look-up table red RAM chip error
3918	Look-up table green RAM chip error
3919	Look-up table blue RAM chip error
3920	Look-up table data latch error
3921	Horizontal display error
3922	Vertical display error
3923	Light-pen error
3924	Unexpected error
3925	Emulator addressing error
3926	Emulator data latch error
3927	Base for error codes 3928-3930 (Emulator RAM)
3928	Emulator RAM error
3929	Emulator RAM error
3930	Emulator RAM error
3931	Emulator horizontal/vertical display problem
3932	Emulator cursor position error
3933	Emulator attribute display problem

Code	Description
3934	Emulator cursor display error
3935	Fundamental emulation RAM problem
3936	Emulation character set problem
3937	Emulation graphics display error
3938	Emulation character display problem
3939	Emulation bank select error
3940	Adapter RAM U2 error
3941	Adapter RAM U4 error
3942	Adapter RAM U6 error
3943	Adapter RAM U8 error
3944	Adapter RAM U10 error
3945	Adapter RAM U1 error
3946	Adapter RAM U3 error
3947	Adapter RAM U5 error
3948	Adapter RAM U7 error
3949	Adapter RAM U9 error
3950	Adapter RAM U12 error
3951	Adapter RAM U14 error
3952	Adapter RAM U16 error
3953	Adapter RAM U18 error
3954	Adapter RAM U20 error
3955	Adapter RAM U11 error
3956	Adapter RAM U13 error
3957	Adapter RAM U15 error
3958	Adapter RAM U17 error
3959	Adapter RAM U19 error
3960	Adapter RAM U22 error
3961	Adapter RAM U24 error
3962	Adapter RAM U26 error
3963	Adapter RAM U28 error
3964	Adapter RAM U30 error
3965	Adapter RAM U21 error
3966	Adapter RAM U23 error
3967	Adapter RAM U25 error
3968	Adapter RAM U27 error
3969	Adapter RAM U29 error
3970	Adapter RAM U32 error
3971	Adapter RAM U34 error
3972	Adapter RAM U36 error

(continues)

Table A.21 Continued	
Code	**Description**
3973	Adapter RAM U38 error
3974	Adapter RAM U40 error
3975	Adapter RAM U31 error
3976	Adapter RAM U33 error
3977	Adapter RAM U35 error
3978	Adapter RAM U37 error
3979	Adapter RAM U39 error
3980	Graphics controller RAM timing error
3981	Graphics controller read/write latch error
3982	Shift register bus output latches error
3983	Addressing error (vertical column of memory; U2 at top)
3984	Addressing error (vertical column of memory; U4 at top)
3985	Addressing error (vertical column of memory; U6 at top)
3986	Addressing error (vertical column of memory; U8 at top)
3987	Addressing error (vertical column of memory; U10 at top)
3988	Base for error codes 3989-3991 (horizontal bank latch errors)
3989	Horizontal bank latch errors
3990	Horizontal bank latch errors
3991	Horizontal bank latch errors
3992	RAG/CAG graphics controller error
3993	Multiple write modes, nibble mask errors
3994	Row nibble (display RAM) error
3995	Graphics controller addressing error
44xx	5278 Display Attachment Unit and 5279 Display errors
45xx	IEEE Interface Adapter (IEEE-488) errors
46xx	A Real-Time Interface Coprocessor (ARTIC) Multiport/2 adapter errors
4611	ARTIC adapter error
4612	Memory module error
4613	Memory module error
4630	ARTIC adapter error
4640	Memory module error
4641	Memory module error
4650	ARTIC interface cable error
48xx	Internal Modem errors
49xx	Alternate Internal Modem errors
50xx	PC Convertible LCD errors
5001	LCD display buffer failure
5002	LCD font buffer failure
5003	LCD controller failure

Code	Description
5004	User indicated PEL/drive test failed
5008	User indicated display attribute test failed
5016	User indicated character set test failed
5020	User indicated alternate character set test failure
5024	User indicated 80x25 mode test failure
5032	User indicated 40x25 mode test failure
5040	User indicated 320x200 graphics test failure
5048	User indicated 640x200 graphics test failure
5064	User indicated paging test failure
51xx	PC Convertible Portable Printer errors
5101	Portable printer interface failure
5102	Portable printer busy error
5103	Portable printer paper or ribbon error
5104	Portable printer time-out
5105	User indicated print-pattern test error
56xx	Financial communication system errors
70xx	Phoenix BIOS/chipset unique error codes
7000	Chipset CMOS failure
7001	Chipset shadow RAM failure
7002	Chipset CMOS configuration error
71xx	Voice Communications Adapter (VCA) errors
7101	Adapter test failure
7102	Instruction or external data memory error
7103	PC to VCA interrupt error
7104	Internal data memory error
7105	Direct memory access (DMA) error
7106	Internal registers error
7107	Interactive shared memory error
7108	VCA to PC interrupt error
7109	DC wrap error
7111	External analog wrap and tone-output error
7112	Microphone to speaker wrap error
7114	Telephone attachment test failure
73xx	3 1/2-inch External Diskette Drive errors
7301	Diskette drive/adapter test failure
7306	Disk Changeline failure
7307	Diskette is write protected
7308	Drive command error
7310	Diskette initialization failure; track 0 bad

(continues)

Table A.21 Continued	
Code	**Description**
7311	Drive time-out error
7312	Controller chip (NEC) error
7313	Direct memory access (DMA) error
7314	Direct memory access (DMA) boundary overrun
7315	Drive index timing error
7316	Drive speed error
7321	Drive seek error
7322	Drive cyclic redundancy check (CRC) error
7323	Sector not found error
7324	Address mark error
7325	Controller chip (NEC) seek error
74xx	IBM PS/2 Display Adapter (VGA card) errors
74xx	8514/A Display Adapter errors
7426	8514 display error
7440	8514/A memory module 31 error
7441	8514/A memory module 30 error
7442	8514/A memory module 29 error
7443	8514/A memory module 28 error
7444	8514/A memory module 22 error
7445	8514/A memory module 21 error
7446	8514/A memory module 18 error
7447	8514/A memory module 17 error
7448	8514/A memory module 32 error
7449	8514/A memory module 14 error
7450	8514/A memory module 13 error
7451	8514/A memory module 12 error
7452	8514/A memory module 06 error
7453	8514/A memory module 05 error
7454	8514/A memory module 02 error
7455	8514/A memory module 01 error
7460	8514/A memory module 16 error
7461	8514/A memory module 27 error
7462	8514/A memory module 26 error
7463	8514/A memory module 25 error
7464	8514/A memory module 24 error
7465	8514/A memory module 23 error
7466	8514/A memory module 20 error
7467	8514/A memory module 19 error
7468	8514/A memory module 15 error

Code	Description
7469	8514/A memory module 11 error
7470	8514/A memory module 10 error
7471	8514/A memory module 09 error
7472	8514/A memory module 08 error
7473	8514/A memory module 07 error
7474	8514/A memory module 04 error
7475	8514/A memory module 03 error
76xx	4216 PagePrinter Adapter errors
7601	Adapter test failure
7602	Adapter error
7603	Printer error
7604	Printer cable error
84xx	PS/2 Speech Adapter errors
85xx	2MB XMA Memory Adapter or XMA Adapter/A errors
850x	Adapter error
851x	Adapter error
852x	Memory module error
8599	Unusable memory segment found
86xx	PS/2 Pointing Device (Mouse) errors
8601	Pointing device error; mouse time-out
8602	Pointing device error; mouse interface
8603	Pointing device or system-bus failure; mouse interrupt
8604	Pointing device or system-board error
8611	System bus error - I/F between 8042 and TrackPoint II
8612	TrackPoint II error
8613	System bus error or TrackPoint II error
89xx	Musical Instrument Digital Interface (MIDI) Adapter errors
91xx	IBM 3363 Write-Once Read Multiple (WORM) Optical Drive/Adapter errors
96xx	SCSI Adapter with Cache (32-bit) errors
100xx	Multiprotocol Adapter/A errors
10001	Presence test failure
10002	Card selected feedback error
10003	Port 102h register rest failure
10004	Port 103h register rest failure
10006	Serial option cannot be put to sleep
10007	Cable error
10008	Interrupt request (IRQ) 3 error
10009	Interrupt request (IRQ) 4 error
10010	16550 chip register failure

(continues)

Table A.21 Continued

Code	Description
10011	Internal wrap test of 16550 chip modem control line failure
10012	External wrap test of 16550 chip modem control line failure
10013	16550 chip transmit error
10014	16550 chip receive error
10015	16550 chip receive error; data not equal to transmit data
10016	16550 chip interrupt function error
10017	16550 chip baud rate test failure
10018	16550 chip receive external data wrap test failure
10019	16550 chip first-in first-out (FIFO) buffer failure
10026	8255 Port A error
10027	8255 Port B error
10028	8255 Port C error
10029	8254 timer 0 error
10030	8254 timer 1 error
10031	8254 timer 2 error
10032	Binary sync data set ready response to data terminal ready error
10033	Binary sync clear to send response to ready to send error
10034	8251 hardware reset test failed
10035	8251 function error
10036	8251 status error
10037	Binary sync timer interrupt error
10038	Binary sync transmit interrupt error
10039	Binary sync receive interrupt error
10040	Stray interrupt request (IRQ) 3 error
10041	Stray interrupt request (IRQ) 4 error
10042	Binary sync external wrap error
10044	Binary sync data wrap error
10045	Binary sync line status/condition error
10046	Binary sync time-out error during data wrap test
10050	8273 command acceptance or results ready time-out error
10051	8273 Port A error
10052	8273 Port B error
10053	SDLC modem status change logic error
10054	SDLC timer interrupt request (IRQ) 4 error
10055	SDLC modem status change interrupt request (IRQ) 4 error
10056	SDLC external wrap error
10057	SDLC interrupt results error
10058	SDLC data wrap error
10059	SDLC transmit interrupt error

Code	Description
10060	SDLC receive interrupt error
10061	Direct memory access (DMA) channel 1 transmit error
10062	Direct memory access (DMA) channel 1 receive error
10063	8273 status detect failure
10064	8273 error detect failure
101xx	300/1200bps Internal Modem/A
10101	Presence test failure
10102	Card selected feedback error
10103	Port 102h register test failure
10106	Serial option cannot be put to sleep
10108	Interrupt request (IRQ) 3 error
10109	Interrupt request (IRQ) 4 error
10110	16450 chip register failure
10111	Internal wrap test of 16450 modem control line failure
10113	16450 transmit error
10114	16450 receive error
10115	16450 receive error data not equal transmit data
10116	16450 interrupt function error
10117	16450 baud rate test failure
10118	16450 receive external data wrap test failure
10125	Modem reset result code error
10126	Modem general result code error
10127	Modem S registers write/read error
10128	Modem turn echo on/off error
10129	Modem enable/disable result codes error
10130	Modem enable number/word result codes error
10133	Connect results for 300 baud not received
10134	Connect results for 1200 baud not received
10135	Modem fails local analog loopback test at 300 baud
10136	Modem fails local analog loopback test at 1200 baud
10137	Modem does not respond to escape/reset sequence
10138	S-Register 13 does not show correct parity or number of data bits
10139	S-Register 15 does not reflect correct bit rate
104xx	ESDI or MCA IDE Fixed Disk or Adapter errors
10450	Read/write test failed
10451	Read verify test failed
10452	Seek test failed
10453	Wrong drive type indicated
10454	Controller sector buffer test failure

(continues)

Table A.21 Continued	
Code	**Description**
10455	Controller invalid failure
10456	Controller diagnostic command failure
10461	Drive format error
10462	Controller head select error
10463	Drive read/write sector error
10464	Drive primary defect map unreadable
10465	Controller; error-correction code (ECC) 8-bit error
10466	Controller; error-correction code (ECC) 9-bit error
10467	Drive soft seek error
10468	Drive hard seek error
10469	Drive soft error count exceeded
10470	Controller attachment diagnostic error
10471	Controller wrap mode interface error
10472	Controller wrap mode drive select error
10473	Read verify test errors
10480	Seek failure; drive 0
10481	Seek failure; drive 1
10482	Controller transfer acknowledge error
10483	Controller reset failure
10484	Controller; head select 3 error
10485	Controller; head select 2 error
10486	Controller; head select 1 error
10487	Controller; head select 0 error
10488	Controller; read gate - command complete 2 error
10489	Controller; write gate - command complete 1 error
10490	Diagnostic area read error; drive 0
10491	Diagnostic area read error; drive 1
10492	Controller error, drive 1
10493	Reset error, drive 1
10499	Controller failure
107xx	5 1/4-inch External Diskette Drive or Adapter errors
112xx	SCSI Adapter (16-bit without Cache) errors
113xx	System Board SCSI Adapter (16-bit) errors
129xx	Processor Complex (CPU Board) errors
129005	DMA error
12901	Processor board; processor test failed
12902	Processor board; cache test failed
12904	Second level cache failure
12905	Cache enable/disable errors

Code	Description
12907	Cache fatal error
12908	Cache POST program error
12912x	Hardware failure
12913x	Micro channel bus timeout
12914x	Software failure
12915x	Processor complex error
12916x	Processor complex error
12917x	Processor complex error
12918x	Processor complex error
12919x	Processor complex error
12940x	Processor complex failure
12950x	Processor complex failure
129900	Processor complex serial-number mismatch
149xx	P70/P75 Plasma Display and Adapter errors
14901	Plasma Display Adapter failure
14902	Plasma Display Adapter failure
14922	Plasma display failure
14932	External display failure
152xx	XGA Display Adapter/A errors
164xx	120M Internal Tape Drive errors
165xx	6157 Streaming Tape Drive or Tape Attachment Adapter errors
16520	Streaming tape drive failure
16540	Tape attachment adapter failure
166xx	Primary Token Ring Network Adapter errors
167xx	Alternate Token Ring Network Adapter errors
180xx	PS/2 Wizard Adapter errors
18001	Interrupt controller failure
18002	Incorrect timer count
18003	Timer interrupt failure
18004	Sync check interrupt failure
18005	Parity check interrupt failure
18006	Access error interrupt failure
18012	Bad checksum error
18013	Micro Channel interface error
18021	Wizard memory compare or parity error
18022	Wizard memory address line error
18023	Dynamic RAM controller failure
18029	Wizard memory byte enable error
18031	Wizard memory-expansion module memory compare or parity error

(continues)

Table A.21 Continued

Code	Description
18032	Wizard memory-expansion module address line error
18039	Wizard memory-expansion module byte enable error
185xx	DBCS Japanese Display Adapter/A errors
194xx	80286 Memory-Expansion Option Memory-Module errors
200xx	Image Adapter/A errors
208xx	Unknown SCSI Device errors
209xx	SCSI Removable Disk errors
210xx	SCSI Fixed Disk errors
210PLSC	PLSC codes indicate errors P = SCSI ID number (Physical Unit Number or PUN) L = Logical unit number (LUN, usually 0) S = Host Adapter slot number C = SCSI Drive capacity: A = 60M B = 80M C = 120M D = 160M E = 320M F = 400M H = 1,024M (1G) I = 104M J = 212M U = Undetermined or Non-IBM OEM Drive
211xx	SCSI Tape Drive errors
212xx	SCSI Printer errors
213xx	SCSI Processor errors
214xx	SCSI Write-Once Read Multiple (WORM) Drive errors
215xx	SCSI CD-ROM Drive errors
216xx	SCSI Scanner errors
217xx	SCSI Magneto Optical Drive errors
218xx	SCSI Jukebox Changer errors
219xx	SCSI Communications errors
243xxxx	XGA-2 Adapter/A errors
I998xxxx	Dynamic Configuration Select (DCS) information codes
I998001x	Bad integrity of DCS master boot record
I988002x	Read failure of DCS master boot record
I988003x	DCS master boot record is not compatible with the planar ID
I988004x	DCS master boot record is not compatible with the model/submodel byte
I988005x	Bad integrity of CMOS/NVRAM (or internal process error)
I988006x	Read failure of header/mask/configuration record
I988007x	Bad integrity of header/mask/configuration record
I988008x	Hard disk does not support the command to set the maximum RBA
I988009x	DCS master boot record is older than system ROM

Code	Description
I9880402	Copyright notice in E000 segment does not match the one in DCS MBR
I9880403	DCS MBR is not compatible with the system board ID or model/submodel byte
I99900xx	Initial Microcode Load (IML) error
I999001x	Invalid disk IML record
I999002x	Disk IML record load error
I999003x	Disk IML record incompatible with system board
I999004x	Disk IML record incompatible with processor/processor card
I999005x	Disk IML not attempted
I999006x	Disk stage II System Image load error
I999007x	Disk stage II image checksum error
I999008x	IML not supported on priamry disk drive
I999009x	Disk IML record is older than ROM
I99900x1	Invalid diskette IML record
I99900x2	Diskette IML record load error
I99900x3	Diskette IML record incompatible with system board
I99900x4	Diskette IML record incompatible with processor card
I99900x5	Diskette IML recovery prevented (valid password and CE override not set)
I99900x6	Diskette stage II image load error
I99900x7	Diskette stage II image checksum error
I99900x9	Diskette IML record older than ROM
I99903xx	No bootable device, Initial Program Load (IPL) errors
I9990302	Invalid disk boot record, unable to read IPL boot record from disk.
I9990303	IML System Partition boot failure
I9990304	No bootable device with ASCII console
I9990305	No bootable media found
I9990306	Invalid SCSI Device boot record
I99904xx	IML-to-System mismatch
I9990401	Unauthorized access (manufacturing boot request with valid password)
I9990402	Missing ROM IBM Copyright notice
I9990403	IML Boot Record incompatible with system board/processor card.
I99906xx	IML errors

IBM SCSI Error Codes

With the new IBM SCSI adapter and SCSI devices comes a new set of error codes. This section contains tables describing all the known IBM SCSI Power-On Self Test (POST) and advanced diagnostics error codes. These codes can be used to determine the meaning of errors that occur on the IBM SCSI adapters and any attached SCSI devices. The error codes that occur during POST and diagnostics tests have the format shown in figure A.5.

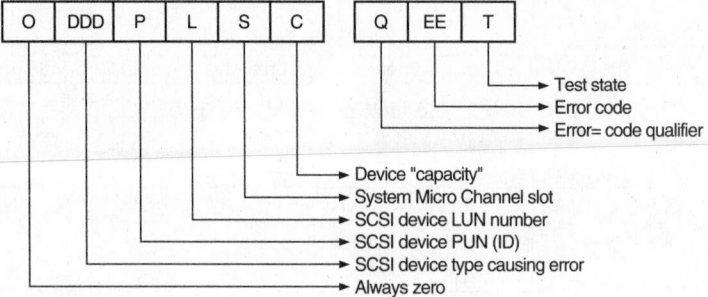

Fig. A.5

IBM SCSI POST and diagnostics error code format.

This section shows what each part of the error code indicates.

The DDD field in figure A.5 indicates the SCSI device causing the error. Table A.22 shows the device codes.

The P field indicates the SCSI device physical unit number (PUN) or SCSI ID. This value is between 0 and 7, with the host adapter normally set to 7 and the first (bootable) SCSI hard disk set to 6.

The L field indicates the SCSI device logical unit number (LUN). For most SCSI devices it is 0 because normally there is only a single LUN per physical unit or SCSI ID.

The S field indicates the system Micro Channel Architecture (MCA) slot number containing the SCSI host adapter to which the device in error is connected. If S equals 0, the error is an adapter initialization error (there is no MCA slot 0). In this case, the DDD number is 096, 112, or 113, and you must use the following adapter initialization error chart to determine the error. The specific errors in this chart are indicated by the value in the L field, which immediately precedes the S field. In this case, the L does *not* represent the logical unit number (as it normally does), but instead shows a specific initialization error for the adapter. If S is not equal to 0, no error is on the adapter (or device attached to the adapter) in slot S. You can determine these standard errors by using the rest of the tables in this section.

The C field indicates the capacity of the device originating the error code. In the case of error codes from a device with no capacity (such as a SCSI adapter or printer), this field is 0.

Table A.22 SCSI Device Error Codes	
DDDxxxx xxxx	**Error**
096xxxx xxxx	32-bit cached SCSI host adapter
112xxxx xxxx	16-bit non-cached SCSI host adapter
113xxxx xxxx	System board SCSI host adapter
208xxxx xxxx	Unknown SCSI device type
209xxxx xxxx	Direct access (disk) device with removable media and/or other than 512 byte blocks

DDDxxxx xxxx	Error
210xxxx xxxx	Direct access (disk) device with nonremovable media and 512 byte blocks (hard disk)
211xxxx xxxx	Sequential access device (magnetic tape)
212xxxx xxxx	Printer device
213xxxx xxxx	Processor device (host to host)
214xxxx xxxx	Write-Once, Read Multiple device (optical WORM drive)
215xxxx xxxx	Read-only device (CD-ROM drive)
216xxxx xxxx	Scanner device
217xxxx xxxx	Optical memory device (optical drive)
218xxxx xxxx	Media changer device (multiple tray CD-ROM or jukebox)
219xxxx xxxx	Communications device (LAN bridge)
DDD0LS0 0000	SCSI adapter initialization errors, where S = 0
DDD0100 0000	No extended CMOS setup data available. On systems with Non-Volatile RAM (NVRAM), this means that SCSI setup data was not located or the checksum did not verify. On systems without NVRAM (Model 50, for example), the setup data must be on the first non-SCSI fixed disk.
DDD0200 0000	No hard disk at PUN 6, LUN 0. (Also expect to see 161, 162, or 165 errors.)
DDD0300 0000	No space available in extended BIOS data area for SCSI data table
DDD0400 0000	ROM modules not found on SCSI adapter
DDD0500 0000	ROM checksum error in the second 16K portion of 32K SCSI adapter ROM space

A value of x *indicates any number or character.*

Table A.23 SCSI Device Capacity Codes

DDDxxxC xxxx	SCSI device capacity
DDDxxx0 xxxx	Not a storage device
DDDxxxA xxxx	60M
DDDxxxB xxxx	80M
DDDxxxC xxxx	120M
DDDxxxD xxxx	160M
DDDxxxE xxxx	320M
DDDxxxF xxxx	400M
DDDxxxH xxxx	1,024M (1G)
DDDxxxI xxxx	104M
DDDxxxJ xxxx	212M
DDDxxxU xxxx	Undetermined Device Capacity or Non-IBM OEM Drive

The Q field is the error code (EE field) qualifier. Q can have a value from 0 through 7. Depending on the value of Q, the error codes take on different meanings, because Q indicates what class of error occurred or what part of the SCSI system the error is coming from. To determine the error code meaning, use one of the following tables that correspond to the value of Q you have.

The Q value defines the origin of the EE code reported. Error codes with Q = 0 or 1 are generated by the SCSI host adapter, and all error codes with Q greater than 1 are developed using information returned by the adapter or a SCSI device. If Q = 2, the EE code indicates the value returned in the Command Error field (word 8, bits 15-8) of the SCSI Command Complete Status Block (CCSB) for values indicating hardware problems (codes of 20h or greater). If Q = 3, then EE also indicates the value returned in the Command Error field (word 8, bits 15-8) of the Command Complete Status Block (CCSB), but for values indicating software problems (codes less than 20h). If Q = 4, then EE indicates the value returned in the Sense Key field (byte 2, bits 3-0) of a Sense Data Block returned to the SCSI host adapter by a device following a SCSI Request Sense command. If Q = 5, then EE indicates the value returned in the Additional Sense Code field (byte 12) of a Sense Data Block returned by a Direct Access (Disk) device following a SCSI Request Sense command. If Q = 6, then EE indicates the value returned in the Device Error Code field (word 8, bits 7-0) of the Command Complete Status Block (CCSB). If Q = 7, a device error has occurred that normally would not be considered an error, but is now considered an error based on when the code was returned—for example, a Medium Corrupted error from a device with nonremovable media.

Although IBM has a unique format for displaying SCSI error codes, almost all except the adapter-specific errors are part of the SCSI specification. Because many of these codes come from the devices attached to the SCSI bus and not the host adapter, a new code not listed here possibly could appear because some errors can be dependent on the particular device, and some devices send manufacturer-specific errors. You then can look up the error code in the manufacturers documentation for the device to determine the meaning. The tables in this section are standard as defined in the SCSI Common Command Set (CCS) of the ANSI SCSI-1 specification. Further information is in the IBM hardware-maintenance and service manual for the IBM SCSI adapter and the various SCSI devices.

Table A.24 SCSI Host Adapter Error Codes with Q = 0	
DDDxxxx QEEx	**Error code**
96xxxx 001x	80188 ROM test failure
96xxxx 002x	Local RAM test failure
96xxxx 003x	Power protection error (terminator or fuse)
96xxxx 004x	80188 internal peripheral test failure
96xxxx 005x	Buffer control chip test failure
96xxxx 006x	Buffer RAM test failure
96xxxx 007x	System interface control chip test failure

DDDxxxx QEEx	Error code
96xxxx 008x	SCSI interface test failure
112xxxx 001x	8032 ROM test failure
112xxxx 002x	Local RAM test failure
112xxxx 003x	Power protection device error (terminator or fuse)
112xxxx 004x	8032 internal peripheral test failure
112xxxx 005x	Buffer control chip test failure
112xxxx 006x	Undefined error condition
112xxxx 007x	System interface control chip test failure
112xxxx 008x	SCSI interface test failure
113xxxx 001x	Microprocessor ROM test failure
113xxxx 002x	Local RAM test failure
113xxxx 003x	Power protection device error (terminator or fuse)
113xxxx 004x	Microprocessor internal peripheral test failure
113xxxx 005x	Buffer control chip test failure
113xxxx 006x	Undefined error condition
113xxxx 007x	System interface control chip test failure
113xxxx 008x	SCSI interface test failure

Table A.25 SCSI Adapter Error Codes with Q = 1

DDDxxxx QEEx	Error code
DDDxxxx 107x	Adapter hardware failure
DDDxxxx 10Cx	Command completed with failure
DDDxxxx 10Ex	Command error (invalid command or parameter)
DDDxxxx 10Fx	Software sequencing error
DDDxxxx 180x	Time out
DDDxxxx 181x	Adapter busy error
DDDxxxx 182x	Unexpected interrupt presented by adapter
DDDxxxx 183x	Adapter register test failure
DDDxxxx 184x	Adapter reset (via basic control register) failure
DDDxxxx 185x	Adapter buffer test failure (cached adapter only)
DDDxxxx 186x	Adapter reset count expired
DDDxxxx 187x	Adapter registers not cleared on reset (power-on or channel reset)
DDDxxxx 188x	Card ID in adapter microcode did not match ID in POS registers
DDDxxxx 190x	Expected device did not respond (target device not powered on)
DDDxxxx 190x	DMA arbitration level conflict (if device number is 096, 112, or 113)

Table A.26 SCSI Hardware Error Codes with Q = 2

DDDxxxx QEEx	Error code
DDDxxxx 220x	Adapter hardware error
DDDxxxx 221x	Global command time-out on adapter (device did not respond)
DDDxxxx 222x	Adapter DMA error
DDDxxxx 223x	Adapter buffer defective
DDDxxxx 224x	Command aborted by adapter
DDDxxxx 280x	Adapter microprocessor detected error

Table A.27 SCSI Software Error Codes with Q = 3

DDDxxxx QEEx	Error code
DDDxxxx 301x	Invalid parameter in subsystem control block
DDDxxxx 302x	Reserved
DDDxxxx 303x	Command not supported
DDDxxxx 304x	Command aborted by system
DDDxxxx 305x	Command rejected (buffer not disabled)
DDDxxxx 306x	Command rejected (adapter diagnostic failure)
DDDxxxx 307x	Format rejected (sequence error)
DDDxxxx 308x	Assign rejected (command in progress on device)
DDDxxxx 309x	Assign rejected (device already assigned)
DDDxxxx 30Ax	Command rejected (device not assigned)
DDDxxxx 30Bx	Maximum logical block address exceeded
DDDxxxx 30Cx	16-bit card slot address range exceeded
DDDxxxx 313x	Invalid device for command
DDDxxxx 3FFx	Status not returned by adapter

Table A.28 SCSI Device Sense Key Error Codes with Q = 4

DDDxxxx QEEx	Error code
DDDxxxx 401x	Recovered error (not considered an error condition)
DDDxxxx 402x	Device not ready
DDDxxxx 403x	Device media error
DDDxxxx 404x	Device hardware error
DDDxxxx 405x	Illegal request for device
DDDxxxx 406x	Device unit attention would not clear
DDDxxxx 407x	Device data protect error
DDDxxxx 408x	Device blank check error
DDDxxxx 409x	Device vendor unique error
DDDxxxx 40Ax	Device copy aborted

DDDxxxx QEEx	Error code
DDDxxxx 40Bx	Command aborted by device
DDDxxxx 40Cx	Device search data command satisfied
DDDxxxx 40Dx	Device volume overflow (residual data still in buffer)
DDDxxxx 40Ex	Device miscompare (source and medium data don't match)
DDDxxxx 40Fx	Reserved

Table A.29 SCSI Device Extended Sense Error Codes with Q = 5

DDDxxxx QEEx	Error code
DDDxxxx 501x	No index or sector signal
DDDxxxx 502x	Seek incomplete
DDDxxxx 503x	Write fault
DDDxxxx 504x	Drive not ready
DDDxxxx 505x	Drive not selected
DDDxxxx 506x	No track 0 found
DDDxxxx 507x	Multiple drives selected
DDDxxxx 508x	Logical unit communication failure
DDDxxxx 509x	Head positioning error (track following error)
DDDxxxx 50Ax	Error log overflow
DDDxxxx 50Cx	Write error
DDDxxxx 510x	CRC or ECC error on ID field
DDDxxxx 511x	Unrecoverable read error
DDDxxxx 512x	Address mark not found for ID field
DDDxxxx 513x	Address mark not found for data field
DDDxxxx 514x	Record not found
DDDxxxx 515x	Seek error
DDDxxxx 516x	Data synchronization mark error
DDDxxxx 517x	Recovered read data with retries (without ECC)
DDDxxxx 518x	Recovered read data with ECC correction
DDDxxxx 519x	Defect list error
DDDxxxx 51Ax	Parameter list length overrun
DDDxxxx 51Bx	Synchronous data transfer error
DDDxxxx 51Cx	Primary defect list not found
DDDxxxx 51Dx	Data miscompare during verify
DDDxxxx 51Ex	Recovered ID read with ECC correction
DDDxxxx 520x	Invalid command operation code
DDDxxxx 521x	Illegal logical block address (out of range)
DDDxxxx 522x	Illegal function for device type
DDDxxxx 524x	Invalid field in command descriptor block

(continues)

Table A.29 Continued

DDDxxxx QEEx	Error code
DDDxxxx 525x	Invalid logical unit number (LUN not supported)
DDDxxxx 526x	Invalid field in parameter list
DDDxxxx 527x	Media write protected
DDDxxxx 528x	Media changed error (ready went true)
DDDxxxx 529x	Power-on or bus device reset occurred (not an error)
DDDxxxx 52Ax	Mode select parameters changed (not an error)
DDDxxxx 52Bx	Copy command can't execute because host can't disconnect
DDDxxxx 52Cx	Command sequence error
DDDxxxx 52Fx	Tagged commands cleared by another initiator
DDDxxxx 530x	Incompatible media (unknown or incompatible format)
DDDxxxx 531x	Medium format corrupted
DDDxxxx 532x	Defect spare location unavailable
DDDxxxx 537x	Rounded parameter error
DDDxxxx 539x	Saving parameters not supported
DDDxxxx 53Ax	Media not present
DDDxxxx 53Cx	Link flag bit not supported
DDDxxxx 53Dx	Invalid bits in identify message
DDDxxxx 53Ex	Logical unit has not self-configured
DDDxxxx 53Fx	Target operating conditions have changed
DDDxxxx 540x	Device RAM failure
DDDxxxx 541x	Data path diagnostic failure
DDDxxxx 542x	Device power-on diagnostic failure
DDDxxxx 543x	Device message rejected
DDDxxxx 544x	Target device internal controller error
DDDxxxx 545x	Select/reselect failure (device unable to reconnect)
DDDxxxx 546x	Device soft reset unsuccessful
DDDxxxx 547x	SCSI interface parity error
DDDxxxx 548x	Initiator detected error
DDDxxxx 549x	Illegal command or command out of sequence error
DDDxxxx 54Ax	SCSI command phase error
DDDxxxx 54Bx	SCSI data phase error
DDDxxxx 54Cx	Logical unit failed self-configuration
DDDxxxx 54Ex	Overlapped commands attempted
DDDxxxx 560x	Status error from second-party copy command
DDDxxxx 588x	Not digital audio track
DDDxxxx 589x	Not CD-ROM data track
DDDxxxx 58Ax	Drive not in play audio state
DDDxxxx 5F0x	Format in progress (not an error)
DDDxxxx 5F1x	Spinup in progress

Table A.30 SCSI Command Complete Status Block Errors with Q = 6

DDDxxxx QEEx	Error
DDDxxxx 601x	SCSI bus reset occurred
DDDxxxx 602x	SCSI interface fault
DDDxxxx 610x	SCSI selection time-out (device not available)
DDDxxxx 611x	Unexpected SCSI bus free
DDDxxxx 612x	Mandatory SCSI message rejected
DDDxxxx 613x	Invalid SCSI phase sequence
DDDxxxx 620x	Short length record error

Table A.31 SCSI Device Condition Error Codes with Q = 7

DDDxxxx QEEx	Error code
DDDxxxx 702x	Device not ready (removable media devices)
DDDxxxx 704x	Device not ready (nonremovable media devices)
DDDxxxx 728x	Media changed error would not clear
DDDxxxx 731x	Medium format corrupted (format unit interrupted—reissue format)
DDDxxxx 7F0x	Format in progress (prior format unit command being completed)
DDDxxxx 7F1x	Spinup in progress

Table A.32 shows the diagnostics test state codes used when a failure occurs. Position *T* indicates the POST *or* diagnostics test state in which the failure occurred.

Table A.32 SCSI Diagnostics Test State Codes

DDDxxxx xxxT	Test state code
DDDxxxx xxx0	Not applicable for error code
DDDxxxx xxxA	Adapter initialization
DDDxxxx xxxB	Adapter reset
DDDxxxx xxxC	Adapter register test
DDDxxxx xxxD	Adapter buffer test Phase 1 (cached adapter only)
DDDxxxx xxxE	Adapter buffer test Phase 2 (cached adapter only)
DDDxxxx xxxF	Adapter buffer test Phase 3 (cached adapter only)
DDDxxxx xxxG	Adapter buffer test Phase 4 (cached adapter only)
DDDxxxx xxxH	Adapter information test state (buffer enable/size, retry enable, etc.)
DDDxxxx xxxI	Device assignment sequence
DDDxxxx xxxJ	Device not ready (also initial unit attention clearing)
DDDxxxx xxxK	Device reset
DDDxxxx xxxL	Device starting phase (appropriate devices only)
DDDxxxx xxxM	Device in process of starting (wait for device to become ready)

(continues)

Table A.32 SCSI Diagnostics Test State Codes	
DDDxxxx xxxT	**Test state code**
DDDxxxx xxxN	Device block size determination
DDDxxxx xxxO	Device self test
DDDxxxx xxxP	Device single block (logical block address) read
DDDxxxx xxxQ	Device double block (logical block address) read
DDDxxxx xxxS	Error occurred after device testing had completed

System Memory Maps

The following maps show where memory is located logically within a system. The first map shows the processor-addressable memory in real mode. The second map shows processor-addressable memory in protected mode. The third map shows how expanded memory fits into the reserved space between 640K and 1M, and how it is not directly addressable by the processor. Expanded memory can be addressed only a small piece (*page*) at a time through a small window of memory. These maps can be useful for mapping out the logical locations of any adapter in your system. All memory locations must be uniquely supplied by a single device; the potential for conflicts does exist if two devices are mapped into the same logical locations.

1-M Conventional Memory Map Template. The following map shows the logical address locations for an Intel processor running in real mode. In this mode, the processor can see only 1 megabyte of memory, which is mapped in the following way.

. = Program-accessible memory (standard RAM)

v = Video RAM

a = Adapter board ROM and special-purpose RAM

r = Motherboard ROM BIOS

b = IBM Cassette BASIC (would be "r" in compatibles)

h = High memory area (HMA)

Conventional (base) memory

```
        : 0---1---2---3---4---5---6---7---8---9---A---B---C---D---E---F---
000000: ................................................................
010000: ................................................................
020000: ................................................................
030000: ................................................................
040000: ................................................................
050000: ................................................................
060000: ................................................................
070000: ................................................................
080000: ................................................................
090000: ................................................................
```

Upper memory area (UMA)

```
0A0000: vvvvvvvvvvvvvvvvvvvvvvvvvvvvvvvvvvvvvvvvvvvvvvvvvvvvvvvvvvvvvvvv
0B0000: vvvvvvvvvvvvvvvvvvvvvvvvvvvvvvvvvvvvvvvvvvvvvvvvvvvvvvvvvvvvvvvv
0C0000: aaaaaaaaaaaaaaaaaaaaaaaaaaaaaaaaaaaaaaaaaaaaaaaaaaaaaaaaaaaaaaaa
0D0000: aaaaaaaaaaaaaaaaaaaaaaaaaaaaaaaaaaaaaaaaaaaaaaaaaaaaaaaaaaaaaaaa
0E0000: rrrrrrrrrrrrrrrrrrrrrrrrrrrrrrrrrrrrrrrrrrrrrrrrrrrrrrrrrrrrrrrr
0F0000: rrrrrrrrrrrrrrrrrrrrrrrrbbbbbbbbbbbbbbbbbbbbbbbbbbbbbrrrrrrrrr
```

Extended memory

```
      : 0---1---2---3---4---5---6---7---8---9---A---B---C---D---E---F---
100000: hhhhhhhhhhhhhhhhhhhhhhhhhhhhhhhhhhhhhhhhhhhhhhhhhhhhhhhhhhhhhhhh
```

Note that because the first 64K of extended memory is acessable in real mode, a system with a 286 or better processor can access the high memory area (HMA).

16-M Conventional and Extended Memory Map Template. The following map shows the logical address locations for an Intel processor running in protected mode. In this mode, the processor can see a full 16 megabytes of memory, which is mapped in the following way.

. = Program-accessible memory (standard RAM)

v = Video RAM

a = Adapter board ROM and special-purpose RAM

r = Motherboard ROM BIOS

b = IBM Cassette BASIC (would be "r" in compatibles)

h = High memory area (HMA)

Conventional (base) memory:

```
      : 0---1---2---3---4---5---6---7---8---9---A---B---C---D---E---F---
000000: ..............................................................
010000: ..............................................................
020000: ..............................................................
030000: ..............................................................
040000: ..............................................................
050000: ..............................................................
060000: ..............................................................
070000: ..............................................................
080000: ..............................................................
090000: ..............................................................
```

Upper memory area (UMA)

```
0A0000: vvvvvvvvvvvvvvvvvvvvvvvvvvvvvvvvvvvvvvvvvvvvvvvvvvvvvvvvvvvvvvvv
0B0000: vvvvvvvvvvvvvvvvvvvvvvvvvvvvvvvvvvvvvvvvvvvvvvvvvvvvvvvvvvvvvvvv
0C0000: aaaaaaaaaaaaaaaaaaaaaaaaaaaaaaaaaaaaaaaaaaaaaaaaaaaaaaaaaaaaaaaa
0D0000: aaaaaaaaaaaaaaaaaaaaaaaaaaaaaaaaaaaaaaaaaaaaaaaaaaaaaaaaaaaaaaaa
0E0000: rrrrrrrrrrrrrrrrrrrrrrrrrrrrrrrrrrrrrrrrrrrrrrrrrrrrrrrrrrrrrrrr
0F0000: rrrrrrrrrrrrrrrrrrrrrrrrbbbbbbbbbbbbbbbbbbbbbbbbbbbbbrrrrrrrrr
```

Extended memory

```
         : 0---1---2---3---4---5---6---7---8---9---A---B---C---D---E---F---
  100000: hhhhhhhhhhhhhhhhhhhhhhhhhhhhhhhhhhhhhhhhhhhhhhhhhhhhhhhhhhhhhhhh
```

XMS extended memory

```
  110000: ..............................................................
  120000: ..............................................................
  130000: ..............................................................
  140000: ..............................................................
  150000: ..............................................................
  160000: ..............................................................
  170000: ..............................................................
  180000: ..............................................................
  190000: ..............................................................
  1A0000: ..............................................................
  1B0000: ..............................................................
  1C0000: ..............................................................
  1D0000: ..............................................................
  1E0000: ..............................................................
  1F0000: ..............................................................
         : 0---1---2---3---4---5---6---7---8---9---A---B---C---D---E---F---
  200000: ..............................................................
  210000: ..............................................................
  220000: ..............................................................
  230000: ..............................................................
  240000: ..............................................................
  250000: ..............................................................
  260000: ..............................................................
  270000: ..............................................................
  280000: ..............................................................
  290000: ..............................................................
  2A0000: ..............................................................
  2B0000: ..............................................................
  2C0000: ..............................................................
  2D0000: ..............................................................
  2E0000: ..............................................................
  2F0000: ..............................................................
         : 0---1---2---3---4---5---6---7---8---9---A---B---C---D---E---F---
  300000: ..............................................................
  310000: ..............................................................
  320000: ..............................................................
  330000: ..............................................................
  340000: ..............................................................
  350000: ..............................................................
  360000: ..............................................................
  370000: ..............................................................
  380000: ..............................................................
  390000: ..............................................................
  3A0000: ..............................................................
  3B0000: ..............................................................
  3C0000: ..............................................................
  3D0000: ..............................................................
  3E0000: ..............................................................
  3F0000: ..............................................................
```

```
        : 0---1---2---3---4---5---6---7---8---9---A---B---C---D---E---F---
400000: ................................................................
410000: ................................................................
420000: ................................................................
430000: ................................................................
440000: ................................................................
450000: ................................................................
460000: ................................................................
470000: ................................................................
480000: ................................................................
490000: ................................................................
4A0000: ................................................................
4B0000: ................................................................
4C0000: ................................................................
4D0000: ................................................................
4E0000: ................................................................
4F0000: ................................................................
        : 0---1---2---3---4---5---6---7---8---9---A---B---C---D---E---F---
500000: ................................................................
510000: ................................................................
520000: ................................................................
530000: ................................................................
540000: ................................................................
550000: ................................................................
560000: ................................................................
570000: ................................................................
580000: ................................................................
590000: ................................................................
5A0000: ................................................................
5B0000: ................................................................
5C0000: ................................................................
5D0000: ................................................................
5E0000: ................................................................
5F0000: ................................................................
        : 0---1---2---3---4---5---6---7---8---9---A---B---C---D---E---F---
600000: ................................................................
610000: ................................................................
620000: ................................................................
630000: ................................................................
640000: ................................................................
650000: ................................................................
660000: ................................................................
670000: ................................................................
680000: ................................................................
690000: ................................................................
6A0000: ................................................................
6B0000: ................................................................
6C0000: ................................................................
6D0000: ................................................................
6E0000: ................................................................
6F0000: ................................................................
        : 0---1---2---3---4---5---6---7---8---9---A---B---C---D---E---F---
700000: ................................................................
710000: ................................................................
720000: ................................................................
730000: ................................................................
740000: ................................................................
```

```
750000: ................................................................
760000: ................................................................
770000: ................................................................
780000: ................................................................
790000: ................................................................
7A0000: ................................................................
7B0000: ................................................................
7C0000: ................................................................
7D0000: ................................................................
7E0000: ................................................................
7F0000: ................................................................
      : 0---1---2---3---4---5---6---7---8---9---A---B---C---D---E---F---
800000: ................................................................
810000: ................................................................
820000: ................................................................
830000: ................................................................
840000: ................................................................
850000: ................................................................
860000: ................................................................
870000: ................................................................
880000: ................................................................
890000: ................................................................
8A0000: ................................................................
8B0000: ................................................................
8C0000: ................................................................
8D0000: ................................................................
8E0000: ................................................................
8F0000: ................................................................
      : 0---1---2---3---4---5---6---7---8---9---A---B---C---D---E---F---
900000: ................................................................
910000: ................................................................
920000: ................................................................
930000: ................................................................
940000: ................................................................
950000: ................................................................
960000: ................................................................
970000: ................................................................
980000: ................................................................
990000: ................................................................
9A0000: ................................................................
9B0000: ................................................................
9C0000: ................................................................
9D0000: ................................................................
9E0000: ................................................................
9F0000: ................................................................
      : 0---1---2---3---4---5---6---7---8---9---A---B---C---D---E---F---
A00000: ................................................................
A10000: ................................................................
A20000: ................................................................
A30000: ................................................................
A40000: ................................................................
A50000: ................................................................
A60000: ................................................................
A70000: ................................................................
A80000: ................................................................
A90000: ................................................................
AA0000: ................................................................
```

```
AB0000: ................................................................
AC0000: ................................................................
AD0000: ................................................................
AE0000: ................................................................
AF0000: ................................................................
      : 0---1---2---3---4---5---6---7---8---9---A---B---C---D---E---F---
B00000: ................................................................
B10000: ................................................................
B20000: ................................................................
B30000: ................................................................
B40000: ................................................................
B50000: ................................................................
B60000: ................................................................
B70000: ................................................................
B80000: ................................................................
B90000: ................................................................
BA0000: ................................................................
BB0000: ................................................................
BC0000: ................................................................
BD0000: ................................................................
BE0000: ................................................................
BF0000: ................................................................
      : 0---1---2---3---4---5---6---7---8---9---A---B---C---D---E---F---
C00000: ................................................................
C10000: ................................................................
C20000: ................................................................
C30000: ................................................................
C40000: ................................................................
C50000: ................................................................
C60000: ................................................................
C70000: ................................................................
C80000: ................................................................
C90000: ................................................................
CA0000: ................................................................
CB0000: ................................................................
CC0000: ................................................................
CD0000: ................................................................
CE0000: ................................................................
CF0000: ................................................................
      : 0---1---2---3---4---5---6---7---8---9---A---B---C---D---E---F---
D00000: ................................................................
D10000: ................................................................
D20000: ................................................................
D30000: ................................................................
D40000: ................................................................
D50000: ................................................................
D60000: ................................................................
D70000: ................................................................
D80000: ................................................................
D90000: ................................................................
DA0000: ................................................................
DB0000: ................................................................
DC0000: ................................................................
DD0000: ................................................................
DE0000: ................................................................
DF0000: ................................................................
```

```
            : 0---1---2---3---4---5---6---7---8---9---A---B---C---D---E---F---
    E00000: ................................................................
    E10000: ................................................................
    E20000: ................................................................
    E30000: ................................................................
    E40000: ................................................................
    E50000: ................................................................
    E60000: ................................................................
    E70000: ................................................................
    E80000: ................................................................
    E90000: ................................................................
    EA0000: ................................................................
    EB0000: ................................................................
    EC0000: ................................................................
    ED0000: ................................................................
    EE0000: ................................................................
    EF0000: ................................................................
            : 0---1---2---3---4---5---6---7---8---9---A---B---C---D---E---F---
    F00000: ................................................................
    F10000: ................................................................
    F20000: ................................................................
    F30000: ................................................................
    F40000: ................................................................
    F50000: ................................................................
    F60000: ................................................................
    F70000: ................................................................
    F80000: ................................................................
    F90000: ................................................................
    FA0000: ................................................................
    FB0000: ................................................................
    FC0000: ................................................................
    FD0000: ................................................................
    FE0000: rrrrrrrrrrrrrrrrrrrrrrrrrrrrrrrrrrrrrrrrrrrrrrrrrrrrrrrrrrrrrrrr
    FF0000: rrrrrrrrrrrrrrrrrrrrrrrrbbbbbbbbbbbbbbbbbbbbbbbbbbbbbbbbrrrrrrrr
```

The motherboard ROM BIOS has a duplicated address space that makes it appear both at the end of the 1M real mode space and at the end of the 16M or 4,096M protected mode space.

The addresses from 0E0000-0FFFFF are equal to FE0000-FFFFFF. This is necessary because of differences in the memory addressing during the shift between real and protected modes.

Expanded Memory. The map in figure A.6 shows how expanded memory fits with conventional and extended memory.

Hardware and ROM BIOS Data

This section has an enormous amount of detailed reference information covering a variety of hardware and ROM BIOS topics. These figures and tables cover very useful information, such as IBM PC and XT mother-board switch settings AT CMOS RAM addresses, and diagnostic status-byte information. This section also has a variety of other hardware information, such as BIOS version data, keyboard scan codes, and a great deal of information about the expansion buses—pinouts, resources such as interrupts, DMA channels, and I/O port addresses. Finally, this section has a number of connector pinouts for serial, parallel, keyboard, video, and other connectors (see fig. A.7).

CMOS RAM Addresses. Table A.33 shows the information maintained in the 64-byte AT CMOS RAM module. This information controls the configuration of the system much like the switches control the PC and XT configurations. This memory is read and written by the system SETUP program.

Table A.34 shows the values that may be stored by your system BIOS in a special CMOS byte called the *diagnostics status byte*. By examining this location with a diagnostics program, you can determine whether your system has set trouble codes, which indicates that a problem previously has occurred.

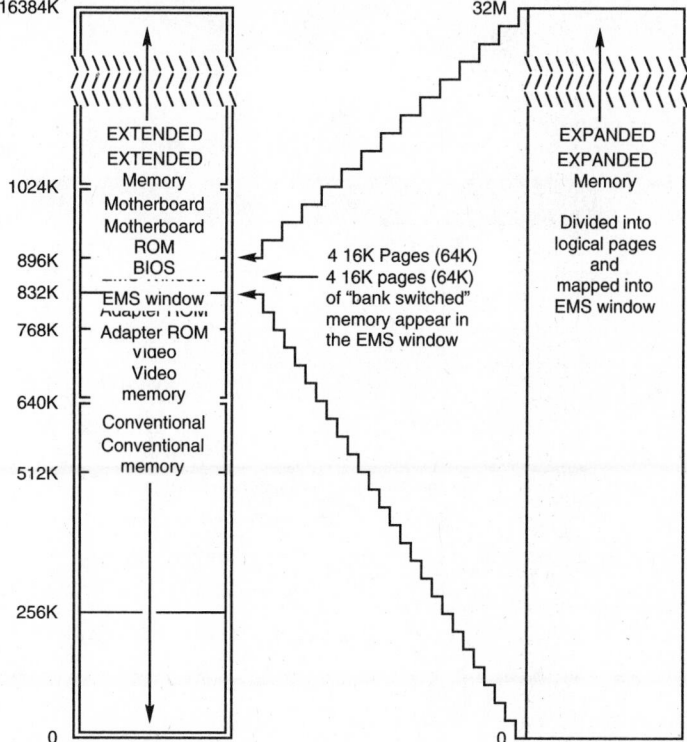

Fig. A.6

The relationship between conventional, extended, and expanded memory.

A. IBM PC and XT Motherboard Switch Settings

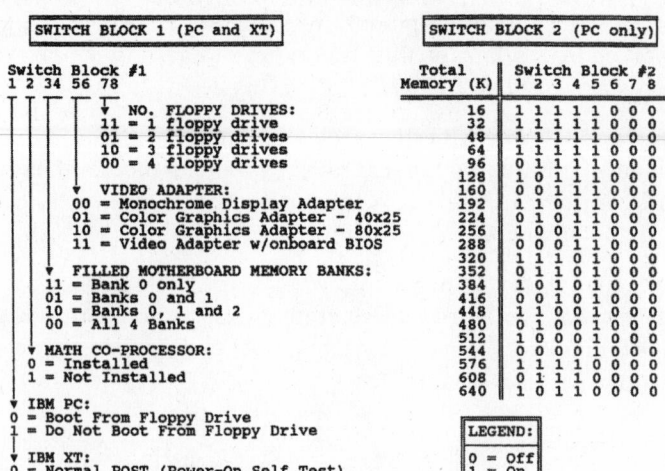

Fig. A.7

IBM PC and XT motherboard switch settings.

Table A.33 AT CMOS RAM Addresses			
Offset Hex	**Offset Dec**	**Field size**	**Function**
00h	0	1 byte	Current second in binary coded decimal (BCD)
01h	1	1 byte	Alarm second in BCD
02h	2	1 byte	Current minute in BCD
03h	3	1 byte	Alarm minute in BCD
04h	4	1 byte	Current hour in BCD
05h	5	1 byte	Alarm hour in BCD
06h	6	1 byte	Current day of week in BCD
07h	7	1 byte	Current day in BCD
08h	8	1 byte	Current month in BCD
09h	9	1 byte	Current year in BCD
0Ah	10	1 byte	Status register A
			Bit 7 = Update in progress
			0 = Date and time can be read
			1 = Time update in progress
			Bits 6-4 = Time frequency divider
			010 = 32.768KHz
			Bits 3-0 = Rate selection frequency
			0110 = 1.024KHz square wave frequency
0Bh	11	1 byte	Status register B

Offset Hex	Offset Dec	Field size	Function
	Bit 7 = Clock update cycle		
		0 = Update normally	
		1 = Abort update in progress	
	Bit 6 = Periodic interrupt		
		0 = Disable interrupt (default)	
		1 = Enable interrupt	
	Bit 5 = Alarm interrupt		
		0 = Disable interrupt (default)	
		0 = Disable interrupt (default)	
		1 = Enable interrupt	
	Bit 4 = Update-ended interrupt		
		0 = Disable interrupt (default)	
		1 = Enable interrupt	
	Bit 3 = Status register A square wave frequency		
		0 = Disable square wave (default)	
		1 = Enable square wave	
	Bit 2 = Date format		
		0 = Calendar in BCD format (default)	
		1 = Calendar in binary format	
	Bit 1 = 24-hour clock		
		0 = 24-hour mode (default)	
		1 = 12-hour mode	
	Bit 0 = Daylight Savings Time		
		0 = Disable Daylight Savings (default)	
		1 = Enable Daylight Savings	
0Ch	12	1 byte	Status register C
	Bit 7 = IRQF flag		
	Bit 6 = PF flag		
	Bit 5 = AF flag		
	Bit 4 = UF flag		
	Bits 3-0 = Reserved		
0Dh	13	1 byte	Status register D
	Bit 7 = Valid CMOS RAM bit		
		0 = CMOS battery dead	
		1 = CMOS battery power good	
	Bits 6-0 = Reserved		
0Eh	14	1 byte	Diagnostic status
	Bit 7 = Real-time clock power status		
		0 = CMOS *has not* lost power	
		1 = CMOS *has* lost power	
	Bit 6 = CMOS checksum status		
		0 = Checksum is good	
		1 = Checksum is bad	
	Bit 5 = POST configuration information status		
		0 = Configuration information is valid	
		1 = Configuration information is invalid	
	Bit 4 = Memory size compare during POST		
		0 = POST memory equals configuration	
		1 = POST memory *not equal* to configuration	
	Bit 3 = Fixed disk/adapter initialization		
		0 = Initialization good	
		1 = Initialization failed	
	Bit 2 = CMOS time status indicator		
		0 = Time is valid	
		1 = Time is Invalid	
	Bits 1-0 = Reserved		

(continues)

Table A.33 Continued

Offset Hex	Offset Dec	Field size	Function
0Fh	15	1 byte	Shutdown code
	00h = Power on or soft reset		
	04h = POST end; boot system		
	05h = JMP double word pointer with EOI		
	06h = Protected mode tests pass		
	07h = Protected mode tests fail		
	07h = Protected mode tests fail		
	08h = Memory size fail		
	09h = Int 15h block move		
	0Ah = JMP double word pointer without EOI		
	0Bh = used by 80386		
10h	16	1 byte	Floppy disk drive types
	Bits 7-4 = Drive 0 type		
	Bits 3-0 = Drive 1 type		
	0000 = None		
	0001 = 360K		
	0010 = 1.2M		
	0011 = 720K		
	0100 = 1.44M		
11h	17	1 byte	Reserved
12h	18	1 byte	Hard disk types
	Bits 7-4 = Hard disk 0 type (0-15)		
	Bits 3-0 = Hard disk 1 type (0-15)		
13h	19	1 byte	Reserved
14h	20	1 byte	Installed equipment
	Bits 7-6 = Number of floppy disk drives		
	00 = 1 floppy disk drive		
	01 = 2 floppy disk drives		
	Bits 5-4 = Primary display		
	00 = Use display adapter BIOS		
	01 = CGA 40-column		
	10 = CGA 80-column		
	11 = Monochrome Display Adapter		
	Bits 3-2 = Reserved		
	Bit 1 = Math coprocessor present		
	Bit 0 = Floppy disk drive present		
15h	21	1 byte	Base memory low-order byte
16h	22	1 byte	Base memory high-order byte
17h	23	1 byte	Extended memory low-order byte
18h	24	1 byte	Extended memory high-order byte
19h	25	1 byte	Hard Disk 0 Extended Type (0-255)
1Ah	26	1 byte	Hard Disk 1 Extended Type (0-255)
1Bh	27	9 bytes	Reserved
2Eh	46	1 byte	CMOS checksum high-order byte
2Fh	47	1 byte	CMOS checksum low-order byte

Offset Hex	Offset Dec	Field size	Function
30h	48	1 byte	Actual extended memory low-order byte
31h	49	1 byte	Actual extended memory high-order byte
32h	50	1 byte	Date century in BCD
33h	51	1 byte	POST information flag

Bit 7 = Top 128K base memory status
    0 = Top 128K base memory not installed
    1 = Top 128K base memory installed
Bit 6 = Setup program flag
    0 = Normal (default)
    1 = Put out first user message
Bits 5-0 = Reserved

Offset Hex	Offset Dec	Field size	Function
34h	52	2 bytes	Reserved

Table A.34 CMOS RAM (AT and PS/2) Diagnostic Status Byte Codes

Bit number 7 6 5 4 3 2 1 0	Hex	Function
1	80	Real-time clock (RTC) chip lost power
. 1	40	CMOS RAM checksum is bad
. . 1	20	Invalid configuration information found at POST
. . . 1	10	Memory size compare error at POST
. . . . 1 . . .	08	Fixed disk or adapter failed initialization
. . . . . 1 . .	04	Real-time clock (RTC) time found invalid
. . . . . . 1 .	02	Adapters do not match configuration
. . . . 1	01	Time-out reading an adapter ID
. . . .	00	No errors found (Normal)

IBM BIOS Model, Submodel, and Revison Codes. Table A.35 shows information about the different ROM BIOS versions that have appeared in various IBM systems.

Table A.35 IBM BIOS Model, Submodel, and Revision Codes

System description	CPU	Clock speed	Bus type/ width	ROM BIOS date
PC	8088	4.77 MHz	ISA/8	04/24/81
PC	8088	4.77 MHz	ISA/8	10/19/81
PC	8088	4.77 MHz	ISA/8	10/27/82
PC-XT	8088	4.77 MHz	ISA/8	11/08/82
PC-XT	8088	4.77 MHz	ISA/8	01/10/86
PC-XT	8088	4.77 MHz	ISA/8	05/09/86
PCjr	8088	4.77 MHz	ISA/8	06/01/83
PC Convertible	80C8	4.77 MHz	ISA/8	09/13/85
PS/2 25	8086	8 MHz	ISA/8	06/26/87
PS/2 30	8086	8 MHz	ISA/8	09/02/86
PS/2 30	8086	8 MHz	ISA/8	12/12/86
PS/2 30	8086	8 MHz	ISA/8	02/05/87
PC-AT	286	6 MHz	ISA/16	01/10/84
PC-AT	286	6 MHz	ISA/16	06/10/85
PC-AT	286	8 MHz	ISA/16	11/15/85
PC-XT 286	286	6 MHz	ISA/16	04/21/86
PS/1	286	10 MHz	ISA/16	12/01/89
PS/2 25 286	286	10 MHz	ISA/16	06/28/89
PS/2 30 286	286	10 MHz	ISA/16	08/25/88
PS/2 30 286	286	10 MHz	ISA/16	06/28/89
PS/2 35 SX	386SX	20 MHz	ISA/16	03/15/91
PS/2 35 SX	386SX	20 MHz	ISA/16	04/04/91
PS/2 40 SX	386SX	20 MHz	ISA/16	03/15/91
PS/2 40 SX	386SX	20 MHz	ISA/16	04/04/91
PS/2 L40 SX	386SX	20 MHz	ISA/16	02/27/91
PS/2 50	286	10 MHz	MCA/16	02/13/87
PS/2 50	286	10 MHz	MCA/16	05/09/87
PS/2 50Z	286	10 MHz	MCA/16	01/28/88
PS/2 50Z	286	10 MHz	MCA/16	04/18/88
PS/2 55 SX	386SX	16 MHz	MCA/16	11/02/88
PS/2 55 LS	386SX	16 MHz	MCA/16	?
PS/2 57 SX	386SX	20 MHz	MCA/16	07/03/91
PS/2 60	286	10 MHz	MCA/16	02/13/87
PS/2 65 SX	386SX	16 MHz	MCA/16	02/08/90
PS/2 70 386	386DX	16 MHz	MCA/32	01/29/88
PS/2 70 386	386DX	16 MHz	MCA/32	04/11/88
PS/2 70 386	386DX	16 MHz	MCA/32	12/15/89
PS/2 70 386	386DX	20 MHz	MCA/32	01/29/88

ID byte	Sub-model byte	Rev.	ST506 drive types
FF	—	—	—
FF	—	—	—
FF	—	—	—
FE	—	—	—
FB	00	01	—
FB	00	02	—
FD	—	—	—
F9	00	00	—
FA	01	00	26
FA	00	00	26
FA	00	01	26
FA	00	02	26
FC	—	—	15
FC	00	01	23
FC	01	00	23
FC	02	00	24
FC	0B	00	44
FC	09	02	37
FC	09	00	37
FC	09	02	37
F8	19	05	37
F8	19	06	37
F8	19	05	37
F8	19	06	37
F8	23	02	37
FC	04	00	32
FC	04	01	32
FC	04	02	33
FC	04	03	33
F8	0C	00	33
F8	1E	00	33
F8	26	02	None
FC	05	00	32
F8	1C	00	33
F8	09	00	33
F8	09	02	33
F8	09	04	33
F8	04	00	33

(continues)

Table A.35 Continued

System description	CPU	Clock speed	Bus type/ width	ROM BIOS date
PS/2 70 386	386DX	20 MHz	MCA/32	04/11/88
PS/2 70 386	386DX	20 MHz	MCA/32	12/15/89
PS/2 70 386	386DX	25 MHz	MCA/32	06/08/88
PS/2 70 386	386DX	25 MHz	MCA/32	02/20/89
PS/2 70 486	486DX	25 MHz	MCA/32	12/01/89
PS/2 70 486	486DX			
		16 MHz	MCA/32	?
PS/2 P70 386	386DX	20 MHz	MCA/32	01/18/89
PS/2 P75 486	486DX	33 MHz	MCA/32	10/05/90
PS/2 80 386	386DX	16 MHz	MCA/32	03/30/87
PS/2 80 386	386DX	20 MHz	MCA/32	10/07/87
PS/2 80 386	386DX	25 MHz	MCA/32	11/21/89
PS/2 90 XP 486	486SX	20 MHz	MCA/32	?
PS/2 90 XP 486	487SX	20 MHz	MCA/32	?
PS/2 90 XP 486	486DX	25 MHz	MCA/32	?
PS/2 90 XP 486	486DX	33 MHz	MCA/32	?
PS/2 90 XP 486	486DX	50 MHz	MCA/32	?
PS/2 95 XP 486	486SX	20 MHz	MCA/32	?
PS/2 95 XP 486	487SX	20 MHz	MCA/32	?
PS/2 95 XP 486	486DX	25 MHz	MCA/32	?
PS/2 95 XP 486	486DX	33 MHz	MCA/32	?
PS/2 95 XP 486	486DX	50 MHz	MCA/32	?

The ID byte, Submodel byte, and Revision numbers are in hexadecimal.
— = This feature is not supported.
None = Only SCSI drives are supported.
? = Information unavailable.

ID byte	Sub-model byte	Rev.	ST506 drive types
F8	04	02	33
F8	04	04	33
F8	0D	00	33
F8	0D	01	33
F8	0D	?	?
F8	50	00	?
F8	0B	00	33
F8	52	00	33
F8	00	00	32
F8	01	00	32
F8	80	01	?
F8	2D	00	?
F8	2F	00	?
F8	11	00	?
F8	13	00	?
F8	2B	00	?
F8	2C	00	?
F8	2E	00	?
F8	14	00	?
F8	16	00	?
F8	2A	00	?

Keyboard Key Numbers and Scan Codes

When a keyswitch on the keyboard fails, the scan code of the failed keyswitch is reported by diagnostics software, such as the POST. The tables in this section list all the scan codes for every key on the 83-, 84-, and 101-key keyboards. By looking up the reported scan code on these charts, you can determine which keyswitch is defective or needs to be cleaned. Note that the 101-key enhanced keyboards are capable of 3 different scan code sets, with set 1 being the default.

Table A.36 83-Key (PC/XT) Keyboard Key Numbers and Scan Codes

Key number	Scan code	Key
1	01	Escape
2	02	1
3	03	2
4	04	3
5	05	4
6	06	5
7	07	6
8	08	7
9	09	8
10	0A	9
11	0B	0
12	0C	-
13	0D	=
14	0E	Backspace
15	0F	Tab
16	10	q
17	11	w
18	12	e
19	13	r
20	14	t
21	15	y
22	16	u
23	17	i
24	18	o
25	19	p
26	1A	[
27	1B	]
28	1C	Enter
29	1D	Ctrl
30	1E	a
31	1F	s
32	20	d
33	21	f
34	22	g
35	23	h
36	24	j
37	25	k
38	26	l
39	27	;

Key number	Scan code	Key
40	28	'
41	29	´
42	2A	Left Shift
43	2B	\
44	2C	z
45	2D	x
46	2E	c
47	2F	v
48	30	b
49	31	n
50	32	m
51	33	,
52	34	.
53	35	/
54	36	Right Shift
55	37	*
56	38	Alt
57	39	Space bar
58	3A	Caps Lock
59	3B	F1
60	3C	F2
61	3D	F3
62	3E	F4
63	3F	F5
64	40	F6
65	41	F7
66	42	F8
67	43	F9
68	44	F10
69	45	Num Lock
70	46	Scroll Lock
71	47	Keypad 7 (Home)
72	48	Keypad 8 (Up arrow)
73	49	Keypad 9 (PgUp)
74	4A	Keypad -
75	4B	Keypad 4 (Left arrow)
76	4C	Keypad 5
77	4D	Keypad 6 (Right arrow)
78	4E	Keypad +

(continues)

Table A.36 Continued

Key number	Scan code	Key
79	4F	Keypad 1 (End)
80	50	Keypad 2 (Down arrow)
81	51	Keypad 3 (PgDn)
82	52	Keypad 0 (Ins)
83	53	Keypad . (Del)

Table A.37 84-Key (AT) Keyboard Key Numbers and Scan Codes

Key number	Scan code	Key
1	29	´
2	02	1
3	03	2
4	04	3
5	05	4
6	06	5
7	07	6
8	08	7
9	09	8
10	0A	9
11	0B	0
12	0C	-
13	0D	=
14	2B	\
15	0E	Backspace
16	0F	Tab
17	10	q
18	11	w
19	12	e
20	13	r
21	14	t
22	15	y
23	16	u
24	17	i
25	18	o
26	19	p
27	1A	[
28	1B	]
30	1D	Ctrl

Key number	Scan code	Key
31	1E	a
32	1F	s
33	20	d
34	21	f
35	22	g
36	23	h
37	24	j
38	25	k
39	26	l
40	27	;
41	28	'
43	1C	Enter
44	2A	Left Shift
46	2C	z
47	2D	x
48	2E	c
49	2F	v
50	30	b
51	31	n
52	32	m
53	33	,
54	34	.
55	35	/
57	36	Right Shift
58	38	Alt
61	39	Space bar
64	3A	Caps Lock
65	3C	F2
66	3E	F4
67	40	F6
68	42	F8
69	44	F10
70	3B	F1
71	3D	F3
72	3F	F5
73	41	F7
74	43	F9
90	01	Escape
91	47	Keypad 7 (Home)

(continues)

Table A.37 Continued

Key number	Scan code	Key
92	4B	Keypad 4 (Left arrow)
93	4F	Keypad 1 (End)
95	45	Num Lock
96	48	Keypad 8 (Up arrow)
97	4C	Keypad 5
98	50	Keypad 2 (Down arrow)
99	52	Keypad 0 (Ins)
100	46	Scroll Lock
101	49	Keypad 9 (PgUp)
102	4D	Keypad 6 (Right arrow)
103	51	Keypad 3 (PgDn)
104	53	Keypad . (Del)
105	54	SysRq
106	37	Keypad *
107	4A	Keypad –
108	4E	Keypad +

Table A.38 101/102-Key (Enhanced) Keyboard Key Numbers and Scan Codes (Set 1)

Key number	Scan code	Key
1	29	`
2	02	1
3	03	2
4	04	3
5	05	4
6	06	5
7	07	6
8	08	7
9	09	8
10	0A	9
11	0B	0
12	0C	-
13	0D	=
15	0E	Backspace
16	0F	Tab
17	10	q
18	11	w
19	12	e

Key number	Scan code	Key
20	13	r
21	14	t
22	15	y
23	16	u
24	17	i
25	18	o
26	19	p
27	1A	[
28	1B	]
29	2B	\ (101-key *only*)
30	3A	Caps Lock
31	1E	a
32	1F	s
33	20	d
34	21	f
35	22	g
36	23	h
37	24	j
38	25	k
39	26	l
40	27	;
41	28	'
42	2B	# (102-key only)
43	1C	Enter
44	2A	Left Shift
45	56	\ (102-key only)
46	2C	z
47	2D	x
48	2E	c
49	2F	v
50	30	b
51	31	n
52	32	m
53	33	,
54	34	.
55	35	/
57	36	Right Shift
58	1D	Left Ctrl
60	38	Left Alt

(continues)

Table A.38 Continued

Key number	Scan code	Key
61	39	Space bar
62	E0,38	Right Alt
64	E0,1D	Right Ctrl
75	E0,52	Insert
76	E0,53	Delete
79	E0,4B	Left arrow
80	E0,47	Home
81	E0,4F	End
83	E0,48	Up arrow
84	E0,50	Down arrow
85	E0,49	Page Up
86	E0,51	Page Down
89	E0,4D	Right arrow
90	45	Num Lock
91	47	Keypad 7 (Home)
92	4B	Keypad 4 (Left arrow)
93	4F	Keypad 1 (End)
95	E0,35	Keypad /
96	48	Keypad 8 (Up arrow)
97	4C	Keypad 5
98	50	Keypad 2 (Down arrow)
99	52	Keypad 0 (Ins)
100	37	Keypad *
101	49	Keypad 9 (PgUp)
102	4D	Keypad 6 (Left arrow)
103	51	Keypad 3 (PgDn)
104	53	Keypad . (Del)
105	4A	Keypad -
106	4E	Keypad +
108	E0,1C	Keypad Enter
110	01	Escape
112	3B	F1
113	3C	F2
114	3D	F3
115	3E	F4
116	3F	F5
117	40	F6
118	41	F7
119	42	F8

Key number	Scan code	Key
120	43	F9
121	44	F10
122	57	F11
123	58	F12
124	E0,2A,E0,37	Print Screen
125	46	Scroll Lock
126	E1,1D,45,E1,9D,C5	Pause

Table A.39   101/102-Key (Enhanced) Keyboard Key Numbers and Scan Codes (Set 2)

Key number	Scan Code	Key
1	0E	'
2	16	1
3	1E	2
4	26	3
5	25	4
6	2E	5
7	36	6
8	3D	7
9	3E	8
10	46	9
11	45	0
12	4E	-
13	55	=
15	66	Backspace
16	0D	Tab
17	15	q
18	1D	w
19	24	e
20	2D	r
21	2C	t
22	35	y
23	3C	u
24	43	i
25	44	o
26	4D	p
27	54	[
28	5B	]

(continues)

Table A.39 Continued

Key number	Scan Code	Key
29	5D	\ (101-key *only*)
30	58	Caps Lock
31	1C	a
32	1B	s
33	23	d
34	2B	f
35	34	g
36	33	h
37	3B	j
38	42	k
39	4B	l
40	4C	;
41	52	'
42	5D	# (102-key *only*)
43	5A	Enter
44	12	Left Shift
45	61	\ (102-key *only*)
46	1A	z
47	22	x
48	21	c
49	2A	v
50	32	b
51	31	n
52	3A	m
53	41	,
54	49	.
55	4A	/
57	59	Right Shift
58	14	Left Ctrl
60	11	Left Alt
61	29	Space bar
62	E0,11	Right Alt
64	E0,14	Right Ctrl
75	E0,70	Insert
76	E0,71	Delete
79	E0,6B	Left arrow
80	E0,6C	Home
81	E0,69	End

Key number	Scan Code	Key
83	E0,75	Up arrow
84	E0,72	Down arrow
85	E0,7D	Page Up
86	E0,7A	Page Down
89	E0,74	Right arrow
90	77	Num Lock
91	6C	Keypad 7 (Home)
92	6B	Keypad 4 (Left arrow)
93	69	Keypad 1 (End)
95	E0,4A	Keypad /
96	75	Keypad 8 (Up arrow)
97	73	Keypad 5
98	72	Keypad 2 (Down arrow)
99	70	Keypad 0 (Ins)
100	7C	Keypad *
101	7D	Keypad 9 (PgUp)
102	74	Keypad 6 (Left arrow)
103	7A	Keypad 3 (PgDn)
104	71	Keypad . (Del)
105	7B	Keypad -
106	E0,5A	Keypad +
108	E0,5A	Keypad Enter
110	76	Escape
112	05	F1
113	06	F2
114	04	F3
115	0C	F4
116	03	F5
117	0B	F6
118	83	F7
119	0A	F8
120	01	F9
121	09	F10
122	78	F11
123	07	F12
124	E0,12,E0,7C	Print Screen
125	7E	Scroll Lock
126	E1,14,77,E1,F0,14,F0,77	Pause

Table A.40 101/102-Key (Enhanced) Keyboard Key Numbers and Scan Codes (Set 3)

Key number	Scan Code	Key
1	0E	`
2	16	1
3	1E	2
4	26	3
5	25	4
6	2E	5
7	36	6
8	3D	7
9	3E	8
10	46	9
11	45	0
12	4E	-
13	55	=
15	66	Backspace
16	0D	Tab
17	15	q
18	1D	w
19	24	e
20	2D	r
21	2C	t
22	35	y
23	3C	u
24	43	i
25	44	o
26	4D	p
27	54	[
28	5B	]
29	5C	\ (101-key *only*)
30	14	Caps Lock
31	1C	a
32	1B	s
33	23	d
34	2B	f
35	34	g
36	33	h
37	3B	j
38	42	k
39	4B	l

Key number	Scan Code	Key
40	4C	;
41	52	'
42	53	# (102-key *only*)
43	5A	Enter
44	12	Left Shift
45	13	\ (102-key *only*)
46	1A	z
47	22	x
48	21	c
49	2A	v
50	32	b
51	31	n
52	3A	m
53	41	,
54	49	.
55	4A	/
57	59	Right Shift
58	11	Left Ctrl
60	19	Left Alt
61	29	Space bar
62	39	Right Alt
64	58	Right Ctrl
75	67	Insert
76	64	Delete
79	61	Left arrow
80	6E	Home
81	65	End
83	63	Up arrow
84	60	Down arrow
85	6F	Page Up
86	6D	Page Down
89	6A	Right arrow
90	76	Num Lock
91	6C	Keypad 7 (Home)
92	6B	Keypad 4 (Left arrow)
93	69	Keypad 1 (End)
95	77	Keypad /
96	75	Keypad 8 (Up arrow)
97	73	Keypad 5

(continues)

Table A.40 Continued

Key number	Scan Code	Key
98	72	Keypad 2 (Down arrow)
99	70	Keypad 0 (Ins)
100	7E	Keypad *
101	7D	Keypad 9 (PgUp)
102	74	Keypad 6 (Left arrow)
103	7A	Keypad 3 (PgDn)
104	71	Keypad . (Del)
105	84	Keypad -
106	7C	Keypad +
108	79	Keypad Enter
110	08	Escape
112	07	F1
113	0F	F2
114	17	F3
115	1F	F4
116	27	F5
117	2F	F6
118	37	F7
119	3F	F8
120	47	F9
121	4F	F10
122	56	F11
123	5E	F12
124	57	Print Screen
125	5F	Scroll Lock
126	62	Pause

Hardware Interrupts

Interrupt request channels (IRQ), or hardware interrupts, are used by various hardware devices to signal the motherboard that a request must be fulfilled. These channels are represented by wires on the motherboard and in the slot connectors. When a particular interrupt is invoked, a special routine takes over the system, which first saves all the CPU register contents on a stack and then directs the system to the interrupt vector table. In this vector table is a list of program locations or addresses that correspond to each interrupt channel. Depending on which interrupt was invoked, the program corresponding to that channel is run. The pointers in this vector table point to the address of whatever software driver is used to service the card that generated the interrupt. For a network card, for example, the vector may point to the address of the network drivers that have been loaded to operate the card; for a hard disk controller, the vector may point to the ROM BIOS code that operates the controller. After the particular software routine is finished performing whatever function the card needed, the interrupt control software returns the stack contents to the CPU registers, and the system then continues whatever it was doing before the interrupt occurred.

By using interrupts, your system can respond in a timely fashion to external events. Each time a serial port presents a byte to your system, an interrupt is generated to ensure that the system responds immediately to read that byte before another comes in. Hardware interrupts are prioritized by their number, with the highest-priority interrupts having the lowest numbers. Higher-priority interrupts take precedence over lower-priority interrupts by interrupting them. In this way, several interrupts can occur concurrently in your system, each nesting within the other. If you overload the system, in this case by running out of stack resources, an Internal stack overflow message results. By increasing the available stack resources through the STACKS parameter in CONFIG.SYS, you can handle such situations.

The Industry Standard Architecture (ISA) bus uses *edge-triggered interrupt sensing*, in which the interrupt is sensed by a signal sent on a particular wire located in the slot connector. A different wire corresponds to each hardware interrupt. Because the motherboard cannot recognize which slot contains the card that signalled the interrupt line and therefore generated the interrupt, if more than one card were set to use a particular interrupt, confusion would result. Each interrupt, therefore, usually is designated for a single hardware device, and most of the time cannot be shared.

A device can be designed to share interrupts, and a few devices allow this; most cannot, however, because of the way interrupts are signaled in the ISA bus. Systems with the Micro Channel Architecture (MCA) bus use *level-sensitive interrupts*, which allows complete interrupt sharing to occur. In fact, all boards could be set to the same interrupt with no conflicts or problems. For maximum performance, however, interrupts should be staggered as much as possible. By eliminating interrupt conflicts as a problem, the MCA bus makes configuring boards much simpler than the ISA bus, and allows for more expansion, because you can never run out of interrupts.

Because interrupts usually cannot be shared in the ISA bus systems, you often will run out of interrupts when you are adding boards to a system. If two boards use the same interrupt level to signal the system, a conflict causes neither board to operate properly. The tables in the following sections show you the interrupt channels (IRQ) any standard devices use, and what may be free in your system. The AT systems have twice the number of interrupts and usually can be expanded much more easily than 8-bit ISA (PC or XT) systems.

8-Bit ISA Bus Interrupts. The PC and XT have eight standard prioritized levels of interrupt, with the lower priority 6 (numbered 2-7) being bused to the system expansion slots. A special Non-Maskable Interrupt (NMI) has the highest priority. The interrupts are used as follows, in order of priority:

Table A.41 XT-bus (8-bit ISA) Default Interrupt Assignments

IRQ	Function	Bus Slot
0	System Timer	No
1	Keyboard Controller	No
2	Available	No
3	Serial Port 2 (COM2:)	Yes (8-bit)
4	Serial Port 1 (COM1:)	Yes (8-bit)
5	Hard Disk Controller	Yes (8-bit)
6	Floppy Disk Controller	Yes (8-bit)
7	Parallel Port 1 (LPT1:)	Yes (8-bit)

ISA (16-bit), EISA, and MCA Bus Interrupts. The AT supports 16 standard levels of interrupts, with 11 channels bused to the expansion slots. A special Non-Maskable Interrupt (NMI) has the highest priority. Two Intel 8259A controllers are used, with 8 channels per chip. The interrupts from the second chip are cascaded through IRQ 2 on the first chip.

Because IRQ 2 now is used directly by the motherboard, the wire for IRQ 9 has been rerouted to the same position in the slot that IRQ 2 normally would occupy. Therefore, any board you install that is set to IRQ 2 is really using IRQ 9. The interrupt vector table has been adjusted accordingly to enable this deception to work. This adjustment to the system enables greater compatibility with the PC interrupt structure and enables cards set to IRQ 2 to work properly. Note that Interrupts 0, 1, 2, 8, and 13 are *not* on the bus connectors and are not accessible to adapter cards. Interrupts 8, 10, 11, 12, 13, 14, and 15 are from the second interrupt controller and are accessible only by boards that use the 16-bit extension connector, because this is where these wires are found. IRQ 9 is rewired to the 8-bit slot connector in place of IRQ 2, which means that IRQ 9 replaces IRQ 2 and therefore is available to 8-bit cards (as IRQ 2). Although the 16-bit ISA bus has twice as many interrupts as systems with the 8-bit ISA bus, you still will run out of available interrupts because only 16-bit adapters can use any of the new interrupts.

As before, although the MCA bus does follow this scheme, the interrupts can be shared without conflict. The interrupts are used as shown in this table:

Table A.42 ISA, EISA, and MCA Default Interrupt Assignments

IRQ	Standard Function	Bus Slot
0	System Timer	No
1	Keyboard Controller	No
2	Second IRQ Controller	No
8	Real-Time Clock	No
9	Available (appears as IRQ 2)	Yes (8-bit)
10	Available	Yes (16-bit)
11	Available	Yes (16-bit)
12	Motherboard Mouse Port	Yes (16-bit)
13	Math Coprocessor	No
14	Hard Disk Controller	Yes (16-bit)
15	Available	Yes (16-bit)
3	Serial Port 2 (COM2:)	Yes (8-bit)
4	Serial Port 1 (COM1:)	Yes (8-bit)
5	Parallel Port 2 (LPT2:)	Yes (8-bit)
6	Floppy Disk Controller	Yes (8-bit)
7	Parallel Port 1 (LPT1:)	Yes (8-bit)

DMA Channels

DMA channels are used by any high-speed communications devices that must send and receive information at high speed with the motherboard. A serial or parallel port does not use a DMA channel, but a network adapter often does. DMA channels sometimes can be shared if the devices are not of the type that would need them simultaneously. For example, you can have a network adapter and a tape backup adapter both sharing DMA channel 1, but you cannot back up while the network is running. To back up during network operation, you must ensure that each adapter used a unique DMA channel. Note that twice as many DMA channels are available in an AT-type system.

8-Bit ISA DMA Channels. Four DMA (direct memory access) channels support high-speed data transfers between I/O devices and memory. Three of the channels are bused to the expansion slots, and are used as follows:

Table A.43 XT-bus (8-bit ISA) Default DMA Channel Assignments

DMA	Standard Function	Bus Slot
0	Dynamic RAM Refresh	No
1	Available	Yes (8-bit)
2	Floppy disk controller	Yes (8-bit)
3	Hard disk controller	Yes (8-bit)

ISA (16-bit), EISA, and MCA Bus DMA Channels. The system supports seven direct memory access (DMA) channels, with six bused to the expansion slots. DMA channel 4 is used to cascade channels 0 through 3 to the microprocessor. Channels 1-3 are available for 8-bit transfers, and DMA 0 and 5-7 are for 16-bit transfers only. The channels are used as shown in this table:

Table A.44 ISA, EISA, and MCA Default DMA Channel Assignments

DMA	Standard Function	Bus Slot
0	Available	Yes (16-bit)
1	Available	Yes (8-bit)
2	Floppy disk controller	Yes (8-bit)
3	Available	Yes (8-bit)
4	First DMA controller	No
5	Available	Yes(16-bit)
6	Available	Yes(16-bit)
7	Available	Yes(16-bit)

I/O Port Addresses

Input-output ports are addresses used by the processor to communicate directly with devices. These addresses are like memory addresses but are not for storage; 1,024 I/O ports are available in the IBM system design for both XT- and AT-type systems. Because the ports must be uniquely assigned to only a single board or device, the potential for conflicts exists. Plenty of I/O ports generally are available, but many boards do not allow their default port addresses to be changed.

Table A.45 lists all the default port addresses for any PC-type system. Note that the I/O addresses hex 000 to 0FF are reserved for the system board. Ports hex 100 to 3FF are available on the I/O channel.

Table A.45 8-Bit ISA I/O Port Addresses

Hex range	Device
000-00F	8237 DMA chip
020-021	8259 interrupt chip
040-043	8253 timer chip
060-063	8255 programmable peripheral interface chip
080	Manufacturer POST code port
080-083	DMA page registers
0A0	NMI mask register
0Cx	Reserved
0Ex	Reserved

Hex range	Device
200-20F	Game control
201	Game I/O
210-217	Expansion unit
278-27F	Parallel printer port 2
2B0-2DF	Alternate Enhanced Graphics Adapter
2E1	GPIB (Adapter 0)
2E2-2E3	Data acquisition (Adapter 0)
2F8-2FF	Serial port 2
300-31F	Prototype card
320-32F	Hard disk controller
348-357	DCA 3278
360-367	PC network (low address)
368-36F	PC network (high address)
378-37F	Parallel printer port 1
380-38F	SDLC, bisynchronous 2
390-393	Cluster
3A0-3AF	Bisynchronous 1
3B0-3BF	Monochrome Display and Printer Adapter
3C0-3CF	Enhanced Graphics Adapter
3D0-3DF	Color/Graphics Monitor Adapter
3F0-3F7	Floppy disk controller
3F8-3FF	Serial port 1
6E2-6E3	Data acquisition (Adapter 1)
790-793	Cluster (Adapter 1)
AE2-AE3	Data acquisition (Adapter 2)
B90-B93	Cluster (Adapter 2)
EE2-EE3	Data acquisition (Adapter 3)
1390-1393	Cluster (Adapter 3)
22E1	GPIB (Adapter 1)
2390-2393	Cluster (Adapter 4)
42E1	GPIB (Adapter 2)
62E1	GPIB (Adapter 3)
82E1	GPIB (Adapter 4)
A2E1	GPIB (Adapter 5)
C2E1	GPIB (Adapter 6)
E2E1	GPIB (Adapter 7)

Table A.46 lists all the default port addresses for any AT-type system. Note that the I/O addresses hex 000 to 0FF are reserved for the system board. Ports hex 100 to 3FF are available on the I/O channel.

Table A.46 16-bit ISA I/O Port Addresses

Hex range	Device
000-91F	DMA controller 1, 8237A-5
020-03F	Interrupt controller 1, 8259A, master
040-05F	Timer, 8254-2
060	8042 Keyboard/Auxiliary Device (mouse) controller
061	System board I/O port
064	8042 Keyboard/Auxiliary Device (mouse) controller
070-07F	Real-time clock, NMI (Non-Maskable Interrupt) mask
080	Manufacturer POST code port
080-09F	DMA page registers, 74LS612
0A0-0BF	Interrupt controller 2, 8237A-5
0F0	Clear math coprocessor busy
0F1	Reset math coprocessor
0F8-0FF	Math coprocessor
1F0-1F8	Hard disk controller
21F	Voice communications adapter
278-27F	Parallel printer port 2
2B0-2DF	Alternate Enhanced Graphics Adapter
2E1	GPIB (Adapter 0)
2E2-2E3	Data acquisition (Adapter 0)
2F8-2FF	Serial Port 2
300-31F	Prototype adapter
360-363	PC network (low address)
368-36B	PC network (high address)
378-37F	Parallel printer port 1
380-38F	SDLC, bisynchronous 2
3A0-3AF	Bisynchronous 1
3B0-3BF	Monochrome Display and Printer Adapter
3C0-3CF	Enhanced Graphics Adapter
3D0-3DF	Color/Graphics Monitor Adapter
3F0-3F7	Floppy disk controller
3F8-3FF	Serial Port 1
6E2-6E3	Data acquisition (Adapter 1)
AE2-AE3	Data acquisition (Adapter 2)
EE2-EE3	Data acquisition (Adapter 3)
22E1	GPIB (Adapter 1)
42E1	GPIB (Adapter 2)
62E1	GPIB (Adapter 3)
82E1	GPIB (Adapter 4)

Hex range	Device
A2E1	GPIB (Adapter 5)
C2E1	GPIB (Adapter 6)
E2E1	GPIB (Adapter 7)

Connector Pinouts

This section lists the connector pinout specifications for a variety of connectors from the ISA and MCA bus connectors to serial and parallel ports as well as video display, keyboard, and even power-supply connectors. This information can be useful in troubleshooting cables or connections between devices.

System Bus Pinouts

The following section details the interface connector pinouts for all of the PC bus architectures available today. These pinout tables can be useful when troubleshooting problems with devices plugged into the bus.

ISA Bus (8-Bit and 16-Bit) Interface Connectors. The following tables show the pinouts for the Industry Standard Architecture (ISA) PC, XT, and AT 8-bit and 16-bit expansion slot connectors.

Table A.47 ISA (Industry Standard Architecture) 8-Bit Bus Connector

Signal	Pin	Pin	Signal	Signal	Pin	Pin	Signal
GROUND	— B1	A1 —	-I/O CH CHK	GROUND	— B1	A1 —	-I/O CH CHK
RESET DRV	— B2	A2 —	Data Bit 7	RESET DRV	— B2	A2 —	Data Bit 7
+5 Vdc	— B3	A3 —	Data Bit 6	+5 Vdc	— B3	A3 —	Data Bit 6
IRQ 2	— B4	A4 —	Data Bit 5	IRQ 9	— B4	A4 —	Data Bit 5
-5 Vdc	— B5	A5 —	Data Bit 4	-5 Vdc	— B5	A5 —	Data Bit 4
DRQ 2	— B6	A6 —	Data Bit 3	DRQ 2	— B6	A6 —	Data Bit 3
-12 Vdc	— B7	A7 —	Data Bit 2	-12 Vdc	— B7	A7 —	Data Bit 2
-CARD SLCTD	— B8	A8 —	Data Bit 1	-0 WAIT	— B8	A8 —	Data Bit 1
+12 Vdc	— B9	A9 —	Data Bit 0	+12 Vdc	— B9	A9 —	Data Bit 0
GROUND	— B10	A10 —	-I/O CH RDY	GROUND	— B10	A10 —	-I/O CH RDY
-SMEMW	— B11	A11 —	AEN	-SMEMW	— B11	A11 —	AEN
-SMEMR	— B12	A12 —	Address 19	-SMEMR	— B12	A12 —	Address 19
-IOW	— B13	A13 —	Address 18	-IOW	— B13	A13 —	Address 18
-IOR	— B14	A14 —	Address 17	-IOR	— B14	A14 —	Address 17
-DACK 3	— B15	A15 —	Address 16	-DACK 3	— B15	A15 —	Address 16
DRQ 3	— B16	A16 —	Address 15	DRQ 3	— B16	A16 —	Address 15
-DACK 1	— B17	A17 —	Address 14	-DACK 1	— B17	A17 —	Address 14

(continues)

Table A.47 Continued

Signal	Pin	Pin	Signal	Signal	Pin	Pin	Signal
DRQ 1	— B18	A18 —	Address 13	DRQ 1	— B18	A18 —	Address 13
-REFRESH	— B19	A19 —	Address 12	-REFRESH	— B19	A19 —	Address 12
CLK(4.77MHz)	— B20	A20 —	Address 11	CLK(8.33MHz)	— B20	A20 —	Address 11
IRQ 7	— B21	A21 —	Address 10	IRQ 7	— B21	A21 —	Address 10
IRQ 6	— B22	A22 —	Address 9	IRQ 6	— B22	A22 —	Address 9
IRQ 5	— B23	A23 —	Address 8	IRQ 5	— B23	A23 —	Address 8
IRQ 4	— B24	A24 —	Address 7	IRQ 4	— B24	A24 —	Address 7
IRQ 3	— B25	A25 —	Address 6	IRQ 3	— B25	A25 —	Address 6
-DACK 2	— B26	A26 —	Address 5	-DACK2	— B26	A26 —	Address 5
T/C	— B27	A27 —	Address 4	T/C	— B27	A27 —	Address 4
BALE	— B28	A28 —	Address 3	BALE	— B28	A28 —	Address 3
+5 Vdc	— B29	A29 —	Address 2	+5 Vdc	— B29	A29 —	Address 2
OSC(14.3MHz)	— B30	A30 —	Address 1	OSC(14.3MHz)	— B30	A30 —	Address 1
GROUND	— B31	A31 —	Address 0	GROUND	— B31	A31 —	Address 0
				KEY	**KEY**	**KEY**	**KEY**
				-MEM CS16	— D1	C1 —	-SBHE
				-I/O CS16	— D2	C2 —	Latch Address 23
				IRQ 10	— D3	C3 —	Latch Address 22
				IRQ 11	— D4	C4 —	Latch Address 21
				IRQ 12	— D5	C5 —	Latch Address 20
				IRQ 15	— D6	C6 —	Latch Address 19
				IRQ 14	— D7	C7 —	Latch Address 18
				-DACK 0	— D8	C8 —	Latch Address 17
				DRQ 0	— D9	C9 —	-MEMR
				-DACK 5	— D10	C10 —	-MEMW
				DRQ 5	— D11	C11 —	Data Bit 8
				-DACK 6	— D12	C12 —	Data Bit 9
				DRQ 6	— D13	C13 —	Data Bit 10
				-DACK 7	— D14	C14 —	Data Bit 11
				DRQ 7	— D15	C15 —	Data Bit 12
				+5 Vdc	— D16	C16 —	Data Bit 13
				-MASTER	— D17	C17 —	Data Bit 14
				Ground	— D18	C18 —	Data Bit 15

EISA Bus (32-Bit) Interface Connectors

Table A.48 EISA (Extended Industry Standard Architecture) 32-Bit Bus Connector					
Upper Signal	**Lower Signal**	**Pin**	**Pin**	**Lower Signal**	**Upper Signal**
GROUND	GROUND	B1	A1	-I/O CH CHK	-CMD
+5 Vdc	RESET DRV	B2	A2	Data Bit 7	-START
+5 Vdc	+5 Vdc	B3	A3	Data Bit 6	EXRDY
RESERVED	IRQ 9	B4	A4	Data Bit 5	-EX32
RESERVED	-5 Vdc	B5	A5	Data Bit 4	GROUND
KEY	DRQ 2	B6	A6	Data Bit 3	KEY
RESERVED	-12 Vdc	B7	A7	Data Bit 2	-EX16
RESERVED	-0 WAIT	B8	A8	Data Bit 1	-SLBURST
+12 Vdc	+12 Vdc	B9	A9	Data Bit 0	-MSBURST
M-IO	GROUND	B10	A10	-I/O CH RDY	W-R
-LOCK	-SMEMW	B11	A11	AEN	GROUND
RESERVED	-SMEMR	B12	A12	Address 19	RESERVED
GROUND	-IOW	B13	A13	Address 18	RESERVED
RESERVED	-IOR	B14	A14	Address 17	RESERVED
-BE3	-DACK 3	B15	A15	Address 16	GROUND
KEY	DRQ 3	B16	A16	Address 15	KEY
-BE2	-DACK 1	B17	A17	Address 14	-BE1
-BE0	DRQ 1	B18	A18	Address 13	-LAddress31
GROUND	-REFRESH	B19	A19	Address 12	GROUND
+5 Vdc	CLK (8.33MHz)	B20	A20	Address 11	-LAddress30
-LAddress 29	IRQ 7	B21	A21	Address 10	-LAddress28
GROUND	IRQ 6	B22	A22	Address 9	-LAddress27
-LAddress 26	IRQ 5	B23	A23	Address 8	-LAddress 25
-LAddress 24	IRQ 4	B24	A24	Address 7	GROUND
KEY	IRQ 3	B25	A25	Address 6	KEY
LAddress 16	-DACK2	B26	A26	Address 5	LAddress 15
LAddress 14	T/C	B27	A27	Address 4	LAddress 13
+5 Vdc	BALE	B28	A28	Address 3	LAddress12
+5 Vdc	+5 Vdc	B29	A29	Address 2	LAddress 11
GROUND	OSC (14.3MHz)	B30	A30	Address 1	GROUND
LAddress 10	GROUND	B31	A31	Address 0	LAddress 9
KEY	KEY	KEY	KEY	KEY	KEY
LAddress 8	-MEM CS16	D1	C1	-SBHE	LAddress 7
LAddress 6	-I/O CS16	D2	C2	LAddress 23	GROUND
LAddress 5	IRQ 10	D3	C3	LAddress 22	LAddress 4
+5 Vdc	IRQ 11	D4	C4	LAddress 21	LAddress 3

(continues)

Table A.48 Continued

Upper Signal	Lower Signal	Pin	Pin	Lower Signal	Upper Signal
LAddress 2	IRQ 12	D5	C5	LAddress 20	GROUND
KEY	IRQ 15	D6	C6	LAddress 19	KEY
Data Bit 16	IRQ 14	D7	C7	LAddress 18	Data Bit 17
Data Bit 18	-DACK 0	D8	C8	LAddress 17	Data Bit19
GROUND	DRQ 0	D9	C9	-MEMR	Data Bit 20
Data Bit 21	-DACK 5	D10	C10	-MEMW	Data Bit 22
Data Bit 23	DRQ 5	D11	C11	Data Bit 8	GROUND
Data Bit 24	-DACK 6	D12	C12	Data Bit 9	Data Bit 25
GROUND	DRQ 6	D13	C13	Data Bit 10	Data Bit 26
Data Bit 27	-DACK 7	D14	C14	Data Bit 11	Data Bit 28
KEY	DRQ 7	D15	C15	Data Bit 12	KEY
Data Bit 29	+5 Vdc	D16	C16	Data Bit 13	GROUND
+5 Vdc	-MASTER	D17	C17	Data Bit 14	Data Bit 30
+5 Vdc	Ground	D18	C18	Data Bit 15	Data Bit 31
-MAKx		D19	C19		-MREQx

VESA VL-Bus Interface Connectors

Table A.49 VESA VL-Bus (Video Local-Bus) Connector Pinouts (Rev. 2.0p)

64-Bit	32-Bit	Pin	Pin	32-Bit	64-Bit
	DAT00	A01	B01	DAT01	
	DAT02	A02	B02	DAT03	
	DAT04	A03	B03	GND	
	DAT06	A04	B04	DAT05	
	DAT08	A05	B05	DAT07	
	GND	A06	B06	DAT09	
	DAT10	A07	B07	DAT11	
	DAT12	A08	B08	DAT13	
	VCC	A09	B09	DAT15	
	DAT14	A10	B10	GND	
	DAT16	A11	B11	DAT17	
	DAT18	A12	B12	VCC	
	DAT20	A13	B13	DAT19	
	GND	A14	B14	DAT21	
	DAT22	A15	B15	DAT23	
	DAT24	A16	B16	DAT25	
	DAT26	A17	B17	GND	
	DAT28	A18	B18	DAT27	

64-Bit	32-Bit	Pin	Pin	32-Bit	64-Bit
	DAT30	A19	B19	DAT29	
	VCC	A20	B20	DAT31	
DAT63	ADR31	A21	B21	ADR30	DAT62
	GND	A22	B22	ADR28	DAT60
DAT61	ADR29	A23	B23	ADR26	DAT58
DAT59	ADR27	A24	B24	GND	
DAT57	ADR25	A25	B25	ADR24	DAT56
DAT55	ADR23	A26	B26	ADR22	DAT54
DAT53	ADR21	A27	B27	VCC	
DAT51	ADR19	A28	B28	ADR20	DAT52
	GND	A29	B29	ADR18	DAT50
DAT49	ADR17	A30	B30	ADR16	DAT48
DAT47	ADR15	A31	B31	ADR14	DAT46
	VCC	A32	B32	ADR12	DAT44
DAT45	ADR13	A33	B33	ADR10	DAT42
DAT43	ADR11	A34	B34	ADR08	DAT40
DAT41	ADR09	A35	B35	GND	
DAT39	ADR07	A36	B36	ADR06	DAT38
DAT37	ADR05	A37	B37	ADR04	DAT36
	GND	A38	B38	WBACK#	
DAT35	ADR03	A39	B39	BE0#	BE4#
DAT34	ADR02	A40	B40	VCC	
LBS64#	NC	A41	B41	BE1#	BE5#
	RESET#	A42	B42	BE2#	BE6#
	D/C#	A43	B43	GND	
	M/IO#	A44	B44	BE3#	BE7#
	W/R#	A45	B45	ADS#	
KEY	KEY	A46	B46	KEY	KEY
KEY	KEY	A47	B47	KEY	KEY
	RDYRTN#	A48	B48	LRDY#	
	GND	A49	B49	LDEV<x>#	
	IRQ9	A50	B50	LREQ<x>#	
	BRDY#	A51	B51	GND	
	BLAST#	A52	B52	LGNT<x>#	
DAT32	ID0	A53	B53	VCC	
DAT33	ID1	A54	B54	ID2	
	GND	A55	B55	ID3	
	LCLK	A56	B56	ID4	ACK64#
	VCC	A57	B57	NC	
	LBS16#	A58	B58	LEADS#	

PCI Local Bus Interface Connectors

Pin	5V Side-B	5V Side-A	3.3V Side-B	3.3V Side-A	Comments
Table A.50 PCI Local Bus Connector Pinouts (Rev 2.0)					
1	-12V	TRST#	-12V	TRST#	32-bit connector start
2	TCK	+12V	TCK	+12V	
3	Ground	TMS	Ground	TMS	
4	TDO	TDI	TDO	TDI	
5	+5V	+5V	+5V	+5V	
6	+5V	INTA#	+5V	INTA#	
7	INTB#	INTC#	INTB#	INTC#	
8	INTD#	+5V	INTD#	+5V	
9	PRSNT1#	Reserved	PRSNT1#	Reserved	
10	Reserved	+5V (I/O)	Reserved	+3.3V (I/O)	
11	PRSNT2#	Reserved	PRSNT2#	Reserved	
12	Ground	Ground	KEY	KEY	3.3 volt key
13	Ground	Ground	KEY	KEY	3.3 volt key
14	Reserved	Reserved	Reserved	Reserved	
15	Ground	RST#	Ground	RST#	
16	CLK	+5V (I/O)	CLK	+3.3V (I/O)	
17	Ground	GNT#	Ground	GNT#	
18	REQ#	Ground	REQ#	Ground	
19	+5V (I/O)	Reserved	+3.3V (I/O)	Reserved	
20	AD[31]	AD[30]	AD[31]	AD[30]	
21	AD[29]	+3.3V	AD[29]	+3.3V	
22	Ground	AD[28]	Ground	AD[28]	
23	AD[27]	AD[26]	AD[27]	AD[26]	
24	AD[25]	Ground	AD[25]	Ground	
25	+3.3V	AD[24]	+3.3V	AD[24]	
26	C/BE[3]#	IDSEL	C/BE[3]#	IDSEL	
27	AD[23]	+3.3V	AD[23]	+3.3V	
28	Ground	AD[22]	Ground	AD[22]	
29	AD[21]	AD[20]	AD[21]	AD[20]	
30	AD[19]	Ground	AD[19]	Ground	
31	+3.3V	AD[18]	+3.3V	AD[18]	
32	AD[17]	AD[16]	AD[17]	AD[16]	
33	C/BE[2]#	+3.3V	C/BE[2]#	+3.3V	
34	Ground	FRAME#	Ground	FRAME#	
35	IRDY#	Ground	IRDY#	Ground	
36	+3.3V	TRDY#	+3.3V	TRDY#	
37	DEVSEL#	Ground	DEVSEL#	Ground	

Pin	5V Side-B	5V Side-A	3.3V Side-B	3.3V Side-A	Comments
38	Ground	STOP#	Ground	STOP#	
39	LOCK#	+3.3V	LOCK#	+3.3V	
40	PERR#	SDONE	PERR#	SDONE	
41	+3.3V	SBO#	+3.3V	SBO#	
42	SERR#	Ground	SERR#	Ground	
43	+3.3V	PAR	+3.3V	PAR	
44	C/BE[1]#	AD[15]	C/BE[1]#	AD[15]	
45	AD[14]	+3.3V	AD[14]	+3.3V	
46	Ground	AD[13]	Ground	AD[13]	
47	AD[12]	AD[11]	AD[12]	AD[11]	
48	AD[10]	Ground	AD[10]	Ground	
49	Ground	AD[09]	Ground	AD[09]	
50	KEY	KEY	Ground	Ground	5 volt key
51	KEY	KEY	Ground	Ground	5 volt key
52	AD[08]	C/BE[0]#	AD[08]	C/BE[0]#	
53	AD[07]	+3.3V	AD[07]	+3.3V	
54	+3.3V	AD[06]	+3.3V	AD[06]	
55	AD[05]	AD[04]	AD[05]	AD[04]	
56	AD[03]	Ground	AD[03]	Ground	
57	Ground	AD[02]	Ground	AD[02]	
58	AD[01]	AD[00]	AD[01]	AD[00]	
59	+5V (I/O)	+5V (I/O)	+3.3V (I/O)	+3.3V (I/O)	
60	ACK64#	REQ64#	ACK64#	REQ64#	
61	+5V	+5V	+5V	+5V	
62	+5V	+5V	+5V	+5V	32-bit connector end
	KEY	KEY	KEY	KEY	64-bit spacer
	KEY	KEY	KEY	KEY	64-bit spacer
63	Reserved	Ground	Reserved	Ground	64-bit connector start
64	Ground	C/BE[7]#	Ground	C/BE[7]#	
65	C/BE[6]#	C/BE[5]#	C/BE[6]#	C/BE[5]#	
66	C/BE[4]#	+5V (I/O)	C/BE[4]#	+3.3V (I/O)	
67	Ground	PAR64	Ground	PAR64	
68	AD[63]	AD[62]	AD[63]	AD[62]	
69	AD[61]	Ground	AD[61]	Ground	
70	+5V (I/O)	AD[60]	+3.3V (I/O)	AD[60]	
71	AD[59]	AD[58]	AD[59]	AD[58]	
72	AD[57]	Ground	AD[57]	Ground	
73	Ground	AD[56]	Ground	AD[56]	

(continues)

Pin	5V Side-B	5V Side-A	3.3V Side-B	3.3V Side-A	Comments
Table A.50 Continued					
74	AD[55]	AD[54]	AD[55]	AD[54]	
75	AD[53]	+5V (I/O)	AD[53]	+5V (I/O)	
76	Ground	AD[52]	Ground	AD[52]	
77	AD[51]	AD[50]	AD[51]	AD[50]	
78	AD[49]	Ground	AD[49]	Ground	
79	+5V (I/O)	AD[48]	+3.3V (I/O)	AD[48]	
80	AD[47]	AD[46]	AD[47]	AD[46]	
81	AD[45]	Ground	AD[45]	Ground	
82	Ground	AD[44]	Ground	AD[44]	
83	AD[43]	AD[42]	AD[43]	AD[42]	
84	AD[41]	+5V (I/O)	AD[41]	+3.3V (I/O)	
85	Ground	AD[40]	Ground	AD[40]	
86	AD[39]	AD[38]	AD[39]	AD[38]	
87	AD[37]	Ground	AD[37]	Ground	
88	+5V (I/O)	AD[36]	+3.3V (I/O)	AD[36]	
89	AD[35]	AD[34]	AD[35]	AD[34]	
90	AD[33]	Ground	AD[33]	Ground	
91	Ground	AD[32]	Ground	AD[32]	
92	Reserved	Reserved	Reserved	Reserved	
93	Reserved	Ground	Reserved	Ground	
94	Ground	Reserved	Ground	Reserved	64-bit connector end

MCA (16-Bit and 32-Bit) Interface Connectors. The following tables show the pinouts for the Micro Channel Architecture (MCA) bus connectors in the PS/2 systems. The 16-bit connector with an optional auxiliary video-extension connector (AVEC) and the 32-bit connector with the optional matched memory extension are shown.

Table A.51 MCA 16-Bit Connector with Optional Auxiliary Video Extension			
Signal	**Pin**	**Pin**	**Signal**
ESYNC	BV10	AV10	VSYNC
Ground	BV9	AV9	HSYNC
P5	BV8	AV8	BLANK
P4	BV7	AV7	Ground
P3	BV6	AV6	P6
Ground	BV5	AV5	EDCLK
P2	BV4	AV4	DCLK
P1	BV3	AV3	Ground
P0	BV2	AV2	P7

Pin	5V Side-B	5V Side-A	3.3V Side-B	3.3V Side-A	Comments
Ground	BV1	AV1	EVIDEO		
KEY	KEY	KEY	KEY		
AUDIO GND	B1	A1	-CD SETUP		
AUDIO	B2	A2	MADE 24		
Ground	B3	A3	Ground		
OSC (14.3MHz)	B4	A4	Address 11		
Ground	B5	A5	Address 10		
Address 23	B6	A6	Address 9		
Address 22	B7	A7	+5 Vdc		
Address 21	B8	A8	Address 8		
Ground	B9	A9	Address 7		
Address 20	B10	A10	Address 6		
Address 19	B11	A11	+5 Vdc		
Address 18	B12	A12	Address 5		
Ground	B13	A13	Address 4		
Address 17	B14	A14	Address 3		
Address 16	B15	A15	+5 Vdc		
Address 15	B16	A16	Address 2		
Ground	B17	A17	Address 1		
Address 14	B18	A18	Address 0		
Address 13	B19	A19	+12 Vdc		
Address 12	B20	A20	-ADL		
Ground	B21	A21	-PREEMPT		
-IRQ 9	B22	A22	-BURST		
-IRQ 3	B23	A23	-12 Vdc		
-IRQ 4	B24	A24	ARB 00		
Ground	B25	A25	ARB 01		
-IRQ 5	B26	A26	ARB 02		
-IRQ 6	B27	A27	-12 Vdc		
-IRQ 7	B28	A28	ARB 03		
Ground	B29	A29	ARB/-GNT		
RESERVED	B30	A30	-TC		
RESERVED	B31	A31	+5 Vdc		
-CHCK	B32	A32	-SO		
Ground	B33	A33	-S1		
-CMD	B34	A34	M/-IO		
CHRDYRTN	B35	A35	+12 Vdc		
-CD SFDBK	B36	A36	CD CHRDY		
Ground	B37	A37	Data Bit 0		
Data Bit 1	B38	A38	Data Bit 2		

(continues)

Table A.51 Continued

Signal	Pin	Pin	Signal
Data Bit 3	B39	A39	+5 Vdc
Data Bit 4	B40	A40	Data Bit 5
Ground	B41	A41	Data Bit 6
CHRESET	B42	A42	Data Bit 7
RESERVED	B43	A43	Ground
RESERVED	B44	A44	-DS 16 RTN
Ground	B45	A45	-REFRESH
KEY	B46	A46	KEY
KEY	B47	A47	KEY
Data Bit 8	B48	A48	+5 Vdc
Data Bit 9	B49	A49	D10
Ground	B50	A50	D11
Data Bit 12	B51	A51	D13
Data Bit 14	B52	A52	+12 Vdc
Data Bit 15	B53	A53	RESERVED
Ground	B54	A54	-SBHE
-IRQ 10	B55	A55	-CD DS 16
-IRQ 11	B56	A56	+5 Vdc
-IRQ 12	B57	A57	-IRQ 14
Ground	B58	A58	-IRQ 15
Reserved	B59	A59	Reserved
Reserved	B60	A60	Reserved

Table A.52 MCA 32-Bit Connector with Optional Matched Memory Extension

Signal	Pin	Pin	Signal
Ground	BM4	AM4	Reserved
Reserved	BM3	AM3	-MMC CMD
-MMCR	BM2	AM2	Ground
Reserved	BM1	AM1	-MMC
AUDIO GND	B1	A1	-CD SETUP
AUDIO	B2	A2	MADE 24
Ground	B3	A3	Ground
OSC (14.3MHz)	B4	A4	Address 11
Ground	B5	A5	Address 10
Address 23	B6	A6	Address 9
Address 22	B7	A7	+5 Vdc
Address 21	B8	A8	Address 8

Signal	Pin	Pin	Signal
Ground	B9	A9	Address 7
Address 20	B10	A10	Address 6
Address 19	B11	A11	+5 Vdc
Address 18	B12	A12	Address 5
Ground	B13	A13	Address 4
Address 17	B14	A14	Address 3
Address 16	B15	A15	+5 Vdc
Address 15	B16	A16	Address 2
Ground	B17	A17	Address 1
Address 14	B18	A18	Address 0
Address 13	B19	A19	+12 Vdc
Address 12	B20	A20	-ADL
Ground	B21	A21	-PREEMPT
-IRQ 9	B22	A22	-BURST
-IRQ 3	B23	A23	-12 Vdc
-IRQ 4	B24	A24	ARB 00
Ground	B25	A25	ARB 01
-IRQ 5	B26	A26	ARB 02
-IRQ 6	B27	A27	-12 Vdc
-IRQ 7	B28	A28	ARB 03
Ground	B29	A29	ARB/-GNT
RESERVED	B30	A30	-TC
RESERVED	B31	A31	+5 Vdc
-CHCK	B32	A32	-SO
Ground	B33	A33	-S1
-CMD	B34	A34	M/-IO
CHRDYRTN	B35	A35	+12 Vdc
-CD SFDBK	B36	A36	CD CHRDY
Ground	B37	A37	Data Bit 0
Data Bit 1	B38	A38	Data Bit 2
Data Bit 3	B39	A39	+5 Vdc
Data Bit 4	B40	A40	Data Bit 5
Ground	B41	A41	Data Bit 6
CHRESET	B42	A42	Data Bit 7
RESERVED	B43	A43	Ground
RESERVED	B44	A44	-DS 16 RTN
Ground	B45	A45	-REFRESH
KEY	B46	A46	KEY
KEY	B47	A47	KEY

(continues)

Table A.52 Continued

Signal	Pin	Pin	Signal
Data Bit 8	B48	A48	+5 Vdc
Data Bit 9	B49	A49	D10
Ground	B50	A50	D11
Data Bit 12	B51	A51	D13
Data Bit 14	B52	A52	+12 Vdc
Data Bit 15	B53	A53	RESERVED
Ground	B54	A54	-SBHE
-IRQ 10	B55	A55	-CD DS 16
-IRQ 11	B56	A56	+5 Vdc
-IRQ 12	B57	A57	-IRQ 14
Ground	B58	A58	-IRQ 15
Reserved	B59	A59	Reserved
Reserved	B60	A60	Reserved
Reserved	B61	A61	Ground
Reserved	B62	A63	Reserved
Ground	B63	A63	Reserved
Data Bit 16	B64	A64	Reserved
Data Bit 17	B65	A65	+12 Vdc
Data Bit 18	B66	A66	Data Bit 19
Ground	B67	A67	Data Bit 20
Data Bit 22	B68	A68	Data Bit 21
Data Bit 23	B69	A69	+5 Vdc
Reserved	B70	A70	Data Bit 24
Ground	B71	A71	Data Bit 25
Data Bit 27	B72	A72	Data Bit 26
Data Bit 28	B73	A73	+5 Vdc
Data Bit 29	B74	A74	Data Bit 30
Ground	B75	A75	Data Bit 31
-BE 0	B76	A76	Reserved
-BE 1	B77	A77	+12 Vdc
-BE 2	B78	A78	-BE 3
Ground	B79	A79	-DS 32 RTN
TR 32	B80	A80	-CD DS 32
Address 24	B81	A81	+5 Vdc
Address 25	B82	A82	Address 26
Ground	B83	A83	Address 27
Address 29	B84	A84	Address 28
Address 30	B85	A85	+5 Vdc

Signal	Pin	Pin	Signal
Address 31	B86	A86	Reserved
Ground	B87	A87	Reserved
Reserved	B88	A88	Reserved
Reserved	B89	A89	Ground

PCMCIA Interface Connector. The PCMCIA (Personal Computer Memory Card International Association) bus is also known as the credit card adapter bus since the cards are approximately the same shape and size as a credit card. Although originally designed for memory cards only, the PCMCIA has been adapted to work with virtually any type of peripheral. The following table shows the PCMCIA Interface connector specification.

Table A.53 PCMCIA Bus Pinout	
Pin	**PCMCIA Signal**
1	Ground
2	Data Bit 3
3	Data Bit 4
4	Data Bit 5
5	Data Bit 6
6	Data Bit 7
7	-Card Enable 1
8	Address Bit 10
9	-Output Enable
10	Address Bit 11
11	Address Bit 9
12	Address Bit 8
13	Address Bit 13
14	Address Bit 14
15	-Write Enable /-Program
16	Ready/-Busy (IREQ)
17	+5 Vdc
18	Vpp1
19	Address Bit 16
20	Address Bit 15
21	Address Bit 12
22	Address Bit 7
23	Address Bit 6
24	Address Bit 5
25	Address Bit 4
26	Address Bit 3

(continues)

Table A.53 Continued	
Pin	**PCMCIA Signal**
27	Address Bit 2
28	Address Bit 1
29	Address Bit 0
30	Data Bit 0
31	Data Bit 1
32	Data Bit 2
33	Write Protect (-IOIS16)
34	Ground
35	Ground
36	-Card Detect 1
37	Data Bit 11
38	Data Bit 12
39	Data Bit 13
40	Data Bit 14
41	Data Bit 15
42	-Card Enable 2
43	Refresh
44	RFU (-IOR)
45	RFU (-IOW)
46	Address Bit 17
47	Address Bit 18
48	Address Bit 19
49	Address Bit 20
50	Address Bit 21
51	+5 Vdc
52	Vpp2
53	Address Bit 22
54	Address Bit 23
55	Address Bit 24
56	Address Bit 25
57	RFU
58	RESET
59	-WAIT
60	RFU (-INPACK)
61	-Register Select
62	Battery Voltage Detect 2 (-SPKR)
63	Battery Voltage Detect 1 (-STSCHG)
64	Data Bit 8
65	Data Bit 9

Pin	PCMCIA Signal
66	Data Bit 10
67	-Card Detect 2
68	Ground

SIMM Interface Connectors

There are two main types of SIMM (Single In-line Memory Modules) found in PC systems today with regard to the interface. These are:

- 9-Bit (30-Pin) SIMMs

- 36-Bit (72-Pin) SIMMs

There are two different styles of 9-bit (30-pin) SIMMs, there is an industry standard version that is used by most PC compatible systems, and then there is a version used by IBM in some of the older PS/2 systems. The IBM 9-bit variant is no longer used by IBM, as they now use only industry standard 36-bit (72-pin) SIMMs in their systems today.

The 36-bit (72-pin) SIMMs are available in one common connector type, which is an industry standard. These SIMMs are vastly preferred over the 9-bit variety, because with 36-bits, they contain an entire bank of memory for a 32-bit system (32 data bits plus 4 parity bits). This means that in most 386, 486, or Pentium systems, these SIMMs can be installed or removed one at a time. This is unlike the 9-bit SIMMs, which must be used in groups of 4 to make up a full bank in a 32-bit system. This makes the 9-bit SIMMs clumsy, and much more difficult to work with, plus they take up much more motherboard real estate. I only recommend purchasing systems today that use the 36-bit SIMMs.

The following tables show the interface connector pinouts for both 9-bit (30-pin) varieties, and the standard 36-bit SIMM. Also included is a special presence detect table that shows the configuration of the presence detect pins on various 36-bit SIMMs. The presence detect pins are used by the motherboard to detect exactly what size and speed SIMM is installed. Industry standard 9-bit SIMMs do not have a presence detect feature.

Pin	Standard SIMM Signal Names	IBM SIMM Signal Names
1	+5 Vdc	+5 Vdc
2	Column Address Strobe	Column Address Strobe
3	Data Bit 0	Data Bit 0
4	Address Bit 0	Address Bit 0
5	Address Bit 1	Address Bit 1
6	Data Bit 1	Data Bit 1
7	Address Bit 2	Address Bit 2
8	Address Bit 3	Address Bit 3

Table A.54 Industry Standard and IBM 30-Pin (9-bit) SIMM Pinouts

(continues)

Table A.54 Continued

Pin	Standard SIMM Signal Names	IBM SIMM Signal Names
9	Ground	Ground
10	Data Bit 2	Data Bit 2
11	Address Bit 4	Address Bit 4
12	Address Bit 5	Address Bit 5
13	Data Bit 3	Data Bit 3
14	Address Bit 6	Address Bit 6
15	Address Bit 7	Address Bit 7
16	Data Bit 4	Data Bit 4
17	Address Bit 8	Address Bit 8
18	Address Bit 9	Address Bit 9
19	Address Bit 10	Row Address Strobe 1
20	Data Bit 5	Data Bit 5
21	Write Enable	Write Enable
22	Ground	Ground
23	Data Bit 6	Data Bit 6
24	No Connection	Presence Detect (Ground)
25	Data Bit 7	Data Bit 7
26	Data Bit 8 (Parity) Out	Presence Detect (1M = Ground)
27	Row Address Strobe	Row Address Strobe
28	Column Address Strobe Parity	No Connection
29	Data Bit 8 (Parity) In	Data Bit 8 (Parity) I/O
30	+5 Vdc	+5 Vdc

Table A.55 Standard 72-Pin (36-bit) SIMM Pinout

Pin	SIMM Signal Name
1	Ground
2	Data Bit 0
3	Data Bit 16
4	Data Bit 1
5	Data Bit 17
6	Data Bit 2
7	Data Bit 18
8	Data Bit 3
9	Data Bit 18
10	+5 Vdc
11	Column Address Strobe Parity
12	Address Bit 0

Pin	Standard SIMM Signal Names	IBM SIMM Signal Names
13	Address Bit 1	
14	Address Bit 2	
15	Address Bit 3	
16	Address Bit 4	
17	Address Bit 5	
18	Address Bit 6	
19	Reserved	
20	Data Bit 4	
21	Data Bit 20	
22	Data Bit 5	
23	Data Bit 21	
24	Data Bit 6	
25	Data Bit 22	
26	Data Bit 7	
27	Data Bit 23	
28	Address Bit 7	
29	Block Select 0	
30	+5 Vdc	
31	Address Bit 8	
32	Address Bit 9	
33	Row Address Strobe 3	
34	Row Address Strobe 2	
35	Parity Data Bit 2	
36	Parity Data Bit 0	
37	Parity Data Bit 1	
38	Parity Data Bit 3	
39	Ground	
40	Column Address Strobe 0	
41	Column Address Strobe 2	
42	Column Address Strobe 3	
43	Column Address Strobe 1	
44	Row Address Strobe 0	
45	Row Address Strobe 1	
46	Block Select 1	
47	Write Enable	
48	Reserved	
49	Data Bit 8	
50	Data Bit 24	
51	Data Bit 9	
52	Data Bit 25	

(continues)

Table A.55 Continued

Pin	SIMM Signal Name
53	Data Bit 10
54	Data Bit 26
55	Data Bit 11
56	Data Bit 27
57	Data Bit 12
58	Data Bit 28
59	+5 Vdc
60	Data Bit 29
61	Data Bit 13
62	Data Bit 30
63	Data Bit 14
64	Data Bit 31
65	Data Bit 15
66	Block Select 2
67	Presence Detect Bit 0
68	Presence Detect Bit 1
69	Presence Detect Bit 2
70	Presence Detect Bit 3
71	Block Select 3
72	Ground

Table A.56 72-Pin (36-bit) SIMM Presence Detect Pins

70	69	68	67	SIMM Type	IBM Part Number
N/C	N/C	N/C	N/C	Not a valid SIMM	N/A
N/C	N/C	N/C	Gnd	1 MB 120ns	N/A
N/C	N/C	Gnd	N/C	2 MB 120ns	N/A
N/C	N/C	Gnd	Gnd	2 MB 70ns	92F0102
N/C	Gnd	N/C	N/C	8 MB 70ns	64F3606
N/C	Gnd	N/C	Gnd	Reserved	N/A
N/C	Gnd	Gnd	N/C	2 MB 80ns	92F0103
N/C	Gnd	Gnd	Gnd	8 MB 80ns	64F3607
Gnd	N/C	N/C	N/C	Reserved	N/A
Gnd	N/C	N/C	Gnd	1 MB 85ns	90X8624
Gnd	N/C	Gnd	N/C	2 MB 85ns	92F0104
Gnd	N/C	Gnd	Gnd	4 MB 70ns	92F0105
Gnd	Gnd	N/C	N/C	4 MB 85ns	79F1003 (square notch) L40-SX
Gnd	Gnd	N/C	Gnd	1 MB 100ns	N/A

Pin	SIMM Signal Name				
Gnd	Gnd	N/C	Gnd	8 MB 80ns	79F1004 (square notch) L40-SX
Gnd	Gnd	Gnd	N/C	2 MB 100ns	N/A
Gnd	Gnd	Gnd	Gnd	4 MB 80ns	87F9980
Gnd	Gnd	Gnd	Gnd	2 MB 85ns	79F1003 (square notch) L40SX

Notes:
N/C = No Connection (open)
Gnd = Ground
Pin 67 = Presence detect bit 0
Pin 68 = Presence detect bit 1
Pin 69 = Presence detect bit 2
Pin 70 = Presence detect bit 3
Serial and Parallel Connector Pinouts

The tables in this section show the pinouts for all the different types of serial and parallel port connectors.

Table A.57 9-Pin (AT) Serial Port Connector

Pin	Signal	Description	I/O
1	CD	Carrier detect	In
2	RD	Receive data	In
3	TD	Transmit data	Out
4	DTR	Data terminal ready	Out
5	SG	Signal ground	—
6	DSR	Data set ready	In
7	RTS	Request to send	Out
8	CTS	Clear to send	In
9	RI	Ring indicator	In

Table A.58 25-Pin (PC, XT, and PS/2) Serial Port Connector

Pin	Signal	Description	I/O
1	—	Chassis Ground	—
2	TD	Transmit Data	Out
3	RD	Receive Data	In
4	RTS	Request to Send	Out
5	CTS	Clear to Send	In
6	DSR	Data Set Ready	In
7	SG	Signal Ground	—
8	CD	Carrier Detect	In

(continues)

Pin	Signal	Description	I/O
Table A.58 Continued			
Pin	Signal	Description	I/O
9	—	+Transmit Current Loop Return	Out
11	—	−Transmit Current Loop Data	Out
18	—	+Receive Current Loop Data	In
20	DTR	Data Terminal Ready	Out
22	RI	Ring Indicator	In
25	—	−Receive Current Loop Return	In

Pins 9, 11, 18, and 25 are used for a Current Loop interface only. Current Loop is not supported on the AT Serial/Parallel Adapter or PS/2 systems.

Table A.59 9-Pin to 25-Pin Serial Cable Adapter Connections

9-pin	25-pin	Signal	Description
1	8	CD	Carrier Detect
2	3	RD	Receive Data
3	2	TD	Transmit Data
4	20	DTR	Data Terminal Ready
5	7	SG	Signal Ground
6	6	DSR	Data Set Ready
7	4	RTS	Request to Send
8	5	CTS	Clear to Send
9	22	RI	Ring Indicator

Table A.60 25-Pin PC-Compatible Parallel Port Connector

Pin	Description	I/O
1	−Strobe	Out
2	+Data Bit 0	Out
3	+Data Bit 1	Out
4	+Data Bit 2	Out
5	+Data Bit 3	Out
6	+Data Bit 4	Out
7	+Data Bit 5	Out
8	+Data Bit 6	Out
9	+Data Bit 7	Out
10	−Acknowledge	In
11	+Busy	In

Pin	Description	I/O
12	+Paper End	In
13	+Select	In
14	–Auto Feed	Out
15	–Error	In
16	–Initialize Printer	Out
17	–Select Input	Out
18	–Data Bit 0 Return (GND)	In
19	–Data Bit 1 Return (GND)	In
20	–Data Bit 2 Return (GND)	In
21	–Data Bit 3 Return (GND)	In
22	–Data Bit 4 Return (GND)	In
23	–Data Bit 5 Return (GND)	In
24	–Data Bit 6 Return (GND)	In
25	–Data Bit 7 Return (GND)	In

Wrap Plug (Loopback) Wiring

Many third-party diagnostics packages do not have correctly wired wrap plugs. These plugs may pass their own tests, but fail tests by other diagnostics, especially IBMs Advanced Diagnostics. The following figures show the wiring of IBMs tri-connector wrap plug P/N 72X8546. These plugs pass IBM's Advanced Diagnostics as well as virtually all compatible diagnostics software tests that check serial and parallel ports.

The following table shows the Monochrome Display Adapter connector pinout.

Table A.61 9-Pin Monochrome Display Adapter (MDA) Connector		
Pin	**Description**	**I/O**
1	Ground	—
2	Ground	—
3	Not Used	—
4	Not Used	—
5	Not Used	—
6	+Intensity	Out
7	+Video	Out
8	+Horizontal	Out
9	–Vertical	Out

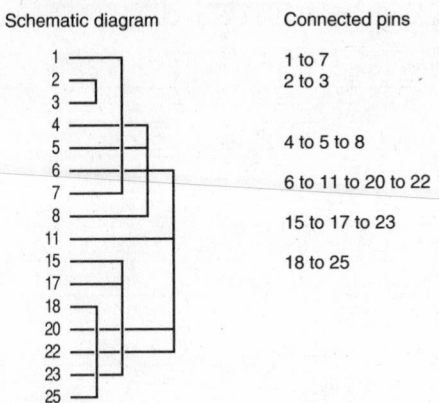

Schematic diagram   Connected pins

1 to 7
2 to 3

4 to 5 to 8

6 to 11 to 20 to 22

15 to 17 to 23

18 to 25

Fig. A.8
Twenty-five-pin serial loopback connector (wrap plug) wiring.

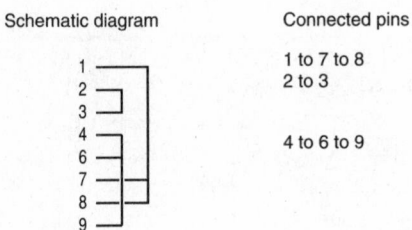

Schematic diagram   Connected pins

1 to 7 to 8
2 to 3

4 to 6 to 9

Fig. A.9
Nine-pin serial loopback connector (wrap plug) wiring.

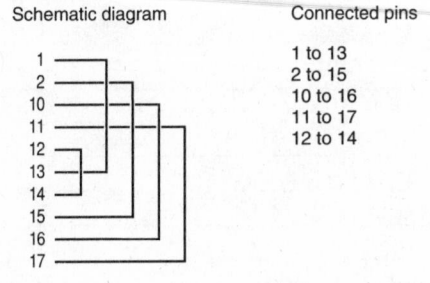

Schematic diagram   Connected pins

1 to 13
2 to 15
10 to 16
11 to 17
12 to 14

Fig. A.10
Seventeen-pin parallel loopback connector (wrap plug) wiring.

The following table shows the Color Graphics Adapter connector pinout.

Table A.62 9-Pin Color Graphics Adapter (CGA) Connector		
Pin	**Description**	**I/O**
1	Ground	—
2	Ground	—
3	Red	Out
4	Green	Out
5	Blue	Out
6	+Intensity	Out
7	RESERVED	—
8	+Horizontal drive	Out
9	–Vertical drive	Out

The following table shows the EGA (Enhanced Graphics Adapter) connector pinout.

Table A.63 9-Pin Enhanced Graphics Adapter (EGA) Connector		
Pin	**Description**	**I/O**
1	Ground	—
2	Secondary Red	Out
3	Red	Out
4	Green	Out
5	Blue	Out
6	Secondary Green/Intensity	Out
7	Secondary Blue/Mono	Out
8	Horizontal Retrace	Out
9	Vertical Retrace	Out

The following table shows the VGA (Video Graphics Array) or XGA (eXtended Graphics Array) connector pinouts. Also shown are typical pinouts for Monochrome or Color Displays which may be attached to the video adapter. Note that when the display adapter detects a monochrome display, it performs a color summing function and sends the sum signal out pin 2 (green). This is how the monochrome displays can display colors as different shades.

Table A.64 15-Pin Video Graphics Array (VGA) Connector				
Pin	**VGA Signal**	**I/O**	**Mono Display**	**Color Display**
1	Red	Out	No Pin	Red
2	Green	Out	Mono	Green
3	Blue	Out	No Pin	Blue

(continues)

Table A.64 Continued

Pin	VGA Signal	I/O	Mono Display	Color Display
4	Monitor ID 2	In	No Pin	No Pin/Ground
5	Digital Ground	—	Self Test	Self Test
6	Red Ground	—	Not Connected	Red Ground
7	Green Ground	—	Mono Ground	Green Ground
8	Blue Ground	—	No Pin	Blue Ground
9	KEY (plug)	—	KEY (No Pin)	KEY (No Pin)
10	Sync Ground	—	Ground	Ground
11	Monitor ID 0	In	Ground	No Pin
13	Horizontal Sync	Out	Horizontal Sync	Horizontal Sync
14	Vertical Sync	Out	Vertical Sync	Vertical Sync
15	Monitor ID 3	In	No Pin	No Pin/Ground

The following table shows the settings used for the Monitor ID bits for several different IBM displays. By sensing which of these 4 pins are grounded, the video adapter can determine what type of display is attached. This is especially used with regards to Monochrome or Color display detection. In this manner, the VGA or XGA circuitry can properly select the color mapping and image size to suit the display.

Table A.65 IBM Display Monitor ID Settings

Display	Size	Type	ID0	ID1	ID2	ID3
8503	12-inch	Mono	No Pin	Ground	No Pin	No Pin
8512	13-inch	Color	Ground	No Pin	No Pin	No Pin
8513	12-inch	Color	Ground	No Pin	No Pin	No Pin
8514	15-inch	Color	Ground	No Pin	Ground	No Pin
8515	14-inch	Color	No Pin	No Pin	Ground	No Pin
9515	14-inch	Color	No Pin	No Pin	Ground	No Pin
9517	17-inch	Color	Ground	No Pin	Ground	Ground
9518	14-inch	Color	Ground	No Pin	Ground	No Pin

Table A.66 shows connector pinouts for each keyboard cable connectors.

Table A.66 Keyboard Connector Signals

Signal Name	5-pin DIN	6-pin mini-DIN	6-pin SDL
Keyboard data	2	1	B
Ground	4	3	C
+5v	5	4	E
Keyboard clock	1	5	D

Signal Name	5-pin DIN	6-pin mini-DIN	6-pin SDL
Not connected	—	2	A
Not connected	—	6	F
Not connected	3	—	—

DIN = German Industrial Norm (Deutsche Industrie Norm), a committee that sets German dimensional standards.
SDL = Shielded Data Link, a type of shielded connector created by AMP and used by IBM and others for keyboard cables.

The following table shows the pinouts for most standard AT or PC/XT compatible systems. Some systems may have more or fewer drive connectors, for example, IBM's AT system power supplies only had three disk drive power connectors, although most compatible power supplies have 4. If you are adding drives and need additional disk drive power connectors, "Y" splitter cables are available from many electronics supply houses (including Radio Shack) that will adapt a single power connector to serve two drives. Be sure that your total power supply output is capable of supplying the additional power as a precaution.

Table A.67 Typical PC-Compatible Power-Supply Connections

Connector	AT Type	PC/XT Type
P8-1	Power Good (+5 Vdc)	Power Good (+5 Vdc)
P8-2	+5 Vdc	Key (No connect)
P8-3	+12 Vdc	+12 Vdc
P8-4	–12 Vdc	–12 Vdc
P8-5	Ground (0)	Ground (0)
P8-6	Ground (0)	Ground (0)
P9-1	Ground (0)	Ground (0)
P9-2	Ground (0)	Ground (0)
P9-3	–5 Vdc	–5 Vdc
P9-4	+5 Vdc	+5 Vdc
P9-5	+5 Vdc	+5 Vdc
P9-6	+5 Vdc	+5 Vdc
P10-1	+12 Vdc	+12 Vdc
P10-2	Ground (0)	Ground (0)
P10-3	Ground (0)	Ground (0)
P10-4	+5 Vdc	+5 Vdc
P11-1	+12 Vdc	+12 Vdc
P11-2	Ground (0)	Ground (0)
P11-3	Ground (0)	Ground (0)
P11-4	+5 Vdc	+5 Vdc

(continues)

Table A.67 Continued		
Connector	**AT Type**	**PC/XT Type**
P12-1	+12 Vdc	—
P12-2	Ground (0)	—
P12-3	Ground (0)	—
P12-4	+5 Vdc	—
P13-1	+12 Vdc	—
P13-2	Ground (0)	—
P13-3	Ground (0)	—
P13-4	+5 Vdc	—

Acceptable voltage ranges are 4.5 to 5.4 for 5 volts, and 10.8 to 12.9 for 12 volts.

PC Compatible Game (Joystick) Interface. The following table shows the interface connector specification for a PC compatible Game Adapter. These adapters normally have a 15-pin D shell connector that is used to connect joysticks or paddles for controlling games. Because this adapter actually reads resistance and can easily be manipulated with standard programming languages, the game adapter serves as a poor man's data acquisition board or realtime interface card. With it, you can hook up sensors and easily read the data in the PC.

Table A.68 PC-Compatible Game Adapter Connector			
Pin	**Signal**	**Function**	**I/O**
1	+5 Vdc		Out
2	Button 4	Paddle 1 button, joystick A button	In
3	Position 0	Paddle 1 position, joystick A x-coordinate	In
4	Ground		
5	Ground		
6	Position 1	Paddle 2 position, joystick a y-coordinate	In
7	Button 5	Paddle 2 button	In
8	+5 Vdc		Out
9	+5 Vdc		Out
10	Button 6	Paddle 3 button, joystick B button	In
11	Position 2	Paddle 3 position, joystick B x-coordinate	In
12	Ground		
13	Position 3	Paddle 4 position, joystick B y-coordinate	In

Pin	Signal	Function	I/O
14	Button 7	Paddle 4 button	In
15	+5 Vdc		Out

Disk Drives

This section has tables of information that pertain to disk drives. You can find a wealth of information here, including floppy and hard disk drive specifications and parameter data, information on the different disk interfaces from the ROM BIOS and DOS perspective, and even pinouts of the different hard disk interfaces.

Disk Software Interfaces

The following figure shows a representation of the relationship between the different disk software interfaces at work in an IBM-compatible system. This figure shows the chain of command from the hardware, which is the drive controller, to the ROM BIOS, DOS, and, finally, an application program.

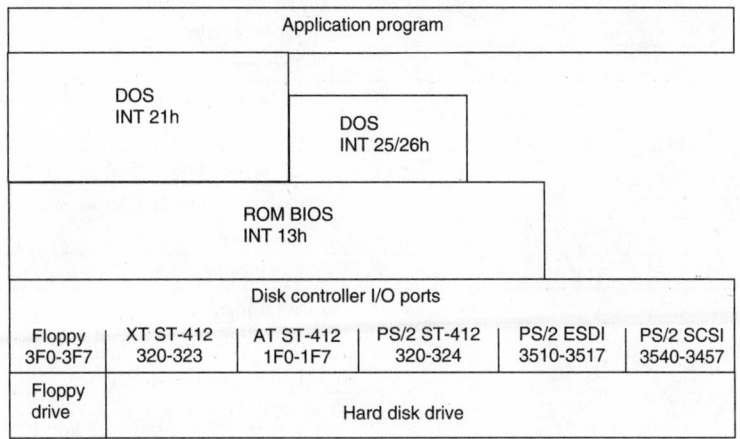

Fig. A.11

Disk Software Interface levels and relationships.

The following table shows the different functions available at the Interrupt 13h BIOS interface. Some functions are available to floppy drives or hard drives only, while others are available to both types of drives.

Table A.69 Int 13h BIOS Disk Functions			
Function	**Floppy disk**	**Hard disk**	**Description**
00h	X	X	Reset disk system
01h	X	X	Get status of last operation
02h	X	X	Read sectors
03h	X	X	Write sectors
04h	X	X	Verify sectors
05h	X	X	Format track
06h		X	Format bad track
07h		X	Format drive
08h	X	X	Read drive parameters
09h		X	Initialize drive characteristics
0Ah		X	Read long
0Bh		X	Write long
0Ch		X	Seek
0Dh		X	Alternate hard disk reset
0Eh		X	Read sector buffer
0Fh		X	Write sector buffer
10h		X	Test for drive ready
11h		X	Recalibrate drive
12h		X	Controller RAM diagnostic
13h		X	Controller drive diagnostic
14h		X	Controller internal diagnostic
15h	X	X	Get disk type
16h	X		Get floppy disk change status
17h	X		Set floppy disk type for format
18h	X		Set media type for format
19h		X	Park hard disk heads
1Ah		X	ESDI—Low-level format
1Bh		X	ESDI—Get manufacturing header
1Ch		X	ESDI—Get configuration

The following table shows the error codes that may be returned by the BIOS INT 13h routines. In some cases you may see these codes be referred to when running a Low Level Format program, disk editor, or other program that can directly access a disk drive through the BIOS.

Table A.70 INT13h BIOS Error Codes

Code	Description
00h	No error
01h	Bad command
02h	Address mark not found
03h	Write protect
04h	Request sector not found
05h	Reset failed
06h	Media change error
07h	Initialization failed
09h	Cross 64K DMA boundary
0Ah	Bad sector flag detected
0Bh	Bad track flag detected
10h	Bad ECC on disk read
11h	ECC corrected data error
20h	Controller has failed
40h	Seek operation failed
80h	Drive failed to respond
AAh	Drive not ready
BBh	Undefined error
CCh	Write fault
0Eh	Register error
FFh	Sense operation failed

The following table shows how the sectors on a typical disk are layed out. In this example, an MFM 17-Sector per track hard disk is used, but these structures are similar on all types of drives, including floppy drives. This table shows the true structure of a track on a disk, and demonstrates why the formatted capacity of a disk is lower than the unformatted capacity.

Table A.71 Typical MFM Disk Sector Format

Bytes	Name	Description
16	POST INDEX GAP	All 4Eh, at the track beginning after the Index mark Sector data; repeated 17 times for an MFM encoded track.
13	ID VFO LOCK	All 00h; synchronizes the VFO for the sector ID
1	SYNC BYTE	A1h; notifies the controller that data follows
1	ADDRESS MARK	FEh; defines that ID field data follows
2	CYLINDER NUMBER	A value that defines the actuator position
1	HEAD NUMBER	A value that defines the head selected
1	SECTOR NUMBER	A value that defines the sector

(continues)

Table A.71 Continued		
Bytes	**Name**	**Description**
2	CRC	Cyclic Redundancy Check to verify ID data
3	WRITE TURN-ON GAP	00h written by format to isolate the ID from DATA
13	DATA SYNC VFO LOCK	All 00h; synchronizes the VFO for the DATA
1	SYNC BYTE	A1h; notifies the controller that data follows
1	ADDRESS MARK	F8h; defines that user DATA field follows
512	DATA	The area for user DATA
2	CRC	Cyclic Redundancy Check to verify DATA
3	WRITE TURN-OFF GAP	00h; written by DATA update to isolate DATA
15	INTER-RECORD GAP	All 00h; a buffer for spindle speed variation
693	PRE-INDEX GAP	All 4Eh, at track end before Index mark

571	*Total bytes per sector*
512	*Data bytes per sector*
10416	*Total bytes per track*
8704	*Data bytes per track*

Characteristics of Floppy Drives and Disks

This section provides information about the physical properties of floppy disks and drives. This information shows how one type of disk or drive differs from the others in operation and use. The tables in this section explain the difference between floppy disk formats, how data is written to a disk, and how one type of media differs from the others. Knowing this information helps you prevent improper use and formatting of floppy disks, thereby preventing unnecessary future data loss.

Floppy Disk Physical Layout. The following table indicates the physical geometry of each standard floppy disk format. From this information, you can see how the storage capacity of each type of disk is derived.

Table A.72 5 1/4-inch Floppy Disk Drive Formats		
5 1/4-inch Disk	**Double Density 360K (DD)**	**High Density 1.2M (HD)**
Bytes per Sector	512	512
Sectors per Track	9	15
Tracks per Side	40	80
Sides	2	2
Capacity (K)	360	1,200
Capacity (M)	0.352	1.172
Capacity (M)	0.369	1.229

Table A.73 3 1/2-inch Floppy Disk Drive Formats

3 1/2-inch Disk	Double Density 720K (DD)	High Density 1.44M (HD)	Extra-High Density 2.88M (ED)
Bytes per Sector	512	512	512
Sectors per Track	9	18	36
Tracks per Side	80	80	80
Sides	2	2	2
Capacity (K)	720	1,440	2,880
Capacity (M)	0.703	1.406	2.813
Capacity (M)	0.737	1.475	2.949

The following table indicates the width of the magnetic track written by each of the standard floppy drives. Understanding this information helps you recognize when exchanging disks between two different drives is improper.

Table A.74 Floppy Disk Drive Track Width

Drive type	No. of tracks	Track width	
5 1/4-inch 360K	40 per side	0.300 mm	0.0118 in.
5 1/4-inch 1.2M	80 per side	0.155 mm	0.0061 in.
3 1/2-inch 720K	80 per side	0.115 mm	0.0045 in.
3 1/2-inch 1.44M	80 per side	0.115 mm	0.0045 in.
3 1/2-inch 2.88M	80 per side	0.115 mm	0.0045 in.

For example, this table shows that because the 360K drive writes a track that is .330 millimeters wide, overwriting such a track using a 1.2M drive probably would result in a problem: when a wider track is overwritten by a narrower one, the overwrite will not be complete. Usually the 360K drive cannot further read a disk written on in this way. You also should be able to derive that full read-and-write interchangeability occurs between *all* the 3 1/2-inch drives. In other words, a 2.88M drive can write perfectly on 720K or 1.44M formatted floppy disks with no problems because the written track widths are the same between all of the standard 3 1/2-inch drives.

Floppy Disk Media Specifications. The following table shows the physical differences between the various standard floppy disk media. A common misconception seems to exist among some users that double-density (DD) and high-density (HD) floppy disks are the same, especially in the 3 1/2-inch media. This is absolutely untrue! Many users who believe this myth are improperly formatting DD floppy disks as HD disks. These floppy disks are in fact very different physically and magnetically, as outlined here.

Table A.75 Floppy Disk Media Specifications

| Media Parameters | 5 1/4-inch | | | 3 1/2-inch | | |
	Double Density (DD)	Quad Density (QD)	High Density (HD)	Double Density (DD)	High Density (HD)	Extra-High Density (ED)
Tracks Per Inch (TPI)	48	96	96	135	135	135
Bits Per Inch (BPI)	5,876	5,876	9,646	8,717	17,434	34,868
Media Formulation	Ferrite	Ferrite	Cobalt	Cobalt	Cobalt	Barium
Coercivity (Oersteds)	300	300	600	600	720	750
Thickness (Micro-In.)	100	100	50	70	40	100
Recording Polarity	Horiz.	Horiz.	Horiz.	Horiz.	Horiz.	Vert.

This information should be used to discourage the use of hole punchers or other devices designed to allow someone to fool a drive into believing that a DD floppy disk is really a HD floppy disk. Improper formatting and use of such floppy disks causes data loss after the disk has been stored a while (usually six months to a year later) because of the inability of the lower-coercivity media to hold the magnetic patterns stable. Using devices or techniques to improperly format floppy disks in this fashion should be discouraged.

The following table shows the logical parameters and structure for each of the possible floppy drive formats. DOS uses and writes this information when it formats a floppy disk.

Table A.76 Floppy Disk Logical (DOS) Parameters

| Disk Size (in.) / Disk Capacity (KB) | Current Formats | | | | | Obsolete Formats | | |
	3 1/2" 2,880	3 1/2" 1,440	3 1/2" 720	5 1/4" 1,200	5 1/4" 360	5 1/4" 320	5 1/4" 180	5 1/4" 160
Media Descriptor Byte	F0h	F0h	F9h	F9h	FDh	FFh	FCh	FEh
Sides (Heads)	2	2	2	2	2	2	1	1
Tracks per Side	80	80	80	80	40	40	40	40
Sectors per Track	36	18	9	15	9	8	9	8
Bytes per Sector	512	512	512	512	512	512	512	512
Sectors per Cluster	2	1	2	1	2	2	1	1
FAT Length (Sectors)	9	9	3	7	2	1	2	1
Number of FATs	2	2	2	2	2	2	2	2
Root Dir. Length (Sectors)	15	14	7	14	7	7	4	4
Maximum Root Entries	240	224	112	224	112	112	64	64
Total Sectors per Disk	5,760	2,880	1,440	2,400	720	640	360	320
Total Available Sectors	5,726	2,847	1,426	2,371	708	630	351	313
Total Available Clusters	2,863	2,847	713	2,371	354	315	351	313

Floppy Controller Interface. The following table shows the pinout of the standard 34-pin floppy controller interface connector.

Table A.77 IBM-Compatible Floppy Controller Interface Connector pinout			
Signal Name	**Pin**	**Pin**	**Signal Name**
GROUND	1	2	-Reduced Write
GROUND	3	4	Not Connected
KEY (no pin)	5	6	Not Connected
GROUND	7	8	-Index
GROUND	9	10	-Motor Enable 0
GROUND	11	12	-Drive Select 0
GROUND	13	14	-Drive Select 1
GROUND	15	16	-Motor Enable 1
GROUND	17	18	-Direction Select
GROUND	19	20	-Step
GROUND	21	22	-Write Data
GROUND	23	24	-Write Enable
GROUND	25	26	-Track 0
GROUND	27	28	-Write Protect
GROUND	29	30	-Read Data
GROUND	31	32	-Head 1 Select
GROUND	33	34	-Diskette Change

Hard Disk Drives

This section has a great deal of information concerning all aspects of hard disk drives, including a table that lists a large number of different drive parameters, organized by manufacturer. Because Seagate is the largest supplier of hard disks in the world, and its product line is so extensive, a separate table references Seagate's hard disk product line, which shows the parameters of all of its drives. This section also shows BIOS hard drive parameter tables for a number of different ROM BIOS versions, including those from IBM, Compaq, AMI, Award, Phoenix, and Zenith. Finally, this section includes the pinouts of popular hard disk interfaces such as ST-506/412, ESDI, IDE, and SCSI.

The following table shows parameters and specifications for a large number of different hard disk drives. This table can be very helpful when you are trying to install one of these drives in a system with no documentation for the drive.

Table A.78 Hard Disk Drive Specifications

Make/Model	Capacity (MB)	Cyls	Hds	Sectors per Track	Write Pre-comp	Park Cyl
Atasi						
502	46.0	755	7	17	—	—
504	46.0	755	7	17	—	—
514	117.2	1,224	11	17	—	—
519MFM	159.8	1,224	15	17	—	—
519RLL	244.4	1,224	15	26	—	—
617	149.0	1,223	7	34	—	—
628	234.2	1,223	11	34	—	—
638	319.3	1,223	15	34	—	—
3046	39.3	645	7	17	323	644
3051	42.9	704	7	17	352	703
3051+	44.7	733	7	17	368	732
3085	71.3	1,024	8	17	0	—
V130	25.8	987	3	17	128	—
V150	43.0	987	5	17	128	—
V170	60.1	987	7	17	128	—
V185	71.0	1,166	7	17	128	—
Brand Technology						
BT8085	71.3	1,024	8	17	512	—
BT8128	109.1	1,024	8	26	—	—
BT8170E	142.5	1,023	8	34	—	—
Conner Peripherals						
CP-342	42.7	981	5	17	—	—
CP-344	42.9	805	4	26	—	—
CP-3024	21.4	634	2	33	—	—
CP-3044	43.1	526	4	40	—	—
CP-3102-A	104.9	776	8	33	—	—
CP-3102-B	104.3	772	8	33	—	—
CP-3104	104.9	776	8	33	—	—
CP-3184	84.3	832	6	33	—	—
CP-3204	209.8	1,348	8	38	—	—
CP-3204F	212.9	684	16	38	—	—
CP-30104	121.6	1,522	4	39	—	—
CMI						
CM-6626	22.3	640	4	17	256	615
CM-6640	33.4	640	6	17	256	615

Make/Model	Capacity (MB)	Cyls	Hds	Sectors per Track	Write Pre-comp	Park Cyl
Data-Tech Memories						
DTM-553	44.6	1,024	5	17	850	—
DTM-853	44.6	640	8	17	256	—
DTM-885	71.3	1,024	8	17	850	—
Fujitsu						
M2225D	21.4	615	4	17	—	615
M2227D	42.8	615	8	17	—	615
M2241AS	26.3	754	4	17	128	—
M2242AS	45.9	754	7	17	128	—
M2243AS	72.2	754	11	17	128	—
M2244E	71.5	822	5	34	—	—
M2245E	100.2	822	7	34	—	—
M2246E	143.1	822	10	34	—	—
M2247E	151.3	1,242	7	34	—	—
M2248E	237.8	1,242	11	34	—	—
M2249E	324.3	1,242	15	34	—	—
M2261E	359.7	1,657	8	53	—	—
M2263E	674.5	1,657	15	53	—	—
M2611T	45.1	1,334	2	33	—	—
M2612T	90.2	1,334	4	33	—	—
M2613T	135.2	1,334	6	33	—	—
M2614T	180.3	1,334	8	33	—	—
Hewlett-Packard						
97544EF	339.9	1,456	8	57	128	—
97548EF	679.9	1,456	16	57	128	—
Hitachi						
DK511-3	30.4	699	5	17	300	699
DK511-5	42.6	699	7	17	300	699
DK511-8	71.6	823	10	17	256	—
DK512-8	71.5	822	5	34	—	—
DK512-10	85.9	822	6	34	—	—
DK512-12	100.2	822	7	34	—	—
DK512-17	143.1	822	10	34	—	—
DK514-38	329.7	902	14	51	—	—
DK522-10	85.9	822	6	34	—	—
Imprimis (CDC)						
9415-519	18.2	697	3	17	128	—
9415-536	30.3	697	5	17	128	—

(continues)

Table A.78 Continued

Make/Model	Capacity (MB)	Cyls	Hds	Sectors per Track	Write Pre-comp	Park Cyl
9415-538	31.9	733	5	17	128	—
94155-48	40.3	925	5	17	128	—
94155-57	48.3	925	6	17	128	—
94155-67	56.4	925	7	17	128	—
94155-77	64.4	925	8	17	128	—
94155-85	71.3	1,024	8	17	—	—
94155-85P	71.3	1,024	8	17	128	—
94155-86	72.5	925	9	17	128	—
94155-96	80.2	1,024	9	17	—	—
94155-96P	80.2	1,024	9	17	128	—
94155-120	102.2	960	8	26	—	—
94155-120P	102.2	960	8	26	128	—
94155-135	115.0	960	9	26	—	—
94155-135P	115.0	960	9	26	128	—
94156-48	40.3	925	5	17	128	—
94156-67	56.4	925	7	17	128	—
94156-86	72.5	925	9	17	128	—
94166-101	84.3	968	5	34	—	—
94166-141	118.0	968	7	34	—	—
94166-182	151.7	968	9	34	—	—
94186-383	319.3	1,411	13	34	—	—
94186-383H	319.3	1,223	15	34	—	—
94186-442H	368.4	1,411	15	34	—	—
94196-766	663.9	1,631	15	53	—	—
94204-65	65.5	941	8	17	128	—
94204-71	71.3	1,024	8	17	128	—
94205-51	43.0	989	5	17	128	—
94205-77	65.8	989	5	26	128	—
94211-106	89.0	1,023	5	34	—	—
94244-383	338.1	1,747	7	54	—	—
94246-383	331.7	1,746	7	53	—	—
94354-160	143.3	1,072	9	29	128	—
94354-200	177.8	1,072	9	36	—	—
94354-230	211.0	1,272	9	36	—	—
94355-100	84.0	1,072	9	17	128	—
94355-150	128.4	1,072	9	26	128	—
94356-111	93.2	1,071	5	34	—	—
94356-155	130.5	1,071	7	34	—	—
94356-200	167.8	1,071	9	34	—	—

Make/Model	Capacity (MB)	Cyls	Hds	Sectors per Track	Write Pre-comp	Park Cyl
Kalok						
KL320	21.4	615	4	17	—	660
KL330	32.7	615	4	26	—	660
KL343	42.5	670	4	31	—	669
Kyocera						
KC20A	21.4	616	4	17	0	—
KC20B	21.4	615	4	17	0	664
KC30A	32.8	616	4	26	0	—
KC30B	32.7	615	4	26	0	664
KC40GA	42.5	977	5	17	0	980
Lapine						
TITAN20	21.4	615	4	17	0	615
Maxtor						
LXT50S	48.0	733	4	32	—	—
LXT100S	96.1	733	8	32	—	—
LXT200A	200.5	816	15	32	—	—
LXT200S	212.9	1,320	7	45	—	—
LXT213A	212.6	683	16	38	—	—
LXT340S	352.2	1,560	7	63	—	—
LXT340AT	352.2	1,560	7	63	—	—
XT1050	39.3	902	5	17	—	—
XT1065	55.9	918	7	17	—	—
XT1085	71.3	1,024	8	17	—	—
XT1105	87.9	918	11	17	—	—
XT1120R	109.1	1,024	8	26	—	—
XT1140	119.9	918	15	17	—	—
XT1160	133.7	1,024	15	17	—	—
XT1240R	204.5	1,024	15	26	—	—
XT2085	74.6	1,224	7	17	—	—
XT2140	117.2	1,224	11	17	—	—
XT2190	159.8	1,224	15	17	—	—
XT4170E	149.2	1,224	7	34	—	—
XT4170S	149.2	1,224	7	34	—	—
XT4175	149.2	1,224	7	34	—	—
XT4230E	203.0	1,224	9	36	—	—
XT4280	234.4	1,224	11	34	—	—
XT4380E	338.4	1,224	15	36	—	—
XT4380S	338.4	1,224	15	36	—	—

(continues)

Make/Model	Capacity (MB)	Cyls	Hds	Sectors per Track	Write Pre-comp	Park Cyl
Table A.78 Continued						
XT8380E	361.0	1,632	8	54	—	—
XT8380S	361.0	1,632	8	54	—	—
XT8610E	541.5	1,632	12	54	—	—
XT8760E	676.8	1,632	15	54	—	—
XT8760S	676.8	1,632	15	54	—	—
XT8702S	617.9	1,490	15	54	—	—
XT8800E	694.7	1,274	15	71	—	—
Micropolis						
1323	35.7	1,024	4	17	—	—
1323A	44.6	1,024	5	17	—	—
1324	53.5	1,024	6	17	—	—
1324A	62.4	1,024	7	17	—	—
1325	71.3	1,024	8	17	—	—
1333	35.7	1,024	4	17	—	—
1333A	44.6	1,024	5	17	—	—
1334	53.5	1,024	6	17	—	—
1334A	62.4	1,024	7	17	—	—
1335	71.3	1,024	8	17	—	—
1353	71.2	1,023	4	34	—	—
1353A	89.0	1,023	5	34	—	—
1354	106.9	1,023	6	34	—	—
1354A	124.7	1,023	7	34	—	—
1355	142.5	1,023	8	34	—	—
1551	149.0	1,223	7	34	—	—
1554	234.2	1,223	11	34	—	—
1555	255.5	1,223	12	34	—	—
1556	276.8	1,223	13	34	—	—
1557	298.1	1,223	14	34	—	—
1558	319.3	1,223	15	34	—	—
1568-15	663.9	1,631	15	53	—	—
1653-4	86.9	1,248	4	34	—	—
1653-5	108.6	1,248	5	34	—	—
1654-6	130.4	1,248	6	34	—	—
1654-7	152.1	1,248	7	34	—	—
1664-7	337.9	1,779	7	53	—	—
1743-5	110.9	1,140	5	38	—	—

Make/Model	Capacity (MB)	Cyls	Hds	Sectors per Track	Write Pre-comp	Park Cyl
Microscience						
HH-325	21.4	615	4	17	—	615
HH-725	21.4	615	4	17	—	615
HH-1050	44.6	1,024	5	17	—	—
HH-1060	68.2	1,024	5	26	—	—
HH-1075	62.4	1,024	7	17	—	—
HH-1090	80.1	1,314	7	17	—	—
HH-1095	95.4	1,024	7	26	—	—
HH-1120	122.4	1,314	7	26	—	—
HH-2120	124.7	1,023	7	34	—	—
HH-2160	155.4	1,275	7	34	—	—
4050	44.6	1,024	5	17	768	—
4060	68.2	1,024	5	26	768	—
4070	62.4	1,024	7	17	768	—
4090	95.4	1,024	7	26	768	—
5040-00	45.9	854	3	35	—	—
5070-00	76.5	854	5	35	—	—
5070-20	85.9	959	5	35	—	—
5100-00	107.1	854	7	35	—	—
5100-20	120.3	959	7	35	—	—
5160-00	159.3	1,270	7	35	—	—
7040-00	46.0	855	3	35	—	—
7070-00	76.6	855	5	35	—	—
7070-20	86.0	960	5	35	—	—
7100-00	107.3	855	7	35	—	—
7100-20	120.4	960	7	35	—	—
Miniscribe						
1006	5.3	306	2	17	128	336
1012	10.7	306	4	17	128	336
2006	5.3	306	2	17	128	336
2012	10.7	306	4	17	128	336
3012	10.7	612	2	17	128	656
3053	44.6	1,024	5	17	512	—
3085	71.3	1,170	7	17	512	—
3130E	112.0	1,250	5	35	—	—
3180E	156.8	1,250	7	35	—	—
3180S	161.9	1,255	7	36	—	—
3212	10.7	612	2	17	128	656

(continues)

Table A.78 Continued

Make/Model	Capacity (MB)	Cyls	Hds	Sectors per Track	Write Pre-comp	Park Cyl
3412	10.7	306	4	17	128	336
3425	21.4	615	4	17	128	656
3425P	21.4	615	4	17	128	656
3438	32.7	615	4	26	128	656
3438P	32.7	615	4	26	128	656
3650	42.2	809	6	17	128	852
3650R	64.6	809	6	26	128	852
3675	64.6	809	6	26	128	852
4010	8.4	480	2	17	128	522
4020	16.7	480	4	17	128	522
6032	26.7	1,024	3	17	512	—
6053	44.6	1,024	5	17	512	—
6079	68.2	1,024	5	26	512	—
6085	71.3	1,024	8	17	512	—
6128	109.1	1,024	8	26	512	—
7040A	42.7	981	5	17	—	—
7080A	85.4	981	10	17	—	—
8051A	42.7	745	4	28	—	—
8051S	42.7	745	4	28	—	—
8212	10.7	615	2	17	128	656
8225	20.5	771	2	26	128	810
8225A	21.4	615	4	17	—	810
8225XT	21.4	805	2	26	—	820
8412	10.7	306	4	17	128	336
8425	21.4	615	4	17	128	664
8425F	21.4	615	4	17	128	664
8425S	21.4	615	4	17	—	664
8425XT	21.4	615	4	17	—	664
8438	32.7	615	4	26	128	664
8438F	32.7	615	4	26	128	664
8450	41.1	771	4	26	128	810
8450A	42.7	745	4	28	—	810
8450XT	42.9	805	4	26	—	820
9380E	329.0	1,224	15	35	—	—
9380S	336.8	1,218	15	36	—	—
9780E	676.1	1,661	15	53	—	—

Make/Model	Capacity (MB)	Cyls	Hds	Sectors per Track	Write Pre-comp	Park Cyl
Mitsubishi						
MR522	21.3	612	4	17	300	612
MR535	42.5	977	5	17	0	—
MR535RLL	65.0	977	5	26	0	—
MR5310E	85.0	976	5	34	—	—
NEC						
D3126	21.4	615	4	17	256	664
D3142	44.7	642	8	17	128	664
D3146H	42.8	615	8	17	256	664
D3661	111.4	914	7	34	—	—
D3741	45.0	423	8	26	—	423
D5126	21.4	615	4	17	128	664
D5126H	21.4	615	4	17	128	664
D5127H	32.7	615	4	26	128	664
D5128	21.4	615	4	17	128	664
D5146H	42.8	615	8	17	128	664
D5147H	65.5	615	8	26	128	664
D5452	71.6	823	10	17	512	—
D5652	143.1	822	10	34	—	—
D5655	149.0	1,223	7	34	—	—
D5662	319.3	1,223	15	34	—	—
D5682	664.3	1,632	15	53	—	—
Newbury						
NDR320	21.4	615	4	17	—	615
NDR340	42.8	615	8	17	—	615
NDR360	65.5	615	8	26	—	615
NDR1065	55.9	918	7	17	—	—
NDR1085	71.3	1,024	8	17	—	—
NDR1105	87.9	918	11	17	—	—
NDR1140	119.9	918	15	17	—	—
NDR2190	159.8	1,224	15	17	—	—
NDR4170	149.0	1,223	7	34	—	—
NDR4380	319.3	1,223	15	34	—	—
Pacific Magtron						
4115E	114.6	1,599	4	35	—	—
4140E	143.3	1,599	5	35	—	—
4170E	171.9	1,599	6	35	—	—

(continues)

Table A.78 Continued

Make/Model	Capacity (MB)	Cyls	Hds	Sectors per Track	Write Pre-comp	Park Cyl
Plus Development						
40AT	42.0	965	5	17	—	—
80AT	84.0	965	10	17	—	—
120AT	120.0	814	9	32	—	—
170AT	168.5	968	10	34	—	—
210AT	209.2	873	13	36	—	—
52AT/LP	52.3	751	8	17	—	—
80AT/LP	85.8	616	16	17	—	—
105AT/LP	105.1	755	16	17	—	—
Priam						
502	46.0	755	7	17	—	—
504	46.0	755	7	17	—	—
514	117.2	1,224	11	17	—	—
519	159.8	1,224	15	17	—	—
617	143.8	751	11	34	—	—
623	196.1	751	15	34	—	—
638	319.3	1,223	15	34	—	—
V130	25.8	987	3	17	128	—
V150	43.0	987	5	17	128	—
V170	60.1	987	7	17	128	—
V185	71.0	1,166	7	17	128	—
PTI						
PT225	21.4	615	4	17	410	—
PT234	28.5	820	4	17	547	—
PT338	32.1	615	6	17	410	—
PT351	42.8	820	6	17	547	—
PT238R	32.7	615	4	26	410	—
PT251R	43.7	820	4	26	547	—
PT357R	49.1	615	6	26	410	—
PT376R	65.5	820	6	26	547	—
Quantum						
40AT	42.0	965	5	17	—	—
80AT	84.0	965	10	17	—	—
120AT	120.0	814	9	32	—	—
170AT	168.5	968	10	34	—	—
210AT	209.2	873	13	36	—	—

Make/Model	Capacity (MB)	Cyls	Hds	Sectors per Track	Write Pre-comp	Park Cyl
LPS52	52.3	751	8	17	—	—
LPS80	85.8	616	16	17	—	—
LPS105	105.1	755	16	17	—	—
Q520	17.8	512	4	17	256	512
Q530	26.7	512	6	17	256	512
Q540	35.7	512	8	17	256	512
Rodime						
203	16.8	321	6	17	132	321
204	22.4	321	8	17	132	321
202E	22.3	640	4	17	0	640
203E	33.4	640	6	17	0	640
204E	44.6	640	8	17	0	640
3099A	80.2	373	15	28	—	—
3139A	112.5	523	15	28	—	—
3259A	212.9	990	15	28	—	—
3000A-NAT	43.2	625	5	27	0	—
3000A-XLAT	43.2	992	5	17	0	—
3060R	49.9	750	5	26	0	—
3075R	59.9	750	6	26	0	—
3085R	69.9	750	7	26	0	—
5040	32.0	1,224	3	17	0	—
5065	53.3	1,224	5	17	0	—
5090	74.6	1,224	7	17	0	—
Samsung						
SHD2020	21.8	820	2	26	—	—
SHD2021	23.5	820	2	28	—	—
SHD2030	28.5	820	4	17	—	—
SHD2040	43.7	820	4	26	—	—
SHD2041	47.0	820	4	28	—	—
Siemens						
MF-1200	169.2	1,215	8	34	—	—
MF-1300	253.8	1,215	12	34	—	—
MF-4410	321.9	1,099	11	52	—	—
Syquest						
SQ312RD	10.7	612	2	17	0	615
SQ315F	21.3	612	4	17	0	615
SQ338F	32.0	612	6	17	0	615

(continues)

Table A.78 Continued

Make/Model	Capacity (MB)	Cyls	Hds	Sectors per Track	Write Pre-comp	Park Cyl
Tandon						
TN262	21.4	615	4	17	0	615
TN362	21.4	615	4	17	0	615
TN703	25.2	578	5	17	0	615
TN703AT	31.9	733	5	17	0	733
TN705	41.9	962	5	17	0	962
TN755	42.7	981	5	17	128	981
Toshiba						
MK-53F	36.1	830	5	17	—	—
MK-53FRLL	55.2	830	5	26	—	—
MK-54F	50.6	830	7	17	—	—
MK-54FRLL	77.3	830	7	26	—	—
MK-56F	72.2	830	10	17	—	—
MK-56FRLL	110.5	830	10	26	—	—
MK-72PCMFM	72.2	830	10	17	—	—
MK-72PCRLL	110.5	830	10	26	512	—
MK-134FAMFM	44.7	733	7	17	—	—
MK-134FARLL	68.3	733	7	26	512	—
MK-153FA	72.2	829	5	34	—	—
MK-154FA	101.0	829	7	34	—	—
MK-156FA	144.3	829	10	34	—	—
MK-232FC	45.4	845	3	35	—	—
MK-234FC-I	106.0	845	7	35	—	—
MK-355FA	398.3	1,631	9	53	—	—
MK-358FA	663.9	1,631	15	53	—	—
MK-538FB	1229.0	1,980	15	80	—	—
Tulin						
TL226	22.3	640	4	17	—	640
TL240	33.4	640	6	17	—	640
Vertex						
V130	25.8	987	3	17	128	—
V150	43.0	987	5	17	128	—
V170	60.1	987	7	17	128	—
V185	71.0	1,166	7	17	128	—
Western Digital						
WD-93024A	21.6	782	2	27	—	—
WD-93028A	21.6	782	2	27	—	—
WD-93044A	43.2	782	4	27	—	—

Make/Model	Capacity (MB)	Cyls	Hds	Sectors per Track	Write Pre-comp	Park Cyl
WD-93048A	43.2	782	4	27	—	—
WD-95028A	21.6	782	2	27	—	—
WD-95044A	43.2	782	4	27	—	—
WD-95048A	43.2	782	4	27	—	—
WD-AC140	42.6	980	5	17	—	—
WD-AC280	85.3	980	10	17	—	—
WD-AP4200	212.2	987	12	35	—	—
WD-SP4200	209.7	1,280	8	40	—	—
WD-SC8320	326.5	949	14	48	—	—
WD-SC8400	413.2	1,201	14	48	—	—

—No write precompensation required, or no parking cylinder required (autopark).

Table A.79 Seagate Hard Disk Drive Specifications

Seagate Model #	Imprimis Model #	Cyls	Hds	WPC	Park Cyl	Sectors per track	Capacity (MB)	Total Sectors
ST1057		1024	6	-1	1024	17*	53.5	104448
ST1090A	94354-90	1072	5	-1	1072	29	79.6	155440
Opt. CMOS Values:		335	16	335	335	29	79.6	155440
ST1090n	94351-90	1068	5	-1	1068	29	79.3	154860
ST1096n		906	7	-1	906	26	84.4	164892
ST110	94355-100	1072	9	-1	1072	17	84.0	164016
ST1102a		1024	10	-1	1024	17*	89.1	174080
ST1106r		977	7	-1	977	26	91.0	177814
ST1111a	94354-111	1072	5	-1	1072	36	98.8	192960
Opt. CMOS Values:		402	10	402	402	48	98.8	192960
ST1111e	94356-111	1072	5	-1	1072	36	98.8	192960
ST1111n	94351-111	1068	5	-1	1068	36	98.4	192240
ST11200n		1872	15	-1	1872	73*	1049.5	2049840
ST1126a	94354-126	1072	7	-1	1072	29	111.4	217616
Opt. CMOS Values:		469	16	469	469	29	111.4	217616
ST1126n	94351-125	1068	7	-1	1068	29	111.0	216804
ST1133a	94354-133	1272	5	-1	1272	36	117.2	228960
Opt. CMOS Values:		477	8	477	477	60	117.2	228960

(continues)

Table A.79 Continued

Seagate Model #	Imprimis Model #	Cyls	Hds	WPC	Park Cyl	Sectors per track	Capacity (MB)	Total Sectors
ST1133n	943551-133s	1268	5	-1	1268	36	116.9	228240
ST1144a		1001	15	-1	1001	17*	130.7	255255
ST1150r	94355-150	1072	9	300	1072	26	128.4	250848
ST1156a	94354-156	1072	7	-1	1072	36	138.3	270144
Opt. CMOS Values:		536	9	536	536	56	138.3	270144
ST1156e	94356-156	1072	7	-1	1072	36	138.3	270144
ST1156n	94351-155	1068	7	-1	1068	36	137.8	269136
ST1156r	94355-156	1072	7	300	1072	36	138.3	270144
ST1162a	94354-162	1072	9	-1	1072	29	143.3	279792
Opt. CMOS Values:		603	16	603	603	29	143.3	279792
ST1162n	94351-160	1068	9	-1	1068	29	142.7	278748
ST1182e		972	9	-1	972	36	161.2	314298
ST1186a	94354-186	1272	7	-1	1272	36	164.1	320544
Opt. CMOS Values:		636	9	636	636	56	164.1	320544
ST1186n	94351-186	1268	7	-1	1268	36	163.6	319536
ST11950n		2706	15	-1	2706	99*	2057.4	4018410
ST1201a	94354-201	1072	9	-1	1072	36	177.8	347328
Opt. CMOS Values:		804	9	804	804	48	177.8	347328
ST1201e	94356-201	1072	9	-1	1072	36	177.8	347328
ST120n	94351-200	1068	9	-1	1068	36	177.2	346032
ST1239a	94354-239	1272	9	-1	1272	36	211.0	412128
Opt. CMOS Values:		848	9	848	848	54	211.0	412128
ST1239n	94351-230	1268	9	-1	1268	36	210.3	410832
ST124		615	4	-1	670	17	21.4	41820
ST12400n		2626	19	-1	2626	82*	2094.7	4091308
ST125		615	4	-1	615	17	21.4	41820
ST125-1		615	4	-1	615	17	21.4	41820
ST12550n		2707	19	-1	2707	99*	2607.0	5091867
ST125a		404	4	-1	404	26	21.5	42016
Opt. CMOS Values:		615	4	615	615	17	2.14	41820
ST125n		407	4	-1	408	26	21.7	42328
ST137r		615	6	-1	670	26	49.1	95940
ST138		615	6	-1	615	17	32.1	62730
ST138a		604	4	-1	604	26	32.2	62816

Seagate Model #	Imprimis Model #	Cyls	Hds	WPC	Park Cyl	Sectors per track	Capacity (MB)	Total Sectors
Opt. CMOS Values:		615	6	615	615	17	32.1	62730
ST138n		615	4	-1	615	26	32.7	63960
ST138r		615	4	-1	615	26	32.7	63960
ST1400a		1018	12	-1	1018	53*	331.5	647448
ST1400n		1476	7	-1	1476	62*	328.0	640584
ST1400ns		1476	7	-1	1476	62*	328.0	640584
ST1401a		726	15	-1	726	61*	340.1	664290
ST1401n		1100	9	-1	1100	66*	334.5	653400
ST1401ns		1100	9	-1	1100	66*	334.5	653400
ST15480a		1474	9	-1	1474	62*	421.1	822492
Opt. CMOS Values:		1015	15	1015	1015	54*	420.9	822150
ST1480n		1476	9	-1	1476	62*	421.7	823608
ST1480ns		1476	9	-1	1476	62*	4217	823608
ST1481n		1476	9	-1	1476	62*	4217	823608
ST151		977	5	-1	977	17	42.5	83045
ST157a		560	6	-1	560	26	44.7	87360
Opt. CMOS Values:		733	7	733	733	17	44.7	87227
ST157n		615	6	-1	615	26	49.1	95940
ST157r		615	6	-1	615	26	49.1	95940
ST1581n		1476	9	-1	1476	77*	523.7	1022868
ST177n		921	5	-1	921	26	61.3	119730
ST1980n		1730	13	-1	1730	74*	852.1	1664260
ST2106e	94216-106	1024	5	-1	1024	36	94.4	184320
ST2106n	94211-091	1024	5	-1	1024	36	94.4	184320
ST2106n	94211-106	1024	5	-1	1024	36	94.4	184320
ST2106nm	94211-106	1024	5	-1	1024	36	94.4	184320
ST212		306	4	128	319	17	10.7	20808
ST2125n	94221-125	1544	3	-1	1544	45*	106.7	208440
ST2125nm	94221-125	1544	3	-1	1544	45*	106.7	208440
ST2125nv	94221-125	1544	3	-1	1544	45*	106.7	208440
ST213		6156	2	300	670	17	10.7	20910
ST2182e	94246-182	1453	4	-1	1453	54	160.7	313848
ST2209n	94221-209	1544	5	-1	1544	45*	177.9	347400
ST2209nm	94221-209m	1544	5	-1	1544	45*	177.9	347400
ST2209nv	94221-209	1544	5	-1	1544	45*	177.9	347400
ST224n		615	2	-1	615	17	10.7	20910
ST225		615	4	300	670	17	21.4	41820

(continues)

Table A.79 Continued

Seagate Model #	Imprimis Model #	Cyls	Hds	WPC	Park Cyl	Sectors per track	Capacity (MB)	Total Sectors
ST225n		615	4	-1	615	17	21.4	41820
ST225r		667	2	-1	670	31	21.2	41354
ST2274a	94244-274	1747	5	-1	1747	54	241.5	471690
Opt. CMOS Values:		536	16	536	536	55	241.5	471680
ST238		615	4	-1	670	26	32.7	63960
ST2383a	94244-383	1747	7	-1	1747	54	338.1	660366
Opt. CMOS Values:		737	16	737	737	56	338.1	660352
ST2383e	94246-383	1747	7	-1	1747	54	338.1	660366
ST2383n	94241-383	1260	7	-1	1260	74*	334.2	652680
ST2383nm	94241-383	1260	7	-1	1260	74*	334.2	652680
ST238r		615	4	-1	670	26	32.7	63960
ST2502n	94241-502	1756	7	-1	1755	69*	434.3	848148
ST2502nm	94241-502	1756	7	-1	1755	69*	434.3	848148
ST2502nv	94241-502	1756	7	-1	1755	69*	434.3	848148
ST250n		667	4	-1	670	31	42.3	82708
ST250r		667	4	-1	670	31	42.3	82708
ST251		820	6	-1	820	17	42.8	83640
ST251n-0		820	4	-1	820	26	43.7	85280
ST251n-1		630	4	-1	630	34	43.9	85680
ST252		820	6	-1	820	17	42.8	83640
ST253	94205-51	989	5	128	989	17	43.0	84065
ST247a	94204-74	948	5	-1	948	27	65.5	127980
ST277n-0		820	6	-1	820	26	65.5	127920
ST277n-1		628	6	-1	628	34	65.6	128112
ST277r		820	6	-1	820	26	65.5	127920
ST278r		820	6	-1	820	26	65.5	127920
ST279r	94205-77	989	5	-1	989	26	65.8	128570
ST280A	94204-71	1032	5	-1	1032	27	71.3	139320
Opt. CMOS Values:		1024	8	1024	1024	17	71.3	139264
ST280a	94204-81	1032	5	-1	1032	27	71.3	139320
Opt. CMOS Values:		1024	8	1024	1024	17	71.3	139264
ST296n		820	6	-1	820	34	85.6	167280
ST3051a		820	6	-1	820	17	42.8	83640
ST3096a		1024	10	-1	1024	17	89.1	174080
ST31200n		2626	9	-1	2626	79*	955.9	1867086

Seagate Model #	Imprimis Model #	Cyls	Hds	WPC	Park Cyl	Sectors per track	Capacity (MB)	Total Sectors
ST3120a		1024	12	-1	1024	17*	107.0	208896
ST3123a		1024	12	-1	1024	17*	107.0	208896
ST3144a		1001	15	-1	1001	17*	130.7	255255
ST3145a		1001	15	-1	1001	17*	130.7	255255
ST3195a		981	10	-1	981	34*	170.8	333540
ST3243a		1024	12	-1	1024	34*	213.9	417792
ST325a		615	4	-1	615	17	21.4	41820
ST325a/x		615	4	-1	615	17	21.4	41820
ST325n		654	2	-1	654	32	21.4	41856
ST325x		615	4	-1	615	17	21.4	41820
ST3283a		978	14	-1	978	35*	245.4	479220
ST3283n		1689	5	-1	1689	57*	246.5	481365
ST3290a		1001	15	-1	1001	34*	261.4	510510
ST3385a		767	14	-1	767	62*	340.9	665756
ST3390a		768	14	-1	768	62*	341.3	666624
ST3390n		2676	3	-1	2676	83*	341.2	666324
ST3500a		895	15	-1	895	62*	426.2	832350
ST351a		820	6	-1	820	17	42.8	83640
ST351a/x		820	6	-1	820	17	42.8	83640
ST351x		820	6	-1	820	17	42.8	83640
ST3550a		1018	14	-1	1018	62*	452.4	883624
ST3550n		2126	5	-1	2126	83*	451.7	882290
ST3600a		1872	7	-1	1872	79*	530.0	1035216
Opt. CMOS Values:		1024	16	1024	1024	63*	528.5	1032192
ST3600n		1872	7	-1	1872	79*	530.0	1035216
ST3610n		1872	7	-1	1872	52*	348.9	681408
ST3655a		1024	16	-1	1024	63*	528.5	1032192
ST3655n		2676	5	-1	2676	79*	541.2	1057020
ST4026		615	4	-1	670	17	21.4	41820
ST4038		733	5	-1	733	17	31.9	62305
ST4038m		733	5	-1	733	17	31.9	62305
ST4051		977	5	-1	977	17	42.5	83045
ST4053		1024	5	-1	1024	17	44.6	87040
ST406		306	2	128	319	17	5.3	10404
ST4085		1024	8	-1	1024	17	71.3	39264
ST4086	94155-86	925	9	-1	925	17	72.5	141525
ST4086p	94155-86p	925	9	128	925	17	72.5	141525
ST4096		1024	9	-1	1024	17	80.2	156672

(continues)

Table A.79 Continued

Seagate Model #	Imprimis Model #	Cyls	Hds	WPC	Park Cyl	Sectors per track	Capacity (MB)	Total Sectors
ST4097	91455-96	1024	9	-1	1024	17	80.2	156672
ST4097p	94155-96p	1024	9	128	1024	17	80.2	156672
ST412		306	4	128	319	17	10.7	20808
ST41200n	94601-12g	1931	15	-1	1931	71*	1052.9	2056515
ST41200nm	94601-12g	1931	15	-1	1931	71*	1052.9	2056515
ST41200nv	94601-12g	1931	15	-1	1931	71*	1052.9	2056515
ST4135r	94155-135	960	9	-1	960	26	115.0	224640
ST4144r		1024	9	-1	1024	26	122.7	239616
ST41520n		2101	17	-1	2101	77*	1408.1	2750209
ST41600n		2098	17	-1	2098	74*	1351.1	2639284
ST41650n		2110	15	-1	2110	88*	1426.8	2785200
ST42651n		2107	15	-1	2107	87*	1407.8	2749635
ST4182e	94166-155	969	9	-1	969	36	160.7	313956
ST4182e	94166-155	969	9	-1	969	36	160.7	313956
ST4182n	94161-182	967	9	-1	967	36	160.4	313308
ST4182nm	94161-182	997	9	-1	967	36	160.4	313308
ST419		306	6	128	319	17	16.0	31212
ST42000n		2624	16	-1	2624	83*	1784.2	3484672
ST42100n		2573	15	-1	2573	96*	1897.0	3705120
ST42400n		2624	19	-1	2624	83*	2118.7	4138048
ST425		306	8	128	319	17	21.3	41616
ST43400n		2735	21	-1	2735	99*	2911.3	5686065
ST4350n	94171-300	1412	9	-1	1412	46*	299.3	584568
ST4350n	94171-307	1412	9	-1	1412	46*	299.3	584568
ST4350n	94171-327	1412	9	-1	1412	46*	299.3	584568
ST4350n	94171-350	1412	9	-1	1412	46*	299.3	584568
ST4350nm	94171-327	1412	9	-1	1412	46*	299.3	528468
ST4376n	94171-344	1549	9	-1	1549	45*	321.2	627345
ST4376n	94171-376	1549	9	-1	1549	45*	321.2	627345
ST4376nm	94171-344	1549	9	-1	1549	45*	321.2	627345
ST4376nv	94171-344	1549	9	-1	1549	45*	321.2	627345
ST4383e	94186-383	1412	13	-1	1412	36	338.3	660816
ST4384e	94186-383h	1224	15	-1	1224	36	338.4	660690
ST4385n	94181-385h	791	15	-1	791	55*	334.1	652575
ST4385nm	94181-385h	791	15	-1	791	55*	334.1	652575
SST4385nv	94181-385h	791	15	-1	791	55*	334.1	652575
ST442e	94186-442	1412	15	-1	1412	36	390.4	762480
ST4702n	94181-702	1546	15	-1	1546	50*	593.7	1159500
ST4702nm	94181-702	15496	15	-1	1546	50*	593.7	1159500

Seagate Model #	Imprimis Model #	Cyls	Hds	WPC	Park Cyl	Sectors per track	Capacity (MB)	Total Sectors
ST4766e	94196-766	1632	15	-1	1632	54	676.8	1321920
ST4766n	94191-766	1632	15	-1	1632	54	676.8	1321920
ST4766nm	94191-766	1632	15	-1	1632	54	676.8	1321920
ST4766nv	94191-766	1632	15	-1	1632	54	676.8	1321920
ST4767e		1399	15	-1	1399	63	676.9	1322055
St4767n	94601-767h	1356	15	-1	1356	64*	666.5	1301760
ST4767nm	94601-767h	1356	15	-1	1356	64*	666.5	1301760
ST4767nv	94601-767h	1356	15	-1	1356	64*	666.5	1301760
ST4769e		1552	15	-1	1552	58	691.3	1350240
ST506		153	4	128	157	17	5.3	10404
ST9025a		1024	4	-1	1024	17	35.7	69632
ST9051a		1024	6	-1	1024	17	53.5	104448
ST9052a		980	5	-1	980	17*	42.6	83300
ST9077a		669	11	-1	669	17	64.1	125103
ST9080a		823	4	-1	823	38*	64.0	125096
ST9096a		980	10	-1	980	17*	85.3	166600
ST9100a		748	14	-1	748	16*	85.8	167552
ST9140a		980	15	-1	980	17*	127.9	249900
ST9144a		980	15	-1	980	17*	127.9	249900
ST9145a		980	15	-1	980	17*	127.9	249900
ST9190a		873	16	-1	873	24*	171.6	335232
ST9235a		985	13	-1	985	32*	209.8	409760
ST9235n		985	13	-1	985	32*	209.8	409760
ST----	9415-521	697	3	0	697	17	18.2	35547
ST----	9415-525	697	4	0	697	17	24.3	47396
ST----	9415-536	697	5	0	697	17	30.3	59245
ST----	9415-538	733	5	0	733	17	31.9	62305
ST----	94151-42	921	5	-1	921	17	40.1	78285
ST----	94151-62	921	7	-1	921	17	56.1	109599
ST----	94151-80	921	9	-1	921	17	72.1	140913
ST----	94155-48	925	5	-1	925	17	40.3	78625
ST----	94155-48p	925	5	128	925	17	40.3	78625
ST----	94155-57	925	6	-1	925	17	48.3	94350
ST----	94155-57p	925	6	128	925	17	48.3	94350
ST----	94155-67	925	7	-1	925	17	56.4	110075
ST----	94155-67p	925	7	128	925	17	56.4	110075
ST----	94155-92	989	9	-1	989	17	77.5	151317
ST----	94155-92p	989	9	128	989	17	77.5	151317
ST----	94155-130	024	9	128	1024	26	122.7	239616

(continues)

Table A.79 Continued								
Seagate Model #	Imprimis Model #	Cyls	Hds	WPC	Park Cyl	Sectors per track	Capacity (MB)	Total Sectors
ST----	94156-48	925	9	-1	925	17	72.5	141525
ST----	94156-67	925	7	-1	925	17	56.4	110075
ST----	94156-86	925	7	-1	925	17	56.4	110075
ST----	94161-86	969	5	-1	969	35	86.8	169575
ST----	94161-103	969	6	-1	969	35	104.2	203490
ST----	94161-121	969	7	-1	969	35	121.6	237405
ST----	94161-138	969	8	-1	969	35	138.9	271320
ST----	94166-86	969	5	-1	969	35	86.8	169575
ST----	94166-103	969	6	-1	969	35	104.2	203490
ST----	94166-121	969	7	-1	969	35	121.6	237405
ST----	94166-138	969	8	-1	969	35	138.9	271320
ST----	94244-219	1747	4	-1	1747	54	193.2	377352
Opt. CMOS Values:		536	16	536	536	44	193.2	377344

* Because these drives use zoned recording, the sectors-per-track value is an average, rounded down to the next-lower integer.
* Opt. CMOS Values indicates optional translated values for the preceding drive in the table which can be entered if the CMOS Setup program will not accept the actual values for the drive.

Seagate Model designations follow a specific format shown as follows:

ST-FXXXI PR-A

The various parts of each model number designation have meanings according to the following tables.

Code	Description
ST	Seagate Technologies
F	Form Factor (see following table)
XXX	Unformatted Capacity in M
I	Interface Type (see following table)
PR	Paired Solution (shipped with controller and installation software)
A	Access time; 0 = Standard, 1= Fast

F-Code	Description
1	3.5-inch Half Height (41mm)
2	5.25-inch Half Height (41mm)
3	3.5-inch 1-inch High (25mm)

F-Code	Description
4	5.25-inch Full Height (82mm)
6	9-inch
8	8-inch
9	2.5-inch .75-inch High (19mm)

I-Code	Description
None	ST-412 MFM interface
R	ST-412 (RLL certified) interface
E	ESDI interface
A	ATA (AT Attachment) IDE interface
X	XT-Bus (8-bit) IDE interface
A/X	Switchable ATA IDE or XT-Bus interface
M or P	Modified Precompensation
N	SCSI Single Ended (SE) interface
NM	SCSI SE interface (Macintosh Plus)
NV	SCSI SE interface (Novell NetWare)
NS	SCSI SE interface (Synchronized Spindle)
ND	SCSI Differential interface

For example, the model designation ST112550N equates to a 3.5-inch Half Height drive with an unformatted capacity of about 2550M, and a SCSI Single Ended interface.

Hard Disk Interface Connector Pinouts

This section details the interface connector pinouts of each of the popular hard disk drive interfaces, including ST-506/412, ESDI, IDE, and SCSI.

ST-506/412 Interface Connectors. The ST-506/412 Interface uses two connections, a 34-pin Control connector and a 20-pin Data connector. The following tables show the pinouts for these connectors.

Table A.80 ST-506/412 Hard Disk Interface 34-Pin Control Connector Pinout			
Signal Name	**Pin**	**Pin**	**Signal Name**
GROUND	1	2	-HD SLCT 3
GROUND	3	4	-HD SLCT 2
GROUND	5	6	-WRITE GATE
GROUND	7	8	-SEEK CMPLT
GROUND	9	10	-TRACK 0
GROUND	11	12	-WRITE FAULT
GROUND	13	14	-HD SLCT 0

(continues)

Table A.80 Continued

Signal Name	Pin	Pin	Signal Name
KEY (no pin)	15	16	Not Connected
GROUND	17	18	-HD SLCT 1
GROUND	19	20	-INDEX
GROUND	21	22	-READY
GROUND	23	24	-STEP
GROUND	25	26	-DRV SLCT 0
GROUND	27	28	-DRV SLCT 1
GROUND	29	30	Not Connected
GROUND	31	32	Not Connected
GROUND	33	34	-DIRECTION IN

Table A.81 ST-506/412 Hard Disk Interface 20-Pin Data Connector Pinout

Signal Name	Pin	Pin	Signal Name
-DRV SLCTD	1	2	GROUND
Not Connected	3	4	GROUND
Not Connected	5	6	GROUND
Not Connected	7	8	KEY (no pin)
Not Connected	9	10	Not Connected
GROUND	11	12	GROUND
+MFM WRITE	13	14	-MFM WRITE
GROUND	15	16	GROUND
+MFM READ	17	18	-MFM READ
GROUND	19	20	GROUND

ESDI Interface Connectors. ESDI (Enhanced Small Device Interface) uses two connections, a 34-pin Control connector and a 20-pin Data connector. The following tables show the pinouts for these connectors.

Table A.82 ESDI 34-Pin Control Connector Pinout

Signal Name	Pin	Pin	Signal Name
GROUND	1	2	-HD SLCT 3
GROUND	3	4	-HD SLCT 2
GROUND	5	6	-WRITE GATE
GROUND	7	8	-CNFG/STATUS
GROUND	9	10	-XFER ACK
GROUND	11	12	-ATTENTION
GROUND	13	14	-HD SLCT 0

Signal Name	Pin	Pin	Signal Name
KEY (no pin)	15	16	-SECTOR
GROUND	17	18	-HD SLCT 1
GROUND	19	20	-INDEX
GROUND	21	22	-READY
GROUND	23	24	-XFER REQ
GROUND	25	26	-DRV SLCT 0
GROUND	27	28	-DRV SLCT 1
GROUND	29	30	Reserved
GROUND	31	32	-READ GATE
GROUND	33	34	-CMD DATA

Table A.83 ESDI 20-Pin Data Connector Pinout

Signal Name	Pin	Pin	Signal Name
-DRV SLCTD	1	2	-SECTOR
-CMD COMPL	3	4	-ADDR MK EN
GROUND	5	6	GROUND
+WRITE CLK	7	8	-WRITE CLK
GROUND	9	10	+RD/REF CLK
-RD/REF CLK	11	12	GROUND
+NRZ WRITE	13	14	-NRZ WRITE
GROUND	15	16	GROUND
+NRZ READ	17	18	-NRZ READ
GROUND	19	20	-INDEX

IDE (Integrated Drive Electronics) Connector Pinouts. There are a number of different IDE (Integrated Drive Electronics) interfaces that have been used in PC systems. There are four that have been most widely used:

■ ATA (AT Attachment) IDE

■ XT-Bus IDE

■ IBM XT-Bus IDE

■ IBM MCA (Micro Channel Architecture) IDE

The most common would be the ATA (AT Attachment) version, which is an ANSI standard interface that is by far the most popular IDE interface, and the only one of these still being used in new systems today. When the term "IDE" is used, you can usually assume it means ATA IDE. Since the ATA IDE interface is a 16-bit design, it could not be used in 8-bit (XT type) systems, so some of the drive manufacturers standardized on an XT-Bus (8-bit) IDE interface for XT class systems. These drives were never very popular, and were usually only available in capacities from 20M to 40M. IBM used a custom version of the XT-Bus IDE interface in the PS/2 Model 25 and Model 30 systems. IBM also developed an MCA (Micro Channel Architecture) IDE interface for use in the Micro Channel based PS/2 systems. MCA IDE was used in many of the desktop PS/2s, including the Model 50Z, 55, 70, and P70 systems, and were available in capacities ranging from 30M to 160M.

The following tables show each of the the IDE interface connector pinouts.

ATA IDE

Table A.84 ATA (AT Attachment) IDE Connector Pinout			
Signal Name	**Pin**	**Pin**	**Signal Name**
-RESET	1	2	GROUND
Data Bit 7	3	4	Data Bit 8
Data Bit 6	5	6	Data Bit 9
Data Bit 5	7	8	Data Bit 10
Data Bit 4	9	10	Data Bit 11
Data Bit 3	11	12	Data Bit 12
Data Bit 2	13	14	Data Bit 13
Data Bit 1	15	16	Data Bit 14
Data Bit 0	17	18	Data Bit 15
GROUND	19	20	KEY (pin missing)
DRQ 3	21	22	GROUND
-IOW	23	24	GROUND
-IOR	25	26	GROUND
I/O CH RDY	27	28	SPSYNC:CSEL
-DACK 3	29	30	GROUND
IRQ 14	31	32	-IOCS16
Address Bit 1	33	34	-PDIAG
Address Bit 0	35	36	Address Bit 2
-CS1FX	37	38	-CS3FX
-DA/SP	39	40	GROUND
+5 Vdc (Logic)	41	42	+5 Vdc (Motor)
GROUND	43	44	-TYPE (0=ATA)

XT-Bus IDE

Table A.85 XT-Bus IDE (Integrated Drive Electronics) Connector Pinout			
Signal Name	**Pin**	**Pin**	**Signal Name**
-RESET	1	2	GROUND
Data Bit 7	3	4	GROUND
Data Bit 6	5	6	GROUND
Data Bit 5	7	8	GROUND
Data Bit 4	9	10	GROUND
Data Bit 3	11	12	GROUND
Data Bit 2	13	14	GROUND
Data Bit 1	15	16	GROUND
Data Bit 0	17	18	GROUND
GROUND	19	20	KEY (pin missing)
AEN	21	22	GROUND
-IOW	23	24	GROUND
-IOR	25	26	GROUND
-DACK 3	27	28	GROUND
DRQ 3	29	30	GROUND
IRQ 5	31	32	GROUND
Address Bit 1	33	34	GROUND
Address Bit 0	35	36	GROUND
-CS1FX	37	38	GROUND
-Drive Active	39	40	GROUND

IBM XT-Bus IDE

Table A.86 IBM Unique XT-Bus (PS/2 Model 25 and 30) IDE Connector Pinout			
Signal Name	**Pin**	**Pin**	**Signal Name**
-RESET	1	2	-Disk Installed
Data Bit 0	3	4	GROUND
Data Bit 1	5	6	GROUND
Data Bit 2	7	8	GROUND
Data Bit 3	9	10	GROUND
Data Bit 4	11	12	GROUND
Data Bit 5	13	14	GROUND
Data Bit 6	15	16	GROUND
Data Bit 7	17	18	GROUND
-IOR	19	20	GROUND
-IOW	21	22	GROUND

(continues)

Table A.86 Continued			
Signal Name	**Pin**	**Pin**	**Signal Name**
-CS1FX	23	24	GROUND
Address Bit 0	25	26	GROUND
Address Bit 1	27	28	GROUND
Address Bit 2	29	30	+5 Vdc
RESERVED	31	32	+5 Vdc
-DACK 3	33	34	GROUND
DRQ 3	35	36	GROUND
IRQ 5	37	38	GROUND
I/O CH RDY	39	40	+ 12 Vdc
Spare	41	42	+ 12 Vdc
Spare	39	44	+ 12 Vdc

MCA IDE

Table A.87 MCA (Micro Channel Architecture) IDE Connector Pinout			
Signal Name	**Pin**	**Pin**	**Signal Name**
-CD SETUP	A1	B1	Address Bit 15
Address Bit 13	A2	B2	Address Bit 14
GROUND	A3	B3	GROUND
Address Bit 11	A4	B4	OSC (14.3MHz)
Address Bit 10	A5	B5	GROUND
Address Bit 9	A6	B6	Address Bit 12
+5 Vdc	A7	B7	-CMD
Address Bit 8	A8	B8	-CD SFDBK
Address Bit 7	A9	B9	GROUND
Address Bit 6	A10	B10	Data Bit 1
+5 Vdc	A11	B11	Data Bit 3
Address Bit 5	A12	B12	Data Bit 4
Address Bit 4	A13	B13	GROUND
Address Bit 3	A14	B14	CHRESET
+5 Vdc	A15	B15	Data Bit 8
Address Bit 2	A16	B16	Data Bit 9
Address Bit 1	A17	B17	GROUND
Address Bit 0	A18	B18	Data Bit 12
+12 Vdc	A19	B19	Data Bit 14
-ADL	A20	B20	Data Bit 15
-PREEMPT	A21	B21	GROUND
-BURST	A22	B22	Data Bit 0
+5 Vdc	A23	B23	Data Bit 2

Signal Name	Pin	Pin	Signal Name
ARB 0	A24	B24	Data Bit 5
ARB 1	A25	B25	GROUND
ARB 2	A26	B26	Data Bit 6
+12 Vdc	A27	B27	Data Bit 7
ARB 3	A28	B28	Data Bit 10
+ARB/-GRANT	A29	B29	GROUND
-TC	A30	B30	Data Bit 11
+5 Vdc	A31	B31	Data Bit 13
-S0	A32	B32	-SBHE
-S1	A33	B33	GROUND
+M/-IO	A34	B34	-CD DS 16
GROUND	A35	B35	-IRQ 14
CD CHRDY	A36	B36	GROUND

SCSI Interface Pinouts. The following section details the pinouts of the various SCSI cables and connectors. There are two electrically different versions of SCSI, Single Ended and Differential. These two versions are electrically incompatible, and must not be inter-connected or damage will result. Fortunately, there are very few Differential SCSI applications available in the PC industry, so you will rarely (if ever) encounter it. Within each electrical type (Single Ended or Differential), there are basically three SCSI cable types:

- A-Cable (Standard SCSI)
- P-Cable (Wide SCSI)
- Q-Cable (32-bit Wide SCSI)

The A-Cable is used in most SCSI-1 and SCSI-2 installations, and is the standard one you will encounter. SCSI-2 Wide (16-bit) applications use a P-Cable instead, which com-pletely replaces the A-Cable. You can intermix standard and wide SCSI devices on a single SCSI bus by interconnecting A- and P-Cables with special adapters. 32-bit wide SCSI-3 applications use both the P- and Q-Cables in parallel to each 32-bit device. Today there are virtually no PC applications for 32-bit Wide SCSI-3, and because of the two cable requirement, it is not likely to catch on.

The A-Cables can have Pin Header (Internal) type connectors or External Shielded con-nectors, each with a different pinout. The P- and Q-Cables feature the same connector pinout on either Internal or External cable connections.

The following tables shows all of the possible interface, cable, and connector pinout specifications. A hyphen preceding a signal name indicates the signal is Active Low. The RESERVED lines have continuity from one end of the SCSI bus to the other. In an A-Cable bus, the RESERVED lines should be left open in SCSI devices (but may be connected to ground), and are connected to ground in the bus terminator assemblies. In the P- and Q-Cables, the RESERVED lines are left open in SCSI devices as well as in the bus terminator assemblies.

Single Ended SCSI

A-Cable (Single-Ended) Connectors

Table A.88 A-Cable (Single Ended) Internal Unshielded Header Connector Pinout

Signal Name	Pin	Pin	Signal Name
GROUND	1	2	-DB(0)
GROUND	3	4	-DB(1)
GROUND	5	6	-DB(2)
GROUND	7	8	-DB(3)
GROUND	9	10	-DB(4)
GROUND	11	12	-DB(5)
GROUND	13	14	-DB(6)
GROUND	15	16	-DB(7)
GROUND	17	18	-DB(Parity)
GROUND	19	20	GROUND
GROUND	21	22	GROUND
RESERVED	23	24	RESERVED
Open	25	26	TERMPWR
RESERVED	27	28	RESERVED
GROUND	29	30	GROUND
GROUND	31	32	-ATN
GROUND	33	34	GROUND
GROUND	35	36	-BSY
GROUND	37	38	-ACK
GROUND	39	40	-RST
GROUND	41	42	-MSG
GROUND	43	44	-SEL
GROUND	45	46	-C/D
GROUND	47	48	-REQ
GROUND	49	50	-I/O

Table A.89 A-Cable (Single Ended) External Shielded Connector Pinout

Signal Name	Pin	Pin	Signal Name
GROUND	1	26	-DB(0)
GROUND	2	27	-DB(1)
GROUND	3	28	-DB(2)

Signal Name	Pin	Pin	Signal Name
GROUND	4	29	-DB(3)
GROUND	5	30	-DB(4)
GROUND	6	31	-DB(5)
GROUND	7	32	-DB(6)
GROUND	8	33	-DB(7)
GROUND	9	34	-DB(Parity)
GROUND	10	35	GROUND
GROUND	11	36	GROUND
RESERVED	12	37	RESERVED
Open	13	38	TERMPWR
RESERVED	14	39	RESERVED
GROUND	15	40	GROUND
GROUND	16	41	-ATN
GROUND	17	42	GROUND
GROUND	18	43	-BSY
GROUND	19	44	-ACK
GROUND	20	45	-RST
GROUND	21	46	-MSG
GROUND	22	47	-SEL
GROUND	23	48	-C/D
GROUND	24	49	-REQ
GROUND	25	50	-I/O

IBM has standardized on the SCSI interface for virtually all PS/2 systems introduced since 1990. These systems use a Micro Channel SCSI adapter or have the SCSI Host Adapter built into the motherboard. In either case, IBM's SCSI interface uses a special 60-pin mini-Centronics type external shielded connector that is unique in the industry. A special IBM cable is required to adapt this connector to the standard 50-pin Centronics style connector used on most external SCSI devices. The pinout of the IBM 60-pin mini-Centronics style External Shielded connector is shown in the following table. Note that although the pin arrangement is unique, the pin number to signal designations correspond with the standard unshielded internal pin header type of SCSI connector.

Table A.90 IBM PS/2 SCSI External Shielded 60-Pin Connector Pinout			
Signal Name	**Pin**	**Pin**	**Signal Name**
GROUND	1	60	Not Connected
-DB(0)	2	59	Not Connected
GROUND	3	58	Not Connected
-DB(1)	4	57	Not Connected
GROUND	5	56	Not Connected

(continues)

Table A.90 Continued			
Signal Name	**Pin**	**Pin**	**Signal Name**
-DB(2)	6	55	Not Connected
GROUND	7	54	Not Connected
-DB(3)	8	53	Not Connected
GROUND	9	52	Not Connected
-DB(4)	10	51	GROUND
GROUND	11	50	-I/O
-DB(5)	12	49	GROUND
GROUND	13	48	-REQ
-DB(6)	14	47	GROUND
GROUND	15	46	-C/D
-DB(7)	16	45	GROUND
GROUND	17	44	-SEL
-DB(Parity)	18	43	GROUND
GROUND	19	42	-MSG
GROUND	20	41	GROUND
GROUND	21	40	-RST
GROUND	22	39	GROUND
RESERVED	23	38	-ACK
RESERVED	24	37	GROUND
Open	25	36	-BSY
TERMPWR	26	35	GROUND
RESERVED	27	34	GROUND
RESERVED	28	33	GROUND
GROUND	29	32	-ATN
GROUND	30	31	GROUND

P-Cable (Single-Ended) Connector

Table A.91 P-Cable (Single Ended) Internal or External Shielded Connector Pinout			
Signal Name	**Pin**	**Pin**	**Signal Name**
GROUND	1	35	-DB(12)
GROUND	2	36	-DB(13)
GROUND	3	37	-DB(14)
GROUND	4	38	-DB(15)
GROUND	5	39	-DB(Parity 1)
GROUND	6	40	-DB(0)
GROUND	7	41	-DB(1)
GROUND	8	42	-DB(2)
GROUND	9	43	-DB(3)

Signal Name	Pin	Pin	Signal Name
GROUND	10	44	-DB(4)
GROUND	11	45	-DB(5)
GROUND	12	46	-DB(6)
GROUND	13	47	-DB(7)
GROUND	14	48	-DB(Parity 0)
GROUND	15	49	GROUND
GROUND	16	50	GROUND
TERMPWR	17	51	TERMPWR
TERMPWR	18	52	TERMPWR
RESERVED	19	53	RESERVED
GROUND	20	54	GROUND
GROUND	21	55	-ATN
GROUND	22	56	GROUND
GROUND	23	57	-BSY
GROUND	24	58	-ACK
GROUND	25	59	-RST
GROUND	26	60	-MSG
GROUND	27	61	-SEL
GROUND	28	62	-C/D
GROUND	29	63	-REQ
GROUND	30	64	-I/O
GROUND	31	65	-DB(8)
GROUND	32	66	-DB(9)
GROUND	33	67	-DB(10)
GROUND	34	68	-DB(11)

Q-Cable (Single Ended) Connector

Table A.92 P-Cable (Single Ended) Internal or External Shielded Connector Pinout			
Signal Name	Pin	Pin	Signal Name
GROUND	1	35	-DB(28)
GROUND	2	36	-DB(29)
GROUND	3	37	-DB(30)
GROUND	4	38	-DB(31)
GROUND	5	39	-DB(Parity 3)
GROUND	6	40	-DB(16)
GROUND	7	41	-DB(17)
GROUND	8	42	-DB(18)
GROUND	9	43	-DB(19)

(continues)

Table A.92 Continued			
Signal Name	**Pin**	**Pin**	**Signal Name**
GROUND	10	44	-DB(20)
GROUND	11	45	-DB(21)
GROUND	12	46	-DB(22)
GROUND	13	47	-DB(23)
GROUND	14	48	-DB(Parity 2)
GROUND	15	49	GROUND
GROUND	16	50	GROUND
TERMPWRQ	17	51	TERMPWRQ
TERMPWRQ	18	52	TERMPWRQ
RESERVED	19	53	RESERVED
GROUND	20	54	GROUND
GROUND	21	55	TERMINATED
GROUND	22	56	GROUND
GROUND	23	57	TERMINATED
GROUND	24	58	-ACKQ
GROUND	25	59	TERMINATED
GROUND	26	60	TERMINATED
GROUND	27	61	TERMINATED
GROUND	28	62	TERMINATED
GROUND	29	63	-REQQ
GROUND	30	64	TERMINATED
GROUND	31	65	-DB(24)
GROUND	32	66	-DB(25)
GROUND	33	67	-DB(26)
GROUND	34	68	-DB(27)

Differential SCSI. Differential SCSI is not normally used in a PC environment, however the interface connector specifications are shown here for reference.

A-Cable (Differential) Connectors

Table A.93 A-Cable (Differential) Internal Unshielded Header Connector Pinout			
Signal Name	**Pin**	**Pin**	**Signal Name**
GROUND	1	2	GROUND
+DB(0)	3	4	-DB(0)
+DB(1)	5	6	-DB(1)
+DB(2)	7	8	-DB(2)
+DB(3)	9	10	-DB(3)
+DB(4)	11	12	-DB(4)

Signal Name	Pin	Pin	Signal Name
+DB(5)	13	14	-DB(5)
+DB(6)	15	16	-DB(6)
+DB(7)	17	18	-DB(7)
+DB(Parity)	19	20	-DP(Parity)
DIFFSENS	21	22	GROUND
RESERVED	23	24	RESERVED
TERMPWR	25	26	TERMPWR
RESERVED	27	28	RESERVED
+ATN	29	30	-ATN
GROUND	31	32	GROUND
+BSY	33	34	-BSY
+ACK	35	36	-ACK
+RST	37	38	-RST
+MSG	39	40	-MSG
+SEL	41	42	-SEL
+C/D	43	44	-C/D
+REQ	45	46	-REQ
+I/O	47	48	-I/O
GROUND	49	50	GROUND

Table A.94 A-Cable (Differential) External Shielded Connector Pinout

Signal Name	Pin	Pin	Signal Name
GROUND	1	26	GROUND
+DB(0)	2	27	-DB(0)
+DB(1)	3	28	-DB(1)
+DB(2)	4	29	-DB(2)
+DB(3)	5	30	-DB(3)
+DB(4)	6	31	-DB(4)
+DB(5)	7	32	-DB(5)
+DB(6)	8	33	-DB(6)
+DB(7)	9	34	-DB(7)
+DB(Parity)	10	35	-DP(Parity)
DIFFSENS	11	36	GROUND
RESERVED	12	37	RESERVED
TERMPWR	13	38	TERMPWR
RESERVED	14	39	RESERVED
+ATN	15	40	-ATN
GROUND	16	41	GROUND

(continues)

Table A.94 Continued

Signal Name	Pin	Pin	Signal Name
+BSY	17	42	-BSY
+ACK	18	43	-ACK
+RST	18	44	-RST
+MSG	20	45	-MSG
+SEL	21	46	-SEL
+C/D	22	47	-C/D
+REQ	23	48	-REQ
+I/O	24	49	-I/O
GROUND	25	50	GROUND

P-Cable (Differential) Connector

Table A.95 P-Cable (Differential) Internal or External Shielded Connector Pinout

Signal Name	Pin	Pin	Signal Name
+DB(12)	1	35	-DB(12)
+DB(13)	2	36	-DB(13)
+DB(14)	3	37	-DB(14)
+DB(15)	4	38	-DB(15)
+DB(Parity 1)	5	39	-DB(Parity 1)
GROUND	6	40	GROUND
+DB(0)	7	41	-DB(0)
+DB(1)	8	42	-DB(1)
+DB(2)	9	43	-DB(2)
+DB(3)	10	44	-DP(3)
+DB(4)	11	45	-DB(4)
+DB(5)	12	46	-DB(5)
+DB(6)	13	47	-DB(6)
+DB(7)	14	48	-DB(7)
+DB(Parity 0)	15	49	-DB(Parity 0)
DIFFSENS	16	50	GROUND
TERMPWR	17	51	TERMPWR
TERMPWR	18	52	TERMPWR
RESERVED	19	53	RESERVED
+ATN	20	54	-ATN
GROUND	21	55	GROUND
+BSY	22	56	-BSY
+ACK	23	57	-ACK
+RST	24	58	-RST
+MSG	25	59	-MSG

Signal Name	Pin	Pin	Signal Name
+SEL	26	60	-SEL
+C/D	27	61	-C/D
+REQ	28	62	-REQ
+I/O	29	63	-I/O
GROUND	30	64	GROUND
+DB(8)	31	65	-DB(8)
+DB(9)	32	66	-DB(9)
+DB(10)	33	67	-DB(10)
+DB(11)	34	68	-DB(11)

Q-Cable (Differential) Connector

Table A.96 Q-Cable (Differential) Internal or External Shielded Connector Pinout

Signal Name	Pin	Pin	Signal Name
+DB(28)	1	35	-DB(28)
+DB(29)	2	36	-DB(29)
+DB(30)	3	37	-DB(30)
+DB(31)	4	38	-DB(31)
+DB(Parity 3)	5	39	-DB(Parity 3)
GROUND	6	40	GROUND
+DB(16)	7	41	-DB(16)
+DB(17)	8	42	-DB(17)
+DB(18)	9	43	-DB(18)
+DB(19)	10	44	-DP(19)
+DB(20)	11	45	-DB(20)
+DB(21)	12	46	-DB(21)
+DB(22)	13	47	-DB(22)
+DB(23)	14	48	-DB(23)
+DB(Parity 2)	15	49	-DB(Parity 2)
DIFFSENS	16	50	GROUND
TERMPWRQ	17	51	TERMPWRQ
TERMPWRQ	18	52	TERMPWRQ
RESERVED	19	53	RESERVED
TERMINATED	20	54	TERMINATED
GROUND	21	55	GROUND
TERMINATED	22	56	TERMINATED
+ACKQ	23	57	-ACKQ
TERMINATED	24	58	TERMINATED
TERMINATED	25	59	TERMINATED

(continues)

Table A.96 Continued

Signal Name	Pin	Pin	Signal Name
TERMINATED	26	60	TERMINATED
TERMINATED	27	61	TERMINATED
+REQQ	28	62	-REQQ
TERMINATED	29	63	TERMINATED
GROUND	30	64	GROUND
+DB(24)	31	65	-DB(24)
+DB(25)	32	66	-DB(25)
+DB(26)	33	67	-DB(26)
+DB(27)	34	68	-DB(27)

Hard Disk Parameter Tables

When a hard disk drive is installed in a system, the system BIOS must be informed about the physical geometry of the drive in order for the Int 13h BIOS functions to work. Usually, the BIOS is informed through a table contained in the motherboard or controller BIOS that has entries defining various drive geometries. The disk installer then selects the entry that matches the drive being installed and normally informs the BIOS through the systems SETUP utility. After entering the drive type through SETUP, the type information usually is maintained in CMOS RAM by virtue of a long-life lithium battery. With XT-class systems, the Int 13h BIOS support usually is found directly on the hard disk controller in a built-in BIOS. In this case, selection of a specific drive type usually is done by moving jumpers on the controller card.

In the case of the battery-maintained CMOS memory, this Setup procedure usually is performed only during these conditions:

- The system is new and has not yet been set up.

- A new peripheral is installed. CMOS normally stores information about these items only:

  Floppy drive types
  Hard drive types
  Base and extended memory amount
  Video Display Adapter and mode
  Math coprocessor—installed or not
  Date and time

- The battery is dead or dying.

The Setup program comes on a disk for systems made by IBM or COMPAQ; most compatibles made after 1987, however, have the Setup program built directly into the BIOS. As a feature of some of the newer PS/2 systems (Models 57, 90, and 95), the Setup program, as well as the entire ROM BIOS, is stored on the hard disk in a special hidden, 3-megabyte partition—the system partition. Having the Setup built into the motherboard

BIOS or loaded from a system partition as in the newer PS/2 systems is very convenient, and eliminates the need for a separate floppy disk containing the Setup program. Most of the time these BIOS-based Setup programs are activated by a particular keystroke sequence either at any time or only during the Power-On Self Test. The four popular compatible BIOS manufacturers use these keystrokes to activate Setup:

Phoenix BIOS	Ctrl-Alt-Esc or Ctrl-Alt-S
AMI BIOS	Del key during the POST
Award BIOS	Ctrl-Alt-Esc
IBM PS/2 BIOS	Ctrl-Alt-Ins after Ctrl-Alt-Del

With the Phoenix, Award, or IBM BIOS, you must hold the three keys down simultaneously to invoke Setup. With AMI, you just press the Del key during the POST. Note that only certain PS/2 models support Initial Microcode Load (IML) from the hard disk, which means that the BIOS and Reference disk (Setup) can be invoked with the indicated keystrokes.

To select the correct hard disk type for most ST-506/412, IDE, or ESDI type drives, you first must know your drive's physical characteristics. With most IDE drives, you need to know just the total number of sectors on the drive. SCSI drives almost always automatically configure to the system by entering a disk type of 0.

This step enables the SCSI BIOS to execute a SCSI Read Capacity command and supply the parameters to the system on the fly.

Drive-parameter information can be found in the technical-reference documentation that came with your drive or system. If you did not get this documentation, call your vendor and demand it. After knowing the parameters for your drive, you need to find a table entry in your specific BIOS that matches the drive parameters. If none is an exact match, in some cases you can use an entry that is close as long as the entries for cylinders, heads, or sectors per track are not more than the drive is capable of. You also should match as close as possible the Write Precompensation starting cylinder value for reliable operation on the drives inner cylinders. See Chapter 10, "Hard Disk Drives," for more information on selecting a correct type.

Because a variety of BIOS manufacturers are available in the marketplace, your systems may contain different tables. Each BIOS manufacturer has defined its own drive tables, usually starting with entries that are the same as IBM's. Most BIOS drive tables are similar to IBM for the first 15 or 23 entries, but from there they vary from manufacturer to manufacturer. For this reason, a drive manufacturer cannot simply stamp the drive type on the drive itself. For example, the correct drive type used for a Seagate ST-251 drive varies according to the BIOS manufacturer:

IBM BIOS	Type 8
COMPAQ BIOS	Type 5
AMI BIOS	Type 40
Award BIOS	Type 40
Phoenix BIOS	Type 44

Note that because of the lack of a user-definable type in the IBM and COMPAQ BIOS, this drive is not used to full capacity in those systems (especially in the IBM). So, if Seagate were to put the drive type on the drive, which number should it use? Obviously, it cannot do so, and the installer or data-recovery specialist must make the correct selection.

The tables in this section show the contents of the disk tables for a variety of BIOS manufacturers including IBM, COMPAQ, Phoenix, AMI, and Award. This information is helpful in determining the correct drive type for a particular drive and system combination. Note that some BIOS vendors now provide user-definable entries in their tables, which means that the values in the table can be typed directly from the keyboard, thereby allowing for virtually infinite customization without having to modify the BIOS itself.

Also included are tables for IBM's XT controllers, whose table format differs slightly from the tables in AT-class systems.

Table A.97 IBM 10M Hard Disk Controller (Xebec 1210) Drive Parameter Tables

Entry	Type	Cyls	Heads	WPC	Ctrl	LZ	S/T	Meg	MB
0	_	306	2	0	00h	00h	00h	5.08	5.33
1	_	375	8	0	05h	00h	00h	24.90	26.11
2	_	306	6	256	05h	00h	00h	15.24	15.98
3	_	306	4	0	05h	00h	00h	10.16	10.65

Table A.98 IBM 20M Hard Disk Controller (Xebec 1210) Drive Parameter Tables

Entry	Type	Cyls	Heads	WPC	Ctrl	LZ	S/T	Meg	MB
0	1	306	4	0	05h	305	17	10.16	10.65
1	16	612	4	0	05h	663	17	20.32	21.31
2	2	615	4	300	05h	615	17	20.42	21.41
3	13	306	8	128	05h	319	17	20.32	21.31

Entry = Controller table position
Type = Drive type number
Cyls = Total number of cylinders
Heads = Total number of heads
WPC = Write precompensation starting cylinder
Ctrl = Control byte, values as follows:

Bit 0	*01h, drive step rate*
Bit 1	*02h, drive step rate*
Bit 2	*04h, drive step rate*
Bit 3	*08h, more than eight heads*
Bit 4	*10h, embedded servo drive*
Bit 5	*20h, OEM defect map at (Cyls + 1)*

Bit 6   *40h, disable ECC retries*
Bit 7   *80h, disable disk access retries*
Xebec 1210 Drive Step Rate Coding (Control Byte bits 0-3)
00h, 3-millisecond step rate
04h, 200-microsecond buffered step
05h, 70-microsecond buffered step
06h, 30-microsecond buffered step
07h, 15-microsecond buffered step
LZ = Landing zone cylinder for head parking
S/T = Number of sectors per track
Meg = Drive capacity in megabytes
M = Drive capacity in millions of bytes
The Landing Zone field and Sectors per Track fields are not used in the 10M (original) controller and contain 00h values for each entry.

Note

MB and Meg sometimes are used interchangeably, but this is not exactly correct. MB is one Million Bytes, or 1,000,000 bytes. Meg (or M) is one Megabyte, which is equal to 1,048,576 bytes. (1 megabyte = 1 kilobyte times 1 kilobyte, and 1 kilobyte = 1024 bytes. Thus, 1 megabyte = 1024 times 1024 = 1,048,576.)

To select one of the drive table entries in the IBM XT controllers (Xebec 1210), you would set the drive table selection jumper (Jumper W5). The following table shows how these jumpers should be set to select a particular table entry For example, to select table entry 2 for drive 0 (C:), you would set the jumper Off at position 1 and On at position 2.

Table A.99 IBM XT Controller (Xebec 1210) Drive Table Jumper (W5) Settings

Drive 0 Table Entry	1	2	3	4
Jumper 1	On	On	Off	Off
Jumper 2	On	Off	On	Off
Drive 1 Table Entry	**1**	**2**	**3**	**4**
Jumper 3	On	On	Off	Off
Jumper 4	On	Off	On	Off

Motherboard BIOS Hard Drive Tables

The following table shows the IBM motherboard ROM BIOS hard disk parameters for AT or PS/2 systems using ST-506/412 (standard or IDE) controllers.

Table A.100 IBM AT and PS/2 BIOS Hard Disk Table

Type	Cylinders	Heads	WPC	Ctrl	LZ	S/T	Meg	MB
1	306	4	128	00h	305	17	10.16	10.65
2	615	4	300	00h	615	17	20.42	21.41
3	615	6	300	00h	615	17	30.63	32.12
4	940	8	512	00h	940	17	62.42	65.45
5	940	6	512	00h	940	17	46.82	49.09
6	615	4	65535	00h	615	17	20.42	21.41
7	462	8	256	00h	511	17	30.68	32.17
8	733	5	65535	00h	733	17	30.42	31.90
9	900	15	65535	08h	901	17	112.06	117.50
10	820	3	65535	00h	820	17	20.42	21.41
11	855	5	65535	00h	855	17	35.49	37.21
12	855	7	65535	00h	855	17	49.68	52.09
13	306	8	128	00h	319	17	20.32	21.31
14	733	7	65535	00h	733	17	42.59	44.66
15	0	0	0	00h	0	0	0	0
16	612	4	0	00h	663	17	20.32	21.31
17	977	5	300	00h	977	17	40.55	42.52
18	977	7	65535	00h	977	17	56.77	59.53
19	1024	7	512	00h	1023	17	59.50	62.39
20	733	5	300	00h	732	17	30.42	31.90
21	733	7	300	00h	732	17	42.59	44.66
22	733	5	300	00h	733	17	30.42	31.90
23	306	4	0	00h	336	17	10.16	10.65
24	612	4	305	00h	663	17	20.32	21.31
25	306	4	65535	00h	340	17	10.16	10.65
26	612	4	65535	00h	670	17	20.32	21.31
27	698	7	300	20h	732	17	40.56	42.53
28	976	5	488	20h	977	17	40.51	42.48
29	306	4	0	00h	340	17	10.16	10.65
30	611	4	306	20h	663	17	20.29	21.27
31	732	7	300	20h	732	17	42.53	44.60
32	1023	5	65535	20h	1023	17	42.46	44.52
33	614	4	65535	20h	663	25	29.98	31.44
34	775	2	65535	20h	900	27	20.43	21.43
35	921	2	65535	20h	1000	33	29.68	31.12
36	402	4	65535	20h	460	26	20.41	21.41
37	580	6	65535	20h	640	26	44.18	46.33
38	845	2	65535	20h	1023	36	29.71	31.15
39	769	3	65535	20h	1023	36	40.55	42.52

Type	Cylinders	Heads	WPC	Ctrl	LZ	S/T	Meg	MB
40	531	4	65535	20h	532	39	40.45	42.41
41	577	2	65535	20h	1023	36	20.29	21.27
42	654	2	65535	20h	674	32	20.44	21.43
43	923	5	65535	20h	1023	36	81.12	85.06
44	531	8	65535	20h	532	39	80.89	84.82
45	0	0	0	00h	0	0	0.00	0.00
46	0	0	0	00h	0	0	0.00	0.00
47	0	0	0	00h	0	0	0.00	0.00

LZ = Landing zone cylinder for head parking
S/T = Number of sectors per track
Meg = Drive capacity in megabytes
MB = Drive capacity in millions of bytes
The Landing zone and Sectors per Track fields are not used in the 10MB (original) controller and contain 00h values for each entry.

Table entry 15 is reserved to act as a pointer to indicate that the type is greater than 15. Most IBM systems do not have every entry in this table. The maximum usable type number varies for each particular ROM version. The maximum usable type for each IBM ROM is indicated in the table on IBM ROM versions, earlier in this appendix. If you have a compatible, this table may be inaccurate for many of the entries past type 15. Instead, you should see whether one of the other tables listed here applies to your specific compatible ROM. Most compatibles follow the IBM table for at least the first 15 entries.

Most IBM PS/2 systems now are supplied with hard disk drives that have the defect map written as data on the cylinder one cylinder beyond the highest reported cylinder. This special data is read by the IBM PS/2 Advanced Diagnostics low-level format program. This process automates the entry of the defect list and eliminates the chance of human error, as long as you use only the IBM PS/2 Advanced Diagnostics for hard disk low-level formatting.

This type of table does not apply to IBM ESDI or SCSI hard disk controllers, host adapters, and drives. Because the ESDI and SCSI controllers or host adapters query the drive directly for the required parameters, no table-entry selection is necessary. Note, however, that the table for the ST-506/412 drives can still be found currently in the ROM BIOS of most of the PS/2 systems, even if the model came standard with an ESDI or SCSI disk subsystem.

Table A.101 shows the COMPAQ motherboard ROM BIOS hard disk parameters for the COMPAQ Deskpro 386.

Table A.101 COMPAQ Deskpro 386 Hard Disk Table								
Type	**Cylinders**	**Heads**	**WPC**	**Ctrl**	**LZ**	**S/T**	**Meg**	**MB**
1	306	4	128	00h	305	17	10.16	10.65
2	615	4	128	00h	638	17	20.42	21.41
3	615	6	128	00h	615	17	30.63	32.12
4	1024	6	512	00h	939	17	46.82	49.09
6	697	5	128	00h	696	17	28.93	30.33
7	462	8	256	00h	511	17	30.68	32.17
8	925	5	128	00h	924	17	38.39	40.26
9	900	15	65535	08h	899	17	112.06	117.50
10	980	5	65535	00h	980	17	40.67	42.65
11	925	7	128	00h	924	17	53.75	56.36
12	925	9	128	08h	924	17	69.10	72.46
13	612	8	256	00h	611	17	40.64	42.61
14	980	4	128	00h	980	17	32.54	34.12
15	0	0	0	00h	0	0	0	0
16	612	4	0	00h	612	17	20.32	21.31
17	980	5	128	00h	980	17	40.67	42.65
18	966	6	128	00h	966	17	48.11	50.45
19	1023	8	65535	00h	1023	17	67.93	71.23
20	733	5	256	00h	732	17	30.42	31.90
21	733	7	256	00h	732	17	42.59	44.66
22	805	6	65535	00h	805	17	40.09	42.04
23	924	8	65535	00h	924	17	61.36	64.34
24	966	14	65535	08h	966	17	112.26	117.71
25	966	16	65535	08h	966	17	128.30	134.53
26	1023	14	65535	08h	1023	17	118.88	124.66
27	966	10	65535	08h	966	17	80.19	84.08
28	748	16	65535	08h	748	17	99.34	104.17
29	805	6	65535	00h	805	26	61.32	64.30
30	615	4	128	00h	615	25	30.03	31.49
31	615	8	128	00h	615	25	60.06	62.98
32	905	9	128	08h	905	25	99.43	104.26
33	748	8	65535	00h	748	34	99.34	104.17
34	966	7	65535	00h	966	34	112.26	117.71
35	966	8	65535	00h	966	34	128.30	134.53
36	966	9	65535	08h	966	34	144.33	151.35
37	966	5	65535	00h	966	34	80.19	84.08
38	611	16	65535	08h	611	63	300.73	315.33
39	1023	11	65535	08h	1023	33	181.32	190.13

Type	Cylinders	Heads	WPC	Ctrl	LZ	S/T	Meg	MB
40	1023	15	65535	08h	1023	34	254.75	267.13
41	1023	15	65535	08h	1023	33	247.26	259.27
42	1023	16	65535	08h	1023	63	503.51	527.97
43	805	4	65535	00h	805	26	40.88	42.86
44	805	2	65535	00h	805	26	20.44	21.43
45	748	8	65535	00h	748	33	96.42	101.11
46	748	6	65535	00h	748	33	72.32	75.83
47	966	5	128	00h	966	25	58.96	61.82

Table entry 15 is reserved to act as a pointer to indicate that the type is greater than 15.

Table A.102 shows the COMPAQ motherboard ROM BIOS hard disk parameters for the COMPAQ Deskpro 286 Revision F.

Table A.102 COMPAQ Deskpro 286 Revision F Hard Disk Table								
Type	Cylinders	Heads	WPC	Ctrl	LZ	S/T	Meg	MB
1	306	4	128	00h	305	17	10.16	10.65
2	615	4	128	00h	638	17	20.42	21.41
3	615	6	128	00h	615	17	30.63	32.12
4	1024	8	512	00h	1023	17	68.00	71.30
5	940	6	512	00h	939	17	46.82	49.09
6	697	5	128	00h	696	17	28.93	30.33
7	462	8	256	00h	511	17	30.68	32.17
8	925	5	128	00h	924	17	38.39	40.26
9	900	15	65535	08h	899	17	112.06	117.50
10	980	5	65535	00h	980	17	40.67	42.65
11	925	7	128	00h	924	17	53.75	56.36
12	925	9	128	08h	924	17	69.10	72.46
13	612	8	256	00h	611	17	40.64	42.61
14	980	4	128	00h	980	17	32.54	34.12
15	0	0	0	00h	0	0	0	0
16	612	4	0	00h	612	17	20.32	21.31
17	980	5	128	00h	980	17	40.67	42.65
18	966	6	128	00h	966	17	48.11	50.45
19	1023	8	65535	00h	1023	17	67.93	71.23
20	733	5	256	00h	732	17	30.42	31.90
21	733	7	256	00h	732	17	42.59	44.66
22	768	6	65535	00h	768	17	38.25	40.11

(continues)

Table A.102 Continued								
Type	**Cylinders**	**Heads**	**WPC**	**Ctrl**	**LZ**	**S/T**	**Meg**	**MB**
23	771	6	65535	00h	771	17	38.40	40.26
24	966	14	65535	08h	966	17	112.26	117.71
25	966	16	65535	08h	966	17	128.30	134.53
26	1023	14	65535	08h	1023	17	118.88	124.66
27	966	10	65535	08h	966	17	80.19	84.08
28	771	3	65535	00h	771	17	19.20	20.13
29	578	4	65535	00h	578	17	19.19	20.12
30	615	4	128	00h	615	25	30.03	31.49
31	615	8	128	00h	615	25	60.06	62.98
32	966	3	65535	00h	966	34	48.11	50.45
33	966	5	65535	00h	966	34	80.19	84.08
34	966	7	65535	00h	966	34	112.26	117.71
35	966	8	65535	00h	966	34	128.30	134.53
36	966	9	65535	08h	966	34	144.33	151.35
37	966	5	65535	00h	966	34	80.19	84.08
38	1023	9	65535	08h	1023	33	148.35	155.56
39	1023	11	65535	08h	1023	33	181.32	190.13
40	1023	13	65535	08h	1023	33	214.29	224.70
41	1023	15	65535	08h	1023	33	247.26	259.27
42	1023	16	65535	08h	1023	34	271.73	284.93
43	756	4	65535	00h	756	26	38.39	40.26
44	756	2	65535	00h	756	26	19.20	20.13
45	768	4	65535	00h	768	26	39.00	40.89
46	768	2	65535	00h	768	26	19.50	20.45
47	966	5	128	00h	966	25	58.96	61.82

Table entry 15 is reserved to act as a pointer to indicate that the type is greater than 15.

Table A.103 shows the COMPAQ motherboard ROM BIOS hard disk parameters for the COMPAQ Deskpro 286e Revision B (03/22/89).

Table A.103 COMPAQ Deskpro 286e Revision B Hard Disk Table								
Type	**Cylinders**	**Heads**	**WPC**	**Ctrl**	**LZ**	**S/T**	**Meg**	**MB**
1	306	4	128	00h	305	17	10.16	10.65
2	615	4	128	00h	638	17	20.42	21.41
3	615	6	128	00h	615	17	30.63	32.12
4	1024	8	512	00h	1023	17	68.00	71.30
5	805	6	65535	00h	805	17	40.09	42.04

Type	Cylinders	Heads	WPC	Ctrl	LZ	S/T	Meg	MB
6	697	5	128	00h	696	17	28.93	30.33
7	462	8	256	00h	511	17	30.68	32.17
8	925	5	128	00h	924	17	38.39	40.26
9	900	15	65535	08h	899	17	112.06	117.50
10	980	5	65535	00h	980	17	40.67	42.65
11	925	7	128	00h	924	17	53.75	56.36
12	925	9	128	08h	924	17	69.10	72.46
13	612	8	256	00h	611	17	40.64	42.61
14	980	4	128	00h	980	17	32.54	34.12
15	0	0	0	00h	0	0	0	0
16	612	4	0	00h	612	17	20.32	21.31
17	980	5	128	00h	980	17	40.67	42.65
18	966	5	128	00h	966	17	40.09	42.04
19	754	11	65535	08h	753	17	68.85	72.19
20	733	5	256	00h	732	17	30.42	31.90
21	733	7	256	00h	732	17	42.59	44.66
22	524	4	65535	00h	524	40	40.94	42.93
23	924	8	65535	00h	924	17	61.36	64.34
24	966	14	65535	08h	966	17	112.26	117.71
25	966	16	65535	08h	966	17	128.30	134.53
26	1023	14	65535	08h	1023	17	118.88	124.66
27	832	6	65535	00h	832	33	80.44	84.34
28	1222	15	65535	08h	1222	34	304.31	319.09
29	1240	7	65535	00h	1240	34	144.10	151.10
30	615	4	128	00h	615	25	30.03	31.49
31	615	8	128	00h	615	25	60.06	62.98
32	905	9	128	08h	905	25	99.43	104.26
33	832	8	65535	00h	832	33	107.25	112.46
34	966	7	65535	00h	966	34	112.26	117.71
35	966	8	65535	00h	966	34	128.30	134.53
36	966	9	65535	08h	966	34	144.33	151.35
37	966	5	65535	00h	966	34	80.19	84.08
38	611	16	65535	08h	611	63	300.73	315.33
39	1023	11	65535	08h	1023	33	181.32	190.13
40	1023	15	65535	08h	1023	34	254.75	267.13
41	1630	15	65535	08h	1630	52	620.80	650.96
42	1023	16	65535	08h	1023	63	503.51	527.97
43	805	4	65535	00h	805	26	40.88	42.86
44	805	2	65535	00h	805	26	20.44	21.43

(continues)

Table A.103 Continued								
Type	**Cylinders**	**Heads**	**WPC**	**Ctrl**	**LZ**	**S/T**	**Meg**	**MB**
45	748	8	65535	00h	748	33	96.42	101.11
46	748	6	65535	00h	748	33	72.32	75.83
47	966	5	128	00h	966	25	58.96	61.82

Table entry 15 is reserved to act as a pointer to indicate that the type is greater than 15.

Table A.104 shows the AMI ROM BIOS (286 BIOS Version 04/30/89) hard disk parameters.

Table A.104 AMI ROM BIOS (286 BIOS Version 04/30/89) Hard Disk Table								
Type	**Cylinders**	**Heads**	**WPC**	**Ctrl**	**LZ**	**S/T**	**Meg**	**MB**
1	306	4	128	00h	305	17	10.16	10.65
2	615	4	300	00h	615	17	20.42	21.41
3	615	6	300	00h	615	17	30.63	32.12
4	940	8	512	00h	940	17	62.42	65.45
5	940	6	512	00h	940	17	46.82	49.09
6	615	4	65535	00h	615	17	20.42	21.41
7	462	8	256	00h	511	17	30.68	32.17
8	733	5	65535	00h	733	17	30.42	31.90
9	900	15	65535	08h	901	17	112.06	117.50
10	820	3	65535	00h	820	17	20.42	21.41
11	855	5	65535	00h	855	17	35.49	37.21
12	855	7	65535	00h	855	17	49.68	52.09
13	306	8	128	00h	319	17	20.32	21.31
14	733	7	65535	00h	733	17	42.59	44.66
15	0	0	0	00h	0	0	0	0
16	612	4	0	00h	663	17	20.32	21.31
17	977	5	300	00h	977	17	40.55	42.52
18	977	7	65535	00h	977	17	56.77	59.53
19	1024	7	512	00h	1023	17	59.50	62.39
20	733	5	300	00h	732	17	30.42	31.90
21	733	7	300	00h	732	17	42.59	44.66
22	733	5	300	00h	733	17	30.42	31.90
23	306	4	0	00h	336	17	10.16	10.65
24	925	7	0	00h	925	17	53.75	56.36
25	925	9	65535	08h	925	17	69.10	72.46
26	754	7	526	00h	754	17	43.81	45.94
27	754	11	65535	08h	754	17	68.85	72.19
28	699	7	256	00h	699	17	40.62	42.59

Type	Cylinders	Heads	WPC	Ctrl	LZ	S/T	Meg	MB
29	823	10	65535	08h	823	17	68.32	71.63
30	918	7	874	00h	918	17	53.34	55.93
31	1024	11	65535	08h	1024	17	93.50	98.04
32	1024	15	65535	08h	1024	17	127.50	133.69
33	1024	5	1024	00h	1024	17	42.50	44.56
34	612	2	128	00h	612	17	10.16	10.65
35	1024	9	65535	08h	1024	17	76.50	80.22
36	1024	8	512	00h	1024	17	68.00	71.30
37	615	8	128	00h	615	17	40.84	42.82
38	987	3	805	00h	987	17	24.58	25.77
39	987	7	805	00h	987	17	57.35	60.14
40	820	6	820	00h	820	17	40.84	42.82
41	977	5	815	00h	977	17	40.55	42.52
42	981	5	811	00h	981	17	40.72	42.69
43	830	7	512	00h	830	17	48.23	50.57
44	830	10	65535	08h	830	17	68.90	72.24
45	917	15	65535	08h	918	17	114.18	119.72
46	1224	15	65535	08h	1223	17	152.40	159.81
47	0	0	0	00h	0	0	0.00	0.00

Table entry 15 is reserved to act as a pointer to indicate that the type is greater than 15.
This BIOS uses type 47 as a user-definable entry.

Table A.105 shows the Award ROM BIOS (286 BIOS Version 04/30/89) (Modular 286, 386SX, and 386 BIOS Version 3.05) hard disk parameters.

Table A.105 Award ROM BIOS Version 3.05 Hard Disk Table								
Type	**Cylinders**	**Heads**	**WPC**	**Ctrl**	**LZ**	**S/T**	**Meg**	**MB**
1	306	4	128	00h	305	17	10.16	10.65
2	615	4	300	00h	615	17	20.42	21.41
3	615	6	300	00h	615	17	30.63	32.12
4	940	8	512	00h	940	17	62.42	65.45
5	940	6	512	00h	940	17	46.82	49.09
6	615	4	65535	00h	615	17	20.42	21.41
7	462	8	256	00h	511	17	30.68	32.17
8	733	5	65535	00h	733	17	30.42	31.90
9	900	15	65535	08h	901	17	112.06	117.50
10	820	3	65535	00h	820	17	20.42	21.41
11	855	5	65535	00h	855	17	35.49	37.21

(continues)

Type	Cylinders	Heads	WPC	Ctrl	LZ	S/T	Meg	MB
12	855	7	65535	00h	855	17	49.68	52.09
13	306	8	128	00h	319	17	20.32	21.31
14	733	7	65535	00h	733	17	42.59	44.66
15	0	0	0	00h	0	0	0	0
16	612	4	0	00h	663	17	20.32	21.31
17	977	5	300	00h	977	17	40.55	42.52
18	977	7	65535	00h	977	17	56.77	59.53
19	1024	7	512	00h	1023	17	59.50	62.39
20	733	5	300	00h	732	17	30.42	31.90
21	733	7	300	00h	732	17	42.59	44.66
22	733	5	300	00h	733	17	30.42	31.90
23	306	4	0	00h	336	17	10.16	10.65
24	977	5	65535	00h	976	17	40.55	42.52
25	1024	9	65535	08h	1023	17	76.50	80.22
26	1224	7	65535	00h	1223	17	71.12	74.58
27	1224	11	65535	08h	1223	17	111.76	117.19
28	1224	15	65535	08h	1223	17	152.40	159.81
29	1024	8	65535	00h	1023	17	68.00	71.30
30	1024	11	65535	08h	1023	17	93.50	98.04
31	918	11	65535	08h	1023	17	83.82	87.89
32	925	9	65535	08h	926	17	69.10	72.46
33	1024	10	65535	08h	1023	17	85.00	89.13
34	1024	12	65535	08h	1023	17	102.00	106.95
35	1024	13	65535	08h	1023	17	110.50	115.87
36	1024	14	65535	08h	1023	17	119.00	124.78
37	1024	16	65535	08h	1023	17	136.00	142.61
39	918	15	65535	08h	1023	17	114.30	119.85
40	820	6	65535	00h	820	17	40.84	42.82
41	1024	5	65535	00h	1023	17	42.50	44.56
42	1024	5	65535	00h	1023	26	65.00	68.16
43	809	6	65535	00h	808	17	40.29	42.25
44	820	6	65535	00h	819	26	62.46	65.50
45	776	8	65535	00h	775	33	100.03	104.89
46	0	0	0	00h	0	0	0.00	0.00
47	0	0	0	00h	0	0	0.00	0.00

Table A.105 Continued

Table entry 15 is reserved to act as a pointer to indicate that the type is greater than 15.
This BIOS uses types 46 and 47 as user-definable entries.

Table A.106 shows the Award ROM BIOS hard disk parameters (modular 286, 386SX, and 386 BIOS Version 3.1).

Table A.106 Award ROM BIOS Version 3.1 Hard Disk Table								
Type	**Cylinders**	**Heads**	**WPC**	**Ctrl**	**LZ**	**S/T**	**Meg**	**MB**
1	306	4	128	00h	305	17	10.16	10.65
2	615	4	300	00h	615	17	20.42	21.41
3	615	6	300	00h	615	17	30.63	32.12
4	940	8	512	00h	940	17	62.42	65.45
5	940	6	512	00h	940	17	46.82	49.09
6	615	4	65535	00h	615	17	20.42	21.41
7	462	8	256	00h	511	17	30.68	32.17
8	733	5	65535	00h	733	17	30.42	31.90
9	900	15	65535	08h	901	17	112.06	117.50
10	820	3	65535	00h	820	17	20.42	21.41
11	855	5	65535	00h	855	17	35.49	37.21
12	855	7	65535	00h	855	17	49.68	52.09
13	306	8	128	00h	319	17	20.32	21.31
14	733	7	65535	00h	733	17	42.59	44.66
15	0	0	0	00h	0	0	0	0
16	612	4	0	00h	663	17	20.32	21.31
17	977	5	300	00h	977	17	40.55	42.52
18	977	7	65535	00h	977	17	56.77	59.53
19	1024	7	512	00h	1023	17	59.50	62.39
20	733	5	300	00h	732	17	30.42	31.90
21	733	7	300	00h	732	17	42.59	44.66
22	733	5	300	00h	733	17	30.42	31.90
23	306	4	0	00h	336	17	10.16	10.65
24	977	5	65535	00h	976	17	40.55	42.52
25	1024	9	65535	08h	1023	17	76.50	80.22
26	1224	7	65535	00h	1223	17	71.12	74.58
27	1224	11	65535	08h	1223	17	111.76	117.19
28	1224	15	65535	08h	1223	17	152.40	159.81
29	1024	8	65535	00h	1023	17	68.00	71.30
30	1024	11	65535	08h	1023	17	93.50	98.04
31	918	11	65535	08h	1023	17	83.82	87.89
32	925	9	65535	08h	926	17	69.10	72.46
33	1024	10	65535	08h	1023	17	85.00	89.13
34	1024	12	65535	08h	1023	17	102.00	106.95
35	1024	13	65535	08h	1023	17	110.50	115.87

(continues)

Table A.106 Continued								
Type	**Cylinders**	**Heads**	**WPC**	**Ctrl**	**LZ**	**S/T**	**Meg**	**MB**
36	1024	14	65535	08h	1023	17	119.00	124.78
37	1024	2	65535	00h	1023	17	17.00	17.83
38	1024	16	65535	08h	1023	17	136.00	142.61
39	918	15	65535	08h	1023	17	114.30	119.85
40	820	6	65535	00h	820	17	40.84	42.82
41	1024	5	65535	00h	1023	17	42.50	44.56
42	1024	5	65535	00h	1023	26	65.00	68.16
43	809	6	65535	00h	852	17	40.29	42.25
44	809	6	65535	00h	852	26	61.62	64.62
45	776	8	65535	00h	775	33	100.03	104.89
46	684	16	65535	08h	685	38	203.06	212.93
47	615	6	65535	00h	615	17	30.63	32.12

Table entry 15 is reserved to act as a pointer to indicate that the type is greater than 15.
This BIOS uses types 48 and 49 as user-definable entries.

Table A.107 shows the Phoenix 286 ROM BIOS (80286 ROM BIOS Version 3.01, dated 11/01/86) hard disk parameters.

Table A.107 Phoenix 286 (80286 ROM BIOS Version 3.01) Hard Disk Table								
Type	**Cylinders**	**Heads**	**WPC**	**Ctrl**	**LZ**	**S/T**	**Meg**	**MB**
1	306	4	128	00h	305	17	10.16	10.65
2	615	4	300	00h	638	17	20.42	21.41
3	615	6	300	00h	615	17	30.63	32.12
4	940	8	512	00h	940	17	62.42	65.45
5	940	6	512	00h	940	17	46.82	49.09
6	615	4	65535	00h	615	17	20.42	21.41
7	462	8	256	00h	511	17	30.68	32.17
8	733	5	65535	00h	733	17	30.42	31.90
9	900	15	65535	08h	901	17	112.06	117.50
10	820	3	65535	00h	820	17	20.42	21.41
11	855	5	65535	00h	855	17	35.49	37.21
12	855	7	65535	00h	855	17	49.68	52.09
13	306	8	128	00h	319	17	20.32	21.31
14	733	7	65535	00h	733	17	42.59	44.66
15	0	0	0	00h	0	0	0.00	0.00
16	612	4	0	00h	633	17	20.32	21.31
17	977	5	300	00h	977	17	40.55	42.52
18	977	7	65535	00h	977	17	56.77	59.53

Type	Cylinders	Heads	WPC	Ctrl	LZ	S/T	Meg	MB
19	1024	7	512	00h	1023	17	59.50	62.39
20	733	5	300	00h	732	17	30.42	31.90
21	733	7	300	00h	733	17	42.59	44.66
22	733	5	300	00h	733	17	30.42	31.90
23	0	0	0	00h	0	0	0.00	0.00
24	0	0	0	00h	0	0	0.00	0.00
25	0	0	0	00h	0	0	0.00	0.00
26	0	0	0	00h	0	0	0.00	0.00
27	0	0	0	00h	0	0	0.00	0.00
28	0	0	0	00h	0	0	0.00	0.00
29	0	0	0	00h	0	0	0.00	0.00
30	0	0	0	00h	0	0	0.00	0.00
31	0	0	0	00h	0	0	0.00	0.00
32	0	0	0	00h	0	0	0.00	0.00
33	0	0	0	00h	0	0	0.00	0.00
34	0	0	0	00h	0	0	0.00	0.00
35	0	0	0	00h	0	0	0.00	0.00
36	1024	5	512	00h	1024	17	42.50	44.56
37	830	10	65535	08h	830	17	68.90	72.24
38	823	10	256	08h	824	17	68.32	71.63
39	615	4	128	00h	664	17	20.42	21.41
40	615	8	128	00h	664	17	40.84	42.82
41	917	15	65535	08h	918	17	114.18	119.72
42	1023	15	65535	08h	1024	17	127.38	133.56
43	823	10	512	08h	823	17	68.32	71.63
44	820	6	65535	00h	820	17	40.84	42.82
45	1024	8	65535	00h	1024	17	68.00	71.30
46	925	9	65535	08h	925	17	69.10	72.46
47	1024	5	65535	00h	1024	17	42.50	44.56

Table entry 15 is reserved to act as a pointer to indicate that the type is greater than 15.

Table A.108 shows the Phoenix 286 ROM BIOS (286 BIOS Plus, Version 3.10) hard disk parameters.

Table A.108 Phoenix 286 ROM BIOS (286 BIOS Plus Version 3.10) Hard Disk Table								
Type	Cylinders	Heads	WPC	Ctrl	LZ	S/T	Meg	MB
1	306	4	128	00h	305	17	10.16	10.65
2	615	4	300	00h	615	17	20.42	21.41

(continues)

	Table A.108 Continued							
Type	**Cylinders**	**Heads**	**WPC**	**Ctrl**	**LZ**	**S/T**	**Meg**	**MB**
3	615	6	300	00h	615	17	30.63	32.12
4	940	8	512	00h	940	17	62.42	65.45
5	940	6	512	00h	940	17	46.82	49.09
6	615	4	65535	00h	615	17	20.42	21.41
7	462	8	256	00h	511	17	30.68	32.17
8	733	5	65535	00h	733	17	30.42	31.90
9	900	15	65535	08h	901	17	112.06	117.50
10	820	3	65535	00h	820	17	20.42	21.41
11	855	5	65535	00h	855	17	35.49	37.21
12	855	7	65535	00h	855	17	49.68	52.09
13	306	8	128	00h	319	17	20.32	21.31
14	733	7	65535	00h	733	17	42.59	44.66
15	0	0	0	00h	0	0	0	0
16	612	4	0	00h	663	17	20.32	21.31
17	977	5	300	00h	977	17	40.55	42.52
18	977	7	65535	00h	977	17	56.77	59.53
19	1024	7	512	00h	1023	17	59.50	62.39
20	733	5	300	00h	732	17	30.42	31.90
21	733	7	300	00h	732	17	42.59	44.66
22	733	5	300	00h	733	17	30.42	31.90
23	306	4	0	00h	336	17	10.16	10.65
24	0	0	0	00h	0	0	0.00	0.00
25	615	4	0	00h	615	17	20.42	21.41
26	1024	4	65535	00h	1023	17	34.00	35.65
27	1024	5	65535	00h	1023	17	42.50	44.56
28	1024	8	65535	00h	1023	17	68.00	71.30
29	512	8	256	00h	512	17	34.00	35.65
30	615	2	615	00h	615	17	10.21	10.71
31	989	5	0	00h	989	17	41.05	43.04
32	1020	15	65535	08h	1024	17	127.00	133.17
33	0	0	0	00h	0	0	0.00	0.00
34	0	0	0	00h	0	0	0.00	0.00
35	1024	9	1024	08h	1024	17	76.50	80.22
36	1024	5	512	00h	1024	17	42.50	44.56
37	830	10	65535	08h	830	17	68.90	72.24
38	823	10	256	08h	824	17	68.32	71.63
39	615	4	128	00h	664	17	20.42	21.41
40	615	8	128	00h	664	17	40.84	42.82
41	917	15	65535	08h	918	17	114.18	119.72

Type	Cylinders	Heads	WPC	Ctrl	LZ	S/T	Meg	MB
42	1023	15	65535	08h	1024	17	127.38	133.56
43	823	10	512	08h	823	17	68.32	71.63
44	820	6	65535	00h	820	17	40.84	42.82
45	1024	8	65535	00h	1024	17	68.00	71.30
46	925	9	65535	08h	925	17	69.10	72.46
47	699	7	256	00h	700	17	40.62	42.59

Table entry 15 is reserved to act as a pointer to indicate that the type is greater than 15.
This BIOS uses types 48 and 49 as user-definable entries.

Table A.109 shows the Pheonix 386 ROM BIOS (A386 BIOS 1.01 Reference ID 08, dated 04/19/90) hard disk parameters.

Table A.109 Phoenix 386 ROM BIOS (A386 BIOS 1.01) Hard Disk Table								
Type	**Cylinders**	**Heads**	**WPC**	**Ctrl**	**LZ**	**S/T**	**Meg**	**MB**
1	306	4	128	00h	305	17	10.16	10.65
2	615	4	300	00h	615	17	20.42	21.41
3	615	6	300	00h	615	17	30.63	32.12
4	940	8	512	00h	940	17	62.42	65.45
5	940	6	512	00h	940	17	46.82	49.09
6	615	4	65535	00h	615	17	20.42	21.41
7	462	8	256	00h	511	17	30.68	32.17
8	733	5	65535	00h	733	17	30.42	31.90
9	900	15	65535	08h	901	17	112.06	117.50
10	820	3	65535	00h	820	17	20.42	21.41
11	855	5	65535	00h	855	17	35.49	37.21
12	855	7	65535	00h	855	17	49.68	52.09
13	306	8	128	00h	319	17	20.32	21.31
14	733	7	65535	00h	733	17	42.59	44.66
15	0	0	0	00h	0	0	0	0
16	987	12	65535	08h	988	35	202.41	212.24
17	977	5	300	00h	977	17	40.55	42.52
18	977	7	65535	00h	977	17	56.77	59.53
19	1024	7	512	00h	1023	17	59.50	62.39
20	733	5	300	00h	732	17	30.42	31.90
21	733	7	300	00h	732	17	42.59	44.66
22	1024	16	0	08h	0	17	136.00	142.61
23	914	14	0	08h	0	17	106.22	111.38
24	1001	15	0	08h	0	17	124.64	130.69

(continues)

Type	Cylinders	Heads	WPC	Ctrl	LZ	S/T	Meg	MB
25	977	7	815	00h	977	26	86.82	91.04
26	1024	4	65535	00h	1023	17	34.00	35.65
27	1024	5	65535	00h	1023	17	42.50	44.56
28	1024	8	65535	00h	1023	17	68.00	71.30
29	980	10	812	08h	990	17	81.35	85.30
30	1024	10	0	08h	0	17	85.00	89.13
31	832	6	832	00h	832	33	80.44	84.34
32	1020	15	65535	08h	1024	17	127.00	133.17
33	776	8	0	00h	0	33	100.03	104.89
34	782	4	0	00h	862	27	41.24	43.24
35	1024	9	1024	08h	1024	17	76.50	80.22
36	1024	5	512	00h	1024	17	42.50	44.56
37	830	10	65535	08h	830	17	68.90	72.24
38	823	10	256	08h	824	17	68.32	71.63
39	980	14	65535	08h	990	30	200.98	210.74
40	615	8	128	00h	664	17	40.84	42.82
41	917	15	65535	08h	918	17	114.18	119.72
42	1023	15	65535	08h	1024	17	127.38	133.56
43	823	10	512	08h	823	17	68.32	71.63
44	820	6	65535	00h	820	17	40.84	42.82
45	1024	8	65535	00h	1024	17	68.00	71.30
46	0	0	0	00h	0	0	0.00	0.00
47	0	0	0	00h	0	0	0.00	0.00

Table entry 15 is reserved to act as a pointer to indicate that the type is greater than 15.
This BIOS uses types 46 and 47 as user-definable entries.

Table A.110 shows the Zenith motherboard BIOS (80286 Technical Reference 1988) hard disk parameters.

Table A.110 Zenith BIOS Hard Disk Table

Type	Cylinders	Heads	WPC	Ctrl	LZ	S/T	Meg	MB
1	306	4	128	00h	305	17	10.16	10.65
2	615	4	300	00h	615	17	20.42	21.41
3	699	5	256	00h	710	17	29.01	30.42
4	940	8	512	00h	940	17	62.42	65.45
5	940	6	512	00h	940	17	46.82	49.09

Type	Cylinders	Heads	WPC	Ctrl	LZ	S/T	Meg	MB
6	615	4	65535	00h	615	17	20.42	21.41
7	699	7	256	00h	710	17	40.62	42.59
8	733	5	65535	00h	733	17	30.42	31.90
9	900	15	65535	08h	901	17	112.06	117.50
10	925	5	0	00h	926	17	38.39	40.26
11	855	5	65535	00h	855	17	35.49	37.21
12	855	7	65535	00h	855	17	49.68	52.09
13	306	8	128	00h	319	17	20.32	21.31
14	733	7	65535	00h	733	17	42.59	44.66
15	0	0	0	00h	0	0	0	0
16	612	4	0	00h	663	17	20.32	21.31
17	977	5	300	00h	977	17	40.55	42.52
18	977	7	65535	00h	977	17	56.77	59.53
19	1024	7	512	00h	1023	17	59.50	62.39
20	733	5	300	00h	732	17	30.42	31.90
21	733	7	300	00h	732	17	42.59	44.66
22	733	5	300	00h	733	17	30.42	31.90
23	306	4	0	00h	336	17	10.16	10.65
24	612	2	65535	00h	611	17	10.16	10.65
25	615	6	300	00h	615	17	30.63	32.12
26	462	8	256	00h	511	17	30.68	32.17
27	820	3	65535	00h	820	17	20.42	21.41
28	981	7	65535	00h	986	17	57.00	59.77
29	754	11	65535	08h	754	17	68.85	72.19
30	918	15	65535	08h	918	17	114.30	119.85
31	987	5	65535	00h	987	17	40.96	42.95
32	830	6	400	00h	830	17	41.34	43.35
33	697	4	0	00h	696	17	23.14	24.27
34	615	4	65535	00h	615	17	20.42	21.41
35	615	4	128	00h	663	17	20.42	21.41
36	1024	9	65535	08h	1024	17	76.50	80.22
37	1024	5	512	00h	1024	17	42.50	44.56
38	820	6	65535	00h	910	17	40.84	42.82
39	615	4	306	00h	684	17	20.42	21.41
40	925	9	0	08h	924	17	69.10	72.46
41	1024	8	512	00h	1023	17	68.00	71.30
42	1024	5	1024	00h	1023	17	42.50	44.56
43	615	8	300	00h	615	17	40.84	42.82

(continues)

Type	Cylinders	Heads	WPC	Ctrl	LZ	S/T	Meg	MB
44	989	5	0	00h	988	17	41.05	43.04
45	0	0	0	00h	0	0	0.00	0.00
46	0	0	0	00h	0	0	0.00	0.00
47	0	0	0	00h	0	0	0.00	0.00

Table A.110 Continued

Table entry 15 is reserved to act as a pointer to indicate that the type is greater than 15.
Type = Drive type number
Cyls = Total number of cylinders
Heads = Total number of heads
WPC = Write precompensation starting cylinder
      65535 = No Write precompensation
          0 = Write precompensation on all cylinders
Ctrl = Control byte, with values according to the following table:

Bit number	Hex	Meaning
Bit 0	01h	Not used (XT = drive step rate)
Bit 1	02h	Not used (XT = drive step rate)
Bit 2	04h	Not used (XT = drive step rate)
Bit 3	08h	More than eight heads
Bit 4	10h	Not used (XT = imbedded servo drive)
Bit 5	20h	OEM defect map at (cyls + 1)
Bit 6	40h	Disable ECC retries
Bit 7	80h	Disable disk access retries

LZ = Landing-zone cylinder for head parking
S/T = Number of sectors per track
Meg = Drive capacity in megabytes
MB = Drive capacity in millions of bytes

Printer and Modem Codes

This section lists the command and control codes for popular printers and modems. If you ever have had to work with these devices without the original documentation, you will appreciate these tables.

Table A.111 IBM Printer-Control Codes

Function	Codes in ASCII	Codes in Hex	Pro-printer	Graphics-printer	Color-printer
Job-control commands:					
Escape (command start)	<ESC>	1B	X	X	X
Null (command end)	<NUL>	00	X	X	X
Ring bell	<BELL>	07	X	X	X
Cancel (clear printer buffer)	<CAN>	18	X	X	X
Select printer	<DC1>	11	X		X
Deselect printer n	<ESC>Q#	1B 51#	X		X
Deselect printer	<DC3>	13	X		X
Automatic ribbon band shift	<ESC>a	1B 61			X
Select ribbon band 1	<ESC>y	1B 79			X
Select ribbon band 2	<ESC>m	1B 6D			X
Select ribbon band 3	<ESC>c	1B 63			X
Select ribbon band 4 (black)	<ESC>b	1B 62			X
Home print head	<ESC><	1B 3C		X	X
Form feed	<FF>	0C	X	X	X
Horizontal tab	<HT>	09	X	X	X
Backspace	<BS>	08	X		X
Initialize function On	<ESC>?<SOH>	1B 3F 01			X
Initialize function Off	<ESC>?<NUL>	1B 3F 00			X
Unidirectional printing On	<ESC>U<SOH>	1B 55 01	X	X	X
Unidirectional printing Off	<ESC>U<NUL>	1B 55 00	X	X	X
Space #/120 fwd to next character	<ESC>d#	1B 64 #			X
Space #/120 bwd to next character	<ESC>e#	1B 65 #			X
Set aspect ratio to 1:1	<ESC>n<SOH>	1B 6E 01			X
Set aspect ratio to 5:6	<ESC>n<NUL>	1B 6E 00			X
Select control values = binary	<ESC>@#<NUL>	1B 40 # 00			X
Select control values = ASCII	<ESC>@<SOH>	1B 40 01			X
Printer-control commands:					
Ignore paper end On	<ESC>8	1B 38		X	
Ignore paper end Off	<ESC>9	1B 39		X	
Set length of page in lines (1-127)	<ESC>C#	1B 43 #	X	X	X
Set length of page in inches (1-22)	<ESC>C<SOH>#	1B 43 01 #	X	X	X
Automatic line justification On	<ESC>M<SOH>	1B 4D 01			X

(continues)

Table A.111 Continued

Function	Codes in ASCII	Codes in Hex	Pro-printer	Graphics-printer	Color-printer
Automatic line justification Off	<ESC>M<NUL>	1B 4D 00			X
Perforation skip On (1-127)	<ESC>N #	1B 4E #	X	X	X
Perforation skip Off	<ESC>O	1B 4F	X	X	X
Set top of page (form)	<ESC>4	1B 34	X		X
Set left and right margins	<ESC>X #	1B 58 #			X
Clear tabs (set to power-on defaults)	<ESC>R	1B 52	X		X
Set horizontal tab stops	<ESC>D # <NUL>	1B 44 # 00	X	X	X
Set vertical tab stops	<ESC>B # <NUL>	1B 42 # 00	X	X	X
Carriage return	<CR>	0D	X	X	X
Line feed	<LF>	0A		X	X
Set n/72 lines per inch	<ESC>A #	1B 41 #	X	X	X
Set n/216 lines per inch	<ESC>3 #	1B 33 #	X	X	#/144"
Set 8 lines per inch	<ESC>0	1B 30	X	X	X
Set 7/72nd line per inch	<ESC>1	1B 31	X	X	6/72"
Start new line spacing	<ESC>2	1B 32	X	X	X
Vertical tab	<VT>	0B	X	X	X
Reverse line feed	<ESC>]	1B 5D			X
Automatic line feed On	<ESC>5<SOH>	1B 35 01	X		X
Automatic line feed Off	<ESC>5<NUL>	1B 35 00	X		X
Font selection:					
Select character set 1	<ESC>7	1B 37	X	X	X
Select character set 2	<ESC>6	1B 36	X	X	X
10 cpi (compressed Off)	<DC2>	12	X	X	X
17.1 cpi (compressed On)	<SI>	0F	X	X	X
Doublestrike On	<ESC>G	1B 47	X	X	X
Doublestrike Off	<ESC>H	1B 48	X	X	X
Doublewidth On (lines)	<ESC>W<SOH>	1B 57 01	X	X	X
Doublewidth Off (lines)	<ESC>W<NUL>	1B 57 00	X	X	X
Doublewidth by line On	<SO>	0E	X	X	X
Doublewidth by line Off	<DC4>	14	X	X	X
Emphasized printing On	<ESC>E	1B 45	X	X	X
Emphasized printing Off	<ESC>F	1B 46	X	X	X
Subscript On	<ESC>S<SOH>	1B 53 01	X	X	X
Superscript On	<ESC>S<NUL>	1B 53 00	X	X	X
Subscript/superscript Off	<ESC>T	1B 54	X	X	X
Set draft quality	<ESC>I<SOH>	1B 49 01			X

Function	Codes in ASCII	Codes in Hex	Pro-printer	Graphics-printer	Color-printer
Set text quality (near-letter quality)	<ESC>I<STX>	1B 49 02	X		X
Set letter quality	<ESC>I<ETX>	1B 49 03			X
Proportional spacing On	<ESC>P<SOH>	1B 50 01			X
Proportional spacing Off	<ESC>P<NUL>	1B 50 00			X
12-characters-per-inch spacing	<ESC>:	1B 3A	X		X
Print all characters	<ESC>\ #	1B 5C #	X		X
Print next character	<ESC>^	1B 5E	X		X
Underline On	<ESC>-<SOH>	1B 2D 01	X	X	X
Underline Off	<ESC>-<NUL>	1B 2D 00	X	X	X
Graphics:					
Graphics, 60 dots per inch (DPI)	<ESC>K #	1B 4B #	X	X	
Graphics, 70/84 DPI	<ESC>K #	1B 4B #			X
Graphics, 120 DPI half speed	<ESC>L #	1B 4C #	X	X	
Graphics, 140/168 DPI half speed	<ESC>L #	1B 4C #			X
Graphics, 120 DPI normal speed	<ESC>Y #	1B 59 #	X	X	
Graphics, 140/168 DPI normal speed	<ESC>Y #	1B 59 #			X
Graphics, 240 DPI half speed	<ESC>Z #	1B 5A #	X	X	
Graphics, 280/336 DPI half speed	<ESC>Z #	1B 5A #			X

 # indicates a variable number in the code.

Table A.112 Epson Printer-Control Codes

Function	Codes in ASCII	Codes in Hex
Job-control commands:		
Ring bell	<BELL>	07
Clear line	<CAN>	18
Select printer	<DC1>	11
Deselect printer	<DC3>	13
Set justification	<ESC>a	1B 61
Cut sheet-feeder control	<ESC>	EM1B 19
Select character space	<ESC>	SP1B 20
Select mode combinations	<ESC>!	1B 21
Select active character set	<ESC>%	1B 25
Copies ROM to user RAM	<ESC>:	1B 3A

(continues)

Table A.112 Continued

Function	Codes in ASCII	Codes in Hex
Defines user characters	<ESC>&	1B 26
Set MSB = 0	<ESC>>	1B 3E
Set MSB = 1	<ESC>=	1B 3D
Select international character set	<ESC>R#	1B 72#
Select 15 width	<ESC>g	1B 67
Select immediate print (typewriter mode)	<ESC>i	1B 69
Half-speed printing Off	<ESC>s<NUL>	1B 73 00
Half-speed printing On	<ESC>s<SOH>	1B 73 01
Set horizontal tab unit	<ESC>e<NUL>	1B 65 00
Set vertical tab unit	<ESC>e<SOH>	1B 6D 01
Special character-generator selection (control codes accepted)	<ESC>m<NUL>	1B 6D 00
Special character-generator selection (graphic characters accepted)	<ESC>m<SOH>	1B 6D 01
Unidirectional printing On	<ESC>U<SOH>	1B 55 01
Unidirectional printing Off	<ESC>U<NUL>	1B 55 00
Turn unidirectional (left to right) On	<ESC><	1B 3C
Form feed	<FF>	0C
Horizontal tab	<HT>	09
Initialize printer	<ESC>@	1B 40
Backspace	<BS>	08
Printer-control commands:		
Ignore paper end On	<ESC>8	1B 38
Ignore paper end Off	<ESC>9	1B 39
Set length of page in lines (1-127)	<ESC>C#	1B 43#
Set length of page in inches (1-22)	<ESC>C<NUL>#	1B 43 00#
Set absolute tab	<ESC>$	1B 24
Set vertical tab	<ESC>/	1B 2F
Set vertical tab	<ESC>b	1B 62
Set horizontal tab unit	<ESC>e<NUL>	1B 65 00
Set vertical tab unit	<ESC>e<SOH>	1B 65 01
Set horizontal skip position	<ESC>f<NUL>	1B 66 00
Set vertical skip position	<ESC>f<SOH>	1B 66 01
Perforation skip On (1-127)	<ESC>N#	1B 4E#
Perforation skip Off	<ESC>O	1B 4F
Set horizontal tab stop	<ESC>D	1B 44
Set vertical tab stop	<ESC>B	1B 42
Carriage return	<CR>	0D

Function	Codes in ASCII	Codes in Hex
Line feed	<LF>	0A
Set variable line feed to #/72 inch (1-85)	<ESC>A#	1B 41#
Set variable line feed to #/216 inch	<ESC>J#	1B 4A#
Set spacing at 1/8 inch	<ESC>0	1B 30
Set spacing at 7/72 inch	<ESC>1	1B 31
Set line spacing at 1/6 inch	<ESC>2	1B 32
Set #/216 inch line feed (0-225)	<ESC>3#	1B 33#
Vertical tab	<VT>	0B
Font selection:		
Deactivate high-order control codes	<ESC>6	1B 36
Turn alternate character (italics) On	<ESC>4	1B 34
10 CPI (compressed Off) spacing	<DC2>	12
17.1 CPI (compressed On) spacing	<SI>	0F
Doublestrike On	<ESC>G	1B 47
Doublestrike Off	<ESC>H	1B 48
Doublewidth On (lines)	<ESC>W<SOH>	1B 57 01
Doublewidth Off (lines)	<ESC>W<NUL>	1B 57 00
Enlarged print mode On	<SO>	0E
Enlarged print mode Off	<DC4>	14
Emphasized printing On	<ESC>E	1B 45
Emphasized printing Off	<ESC>F	1B 46
Turn alternate character (italics) On	<ESC>4	1B 34
Turn alternate character (italics) Off	<ESC>5	1B 35
Elite mode On (Pica mode off)	<ESC>M	1B 4D
Select family of type styles	<ESC>k	1B 6B
Proportional printing Off	<ESC>p<NUL>	1B 70 00
Proportional printing On	<ESC>p<SOH>	1B 70 01
Select letter- or draft-quality printing	<ESC>z	1B 7A
Subscript On	<ESC>S<SOH>	1B 53 01
Superscript On	<ESC>S<NUL>	1B 53 00
Subscript/superscript Off	<ESC>T	1B 54
Control code select	<ESC>I	1B 49
Elite mode Off (Pica mode On)	<ESC>P	1B 50
Nine-pin graphics mode	<ESC>^	1B 5E
Underline On	<ESC>-<SOH>	1B 2D 01
Underline Off	<ESC>-<NUL>	1B 2D 00

(continues)

Table A.112 Continued		
Function	**Codes in ASCII**	**Codes in Hex**
Graphics:		
Normal-density bit image	<ESC>K	1B 4B##
Dual-density bit image	<ESC>L	1B 4C##
Double-speed, dual-density bit image	<ESC>Y	1B 59##
Quadruple-density bit image	<ESC>Z	1B 5A##

International character sets:
0 = U.S.
1 = France
2 = Germany
3 = England
4 = Denmark
5 = Sweden
6 = Italy
7 = Spain
8 = Japan
9 = Norway
10 = Denmark II
Characters in brackets are ASCII code names.
 # indicates a variable numeric value.

Table A.113 HP LaserJet Printer-Control Codes			
Function type	**Function**	**Codes in ASCII**	**Codes in Hex**
Job-control commands:			
Printer control	Reset printer	<ESC>E	1B 45
	Self test mode	<ESC>z	1B 7A
	Number of copies	<ESC>&l#X	1B 26 6C # 58
	Long-edge (left) offset registration	<ESC>&l#U	1B 26 6C # 55
	Short-edge (top) offset registration	<ESC>&l#Z	1B 26 6C # 5A
Printer-control commands:			
Paper source	Eject page	<ESC>&l0H	1B 26 6C 30 48
	Paper-tray auto feed	<ESC>&l1H	1B 26 6C 31 48
	Manual feed	<ESC>&l2H	1B 26 6C 32 48
	Manual envelope feed	<ESC>&l3H	1B 26 6C 33 48
	Feed from lower cassette	<ESC>&l4H	1B 26 6C 34 48
Page size	Executive	<ESC>&l1A	1B 26 6C 31 41
	Letter	<ESC>&l2A	1B 26 6C 32 41
	Legal	<ESC>&l3A	1B 26 6C 33 41
	A4	<ESC>&l26A	1B 26 6C 32 36 41
	Monarch (envelope)	<ESC>&l80A	1B 26 6C 38 30 41

Function type	Function	Codes in ASCII	Codes in Hex
	COM 10 (envelope)	<ESC>&l81A	1B 26 6C 38 31 41
	DL (envelope)	<ESC>&l90A	1B 26 6C 39 30 41
	C5 (envelope)	<ESC>&l91A	1B 26 6C 39 31 41
Orientation	Portrait mode	<ESC>&l0O	1B 26 6C 30 4F
	Landscape mode	<ESC>&l1O	1B 26 6C 31 4F
	Reverse portrait	<ESC>&l2O	1B 26 6C 32 4F
	Reverse landscape	<ESC>&l3O	1B 26 6C 33 4F
	Print direction	<ESC>&a#P	1B 26 61 # 50
Page settings	Page length	<ESC>&l#P	1B 26 6C # 50
	Top margin	<ESC>&l#E	1B 26 6C # 45
	Text length	<ESC>&l#F	1B 26 6C # 46
	Clear horizontal margins	<ESC>9	1B 39
	Set left margin	<ESC>&a#L	1B 26 61 # 4C
	Set right margin	<ESC>&a#M	1B 26 61 # 4D
	Perforation skip enable	<ESC>&l1L	1B 26 6C 31 4C
	Perforation skip disable	<ESC>&l0L	1B 26 6C 30 4C
Line spacing	Vertical motion index	<ESC>&l#C	1B 26 6C # 43
	Horizontal motion index	<ESC>&k#H	1B 26 6B # 4B
	1 line/inch	<ESC>&l1D	1B 26 6C 31 44
	2 lines/inch	<ESC>&l2D	1B 26 6C 32 44
	3 lines/inch	<ESC>&l3D	1B 26 6C 33 44
	4 lines/inch	<ESC>&l4D	1B 26 6C 34 44
	6 lines/inch	<ESC>&l6D	1B 26 6C 36 44
	8 lines/inch	<ESC>&l8D	1B 26 6C 38 44
	12 lines/inch	<ESC>&l12D	1B 26 6C 31 32 44
	16 lines/inch	<ESC>&l16D	1B 26 6C 31 36 44
	24 lines/inch	<ESC>&l24D	1B 26 6C 32 34 44
	48 lines/inch	<ESC>&l48D	1B 26 6C 34 38 44
	Half line feed	<ESC>=	1B 3D
Stacking position	Default	<ESC>&l0T	1B 26 6C 30 54
	Toggle	<ESC>&l1T	1B 26 6C 31 54
Cursor positioning:			
Vertical position	Number of rows	<ESC>&a#R	1B 26 61 # 52
	Number of dots	<ESC>*p#Y	1B 2A 70 # 59
	Number of decipoints	<ESC>&a#V	1B 26 61 # 56
Horizontal position	Number of rows	<ESC>&a#C	1B 26 61 # 43
	Number of dots	<ESC>*p#X	1B 2A 70 # 58
	Number of decipoints	<ESC>&a#H	1B 26 61 # 48
End-of-line	CR=CR; LF=LF; FF=FF	<ESC>&k0G	1B 26 6B 30 47
	CR=CR+LF; LF=LF; FF=FF	<ESC>&k1G	1B 26 6B 31 47

(continues)

Table A.113 Continued

Function type	Function	Codes in ASCII	Codes in Hex
	CR=CR; LF=CR+LF; FF=CR+FF	<ESC>&k2G	1B 26 6B 32 47
	CR=CR+LF; LF=CR+LF; FF=CR+FF	<ESC>&k3G	1B 26 6B 33 47
Push/Pop position	Push position	<ESC>&f0S	1B 26 66 30 53
	Pop position	<ESC>&f1S	1B 26 66 31 53
Font selection:			
Font symbol set	Roman-8	<ESC>(8U	1B 28 38 55
	USASCII	<ESC>(0U	1B 28 30 55
	Danish/Norwegian	<ESC>(0D	1B 28 30 44
	British (U.K.)	<ESC>(1E	1B 28 31 45
	French	<ESC>(1F	1B 28 31 46
	German	<ESC>(1G	1B 28 31 47
	Italian	<ESC>(0I	1B 28 30 49
	Swedish/Finnish	<ESC>(0S	1B 28 30 53
	Spanish	<ESC>(2S	1B 28 32 53
	Legal	<ESC>(1U	1B 28 31 55
	Linedraw	<ESC>(0B	1B 28 30 42
	Math8	<ESC>(8M	1B 28 38 4D
	Math7	<ESC>(0A	1B 28 30 41
	PiFont	<ESC>(15U	1B 28 31 35 55
	ECMA-94 Latin	<ESC>(0N	1B 28 30 4E
	PC-8	<ESC>(10U	1B 28 31 30 55
	PC-8 D/N	<ESC>(11U	1B 28 31 31 55
	PC 850	<ESC>(12U	1B 28 31 32 55
Primary spacing	Proportional	<ESC>(s1P	1B 28 73 31 50
	Fixed	<ESC>(s0P	1B 28 73 30 50
Character pitch	10 characters per inch	<ESC>(s10H	1B 28 73 31 30 48
	12 characters per inch	<ESC>(s12H	1B 28 73 31 32 48
	16.6 characters per inch	<ESC>(s16.6H	1B 28 73 31 36 2E 36 48
	Standard pitch (10 cpi)	<ESC>&k0S	1B 26 6B 30 53
	Compressed pitch (16.6 cpi)	<ESC>&k2S	1B 26 6B 32 53
	Elite (12.0)	<ESC>&k4s	1B 26 6B 34 53
Character point size	7 point	<ESC>(s7V	1B 28 73 37 56
	8 point	<ESC>(s8V	1B 28 73 38 56
	8.5 point	<ESC>(s8.5V	1B 28 73 38 2E 35 56
	10 point	<ESC>(s10V	1B 28 73 31 30 56
	12 point	<ESC>(s12V	1B 28 73 31 32 56

Function type	Function	Codes in ASCII	Codes in Hex
	14.4 point	<ESC>(s14.4V	1B 28 73 31 34 2E 34 56
Character style	Upright	<ESC>(s0S	1B 28 73 30 53
	Italic	<ESC>(s1S	1B 28 73 31 53
Character weight	Ultra thin	<ESC>(s-7B	1B 28 73 -37 42
	Extra thin	<ESC>(s-6B	1B 28 73 -36 42
	Thin	<ESC>(s-5B	1B 28 73 -35 42
	Extra light	<ESC>(s-4B	1B 28 73 -34 42
	Light	<ESC>(s-3B	1B 28 73 -33 42
	Demi light	<ESC>(s-2B	1B 28 73 -32 42
	Semi light	<ESC>(s-1B	1B 28 73 -31 42
	Medium (normal)	<ESC>(s0B	1B 28 73 30 42
	Semi bold	<ESC>(s1B	1B 28 73 31 42
	Demi bold	<ESC>(s2B	1B 28 73 32 42
	Bold	<ESC>(s3B	1B 28 73 33 42
	Extra bold	<ESC>(s4B	1B 28 73 34 42
	Black	<ESC>(s5B	1B 28 73 35 42
	Extra black	<ESC>(s6B	1B 28 73 36 42
	Ultra black	<ESC>(s7B	1B 28 73 37 42
Character typeface	Courier	<ESC>(s3T	1B 28 73 33 54
	Univers	<ESC>(s52T	1B 28 73 35 32 54
	Line printer	<ESC>(s0T	1B 28 73 30 54
	CG Times	<ESC>(s4101T	1B 28 73 34 31 30 31 54
	Helvetica	<ESC>(s4T	1B 28 73 34 54
	TMS RMN	<ESC>(s5T	1B 28 73 33 54
Font default	Primary font	<ESC>(3@	1B 28 33 40
	Secondary font	<ESC>)3@	1B 29 33 40
Underlining	Underline On	<ESC>&d#D	1B 26 64 30 44
	Underline floating	<ESC>&d3D	1B 26 64 33 44
	Underline Off	<ESC>&d@	1B 26 64 40
Transparent print	Number of bytes	<ESC>&p#X[Data]	1B 26 70 # 58
Font management:			
Assign font ID	Font ID number	<ESC>*c#D	1B 2A 63 # 44
Font and character control	Delete all fonts	<ESC>*c0F	1B 2A 63 30 46
	Delete all temporary fonts	<ESC>*c1F	1B 2A 63 31 46
	Delete last font ID specified	<ESC>*c2F	1B 2A 63 32 46
	Delete last font ID and char code	<ESC>*c3F	1B 2A 63 33 46
	Make temporary font	<ESC>*c4F	1B 2A 63 34 46

(continues)

Table A.113 Continued			
Function type	**Function**	**Codes in ASCII**	**Codes in Hex**
	Make permanent font	<ESC>*c5F	1B 2A 63 35 46
	Copy/assign font	<ESC>*c6F	1B 2A 63 36 46
Select font (ID)	Primary font ID number	<ESC>(#X	1B 28 # 58
	Secondary font ID number	<ESC>)#X	1B 29 # 58
Soft font creation:			
Font descriptor	Create font	<ESC>)s#W[Data]	1B 29 73 # 57
	Download character	<ESC>(s#W[Data]	1B 28 73 # 57
	ASCII character code number	<ESC>*c#E	1B 2A 63 # 45
Graphics:			
Vector graphics	Enter HP-GL/2 mode	<ESC>%0B	1B 25 30 42
	HP-GL/2 plot horizontal size	<ESC>%1B	1B 25 31 42
	HP-GL/2 plot vertical size	<ESC>*c#K	1B 2A 63 # 4B
	Set picture frame	<ESC>*0T	1B 2A 63 30 54
	Picture frame horizontal size	<ESC>*c#X	1B 2A 63 # 58
	Picture frame vertical size	<ESC>*c#Y	1B 2A 63 # 59
Raster resolution	75 dpi resolution	<ESC>*t75R	1B 2A 74 37 35 52
	100 dpi resolution	<ESC>*t100R	1B 2A 74 31 30 30 52
	150 dpi resolution	<ESC>*t150R	1B 2A 74 31 35 30 52
	300 dpi resolution	<ESC>*t300R	1B 2A 74 33 30 30 52
	Start at leftmost position	<ESC>*r0A	1B 2A 72 30 41
	Start at current cursor	<ESC>*r1A	1B 2A 72 31 41
Raster graphics presentation	Rotate image	<ESC>*r0F	1B 2A 72 30 46
	LaserJet landscape compatible	<ESC>*r3F	1B 2A 72 33 46
	Left raster graphics margin	<ESC>*r0A	1B 2A 72 30 41
	Current cursor	<ESC>*r1A	1B 2A 72 31 41
	Raster Y offset	<ESC>*b0M	1B 2A 62 # 59
Set raster compression	Uncoded	<ESC>*b0M	1B 2A 62 30 41
	Mode run-length encoded	<ESC>*b1M	1B 2A 62 31 41
	Tagged image file format	<ESC>*b2M	1B 2A 62 32 41
	Delta row	<ESC>*b3M	1B 2A 62 33 41
	Transfer graphic rows	<ESC>*b#W[Data]	1B 2A 62 # 57
	End graphics	<ESC>*rB	1B 2A 72 42
	Raster height	<ESC>*r#T	1B 2A 72 # 54
	Raster width	<ESC>*r#S	1B 2A 72 # 53

Function type	Function	Codes in ASCII	Codes in Hex
The print model:			
Select pattern	Solid black (default)	<ESC>*v0T	1B 2A 76 30 54
	Solid white	<ESC>*v1T	1B 2A 76 31 54
	HP-defined shading pattern	<ESC>*v2T	1B 2A 76 32 54
	HP-defined cross-hatched pattern	<ESC>*v3T	1B 2A 76 33 54
Select source	Transparent	<ESC>*v0N	1B 2A 76 30 42
Transparency	Opaque	<ESC>*v1N	1B 2A 76 31 42
Select pattern	Transparent	<ESC>*v0O	1B 2A 76 30 43
Transparency	Opaque	<ESC>*v1O	1B 2A 76 31 43
Rectangle width	Horizontal # dots in pattern	<ESC>*c#A	1B 2A 63 # 41
	Horizontal # decipoints in pattern	<ESC>*c#H	1B 2A 63 # 48
Rectangle height	Vertical # dots in pattern	<ESC>*c#B	1B 2A 63 # 42
	Vertical # decipoints in pattern	<ESC>*c#V	1B 2A 63 # 56
Fill rectangular	Solid black	<ESC>*c0P	1B 2A 63 30 50
Area	Erase (solid white area fill)	<ESC>*c1P	1B 2A 63 31 50
	Shade fill	<ESC>*c2P	1B 2A 63 32 50
	Cross-hatched fill	<ESC>*c3P	1B 2A 63 33 50
	User defined	<ESC>*c4P	1B 2A 63 34 50
	Current pattern	<ESC>*c5P	1B 2A 63 35 50
Pattern ID	Percent of shading or type of pattern	<ESC>*c#G	1B 2A 63 # 47
Shading	Print 2% gray scale	<ESC>*c2G	1B 2A 63 32 47
	Print 10% gray scale	<ESC>*c10G	1B 2A 63 31 30 47
	Print 15% gray scale	<ESC>*c15G	1B 2A 63 31 35 47
	Print 30% gray scale	<ESC>*c30G	1B 2A 63 33 30 47
	Print 45% gray scale	<ESC>*c45G	1B 2A 63 34 35 47
	Print 70% gray scale	<ESC>*c70G	1B 2A 63 37 30 47
	Print 90% gray scale	<ESC>*c90G	1B 2A 63 39 30 47
	Print 100% gray scale	<ESC>*c100G	1B 2A 63 31 30 30 47
Pattern	1 horizontal line	<ESC>*c1G	1B 2A 63 31 47
	2 vertical lines	<ESC>*c2G	1B 2A 63 32 47
	3 diagonal lines	<ESC>*c3G	1B 2A 63 33 47
	4 diagonal lines	<ESC>*c4G	1B 2A 63 34 47
	5 square grid	<ESC>*c5G	1B 2A 63 35 47
	6 diagonal grid	<ESC>*c6G	1B 2A 63 36 47
Macros:			
Macro ID	Macro ID number	<ESC>&f#Y	1B 26 66 # 59
Macro control	Start macro	<ESC>&f0X	1B 26 66 30 58
	Stop macro definition	<ESC>&f1X	1B 26 66 31 58

(continues)

Table A.113 Continued			
Function type	**Function**	**Codes in ASCII**	**Codes in Hex**
	Execute macro	<ESC>&f2X	1B 26 66 32 58
	Call macro	<ESC>&f3X	1B 26 66 33 58
	Enable overlay	<ESC>&f4X	1B 26 66 34 58
	Disable overlay	<ESC>&f5X	1B 26 66 35 58
	Delete macros	<ESC>&f6X	1B 26 66 36 58
	Delete all temporary macros	<ESC>&f7X	1B 26 66 37 58
	Delete macro ID	<ESC>&f8X	1B 26 66 38 58
	Make temporary	<ESC>&f9X	1B 26 66 39 58
	Make permanent	<ESC>&f10X	1B 26 66 31 30 58
Programming hints:			
Display functions	Display functions On	<ESC>Y	1B 59
	Display functions Off	<ESC>Z	1B 5A
End-of-line wrap	Enable	<ESC>&s0C	1B 26 73 30 43
	Disable	<ESC>&s1C	1B 26 73 31 43

 # indicates a variable numeric value.
[Data] indicates a bitstream of appropriate data.

The following table shows the commands recognized by the popular Hayes and USRobotics modems. These modems have a standard command set that can get quite complicated in the higher-end models. This table comes in handy when you need to reconfigure a modem without the original manual. Even if your modem is not Hayes or USRobotics, it probably follows most of these commands because this command set has become somewhat of a standard.

Table A.114 USRobotics and Hayes Modem Commands and Supported Features					
Command	**Modem Functions and Options**	**USR Dual**	**2400**	**Hayes 2400**	**1200**
&	See Extended Command Set	X			
%	See Extended Command Set	X			
A	Force Answer mode when modem has not received an incoming call	X	X	X	X
A/	Re-execute last command once	X	X	X	X
A>	Repeat last command continuously	X			
Any key	Terminate current connection attempt; exit Repeat mode	X	X		
AT	Attention: must precede all other commands except A/, A>, and +++	X	X	X	X
BN	HANDSHAKE OPTIONS	X		X	
	BO CCITT answer sequence	X		X	

Command	Modem Functions and Options		USR Dual	2400	Hayes 2400	1200
	B1	Bell answer tone	X		X	
Cn	Transmitter On/Off		X	X	X	X
	C0	Transmitter Off	X	X	X	X
	C1	Transmitter On-Default	X	X	X	X
Dn	Dial number n and go into orginate mode					
	Use any of these options:		X	X	X	X
	P	Pulse dial-Default	X	X	X	X
	T	Touch-Tone dial	X	X	X	X
	,	(Comma) Pause for 2 seconds	X	X	X	X
	;	Return to command state after dialing	X	X	X	X
	"...	Dial the letters that follow	X	X		
	!	Flash switch-hook to transfer call	X	X	X	
	W	Wait for 2nd dial tone (if X3 or higher is set)	X	X	X	
	@	Wait for an answer (if X3 or higher is set)	X	X	X	
	R	Reverse frequencies	X	X	X	X
	S	Dial stored number			X	
DL	Dial the last-dialed number		X			
DSn	Dial number stored in NVRAM at position n		X			
En	Command mode local echo; not applicable after a connection has been made		X	X	X	X
	E0	Echo Off	X	X	X	X
	E1	Echo On	X	X	X	X
Fn	Local echo On/Off when a connection has been made		X	X	X	X
	F0	Echo On (Half duplex)	X	X	X	X
	F1	Echo Off (Full duplex)-Default	X	X	X	X
Hn	On/Off hook control		X	X	X	X
	H0	Hang up (go on hook)-Default	X	X	X	X
	H1	Go off hook	X	X	X	X
In	Inquiry		X	X	X	X
	I0	Return product code	X	X	X	X
	I1	Return memory (ROM) checksum	X	X	X	X
	I2	Run memory (RAM) test	X	X	X	
	I3	Return call duration/real time	X	X		
	I4	Return current modem settings	X	X		
	I5	Return NVRAM settings	X			
	I6	Return link diagnostics	X			

(continues)

Table A.114 Continued

Command	Modem Functions and Options		USR Dual	2400	Hayes 2400	1200
	I7	Return product configuration	X			
Kn	Modem clock operation		X			
	K0	ATI3 displays call duration-Default	X			
	K1	ATI3 displays real time; set with ATI3=HH:MM:SSK1	X			
Ln	Loudness of speaker volume;				X	
	L0	Low			X	
	L1	Low			X	
	L2	Medium			X	
	L3	High			X	
Mn	Monitor (speaker) control		X	X	X	X
	M0	Speaker always Off	X	X	X	X
	M1	Speaker On until carrier is established-Default	X	X	X	X
	M2	Speaker always On	X	X	X	X
	M3	Speaker On after last digit dialed, Off at carrier detect	X	X	X	X
O	Return on-line after command execution		X	X	X	X
	O0	Return on-line, normal	X	X	X	X
	O1	Return on-line, retrain	X	X	X	X
P	Pulse dial		X	X	X	X
Qn	Result codes display		X	X	X	X
	Q0	Result codes displayed	X	X	X	X
	Q1	Result codes suppressed (quiet mode)	X	X	X	X
	Q2	Quiet in answer mode only	X			
Sr=n	Set register commands: r is any S-register; n must be a decimal number between 0 and 255.		X	X	X	X
Sr.b=n	Set bit .b of register r to n (0/Off or 1/On)		X			
Sr?	Query register r		X	X	X	X
T	Tone dial		X	X	X	X
Vn	Verbal/Numeric result codes		X	X	X	X
	V0	Numeric mode	X	X	X	X
	V1	Verbal mode	X	X	X	X
Xn	Result code options		X	X	X	X
Yn	Long space disconnect				X	
	Y0	Numeric mode			X	
	Y1	Enabled; disconnects after 1.5-second break			X	
Z	Software reset		X	X	X	X

Command	Modem Functions and Options	USR Dual	2400	Hayes 2400	1200
+++	Escape code sequence, preceded and followed by at least one second of no data transmission	X	X		
/(Slash)	Pause for 125 msec	X			
>	Repeat command continuously or up to 10 dial attempts; cancel by pressing any key	X	X		
$	Online Help - Basic command summary	X	X		
&$	Online Help - Ampersand command summary	X			
%$	Online Help - Percent command summary	X			
D$	Online Help - Dial command summary	X	X		
S$	Online Help - S-register summary	X	X		
<Ctrl>-S	Stop/restart display of HELP screens		X		
<Ctrl>-C	Cancel display HELP screens		X		
<Ctrl>-K	Cancel display HELP screens		X		
Extended command set					
&An	ARQ result codes 14-17, 19	X			
	&A0 Supppress ARQ result codes	X			
	&A1 Display ARQ result codes-Default	X			
	&A2 Display HST and V.32 result codes	X			
	&A3 Display protocol result codes	X			
&Bn	Data Rate, terminal-to-modem (DTE/DCE)	X			
	&B0 DTE rate follows connection rate-Default	X			
	&B1 Fixed DTE rate	X			
	&B2 Fixed DTE rate in ARQ mode; variable DTE rate in non-ARQ mode	X			
&Cn	Carrier Detect (CD) operations	X		X	
	&C0 CD override	X		X	
	&C1 Normal CD operations	X		X	
&Dn	Data Terminal Ready (DTR) operations	X		X	
	&D0 DTR override	X		X	
	&D1 DTR Off; goes to command state			X	
	&D2 DTR Off; goes to command state and on hook	X		X	
	&D3 DTR Off; resets modem			X	
&F	Load factory settings into RAM	X		X	
&Gn	Guard tone	X		X	
	&G0 No guard tone; U.S., Canada-Default	X		X	
	&G1 Guard tone; some European countries	X		X	
	&G2 Guard tone; U.K., requires B0	X		X	
&Hn	Transmit Data flow control	X			

(continues)

Table A.114 Continued

Command	Modem Functions and Options	USR Dual	2400	Hayes 2400	1200
	&H0 Flow control disabled-Default	X			
	&H1 Hardware (CTS) flow control	X			
	&H2 Software (XON/XOFF) flow control	X			
	&H3 Hardware and software control	X			
&In	Received Data software flow control	X			
	&I0 Flow control disabled-Default	X			
	&I1 XON/XOFF to local modem and remote computer	X			
	&I2 XON/XOFF to local modem only	X			
	&I3 Host mode, Hewlett-Packard protocol	X			
	&I4 Terminal mode, Hewlett-Packard protocol	X			
	&I5 ARQ mode-same as &I2; non-ARQ mode; look for incoming XON/XOFF	X			
&Jn	Telephone Jack selection			X	
	&J0 RJ-11/RJ-41S/RJ-45S			X	
	&J1 RJ-12/RJ-13			X	
&Kn	Data compression	X			
	&K0 Disabled	X			
	&K1 Auto enable/disable-Default	X			
	&K2 Enabled	X			
	&K3 V.42bis only	X			
&Ln	Normal/Leased line operation	X		X	
	&L0 Normal phone line-Default	X		X	
	&L1 Leased line	X		X	
&Mn	Error Cotnrol/Synchronous Options	X		X	
	&M0 Normal mode, no error control	X		X	
	&M1 Synch mode	X		X	
	&M2 Synch mode 2 - stored number dialing			X	
	&M3 Synch mode 3 - manual dialing	X			
	&M4 Normal/ARQ mode-Normal if ARQ connection cannot be made-Default	X			
	&M5 ARQ mode-hang up if ARQ connection cannot be made	X			
&Nn	Data Rate, data link (DCE/DCE)	X			
	&N0 Normal link operations-Default	X			
	&N1 300 bps	X			
	&N2 1200 bps	X			
	&N3 2400 bps	X			

Command	Modem Functions and Options	USR Dual	2400	Hayes 2400	1200
	&N4 4800 bps	X			
	&N5 7200 bps	X			
	&N6 9600 bps	X			
	&N7 12K bps	X			
	&N8 14.4K bps	X			
&Pn	Pulse dial make/break ratio	X		X	
	&P0 North America-Default	X		X	
	&P1 British Commonwealth	X		X	
&Rn	Received Data hardware (RTS) flow control	X		X	
	&R0 CTS tracks RTS	X		X	
	&R1 Ignore RTS-Default	X		X	
	&R2 Pass received data on RTS high; used Pass received data on RTS high; used	X			
&Sn	Data Set Ready (DSR) override	X		X	
	&S0 DSR override (always On-Default)	X		X	
	&S1 Modem controls DSR	X		X	
	&S2 Pulsed DSR; CTS follows CD	X			
	&S3 Pulsed DSR	X			
&Tn	Modem Testing	X		X	
	&T0 End testing	X		X	
	&T1 Analog loopback	X		X	
	&T2 Reserved	X			
	&T3 Digital loopback	X		X	
	&T4 Grant remote digital loopback	X		X	
	&T5 Deny remote digital loopback	X		X	
	&T6 Initiate remote digital loopback	X		X	
	&T7 Remote digital loopback with self test	X		X	
	&T8 Analog loopback with self test	X		X	
&W	Write current settings to NVRAM	X		X	
&Xn	Synchronous timing source	X		X	
	&X0 Modem's transmit clock-Default	X		X	
	&X1 Terminal equipment	X		X	
	&X2 Modem's receiver clock	X		X	
&Yn	Break handling. Destructive breaks clear the buffer; expedited Breaks are sent immediately to remote system.	X			
	&Y0 Destructive, but don't send break	X			
	&Y1 Destructive, expedited-Default	X			
	&Y2 Nondestructive, expedited	X			

(continues)

Table A.114 Continued

Command	Modem Functions and Options	USR Dual	2400	Hayes 2400	1200
	&Y3 Nondestructive, unexpedited	X			
&Zn=L	Store last-dialed phone number in NVRAM at position n	X			
&Zn=s	Write phone number(s) to NVRAM at position n (0-3); 36 characters maximum	X			
&Zn?	Display phone number in NVRAM at position n (n=0-3)	X		X	
%Rn	Remote access to Rack Controller Unit (RCU)	X			
	%R0 Disabled	X			
	%R1 Enabled	X			
%T	Enable Touch-Tone recognition	X			

Modem S-Register Functions and Defaults

Command	Modem Functions and Options	USR Dual	2400	Hayes 2400	1200
S0	Number of rings before automatic answering when DIP switch 5 is UP. Default = 1. S0 = 0 disables Auto Answer, equivalent to DIP switch 5 Down	SW5	SW5	0	SW5
S1	Counts and stores number of rings from incoming call	0	0	0	0
S2	Define escape code character. Default = +.	43	43	43	43
S3	Define ASCII carriage return	13	13	13	13
S4	Define ASCII line feed	10	10	10	10
S5	Define ASCII Backspace	8	8	8	8
S6	Number of seconds modem waits before dialing	2	2	2	2
S7	Number of seconds modem waits for a carrier	60	30	30	30
S8	Duration (sec) for pause (,) option in Dial command and pause between command reexecutions for Repeat (>) command	2	2	2	2
S9	Duration (.1 sec units) of remote carrier signal before recognition	6	6	6	6
S10	Duration (.1 sec units) modem waits after loss of carrier before hanging up	7	7	7	7
S11	Duration and spacing (ms) of dialed Touch-Tones	70	70	70	70
S12	Guard time (in .02 sec units) for escape code sequence	50	50	50	50
S13	Bit-mapped register:	0			
	1 Reset when DTR drops				
	2 Auto answer in originate mode				
	4 Disable result code pause				
	8 DS0 on DTR low-to-high				

Command	Modem Functions and Options	USR Dual	2400	Hayes 2400	1200
	16 DS0 on power up, ATZ				
	32 Disable HST modulation				
	64 Disable MNP Level 3				
	128 Watchdog hardware reset				
S15	Bit-mapped register:	0			
	1 Disable high-frequency equalization				
	2 Disable on-line fallback				
	4 Force 300-bps back channel				
	8 Set non-ARQ transmit buffer to 128 bytes				
	16 Disable MNP Level 4				
	32 Set Del as Backspace key				
	64 Unusual MNP incompatibilty				
	128 Custom applications only				
S16	Bit-mapped register:	0	0	0	
	1 Analog loopback				
	2 Dial test				
	4 Test pattern				
	8 Initiate remote digital loopback				
	16 Reserved				
	32 Reserved				
	64 Reserved				
	128 Reserved				
S18	&Tn Test timer, disabled when set to 0	0		0	
S19	Set inactivity timer in minutes	0			
S21	Length of Break, DCE to DTE, in 10ms units	10		0	
S22	Define ASCII XON	17		17	
S23	Define ASCII XOFF	19		19	
S24	Duration (20ms units) of pulsed DSR when modem is set to &S2 or &S3	150			
S25	Delay to DTR	5			
S26	Duration (10ms units) of delay between RTS and CTS, synchronous mode	1		1	
S27	Bit-mapped register:	0			
	1 Enable V.21 modulation, 300 bps				
	2 Enable unencoded V.32 modulation				
	4 Disable V.32 modulation				
	8 Disable 2100 Hz answer tone				
	16 Disable MNP handshake				
	32 Disable V.42 Detect phase				

(continues)

Table A.114 Continued

Command	Modem Functions and Options		USR Dual	2400	Hayes 2400	1200
	64	Reserved				
	128	Unusual software incompatibility				
S28	Duration (.1 sec units) of V.21/V.23 handshake delay		8			
S32	Voice/Data switch options:		1			
	0	Disabled				
	1	Go off hook in originate mode				
	2	Go off hook in answer mode				
	3	Redial last-dialed number				
	4	Dial number stored at position 0				
	5	Auto answer toggle On/Off				
	6	Reset modem				
	7	Initiate remote digital loopback				
S34	Bit-mapped register:		0			
	1	Disable V.32bis				
	2	Disable enhanced V.32 mode				
	4	Disable quick V.32 retrain				
	8	Enable V.23 modulation				
	16	Change MR LED to DSR				
	32	Enable MI/MIC				
	64	Reserved				
	128	Reserved				
S38	Duration (sec) before disconnect when DTR drops during an ARQ call		0			

ARQ = Automatic repeat request
ASCII = American Standard Code for Information Interchange
BPS = Bits per second
CCITT = Consultative Committee for International Telephone and Telegraph
CD = Carrier detect
CRC = Cyclic redundancy check
DCE = Data communications equipment
DTE = Data terminal equipment
EIA = Electronic Industries Association
HDLC = High-level data link control
HST = High-speed technology
Hz = Hertz
LAPM = Link access procedure for modems
MI/MIC = Mode indicate/Mode indicate common
MNP = Microcom networking protocol
NVRAM = Non-volatile memory
RAM = Random-access memory

ROM = Read-only memory
SDLC = Synchronous Data Link Control
MR = Modem ready
LED = Light-emitting diode
DTR = Data terminal ready
CTS = Clear to send
RTS = Ready to send
DSR = Data set ready

Industry and Worldwide Standards Information

The following list shows official sources for documentation on industry and worldwide standards that relate to the computer industry.

FIPS or CCITT Recommendations:
National Technical Information Service
Springfield, VA 22161
(703) 487-4650

Standard Reference Materials (SRMs):
Office of Standards Reference Materials
National Bureau of Standards
Room B311, Chemistry Building
Gaithersburg, MD 20899
(301) 975-6776

ANSI or ISO Standards:
National Standards Institute
1430 Broadway, New York, NY 10018
(212) 642-4900

X3 Standards:
X3 Secretariat
CBEMA
311 First Street, N.W., Suite 500
Washington, DC 20001
(202) 737-8888

or
Global Engineering Documents
15 Inverness Way East
Englewood, CO 80112-5704
(303) 792-2181
(800) 854-7179
(303) 792-2192 FAX

EIA Standards:
Electronic Industries Association
Engineering Department
2001 Eye Street N.W.
Washington, DC 20006
(202) 457-4500

MIL Standards:
Navy Publication Center
Philadelphia, PA
(215) 697-2667 orders
(215) 697-2191 publications
(215) 697-4834 customer services

IEEE Standards:
IEEE Service Center,
445 Hoes Lane,
Piscataway, NJ 08854
(201) 981-0060

or
IEEE Computer Society Press
Worldway Postal Center
Los Angeles, CA 90080
(714) 821-8380

Federal Telecommunications Standards (FED-STD):
General Services Administration
Specifications Sales (WFRI)
7th and D Streets, S.W.
Washington, DC 20407
(202) 472-2205

ECMA standards:
European Computer Manufacturers Association
114 Rue de Rhone
CH-1204 Geneva, Switzerland

Recommended Vendor List

One of the most frustrating things about supporting PCs is finding a specific adapter board, part, driver program, or whatever you need to make a system work. If you are supporting or installing products, you will often need access to technical support or documentation for products that you may not have purchased yourself. Over the years I have compiled a list of companies whose products are popular or that I have found to work exceptionally well. I use these contacts regularly to provide information and components to enable me to support PC systems effectively.

This list is as up-to-date as possible, but companies move or go out of business all the time. If you find any information in this list that no longer is accurate, please call me or leave me a message on CompuServe. My address, phone number, and CIS ID are under the listing for Mueller Technical Research.

Many of the companies listed also provide support via electronic Bulletin Board Systems (BBSs). While originally exclusively the domain of computer enthusiasts, today many companies use BBS systems to provide a high level of technical support. Through a company run BBS you can often receive detailed technical support on that company's products, as well as download product literature and reference materials. I usually find that the level of support that I can obtain through a BBS is superior to traditional phone support, especially since you don't have to wait on hold!

Many of these companies also provide on-line support and services through the CompuServe Information System (CIS). You will find many major hardware and software companies on CIS, however most of these same companies also run standard BBS systems as well. Access to CIS is charged by the hour based on the connect speed (up to 9600bps), but the phone call itself is usually a local one. If you wish to access CIS, you can contact them via a voice line (see the vendor list) and request a startup kit.

With each company listing, I have included both standard phone numbers as well as 800 numbers where possible, so that U.S. and international readers can easily contact these companies. Also included are FAX and Bulletin Board System (BBS) numbers where available. I have not included any communications parameter settings, but virtually all BBS systems will work with at least 2400bps (V.22bis), 8 data bits, no parity, and 1 stop bit. Many of these systems will also support faster communications rates up to 14400bps (V.32bis), or even 28800bps (V.32fast). Some companies run a FAXback system, which is an automated system through which you can request product and technical information to be send directly to your own FAX machine. FAXback systems are an excellent way to get immediate documentation or technical support to solve tough problems.

Finally, each listing also includes a short description of the products or services that the company provides. I use this vendor list constantly myself, I hope that you find this list as useful as I do!

3M Data Storage Products Division

#223-5S-01 3M Center Building
St. Paul, MN 55144
(612)736-1866
Manufactures magnetic disk and tape media. DC-600 and DC-2000 media are standards for tape-backup data cartridges.

Accurite Technologies, Inc.

231 Charcot Ave.
San Jose, CA 95131-1107
(408)433-1980
Manufactures Accurite Drive Probe floppy disk diagnostics program, as well as HRD, DDD, and ADD industry-standard test disks.

Acer Technologies Corporation

2641 Orchard Park Way
San Jose, CA 95134
(408)432-6200
(800)733-2237
(408)922-2933 FAX
(408)428-0140 BBS
Manufactures PC-compatible systems, monitors, and printers.

Acme Electric/Safe Power

20 Water Street
Cuba, NY 14727
(716)968-2400
(800)325-5848
Manufactures uninterruptible power supplies (UPS) systems and power conditioners.

Adaptec

691 S. Milpitas Boulevard
Milpitas, CA 95035
(408)945-8600
(408)945-2550 Technical Support
(800)959-7274 Technical Support
(800)934-2766 Literature
(408)945-7727 BBS

Manufactures a variety of excellent hard disk controllers and SCSI host adapters. Their SCSI Host Adapters have become a defacto standard and have an enormous amount of 3rd party support.

Adaptive Technologies

127 N. Ventura Blvd.
Port Hueneme, CA 93041
(805)488-8832
(805)488-4890 FAX
Manufactures and sells the PROMPAQ automobile ECM chip selector. This is a device that installs in General Motors automobiles and allows for switching among as many as 4 EPROMS with different vehicle operating programs.

Addison-Wesley Publishing Co, Inc.

1 Jacob Way
Reading, MA 01867
(617)944-3700
Publishes technical publications and books.

Adobe Systems, Inc.

1585 Charleston Road
Box 7900
Mountain View, CA 94039
(408)986-6500
(800)447-3577
Manufactures and created the PostScript language and a variety of graphics software.

Advanced Digital Information Corporation

14737 NE 87th Street
Box 97057
Redmond, WA 98073-2966
(206)881-8004
(800)336-1233
(206)881-2296 FAX
(714)894-0893 BBS
Manufactures high-capacity tape-backup subsystems.

Advanced Logic Research (ALR)

9401 Jeronimo Street
Irvine, CA 92718
(714)581-6770
(800)444-4257
(714)581-0532 FAX
(714)458-1952 Technical Support
(714)458-6834 BBS
Manufactures PC compatibles featuring ISA, EISA, and MCA buses.

Advanced Micro Devices (AMD)

Box 3453
Sunnyvale, CA 94088-3453
(408)732-2400
Manufactures 386-compatible chips and math coprocessors.

Aeronics, Inc.

12741 Research Blvd.
Suite #500
Austin, TX 78759
(512)258-2303
(512)258-4392 FAX
Manufactures the highest quality Active and Forced Perfect Terminators for use in SCSI bus systems. They are known for solving problems with longer distances or multiple SCSI devices.

Aldus Corporation

411 1st Avenue South
Seattle, WA 98104
(206)622-5500
(800)333-2538
Manufactures PageMaker desktop publishing software and a variety of other graphical programs.

ALL Computers, Inc.

1220 Yonge Street
Second Floor
Toronto, ONT M4T1W1
(416)960-0111
(800)387-2744
(416)960-0111 Technical Support
(416)960-5426 FAX
(416)960-8679 BBS
Manufactures the ALL Chargecard memory coprocessor.

Allied Computer Services, Inc.

3417 Center Point Road N.E.
Cedar Rapids, IA 52402
(319)378-1383
(319)378-1489 FAX
Manufactures and sells the Trapcard II IRQ and DMA diagnostic board.

AllMicro, Inc.

18820 US Highway 19 North
Suite 215
Clearwater, FL 34624
(813)539-7283
(813) 531-0200 FAX
(800)653-4933
Manufacturer and distributor of the Rescue data recovery software and various other hardware and software diagnostic and troubleshooting tools.

Alloy Computer Products

25 Porter Road
Littleton, MA 01460
(800)544-7551
(508)486-0001 Technical Support
(508)481-7711 FAX
(508)460-8140 BBS
Manufactures tape-backup subsystems.

Alpha Research Corporation

10435 Bernet Road
Suite 107
Austin, TX 78758
(512)836-0709
(512)836-0944
(512)345-6496 FAX
Manufactures a complete line of caching and non-caching disk controllers, local bus motherboards, and video cards. Specializes in IDE and SCSI adapters that are fast and flexible.

ALPS America

3553 N. First Street
San Jose, CA 95134
(408)432-6000
Supplies 5 1/4-inch and 3 1/2-inch
floppy drives to IBM for use in the
original XT, AT, and now the PS/2
systems. Also manufactures a line of
printers and scanners.

Altex Electronics, Inc.

11342 IH 35 N
San Antonio, TX 78233
(210)655-8882
(800)531-5369
Supplies mail-order electronics parts.

Ambra Computer Corporation

3200 Beechleaf Court
Raleigh, NC 27604-1063
(919)713-1550
(800)25-AMBRA
(919)713-1599 FAX
An IBM company that manufactures
and sells low cost, high performance
compatible systems featuring Pentium
and IBM Blue Lightning processors.

Amdek Corporation

3471 N. First Street
San Jose, CA 95134-1803
(408)473-1200
(800)722-6335
(408)435-2770 Technical Support
(408)922-5729 FAX
(408)922-4400 BBS
Division of Wyse Technology that
manufactures monitors.

American Megatrends, Inc. (AMI)

6145-F Northbelt Parkway
Norcross, GA 30071
(404)263-8181
(800)828-9264
(404)246-8780 BBS

Manufactures the most popular IBM-
compatible BIOS, excellent ISA, EISA,
VL-Bus, and PCI Local bus
motherboards, and diagnostic software
such as AMIDIAG, SCSI DIAG, and
Remote.

American National Standards Institute

11 West 42nd Street
13th Floor
New York, NY 10036
(212)642-4900
ANSI committees set standards
throughout the computer industry.
Copies of any ANSI-approved standard
can be ordered here.

AMP, Inc.

P.O. Box 3608
Harrisburg, PA 17105
(717)564-0100
(800)522-6752
Manufactures a variety of computer
connectors, sockets, and cables used by
many OEMs, including IBM.

Andromeda Research

P.O. Box 222
Milford, OH 45150
(513)831-9708
(513)831-7562 FAX
Manufactures an excellent EPROM
programmer that runs from a PC
parallel port.

Annabooks

11848 Bernardo Plaza Court
Suite 110
San Diego, CA 92128-2417
(619) 673-0870
(800) 462-1042
(619)673-1432 FAX
Publishes and sells an excellent line of
technical publications and books especially for those in PC hardware and
software design.

Anthem Technology Systems (ATS)

1160 Ridder Park Drive
San Jose, CA 95131
(408)441-7177
(800)359-3580
(408)441-4503 FAX
A large distributor of Hewlett-Packard
DAT Tape and Hard Disk drives. They
also distribute other hard disk and
storage products.

Anvil Cases

15650 Salt Lake Avenue
Industry, CA 91745
(818)968-4100
(800)359-2684
Manufactures heavy-duty equipment
cases.

AOX, Inc.

100 Fifth
7th Floor
Waltham, MA 02154
(617)684-1400
(800)726-0269
Manufactures PS/2 MCA bus master
386 and 486 processor upgrade boards.

Apple Computer, Inc.

20525 Mariani Avenue
Cupertino, CA 95014
(408)996-1010
(800)538-9696

Archive Technology/Ardat, Inc.

1650 Sunflower Avenue
Costa Mesa, CA 92626
(714)641-1230
(800)537-2724
Manufactures high-capacity tape
drives.

Arco Electronics, Inc.

2750 N. 29th Ave.
Suite 316
Hollywood, FL 33020
(305)925-2688
(305)925-2889 FAX
(305)925-2791 BBS
Manufactures a complete line of Micro
Channel ATA IDE adapters which can
be used to upgrade IBM PS/2 systems.

Areal Technology, Inc.

2075 Zanker Road
San Jose, CA 95131
(408)436-6800
Manufactures high-capacity 3 1/2-inch
hard disk drives.

Arrow Electronics, Inc.

25 Hub Drive
Melville, NY 11747
(516)391-1300
(800)447-5270
System and peripheral distributor.

Arrowfield International, Inc.

2822-C Walnut Ave.
Tustin, CA 92680
(714)669-0101
(714)669-0526 FAX
Manufactures an incredible array of
disk drive brackets, rails, slides, cable
adapters, bezels, cabinets, and complete drive upgrade and repair assemblies for most IBM compatible systems.

AST Research, Inc.

16215 Alton Parkway
Irvine, CA 92718-9658
(714)727-4141
(800)876-4278
(714)727-4723 BBS
Manufactures an extensive line of
adapter boards and peripherals, as well
as a line of IBM-compatible systems.

Astec Standard Power

Division of Astec America, Inc.
401 Jones Road
Oceanside, CA 92054-1216
(619)757-1880
(619)439-4243 FAX
Manufactures high end power supplies
for PC systems as well as many other
applications. Astec power supplies are
used as OEM equipment in many of
the top manufacturer's systems including IBM and others.

ATI Technologies, Inc.

33 Commerce Valley Drive East
Thornhill, ONT L3T7N6
(416)882-2600
(416)882-2626 Technical Support
(416)882-2620 FAX
(416)764-9404 BBS
Manufactures an excellent line of high
performance standard and Local Bus
video cards and chipsets.

Autodesk, Inc.

2320 Marinship Way
Sausalito, CA 94965
(415)332-2344
(800)964-6432
Manufactures AutoCAD software.

Award Software, Inc.

777 E. Middlefield Road
Mountain View, CA 94043
(415)968-4433
(415)968-0274 FAX
(415)968-0249 BBS
Manufactures a line of IBM-compatible
ROM BIOS software.

Beckman Industrial

3883 Ruffin Road
San Diego, CA 92123
(619)495-3200
(800)854-2708
Manufactures diagnostics and test
equipment.

Belden Wire and Cable

2200 U.S. Highway 275
Richmond, IN 47375
(317)983-5200
(800)235-3361
Manufactures cable and wire products.

Berkshire Products, Inc.

2180 Pleasant Hill Road
Suite A-5185
Duluth, GA 30136-4663
(404)271-0088
(404)932-0082 FAX
Manufactures a diagnostic monitoring
product called System Sentry, which
continuously monitors power supply
performance and system internal temperature as well as CMOS battery voltage, and BIOS POST codes. They also
make a high speed buffered parallel
port adapter.

Best Power Technology, Inc.

P.O. Box 280
Necedah, WI 54646
(608)565-7200
(800)356-5794
(608)565-2221 FAX
Manufactures an excellent line of computer power protection equipment
from high end Ferroresonent UPS systems to Line Conditioners and Standby
Power Protection systems.

Bitstream, Inc.

215 1st Street
Cambridge, MA 02142
(617)497-6222
(800)522-3668
Manufactures fonts and font software.

Black Box Corporation

P.O. Box 12800
Pittsburgh, PA 15241
(412)746-5530
Manufactures and distributes a variety
of communications products including
network adapters, cables, and connectors for a variety of applications.

Boca Research, Inc.

6413 Congress Avenue
Boca Raton, FL 33487-2841
(407)997-6227
(407)241-8088 Technical Support
(407)997-0918 FAX
(407)241-1601 BBS
Manufactures a low-cost line of adapter
card products for IBM-compatibles.

Bondwell Industrial Company, Inc.

47485 Seabridge Drive
Fremont, CA 94538
(415)490-4300
Manufactures a line of laptop systems.

Borland International

100 Borland Way
Scotts Valley, CA 95067
(408)431-1000
(800)841-8180 Technical Support
(408)439-9119 FAX orders
(408)439-9096 BBS (1200 or 2400 BPS,
8 bits, no parity, 1 stop bit)
Software manufacturer that features
Turbo language products, Paradox, and
Quattro Pro, as well as dBASE IV,
acquired from Ashton-Tate.

Boston Computer Exchange

55 Temple Place
Boston, MA 02111
(617)542-4414
A broker for used IBM and compatible
computers.

Bracking, Jim

967 Pinewood Drive
San Jose, CA 95129
(408)725-0628
Manufactures the HDtest hard disk test
and format program. This program,
distributed as shareware, is excellent
for testing and educational use.

Buerg, Vernon D.

139 White Oak Circle
Petaluma, CA 94952
(707)778-1811
(707)778-8728 FAX
(707)778-8944 BBS
Manufactures an excellent line of utility programs including the popular
LIST program. Buerg Software is
distributed through BBS systems
and CompuServe.

Bureau of Electronic Publishing

141 New Road
Parsippany, NJ 07054
(201)808-2700
(800)828-4766
Distributes and publishes software on
CD-ROM disks.

Byte Information Exchange (BIX)

1030 Massachussets Avenue
Fourth Floor
Cambridge, MA 01238
(800)695-4775
(800)695-4882 BBS
(617)491-6642 FAX
An on-line computer information and
messaging system.

Byte Magazine

One Phoenix Mill Lane
Peterborough, NH 03458
(603)924-9281
(617)861-9764 BBS
A monthly magazine covering all lines
of microcomputers.

Cable Connection

557 Salmar Avenue
Suite B
Campbell, CA 95008
(408)354-0710
Manufactures a variety of cable,
connector, and switch products.

Cables To Go

1501 Webster Street
Dayton, OH 45404-9914
(513)224-8646
(800)826-7904
Manufactures a variety of cable,
connector, and switch products.

Cache Computers, Inc.

46600 Landing Parkway
Fremont, CA 94538
(510)226-9922
Manufactures a line of 386 and 486
motherboards.

Cal-Abco

6041 Variel Avenue
Woodland Hills, CA 91367
(818)704-7733
(800)669-2226
Distributes computer systems and
peripherals.

Canon USA, Inc.

One Canon Plaza
Lake Success, NY 11042
(516)488-6700 or
(516)328-5960
(800)221-3333
(516)354-5805 FAX
(516)488-6528 BBS
Manufactures a line of printer and
video equipment as well as floppy
drives. Supplies floppy drives to
Compaq and IBM.

Casio, Inc.

15 Gardner Road
Fairfield, NJ 07006
(201)361-5400
Manufactures personal data systems
and digital watches.

Central Point Software, Inc.

15220 NW Greenbrier Parkway
Suite 200
Beaverton, OR 97006-9937
(503)690-8088
(800)445-4208
(503)690-8083 FAX
(503)690-6650 BBS
Manufactures the PC Tools, Copy II PC,
and Central Point Backup software.
Central Point supplies many of the
utilities found in IBM and MS DOS 5.0
and higher.

Chemtronics, Inc.

8125 Cobb Center Drive
Kennesaw, GA 30144
(404)424-4888
(404)424-4267 FAX
Manufactures and sells a complete line
of computer and electronic grade
chemicals, materials, and supplies.

Cherry Electrical Products

3600 Sunset Avenue
Waukegan, IL 60087
(708)662-9200
Manufactures a line of high quality
keyboards for IBM-compatible systems.

Chicago Case Company

4446 S. Ashland Avenue
Chicago, IL 60609
(312)927-1600
Manufactures equipment-shipping and
travel cases.

Chinon America, Inc.

615 Hawaii Avenue
Torrance, CA 90503
(310)533-0274
(800)441-0222
Manufactures a line of floppy disk and
CD-ROM drives.

Chips & Technologies, Inc.

3050 Zanker Road
San Jose, CA 95134
(408)434-0600
(800)944-6284
Manufactures specialized chipsets
for compatible motherboard
manufacturers.

Ci Design Company

1711 Langley Avenue
Irvine, CA 92714
(714)261-5524
Manufactures custom-made 3 1/2-inch
drive mounting kits used by Toshiba,
Panasonic, and NEC for their drive
products. Also makes drive faceplates,
enclosures, and custom cable assemblies.

Cipher Data Products, Inc.

10101 Old Grove Road
San Diego, CA 92131
(619)578-9100
(800)424-7437
Manufactures a line of tape-backup
products. Also supplies tape-backup
systems to IBM.

Ciprico, Inc.

2800 Campus Drive
Plymouth, MN 55441
(612)551-4000
(800)727-4669
Manufactures high-performance SCSI
host adapters.

Citizen America Corporation

2450 Broadway
Suite 600
Santa Monica, CA 90404
(310)453-0614
(800)556-1234
(310)453-2814 FAX
(310)453-7564 BBS
Manufactures a line of printers and
floppy disk drives.

CMD Technology, Inc.

1 Vanderbilt
Irvine, CA 92718
(714)454-0800
(800)426-3832
(714)455-1656 FAX
Manufactures EISA adapters, PCI and
VL-Bus, IDE and SCSI disk adapters.

CMS Enhancements, Inc.

2722 Michelson Drive
Irvine, CA 92715
(714)222-6000
Distributes a variety of system and
peripheral products, and specializes in
hard disk drives.

Colorado Memory Systems, Inc.

800 S. Taft Avenue
Loveland, CO 80537
(303)669-8000
(800)346-9881
(303)635-1500 Customer Support
(303)667-0997 FAX
(303)635-0650 BBS
Manufactures tape-backup subsystems
specializing in QIC-80 and QIC-40
systems that attach through an interface card, floppy controller, or parallel
port connection.

Columbia Data Products

1070B Rainer Drive
Altamonte Springs, FL 32714
(407)869-6700
(407)862-4725 FAX
(407)862-4724 BBS
Manufactures SCSI drivers for Western
Digital FASST host adapters.

Comb

7101 Winnetka Avenue N.
P.O. Box 299 DO
Minneapolis, MN 55429-0900
(612)535-4944
(800)328-0609
Liquidates and distributes a variety of
discontinued products, including PC
compatible systems and peripherals.

COMPAQ Computer Corporation

20555 State Hwy. 249
P.O. Box 692000
Houston, TX 77269-2000
(713)370-0670
(800)231-0900
(800)345-1518 Technical Support
(713)374-1518 BBS
Manufactures high end IBM-
compatible computer systems.

CompUSA, Inc.

15167 Business Avenue
Dallas, TX 75244
(214)888-5700
(800)932-2667
Computer retail superstore and mail-
order outlet.

CompuServe Information Service (CIS)

5000 Arlington Centre Boulevard
Columbus, OH 43220
(614)457-8600
(800)848-8199
Largest on-line information and messaging service; offers manufacturer-
and vendor-sponsored forums for
technical support.

Computer Component Source, Inc.

135 Eileen Way
Syosset, NY 11791-9022
(516)496-8727
(800)356-1227
(516)496-8984 FAX
(800)926-2062 FAX
Distributes a large number of computer
components for repair. Specializes in
display parts such as flyback transformers and other components.

Computer Hotline Magazine

15400 Knoll Trail
#500
Dallas, TX 75248
(214)233-5131
(800)866-3241
Publication featuring advertisers offering excellent sources of replacement
and repair parts as well as new and
used equipment at wholesale prices.

Computer Reseller News Magazine

CMP Publications, Inc.
600 Community Drive
Manhasset, NY 11030-3875
(516)562-5000
(516)562-5468 FAX Subscriptions
An excellent industry trade weekly
news magazine featuring news for
computer professionals involved in
value added reselling of computer
equipment.

Computer Retail Week Magazine

CMP Publications, Inc.
600 Community Drive
Manhasset, NY 11030-3875
(516)562-5000
(516)562-5468 FAX Subscriptions
An excellent industry trade weekly
news magazine featuring news for
computer superstores, mass merchants,
and retailers.

Computer Shopper Magazine

5211 S. Washington Avenue
Titusville, FL 32780
(407)269-3211
Monthly magazine for experimenters
and bargain hunters that features a
large number of advertisements.

Computer Technology Review Magazine

West World Productions, Inc.
924 Westwood Blvd.
Suite 650
Los Angeles, CA 90024-2910
(213)208-1335
An excellent monthly technical magazine for systems integrators, Value
Added Resellers, and Original Equipment Manufacturers.

Comtech Publishing Ltd.

P.O. Box 12340
Reno, NV 89510
(702)825-9000
(800)456-7005
(702)825-1818 FAX
Manufactures dSalvage Professional,
the best and most comprehensive
xBASE data-recovery and file repair
software available.

Connector Resources Unlimited (CRU)

1005 Ames Avenue
Milpitas, CA 95035
(408)942-9077
Manufactures a large variety of disk
enclosures, mounting kits, cables, and
connectors for IBM and Mac systems.

Conner Peripherals, Inc.

3081 Zanker Road
San Jose, CA 95134
(408)456-4500
(800)426-6637
(408)456-3388 Technical Support
(408)456-4501 FAX
(800)4CONNER (426-6637) FAXback
Information System

(408)456-4415 BBS
Manufactures 3 1/2-inch IDE and SCSI
hard disk drives, and a line of tape-
backup products from DC-2000 to DAT
and 8mm units.

Conner Tapes Products

1650 Sunflower Avenue
Costa Mesa, CA 92626
(714)641-1230
(800)537-2724
Manufactures high-capacity tape
drives.

Core International, Inc.

7171 North Federal Hwy.
Boca Raton, FL 33487
(407)997-6055
(407)241-2929 BBS
Distributes a variety of different manufacturers hard disk drives including
Seagate and Western Digital.

Corel Systems, Inc.

1600 Carling Avenue
Ottawa, ONT, K1Z8R7
(613)728-8200
(800)772-6735 Service Only
(613)728-9790 FAX
(613)728-4752 BBS
Manufactures the CorelDraw graphics
program as well as Corel SCSI, a SCSI
driver kit featuring drivers for a variety
of SCSI host adapters and devices.

Creative Labs, Inc.

1901 McCarthy Boulevard
Miltitas, CA 95035
(408)428-6600
(800)544-6146
(405)742-6622 Technical Support
(408)428-6011 FAX
(408)428-6660 BBS
Manufactures the Soundblaster series
audio cards for multimedia and sound
applications.

CS Electronics

1342 Bell Avenue
Suite 3C
Tustin, CA 92680
(714)259-9100
(714)259-0911 FAX
Manufactures a very high quality line of disk and tape drive cables, specializing in SCSI-1, SCSI-2, and SCSI-3 applications. They offer custom lengths, connectors, and impedances for a proper match with an existing installation, and use the highest quality raw cable available.

Cumulus Corporation

23500 Mercantile Road
Cleveland, OH 44120
(216)464-3019 BBS
Manufactures processor-upgrade products and clone systems.

Curtis Manufacturing Co, Inc.

30 Fitzgerald Drive
Jaffrey, NH 03452
(603)532-4123
(800)955-5544
Manufactures a line of computer accessories, cables, and toolkits.

Cyrix Corporation

2703 N. Central Expressway
Richardson, TX 75080
(214)994-8387
(800)327-6284
(214)699-9857 FAX
Manufactures fast Intel-compatible processors and math coprocessors for 286-, 386SX-, and 386DX-based systems. One product they make is the 486DRx2, a clock-doubled 486 processor that is pin compatible with the Intel 386DX, and which can be used to upgrade existing 386DX systems.

Dak Industries, Inc.

8200 Remmet Avenue
Canoga Park, CA 91304
(818)888-8220
(800)325-0800
(818)715-7153 BBS
Liquidates and distributes a variety of discontinued and/or unique products, including PC compatible systems and peripherals.

Dallas Semiconductor

4401 S. Beltwood Parkway
Dallas, TX 75244-3292
(214)450-0400
Manufactures real-time clock and non-volatile RAM modules used by a number of OEMs including IBM, Compaq, and others.

Damark International, Inc.

7101 Winnetka Avenue North
Minneapolis, MN 55429
(612)531-0066
(800)729-9000
Liquidates and distributes a variety of discontinued products, including PC compatible systems and peripherals.

Data Depot

1710 Drew Street
Clearwater, FL 34615-2151
(813)446-3402
(800)275-1913
(800)SOS-DIAGnostics (767-3424)
(813)443-4377 FAX
Manufactures the PocketPOST diagnostic card for ISA and EISA systems, as well as several other excellent diagnostics hardware and software products.

Data Spec

9410 Owens Mouth Avenue
Chatsworth, CA 91311
(818)772-2700
(800)431-8124
Manufactures a complete line of switch
boxes for parallel, serial, video, and
many other connections.

Data Technology Corporation (DTC)

1515 Centre Pointe Drive
Milpitas, CA 95035-8010
(408)942-4000
(408)942-4027 FAX
(408)942-4197 BBS
Manufactures a complete line of hard
disk controllers for ISA and EISA bus
systems.

Datastorm Technologies, Inc.

3212 Lemone Boulevard
Columbia, MO 65201
(314)443-3282
(314)875-0530 Technical Support
(314)443-3282 BBS
Manufactures ProCOMM and
ProCOMM Plus communications
software.

Dell Computer Corporation

9505 Arboretum Boulevard
Austin, TX 78759
(512)338-4400
(800)426-5150
(512)338-8528 BBS
Manufactures a line of low-cost, high-
performance IBM-compatible computer
systems.

DiagSoft, Inc.

5615 Scotts Valley Drive
Suite 140
Scotts Valley, CA 95066
(408)438-8247
(800)342-4763
(408)438-7113 FAX

Manufactures the QAPlus user level PC
diagnostics software, as well as the
high end QAPlus/FE (Field Engineer)
software.

Digi-Key Corporation

701 Brooks Ave. South
P.O. Box 677
Thief River Falls, MN 56701-0677
(218)681-6674
(800)344-4539
(218)681-3380 FAX
Sells an enormous variety of electronic
and computer components, tools, and
test equipment. Publishes a complete
catalog listing all items.

Digital Research, Inc. (Now known as Novell, Inc.)

70 Garden Court
Monterey, CA 93940
(408)649-3896
(800)NET-WARE (638-9273)
(408)649-2344 FAXback Information
Line
(408)649-3696 BBS (9600bps)
(408)649-3443 BBS all others
1-801-429-5588 International number
(goes to corporate offices in Provo,
Utah)
Manufactures the DR DOS operating
system.

Direct Drives

1107 Euclid Lane
Richton Park, IL 60471
(708)481-1111
Distributes an incredible selection of
hard disk drives and controllers. Also
publishes the *Hard Drive Buyer's Resource Guide*, a comprehensive and
accurate listing of drive and controller
specifications available.

Distributed Processing Tech. (DPT)

140 Candace Drive
Maitland, FL 32751
(407)830-5522
(407)831-6432 BBS
Manufactures high-performance caching SCSI host adapters.

Diversified Technology

112 E. State Street
Ridgeland, MS 39158
(601)856-4121
(800)443-2667
Manufactures industrial and rackmount PC compatible systems as well as a variety of backplane-design CPU boards and multifunction adapters.

Dolphin Data Products, Inc.

1938 Souvenir Drive
Clearwater, FL 34615
(813)461-2064
(800)393-2064

DTK Computer, Inc.

17700 Castleton Street
Suite #160
Industry, CA 91748
(818)810-8880
(818)333-6548 BBS
Manufactures PC-compatible systems and BIOS software.

Dukane Corporation

2900 Dukane Drive
St. Charles, IL 60174
(708)584-2300
(708)584-5156 FAX
Manufactures the best Audio Visual overhead projectors on the market today.

Dynatech Computer Power Inc.

5800 Butler Lane
Scotts Valley, CA 95066
(408)438-5760
(800)638-9098

Manufactures a line of computer power-protection devices.

Edmund Scientific

101 E. Gloucester Pike
Barrington, NJ 08007
(609)573-6250
Supplies scientific supplies including optical equipment and components, test equipment, and a variety of electronic components and gadgets. Their catalog is an experimenter's dream!

***Electronic Buyers' News* Magazine**

CMP Publications, Inc.
600 Community Drive
Manhasset, NY 11030-3875
(516)562-5000
(516)562-5468 FAX Circulation
An excellent industry trade weekly magazine featuring news and information for those involved in electronics purchasing, materials and management.

***Electronic Engineering Times* Magazine**

CMP Publications, Inc.
600 Community Drive
Manhasset, NY 11030-3875
(516)562-5000
(516)562-5468 FAX Circulation
An excellent industry trade weekly news magazine featuring news for engineers and technical management.

***Electronic Products* Magazine**

Hearst Business Communications, Inc.
645 Stewart Ave.
Garden City, NY 11530
(516)227-1300
(516)227-1444 FAX
An excellent industry trade magazine featuring engineering type information on electronic and computer components and in-depth technical articles.

Elek-Tek, Inc.

7350 North Linder Avenue
Skokie, IL 60077
(708)677-7660
(800)395-1000
Computer retail superstore offering a large selection of brand-name equipment at discount pricing.

Emerson Computer Power

9650 Jeronimo
Irvine, CA 92718
(714)457-3600
(800)222-5877
Manufactures a line of computer power-protection devices.

Endl Publications

14426 Black Walnut Court
Saratoga, CA 95070
(408)867-6642
Publishes SCSI technical documentation such as *The SCSI Bench Reference* and *The SCSI Encyclopedia*.

Epson America, Inc. OEM Division

20770 Madrona Avenue
Torrance, CA 90503
(310)782-0770
(310)782-5220 FAX
(800)922-8911 FAXback Information Line
(408)946-8777 BBS
Manufactures printers, floppy disk drives, and complete PC-compatible systems.

Everex Systems, Inc.

48431 Milmont Drive
Fremont, CA 94538
(415)498-1111
(800)922-8911
(510)683-2984 BBS
Manufactures PC-compatible systems and peripherals.

Exabyte Corporation

1685 38th Street
Boulder, CO 80301
(303)447-7359
Manufactures high-performance 8mm tape-backup systems.

Excel, Inc.

2200 Brighton-Henrietta Townline Road
Rochester, NY 14623
Distributes refurbished IBM PC, XT, AT, and PS/2 systems and peripherals.

Fedco Electronics, Inc.

184 W. 2nd Street or
P.O. Box 1403
Fond du Lac, WI 54936-1403
(414)922-6490
(800)542-9761
Manufactures and supplies a large variety of computer batteries.

Fessenden Technologies

116 N. 3rd Street
Ozark, MO 65721
(417)485-2501
Service company that offers hard disk drive and monitor repair and reconditioning. Also offers floppy disk and hard disk test equipment.

Fifth Generation Systems, Inc.

10049 N. Reiger Road
Baton Rouge, LA 70809
(504)291-7221
(800)873-4384
(504)295-3344 BBS
Manufactures a variety of software utility products including FASTBACK, the Mace Utilities, and the Brooklyn Bridge. Recently acquired by Symantec.

Fluke, John Manufacturing Company, Inc.

P.O. Box 9090
Everett, WA 98206-9090
(206)347-6100
(800)443-5853
(206)356-5116 FAX
Manufactures a line of high-end digital troubleshooting tools including the 9000 series products that are designed to troubleshoot PC motherboards down to the component level. These systems are used by many motherboard manufacturers for design and manufacturing troubleshooting.

Forbin Project

P.O. Box 702
Cedar Falls, IA 50613
(319)266-0540
Manufactures the Qmodem communications software.

Fujitsu America, Inc.

3055 Orchard Drive
San Jose, CA 95134
(408)432-1300
(800)626-4686
(408)944-9899 BBS
Manufactures a line of high-capacity hard disk drives.

Future Domain Corporation

2801 McGaw Avenue
Irvine, CA 92714
(714)253-0400
(714)253-0913 FAX
(714)253-0432 BBS
Manufactures a line of high-performance SCSI host adapters and software.

Gateway 2000

610 Gateway Drive
North Sioux City, SD 57049
(605)232-2000
(800)523-2000
(605)232-2109 BBS
Manufactures a popular line of PC-compatible systems sold by mail order.

Gazelle

305 North 500 West
Provo, Utah 84601
(801)377-1288
(800)RUN-FAST (786-3278)
(801)373-6933 FAX
Manufactures the Optune disk defragmenter and disk performance utility program.

GigaTrend, Inc.

2234 Rutherford Road
Carlsbad, CA 92008
(619)931-9122
Manufactures high-capacity tape drives.

Global Engineering Documents

15 Inverness Way East
Englewood, CO 80112-5704
(303)792-2181
(800)854-7179
(303) 792-2192 FAX or
7730 Carondelet Avenue
Suite 407
Clayton, MI 63105
(314)726-6444
A source for various ANSI and other industry standard documents, including SCSI-1, 2, and 3, ATA IDE, ESDI, and many others. Unlike ANSI, they sell draft documents of standards that are not yet fully ANSI approved.

Globe Manufacturing, Inc.

1159 Route 22
Mountainside, NJ 07092
(908)232-7301
(800)227-3258
Manufactures assorted PC adapter card brackets.

Golden Bow Systems

842 B. Washington Street
San Diego, CA 92103
(619)298-9349
(800)284-3269
Manufactures VOPT, the best and fastest disk optimizer software available.

GoldStar Technology, Inc.

3003 N. First Street
San Jose, CA 95134
(408)432-1331
(408)432-0236 BBS
Manufactures a line of PC systems, monitors, and fax machines.

GRACE Electronic Materials

77 Dragon Court
Woburn, MA 01888
(617)935-4850
(617)933-4318 FAX
Manufactures thermally conductive tapes and heat sinks.

Great Falls Computer Corp.

505 Innsbruck Ave.
Great Falls, VA 22066
(703)759-5570
(703)759-7152 FAX
A service company specializing in computer repair and data recovery.

GSI (Great Software Ideas), Inc.

17951-H Skypark Circle
Irvine, CA 92714-6343
(714)261-7949
(800)486-7800
(714)757-1778 FAX
Manufactures an extremely flexible and powerful line of IDE adapters and floppy controllers, including units with security locks, and support for 2.88M drives. Also offers complete 2.88M drive upgrade kits. Their IDE controllers have a flexible on-board BIOS that allows them to coexist with other drive interfaces.

Harbor Electronics

650 Danbury Road
Ridgefield, CT 06877
(203)438-9625
(203)431-3001 FAX
Manufactures a line of high quality SCSI-1. -2, and -3 interconnect cables.

Hauppauge Computer Works, Inc.

91 Cabot Court
Hauppauge, NY 11788
(516)434-1600
(800)443-6284
Manufactures upgrade motherboards for PC-compatible systems.

Hayes Microcomputer Products

P.O Box 105203
Atlanta, GA 30348
(404)840-9200
(404)446-6336 BBS
Manufactures a complete line of modems.

Heathkit

Heath Company
455 Riverview Drive
P.O. Box 1288
Benton Harbor, MI 49022
(800)253-0570
Manufactures various kits for learning electronics and computer design. Also sells Zenith computers and technical documentation.

Hermann Marketing

1400 North Price Road
St. Louis, MO 63132-2308
(800)523-9009
(314)432-1818 FAX
Distributes a line of "Uniquely Intel" products and accessories.

Hewlett-Packard

16399 W. Bernardo Drive
San Diego, CA 92127
(619)592-4522
(800)333-1917 HP FIRST (Fax Information Retrieval System)
(208)344-4809 HP FIRST (Fax Information Retrieval System)
Manufactures an extensive line of excellent printers and PC-compatible systems.

Hewlett-Packard, Disk Memory Division

11311 Chinden Boulevard
Boise, ID 83714
(208)396-6000
Manufactures high-capacity 3 1/2-inch hard disk drives.

Hitatchi America, Ltd.

50 Prospect Avenue
Tarrytown, NY 10591
(914)332-5800
Manufactures computer peripherals, including hard disks and LCD devices.

Hyundai Electronics America

166 Baypointe Parkway
San Jose, CA 95134
(408)473-9200
Manufactures PC-compatible systems.

IBM Desktop Software

472 Wheelers Farm Road
Milford, CT 06460
(203)783-7000
Supports IBM PC applications software such as DisplayWrite and PC Storyboard.

IBM National Distribution Division (NDD)

101 Paragpn Drive
Montvale, NJ 07645
(800)426-9397
Manufactures and supports IBM DOS and OS/2.

IBM OEM Division

1133 Westchester Avenue
White Plains, NY 10604
(914)288-3000
Manufactures and distributes IBM products such as high-capacity 3 1/2-inch hard disk drives, networking and chipset products.

IBM Parts Order Center

Dept. E54
P.O. Box 9022
Boulder, CO 80301
(303)924-4100 Orders
(303)924-4015 Part Number ID and Lookup
IBM's nationwide service parts ordering center.

IBM PC Company

11400 Burnet Road
Austin, TX 78758
(512)823-2851
(800)IBM-3333
(800)426-7015 IBM PC Co. Factory Outlet (discontinued/used equipment)
(800)426-4329 IBM FAX Information Service (FAXback system)
(800)426-3395 IBM Tech Support FAX Information (FAXback system)
(919)517-0001 IBM National Support Center BBS
(919)517-0095 IBM NSC BBS Status Line (voice)
Manufactures and supports IBM's PS/2, PS/Valuepoint, and PS/1 products.

IBM PC Direct

3039 Cornwallis Road
Building 203
Research Triangle Park, NC 27709-9766
(800)IBM-2YOU (426-2968)
(800)465-7999 Canada
(919)517-2050 FAX
IBM PC Company direct mail order catalog sales division.

IBM Personal Systems Technical Solutions Magazine

The TDA Group
175 Galli Drive
Los Altos, CA 94022
(800)551-2832
(415)948-4280 FAX
Publishes an excellent bimonthly magazine covering IBM Personal Computer systems and software.

IBM Technical Directory

P.O. Box 2009
Racine, WI 53404
(800)426-7282
The source for books, reference manuals, documentation, software toolkits, and language products for IBM systems.

Illinois Lock

301 West Hintz Road
Wheeling, IL 60090-5754
(708)537-1800
(708)537-1881 FAX
Manufactures keylocks used in many different IBM and IBM-compatible computer systems.

InfoChip Systems, Inc.

2840 San Tomas Expressway
Santa Clara, CA 95051
(408)727-0514
(408)727-2496 BBS
Manufactures the Expanz data-compression coprocessor products.

InfoWorld Magazine

4 Chrysler Road
Natick, MA 01760
(508)879-0700
(800)343-6474
Publishes InfoWorld magazine, featuring excellent product reviews.

Inline, Inc.

1901 E. Lambert Road
Suite 110
La Habra, CA 90631
(213)690-6767
(800)882-7117
Manufactures a complete line of video-connection accessories.

Inmac

2465 Augustine Drive
Santa Clara, CA 95052
(800)547-5444
(800)972-3210 FAX
(800)972-9233 Technical Support
Distributes a large variety of computer supplies, floppy disks, cables, and so on.

Integrated Information Technology (IIT)

2445 Mission College Boulevard
Santa Clara, CA 95054
(408)727-1885
(800)832-0770
Manufactures fast Intel-compatible math coprocessors for 286-, 386SX-, and 386DX-based systems.

Intel Corporation

3065 Bowers Avenue
Santa Clara, CA 95051
(408)765-8080
(800)548-4725
Manufactures microprocessors used in IBM and compatible systems. Also makes a line of memory and accelerator boards.

Intel PC Enhancement Operations

5200 NE Elam Young Parkway
Hillsboro, OR 97124
(503)629-7354
(800)538-3373

(503)645-6275 BBS
Manufactures a variety of PC upgrade
products and expansion boards including Overdrive CPU upgrades,
AboveBoard memory adapters, SIMM
memory modules, and modems.

Interface Group

300 First Avenue
Needham, MA 02194
(617)449-6600
Produces the annual COMDEX/Fall
and COMDEX/Spring computer shows.

International Electronic Research Corp. (IERC)

135 W. Magnolia Boulevard
Burbank, CA 91502
(213)849-2481
(818)848-8872 FAX
Manufactures a line of excellent CPU
heat sink products.

Intex Solutions, Inc.

35 Highland Circle
Needham, MA 02194
(617)449-6222
(617)444-2318 FAX
Manufactures and distributes software,
especially Lotus enhancement products
such as the Rescue Plus Lotus spreadsheet Data Recovery program. Rescue is
the most comprehensive and capable
data recovery program for Lotus
spreadsheet files.

Iomega Corporation

1821 West 4000 South
Roy, UT 84067
(801)778-1000
(800)456-5522
(801)778-4400 BBS
Manufactures the Bernoulli box
removable-cartridge drive.

IQ Technologies, Inc.

13625 NE 126th Place
Suite 400
Kirkland, WA 98034
(206)823-2273
(800)752-6526
Manufactures PC interconnect cables
and devices, including the SmartCable
RS232 devices.

Jameco Computer Products

1355 Shoreway Road
Belmont, CA 94002
(415)592-8097
Supplies computer components, parts,
and peripherals by way of mail order.

JDR Microdevices

2233 Simartian Drive
San Jose, CA 95124
(408)559-1200
(800)538-5000
(408)559-0253 BBS
A vendor for chips, disk drives, and
various computer and electronic parts
and components.

Jensen Tools

7815 S. 46th Street
Phoenix, AZ 85044-5399
(602)968-6231
(800)426-1194
(800)366-9662 FAX
Supplies and manufactures high-
quality tools and test equipment.

Kalok Corporation

1289 Anvilwood Avenue
Sunnyvale, CA 94089
(408)747-1315
Manufactures a line of low-cost 3 1/2-
inch hard disk drives.

Kenfil Distribution

16745 Saticoy Street
Van Nuys, CA 91406
(818)785-1181
A major software distributor.

Kensington Microware, Ltd.

2855 Campus Drive
San Mateo, CA 94403
(415)572-2700
(800)535-4242
Manufactures and supplies computer
accessories.

Key Tronic Corporation

Mailing Address:
P.O. Box 14687
Spokane, WA 99214-0687
Shipping Address:
North 4424 Sullivan Road
Spokane, WA 99216
(509)928-8000
(800)262-6006
Manufactures a variety of high-quality
keyboards and mice for PC-compatible
systems.

Kingston Technology Corporation

17600 Newhope Street
Fountain Valley, CA 92708
(714)435-2600
(714)435-2699 FAX
(800)835-6575
Manufactures an excellent line of processor upgrade products for 286 and
386 IBM and Compaq systems.

Labconco Corporation

8811 Prospect
Kansas City, MO 64132
(816)333-8811
(800)821-5525
(816)363-0130 FAX
Manufactures a variety of clean room
cabinets and clean benches for use in
hard disk drive and other sensitive
component repair.

Landmark Research International

703 Grand Central Street
Clearwater, FL 34616
(813)443-1331
(800)683-6696
Manufactures the excellent Service
Diagnostics PC diagnostics program, as
well as the Kickstart diagnostic adapter
cards. Known also for the Landmark
System Speed Test program.

Laser Magnetic Storage

4425 Arrowswest Drive
Colorado Springs, CO 80907
(719)593-7900
Manufactures a variety of optical disk
products.

Lexmark

740 New Circle Road
Lexington, KY 40511
(606)232-6814
(606)232-5653 BBS
Manufactures IBM keyboards and
printers for retail distribution. Spun off
from IBM in 1991, now sells to other
OEMs and distributors.

Liuski International, Inc.

10 Hub Drive
Melville, NY 11747
(516)454-8220
(800)347-5454
Hardware distributor that carries a
variety of peripherals and systems.

Longshine Computer, Inc.

2013 N. Capitol Avenue
San Jose, CA 95132
(408)942-1746
Manufactures various PC adapters in-
cluding floppy, hard disk, SCSI, Token
Ring, Ethernet, and so on.

Lotus Development Corporation

55 Cambridge Parkway
Cambridge, MA 02142
(617)577-8500
(800)343-5414
Manufactures Lotus 1-2-3, Symphony,
and Magellan software.

LSI Logic, Inc.

1551 McCarthy Boulevard
Milpitas, CA 95035
(408)433-8000
Manufactures motherboard logic and
chipsets.

Manzana Microsystems, Inc.

P.O. Box 2117
Goleta, CA 93118
(805)968-1387
Manufactures floppy disk upgrade
subsystems and controllers.

Mastersoft, Inc.

8737 E. Via de Commercio
6991 E. Camelback Road (Business)
Scottsdale, AZ 85258
(602)948-4888
(800)624-6107 Sales and product information
Manufactures Word for Word, a word
processing file-conversion program.

Maxell Corporation of America

22-08 Route 208
Fair Lawn, NJ 07410
(201)795-5900
(800)533-2836
Manufactures magnetic media products
including disks and tape cartridges.

Maxi Switch, Inc.

2901 East Elvira Road
Tuscon, AZ 85706
(602)294-5450
(602)294-6890 FAX

Manufactures a line of high quality PC
keyboards, including some designed for
harsh or industrial environments.

Maxoptix

2520 Junction Avenue
San Jose, CA 95134
(408)954-9700
(800)848-3092
Manufactures a line of optical WORM
and magneto-optical drives. Joint ven-
ture with Maxtor Corporation and
Kubota Corporation.

Maxtor Corporation

211 River Oaks Parkway
San Jose, CA 95134
(408)432-1700
(800)262-9867
(303)678-2222 BBS (2400bps)
(303)678-2020 BBS (9600+bps)
Manufactures a line of large-capacity,
high-quality hard disk drives.

Maynard Electronics, Inc. (Division of Conner Peripherals, Inc.)

36 Skyline Drive
Lake Mary, FL 32746
(407)263-3500
(800)821-8782
(407)263-3502 BBS
Manufactures a line of tape-backup
products.

McAfee Associates

2710 Walsh Avenue, Suite 200
Santa Clara, CA 95051-0963
(408)988-3832
(408)988-4044 BBS
Manufactures the SCAN virus-scanning
software, which is nonresident and
updated frequently to handle new
viruses as they are discovered.

McGraw-Hill, Inc.

1311 Monterey Lane
Blue Ridge Summit, PA 17294
(800)822-8158 or
(800)233-1128
Publishes technical information and
books.

McTronic Systems

7426 Cornwall Bridge Lane
Houston, TX 77041-1709
(713)462-7687
Manufactures the excellent Port Finder
serial and parallel port diagnostic and
utility program. This is a shareware
utility available direct from them as
well as through downloading from the
IBMHW forum on CompuServe.

Megahertz Corporation

4505 S. Wasatch Boulevard
Salt Lake City, UT 84124
(801)272-6000
(800)527-8677
Manufactures laptop modems and
external network adapters. Also makes
AT-speedup products.

Memorex Computer Supplies

1200 Memorex Drive
Santa Clara, CA 95050
(408)957-1000
Manufactures a line of computer diskette media, tape cartridges, and various other supplies.

Mentor Electronics, Inc.

7560 Tylor Boulevard
#E
Mentor, OH 44060
(216)951-1884
Supplies surplus IBM PC (10/27/82)
ROM BIOS update chips.

Merisel

200 Continental Boulevard
El Segundo, CA 90245
(310)615-3080
(800)645-7778
A large distributor of PC hardware and
software products from many manufacturers.

Meritec

1359 West Jackson Street
P.O. Box 8003
Painesville, OH 44077
(216)354-3148
(216)354-0509 FAX
Manufactures a line of SCSI 8-bit to 16-
bit (Wide SCSI) adapters in a variety of
configurations. These adapters allow
Wide SCSI devices to be installed in a
standard 8-bit SCSI bus and vice versa.

Merritt Computer Products, Inc.

5565 Red Bird Center Drive
#150
Dallas, TX 75237
(214)339-0753
Manufactures the SafeSkin keyboard
protector.

Methode Electronics, Inc.

DataMate Division
7444 W. Wilson Ave.
Chicago, IL 60656
(708)867-9600
(708)867-3149 FAX
Manufactures and sells a complete line
of SCSI terminators.

Micro 2000, Inc.

1100 E. Broadway
Third Floor
Glendale, CA 91205
(818)547-0125

Manufactures the MicroScope PC diagnostics program, as well as the POSTProbe ISA, EISA, and MCA POST diagnostics card. Is extending 25 percent discount to anyone who mentions this book when purchasing.

Micro Accessories, Inc.

6086 Stewart Avenue
Fremont, CA 94538
(408)441-1242
(800)777-6687
Manufactures a variety of cables and disk drive mounting brackets and accessories, including PS/2 adapter kits.

Micro Channel Developers Association

2 Greenwich Plaza
#100
Greenwich, CT 06830
(203)622-7614
An independent organization that facilitates evolution of the Micro Channel Architecture.

Micro Computer Cable Company, Inc.

12200 Delta Drive
Taylor, MI 48180
(313)946-9700
(313)946-9645 FAX
Manufactures and sells a complete line of computer cables, and cabling accessories.

Micro Design International

6985 University Boulevard
Winter Park, FL 32792
(407)677-8333
(800)228-0891
Manufactures the SCSI Express driver software for integration of SCSI peripherals in a variety of environments.

Micro House International

4900 Pearl East Circle
Suite 101
Boulder, CO 80301
(303)443-3389
(800)926-8299
(303)443-3323 FAX
(303)443-9957 BBS
Publishes the *Encyclopedia of Hard Disks*, an excellent reference book that shows hard disk drive and controller jumper settings.

Micro Solutions, Inc.

132 W. Lincoln Hwy.
DeKalb, IL 60115
(815)756-3411
(815)756-9100 BBS
Manufactures a complete line of floppy controllers and subsystems including 2.88M versions. Also offers floppy drive and tape-backup systems that run from a standard parallel port, using no expansion slots.

Microcom, Inc.

500 River Ridge Drive
Norwood, MA 02062
(617)551-1000
(800)822-8224
Manufactures error-correcting modems, and develops the MNP communications protocols.

MicroComputer Accessories, Inc.

5405 Jandy Place
Los Angeles, CA 90066
(213)301-9400
Manufactures a variety of computer and office accessories.

Micrografx, Inc.

1303 E. Arapaho
Richardson, TX 75081
(214)994-6431
(800)733-3729 Sales department
Manufactures the Micrografx Designer,
Draw Plus, and Charisma software.
Specializes in Windows and OS/2
development.

Microid Research, Inc.

2336 Walsh Ave
Suite D
Santa Clara, CA 95051
(408)727-6991
(408)727-6996 FAX
Manufactures the MR BIOS, one of the
most flexible and configurable BIOS
versions available. They have versions
available for a variety of different chip
sets and motherboards.

Microlink/Micro Firmware, Inc.

Mailing Address:
330 West Gray St.
Suite 170
Norman, OK 73069-7111
(405)321-8333
(405)321-3553 BBS
The largest distributor of Phoenix ROM
BIOS upgrades. Develops custom versions for specific motherboards and
supplies many other BIOS vendors with
products.

Micron Technologies

2805 E. Columbia Road
Boise, ID 83706
(208)368-3900
(800)642-7661
(208)368-4530 BBS
Manufactures various memory chips,
SIMMs, and memory boards, as well as
a line of IBM-compatible systems.

Micronics Computers, Inc.

232 E. Warren Avenue
Fremont, CA 94539
(510)651-2300
(510)651-6837 BBS
Manufactures PC-compatible
motherboards and complete laptop
and portable systems. Micronics
motherboards feature the Phoenix
BIOS.

Micropolis Corporation

21211 Nordhoff Street
Chatsworth, CA 91311
(818)709-3300
(818)709-3310 BBS
Manufactures a line of high-capacity
5 1/4- and 3 1/2-inch hard disk drives.

Microprocessors Unlimited, Inc.

24000 S. Peoria Avenue
Beggs, OK 74421
(918)267-4961
Distributes memory chips, SIMMs,
math coprocessors, UART chips, and
other integrated circuits.

Microscience International Corporation

90 Headquarters Drive
San Jose, CA 95134
Manufactures hard disk drives.

Microsoft Corporation

One Microsoft Way
Redmond, WA 98052-6399
(206)882-8080
(800)426-9400 Consumer Sales Line
(206)936-6735 BBS
Manufactures MS-DOS, Windows, Windows NT, and a variety of applications
software.

MicroSystems Development (MSD)

4100 Moorpark Avenue
Suite 104
San Jose, CA 95117
(408)269-4000
(408)296-5877 FAX
(408)296-4200 BBS
Manufactures the Port Test serial and parallel diagnostics test kit and the Post Code Master POST diagnostics card.

MicroWay, Inc.

Mailing Address:
Research Park
Box 79
Kingston, MA 02364
(508)746-7341
Manufactures a line of accelerator products for IBM and compatible systems. Also specializes in math coprocessor chips, math chip accelerators, and language products.

Mitsubishi Electronics America, Inc.

565 Plaza Drive
P.O. Box 6007
Cypress, CA 90630
(714)220-2500
(800)843-2515
(213)324-3092 BBS
Manufactures monitors, printers, hard disks, and floppy disk storage products.

Motorola, Inc.

6501 William Cannon Drive West
Austin, TX 78735
(512)891-2000
Manufactures microprocessors, memory components, real-time clocks, controller chips, and so on.

Mountain Network Solutions, Inc.

360 El Pueblo Road
Scotts Valley, CA 95066
(408)438-6650
(800)458-0300
(408)438-2665 BBS
Manufactures tape drives and backup subsystems including hardware and software.

Mueller Technical Research

21718 Mayfield Lane
Barrington, IL 60010-9733
(708)726-0709
(708)726-0710 FAX
You found me! I run a service company that offers the best in PC hardware and software technical seminars and training, specializing in PC hardware and software troubleshooting and data recovery. My CompuServe ID is 73145,1566 (Scott Mueller).

Mustang Software

Mailing Address:
P.O. Box 2264
Bakersfield, CA 93303
Shipping Address:
915 17th Street
Bakersfield, CA 93303
(805)395-0223
(800)999-9619
(805)395-0650 BBS
Manufactures Wildcat! BBS software.

Mylex Corporation

34551 Ardenwood Boulevard
Fremont, CA 94555
(510)796-6100
(800)776-9539
Manufactures high-performance ISA and EISA motherboards and SCSI host adapters.

National Semiconductor Corporation

2900 Semiconductor Drive
Santa Clara, CA 95052
(408)721-5151
(408)245-0671 BBS
Manufactures a variety of chips for PC
circuit applications. Known especially
for its UART chips.

NCL America, Inc.

574 Weddell Drive
Suite #4
Sunnyvale, CA 94089
(408)734-1006
Manufactures high-performance SCSI
host adapters.

NCR (Computer Division)

1700 S. Patterson Boulevard
Dayton, OH 45479
(800)CALL-NCR (225-5627)
(201)769-6397 BBS
Manufactures a line of IBM-compatible
computer systems.

NCR Microelectronics

1635 Aeroplaza
Colorado Springs, CO 80916
(719)596-5795
(800)334-5454
(719)574-0424 BBS
Manufactures a variety of integrated
circuits for PC systems including SCSI
protocol chips used by many OEMs.
They also sponsor the SCSI BBS, an
excellent source for standard documents covering SCSI, IDE, and other
interfaces.

NEC Technologies, Inc.

1414 Massachusetts Avenue
Boxborough, MA 01719
(508)264-8000
(800)632-4636
(708)860-2602 BBS

Manufactures Multisync monitors, CD-
ROM drives, video adapters, printers,
and other peripherals as well as complete PC-compatible systems.

Northgate Computer Systems, Inc.

7075 Flying Cloud Drive
Eden Prairie, MN 55344
(800)548-1993
Manufactures PC-compatible systems
sold through mail order.

NovaStor Corporation

30961 Agoura Road
Suite 109
Westlake Village, CA 91361
(818)707-9900
(818)707-9902 FAX
Manufactures the Novaback tape
backup software for SCSI Tape drives.
Supports 8mm, 4mm (DAT), 1/4 inch
cartridge (QIC), IBM 3480, and 9-track
tape drives.

Novell, Inc.

122 E. 1700 South
Provo, UT 84601
(801)429-7000
(800)526-7937
(800)NET-WARE (638-9273)
(801)429-3030 BBS
Manufactures the NetWare LAN operating system.

Okidata

532 Fellowship Road
Mount Laurel, NJ 08054
(609)235-2600
(800)654-3282
(800)283-5474 BBS (dealers only)
(609)234-5344 BBS (customers)
(609)778-4184 FAX
(609)273-0300 Technical Support
Manufactures printers and modems.

Olivetti

765 US Hwy. 202
Somerville, NJ 08807
(908)526-8200
(800)527-2960
(908)526-8405 FAX
(800)222-2310 Technical Support
Manufactures Olivetti and many AT&T
PC systems.

Ontrack Computer Systems, Inc.

6321 Bury Drive
Suites #15-19
Eden Prairie, MN 55346
(612)937-1107
(800)752-1333
(612)937-2121 Technical Support
(612)937-5161 Ontrack Data Recovery
(800)872-2599 Ontrack Data Recovery
(612)937-5750 FAX
(612)937-0860 BBS (2400bps)
(612)937-8567 BBS (9600+bps)
Manufactures the Disk Manager
hard disk utilities for PC, PS/2, and
Macintosh. Disk Manager is the most
comprehensive and flexible low level
format program available, supporting
even IDE drives. Also provides extensive data recovery services.

Orchid Technology

45365 Northport Loop West
Fremont, CA 94538
(510)683-0300
(800)767-2443
(510)683-0329 BBS
Manufactures a line of video and
memory board products for IBM and
compatible systems.

Osborne/McGraw Hill

2600 10th Street
Berkeley, CA 94710
(415)549-6618
(800)227-0900
Publishes computer books.

Pacific Data Products

9125 Rehco Road
San Diego, CA 92121
(619)552-0880
(619)452-6329 BBS
Manufactures the Pacific Page XL and
PacificPage PE Postscript-compatible
enhancement products for HP LaserJet
printers.

Pacific Magtron, Inc.

568-8 Weddell Drive
Sunnyvale, CA 94089
(408)774-1188
Manufactures hard disk drives.

Packard Bell

9425 Canoga Avenue
Chatsworth, CA 91311
(818)886-4600
(800)733-4411 Hardware Technical
Support
(818)773-7207 BBS
Manufactures an excellent line of low-
cost PC-compatible computer systems.

Panasonic Communications & Systems

2 Panasonic Way
Secaucus, NJ 07094
(201)348-7000
(201)863-7845 BBS
(800)545-2672 Authorized dealers
(800)332-5368 Accessories
(800)922-0028 Phone Assistance
(800)435-7329 FAX
(800)225-5329 FAX
Manufactures monitors, optical drive
products, floppy drives, printers, and
PC-compatible laptop systems.

Parts Now, Inc.
810 Stewart Street
Madison, WI 53713
(608)276-8688
(800)886-6688
Sells a large variety of laser printer parts
for HP, Canon, Apple, and other laser
printers using Canon engines.

PC Connection
6 Mill Street
Marlow, NH 03456
(603)446-7721
(800)800-5555
Distributes many different hardware
and software packages by way of mail
order.

PC Magazine
One Park Avenue
Fourth Floor
New York, NY 10016
(212)503-5446
(212)503-5921
(212)503-5116
Magazine featuring product reviews
and comparisons.

**PCMCIA — Personal Computer
Memory Card International
Association**
1030G East Duane Avenue
Sunnyvale, CA 94086
(408)720-0107
An independent organization that
maintains the PCMCIA bus standard
for credit card sized expansion adapters.

PC Power & Cooling, Inc.
5995 Avenida Encinas
Carlsbad, CA 92008
(619)931-5700
(800)722-6555
(619)931-6988

Manufactures a line of high-quality,
high-output power supplies for IBM
and compatible systems.

PC Repair Corporation
2010 State Street
Harrisburg, PA 17103
(717)232-7272
(800)727-3724
Service company and parts distributor
that performs board repair of IBM PCs
and PS/2s, printers, and typewriters as
well as COMPAQ systems repair. Also
offers an extensive parts line for these
systems.

PC *Week* Magazine
10 Presidents Landing
Medford, MA 02155
(617)393-3000
Weekly magazine featuring industry
news and information.

PC *World* Magazine
375 Chochituate Road
Framingham, MA 01701
(508)879-0700
(800)435-7766
A monthly magazine featuring product
reviews and comparisons.

PC-Kwik Corporation
15100 S.W. Koll Parkway
Suite P
Beaverton, OR 97006-6026
(503)644-5644
(800)759-5945
(503)646-8267 FAX
Formerly Multisoft, they manufacture
the PC-Kwik Power Pak system performance utilities, Super PC-Kwik disk
cache, and WinMaster Windows utility
programs.

PC-SIG/Spectra Publishing

1030 E. Duane Avenue
#D
Sunnyvale, CA 94086
(408)730-9291
(800)245-6717
Publishes public-domain software and
shareware available on CD-ROM.

PCI Special Interest Group

P.O. Box 14070
Portland, OR 97214
(503)696-2000
(800)433-5177 Order Revisions
(503)693-0920 FAX
An independent group that owns and
manages the PCI (Peripheral Component Interconnect) Local Bus architecture.

Philips Consumer Electronics

One Philips Drive
Knoxville, TN 37914
(615)521-4366
Manufactures Magnavox PCs, monitors, and CD-ROM drives.

Phoenix Technologies, Ltd.

846 University Avenue
Norwood, MA 02062
(617)551-4000
Manufactures IBM-compatible BIOS
software for a number of ISA, EISA, and
MCA systems.

Pivar Computing Services, Inc.

165 Arlington Heights Road
Buffalo Grove, IL 60089
(708)459-6010
(800)266-8378
Service company that specializes in
data and media conversion.

PKWare, Inc.

9025 N. Deerwood Drive
Brown Deer, WI 53223
(414)354-8699
(414)354-8559 FAX
(414)354-8670 BBS
Manufactures the PKZIP, PKUNZIP,
PKLite, and PKZMENU data compression software. Widely used on BBS
systems and by manufacturers for software distribution.

Priam Systems Corporation

1140 Ringwood Court
San Jose, CA 95131
(408)263-9994
(408)434-1646 BBS
Provides service and repair for Priam
drives; original Priam has gone out of
business.

Processor Magazine

P.O. Box 85518
Lincoln, NE 68501
(800)247-4880
Publication that offers excellent
sources of replacement and repair parts
as well as new equipment at wholesale
prices.

Programmers Shop

90 Industrial Park Road
Hingham, MA 02043
(617)740-2510
(800)421-8006
Distributes programming tools and
utility software.

PTI Industries

269 Mount Hermon Road
Scott Valley, CA 95066
Manufactures a line of computer
power-protection devices.

Public Brand Software

P.O. Box 51315
Indianapolis, IN 46251
(317)856-7571
(800)426-3475
Publishes a public domain and
shareware library.

Public Software Library

P.O. Box 35705-F
Houston, TX 77235
(713)524-6394
(800)242-4775
Top-notch distributor of high-quality
public domain and shareware software.

Quaid Software Limited

45 Charles Street East
Third Floor
Toronto, ON, M4Y1S2,
(519)942-0832
Manufactures the Quaid Copywrite
disk copy program and other disk
utilities.

Qualitas, Inc.

7101 Wisconsin Avenue
#1386
Bethesda, MD 20814
(301)907-6700
(301)907-8030 BBS
Manufactures the 386Max and
BlueMax memory-manager utility
programs.

Quantum Corporation

500 McCarthy Boulevard
Milpitas, CA 95035
(408)894-4000
(408)434-1664 BBS
(800)624-5545 Sales
(800)826-8022 Technical Support
(800)894-3282 FAX
(800)894-3214 BBS

Manufactures a line of 3 1/2-inch hard
disk drives, and the Plus Hardcard line.
Supplies drives to Apple Computer.

Quarter-Inch Cartridge Drive Standards, Inc. (QIC)

311 East Carrillo Street
Santa Barbara, CA 93101
(805)963-3853
(805)962-1541 FAX
An independent industry group that
sets and maintains Quarter Inch Cartridge (QIC) tape drive standards for
backup and archiving purposes.

Quarterdeck Office Systems

150 Pico Boulevard
Santa Monica, CA 90405
(213)392-9851
(213)396-3904 BBS
Manufactures the popular DESQview,
QEMM, and QRAM memory-manager
products.

Que Corporation

201 West 103rd Street
Indianapolis, IN 46290
(317)581-3500
(800)428-5331 Order Line
(800)448-3804 Sales FAX
Publishes the highest-quality computer
applications software and hardware
books in the industry, including this
one!

Qume Peripherals, Inc.

2605 Malpitas Boulevard
Milpitas, CA 95035
(408)942-4000
Manufactures a variety of peripherals
including displays, printers, and
printer supplies such as toner cartridges. Qume owns DTC, a disk controller manufacturer.

Radio Shack

Division of Tandy Corporation
1800 One Tandy Center
Fort Worth, TX 76102
(817)390-3011
(817)390-2774 FAX
Sells numerous electronic devices, parts and supplies, and manufactures a line of PC-compatible computers and accessories.

Rancho Technology, Inc.

Mailing Address:
P.O. Box 923
Rancho Cucamonga, CA 91730
Shipping Address:
10783 Bell Court
Rancho Cucamonga, CA 91730
(714)987-3966
Manufactures an extensive line of SCSI products including host adapters for ISA, EISA, and MCA bus systems, SCSI extenders, and interface software.

Renasonce Group, Inc.

5173 Waring Road
Suite 115
San Diego, CA 92120
(619)287-3348
(619)287-3554 FAX
Manufactures the excellent InfoSpotter system inspection and diagnostics program, as well as RemoteRX and the Skylight Windows troubleshooting program.

Reply Corporation

4435 Fortran Drive
San Jose, CA 95134
(408)942-4804
(800)955-5295
(408)942-4897 FAX
Designs and sells an exclusive line of complete 386 and 486 motherboard upgrades for IBM PS/2 systems, with integrated local bus SVGA adapters, Pentium Overdrive support, 2.88M floppy controller, Flash BIOS, built-in ATA IDE adapter, support for up to 32M of motherboard memory, and numerous other features. These upgrade boards are actually manufactured for Reply by IBM, and are fully IBM compatible.

Rotating Memory Repair, Inc.

23382-J Madero Road
Mission Viejo, CA 92691
(714)472-0159
Repair company that specializes in hard drive and floppy drive repair. Also repairs power supplies and displays.

Rotating Memory Services

5075 Hilldale
Suite C
El Dorado Hills, CA 95762
(916)939-7500
Repair company that specializes in hard disk drives.

Rupp Corporation

7285 Franklin Avenue
Los Angeles, CA 90046
(213)850-5394
Manufactures the FastLynx program, which performs system-to-system transfers over serial or parallel ports.

Safeware Insurance Agency, Inc.

2929 N. High Street
Columbus, OH 43202
(614)262-0559
(800)848-3469
Insurance company that specializes in insurance for computer equipment.

SAMS

201 West 103rd Street
Indianapolis, IN 46290
(317)581-3500
Publishes technical books on computers and electronic equipment.

Seagate Technology

920 Disc Drive
Scotts Valley, CA 95067
(408)438-6550
(408)429-6356 FAX
(408)438-8111 Sales
(800)468-3472 Service
(405)491-6260 Service
(405)491-6261 Service FAX
(408)438-2620 FAXback Information
Line
(408)438-8771 BBS
The largest hard disk manufacturer in
the world. Offers the most extensive
product line of any disk manufacturer,
ranging from low-cost units to the
highest-performance, capacity, and
quality drives available.

Service News **Magazine**

United Publications Inc.
38 Lafayette St.
P.O. Box 995
Yarmouth, ME 04096
(207)846-0600
(207)846-0657 FAX
An excellent monthly newspaper for
computer service and support person-
nel featuring articles covering PC service and repair products.

SGS-Thomson Microelectronics/Inmos

1000 E. Bell Road
Phoenix, AZ 85022
(602)867-6100
Manufactures custom chipsets, and has
been licensed by IBM to produce IBM-
designed XGA chipsets for ISA, EISA,
and MCA bus systems.

Sharp Electronics Corporation

Sharp Plaza
Mahwah, NJ 07430-2135
(201)529-8200
(201)529-8731 Sales Hotline
(201)529-9636 FAX

Manufactures a wide variety of electronic and computer equipment including the best LCD monochrome
and Active Matrix color displays and
panels, as well as scanners, printers,
and complete laptop and notebook
systems.

Shugart Corporation

9292 Jeronimo Road
Building #103
Irvine, CA 92714
(714)770-1100
Manufactures hard disk, floppy disk,
and tape drives.

Sigma Data

Scytheville Row
P.O. Box 1790
New London, NH 03257
(603)526-6909
(800)446-4525
(603)526-6915 FAX
Distributes a complete line of SIMM
memory modules, hard drive, and
processor upgrades. They are the
sole distributor of a unique line of
"Hyperace" direct processor upgrades
for 286- and 386-based IBM PS/2 systems. They also have a line of ATA IDE
adapters and no slot hard disk upgrades
for IBM PS/2 systems as well.

Silicon Valley Computer

441 N Whisman Road
Building 13
Mountain View, CA 94043
(415)967-1100
(415)967-0770 FAX
(415)967-8081 BBS
Manufactures a complete line of IDE
interface adapters, including a unique
model that supports 16-bit IDE (ATA)
drives on PC and XT systems (8-bit ISA
bus) and models including floppy drive
support as well as serial and parallel
ports.

SMS Technology, Inc.

550 E. Brokaw Road
Box 49048
San Jose, CA 95161-9048
(408)954-1633
(510)964-5700 BBS
Manufactures the OMTi disk control-
lers, formerly known as Scientific
Micro Systems.

SofTouch Systems, Inc.

1300 S. Meridian
Suite 600
Oklahoma city, OK 73108-1751
(405)947-8080
(405)632-6537 FAX
Manufactures the GammaTech Utilities
for OS/2, which can undelete and recover files running under OS/2 even on
an OS/2 HPFS partition.

Sola Electric

1717 Busse Road
Elk Grove, IL 60007
(708)439-2800
(800)289-7652
Manufactures a line of computer
power-protection devices.

Sonera Technologies

P.O. Box 565
Rumson, NJ 07760
(908)747-6886
(800)932-6323
(908)747-4523 FAX
Manufactures the DisplayMate video
display utility and diagnostic program.
Displaymate exercises, troubleshoots,
and diagnoses video display adapter
and monitor problems.

Sony Corporation of America

1 Sony Drive
Park Ridge, NJ 07656-8003
(201)930-1000

Manufactures all types of high-quality
electronic and computer equipment
including displays and magnetic- and
optical-storage devices.

Specialized Products Company

3131 Premier Drive
Irving, TX 75063
(214)550-1923
(800)527-5018
Distributes a variety of tools and test
equipment.

Sprague Magnetics, Inc.

15720 Stagg Street
Van Nuys, CA 91406
(818)994-6602
(800)553-8712
Manufactures a unique and interesting
magnetic developer fluid that can be
used to view sectors and tracks on a
magnetic disk or tape. Also repairs tape
drives.

Stac Electronics

5993 Avenida Encinas
Carlsbad, CA 92008
(619)431-7474
(800)522-7822
(619)431-5956 BBS
Manufactures the Stacker real-time
data-compression adapter and software
for OS/2 and DOS.

Standard Microsystems Corporation

35 Marcus Boulevard
Hauppauge, NY 11788
Mailing Address:
80 Arkay Drive
Hauppauge, NY 11788
(516)273-3100
(800)992-4762
Manufactures ARCnet and EtherNet
network adapters.

Star Micronics America, Inc.

420 Lexington Avenue
Suite 2702
New York, NY 10170
(212)986-6770
(800)447-4700
Manufactures a line of low-cost
printers.

STB Systems, Inc.

1651 N. Glenville
Suite #210
Richardson, TX 75081
(214)234-8750
(214)437-9615 BBS
Manufactures various adapter boards,
and specializes in a line of high-
resolution VGA video adapters.

Storage Dimensions, Inc.

1656 McCarthy
Milpitas, CA 95035
(408)954-0710
(800)765-7895
(408)944-1220 BBS
Distributes Maxtor hard disk and optical drives as complete subsystems. Also
manufactures the Speedstor hard disk
utility software.

Symantec Corporation

10201 Torre Avenue
Cupertino, CA 95014
(408)253-9600
(800)441-7234 Customer service
(408)973-9598 BBS
Manufactures a line of utility and applications software featuring the Norton
Utilities for IBM and Apple systems.

SyQuest Technology

47071 Bayside Parkway
Fremont, CA 94538
(415)226-4000
(800)245-2278
(415)656-0470 BBS

Manufactures removable-cartridge hard
disk drives.

Sysgen, Inc.

556 Gibraltar Drive
Milpitas, CA 95035
(408)263-4411
(800)821-2151
(408)946-5032 BBS
Manufactures a line of tape-backup
storage devices.

Sytron

134 Flanders Road
P.O. Box 5025
Westboro, MA 01581-5025
(508)898-0100
(800)877-0016
(508)898-2677 FAX
Manufactures the SyTOS tape-backup
software for DOS and OS/2, the most
widely used tape software in the
industry.

Tadiran

2975 Bowers Avenue
#203
Santa Clara, CA 95051
(408)727-0300
Manufactures a variety of batteries for
computer applications.

Tandon Corporation

405 Science Drive
Moorpark, CA 93021
(805)523-0340
Manufactures IBM-compatible computer systems and disk drives. Supplied
to IBM most of the full-height floppy
drives used in the original PC and XT
systems.

Tandy Corporation/Radio Shack

1800 One Tandy Center
Fort Worth, TX 76102
(817)390-3700
(817)390-3011
Manufactures a line of IBM-compatible
systems, peripherals, and accessories.
Also distributes electronic parts and
supplies.

Tatung Company of America, Inc.

2850 El Presidio Street
Long Beach, CA 90810
(213)979-7055
(800)827-2850
Manufactures monitors and complete
compatible systems.

TCE Company

35 Fountain Square Plaza
5th Floor, Suite 500
Elgin, IL 60120
(708)741-7200
(800)383-8001
(708)741-1801 FAX
Manufactures an IDE drive formatter
specifically for Conner Peripherals
drives called "The Conner," consisting
of a special hardware connector that
plugs into the diagnostic port on
Conner IDE drives, as well as special
software to format the drive. They also
specialize in power supply and power
line monitoring and test equipment,
and make one of the best PC power
supply test machines available.

TDK Electronics Corporation

12 Harbor Park Drive
Port Washington, NY 11050
(516)625-0100
Manufactures a line of magnetic and
optical media including disk and tape
cartridges.

Teac America, Inc.

7733 Telegraph Road
Montebello, CA 90640
(213)726-0303
Manufactures a line of floppy and tape
drives, including a unit that combines
both 3 1/2-inch and 5 1/4-inch drives
in one half-height package.

Tech Data Corporation

5350 Tech Data Drive
Clearwater, FL 34620
(813)539-7429
(800)237-8931
Distributes computer equipment and
supplies.

Tech Spray Inc.

88 N. Hughs
P.O. Box 949
Amarillo, TX 79102
(806)372-8523
Manufactures a complete line of computer and electronic cleaning chemicals and products.

Tecmar, Inc.

6225 Cochran Road
Solon, OH 44139
(216)349-0600
(800)344-4463
(216)349-0853 BBS
Manufactures a variety of adapter
boards for IBM and compatible
systems.

Thermalloy Inc.

2021 W. Valley View Lane
P.O. Box 810839
Dallas, TX 75381-0839
(214)243-4321
(214)241-4656 FAX
Manufactures a line of excellent CPU
heat sink products including versions
with built-in fan modules.

Toshiba America, Inc.

9740 Irvine Boulevard
Irvine, CA 92718
(714)583-3000
(800)999-4823
(714)837-2116 BBS
Manufactures a complete line of 5 1/4-
and 3 1/2-inch floppy and hard disk
drives, CD-ROM drives, display products, printers, and a popular line of
laptop and notebook IBM-compatible
systems.

TouchStone Software Corporation

2130 Main Street
Suite 250
Huntington Beach, CA 92648
(714)969-7746
(800)531-0450
(714)960-1886 FAX
Manufactures the CheckIt user level
and CheckIt Pro Deluxe high-end PC
diagnostics and troubleshooting
programs.

Trantor Systems, Ltd.

5415 Randall Place
Fremont, CA 94538
(510)770-1400
(415)656-5159 BBS
Manufactures the MiniSCSI and
MiniSCSI Plus Parallel Port SCSI adapters, including hard disk and CD-ROM
drivers for a variety of devices.

Traveling Software, Inc.

18702 N. Creek Parkway
Bothell, WA 98011
(206)483-8088
(800)662-2652
Manufactures the LapLink file-transfer
program for PC and Mac systems as
well as several other utility programs.

Tripp Lite Manufacturing

500 N. Orleans
Chicago, IL 60610
(312)329-1777
Manufactures a complete line of computer power-protection devices.

Tseng Labs, Inc.

6 Terry Drive
Newtown Commons
Newtown, PA 18940
(215)968-0502
Manufactures video controller chipsets,
BIOS, and board design for OEMs.

U.S. Robotics, Inc.

8100 N. McCormick Boulevard
Skokie, IL 60076
(708)982-5010
(800)982-5151
(708)982-5092 BBS
Manufactures a complete line of modems and communications products.
Its modems support more protocols
than most others, including V.32bis,
HST, and MNP protocols.

Ultra-X, Inc.

2005 De La Cruz Boulevard
Suite 115
San Jose, CA 95050 or
P.O. Box 730010
San Jose, CA 95173-0010
(408)988-4721
(800)722-3789
(408)988-4849 FAX
Manufactures the excellent QuickPost
PC, QuickPost PS/2, and Racer II diagnostic cards, as well as the Quicktech
and Diagnostic Reference software
packages. The Racer II is one of the
most complete troubleshooting hardware cards on the market today.

Ultrastor Corporation

15 Hammond Street
#310
Irvine, CA 92718
(714)581-4100
Manufactures a complete line of high-performance ESDI, SCSI, and IDE disk controllers for ISA and EISA bus systems.

UNISYS

Township Line and Union Meeting Roads
Blue Bell, PA 19424
(215)986-4011
(800)448-1424
(800)328-0440 Technical Support
Manufactures PC-compatible systems that are part of the government Desktop IV contract.

Universal Memory Products

1378 Logan Avenue #F
Costa Mesa, CA 92626
Distributes memory components including chip and SIMM modules.

Upgrades Etc.

1445 Donlon Street
Suite #9
Ventura, CA 93003
(800)541-1943
Distributes AMI, Award, and Phoenix BIOS upgrades.

V Communications, Inc.

4320 Stevens Creek Boulevard
#275
San Jose, CA 95129
(408)296-4224
Manufactures the Sourcer disassembler and other programming tools.

Varta Batteries, Inc.

300 Executive Boulevard
Elmsford, NY 10523
(914)592-2500
Manufactures a complete line of computer batteries.

Verbatim Corporation

1200 WT Harris Boulevard
Charlotte, NC 28262
(704)547-6500
Manufactures a line of storage media including optical and magnetic disks and tapes.

VESA - Video Electronic Standards Association

2150 North First St.
Suite 440
San Jose, CA 95131-2029
(408)435-0333
(408)435-8225 FAX
An organization of manufacturers dedicated to setting and maintaining video display, adapter and bus standards.

Visiflex Seels

16 E. Lafayette Street
Hackensack, NJ 07601
(201)487-8080
Manufactures form-fitting clear keyboard covers and other computer accessories.

VLSI Technology, Inc.

8375 S. River Parkway
Tempe, AZ 85284
(602)752-8574
Manufactures chipsets and circuits for PC-compatible motherboards and adapters. IBM uses these chipsets in some of the PS/2 system designs.

Volpe, Hank

P.O. Box 43214
Baltimore, MD 21236
(410)256-5767
(410)256-3631 BBS
Manufactures the Modem Doctor serial
port and modem diagnostics program.

Walling Company

4401 S. Juniper
Tempe, AZ 85282
(602)838-1277
(800)338-9813
Manufactures the DataRase EPROM
eraser, which can erase as many as four
EPROM chips simultaneously using
ultraviolet light.

Wang Laboratories, Inc.

One Industrial Avenue
Lowell, MA 01851
(800)225-0654
Manufactures a variety of PC-compatible systems including some with MCA
bus slots.

Wangtek, Inc.

41 Moreland Road
Simi Valley, CA 93065
(805)582-3300
(800)992-9916
(805)582-3370 BBS
Manufactures a complete line of tape-
backup drives including QIC, DAT, and
8mm drives for ISA, EISA, and MCA
bus systems.

S.L. Waper Inc.

1160 W. Industrial Park Drive
Nogales, AZ 85621
(602)761-1028
(800)638-9098
Manufactures a line of computer
power-protection devices.

Warshawski/Whitney & Co.

1916 S. State Street
Chicago, IL 60680
(312)431-6100
Distributes an enormous collection of
bargain-priced tools and equipment. Its
products are primarily for automotive
applications, but many of the tools
have universal uses.

Washburn & Co.

3800 Monroe Avenue
Pittsford, NY 14534
(716)248-3627
(800)836-8026
The largest distributor of AMI BIOS and
AMI motherboard products, known for
providing very high end technical
information and support.

Watergate Software

2000 Powell Street
Suite 1200
Emeryville, CA 94608
(510)596-1770
(510)653-4784 FAX
Manufactures the excellent PC Doctor
diagnostic program for PC troubleshooting and repair.

Wave Mate Inc.

22750 Hawthorne Boulevard
Suite 207
Torrance, CA 90501
(310)791-2860
Manufactures a line of high-speed replacement motherboards for IBM and
compatible systems.

Wavetech Instruments

9145 Balboa Street or
9045 Balboa Avenue (Mailing Address)
or
P.O. Box 85434
San Diego, CA 92123

(619)495-3200
(800)854-2708
Manufactures diagnostics and test equipment.

Weitek Corporation
1060 E. Arques
Sunnyvale, CA 94086
(408)738-8400
Manufactures high-performance math coprocessor chips.

Western Digital Corporation
8105 Irvine Center Drive
Irvine, CA 92718
(714)932-5000
(800)832-4778
(714)753-1234 BBS (2400bps)
(714)753-1068 BBS (9600+bps)
Manufactures many products including IDE and SCSI hard drives; SCSI and ESDI adapters for ISA, EISA, and MCA bus systems; and EtherNet, Token Ring, and Paradise video adapters. Supplies IBM with IDE and SCSI drives for PS/2 systems.

Windsor Technologies, Inc.
130 Alto Street
San Rafael, CA 94901
(415)456-2200
(415)456-2244 FAX
Manufactures PC Technician, an excellent high end technician level PC diagnostics and troubleshooting program.

WordPerfect Corporation
1555 N. Technology Way
Orem, UT 84057-2399
(801)225-5000
(800)451-5151
(801)225-4414 BBS
Manufactures the popular WordPerfect word processing program.

WordStar International, Inc.
201 Alameda del Prado
Novato, CA 94949
(415)382-8000
(800)227-5609
Manufactures the WordStar and WordStar 2000 programs.

Wyse Technology
3471 N. 1st Street
San Jose, CA 95134
(408)473-1200
(800)438-9973
(408)922-4400 BBS
Manufactures PC-compatible systems and terminals.

Xebec
3579 Gordon
Carson City, NV 89701
(702)883-4000
(702)883-9264 BBS
Manufactures ISA disk controllers originally used by IBM in the XT.

Xerox Corporation
Xerox Square
Rochester, NY 14644
(716)423-5078
Manufactures the Ventura desktop publishing software as well as an extensive line of computer equipment, copiers, and printers.

Xidex Corporation
5100 Patrick Henry Drive
Santa Clara, CA 95050
(408)970-6574
Manufactures disk and tape media.

Xircom

26025 Mureau Road
Calbasas, CA 91302
(818)878-7600
(800)874-7875
(818)878-7618 BBS
Manufactures external Token Ring and
EtherNet adapters that attach to a parallel port.

Y-E Data America, Inc.

5824 Peachtree Corners E.
Suite A
Norcross, GA 30092
(404)446-8655
Manufactures a line of floppy disk
drives, tape drives, and printers. Supplied 5 1/4-inch floppy drives to IBM
for use in XT, AT, and PS/2 systems.

Zenith Data Systems

2150 E. Lake Cook Road
Buffalo Grove, IL 60089
(708)508-5000
(800)553-0331
Manufactures a line of IBM-compatible
systems.

Zeos International, Ltd.

1301 Industrial Boulevard
Minneapolis, MN 55413
(612)633-4591
(800)423-5891
Manufactures a line of good, low-cost
PC-compatible ISA and EISA bus systems sold by way of mail order.

Glossary

The glossary contains computer and electronics terms that are applicable to the subject matter in this book. The glossary is meant to be as comprehensive as possible on the subject of upgrading or repairing PCs. Many terms correspond to the latest technology in disk interfaces, modems, video and display equipment, and many standards that govern the PC industry. Although a glossary is a resource not designed to be read from beginning to end, you should find that scanning through this one is interesting, if not enlightening, with respect to some of the newer PC technology.

The computer industry is filled with acronyms used as shorthand for a number of terms. This glossary defines many acronyms, as well as the term on which the acronym is based. The definition of an acronym usually is included under the acronym. For example, Video Graphics Array is defined under the acronym VGA rather than under Video Graphics Array. This organization makes it easier to look up a term—IDE, for example—even if you do not know in advance what it stands for (integrated drive electronics).

For additional reference, *Que's Computer User's Dictionary* is a comprehensive, general-purpose computer dictionary of computer terminology.

80286

An Intel microprocessor with 16-bit registers, a 16-bit data bus, and a 24-bit address bus. Can operate in real and protected virtual modes.

80287

An Intel math coprocessor designed to perform floating-point math with much greater speed and precision than the main CPU. The 80287 can be installed in most 286- and some 386DX-based systems, and adds more than 50 new instructions to what is available in the primary CPU alone.

80386

See 80386DX.

80386DX

An Intel microprocessor with 32-bit registers, a 32-bit data bus, and a 32-bit address bus. This processor can operate in real, protected virtual, and virtual real modes.

80386SX

An Intel microprocessor with 32-bit registers, a 16-bit data bus, and a 24-bit address bus. This processor, designed as a low-cost version of the 386DX, can operate in real, protected virtual, and virtual real modes.

80387DX

An Intel math coprocessor designed to perform floating-point math with much greater speed and precision than the main CPU. The 80387DX can be installed in most 386DX-based systems, and adds more than 50 new instructions to what is available in the primary CPU alone.

80387SX

An Intel math coprocessor designed to perform floating-point math with much greater speed and precision than the main CPU. The 80387SX can be installed in most 386SX-based systems, and adds more than 50 new instructions to what is available in the primary CPU alone.

80486

See 80486DX.

80486DX

An Intel microprocessor with 32-bit registers, a 32-bit data bus, and a 32-bit address bus. The 486DX has a built-in cache controller with 8K of cache memory as well as a built-in math coprocessor equivalent to a 387DX. The 486DX can operate in real, protected virtual, and virtual real modes.

80486DX2

A version of the 486DX with an internal clock doubling circuit that causes the chip to run at twice the motherboard clock speed. If the motherboard clock is 33MHz, then the DX2 chip will run at 66MHz. The DX2 designation applies to chips sold through the OEM market, while a retail version of the DX2 is sold as an Overdrive processor.

80486SX

An Intel microprocessor with 32-bit registers, a 32-bit data bus, and a 32-bit address bus. The 486SX is the same as the 486DX except that it lacks the built-in math coprocessor function, and was designed as a low-cost version of the 486DX. The 486SX can operate in real, protected virtual, and virtual real modes.

80487SX

An Intel microprocessor with 32-bit registers, a 32-bit data bus, and a 32-bit address bus. The 487SX has a built-in cache controller with 8K of cache memory as well as a built-in math coprocessor equivalent to a 387DX. The 486DX can operate in real, protected virtual, and virtual real modes. This processor is a complete processor and math coprocessor unit, not just a math coprocessor. The 487SX is designed to upgrade systems with the 486SX processor, which lacks the math coprocessor function. When a 487SX is installed in a system, it shuts down the 486SX and takes over the system. In effect, the 487SX is a full-blown 486DX modified to be installed as an upgrade for 486SX systems.

8086

An Intel microprocessor with 16-bit registers, a 16-bit data bus, and a 20-bit address bus. This processor can operate only in real mode.

8087

An Intel math coprocessor designed to perform floating-point math with much greater speed and precision than the main CPU. The 8087 can be installed in most 8086- and 8088-based systems, and adds more than 50 new instructions to what is available in the primary CPU alone.

8088

An Intel microprocessor with 16-bit registers, an 8-bit data bus, and a 20-bit address bus. This processor can operate only in real mode, and was designed as a low-cost version of the 8086.

8514/A

An analog video display adapter from IBM for the PS/2 line of personal computers. Compared to previous display adapters such as EGA and VGA, it provides a high resolution of 1024x768 pixels with as many as 256 colors or 64 shades of gray. It provides a video coprocessor that performs two-dimensional graphics functions internally, thus relieving the CPU of graphics tasks. It is an interlaced monitor: It scans every other line every time the screen is refreshed.

abend

Short for *abnormal end*. Used when the execution of a program or task is terminated unexpectedly because of a bug or crash.

AC

Alternating current. The frequency is measured in cycles per seconds (cps), or hertz. The standard value running through the wall outlet is 120 volts at 60 Hertz, through a fuse or circuit breaker that usually can handle about 20 amps.

accelerator board

An add-in board replacing the computer's CPU with circuitry that enables the system to run faster.

access time

The time that elapses from the instant information is requested to the point that delivery is completed. Usually described in nanoseconds for memory chips. The IBM PC requires memory chips with an access time of 200 nano-seconds, and the AT requires 150-nanosecond chips. For hard disk drives, access time is described in milliseconds. Most manufacturers rate average access time on a hard disk as the time required for a seek across one-third of the total number of cylinders plus one-half of the time for a single revolution of the disk platters (latency).

accumulator

A register (temporary storage) in which the result of an operation is formed.

acronym

An acronym is a word or group of letters formed from the first or first few letters of a series of words. For example, CPU is an acronym for Central Processing Unit. This glossary contains definitions for many acronyms popular in the personal computer industry.

active high

Designates a digital signal that has to go to a high value to produce an effect. Synonymous with positive true.

active low

Designates a digital signal that has to go to a low value to produce an effect. Synonymous with negative true.

actuator

The device that moves a disk drive's read/write heads across the platter surfaces. Also known as an access mechanism.

adapter

The device that serves as an interface between the system unit and the devices attached to it. Used by IBM to be synonymous with circuit board, circuit card, or card.

address

Refers to where a particular piece of data or other information is found in the computer. Also can refer to the location of a set of instructions.

address bus

One or more electrical conductors used to carry the binary-coded address from the microprocessor throughout the rest of the system.

alphanumeric characters

A character set that contains only letters (A-Z) and digits (0-9). Other characters, such as punctuation marks, also may be allowed.

ampere

The basic unit for measuring electrical current. Also called amp.

analog loopback

A modem self-test in which data from the keyboard is sent to the modem's transmitter, modulated into analog form, looped back to the receiver, demodulated into digital form, and returned to the screen for verification.

analog signals

Continuously variable signals in which the slightest change may be significant. Analog circuits are more subject to distortion and noise but are capable of handling complex signals with relatively simple circuitry. An alternative to analog is digital, in which signals are in only one of two states.

AND

A logic operator having the property that if P is a statement, Q is a statement, R is a statement,..., then the AND of P,Q,R,... is true if all statements are true and is false if any statement is false.

AND gate

A logic gate in which the output is 1 only if all inputs are 1.

ANSI

Acronym for American National Standards Institute, a nongovernmental organization founded in 1918 to propose, modify, approve, and publish data processing standards for voluntary use in the United States. Also the U.S. representative to the International Standards Organization (ISO) in Paris and the International Electrotechnical Commission (IEC). For more information, contact ANSI, 1430 Broadway, New York, NY 10018.

answer mode

A state in which the modem transmits at the predefined high frequency of the communications channel and receives at the low frequency. The transmit/receive frequencies are the reverse of the calling modem, which is in originate mode.

APA

All points addressable. A mode in which all points of a displayable image can be controlled by the user or a program.

API

An acronym for application program interface. A system call (routine) that gives programmers access to the services provided by the operating system. In IBM-compatible systems, the ROM BIOS and DOS together present an API that a programmer can use to control the system hardware.

arbitration

A method by which multiple devices attached to a single bus can bid or arbitrate to get control of that bus.

archive bit

The bit in a file's attribute byte that sets the archive attribute. Tells whether the file has been changed since it last was backed up.

archive medium

A storage medium (floppy disk, tape cartridge, or removable cartridge) to hold files that need not be accessible instantly.

ARCnet

An acronym for *Attached Resource Computer Network*, a baseband, token-passing local area network technology offering a flexible bus/star topology for connecting personal computers. Operates at 2.5 megabits per second, is one of the oldest LAN systems, and has become popular in low-cost networks. Originally developed by John Murphy, of Datapoint Corporation, although ARCnet interface cards are available from a variety of vendors.

Areal Density

Areal Density is a calculation of the Bit Density (Bits Per Inch, or BPI) multiplied by the Track Density (Tracks Per Inch, or TPI), which results in a figure indicating how many bits per square inch are present on the disk surface.

ARQ

*A*utomatic *r*epeat *re*quest. A general term for error-control protocols that feature error detection and automatic retransmission of defective blocks of data.

ASCII

An acronym for American Standard Code for Information Interchange, a standard 7-bit code created in 1965 by Robert W. Bemer to achieve compatibility among various types of data processing equipment. The standard ASCII character set consists of 128 decimal numbers, ranging from 0 through 127, assigned to letters, numbers, punctuation marks, and the most common special characters. In 1981 IBM introduced the extended ASCII character set with the IBM PC, extending the code to eight bits and adding characters from 128 through 255 to represent additional special mathematical, graphics, and foreign characters.

ASCII character

A 1-byte character from the ASCII character set, including alphabetic and numeric characters, punctuation symbols, and various graphics characters.

ASME

An acronym for the American Society of Mechanical Engineers.

assemble

To translate a program expressed in an assembler language into a computer machine language.

assembler language

A computer-oriented language whose instructions are usually in one-to-one correspondence with machine language instructions.

asymmetrical modulation

A duplex transmission technique that splits the communications channel into one high-speed channel and one slower channel. During a call under asymmetrical modulation, the modem with the greatest amount of data to transmit is allocated the high-speed channel. The modem with less data is allocated the slow, or back, channel (450 bps). The modems dynamically reverse the channels during a call if the volume of data transfer changes.

asynchronous communication

Data transmission in which the length of time between transmitted characters may vary. Timing is dependent on the actual time for the transfer to take place, as opposed to synchronous communication, which is timed rigidly by an external clock signal. Because the receiving modem must be signaled about when the data bits of a character begin and end, start and stop bits are added to each character.

ATA

An acronym for AT Attachment interface, an IDE disk interface standard introduced in March 1989 that defines a compatible register set and a 40-pin connector and its associated signals. *See also* IDE.

attribute byte

A byte of information, held in the directory entry of any file, that describes various attributes of the file, such as whether it is read-only or has been backed up since it last was changed. Attributes can be set by the DOS ATTRIB command.

audio

A signal that can be heard, such as through the speaker of the PC. Many PC diagnostics tests use both visual (on-screen) codes and audio signals.

audio frequencies

Frequencies that can be heard by the human ear (approximately 20 to 20,000 hertz).

auto answer

A feature in modems enabling them to answer incoming calls over the phone lines without the use of a telephone receiver.

auto dial

A feature in modems enabling them to dial phone numbers without the use of a telephone transmitter.

AUTOEXEC.BAT

A special batch file that DOS executes at start-up. Contains any number of DOS commands that are executed automatically.

automatic head parking

Disk drive head parking performed whenever the drive is powered off. Found in all hard disk drives with a voice-coil actuator.

Average Access Time

The average time it takes a disk drive to begin reading any data placed anywhere on the drive. This includes the Average Seek Time, which is when the heads are moved, as well as the Latency, which is the average amount of time required for any given data sector to pass underneath the heads. Together these make up the Average Access Time.

average latency

The average time required for any byte of data stored on a disk to rotate under the disk drive's read/write head. Equal to one-half the time required for a single rotation of a platter.

Average Seek Time

Average Seek Time for a drive is the average amount of time it takes to move the heads from one random cylinder location to another, usually including any head settling time. In many cases, the average seek is tested across one-third of the total number of cylinders for consistency in measurement.

AVI

AVI is an acronym for Audio Video Interleave, a storage technique developed by Microsoft for its "Video for Windows" product that combines audio and video into a single frame or track, saving valuable disk space and keeping audio in synchronization with the corresponding video.

backup

The process of duplicating a file or library onto a separate piece of media. Good insurance against loss of an original.

backup disk

Contains information copied from another disk. Used to make sure that original information is not destroyed or altered.

bad sector

A disk sector that cannot hold data reliably because of a media flaw or damaged format markings.

bad track table

A label affixed to the casing of a hard disk drive that tells which tracks are flawed and cannot hold data. The listing is entered into the low-level formatting program.

balanced signal

A term referring to signals consisting of equal currents moving in opposite directions. When balanced or nearly balanced signals pass through twisted pair lines, the electromagnetic interference effects such as cross talk caused by the two opposite currents largely cancel each other out. Differential signaling is a method that uses balanced signals.

balun

Short for *bal*anced/*un*balanced. A type of transformer that enables balanced cables to be joined with unbalanced cables. Twisted pair (balanced) cables, for example, can be joined with coaxial (unbalanced) cables if the proper balun transformer is used.

bandwidth

Generally the measure of the range of frequencies within a radiation band required to transmit a particular signal. Measures in millions of cycles per second the difference between the lowest and highest signal frequencies. The bandwidth of a computer monitor is a measure of the rate that a monitor can handle information from the display adapter. The wider the bandwidth, the more information the monitor can carry, and the greater the resolution.

bank

The collection of memory chips that make up a block of memory readable by the processor in a single bus cycle. This block therefore must be as large as the data bus of the particular microprocessor. In IBM systems, the processor data bus is usually 8, 16, or 32 bits, plus a parity bit for each 8 bits, resulting in a total of 9, 18, or 36 bits for each bank.

bar code

The code used on consumer products and inventory parts for identification purposes. Consists of bars of varying thicknesses to represent characters and numerals that are read with an optical reader. The most common version is called the Universal Product Code (UPC).

baseband

The transmission of digital signals over a limited distance. ARCnet and EtherNet local area networks utilize baseband signaling. Contrasts with broadband transmission, which refers to the transmission of analog signals over a greater distance.

BASIC

An acronym for Beginner's All-purpose Symbolic Instruction Code, a popular computer programming language. Originally developed by John Kemeny and Thomas Kurtz, in the mid-1960s at Dartmouth College. Normally an interpretive language, meaning that each statement is translated and executed as it is encountered; but can be a compiled language, in which all the program statements are compiled before execution.

batch file

A set of commands stored in a disk file for execution by the operating system. A special batch file called AUTOEXEC.BAT is executed by IBM DOS each time the system is started. All DOS batch files have a BAT file extension.

baud

A unit of signaling speed denoting the number of discrete signal elements that can be transmitted per second. The word *baud* is derived from the name of J.M.E. Baudot (1845-1903), a French pioneer in the field of printing telegraphy and the inventor of Baudot code. Although technically inaccurate, baud rate commonly is used to mean *bit rate*. Because each signal element or baud may translate into many individual bits, bits per second (bps) normally differs from baud rate. A rate of 2400 baud means that 2400 frequency or signal changes per second are being sent, but each frequency change may signal several bits of information. Most people are surprised to learn that 2400 and 1200 bps modems transmit at 600 baud, and that 9600 and 14400 bps modems transmit at 2400 baud.

baud rate

See baud.

Baudot code

A 5-bit code used in many types of data communications including teletype (TTY), radio teletype (RTTY), and telecommunications devices for the deaf (TDD). Baudot code has been revised and extended several times.

bay

An opening in a computer cabinet that holds disk drives.

BBS

An acronym for bulletin board system, a computer that operates with a program and a modem to enable other computers with modems to communicate with it, often on a round-the-clock basis. Thousands of IBM- and Apple-related bulletin board systems offer a wealth of information and public-domain software that can be downloaded.

bezel

A cosmetic panel that covers the face of a drive or some other device.

Bézier curve

A mathematical method for describing a curve, often used in illustration and CAD programs to draw complex shapes.

bidirectional

Refers to lines over which data can move in two directions, like a data bus or a telephone line. Also refers to the capability of a printer to print from right to left and from left to right alternately.

binary

Refers to the computer numbering system that consists of two numerals, 0 and 1. Also called base-2.

BIOS

Basic input-output system. The part of an operating system that handles the communications between the computer and its peripherals. Often burned into read-only memory (ROM) chips.

bisynchronous

Binary synchronous control. An earlier protocol developed by IBM for software applications and communicating devices operation in synchronous environments. The protocol defines operations at the link level of communications— for example, the format of data frames exchanged between modems over a phone line.

bit

Binary digit. Represented logically by 0 or 1 and electrically by 0 volts and (typically) 5 volts. Other methods are used to represent binary digits physically (tones, different voltages, lights, and so on), but the logic is always the same.

Bit Density

Expressed as Bits Per Inch (BPI), Bit Density defines how many bits can be written onto one linear inch of a track. Sometimes also called linear density.

bit map

A method of storing graphics information in memory in which a bit devoted to each pixel (picture element) on-screen indicates whether that pixel is on or off. A bit map contains a bit for each point or dot on a video display screen and allows for fine resolution because any point or pixel on-screen can be addressed. A greater number of bits can be used to describe each pixel's color, intensity, and other display characteristics.

block

A string of records, words, or characters formed for technical or logic reasons and to be treated as an entity.

block diagram

The logical structure or layout of a system in graphics form. Does not necessarily match the physical layout and does not specify all the components and their interconnections.

BNC

An acronym for British National Connector, a type of connector plug and jack system. Originally designed in England for television set antennas, the BNC is a type of connector designed for use with coaxial cabling. Male and female BNCs are available. Although the term is redundant, BNCs usually are referred to as *BNC connectors*. Often used in local area network cabling systems that use coaxial cable, such as EtherNet and ARCnet, and also used frequently for video cabling systems.

Boolean operation

Any operation in which each of the operands and the result take one of two values.

boot

Load a program into the computer. The term comes from the phrase "pulling a boot on by the bootstrap."

boot record

A one-sector record that tells the computer's built-in operating system (BIOS) the most fundamental facts about a disk and DOS. Instructs the computer how to load the operating system files into memory, thus booting the machine.

bootstrap

A technique or device designed to bring itself into a desired state by means of its own action.

bps

Bits per second. The number of binary digits, or bits, transmitted per second. Sometimes confused with baud.

bridge

In local area networks, an interconnection between two networks. Also, the hardware equipment used to establish such an interconnection.

broadband

A term used to describe analog transmission. Requires modems for connecting terminals and computers to the network. Using frequency division multiplexing, many different signals or sets of data can be transmitted simultaneously. The alternate transmission scheme is baseband, or digital, transmission.

bubble memory

A special type of nonvolatile read/write memory introduced by Intel in which magnetic regions are suspended in crystal film and data is maintained when the power is off. A typical bubble memory chip contains about 512K, or more than four million bubbles. Failed to catch on because of slow access times measured in several milliseconds. Has found a niche use as solid-state "disk" emulators in environments in which conventional drives are unacceptable, such as military or factory use.

buffer

A block of memory used as a holding tank to store data temporarily. Often positioned between a slower peripheral device and the faster computer. All data moving between the peripheral and the computer passes through the buffer. A buffer enables the data to be read from or written to the peripheral in larger chunks, which improves performance. A buffer that is x bytes in size usually holds the last x bytes of data that moved between the peripheral and CPU. This method contrasts with that of a cache, which adds intelligence to the buffer so that the most often accessed data rather than the last accessed data remains in the buffer (cache). A cache can improve performance greatly over a plain buffer.

bug

An error or defect in a program.

burn-in

The operation of a circuit or equipment to stabilize components and to screen for failures.

bus

A linear electrical signal pathway over which power, data, and other signals travel and are capable of connection to three or more attachments. A bus is generally considered to be distinct from radial or point-to-point signal connections. The term *bus* comes from the Latin "omnibus" meaning "for all." When used to describe a topology, bus always implies a linear structure.

bus master

An intelligent device that when attached to the Micro Channel bus can bid for and gain control of the bus to perform its specific task.

byte

A collection of bits that makes up a character or other designation. Generally, a byte is 8 data bits plus one parity (error-checking) bit.

cache

An intelligent buffer. By using an intelligent algorithm, a cache contains the data that is accessed most often between a slower peripheral device and the faster CPU.

CAM

An acronym for Common Access Method, a committee formed in 1988 consisting of a number of computer peripheral suppliers and dedicated to developing standards for a common software interface between SCSI peripherals and host adapters. The CAM committee also has set a standard for IDE drives called the ATA interface.

capacitor

A device consisting of two plates separated by insulating material and designed to store an electrical charge.

card

A printed circuit board containing electronic components that form an entire circuit, usually designed to plug into a connector or slot. Sometimes also called an adapter.

carpal tunnel syndrome

A painful hand injury that gets its name from the narrow tunnel in the wrist which connects ligament and bone. When undue pressure is put on the tendons, they can swell and compress the median nerve, which carries impulses from the brain to the hand, causing numbness, weakness, tingling, and burning in the fingers and hands. Computer users get carpal tunnel syndrome primarily from improper keyboard ergonomics that result in undue strain on the wrist and hand.

carrier

A continuous frequency signal capable of being either modulated or impressed with another information-carrying signal. The reference signal used for the transmission or reception of data. The most common use of this signal with computers involves modem communications over phone lines. The carrier is used as a signal on which the information is superimposed.

carrier detect signal

A modem interface signal which indicates to the attached data terminal equipment (DTE) that it is receiving a signal from the distant modem. Defined in the RS-232 specification. Same as the received line-signal detector.

cathode ray tube

A device that contains electrodes surrounded by a glass sphere or cylinder and displays information by creating a beam of electrons that strike a phosphor coating inside the display unit.

CAV

CAV is an acronym for Constant Angular Velocity, an optical disk recording format where the data is recorded on the disk in concentric circles. CAV disks are rotated at a constant speed. This is similar to the recording technique used on floppy disk drives. CAV limits the total recorded capacity compared to CLV (Constant Linear Velocity), which is also used in optical recording.

CCITT

An acronym for the Comité Consultatif Internationale de Télégraphique et Téléphonique (in English, the International Telegraph and Telephone Consultative Committee or the Consultative Committee for International Telegraph and Telephone). An international committee organized by the United Nations to set international communications recommendations, which frequently are adopted as standards, and to develop interface, modem, and data network recommendations. The Bell 212A standard for 1200 bps communication in North America, for example, is observed internationally as CCITT

V.22. For 2400 bps communication, most U.S. manufacturers observe V.22bis, and V.32 and V.32bis are standards for 9600 and 14400 bps, respectively. Work is now under way to define a new standard for 19200 bps called V.32fast.

CCS

An acronym for the Common Command Set, a set of SCSI commands specified in the ANSI SCSI-1 Standard X3.131-1986 Addendum 4.B. All SCSI devices must be capable of using the CCS in order to be fully compatible with the ANSI SCSI-1 standard.

CD-DA

CD-DA is an acronym for Compact Disc Digital Audio. CD-DA is also known as "Red Book Audio," and is the digital sound format used by audio CDs. CD-DA uses a sampling rate of 44.1KHz and stores 16 bits of information for each sample. CD audio is not played through the computer, but through a special chip in the CD-ROM drive. Fifteen minutes of CD-DA sound can require about 80 MB. The highest quality sound that can be utilized by Multimedia PC is the CD-DA format at 44.1KHz sample rate.

CD-R

CD-R is an acronym for Compact Disk Recordable, sometimes also called CD-Writable. CD-R disks are compact disks that can be recorded several times and read as many times as desired. CD-R is part of the Orange Book Standard defined by ISO. CD-R technology is used for mass production of multimedia applications. CD-R disks can be compatible with CD-ROM, CD-ROM XA, and CD audio. Orange Book specifies multi-session capabilities, which allows data recording on the disk at different times in several recording sessions. Kodak's Photo CD is an example of CD-R technology, and fits up to 100 digital photographs on a single CD. Multi-session capability allows several rolls of 35mm film to be added to a single disk on different occasions.

CD-ROM

An acronym for compact disc read-only memory. A computer peripheral device that employs compact disc (CD) technology to store large amounts of data for later retrieval. Phillips and Sony developed CD-ROM in 1983. Current CD-ROM discs hold approximately 600M of information. CD-ROM drives are much slower than conventional hard disks, with normal average-access times of 380 milliseconds or greater and data transfer rates of about 1.2 megabits per second. Most CD-ROM drives use the SCSI (Small Computer Systems Interface) bus for connection to a system.

CD-ROM XA

CD-ROM XA is an acronym for Compact Disk Read Only Memory eXtended Architecture. The XA standard was developed jointly by Sony, Philips, and Microsoft in 1988 and is now part of the Yellow Book Standard. XA is a built-in feature of newer CD-ROM drives which supports simultaneous sound playback with data transfer. Non-XA drives support either sound playback OR data transfer, but not both simultaneously. XA also provides for data compression right on the disk, which can also increase data transfer rates.

ceramic substrate

A thin, flat, fired ceramic part used to hold an IC chip (usually made of beryllium oxide or aluminum oxide).

CGA

An acronym for Color Graphics Adapter, a type of PC video display adapter introduced by IBM on August 12, 1981, that supports text and graphics. Text is supported at a maximum resolution of 80x25 characters in 16 colors with a character box of 8x8 pixels. Graphics is supported at a maximum resolution of 320x200 pixels in 16 colors or 640x200 pixels in two colors. The CGA outputs a TTL (digital) signal with a horizontal scanning frequency of 15.75KHz, and supports TTL color or NTSC composite displays.

channel

A path along which signals can be sent.

character

A representation, coded in binary digits, of a letter, number, or other symbol.

checksum

Short for *summation check*, a technique for determining whether a package of data is valid. The package, a string of binary digits, is added up and compared with the expected number.

chip

Another name for an IC, or integrated circuit. Housed in a plastic or ceramic carrier device with pins for making electrical connections.

chip carrier

A ceramic or plastic package that carries an integrated circuit.

circuit

A complete electronic path.

circuit board

The collection of circuits gathered on a sheet of plastic, usually with all contacts made through a strip of pins. The circuit board usually is made by chemically etching metal-coated plastic.

CISC

An acronym for complex instruction-set computer. Refers to traditional computers that operate with large sets of processor instructions. Most modern computers, including the Intel 80xxx processors, are in this category. CISC processors have expanded instruction sets that are complex in nature and require several to many execution cycles to complete. This structure contrasts with RISC (reduced instruction-set computer) processors, which have far fewer instructions that execute quickly.

clean room

A dust-free room in which certain electronic components (such as hard disk drives) must be manufactured and serviced to prevent contamination. Rooms are rated by Class numbers. A Class 100 clean room must have fewer than 100 particles larger than .5 microns per cubic foot of space.

clock

The source of a computer's timing signals. Synchronizes every operation of the CPU.

clock speed

A measurement of the rate at which the clock signal for a device oscillates, usually expressed in millions of cycles per second (MHz).

clone

An IBM-compatible computer system that physically as well as electrically emulates the design of one of IBM's personal computer systems, usually the AT or XT. For example, an AT clone has parts (motherboard, power supply, and so on) that are physically interchangeable with the same parts in the IBM AT system.

cluster

Also called allocation unit. A group of sectors on a disk that forms a fundamental unit of storage to the operating system. Cluster or allocation unit size is determined by DOS when the disk is formatted.

CLV

CLV is an acronym for Constant Linear Velocity, an optical recording format where the spacing of data is consistent throughout the disk, and the rotational speed of the disk varies depending on what track is being read. Additionally, more sectors of data are placed on the outer tracks compared to the inner tracks of the disk, which is similar to Zone Recording on hard drives. CLV drives will adjust the rotational speed to maintain a constant track velocity as the diameter of the track changes. CLV drives rotate faster near the center of the disk and slower towards the edge. Rotational adjustment maximizes the amount of data that can be stored on a disk. CD audio and CD-ROM use CLV recording.

CMOS

Complementary Metal-Oxide Semiconductor. A type of chip design that requires little power to operate. In an AT-type system, a battery-powered CMOS memory and clock chip is used to store and maintain the clock setting and system configuration information.

coated media

Hard disk platters coated with a reddish iron-oxide medium on which data is recorded.

coaxial cable

Also called coax cable. A data-transmission medium noted for its wide bandwidth, immunity to interference, and high cost compared to twisted-pair wire. Signals are transmitted inside a fully shielded environment, in which an inner conductor is surrounded by a solid insulating material and then an outer conductor or shield. Used in many local area network systems such as EtherNet and ARCnet.

COBOL

An acronym for Common business-oriented language, a high-level computer programming language. The business world's preferred programming language on mainframe computer systems, it has never achieved popularity on smaller computers.

code page switching

A DOS feature in versions 3.3 and later that changes the characters displayed on-screen or printed on an output device. Primarily used to support foreign-language characters. Requires an EGA or better video system and an IBM-compatible graphics printer.

coercivity

A measurement in units of oersteads of the amount of magnetic energy to switch or "coerce" the flux change in the magnetic recording media. High-coercivity disk media requires a stronger write current.

Color Graphics Adapter

See CGA.

COM port

A serial port on a PC that conforms to the RS-232 standard. *See also* RS-232.

COMDEX

The largest international computer trade show and conference in the world. COMDEX/Fall is held in Las Vegas during October, and COMDEX/Spring usually is held in Chicago or Atlanta during April. The 16th annual COMDEX/Fall is in 1994.

command

An instruction that tells the computer to start, stop, or continue an operation.

COMMAND.COM

An operating system file that is loaded last when the computer is booted. The command interpreter or user interface and program-loader portion of DOS.

common

The ground or return path for an electrical signal. If a wire, usually is colored black.

common mode noise

Noise or electrical disturbances that can be measured between a current- or signal-carrying line and its associated ground. Common mode noise is frequently introduced to signals between separate computer equipment components through the power distribution circuits. It can be a problem when single-ended signals are used to connect different equipment or components that are powered by different circuits.

compiler

A program that translates a program written in a high-level language into its equivalent machine language. The output from a compiler is called an object program.

composite video

Television picture information and sync pulses combined. The IBM Color Graphics Adapter (CGA) outputs a composite video signal.

computer

Device capable of accepting data, applying prescribed processes to this data, and displaying the results or information produced.

CONFIG.SYS

A file that can be created to tell DOS how to configure itself when the machine starts up. Can load device drivers, set the number of DOS buffers, and so on.

configuration file

A file kept by application software to record various aspects of the software's configuration, such as the printer it uses.

console

The unit, such as a terminal or a keyboard, in your system with which you communicate with the computer.

contiguous

Touching or joined at the edge or boundary, in one piece.

continuity

In electronics, an unbroken pathway. Testing for continuity normally means testing to determine whether a wire or other conductor is complete and unbroken (by measuring 0 ohms). A broken wire shows infinite resistance (or infinite ohms).

control cable

The wider of the two cables that connect an ST-506/412 or ESDI hard disk drive to a controller card. A 34-pin cable that carries commands and acknowledgments between the drive and controller.

controller

The electronics that control a device such as a hard disk drive and intermediate the passage of data between the device and the computer.

controller card

An adapter holding the control electronics for one or more devices such as hard disks. Ordinarily occupies one of the computer's slots.

convergence

Describes the capability of a color monitor to focus the three colored electron beams on a single point. Poor convergence causes the characters on-screen to appear fuzzy and can cause headaches and eyestrain.

coprocessor

An additional computer processing unit designed to handle specific tasks in conjunction with the main or central processing unit.

core

An "old-fashioned" term for computer memory.

CP/M

An acronym for Control Program/Microcomputer, an operating system created by Gary Kildall, the founder of Digital Research. Created for the old 8-bit microcomputers that used the 8080, 8085, and Z-80 microprocessors. Was the dominant operating system in the late 1970s and early 1980s for small computers used in a business environment.

cps

Characters per second. A data transfer rate generally estimated from the bit rate and the character length. At 2400 bps, for example, 8-bit characters with start and stop bits (for a total of 10 bits per character) are transmitted at a rate of approximately 240 characters per second (cps). Some protocols, such as V.42 and MNP, employ advanced techniques such as longer transmission frames and data compression to increase cps.

CPU

Central processing unit. The computer's microprocessor chip, the brains of the outfit. Typically, an IC using VLSI (very-large-scale integration) technology to pack several different functions into a tiny area. The most common electronic device in the CPU is the transistor, of which several thousand to several million or more are found.

crash

A malfunction that brings work to a halt. A system crash usually is caused by a software malfunction, and ordinarily you can restart the system by rebooting the machine. A head crash, however, entails physical damage to a disk and probable data loss.

CRC

An acronym for cyclic redundancy checking, an error-detection technique consisting of a cyclic algorithm performed on each block or frame of data by both sending and receiving modems. The sending modem inserts the results of its computation in each data block in the form of a CRC code. The receiving modem compares its results with the received CRC code and responds with either a positive or negative acknowledgment. In the ARQ protocol implemented in high-speed modems, the receiving modem accepts no more data until a defective block is received correctly.

cross talk

The electromagnetic coupling of a signal on one line with another nearby signal line. Cross talk is caused by electromagnetic induction, where a signal traveling through a wire creates a magnetic field that then induces a current in other nearby wires.

CRT

Cathode-ray tube. A term used to describe a television or monitor screen tube.

current

The flow of electrons, measured in amperes.

cursor

The small flashing hyphen that appears on-screen to indicate the point at which any input from the keyboard will be placed.

cyclic redundancy checking

See CRC.

cylinder

The set of tracks on a disk that are on each side of all the disk platters in a stack and are the same distance from the center of the disk. The total number of tracks that can be read without moving the heads. A floppy drive with two heads usually has 160 tracks, which are accessible as 80 cylinders. A typical 20M hard disk has two platters with four heads and 615 cylinders, in which each cylinder is four tracks.

daisy chain

Stringing up components in such a manner that the signals move serially from one to the other. Most microcomputer multiple disk drive systems are daisy-chained. The SCSI bus system is a daisy-chain arrangement, in which the signals move from computer to disk drives to tape units, and so on.

daisywheel printer

An impact printer that prints fully formed characters one at a time by rotating a circular print element composed of a series of individual spokes, each containing two characters that radiate from a center hub. Produces letter-quality output.

DAT

An acronym for Digital Audio Tape, a small cassette tape for storing large amounts of digital information. Also sometimes called 4mm tape. DAT technology emerged in Europe and Japan in 1986 as a way to produce high-quality, digital audio recordings. One DAT cassette can hold approximately 1.3 gigabytes of data.

data

Groups of facts processed into information. A graphic or textural representation of facts, concepts, numbers, letters, symbols, or instructions used for communication or processing.

Also, an android from the 24th century with a processing speed of 60 trillion operations per second and 80 quadrillion bits of storage who serves on the USS Enterprise NCC-1701-D with the rank of lieutenant commander.

data cable

The narrower of two cables that connects a hard disk drive to a controller card.

data communications

A type of communication in which computers and terminals can exchange data over an electronic medium.

data compression

Data compression is a technique where mathematical algorithms are applied to the data in a file to eliminate redundancies and therefore reduce the size of the file. There are two types of compression: lossy and lossless. Lossy compression deletes some of the original (uncompressed) data needed to reconstruct a file, and is normally used only for graphic image or sound files, where the loss of some resolution or information is acceptable. Lossless compression maintains completely the integrity of the original file, allowing it to be reconstructed exactly, and is most commonly used for program or data files.

data separator

A device that separates data and clock signals from a single encoded signal pattern. Usually the same device does both data separation and combination and is sometimes called an "endec" for Encoder/Decoder.

data transfer rate

The maximum rate at which data can be transferred from one device to another.

DC

Direct current, such as that provided by a power supply or batteries.

DC-600

Data Cartridge 600, a data-storage medium invented by 3M in 1971 that uses a quarter-inch-wide tape 600 feet in length.

DCE

Data communications equipment. The hardware that does the communication—usually a dial-up modem that establishes and controls the data link through the telephone network. *See also* DTE.

DDE

An acronym for Dynamic Data Exchange, a form of interprocess communications used by Microsoft Windows to support the exchange of commands and data between two applications running simultaneously. This capability has been enhanced further with Object Linking and Embedding (OLE).

DEBUG

The name of a utility program included with DOS and used for specialized purposes such as altering memory locations, tracing program execution, patching programs and disk sectors, and performing other low-level tasks.

dedicated line

A user-installed telephone line used to connect a specified number of computers or terminals within a limited area, such as a single building. The line is a cable rather than a public-access telephone line. The communications channel also may be referred to as nonswitched because calls do not go through telephone company switching equipment.

dedicated servo surface

In voice-coil-actuated hard disk drives, one side of one platter given over to servo data that is used to guide and position the read/write heads.

default

Any setting assumed at start-up or reset by the computer's software and attached devices and operational until changed by the user. An assumption the
computer makes when no other parameters are specified. When you type `DIR`
without specifying the drive to search, for example, the computer assumes
that you want it to search the default drive. The term is used in software to
describe any action the computer or program takes on its own with imbedded
values.

density

The amount of data that can be packed into a certain area on a specific storage media.

device driver

A memory-resident program, loaded by CONFIG.SYS, that controls an unusual device, such as an expanded memory board.

Dhrystone

A benchmark program used as a standard figure of merit indicating aspects of
a computer system's performance in areas other than floating-point math
performance. Because the program does not use any floating-point operations, performs no I/O, and makes no operating system calls, it is most applicable to measuring the processor performance of a system. The original
Dhrystone program was developed in 1984 and was written in Ada, although
the C and Pascal versions became more popular by 1989.

diagnostics

Programs used to check the operation of a computer system. These programs
enable the operator to check the entire system for any problems and to indicate in what area the problems lie.

differential

An electrical signaling method where a pair of lines are used for each signal
in "push-pull" fashion. In most cases differential signals are balanced so that
the same current flows on each line in opposite directions. This is unlike
single-ended signals which use only one line per signal referenced to a single
ground. Differential signals have a large tolerance for common-mode noise,
and little cross talk when used with twisted pair wires even in long cables.
Differential signaling is expensive because two pins are required for each
signal.

digital loopback

A test that checks the modem's RS-232 interface and the cable that connects the terminal or computer and the modem. The modem receives data (in the form of digital signals) from the computer or terminal and immediately returns the data to the screen for verification.

digital signals

Discrete, uniform signals. In this book, the term refers to the binary digits 0 and 1.

digitize

Digitizing refers to transforming an analog wave to a digital signal that a computer can store. Conversion to digital data and back is performed by a Digital to Analog Converter (DAC), often a single chip device. How closely a digitized sample represents an analog wave depends on the number of times the amplitude of a wave is measured and recorded, or the rate of digitization, as well as the number of different levels that can be specified at each instance. The number of possible signal levels is dictated by the resolution in bits.

DIP

Dual In-line Package. A family of rectangular, integrated-circuit flat packages that have leads on the two longer sides. Package material is plastic or ceramic.

DIP switch

A tiny switch (or group of switches) on a circuit board. Named for the form factor of the carrier device in which the switch is housed.

direct memory access

A process by which data moves between a disk drive (or other device) and system memory without direct control of the central processing unit, thus freeing it up for other tasks.

directory

An area of a disk that stores the titles given to the files saved on the disk and serves as a table of contents for those files. Contains data that identifies the name of a file, the size, the attributes (system, hidden, read-only, and so on), the date and time of creation, and a pointer to the location of the file. Each entry in a directory is 32 bytes long.

disk operating system

DOS. A collection of programs stored on the DOS disk that contain routines enabling the system and user to manage information and the hardware resources of the computer. DOS must be loaded into the computer before other programs can be started.

diskette

A floppy disk. Made of a flexible material coated with a magnetic substance, the disk spins inside its protective jacket, and the read/write head comes in contact with the recording surface to read or write data.

dithering

Dithering is the process of creating more colors and shades from a given color palette. In monochrome displays or printers, dithering will vary the black and white dot patterns to simulate shades of gray. Gray-scale dithering is used to produce different shades of gray when the device can only produce limited levels of black or white outputs. Color screens or printers use dithering to create colors by mixing and varying the dot sizing and spacing.

DLL

An acronym for Dynamic Link Library, an executable driver program module for Microsoft Windows that can be loaded on demand and linked in at run time, and subsequently unloaded when the driver is no longer needed.

DMA

Direct memory access. A circuit by which a high-speed transfer of information may be facilitated between a device and system memory. This transfer is managed by a specialized processor that relieves the burden of managing the transfer from the main CPU.

dot pitch

A measurement of the width of the dots that make up a pixel. The smaller the dot pitch, the sharper the image.

dot-matrix printer

An impact printer that prints characters composed of dots. Prints characters one at a time by pressing the ends of selected wires against an inked ribbon and paper.

double density (DD)

An indication of the storage capacity of a floppy drive or disk in which eight or nine sectors per track are recorded using MFM encoding.

down-time

Operating time lost because of a computer malfunction.

DPMI

An acronym for DOS Protected Mode Interface, an industry standard interface that allows DOS applications to execute program code in the protected mode of the 286 or higher Intel processor. The DPMI specification is available from Intel.

drive

A mechanical device that manipulates data storage media.

DTE

Data terminal (or terminating) equipment. The device, usually a computer or terminal, that generates or is the final destination of data. *See also* DCE.

duplex

Indicates a communications channel capable of carrying signals in both directions.

DVI

DVI is an acronym for Digital Video Interactive, a standard that was originally developed at RCA Laboratories, and sold to Intel in 1988. DVI integrates digital motion, still video, sound, graphics, and special effects in a compressed format. DVI is a highly sophisticated hardware compression technique used in interactive multimedia applications.

Dvorak keyboard

A keyboard design by August Dvorak that was patented in 1936 and approved by ANSI in 1982. Provides increased speed and comfort and reduces the rate of errors by placing the most frequently used letters in the center for use by the strongest fingers. Finger motions and awkward strokes are reduced by more than 90 percent in comparison with the familiar QWERTY keyboard. The Dvorak keyboard has the five vowel keys, AOEUI, together under the left hand in the center row, and the five most frequently used consonants, DHTNS, under the fingers of the right hand.

EBCDIC

An acronym for Extended Binary Coded Decimal Interchange Code, an IBM developed 8-bit code for the representation of characters. It allows 256 possible character combinations within a single byte. EBCDIC is the standard code on IBM mini-computers and mainframes, but not on the IBM micro-computers, where ASCII is used instead.

edit

The process of rearranging data or information.

EGA

An acronym for Enhanced Graphics Adapter, a type of PC video display adapter first introduced by IBM on September 10, 1984, that supports text and graphics. Text is supported at a maximum resolution of 80x25 characters in 16 colors with a character box of 8x14 pixels. Graphics is supported at a maximum resolution of 640x350 pixels in 16 (from a palette of 64) colors. The EGA outputs a TTL (digital) signal with a horizontal scanning frequency of 15.75, 18.432, or 21.85KHz, and supports TTL color or TTL monochrome displays.

EIA

Electronic Industries Association, which defines electronic standards in the United States.

EISA

An acronym for Extended Industry Standard Architecture, an extension of the Industry Standard Architecture (ISA) bus developed by IBM for the AT. The EISA design was led by COMPAQ Corporation. Later, eight other manufacturers (AST, Epson, Hewlett-Packard, NEC, Olivetti, Tandy, Wyse, and Zenith) joined COMPAQ in a consortium founded September 13, 1988. This group became known as the "gang of nine." The EISA design was patterned largely after IBM's Micro Channel Architecture (MCA) in the PS/2 systems, but unlike MCA, EISA allows for backward compatibility with older plug-in adapters.

electronic mail

A method of transferring messages form one computer to another.

electrostatic discharge (ESD)

Static electricity, a sudden flow of electricity between two objects at different electrical potentials. ESD is a primary cause of integrated circuit damage or failure.

embedded servo data

Magnetic markings embedded between or inside tracks on disk drives that use voice-coil actuators. These markings enable the actuator to fine-tune the position of the read/write heads.

EMM

An acronym for Expanded Memory Manager, a driver that provides a software interface to expanded memory. EMMs were originally created for Expanded Memory boards, but can also use the memory management capabilities of the 386 or higher processors to emulate an Expanded Memory board. EMM386.EXE is an example of an EMM that comes with DOS.

EMS

An acronym for Expanded Memory Specification. Sometimes also called the LIM spec. because it was developed by Lotus, Intel, and Microsoft. Provides a way for microcomputers running under DOS to access additional memory. EMS memory management provides access to a maximum of 32M of expanded memory through a small (usually 64K) window in conventional memory. EMS is a cumbersome access scheme designed primarily for pre-286 systems that could not access extended memory.

emulator

A piece of test apparatus that emulates or imitates the function of a particular chip.

encoding

The protocol by which data is carried or stored by a medium.

encryption

The translation of data into unreadable codes to maintain security.

Endec (Encoder/Decoder)

A device that takes data and clock signals and combines or encodes them using a particular encoding scheme into a single signal for transmission or storage. The same device also later separates or decodes the data and clock signals during a receive or read operation. Sometimes called a data separator.

Enhanced Graphics Adapter

See EGA.

Enhanced Small Device Interface

See ESDI.

EPROM

Erasable programmable read-only memory. A type of read-only memory (ROM) in which the data pattern can be erased to allow a new pattern. Usually is erased by ultraviolet light and recorded by a higher than normal voltage programming signal.

equalization

A compensation circuit designed into modems to counteract certain distortions introduced by the telephone channel. Two types are used: fixed (compromise) equalizers and those that adapt to channel conditions (adaptive). Good-quality modems use adaptive equalization.

error control

Various techniques that check the reliability of characters (parity) or blocks of data. V.42, MNP, and HST error-control protocols use error detection (CRC) and retransmission of errored frames (ARQ).

error message

A word or combination of words to indicate to the user that an error has occurred somewhere in the program.

ESDI

An acronym for Enhanced Small Device Interface, a hardware standard developed by Maxtor and standardized by a consortium of 22 disk drive manufacturers on Jan. 26, 1983. A group of 27 manufacturers formed the ESDI steering committee on Sept. 15, 1986, to enhance and improve the specification. A high-performance interface used primarily with hard disks, ESDI provides for a maximum data transfer rate to and from a hard disk of between 10 and 24 megabits per second.

EtherNet

A type of network protocol developed in the late 1970s by Bob Metcalf, at Xerox Corporation, and endorsed by the IEEE. One of the oldest LAN communications protocols in the personal computing industry. EtherNet networks use a collision-detection protocol to manage contention.

expanded memory

Otherwise known as EMS memory, memory that conforms to the EMS specification. Requires a special device driver and conforms to a standard developed by Lotus, Intel, and Microsoft.

eXtended graphics array

See XGA.

extended memory

Direct processor-addressable memory that is addressed by an Intel (or compatible) 286, 386, or 486 processor in the region beyond the first megabyte. Addressable only in the processor's protected mode of operation.

extended partition

A nonbootable DOS partition containing DOS volumes. Starting with DOS V3.3, the DOS FDISK program can create two partitions that serve DOS: an ordinary, bootable partition (called the primary partition) and an extended partition, which may contain as many as 23 volumes from D: through Z:.

extra-high density (ED)

An indication of the storage capacity of a floppy drive or disk in which 36 sectors per track are recorded using a vertical recording technique with MFM encoding.

FIFO

An acronym for *first-in first-out*, a method of storing and retrieving items from a list, table, or stack such that the first element stored is the first one retrieved.

file

A collection of information kept somewhere other than in random-access memory.

file allocation table

A table held near the outer edge of a disk that tells which sectors are allocated to each file and in what order.

file attribute

Information held in the attribute byte of a file's directory entry.

file defragmentation

The process of rearranging disk sectors so that files are compacted on consecutive sectors in adjacent tracks.

file name

The name given to the disk file. Must be one to eight characters long and may be followed by a file-name extension, which can be one to three characters long. Can be made up of any combination of letters and numbers but should be descriptive of the information contained in the file.

firmware

Software contained in a read-only memory (ROM) device. A cross between hardware and software.

fixed disk

Also called a hard disk, a disk that cannot be removed from its controlling hardware or housing. Made of rigid material with a magnetic coating and used for the mass storage and retrieval of data.

floppy tape

A tape standard that uses drives connecting to an ordinary floppy disk controller.

flow control

A mechanism that compensates for differences in the flow of data input to and output from a modem or other device.

FM encoding

Frequency modulation encoding. An outdated method of encoding data on the disk surface that uses up half the disk space with timing signals.

form factor

The physical dimensions of a device. Two devices with the same form factor are physically interchangeable. The IBM PC, XT, and XT Model 286, for example, all use power supplies that are internally different but have exactly the same form factor.

FORMAT.COM

The DOS format program that performs both low- and high-level formatting on floppy disks but only high-level formatting on hard disks.

formatted capacity

The total number of bytes of data that can fit on a formatted disk. The unformatted capacity is higher because space is lost defining the boundaries between sectors.

formatting

Preparing a disk so that the computer can read or write to it. Checks the disk for defects and constructs an organizational system to manage information on the disk.

FORTRAN

An acronym for *formula tran*slator, a high-level programming language for programs dealing primarily with mathematical formulas and expressions, similar to algebra and used primarily in scientific and technical applications. One of the oldest languages but still widely used because of its compact notation, the many mathematical subroutines available, and the ease with which arrays, matrices, and loops can be handled. FORTRAN was written in 1954 by John Backus at IBM, and the first successful FORTRAN program was executed by Harlan Herrick.

frame

A data communications term for a block of data with header and trailer information attached. The added information usually includes a frame number, block size data, error-check codes, and start/end indicators.

full duplex

Signal flow in both directions at the same time. In microcomputer communications, also may refer to the suppression of the on-line local echo.

full-height drive

A drive unit that is 3.25 inches high, 5.75 inches wide, and 8 inches deep.

function keys

Special-purpose keys that can be programmed to perform various operations. Serve many different functions depending on the program being used.

gas-plasma display

Commonly used in portable systems, a type of display that operates by exciting a gas, usually neon or an argon-neon mixture, through the application of a voltage. When sufficient voltage is applied at the intersection of two electrodes, the gas glows an orange-red. Because gas-plasma displays generate light, it requires no backlighting.

giga

A multiplier indicating 1 billion (1,000,000,000) of some unit. Abbreviated as *g* or *G*. When used to indicate a number of bytes of memory storage, the multiplier definition changes to 1,073,741,824. One gigabit, for example, equals 1,000,000,000 bits, and one gigabyte equals 1,073,741,824 bytes.

gigabyte

A unit of information storage equal to 1,073,741,824 bytes.

global backup

A backup of all information on a hard disk, including the directory tree structure.

Green Book

Green Book is the standard for Compact Disc-Interactive (CD-I). Philips developed CD-I technology for the consumer market, to be connected to a television instead of a computer monitor. CD-I is not a computer system, but a consumer device. CD-I disks require special code and are not compatible with standard CD ROMs. A CD-ROM cannot be played on the CD-I machine, but Red Book audio can be played on CD-I devices.

GUI

An acronym for Graphical User Interface, a type of program interface that allows users to choose commands and functions by pointing to a graphical icon using either a keyboard or pointing device such as a mouse. Windows and OS/2 are the most popular GUIs available for PC systems.

half duplex

Signal flow in both directions but only one way at a time. In microcomputer communications, may refer to activation of the on-line local echo, which causes the modem to send a copy of the transmitted data to the screen of the sending computer.

half-height drive

A drive unit that is 1.625 inches high, and either 5.75 or 4 inches wide and 4 or 8 inches deep.

halftone

Halftoning is a process that uses dithering to simulate a continuous tone image such as a photograph or shaded drawing using various sizes of dots. Newspapers, magazines, and many books use halftoning. The human eye will merge the dots to give the impression of gray shades.

hard disk

A high-capacity disk storage unit characterized by a normally nonremovable rigid substrate media. The platters in a hard disk normally are constructed of aluminum or glass.

hard error

An error in reading or writing data that is caused by damaged hardware.

hardware

Physical components that make up a microcomputer, monitor, printer, and so on.

HDLC

High-Level Data Link Control. A standard protocol developed by the International Standards Organization for software applications and communicating devices operating in synchronous environments. Defines operations at the link level of communications—for example, the format of data frames exchanged between modems over a phone line.

head

A small electromagnetic device inside a drive that reads, records, and erases data on the media.

head actuator

The device that moves read/write heads across a disk drive's platters. Most drives use a stepper-motor or a voice-coil actuator.

head crash

A (usually) rare occurrence in which a read/write head strikes a platter surface with sufficient force to damage the magnetic medium.

head parking

A procedure in which a disk drive's read/write heads are moved to an unused track so that they will not damage data in the event of a head crash or other failure.

head seek

The movement of a drive's read/write heads to a particular track.

heat sink

A mass of metal attached to a chip carrier or socket for the purpose of dissipating heat.

helical scan

A type of recording technology that has vastly increased the capacity of tape drives. Invented for use in broadcast systems and now used in VCRs. Conventional longitudinal recording records a track of data straight across the width of a single-track tape. Helical scan recording packs more data on the tape by positioning the tape at an angle to the recording heads. The heads spin to record diagonal stripes of information on the tape.

hexadecimal number

A number encoded in base-16, such that digits include the letters A through F as well as the numerals 0 through 9 (for example, 8BF3, which equals 35,827 in base-10).

hidden file

A file that is not displayed in DOS directory listings because the file's attribute byte holds a special setting.

high density (HD)
An indication of the storage capacity of a floppy drive or disk in which 15 or 18 sectors per track are recorded using MFM encoding.

high-level formatting
Formatting performed by the DOS FORMAT program. Among other things, it creates the root directory and file allocation tables.

history file
A file created by utility software to keep track of earlier use of the software. Many backup programs, for example, keep history files describing earlier backup sessions.

HMA
An acronym for High Memory Area, the first 64K of extended memory which is controlled typically by the HIMEM.SYS device driver. Real mode programs can be loaded into the HMA to conserve conventional memory. Normally DOS 5.0 and higher use the HMA exclusively to reduce the DOS conventional memory footprint.

HPT
High-pressure tin. A PLCC socket that promotes high forces between socket contacts and PLCC contacts for a good connection.

HST
High-speed technology. The USRobotics proprietary high-speed modem-signaling scheme, developed as an interim protocol until the V.32 protocol could be implemented in a cost-effective manner. Incorporates trellis-coded modulation for greater immunity from variable phone-line conditions, and asymmetrical modulation for more efficient use of the phone channel at speeds of 4800 bps and above. The forward channel transmits at either 9600 bps (older designs) or 14400 bps, and the reverse channel transmits at 450 bps. This technique eliminated the need for the V.32 echo-cancellation hardware that was more costly at the time HST was developed. HST also incorporates MNP-compatible error-control procedures adapted to the asymmetrical modulation.

Hz
A mnemonic for *hertz*, a frequency measurement unit used internationally to indicate one cycle per second.

I/O

Input/output. A circuit path that enables independent communications between the processor and external devices.

IBMBIO.COM

One of the DOS system files required to boot the machine. The first file loaded from disk during the boot. Contains extensions to the ROM BIOS.

IBMDOS.COM

One of the DOS system files required to boot the machine. Contains the primary DOS routines. Loaded by IBMBIO.COM, it in turns loads COMMAND.COM.

IC

An acronym for integrated circuit, a complete electronic circuit contained on a single chip. May consist of only a few transistors, capacitors, diodes, or resistors, or thousands of them, and generally is classified according to the complexity of the circuitry and the approximate number of circuits on the chip. SSI (small-scale integration) equals two to 10 circuits. MSI (medium-scale integration) equals 10 to 100 circuits. LSI (large-scale integration) equals 100 to 1,000 circuits. VLSI (very-large-scale integration) equals 1,000 to 10,000 circuits. ULSI (ultra-large-scale integration) equals more than 10,000 circuits.

IDE

An acronym for integrated drive electronics. Describes a hard disk with the disk controller circuitry integrated within it. The first IDE drives commonly were called hard cards. Also refers to the ATA interface standard, the standard for attaching hard disk drives to ISA bus IBM-compatible computers. IDE drives typically operate as though they were standard ST-506/412 drives. *See also* ATA.

incremental backup

A backup of all files that have changed since the last backup.

initiator

A device attached to the SCSI bus that sends a command to another device (the target) on the SCSI bus. The SCSI host adapter plugged into the system bus is an example of an SCSI initiator.

inkjet printer

A type of printer that sprays one or more colors of ink on the paper. Can produce output with quality approaching that of a laser printer at a lower cost.

input

Data sent to the computer from the keyboard, the telephone, the video camera, another computer, paddles, joysticks, and so on.

instruction

Program step that tells the computer what to do for a single operation.

integrated circuit

See IC.

interface

A communications device or protocol that enables one device to communicate with another. Matches the output of one device to the input of the other device.

interlacing

Interlacing is a method of scanning alternate lines of pixels on a display screen. The odd lines are scanned first from top to bottom and left to right. The electron gun goes back to the top and makes a second pass scanning the even lines. Interlacing requires two scan passes to construct a single image. Because of this additional scanning, interlaced screens are often seen to flicker unless a long persistence phosphor is used in the display.

interleave ratio

The number of sectors that pass beneath the read/write heads before the "next" numbered sector arrives. When the interleave ratio is 3:1, for example, a sector is read, two pass by, and then the next is read. A proper interleave ratio, laid down during low-level formatting, enables the disk to transfer information without excessive revolutions due to missed sectors.

internal command

In DOS, a command contained in COMMAND.COM so that no other file must be loaded in order to perform the command. DIR and COPY are two examples of internal commands.

internal drive

A disk or tape drive mounted inside one of a computer's disk drive bays (or a hard disk card, which is installed in one of the computer's slots).

interpreter

A translator program for a high-level language that translates and executes the program at the same time. The program statements that are interpreted remain in their original source language, the way the programmer wrote them—that is, the program does not need to be compiled before execution. Interpreted programs run slower than compiled programs and always must be run with the interpreter loaded in memory.

interrupt

A suspension of a process, such as the execution of a computer program, caused by an event external to that process and performed in such a way that the process can be resumed. An interrupt can be caused by internal or external conditions such as a signal indicating that a device or program has completed a transfer of data.

interrupt vector

A pointer in a table that gives the location of a set of instructions that the computer should execute when a particular interrupt occurs.

IRQ

An acronym for *interrupt request*. Physical connections between external hardware devices and the interrupt controllers. When a device such as a floppy controller or a printer needs the attention of the CPU, an IRQ line is used to get the attention of the system to perform a task. On PC and XT IBM-compatible systems, 8 IRQ lines are included, numbered IRQ0 through IRQ7. On the AT and PS/2 systems, 16 IRQ lines are numbered IRQ0 through IRQ15. IRQ lines must be used by only a single adapter in the ISA bus systems, but Micro Channel Architecture (MCA) adapters can share interrupts.

ISDN

An acronym for Integrated Services Digital Network, an international telecommunications standard that enables a communications channel to carry digital data simultaneously with voice and video information.

ISO

An acronym for International Standards Organization. The ISO, based in Paris, develops standards for international and national data communications. The U.S. representative to the ISO is the American National Standards Institute (ANSI).

ISO 9660

ISO 9660 is an international standard that defines file systems for CD-ROM disks, independent of the operating system. ISO (International Standards Organization) 9660 has two levels. Level one provides for DOS file system compatibility, while Level two allows file names of up to 32 characters.

J-lead

J-shaped leads on chip carriers. Can be surface-mounted on a PC board or plugged into a socket that then is mounted on a PC board, usually on .050-inch centers.

JEDEC

Joint Electron Devices Engineering Council. A group that establishes standards for the electronics industry.

JPEG

JPEG is an acronym for the Joint Photographic Experts Group, a lossy data compression standard that was originally designed for still images, but can also compress real-time video (30 frames per second) and animation. Lossy compression permanently discards unnecessary data, resulting in some loss of precision.

jumper

A small, plastic-covered, metal clip that slips over two pins protruding from a circuit board. Sometimes also called a *shunt*. When in place, the jumper connects the pins electrically and closes the circuit. By doing so, it connects the two terminals of a switch, turning it "on."

Kermit

A protocol designed for transferring files between microcomputers and mainframes. Developed by Frank DaCruz and Bill Catchings, at Columbia University (and named after the talking frog on *The Muppet Show*). Widely accepted in the academic world. The complete Kermit protocol manual and the source for various versions is available from Kermit Distribution, Columbia University Center for Computing Activities, 612 West 115 Street, New York, NY 10025, (212) 854-3703.

key disk

In software copy protection, a distribution floppy disk that must be present in a floppy disk drive for an application program to run.

keyboard macro

A series of keystrokes automatically input when a single key is pressed.

kilo

A multiplier indicating one thousand (1000) of some unit. Abbreviated as *k* or *K*. When used to indicate a number of bytes of memory storage, the multiplier definition changes to 1024. One kilobit, for example, equals 1000 bits, and one kilobyte equals 1024 bytes.

kilobyte

A unit of information storage equal to 1024 bytes.

landing zone

An unused track on a disk surface on which the read/write heads can land when power is shut off. The place that a parking program or a drive with an autopark mechanism parks the heads.

LAPM

Link-access procedure for modems, an error-control protocol incorporated in CCITT Recommendation V.42. Like the MNP and HST protocols, uses cyclic redundancy checking (CRC) and retransmission of corrupted data (ARQ) to ensure data reliability.

laptop computer

A computer system smaller than a briefcase but larger than a notebook, and that usually has a clamshell design in which the keyboard and display are on separate halves of the system, which are hinged together. These systems normally run on battery power.

laser printer

A type of printer that is a combination of an electrostatic copying machine and a computer printer. The output data from the computer is converted by an interface into a raster feed, similar to the impulses that a TV picture tube receives. The impulses cause the laser beam to scan a small drum that carries a positive electrical charge. Where the laser hits, the drum is discharged. A toner, which also carries a positive charge, then is applied to the drum. This toner, a fine black powder, sticks only to the areas of the drum that have been discharged electrically. As it rotates, the drum deposits the toner on a negatively charged sheet of paper. Another roller then heats and bonds the toner to the page.

latency

The amount of time required for a disk drive to rotate half of a revolution. Represents the average amount of time to locate a specific sector after the heads have arrived at a specific track. Latency is part of the average access time for a drive.

LCC

Leadless chip carrier. A type of integrated circuit package that has input and output pads rather than leads on its perimeter.

LCD

An acronym for liquid crystal display, a display that uses liquid crystal sealed between two pieces of polarized glass. The polarity of the liquid crystal is changed by an electric current to vary the amount of light that can pass through. Because LCD displays do not generate light, they depend on either the reflection of ambient light or backlighting the screen. The best type of LCD, the active-matrix or thin-film transistor (TFT) LCD, offers fast screen updates and true color capability.

LED

An acronym for light-emitting diode, a semiconductor diode that emits light when a current is passed through it.

LIF

Low insertion force. A type of socket that requires only a minimum of force to insert a chip carrier.

light pen

A hand-held input device with a light-sensitive probe or stylus, connected to the computer's graphics adapter board by a cable. Used for writing or sketching on-screen or as a pointing device tool for making selections. Unlike mice, not widely supported by software applications.

local echo

A modem feature that enables the modem to send copies of keyboard commands and transmitted data to the screen. When the modem is in command mode (not on-line to another system), the local echo normally is invoked through an ATE1 command, which causes the modem to display your typed commands. When the modem is on-line to another system, the local echo is invoked by an ATF0 command, which causes the modem to display the data it transmits to the remote system.

logical drive

A drive as named by a DOS drive specifier, such as C: or D:. Under DOS 3.3 or later, a single physical drive can act as several logical drives, each with its own specifier.

logical unit number

See LUN.

lost clusters

Clusters that have been marked accidentally as "unavailable" in the file allocation table even though they belong to no file listed in a directory.

low-level formatting

Formatting that divides tracks into sectors on the platter surfaces. Places sector-identifying information before and after each sector and fills each sector with null data (usually hex F6). Specifies the sector interleave and marks defective tracks by placing invalid checksum figures in each sector on a defective track.

LUN

An acronym for logical unit number, a number given to a device (a logical unit) attached to a SCSI physical unit and not directly to the SCSI bus. Although as many as eight logical units can be attached to a single physical unit, normally a single logical unit is a built-in part of a single physical unit. A SCSI hard disk, for example, has a built-in SCSI bus adapter that is assigned a physical unit number or SCSI ID, and the controller and drive portions of the hard disk are assigned a logical unit number (usually 0).

magnetic domain

A tiny segment of a track just large enough to hold one of the magnetic flux reversals that encode data on a disk surface.

magneto-optical recording

An erasable optical disk recording technique that uses a laser beam to heat pits on the disk surface to the point at which a magnet can make flux changes.

master partition boot sector

On hard disks, a one-sector record that gives essential information about the disk and tells the starting locations of the various partitions. Always the first physical sector of the disk.

MCA

An acronym for Micro Channel Architecture. Developed by IBM for the PS/2 line of computers and introduced on April 2, 1987. Features include a 16- or 32-bit bus width and multiple master control. By allowing several processors to arbitrate for resources on a single bus, the MCA is optimized for multitasking, multiprocessor systems. Offers switchless configuration of adapters, which eliminates one of the biggest headaches of installing older adapters.

MCGA

An acronym for MultiColor Graphics Array, a type of PC video display circuit introduced by IBM on April 2, 1987, that supports text and graphics. Text is supported at a maximum resolution of 80x25 characters in 16 colors with a character box of 8x16 pixels. Graphics is supported at a maximum resolution of 320x200 pixels in 256 (from a palette of 262,144) colors or 640x480 pixels in two colors. The MCGA outputs an analog signal with a horizontal scanning frequency of 31.5KHz, and supports analog color or analog monochrome displays.

MCI

MCI is an acronym that stands for Media Control Interface, a device-independent specification for controlling multimedia devices and files. MCI is a part of the multimedia extensions and offers a standard interface set of device control commands, making it easy to program multimedia applications. MCI commands are used for audio recording and playback and animation playback. Videodisk players and other optional devices are controlled by MCI. Device types include CD audio, digital audio tape players, scanners, MIDI sequencers, videotape players or recorder and audio devices that play digitized waveform files. MCI classifies compound and simple device drivers. Compound drivers require a device element (usually a file and a path) during operation. Simple devices do not require a device element for playback.

MDA

An acronym for Monochrome Display Adapter, a type of PC video display adapter introduced by IBM on August 12, 1981, that supports text only. Text is supported at a maximum resolution of 80x25 characters in four colors with a character box of 9x14 pixels. *Colors*, in this case, indicates black, white, bright white, and underlined. Graphics modes are not supported. The MDA outputs a digital signal with a horizontal scanning frequency of 18.432KHz, and supports TTL monochrome displays. The IBM MDA also included a parallel printer port.

mean time between failure

See MTBF.

mean time to repair

See MTTR.

medium

The magnetic coating or plating that covers a disk or tape.

mega

A multiplier indicating 1 million (1,000,000) of some unit. Abbreviated as *m* or *M*. When used to indicate a number of bytes of memory storage, the multiplier definition changes to 1,048,576. One megabit, for example, equals 1,000,000 bits, and one megabyte equals 1,048,576 bytes.

megabyte

A unit of information storage equal to 1,048,576 bytes.

memory

Any component in a computer system that stores information for future use.

memory caching

A service provided by extremely fast memory chips that keeps copies of the most recent memory accesses. When the CPU makes a subsequent access, the value is supplied by the fast memory rather than by relatively slow system memory.

memory-resident program

A program that remains in memory after it has been loaded, consuming memory that otherwise might be used by application software.

menu software

Utility software that makes a computer easier to use by replacing DOS commands with a series of menu selections.

MFM

Modified Frequency Modulation encoding. A method of encoding data on the surface of a disk. The coding of a bit of data varies by the coding of the preceding bit to preserve clocking information.

MHz

An abbreviation for *m*ega*h*ertz, a unit of measurement for indicating the frequency of one million cycles per second. One hertz (Hz) is equal to one cycle per second. Named after Heinrich R. Hertz, a German physicist who first detected electromagnetic waves in 1883.

MI/MIC

Mode Indicate/Mode Indicate Common, also called forced or manual originate. Provided for installations in which equipment other than the modem does the dialing. In such installations, the modem operates in dumb mode (no auto-dial capability) yet must go off-hook in originate mode to connect with answering modems.

micro

A prefix indicating one millionth (1/1,000,000 or .000001) of some unit. Abbreviated as *u*.

microprocessor

A solid-state central processing unit much like a computer on a chip. An integrated circuit that accepts coded instructions for execution.

microsecond

A unit of time equal to one millionth (1/1,000,000 or .000001) of a second. Abbreviated as *us*.

MIDI

An acronym for Musical Instrument Digital Interface, an interface and file format standard for connecting a musical instrument to a microcomputer and storing musical instrument data. Multiple musical instruments can be daisy-chained and played simultaneously with the help of the computer and related software. The various operations of the instruments can be captured, saved, edited, and played back. A MIDI file contains note information, timing (how long a note is held), volume and instrument type for as many as 16 channels. Sequencer programs are used to control MIDI functions such as recording, playback, and editing. MIDI files store only note instructions and not actual sound data.

milli

A prefix indicating one thousandth (1/1,000 or .001) of some unit. Abbreviated as *m*.

millisecond

A unit of time equal to one thousandth (1/1,000 or .001) of a second. Abbreviated as *ms*.

MIPS

An acronym for million instructions per second. Refers to the average number of machine-language instructions a computer can perform or execute in one second. Because different processors can perform different functions in a single instruction, MIPS should be used only as a general measure of performance among different types of computers.

mnemonic

A mnemonic is an abbreviated name for something, which is used in a manner similar to an acronym. Computer processor instructions are often abbreviated with a mnemonic such as JMP (Jump), CLR (Clear), STO (Store), INIT

(Initialize). A mnemonic name for an instruction or an operation makes it easy to remember and convenient to use.

MNP

Microcom Networking Protocol. Asynchronous error-control and data-compression protocols developed by Microcom, Inc. and now in the public domain. Ensure error-free transmission through error detection (CRC) and retransmission of errored frames. MNP Levels 1 through 4 cover error control and have been incorporated into CCITT Recommendation V.42. MNP Level 5 includes data compression but is eclipsed in superiority by V.42bis, an international standard that is more efficient. Most high-speed modems will connect with MNP Level 5 if V.42bis is unavailable.

MO

MO is an acronym for Magneto Optical. MO drives utilize both magnetic and optical storage properties. MO technology is erasable and recordable, as opposed to CD-ROM (Read Only) and WORM (Write Once) drives. MO uses laser and magnetic field technology to record and erase data. The laser is used to heat an area on the disk which can then be recorded magnetically. MO drives are most commonly used in removable storage applications.

modem

*Modulator-dem*odulator. A device that converts electrical signals from a computer into an audio form transmittable over telephone lines, or vice versa. Modulates, or transforms, digital signals from a computer into the analog form that can be carried successfully on a phone line; also demodulates signals received from the phone line back to digital signals before passing them to the receiving computer.

module

An assembly that contains a complete circuit or subcircuit.

Monochrome Display Adapter

See MDA.

morphing

Morphing is a pseudo slang term for metamorphosis, the transformation of one object into another. Morphing is performed by software that analyzes an two images and creates several in-between images such that one image appears to become the other. Originally requiring expensive, high-powered computer hardware, morphing can now be done on PC systems with sophisticated software now available.

MOS

An acronym for Metal-Oxide Semiconductor. Refers to the three layers used in forming the gate structure of a field-effect transistor (FET). MOS circuits offer low-power dissipation and enable transistors to be jammed close together before a critical heat problem arises. PMOS, the oldest type of MOS circuit, is a silicon-gate P-channel MOS process that uses currents made up of positive charges. NMOS is a silicon-gate N-channel MOS process that uses currents made up of negative charges and is at least twice as fast as PMOS. CMOS, Complementary MOS, is nearly immune to noise, runs off almost any power supply, and is an extremely low-power circuit technique.

motherboard

The main circuit board in the computer. Also called planar, system board, or backplane.

MPEG

MPEG is an acronym for the Moving Pictures Experts Group, a lossy data compression standard for motion-video and audio. Lossy compression permanently discards unnecessary data, resulting in some loss of precision. MPEG compression produces about a 50 percent volume reduction in file size.

MTBF

An acronym for *m*ean *t*ime *b*etween *f*ailure, a statistically derived measure of the probable time a device will continue to operate before a hardware failure occurs, usually given in hours. Because no standard technique exists for measuring MTBF, a device from one manufacturer can be significantly more or significantly less reliable than a device with the same MTBF rating from another manufacturer.

MTTR

An acronym for *m*ean *t*ime *t*o *r*epair, a measure of the probable time it will take a technician to service or repair a specific device, usually given in hours.

MultiColor Graphics Array

See MCGA.

Multimedia

Multimedia is the integration of sound, graphic images, animation, motion video and/or text in one environment on a computer. It is a set of hardware and software technologies that is rapidly changing and enhancing the computing environment.

multitask

Run several programs simultaneously.

multiuser system

A system in which several computer terminals share the same central processing unit (CPU).

nano

A prefix indicating one billionth (1/1,000,000,000 or .000000001) of some unit. Abbreviated as *n*.

nanosecond

A unit of time equal to one billionth (1/1,000,000,000 or .000000001) of a second. Abbreviated as *ns*.

network

A system in which a number of independent computers are linked in order to share data and peripherals, such as hard disks and printers.

nonvolatile memory (NVRAM)

Random-access memory whose data is retained when power is turned off. Sometimes nonvolatile RAM is retained without any power whatsoever, as in EEPROM or flash memory devices. In other cases the memory is maintained by a small battery. Nonvolatile RAM that is battery maintained is sometimes also called CMOS memory. CMOS NVRAM is used in IBM-compatible systems to store configuration information. True NVRAM often is used in intelligent modems to store a user-defined default configuration loaded into normal modem RAM at power-up.

nonvolatile RAM disk

A RAM disk powered by a battery supply so that it continues to hold its data during a power outage.

NTSC

An acronym for the National Television Standards Committee, which governs the standard for television and video playback and recording in the United States. The NTSC was originally organized in 1941 when TV broadcasting first began on a wide scale. The original standard it created was called RS-170A, which is now simply referred to as NTSC. The NTSC standard provides for 525 scan lines of resolution and is transmitted at 60 half-frames per second. It is an interlaced signal, which means that it scans every other line each time the screen is refreshed. The signal is generated as a composite of red, green, and blue signals for color and includes an FM frequency for audio and a signal for stereo. Twenty years later, higher standards were adopted in Europe with the PAL and SECAM systems, both incompatible with the NTSC standard of North America. NTSC is also called composite video.

null modem

A serial cable wired so that two data terminal equipment (DTE) devices, such as personal computers, or two data communication equipment (DCE) devices, such as modems or mice, can be connected. Also sometimes called a modem-eliminator. To make a null-modem cable with DB-25 connectors, you wire these pins together: 1-1, 2-3, 3-2, 4-5, 5-4, 6-20, 20-6, and 7-7.

object hierarchy

Object hierarchy occurs in a graphical program when two or more objects are linked and one object's movement is dependent on the other object. This is known as a parent-child hierarchy. In an example using a human figure, the fingers would be child objects to the hand, which is a child object to the arm, which is a child to the shoulder and so on. Object hierarchy provides much control for an animator in moving complex figures.

OCR

An acronym for optical character recognition, an information-processing technology that converts human-readable text into computer data. Usually a scanner is used to read the text on a page, and OCR software converts the images to characters.

OEM

An acronym for Original Equipment Manufacturer, any manufacturer that sells its product to a reseller. Usually refers to the original manufacturer of a particular device or component. Most COMPAQ hard disks, for example, are made by Conner Peripherals, who is considered the OEM.

OLE

An acronym for Object Linking and Embedding, an enhancement to the original Dynamic Data Exchange (DDE) protocol that allows you to embed or link data created in one application in a document created in another application, and subsequently edit that data directly from the final document.

on-line fallback

A feature that enables high-speed error-control modems to monitor line quality and fall back to the next lower speed if line quality degrades. The modems fall forward as line quality improves.

operating system

A collection of programs for operating the computer. Operating systems perform housekeeping tasks such as input and output between the computer and peripherals and accepting and interpreting information from the keyboard. DOS and OS/2 are examples of popular operating systems.

optical disk

A disk that encodes data as a series of reflective pits that are read (and sometimes written) by a laser beam.

Orange Book

Orange Book is the standard for recordable compact disks (like CD-ROM, but recordable instead of Read Only). Recordable compact disks are called CD-R and are becoming popular with the widespread use of multimedia. Publishers use CD-R when transferring paper books to electronic publishing tools. Part of the Orange Book standard defines rewritable Magneto Optical disks and another section defines optical Write Once Read Many (WORM) disks. Publishers usually record a master onto a CD-R WORM disk prior to mass distribution. Titles recorded on WORM can be played by any standard CD-ROM drive (Yellow Book).

originate mode

A state in which the modem transmits at the predefined low frequency of the communications channel and receives at the high frequency. The transmit/receive frequencies are the reverse of the called modem, which is in answer mode.

OS/2

A universal operating system developed through a joint effort by IBM and Microsoft Corporation. The latest operating system for microcomputers using the Intel 80286 or better microprocessors, OS/2 is the successor to DOS (developed also by Microsoft and IBM) and Windows. OS/2 uses the protected mode operation of the processor to expand memory from 1M to 16M and to support fast, efficient multitasking. The OS/2 Presentation Manager, an integral part of the system, is a graphical interface similar to Microsoft Windows and the Apple Macintosh system. The latest version runs DOS, Windows, and OS/2-specific software.

output

Information processed by the computer; or the act of sending that information to a mass storage device such as a video display, a printer, or a modem.

overlay

Part of a program that is loaded into memory only when it is required.

overrun

A situation in which data moves from one device faster than a second device can accept it.

overwrite

To write data on top of existing data, thus erasing the existing data.

package

A device that includes a chip mounted on a carrier and sealed.

PAL

An acronym for phase alternating line system. Invented in 1961 and refers to a system of TV broadcasting used in England and other European countries. With its 625-line picture delivered at 25 frames/second, PAL provides a better image and an improved color transmission over the NTSC system used in North America. PAL also can stand for Programmable Array Logic, a type of chip that has logic gates specified by a device programmer.

palmtop computer

A computer system smaller than a notebook that is designed so that it can be held in one hand while being operated by the other.

parallel

A method of transferring data characters in which the bits travel down parallel electrical paths simultaneously—for example, eight paths for eight-bit characters. Data is stored in computers in parallel form but may be converted to serial form for certain operations.

parity

A method of error checking in which an extra bit is sent to the receiving device to indicate whether an even or odd number of binary 1 bits were transmitted. The receiving unit compares the received information with this bit and can obtain a reasonable judgment about the validity of the character. The same type of parity (even or odd) must be used by two communicating computers, or both may omit parity. When parity is used, a parity bit is added to each transmitted character. The bit's value is 0 or 1, to make the total number of 1s in the character even or odd, depending on which type of parity is used.

park program

A program that executes a seek to the highest cylinder or just past the highest cylinder of a drive so that the potential of data loss is minimized if the drive is moved.

partition

A section of a hard disk devoted to a particular operating system. Most hard disks have only one partition, devoted to DOS. A hard disk can have as many as four partitions, each occupied by a different operating system. DOS V3.3 or higher can occupy two of these four partitions.

Pascal

A high-level programming language named for the French mathematician Blaise Pascal (1623-1662). Developed in the early 1970s by Niklaus Wirth for teaching programming and designed to support the concepts of structured programming. Easy to learn and often the first language taught in schools.

peripheral

Any piece of equipment used in computer systems that is an attachment to the computer. Disk drives, terminals, and printers are all examples of peripherals.

PGA

Pin-grid array. A chip package that has a large number of pins on the bottom designed for socket mounting. Also can mean Professional Graphics Adapter, a limited-production, high-resolution graphics card for XT and AT systems from IBM.

Photo CD

Photo CD is a technology developed by Eastman Kodak and Philips that provides for storing photographic images from 35mm film on a CD-R recordable compact disk. Images stored on the Photo CD may have resolutions as high as 2048 x 3072 pixels. Up to 100 true-color images (24-bit color) can be stored on one disk. Photo CD images are created by scanning 35mm film and digitally recording the images on compact disks (CDs). The digitized images are indexed (given a four-digit code) and thumbnails of each image on the disk are shown on the front of the case along with its index number. Multi-session capability allows several rolls of 35mm film to be added to a single disk on different occasions.

physical drive

A single disk drive. DOS defines logical drives, which are given a specifier, such as C: or D:. A single physical drive may be divided into multiple logical drives. Conversely, special software can span a single logical drive across two physical drives.

physical unit number

See PUN.

PIF

An acronym for Program Information File, a file that contains information about a non-Windows application specifying optimum settings for running the program under Windows.

pixel

A mnemonic term meaning picture element. Any of the tiny elements that form a picture on a video display screen. Also called a pel.

planar board

A term equivalent to motherboard, used by IBM in some of its literature.

plated media

Hard disk platters plated with a form of thin metal film media on which data is recorded.

platter

A disk contained in a hard disk drive. Most drives have two or more platters, each with data recorded on both sides.

PLCC

Plastic leaded-chip carrier. A popular chip-carrier package with J-leads around the perimeter of the package.

port

Plug or socket that enables an external device such as a printer to be attached to the adapter card in the computer. Also a logical address used by a micro-processor for communications between itself and various devices.

port address

One of a system of addresses used by the computer to access devices such as disk drives or printer ports. You may need to specify an unused port address when installing any adapter boards in a system unit.

portable computer

A computer system smaller than a transportable system, but larger than a laptop system. Most portable systems conform to the lunchbox style popularized by COMPAQ, or the briefcase style popularized by IBM, each with a fold-down (removable) keyboard and built-in display. These systems characteristically run on AC power and not on batteries, include several expansion slots, and can be as powerful as full-blown desktop systems.

POS

An acronym for Programmable Option Select. The Micro Channel Architecture's POS eliminates switches and jumpers from the system board and adapters by replacing them with programmable registers. Automatic configuration routines store the POS data in a battery-powered CMOS memory for system configuration and operations. The configuration utilities rely on adapter description (ADF) files that contain the setup data for each card.

POST

Power-On Self Test. A series of tests run by the computer at power-on. Most computers scan and test many of their circuits and sound a beep from the internal speaker if this initial test indicates proper system performance.

PostScript

A page-description language developed primarily by John Warnock, of Adobe Systems, for converting and moving data to the laser-printed page. Instead of using the standard method of transmitting graphics or character information to a printer, telling it where to place dots one-by-one on a page, PostScript provides a way for the laser printer to interpret mathematically a full page of shapes and curves.

power supply

An electrical/electronic circuit that supplies all operating voltage and current to the computer system.

Presentation Manager

The graphical, icon- and window-based software interface offered with OS/2.

primary partition

An ordinary, single-volume bootable partition. *See also* extended partition.

processor speed

The clock rate at which a microprocessor processes data. A standard IBM PC, for example, operates at 4.77 MHz (4.77 million cycles per second).

program

A set of instructions or steps telling the computer how to handle a problem or task.

PROM

Programmable read-only memory. A type of memory chip that can be programmed to store information permanently—information that cannot be erased.

proprietary

Anything invented by a company and not used by any other company. Especially applies to cases in which the inventing company goes to lengths to hide the specifications of the new invention. The opposite of standard.

protected mode

A mode available in all Intel 80286- or 80386-compatible processors. In this mode, memory addressing is extended to 16 or 4096 megabytes, and restricted protection levels can be set to trap software crashes and control the system.

protocol

A system of rules and procedures governing communications between two or more devices. Protocols vary, but communicating devices must follow the same protocol in order to exchange data. The data format, readiness to receive or send, error detection, and error correction are some of the operations that may be defined in protocols.

PUN

An acronym for *physical unit number*, a term used to describe a device attached directly to the SCSI bus. Also known as a SCSI ID. As many as eight SCSI devices can be attached to a single SCSI bus, and each must have a unique PUN or ID assigned from 7 to 0. Normally the SCSI host adapter is assigned the highest-priority ID, which is 7. A bootable hard disk is assigned an ID of 6, and other nonbootable drives are assigned lower priorities.

QAM

An acronym for quadrature amplitude modulation, a modulation technique used by high-speed modems that combines both phase and amplitude modulation. This technique enables multiple bits to be encoded in a single time interval. The V.32bis standard-codes six data bits plus an additional trellis coding bit for each signal change. An individual signal is evaluated with respect to phase and amplitude compared to the carrier wave. A plot of all possible QAM signal points is referred to as the signal constellation pattern. The V.32bis constellation pattern has 128 discrete signal points.

QIC

Quarter-Inch Committee. An industry association that sets hardware and software standards for tape-backup units that use quarter-inch-wide tapes.

QWERTY keyboard

The standard typewriter or computer keyboard, with the characters Q, W, E, R, T, and Y on the top row of alpha keys. Because of the haphazard placement of characters, this keyboard can hinder fast typing.

rails

Plastic strips attached to the sides of disk drives mounted in IBM ATs and compatibles so that the drives can slide into place. These rails fit into channels in the side of each disk drive bay position.

RAM

An acronym for random-access memory, all memory accessible at any instant (randomly) by a microprocessor.

RAM disk

A "phantom disk drive" in which a section of system memory (RAM) is set aside to hold data, just as though it were a number of disk sectors. To DOS, a RAM disk looks like and functions like any other drive.

random-access file

A file in which all data elements (or records) are of equal length and written in the file end to end, without delimiting characters between. Any element (or record) in the file can be found directly by calculating the record's offset in the file.

random-access memory

See RAM.

read-only file

A file whose attribute setting in the file's directory entry tells DOS not to allow software to write into or over the file.

read-only memory

See ROM.

read/write head

A tiny magnet that reads and writes data on a disk track.

real mode

A mode available in all Intel 8086-compatible processors that enables compatibility with the original 8086. In this mode, memory addressing is limited to one megabyte.

real time

When something is recorded or processed as it is happening in the outside world.

Red Book

Red Book is more commonly known as Compact Disc Digital Audio (CD-DA) and is one of four compact disk standards. Red Book got its name from the color of the manual used to describe the CD audio specifications. The Red Book audio standard requires that digital audio is sampled at a 44.1 KHz sample rate using 16 bits for each sample. This is the standard used by audio CDs and many CD ROMs. Sample rates this high require enormous amounts of disk space.

refresh cycle

A cycle in which the computer accesses all memory locations stored by dynamic RAM chips so that the information remains intact. Dynamic RAM chips must be accessed several times a second, or else the information fades.

register

Storage area in memory having a specified storage capacity, such as a bit, a byte, or a computer word, and intended for a special purpose.

remote digital loopback

A test that checks the phone link and a remote modem's transmitter and receiver. Data entered from the keyboard is transmitted from the initiating modem, received by the remote modem's receiver, looped through its transmitter, and returned to the local screen for verification.

remote echo

A copy of the data received by the remote system, returned to the sending system, and displayed on-screen. A function of the remote system.

resolution

A reference to the size of the pixels used in graphics. In medium-resolution graphics, pixels are large. In high-resolution graphics, pixels are small.

RFI

An acronym for Radio Frequency Interference, a high frequency signal radiated by improperly shielded conductors, particularly when signal path lengths are comparable to or longer than the signal wavelengths. The FCC now regulates RFI in computer equipment sold in the US under FCC Regulations Part 15, Subpart J.

RISC

An acronym for Reduced Instruction Set Computer, as differentiated from CISC, Complex Instruction Set Computer. RISC processors have simple instruction sets requiring only one or a few execution cycles. These simple instructions can be utilized more effectively than CISC systems with appropriately designed software, resulting in faster operations.

RLL

An acronym for Run-Length Limited, a type of encoding that derives its name from the fact that the techniques used limit the distance (run length) between magnetic flux reversals on the disk platter. Several types of RLL encoding techniques exist, although only two are commonly used. (1,7)RLL encoding increases storage capacity by about 30 percent over MFM encoding and is most popular in the very highest capacity drives due to a better window margin, while (2,7)RLL encoding increases storage capacity by 50 percent over MFM encoding and is used in the majority of RLL implementations. Most IDE, ESDI, and SCSI hard disks use one of these forms of RLL encoding.

RLL

An acronym for Run Length Limited, a data encoding scheme which guarantees that there is some maximum period between signal transitions whatever the data. In this sense, RLL is roughly synonymous with self clocking. Nearly all serial recording is done using some form of RLL code, however the term is usually reserved for those more sophisticated group codes which allow comparatively long maximum runs between transitions, but also guarantee some minimum run length of at least two code bit periods between transitions, allowing higher storage densities.

RMA number

Return-merchandise authorization number. A number given to you by a vendor when you arrange to return an item for repairs. Used to track the item and the repair.

ROM

An acronym for Read-Only Memory, a type of memory that has values permanently or semi-permanently burned in. These locations are used to hold important programs or data that must be available to the computer when the power initially is turned on.

ROM BIOS

An acronym for Read Only Memory-Basic Input Output System. A BIOS encoded in a form of read-only memory for protection. Often applied to important start-up programs that must be present in a system for it to operate.

root directory

The main directory of any hard or floppy disk. Has a fixed size and location for a particular disk volume and cannot be resized dynamically the way subdirectories can.

routine

Set of frequently used instructions. May be considered as a subdivision of a program with two or more instructions that are related functionally.

RS-232

An interface introduced in August 1969 by the Electronic Industries Association. The RS-232 interface standard provides an electrical description for connecting peripheral devices to computers.

S-Video (Y/C)

Y/C video is a video signal in which the luminance and chrominance (Y/C) components are kept separate, providing greater control and quality of each image. The luminance (Y) channel controls light intensity. The greater the luminance, the lighter the color. Chrominance (C) contains hue (color) and saturation (depth) information on an image. Examples of Y/C (S-Video) include S-VHS (Super-VHS) and Hi8 (High band 8mm) video.

scratch disk

A disk that contains no useful information and can be used as a test disk. IBM has a routine on the Advanced Diagnostics disks that creates a specially formatted scratch disk to be used for testing floppy drives.

SCSI

An acronym for Small Computer System Interface, a standard originally developed by Shugart Associates (then called SASI for Shugart Associates System Interface) and later approved by ANSI in 1986. Uses a 50-pin connector and permits multiple devices (up to eight including the host) to be connected in daisy-chain fashion.

SDLC

Synchronous Data Link Control. A protocol developed by IBM for software applications and communicating devices operation in IBM's Systems Network Architecture (SNA). Defines operations at the link level of communications—for example, the format of data frames exchanged between modems over a phone line.

SECAM

A mnemonic term for sequential and memory. Refers to a system of TV broadcasting used in France and in a modified form in the USSR. Uses an 819-line picture that provides a better resolution than the (British) PAL 625-line and (U.S.) NTSC 525-line formats.

sector

A section of one track, defined with identification markings and an identification number. Most sectors hold 512 bytes of data.

security software

Utility software that uses a system of passwords and other devices to restrict an individual's access to subdirectories and files.

seek time

The amount of time required for a disk drive to move the heads across one-third of the total number of cylinders. Represents the average time it takes to move the heads from one cylinder to another randomly selected cylinder. Seek time is a part of the average access time for a drive.

semiconductor

A substance, such as germanium or silicon, whose conductivity is poor at low temperatures but is improved by minute additions of certain substances or by the application of heat, light, or voltage. Depending on the temperature and pressure, a semiconductor can control a flow of electricity. Semiconductors are the basis of modern electronic-circuit technology.

sequencer

A sequencer is a software program that controls MIDI (Musical Instrument Digital Interface) file messages and keeps track of music timing. Since MIDI files store note instructions instead of actual sounds, a sequencer is needed to play, record, and edit MIDI sounds. Sequencer programs allow for recording and playback of MIDI files by storing the instrument, the note pitch (frequency), the duration in real time that each note is held and the loudness (amplitude) of each musical or sound effect note.

sequential file

A file in which varying-length data elements are recorded end to end, with delimiting characters placed between each element. To find a particular element, you must read the whole file up to that element.

serial

The transfer of data characters one bit at a time, sequentially, using a single electrical path.

servo data

Magnetic markings written on disk platters to guide the read/write heads in drives that use voice-coil actuators.

session (single or multi-session)

A term used in CD-ROM recording to describe a recording event. In a single session, data is recorded on a CD-ROM disk and an index is created. If additional space is left on the disk, another session can be used to record additional files along with another index. The original index cannot be updated because recordable CD-ROM drives are normally Write Once Read Many (WORM) type drives. Many CD-ROM drives do not expect additional recording sessions and therefore will be unable to read the additional session data on the disk. The advent of Kodak's Photo CD propelled the desire for multi-session CD-ROM XA (extended architecture) drives. The first generation of XA drives were capable of single-session reads only. Multi-session CD-ROM XA drives will read all the indices created when images are recorded many times on the same CD-ROM XA drive.

settling time

The time required for read/write heads to stop vibrating after they have been moved to a new track.

shadow ROM

A copy of a system's slower access ROM BIOS placed in faster access RAM, usually during the start-up or boot procedure. This setup enables the system to access BIOS code without the penalty of additional wait states required by the slower ROM chips.

shell

The generic name of any user interface software. COMMAND.COM is the standard shell for DOS. OS/2 comes with three shells: a DOS command shell, an OS/2 command shell, and the OS/2 Presentation Manager, a graphical shell.

shock rating

A rating (usually expressed in G force units) of how much shock a disk drive can sustain without damage. Usually two different specifications exist for a drive powered on or off.

SIMM

Single in-line memory module. An array of memory chips on a small PC board with a single row of I/O contacts.

single-ended

An electrical signaling method where a single line is used referenced to a ground path common to other signals. In a single-ended bus intended for moderately long distances there is commonly one ground line between groups of signal lines to provide some resistance to signal cross talk. Single-ended signals only require one driver or receiver pin per signal, plus one ground pin per group of signals. Single-ended signals are vulnerable to common mode noise and cross talk, but are much less expensive than differential signaling methods.

SIP

Single In-line Package. A DIP-like package with only one row of leads.

skinny dip

Twenty-four- and 28-position DIP devices with .300-inch row-to-row centerlines.

SMPTE time code

SMPTE is an acronym for the Society of Motion Picture and Television Engineers. The SMPTE time code is a standard used to identify individual video frames in the video editing process. SMPTE time code controls such functions as play, record, rewind, and forward of videotapes. SMPTE time code displays video in terms of hours, minutes, seconds, and frames for accurate video editing.

SO-J

Small Outline J-lead. A small DIP package with J-shaped leads for surface mounting or socketing.

soft error

An error in reading or writing data that occurs sporadically, usually because of a transient problem such as a power fluctuation.

software

A series of instructions loaded in the computer's memory that instructs the computer in how to accomplish a problem or task.

spindle

The central post on which a disk drive's platters are mounted.

SQL

An acronym for structured query language. A standard relational database language used especially on midrange and mainframe computers.

ST-506/412

A hard disk interface invented by Seagate Technology and introduced in 1980 with the ST-506 5M hard drive. The ST-506 interface requires that the read/write head be stepped or moved across the disk one track at a time by carefully timed pulses. Because these pulses cause the read/write head's stepper motor to advance a notch, they cannot be sent faster than the disk drive can move the heads. The ST-412 interface introduced with the ST-412 10M drive adds buffered seeking, which eliminates this problem. Instead of requiring the controller to slow the pulse rate to whatever the mechanism can handle, ST-412 simply counts the pulses as they come in and then decides how far to step the head to move the required number of tracks. ST-506/412 was formerly the interface of choice for IBM-compatible systems but has since been superseded by the ESDI, IDE, and SCSI interfaces.

standby power supply

A backup power supply that quickly switches into operation during a power outage.

start/stop bits

The signaling bits attached to a character before the character is transmitted during asynchronous transmission.

starting cluster

The number of the first cluster occupied by a file. Listed in the directory entry of every file.

stepper motor actuator

An assembly that moves disk drive read/write heads across platters by a sequence of small partial turns of a stepper motor.

storage

Device or medium on or in which data can be entered or held, and retrieved at a later time. Synonymous with memory.

streaming

In tape backup, a condition in which data is transferred from the hard disk as quickly as the tape drive can record the data so that the drive does not start and stop or waste tape.

string

A sequence of characters.

subdirectory

A directory listed in another directory. Subdirectories themselves exist as files.

subroutine

A segment of a program that can be executed by a single call. Also called program module.

surface mount

Chip carriers and sockets designed to mount to the surface of a PC board.

surge protector

A device in the power line that feeds the computer, that provides minimal protection against voltage spikes and other transients.

synchronous communication

A form of communication in which blocks of data are sent at strictly timed intervals. Because the timing is uniform, no start or stop bits are required. Compare with asynchronous communication. Some mainframes support only synchronous communications unless a synchronous adapter and appropriate software have been installed.

system crash

A situation in which the computer freezes up and refuses to proceed without rebooting. Usually caused by faulty software. Unlike a hard disk crash, no permanent physical damage occurs.

system files

The two hidden DOS files IBMBIO.COM and IBMDOS.COM; they represent the interface between the BIOS and DOS (IBMBIO) and the interface between DOS and other applications (IBMDOS).

system integrator

A computer consultant or vendor who tests available products and combines them into highly optimized systems.

target

A device attached to a SCSI bus that receives and processes commands sent from another device (the initiator) on the SCSI bus. A SCSI hard disk is an example of a target.

TCM

An acronym for trellis-coded modulation, an error-detection and correction technique employed by high-speed modems to enable higher-speed transmissions that are more resistant to line impairments. In TCM encoding, the first two data bits of an encoded group are used to generate a third TCM bit that is added to the group. For example, in V.32bis, the first two bits of a 6-bit group are used to generate the TCM bit, which then is placed as the first bit of a new 7-bit group. By reversing the encoding at the other end, the receiving modem can determine whether the received group is valid.

temporary backup

A second copy of a work file, usually having the extension BAK. Created by application software so that you easily can return to a previous version of your work.

temporary file

A file temporarily (and usually invisibly) created by a program for its own use.

tera

A multiplier indicating 1 trillion (1,000,000,000,000) of some unit. Abbreviated as t or T. When used to indicate a number of bytes of memory storage, the multiplier definition changes to 1,099,511,627,776. One terabit, for example, equals 1,000,000,000,000 bits, and one terabyte equals 1,099,511,627,776 bytes.

terabyte

A unit of information storage equal to 1,099,511,627,776 bytes.

terminal

A device whose keyboard and display are used for sending and receiving data over a communications link. Differs from a microcomputer in that it has no internal processing capabilities. Used to enter data into or retrieve processed data from a system or network.

terminal mode

An operational mode required for microcomputers to transmit data. In terminal mode, the computer acts as though it were a standard terminal such as a teletypewriter rather than a data processor. Keyboard entries go directly to the modem, whether the entry is a modem command or data to be transmitted over the phone lines. Received data is output directly to the screen. The more popular communications software products control terminal mode and enable more complex operations, including file transmission and saving received files.

terminator

A piece of hardware that must be attached to both ends of an electrical bus. Functions to prevent the reflection or echoing of signals that reach the ends of the bus and to ensure that the correct impedance load is placed on the driver circuits on the bus.

thin-film media

Hard disk platters that have a thin film (usually three-millionths of an inch) of medium deposited on the aluminum substrate through a sputtering or plating process.

through-hole

Chip carriers and sockets equipped with leads that extend through holes in a PC board.

throughput

The amount of user data transmitted per second without the overhead of protocol information such as start and stop bits or frame headers and trailers.

TIFF

An acronym for Tagged Image File Format, a way of storing and exchanging digital image data. Developed by Aldus Corporation, Microsoft Corporation, and major scanner vendors to help link scanned images with the popular desktop publishing applications. Supports three main types of image data: black-and-white data, halftones or dithered data, and gray-scale data.

token ring

A type of local area network in which the workstations relay a packet of data called a token in a logical ring configuration. When a station wants to transmit, it takes possession of the token, attaches its data, then frees the token after the data has made a complete circuit of the electrical ring. IBM's token ring system is a standard network hardware implementation supported by many manufacturers. It is currently the highest-performance-standard LAN system and transmits at speeds of 16 million bits per second. Because of the token-passing scheme, access to the network is controlled, unlike the slower EtherNet system, in which collisions of data can occur, wasting time. The token ring network also uses twisted-pair wiring, which is cheaper than the coaxial cable used by EtherNet and ARCnet.

TPI

Tracks per inch. Used as a measurement of magnetic track density. Standard 51/4-inch 360K floppy disks have a density of 48 TPI, and the 1.2M disks have a 96-TPI density. All 31/2-inch disks have a 135.4667-TPI density, and hard disks can have densities greater than 3,000 TPI.

track

One of the many concentric circles that hold data on a disk surface. Consists of a single line of magnetic flux changes and is divided into some number of 512-byte sectors.

Track Density

Expressed as Tracks Per Inch (TPI), Track Density defines how many tracks are recorded in one inch of space measured radially from the center of the disk. Sometimes also called Radial Density.

track-to-track seek time

The time required for read/write heads to move between adjacent tracks.

transportable computer

A computer system larger than a portable system, and similar in size and shape to a portable sewing machine. Most transportables conform to a design similar to the original COMPAQ portable, with a built-in CRT display. These systems are characteristically very heavy, and run only on AC power. Because of advances primarily in LCD and plasma-display technology, these systems are largely obsolete and have been replaced by portable systems.

troubleshooting

The task of determining the cause of a problem.

true-color images

True-color images are also called 24-bit color images since each pixel is represented by 24 bits of data, allowing for 16.7 million colors. The number of colors possible is based on the number of bits used to represent the color. If 8 bits are used, there are 256 possible color values (2 to the 8th power). To obtain 16.7 million colors, each of the primary colors (red, green, and blue) is represented by 8 bits per pixel, which allows for 256 possible shades for each of the primary red, green, and blue colors or 256x256x256 = 16.7 million total colors.

TSR

An acronym for Terminate-and-Stay-Resident, a program that remains in memory after being loaded. Because they remain in memory, TSR programs can be reactivated by a predefined keystroke sequence or other operation while another program is active. Usually called resident programs.

TTL

An acronym for Transistor-to-Transistor Logic. Digital signals often are called TTL signals. A TTL display is a monitor that accepts digital input at standardized signal voltage levels.

tweens

Tweens are the name given to a series of animation or video frames between the key frames. When one object is transformed (morphed) into another, the initial object and the final object are set on the computer. Tweens are the frames that transpose the first object into the final image.

twisted pair

A type of wire in which two small insulated copper wires are wrapped or twisted around each other to minimize interference from other wires in the cable. Two types of twisted-pair cables are available: unshielded and shielded. Unshielded twisted-pair wiring commonly is used in telephone cables and provides little protection against interference. Shielded twisted-pair wiring is used in some networks or any application in which immunity from electrical interference is more important. Twisted-pair wire is much easier to work with than coaxial cable and is cheaper as well.

UART

An acronym for Universal Asynchronous Receiver Transmitter, a chip device that controls the RS-232 serial port in a PC-compatible system. Originally developed by National Semi-conductor, several UART versions are in PC-compatible systems: the 8250B is used in PC- or XT-class systems, and the 16450 and 16550A are used in AT-class systems.

unformatted capacity

The total number of bytes of data that can be fit on a disk. The formatted capacity is lower because space is lost defining the boundaries between sectors.

uninterruptible power supply

Also known as UPS. A device that supplies power to the computer from batteries so that power will not stop, even momentarily, during a power outage. The batteries are recharged constantly from a wall socket.

Universal Asynchronous Receiver Transmitter

See UART.

UPC

An acronym for Universal Product Code, a 10-digit computer-readable bar code used in labeling retail products. The code in the form of vertical bars includes a five-digit manufacturer identification number and a five-digit product code number.

update

To modify information already contained in a file or program with current information.

utility

Programs that carry out routine procedures to make computer use easier.

UTP

An acronym for Unshielded Twisted Pair, a type of wire often used indoors to connect telephones or computer devices. Comes with two or four wires twisted inside a flexible plastic sheath or conduit and utilizes modular plugs and phone jacks.

V.21

A CCITT standard for modem communications at 300 bps. Modems made in the U.S. or Canada follow the Bell 103 standard but can be set to answer V.21 calls from overseas. The actual transmission rate is 300 baud and employs FSK (*f*requency *s*hift *k*eying) modulation, which encodes a single bit per baud.

V.22

A CCITT standard for modem communications at 1200 bps, with an optional fallback to 600 bps. V.22 is partially compatible with the Bell 212A standard observed in the United States and Canada. The actual transmission rate is 600 baud, using DPSK (*d*ifferential-*p*hase *s*hift *k*eying) to encode as much as two bits per baud.

V.22bis

A CCITT standard for modem communications at 2400 bps. Includes an automatic link-negotiation fallback to 1200 bps and compatibility with Bell 212A/V.22 modems. The actual transmission rate is 600 baud, using QAM (quadrature amplitude modulation) to encode as much as four bits per baud.

V.23

A CCITT standard for modem communications at 1200 or 600 bps with a 75-bps back channel. Used in the United Kingdom for some videotext systems.

V.25

A CCITT standard for modem communications that specifies an answer tone different from the Bell answer tone used in the U.S. and Canada. Most intelligent modems can be set with an ATB0 command so that they use the V.25 2100 Hz tone when answering overseas calls.

V.32

A CCITT standard for modem communications at 9600 bps and 4800 bps. V.32 modems fall back to 4800 bps when line quality is impaired and fall forward again to 9600 bps when line quality improves. The actual transmission rate is 2400 baud, using QAM (quadrature amplitude modulation) and optional TCM (trellis-coded modulation) to encode as much as 4 data bits per baud.

V.32bis

A CCITT standard that extends the standard V.32 connection range and supports 4800-, 7200-, 9600-, 12000-, and 14400-bps transmission rates. V.32bis modems fall back to the next lower speed when line quality is impaired, fall back further as necessary, and fall forward to the next higher speed when line quality improves. The actual transmission rate is 2400 baud, using QAM (quadrature amplitude modulation) and TCM (trellis-coded modulation) to encode as much as 6 data bits per baud.

V.32fast

A CCITT standard that extends the standard V.32bis connection range, supporting 28800-bps transmission rates as well as all the functions and rates of V.32bis. Products following this standard are now available.

V.32terbo

A proprietary standard proposed by several modem manufacturers which will be cheaper to implement than the standard V.32 fast protocol, but which will only support transmission speeds of up to 18800 bps. Since it is not an industry standard, it is not likely to have widespread industry support.

V.42

A CCITT standard for modem communications that defines a two-stage process of detection and negotiation for LAPM error control. Also supports MNP error-control protocol, Levels 1 through 4.

V.42bis

An extension of CCITT V.42 that defines a specific data-compression scheme for use with V.42 and MNP error control.

vaccine

A type of program used to locate and eradicate virus code from infected programs or systems.

VCPI

An acronym for Virtual Control Program Interface, a 386 and higher processor memory management standard created by Phar Lap software in conjunction with other software developers. VCPI provides an interface between applications using DOS extenders and 386 memory managers.

VESA

An acronym for the Video Electronics Standards Association. Founded in the late 1980s by NEC Home Electronics and eight other leading video board manufacturers, with the main goal to standardize the electrical, timing, and programming issues surrounding 800-by-600 resolution video displays, commonly known as Super VGA. VESA has also developed the Video Local Bus (VL-Bus) standard for connecting high speed adapters directly to the local processor bus.

VGA

An acronym for Video Graphics Array, a type of PC video display circuit (and adapter) first introduced by IBM on April 2, 1987, that supports text and graphics. Text is supported at a maximum resolution of 80x25 characters in 16 colors with a character box of 9x16 pixels. Graphics is supported at a maximum resolution of 320x200 pixels in 256 (from a palette of 262,144) colors or 640x480 pixels in 16 colors. The VGA outputs an analog signal with a horizontal scanning frequency of 31.5 KHz, and supports analog color or analog monochrome displays.

Video Graphics Array

See VGA.

virtual disk

A RAM disk or "phantom disk drive" in which a section of system memory (usually RAM) is set aside to hold data, just as though it were a number of disk sectors. To DOS, a virtual disk looks like and functions like any other "real" drive.

virtual memory

A technique by which operating systems (including OS/2) load more programs and data into memory than they can hold. Parts of the programs and data are kept on disk and constantly swapped back and forth into system memory. The applications software programs are unaware of this setup and act as though a large amount of memory is available.

virtual real mode

A mode available in all Intel 80386-compatible processors. In this mode, memory addressing is limited to 4096 megabytes, restricted protection levels can be set to trap software crashes and control the system, and individual real mode compatible sessions can be set up and maintained separately from one another.

virus

A type of resident program designed to attach itself to other programs. Usually at some later time, when the virus is running, it causes an undesirable action to take place.

VMM

An acronym for Virtual Memory Manager, a facility in Windows enhanced mode that manages the task of swapping data in and out of 386 and higher processor virtual real mode memory space for multiple non-Windows applications running in virtual real mode.

voice-coil actuator

A device that moves read/write heads across hard disk platters by magnetic interaction between coils of wire and a magnet. Functions somewhat like an audio speaker, from which the name originated.

voltage regulator

A device that smoothes out voltage irregularities in the power fed to the computer.

volume

A portion of a disk signified by a single drive specifier. Under DOS V3.3 and later, a single hard disk can be partitioned into several volumes, each with its own logical drive specifier (C:,D:,E:, and so on).

volume label

An identifier or name of up to 11 characters that names a disk.

VRAM

An acronym for Video Random-Access Memory. VRAM chips are modified DRAMs on video boards that enable simultaneous access by the host system's processor and the processor on the video board. A large amount of information thus can be transferred quickly between the video board and the system processor. Sometimes also called dual-ported RAM.

wait states

Pause cycles during system operation that require the processor to wait one or more clock cycles until memory can respond to the processor's request. Enables the microprocessor to synchronize with lower-cost, slower memory. A system that runs with "zero wait states" requires none of these cycles because of the use of faster memory or a memory cache system.

Whetstone

A benchmark program developed in 1976 and designed to simulate arithmetic-intensive programs used in scientific computing. Remains completely CPU-bound and performs no I/O or system calls. Originally written in ALGOL, although the C and Pascal versions became more popular by the late 1980s. The speed at which a system performs floating-point operations often is measured in units of Whetstones.

Whitney technology

A term referring to a magnetic disk design which usually has oxide or thin film media, thin film read/write heads, low floating height sliders, and low mass actuator arms that together allow higher bit densities than the older Winchester technology. Whitney technology was first introduced with the IBM 3370 disk drive circa 1979.

Winchester drive

Any ordinary, nonremovable (or fixed) hard disk drive. The name originates from a particular IBM drive in the 1960s that had 30M of fixed and 30M of removable storage. This 30-30 drive matched the caliber figure for a popular series of rifles made by Winchester, so the slang term Winchester was applied to any fixed platter hard disk.

Winchester technology

The term "winchester" is loosely applied to mean any disk with a fixed or non-removable recording medium. More precisely, the term applies to a ferrite read/write head and slider design with oxide media that was first employed in the IBM 3340 disk drive, circa 1973. Most drives today actually use Whitney technology.

wire frames

Wire frame is the most common technique used to construct a 3-dimensional object for animation. A wire frame is given coordinates of length, height, and width. Wire frames are then filled with textures, colors, and movement. Transforming a wire frame into a textured object is called "rendering."

word length

The number of bits in a data character without parity, start, or stop bits.

WORM

An acronym for write once, read many (or multiple). An optical mass-storage device capable of storing many megabytes of information but that can be written to only once on any given area of the disk. A WORM disk typically holds more than 200M of data. Because a WORM drive cannot write over an old version of a file, new copies of files are made and stored on other parts of the disk whenever a file is revised. WORM disks are used to store information when a history of older versions must be maintained. Recording on a WORM disk is performed by a laser writer that burns pits in a thin metallic film (usually tellurium) embedded in the disk. This burning process is called "ablation." WORM drives are frequently used for archiving data.

write precompensation

A modification applied to write data by a controller in order to alleviate partially the problem of bit shift, which causes adjacent 1s written on magnetic media to read as though they were further apart. When adjacent 1s are sensed by the controller, precompensation is used to write them closer together on the disk, thus enabling them to be read in the proper bit cell window. Drives with built-in controllers normally handle precompensation automatically. Precompensation normally is required for the inner cylinders of oxide media drives.

XGA

An acronym for eXtended Graphics Array, a type of PC video display circuit (and adapter) first introduced by IBM on October 30, 1990, that supports text and graphics. Text is supported at a maximum resolution of 132x60 characters in 16 colors with a character box of 8x6 pixels. Graphics is supported at a maximum resolution of 1024x768 pixels in 256 (from a palette of 262,144) colors or 640x480 pixels in 65,536 colors. The XGA outputs an analog signal with a horizontal scanning frequency of 31.5 or 35.52 KHz, and supports analog color or analog monochrome displays.

XMM

An acronym for eXtended Memory Manager, a driver that controls access to Extended Memory on 286 and higher processor systems. HIMEM.SYS is an example of an XMM that comes with DOS.

Xmodem

A file-transfer protocol—with error checking—developed by Ward Christensen in the mid-1970s and placed in the public domain. Designed to transfer files between machines running the CP/M operating system and using 300- or 1200-bps modems. Until the late 1980s, because of its simplicity and public-domain status, Xmodem remained the most widely used microcomputer file-transfer protocol. In standard Xmodem, the transmitted blocks are 128 bytes. 1K-Xmodem is an extension to Xmodem that increases the block size to 1024 bytes. Many newer file-transfer protocols that are much faster and more accurate than Xmodem have been developed, such as Ymodem and Zmodem.

XMS

An acronym for eXtended Memory Specification, a Microsoft developed standard that provides a way for real mode applications to access extended memory in a controlled fashion. The XMS standard is available from Microsoft.

XON/XOFF

Standard ASCII control characters used to tell an intelligent device to stop or resume transmitting data. In most systems, typing Ctrl-S sends the XOFF character. Most devices understand Ctrl-Q as XON; others interpret the pressing of any key after Ctrl-S as XON.

Y-connector

A Y-shaped splitter cable that divides a source input into two output signals.

Yellow Book

Yellow Book is the standard used by Compact Disc Read Only Memory (CD-ROM). Multimedia applications most commonly use the Yellow Book standard, which specifies how digital information is to be stored on the CD-ROM and read by a computer. EXtended Architecture (XA) is currently an extension of the Yellow Book which allows for the combination of different data types (audio and video, for example) onto one track in a CD-ROM. Without XA, a CD-ROM can only access one data type at a time. Many CD-ROM drives are now XA capable.

Ymodem

A file-transfer protocol first released as part of Chuck Forsberg's YAM (*y*et *a*nother *m*odem) program. An extension to Xmodem, designed to overcome some of the limitations of the original. Enables information about the transmitted file, such as the file name and length, to be sent along with the file data and increases the size of a block from 128 to 1024 bytes. Ymodem-batch adds the capability to transmit "batches" or groups of files without operator interruption. YmodemG is a variation that sends the entire file before waiting for an acknowledgment. If the receiving side detects an error in midstream, the transfer is aborted. YmodemG is designed for use with modems that have built-in, error-correcting capabilities.

ZIF

Zero insertion force. Sockets that require no force for the insertion of a chip carrier. Usually accomplished through movable contacts and used primarily in test devices in which chips will be inserted and removed many times.

ZIP

Zigzag in-line package. A DIP package that has all leads on one edge in a zigzag pattern and mounts in a vertical plane.

Zmodem

A file-transfer protocol commissioned by Telenet and placed in the public domain. Like Ymodem, designed by Chuck Forsberg, and developed as an extension to Xmodem to overcome some of that original protocol's limitations. Among the key features are a 32-bit CRC offering a degree of error detection many times greater than Xmodem CRC, a server facility, batch transfers, and fast error recovery. One feature of Zmodem is the capability to continue transmitting a file from where it left off if the connection has been broken. Zmodem also was engineered specifically to avoid sending certain sequences, such as ESCape-carriage return-ESCape, that the Telenet network uses to control the connection. Its speed, accuracy, and file-recovery capabilities make Zmodem the leading protocol for high-speed modem file transfers.

Index

Symbols

I

GO AHEAD. PLUG YOURSELF INTO
PRENTICE HALL COMPUTER PUBLISHING.

Introducing the PHCP Forum on CompuServe®

Yes, it's true. Now, you can have CompuServe access to the same professional, friendly folks who have made computers easier for years. On the PHCP Forum, you'll find additional information on the topics covered by every PHCP imprint—including Que, Sams Publishing, New Riders Publishing, Alpha Books, Brady Books, Hayden Books, and Adobe Press. In addition, you'll be able to receive technical support and disk updates for the software produced by Que Software and Paramount Interactive, a division of the Paramount Technology Group. It's a great way to supplement the best information in the business.

WHAT CAN YOU DO ON THE PHCP FORUM?

Play an important role in the publishing process—and make our books better while you make your work easier:

- Leave messages and ask questions about PHCP books and software—you're guaranteed a response within 24 hours
- Download helpful tips and software to help you get the most out of your computer
- Contact authors of your favorite PHCP books through electronic mail
- Present your own book ideas
- Keep up to date on all the latest books available from each of PHCP's exciting imprints

JOIN NOW AND GET A FREE COMPUSERVE STARTER KIT!

To receive your free CompuServe Introductory Membership, call toll-free, **1-800-848-8199** and ask for representative **#597**. The Starter Kit Includes:

- Personal ID number and password
- $15 credit on the system
- Subscription to CompuServe Magazine

HERE'S HOW TO PLUG INTO PHCP:

Once on the CompuServe System, type any of these phrases to access the PHCP Forum:

GO PHCP
GO QUEBOOKS
GO SAMS
GO NEWRIDERS
GO ALPHA

GO BRADY
GO HAYDEN
GO QUESOFT
GO PARAMOUNTINTER

Once you're on the CompuServe Information Service, be sure to take advantage of all of CompuServe's resources. CompuServe is home to more than 1,700 products and services—plus it has over 1.5 million members worldwide. You'll find valuable online reference materials, travel and investor services, electronic mail, weather updates, leisure-time games and hassle-free shopping (no jam-packed parking lots or crowded stores).

Seek out the hundreds of other forums that populate CompuServe. Covering diverse topics such as pet care, rock music, cooking, and political issues, you're sure to find others with the sames concerns as you—and expand your knowledge at the same time.

Only Que gives you the most comprehensive programming guides!

DOS Programmer's Reference, 3rd Edition
Through DOS 5.0
$29.95 USA
0-88022-790-7, 1,000 pp., 7³/₈ x 9¹/₈

Borland C++ 3.1Programmer's Reference2nd Edition
Latest Versions of Borland C++ and Turbo C++
$29.95 USA
1-56529-082-8, 900 pp., 7³/₈ x 9¹/₈

FoxPro 2.5 Programmer's Reference
Version 2.5
$35.00 USA
1-56529-210-3, 1,258 pp., 7³/₈ x 9¹/₈

Paradox 4 Developer's Guide
Latest Version
$44.95 USA
0-88022-705-2, 800 pp., 7³/₈ x 9¹/₈

Using Visual Basic 3
Version 3
$34.95 USA
0-88022-763-x, 650 pp., 7³/₈ x 9¹/₈

To Order, Call: (800) 428-5331 OR (317) 581-3500

Using WordPerfect Is Easy When You're Using Que

Using WordPerfect Version 6 for DOS, Special Edition

Que Development Group

The classic, #1 best-selling word processing book—only from Que! Includes tear-out command map, icons, margin notes, and cautions.
WordPerfect 6

$27.95 USA

1-56529-077-1, 1,200pp., 7³/₈ x 9¹/₈

WordPerfect 6 QuickStart

Que Development Group

A graphics-based, fast-paced introduction to 6 essentials! Numerous illustrations demonstrate document production, table design, equation editing, and more.
WordPerfect 6

$21.95 USA

1-56529-085-2, 600 pp., 7³/₈ x 9¹/₈

WordPerfect 6 Quick Reference

Que Development Group

Instant reference for the operations of WordPerfect 6. Alphabetical listings make information easy to find!
WordPerfect 6

$9.95 USA

1-56529-084-4, 160 pp., 4³/₄ x 8

Check Out These Other Great Titles!

Using WordPerfect 5.1, Special Edition

Que Development Group
WordPerfect 5.1

$27.95 USA

0-88022-554-8, 900 pp., 7³/₈ x 9¹/₈

WordPerfect 5.1 QuickStart

Que Development Group
WordPerfect 5.1

$21.95 USA

0-88022-558-0, 427 pp., 7³/₈ x 9¹/₈

WordPerfect 5.1 Quick Reference

Que Development Group
WordPerfect 5.1

$9.95 USA

0-88022-576-9, 160 pp., 4³/₄ x 8

WordPerfect 5.1 Tips, Tricks, and Traps

Charles O. Stewart III, Daniel J. Rosenbaum, & Joel Shore
WordPerfect 5.1

$24.95 USA

0-88022-557-2, 743 pp., 7³/₈ x 9¹/₈

Easy WordPerfect

Shelley O'Hara
WordPerfect 5.1

$19.95 USA

0-88022-797-4, 200 pp., 8 x 10

WordPerfect 5.1 Office Solutions

Ralph Blodgett
Version 5.1

$49.95 USA

0-88022-838-5, 850 pp., 8 x 10

Easy WordPerfect for Version 6

Shelley O'Hara

The perfect introduction for new WordPerfect users—or those upgrading to Version 6.
WordPerfect 6

$16.95 USA

1-56529-087-9, 256 pp., 8 x 10

 **To Order, Call: (800) 428-5331 OR (317) 581-3500**